March 3–6, 2014
Bielefeld, Germany

Association for Computing Machinery

Advancing Computing as a Science & Profession

HRI'14

Proceedings of the 2014 ACM/IEEE International Conference on Human-Robot Interaction

Sponsored by:

ACM SIGCHI, ACM SIGAI and IEEE Robotics & Automation

In-cooperation with:

HFES and AAAI

Supported by:

ALDEBARAN Robotics, Disney Research, Engineered Arts limited, Kinova, Shadow Robot Company, Google, it's owl and The MIT Press

Association for
Computing Machinery

Advancing Computing as a Science & Profession

The Association for Computing Machinery
2 Penn Plaza, Suite 701
New York, New York 10121-0701

ISBN: 978-1-4503-2658-2 (Digital)

ISBN: 978-1-4503-3102-9 (Print)

Additional copies may be ordered prepaid from:

ACM Order Department
PO Box 30777
New York, NY 10087-0777, USA

Phone: 1-800-342-6626 (USA and Canada)
+1-212-626-0500 (Global)
Fax: +1-212-944-1318
E-mail: acmhelp@acm.org
Hours of Operation: 8:30 am – 4:30 pm ET

Printed in the USA

HRI 2014 Chairs' Welcome

It is our great pleasure to welcome you to the Ninth Annual ACM/IEEE International Conference on Human-Robot Interaction. HRI 2014 is a highly selective conference that aims to showcase the very best interdisciplinary and multidisciplinary research in human-robot interaction with roots in robotics, social psychology, cognitive science, HCI, human factors, artificial intelligence, design, engineering, and many more. We invite broad participation and encourage discussion and sharing of ideas across a diverse audience.

Robotics is growing increasingly multidisciplinary as it moves towards realizing capable and collaborative robots that are studied in both laboratory and real world settings. Concurrent development of technical, social, and designed aspects of systems, with a concern for how they will improve the world, is needed.

This year's theme "(E)Merging Perspectives" seeks to combine both user and system perspectives to advance new and possibly unorthodox methodologies. To extend the current singular approaches, our program demonstrates the usage of novel empirical methods, the integration of empirical findings into complex robot systems, and holistic approaches in system evaluation.

The call for papers attracted 132 submissions from Asia, Canada, Europe, Africa, and the United States. Full Papers submitted to the conference were thoroughly reviewed and discussed. The process utilized a rebuttal process and a worldwide team of dedicated, interdisciplinary reviewers. This year's conference continues the tradition of selectivity, the program committee selected 32 of the submissions (24%). Due to the joint sponsorship of ACM and IEEE, papers are archived in both the ACM Digital Library and IEEE Xplore.

For the second year, the conference also features papers from a journal special issue. Six papers were accepted for the Journal of Human-Robot Interaction's special issue on Design, and will be presented throughout the conference program. Accompanying the full papers are the Late Breaking Reports, Videos, and Demos. For the LBR, 109 of 127 two-page papers were accepted and will be presented at the conference poster session. 14 short videos were accepted and will be presented during the video session, and we have 7 demos of robot systems for all participants to be able to interact with during the conference. Rounding out the program are three keynote speakers who will discuss topics relevant to HRI: Dr. Maja Mataric, Dr. Maja Pantic, and Dr. Helge Ritter.

The conference could not have occurred without the extensive volunteer effort put forth by the organizing committee, program committee, and reviewers. We would also like to thank the keynote speakers and panelists for their participation and attendance. The sponsors of the conference are ACM SIGCHI, ACM SIGAI, and IEEE Robotics and Automation. The conference is in cooperation with AAAI and HFES.

We hope that you will find this program interesting and thought-provoking and that the conference will provide you with a valuable opportunity to share ideas with other researchers and practitioners from institutions around the world.

Gerhard Sagerer
HRI'14 General Co-Chair
Bielefeld University, Germany

Michita Imai
HRI'14 General Co-Chair
Keio University, Japan

Tony Belpaeme
HRI'14 Program Co-Chair
Plymouth University, UK

Andrea Thomaz
HRI'14 Program Co-Chair
Georgia Institute of Technology, USA

Table of Contents

Session 5: Human-Robot Teams

Session Chair: Tamim Asfour *(Karlsruhe Institute of Technology)*

Session 6: Video Session

Session Chair: Lars Schillingmann *(Osaka University)*

Session 7: HRI 2014 Late Breaking Reports Poster

Session 11: Living with Robots

Session Chair: Guy Hoffman *(Interdisciplinary Center Herzliya)*

Session 12: Keynote:

(Imperial College London)

Session 13: Robot Teachers and Learners

Session Chair: Julie Shah *(Massachusetts Institute of Technology)*

Session 14: Motivation and Assistive Robotics

Session Chair: Tamim Asfour *(Karlsruhe Institute of Technology)*

Session 15: Proxemics

Session Chair: Yukie Nagai *(Osaka University)*

Session 16: Workshops

HRI 2014 Conference Organization

General Chairs:	Gerhard Sagerer *(Bielefeld University, Germany)* Michita Imai *(Keio University, Japan)*
Program Chairs:	Tony Belpaeme *(Plymouth University, UK)* Andrea Thomaz *(Georgia Institute of Technology, USA)*
Panel Chairs:	Vanessa Evers *(University of Twente, Netherlands)* Maarten Sierhuis *(Nissan Research Center, USA)*
Publication Chairs:	Selma Sabanovic *(Indiana University, USA)* Yukie Nagai *(Osaka University, Japan)*
Local Arrangement Chairs:	Britta Wrede *(Bielefeld University, Germany)* Friederike Eyssel *(Bielefeld University, Germany)*
Financial Chairs:	Franz Kummert *(Bielefeld University, Germany)* Masahiro Shiomi *(ATR, Japan)*
Fundraising Chairs:	Maya Cakmak *(University of Washington, USA)* Gunter Korder *(Leading-Edge Cluster it's OWL, Germany)*
Publicity Chair:	Vanessa Evers *(University of Twente, Netherlands)*
Registration Chairs:	Raquel Ros Espinoza *(Imperial College London, UK)* Joshua M. Peschel *(University of Illinois, USA)*
Workshop & Tutorial Chairs:	Brenna Argall *(Northwestern University, USA)* Marc Hanheide *(University of Lincoln, UK)*
Demonstration Chairs:	Sven Wachsmuth *(Bielefeld University, Germany)* Michael Beetz *(University of Bremen, Germany)*
Late Breaking Reports Chairs:	Cindy Bethel *(Mississippi State University, USA)* Hagen Lehmann *(University of Hertfordshire, UK)*
Video Chairs:	Lars Schillingmann *(Osaka University, Japan)* Anna-Lisa Vollmer *(Plymouth University, UK)*
Design Chair:	Frank Hegel *(Bielefeld University, Germany)*
Web Chair:	Frank Hegel *(Bielefeld University, Germany)*

Steering Committee Chairs: Vanessa Evers *(University of Twente, The Netherlands)*
Holly Yanco *(University of Massachusetts–Lowell, USA)*

Steering Committee: Julie A. Adams *(Vanderbilt University, USA)*
Kai Oliver Arras *(Freiburg University, Germany)*
Tony Belpaeme *(University of Plymouth, UK)*
Sonia Chernova *(Worcester Polytechnic Institute, USA)*
Jodi Forlizzi *(Carnegie Mellon University, USA)*
Jeonghye Han *(Cheongju National University of Education, Korea)*
Michita Imai *(Keio University, Japan)*
Hideaki Kazuoka *(University of Tsukuba, Japan)*
Sara Kiesler *(Carnegie Mellon University, USA)*
Franz Kummert *(Bielefeld University, Germany)*
Bilge Mutlu *(University of Wisconsin–Madison, USA)*
Gerhard Sagerer *(University of Bielefeld, Germany)*
Brian Scassellatti *(Yale University, USA)*
Masahiro Shiomi *(ATR, Japan)*
Bill Smart *(Oregon State University, USA)*
Leila Takayama *(Willow Garage, Inc., USA)*
Fumihide Tanaka *(The University of Tokyo, Japan)*
Andrea Thomaz *(Georgia Institute of Technology, USA)*
Manfred Tscheligi *(University of Salzburg, Austria)*

Program Committee: Julie Adams *(Vanderbilt University, USA)*
Kai Oliver Arras *(Freiburg University, Germany)*
Tamim Asfour *(Karlsruhe Institute of Technology, Germany)*
Cindy Bethel *(Mississippi State University, USA)*
Maya Cakmak *(University of Washington, USA)*
Vanessa Evers *(University of Twente, The Netherlands)*
Kerstin Fisher *(South Denmark University, Denmark)*
Jodi Forlizzi *(Carnegie Mellon University, USA)*
Guy Hoffman *(Interdisciplinary Center Herzliya, Israel)*
Takayuki Kanda *(ATR, Japan)*
Tom Kollar *(Carnegie Mellon University, USA)*
Sonia Kwak *(Ewha Womans University, South Korea)*
Bilge Mutlu *(University of Wisconsin-Madison, USA)*
Yukie Nagai *(Osaka University, Japan)*
Katharina Rohlfing *(Bielefeld University, Germany)*
Selma Sabanovic *(Indiana University, USA)*
Gerhard Sagerer *(Bielefeld University, Germany)*
Majd Sakr *(Carnegie Mellon University, Qatar)*
Julie Shah *(Massachusetts Institute of Technology, USA)*
Sidd Srinivasa *(Carnegie Mellon University, USA)*
Leila Takayama *(Google, USA)*
Fumihide Tanaka *(University of Tokyo, Japan)*
Adriana Tapus *(ENSTA-ParisTech, France)*
Greg Trafton *(Naval Research Laboratory, USA)*

Additional reviewers:

Admoni, Henny
Adorno, Bruno
Akiko, Yamazaki
Alissandrakis, Aris
Allen, Colin
Amanda, Sharkey
Andrist, Sean
Argall, Brenna
Argyros, Antonis
Bartneck, Christoph
Bateman, John
Baxter, Paul
Becker-Asano, Christian
Beer, Jenay
Behnke, Sven
Bellotto, Nicola
Bergmann, Kirsten
Berlin, Matt
Bernardino, Alexandre
Birnbaum, Gurit E.
Bodenheimer, Bobby
Briggs, Gordon
Broz, Frank
Burke, Jennifer
Bustos, Pablo
Castellano, Ginevra
Cha, Elizabeth
Chan, Wesley
Chao, Crystal
Chatterjee, Amitava
Chen, Tiffany
Chernova, Sonia
Chetouani, Mohamed
Cho, Kwangsu
Choi, Jung Ju
Chung, Michael Jae-Yoon
Clavel, Celine
Cramer, Henriette
Crandall, Jacob
Crick, Christopher
Crowell, Charles R.
Crumpton, Joseph
Cuijpers, Raymond H.
Dahl, Torbjorn
Dang, Thi-Hai-Ha
Das, Dipankar
de Greeff, Joachim
de Visser, Ewart
Delaunay, Frederic
Destephe, Matthieu
Dias, Jorge
Dong, Shuonan
Dragan, Anca
Duvallet, Felix
Erdemir, Gokhan
Eyssel, Friederike
Feil-Seifer, David
Fincannon, Thomas
Fink, Julia
Flacco, Fabrizzio
Foltz, Anouschka
Foth, Kilian
Fritsch, Jannik
Fussell, Susan
Gartenberg, Dan
Giannopulu, Irini
Giuliani, Manuel
Glas, Dylan
Goodrich, Michael
Griffiths, Sascha
Grollman, Daniel
Gweon, Gahgene
Hafner, Verena
Ham, Jaap
Han, Jeonghye
Hanheide, Marc
Harriott, Caroline
Hart, Justin
Hasler, Beatrice
Hawes, Nick
Hayes, Brad
Hayes, Sean
Heerink, Marcel
Hegel, Frank
Henkel, Zachary
Hiatt, Laura
Hodgins, Jessica
Hooten, Eli
Howard, Ayanna
Huang, Chien-Ming
Hyon, Sang-Ho
Iio, Takamasa

Additional reviewers:

Jensen, Lars Christian
Jirak, Doreen
Johnson, Michelle
Jost, Celine
Jung, Malte
Kamide, Hiroko
Kennedy, James
Kidd, Cory
Kiesler, Sara
Kim, Eun Ho
Kim, Yunkyung
Kirchner, Nathan
Kirsch, Alexandra
Knepper, Ross A.
Knox, W. Bradley
Koay, Kheng Lee
Kolling, Andreas
Komatsu, Takanori
Kopp, Stefan
Kose-Bagci, Hatice
Kuchenbecker, Katherine
Kuchenbrandt, Dieta Kuchenbrandt
Kuzuoka, Hideaki
Lutkebohle, Ingo
Lanir, Joel
Larradet, Fanny
Lee, Jin Joo
Lee, Kyuhwa
Lee, Min Kyung
Leite, Iolanda
Lewis, Michael
Leyzberg, Dan
Lin, Lanny
Lindner, Felix
Liu, Changchun
Lohan, Katrin Solveig
Looije, Rosemarijn
Lopes, Manuel
Lu, David
MacDorman, Karl
Mainprice, Jim
Makatchev, Maxim
Marayong, Panadda
Martin, Jean-Claude
Martinson, Eric
Matuszek, Cynthia
McCann, Eric
McCrae, Patrick
Mead, Ross
Meddeb, Elizabeth
Meisner, Eric
Menegatti, Emanuele
Meyer, Joachim
Michaud, Francois
Minato, Takashi
Mirnig, Nicole
Mistry, Michael
Mitzel, Daniel
Mohammad, Yasser
Moon, AJung
Mower Provost, Emily
Mubin, Omar
Nalin, Marco
Neerincx, Mark
Nehaniv, Chrystopher L.
Nikolaidis, Stefanos
Novak, Domen
Nunnally, Steven
Obaid, Mohammad
Okita, Sandra
Osentoski, Sarah
Otero, Nuno
Perez-D'Arpino, Claudia
Park, Chung Hyuk
Park, Sung-Kee
Peer, Angelika
Petrick, Ron
Pitsch, Karola
Read, Robin
Ribeiro, Tiago
Riek, Laurel D.
Rogers, John
Rosenthal, Stephanie
Sahin, Erol
Salem, Maha
Satake, Satoru
Scassellati, Brian
Schillingmann, Lars
Schultz, Alan
Sen, Sayan
Severinson-Eklundh, Kerstin
Sharlin, Ehud

Additional reviewers:

Shei, Irene
Shi, Chao
Shiomi, Masahiro
Shomin, Michael
Short, Elaine
Sidner, Candace
Simmons, Reid
Sinapov, Jivko
Sklar, Elizabeth
Slyper, Ronit
Smart, Bill
Spalanzani, Anne
Spinello, Luciano
Sreenath, Koushil
srinivasan, vasant
St. Clair, Aaron
Stachniss, Cyrill
Steinfeld, Aaron
Sundar, S. Shyam
Sung, Ja-Young
Syrdal, Dag Sverre
Tellex, Stefanie
Terada, Kazunori
Toris, Russell
Trickett, Susan
Tsui, Katherine
Vazquez, Marynel
Vallance, Michael
Valstar, Michel
Vanderborght, Bram
Verschae, Rodrigo
Vincze, Markus
Vitiello, Nicola
Vollmer, Anna-Lisa
Walker, Erin
Walter, Matthew
Walters, Michael
Weiss, Astrid
Williams, Andrew
Wrede, Britta
Yamane, Katsu
Yanco, Holly
Yohanan, Steve
Yoshikawa, Yuichiro
Young, James
Zeglin, Garth
Ziemke, Tom
Zuckerman, Oren

HRI 2014 Sponsors & Supporters

Sponsors:

SIGCHI

acm SIGART

IEEE

Technical Co-sponsors:

HF ES

aaai

Gold Level Supporter:

ALDEBARAN Robotics

Silver Level Supporters:

Disney Research

Engineered Arts limite

Bronze Level Supporters:

kinova

Shadow Robot Company

Google™

The Technology-Network:
Intelligent Technical Systems OstWestfalenLippe . Germany
it's owl

The MIT Press

Robot Responsiveness to Human Disclosure Affects Social Impression and Appeal

Guy Hoffman*, Gurit E. Birnbaum†,
Keinan Vanunu*†, Omri Sass†
*Media Innovation Lab / School of Communication, †School of Psychology
IDC Herzliya
P.O.B 167, Herzliya 46150, Israel
{hoffman,birnbag,kvanunu,osass}@idc.ac.il

Harry T. Reis
Department of Clinical and Social Sciences in Psychology
University of Rochester
P.O.B 270266, Rochester, NY 14627, USA
reis@psych.rochester.edu

ABSTRACT

In human relationships, *responsiveness*—behaving in a sensitive manner that is supportive of another person's needs—plays a major role in any interaction that involves effective communication, caregiving, and social support. Perceiving one's partner as responsive has been tied to both personal and relationship well-being. In this work, we examine whether and how a robot's behavior can instill a sense of responsiveness, and the effects of a robot's perceived responsiveness on the human's perception of the robot. In an experimental between-subject study (n=34), a desktop non-anthropomorphic robot performed either positive or negative responsiveness behaviors across two modalities (simple gestures and written text) in response to participants' negative event disclosure. We found that perceived partner responsiveness, positive human-like traits, and robot attractiveness were higher in the positively responsive condition. This has design implications for interactive robots, in particular for robots in caregiving roles.

Categories and Subject Descriptors

H.1.2 [**Models and Principles**]: User/Machine Systems; J.4 [**Computer Applications**]: Social and Behavioral Sciences—*psychology*

General Terms

Human-robot interaction; responsiveness; agent impression; affective & emotional responses; Wizard-of-Oz; care robots; socially assistive robotics; modeling social situations.

1. INTRODUCTION

Robots are predicted to serve in a variety of caregiving roles, such as nursing, childcare, education, and elderly care. There, they would operate in personally meaningful relationships vis-a-vis a wide variety of age and social groups, from children, through teenagers, to adults and the elderly. In addition to their functional operation, robots may be required to monitor their human interlocutors, listen to their experiences, and engage in supportive conversation. For example, a robot serving in an elderly care facility might provide support by listening to life experiences of the caretaker.

In such scenarios, the way a robot responds to the human's communication can have a profound effect on a number of personal and interpersonal outcomes, including the human's perception of the robot, the human's sense of support, the human's mental health, the bond between the human and the robot, the human's willingness to continue to confide in the robot, and the human's overall well-being.

A large body of research in the social psychology literature has investigated the relationship outcomes of human responsiveness—behaving in a sensitive manner that is supportive of another person's needs. Responsiveness has been studied in the context of parent-child relationships, adult close relationships, and therapeutic relationships, as well as in educational, organizational, and healthcare settings. Responsiveness has been shown to play a key role in the provision of caregiving and social support and to be associated with personal and relational well-being [4, 17, 20, 21].

We were interested how some of these findings might carry over to a robot behaving, or not behaving, in a responsive manner to a human's personal event disclosure. We focused on negative event disclosure, because it constitutes a prototypical responsiveness scenario that calls for distress regulation and elicits proximity seeking.

To approach this question, we evaluated whether and how a desktop-scale non-anthropomorphic robot could appear responsive, using simple gestures such as nodding or looking away, in combination with written text associated with the robot, and how this affects the human interlocutor's sense of the robot's character traits and attractiveness.

1.1 Robots in Caregiving Roles

One of the main drivers of personal robotics research is the prospect of using robots in caregiving roles, such as elderly care, health and nursing care, and childcare. A specific class of care robots is denoted as "socially assistive" [6], when in addition to the functional requirements, the robotic agent includes a socially communicative aspect.

Socially assistive robots have been widely researched in the elderly care sub-field of HRI [7]. One example is Paro, a robotic seal designed to be held and touched, which has been

HRI'14, March 3–6, 2014, Bielefeld, Germany.

http://dx.doi.org/10.1145/2559636.2559660.

shown to have positive effects on patients with dementia [30]. Another is USC's humanoid, which showed promising results in therapy for elderly with cognitive impairments, through a musical game [28].

In the healthcare field, a humanoid robot was used in a longitudinal study of children with autism [24]; robotic dogs have been explored in the field of animal-assisted therapy to treat loneliness and depression [1]; and socially assistive robots were used to treat stroke survivors [5].

Robots are also developed for childcare roles, as teachers, learners, and companions. For example, Tanaka studied robots in classrooms as learners, with the intent that students would learn better by teaching the robot [27]. Kanda's work shows that a robot could foster social interaction among elementary school children [14].

We argue that in all of these care roles, robots will need to be psychologically sensitive to their care-receivers and behave in a manner that is supportive of their needs.

1.2 Responsiveness in Human Relationships

Social psychology has long acknowledged the importance of "Perceived Partner Responsiveness" (PPR) for individual well-being and for relationship intimacy. PPR is conceptualized as the "belief that a relationship partner understands, values, and supports important aspects of the self" [3]. Often, PPR is evaluated in the context of disclosure, where one of the conversation partners recounts an event that is important to him or her, and the listening partner responds to this self-disclosure.

PPR has important outcomes for dyadic relationships. It is the linchpin of the development of intimate relationships, and as such, it promotes personal and interpersonal well-being in close relationships. Moreover, PPR has been tied to a large number of other positive outcomes, including mortality, morbidity, happiness, emotional distress, psychological development, and economic success [20].

PPR also plays a crucial role in many relational processes outside of the realm of romantic or couple relationships. For example, perceived parental responsiveness encourages cooperative and exploratory behaviors and is associated with social skills, parent-child relationship quality, and levels of motivation and academic achievement [17]. PPR of physicians towards their patients has been found to positively affect subjective health status in the patient [20]. These findings are particularly interesting to designers of companion robots in the educational, health, and elderly care areas.

Furthermore, PPR has beneficial effects on emotional expression and other emotional outcomes. For example, it has been shown to positively affect self-regulation, which is an important executive function, and has been related to the setting of goals and pursuing them [20].

1.2.1 Responsiveness to Negative Event Disclosures

An established way to study PPR in a lab environment is by using a responsiveness to disclosure protocol. Maisel *et al.* studied responsiveness by asking established romantic couples to discuss personal positive and negative events. Then, they developed a coding guide that assessed responsive behaviors in various interpersonal situations and related PPR to behavioral measures (e.g., expressing empathy, reassurance, providing support) and subjective sense of self-esteem [19].

In another series of three studies, Birnbaum and Reis had couples of opposite-sex strangers interact, and then they related reported PPR to sexual attraction [3]. In the first study, they examined the association between perceived partner responsiveness and sexual attraction in randomly paired strangers. Then, in the second study, the researchers set up an experimental procedure, where they had participants believe that they interacted via textual chat with conversation partners in a different room, whereas they really were chatting with a confederate, in either a positive or a negative responsiveness condition. In this case, they used only negative event disclosure. Given that the second study did not include any nonverbal behavior, a third study replicated the above procedure, but instead of text chat, it employed a face-to-face interview methodology. Results indicated that perceiving a partner as responsive was associated with heightened sexual attraction toward this partner, primarily among men and among less avoidant participants.

The current study is based on the above studies, using the same protocol for negative event disclosure. However, because this is a human-robot conversation, we expand the scope of the previously investigated scenarios by combining face-to-face (the human and the robot are in the same room) with nonverbal behavior (the robot gestures and moves), with mediated communication (a robot is by definition a medium), with textual chat (the robot's response is conveyed not through speech, but through textual chat).

1.2.2 Perceived Responsiveness and Attraction

The studies reported above primarily evaluate the impact of PPR on sexual attraction. In the robot case, however, we were interested in a more general notion of attraction and impression of the agent, especially because the robot was not a potential romantic partner for the disclosers. We therefore evaluated attraction in a more general sense and combined this metric with measures that assessed people's impression of the robot's positive character traits.

2. HOW CAN A ROBOT BE RESPONSIVE?

Human responsiveness research has extensively investigated what behaviors instill a sense of responsiveness in conversation partners. But can a robot also behave in a way that will make it seem responsive to the human?

To answer this question, we look at three components of responsiveness behaviors examined by Maisel *et al.*: understanding, validation, and caring [19]. They based this on Reis and Patrick's theoretical model of responsiveness [22]. *Understanding* includes "active listening", showing attention, interest in the conversation, and understanding of the discloser's words. *Validation* is aimed to make the conversation partner feel respected and to reinforce their self-views. This includes behaviors that acknowledge the significance of the events described. *Caring* includes expressions of love, care about the other's well-being, and showing a joint stake in the issues discussed.

Each of these components of responsiveness behavior could be translated into the human-robot domain; Some of them are sophisticated and require complex AI, but others can be readily implemented on a conversational robot with state-of-the-art technology. A robot can, for example, direct its gaze, nod, and summarize human speech to display understanding, or touch a human gently to show caring. In Table 1 we tried to list possible behaviors a robot could display for the different components of Reis's model of responsiveness.

Table 1: Three components of responsiveness behaviors implementable by robots conversing with humans

Responsiveness component	Behavioral elements adaptable for robot behavior
Understanding	Nodding; backchannel signals; directing gaze attention; summarizing human speech
Validation	Relating events to the resulting feelings; affirming discloser's positive traits
Caring	Affective touch; affirming emotional caring verbally

That said, there are also challenges that arise when we consider the possibility of a robot being perceived as responsive: Humans' expectations of other humans' appropriate behavior might not translate to a robot listening to a human's disclosure; the relationship context (e.g., strangers, peers, partners) might not be as clear in a human-robot dyad as in the human-human case; human nonverbal behavior is tied to a common biological morphology, making it predictably interpreted by a human conspecific, while robotic morphologies are more varied; and finally, being a machine, a robot might never be perceived as positively or negatively responsive, because this could be a human-specific relation.

Thus, it is not clear whether it is possible for a robot to be responsive, and what behaviors would be perceived as responsive. All this before even asking about downstream outcomes of robot responsiveness.

2.1 Robots Listening to Humans

Several HRI research projects have been concerned with robots listening to humans, and how the robot's behavior affects the interaction. Kobayashi *et al.* tackle the analysis of human speech with the intention of the robot providing active listening [8, 15]. The latter paper, in particular, highlights the difficulty of accurately providing responsiveness behaviors of the "understanding" kind.

Research in robots listening to children has shown that children were as likely to share a secret with a robot as with a human, when these use a similar amount of prompting [2]. Similarly, it was demonstrated that 7 to 9 year olds respond very similarly to a robot interviewer as they would to a human interviewer [31]. In another study, researchers have implemented empathy behaviors in a persuasive setting with both robots and virtual characters [18], including a methodological implementation of techniques drawn from the client-therapist literature.

Our work extends the literature of attentive robots by providing the first systematic investigation into the notion of robot responsiveness, proposing possibilities for designing responsive behaviors in non-anthropomorphic robots, and investigating how perceived robot responsiveness relates to personal event disclosure.

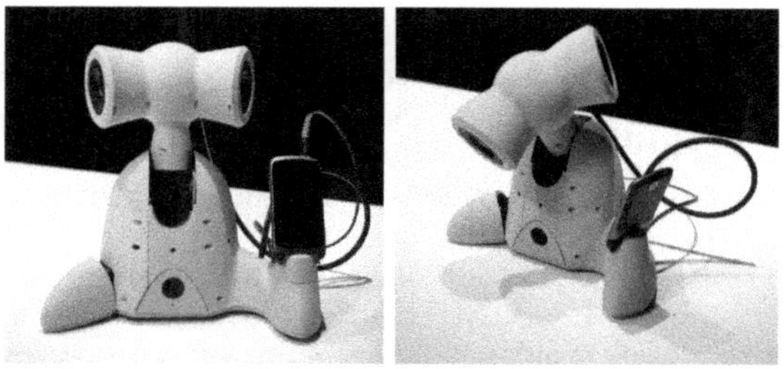

Figure 1: Travis, the robot used in the experiments. Left: in an attentive position; right: in a distracted position, looking at its mobile phone.

2.2 Designing Robot Responsiveness

The responsiveness behaviors in our study were implemented on a non-anthropomorphic desktop robot (Fig 1). We have long been interested in in the social capabilities of simple low-DoF robots with no apparent human-like features [12, 10], as these robots best model commercially plausible machines, with near-term potential for real-world availability. Non-anthropomorphic robots have been shown to be socially and emotionally expressive and readable in a number of HRI studies [16, 25]. But can a robot with minimal DoFs, no face, and no human shape fulfill a socially sensitive function such as responsiveness to human disclosure?

In our attempt to design responsiveness, we combined two modalities: nonverbal gestures and textual responses. The nonverbal channel mostly corresponds with the "Understanding" component of responsiveness in Table 1. The textual modality corresponded to the "Validation" component. We did not attempt supporting "Caring" as a responsiveness component in this study, although people may perceive the robot as caring, because they may interpret his gestures and verbal reactions as expressions of intimacy.

We tried to keep the nonverbal modality to a minimum. To display positive responsiveness, we had the robot maintain a forward focus towards the human, gently sway to display animacy, and implemented short affirmative nods in response to human speech. In the negative case, the robot's would show decreased animacy, no confirmation gestures, and occasional distraction behaviors, in the form of looking away from the human conversation partner (Fig 1, right).

On the verbal channel, we used positively and negatively responsive speech acts, following a previously established protocol of human responsiveness to negative event disclosure [3]. Our responsiveness behaviors are detailed in Section 5.1 and in Table 2.

We found in a pretest, that several participants perceived any movement of the robot as responsive. This could be because the robot did not have a face or eyes, or perhaps because even the robot's sideways gaze could be interpreted as a "lending an ear" gesture. These findings also emphasize the difficulty of designing nonverbal responsiveness behaviors for low-DoF non-anthropomorphic robots.

3. RESEARCH QUESTIONS

To summarize, in this study, we were interested whether the notion of responsiveness carries over from the human-human to the human-robot domain; whether it is possible for an abstract non-anthropomorphic robot to be responsive; how that robot's responsiveness would affect people's impression of the robot; and whether known outcomes from human responsiveness also occur with robot responsiveness.

3.1 Hypotheses

To evaluate the above, we tested the following hypotheses:

Hypothesis 1 (Perceived Partner Responsiveness) — A robot performing positive responsive behaviors to negative event disclosure would be perceived as more responsive on the PPR scale by the disclosing human than a robot displaying negative responsive behaviors.

Hypothesis 2 (Impression of Agent) — A robot performing positive responsive behaviors to negative event disclosure would cause the disclosing human to attach more positive character traits to the robot than a robot displaying negative responsive behaviors.

Hypothesis 2a (Social Perception) — A robot performing positive responsive behaviors to negative event disclosure would be perceived as more social than a robot displaying negative responsive behaviors. Namely, the robot would be perceived as more cooperative, warm, and friendly.

Hypothesis 2b (Competence Perception) — A robot performing positive responsive behaviors to negative event disclosure would be perceived as more competent than a robot displaying negative responsive behaviors. Namely, the robot would be perceived as more intelligent, reliable, and knowledgeable.

Hypothesis 3 (Attraction) — A robot performing positive responsive behaviors to negative event disclosure would be more attractive to the disclosing human than a robot displaying negative responsive behaviors.

To estimate these variables, we manipulated the robot's behavior in two conditions: positive responsiveness and negative responsiveness, and conducted a Wizard-of-Oz between subject experimental study.

4. ROBOTIC PLATFORM

We used the robot *Travis* [10, 13], a research platform we developed to examine HRI as it relates to nonverbal behavior, timing, and physical presence (Fig 1). Travis is a small non-anthropomorphic robot with a vaguely creature-like structure, but without a face. The robot stands about 28cm tall, sized so that, when placed on a desk, its head is roughly in line with a seated person's head in front of it. The robot is capable of basic gesturing, using five degrees-of-freedom. Three DoFs are in the head, one in the "hand" holding the phone, and one in the foot.

All the robot's software runs on an Android smartphone, communicating positions and velocities to an ADK board, which then bridges those to the motors. A detailed description of the robot's design, hardware, and software modules is provided in a separate publication [10].

Part of the robot's design is that it "holds" the smartphone which runs it, allowing for the device to serve as an object of common ground and joint attention [11] between the human and the robot. Importantly for this experiment, this design enabled us to have the robot look at the phone as a non-responsive behavior indicating distraction or boredom.

To eliminate the possibility for estrangement associated with a robotic voice, we opted for the robot to display the text it "says" on a small screen leaning against the robot's body, instead of using audible speech. This screen was completely black except when the robot presented text. Then, a single sentence appeared on the screen for five seconds, before disappearing. We pre-tested the duration of the text display and found it adequate to read all the sentences that were part of the experimental protocol.

4.1 Wizard-of-Oz Setup

In this experiment, the robot was controlled remotely in a Wizard-of-Oz (WoZ) setup [23].We use WoZ here in place of automated speech recognition. While in our case, speech detection and recognition could have been acceptable to time and select the required gestures, and the gestures we used were simple and fixed, we did not want to risk "breaking the fourth wall" (revealing the WoZ deception) while participants were opening up about personally meaningful life events.

The setup had three main control components networked through a wireless network. In the control room, a PC was running a graphical user interface, which sent commands to the smartphone controlling the robot, and the tablet displaying the text the robot produced. The commands were sent in form of pre-programmed gestures to the phone, which ran a behavior system that arbitrated the gestures with the robot's breathing behavior, and translated them into timed motor commands (see: [13]). The robot's responses were sent as text strings to the tablet for display.

In addition to the control software, two cameras were monitoring the control room for the experimenter to be able to time the robot's behaviors to the participant's speech acts.

The control software included two parts: on top there were buttons enabling the experimenter to remotely select behaviors for the robot. At the bottom part of the screen, there was a free-text field, allowing the experimenter to type in responses that would appear on the robot's output screen. A history of ten phrases was kept for quick recall.

5. METHOD

We conducted a controlled laboratory experiment, in which participants were asked to disclose a personally negative event to the robot in front of them. The participants were told that we were testing a new speech understanding algorithm, and that the robot would try to respond to their story as best it could. The robot then behaved with either positive or negative responsiveness. We then had participants evaluate the robot's behavior.

5.1 Design

The robot's behavior was controlled by an experienced operator familiar with the research and the experimental protocol. We made an effort to keep the behaviors as constant as possible within conditions, by closely following a textual protocol, and fixed gestures. However, this had to be balanced with actually responding to the content of the discloser's story. For the textual responses, we adhered to an established protocol used for responsiveness behavior in online chat [3]. The wizard operator selected a single text response at the end of each paragraph from a bank of preset phrases, and only adjusted the phrases slightly to fit the context, if necessary. The same behaviors were used consistently, approximately three times per interaction, and roughly at the same time points in the disclosure.

We manipulated one between-subject variable, the robot's level of responsiveness, based on the behaviors described in Section 2.2. In the *POSITIVE* condition, the robot swayed gently forward and backward, and acknowledged the speaker's end-of-speech with either a single nod, or a double nod. In the *NEGATIVE* condition, the robot swayed, but with a smaller amplitude, and occasionally glanced at the smartphone in its hand, or at the wall clock hanging on the wall between the participants and the robot. In the *POSITIVE* condition, the robot displayed supportive text responses. In the *NEGATIVE* condition, the robot displayed slightly dismissive text responses. Table 2 summarizes the difference in behavior between the two conditions, including samples from the text response repertoire.

Table 2: Responsiveness behaviors used in the current experiment

Cond	Gestures	Speech act samples
POS	Nodding; deep sway	"You must have gone through a very difficult time"; "I completely understand what you've been through"
NEG	Glance at phone / clock; shallow sway	"That doesn't sound so bad to me"; "Are you sure that's the worst thing you can think of?"

After the participants were done, a questionnaire measured the participant's overall perceived robot responsiveness, their impression of the robot's positive human-like characteristics, and the participants' attraction to the robot.

Through video recording, we captured the participant's physical reaction to the experience. These recordings were not used in the currently presented results.

5.2 Participants

A total of 36 (21 female) undergraduate students participated in the experiment. The participants were students from a university in central Israel, and all communication was done in Hebrew. Participants were recruited from several departments voluntarily, or in return for class credit. Participants ranged from 21 to 27 ($M = 24.11$, $SD = 1.53$).

No significant differences were found between the experimental conditions for any of the sociodemographic variables we measured (age, gender, marital status, and past experience with robots or with artificial intelligence).

5.3 Procedure

The experiment was conducted in two experiment rooms with controlled lighting, no windows, and no outside distractions. Upon arrival, each participant was welcomed into the first room, where the experimenter explained the initial experimental guidelines. Each participant filled an informed consent form, and the demographic questionnaire. Next, participants were guided to the adjacent room, were asked to sit on the couch, facing the robot, and received a detailed explanation regarding the remainder of the experiment (Fig 2). The robot was raised from the table by circa 20cm, to make its head level with the seated human's head.

Based on [3], each participant was asked to "choose some current problem, concern, or stressor [they] are facing", such as "a recent argument with a friend or a family member, a grade in class, work or financial problems, or personal illness". They were told that the robot would try to understand what they say and respond with a relevant response, using artificial intelligence and speech recognition.

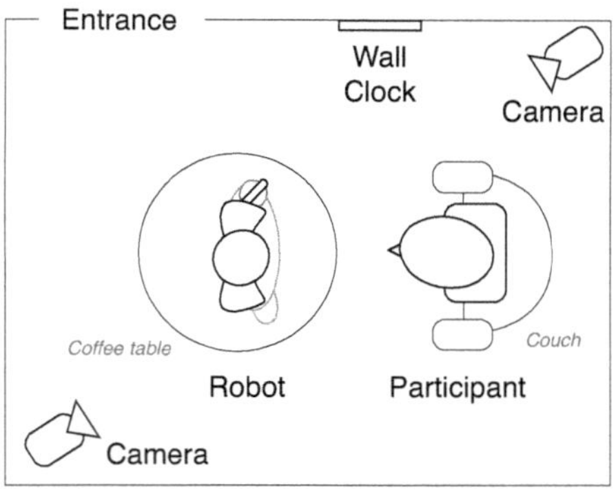

Figure 2: Experimental room layout diagram. The robot's head height is roughly in line with the seated human's eyes.

The participants were asked to divide the message into three "paragraphs": (a) the facts of the event; (b) the emotions and thoughts that arose in them during the event; and (c) the implications of the event on their life afterwards. At the end of each paragraph, participants were asked to use the statement "and that's it", which, according to the cover story, would signal to the robot that the part is done and that speech recognition can begin. This served two goals: The first was to make the robotic cover story more reliable in terms of its speech processing. The second was to provide more time for the experimenter to form a reply and choose a gesture. After indicating that he or she understood these instructions, the participant was left alone in the room to interact with the robot.

Upon completion of the interaction stage, the experimenter re-entered the room, and asked the participant to fill out the post-procedure questionnaires. Then, participants were interviewed by the experimenter, and were asked three open-ended questions about their experience ("How was the experience?", "What did it make you feel?", and "How did you interpret the robot's behavior?").

Participants were then fully debriefed, and were told that the robot was controlled by the experimenter. We made sure, especially in the negative responsiveness condition, that they felt good about their participation in the study before concluding the experiment.

6. MEASURES

All measures are on a 7-point Likert scale (from "strongly disagree" to "strongly agree").

6.1 Perceived Partner Responsiveness

We estimated the PPR of the robot using a composite instrument adapted from Birnbaum and Reis [3]. The scale has been validated and found reliable in prior studies. The current version used assessed perceptions of how understood, validated, and cared for the discloser felt when interacting with the robot. Participants rated nine statements, such as "The robot was aware of what I am thinking and feeling" or "The robot really listened to me." This scale is factorally unidimensional and internally consistent in our sample as well (Cronbach's $\alpha = .92$).

6.2 Impression of Agent

Participants rated their impression of the robotic agent on a composite measure of ten items indicating positive character traits, including the robot's perceived friendliness, intelligence, confidence, warmth, cooperativeness, and sociability. This measure was validated and found reliable in previous studies [26, 9, 13], Cronbach's α was good for this scale (.83).

6.2.1 *Social Perception*

Social perception of the robot is as a sub-scale of the "Impression of Agent" scale, and consists of the four items that measured social aspects of the robot's traits (friendliness, cooperativeness, sociability, and warmth). Cronbach's α for this measure was good (.88).

6.2.2 *Competence Perception*

Competence perception of the robot is a complementary sub-scale of the "Impression of Agent" scale, consisting of five items that measure competence aspects of the robot's traits (intelligence, capability, reliability, knowledgeability, and sensibility). Cronbach's α for this measure was acceptable (.72).

6.3 Attraction to Robot

Responsiveness is known to affect attraction in human relationships. To assess whether similar social mechanisms come into play between humans and robots we implemented an attraction to robot measurement, which measured how attractive participants perceived the robot to be. This measure composite was a seven-item scale, and consisted of items such as "How attractive is the robot?", and "How sophisticated is the robot?". One item was excluded from the measure due to inadequate correlation levels. Cronbach's α for the remaining measure was found to be good (.81).

7. RESULTS

Participants were randomly assigned to interact with either a positively or a negatively responsive robot. Two participants were switched over from the negative to the positive responsiveness condition mid-way, due to the sensitive nature of their disclosed experience, and were excluded from further analysis.

Manipulation check. An independent means t-test on perceived partner responsiveness (PPR) yielded a significant effect, $t(32)$=2.79, $p < .01$. Perceived partner responsiveness was higher in the positively responsive robot condition (M = 3.13, SD = 1.09) than in the negatively responsive robot condition ($M = 2.24$, $SD = .69$).

Impression of Agent An independent means t-test on the impression of agent scale yielded significant results, $t(32) = 3.82, p < .01$. The robot was rated higher in the positively responsive condition (M = 5.01, SD = .92), than in the negatively responsive condition ($M = 3.91$, $SD = .71$).

Social Perception An independent means t-test for the social perception sub-scale yielded significant results, $t(32) = 6.08, p < .001$. Participants in the positive response condition ($M = 5.72$, $SD = .72$) rated the robot more positively regarding social traits, as compared to participants in the negative response condition ($M = 3.72$, $SD = 1.17$).

Competence Perception An independent means t-test for the competence perception sub-scale yielded no significant differences between the conditions $t(32) = 1.29$, ns.

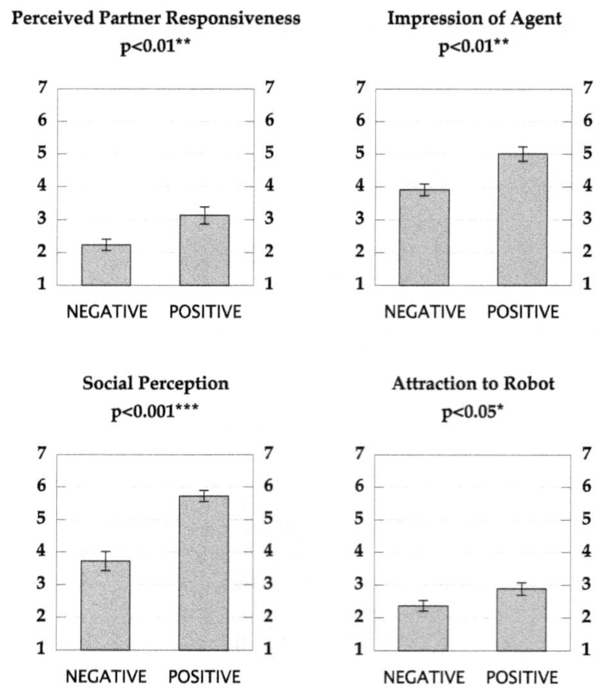

Figure 3: Perceived Partner Responsiveness, Impression of Agent, Social Perception, and Attraction to Robot by condition. Error bars denote standard errors from mean.

Attraction to Robot An independent means t-test for attraction to the robot yielded significant results, $t(32) = 2.06, p < .05$. It was perceived as more attractive when it was positively responsive ($M = 2.89$, $SD = .80$), than when it was negatively responsive ($M = 2.37$, $SD = .66$).

8. DISCUSSION

Our results show support for Hypothesis 1: A robot using positive responsiveness behaviors to negative event disclosure is perceived as more responsive by the human than a robot showing negative behaviors. We can say that our design for responsiveness was effective: Nodding and affirmative texts caused a significant increase in a validated PPR scale when compared to distraction behavior and slightly dismissive text. Indeed the levels and effect sizes we measured with perceived robot responsiveness were on par with those found in perceived human responsiveness. We thus show that PPR can transfer from human-human to human-robot interacting using extremely simple cues from a non-anthropomorphic robot, laying out promising design implications for robotic companions.

Hypothesis 2 was also supported: Positive responsiveness causes people to evaluate the robot's character traits higher than when the robot behaves with negative responsiveness. This relates to our previous findings which show that a joint experience can cause higher impression of the robot [13], adding responsiveness to the robotic behaviors that can positively impact this scale.

Out of the overall agent impression, social perception was significantly affected by the robot's responsiveness (Hypothesis 2a), but the robot's competence impression (Hypothesis

2b) was not. This indicates that responsiveness does not make the robot more positively evaluated across all traits, but that it is specifically related to the social aspects of its perceived character. People found the negatively responsive robot as competent as the positively responsive one. This finding partially rules out a sentiment override (i.e., global, nonspecific positivity or negativity) explanation.

When looking at the robot's desirability, we find support for Hypothesis 3. People find the responsive robot more attractive than the non-responsive one, albeit with a small effect size. Increased desirability or attraction could have implications on the robot's value to people, including monitory value, perhaps their willingness to interact with the robot, and the amount of time people would want to spend with it. These outcomes have implications for long-term human-robot relationships with caregiving robots.

These results were elicited with a minimal set of behaviors, using a simple non-anthropomorphic robot with no face and no audible speech. Indeed, all of the behaviors we used can be easily programmed into a social robotic system, and the robot we used is a commercially feasible device, lending the results near-term practical implications.

Our study, however, raises the question: Why even examine a negatively responsive robot? Clearly, no robot developer would want to program negatively responsive behaviors into a robot, especially one intended for caregiving roles. The response to this question is threefold: While it may be true that we do not want to design robots that are negatively responsive, we do want to determine whether or not humans perceive robots in the same manner as human partners in conversation. In order to understand the effects of a robot's responsiveness, we need to compare different kinds of responsive behavior.

Second, the kind of negative responsiveness displayed in our study is by no means different from what many consider appropriate behavior. Our negative manipulation was not extreme, but more of a cold shoulder, similar to how people intuitively respond to negative event disclosures. Trying to encourage people by telling them that one "doesn't need to take it so badly" is often considered a helpful response. Finally, a robot might need to look away from the user for practical purposes, making it worthwhile to understand the effects this behavior may have on a disclosing individual.

The use of robots listening to humans and displaying appropriate responsiveness behavior can be particularly important in scenarios in which a person cannot, or will not, talk to another human. Specifically, a person's situation could be so sensitive that they prefer to confide in a machine rather than a human. As Turkle points out, people's trust when confiding in a machine does not necessarily "speak to what they thought [the computer] would understand but to their lack of trust in the people who would understand." [29]. There are many populations (e.g., children who suffered abuse, hospitalized, isolated or confined people) who would perhaps prefer to disclose to a robot with limited understanding of the conversation's content, but which can evoke the appropriate sense of responsiveness necessary to support their disclosure in a positive way.

9. CONCLUSION AND FUTURE WORK

In this study we examined the notion of perceived partner responsiveness (PPR) of a robot to a human's negative event disclosure. PPR, the sense that one's partner is supportive of one's needs, is a central concept in human relationships, with positive effects on relationship and personal well-being. As such it is a crucial concept to design for when building robots for caregiving roles.

Our study demonstrates that even using a desktop-size non-anthropomorphic robot with abstract geometric components and no facial features or audible speech, we can design simple behaviors that significantly induce more PPR, at levels comparable with perceived human responsiveness measured in a similar context.

In addition to demonstrating robot PPR, we also showed significant outcomes of the robot's behavior on the agent's perceived positive human-like character traits, and in particular on the social subset of these traits. We also found a significant, if small, effect on the human's attraction to the robot as rated by a validated attraction scale.

In future work, we would like to tease out the relative contribution of the robot's textual responsiveness and the PPR induced by its gestures. In addition, we would like to look at a more varied demographic, as well as at age effects, in particular with robots for elderly care in mind.

Individual differences in personality (such as attachment style) have been shown to mediate PPR effects. We would like to evaluate these in the context of robotic PPR as well.

One limitation of this work was the absence of a neutral responsiveness control condition, in which the robot does not engage in any nonverbal behavior, and does not comment verbally beyond asking the participant to continue to the next paragraph. In our follow-up study, currently underway, we have included such a neutral condition in addition to the two conditions described above.

This work also only looked at responsiveness to negative event disclosure in a laboratory setting. It makes sense to study responsiveness in other contexts, for example positive event disclosure, health-care relationship, and in educational settings. Of course, effects of responsiveness in long-term human-robot relations, and the resulting effects on people's well-being, are an ambitious further step.

Finally, here we only evaluated self-report metrics. We would like to study behavioral outcomes of robot PPR. Does robotic PPR encourage more human disclosure, or reciprocating responsiveness by the human towards the robot?

Nonetheless, this is an important onset to understanding the notion of robot responsiveness to humans, which can inform the design of robots for healthcare, elderly care, education, and other personally meaningful human-robot relationships.

Acknowledgment

This research was supported by FP7 Marie Curie CIG #293733, and Binational Science Foundation Grant #2011381.

10. REFERENCES

[1] M. R. Banks, L. M. Willoughby, and W. A. Banks. Animal-assisted therapy and loneliness in nursing homes: use of robotic versus living dogs. *Journal of the American Medical Directors Association*, 9(3):173–177, 2008.

[2] C. L. Bethel, M. R. Stevenson, and B. Scassellati. Secret-sharing: Interactions between a child, robot, and adult. In *2011 IEEE Int'l Conf on Systems, Man, and Cybernetics*, pages 2489–2494. Ieee, Oct. 2011.

[3] G. E. Birnbaum and H. T. Reis. When does responsiveness pique sexual interest? Attachment and sexual desire in initial acquaintanceships. *Personality & Social Psychology Bulletin*, 38(7):946–58, July 2012.

[4] M. S. Clark and E. P. J. Lemay. Close relationships. In S. T. Fiske, D. T. Gilbert, and G. Lindzey, editors, *Handbook of social psychology*, pages 898–940. Wiley, New York, 5 vol 2 edition, 2010.

[5] J. Fasola and M. J. Mataric. Using socially assistive human–robot interaction to motivate physical exercise for older adults. *Proceedings of the IEEE*, 100(8):2512–2526, 2012.

[6] D. Feil-Seifer and M. Mataric. Socially Assistive Robotics. *IEEE Robotics & Automation Magazine*, 18(1):24–31, Mar. 2011.

[7] J. Forlizzi. Robotic products to assist the aging population. *interactions*, 12(2):16, Mar. 2005.

[8] S. Fujie, K. Fukushima, and T. Kobayashi. A conversation robot with back-channel feedback function based on linguistic and nonlinguistic information. In *Proc. ICARA Int. Conference on Autonomous Robots and Agents*, pages 379–384, 2004.

[9] R. E. Guadagno and R. B. Cialdini. Online persuasion: An examination of gender differences in computer-mediated interpersonal influence. *Group Dynamics: Theory, Research, and Practice*, 6(1):38–51, 2002.

[10] G. Hoffman. Dumb Robots , Smart Phones : a Case Study of Music Listening Companionship. In *RO-MAN 2012 - The IEEE Int'l Symposium on Robot and Human Interactive Communication*, 2012.

[11] G. Hoffman and C. Breazeal. Collaboration in Human-Robot Teams. In *Proc. of the AIAA 1st Intelligent Systems Technical Conference*, Chicago, IL, USA, Sept. 2004. AIAA.

[12] G. Hoffman, R. R. Kubat, and C. Breazeal. A hybrid control system for puppeterring a live robotic stage actor. In *Proceedings of the17th IEEE International Symposium on Robot and Human Interactive Communication (RO-MAN 2008)*, 2008.

[13] G. Hoffman and K. Vanunu. Effects of robotic companionship on music enjoyment and agent perception. In *Proceedings of the 8th ACM/IEEE international conference on Human-robot interaction (HRI)*, 2013.

[14] T. Kanda, H. Ishiguro, M. Imai, and T. Ono. Body Movement Analysis of Human-Robot Interaction. In *Proceedings of theIJCAI-03, Eighteenth International Joint Conference on Artificial Intelligence*, pages 177–182, Acapulco, Mexico, Aug. 2003.

[15] Y. Kobayashi, D. Yamamoto, T. Koga, S. Yokoyama, and Others. Design targeting voice interface robot capable of active listening. In *Human-Robot Interaction (HRI), 2010 5th ACM/IEEE International Conference on*, pages 161–162. IEEE, 2010.

[16] H. Kozima, M. P. Michalowski, and C. Nakagawa. Keepon: A playful robot for research, therapy, and entertainment. *International Journal of Social Robotics*, 1(1):3–18, Nov. 2009.

[17] S. H. Landry, K. E. Smith, and P. R. Swank. Responsive parenting: Establishing early foundations for social, communication, and independent problem-solving skills. *Developmental Psychology*, 42(627–642), 2006.

[18] R. Looije, M. A. Neerincx, and F. Cnossen. Persuasive robotic assistant for health self-management of older adults : Design and evaluation of social behaviors. *Journal of Human Computer Studies*, 68(6):386–397, 2010.

[19] N. C. Maisel, S. L. Gable, and A. Strachman. Responsive behaviors in good times and in bad. *Personal Relationships*, 15(3):317–338, Sept. 2008.

[20] H. T. Reis. Steps toward the ripening of relationship science. *Personal Relationships*, 14(1):1–23, Mar. 2007.

[21] H. T. Reis. Perceived partner responsiveness as an organizing theme for the study of relationships and well-being. In L. Campbell and T. J. Loving, editors, *Interdisciplinary research on close relationships: The case for integration*, pages 27–52. American Psychological Association, US, 2012.

[22] H. T. Reis and B. C. Patrick. Attachment and intimacy: component processes. 1996.

[23] L. D. Riek. Wizard of oz studies in hri: a systematic review and new reporting guidelines. *Journal of Human-Robot Interaction*, 1(1), 2012.

[24] B. Robins, K. Dautenhahn, R. Te Boekhorst, and A. Billard. Robotic assistants in therapy and education of children with autism: Can a small humanoid robot help encourage social interaction skills? *Universal Access in the Information Society*, 4(2):105–120, 2005.

[25] M. Sharma, D. Hildebrandt, G. Newman, J. E. Young, and R. Eskicioglu. Communicating affect via flight path Exploring use of the Laban Effort System for designing affective locomotion paths. In *Human-Robot Interaction (HRI), 2013 8th ACM/IEEE International Conference on*, pages 293–300. IEEE, 2013.

[26] M. Slater, A. Sadagic, M. Usoh, and R. Schroeder. Small Group Behaviour in a Virtual and Real Environment : A Comparative Study. *PRESENCE: Teleoperators & Virtual Environments*, 9:37–51, 2000.

[27] F. Tanaka and M. Ghosh. The implementation of care-receiving robot at an English learning school for children. In *Human-Robot Interaction (HRI), 2011 6th ACM/IEEE International Conference on*, pages 265–266. IEEE, 2011.

[28] A. Tapus, C. Tapus, and M. J. Mataric. The use of socially assistive robots in the design of intelligent cognitive therapies for people with dementia. In *Rehabilitation Robotics, 2009. ICORR 2009. IEEE International Conference on*, pages 924–929. IEEE, Ieee, June 2009.

[29] S. Turkle. Authenticity in the age of digital companions. *Interaction Studies*, 2007.

[30] K. Wada, T. Shibata, T. Musha, and S. Kimura. Robot therapy for elders affected by dementia. *IEEE Engineering in Medicine and Biology Magazine*, 27(4):53–60, 2008.

[31] L. J. Wood, K. Dautenhahn, H. Lehmann, B. Robins, A. Rainer, and D. S. Syrdal. Robot-Mediated Interviews: Does a Robotic Interviewer Impact Question Difficulty and Information Recovery? *Assistive Technology: From Research to Practice: AAATE 2013*, 33:131, 2013.

Would You Like to Play with Me? How Robots' Group Membership and Task Features Influence Human–Robot Interaction

Markus Häring
Human Centered Multimedia
Institute for Computer Science
Augsburg University, Germany
haering@hcm-lab.de

Dieta Kuchenbrandt*
Center of Excellence in
Cognitive Interaction
Technology (CITEC)
Bielefeld
Germany
dkuchenb@cit-ec.uni-bielefeld.de

Elisabeth André
Human Centered Multimedia
Institute for Computer Science
Augsburg University, Germany
andre@hcm-lab.de

ABSTRACT

In the present experiment, we investigated how robots' social category membership and characteristics of an HRI task affect humans' evaluative and behavioral reactions toward robots. Participants ($N = 38$) played a card game together with two robots, one belonging to participants' social in-group and the other one being a social out-group member. Furthermore, participants were either asked to cooperate with the in- and to compete with the out-group robot (congruent condition), or they were asked to cooperate with the out-group robot while competing with the in-group robot (incongruent condition). The results largely support our hypotheses: Participants showed more positive evaluative reactions toward the in-group (vs. the out-group) robot and they anthropomorphized it more strongly, independent of the congruency or incongruence of the HRI. Moreover, if required, participants cooperated with both the in- and the out-group robot, whereas their cooperativeness was more pronounced toward the in-group robot. Finally, participants indicated more difficulties with the HRI in the incongruent vs. the congruent condition. The theoretical and practical implications of the findings are discussed.

1. INTRODUCTION

Nowadays robots are more and more deployed as (semi-) autonomous tools or servants, for instance, in manufacturing, search-and-rescue scenarios, or in the military (e.g., [11, 2, 26]. For the near future, however, scientists and developers envision robots in more socially interactive contexts such as assisting humans in their daily household chores or serving as co-workers and team partners in a work environment (e.g., [24]). However, how do humans react to and interact with socially active robots? Which factors determine whether humans are willing to accept a robot's assistance or to work together with a robot team partner? With the present research we aim to provide some more insights into these still open research questions. More specifically, we wanted to investigate the effects of a robot's social group membership and task features on human–robot interactions (HRI) and humans' perceptions of social robots.

*The first and second author contributed equally to the presented work and the manuscript. The authors therefore share the first authorship.

HRI'14, March 3–6, 2014, Bielefeld, Germany.

ACM 978-1-4503-2658-2/14/03...$15.00.
http://dx.doi.org/10.1145/2559636.2559673.

2. RELATED WORK

How humans perceive social robots and how they interact with these non-human agents is a crucial question in HRI research. In the context of human-computer interaction, Reeves and Nass [21] observed that humans tend to treat computers and virtual agents like human beings (see also [16, 17]). For instance, they found that people mindlessly apply human social categories such as ethnicity to them: Participants in their studies evaluated a computer that ostensibly belonged to the participants' ethnic in-group more positively than a computer that was equipped with out-group cues [18]. This resembles the well-documented phenomenon of intergroup bias in human-human contexts [25]: When we perceive others as members of a social in- or out-group (e.g., in terms of ethnicity, religion, or gender), we treat and evaluate them differentially, favoring in-group members and derogating social out-groupers. Importantly, not only in the human-human or human-computer context but also in the field of HRI, research has documented such intergroup bias towards robots. Accordingly, humans base their perceptions and judgments of robots on cues indicating a robot's social category membership [5, 12]. To illustrate, Eyssel and Kuchenbrandt [5] found that people favored a robot that ostensibly belonged to their national in-group over a robot allegedly being a member of a national out-group. The in-group robot was evaluated more positively as well as anthropomorphized more strongly (i.e., attributed more human qualities) than the national out-group robot. Similar effects could be demonstrated even with arbitrary social categories that were irrelevant for participants' social identity [12, 18].

Importantly, humans' tendency to apply social categories to robots not only has perceptual and evaluative but also behavioral consequences. In a study by Powers and colleagues [20], participants used knowledge about gender roles when interacting with a gendered robot: They elaborated less on a typically female topic (i.e., dating norms) when talking to an ostensibly female robot than when talking to a male robot. Furthermore, research by Siegel, Brezeal, and Norton [23] has shown that humans evaluated a robot of the opposite gender more positively than a same–gender robot, and they even tended to behave more positively toward a robot of the opposite gender. Consequently, alleged social category membership of robots plays a key role in how humans react toward robots and thus clearly needs to be considered when developing robots for different fields of applications.

In order to better understand humans' perceptions of robots and the way humans and robots interact with each other, it is necessary to go beyond the investigation of robot or user features. An HRI is likewise characterized by features of the HRI task that, in turn, could influence humans' perceptions of and behavior toward robots. In line with this reasoning, Mutlu and colleagues [15] yielded empirical evidence for the influence of the structure of an HRI task (i.e. competitive vs. cooperative structure) on the interaction itself and on perceptions of robots. In their experiment, males and females played an interactive video game with a robot, and they did so either in a cooperative or in a competitive way. The results showed that men based their evaluation of the robot to a large extent on the task structure, whereas women were more influenced by the characteristics of the robot. In a different set of studies [8], participants found a robot more suitable for a task when the degree of the robot's humanlikeness matched the degree of sociability required by the task (see also [3]). In contrast, Kuchenbrandt et al. [13] present findings that suggest that a mismatch between robot characteristics (male vs. female robot) and the task type (male vs. female task type) could be beneficial for HRI: Females evaluated an ostensibly female robot more positively when they interacted with it on a typically male task than on a female task, whereas no such effect could be observed for male participants [13]. In sum, research investigating the impact of task features such as task type or task structure and their interplay with robot and user characteristics is still in its infancy and so far yielded inconclusive results. Consequently, more research is needed to shed light on the influence of robot and task features on HRI outcomes.

With the present research we aim to examine for the first time how robots' social category membership in-group vs. out-group robot) and the structure of an HRI task (cooperative vs. competitive) in an HRI affect humans' perceptions of and behavior toward robots. In line with the research reviewed above, we hypothesize that 1) participants will perceive a robot that ostensibly belongs to their social in-group more positively than an out-group robot. That is, they will perceive it as more competent, anthropomorphize it to a greater extent, and perceive it as psychologically more close to themselves. However, according to the contact hypothesis [1], cooperative contact with human out-group members improves our evaluative reactions toward these persons and toward the whole out-group. Consequently, we 2) assume that a cooperative HRI with an out-group robot should result in improved reactions toward that robot compared to competing with a robot target that ostensibly belongs to a social out-group. Social psychological findings further indicate that people are more willing to cooperate with members of social in-groups than with out-group members [7], while out-group members are often perceived as competitors [22]. Competing with an out-group member and cooperating with an in-group member could therefore be regarded as humans' behavioral default. Consistent with this reasoning, we 3) suppose that participants will cooperate with an in-group robot to a greater extent than with an out-group robot. Related to this, competing with a human in-group member and cooperating with an out-group member should, at least in part, contradict humans' behavioral scripts regarding intra- and intergroup interactions, and should thus be more challenging and demanding. Likewise, within the context of an HRI we 4) assume that participants will perceive an HRI as more demanding when they have to cooperate with an out-group robot and compete with an in-group robot (incongruent interaction) than when an in-group robot serves as a cooperation partner and the out-group robot represents the competitor (congruent interaction).

3. METHOD

3.1 Participants and Design

$N = 38$ Germans (23 males, 15 females) took part in the experiment[1]. Their age ranged from 21 to 62 years ($M = 28.21, SD = 7.52$). Participants were randomly allocated to one of two conditions resulting from a 2 (robot–task congruency: congruent vs. incongruent) by 2 (robot group membership: in-group vs. out-group) experimental design with the first factor as a between-subjects factor and the latter one as a within-subjects factor. That is, participants simultaneously interacted with both an in-group and an out-group robot. However, they either played a game together with the in-group robot as a cooperation partner and the out-group robot as a competitor (congruent). Or they played the game having the in-group robot as a competitor while the out-group robot served as the cooperation partner (incongruent).

3.2 Procedure

Participants were tested individually in a laboratory at Augsburg University. They were told that they would play a card game with two different robots. In this card game, all players were supposed to find the best fitting pairs of words that were displayed on the cards. The experimenter introduced the two robots to the participants by mentioning their alleged names (MAIK and MALIK, see section 3.3). Moreover, participants learned that the artificial intelligence (A.I.) of the two robots was programmed by two different student groups (a group of German students and a group of Egyptian guest-students, see section 3.3). Following the introduction, participants received written instructions and information about the course and the rules of the card game (see section 3.2.1). Importantly, at this point participants learned that one of the two robots would be their cooperation partner while the other robot would serve as their com-

[1]Originally, 43 participants (26 male, 17 female, age $M = 27.84, SD = 7.16$) took part in the experiment. Five participants had to be excluded from further analyses, as they did not correctly remember the group membership of the two robots. However, including these five participants in all analyses did not significantly affect our results.

Figure 1: Experimental set-up with the in-group robot MAIK as the cooperation partner and the out-group robot MALIK as the competitor

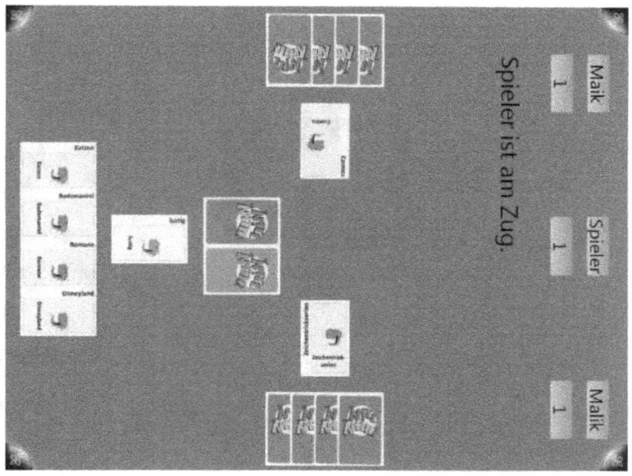

Figure 2: Hand cards, card decks, and each player's current points displayed on the touch-table screen

petitor in the game. After playing the card game together with the two robots, the participants completed a computerized questionnaire containing our dependent variables, were thanked, debriefed, and dismissed.

3.2.1 *Experimental set-up*

Participants were sitting in front of a Microsoft Surface (V1.0)[2] touch-screen table. Two robots (NAO, Academic Edition V4.0, Aldebaran Robotics) were sitting on both sides of the table. One robot served as the participants' cooperation partner and was always placed at the left hand side of the table (as seen from the participant) while the other robot (the competitor) was placed at the right hand side (see Fig. 1).

On the touch-screen table the participants could see two decks of red and green cards as well as three sets of four red cards that were placed in front of each player. These sets represented the players' hand cards (see Fig. 2). The participants' hand cards were face up, so that the participants could see the content of their cards. The robots' cards were displayed face down. Red cards always displayed a noun, while green cards contained adjectives.

Each round of the game followed the same pattern (see Fig. 3): One of the players (active player) draws a green adjective-card from the green deck. The drawn card is then automatically displayed face up. Subsequently, each of the two remaining players (passive players) suggests a noun from the four hand cards that could fit the adjective on the green card. Finally, the active player decides whether to take the noun suggested by passive player one or by passive player two. The player whose suggested noun has been chosen gains a point. A round is finished with the played cards being removed and the passive players' red cards being refilled. For each round, the active player changed clockwise. The complete game consisted of 21 rounds; therefore, each player served as the active player for seven rounds. The player with the highest number of points is considered as the winner of the game.

Irrespective of the information given to the participants, the robots were not equipped with an A.I. but instead followed a predefined script. Accordingly, the sequence of the green and red cards as well as the robots' moves in the game were equal in every game. The robots' decisions regarding whose suggested noun to choose followed a fixed random order and was independent of what participants actually suggested.

To sustain the impression that the participants were actually playing with intelligent robots, both robots were showing simple gaze and pointing behaviors. Moreover, the robots uttered sentences such as "Let's see what the next adjective is", or they gave feedback when receiving a point (e.g., "I also thought that my card was the better one"). This behavior did not differ amongst the two robots. Importantly, independent of their actual role as cooperation partner or competitor, both robots favored the participant over the other robot. That is, both robots chose the nouns that have been suggested by the participant four times (i.e., the participant always received four points by each robot) while choosing the suggestions of the other robot three times. With this, we aimed to assure that every difference in how participants perceived and interacted with the robots solely depended on the robots' ostensible group membership and their assigned role as cooperation partner versus competitor and thus were not affected by differences in the robots' behavior.

To interact with the table and the robots (picking green cards, making suggestions, choosing a suggested noun), the participants had to briefly touch the relevant cards with their fingers. The robots did not touch the table-top. Instead, the respective cards have been displayed automatically following a fixed script. However, the robots commented their 'moves' in the game verbally and showed gaze behavior toward the relevant cards. When the robots had to choose a noun from the two suggestions, they announced their choice verbally and pointed and looked at the player whose suggestion has been chosen.

3.3 Independent Variables

In order to manipulate *group membership* of the two robots, we varied three aspects: First, we named the in-group robot MAIK (a typically German name) and the out-group robot MALIK (a typically Arab name). Second, we told participants that German students have developed MAIK's artificial intelligence. In contrast, Egyptian guest students al-

[2]The tabletop was renamed in June 2012 with V2.0 to PixelSense, www.pixelsense.de

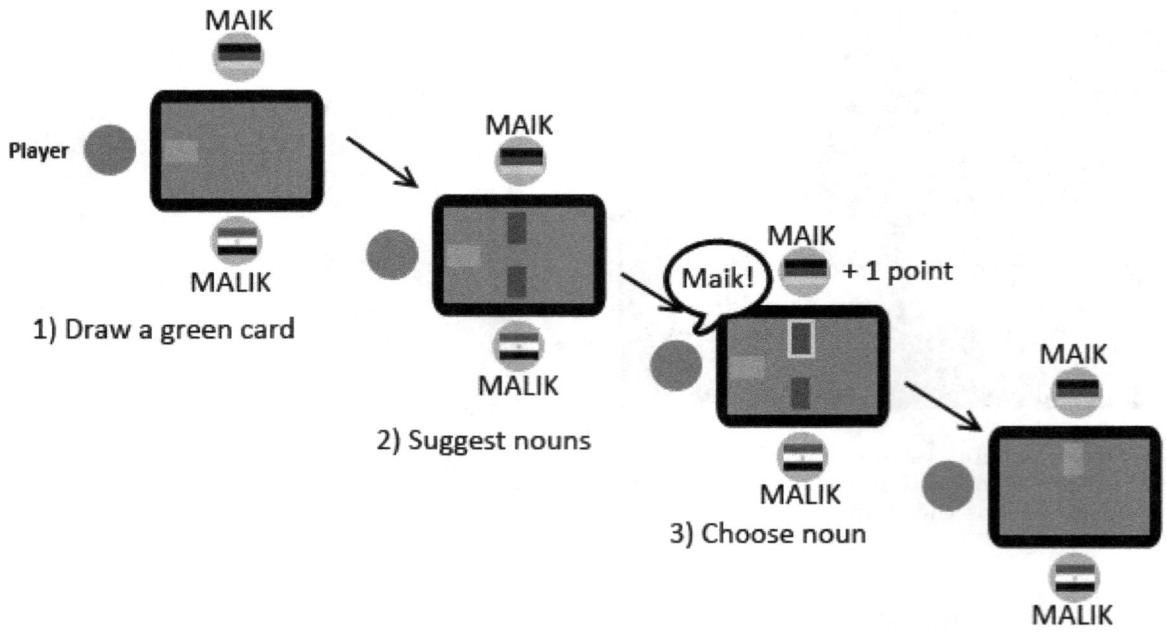

Figure 3: Three steps of a round : 1) the active player draws a green card, 2) the passive players suggest nouns, 3) the active player chooses a noun, the passive player with the chosen noun gets a point. Finally the active player changes clockwise.

legedly developed MALIK's artificial intelligence[3]. Third, MAIK was equipped with a sticker displaying the German national flag, whereas MALIK was provided with the Egyptian flag.

The *robot–task congruency* was manipulated by forcing participants to cooperate either with the in- or with the out-group robot. In the *congruent condition*, participants were told that they could take part in a lottery and have the chance to win 50 Euro if their own points in the game plus MAIK's points together exceed double the points of MALIK. We thus presented the in-group robot MAIK as the cooperation partner in the game while the out-group robot MALIK was presented as a competitor. In the *incongruent condition*, in contrast, the out-group robot served as the cooperation partner and the in-group robot was introduced as the competitor. Consequently, participants were informed that they could participate in the lottery if their own points and MALIK's points together exceed double the points of MAIK. The opportunity to participate in the lottery was given in order to increase the incentive to cooperate (vs. compete) with the respective robot.

3.4 Dependent Variables

The ratings regarding the two robots were always completed en bloc for each robot, whereby the two blocs were presented in random order. To assess the endorsement of the dependent variables, we used seven-point Likert scales (ranging from 1 = *not at all* to 7 = *very*). High values reflect high endorsement of the assessed dimension.

[3]Egyptian students actually visited the lab the first author belongs to during the time the study was conducted. This contributed to the credibility of the cover story.

Manipulation check. As a manipulation check we asked participants to indicate how strongly they perceived MAIK and MALIK as a team partner.

Perceived competence. Participants were asked to rate MAIK and MALIK with regard to four competence-related traits (efficient, skillful, confident, competent; see [6]). The four items were combined to form an acceptably reliable index for the perceived in-group robot's ($\alpha = .69$) and out-group robot's competence ($\alpha = .74$).

Mind attribution. Participants completed nine items with regard to MAIK's and MALIK's mental capabilities. The items were adapted from Gray, Gray, and Wegner ([9], see also [5]): 'To what extent is the robot capable of feeling hungry/joy/pain/fear?'; 'To what extent is the robot capable of hoping for things?'; 'How likely is it that the robot has a personality/own will?'; 'To what extent is the robot capable of being aware of things?'; 'How likely is it that the robot has a soul?'. These items formed reliable indexes for both robots ($\alpha = .88$ for the in-group robot; $\alpha = .87$ for the out-group robot) and were used as an indicator of anthropomorphism [5].

Psychological closeness. To assess the degree of perceived psychological closeness between the participants and MAIK or MALIK, respectively, participants were asked to respond to the following five items: 'To what extent do you feel close / connected / similar to MAIK (MALIK) / on the same wavelength with MAIK (MALIK)' and 'Do you share many commonalities with MAIK (MALIK)?' [4]. This measure was reliable for both robots ($\alpha = .93$ for the in-group robot; $\alpha = .93$ for the out-group robot).

Perceived task difficulty. To assess whether participants perceived the game as differentially demanding depending on the experimental condition, they were asked to indicate how difficult it was for them to play the game.

Perceived stress. Participants were further asked to indicate how much they felt stress during playing the game.

Cooperative behavior. We defined cooperative behavior as favoring the cooperation partner over the competitor. That is, in order to cooperate with one of the robots, the participants had to give more points to the robot cooperation partner (i.e., choosing more often the nouns suggested by this robot) than to the robot competitor. To built a cooperation index, we subtracted the points that participants allocated to the out-group robot MALIK from the points participants allocated to the in-group robot MAIK. Consequently, a positive value of the index indicates cooperation with the in-group robot (more points were allocated to MAIK than to MALIK), while a negative value indicates cooperation with the out-group robot MALIK.

4. RESULTS

4.1 Manipulation Check

As a manipulation check, we first tested whether participants perceived the in-group robot MAIK and the out-group robot MALIK as a team partner as a function of the experimental condition. The results of t-tests show that the in-group robot indeed was perceived as a team partner to a greater extent in the congruent ($M = 3.67, SD = 0.91$) compared to the incongruent condition ($M = 1.40, SD = 0.60$), $t(36) = 9.18, p < .001$. Similarly, participants perceived the out-group robot more strongly as a team partner in the incongruent ($M = 3.20, SD = 1.20$) than in the congruent condition, ($M = 1.94, SD = 0.80$), $t(33.41) = 3.83, p = .001$.

4.2 Test of Main Hypotheses

4.2.1 *Ratings of the robots (Hypotheses 1 and 2)*

Perceived competence. Results of a mixed models analysis of variance (ANOVA) with robot–task congruency (congruent vs. incongruent) as the between-subjects factor and robot type (in-group vs. out-group robot) as the within-subjects factor yielded a marginally significant main effect of robot type, $F(1, 36) = 3.31, p = .08, \eta^2 = .08$. No interaction effect was found, $F < 1$. That is, participants tended to ascribe the in-group robot MAIK more competence ($M = 4.84, SD = .96$) than the out-group robot MALIK ($M = 4.58, SD = 1.07$), irrespective of whether they cooperated or competed with the in- or out-group robot, respectively (see Fig. 4).

Mind attribution. Results of a mixed models ANOVA revealed a similar pattern: A main effect of robot type was found, $F(1, 36) = 4.04, p = .05, \eta^2 = .10$, but no interaction effect, $F < 1$. Participants attributed more mind to the in-group ($M = 2.22, SD = 1.13$) than to the out-group robot ($M = 2.06, SD = 0.99$).

Psychological closeness An ANOVA with robot–task congruency (congruent vs. incongruent) as the between-subjects factor and robot type (in-group vs. out-group robot) as the within-subjects factor yielded no main effect of robot type, $F(1, 36) = 1.19, p = .28, \eta^2 = .03$. However, as hypothesized, we found a significant interaction effect of robot type by experimental condition, $F(1, 36) = 6.94, p = .01, \eta^2 = .16$. To inspect this pattern of findings further, we conducted post hoc t-tests and compared the psychological closeness to the in- and the out-group robot between the experimental conditions: Participants in the congruent condition rated the in-group robot MAIK as closer to themselves (M = 3.69, SD = 1.35) than participants in the incongruent condition ($M = 2.89, SD = 1.22$), $t(36) = 1.92, p = .06$, although this difference only approached significance. No such difference between the experimental conditions was found for the out-group robot MALIK (congruent condition: $M = 2.87, SD = 1.16$; incongruent condition: $M = 3.23, SD = 1.50$), $t(36) = -0.82, p = .42$. Moreover, we further compared the perceived closeness to the in-group robot with the perceived closeness to the out-group robot separately for each condition. In the congruent condition, participants perceived the in-group robot as closer to themselves ($M = 3.69, SD = 1.35$) than the out-group robot ($M = 2.87, SD = 1.16$), $t(17) = 3.00, p = .01$. In the incongruent condition, in contrast, no such difference was obtained, $t(19) = -1.01, p = .33$. Results are depicted in Figure 5.

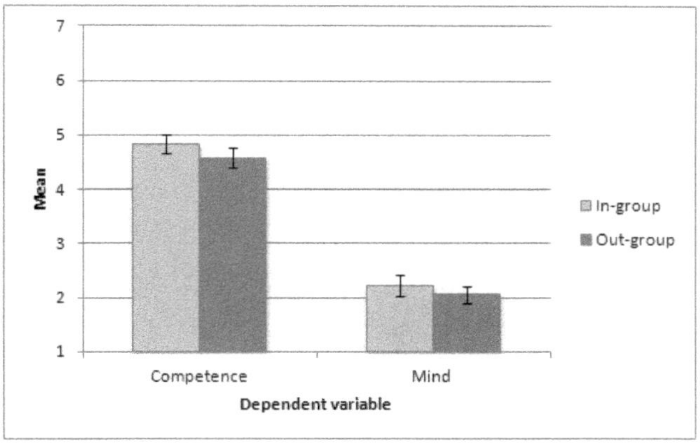

Figure 4: Mean ratings of the robots' competence and mind as a function of the robots' group membership

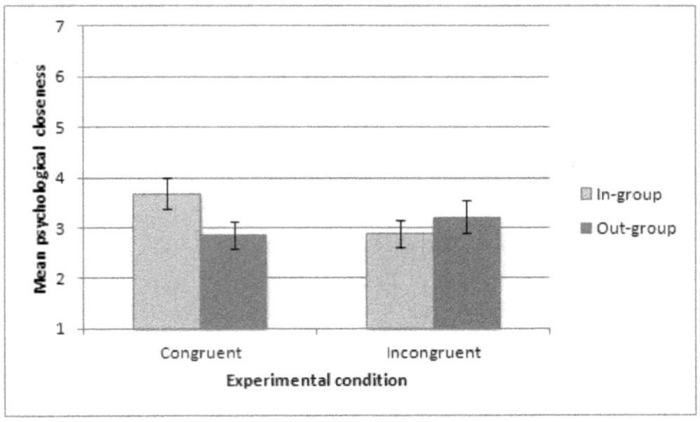

Figure 5: Mean ratings of psychological closeness to the robots as a function of experimental condition

4.2.2 *Ratings of the task (Hypothesis 4)*

Perceived task difficulty. Results of a t-test demonstrate that participants indicated to have more difficulties with the interaction task in the incongruent ($M = 2.15, SD = 1.57$) than in the congruent condition ($M = 1.28, SD = 0.58$), $t(36) = -2.23, p = .03$ (see Fig. 6).

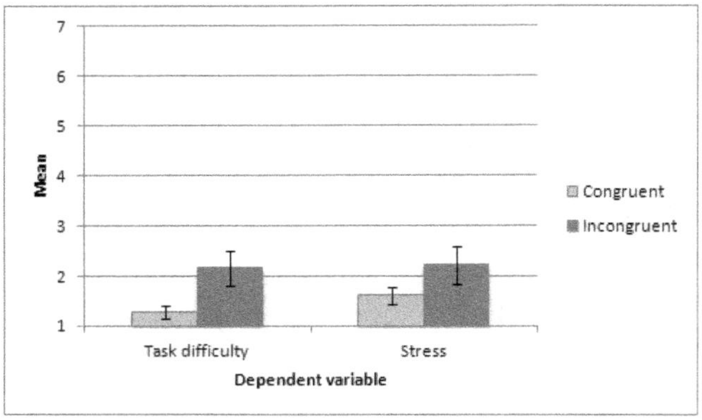

Figure 6: Mean ratings of perceived task difficulty and stress as a function of congruency condition

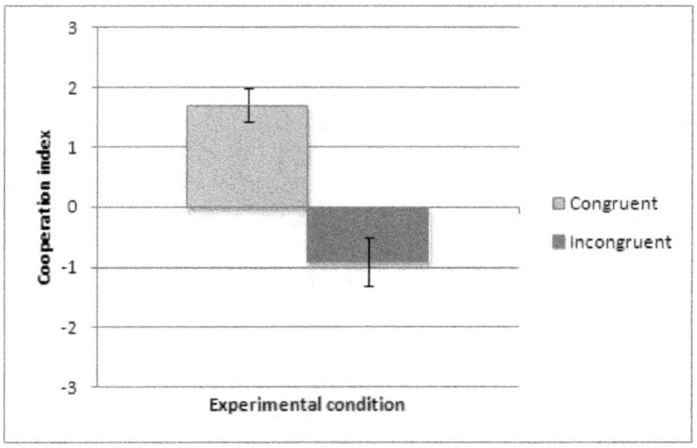

Figure 7: Cooperation index for congruent and incongruent condition

Perceived stress. A comparable pattern of results was obtained for perceived stress during the HRI game. Participants in the incongruent condition in tendency rated the interactive game as more stressful ($M = 2.20, SD = 1.67$) than in the congruent condition ($M = 1.61, SD = 0.70$). However, this was only a non-significant tendency, $t(25.97) = -1.14, p = .16$.

4.2.3 HRI behavior (Hypothesis 3)

Cooperative behavior. With a t-test we tested whether the cooperation index varies as a function of experimental condition. As can be seen in Figure 7, participants cooperated with the in-group robot MAIK in the congruent condition ($M = 1.71, SD = 1.21$) while they cooperated with the out-group robot MALIK in the incongruent condition ($M = -0.90, SD = 1.77$)[4], $t(35) = 5.12, p < .001$. Additionally, we tested whether the cooperation index differs significantly from 1 in the congruent or from -1 in the incongruent condition, respectively. In the congruent condition, a value of 1 would be the minimum value to indicate cooperation with the in-group robot whilst in the incongruent condition a value of -1 represents the minimum value for cooperation with the out-group robot[5]. However, we were interested in whether participants showed cooperative behavior towards the in- or out-group robot over and above the to-be-expected minimum value. Interestingly, participants in the congruent condition clearly showed a cooperative tendency towards the in-group robot over and above the minimum cooperation value of 1, $t(16) = 2.40, p = .03$. In contrast, in the incongruent condition, the cooperation index did not significantly differ from the minimum cooperation value of -1, $t(19) = 0.25, p = .80$. This latter finding demonstrates that although participants cooperated with the out-group robot when the robot served as the cooperation partner, their cooperative behavior did not exceed the to-be-expected minimal cooperative behavior towards the out-group robot.

[4]Remember that a positive value indicates cooperation with the in-group robot while a negative value indicates cooperation with the out-group robot

[5]Participants had to allocate seven points between the two robots. Consequently, one robot always had to have at least one point more (or less) than the other robot, resulting in a minimal difference of 1 or -1 between MAIK's and MALIK's points, respectively.

5. DISCUSSION

With the present research we aimed to contribute to a clearer understanding of the factors that influence how humans react to and interact with social robots. More specifically, we tested whether intergroup bias toward a robot would occur depending on the alleged group membership of the robot. In addition, we examined the effects of HRI task structure (cooperative vs. competitive) on participants' reactions toward the robot and their perception of the HRI. In order to investigate our research questions, participants played a card game with two robots, one belonging to participants' in-group and one being a member of a social outgroup. Furthermore, in the interaction, one of the two robots served as a cooperation partner while the other one was presented as a competitor. Importantly, the study was designed in such a way that half of the participants cooperated with the in-group robot and competed with the out-group robot (congruent condition) whilst for the remaining participants the out-group robot was the cooperation partner and the in-group robot represented the competitor (incongruent condition).

We first of all hypothesized that participants will react more positively toward an alleged in-group versus out-group robot (Hyp. 1). Similar to previous findings [5, 12], participants indeed perceived the in-group robot MAIK as more competent than the out-group robot MALIK. They even anthropomorphized the robot to a greater extent, that is, they attributed more mind to the in-group versus the out-group robot. Interestingly, this latter finding is in line with social psychological research demonstrating that human in-group members are often attributed more humanness compared to human out-groupers [10, 14]; or, to put it differently, members of social out-groups are often dehumanized. Our study substantiates the claim that social categories not only play a key role in the perception of social robots, but social categories lead to similar consequences in HRI as they do in human-human interactions (see also [5, 12]).

We secondly expected that the effects of the robots' group membership would interact with the effects of the HRI task structure. That is, we expected the participants to show improved reactions toward the out-group robot when being forced to cooperate versus to compete with it (Hyp. 2). Our findings do not support this notion: With regard to the robots' perceived competence and mind, the robot–task congruency did not show any influence. Interestingly, our results indicate that the in-group robot MAIK benefitted from being the participants' cooperation partner. Participants perceived MAIK as closer to themselves when they cooperated versus competed with it. In contrast, no such beneficial effects could be found for the out-group robot MALIK. Participants reported similar psychological distance to MALIK irrespective of whether they cooperated or competed with it. These findings contradict results from intergroup contact research in the context of human-human interactions that document the beneficial effects of positive cooperative out-group contact [1, 19] on reactions toward members of social out-groups. Moreover, they again illustrate the importance of social categories in HRI: Intergroup bias toward robots appears to be hard to overcome and the effects of a robot's social category membership even seem to overly the potential impact of a positive social HRI.

Thirdly, we hypothesized that participants would cooperate with the alleged in-group robot to a greater extent than with the out-group robot (Hyp. 3). Previous research in human-human contexts has proven that people more readily cooperate with their in-groupers than with out-group members [7]. The results fully support our third hypothesis. Participants cooperated with both the in- and the out-group robot if requested. However, the cooperation index clearly showed that participants cooperated with the in-group robot to a greater extent (in the congruent condition) than with the out-group robot (in the incongruent condition). For a more refined interpretation of these results, the winning conditions of the game need to be reconsidered: In order to win the game - which could be viewed as the participants' individual goal - participants had to ensure that they obtain the highest overall score compared to each of the two robots. At the same time, participants had to give more points to their robot cooperation partner (i.e., choosing more of the nouns suggested by this robot) than to the robot competitor in order to participate in the lottery - which could be viewed as the mutual goal shared between the participants and the respective robot cooperation partner. However, this cooperation behavior at a certain point involves the risk of not reaching one's individual goal of winning the card game: The more points participants allocated to the cooperation partner, the higher the likelihood that this robot would gain more points than the participant himself/herself, and thus, the higher the likelihood for participants to loose the overall win of the game. Against this background, the present findings suggest that the tendency to cooperate with an in-group robot compared to an out-group robot was so strong that participants even tended to risk their individual win[6]. In contrast, with the out-group robot MALIK as the cooperation partner, participants only showed the minimum of cooperation that was necessary to take part in the lottery. From an applied point of view, this finding is particularly important: Many future applications for social robots involve some degree of cooperation between the human user and the robot partner. The present results suggest that a human–robot cooperation could be reinforced by presenting the robot as an in-group member (i.e., giving the robot a name indicating in-group membership). Likewise, for the purpose of smooth human–robot cooperation cues that signify out-group membership should be avoided.

According to our fourth hypothesis, we expected participants to find an HRI more demanding when robot features and task structure are incongruent, that is, when participants had to cooperate with an out-group robot while competing with an in-group robot (Hyp. 4). Indeed, our results support this assumption: Participants indicated that they had more difficulties in playing the card game in the incongruent than in the congruent experimental condition. Moreover, in tendency, they even felt more stressed in the incongruent interaction. Accordingly, this pattern of results adds to previous research suggesting that a match between robot and task features has a positive impact on how humans perceive a robot and how they interact with it [8, 3]. A match between robot and task features might be in accordance with users' expectations regarding an HRI, which in turn could render the HRI cognitively less effortful for the user. However, other findings [13] suggested that a mismatch could have positive effects, for instance, on how a robot is evaluated. Consequently, future research needs to identify moderating factors that determine when and why a match or mismatch between robot and task features would be advantageous for HRI.

We critically acknowledge that our group manipulation could be confounded with existing stereotypes and expectations about Germans and Egyptians, respectively. However, previous work demonstrated that the mere categorization of the robot as an in- versus out-group member using arbitrary and meaningless categories [12] leads to similar patterns of intergroup bias compared to group manipulations using nationality [4]. This makes us confident that also in the present experiment, the in-group / out-group differentiation was mainly responsible for the reported effects and not only differences in how Egyptians and Germans are perceived.

6. CONCLUSION

In sum, the present study showed that social categories represent core determinants of how we evaluate, perceive, and interact with robots. We demonstrated that perceiving a robot as an in-group member has positive impact on users' reactions toward that robot while categorizing a robot as an out-group member has negative implications for HRI. Importantly, this is the first study documenting that even a positive (cooperative) interaction with an out-group robot does not compensate for the negative impact of out-group category membership. Based on these findings, we conclude that when designing social robots, scientists and developers need to consider various cues of the robot (e.g., voice, appearance, name) that could indicate a robot's social category membership. A robot's alleged group membership together with its supposed application might strongly influence how users react toward and interact with this robot. At the same time, roboticists could make use of social categories in order to make an HRI an intuitive, pleasant and smooth experience for the user.

7. ACKNOWLEDGMENTS

We especially thank Sigfried Depner for his help with the implementation of the game and the robots' behavior.

[6]In the present study, a cooperation index of 2 indicates that the robot cooperation partner gained more points than the participants (who always received eight points). In the congruent condition, the cooperation index of $M = 1.71$ was quite close to this value.

8. REFERENCES

[1] G. W. Allport. *The nature of prejudice.* Oxford,UK: Addison-Wesley, 1954.

[2] A. Davids. Urban search and rescue robots: from tragedy to technology. *Intelligent Systems, IEEE*, 17(2):81–83, 2002.

[3] F. Eyssel and F. Hegel. (s)he's got the look: Gender stereotyping of robots. *Journal of Applied Social Psychology*, 42(9):2213–2230, 2012.

[4] F. Eyssel and D. Kuchenbrandt. My robot is more human than yours: Effects of group membership on anthropomorphic judgments of the social robot flobi. In *Proceedings of the IEEE/RSJ International Conference on Intelligent Robots and Systems (IROS 2011)*, 2011.

[5] F. Eyssel and D. Kuchenbrandt. Social categorization of social robots: Anthropomorphism as a function of robot group membership. *British Journal of Social Psychology*, 51(4):724–731, 2012.

[6] S. T. Fiske, A. J. Cuddy, and P. Glick. Universal dimensions of social cognition: warmth and competence. *Trends in Cognitive Sciences*, 11(2):77 – 83, 2007.

[7] L. Goette, D. Huffman, and S. Meier. The impact of group membership on cooperation and norm enforcement: Evidence using random assignment to real social groups. *The American economic review*, 96(2):212–216, 2006.

[8] J. Goetz, S. Kiesler, and A. Powers. Matching robot appearance and behavior to tasks to improve human-robot cooperation. In *Robot and Human Interactive Communication, 2003. Proceedings. ROMAN 2003. The 12th IEEE International Workshop on*, pages 55–60, 2003.

[9] H. M. Gray, K. Gray, and D. M. Wegner. Dimensions of mind perception. *Science*, 315(5812):619, 2007.

[10] N. Haslam. Dehumanization: An integrative review. *Personality and Social Psychology Review*, 10(3):252–264, 2006.

[11] H. Kitano and S. Tadokoro. Robocup rescue: A grand challenge for multiagent and intelligent systems. *AI Magazine*, 22(1):39, 2001.

[12] D. Kuchenbrandt, F. Eyssel, S. Bobinger, and M. Neufeld. When a robot's group membership matters. *International Journal of Social Robotics*, 5(3):409–417, 2013.

[13] D. Kuchenbrandt, M. Häring, J. Eichberg, and F. Eyssel. Keep an eye on the task! how gender typicality of tasks influence human-robot interactions. In S. Ge, O. Khatib, J.-J. Cabibihan, R. Simmons, and M.-A. Williams, editors, *Social Robotics*, volume 7621 of *Lecture Notes in Computer Science*, pages 448–457. Springer Berlin Heidelberg, 2012.

[14] J.-P. Leyens, P. M. Paladino, R. Rodriguez-Torres, J. Vaes, S. Demoulin, A. Rodriguez-Perez, and R. Gaunt. The emotional side of prejudice: The attribution of secondary emotions to ingroups and outgroups. *Personality and Social Psychology Review*, 4(2):186–197, 2000.

[15] B. Mutlu, S. Osman, J. Forlizzi, J. Hodgins, and S. Kiesler. Task structure and user attributes as elements of human-robot interaction design. In *Robot and Human Interactive Communication, 2006. ROMAN 2006. The 15th IEEE International Symposium on*, pages 74–79, 2006.

[16] C. Nass, B. J. Fogg, and Y. Moon. Can computers be teammates? *Int. J. Hum.-Comput. Stud.*, 45(6):669–678, Dec. 1996.

[17] C. Nass, K. Isbister, and E.-J. Lee. Truth is beauty: researching embodied conversational agents. In *Embodied conversational agents*, pages 374–402. MIT Press, Cambridge, MA, USA, 2000.

[18] C. Nass and Y. Moon. Machines and mindlessness: Social responses to computers. *Journal of social issues*, 56(1):81–103, 2000.

[19] T. F. Pettigrew and L. R. Tropp. A meta-analytic test of intergroup contact theory. *Journal of personality and social psychology*, 90(5):751, 2006.

[20] A. Powers, A. Kramer, S. Lim, J. Kuo, S. lai Lee, and S. Kiesler. Eliciting information from people with a gendered humanoid robot. In *Robot and Human Interactive Communication, 2005. ROMAN 2005. IEEE International Workshop on*, pages 158–163, 2005.

[21] B. Reeves and C. Nass. *How people treat computers, television, and new media like real people and places.* CSLI Publications and Cambridge university press, 1996.

[22] M. Sherif, O. J. Harvey, B. J. White, W. R. Hood, C. W. Sherif, et al. *Intergroup conflict and cooperation: The Robbers Cave experiment*, volume 10. University Book Exchange Norman, OK, 1961.

[23] M. Siegel, C. Breazeal, and M. Norton. Persuasive robotics: The influence of robot gender on human behavior. In *Intelligent Robots and Systems, 2009. IROS 2009. IEEE/RSJ International Conference on*, pages 2563–2568, 2009.

[24] J. Stuckler, D. Holz, and S. Behnke. Robocup@home: Demonstrating everyday manipulation skills in robocup@home. *Robotics Automation Magazine, IEEE*, 19(2):34–42, 2012.

[25] H. Tajfel and J. C. Turner. An integrative theory of intergroup conflict. *The social psychology of intergroup relations*, 33:47, 1979.

[26] D. Voth. A new generation of military robots. *Intelligent Systems, IEEE*, 19(4):2–3, 2004.

Culturally Variable Preferences for Robot Design and Use in South Korea, Turkey, and the United States

Hee Rin Lee
School of Informatics and Computing
901 E. 10th Street
Bloomington IN 47408
hrl@indiana.edu

Selma Šabanović
School of Informatics and Computing
901 E. 10th Street
Bloomington IN 47408
selmas@indiana.edu

ABSTRACT
Based on the results of an online survey conducted with participants in South Korea (N=73), Turkey (N=46), and the United States (N=99), we show that people's perceptions and preferences regarding acceptable designs and uses for robots are culturally variable on a number of dimensions, including general attitudes towards robots, preferences for robot form, interactivity, intelligence, and sociality. We also explore correlations between these design and use characteristics and factors cited as having an effect on user perceptions and acceptance of robots, such as religious beliefs and media exposure. Our research suggests that culturally variable attitudes and preferences toward robots are not simply reducible to these factors, rather they relate to more specific social dynamics and norms. In conclusion, we discuss potential design and research implications of culturally variable and universally accepted user preferences regarding robots.

Categories and Subject Descriptors
H.1.2 [User/Machine Systems]: Human Factors; H.5.2 [User-Centered Design]; I.2.9 [Robotics]: Commercial robots and applications; K.4: Computers and Society

General Terms
Design, Human Factors

Keywords
Cross-cultural study, robots in society, Korea, Turkey, United States, survey, robot design, robot application, user preferences.

1. INTRODUCTION
As the notion of using social robots in everyday contexts with non-expert users gains traction around the world, cultural variability in robot adoption and use has become an important practical problem for developers and a significant research issue. Scholars have shown that our expectations and understandings of technology are "shaped... by the specific cultural and historical resources the world makes available to us" [24]. Culturally variable beliefs, practices, and social norms can therefore be expected to affect robot design, adoption and use.

Both the popular media and scientists are debating cultural differences in the design and projected use of robots in society. East Asian countries like Japan, referred to as a place where robots are "priceless friends" [10], and South Korea, which is implementing service robots as a part of its national information technology policy [14], are expected to readily adopt robots into society. Scholars identify cultural factors such as animism and favorable media representations of robots as possible causes of the positive image of robots in Japan (e.g. [9]; [13]; [15]) and Korea [14]. In contrast, the United States (US) are often described as less accepting of robots due to fears of job loss to automation and threatening media portrayals of robots [3]. Cross-cultural research on people's perceptions of robots challenges the assumption that the Japanese are peerlessly accepting of robots while Americans hold more negative views (e.g. [1]; [20]). Critical studies of robotics in Japan further suggest that positive perceptions of robots are the result of active efforts by the government, industry, and academia to encourage societal acceptance of robotics, rather than of pre-existing cultural predispositions ([11]; [25]).

The development of robotic technologies and applications for global markets requires a deeper understanding of cultural factors that affect robot acceptance and use. It is particularly important to empirically evaluate assumptions about the effects of culture on perceptions of robots. We present the results of a survey performed in the US, S. Korea, and Turkey exploring the incidence and correlations of factors previously identified as relevant to robot design and use, including religious beliefs, popular media portrayals of robots, and preferences for robot appearance and use. Our results show culturally variable perceptions regarding robots design and use, and suggest that culturally variable preferences are not directly explained by previously emphasized factors, such as religious affiliation and media exposure. We identify both culturally specific and universal preferences that can be taken into account in robot design and conclude by discussing the importance of understanding user preferences about robots in the context of situated social norms and practices, rather than generalized cultural characteristics.

2. RELATED WORK
Studies have shown that cultural factors affect the design of robotic technology and researchers' "visions of future possibilities" for robots in society [8]. Shaw-Garlock [22] contrasts the design visions of two social robotics projects, Repliee in Japan and Kismet in the US, to show that history, theology, and popular culture surrounding robots play a role in robot design. Culturally defined conceptions of sociality, such as implicit and explicit displays of affect, also affect the way robots are designed [20]. Suchman [24] suggests that "autonomous, rational agency" is "the prevailing figuration of Euro-American imaginaries" of artificial intelligence and robotics and their role in society. Some Japanese robotics researchers explicitly use notions of cultural specificity and fit to inspire and legitimize the development of socially interactive robots [21].

HRI'14, March 3–6, 2014, Bielefeld, Germany.

ACM 978-1-4503-2658-2/14/03…$15.00.
http://dx.doi.org/10.1145/2559636.2559676

The importance of culture as a framework for making sense of robots in daily life extends to the way users perceive and interact with robots. Bartneck et al [2] find significant cultural variation in negative attitudes towards robots among Dutch, Chinese, German, American, Japanese, and Mexican participants. MacDorman et al show that US and Japanese participants have similar attitudes towards robots, suggesting that factors such as history and religion may affect differences in their willingness to adopt robots [20]. Survey evaluations of the seal-like robot PARO by participants from Japan, the UK, Sweden, Italy, South Korea, Brunei, and the US found that all participants evaluated the robot positively, but identified its most likeable traits differently according to the country [23]. In the context of human-robot teamwork, Evers et al found users from China and the US respond differently to robots [6] and that robots are more effective in influencing the opinions of human team-members when they use culturally appropriate forms of communication [19]. Lee et al. found that culturally variable meanings of the home and collectivist and individualist models of interaction in S. Korea and the US, respectively, affect participants' design preferences for domestic robots [17].

In investigating particular cultural factors that may explain variability in user reception and acceptance of robots, researchers have paid particular attention to the influence of media, religion, and social beliefs. Kaplan identifies animistic beliefs, aesthetic views of nature, and portrayals of robots in popular media as factors that affect positive views of robots in Japan [13]. Kitano suggests that specificities in Japan's social, historical and cultural development led to its unique conceptualization of robot ethics [15]. Robotics research in the US and other Western countries has been described as influenced by Christian beliefs about transcendence and the special nature of humans (e.g. [9]). Media portrayals of robots as positive and friendly or negative and threatening have also been used as explanations for differences in the design and popular image of robots in Japan and the US [3]. The relationship of these factors to user evaluations and preferences has yet to be systematically and empirically studied.

3. STUDY DESIGN

The study presented here contributes to research on cultural differences in user perceptions of robots by using a survey to gauge general user attitudes and preferences toward robots, as well as to explore the correlations between widely discussed cultural factors (e.g. media, religion) and user preferences. The surveys were preformed in three cultural contexts – the US, S. Korea, and Turkey – all of which have moderate to high levels of technological development and are seen as important economic markets. The US is included as a developed Western country, S. Korea is a technologically advanced East Asian country, and Turkey is a swiftly developing Middle Eastern technology market.

3.1 Participants

Our survey was completed by 73 Korean, 99 American and 46 Turkish respondents, all native to and currently living in the participating countries. We recruited participants through word of mouth, resulting in a subject pool with diverse ages and occupations beyond university students and staff, who have been the main participants in prior cross-cultural HRI studies. All participants had at least a high school education. 70/99 US participants were living in Bloomington IN, though their hometowns were distributed across the U.S.; all Korean participants lived in Seoul; all Turkish participants in Istanbul. See Table 1 for other demographic details.

Table 1. Demographic information on participants

		Korea M N=73	US N=99	Turkey N=46
Average age [M(sd)]		34 (11.47)	35 (15.77)	34 (8.31)
Gender	Male (N)	44	38	29
	Female (N)	29	57	17
	Other (N)	0	4	0
Education	High school	19	21	6
	College	42	41	16
	Graduate	12	37	24
Technological expertise 1: Beginner – 7: expert [M(sd)]		3.8 (1.47)	5.0 (1.17)	5.0 (1.16)

3.2 Method

Our survey explored general patterns in people's perceptions and preferences regarding robots. After signing the online consent form, participants answered questions on nine topics: 1) *general views about robots* (e.g. acceptance of robots in various use contexts, 2) *form factors* (e.g., materials, size, level of human-likeness), 3) *intelligence* (e.g., social awareness, level of autonomy), 4) *sociability* (e.g., social roles, personality), 5) *interactivity* (e.g., interaction modes and capabilities), 6) *religious beliefs and social norms* (e.g., religious affiliation, agreement with statements related to Confucianism, Animism, Christianity, etc.), 7) *media exposure* (e.g., knowledge and evaluation of fictional robots such as Astroboy and Terminator), 8) *evaluation of existing robots* (e.g., Aibo, Geminoid, Roomba), and 9) *demographic questions* (e.g. gender, age, income). The exact format of the questions is described in the Results section. Our questions were based on literature on robot design and acceptance (e.g., [5, 7, 18]) and cultural factors related to user perceptions of robots [2, [2, 17]). Participants received a version of the survey in their native language (English[16], Korean, and Turkish).

In our analysis, we describe the general patterns of user preferences and evaluations of robots within the three cultural groups, investigate the effects of specific cultural factors (e.g. religion, media exposure) on these preferences, and explore other salient factors that affected participant preferences. The statistical analyses presented were all performed using SPSS. Due to the unbalanced nature of our national samples, we used a mixed linear model to test the effects of nationality and the other demographic data (e.g. gender, age) on the design preferences and beliefs about robots of our participants. Subsequent post hoc inter-group comparisons with the Sidak adjustment were used to determine the source of significant differences among groups. We also examined correlations between potentially salient independent variables (e.g., religion, media exposure, previous experiences with robots, age, gender) and participants' design preferences with appropriate correlation tests, as described below.

4. RESULTS

We first describe participants' general attitudes toward robots as well as their preferences regarding various attributes of robots, including form factors, intelligence, sociality, and interactivity. We then discuss participants' explicit expressions of religious belief and their agreement with various social and cultural norms, and explore the correlations between their beliefs and robot design and use preferences. We also analyze participants' knowledge about robots in the media and its effects on their evaluations of actual and fictional robots.

4.1 General Attitudes towards Robots

We asked participants to state the extent to which they would want robots to assist them in different use contexts (e.g. the home, office, hospital). The evaluation was on a 5-point scale (1: "Not at all" to 5: "To a great extent", which we from here on refer to as the "5-point opposition scale"). Participants could also choose "I don't know" as an answer, which we excluded from the analysis. Using mixed-effects analysis for variance, we found a significant effect of nationality on participants' acceptance of robots in different contexts (see Table 2). Post hoc comparisons showed Korean and Turkish participants were more willing to have robots in all contexts in comparison to US participants, except for dangerous locations. US participants were generally unwilling to use robots in everyday spaces, but found factories and dangerous environments to be appropriate use contexts for robots.

While participant nationality did not have a significant effect on participant preferences for using robots in dangerous locations, participants who said the media represent robots as negative or useful were significantly more likely to consider dangerous locations as an appropriate context of use for robots ($p<0.05$).

Table 2. Effect of nationality on desired context of use

Context	sig		Korea N=73	US N=99	Turkey N=46
Home	<0.01	M	4.01	2.78	3.76
		SD	1.03	1.17	1.29
Hotel	<0.01	M	3.79	2.55	3.93
		SD	1.31	1.12	1.15
Museum	<0.01	M	3.82	2.41	3.48
		SD	1.07	1.06	1.30
Shopping center	<0.01	M	3.41	2.49	3.77
		SD	1.31	.93	1.22
Office	0.04	M	3.72	2.70	3.94
		SD	1.22	1.10	1.15
School	0.03	M	3.40	2.52	3.43
		SD	1.30	1.20	1.30
Sports facility	<0.01	M	3.74	3.12	3.28
		SD	1.31	1.32	1.51
Hospital	<0.01	M	4.07	3.02	4.04
		SD	1.20	1.16	1.03
Police station	<0.01	M	3.53	2.17	3.33
		SD	1.31	1.00	1.60
Factory	<0.01	M	4.71	4.19	4.77
		SD	.80	1.07	.50
Dangerous locations	0.08	M	4.55	3.78	4.69
		SD	.91	1.40	.71

4.2 Form factors

To ascertain which robot designs would be acceptable in different countries, we asked participants about their preferences for a robot's gender, materials, facial expression, and morphology. A larger proportion of US participants (US: 34%, KR: 12%, TK: 14%) did not care which form the robot takes across all questions, corroborating findings of a prior study [17].

4.2.1 Gender

We asked participants which gender they would want their robot to be (1: male, 2: female, 3: no gender, 4: no preference), with multiple choices allowed. Answers were scored by making a separate column for each choice with 1(selected)/0(not selected) for each participant prior to statistical analysis. We did not find any significant effects of nationality at $p<0.05$. Prior experience with toy robots, however, had a significant negative effect on preferences for robots with no gender ($p<0.05$).

4.2.2 Material

We also asked participants which materials they prefer to be used in robot design, allowing them to choose multiple answers (See Table 3). We scored each category as (1: selected) or (0: not selected) prior to statistical analysis. The results of a mixed-effect analysis of variance and post hoc comparisons indicated that US participants have stronger preferences for fabric over Koreans, and for plastic more than Turkish participants. US participants also chose metal significantly more often than Turkish participants, and "does not matter" significantly more often than Korean participants.

Respondents who thought media represent robots as useful ($p<0.01$) and those with higher incomes ($p<0.05$) had stronger preferences for robots made of silicon. Experience with functional robots (factory, vacuum, lawn mower) had a positive affect on preferences for having robots made out of plastic ($p<0.05$).

Table 3. Effect of nationality on material preferences

Materials	sig		Korea N=73	US N=99	Turkey N=46
Silicon	0.12	M	.59	.47	.46
		SD	.50	.50	.51
Fabric	<0.01	M	.03	.23	.10
		SD	.17	.42	.30
Plastic	0.03	M	.45	.58	.35
		SD	.50	.50	.48
Metal	0.02	M	.32	.52	.26
		SD	.47	.50	.44
Does not matter	0.02	M	.12	.31	.16
		SD	.33	.48	.37

4.2.3 Facial Expression

Participants also expressed their preferences regarding facial expressions in robots, once again being able to give multiple answers (see Table 4) and scored by giving each category a (1: selected) or (0: not selected) value. A face with dynamic facial expressions was the most commonly preferred option. Mixed-effect analysis of variance and post hoc comparisons showed that US participants preferred robots not to have facial expressions or a face at all to a significantly higher degree than Korean and Turkish participants. US and Korean participants tended to prefer fixed facial expressions more than Turkish participants.

Table 4. Effect of nationality on facial expression preferences

Expression	sig		Korea N=73	US N=99	Turkey N=46
Fixed facial expression	0.06	M	.24	.45	.06
		SD	.43	.50	.24
Changing facial expression	0.47	M	.58	.46	.51
		SD	.50	.50	.51
Does not need facial expression	0.71	M	.14	.33	.11
		SD	.35	.47	.32
Does not need face	<0.01	M	.06	.51	.23
		SD	.23	.50	.43
No preference	0.59	M	.13	.17	.09
		SD	.34	.38	.28

4.2.4 Lifelikeness

We asked participants to evaluate how much they would like to interact with robots that were machine-like, plant-like, animal-like, or human-like on the 5-point opposition scale. Mixed-effects analysis of variance and subsequent comparisons showed Koreans had a strong preference for humanlike robots compared to US participants, US participants had a strong preference for machine-like robots over others, and Turkish participants were neutral on both types (See table 5). Koreans had a significantly higher preference for animal-like robots compared to Turkish participants, and for plant-like robots compared to both US and Turkish participants. Turkish participants were significantly more negative towards plant-like robots than others, though this preference might also have been affected by exposure to robot toys, which had a significant negative effect on preferences for plant-like robots ($p<0.05$). Prior experience with factory robots also increased preference for machine-like ($p<0.05$) and animal-like robots ($p<0.05$), though not as strongly as nationality.

Table 5. Effect of nationality on lifelikeness

Lifelikeness	sig		Korea N=73	US N=99	Turkey N=46
Machine-likeness	<0.01	M	2.88	3.48	3.06
		SD	1.16	1.09	1.31
Human-likeness	0.01	M	3.41	2.83	3.14
		SD	1.14	1.23	1.44
Animal-likeness	0.07	M	3.12	2.71	2.38
		SD	1.20	1.25	1.28
Plant-likeness	0.01	M	2.37	2.39	1.68
		SD	1.15	1.26	.98
		SD	1.14	1.27	.97

4.3 Intelligence

We asked participants their preferences regarding a robot's ability to understand their emotions, to perform tasks autonomously, and to understand social rules and cues. When asked to what extent they wanted robots to be able to *understand the users' emotions* ("1: Does not understand emotion," "2: Partially understands emotion and responds as a tool (e.g. play music)," "3: Fully understands as a friend," "4: No preference"), a majority of participants (KR: 56%, US: 57%, TK: 44%) wanted the robot to partially understand their emotional status, with no significant differences among groups. We also asked participants to *what extent robots should be autonomous* ("1: Do not want any autonomy," "2: Partially autonomous," "3: Fully autonomous," "4: No preference"). Our mixed-effect tests showed participants in all three groups preferred robots with partial autonomy (p=.63, M=1.92, SD=.60). Robots with no autonomy ranked second (24% Korean, 16% US, and 20% Turkish participants), while fully autonomous robots were the least preferred (15% Korean, 13% US, and 11% Turkish participants).

Participants rated robots according to their level of *social intelligence*, such as knowledge of etiquette, social norms, law, humor, social hierarchy, and social cues. Nationality did not have significant effect on these preferences, though age did. Preferences for robots that understand law (p=0.02), etiquette (p=.02), social norms (p=.01), humor (p=.01), and social hierarchy (p=.03) increased significantly with participant age Older participants also responded more negatively to "A robot does not need to understand social norms" (p<0.01).

4.4 Sociability

4.4.1 Expected social role of robots

Participants chose their preferences among various social roles robots could have (see Table 6), with multiple choices allowed and categories scored as (1: selected) or (0: not selected) prior to analysis. Mixed-effects analysis showed a significant effect of nationality on their preferences for robots as assistants, pets, and no social role, and a strong trend regarding robots as servants (see Table 8). All participants gave low evaluations to robots as companions (p=.23, M=.20) and teachers (p=.07, M=.19). Post-hoc comparisons showed Koreans assign social roles to robots significantly more often than other participants. Koreans preferred robots as assistants more than both Turkish and US participants, and as pets more than Turkish participants. Unlike Koreans, the majority of whom believed robots should have social roles (92%), most US participants saw robots as tools (53%).

While there were no significant effects of nationality, we found familiarity with toy robots increased preferences for robots as assistants (p<0.01), companions (p=.02), and teachers (p=.01).

Table 6. Effect of nationality on social role preferences

Social role	sig		Korea N=73	US N=99	Turkey N=46
Assistant	0.02	M	.77	.64	.51
		SD	.42	.48	.50
Companion	0.23	M	.25	.17	.26
		SD	.43	.38	.43
Teacher	0.07	M	.15	.25	.09
		SD	.36	.43	.28
Pet	0.02	M	.32	.15	.09
		SD	.47	.36	.28
Servant	0.05	M	.56	.34	.34
		SD	.50	.48	.48
No social role, robots are just tools	<0.01	M	.08	.53	.37
		SD	.28	.50	.49

4.4.2 Expected Users in Various Social Contexts

To understand the roles participants expect robots to play in different social contexts, we asked them to rate which social actors would be most likely to interact with robots in the home, school, and workplace on a 5-point oppositional scale. For *social actors in the home*, all participants had similar expectation regarding fathers (See Table 7). Preference for interaction with children was also affected by age (p<0.01) and previous experience with robots (p<0.05), so the effect of nationality is not clear. Korean and Turkish participants expected mothers and grandparents to interact with domestic robots significantly more often than US participants. Turkish participants also expected pets to interact with robots more than Korean participants. Nationality also had a significant effect on expected levels of interaction of different *social actors in schools*. Turkish participants expected principals and staff to interact with robots significantly more than Korean participants (See Table 9). Korean and Turkish participants expected more interaction with students and parents than those in the US. Turkish participants expected significantly higher levels of interaction between robots and support staff *in the workplace* compared to Korean participants. Media exposure had significant positive effects on preferences for robots to interact with executives (p<0.05), supervisors (p<0.05), and administrative assistants (p<0.05), while age had negative effects on expectations that robots will interact with administrative assistants (p<0.05) and interns (p<0.01).

Table 7. Effect of nationality on social actors in use contexts

Social actor		sig		Korea N=73	US N=99	Turkey N=46
Home	Father	0.40	M	3.29	3.23	3.53
			SD	.92	1.10	.99
	Mother	0.11	M	3.81	3.27	4.09
			SD	.94	1.11	.93
	Kids	<0.01	M	3.84	2.83	3.74
			SD	1.10	1.25	1.14
	Grandparents	<0.01	M	3.07	2.60	3.82
			SD	1.26	1.20	1.20
	Pets	<0.01	M	1.81	2.20	3.03
			SD	1.12	1.09	1.34
School	Principals	<0.01	M	2.94	3.01	3.65
			SD	1.20	1.14	1.04
	Teachers	0.07	M	3.91	3.33	3.97
			SD	1.03	1.00	.94
	Students	0.04	M	3.81	3.00	3.88
			SD	1.20	1.21	1.01
	Staff	0.02	M	3.35	3.35	3.88
			SD	1.17	1.03	1.2
	Parents	0.04	M	2.78	2.12	2.97
			SD	1.24	.97	1.26
Workplace	Executives	0.12	M	3.03	2.68	3.36
			SD	1.24	1.13	1.14
	Supervisors	0.38	M	3.33	2.96	3.42
			SD	1.15	1.06	1.12
	Administrative assistants	0.05	M	3.63	3.04	3.58
			SD	1.10	1.00	.97
	Interns	0.02	M	3.71	2.96	3.12
			SD	1.07	1.04	1.00
	Supporting staff	0.01	M	3.57	3.55	4.30
			SD	1.13	.96	.88

4.5 Interactivity

Participants were asked to choose different modes of interaction they would like to have with robots using a 5-point oppositional scale. Nationality significantly influenced interaction mode preferences (see Table 8). Korean participants preferred multiple modalities including sound and speech compared to US participants, while Turkish participants preferred smart technologies over both American and Korean participants. Male participants were more positive on using touch ($p<0.05$) and speech ($p<0.05$) as modes of interaction.

Table 8. Effect of nationality on interaction mode

Interaction mode	sig		Korea N=73	US N=99	Turkey N=46
Sound	<0.01	M	3.64	2.88	3.69
		SD	1.10	.95	1.13
Visual cues	0.61	M	3.54	3.34	3.77
		SD	1.13	.84	1.02
Gestures	0.30	M	3.45	2.84	3.63
		SD	1.10	1.10	1.26
Speech	0.01	M	4.18	3.52	3.86
		SD	.98	1.14	1.09
Touch	0.09	M	3.12	2.41	2.91
		SD	1.24	1.25	1.40
Bodily movements	0.10	M	3.41	2.78	3.44
		SD	1.10	1.10	1.21
Smart technology	0.02	M	3.78	3.71	4.49
		SD	1.08	1.07	.78

4.6 Religious and spiritual beliefs

One of our aims in this survey was to see whether participants' explicitly stated religious beliefs, which are commonly seen as an important factor in robot acceptance (e.g. [4]), were correlated with their attitudes towards and evaluations of robots.

4.6.1 Religious affiliation

Participants' explicit religious affiliations are shown in Table 9. The majority of participants in our survey (59%) identified as not religious. We did not find any correlation between participants' stated religious affiliation and their preferences for various robot design criteria (e.g. form, interactivity, intelligence).

Table 9. Effect of nationality on robot personality

Religion	Korea N=73	US N=99	Turkey N=46
Protestant	23	17	0
Catholic	4	9	0
Muslim	0	0	24
Buddhist	2	0	0
Not religious	41	57	18
Other	0	3*	0

*Mormon: 2, Jewish: 1

4.6.2 Spiritual beliefs

Participants rated their agreement with a series of statements that reflect particular beliefs and social norms, as well as their adaptations to future interactions with robots, on a 5-point oppositional scale. The statements reflected animist beliefs ("A tree has a soul," "An animal has a soul," "A robot has a soul"), Confucian social norms ("A robot needs to use the honorific to older adults," "A robot should know how to bow and whom to bow to"), and human exceptionialism ("Humans are unique among the creatures in the world," "A human is the owner of nature and can use it as a tool," "Robots should not be made in human form").

A mixed-effects analysis of variance found Koreans were strongly in agreement with both statements related to *Confucian social norms*, Turkish participants agreed with the statement on the use of the honorific, while US participants did not agree with either statement (See Table 10). *Animism* has been widely discussed as a belief/philosophy that might affect people's acceptance and perceptions of robots. Turkish participants expressed significantly stronger agreement with animist statements compared to Koreans, who agreed weakly, and US participants, who did not agree. Interestingly, these animist beliefs did not extend to robots, as all groups on average disagreed with the notion that a robot might have a soul. Nationality had a significant effect on participants' agreement with the statements that "A human is the owner of nature and can use it as a tool," with which Turkish participants disagreed significantly more than Koreans.

Table 10. Effect of nationality on spiritual beliefs

Beliefs	sig		Korea N=73	US N=99	Turkey N=46
A robot needs to use the honorific to older adults.	<0.01	M	3.73	2.50	3.74
		SD	1.13	1.28	1.29
A robot should know how to bow and whom to bow	<0.01	M	3.31	1.72	2.54
		SD	1.22	1.21	1.48
A tree has a soul.	<0.01	M	2.93	2.14	4.35
		SD	1.22	1.36	1.23
An animal has a soul	<0.01	M	3.34	2.84	4.59
		SD	1.30	1.55	.96
A robot could have a soul	0.54	M	2.09	1.88	2.03
		SD	1.11	1.27	1.33
A human is the owner of nature and can use it as a tool	<0.01	M	2.31	1.93	1.51
		SD	1.44	1.20	1.14
Humans are unique among creatures in the world	0.94	M	3.46	3.38	3.33
		SD	1.28	1.50	.1.73
Robots should not be made in human form	0.38	M	2.30	2.43	2.03
		SD	1.30	1.45	1.29

4.6.3 Correlations with spiritual beliefs

Pearson product-moment correlation coefficients (r) and Spearman's Rank Order (r_s) correlations were computed to assess whether participants' preferences regarding robot design and use were correlated with their religious affiliation and spiritual beliefs. The most common correlations of spiritual beliefs and robot design and use preferences were related to participants' agreement with Confucian values. Agreement with the statement that "A robot should know how to bow and whom to bow to" was positively correlated with participants' acceptance of robots in the home (r_s=.415, n=170, $p<0.01$), museum (r_s=.364, n=159, $p<0.01$), and hotel (r_s=.336, n=168, $p<0.01$); agreement with "A robot needs to use the honorific to older people" was positively correlated with participants' willingness to use robots in the home (r_s=.356, n=174, $p<0.01$), museum (r_s=351, n=164, $p<0.01$), and hotel (r_s=.309, n=170, $p<0.01$). Robot bowing was also positively correlated with preference for female robots (r_s=.354, n=171, $p<0.01$) and human-like appearance (r_s=.424, n=163, $p<0.01$); it was negatively correlated with preference for machine-like robots (r_s=-.346, n=162, $p<0.01$). We found negative correlations between no social role for robots and Confucian beliefs about robots bowing (r=-441, n=171, $p<0.01$) and using the honorific to elders (r=-319, n=180, $p<0.01$). A preference for robots with "no face" correlated negatively with participants' agreement with the need for robots to use the honorific (r=-.366, n=175, $p<0.01$) and bow appropriately (r=-.371, n=171, $p<0.01$). We found a positive correlation between the expected level of emotional intelligence and agreement for robots using the honorific (r=.358, n=165, $p<0.01$), and knowing how to bow (r=.435, n=164, $p<0.01$).

Beliefs in animism (e.g. A tree has a soul) showed no correlation with preferences for human-likeness, contrary to our expectations.

4.7 Media Exposure

Along with religion, media exposure is often mentioned as a defining factor in people's perceptions and acceptance of robots. To gauge media exposure and its effects, we asked participants to evaluate how robots are portrayed in the media using a 7-point semantic differential scale (positive-negative, scary-friendly, mean-kind, useful-useless, and smart-stupid). We also asked them to evaluate five fictional robots on the same scale: Japanese animations Astroboy and Doraemon, Maria from *Metropolis*, R2D2 from *Star Wars*, and Terminator (see Figure 1).

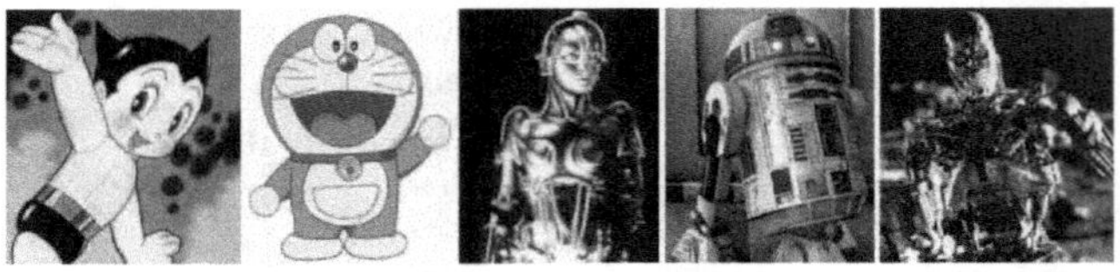

Figure 1. Astroboy, Doraemon, Maria, R2D2, and Terminator

Mixed-effects analysis of variance showed US participants considered portrayals of robots in the media to be significantly more negative, scary and mean than Korean and Turkish participants (See Table 11). All participants thought media portrayed robots as useful and smart. Koreans were more familiar with friendly robots like Astroboy (91%) and Doraemon (76%) than US (66% Astroboy, 3% Doraemon) and Turkish participants (11% Astroboy and 4% Doraemon). We did not find any correlation between being familiar with friendly robots like Astroboy and positivity towards robots, aside from a weak correlation between knowledge of Astroboy and acceptance of robots in the home (r_s =290, n=216, $p<0.01$).

Table 11. Effect of nationality on robots in media

Evaluation	sig		Korea N=73	US N=99	Turkey N=46
Positive - negative	<0.01	M	4.65	3.90	4.77
		SD	1.25	1.25	1.26
Friendly - scary	<0.01	M	4.66	3.72	4.26
		SD	1.16	1.21	1.34
Kind - mean	0.07	M	4.68	4.03	4.40
		SD	1.04	1.08	1.24
Useful - useless	0.69	M	5.65	5.71	5.54
		SD	1.00	.94	1.15
Smart - stupid	0.44	M	5.44	5.66	5.23
		SD	1.41	1.16	1.46

4.8 Evaluation of existing robots

Along with fictional robots, we also asked participants to evaluate existing robots using the same 7-point semantic differential scale. Robots presented were Aibo, Keepon, Wakamaru, Geminoid, Roomba, and Tmsuk (See Figure 2). Prompts to evaluate the robots were accompanied by links to YouTube videos showing their operation and basic movements in a neutral context. As we did not have a way to do physical experiments with so many participants in diverse locations, we included videos to give participants a sense of the robots' embodiment. We discuss only significant differences below due to space constraints.

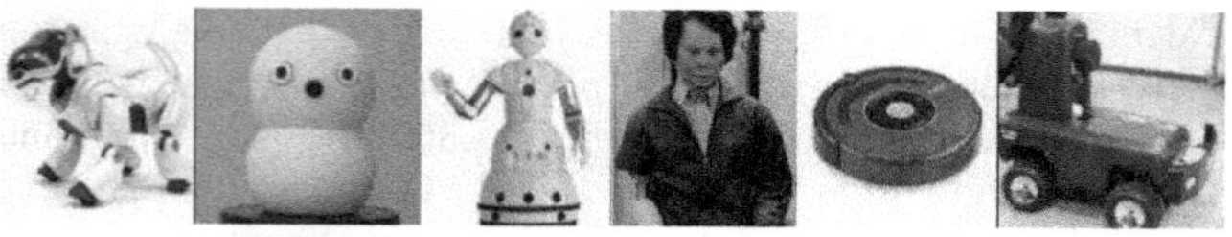

Figure 2. Aibo, Keepon, Wakamaru, Geminoid, Roomba, Tmsuk

Participants regardless of their nationality considered Aibo to be friendly (p=.651, m=5.46, sd=1.28) and kind (p=.338, m=5.12, sd=1.17). Korean and Turkish participants were more likely to evaluate Aibo as positive and useful than US participants, while Koreans saw it as smarter than US participants. Female participants also tended to report Aibo as more positive ($p<0.05$), useful($p<0.01$), and smart ($p<0.01$).

Table 12. Effect of nationality on Aibo evaluation

Types of intelligence	sig		Korea N=73	US N=99	Turkey N=46
Negative - positive	<0.01	M	5.61	4.95	5.77
		SD	1.10	1.23	1.33
Useless - useful	<0.01	M	4.56	2.81	3.80
		SD	1.53	1.36	1.76
Stupid - smart	<0.01	M	4.35	3.38	3.83
		SD	1.35	1.08	1.56

Participants regardless of their nationality evaluated Keepon as positive (m=5.57, sd=1.27), neither smart nor stupid (m=4.07, sd=1.32), friendly (m=5.77, sd=1.11), and kind (m=5.25, sd=1.17). Koreans found Keepon to be more useful than Turkish and US participants.

Table 13. effect of nationality on Keepon evaluation

Types of intelligence	sig		Korea N=73	US N=99	Turkey N=46
Mean - kind	0.11	M	4.96	5.41	5.46
		SD	1.06	1.18	1.27
Useless - useful	<0.01	M	4.24	2.77	3.34
		SD	1.36	1.34	1.73
		SD	1.35	1.33	1.60

Participants regardless of their nationality considered Geminoid is neither smart nor stupid (p=.274, m=4.11, sd=1.14). Both technical expertise and nationality had a significant effect on the negativity of evaluations of Geminoid, with Korean participants showing significantly more negative impressions than US participants. Koreans also thought Geminoid is mean to a significantly greater extent than other participants. Participants with a higher level of technical expertise tended to evaluate Geminoid more positively ($p<0.01$). Also, male participants tended to say Geminoid is more friendly ($p<0.05$)

Table 14. Effect of nationality on Geminoid evaluation

Types of intelligence	sig		Korea N=73	US N=99	Turkey N=46
Negative - positive	<0.01	M	2.48	3.47	2.77
		SD	1.09	1.43	1.48
Scary - friendly	0.043	M	2.58	3.26	3.15
		SD	1.07	1.20	1.40
Mean - kind	<0.01	M	3.34	4.07	4.06
		SD	1.08	.70	.1.03

Overall, the evaluations of existing robots were not conclusive in relation to nationality of the participants due to other factors, which also suggest further avenues for future research.

5. DISCUSSION

Culturally situated studies of technology, such as Bell's ethnography of pervasive technology [4] and Ito's study of mobile phones in Japan [12], showed that cultural factors affect situated practices and sense making about technology in everyday use. Unlike these technologies, robots are not commonly used in everyday life, so we used online surveys rather than ethnographic and observational methods to explore cultural variability in user perceptions and preferences regarding robots. Our results suggest avenues for further experimental and field research as well as factors to consider in designing robots for different cultural contexts.

5.1 Culturally variable user preferences

We found that participants from the three countries surveyed had significantly different preferences regarding how robots should look, act, who they should interact with, and which contexts they should be used in. Korean participants chose robots with design characteristics that were more animate and social than those chosen by US participants, preferring robots with a human-like appearance and expressive faces. US participants, on the other hand, preferred machine-like robots made of metal and without faces or facial expressions. US participants were also more likely to say they had no preference regarding a robot's appearance. Korean participants stated it is appropriate to use robots in social contexts and roles, while US participants did not think robots should be used in everyday contexts and saw them as tools. These results fit the a prior interview study we performed with Korean and US participants [17], in which US participants had a predominantly functional view of robots, while Koreans expected robots to provide social services.

Turkish participants showed a wider diversity of opinions about robot design and use, fitting in somewhere between Korean and US participants. This may have to do with the novelty of robots in Turkey, where specific expectations about their design and use have not yet become culturally dominant. Turkish participants were generally comfortable with having robots serve in various social contexts and roles and with robots having certain human-like characteristics, such as dynamic facial expressions. They equally preferred having machine-like and human-like robots.

These results show that East Asian participants are not alone in accepting socially interactive robots and further suggest that factors beyond religious belief and media exposure, including current social norms and dynamics present across national contexts, might have important effects on this acceptance. Our results also suggest that nationality has a particularly strong effect when participants socially contextualized their preferences regarding robot design and application, such as in choosing appropriate interaction partners and social roles.

5.2 Influence of Media and Religion

Our survey showed that participants varied in terms of their religious beliefs and levels of media exposure, but that these factors did not fully explain the cultural variations in participants' ideas about robots. We did not find any correlations among explicit religious affiliation and user preferences and evaluations of robot design and use. We did, however, find that particular social norms and spiritual beliefs were correlated with participants' statements about robots. Beliefs related to social hierarchy and etiquette (e.g. bowing, use of honorific) were relevant to Korean and Turkish participants who preferred socially interactive robots. Less practice-oriented beliefs (e.g., animal has a soul) did not carry over to user preferences regarding robot design.

Similarly, media portrayals seem to influence user imagination about robots, but did not have significant correlations with participants' acceptance of specific types of robots in society or their preferred design characteristics. Korean participants showed the highest level of exposure to robots in the media, knowing both friendly and threatening robotic characters. US participants were generally familiar with more functional robots, while Turkish participants had a low degree of exposure to the fictional robots we presented. Regardless of their familiarity with diverse robots, Korean participants had a more socially oriented imaginary of robots in society, while US participants thought of robots functionally in line with the nature of their media exposure to robots, and Turkish participants accepted a variety of robots.

Our results suggest that contextually situated social norms and behaviors might be more important for how users view and prefer to use robots than broadly defined religious beliefs and media portrayals of robots, although the latter might affect their general imagination and views. As we saw in prior research [17], users tend to envision robots within specific social contexts, so studying situated interaction and sense making in context will be crucial for developing culturally sensitive robot design.

5.3 Situating robots in social dynamics

Korean and Turkish participants were comfortable with having robots in various everyday settings, while US participants preferred to use robots mainly in industrial settings. Both US and Turkish participants were uncomfortable with having robots used in the police station, which may reflect current events involving police brutality in Turkey, and privacy concerns regarding the use of technology for surveillance in the US.

Cultural variability in participants' preferences for how robots were used further extended to the kinds of social roles they expected robots to take in these contexts. Korean participants envisioned robots as social but subservient to humans, as shown by their preference for robots addressing users with the honorific as well as their desire for robots not to initiate interaction. Korean participants' preference for robots with fixed facial expressions may also be seen as a way of symbolizing actors lower in the social hierarchy, who should not express their emotions directly to others. In their evaluations of robots, Koreans found even simple social robots like Aibo and Keepon to be useful, in contrast to other participants. US participants, who view robots mainly as functional tools, saw such robots as generally useless.

Participant preferences for specific roles of robots also reflected their local social dynamics. The extended family structure in Turkey, in which grandparents participate in the daily life of the family, made them important potential users. In both Turkey and Korea, mothers were the most common users in the home, reflecting the gendered division of domestic labor in those countries. In the US, in contrast, both father and mothers were evenly ranked as the main users of robots.

In summary, our results suggest that, rather than focusing on broad cultural factors such as differences in religious beliefs and media portrayals, researchers and designers need to study the current social dynamics in situated contexts of use to identify salient factors that can inform future robot design.

5.4 Universal design preferences for robots

Regardless of cultural background and other robot design and use preferences, all participants agreed on a few design factors for everyday robots. These were level of autonomy and control over robots. In contrast to the long-term aims of robotics to create autonomous machines, none of our participants wanted fully automated robots. Partial autonomy was preferred for robots as social actors and tools. Participants wanted to retain partial control over robots by making their actions dependent on user commands and instructions. This cross-cultural agreement suggests that appropriate levels of autonomy and modes of user control will be important to consider for robotics developers all over the world.

5.5 Limitations

While our study included a diverse set of participants from three countries, our sample was not representative of the broader population. Our respondents were generally highly educated people living in major cities and a university town. Our respondents, however, fit the profile of potential early adopters of robotic technology, so their views provide a legitimate initial overview of the initial differences that might occur across national cultures. Furthermore, our data was demographically unbalanced across the national samples. A mixed model analysis identified multiple areas of user perceptions of robots in which nationality is a significant factor, as well as additional variables that should be further explored, including gender, age, and prior exposure to robots (the latter in particular will become increasingly salient as exposure to robots in society is more likely). Finally, our use of a survey methodology for studying cross-cultural differences allowed us to pinpoint general differences but did not allow us to isolate specific factors that cause these differences (as might be possible in an experiment) or to study the situated nature of user sense making about robots, which needs to be done to understand the different meanings that users ascribe to robot categories, use contexts, and social roles. Our results point to different areas in which further studies can be performed, such as the focus on studying how robots fit into social norms and dynamics rather than focusing on user characteristics (e.g. religious belief), as well as the study of how cultural meanings may change with broader mediated and face-to-face exposure to robots.

6. CONCLUSION

Through a broad survey of user preferences for robot design and use in the US, Turkey, and S. Korea, we identified culturally variable design characteristics and salient cultural factors that affect user conceptions and evaluations of robots. Our exploratory study emphasizes the importance of performing cross-cultural studies of robots that go beyond general characteristics and delve into more contextually and socially situated dynamics of sense making and interaction to develop technologies for global markets. We particularly suggest focusing not only on cultural difference but also on similarity, and doing situated studies of robot use contexts to clearly identify how culturally variable factors might be incorporated into designing future robots.

7. ACKNOWLEDGMENTS

We appreciate the time and help of all our participants. This work was supported by NSF EAGER grant # IIS-1143712.

8. REFERENCES

[1] Bartneck, C. 2008. Who like androids more: Japanese or US Americans? *Proc. of RO-MAN 2008*, IEEE, 553-557.

[2] Bartneck, C., Nomura, T., Kanda, T., Suzuki, T. and Kensuke, K. 2005. Cultural differences in attitudes towards robots. *Proc. AISB 2005*, 1-4.

[3] Bartneck, C., Suzuki, T., Kanda, T., and Nomura, T., 2007. The influence of people's culture and prior experiences with Aibo on their attitude towards robots. *AI & Society 21*, 1, 217-230.

[4] Bell, G. 2006. The age of the thumb: A cultural reading of mobile technologies from Asia. *Knowledge, Technology & Policy*, *19* (2), 41-57.

[5] Disalvo, C.F., Gemperle, F., Forlizzi, J., and Kiesler, S., 2002. All robots are not created equal: The design and perception of humanoid robot heads. *Proc. of DIS 2002,* ACM, 321-326.

[6] Evers, V., Maldonado, H.C., Brodecki, T.L. and Hinds, P.J. 2008. Relational vs. group self-construal: Untangling the role of national culture in HRI. *Proc.of HRI'08*, ACM, 255-262.

[7] Ezer, N., Fisk, A., and Rogers, W., 2009. Attitudinal and Intentional Acceptance of Domestic Robots by Younger and Older Adults. In *Universal Access in Human-Computer Interaction. Intelligent and Ubiquitous Interaction Environments*, C. Stephanidis Ed. Springer Berlin Heidelberg, 39-48.

[8] Fujimura, J.H., 2005. Postgenomic futures: translations across the machine-nature border in systems biology. *New Genetics and Society 24*, 2, 195-226.

[9] Geraci, R.M., 2006. Spiritual robots: Religion and our scientific view of the natural world. *Theology and Science 4*, 3, 229-246.

[10] Hornyak, T.N. 2007. *Loving the Machine: The art and science of Japanese robots*. Kodansha International, Tokyo.

[11] Ito, K. 2007. Astroboy's Birthday: Robotics and culture in contemporary Japanese society. Paper presented at *EASTS 2007*, from http://stspo.ym.edu.tw/easts/2007/Ito.pdf.

[12] Ito, M., Okabe, D. and Matsuda, M. 2006. *Personal, Portable, Pedestrian: Mobile Phones in Japanese Life*. The MIT Press.

[13] Kaplan, F., 2004. Who is afraid of the humanoid? Investigating cultural differences in the acceptance of robots. *International Journal of Humanoid Robotics 1*, 3, 465-480.

[14] Kim, J.-Y., 2006. Critique of the New Historical Landscape of South Korean Animation. *Animation 1*, 1, 61-81.

[15] Kitano, N., 2006. „Rinri": An Incitement towards the Existence of Robots in Japanese Soci-ety. *Ethics in Robotics 6*, 78.

[16] Lee, H.R., Šabanović, S., English version survey, from http://homes.soic.indiana.edu/hrl/robotsurvey/english_survey .pdf.

[17] Lee, H.R., Sung, J., Šabanović, S., and Han, J., 2012. Cultural design of domestic robots: A study of user expectations in Korea and the United States. *Proc. of RO-MAN 2012,* IEEE, 803-808.

[18] Lee, M.K., Forlizzi, J., Rybski, P.E., Crabbe, F., Chung, W., Finkle, J., Glaser, E., and Kiesler, S., 2009. The Snackbot: Documenting the design of a robot for long-term. *Proc. of HRI'09*, IEEE, 7-14.

[19] Lin, W., Rau, P.L.P., Evers, V., Robinson, B.K., and Hinds, P., 2010. When in Rome: The role of culture & context in adherence to robot recommendations. *Proc. of HRI'10,* ACM, 359-366.

[20] Macdorman, K., Vasudevan, S., and Ho, C.-C., 2009. Does Japan really have robot mania? Comparing attitudes by implicit and explicit measures. *AI & Society 23*, 4, 485-510.

[21] Šabanović, S., In Press. Inventing Japan's "robotics culture:" The repeated assembly of science, technology, and culture in social robotics. *Social Studies of Science.*

[22] Shaw-Garlock, G., 2009. Looking Forward to Sociable Robots. *International Journal of Social Robotics 1*, 3, 249-260.

[23] Shibata, T., Wada, K., Ikeda, Y., and Sabanovic, S., 2009. Cross-Cultural Studies on Subjective Evaluation of a Seal Robot. *Advanced Robotics 23*, 4, 443-458.

[24] Suchman, L., 2007. *Human-machine reconfigurations: Plans and situated actions.* Cambridge University Press.

[25] Wagner, C., 2009.The Japanese way of robotics: Interacting naturally with robots as a national character? *Proc. of RO-MAN 2009,* IEEE, 510-515.

Conversational Gaze Aversion for Humanlike Robots

Sean Andrist, Xiang Zhi Tan, Michael Gleicher, and Bilge Mutlu
Department of Computer Sciences, University of Wisconsin–Madison
1210 West Dayton Street, Madison, WI 53706 USA
{sandrist, xtan, gleicher, bilge}@cs.wisc.edu

ABSTRACT

Gaze aversion—the intentional redirection away from the face of an interlocutor—is an important nonverbal cue that serves a number of conversational functions, including signaling cognitive effort, regulating a conversation's intimacy level, and managing the conversational floor. In prior work, we developed a model of how gaze aversions are employed in conversation to perform these functions. In this paper, we extend the model to apply to conversational robots, enabling them to achieve some of these functions in conversations with people. We present a system that addresses the challenges of adapting human gaze aversion movements to a robot with very different affordances, such as a lack of articulated eyes. This system, implemented on the NAO platform, autonomously generates and combines three distinct types of robot head movements with different purposes: face-tracking movements to engage in mutual gaze, idle head motion to increase lifelikeness, and purposeful gaze aversions to achieve conversational functions. The results of a human-robot interaction study with 30 participants show that gaze aversions implemented with our approach are perceived as intentional, and robots can use gaze aversions to appear more thoughtful and effectively manage the conversational floor.

Categories and Subject Descriptors

H.1.2 [**Models and Principles**]: User/Machine Systems—*human factors, software psychology*; H.5.2 [**Information Interfaces and Presentation**]: User Interfaces—*evaluation/ methodology, user-centered design*

General Terms

Design, Experimentation, Human Factors

1. INTRODUCTION

Gaze is an important nonverbal behavior for social interaction [9]. Research in human-robot interaction (HRI) has investigated the role of gaze behavior across a variety of settings, including open-ended conversation [11], presenting information [16], and storytelling [19]. A recent survey of research on social gaze in HRI proposes a computationally oriented definition of social gaze as a mapping from social functions to the expression of one or more discrete gaze actions [27]. In this paper, we focus on one of these actions—*gaze aversion*—and show they might enable humanlike robots to achieve a number of positive social functions in conversations with humans.

HRI'14, March 3–6, 2014, Bielefeld, Germany.

ACM 978-1-4503-2658-2/14/03 ...$15.00.
http://dx.doi.org/10.1145/2559636.2559666.

Figure 1: A human conversational partner interacting with the NAO robot. Three example gaze aversion directions implemented for the NAO are shown: down, up, and to the side.

Gaze aversion is defined as the intentional redirection of gaze away from the face of an interlocutor, and it is used in conversations to achieve three primary functions: cognitive, intimacy modulation, and floor management. First is the *cognitive* function: speakers spend much more time averting their gaze than listeners in order to better attend to the planning and delivery of their utterances while limiting external distraction [4]. Second is the *intimacy-modulating* function: periodic gaze aversions while speaking or listening can serve to modulate the overall level of intimacy in the conversation [1]. Third is the *floor management* function: looking away while pausing during speech is used to indicate that the conversational floor is being held and the speaker should not be interrupted [13]. These three functions—cognitive, intimacy, and floor management—correspond with three social contexts identified in previous work on social gaze in HRI: projecting mental state, establishing agency, and regulating the interaction process respectively [27].

While the social science literature has highlighted the positive functions of gaze aversion, it does not provide the exact measurements required to synthesize a model of gaze aversion for robots that could achieve these functions. In previous work [3], we analyzed a corpus of human-human conversations to obtain precise spatial and temporal parameters of gaze aversion movements in relation to speech and conversational function. This analysis informed the design of a gaze controller for virtual agents that generated appropriately timed gaze aversions during conversations with people. However, the prior work does not consider the challenges of applying the model to an autonomous robot, nor does it provide any evidence that gaze aversions can be effectively used by robots.

In this paper, we demonstrate that humanlike robots can use gaze aversions to achieve conversational goals. We apply techniques that address the challenges of applying a human-based gaze aversion model to a robot, describe an implementation on the NAO platform, and evaluate the resulting system in a human-robot interaction study. Our work considers three key technical challenges: adapting the human movements to a robot with non-human affordances, making the movements appear lifelike and intentional, and integrating the gaze aversion movements with other head movements. A description of the system, along with a link to downloadable source code, is presented in Section 3.2. In our experimental evaluation, presented in Section 4, human participants interacted with two robots in four conversational tasks (Figure 1). Through this evaluation, we show how the gaze aversions employed by the robot were perceived as intentional, served to make the robot appear more thoughtful, and helped the robot manage the conversational floor.

2. BACKGROUND

In this section, we present an overview of social and cognitive science research on human gaze aversion in conversations, in which three primary functions of gaze aversion have been identified: facilitation of cognitive processing, intimacy modulation, and floor management. We then review related work on designing effective gaze mechanisms for robots.

2.1. Conversational Gaze Aversion

The frequency of speaker gaze aversions in conversation has been shown to be related to the difficulty of *cognitive processing* [10]. When constant mutual gaze is required from someone speaking spontaneously in social interaction, that person's speech becomes significantly impaired [7]. Averting gaze has the practical benefit of improving cognitive performance. This is because an interlocutor's face is rich in social information, and is a cognitively demanding visual target. When people avert their gaze from their interlocutor, they are able to deploy additional cognitive resources to the task of thinking or remembering information. With these aversions, a speaker signals to the listener that cognitive processing is occurring, creating the impression that deep thought or creativity is being undertaken in formulating their speech [4].

Eye contact is a primary contributor to the level of *intimacy* in a conversation along with physical proximity, topic intimacy, amount of smiling, and so on [5]. If one of these dimensions of intimacy is disturbed, compensatory changes will likely occur along the other dimensions. For example, research has shown that children avert their gaze more when answering questions in face-to-face rather than video-mediated conversations [8]. In general, people frequently avert their gaze to alleviate feelings of self-consciousness and, while listening, to make speakers more comfortable and to reduce negative perceptions associated with staring [1].

Gaze is important for facilitating turn-taking and conversational *floor management* [13]. When exchanging speaking turns in conversation, a pattern is frequently observed in which the first speaker finishes speaking, looks toward their interlocutor and engages in momentary mutual gaze, and finally the second speaker averts their gaze and begins their speaking turn [21]. By looking away at the beginning of an utterance, the speaker strengthens his or her claim over the speaking turn. Looking away during a pause in speech is also used to indicate that the conversational floor is being held and that the speaker should not be interrupted [13].

2.2. Robot Gaze Mechanisms

Previous research has shown that robots can greatly benefit from the utilization of humanlike gaze mechanisms [16, 19, 20, 28]. Modeling humanlike gaze mechanisms enables conversational robots to signal different participant roles to human interlocutors, manage turn-exchanges, and shape how users perceive the robot and the conversation [20]. Human comprehension of robot speech is improved when a robot gazes to objects it is speaking about in a similar way and with similar timings as found in human gaze behavior [28]. Robots that use gaze cues are perceived as possessing mental states and intentionality, as evidenced by previous work on gaze leakage in a human-robot guessing game [20].

To be truly effective, a robot's gaze mechanisms need to be employed contingently based on the behaviors of its human interlocutors. A robot that gazes responsively toward a human user is capable of eliciting a stronger feeling of being looked at than a robot that uses non-responsive—i.e., static or random—gaze [30]. In recent work, HRI researchers have developed a responsive, rule-based system for generating robot head nods, tilts, and gazes based on discrete dialogue acts in conversation, such as those associated with turn-taking, backchannels, and conversational fillers [16]. When employing gaze aversions in conversation, robots should do so responsively to the speech behavior of its human interlocutor.

In previous work [3], we showed how to enable virtual agents to effectively use gaze aversions responsively in conversations with people. However, it is not obvious that these results extend to HRI, as the prior work did not consider the technical challenges specific to robots. Robots and virtual agents differ along a number of social dimensions, including realism, social presence, lifelikeness, and physical proximity [24]. Several studies have demonstrated effects of these differences [6, 14, 24].

A fundamental difference between the virtual agents we used in previous work [3] and the robots used in the current work is the difference in physical affordances available for carrying out gaze motions. Overall differences in geometry mean that gaze motions and control laws need to be adapted [22]. Even more critically, the robots lack articulated eyes and must rely solely on head motions to convey gaze motions, making it unclear if they are capable of eliciting the same positive conversational outcomes found in the virtual agent work [3]. Previous research points to the possibility of such capabilities, including work which has shown that people are capable of recognizing a robot's gaze according to its head orientation [11] and that robots can use head motions alone to gaze effectively in a storytelling scenario [19].

3. ROBOT GAZE AVERSION

In prior work [3], we derived a gaze aversion model consisting of precise spatial and temporal parameters—including length, timing, and frequency—in relation to conversational functions and speech. In the next section, we review the data collection and model parameters relevant for the design of a robot gaze controller. Following that, we present our design of gaze aversion motions for humanlike robots without articulated eyes, secondary head motions for achieving mutual gaze and lifelikeness, techniques for combining the different head motions, and the overall system implementation for expressing conversational gaze aversion on the NAO platform.

3.1. Modeling Gaze Aversion

We recruited 24 females and 24 males, aged 18 to 28 and previously unacquainted, for data collection (Figure 2). Each dyad engaged in a structured conversation for approximately five minutes. We analyzed recorded videos of the interactions for participants' gaze and speech. Video coding was carried out by two independent coders with partial overlap. Sequences of time spent speaking and averting gaze were annotated.

Gaze aversions were coded for the conversational function that they were perceived to be supporting: cognitive, intimacy-modulating, or floor management. This coding took place in three passes. In the first pass, the coder marked gaze aversions as cognitive if they occurred near perceived cognitive events, e.g., when a participant appeared to be thinking of a response to a question. In the second pass, gaze aversions were marked as floor management

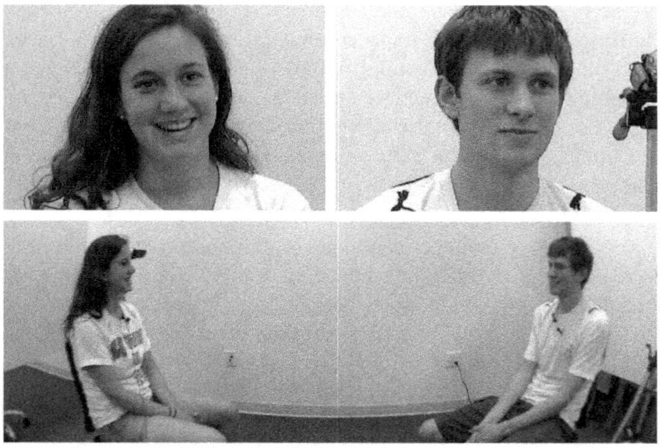

Figure 2: A participant dyad from the data collection. The participants were designated as the *interviewer* and the *interviewee*. The interviewers were instructed to ask interviewees about their movie preferences.

if they occurred near the beginning of a speaking turn or during a pause in speech. In the third pass, all remaining gaze aversions were labeled as intimacy-modulating. An inter-rater reliability analysis showed substantial agreement on the identification of gaze aversions and their conversational function (Cohen's $\kappa = .747$).

From our analysis, we obtained timing statistics for different kinds of gaze aversions. Each of these parameters is modeled as a Gaussian distribution with means and standard deviations derived from the data. For cognitive gaze shifts, we model the length ($M = 3.54s$, $SD = 1.26s$), start time in relation to cognitive events ($M = -1.32s$, $SD = 0.47s$), and end time after cognitive events ($M = 2.23s$, $SD = 0.63s$). A cognitive event is any point in time at which the robot should display a state of deep cognitive processing, e.g., at the beginning of a response to a user's question. For intimacy-modulating gaze aversions, we model the length and time between consecutive gaze aversions while speaking (length: $M = 1.96s$, $SD = 0.32s$; time between: $M = 4.75s$, $SD = 1.39s$), and while listening (length: $M = 1.14s$, $SD = 0.27s$; time between: $M = 7.21s$, $SD = 1.88s$). For floor management gaze aversions, we model the length ($M = 2.30s$, $SD = 1.10s$), start time in relation to the start of the next

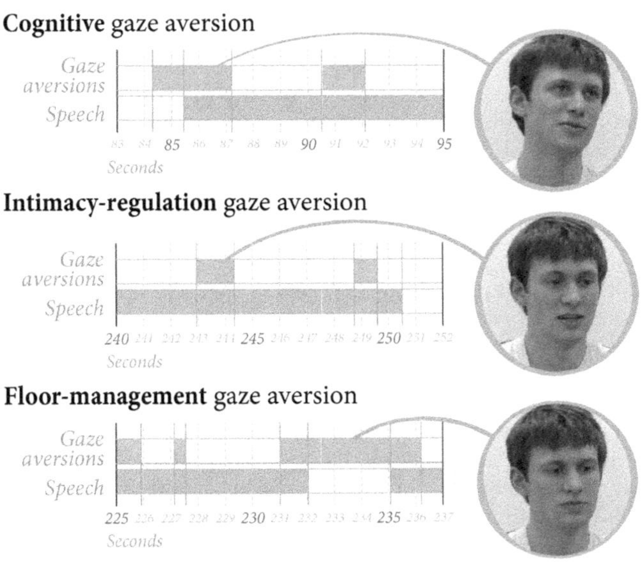

Figure 3: Three examples of gaze aversions from our human-human conversational data. Top: an upward *cognitive* gaze aversion at the beginning of a question response. Middle: a short *intimacy-regulation* gaze aversion while speaking. Bottom: a *floor-management* gaze aversion during a pause.

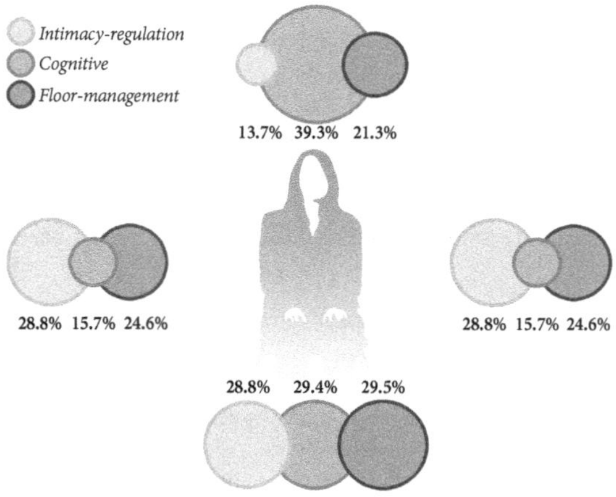

Figure 4: Percentages of gaze aversions directed up, down, and to the side, split by conversational function. Intimacy-regulating and floor-managing gaze aversions are more likely to be directed sideways, while cognitive gaze aversions are more likely to be directed upwards.

utterance ($M = -1.03s$, $SD = 0.39s$), and the end time in relation to that same utterance ($M = 1.27s$, $SD = 0.51s$). Our model also captures the time before the end of a floor-passing utterance at which point mutual gaze is engaged with the interlocutor and no more gaze aversions are generated during that utterance ($M = -2.41s$, $SD = 0.56s$). Figure 3 illustrates each type of gaze aversion.

We also labeled each gaze aversion for its direction as *up*, *down*, and *side* (Figure 4) and found that intimacy-regulating and floor-managing gaze aversions and cognitive gaze aversions were more likely to be directed sideways and upwards, respectively.

3.2. Robot Gaze Aversion Implementation

In this section, we describe methods to overcome three key technical challenges in adapting our gaze aversion model to a head controller for conversational robots: adapting the human movements to a robot with non-human affordances, making the movements appear lifelike and intentional, and integrating the gaze aversion movements with other head movements. To adapt gaze movements to a robot platform without articulated eyes, we substitute head movement for combined eye and head rotations, extending prior work that showed robot head motions to serve as valid gaze signals [19]. To make the movements appear lifelike and intentional, we combine aversion control with face tracking and structured random movements to create idle motion. To realize these behaviors in an autonomous system, we implement them in a predictive filtering framework that affords graceful combination of multiple goals and effective reaction to external events.

3.2.1. Aversion Movement Design

A robot without articulated eyes must rely on head motion alone to carry out gaze aversion motions. There are two considerations when designing these motions: the magnitude and the dynamics.

The appropriate magnitudes for gaze-averting head motions were determined in an iterative process to achieve a natural subjective appearance. Our goal was to generate head movements that are not too extreme yet clearly serve to avert the robot's gaze away from the user. Our system generates vertical gaze-averting head movements with a magnitude of approximately 20 degrees, with horizontal and downward head movements at 28 and 22 degrees respectively. For intimacy-modulating gaze aversions, these angles are scaled by a factor of 0.4, because these gaze aversions occur quite frequently and were observed in our human-human data to be employed with more subtle eyes-only motions.

For the generated gaze aversions, we attempted to recreate the head velocity profile identified in neurophysiological research on human gaze shifts [15]. This profile resembles standard ease-in/ease-out curves found in animation, in which the head rotation starts slow, speeds up during the bulk of the shift, then slows down before coming to a halt. The velocity profile was implemented using programmatically-defined bezier curves. Care was taken to respect both the upper and effective lower limits of the motors' rotational speeds, ensuring smooth motions throughout the robot's gaze shifts.

3.2.2. Achieving Mutual & Lifelike Gaze

In order to interact effectively with humans and accomplish a general feeling of lifelikeness, the robot must use its head for not only gaze aversion, but also mutual gaze. To engage in mutual gaze, the robot must track the user's face. For our system, we use a face-tracking algorithm that used a Microsoft Kinect situated behind the robot. The robot continuously adjusts its head rotation based on the results of the face tracking algorithm, polled every 200*ms*.

At this point the robot is capable of executing gaze aversions and face tracking, however a problem remains in that the transition between statically gazing at the user and engaging in a gaze aversion is still quite abrupt. When the user is sitting still and the robot is not currently engaged in a gaze aversion motion, the robot's head becomes motionless and loses its sense of liveliness. To address this problem, we generate a small amount of idle head motion for the robot to execute at all times. This idle motion was implemented by adding a small amount of structured noise, generated by a Perlin noise function [23], to the results of the face tracking algorithm. A Perlin noise function generates band-limited, pseudorandom signals that are useful for emulating biological forms and motions.

3.2.3. Combining Behaviors

The robot uses its head for three different types of gaze motions: gaze aversions, face tracking, and idle motion. At any point in time, the robot has multiple distinct goals for its target head rotation. These goals must be combined in a natural manner that maintains an ability to be reactive to new goals. To solve this problem, we use a Kalman filter [12], a linear predictive filter used for estimating the state of a system given past states and target goals. The filter predicts the appropriate motion by blending estimated trajectories generated from the current state and current goals, and corrects these estimates as the goals change. The filter gains were chosen empirically to provide an appropriate balance between smoothness and reactivity.

Target head rotations from the three types of motions are streamed through this filter and combined into a single head rotation signal, allowing for graceful transitions between motions. Without this filter, head motions would have to be serially generated and completed, e.g., a head tracking motion to the face of the user would have to be completed before a gaze aversion motion could be executed. The Kalman filter solves this problem by blending estimated trajectories over time, resulting in smooth, interruptible motions.

3.2.4. System Integration

The target platform for this work was the NAO, a programmable humanoid robot manufactured by Aldebaran Robotics. [1] The NAO has 25 degrees of freedom, including two in its neck, and a multitude of sensors. All behaviors for the NAO were implemented using the .NET SDK provided by Aldebaran. Gaze aversion behaviors were implemented on the NAO using two controllers: a high-level *gaze controller* to plan the timing and direction of gaze aversions and a *head controller* to physically execute the gaze shifts. The source code for the entire system has been made available online. [2]

The head controller is situated at the end of an overall system pipeline that also includes a speech recognition system and a dialogue manager. A Microsoft Kinect with the Microsoft Speech Platform [3] are utilized for speech recognition. Recognized speech from the user is passed to a dialogue manager that associates a semantic tag with the utterance and plans the agent's speech accordingly. For example, if the dialogue manager receives a recognized question, it will produce the associated answer. Robot speech is generated in our system by playing pre-recorded audio files, but the NAO's built-in text-to-speech system can also be used.

The dialogue manager sends upcoming speech events and the current conversational state to the gaze controller. As the gaze controller receives these inputs, it continuously plans gaze aversion motions to be executed by the head controller. The exact timings of the gaze aversions are drawn from the parameter distributions reported in the previous section and visually depicted in Figure 3. The direction of each gaze aversion is similarly generated according to its function and the directional likelihoods presented in Figure 4.

Also included in the overall system are a wireless touchpad and the NAO's chest light. The wireless touchpad is used by the user to signal that the NAO can begin the next phase of the interaction, depending on the context. For example, after the user is done giving an open-ended response to a question posed by the NAO, the user would touch the touchpad to signal to the NAO that it can move on to its next question. The NAO's chest light is used to signal to users the beginning (green) and end (red) of the interaction as well as when the NAO is ready to begin a new interaction phase (blue). The chest light was not used during core interaction sequences while gaze aversions were being displayed (i.e., while asking a question, answering a question, or listening to a user's utterance).

[1]http://www.aldebaran-robotics.com/
[2]http://hci.cs.wisc.edu/projects/gaze
[3]http://msdn.microsoft.com

4. EVALUATION

We designed a study to test user perceptions of the generated gaze aversions and their effectiveness in enabling robots to achieve positive conversational functions in human-robot conversations. In this study, participants interacted in multiple conversational tasks with two NAO robots. Each task involved the participant either asking questions to the NAO or responding to questions posed by the NAO.

4.1. Study Design

The experiment involved a single independent variable, *gaze aversion behavior*, with three conditions varying between participants. One condition involved the robots using gaze aversions generated by the controllers described in the previous section, which we call the *good timing* condition. The other two conditions served as baselines for comparison. The first baseline was a *static gaze* condition in which the robots did not employ any gaze aversions. This baseline was included to demonstrate the importance of generating gaze aversion motions regardless of the timing. The second baseline was a *bad timing* condition in which the robot employed just as many gaze aversions as in the *good timing* condition but with reverse timings. More precisely, the *bad timing* condition produced a gaze shift toward the participant—to engage in mutual gaze—every time the *good timing* condition would have triggered a gaze aversion. Similarly, a gaze aversion is triggered every time the *good timing* condition would have produced a shift toward mutual gaze. This third condition was included as a baseline to show that not only the presence, but also the timing of gaze aversions is important for achieving positive social outcomes. Participants were randomly assigned to one of the three gaze aversion conditions, which was then held constant for all tasks (10 participants per condition). Regardless of condition, the robot always tracked the participant's face and utilized a small amount of idle head motion.

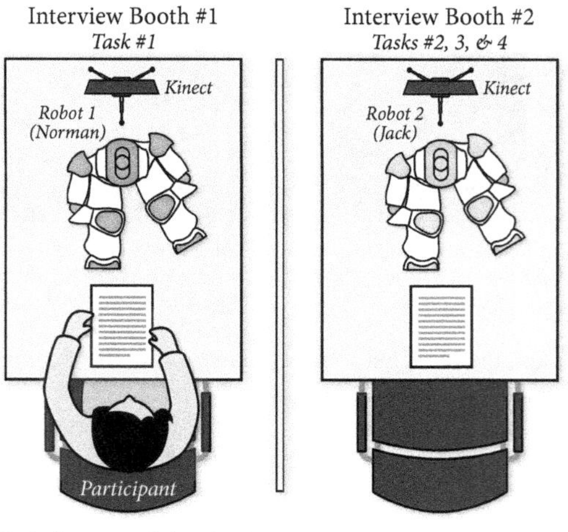

Figure 5: A diagram of the physical setup of the experiment. Participants interacted with Norman for the first task, and Jack for the other three tasks.

4.2. Participants

Thirty participants were recruited for this study (15 females and 15 males)—aged between 20 and 38 ($M = 22.90$, $SD = 4.27$)—from the University of Wisconsin–Madison campus. Participants were primarily University students with a range of fields of study, including biology, computer science, economics, and communication.

4.3. Hypotheses, Tasks, & Measures

We developed two hypotheses related to participants' perceptions of gaze aversions carried out by a robot and how robots might use gaze aversion behaviors to achieve each of the three conversational functions. The second hypothesis is split into three sub-hypotheses, one for each conversational function. Separate tasks and measures were created to test each hypothesis and sub-hypothesis. For clarity, we present each hypothesis together with the task designed to test that hypothesis as well as the primary measure in that task.

Hypothesis 1 – Well-timed robot gaze aversions will be seen as *intentional* motions used to engage in some cognitive processing, rather than randomly generated motions without meaning.

This hypothesis is derived from research that has shown how speaker gaze aversion is recognized by listeners as the speaker's attempt to disengage attention from the listener's face in order to put cognitive effort into organizing a new utterance [8, 10]. Finding support for this hypothesis enables us to conclude that the robot's head movements, which were designed to convey gaze aversion, are indeed perceived as gaze aversions and not as random movements.

Task 1 – The participants were told that the robot was training to work at a library help desk and given five library-related questions to ask the robot. They were instructed to ask each question and listen to the robot's response. The robot paused for 7 to 10 seconds (randomly determined to decrease predictability) before answering each question. Participants were instructed to ask a question again if they thought that the robot did not understand.

Measure 1 – The primary measure was the time participants waited for the robot to respond to questions before interrupting it to ask the question again. Based on our hypothesis, we expected participants to give the robot the most time to respond when it was using gaze aversions in the *good timing* condition, implying that the gaze aversion during its long pause was perceived as an intentional motion to formulate responses to the participants' questions.

Hypothesis 2 – Gaze aversions generated by our model and employed by the robot will enable it to achieve the positive conversational functions observed in human-human interaction. This hypothesis has three sub-hypotheses, one each for the cognitive, intimacy-modulating, and floor management functions of gaze aversion.

Hypothesis 2a – When a robot utilizes cognitive gaze aversions at the start of answers to questions, its answers will be rated as being more *thoughtful* and creative than when it does not display gaze aversions or displays gaze aversions with inappropriate timings.

This hypothesis is derived from research which has shown that people use gaze aversions to signal that cognitive processing is occurring and to create an impression that deep thought or creativity is being undertaken in formulating their utterance [4].

Task 2a – Participants engaged in a mock job interview with the robot, in which the participant was the interviewer and the robot was the interviewee. Participants were instructed to ask a series of five common job interview questions, and the robot was programmed to respond with answers taken from real-world job interviews.

Measure 2a – Participants rated each response immediately after it was given on four seven-point rating items. We constructed a single scale of *thoughtfulness* from the four items, including ratings on perceived thoughtfulness, creativity, disclosure, and naturalness of each response. Internal consistency was good for the items in this scale (Cronbach's $\alpha = .852$). We expected the highest overall ratings to be given by participants when the robot used cognitive gaze aversions at the start of its responses according to our model.

Hypothesis 2b – Robots that display periodic gaze aversions while listening will increase a human interlocutor's comfort and elicit more *disclosure* than robots that do not display gaze aversions or display gaze aversions with inappropriate timings.

Eye contact is one of the factors that shape feelings of intimacy between people. Too much of it results in uncomfortable levels of intimacy [4]. We posit that using gaze aversions appropriately will alleviate this potentially negative outcome.

Task 2b – The robot in this task was introduced to the participant as training to be a therapist's aide that would conduct preliminary interviews with new clients. During the task, the robot asked the participant a series of five questions with increasing levels of intimacy, ranging from "What do you like to do in your free time?" to "What is something you don't like about yourself?," and participants were instructed to respond with as much or as little detail as they wished.

Measure 2b – The primary measure for this task was the *breadth of self-disclosure*, which we obtained using a word count of participants' responses to the robot's questions. Previous research on how computers can elicit self-disclosure from people has validated word count as an appropriate measure of disclosure [17]. We expected that participants would disclose more to a robot that used appropriately timed intimacy-modulating gaze aversions while listening.

Hypothesis 2c – Robots that display gaze aversions during pauses will be perceived as *holding the floor* and will be interrupted less

Figure 6: An experimenter demonstrating the conversational interaction with Jack, one of the NAO robots.

Figure 7: Example of a single question-answer sequence. (a) The participant reads a question from his list in the preparation phase. (b) The participant looks toward the robot, and the robot engages an upward cognitive gaze aversion at the start of its answer. (c) The robot looks back toward the participant during its utterance. (d) The robot engages in a sideways intimacy-modulating gaze aversion. (e) The robot looks back toward the participant to complete its utterance.

than robots that do not display gaze aversions or display gaze aversions with inappropriate timings.

Gaze has been previously shown to be important in regulating conversational turn-taking [13]. By averting its gaze at a pause in speech, we posit that a robot will be able to hold the conversational floor, whereas making eye contact during this pause will result in the robot being interrupted.

Task 2c – Participants were provided with a list of five questions to ask the robot, with the goal of getting to know each other. Participants were instructed to ask each question, listen to the robot's response, and then reciprocate with their own response to the same question. The robot's responses had two parts, separated by a pause between 2 and 4 seconds in length (randomly determined to decrease predictability). If participants started speaking during the pause, the robot refrained from giving the second part of its response.

Measure 2c – The primary measure of this task was the time participants waited for the robot to be silent during the pause in its speech before interrupting or before the robot successfully produced the second part of its utterance. We expected participants to wait longer before interrupting the robot—or to not interrupt the robot at all—when it used appropriate turn-taking gaze aversions during its speech pauses, as specified by our model.

4.4. Setup & Procedure

An orange NAO, given the name Norman, was used for the first task that tested the perceived intentionality of generated gaze shifts. A gray NAO, given the name Jack, was used for the other three tasks. A separate robot was used for the first task due to the unnaturally long pauses present in that task. We did not want negative perceptions associated with these long response times to become associated with the robot during the other three tasks in which conversations proceeded more naturally. Each robot had a unique voice, implemented as pre-recorded audio files from separate male voice actors modulated in pitch to better fit the design of the robot. Participants sat in a chair approximately three feet away from the robot they were currently interacting with. The robot's position was carefully chosen to be at approximately eye-level with the participant and at a comfortable social distance. A black dividing wall was placed between the two robots so that participants could only see a single robot at a time. The setup resembled interview booths commonly used in job fairs (Figure 5 and Figure 6).

Each question-answer interaction sequence, illustrated in Figure 7, began with a *preparation phase*—a common element of human-human interviews—in which the participant looked down and read a question from the list. During this phase, the robot displayed idle gaze movements while staying focused on the participant. Toward the end of the question, the participant redirected their attention toward the robot, at which point the robot began its response, displaying gaze aversions based on the experimental condition. Between gaze aversions, the robot displayed subtle random motions to increase lifelikeness. Upon completing its utterance, the robot always focused back on the participant, displaying subtle idle motion. At this point, the participant looked down to the list, beginning the preparation phase for the next question-answer sequence.

After obtaining informed consent, the experimenter led each participant into the study room and gave a brief introduction to the experiment. The participant first completed the single task with Norman and was then relocated to sit in front of Jack for the other three tasks, which were completed in random order. After completing all four tasks, the participant responded to a survey of demographic characteristics and was debriefed. The study took approximately 30 minutes, and each participant received $5.

4.5. Results

We performed a mixed-design analysis of covariance (ANCOVA) to assess how robot gaze aversion behaviors affected the dependent variable for each task. Participant gender was included as a covariate to control for gender differences. Question ID—five in each task—was included as a covariate to control for learning effects. Question ID was nested within participant ID and modeled as a random effect. This resulted in five observations per participant and 150 total observations in each measure. Planned pairwise comparisons described in our hypotheses were carried out using Tukey's HSD test. A summary of our primary results is presented in Figure 8.

Hypothesis 1 predicted that gaze aversions employed by the robot would be seen as *intentional* motions used to engage in some cognitive processing, rather than randomly generated motions without meaning. Our analysis supported this hypothesis. The time given to the robot before interrupting was significantly higher when the robot used proper gaze aversion with good timing rather than bad timing, $F(1,142) = 7.72, p = .017$, or no gaze aversion at all, $F(1,142) = 5.99, p = .041$.

Hypothesis 2a predicted that when a robot utilized cognitive gaze aversions at the start of answers to participant-provided questions, those answers would be rated as being more *thoughtful* and creative than when the robot did not display gaze aversions or displayed gaze aversions with inappropriate timings. Our analysis supported this hypothesis. Participants assigned higher ratings of thoughtfulness to utterances produced by robots using well-timed gaze aversions over those produced by robots using poorly-timed gaze aversion, $F(1,142) = 27.97, p < .001$, and over those produced by robots using static gaze, $F(1,142) = 10.19, p = .005$.

Hypothesis 2b predicted that robots that displayed periodic gaze aversions while listening would increase a human interlocutor's comfort and elicit more *disclosure* than robots that did not display gaze aversions or displayed gaze aversions with inappropriate timings. Our analysis did not support this hypothesis. The robot using gaze aversions with good timing elicited no more disclosure—measured as word count per response—from participants than when its gaze aversions were badly timed, $F(1,142) = 0.56, p = .735$, or when it used no gaze aversion at all, $F(1,142) = 0.05, p = .972$.

Hypothesis 2c predicted that robots that displayed gaze aversions during pauses would be perceived as *holding the floor* and would be interrupted less than robots that did not display gaze aversions or displayed gaze aversions with inappropriate timings. Our analysis

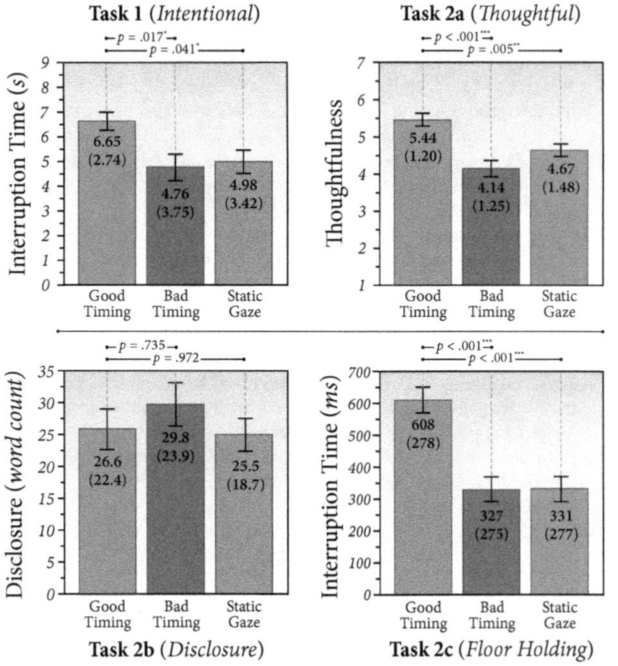

Figure 8: The results of the evaluation. Robot gaze aversions generated by our model were perceived as intentional and enabled the robot to appear more thoughtful and effectively manage the conversational floor. (*), (**), and (***) denote p < .050, p < .010, and p < .001, respectively. Means and standard deviations (in parentheses) are provided inside each bar.

supported this hypothesis. The time given to the robot during its pause before interrupting was significantly higher when the robot used properly-timed gaze aversion than when its gaze aversions were badly timed, $F(1,142)=25.53, p<.001$, or when it did not use gaze aversion at all, $F(1,142)=24.93, p<.001$.

5. DISCUSSION

The goal of the evaluation was to show that gaze aversions generated by our robots are perceived as intentional and meaningful motions, and that robots can use gaze aversions to achieve three conversational functions: signaling that cognitive effort is being spent in producing thoughtful utterances, modulating the overall intimacy level of the conversation, and facilitating floor management.

As shown in the first task, the robot's gaze aversions were perceived as intentional motions to engage in some sort of processing. Participants gave the robot significantly more time to formulate its response to a question when the robot used gaze aversion appropriately. Confirming this first hypothesis is important for interpreting the rest of the results, as we can conclude that the robot's head movements which were designed to convey gaze aversion were indeed perceived as gaze aversions and not as random movements.

As shown in the second task, in which a robot produced responses to a participant's interview-style questions, a robot that uses gaze aversions appropriately is capable of achieving the cognitive conversational function of producing utterances that are perceived as thoughtful and creative. This result is especially interesting as it was not observed when evaluating our previous implementation of gaze aversion behaviors for virtual agents [3]. A potential explanation might be found in the increased social presence of robots over virtual agents, making the generated cognitive gaze aversions more salient cues in this evaluation. That said, a follow-up evaluation that directly compares virtual agents and robots in this task would be required to better explain the observed difference in results.

Robots using well-timed gaze aversions were not successful in eliciting more disclosure from participants, as shown in the third task. A possible explanation is that the intimacy-modulating function of gaze aversion is really about reducing eye-contact and staring and that the precise timing for this type of gaze aversion is not important. Furthermore, the idle Perlin noise motions generated by our robot system in all conditions may have been perceived as small gaze shifts that increased participant comfort without needing more overt gaze aversions. In general, the lack of a significant result is consistent with previous HRI work that also did not find a difference in participant disclosure based on the gaze behavior of a robot [18].

Finally, robots using well-timed gaze aversion behaviors were more successful in managing conversational floor. When the robot used gaze aversions appropriately, participants waited longer during the robot's pause before interrupting it to claim the floor. It should be noted, however, that the robot was never able to hold the conversational floor throughout the entirety of its pause in speech (planned to be 2–4 seconds in length) without being interrupted. When using properly timed gaze aversions, the mean time before interruption was 608*ms*, compared with 329*ms* and 327*ms* in the *static gaze* and *bad timing* conditions, respectively. This is still a noteworthy result, as most gaps between turns in human-human conversations are shorter than 400*ms*, about one-third of them less than 200*ms* [29]. Adding other floor-holding behaviors, such as conversational fillers, might enable the robot to be even more effective in holding the floor during its pause. Previous work in HRI has already demonstrated the usefulness of conversational fillers in alleviating users' negative perceptions to long system response times [26].

5.1. Design Implications

This work has a number of design implications. In general, this work demonstrates the value of gaze aversion as a useful nonverbal conversational cue for designing applications such as an information booth robot that gives suggestions and should appear thoughtful and creative in the production of its utterances or a conversational robot that needs to effectively manage turn-taking with people. That said, gaze aversion motions alone are not sufficient for an autonomous robot system to appear natural and lifelike in its movements. In this paper, we showed how to combine aversion control with face tracking and structured random movements to create lifelike idle motion. A predictive filtering framework was very effective for gracefully combining multiple gaze motions with different goals. We have released online the code for our system of robot gaze aversion, which can be downloaded and run directly on any NAO robot with a Kinect for face tracking and speech recognition.

Another implication concerns the difference between designing social behaviors for virtual agents and physical robots. In this work, we showed how a robot could use gaze aversions effectively in conversations with people, which is similar to what we showed for virtual agents in previous work [3]. However, there are a number of important differences between virtual agents and robots that must be carefully considered when designing behaviors across both modalities, as evidenced by previous work and the difference in results across systems discussed here. It will take careful thought and creativity to develop precise representations of future agent behaviors that achieve targeted conversational functions while still being sufficiently generalizable across virtual and physical platforms.

5.2. Limitations & Future Work

One limitation of this work is that the presented gaze aversion model is static, in that the timings and frequencies of gaze aversions employed by the robot do not change over the course of the conversation or across conversations. In future work, we hope to explore how interaction history might be considered by our model. Previous research has shown that gaze aversions during speech become more common in later conversations between counselors and clients [25].

Another limitation of this work is that the gaze aversions are responsive to the speech of the human user but not to their gaze. By tracking the user's gaze, the robot might be able to more effectively regulate mutual gaze throughout the conversation and recognize gaze aversions of its user. Interactively aligning gaze aversions is particularly important to ensure that the robot's gaze aversions are recognized by the user, for instance, by producing a turn-taking gaze aversion only when the user is looking toward the robot.

When used inappropriately or in excess, gaze aversion can be perceived negatively, as illustrated by our *bad timing* condition. Previous research has linked gaze aversion with avoidance-oriented emotions, such as embarrassment, sorrow, and disgust, and direct gaze with approach-oriented emotions, such as joy, love, and anger [2]. We posit that averting gaze only when it is useful and appropriate maximizes the positive effects of eye contact. The link between gaze aversion and emotion and the tradeoff between the effects of mutual and averted gaze are important directions for future work.

Gaze aversion is only one type of gaze action, but there are many others, including fixations, glances, mutual gaze, and scanning [27]. In future work, we hope to integrate the current work on gaze aversion into a comprehensive gaze controller that implements other gaze models, and test the effectiveness of robot gaze aversion within the context of a richer set of gaze behaviors.

6. CONCLUSION

Gaze aversion—the intentional redirection away from the face of an interlocutor—is an important nonverbal cue that serves cognitive, intimacy-modulating, and floor management functions in conversations. In previous work, we identified precise spatial and temporal parameters of gaze aversion from a video corpus of human-human interactions. In this paper, we presented our work to implement these behaviors on a humanlike robot system. This implementation was designed to overcome the inherent challenges of adapting a human-based gaze model for a robot without articulated eyes. We designed a head controller for the NAO platform that generates and combines head motions with three purposes: purposeful gaze aversions to achieve conversational functions, face tracking for engaging in mutual gaze with a user, and noisy idle head motions to increase lifelikeness. An evaluation of the designed gaze aversion behaviors generated by this system demonstrated that they are perceived as intentional when expressed by a humanlike robot, and that robots can use gaze aversions to appear more thoughtful and effectively manage the conversational floor. These results have important implications for designers of human-robot interactions. Gaze aversions should be considered as an important and useful cue for developing effective conversational interactions between humans and robots.

7. ACKNOWLEDGMENTS

This research was supported by National Science Foundation awards 1017952 and 1208632 and the National Institutes of Health award 1R01HD071089-01A1. We would like to thank Faisal Khan, Brandi Hefty, Ross Luo, Brandon Smith, Catherine Steffel, and Chien-Ming Huang for their contributions to this work.

8. REFERENCES

[1] A. Abele. Functions of gaze in social interaction: Communication and monitoring. *Journal of Nonverbal Behavior*, 10(2):83–101, 1986.

[2] R. B. Adams Jr and R. E. Kleck. Effects of direct and averted gaze on the perception of facially communicated emotion. *Emotion*, 5(1):3–11, 2005.

[3] S. Andrist, B. Mutlu, and M. Gleicher. Conversational gaze aversion for virtual agents. In *Proc. IVA 2013*, pages 249–262, 2013.

[4] M. Argyle and M. Cook. *Gaze and mutual gaze*. Cambridge University Press Cambridge, 1976.

[5] M. Argyle and J. Dean. Eye-contact, distance and affiliation. *Sociometry*, 28(3):289–304, 1965.

[6] W. Bainbridge, J. Hart, E. Kim, and B. Scassellati. The benefits of interactions with physically present robots over video-displayed agents. *International Journal of Social Robotics*, 3(1):41–52, 2011.

[7] G. W. Beattie. A further investigation of the cognitive interference hypothesis of gaze patterns during conversation. *British Journal of Social Psychology*, 20(4):243–248, 1981.

[8] G. Doherty-Sneddon and F. Phelps. Gaze aversion: A response to cognitive or social difficulty? *Memory & Cognition*, 33(4):727–733, 2005.

[9] N. Emery. The eyes have it: the neuroethology, function and evolution of social gaze. *Neuroscience & Biobehavioral Reviews*, 24(6):581–604, 2000.

[10] A. M. Glenberg, J. L. Schroeder, and D. A. Robertson. Averting the gaze disengages the environment and facilitates remembering. *Memory & Cognition*, 26(4):651–658, 1998.

[11] M. Imai, T. Kanda, T. Ono, H. Ishiguro, and K. Mase. Robot mediated round table: Analysis of the effect of robot's gaze. In *Proc. RO-MAN 2002*, pages 411–416, 2002.

[12] R. E. Kalman. A new approach to linear filtering and prediction problems. *Transactions of the ASME–Journal of Basic Engineering*, (82):35–45, 1960.

[13] A. Kendon. Some functions of gaze-direction in social interaction. *Acta psychologica*, 26(1):22–63, 1967.

[14] C. Kidd and C. Breazeal. Effect of a robot on user perceptions. In *Proc. IROS 2004*, volume 4, pages 3559–3564, 2004.

[15] K. H. Kim, R. Brent Gillespie, and B. J. Martin. Head movement control in visually guided tasks: Postural goal and optimality. *Computers in Biology and Medicine*, 37(7):1009–1019, 2007.

[16] C. Liu, C. T. Ishi, H. Ishiguro, and N. Hagita. Generation of nodding, head tilting and eye gazing for human-robot dialogue interaction. In *Proc. HRI 2012*, pages 285–292, 2012.

[17] Y. Moon. Intimate exchanges: Using computers to elicit self-disclosure from consumers. *Journal of Consumer Research*, 26(4):323–339, 2000.

[18] J. Mumm and B. Mutlu. Human-robot proxemics: physical and psychological distancing in human-robot interaction. In *Proc. HRI 2011*, pages 331–338, 2011.

[19] B. Mutlu, J. Forlizzi, and J. Hodgins. A storytelling robot: Modeling and evaluation of human-like gaze behavior. In *Proc. HUMANOIDS 2006*, pages 518–523, 2006.

[20] B. Mutlu, T. Kanda, J. Forlizzi, J. Hodgins, and H. Ishiguro. Conversational gaze mechanisms for humanlike robots. *ACM Transactions on Interactive Intelligent Systems*, 1(2):12:1–12:33, 2012.

[21] D. G. Novick, B. Hansen, and K. Ward. Coordinating turn-taking with gaze. In *Proc. ICSLP 1996*, pages 1888–1891, 1996.

[22] T. Pejsa, B. Mutlu, and M. Gleicher. Stylized and performative gaze for character animation. *Computer Graphics Forum*, 32(2):143–152, 2013.

[23] K. Perlin. Real time responsive animation with personality. *IEEE Transactions on Visualization and Computer Graphics*, 1(1):5–15, 1995.

[24] A. Powers, S. Kiesler, S. Fussell, and C. Torrey. Comparing a computer agent with a humanoid robot. In *Proc. HRI 2007*, pages 145–152, 2007.

[25] D. Schulman and T. Bickmore. Changes in verbal and nonverbal conversational behavior in long-term interaction. In *Proc. ICMI 2012*, pages 11–18, 2012.

[26] T. Shiwa, T. Kanda, M. Imai, H. Ishiguro, and N. Hagita. How quickly should communication robots respond? In *Proc. HRI 2008*, pages 153–160, 2008.

[27] V. Srinivasan and R. Murphy. A survey of social gaze. In *Proc. HRI 2011*, pages 253–254, 2011.

[28] M. Staudte and M. W. Crocker. Visual attention in spoken human-robot interaction. In *Proc. HRI 2009*, pages 77–84, 2009.

[29] T. P. Wilson and D. H. Zimmerman. The structure of silence between turns in two-party conversation. *Discourse Processes*, 9(4):375–390, 1986.

[30] Y. Yoshikawa, K. Shinozawa, H. Ishiguro, N. Hagita, and T. Miyamoto. Responsive robot gaze to interaction partner. In *Proc. RSS 2006*, 2006.

Collaborative Effort towards Common Ground in Situated Human-Robot Dialogue

Joyce Y. Chai, Lanbo She, Rui Fang, Spencer Ottarson, Cody Littley, Changsong Liu and Kenneth Hanson
Department of Computer Science and Engineering
Michigan State University
East Lansing, MI 48824, USA
{jchai, shelanbo, fangrui, ottarso5, littley1, cliu, hanson54 }@cse.msu.edu

ABSTRACT

In situated human-robot dialogue, although humans and robots are co-present in a shared environment, they have significantly mismatched capabilities in perceiving the shared environment. Their representations of the shared world are misaligned. In order for humans and robots to communicate with each other successfully using language, it is important for them to mediate such differences and to establish common ground. To address this issue, this paper describes a dialogue system that aims to mediate a shared perceptual basis during human-robot dialogue. In particular, we present an empirical study that examines the role of the robot's collaborative effort and the performance of natural language processing modules in dialogue grounding. Our empirical results indicate that in situated human-robot dialogue, a low collaborative effort from the robot may lead its human partner to believe a common ground is established. However, such beliefs may not reflect true mutual understanding. To support truly grounded dialogues, the robot should make an extra effort by making its partner aware of its internal representation of the shared world.

Categories and Subject Descriptors: H.5.2 [Information Interfaces and Presentation]:User Interfaces

General Terms: Algorithms, Experimentation

Keywords: Common Ground, Collaboration, Human-Robot Dialogue

1. INTRODUCTION

In human-human communication, when we are co-present, we have the same perceptual access to the shared environment [4] and generally do not have any problem understanding each other's references (e.g., what "the green cup" refers to in the environment). What makes the communication between us successful is the *common ground* we have: mutual beliefs and knowledge about the shared environment [4].

HRI'14, March 3–6, 2014, Bielefeld, Germany.

http://dx.doi.org/10.1145/2559636.2559677.

However, in human-robot dialogue, although a human and a robot are co-present in a shared environment, they have significantly mismatched perceptual capabilities. The "cup" that is easily recognized by the human may not be recognizable to the robot. In addition, the human has much more knowledge about the environment and can infer and represent the environment symbolically and thus be able to communicate with others using language. However the robot's representation of the same environment may not be symbolic and may contain lower level numerical features (such as bounding boxes or color distributions associated with the perceived objects). These phenomena contribute to a gap between the human representation and the robot representation of the shared environment. Therefore, the shared perceptual basis is missing. In order for humans and robots to communicate with each other successfully using language, it is important for them to mediate such differences and establish a common ground.

Despite recent efforts [9, 13, 20, 21], research on situated human-robot dialogue is still in its infancy. It is not clear how the mismatched perceptual basis may affect the use of language and how to mediate such differences. To address this issue, this paper presents a dialogue system implemented in a NAO robot. Our robot can carry natural language dialogue with its human partner and utilize the collaborative discourse to acquire knowledge about the environment and strive to establish common ground. In particular, we present an empirical study that examines the role of the robot's collaborative effort in this process. A *low effort* refers to the robot's minimum effort in accepting or rejecting a presentation from its partner through explicit confirmation. A *high effort* refers to the robot's extra effort in proactively describing what it perceives from the shared environment in addition to an explicit confirmation. Our empirical results have shown that, a low collaborative effort from the robot may lead its human partner to believe a common ground is established. However, such beliefs may not reflect true mutual understanding. To establish a true common ground, the robot should make an extra effort by making its partner aware of its internal representation of the shared world.

2. RELATED WORK

Common ground is essential to the success of communication [24]. It is defined as a collection of "mutual, common, or joint knowledge, beliefs, and suppositions." [5]. In conversation, participants coordinate their mental states based

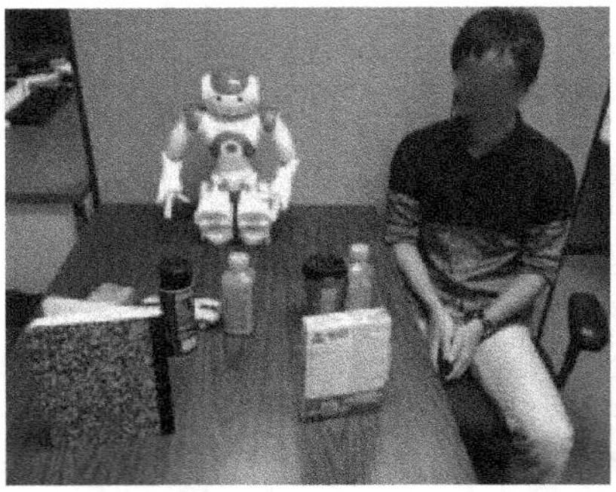

(a) Situated Setup

H1:	The green cup is called Bill.
R1:	Ok, the green cup is Bill. (point to the inferred object)
H2:	Do you see a car?
R2:	Yes, I see a car.
H3:	Do you see a blue can behind it?
R3:	I don't see a blue can. But I see a blue unknown object there. Is that the can you are talking about? (point to the inferred object)
H4:	Yes, it's called Mary.
R4:	Got it, the blue can is Mary.

(b) Sample Dialogue

Figure 1: An example of situated setup and human-robot dialogue

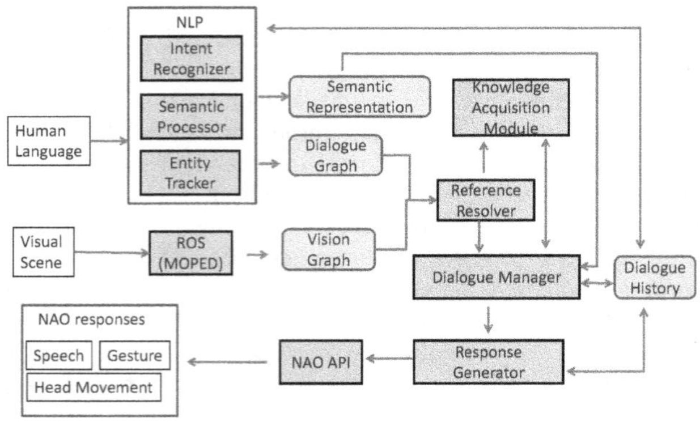

Figure 2: The overall architecture

on their mutual understanding of their intentions, goals, and current tasks [4]. The process to establish common ground is called *grounding*. Clark and colleagues have further characterized this process by defining *contributions*, the basic elements of a conversation [6]. Each contribution has two phases: a *presentation* phase where the speaker presents an utterance to the addressee and an *acceptance* phase where the addressee provides evidence of understanding to the speaker. This grounding process is viewed as a collaborative process where the speaker and the addressee make extra efforts to collaborate with each other to reach a mutual understanding [7]. The notion of common ground and communication grounding have been investigated extensively from human-human communication [5,10], to computational models for spoken dialogue systems [30], and more recently to human-robot interaction [12,18,27,28]. In particular, the recent work that is most relevant here has investigated symbol grounding [17] and feedback and adaptation [2] in human-robot dialogue.

Different from the above previous works, this paper presents a human-robot dialogue system with a specific focus on collaborative efforts. To infer the common ground, *shared bases* such as joint personal experiences, events, or episodes play an important role [4]. However, in situated human-robot dialogue, the human and the robot have disjoint perceptual experiences although they are physically co-present. Therefore, this paper intends to demonstrate how the mismatched perceptual basis may affect the joint tasks in human-robot dialogue, and how collaborative efforts may influence dialogue grounding.

3. HUMAN-ROBOT DIALOGUE SYSTEM

Suppose a human and a robot are co-present as shown in Figure 1(a). The human needs to communicate the secret names of several objects to the robot so that the robot knows which object has what name. Figure 1(b) shows a sample dialogue between the human and the robot. As shown in the example, instead of directly saying "the blue can is called Mary", the human starts with *the car* (i.e., H_2) (right in front of the robot) and makes sure the robot recognizes it and from there goes to the target object (H_3, H_4). This is one type of collaborative behavior referred to as *installment* [6]. The robot accepts the human's presentation by pointing to the intended object. In addition, the robot also describes to the human what it perceives from the environment (e.g., R_3). Through these mechanisms, the human and the robot strive to reach a common ground about the names of objects in the shared world. This is the kind of dialogue our system aims to support. The overall architecture is shown in Figure 2. Next we illustrate several key components of the system.

3.1 NLP Modules

Human language (i.e., the output from an automatic speech recognizer) is processed by a set of NLP modules to create a semantic representation that captures the meaning of each human utterance (e.g., intent of the utterance, focus of attention, etc.) as shown in Figure 3.

More specifically, an `Intent Recognizer` is applied to identify the human intent (represented by `Act`) such as whether it is a request for the robot to identify certain objects (i.e., `Act:RequestIdObject`) or an acceptance of the robot's presentation (i.e., `Act:Accept`). Currently, we only implemented a simple rule-based approach for intent recognition. Since our domain is quite narrow (mainly involving negotiation about the shared environment), it appears sufficient.

Besides human intent, a `Semantic Processor` is applied to identify the focus of attention (represented by `Focus`), as well as linguistic entities (i.e., `Refs`) and their properties mentioned in the utterance (i.e., the corresponding logic forms). Since human utterances can be informal, fragmented, and contain various types of disfluencies, we apply a partial parser based on combinatory categorial grammar (CCG) [26]. We have defined a set of basic CCG lexicon rules, which covers key vocabulary in our domain, such as object colors, shapes, spatial relations and so forth. Given a human utterance, our CCG parser repeatedly searches for the longest sequence covered by the grammar until the end of the utterance. As a result, the `Semantic Processor` creates a list of

H1: Human	**H2: Human**	**H3: Human**	**H4: Human**
Act: DescribeObjectName [Type: Statement]; Focus: x1, Refs: ['x1'] Sem: Color(x1,green)^ Type(x1,cup)^ Name(x1,bill)	Act: RequestIdObject [Type: Question(y/n)]; Focus: x2 Refs: [x2] Sem: Type(x2,car)	Act: RequestIdObject [Type: Question(y/n)] Focus: x3 Refs: [x3, x4| x4->y2] Sem: Color(x3,blue)^ Type(x3,can)^ Spatial-Behind(x3,x4)	Act: Accept [Type: Explicit(yes)]; Act: DescribeObjectName [Type: Statement] Focus: x5 Refs: [x5|x5->y3] Sem: Name(x5,Mary)
R1: Robot	**R2: Robot**	**R3: Robot**	**R4: Robot**
Act: Accept [Type: Explicit]; Act: DescribeObjectName [Type: Statement] Focus: y1 Refs: [y1 | y1->x1] Sem: Color(y1,green)^ Type(y1,cup)^ Name(y1,bill)	Act: Accept [Type: Explict(yes)]; Act: DescribeObjectProperty [Type: Statement] Focus: y2 Refs: [y2 | y2->x2] Sem: Type(y2,car)	Act: Reject [Type: Explicit]; Act: DescribeObjectProperty [Type: Statement]; Act: RequestConfirm [Type: Explicit] Focus: y3 Refs: [y3 | y3->x3] Sem: Color(y3,blue)	Act: Accept [Type: Explicit]; Act: DescribeObjectName [Type: Statement] Focus: y4 Refs: [y4 | y4->x5] Sems: Type(y4,can)^ Color(y4,blue)^ Name(y4,Mary)

Figure 3: Examples of semantic representations

linguistic entities introduced by the utterance, and a list of first order predicates specifying the properties and relations between these entities.

An `Entity Tracker` is used to manage the linguistic entities from the conversation discourse. It determines whether a linguistic entity is newly introduced into the discourse or co-refers to an entity that already exists in the discourse. To arrive at such a decision, the `Entity Tracker` combines linguistic information (e.g., the types of linguistic expressions), recency information (e.g., how long ago linguistic entities are introduced into the discourse), and semantic compatibility between various entities to make a prediction. For example, for H_3 in Figure 3, the linguistic entity x_4 (introduced by the pronoun "it") is predicted to corefer with a linguistic entity created by the robot (i.e., y_2 introduced by the noun phrase "a car" in R_2).

3.2 Reference Resolution

Through entity tracking, the coreferring entities (since they all refer to a same object in the physical world) are merged together to form a node in the `Dialogue Graph` as shown in Figure 4(a). The attributes of a node capture semantic properties of the corresponding linguistic entity. Each edge in the `Dialogue Graph` captures the semantic relations between linguistic entities.

The visual scene received by the robot is processed by a real-time object recognition system MOPED (`http://personalrobotics.ri.cmu.edu/projects/moped.php`). For example, Figure 4(b) shows what is perceived by the robot from the shared environment. The processing results are captured by the `Vision Graph` as shown in Figure 4(c). The `Vision Graph` captures the robot's internal representation of the shared environment. Each node in the vision graph represents a perceived object. The lower level visual properties such as color distributions, size of bounding boxes, etc. are captured as attributes of the nodes.

Given these two graphs, a `Reference Resolver` applies an inexact graph-matching algorithm to match the dialogue graph to the vision graph to infer what objects in its own representation of the world are referred to or described by the human during conversation. Different matching algorithms and issues related to graph-matching have been described in our previous work [14, 15].

3.3 Knowledge Acquisition

Since the dialogue graph represents the human's knowledge of the shared world and the vision graph represents the robot's own internal representation of the perceived world, graph matching allows to bridge the gap between the symbolic representations and lower level numerical features. Based on such matching, a `Knowledge Acquisition Module` attempts to acquire knowledge from the matched nodes and relations to enrich the robot's own representation of the environment. However, graph-matching alone is not sufficient. The robot needs to acquire *correct* descriptions, in other words, descriptions that are mutually agreed upon. Therefore, the `Knowledge Acquisition Module` not only takes the results from the `Reference Resolver`, but also utilizes the `Dialogue Manager` to arrange *confirmation* sub-dialogue with the human. Only when the confirmation is accepted by the human partner, is the corresponding symbolic knowledge added to the robot's internal representation. Because of such confirmation, the knowledge acquired is considered *common ground knowledge.* For example, in Figure 5, the name, color, and type information concerning n_5 and n_7 is acquired and added to the robot's internal representation. In addition, the symbolic description *Behind* is also added to the representation to describe the spatial relation between n_7 and n_0. Through this way, the robot acquires knowledge through dialogue to build up the common ground.

3.4 Dialogue Management

The goal of the `Dialogue Manager` is to decide what actions the robot should take during conversation. Our `Dialogue Manager` has three parts: a representation of the state of the dialogue; an action space for the robot; and a dialogue policy that describes which action to take under which state.

The dialogue states are characterized based on human intent, focus of attention, graph matching results from the `Reference Resolver`, previous actions of the robot maintained in the `Dialogue History`, and pending knowledge to be acquired. The current space of actions allow the robot to greet, explicitly or implicitly confirm a request, accept or reject a presentation from its partner, describe what it perceives, ask for confirmation, and ask for specific information. Our dialogue policy consists of 17 (dialogue state, action) pairs. At execution time, the dialogue manager will

(a) Dialogue Graph (b) Perceived Scene (c) Vision Graph

Figure 4: Examples of graph representation

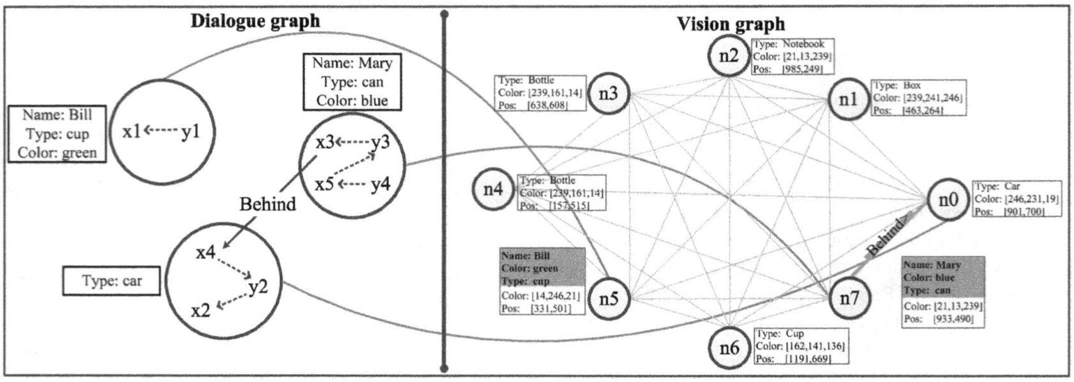

Figure 5: An example of knowledge acquisition through graph matching

go through the dialogue policy and identify a dialogue state that best matches the current state and then take the corresponding actions.

3.5 Response Generation

Once an action is chosen by the `Dialogue Manager`, the `Response Generator` decides how to realize such action using speech, gesture, and head movement. Non-verbal modalities such as gesture and gaze have been investigated extensively in HRI literature, for example, for engagement [1, 19, 23], and turn taking and participation [16]. These are all very important aspects in human-robot dialogue. Currently, we have not addressed these issues in our robot. Similar to previous work [25], we only use hand gesture and head movement to indicate the inferred object (i.e., the object understood by the robot) and the intended object (i.e., the object the robot describes). Occasionally, we also use head nodding or shaking to accept or reject a presentation from the human. For speech responses, several templates are predefined which support parameter passing at the run time. The correspondence between an action and a combination of speech, gesture, and head movement are predefined as a behavior policy. During the run time, given an action passed by the `Dialogue Manager`, the `Response Generator` will check the policy and generate the specified movements.

4. EMPIRICAL STUDIES

Using the dialogue system described above, we conducted an empirical study. The goal was to examine how the robot's collaborative effort may help mediate a shared perceptual basis and establish a common ground.

4.1 Design Factors

Our experiments were designed to take into consideration the following three main issues:

Shared Perceptual Basis. This factor aims to address to what degree mismatched perceptions between humans and robots will affect communication grounding in human-robot dialogue. More specifically, we selected a collection of everyday objects which were easily recognizable by human subjects for our experiments. We trained our robot to recognize these objects. By controlling the recognition results, we were able to manipulate two levels of mismatched perceptual basis:

- **Low-Mismatch** situation, where the robot can recognize most of the objects in the shared environment as its human partner. Either 10% or 30% of the objects in the scene are not recognizable to the robot. Thus the perceptual differences between the human and the robot are low.
- **High-Mismatch** situation, where the robot can *not* recognize most of the objects (either 60% or 90% of the objects are not recognizable). Thus the perceptual differences between the human and the robot are high.

Robot's Collaborative Effort. Our previous work based on human-human dialogue [15] has shown that, when the shared perceptual basis is missing, conversation partners

Confidence	Low Effort	High Effort
[80%..1]	Accept *"Got it"*	Accept and Describe *"Sure, the orange bottle is Eric"*
[25%..80%)	Weak Accept *"I think I see it, is that correct?"*	Weak Accept and Describe *"I see something there, is that orange bottle Eric? "*
[0..25%)	Reject *"I don't see it"*	Reject and Describe *"I don't see it, but I see an orange bottle there"*

Table 1: Definitions of two levels of collaborative effort

tend to make extra effort to collaborate with each other to mediate shared basis. In particular, a prominent collaborative strategy adopted by the robot players (with simulated lower perceptual capability) is to proactively present what he/she perceives from the environment. Such presentation often provides an anchor to his/her partner (with higher perceptual capability) to further expand towards a mutual understanding. Motivated by our earlier findings, we are interested in whether and to what degree the extra effort made by the robot may help with communication grounding. Therefore, in our experiments, we specifically modeled two levels of collaborative effort associated with the robot's acceptance:

- **Low-Effort** represents the minimum effort taken by the robot. It only accepts or rejects a presentation from its human partner explicitly, nothing more.
- **High-Effort** represents an extra collaborative effort taken by the robot. After it accepts or rejects a presentation, the robot proactively describes what it perceives from the environment based on its internal representation of the inferred object.

The decision on whether to accept or to reject is made by the `Dialogue Manager` based on the robot's confidence at identifying the intended object (as a result of graph-matching). Table 1 shows the definition of these two levels of effort, together with examples of the robot's verbal responses. These verbal responses are also accompanied by pointing gestures to the inferred or intended objects.

Automated NLP Processing. The ability to reach a common ground largely depends on how well the robot understands human language. To examine how automated NLP performance may affect dialogue grounding, we also experimented with two different settings:

- **Automatic Run** refers to the condition where all NLP modules are fully automated (as shown in Figure 2) during dialogue.
- **Wizard Run** refers to the condition where the results from NLP modules are verified and possibly updated by a human wizard to ensure correct interpretation.

In both settings, the downstream modules in Figure 2 remain fully automated.

4.2 Experimental Tasks

We designed a naming game for our experiments. Similar to the set up shown in Figure 1(a) a human subject and our NAO robot were positioned in front of a table which held ten everyday objects. The subject was given a printout of the environment at the beginning of each trial/task. The printout showed the secret names of six objects in the environment. The human subject's goal was to communicate these names to the robot so that the robot became aware which object has what name. The subject was also given a pen and instructed to keep track of his/her progress on the sheet. The task is considered *completed* if the subject **believes** he/she has successfully communicated these names to the robot and he/she and the robot have reached a mutual understanding about the object names. In other words, the task is considered completed if the human subject believes he/she and the robot have come to a common ground. So this is a subjective measurement, which we call *perceived task completion*, *perceived common ground*, or *perceived dialogue grounding*.

To avoid interaction deadlock that may result from errors in automated processing, we also defined a *task abort* criterion. During interaction, if the robot failed to acquire any knowledge (i.e., no knowledge updating) as described in Section 3.3 for three minutes, the task would be aborted and considered *incomplete*.

In each trial, the subject was instructed to keep his/her dialogue going with the the robot until either the subject believed the task was completed or the on-going dialogue met the abort criterion.

4.3 Procedures

The perceptual differences were implemented by four levels: 10% and 30% unrecognizable objects for Low-Mismatch, and 60% and 90% for High-Mismatch. To create an experimental configuration, we combined two of the four levels with a low collaborative effort and the other two with a high collaborative effort. For example, one configuration was 10% with a low effort, 30% with a high effort, 60% with a low effort, and 90% with a high effort. Thus there were six different configurations in total. Each of these configurations specified four treatment conditions (i.e., a combination of perception and effort) assigned to one subject.

We also designed four scenes with ten objects each where six objects were assigned secret names. These four scenes were independent from each other (e.g., an apple in two different scenes would have two different names). To each subject, an experimental configuration was first assigned. Each of the four treatment conditions specified in the configuration was randomly assigned to each of the four scenes. The objects from each scene that were deemed un-recognizable were randomly chosen based on the distribution specified by the perception factor.

We recruited a total of 24 human subjects from the MSU campus to participate in our study. These subjects were not aware of any part of the system or the study design. During the experiments, each subject, based on the assigned configuration, performed four naming tasks for four scenes. The order of the scenes was randomized. These four tasks were first performed under the condition of *Automatic Runs*, meaning that the human interacted with a fully automated robot [1]. After the automatic runs, if there were any aborted tasks, we conducted further experiments under the condition of *Wizard Run*. We asked the subjects to take a break and

[1]Speech recognizers (e.g., Sphinx 4) are integrated in our robot. However, to focus our current effort on language understanding and dialogue grounding, in our user studies, human speech was transcribed on the fly by a researcher behind the scene.

	Low-Mismatch		High-Mismatch	
	L-Effort	H-Effort	L-Effort	H-Effort
Num. of Dialogues	24	24	24	24
Perceived Grounding	17	6	14	6
Rate	0.708	0.25	0.583	0.25

Table 2: Rate of perceived common ground

then repeated those aborted tasks in a random order with the same subject. The wizard's responses were reasonably fast. We did not observe any noticeable delay.

4.4 Empirical Results

Our experiments resulted in a total of 96 dialogues with the fully automated robot (i.e., under the condition of *Automatic Run*). Among these, 43 dialogues led to *perceived task completion* or *perceived common ground*. The remaining 53 incompleted tasks were performed again with the help from the wizard, which led to an additional 53 dialogues under the condition of *Wizard Run*.

4.4.1 Perceived Common Ground

Table 2 shows the rate of perceived grounding for all 96 dialogues during automatic runs. There is a significant difference among different settings ($\chi^2 = 15.9649$, $p = 0.001$). Interestingly, the dialogues where the robot made an extra collaborative effort (i.e., *H-Effort*) have a lower rate compared to those where the robot made a low effort (i.e., L-Effort). A Tukey post-hoc test reveals that such difference is significant for the *Low-Mismatch* setting (at $p < 0.05$) and marginal for the *High-Mismatch* setting.

Although it may appear counter-intuitive at first glance, this result demonstrates the role of collaborative effort in the perception of common ground. Note that the *perceived common ground* is defined from the human subject's perspective concerning whether he/she *believes* a common ground is reached. In the case of *L-Effort*, a simple acceptance from the robot (without further describing its internal states) could often lead the human subjects to believe that a mutual understanding has been reached. This is especially the case since the space is crowded and pointing to or looking at an object sometimes cannot be precise. In the case of *H-Effort*, the robot also proactively describes its internal representation of the inferred object. This extra information provides feedback to the human partners on what exactly is grounded. This information can potentially reveal incorrect grounding and thus lower the human's beliefs of mutual understanding.

4.4.2 True Common Ground

A perceived common ground does not mean a true common ground. In the context of our naming game, a true common ground is where the name acquired for each object by the robot at the end of dialogue is indeed the correct name intended by the human for that object. In the best case, the robot should acquire all six names correctly to reach a common ground with its partner. Thus we take a closer look at those dialogues with perceived common ground. These include 43 out of 96 dialogues from the automatic runs and 28 out of 53 dialogues from the wizard runs.

First, we examine the average number of turns in these dialogues as shown in Table 3. For automatic runs (the row marked with "A"), a two-way ANOVA did not find any significant main effects from mismatched perception, collaborative effort, or their interaction. However, for the wizard runs (the row marked with "W"), a two way ANOVA found a significant main effect of mismatched perception ($F(1, 25) = 4.59$, $p < 0.05$, partial $\eta^2 = 0.16$) on the number of turns. This indicates that a higher perceptual mismatch requires a larger number of dialogue turns in order to reach a perceived common ground.

	Low-Mismatch		High-Mismatch	
	L-Effort	H-Effort	L-Effort	H-Effort
A	29.12 ± 10.81	28.33 ± 7.94	31.43 ± 11.08	29.50 ± 8.94
W	17.50 ± 1.00	21.82 ± 4.77	23.60 ± 8.65	25.78 ± 6.28

Table 3: The average number of turns from dialogues with perceived common ground

	Low-Mismatch		High-Mismatch	
	L-Effort	H-Effort	L-Effort	H-Effort
A	3.47 ± 1.13	3.67 ± 1.03	2.36 ± 1.39	3.67 ± 1.37
W	4.75 ± 0.50	4.36 ± 0.51	3.25 ± 1.26	4.50 ± 0.71

Table 4: The average number of correctly acquired names from dialogues with perceived common ground

Next we examine the average number of correctly acquired names (i.e., an objective measure of common ground) for those dialogues as shown in Table 4. For the automatic runs, through a two-way ANOVA, the main effect of collaborative effort on true common ground is marginal ($F(1, 39) = 3.17$, $p = 0.083$, partial $\eta^2 = 0.08$). For the wizard runs, a two-way ANOVA found a significant main effect of perception ($F(1, 25) = 5.363$, $p = 0.029$, partial $\eta^2 = 0.18$) on true common ground. We also found a significant interaction of perception and effort ($F(1, 25) = 7.723$, $p = 0.010$, partial $\eta^2 = 0.236$). The interaction plot is shown in Figure 6. For the low-mismatched perception, whether a low effort or a high effort is applied does not seem to make much difference. However, for the high-mismatched perception, a high effort leads to much better grounding performance than a low effort. This result indicates that while a low effort may work fine when the perceptual basis is mostly aligned, it will not be sufficient when there is a significant perceptual difference between the human and the robot.

4.4.3 Automatic NLP Processing

We conducted a further analysis on how the automatic NLP performance may affect dialogue grounding. Particularly, we are interested in semantic processing and entity tracking since their performance determines the quality of dialogue graphs, which further links to graph matching, essential to our task on grounding names. Among 96 dialogues, the overall accuracy for semantic processing is 81.4%. This means that 81.4% of properties associated with linguistic entities extracted from human utterances are correct. The accuracy on entity tracking is 64.6%. This means that, given a linguistic entity from a human utterance (a total of over 1600 in our data), 64.5% of time the `Entity Tracker` can correctly predict whether it introduces a new entity or it corefers with an existing entity. The performance is further broken down as shown in Table 5.

There is no significant difference in semantic processing performance across different conditions ($\chi^2 = 4.303$, $p = 0.231$). However, there is a significant difference regarding entity tracking performance ($\chi^2 = 20.889$, $p < 0.001$). In particular, a Tukey's post-hoc comparison test indicates that

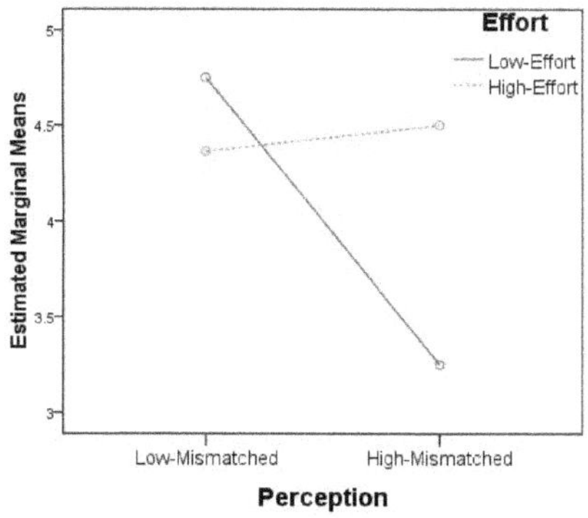

Figure 6: Interaction plot between perception and effort

	Low-Mismatch		High-Mismatch	
	L-effort	H-effort	L-effort	H-effort
semantic processing	0.780	0.814	0.835	0.826
entity tracking	0.651	0.605	0.742	0.605

Table 5: Performance of automated NLP processing

under the high mismatched perception, the entity tracking component performed significantly worse in the high-effort setting compared to the low-effort setting (at $p < 0.05$). This is mainly because in the high-effort setting, the robot proactively describes what it perceives from the environment. Therefore, the robot can introduce new entities into the discourse. So a linguistic entity now can also corefer to the entities introduced by the robot (as opposed to the entities introduced only by the human as in the low-effort case). This may add some complexity to our simple entity tracking algorithm. We are currently developing better algorithms for entity tracking based on the collected data.

To understand how much NLP performance may affect dialogue grounding, we compared the 53 incompleted tasks under the condition of *Automatic Run* with the same tasks under the condition of *Wizard Run*. We examine the average number of correctly acquired names from these tasks as shown in Figure 7. It shows a significant main effect of semantic interpretation on grounding ($F(1,98) = 33.25$, $p < 0.0001$, partial $\eta^2 = 0.253$). A follow up T-test has shown that, wizard runs significantly outperform the automatic runs under both the low mismatch($t = -4.231$, $p < 0.0001$, two-tailed) and the high mismatch ($t = -4.608$, $p < 0.0001$, two-tailed) perception, as well as the low collaborative ($t = -2.578$, $p = 0.015$, two-tailed) and the high collaborative ($t = -5.970$, $p < 0.0001$, two-tailed) effort.

These results confirm that better NLP performance will lead to better common ground. In addition, since the average number of correctly acquired names from the wizard runs (with close-to ground-truth NLP processing) is still short from being perfect (i.e., 6), these results further emphasize the need to improve other modules such as dialogue management and knowledge acquisition.

5. DISCUSSION

It has been long established that common ground is key to communication success. A significant body of work has investigated common ground in human-human communication, for example, how the shared culture background [4] and

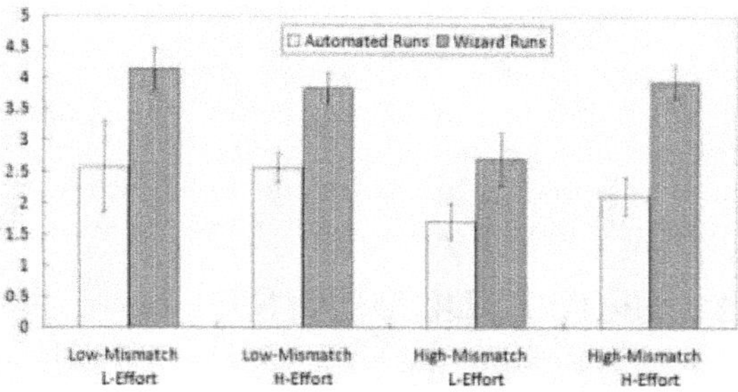

Figure 7: Average number of correctly acquired names from automatic runs and wizard runs

spatial reasoning capabilities [22] affect human-human communication. In spoken dialogue systems, previous work has addressed how automated speech recognition and language understanding affect common ground [11]. Compared to human-human communication or spoken dialogue systems, the issue of common ground is more complex in human-robot dialogue. This is because it involves an additional layer of common ground - a lower level that concerns perception (e.g., visual and tactile) and symbol grounding. Although fundamental to human-robot dialogue, this level generally is not concerned in human-human communication. Thus, as in recent work [2, 17], this paper pays a special attention to this lower level of common ground.

One of the important characteristics of situated interaction is the embodiment. Humans and robots have physical bodies in the shared environment and they can presumably utilize non-verbal modalities and actions to communicate and establish common ground. However, our current work has focused on mediating a shared visual perceptual basis mainly using language. Especially, we have not looked into collaborative non-verbal behaviors such natural gestures or actions (e.g., pointing gestures and picking up an object to teach the robot different attributes) from human partners. These actions will be even more important for a dynamic environment. Our future work will address this limitation by integrating embodiment with language based communication and investigate its role in establishing common ground.

The acquired common ground knowledge will provide a basis for follow-up communications. Furthermore, as knowledge accumulates, it will allow the robot to automatically learn new models, for example, word models for grounded semantics [8]. Our current work has only focused on acquiring knowledge towards common ground through collaborative dialogue. We have not explored the direction where the robot actively learns about the environment [3, 29]. Our future work will extend the current models to address robot learning through dialogue to establish common ground.

6. CONCLUSION

This paper describes a dialogue system that attempts to mediate a shared perceptual basis between the human and the robot through automatic knowledge acquisition. As conversation proceeds, the robot first matches human descriptions to its internal representation of the shared world. It then automatically acquires and confirms through dialogue common ground knowledge about the shared environment. The acquired knowledge is used to enrich the robot's representation of the shared world. In particular, this paper examines the role of the robot's collaborative effort in this grounding process. Our results have shown that an extra effort from the robot to make its human partner aware of its internal representation of the shared world contributes to better common ground. Our future work will build upon the current system and integrate non-verbal behaviors and active learning for common ground knowledge acquisition.

7. ACKNOWLEDGMENTS

This work was supported by N00014-11-1-0410 from the Office of Naval Research and IIS-1208390 from the National Science Foundation.

8. REFERENCES

[1] D. Bohus and E. Horvitz. Models for multiparty engagement in open-world dialog. In *Proceedings of the SIGDIAL 2009 Conference*, pages 225–234, 2009.

[2] H. Buschmeier and S. Kopp. Co-constructing grounded symbols - feedback and incremental adaptation in human-agent dialogue. *Künstliche Intelligenz*, 27:137–143, 2013.

[3] M. Cakmak and A. L. Thomaz. Designing robot learners that ask good questions. In *Proceedings of the HRI12*, pages 17–24, 2012.

[4] H. H. Clark. *Using language*. Cambridge University Press, Cambridge, UK, 1996.

[5] H. H. Clark and S. E. Brennan. Grounding in communication. In L. B. Resnick, R. M. Levine, and S. D. Teasley, editors, *Perspectives on socially shared cognition*, pages 127–149. 1991.

[6] H. H. Clark and E. F. Schaefer. Contributing to discourse. In *Cognitive Science*, number 13, pages 259–294. 1989.

[7] H. H. Clark and D. Wilkes-Gibbs. Referring as a collaborative process. In *Cognition*, number 22, pages 1–39. 1986.

[8] R. Fang, C. Liu, and J. Y. Chai. Integrating word acquisition and referential grounding towards physical world interaction. In *Proceedings of the 14th ACM International Conference on Multimodal Interaction*, ICMI '12, pages 109–116, 2012.

[9] B. Fransen, V. Morariu, E. Martinson, S. Blisard, M. Marge, S. Thomas, A. Schultz, and D. Perzanowski. Using vision, acoustics, and natural language for disambiguation. In *Proceedings of the HRI07*, pages 73–80, 2007.

[10] D. Gergle, R. E. Kraut, and S. R. Fussell. Using visual information for grounding and awareness in collaborative tasks. *Human Computer Interaction*, 28:1–39, 2013.

[11] J. Gordon, R. Passonneau, and S. Epstein. Learning to balance grounding rationales for dialogue systems. In *Proceedings of the SIGDIAL 2011 Conference*, pages 266–271, 2011.

[12] S. Kiesler. Fostering common ground in human-robot interaction. In *Proceedings of the IEEE International Workshop on Robots and Human Interactive Communication (ROMAN)*, pages 729–734, 2005.

[13] G.-J. M. Kruijff, P. Lison, T. Benjamin, H. Jacobsson, and N. Hawes. Incremental, multi-level processing for comprehending situated dialogue in human-robot interaction. In *Symposium on Language and Robots*, 2007.

[14] C. Liu, R. Fang, and J. Y. Chai. Towards mediating shared perceptual basis in situated dialogue. In *Proceedings of the SIGDIAL 2012 Conference*, pages 140–149, 2012.

[15] C. Liu, R. Fang, L. She, and J. Chai. Modeling collaborative referring for situated referential grounding. In *Proceedings of the SIGDIAL 2013 Conference*, pages 78–86, Metz, France, 2013.

[16] B. Mutlu, T. Shiwa, T. Kanda, H. Ishiguro, and N. Hagita. Footing in human-robot conversations: How robots might shape participant roles using gaze cues. *Proceedings of the HRI09*, pages 61–68, 2009.

[17] J. Peltason, H. Rieser, S. Wachsmuth, and B. Wrede. On grounding natural kind terms in human-robot communication. *Künstliche Intelligenz*, 27:107–118, 2013.

[18] A. Powers, A. Kramer, S. Lim, J. Kuo, S.-L. Lee, and S. Kiesler. Common ground in dialogue with a gendered humanoid robot. In *Proceedings of ICRA*, 2005.

[19] C. Rich, B. Ponsleur, A. Holroyd, and C. L. Sidner. Recognizing engagement in human-robot interaction. In *Proceedings of the HRI10*, pages 375–382, 2010.

[20] P. E. Rybski, K. Yoon, J. Stolarz, and M. M. Veloso. Interactive robot task training through dialog and demonstration. In *Proceedings of the HRI07*, pages 49–56, 2007.

[21] M. Scheutz, P. Schermerhorn, J. Kramer, and D. Anderson. Incremental natural language processing for hri. In *Proceedings of the HRI07*, 2007.

[22] M. F. Schober. Spatial dialogue between partners with mismatched abilities. In *Spatial Language and Dialogue*, pages 23–39. Oxford University Press, 2009.

[23] C. Sidner, C. Lee, C. D. Kidd, N. Lesh, and C.Rich. Explorations in engagement for humans and robots. In *Artificial Intelligence*, volume 166(1-2), pages 140–164, 2005.

[24] R. Stalnaker. Common ground. *Linguistics and Philosophy*, 25:701–721, 2002.

[25] M. Staudte and M. W. Crocker. Visual attention in spoken human-robot interaction. In *Proceedings of the HRI09*, pages 77–84, 2009.

[26] M. Steedman and J. Baldridge. Combinatory categorial grammar. *Non-Transformational Syntax Oxford: Blackwell*, pages 181–224, 2011.

[27] K. Stubbs, P. Hinds, and D. Wettergreen. Autonomy and common ground in human-robot interaction. In *IEEE Intelligent Systems*, pages 42–50, 2007.

[28] K. Stubbs, D. Wettergreen, and I. Nourbakhsh. Using a robot proxy to create commmon ground in exploration tasks. In *Proceedings of the HRI08*, pages 375–382, 2008.

[29] S. Tellex, R. Deits, P. Thaker, D. Simeonov, T. Kollar, and N. Roy. Clarifying commands with information-theoretic human-robot dialog. *Journal of Human-Robot Interaction*, 1:78–95, 2012.

[30] D. Traum. *A Computational Theory of Grounding in Natural Language Conversation*. PhD thesis, University of Rochester, 1994.

Situational Context Directs How People Affectively Interpret Robotic Non-Linguistic Utterances

Robin Read
Plymouth University
Centre for Robotics and Neural Systems
Drake Circus, Plymouth, PL4 8AA, UK
robin.read@plymouth.ac.uk

Tony Belpaeme
Plymouth University
Centre for Robotics and Neural Systems
Drake Circus, Plymouth, PL4 8AA, UK
tony.belpaeme@plymouth.ac.uk

ABSTRACT

This paper presents an experiment investigating the influence that a situational context has upon how people affectively interpret Non-Linguistic Utterances made by a social robot. Subjects were presented five video conditions showing the robot making both a *positive* and *negative* utterance, the robot being subject to an action (e.g. receiving a kiss, or a slap), and then two videos showing the combination of the action and the robot reacting with both the positive and negative utterances. For each video an affective rating of valence was provided based upon how the subjects thought the robot *felt* given what had happened in the video. This was repeated for 5 different action scenarios. Results show that the affective interpretation of an action appears to override that of an utterance, regardless of the affective charge of the utterance. Furthermore, it is shown that if the meaning of the action and utterance are aligned, the overall interpretation is *amplified.* These findings are considered with respect to the practical use of utterances during social HRI.

Categories and Subject Descriptors

H.5.2 [**User Interfaces**]: Auditory (non-speech) feedback; H.5.5 [**Sound and Music Computing**]: Systems; I.2.9 [**Robotics**]: Operator interfaces

Keywords

Non-Linguistic Utterances; Social HRI; Situational Context

1. INTRODUCTION

Non-Linguistic Utterances (NLUs) are robotic sounds made by synthetic social agents, as opposed to utterances that resemble natural language, such as artificial languages [4] and Gibberish Speech [5, 12]. While NLUs have been used to great effect within the world of animation and through popular culture/media as a *proto-language* (robots such as R2D2 and WALL-E provide vivid examples of this), few efforts have been made to systematically explore and investigate the potential utility of this modality as applied to real social robots. The work presented here is part of a larger branch of research that does just that.

Currently, fictional robots have been the most prominent beneficiaries of NLUs, however examples of robots that already employ this modality are emerging. For example the Keepon robot [3], with its simplistic aesthetic employs NLUs rather than natural language as a means of expressive communication with autistic children. This use of NLUs has also been extended to the recent commercial cousin, My Keepon. NLUs also have a variety of traits that makes them advantageous for HRI. Firstly, they are not bound to a particular spoken dialect and thus could be used in multi-lingual and multi-cultural settings. Furthermore, as NLUs do not encode linguistic semantic context, there is less need to process spoken input from humans for semantic content, and as such, NLUs may be used in real world settings that pose challenges for Natural Language Processing (NLP) such as noisy environments and settings with multi-speakers (and accents) - NLUs may help robots operating in the *wild* be more expressive through the acoustic modality.

Our previous work has focused on identifying the acoustic parameters of utterances that influence how people affectively interpret NLUs [7] and probing the landscape of these affective interpretations [8], as well as how the morphology of a robot may influence this [6]. As a trend, these results have shown that subjects tend to not be coherent in their affective ratings of utterances, as well as indicating that subjects' interpretations are coarse and subject to a "magnet effect", with utterances being interpreted as belonging to only a few basic emotions.

We hypothesise that this general lack of coherence has been due to the abstract nature of the utterances and the lack of situational context when they were presented to subjects. To tackle this, the experiment presented here probes the influence that a situational context has upon how people affectively interpret NLUs made by a robot (an Aldebaran Nao, in this case), or visa versa. To take a film analogy: if the soundtracks of two scenes in which R2D2 "talks" were swapped, would we notice a difference in meaning?

As most (if not all) HRI has implicit context associated with it, it is vital to have insights into the nature of this influence as it provides guidelines on how NLUs may be utilized by *real* robots in the *wild*, from a practical perspective – i.e. how to generate utterances, and how and when to use them within an interaction.

HRI'14, March 3–6, 2014, Bielefeld, Germany.

ACM 978-1-4503-2658-2/14/03 ...$15.00.
http://dx.doi.org/10.1145/2559636.2559680.

2. EXPERIMENTAL SETUP

The experiment set out to test the following hypotheses:

- H_1: An NLU overrides/biases the interpretation of a situational context.
- H_2: The situational context overrides/biases the interpretation of an NLU.

To test these hypotheses, an online experiment was setup using an online crowd-sourcing service, where subjects were asked to affectively rate videos of a robot across 5 conditions:

- C^P_{NLU}: The robot emitting a *positive* sounding NLU.
- C^N_{NLU}: The robot emitting a *negative* sounding NLU.
- C_{Action}: The robot being subject to an action from a human (e.g. the robot being slapped on the head) and making no NLU response.
- C^P_{Action}: The robot being subject to an action from a human and emitting the *positive* NLU from C^P_{NLU} in reaction.
- C^N_{Action}: The robot being subject to an action from a human and emitting the *negative* NLU from C^N_{NLU} in reaction.

Conditions C^P_{NLU} and C^N_{NLU} provide the base interpretation for the respective NLUs without any situational context: a sanity check to see whether the NLUs are indeed interpreted differently. Similarly, condition C_{Action} obtains the base interpretation for the actions, again necessary before we can measure the relative influence of NLUs on actions. Conditions C^P_{Action} and C^N_{Action} assess the interaction between the NLU and the context when combined.

Relating these conditions to the hypotheses, if H_1 is true, it would be expected that, for example, the ratings for C^P_{Action} and C_{Action} would be significantly different while C^P_{Action} and C^P_{NLU} would have similar ratings - the NLU has been able to *pull* the rating of the action away from the original interpretation. Conversely, if H_2 were true, the opposite would be expected: the ratings for C^P_{Action} and C^P_{NLU} would be significantly different while C_{Action} and C^P_{Action} would have similar ratings - the situational context has been able to *pull* the rating of an utterance away from the original interpretation. These two examples are shown graphically in figure 1.

If either these hypotheses are highly potent, then the same effect should be found when the valance for the action and NLU are opposite. For example, in the case of H_2, if C_{Action} were to show a robot being slapped (likely a negative action), then the rating for C^P_{Action} should be significantly different to that of C^P_{NLU} and close to that of C_{Action}.

Ratings were collected using a 9 point Likert scale representing *valence*, where 1 corresponded to "very negative" and 9 to "very positive". Subjects were asked to watch each video and provide a rating of how they thought the robot felt based upon the action that happened in the video, or the sound that the robot made in the video.

5 different action scenarios (the robot being kissed on the head, slapped in the face, poked on the forehead, stroked on the head and having its eye covered) were selected and videos produced for the conditions C_{Action}, C^P_{Action} and C^N_{Action},

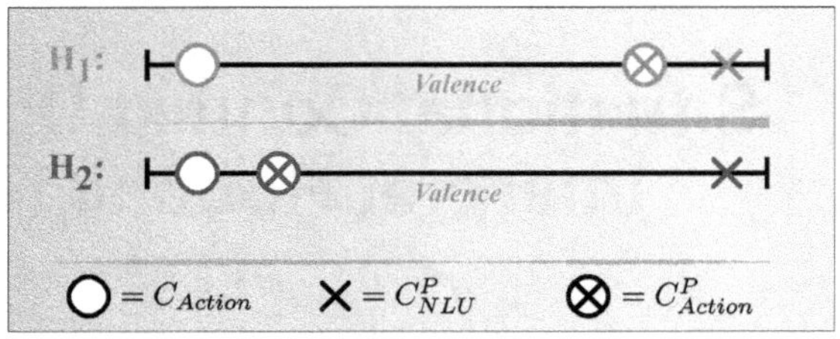

Figure 1: Example of how the video conditions C_{Action}, C^P_{NLU} and C^P_{Action} may hypothetically be rated, for each of the two Hypotheses.

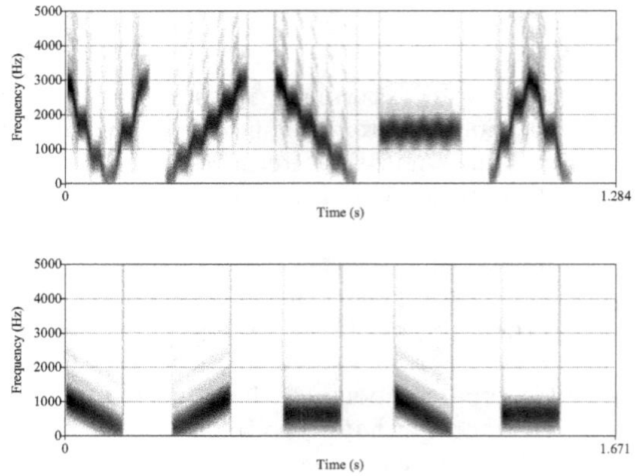

Figure 2: Spectrograms of NLU#1 (top) and NLU#2 (bottom), used as the *positive* and *negative* NLUs respectively.

thus producing 15 videos in total, with the five different actions providing a gradient of affective interpretations across the likert scale. This set of videos is referred to as *Action videos*. Similarly, 5 different NLUs were produced and videos recorded of the robot emitting the utterance. These are referred to as the *NLU videos*. Two of these NLUs were used as the NLUs in conditions C^P_{Action} and C^N_{Action} as they were deemed to be most representative positive and negative respectively[1].

2.1 Stimulus Production

NLUs in the work presented here, consist of a concatenation of single, frequency modulated, sine wave tones of varying duration, separated by pauses also of varying duration. All utterances have a fixed length of 5 sound units and were designed with the aim of providing a broad range of different utterances. NLU#1 was identified via a pilot study as the "positive" utterance, while NLU #2 was identified as the "negative" utterance, and thus represented C^P_{NLU} and C^N_{NLU} respectively (see figure 2 for spectrograms).

Videos were recorded of each of the five actions (see figure 3), without the robot making a sound. Next, professional audio equipment was used to capture the NLUs in high quality. To create the videos showing the robot making an NLU in response to the action, the audio of the particular NLU was added to the audio of the action video using video editing software, thus ensuring that it was only the NLU that

[1] As identified through a pilot study.

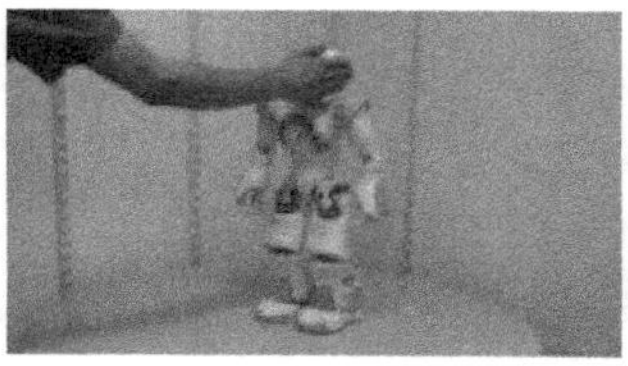

(a) **Slap Action**

(b) **Kiss Action**

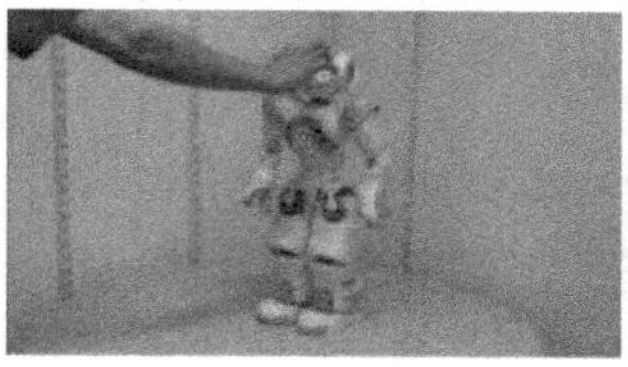

(c) **Flick Action**

(d) **Head Stroke Action**

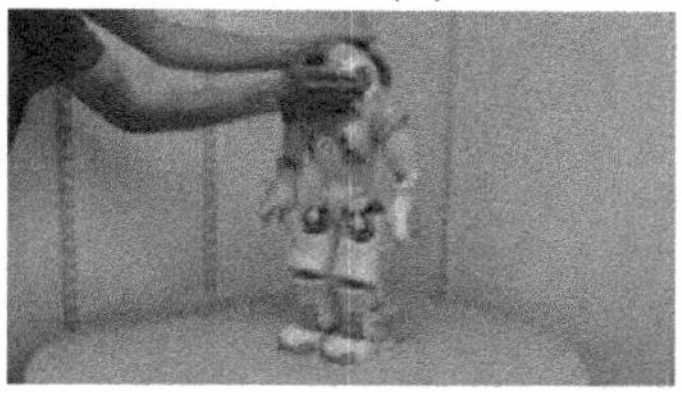

(e) **Eye Cover Action**

Figure 3: Images of the five actions.

was different between the NLU/action conditions for each action[2].

2.2 Experimental Procedure

Online crowd sourcing studies has recently been shown to be a fast and fruitful means to gather information on HRI on a large scale (*cf.* [1]). This work was conducting using an online crowd sourcing service, *CrowdFlower*[3]. Recruitment of subjects was limited to the USA to focus the subject demographics. Subjects were rewarded 0.3$ USD for their participation.

At the start of the online survey, subjects were asked to provide their age and gender. Each video was then presented with all 20 videos in one of three orders (it was not possible to completely randomize the order of the questions using the CrowdFlower service). For each video, subjects were asked to provide an affective (valence) rating indicating how they thought the robot felt based upon what happened to the robot in the video, or by the sound that the robot made. Each video also had a *validation* question, which asked a specific detail regarding the content of the video. This was done to confirm whether the subject had watched the video. Questions queried details such as the colour of the robot's eyes, the colour of the human's t-shirt, whether the robot made a sound in the video and what action happened in the video. All the validation questions were forced choice with either two or three options. Finally subjects where queried over whether they were familiar with the robot (having seen it before somewhere).

Overall, subjects were asked to rate 5 NLU videos, 5 action videos, 10 action/NLU videos, 2 personal questions, and the question regarding whether they had seen the robot before. Thus there were 23 questions in the survey in total. The average time taken to complete the surgery was no more than 6 minutes.

3. RESULTS

In total, 324 people responded via the CrowdFlower service, however, the data for 21 subjects was removed as their accuracy for the validation questions (mean = 93.96%, std = 11.02%) fell below 80%. 330 subjects were thus used in this analysis. Of these subjects, 87 were male (mean age = 32.24, std = 10.27) and 216 were female (mean age = 37.15, std = 11.39). 99 subjects answered to the first order of questions, 101 subjects for the second order and 103 for the third order. 151 subjects reported that they had seen the robot before (53 males, mean age = 32.24, std = 11.12, and 98 females, mean age = 37.71, std = 11.12).

Cronbach's α was used as a measure of internal agreement between subjects. For the videos showing only the NLU conditions (C^P_{NLU} and C^N_{NLU}), the α value for the ratings was 0.973, and for the videos showing only the action (C_{Action}) the α value for the ratings was 0.997. The ratings for the videos showing the Action/NLU combinations (C^P_{Action} and C^N_{Action}) both had an α value of 0.998. Collapsing all the ratings together an α value of 0.997 was obtained. All these α values are high, indicating a strong level of internal agreement between all subjects across all the action scenarios and respective video conditions.

In order to access the base interpretation of the NLUs, the ratings for the NLU videos (C^P_{NLU} and C^N_{NLU}) were subject to a 3-way repeated measures ANOVA (5x2x2) where the factors were the video shown (within subjects), subject gender (between subjects) and robot familiarity (between subjects). The Action Videos (C_{Action}) were subject to the same ANOVA design.

To test the impact of the Action/NLU combinations (C^P_{NLU} and C^N_{NLU}) for each of the 5 different actions the same 3-way repeated measures ANOVA (5x2x2) design was used. The video factor consisted of the videos showing each of the 5 different conditions. The two other factors were again subject gender and robot familiarity. All ANOVA results were also subject to post-hoc multi comparison tests using the Scheffé method with Bonferroni corrections used to identify the relative ratings between the various factors and video conditions.

3.1 Sound only Videos

The ANOVA identified a significant main effect due to the NLU made by the robot ($F(4, 1196) = 32.024$, $MSE = 31.206$, $p \leq 0.001$). This indeed confirms that the NLUs are interpreted differently: a prerequisite for further experiments.

The post-hoc tests showed that NLU#2 (mean = 5.129, 95% CI = [5.053 5.385]) was rated significantly lower than all the other NLUs ($p \leq 0.001$). NLU#1 (mean = 6.100, 95% CI = [5.923 6.277]) and NLU#4 (mean = 6.102, 95% CI = [5.926 6.278]) jointly had the highest rating[4] and received significantly higher ratings than NLU#3 (mean = 5.781, 95% CI = [5.621 5.942]), $p \leq 0.05$. No significant difference was found between NLU#5 (mean = 5.781, 95% CI = [5.621 5.942]) and NLU#3 (mean = 5.866, 95% CI = [5.703 6.029]) while both were found to have statically

[2]The videos can be viewed here: `http://www.youtube.com/playlist?list=PLJwvAKNW4DupOrU4SWSQJMzMbTLsa9T4T`

[3]CrowdFlower can be accessed from `www.crowdflower.com`.

[4]Thus were not significantly different.

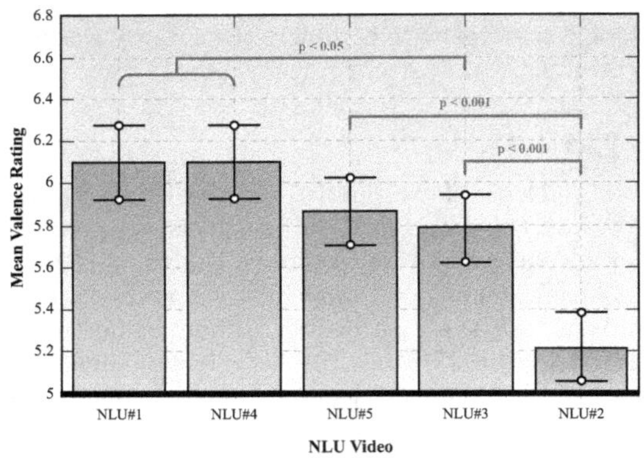

Figure 4: Bar graph showing the mean and 95% Confidence Interval for the valence ratings for each of the 5 NLU videos.

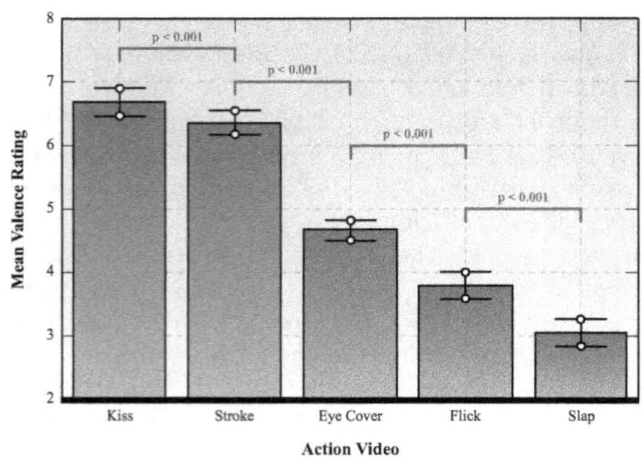

Figure 5: Bar graph showing the mean and 95% Confidence Interval for the valence ratings for each of the 5 Action videos.

higher ratings than NLU#2 ($p \leq 0.001$). These results are shown in figure 4.

3.2 Action Videos

For the action videos a significant main effect was found due to the action that was shown in the video ($F(4, 1196) = 251.833$, $MSE = 601.029$, $p \leq 0.001$), with no other main effects or interaction effects being identified.

The post-hoc tests revealed that the videos indeed represented a gradient of interpretations across the 5 different actions, and that the ratings for all actions were significantly different ($p \leq 0.001$). The video showing the robot being slapped received the lowest rating (mean = 3.045, 95% CI = [2.828 3.262]), followed by the flicking action (mean = 3.787, 95% CI= [3.578 3.995]). The covering of the robot's eyes action (mean = 4.669, 95% CI = [4.517 4.822]) represented the middle action, being interpreted neutrally. The video of the robot being stroked on the head received the second highest rating (mean = 6.361, 95% CI= [6.172 6.549]) while the video showing the robot being kissed on the head received the highest rating (mean = 6.687, 95% CI = [6.469 6.905]). These results are shown in figure 5.

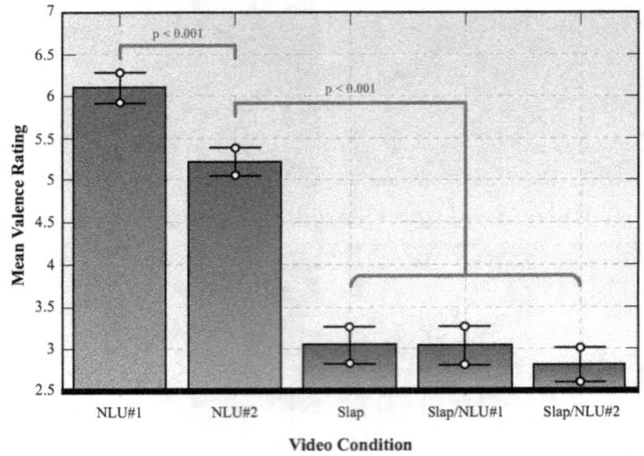

Figure 6: Bar graph showing the mean and 95% Confidence Interval for the valence ratings for each video conditions for the Slap Action scenario.

3.3 Action/NLU combination Videos

This section presents the results of the ANOVA analysis for each of the five action scenarios. The C^P_{NLU} and C^N_{NLU} conditions are present in all the scenarios and thus these two conditions have the same ratings throughout, while the ratings for conditions C_{Action}, C^P_{Action} and C^N_{Action} for each action scenario are different.

3.3.1 Slap Action Scenario

For the slapping action, only a main effect due to the video shown was found ($F(4, 1196) = 301.774$, $MSE = 546.218$, $p \leq 0.001$). No other effects were found.

The post-hoc tests showed that the videos showing condition C^P_{NLU} (mean = 6.100, 95% CI = [5.923 6.277]) and C^N_{NLU} (mean = 5.129, 95% CI = [5.053 5.385]) had a significantly different rating ($p \leq 0.001$), and that the videos showing condition C_{Action} (mean = 3.045, 95% CI = [2.828 3.262]), C^P_{Action}(mean = 3.042, 95% CI = [2.810 3.275]) and C^N_{Action} (mean = 2.805, 95% CI = [2.604 3.007]) had no significant differences in their ratings while they were all rated significantly lower than the video showing C^N_{NLU}, $p \leq 0.001$ (figure 6).

3.3.2 Kiss Action Scenario

For the kissing action, the ANOVA found only a main effect due to the video condition ($F(4, 1196) = 139.445$, $MSE = 191.377$, $p \leq 0.001$) and no interaction effects.

The post-hoc tests revealed that all the videos had significantly different ratings ($p \leq 0.001$). The video showing the C^P_{Action} condition received the highest rating (mean = 7.550, 95% CI = [7.378 7.721]), followed by C^N_{Action} (mean = 7.017, 95% CI = [6.822 7.212]). The C_{Action} condition (mean = 6.687, 95% CI = [6.469 6.905]) has rated higher than C^P_{NLU} (mean = 6.100, 95% CI = [5.923 6.277]) while the C^N_{NLU} condition received the lowest rating (mean = 5.129, 95% CI = [5.053 5.385]). These results are shown in figure 7.

3.3.3 Flicking Action Scenario

It was found, in the flicking scenario, that there was a significant main effect due to the video that was shown ($F(4, 1196) = 184.597$, $MSE = 309.671$, $p \leq 0.001$), as well as an interaction effect between the subject gender and the video shown ($F(4, 1196) = 3.021$, $MSE = 5.069$, $p \leq 0.05$).

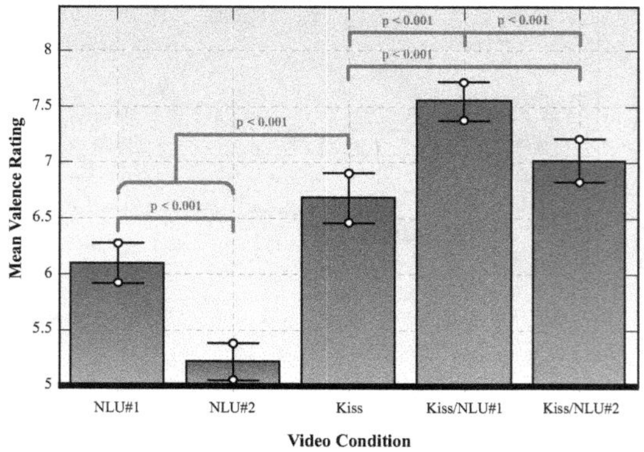

Figure 7: Bar graph showing the mean and 95% Confidence Interval for the valence ratings for each video conditions for the Kiss Action scenario.

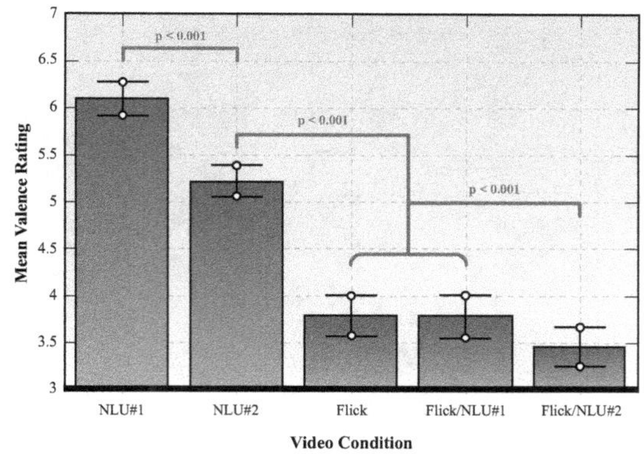

(a) Bar graph showing the mean and 95% Confidence Interval for the valence ratings for each video conditions for the Flick Action scenario.

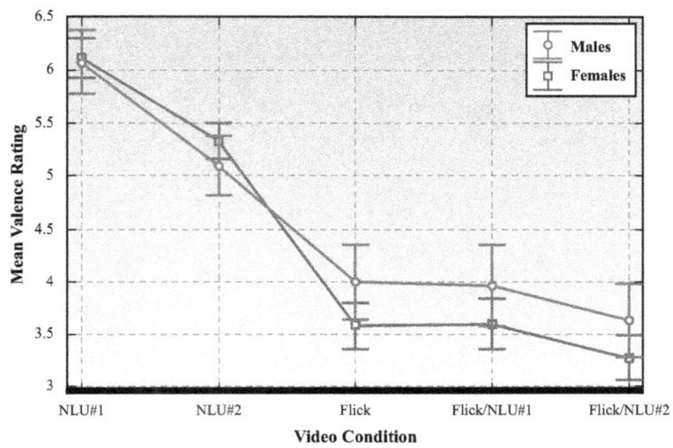

(b) Plot of the Mean Values and 95% Confidence Intervals for the Flick Action ratings, across the male and females subjects.

Figure 8: Plots of the main and interaction effects identified for the Flick Action scenario ratings.

With respect to the main effect due to the video shown, the post-hoc tests revealed that the videos showing the action (C_{Action}) and action/NLU combinations (C^P_{Action} and C^N_{Action}) were rated as significantly lower than the video showing C^N_{NLU} ($p \leq 0.001$), and that there was no difference in the rating between C_{Action} (mean = 3.787, 95% CI = [3.578 3.995]) and the C^P_{Action} (mean = 3.784, 95% CI = [3.556 4.012]). The C^N_{Action} video (mean = 3.456, 95% CI = [3.251 3.661] was rated significantly lower than all other videos ($p \leq 0.001$). These results are shown in figure 8a.

For the interaction effect, the post-hoc tests indicated that for the two NLU videos, females provided marginally higher ratings, while for the flicking action and combination videos the females provided lower ratings (see figure 8b).

3.3.4 Stroke Action Scenario

For the stroking action, the ANOVA found that there were main effects due to the video shown ($F(4, 1196) = 66.843$, $MSE = 98.964$, $p \leq 0.001$) and the subject gender ($F(1, 299) = 11.411$, $MSE = 55.833$, $p \leq 0.001$), as well as an interaction effect between these two factors ($F(4, 1196) = 4.707$, $MSE = 6.968$, $p \leq 0.01$).

With respect to the main effect due to the video condition, the post-hoc tests revealed that the C^P_{Action} had the highest rating and was significantly different ($p \leq 0.001$) to the ratings for C^P_{NLU} (mean = 6.100, 95% CI = [5.923 6.277]) and the video of C_{Action} (mean = 6.361, 95% CI = [6.172 6.549]) while no significant difference was found between the C^P_{Action} and C^N_{Action} (mean = 6.663, 95% CI = [6.464 6.862]) or the C_{Action} and C^N_{Action} videos. The C^N_{NLU} video had the lowest rating (mean = 5.129, 95% CI = [5.053 5.385]) and was significantly different from all the other videos ($p \leq 0.001$). This result is shown in figure 9a.

The tests also revealed that overall the mean rating for the female subjects (mean = 6.459, 95% CI = [6.326 6.592]) was significantly higher ($p \leq 0.01$) than the ratings provided by the male subjects (mean = 6.027, 95% CI = [5.813 6.241).

The interaction effect between the videos and subject gender was identified as female subjects providing higher ratings than the males, with the difference between the ratings being notably larger for the action/NLU combinations than the other videos (see figure 9b).

3.3.5 Eye Cover Action Scenario

It was found that the video shown again had a significant main effect ($F(4, 1196) = 78.989$, $MSE = 105.718$, $p \leq 0.001$), and that there were interaction effects between the subject gender and the video shown ($F(4, 1196) = 2.571$, $MSE = 3.441$, $p \leq 0.05$), and the robot familiarity and the video shown ($F(4, 1196) = 2.871$, $MSE = 3.842$, $p \leq 0.05$).

For the main effect due to the videos shown, the post-hoc tests revealed that C_{Action} video (mean = 4.669, 95% CI = [4.517 4.822]), C^P_{Action} video (mean = 4.611, 95% CI = [4.422 4.799]) and C^N_{Action} video (mean = 4.497, 95% CI = [4.322 4.672]) had no significant difference, but all were rated as significantly lower than the C^N_{NLU} video (mean = 5.129, 95% CI = [5.053 5.385]), $p \leq 0.001$ (see figure 10a).

The interaction effects were identified as the female subjects providing higher ratings than the males for the NLU videos, while providing lower ratings for the action and action/NLU combination videos. Similarly, the subjects whom were familiar with the robot provided higher ratings for the NLU videos than subject unfamiliar with the robot, with the opposite being true for the action and action/NLU com-

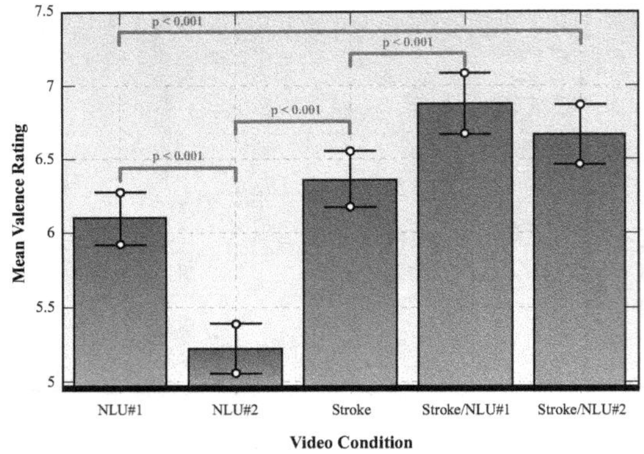

(a) Bar graph showing the mean and 95% Confidence Interval for the valence ratings for each video conditions for the Stroke Action scenario.

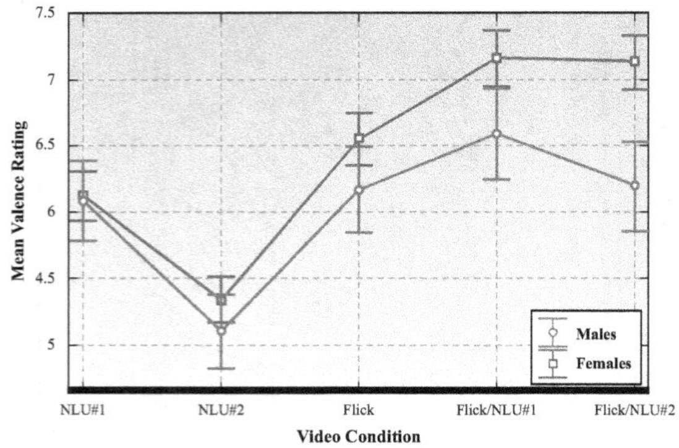

(b) Plot of the Mean Values and 95% Confidence Intervals for the Stroke Action ratings, across the male and females subjects.

Figure 9: Plots of the main and interaction effects identified for the Stroke Action scenario ratings.

bination videos. These results are shown in figures 10b and 10c.

4. DISCUSSION

This section provides a discussion of the experiment and results obtained from a variety of perspectives such as with regard to the Hypotheses outlined at the beginning of the chapter, the drawbacks of the methodology, limitations regarding the interpretation of the results and the implications of how NLUs may be used practically.

4.1 Main Effects

The high Cronbach's α values indicate that overall the subjects were in agreement in their interpretations of the videos presented, and in their use of the Likert scale when interpreting and rating the videos. As a result, this promotes confidence regarding the validity of the results obtained via this measuring scale.

With respect to H_1 (the hypothesis that the interpretation of an NLU overrides that of the action), none of the results provide any support for this hypothesis - no signifi-

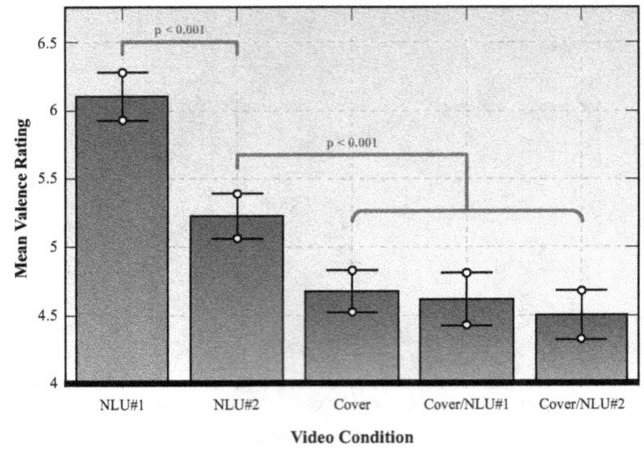

(a) Bar graph showing the mean and 95% Confidence Interval for the valence ratings for each video conditions for the Cover Action scenario.

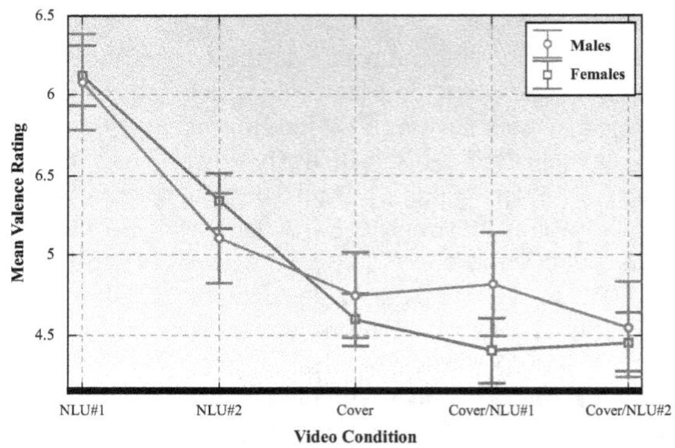

(b) Plot of the Mean Values and 95% Confidence Intervals for the Cover Action ratings, across the male and females subjects.

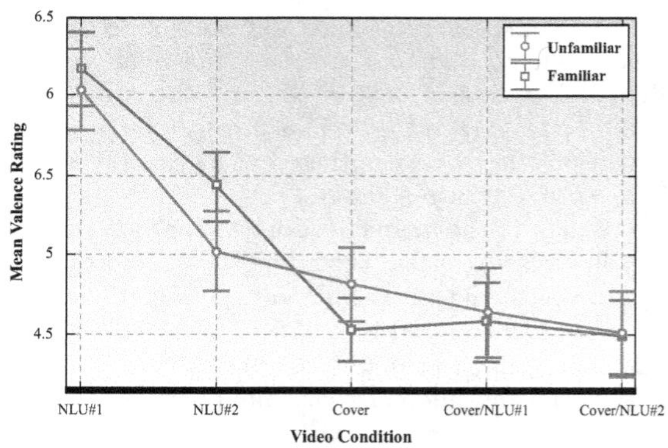

(c) Plot of the Mean Values and 95% Confidence Intervals for the Flick Action ratings, across the subjects whom were familiar and unfamiliar with the robot.

Figure 10: Plots of the main and interaction effects identified for the Eye Cover Action scenario ratings.

cant effects were found, across any of the actions, where the interpretation of either the C^P_{Action} or C^N_{Action} condition was significantly different to the C_{Action} condition *and closer* to the rating of either the C^P_{NLU} or C^N_{NLU} conditions. Thus, it can be reasonably concluded that the NLUs did not have an effect whereby they pulled the interpretation of an Action/NLU combination toward the base interpretation of the NLU.

With respect to H_2 (the hypothesis that the interpretation of an action overrides that of an NLU), all the results provide evidence supporting this hypothesis. In all the action scenarios the videos showing the action/NLU combinations (C^P_{Action} and C^N_{Action}) received ratings that were either not significantly different from the action only video (C_{Action}), or they were significantly different and more *extreme* than the action video rating. Coupling this with the finding that in all but one of the action conditions (the stroking action) the action videos were found to be rated significantly different and more extreme than the NLU only videos, it is clear that the actions provided a strong biasing effect that overrode the base interpretation of a given NLU.

These results did also yield a further insight: the results for the kissing action, stroking action and flicking action all indicate that the alignment in valence between the NLU and the action can actually *enhance* a given rating of an action, pushing it to a more *extreme* interpretation (i.e. C^P_{Action} was significantly more extreme than C_{Action} whereas C^N_{Action} was not). While this is a rather intuitive result, given that the NLU provided a reaction to the action, it also demonstrates that while the action provided a dominant bias, the NLU did contain subtle acoustic cues that subjects were sensitive to. The identification of this sensitivity is important as it highlights the *subtle* degree through which NLUs operate.

4.2 Interaction Effects

Significant interaction effects were identified between the different video conditions and the subject gender, with this being true for the Stroking, Flicking and Eye Covering action scenarios. In all cases if was found that the females provided more extreme ratings than the males overall, with this being a more prominent effect with the Action Videos than the NLU Videos. These effects may be a suggestion that the females subjects are able to empathise more with the robot, something that has been reported in a variety of HRI studies, however with inconsistent results [10].

It is however important to consider the magnitude of the interaction effect and the conditions under which it has been found. The general size of effects due to gender and the familiarity with the Nao are all small (≤ 1.0). These differences cover a small range of the overall rating scale, and more importantly, cover a small promotion of the *working* range of responses (i.e. between the highest and lowest mean ratings). Also, these effects have only been found in the scenarios in which the affective ratings are not extreme (e.g the the kiss and slap actions).

4.3 Methodological Drawbacks & Limitations

While the results have shown support for H_2, there are a number of drawbacks that need to be highlighted with respect to the methodology of the experiment.

There is a clear gender imbalance, which due to the nature of the CrowdFlower service was uncontrollable, and as such it is difficult to disentangle and uncover the relation between the effects found and the size of the gender populations.

The fact that the experiment was conducted online using videos results in somewhat reduced ecological validity. The rational for the use of videos was that you can present subjects with exactly the same stimulus, and given the content of the videos, this is something that could not be achieved when presenting the action scenarios in real life. However, it is possible that the results found may have been different if the experiment were to have been conducted within the *real world* as it is likely that medium of video provides a certain degree of *disconnection* between the subjects and the events shown within the videos, in particular with respect to a subjects ability to empathize with the robot given that the subjects were *observing* the actions and reactions of the robot, rather than being the *cause* of these (however, see [11] for a counter-argument). Future work may seek to conduct a similar experiment within a real world setting, with subjects being both observers of the robot's behaviour as well as the cause of the behaviours.

The actions that were selected in this study may be considered as *iconic*, having little ambiguity compared with other potential physical interactions (for example, moving the robot's arm randomly). As a result, the notion that the situation overrides the NLU is intuitive but may have limited generalization. However, it may be that subjects (consciously or unconsciously) project meaning into the physical interactions with robots that they either observe or engage in, based upon previous experiences which they can draw upon. If this is the case, the underlying insight that physical interaction appears to bias how NLUs are interpreted remains valid. However, this far-reaching notion is yet to be tested.

Finally, all the NLUs covered a small region of the Likert scale with this region being located around what might be considered as "neutral". Given this, it is not overly surprising that the actions override the NLU interpretation, however in this light it is surprising that effect of the alignment in valence between the NLU and action occurs. If the NLUs were to represent and evoke more extreme affective ratings, evidence supporting H_1 may emerge, particularly in the case of a misalignment in the valence of the action and NLU. This could result in the evidence supporting H_2 being less prominent. However, this assumes that it is indeed possible for NLUs to wield interpretations with similar a magnitude as the Kissing and Slapping action scenarios without the inclusion of context. This is a more general assumption about the utility and communicative capabilities of NLUs that has a variety of complex facets (such as how exposure to NLUs through long-term social interaction with the robot may impact how subjects interpret NLUs) that requires further attention and investigation.

4.4 Practical Use of NLUs

The results of this experiment also lend themselves to providing insights as to how NLUs may be used practically in real (social) robotic systems.

What NLU to make: As a general "rule of thumb", if the context is clear, it is likely that any sound (within reason) is likely to produce an adequate alignment to the desired interpretation. However, the subtle sensitivity to NLUs that has been demonstrated here should not be overlooked. If both the valence of the action and the NLU are known, the affective interpretation of the scenario can be amplified to be *more* extreme (and perhaps robust). Though, caution must be drawn to the use of iconic sounds such as single tones with either a rising or falling frequency modulation as these tend to have clear and robust/well established, iconic meanings, and the interaction between iconic actions and iconic sounds has not been studied here.

When to make an NLU: This experiment has used NLUs as a means of animating how a robot reacts to physical actions it is subject to, each with an implied affective valence, rather than a means of replacing natural language interaction (NLI). In a similar light to providing feedback, NLUs that have been used here may potentially be used as reactions/feedback to external events that are encoded in language - NLUs could be used for *back-channelling* also. When a robot experiences salient sensory input, or performs a salient *physical* action, using NLUs will likely enhance how the robot is perceived by a human.

Replacing NLI: Depending on the type of interaction that is desired, NLUs, like Gibberish, may be used to foster natural language responses (and other behaviours, such as gesturing) from a user, without the need to rely on NLP. As an example of this, Chao and Thomaz [2] have used Gibberish Speech to circumvent the need for NLP (and the inherent complexities it adds to a system) while still evoking natural dialogue from subjects when evaluating their model of turn-taking behaviour. In this light, both NLUs and Gibberish might have potential in moving beyond Wizard of Oz (WoZ) approaches in HRI studies to overcome shortcomings in NLP [9], moving closer to fully autonomous social HRI.

5. CONCLUSIONS

This paper has presented the results of an experiment probing the interaction between situational context and Non-Linguistic Utterances in robotics. NLUs have been used with great effect by the animation industry to bring fictional robot characters to life, but there have been few efforts to investigate to what extent the utility of NLUs translates to real world social HRI.

In this experiment, subjects were shown 5 video conditions, showing a robot making a positive NLU, a negative NLU, being subjected to an affect-laden action, being subjected to the action and while uttering the positive or negative NLU. This was done for 5 different actions: a slap, a kiss, a flick, a stroke on the head and the robot's eyes being covered. For each video subjects rated how they thought the robot felt. The results found that the context valence of the action overrode the the valence of the NLUs when the action and NLU were combined in a video. Furthermore, the results indicate that when the valence of the NLU and action were aligned, the affective interpretation was *enhanced*.

These insights help inform guidelines regarding how NLUs may be utilized by roboticists' developing social robots that operate in the real world. For example, while NLUs tend to have rather ambiguous interpretations, when used within a clear context, the meaning of the context is adopted by the NLU. This also appears to be the case for NLUs with a notably different acoustic characteristics. As such, our proposed "rule of thumb" is that to acoustically animate a robot during HRI, selecting/generating a random NLU may suffice, as the utterance only serves to amplify the semantics of the visual context.

6. ACKNOWLEDGMENTS

This work is (partially) funded by the EU FP7 ALIZ-E project (grant 248116).

7. REFERENCES

[1] C. Breazeal, N. Depalma, J. Orkin, and S. Chernova. Crowdsourcing Human-Robot Interaction : New Methods and System Evaluation in a Public Environment. *Journal of Human-Robot Interaction*, 2(1):82–111, 2013.

[2] C. Chao and A. Thomaz. Controlling Social Dynamics with a Parametrized Model of Floor Regulation. *Journal of Human-Robot Interaction*, 2(1):4 – 29, 2013.

[3] H. Kozima, M. P. Michalowski, and C. Nakagawa. Keepon: A Playful Robot for Research, Therapy, and Entertainment. *International Journal of Social Robotics*, 1(1):3–18, Nov. 2009.

[4] O. Mubin, C. Bartneck, L. Leijs, H. Hooft van Huysduynen, J. Hu, and J. Muelver. Improving Speech Recognition with the Robot Interaction Language. *Disruptive Science and Technology*, 1(2):79–88, Dec. 2012.

[5] P.-Y. Oudeyer. The production and recognition of emotions in speech: features and algorithms. *International Journal of Human-Computer Studies*, 59(1-2):157–183, 2003.

[6] R. Read and T. Belpaeme. Interpreting Non-Linguistic Utterances by Robots : Studying the Influence of Physical Appearance. In *Proceedings of the 3rd International Workshop on Affective Interaction in Natural Environments (AFFINE 2010) at ACM Multimedia 2010*, pages 65–70, Firenze, Italy, Oct. 2010. ACM.

[7] R. Read and T. Belpaeme. How to Use Non-Linguistic Utterances to Convey Emotion in Child-Robot Interaction. In *Proceedings of the 7th International Conference on Human-Robot Interaction (HRI'12)*, pages 219–220, Boston, MA, U.S.A., Mar. 2012. ACM/IEEE.

[8] R. Read and T. Belpaeme. People Interpret Robotic Non-Linguistic Utterances Categorically. In *Proceedings of the 8th International Conference on Human-Robot Interaction (HRI'13)*, pages 209–210, Tokyo, Japan, Mar. 2013. ACM/IEEE.

[9] L. Riek. Wizard of Oz Studies in HRI: A Systematic Review and New Reporting Guidelines. *Journal of Human-Robot Interaction*, 1(1):119–136, Aug. 2012.

[10] A. M. Rosenthal-von der Pütten, N. C. Krämer, L. Hoffmann, S. Sobieraj, and S. C. Eimler. An Experimental Study on Emotional Reactions Towards a Robot. *International Journal of Social Robotics*, 5(1):17 – 34, 2012.

[11] S. Woods, M. Walters, K. Koay, and K. Dautenhahn. Methodological Issues in HRI: A Comparison of Live and Video-Based Methods in Robot to Human Approach Direction Trials. *Proceedings of the 15th International Symposium on Robot and Human Interactive Communication (RO-MAN 2006)*, pages 51–58, Sept. 2006.

[12] S. Yilmazyildiz, D. Henderickx, B. Vanderborght, W. Verhelst, E. Soetens, and D. Lefeber. EMOGIB : Emotional Gibberish Speech Database for Affective Human-Robot Interaction. In *Proceedings of the International Conference on Affective Computing and Intelligent Interaction (ACII'11)*, pages 163–172, Memphis, TN, U.S.A., Oct. 2011. Springer-Verlag.

Deliberate Delays During Robot-to-Human Handovers Improve Compliance With Gaze Communication

Henny Admoni[1], Anca Dragan[2], Siddhartha S. Srinivasa[2], Brian Scassellati[1]
[1]Department of Computer Science, Yale University, New Haven, CT 06520
[2]The Robotics Institute, Carnegie Mellon University, Pittsburgh, PA 15213
{henny,scaz}@cs.yale.edu, {adragan,siddh}@cs.cmu.edu

ABSTRACT

As assistive robots become popular in factories and homes, there is greater need for natural, multi-channel communication during collaborative manipulation tasks. Non-verbal communication such as eye gaze can provide information without overloading more taxing channels like speech. However, certain collaborative tasks may draw attention away from these subtle communication modalities. For instance, robot-to-human handovers are primarily manual tasks, and human attention is therefore drawn to robot hands rather than to robot faces during handovers. In this paper, we show that a simple manipulation of a robot's handover behavior can significantly increase both awareness of the robot's eye gaze and compliance with that gaze. When eye gaze communication occurs during the robot's release of an object, delaying object release until the gaze is finished draws attention back to the robot's head, which increases conscious perception of the robot's communication. Furthermore, the handover delay increases peoples' compliance with the robot's communication over a non-delayed handover, even when compliance results in counterintuitive behavior.

1. INTRODUCTION

In the future, assistive robots will help people perform manual tasks more easily and efficiently. These robots may retrieve items from high shelves [23], assist in fine motor manipulations [4], or act as extra hands during physically complex tasks [10]. One of the primary challenges for such robots will be the ability to manipulate objects in collaboration with people [1].

For example, imagine a robot, like the one in Figure 1a, that helps a wheelchair-bound user cook a meal. This robot can move around the kitchen, grabbing the right ingredients and handing them to the user. The robot and user can also prepare parts of the meal simultaneously, passing utensils and ingredients back and forth between them. Finally, the robot can help clean up, taking items from the user and moving them to the sink.

HRI'14, March 3–6, 2014, Bielefeld, Germany.

http://dx.doi.org/10.1145/2559636.2559682.

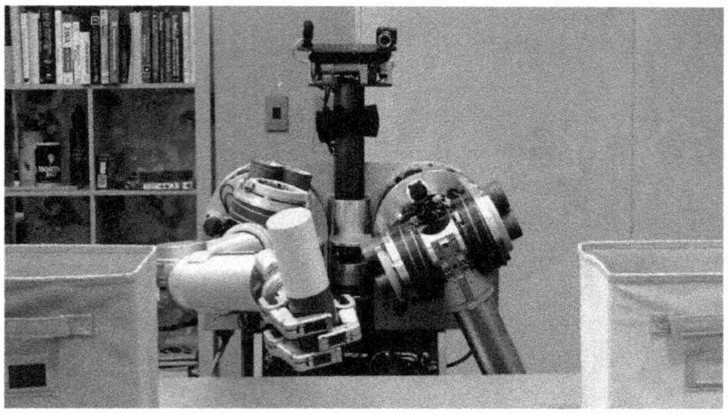

(a) A participant's view of the block sorting task.

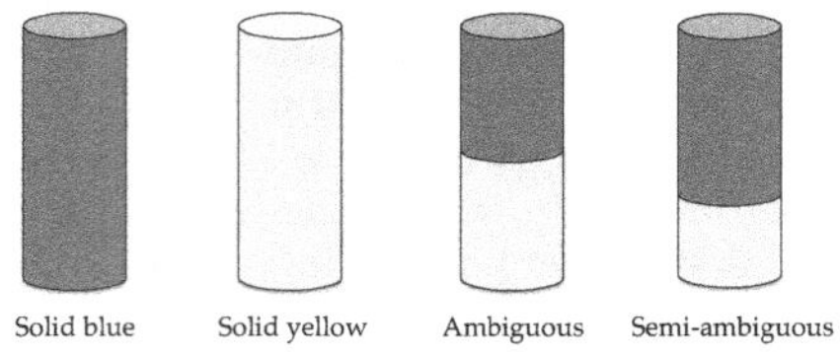

(b) Blocks were fully colored, ambiguously colored (50% of each color) or semi-ambiguously colored (70% of one color).

Figure 1: Participants engage in a collaborative manipulation task with HERB. The robot hands over colored blocks, and participants sort them into colored boxes on the table.

A common task throughout this interaction is the *handover*: the act of transferring an item from one actor to another. For seamless robot-to-human handovers, the robot must generate appropriate social cues that alert the person to the what, when, and where of the handover [7, 28].

But other information, unrelated to the handover itself, may also need to be communicated during a handover. For example, the robot might want to indicate where to put an object after giving it. Speech is an obvious mode of communication for conveying such information, but it may not be available or effective in all situations. For instance, speech may be unavailable in a noisy room, when interacting with the hearing impaired, or when a person is already engaged in a listening task, such as holding a conversation while cooking. Even when speech is available, it is not always the most effective means of communicating: a robot that announced every handover before it occurred would hinder the fluency of interactions involving frequent handovers.

Eye gaze is an alternative means of communication that can be used when speech isn't practical. Typical humans can understand the motor intentions of others based on their gaze [24], and robots are able to influence human motor behavior using gaze (e.g., [22]). Based on this, a natural conclusion is to communicate information about where to put the object using eye gaze.

Because eye gaze requires the user to attend to the cue in order to be effective, it becomes critical to select the right time to exhibit the eye gaze cue. This communication should occur during the *transfer phase* of the handover, which starts from the point at which the giver has finished reaching with the object toward the agreed-upon transfer location, and ends when the receiver has taken hold of the object and retracted it, signaling the end of joint activity [28]. Earlier signals specifying where to put the object may be confused with attempts to establish the what, when, and where features of the handover [28]. Signals sent after the transfer phase may be missed, because the user's attention may have already shifted to the next task location [15]. Thus the transfer phase is the ideal time to indicate temporally relevant but non-handover-related information.

However, handovers are primarily manual tasks that draw attention directly to the robot's hand and away from its eyes. Mutual eye gaze is not a necessary part of handovers [27], and because people fixate their gaze almost exclusively on areas of their environment related to the task [15], attention is often directed somewhere other than the robot's head during a handover. In our first attempts to influence human behavior using eye gaze, we found that drawing attention to the robot's face during the gaze cue was surprisingly difficult. People responded to the unfamiliar experience of robot handovers by focusing intently on the robot's hand, ignoring all non-verbal communication from the robot's head.

To address this, we introduce the idea of a *deliberate delay*—an intentional hiccup in the handover—which prompts users to shift their attention from the robot's hand to its head. In particular, we look at deliberately delaying the transfer phase of the handover by postponing the release of an object from the robot giver to the human receiver until a gaze cue has been delivered. Handovers cause user attention to be focused on the robot's hand. By manipulating the force profile during a handover—deliberately making the robot hold on to an object longer—we can draw attention to other channels like head direction.

In this paper, we present experimental evidence that adding a deliberate delay to a handover is beneficial for communicating non-handover information non-verbally, even though this delay decreases the smoothness of the handover itself. As we show below, a deliberate delay not only increases attention to the robot's head, but also increases the rate at which people comply with the robot when its gaze cue leads to counterintuitive actions.

We test the effect of a handover delay on a simplified collaborative task (Figure 1). In this task, a robot called HERB hands colored blocks to participants, who sort those blocks into one of two colored boxes according to their personal preference. A 6-axis force-torque sensor in the robot's hand identifies when the participant has grasped the block to begin the transfer phase of the handover.

When it enters the transfer phase, the robot gives sorting suggestions by looking at one of the boxes. We manipulate when this gaze cue is executed relative to the object release during transfer: in the "no delay" case, the gaze cue and release occur simultaneously; in the "delay" case, the release is delayed until the gaze cue is complete (Figure 2).

We hypothesize that:

H1 A handover delay will cause people to pay more attention to HERB's gaze communication, and that

H2 Social gaze will lead people to comply more with HERB's counterintuitive suggestion.

Our results validate H1: a deliberate delay during the transfer phase of a handover causes people to pay more attention to the robot's head and to notice the robot's nonverbal gaze suggestion more frequently. More surprisingly, the delay also causes people to comply more often with the robot's sorting suggestion, even when it is contrary to their natural behavior. This compliance effect holds even for people who explicitly notice HERB's suggestion, indicating that the delay itself, and not solely increased attention, is responsible for increased compliance. Interestingly, H2 was not supported: we found no effect of social gaze on compliance.

This work lays the foundation for a new type of robot handover. Instead of working toward seamlessness, researchers can design behaviors that leverage alternate communication channels, such as eye gaze, and introduce targeted, deliberate imperfections to improve communication and efficiency.

2. RELATED WORK

Our work draws from two areas of research in HRI: robot-to-human handovers and robot gaze communication. Though these areas have developed independently, they share considerable overlaps, for instance, using joint attention to signal a handover. Rather than surveying the broad fields individually, we highlight papers in each area that address the overlap between handovers and gaze communication.

Handovers can be divided into three distinct phases [19, 28]: the *approach*, during which a giver moves toward a receiver; the *signal*, during which giver and receiver communicate their readiness for the handover; and the *transfer*, during which the object is transferred from giver to receiver.

Handovers are a primary part of collaborative robotics, and there is strong interest in automatically generating successful robot-to-human handovers [2, 12, 25, 28]. To produce a successful handover, a robot must first convey its intention to execute that handover, which requires both spatial information (a distinct handover pose) and temporal contrast (a distinct movement profile for handovers) [7, 13]. HRI studies have attempted to determine user preferences for optimal handover behavior, such as maximal arm extension [6], minimum jerk motion profiles [17], and legibility of motion [11]. Metrics for determining human preferences range from surveys and observation [6] to physiological measurements like skin conductance and eye movement [9].

The structure of human-human handovers can also be used to inform human-robot handovers [28]. Investigations of human-human handovers identified that object transfer time (from initial contact by the receiver to final release from the giver) is approximately 500 milliseconds [8].

Mutual gaze is not a predictor of handover initiation; confirming the partner's availability through asynchronous fixations is more important to successful handovers than synchronized mutual eye contact [27]. However, taking a human partner's eye gaze into account when planning a handover increases the success of robot-to-human handovers [14]. More generally, human gaze is task driven, and gaze fixations are rarely directed to locations in the world that are not relevant to the task, even if they are visually salient [15]. Fixations are instead guided by the spatio-temporal requirements of

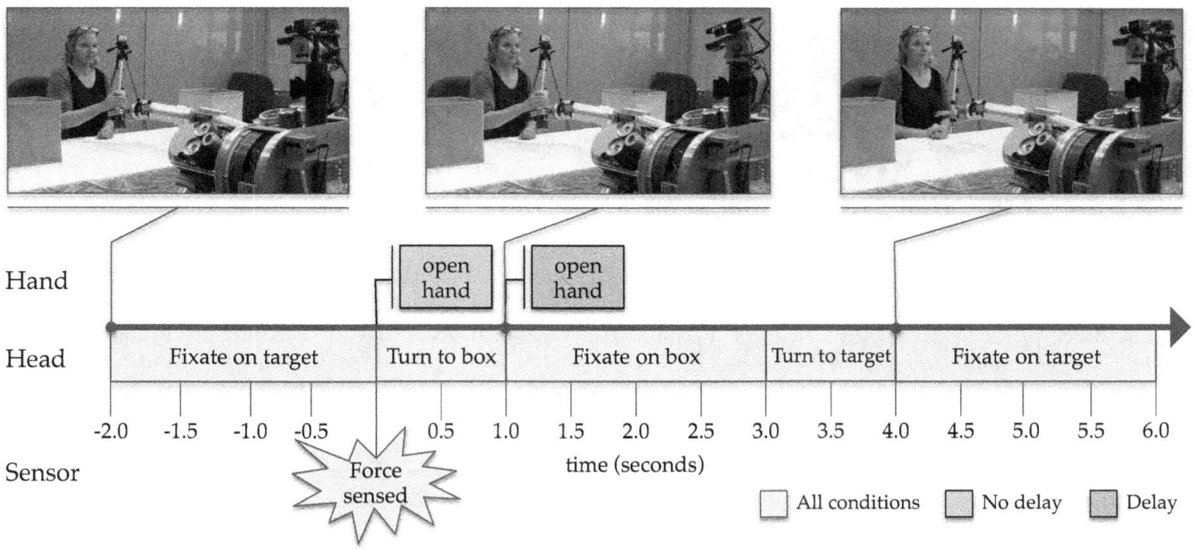

Figure 2: A graphical timeline of HERB's head and hand motions turning the transfer phase of the handover. HERB begins by fixating on a target (the participant's face or a mirrored point, depending on gaze condition), then looks at one of the boxes as a suggestion, and finally returns to fixate on the target. The timing of the block release depends on delay condition; it is either simultaneous with the head turn toward a box, or just after the head turn.

the task, arriving at the relevant location just at the point at which they are needed for task completion [18].

Robot eye gaze, however, is an important communication mode in HRI. Robots can communicate information through gaze during tasks like storytelling [20] and teaching [3]. Robot gaze cues such as joint attention facilitate performance in cooperative tasks [5] and improve perceptions of a robot's competence and naturalness [16]. Robots can even manipulate peoples' behavior using only gaze cues, prompting people to adopt certain conversational roles [21] or select certain objects from a set [22], even without people consciously registering the gaze cue. Robot gaze is clearly an informative communication channel in human-robot handovers, and we leverage this to provide sorting suggestions in the experiment described here.

3. METHODS

Users engage in a simple collaborative manipulation task with HERB: the robot hands blocks to participants, who are asked to sort these blocks into either a yellow box or a blue box on the table in front of them. Most blocks are unambiguously colored (fully yellow or blue), but some blocks are ambiguously colored (50% yellow and 50% blue) or semi-ambiguously colored (70% of one color and 30% of another), as illustrated in Figure 1b.

The main manipulation in this experiment is the deliberate delay between HERB's sorting suggestion and block release (Figure 2). HERB provides a non-verbal sorting suggestion by looking (i.e., orienting its head) toward one of the boxes on the table. On "no delay" trials, HERB simultaneously releases the block to the participant and executes the suggestion behavior by looking at one of the boxes. On "delay" trials, HERB first looks at one of the boxes, and only then releases the block to the participant. The suggestion behavior takes about four seconds to execute: one second for HERB to turn its head toward the box, two seconds to gaze at the box, and one second to return its head to the starting point. Thus, there is a one second difference in when the block is released between no delay and delay conditions.

There are several strategies participants could employ for sorting the blocks. One of the more obvious strategies is to sort by dominant color, putting the primarily yellow blocks in the yellow box and the primarily blue blocks in the blue box. Another strategy is to sort by the first visible color (typically the top color), regardless of how the rest of the block is colored. Other strategies, like sorting randomly or alternating boxes, do not take color into account. There are several possible sorting strategies; our analyses do not rely on participants to follow any particular strategy.

In order to test whether people see and comply with a robot's suggestions, we made HERB's suggestions as counterintuitive as possible. Therefore, when handing over the ambiguous block, HERB always suggested the bottom (i.e., less visible) color when it presented the block, which conflicts with the top color strategy (Figure 3). Because the block was exactly half of each color, however, there was no conflict with the dominant color strategy, so the ambiguous case was only mildly counterintuitive. When handing over the semi-ambiguous block, HERB always presented the block with the dominant color on top and always suggested the less dominant color. HERB's suggestion conflicts with both the dominant color strategy *and* the top color strategy, making this a highly counterintuitive suggestion.

We also manipulated whether HERB engages in social or non-social gaze before the suggestion (Figure 4). In the joint attention condition, HERB first makes eye contact by looking at the participant's face, then down at the block in its hand, and then back to the participant's face as it reaches with the block to begin the handover. After HERB initiates the suggestion by turning its head to one of the boxes, it again returns to look at the participant's face before retracting its hand. In the mirrored condition, HERB's head moves at the same time and for the same distance as in the joint attention condition, but it moves laterally and remains oriented downward throughout this movement, so the gaze

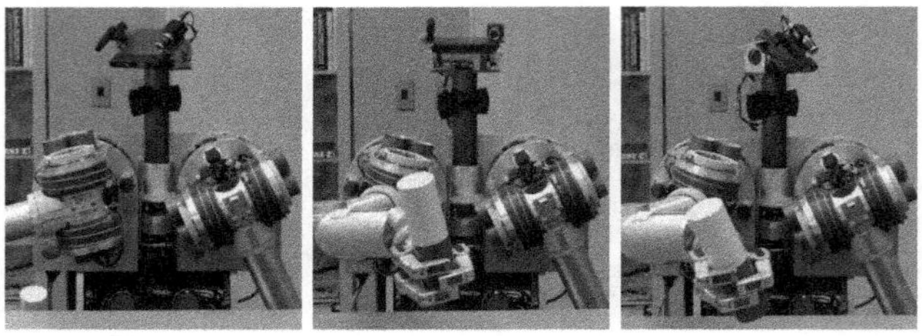

(a) Neutral gaze. (b) Joint attention. (c) Mirrored gaze.

Figure 4: HERB began every trial in a neutral gaze position, looking at the block in its hand. Figures (b) and (c) show HERB in the two gaze conditions from the experiment.

appears non-social. Therefore, we control for total amount of head movement while manipulating whether the gaze is social or non-social. This manipulation explores whether social gaze before the suggestion affects how people respond to a counterintuitive suggestion.

3.1 Robot platform

Our robot HERB (Home Exploring Robot Butler) is a bimanual robot developed for assistive tasks in home environments [26]. HERB has two 7-DOF WAM arms, each with a 4-DOF BH8-series Barrett hand with three fingers. In this experiment, only the right arm was used. HERB's hand has a 6-axis force/torque sensor that can detect external forces applied to the joints, for instance when a participant gently pulls on an object in HERB's hand. Motion trajectories for picking up and handing over blocks were pre-planned using CHOMP [29] and played back during the experiment.

HERB also has a pan-tilt head outfitted with a Microsoft Kinect and a camera, though no real-time vision was used in this experiment. The front of the Kinect has two visible round cameras which serve as HERB's "eyes."

3.2 Procedure

Participants were randomly assigned to either the delay or no delay condition, and to either the joint attention or mirrored condition. There were 32 participants (18 females), eight in each of the four conditions, with a mean age of 34. Participants were recruited from the Pittsburgh area using an online participant pool website through Carnegie Mellon University. They were compensated $10 for their time.

Participants were told that they would play a sorting game with HERB. They were instructed to take the block from HERB's hand once HERB had extended the block to them. Participants were also told that HERB's head would move and that HERB may provide suggestions about how to sort the blocks, but that the final sorting method was up to them. Participants were not informed about the kinds of blocks they would be seeing, and the blocks were kept hidden under the table until HERB handed them to the participant.

On each trial, HERB picked up a block from below the table and handed it to participants by extending its arm forward while grasping the block. Following previous research [6], HERB's arm became fully extended to clearly communicate the handover.

HERB's hand contains a force sensor that identified when participants grasped the block during the handover. When the force sensor in the hand registered the participant's grasp on the block, HERB initiated a suggestion behavior by turning its head to one of the two boxes on the table. Depending on the delay condition, HERB either simultaneously released the block (no delay) or waited until its head was fully turned and then released the block (delay, Figure 2). Once the block was released, HERB withdrew its hand to begin the next trial.

Each participant engaged in five block handovers. The first two handovers involved solid color blocks, one of each color, both to familiarize participants with the task and to establish their preferred sorting method. The third handover involved the ambiguous block, presented with the first block's color on top. HERB always suggested that this block be sorted according to the color on the bottom, which violated the top-color sorting strategy, but was only a mildly counterintuitive suggestion because it did not violate the dominant color strategy (since there was no dominant color on the ambiguous block). The fourth block was again a solid colored block of the same color as the first block, intended to separate the test trials and to balance the number of blocks in each box as well as possible. For example, if the first block was yellow, the second block was blue, and the third block was ambiguous (presented with yellow on top), then the fourth block would be yellow again; the idea was that participants would sort the first and fourth blocks into the yellow box and the second and third blocks into the blue box, though this was not always the case. The final block was the semi-ambiguous block; this was always presented with the dominant color upward, to increase the saliency of the dominant color, but HERB always suggested sorting by the minority color. For example, if the fifth block was 70% blue, HERB oriented its head toward the yellow box.

By handing the ambiguous and semi-ambiguous blocks over with HERB's suggested color on bottom, we made it as easy as possible for participants to use a sorting strategy that would conflict with HERB's suggestions in these cases. Therefore, we expect to see low compliance with HERB's suggestions in the absence of a manipulation.

First block color, dominant color of the semi-ambiguous block, and the arrangement of the boxes on the table were counterbalanced between participants. The experiment ran fully autonomously using pre-scripted trajectories for block pick-ups, block handovers, and head movements. There was real-time force feedback to measure when participants grasped the block during the transfer phase of the handover. The human-robot interactions lasted approximately 2 minutes and 20 seconds, though the particular amount of time varied by how long the participant took to sort the block.

3.3 Data collection

There are four data sources in this experiment. First, task performance was evaluated by whether participants followed HERB's suggestion on ambiguous and semi-ambiguous block trials. This provides a quantitative evaluation of compliance with HERB's counterintuitive suggestions.

Immediately after the interaction, participants completed written questionnaires that asked about their experiences and decisions during the task. These included free-response questions about whether they noticed suggestions from HERB and about their sorting strategy. Questionnaires contained specific questions about the ambiguous and semi-ambiguous blocks (represented with drawings), as well as Likert scale questions about HERB—rating features such as intelligence and friendliness—and about the collaboration—rating statements such as "I felt like HERB and I acted as a team."

(a) Delay

(b) No delay

Figure 3: A comparison of HERB's head and hand movements during the handover's transfer phase in delay and no delay conditions. In the no delay condition, HERB releases the block as it turns its head to a box. In the delay condition, the release occurs only after the head turn (frame 3).

After completing the survey, participants also engaged in a semi-structured interview with an experimenter. They were asked to explain their sorting of the ambiguous and semi-ambiguous blocks. They were also asked whether they noticed any suggestion behavior from HERB. The responses from these interviews are used to support participants' written responses in the surveys.

Finally, the interaction with HERB was video recorded, and these videos were coded for information such as amount of time spent looking at HERB's face and whether or not the participant looked at HERB's head as it executed a suggestion behavior. The videos were annotated by an independent coder naïve to the research hypothesis. We randomly selected 10% of the videos for validatation with a second coder; inter-coder agreement was 87% or higher. Because all of the coding measures were objective and inter-coder agreement was above the accepted 80% threshold, we feel confident analyzing the single coder's annotations.

4. RESULTS

This experiment yielded quantitative results from the task (such as the rate of participants complying with HERB's suggestion), self-reports in the form of Likert scales and free-responses on the post-task questionnaire and semi-structured interview, and objective observations of the interaction from the recorded videos (such as the amount of time participants spent looking at HERB's head).

Manipulation Check. To verify that HERB's sorting suggestion for semi-ambiguous blocks was counterintuitive, we analyzed the rate at which people chose the "counterintuitive" box when they were unaware of HERB's suggestion. Recognizing HERB's head movements as sorting suggestions significantly correlates with sorting the semi-ambiguous block as suggested (Pearson's $\chi^2(1, N = 32) = 11.567, p = 0.007$). Only one participant out of 14 sorted the semi-ambiguous block as HERB suggested without recognizing HERB's suggestion, verifying participants' bias against HERB's sorting suggestion and supporting the semi-ambiguous block as a valid manipulation to test for compliance.

Compliance: Semi-Ambiguous Block. The central research question is whether users comply with HERB's suggestion in the semi-ambiguous case. To test the effects of delay and gaze on correctness, we ran a factorial nominal logistic regression, which found that delay has a significant effect on compliance ($\chi^2(1, N = 32) = 6.77, p = 0.0092$). Without delay, only 19% of users sorted the semi-ambiguous block according to HERB's suggestion; delaying the release leads to 63% of users matching HERB's suggestion (Figure 5a).

When we analyze only participants who reported recognizing HERB's head movements as suggestions, the rate of compliance increases to 83% for participants in the delay condition and 33% for participants in the no delay condition (Figure 5b), with delay playing a significant role in this outcome: a nominal logistic regression for compliance with gaze and delay as factors, on only users who recognized HERB's head motions as suggestions, reveals a significant effect of delay ($\chi^2(1, N = 18) = 4.46, p = 0.0346$).

Compliance: Ambiguous Block. The ambiguous block represents a relatively low-conflict suggestion. Even though HERB always suggests sorting by bottom color, which violates the top-color strategy, most participants (59%) followed HERB's suggestion for sorting the ambiguous block.

An effect likelihood ratio test reveals a borderline significant effect for delay ($\chi^2(1, N = 32) = 3.632, p = 0.0567$), with 75% of participants in the delay condition following the ambiguous block suggestion, but only 56% of participants in the no delay condition following the suggestion (Figure 5c). There was no effect of gaze or an interaction.

Sorting ambiguous and semi-ambiguous blocks by HERB's suggestions are highly correlated (Pearson's $\chi^2(1, N = 32) = 9.85, p = 0.0017$). Ninety-two percent of users who sorted the semi-ambiguous block according to HERB's suggestion also previously sorted the ambiguous block according to HERB's suggestion.

Gaze. Gaze type (joint attention versus mirrored) did not significantly affect compliance, and there was no significant interaction effect. Similarly, the analysis of compliance in only participants who reported recognizing HERB's suggestions found no significant effect of gaze. Joint attention does correspond to a higher probability of following HERB's suggestion (44% with joint attention, 38% with mirrored), but the difference is not statistically significant.

Self-Reports. Participants' free responses on the questionnaire and interview revealed that 75% of participants in the delay condition and 38% of participants in the no delay

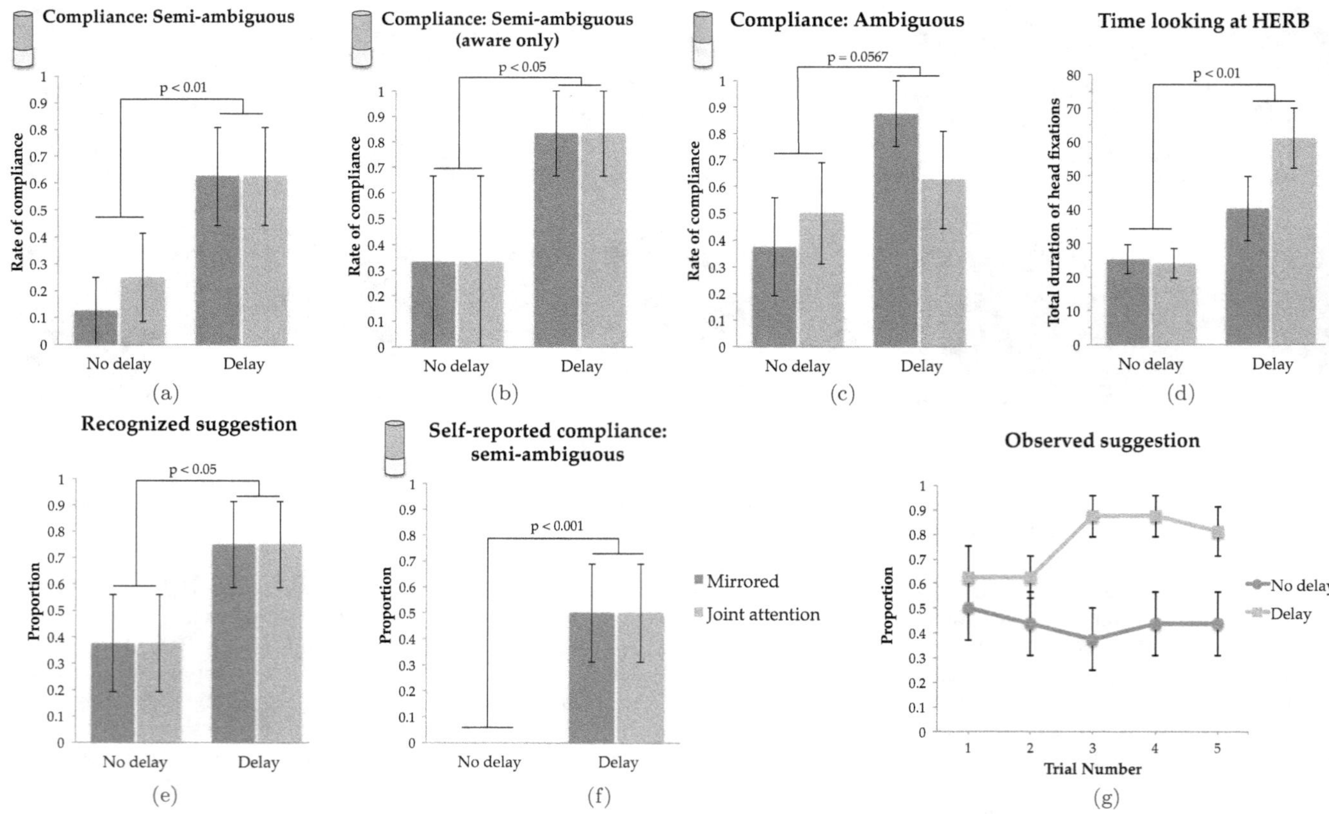

Figure 5: Results of the experiment from task responses, self reports, and video observations. Error bars indicate ±2 SE.

condition noticed and interpreted HERB's head movements as sorting suggestions (Figure 5e). A nominal logistic regression with gaze and delay as factors shows that delay significantly affects whether participants thought HERB had a sorting suggestion ($\chi^2(1, N = 32) = 4.69, p = 0.0302$, Wald test $\chi^2(1, 32) = 4.32, p = 0.0377$). No significant effect was found for gaze, and no interaction was found.

None of the participants in the no delay condition thought they complied with HERB's suggestion on the semi-ambiguous block trial; they either did not state that HERB gave them a suggestion, or they explicitly stated that they did not follow HERB's suggestion (Figure 5f). In the delay condition, 50% of users explicitly stated that they chose their sorting strategy based on HERB's suggestion for the semi-ambiguous block. The effect is significant according to the effect likelihood ratio test ($\chi^2(1, N = 32) = 13.8, p = 0.0002$) but not according to the Wald test.

Video Coding. Videos were coded for how long participants looked at HERB's head, which reveal how much visual attention participants devoted to HERB's head during the task. Videos were also coded for events in which participants looked at HERB's head while HERB looked at one of the boxes, which indicate whether attention was directed to HERB's head at the right time to notice HERB's gaze cues.

A two-factor analysis of variance investigating the effect of delay and gaze on the total amount of time the participant looked at HERB's head showed a significant effect of delay ($F(1, 31) = 12.9828, p = 0.0012$). The handover delay more than doubled the mean looking time, from 24.7 seconds to 50.6 seconds (Figure 5d). There was no significant effect of gaze or an interaction.

To understand whether this additional time spent looking at HERB's head was useful, we ran a nominal logistic regression analyzing the effect of delay and gaze on whether the participant noticed HERB's suggestion in each trial, as measured by whether the participant looked at HERB's head while it was oriented toward one of the boxes (Figure 5g). The test found a significant effect of delay on noticing HERB's suggestion in the third and fourth trials, and a borderline significant effect in the fifth trial, but no significant effect of delay in the first or second trials ($\chi^2(1, N = 32) = 9.113, p = 0.003$ for trial 3, $\chi^2(1, N = 32) = 6.974, p = 0.008$ for trial 4, and $\chi^2(1, N = 32) = 4.993, p = 0.0254$ for trial 5, lowering the α to 0.01 for this analysis based on a Bonferroni correction, the most conservative control for multiple comparisons).

Given that HERB first presents the delay in the third trial, these results show that a deliberate delay led people to attend more to HERB's suggestions, even in subsequent trials when no delay was present (the fourth trial). The analysis did not find any effect of gaze on any trials.

5. DISCUSSION

Our results yield two main findings about the effects of deliberate handover delays.

RESULT 1. *Handover delays increased the amount of attention participants paid to HERB's head, which increased participants' awareness of HERB's non-verbal gaze cues.*

As predicted by hypothesis H1, deliberate delays increased the amount of time participants spent looking at HERB's head in general. This increase was not spurious: deliberate delays also increased time spent looking at HERB's head specifically when HERB made a suggestion. Therefore, a handover delay drew attention to HERB's head even though the head was not involved in the handover. These results are supported by both self-reports and video observations.

RESULT 2. *In addition to increasing recognition of HERB's suggestions, the handover delay also increased compliance with those suggestions.*

In our analysis of just the participants who reported recognizing HERB's head movements as suggestions, there was still a significant effect of delay on compliance. In other words, even once participants are aware that HERB is making a suggestion, they are still more likely to comply with that counterintuitive suggestion if the handover has a delay.

There are several interpretations for this second finding. The non-agentic explanation is that the delay drew peoples' attention to HERB's head which, because it was moving, increased the saliency of the suggestion behavior to the point where people followed it. This explanation does not require participants to attribute any kind of meaning to the handover delay. It is not wholly satisfactory, however, because when we exclude people who do not explicitly report seeing HERB's suggestion, there is *still* an effect of delay on compliance. Because these participants already notice HERB's head movements and explicitly interpret them as suggestions, the saliency of HERB's head movement seems unlikely to have a further effect.

A more agentic explanation is that HERB's handover delay was interpreted as *purposeful*, and that people were more likely to comply with HERB's suggestion when they believed that it came from an intentional agent. In order to test this explanation, we would need to measure peoples' attributions of agency to HERB before and after experiencing the delayed trials, an interesting point for future work.

In the current experiment, when the robot expressed a delay, there was always another meaningful channel of communication (eye gaze) to draw information from. However, it would be interesting to explore the effect of a delay when there is no other salient feature on which to focus attention. Perhaps in that case the delay would be interpreted as less agentic; the robot might even be seen as broken.

Mechanics of Deliberate Delays. We used a handover delay of one second in this study because that was the amount of time it took for HERB to turn its head toward a box. By the strength of the results, this duration was effective for drawing attention back to HERB's head.

A minority of participants in the delay case did not shift their attention in response to the delay; instead, these people seemed to focus more intently on pulling the block from HERB's hand. In these few cases, perhaps the delay was so unexpected that it served to draw attention to the hand, rather than release attention from it. More work is necessary to find the "sweet spot" where the delay is long enough to notice but not so long as to be problematic. This spot may also vary among people and depend on factors such as comfort with the robot.

Tasks for Investigating Compliance. The analysis supports our use of a semi-ambiguous block to investigate compliance. We found a strong correlation between noticing HERB's suggestion and sorting the block according to that suggestion. Of the 14 participants who did not report noticing HERB's suggestions, only one of them sorted the semi-ambiguous block in the same box that HERB suggested, emphasizing the counterintuitive nature of that suggestion. More users overall matched HERB's suggestion in the ambiguous case (59%) than in the semi-ambiguous case (41%). This is expected, as HERB's suggestion for the semi-ambiguous block conflicted with both the dominant color strategy and the top color strategy, whereas the ambiguous suggestion only conflicts with the top color strategy.

A block-sorting task is a useful proxy for other collaborative manipulation tasks because it involves many of the same behaviors in a simplified format. Our task included handovers, object manipulation, classification decisions, joint attention, referential gaze, and mutual gaze. It subtly addressed the issue of compliance and touched upon animacy and intentionality of robot agents. The task was performed in a constrained environment with high repeatability and few distractions, but it remained easy to understand and natural to complete.

Gaze. Our gaze manipulations had little effect on attention and compliance in this handover task. Though people could understand HERB's gaze to the box as a suggestion, there was no difference between joint attention and mirrored gaze conditions in terms of how much attention was directed at HERB's head or the rate at which participants complied with HERB's counterintuitive suggestions. Thus, hypothesis H2 was not supported.

While studies have shown that robot gaze is a strong social cue, many of these studies used tasks in which gaze was a primary component, such as conversation. In these situations, a person attends to the robot's gaze as part of the task, and therefore gaze cues may be more salient or useful.

Furthermore, HERB's "face", as seen in Figure 1a, is relatively abstract: the entire head consists of a flat platform with a pair of cameras for perception and a microphone. It is possible that HERB's non-anthropomorphic head affected how well people actually perceived joint attention, and that the joint attention condition would have yielded different results on a robot with more defined eyes.

In the delay condition, joint attention increased the amount of time spent looking at HERB's head to 61 seconds from 41 seconds for mirrored gaze. Joint attention also doubled the probability of a participant complying with HERB's suggestion in the no delay condition (from 12.5% to 25%). However, neither of these effects reached significance. More research is needed to understand how social gaze affects people in tasks where gaze is not a central component.

Future Work. Speech can be more precise and noticeable than gaze in many situations. Because this study focused on non-verbal communication (handover fluency and eye gaze), adding speech to the system would have been a confound with our current manipulations (handover delay and social gaze). However, future work on a robust human-robot handover system should incorporate spoken cues.

The decision to present the gaze cue during the handover transfer phase was based on a pilot and previous experience with HERB. Future studies can explore the effects of presenting the gaze cue at different points in the interaction.

Implications. The results reported in this paper provide insight into the design of effective robot-to-human handovers. When information needs to be conveyed during handovers, we suggest that seamlessness should be secondary to communication. For instance, by manipulating the force profile of the handover so that the robot deliberately delays releasing an object, robot designers can draw attention to important features like eye gaze and other non-verbal communication. This idea is in line with previous research that has shown that deliberately manipulating other aspects of a handover, like the spatio-temporal motion, can help convey information about the task [6]. The current work is novel because it uses a feature of the handover (the force profile) to convey information toward an unrelated mode of communication (eye gaze) about a subsequent task (block sorting).

6. ACKNOWLEDGMENTS

This work is supported by an Intel PhD Fellowship, NSF-IIS-1139078, NSF-IIS-1117801, NSF-EEC-0540865, ONR-N00014-12-1-0822, ONR-YIP 2012, and Intel Embedded Computing ISTC.

7. REFERENCES

[1] *A Roadmap for U.S. Robotics: From Internet to Robotics.* Robotics Virtual Organization, 2013.

[2] J. Aleotti, V. Micelli, and S. Caselli. Comfortable robot to human object hand-over. In *21st IEEE International Symposium on Robot and Human Interactive Communication (RO-MAN 2012)*, pages 771–776, 2012.

[3] S. Andrist, T. Pejsa, B. Mutlu, and M. Gleicher. Designing effective gaze mechanisms for virtual agents. In *2012 ACM Annual Conference on Human Factors in Computing Systems (CHI '12)*, pages 705–714, 2012.

[4] A. Bicchi and V. Kumar. Robotic grasping and contact: A review. In *IEEE International Conference on Robotics and Automation (ICRA '00)*, volume 1, pages 348–353, 2000.

[5] J.-D. Boucher, U. Pattacini, A. Lelong, G. Bailly, F. Elisei, S. Fagel, P. F. Dominey, and J. Ventre-Dominey. I Reach Faster When I See You Look: Gaze Effects in Human-Human and Human-Robot Face-to-Face Cooperation. *Frontiers in Neurorobotics*, 6:1–11, 2012.

[6] M. Cakmak, S. S. Srinivasa, J. Forlizzi, and S. Kiesler. Human preferences for robot-human hand-over configurations. In *2011 IEEE/RSJ International Conference on Intelligent Robots and Systems (IROS '11)*, pages 1986–1993, 2011.

[7] M. Cakmak, S. S. Srinivasa, M. K. Lee, S. Kiesler, and J. Forlizzi. Using spatial and temporal contrast for fluent robot-human hand-overs. In *6th International Conference on Human-Robot Interaction (HRI '11)*, page 489, 2011.

[8] W. P. Chan, C. A. Parker, H. M. V. der Loos, and E. A. Croft. Grip Forces and Load Forces in Handovers: Implications for Designing Human-Robot Handover Controllers. In *8th ACM/IEEE International Conference on Human-Robot Interaction (HRI 2013)*, pages 9–16, 2012.

[9] F. Dehais, E. A. Sisbot, R. Alami, and M. Causse. Physiological and subjective evaluation of a human-robot object hand-over task. *Applied Ergonomics*, 42:785–791, 2011.

[10] M. Diftler, J. Mehling, M. Abdallah, N. Radford, L. Bridgewater, A. Sanders, R. Askew, D. Linn, J. Yamokoski, F. Permenter, B. Hargrave, R. Platt, R. Savely, and R. Ambrose. Robonaut 2-The First Humanoid Robot in Space. In *2011 IEEE International Conference on Robotics and Automation (ICRA '11)*, pages 2178–2183, 2011.

[11] A. D. Dragan, K. C. T. Lee, and S. S. Srinivasa. Legibility and predictability of robot motion. In *8th ACM/IEEE International Conference on Human-Robot Interaction (HRI 2013)*, pages 301–308, 2013.

[12] A. Edsinger and C. C. Kemp. Human-Robot Interaction for Cooperative Manipulation: Handing Objects to One Another. In *16th IEEE International Symposium on Robot and Human Interactive Communication (RO-MAN 2007)*, pages 1167–1172, 2007.

[13] S. Glasauer, M. Huber, P. Basili, A. Knoll, and T. Brandt. Interacting in time and space: Investigating human-human and human-robot joint action. In *19th International Symposium in Robot and Human Interactive Communication*, pages 252–257, 2010.

[14] E. C. Grigore, K. Eder, A. G. Pipe, C. Melhuish, and U. Leonards. Joint Action Understanding improves Robot-to-Human Object Handover. In *IEEE/RSJ International Conference on Intelligent Robots and Systems (IROS 2013)*, 2013.

[15] M. Hayhoe and D. Ballard. Eye movements in natural behavior. *Trends in Cognitive Sciences*, 9(4):188–194, 2005.

[16] C.-M. Huang and A. L. Thomaz. Effects of responding to, initiating and ensuring joint attention in human-robot interaction. In *20th IEEE International Symposium on Robot and Human Interactive Communication (RO-MAN 2011)*, pages 65–71, 2011.

[17] M. Huber, M. Rickert, A. Knoll, T. Brandt, and S. Glasauer. Human-Robot Interaction in Handing-Over Tasks. In *17th IEEE International Symposium on Robot and Human Interactive Communication (RO-MAN 2008)*, pages 107–112, 2008.

[18] R. S. Johansson, G. Westling, A. Bäckström, and J. R. Flanagan. Eye-hand coordination in object manipulation. *The Journal of Neuroscience*, 21(17):6917–6932, 2001.

[19] M. K. Lee, J. Forlizzi, S. Kiesler, M. Cakmak, and S. Srinivasa. Predictability or Adaptivity? Designing Robot Handoffs Modeled from Trained Dogs and People. In *6th International Conference on Human-Robot Interaction (HRI '11)*, pages 179–180, 2011.

[20] B. Mutlu, J. Forlizzi, and J. Hodgins. A Storytelling Robot: Modeling and Evaluation of Human-like Gaze Behavior. In *6th IEEE/RAS International Conference on Humanoid Robots (Humanoids 06)*, pages 518–523. IEEE, 2006.

[21] B. Mutlu, T. Shiwa, T. Kanda, H. Ishiguro, and N. Hagita. Footing In Human-Robot Conversations : How Robots Might Shape Participant Roles Using Gaze Cues. In *4th ACM/IEEE International Conference on Human Robot Interaction (HRI 09)*, pages 61–68, 2009.

[22] B. Mutlu, F. Yamaoka, T. Kanda, H. Ishiguro, and N. Hagita. Nonverbal Leakage in Robots: Communication of Intentions through Seemingly Unintentional Behavior. In *4th ACM/IEEE International Conference on Human Robot Interaction (HRI 09)*, pages 69–76, 2009.

[23] H. Nguyen, C. Anderson, A. Trevor, A. Jain, Z. Xu, and C. C. Kemp. El-E: An assistive robot that fetches objects from flat surfaces. In *Robotic Helpers Workshop at HRI '08*, 2008.

[24] A. C. Pierno, M. Mari, S. Glover, I. Georgiou, and U. Castiello. Failure to read motor intentions from gaze in children with autism. *Neuropsychologia*, 44(8):1483–1488, 2006.

[25] E. A. Sisbot and R. Alami. A Human-Aware Manipulation Planner. *IEEE Transactions on Robotics*, 28(5):1045–1057, 2012.

[26] S. S. Srinivasa, D. Berenson, M. Cakmak, A. Collet, M. R. Dogar, A. D. Dragan, R. A. Knepper, T. Niemueller, K. Strabala, M. V. Weghe, and J. Ziegler. HERB 2.0 : Lessons Learned From Developing a Mobile Manipulator for the Home. *Proceedings of the IEEE*, 100(8):2410–2428, 2012.

[27] K. Strabala, M. K. Lee, A. Dragan, J. Forlizzi, and S. S. Srinivasa. Learning the communication of intent prior to physical collaboration. In *21st IEEE International Symposium on Robot and Human Interactive Communication (RO-MAN 2012)*, pages 968–973, 2012.

[28] K. Strabala, M. K. Lee, A. Dragan, J. Forlizzi, S. S. Srinivasa, M. Cakmak, and V. Micelli. Toward Seamless Human-Robot Handovers. *Journal of Human-Robot Interaction*, 2(1):112–132, 2013.

[29] M. Zucker, N. Ratliff, A. Dragan, M. Pivtoraiko, M. Klingensmith, C. Dellin, J. A. D. Bagnell, and S. Srinivasa. Chomp: Covariant hamiltonian optimization for motion planning. *International Journal of Robotics Research*, 2013.

Learning-Based Modeling of Multimodal Behaviors for Humanlike Robots

Chien-Ming Huang and Bilge Mutlu
Department of Computer Sciences, University of Wisconsin–Madison
1210 West Dayton Street, Madison, WI 53706 USA
{cmhuang, bilge}@cs.wisc.edu

ABSTRACT

In order to communicate with their users in a natural and effective manner, humanlike robots must seamlessly integrate behaviors across multiple modalities, including speech, gaze, and gestures. While researchers and designers have successfully drawn on studies of human interactions to build models of humanlike behavior and to achieve such integration in robot behavior, the development of such models involves a laborious process of inspecting data to identify patterns within each modality or across modalities of behavior and to represent these patterns as "rules" or heuristics that can be used to control the behaviors of a robot, but provides little support for validation, extensibility, and learning. In this paper, we explore how a *learning-based* approach to modeling multimodal behaviors might address these limitations. We demonstrate the use of a *dynamic Bayesian network (DBN)* for modeling how humans coordinate speech, gaze, and gesture behaviors in narration and for achieving such coordination with robots. The evaluation of this approach in a human-robot interaction study shows that this learning-based approach is comparable to conventional modeling approaches in enabling effective robot behaviors while reducing the effort involved in identifying behavioral patterns and providing a probabilistic representation of the dynamics of human behavior. We discuss the implications of this approach for designing natural, effective multimodal robot behaviors.

Categories and Subject Descriptors

H.1.2 [**Models and Principles**]: User/Machine Systems—*human factors, software psychology*; H.5.2 [**Information Interfaces and Presentation**]: User Interfaces—*evaluation/ methodology, user-centered design*

General Terms

Design, Human Factors

1. INTRODUCTION

In communication, people draw on a rich repertoire of behaviors from multiple modalities, including speech, gaze, gestures, and so on. While this repertoire offers a rich design space for creating robot behaviors that achieve natural, effective communication, how behaviors across different modalities are integrated is critical to the success of such robot behaviors. For example, previous work in human-robot interaction has shown that robots that do not employ gaze behaviors that are contingent with their speech impair learning, collaboration, and user experience, while robots that better align their gaze with their speech improve such interaction outcomes [9].

HRI'14, March 3–6, 2014, Bielefeld, Germany.

ACM 978-1-4503-2658-2/14/03 ...$15.00.
http://dx.doi.org/10.1145/2559636.2559668.

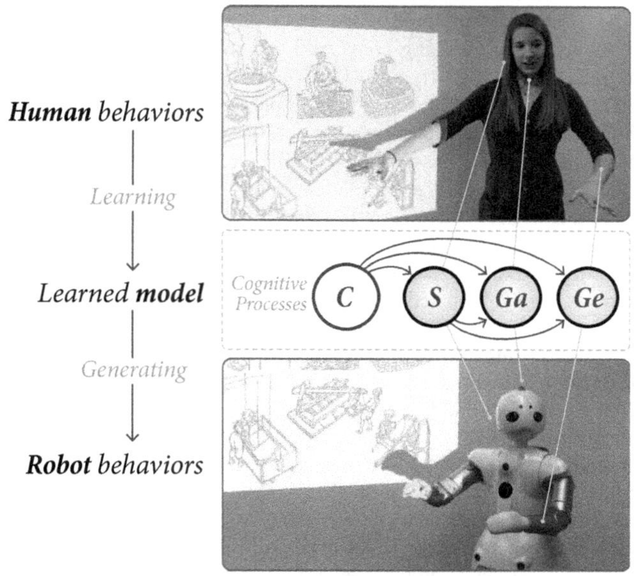

Figure 1: We used a learning-based approach to *model* how humans employ multimodal behaviors involving speech, gaze, and gestures during narration and *generate* multimodal behaviors for a humanlike robot to perform the same narration task.

How might robots employ behaviors across multiple modalities while ensuring proper alignment among them? To achieve such alignment, researchers and designers have developed *multimodal* models of behavior that specify patterns in which behaviors co-occur, such as how speakers coordinate their gaze and speech to manage conversational floor [30] or how gesture and speech are aligned in giving directions [32]. However, the development of such models involves a laborious process of sifting through data to identify and extract distribution and alignment parameters and provides limited support for validation, extensibility, and learning.

To facilitate this process and address its limitations, we propose a *learning-based* approach that involves the use of probabilistic graphical models (PGMs) to automatically learn distribution and alignment parameters from annotated data on human behavior. In this paper, we demonstrate the use of a dynamic Bayesian network (DBN) to model the alignment among speech, gaze, and gesture behaviors in a narration task and to estimate distribution and alignment parameters for these behaviors to enable a humanlike robot to perform the same narration task (Figure 1). We also present an empirical evaluation of the effectiveness of this approach in generating robot behaviors against approaches that generate robot behaviors based on designer-specified parameters, randomly-generated parameters, and no behaviors.

2. BACKGROUND

2.1. Human Multimodal Behavior

Humans naturally use multimodal behaviors involving speech, gaze, and gestures during interaction. While *speech* serves as the main channel to convey information, *gestures* are used to illustrate imagery [21], draw attention from other participants [7], disambiguate unclear speech, and supplement speech with additional information [16]. *Gaze* also supplement speech, facilitating turn-taking in conversation [14], signaling conversational roles [5], and regulating intimacy between participants [1]. These three channels make up a rich repertoire of social behaviors that play a critical role in effective communication in settings such as narration [37] and reenactments of previous events or experiences [38].

Research in human communication has extensively studied the relationship between speech and gesture [15, 21], particularly the four common types of gestures: (1) *deictic* gestures, which involve pointing toward a shared reference, (2) *iconic* gestures that illustrate concrete objects or actions, (3) *metaphoric* gestures, which use concrete metaphors to represent abstract concepts such as time, and (4) *beat* gestures, which are rhythmic movements that mark the structure of the speaker's discourse. Gestures and speech are tightly linked at both semantic and structural levels. Deictic, iconic, and metaphoric gestures are closely related to the semantics in speech through *lexical affiliates*—the words or phrases with which gestures co-express semantic meaning [35]. Beat gestures are linked to speech at a structural level and indicate significant points in speech, such as connecting discontinuous parts in speech and introducing a new topic [21]. Research has also studied the relationship between speech and gaze [6, 14, 23], identifying a close coupling between these two channels, such as a tendency to gaze toward referents before they refer to them in speech [6, 23] and the use of gaze cues to signal opportunities for exchanging conversation floor [14].

2.2. Multimodal Behaviors in Robots

Previous research in human-robot interaction has explored the development of mechanisms for achieving natural and effective multimodal behaviors for robots, such as the development of models of gaze for displaying appropriate head movements at meaningful speech points for a museum guide robot [40], aligning gaze shifts with discourse structure for a storytelling robot [29], and synchronizing deictic verbal and gaze references for an instructional robot [9]. These examples highlight the importance of temporal alignment among different modalities of behavior to improve human-robot collaboration, perceptions of the robot, and overall user experience. Researchers have also developed models of gesture to improve human-robot interaction, including a probabilistic model to generate the four common types of gestures that are aligned with speech and achieve varying levels of expressiveness for robots [31] and a method for aligning speech and gesture strokes and smoothing transitions between gestures to produce more fluent behavior [34]. Robot that appropriately align their speech and gesture using such models were found to be more natural [32].

In our prior work, we explored how robots might display coherent multimodal behaviors involving speech, gaze, and gestures [10]. We explicitly specified the semantic link between speech and gestures and empirically obtained parameters to quantify the temporal speech-gesture and gaze-gesture alignments. Specifically, the speech-gesture associations were hand-coded by identifying the lexical affiliate for each gesture according to literature on human communication [21] and quantifying the alignment between them. We also modeled the link between gaze and gestures by obtaining distributions of where the speaker looked while performing different types of gestures. While this approach yielded acceptable behaviors, enabling us to study how gestures might shape interaction outcomes, it required a deliberate selection of alignment parameters.

Additionally, while such inspection-based approaches might be feasible for modeling a small number of behaviors from small datasets, this feasibility diminishes when a larger number of behaviors or large datasets are considered. The models built by these approaches are also highly sensitive to the decisions made and inspection methods used by the researcher or the designer in the modeling process. To address these limitations, we propose a learning-based approach to automatically learn these parameters from data.

2.3. Learning-based Modeling

Previous research in human-robot interaction has used learning-based approaches primarily to achieve autonomous human-robot interaction. Examples of such uses include unsupervised learning of associations between human gestural commands and robot actions using graphical models [24, 25] and using a multilayer Bayesian approach to realize active perception [4].

Learning-based approaches have commonly been used to build predictive models of human behavior and to control behaviors of embodied conversational agents (e.g., [19, 26, 33]). These approaches frequently use probabilistic graphical models (PGMs) for their support for modeling complex relationships under uncertainty.

Building on these approaches, the current work seeks to use PGMs to represent human multimodal behaviors, learn model parameters from annotated data on human behaviors, and draw on the learned model to achieve natural, humanlike robot behaviors.

3. DESIGNING MULTIMODAL BEHAVIOR

We conceptualized the problem of generating multimodal robot behaviors into two levels—the *feature* level and the *domain* level. Figure 2 illustrates this conceptualization for the process of generating speech, gaze, and gestures. The feature level represents high-level behavioral features of the target channel, such as "iconic gesture" for gesture type and "listener" for gaze target. At the domain level, behavioral features are associated with specific motions, such as specific arm motions for an iconic gesture and gaze shifts toward the listener. This separation allows us to modularize the problem space and develop and improve different components in isolation. In this work, we focus on learning and inference at the feature level and employ simple mechanisms to bridge the feature and domain levels. The following sections describe how human data was collected and annotated for learning and how the feature and domain levels were associated to produce robot behaviors.

3.1. Data Collection and Annotation

Our investigation of human multimodal behavior focused on three modalities—speech, gaze, and gestures—as widely observed behaviors in human interaction across various contexts and cultures [1, 21]. We contextualized our investigation in a narration task in which a narrator presents *the process of making paper* to a recipient with the aid of a projected illustration of the process (Figure 1). We chose narration to model the dynamics of human behavior, because narration elicits the use of a wide range of gestures [21], and narrative re-enactments involve a rich interplay between gaze and gestures [37]. Additionally, robots are envisioned to serve in roles similar to

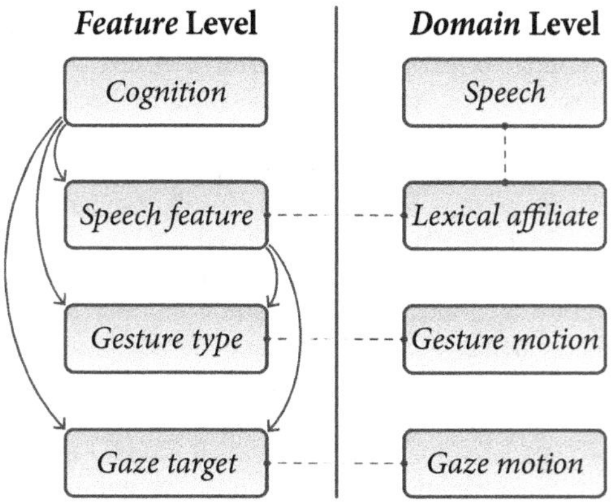

Figure 2: Our conceptualization of the process of generating speech, gaze, and gestures. Learning and inference for high-level features are performed at the *feature* level, while specific motions are defined at the *domain* level.

that of a narrator conveying information to users, such as museums tour guides, shopping assistants, or receptionists [2, 13, 20].

To understand how people concurrently use speech, gaze, and gestures, we conducted a human-human interaction study with 16 participants, recruited from the University of Wisconsin–Madison campus, whose ages ranged 19–26 ($M = 22.00, SD = 2.16$). Dyads were gender-balanced so that two dyads represented each gender combination in the study. Dyadic interactions yielded a total of 37.15 minutes ($M = 4.64, SD = 1.16$) of video data.

The video data was coded for speech, gaze, and gestures features. Four typical types of gestures—*deictics*, *iconics*, *metaphorics*, and *beats*—were coded according to the guidelines provided by McNeill [21]. Instances of no gestures were also coded. Four clusters of gaze targets—*reference*, *recipient*, *narrator's own gesture*, and *other places*—were observed in the collected data and used for coding to represent features of gaze behavior. Additionally, we coded speech for lexical affiliates for deictic, iconic, and metaphoric gestures and significant structural points for beat gestures. Used affinity diagramming, we categorized lexical affiliates and significant points in speech. The top three categories for each type of gesture served as speech features (Figure 3). A primary coder coded the eight interaction episodes, and a secondary coder coded 10% of the data to ensure inter-coder reliability. The reliability analysis showed almost perfect agreement for speech features (Cohen's κ = .870), gesture type (Cohen's κ = .845) and gaze target (Cohen's κ = .916) based on guidelines suggested by Landis and Koch [18].

3.2. Dynamic Bayesian Network

A dynamic Bayesian network (DBN) is a type of probabilistic graphical model (PGM) that provides compact representations of conditional independence among random variables [17]. DBNs generalize hidden Markov models (HMMs) to represent the hidden state and the observation as a set of random variables. In their basic form, DBNs are directed acyclic graphs in which nodes represent random variables and edges represent conditional dependencies (e.g., Figure 4). Semantically, an edge from a parent node A to a child node B means that node A has influence over node B. A dynamic Bayesian network extends static Bayesian nets (BNs) to incorporate the temporal dependencies among variables. These characteristics for dealing with *uncertain* and *temporal* relations among random variables make dynamic Bayesian networks particularly useful in modeling the dynamics of multimodal behaviors. Murphy [28] provides an extensive introduction to representation, learning, and inference in DBNs.

Gesture Type	Speech Features		
Deictic gestures	Concrete reference *"a big pot"*	Abstract reference *"the first step"*	Pronoun *"this person"*
Iconic gestures	Concrete object *"two boards"*	Descriptive verb *"peel it off"*	Non-descriptive action *"make it"*
Metaphoric gestures	Abstract concept *"for six hours"*	Abstract process *"how paper is made"*	Abstract object *"the water soluble elements"*
Beat gestures	Important information *"at least ten times of water"*	New information *"for example"*	Connector *"so that"*

Figure 3: Speech features for gestures. Features were identified through affinity diagramming of human data and by using the guideline suggested by McNeill [21]. An example of each type of feature is also provided.

3.3. Model Representation

Informed by literature in human communication [8, 11, 21], we propose a network structure, shown in Figure 4, to represent the relationships among speech, gaze, and gestures. In developing this network, we included a *hidden random variable* denoting a cognitive process (C) that directs how humans coordinate speech (S), gaze (Ga), and gestures (Ge), which were considered *observations*. We assumed the latent cognitive process was a discrete-time Markov process. This assumption is consistent with psycholinguistic models of speech production [8, 11]. Additionally, we assumed that speech influences gaze and gestures, as research suggests that nonverbal behaviors might be contingent on verbal utterances [21]. Based on our exploratory tests, we empirically determined there were three hidden states and that the discrete time window of the Markov process was 500 ms.

3.4. Learning and Inference

To learn the parameters of each conditional probability distribution (CPD) in the DBN (Figure 4), the expectation-maximization (EM) algorithm [3] was used. The eight coded episodes of interaction were used as the training data.

To control the robot's behaviors using the learned DBN, we assumed that the robot's speech features would be given and the most probable gesture type and gaze target would be inferred at any given time t. To this end, we used a junction tree algorithm to perform offline smoothing [28] and compute the most probable explanation (MPE)—the maximal posterior probability of a set of variables given observations of another set of variables—of gaze and gestures. We used the Bayes Net Toolbox [27] for learning and inference.

The latent cognitive process contained three states ($C = c_i, i = 1,2,3$). Gaze and gestures contained four ($Ga = a_i, i = 1,...,4$) and five ($Ge = e_i, i = 1,...,5$) values, respectively. Speech (S) was represented by 12 boolean variables, each of which corresponded to a speech feature (Figure 3). As a result, the model is characterized by a vector

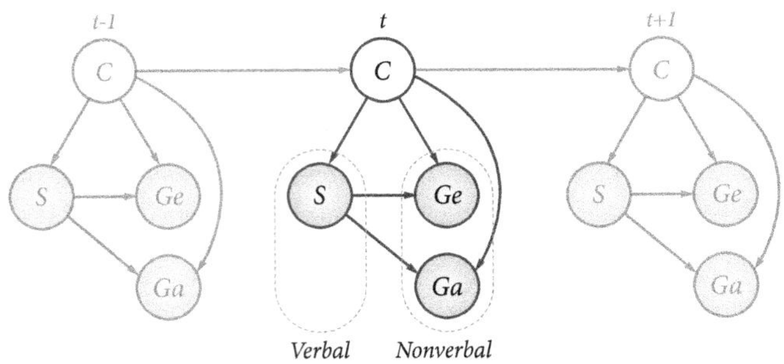

Figure 4: The proposed dynamic Bayesian network for modeling and generating multimodal behaviors. C denotes a latent cognitive process that directs verbal, involving speech (S), and nonverbal, involving gaze (Ga) and gestures (Ge), processes.

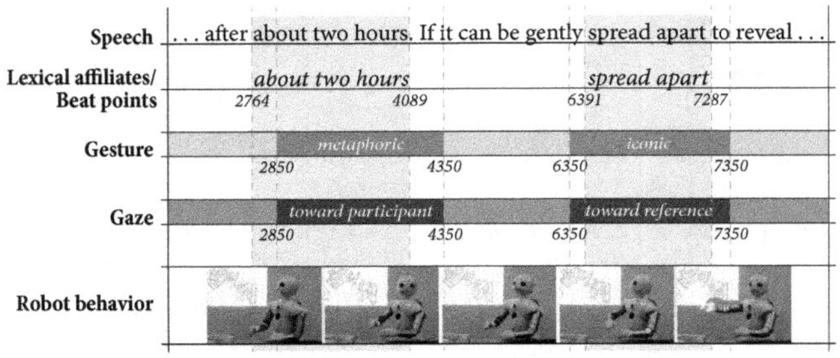

Figure 5: An example of the robot displaying speech, gaze, and gesture behaviors generated by the proposed learning-based approach.

of 15 discrete values at each time step. Given the speech features, the most probable latent cognitive state (C_t), gesture type (Ge_t), and gaze target (Ga_t) at any given time t over the duration of the speech ($S_{1:T}$) can therefore be computed using Equation 1. Here, X represents C, Ga, and Ge, and x represents c, a, and e.

$$\arg\max_i p(X_t = x_i | S_{1:T}) \qquad \forall t \in T \tag{1}$$

The features of the robot's speech were manually marked, and the annotated speech features were discretized into feature sequences at the rate of 500 ms per feature. During inference, the sequences of speech features were used as partial observations, and gaze and gesture were treated as missing values. The consecutive states inferred for each behavior were combined into a sequence of behavior that was considered to be one continuous instance of behavior. For example, six consecutive states of iconic gestures were combined into one iconic gesture lasting 3,000 ms.

3.5. Model Evaluation

An evaluation of the model sought to determine to what extent the DBN model, as illustrated in Figure 4, accurately predicted gaze targets and gesture types when given speech features by comparing gaze and gestures predicted by Equation 1 against the human data. The evaluation was conducted using eight-fold leave-one-out cross validation. We used gaze and gesture data from seven dyads to train the DBN and evaluated the performance of the trained model in predicting gaze targets and gesture types, given speech features from the eighth dyad. While the behaviors are continuous in time, we chose to discretize the data using a window 500 ms and to compare the predicted behavior to the behavior in the test dataset at each discrete window. The accuracy of prediction was on average 54.57% for gaze targets and 62.77% for gesture type. While prediction accuracy is significantly better than chance (25% for gaze and 20% for gestures), it might be further improved by considering more features. Moreover, the highest and lowest accuracies in the cross validation for gaze were 68.23% and 46.48%, respectively, and for gestures were 69.76% and 44.25%, respectively. These results suggest a large variation in how people employed behaviors during narration. Collecting more data to train the model might improve predictive accuracy.

3.6. Generating Robot Behavior

At the *domain* level, the robot's gestures were designed based on our observations of human narrators' gestures. While gesture performance at a given gesture point varied slightly among narrators, narrators displayed semantically similar elements. For example, to describe "beating (paper) with a stick," participants displayed one-handed or two-handed up and down movements, but at different speeds and with different hand angles with respect to the ground. For each unique gesture point, we created one robot gesture that captured the common elements we observed from the human narrators. Robot gestures were created through puppeteering, which involved manually moving the robot's arms while recording key frames of the gestural trajectories. Gesture libraries were created for the four common gesture types to include all the gestures that might be used in the narration task.

To generate robot behaviors, simple mechanisms were used to link components at the feature and domain levels. Lexical affiliates in the robot's speech were manually annotated and tagged with gesture types. The mechanism for linking inferred gesture types to actual robot gestures functioned as follows. For each inferred gesture, we first checked whether the robot's speech included lexical affiliates that temporally overlapped with the gesture within a window of 2,000 ms—1,000 ms before and 1,000 ms after the beginning of the gesture. No lexical affiliates or a lexical affiliate for a gesture type that did not match with the inferred gesture type within this window prompted the robot to randomly select and perform a gesture from the gesture library of the inferred gesture type. If the gesture type of the found lexical affiliate was consistent with the inferred gesture type, the lexical affiliate was linked to an actual gesture using an association mechanism.

Speech and inferred gaze and gesture motions were synchronized using the Robot Behavior Toolkit [9], a Robot Operating System (ROS) module for controlling multimodal robot behaviors. Figure 5 illustrates a sample sequence of speech, gaze, and gesture behaviors that were controlled by the proposed learning-based approach.

4. EVALUATION

In addition to the model evaluation described above, we evaluated how robot behaviors produced by the learning-based approach shaped people's perceptions of the robot in a human-robot interaction study. The evaluation sought to test our central hypothesis that robot behaviors produced by learned parameters would improve interaction outcomes, specifically improved perceptions of the robot in terms of immediacy, naturalness, effectiveness, likability, and credibility and improved ability of the participants to retell the robot's story, over baseline behaviors such as behaviors produced by randomly generated parameters or no behaviors, while resulting in outcomes that are comparable to those elicited by conventional modeling approaches.

4.1. Study Design, Task, and Procedure

The evaluation study used the same narration task as the one used in the modeling study. We manipulated the method used to control the robot's gaze and gesture behaviors while keeping the robot's speech the same across conditions. We designed a between-participants study, in which each participant was randomly assigned to one of the following conditions:

1. In the *learning-based* condition, the learned DBN described in the previous section directed the robot's gaze and gestures.
2. In the *unimodal* condition, the robot only used the speech channel to verbally present the narration topic without gaze or gesture behaviors. This condition served as the experimental control.
3. In the *random* condition, the same network structure as described in the previous section was used to generate behaviors. However, the model instead used randomly generated parameters, introducing temporal and spatial randomness in the produced behavior.
4. The *conventional* condition involved directing the robot's gaze and gestures based on designer-specified parameters for aligning behaviors. In particular, the parameters specified how different types of gestures were aligned with speech features (i.e., lexical affiliates) according to the literature on human

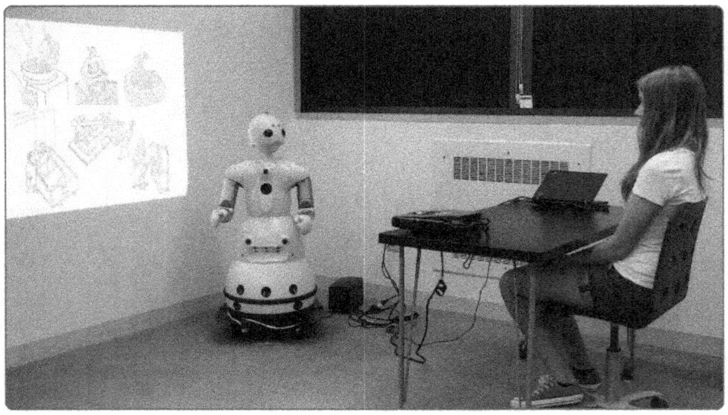

Figure 6: An experimenter demonstrating the setup of the evaluation study.

communication [21]. The parameters also specified gaze-gesture relationships by extracting distributions representing where a speaker looked while performing different types of gestures. Every time its gesture state changed, the robot determined its new gaze target based on these distributions. The behaviors generated using this approach predicted significant improvements in learning and perceptions of the robot [10].

After obtaining informed consent, the experimenter directed participants to a controlled laboratory environment, where each participant listened to the robot narrate the process of making paper (Figure 6). The robot's narration lasted approximately six minutes. Following the narration, participants completed a distractor task that lasted approximately five minutes and then took a quiz on the presented information. Participants then retold the narration and filled out a post-experiment questionnaire that evaluated their perceptions of the robot. Participants received $5 for their participation. The entire experiment took approximately 30 minutes per participant.

4.2. Participants

A total of 29 participants (16 males, 13 females), whose ages ranged 18–38 ($M = 22.62, SD = 4.35$), were recruited from the University of Wisconsin–Madison campus. There were six, eight, seven, and eight participants in the learning-based, unimodal, random, and conventional conditions, respectively. Participants reported relatively low familiarity with robots ($M = 2.48, SD = 1.53$) and with the process of making paper ($M = 1.69, SD = 1.11$) in seven-point rating scales.

4.3. Measurement and Analysis

We used a post-experiment questionnaire to evaluate the participants' perceptions of the robot's behavior. Four measurement scales were developed using seven-point questionnaire items. *Immediacy*, defined as psychological distance between individuals [22], assessed how close participants felt to the robot and how engaging they thought the robot was (3 items, Cronbach's $\alpha = .79$). *Naturalness* gauged how natural the robot's motions were (5 items, Cronbach's $\alpha = .84$). *Effectiveness* measured how participants perceived the robot's effectiveness as a presenter (4 items, Cronbach's $\alpha = .87$). *Likability* evaluated how likable the robot was (8 items, Cronbach's $\alpha = .88$). An additional item measured the robot's *credibility* using a question about whether or not the robot provided sufficient information for the participant to answer the quiz questions. Moreover, we asked participants to choose from a list of 20 adjectives to describe the robot's overall behavior. The list of 20 adjectives consisted of 10 positive and 10 negative adjectives. Two manipulation-check items were included to ensure that manipulations in the trained model to create the unimodal and random conditions were successful.

In addition to questionnaire evaluation, we evaluated participants' performance in retelling the information that the robot presented, calculating measures of *familiarity* with the narration topic, their use of *body language*, and an *overall evaluation* of presenter effectiveness. Three raters who were blind to the experimental conditions rated video recordings of the participants' retelling performance on these measures using seven-point scales. Inter-rater reliability analysis using intra-class correlation coefficient (ICC) [36] as a measure revealed high correlations among the three raters on measures of familiarity of content (ICC(3,3)=.884), use of body language (ICC(3,3)=.897), and overall evaluation (ICC(3,3)=.771).

While we did not develop any hypothesis regarding the effect of the robot's behaviors on participants' learning of the information presented by the robot, we included an exploratory measure that involved a quiz consisting of 18 questions on this information. This measure explored whether or not the manipulations in the robot's behaviors affected participants' recall of the narrated information.

One-way fixed-effects analysis of variance (ANOVA) tests, using the manipulation in the robot's behaviors as the fixed factor, were conducted to analyze the manipulation checks, questionnaire measures, quiz data, and retelling evaluation. Planned many-to-one multiple comparisons used the Dunnett's method, considering the learning-based approach as the comparison baseline, to assess how the unimodal, random, and conventional conditions compared against the learning-based condition. Additionally, we performed Dunnett's tests, considering the unimodal and random conditions as baselines, using data on manipulation checks to verify whether the learned model was successfully manipulated to create the unimodal and random conditions. To determine whether behaviors produced by the learning-based and conventional approaches are comparable, we followed guidelines suggested by Walker and Nowacki [39] and Julnes and Mohr [12], applying a conservative equivalence margin of 0.50 (i.e., $p > .50$) to the comparisons between these two conditions.

4.4. Results

4.4.1. Manipulation checks

To check whether our manipulations to create the unimodal behavior condition was successful, we asked participants whether or not they perceived the robot to be motionless. The analysis of variance found a significant effect of our manipulation on this measure, $F(3,25) = 22.88, p < .001$. Comparisons using the Dunnett's test showed that participants in the unimodal condition perceived the robot to be more motionless than those in the learning-based, $p < .001$, random, $p < .001$, and conventional, $p < .001$, conditions. We also asked participants whether the robot's motions appeared random to verify that we successfully created the random condition. The analysis found a significant effect of our manipulation on this measure, $F(3,25) = 6.12, p = .003$. Comparisons showed that participants in the random condition perceived the robot's motions to be more random than those in the learning-based, $p = .005$, unimodal, $p = .017$, and conventional, $p = .002$, conditions did.

4.4.2. Perceptions of the robot

We found that our manipulation had a significant effect on the perceived immediacy, $F(3,25) = 6.91, p = .002$, naturalness, $F(3,25) = 5.77, p = .004$, effectiveness, $F(3,25) = 4.59, p = .011$, and likability, $F(3,25) = 6.44, p = .002$, of the robot, but not on participants' perceptions of the robot's credibility, $F(3,25) = 2.07, p = .130$. Comparisons further revealed that the learning-based and conventional approaches showed equivalence in measures of perceived immediacy, $p = .923$, naturalness, $p = .917$, effectiveness, $p = .999$, likability, $p = .722$, and credibility, $p = .645$.

Comparisons also showed that participants in the learning-based condition rated the robot to have higher immediacy, $p = .002$, and to be more natural, $p = .003$, more effective, $p = .027$, and more likable, $p = .023$, than those in the unimodal condition. However,

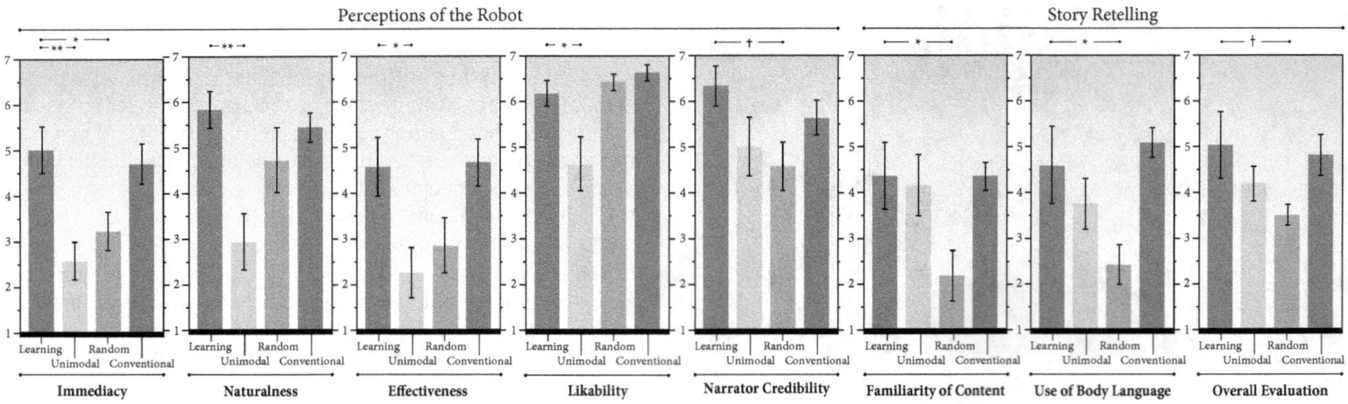

Figure 7: Results on perceptions of the robot and retelling performance. Only significant results are marked. (NS), (†), (*), (**), and (***) denote $p > .10$, $p < .10$, $p < .050$, $p < .010$, and, $p < .001$, respectively.

no significant differences were found between the learning-based and unimodal conditions in perceived credibility, $p = .191$. While the comparisons showed that participants in the learning-based condition perceived the robot to have higher immediacy, $p = .032$, and marginally more credibility than in the random condition, $p = .072$, no differences were found between the learning-based and random conditions in measures of naturalness, $p = .378$, effectiveness, $p = .131$, and likability, $p = .931$. Figure 7 summarizes these results.

Our analysis also found a significant effect of our manipulation on the number of positive adjectives that participants used to describe the robot's behaviors, $F(3,25) = 6.44, p = .002$. Comparisons showed that participants in the learning-based condition used more positive adjectives than those in the unimodal, $p = .013$, and random, $p = .027$, conditions did. The learning-based and conventional conditions demonstrated equivalence in the use of positive adjectives, $p = .999$ (Figure 8) . However, our manipulation did not have a significant effect on the number of negative adjectives used, $F(3,25) = 1.86, p = .162$. Comparisons showed that participants in the unimodal, $p = .354$, random, $p = .460$, and conventional, $p = .947$, conditions used a similar number of negative adjectives in describing the robot's behavior to those in the learning-based condition did. Figure 8 shows the top three adjectives used to describe the robot's behaviors.

4.4.3. *Retelling performance*

We found a significant effect of our manipulation on participants' perceived familiarity with the narration topic, $F(3,25) = 3.37, p = .034$, and effective use of body language, $F(3,25) = 4.67, p = .010$,

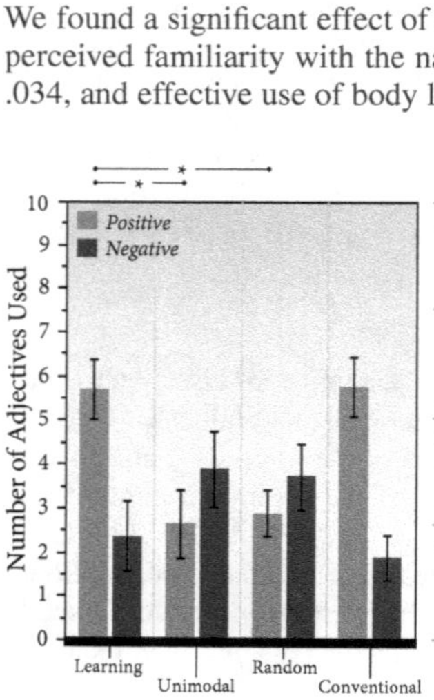

	Positive	Negative
Learning-based (6) *Coherent (5), Scripted (5), Communicative (5), Confident (5)*	70.83%	29.17%
Unimodal (8) *Rigid (6), Precise (5), Robotic (6), Scripted (5), Artificial (5)*	40.38%	59.62%
Random (7) *Artificial (5), Confident (5), Robotic (5)*	43.48%	56.52%
Conventional (8) *Coherent (7), Lively (6), Confident (7), Scripted (6), Communicative (6)*	75.41%	24.59%

Figure 8: Results on participants' use of positive and negative adjectives in describing the robot's behavior. Top three choices of adjectives and percentages of used positive and negative adjectives are listed. Values in parentheses indicate how many participants used the adjective to describe the robot. Only significant results are marked. (*) denote $p < .050$.

but not on the overall evaluation of the participant as an effective presenter, $F(3,25) = 2.16, p = .118$. Comparisons revealed equivalence between the learning-based and conventional approaches with respect to familiarity of the topic, $p = 1.000$, effective use of body language, $p = .848$, and overall evaluation of presenter effectiveness, $p = .977$, as shown in Figure 7.

Comparisons also showed that participants in the learning-based condition were rated to be more familiar with the topic, $p = .042$, and to more effectively use body language, $p = .033$, than those in the random condition. They were also rated marginally higher in overall evaluation than those in the random condition, $p = .084$. However, comparisons did not find significant differences in participants' familiarity with the topic, $p = .986$, effective use of body language, $p = .569$, and overall performance as an effective presenter, $p = .447$, between the learning-based and unimodal conditions (Figure 7).

4.4.4. *Cognitive assessment*

The manipulation in the robot's behaviors did not have a significant effect on participants' information recall in the quiz, $F(3,25) = 0.98, p = .418$. No significant differences were found between the learning-based condition and the unimodal, $p = .621$, random, $p = .866$, and conventional, $p = .986$, conditions in comparisons.

4.4.5. *Summary and Discussion*

Overall, our results showed that participants in the learning-based condition rated the immediacy, naturalness, effectiveness, and likability of the robot higher than those in the unimodal condition did. Participants in the learning-based condition were also rated higher in their retelling of the narration topic compared with those in the random condition. Additionally, the learning-based and conventional conditions showed equivalence in participants' perceptions of the robot and retelling performance.

While behaviors in the unimodal condition negatively affected how participants perceived the robot in terms of immediacy, naturalness, effectiveness, and likability, it did not affect participants' perceived credibility of the robot, retelling performance, or information recall. The following excerpts from post-experiment interviews provide some insight into these results:

> *"The robot didn't particularly move, which I didn't think was realistic, and also it didn't make eye contact with me."*

> *"When it switched steps, it would be more engaging if it would [like] point to the new step..."*

> *"I was more focused on what the robot was saying and the screen..."*

While participants in the unimodal condition noticed that the robot's behaviors were not natural, they still paid attention to the verbal information and the projected illustration to understand the presented information, demonstrating comparable results in perceived credibility, retelling of the topic, and learning.

Participant comments also provided insight into why the random manipulation did not affect their perceptions of the robot but affected their retelling performance, as illustrated in the excerpts below:

> *"The motion was kind of distracting ... sometimes maybe it used hand gestures in a way that I wouldn't necessary to use that ... [but] I feel like people do that sometimes too..."*

> *"It was very distracting... what are you [the robot] trying to do, I don't know what you [the robot] are trying to do. It was just odd."*

Most participants in the random condition found the robot's behaviors to be distracting, which suggests that participants may have found it difficult to focus on the information presented by the robot, potentially leading to poor retelling performance. The discrepancy between quiz results and topic familiarity in retelling may reflect the effects distraction may have had on their learning.

However, while some of the participants in the random condition perceived that the robot's behaviors deviated from social norms, others found these behaviors to be acceptable. These results are consistent with previous work on robots' use of gestures to support speech, which found no differences in participants' ratings of a robot displaying gestures that were semantically incongruent with its speech and one that displayed congruent behaviors in measures of how lively, active, engaged, communicative, and fun-loving they perceived the robot to be [34].

The participants perceived the robot in the learning-based condition as showing higher immediacy—displaying more engagement and psychological closeness—than they did in the unimodal and random conditions. This result is consistent with research in education, which shows that instructors with high immediacy use more gestures and greater eye contact with students [22].

Finally, our results suggested that the behaviors driven by the learning-based and conventional approaches demonstrated similar effectiveness in every measure. Participant comments also highlight similar limitations both approaches have in generating natural, humanlike behaviors, as suggested by the following comments on the robot's gaze behavior, the first by a participant in the learning-based condition and the other two from participants in the conventional condition:

> *"It seemed not to sometimes make eye contact when I expected it to. There were a few periods where it was talking and talking straight at the screen and not making eye contact."*

> *"What it [the robot] could do more is to look as if it is an actual human were presenting. It could look more at the screen [be]cause that's how I feel a lot people do."*

> *"There were a few times I noticed it pointed to the screen without looking at it."*

These comments also highlight the variability in people's expectations of the behaviors of an effective presenter and suggest that gaze behaviors controlled by the learning-based and conventional approaches will require further improvement to meet the expectations of a broader population of users.

5. GENERAL DISCUSSION

5.1. Design Implications

To generate robot behaviors that enable natural and effective human-robot interaction, researchers and designers have constructed models of multimodal behavior from human data through an inspection-based process that identifies behavioral patterns and extracts alignment parameters for behaviors in different modalities. While this process has been successfully used to design robot behaviors that achieve predicted outcomes (e.g., [9, 10, 29, 40]), the inspection-based approach to identifying and extracting behavioral parameters does not scale well to more challenging modeling tasks, such as modeling relationships among a large number of multimodal behaviors from large datasets. The learning-based approach presented in this paper facilitates this process by automatically learning behavioral patterns and alignment parameters from annotated human data and promising greater scalability to large datasets and a large number of behavioral modalities. Additionally, the learning-based approach offers formalisms in the form of probabilistic representations of the design space for robot behaviors, which might facilitate the validation of the learned models and extensions of these models using methods such as active learning. While our results show that the learning-based and conventional approaches reach comparable effectiveness in generating robot behaviors, we expect the learning-based approach to better capture the dynamics of multimodal behavior when more data and behavioral modalities are considered.

5.2. Limitations and Future work

A key limitation of our work is the assumption that the Markov process that underlies the production of multimodal behavior is discrete, following an empirically determined window size of 500 ms. However, human behavior is inherently more continuous. While the use of this discrete window yielded acceptable behaviors, a consideration of human behavior as a continuous process in modeling might yield better outcomes. We also assumed that the duration of state transitions were identical across different behavioral modalities, although different behaviors might have different state duration. For example, gaze behavior might change more frequently than gestures. Methods that explicitly model duration, such as the use of a hidden semi-Markov model (HSMM), might be more appropriate for modeling these temporal characteristics.

In designing robot behaviors, we considered the speaker's behaviors independent of the recipient's behaviors. While this approach might be adequate for a narration scenario, extending our work to more interactive scenarios such as conversations will require jointly modeling recipient and speaker behaviors using modeling approaches such as the coupled hidden Markov model (CHMM). We also focused on gaze and gesture as nonverbal channels, while other nonverbal behaviors, such as head nods and facial expressions, play a key role in communication.

In our proposed approach, the specific network structure of the model, which we constructed based on literature on human communication, has a significant effect on the success of the model in achieving natural, effective humanlike behavior, and alternative network structures or structures that are learned directly from data might achieve different or better results. Finally, this work used simple, proof-of-concept mechanisms to link components in the feature and domain levels (Figure 2). Future work could extend the learning-based approach to jointly learn at both feature and domain levels and the associations between the two levels, which might facilitate the generation of richer and more accurate robot behaviors.

6. CONCLUSION

Human behavior offers a rich space for designing natural and effective behaviors for robots. Researchers and designers have explored ways of capturing the patterns in which humans behave as models and heuristics to control robot behaviors. However, these approaches usually involve a laborious process of inspecting large volumes of data to identify temporal patterns in behaviors and alignments across behaviors in different modalities. To facilitate this process, we proposed a *learning-based* modeling approach that uses probabilistic graphical models (PGMs) to automatically learn distribution and alignment parameters from data on human behavior. In this paper, we demonstrated a specific instantiation of this approach that used a dynamic Bayesian network (DBN) to model speech, gaze, and gesture behaviors in a narration task and to estimate distribution and alignment parameters for these behaviors to enable a humanlike robot to perform the same narration task. We then evaluated the effectiveness of our approach in achieving natural, humanlike robot behaviors by comparing it against a number of baselines. The results showed behaviors generated by a learned model to be more effective than no behavior and random behavior baselines in a number of measures and equally effective as those controlled by a set of heuristics. Our findings suggest that the proposed learning-based approach offers design outcomes that are comparable to those obtained by heuristics-based approaches while promising significant reduction in the effort involved in constructing models of multimodal behavior and greater scalability to more complex modeling tasks toward achieving richer and more natural human-robot interactions.

7. ACKNOWLEDGMENTS

This research was supported by National Science Foundation awards 1017952 and 1149970 and an equipment loan from Mitsubishi Heavy Industries, Ltd. We would like to thank Jilana Boston, Brandi Hefty, Ross Luo, Catherine Steffel, and Lindsay Jacobs for their help in our work.

8. REFERENCES

[1] M. Argyle and M. Cook. *Gaze and mutual gaze*. Cambridge University Press, 1976.

[2] W. Burgard, A. Cremers, D. Fox, D. Hähnel, G. Lakemeyer, D. Schulz, W. Steiner, and S. Thrun. Experiences with an interactive museum tour-guide robot. *Artificial Intelligence*, 114(1):3–55, 1999.

[3] A. P. Dempster, N. M. Laird, and D. B. Rubin. Maximum likelihood from incomplete data via the em algorithm. *Journal of Royal Statistical Society*, pages 1–38, 1977.

[4] J. F. Ferreira, M. Castelo-Branco, and J. Dias. A hierarchical bayesian framework for multimodal active perception. *Adaptive Behavior*, 20(3):172–190, 2012.

[5] C. Goodwin. *Conversational organization: Interaction between speakers and hearers*. Academic Press New York, 1981.

[6] Z. M. Griffin. Gaze durations during speech reflect word selection and phonological encoding. *Cognition*, 82(1):B1–B14, 2001.

[7] C. C. Heath. Gesture's discrete tasks: Multiple relevancies in visual conduct in the contextualization of language. In P. Auer and A. Di Luzio, editors, *The contextualization of language*, pages 102–127. John Benjamins, 1992.

[8] A. Henderson, F. Goldman-Eisler, and A. Skarbek. Sequential temporal patterns in spontaneous speech. *Language and Speech*, 9:207–216, 1966.

[9] C.-M. Huang and B. Mutlu. Robot behavior toolkit: Generating effective social behaviors for robots. In *Proc. HRI 2012*, 2012.

[10] C.-M. Huang and B. Mutlu. Modeling and evaluating narrative gestures for humanlike robots. In *Proc. RSS 2013*, 2013.

[11] J. Jaffe, L. Cassotta, and S. Feldstein. Markovian model of time patterns of speech. *Science*, 144:884–886, 1964.

[12] G. Julnes and L. B. Mohr. Analysis of no-difference findings in evaluation research. *Evaluation Review*, 13(6):628–655, 1989.

[13] T. Kanda, M. Shiomi, Z. Miyashita, H. Ishiguro, and N. Hagita. An affective guide robot in a shopping mall. In *Proc. HRI 2009*, pages 173–180, 2009.

[14] A. Kendon. Looking in conversation and the regulation of turns at talk: A comment on the papers of g. beattie and d. r. rutter et al. *British Journal of Social and Clinical Psychology*, 17:23–24, 1978.

[15] A. Kendon. *Gesticulation and Speech: Two Aspects of the Process of Utterance*. Mouton De Gruyter, 1980.

[16] A. Kendon. Do gestures communicate? a review. *Research on Language and Social Interaction*, pages 175–200, 1994.

[17] D. Kollar and N. Friedman. *Probabilistic graphical models: principles and techniques*. MIT Press, 2009.

[18] J. Landis and G. Koch. The measurement of observer agreement for categorical data. *Biometrics*, 33(1):159–174, 1977.

[19] J. Lee and S. Marsella. Modeling speaker behavior: a comparison of two approaches. In *Proc. IVA 2012*, pages 161–174, 2012.

[20] M. Lee, S. Kiesler, and J. Forlizzi. Receptionist or information kiosk: how do people talk with a robot? In *Proc. HRI 2010*, 2010.

[21] D. McNeill. *Hand and Mind*. The University of Chicago Press, 1992.

[22] A. Mehrabian. *Silent messages*. Wadsworth, 1971.

[23] A. S. Meyer, A. M. Sleiderink, and W. J. M. Levelt. Viewing and naming objects: eye movements during noun phrase production. *Cognition*, 66(2):B25–B33, 1998.

[24] Y. Mohammad and T. Nishida. Learning interaction protocols using augmented baysian networks applied to guided navigation. In *Proc. IROS 2010*, pages 4119–4126, 2010.

[25] Y. Mohammad, T. Nishida, and S. Okada. Unsupervised simultaneous learning of gestures, actions and their associations for human-robot interaction. In *Proc. IROS 2009*, pages 2537–2544, 2009.

[26] L.-P. Morency. Modeling human communication dynamics. *IEEE Signal Processing Magazine*, 27(5):112–116, 2010.

[27] K. Murphy et al. The bayes net toolbox for matlab. *Computing science and statistics*, 33(2):1024–1034, 2001.

[28] K. P. Murphy. *Dynamic bayesian networks: representation, inference and learning*. PhD thesis, University of California, 2002.

[29] B. Mutlu, J. Forlizzi, and J. Hodgins. A storytelling robot: Modeling and evaluation of humanlike gaze behavior. In *Proc. HUMANOIDS 2006*, pages 518–523, 2006.

[30] B. Mutlu, T. Kanda, J. Forlizzi, J. Hodgins, and H. Ishiguro. Conversational gaze mechanisms for humanlike robots. *ACM TiiS*, 1(2):12:1–12:33, 2012.

[31] V. Ng-Thow-Hing, P. Luo, and S. Okita. Synchronized gesture and speech production for humanoid robots. In *Proc. IROS 2010*, pages 4617–4624, 2010.

[32] Y. Okuno, T. Kanda, M. Imai, H. Ishiguro, and N. Hagita. Providing route directions: design of robot's utterance, gesture, and timing. In *Proc. HRI 2009*, pages 53–60, 2009.

[33] K. Otsuka, H. Sawada, and J. Yamato. Automatic inference of cross-modal nonverbal interactions in multiparty conversations: who responds to whom, when, and how? from gaze, head gestures, and utterances. In *Proc. ICMI 2007*, pages 255–262, 2007.

[34] M. Salem, S. Kopp, I. Wachsmuth, K. Rohlfing, and F. Joublin. Generation and evaluation of communicative robot gesture. *International Journal of Social Robotics*, pages 201–217, 2012.

[35] E. Schegloff. On some gestures' relation to speech. In J. M. Atkinson and J. Heritage, editors, *Structures of social action: Studies in conversational analysis*, pages 266–296. Cambridge Univ. Press, 1984.

[36] P. E. Shrout and J. L. Fleiss. Intraclass correlations: uses in assessing rater reliability. *Psychological bulletin*, 86(2):420, 1979.

[37] J. Sidnell. Coordinating gesture, talk, and gaze in reenactments. *Research on Language and Social Interaction*, 39(4):377–409, 2006.

[38] J. Streeck. Gesture as communication i: Its coordination with gaze and speech. *Communication Monographs*, 60(4):275–299, 1993.

[39] E. Walker and A. S. Nowacki. Understanding equivalence and noninferiority testing. *Journal of General Internal Medicine*, 26:192–196, 2011.

[40] A. Yamazaki, K. Yamazaki, Y. Kuno, M. Burdelski, M. Kawashima, and H. Kuzuoka. Precision timing in human-robot interaction: coordination of head movement and utterance. In *Proc. CHI 2008*, pages 131–140, 2008.

From Interaction Science to Cognitive Interaction Technology

Helge Ritter
Cognitive Interaction Technology – Center of Excellence
Bielefeld University
helge@techfak.uni-bielefeld.de

ABSTRACT

A cascade of revolutions has transformed robotics into a new science that begins to link physical concepts of control and interaction with qualities and concepts analyzed so far mainly in disciplines such as psychology, biology, linguistics or the social sciences.

A visible manifestation of this transformation is the rapid evolution of robot body morphologies within the last decade: robots with different degrees of humanoid appearance –ranging from a coarse analogy of humanoid body structure to amazingly detailed replications of human appearance– are now being developed in numerous labs and not few of them have become commercially available.

This has completely reshaped the interface between robots and people: expressive faces require a rethinking of the way robots and humans can interact. Human-like hands offer new levels of interaction provided we can find ways to coordinate their rich degrees of freedom to bring their skills closer to what we see in humans. And progress in processing power, storage density and sensing technologies allows to create and maintain rich representations to cope with contact at all levels from the physical to the social, thereby turning robots from the "contact minimizers" of the past into interactive agents that can assist people in natural ways and in natural environments.

These developments have shaped much of CITEC's vision of cognitive interaction technology and the associated research agenda along the four topic pillars of motion intelligence, attentive systems, situated communication, and memory and learning. We describe some of the underlying methodology and how we have mapped it into a dedicated lab infrastructure to investigate cognitive interaction processes across a wide spectrum of spatial and temporal scales. We present selected examples of cognitive interaction that are in the focus of major CITEC research lines: the Bielefeld expressive robot head Flobi that offers a versatile platform to find new ways to make human robot interaction more natural and to enrich it with new layers of usefulness; the advancement of touch as the modality where social and physical contact come together, for instance, through sensors that are more skin-like and ways of how to use such sensors for haptic exploration of surfaces or as research tools for studying human haptics; and interdisciplinary work towards a deeper understanding of "manual intelligence" and its replication in bimanual robots to enable them to flexibly manipulate everyday objects and to cooperate more naturally with people. Finally, we report on the status of the newly started project FAMULA that connects 10 CITEC groups to study and replicate the process of familiarization with novel objects through combined use of embodied manipulation and language.
Turning to the perspectives of our field into the future, we argue that we can take inspiration from the systematic elucidation of principles and mechanisms of interaction that enabled physics to advance to a new level. Taking guidance from this success story may put us on a similarly grand path: creating a science for elucidating the inner workings of cognitive interaction that arises when we take the step from physical particles to cognitive agents and using our insights to create better bridges between humans and tomorrow's technology.

HRI'14, March 3–6, 2014, Bielefeld, Germany.
ACM 978-1-4503-2658-2/14/03.
http://dx.doi.org/10.1145/2559636.2566688

Categories and Subject Descriptors
H.1.2 User/Machine Systems

Keywords
ACM SIGCHI; computing; human-robot interaction

Bio
Helge Ritter studied physics and mathematics at the Universities of Bayreuth, Heidelberg and Munich and received a Ph.D. in Physics from the Technical University of Munich in 1988. Since 1985, he has been engaged in research in the field of neural networks. In 1989 he moved as a guest scientist to the Laboratory of Computer and Information Science at Helsinki University of Technology. Subsequently he was assistant research professor at the then newly established Beckman Institute for Advanced Science and Technology and the Department of Physics at the University of Illinois at Urbana-Champaign. Since 1990, he is professor at the Department of Information Science, University of Bielefeld. In 1995, Helge Ritter spent one year as a fellow at the Institute of Advanced Studies in Berlin. His main interests are principles of neural computation, in particular self-organizing and learning systems, and their application to robot cognition, data analysis and interactive man-machine interfaces. In 1999, Helge Ritter was awarded the SEL Alcatel Research Prize and in 2001 the Leibniz Prize of the German Research Foundation DFG. Helge Ritter is co-founder and one of the directors of the Bielefeld Institute of Cognition and Robotics (CoR-Lab) and coordinator of the excellence cluster "Cognitive Interaction Technology".

Dimensions of Anthropomorphism

From Humanness to Humanlikeness

Jakub Złotowski[1], Ewald Strasser[2], Christoph Bartneck[1]
[1]HIT Lab NZ, University of Canterbury, Christchurch, New Zealand
[2]HCI & Usability Unit, ICT&S Center, University of Salzburg, Salzburg, Austria
jakub.zlotowski@pg.canterbury.ac.nz, christoph.bartneck@canterbury.ac.nz
ewald.strasser@sbg.ac.at

ABSTRACT

In HRI anthropomorphism has been considered to be a unidimensional construct. However, social psychological studies of the potentially reverse process to anthropomorphisation - known as dehumanization - indicate that there are two distinct senses of humanness with different consequences for people who are dehumanized by deprivation of some of the aspects of these dimensions. These attributes are crucial for perception of others as humans. Therefore, we hypothesized that the same attributes could be used to anthropomorphize a robot in HRI and only a two-dimensional measures would be suitable to distinguish between different forms of making a robot more humanlike. In a study where participants played a quiz based on the TV show "Jeopardy!" we manipulated a NAO robot's intelligence and emotionality. The results suggest that only emotionality, not intelligence, makes robots be perceived as more humanlike. Furthermore, we found some evidence that anthropomorphism is a multidimensional phenomenon.

Categories and Subject Descriptors

I.2.9 [**Computing Methodologies**]: ARTIFICIAL INTELLIGENCE—*Robotics*

1. INTRODUCTION

Anthropomorphism, understood as the attribution of humanlike properties or characteristics to real or imagined nonhuman agents and objects [4], is a common theme appearing regularly in the field of HRI. However, it was described for the first time a long time ago by Xenophanes in the 6th century BC [18]. It has been proposed that anthropomorphism in those times had an adaptive function as it allowed early humans to interpret ambiguous shapes as human in order to minimize the risk of being killed by enemy or increase the chances of finding companions [12]. In today's society, despite the widespread tendency to anthropomorphize other objects, it has been suggested that people's mental models of autonomous robots are especially anthropomorphic [8].

HRI'14, March 03 - 06 2014, Bielefeld, Germany.

ACM 978-1-4503-2658-2/14/03...$15.00.
http://dx.doi.org/10.1145/2559636.2559679

A good example of this is the 2012 science fiction movie "Prometheus" that started its promotional marketing campaign in the form of short viral videos showing a fictional future and products developed by a company known as Wayland Corporation. One of these viral ads presented the latest generation of robots known as "David 8" that are almost indistinguishable from mankind itself in a Wayland Corporation's commercial recommending this technology. The commercial ends with a slogan "Technological, intellectual, physical, emotional", referring to the robot. In other words, in the fictional future, the key aspects that make a machine humanlike are intelligence, physical appearance and emotions.

This is a science fiction vision of the future, but the interest in understanding what makes robots anthropomorphic is not new in the field of HRI. Previous studies proposed multiple factors as affecting humanlikeness of robots: embodiment [7], movement [25], verbal communication [23, 24], emotions [5], and gestures [22]. However, all of these factors were investigated separately and there is no unifying theory of anthropomorphism that could explain what robot specific attributes will lead people to perceive a robot as more humanlike. Epley and colleagues [4] proposed a three-factor theory of anthropomorphism that identified three psychological determinants that affect the likelihood of anthropomorphizing an object: elicited agent knowledge (accessibility and applicability of anthropocentric knowledge), effectance motivation (motivation of a person for being an effective social agent) and sociality motivation (desire for engaging in social contact). This general theory of anthropomorphism is also applicable for robots. However, only some of these factors can be applied to a robot's design in order to affect its humanlikeness and this theory does not accommodate the above mentioned factors affecting anthropomorphism in HRI. Since the core aspect of anthropomorphism is humanness, instead of looking at what makes an object humanlike, we could look at what makes a human less humanlike. We thereby take the opposite approach to the problem as humanness can be a key to understanding why these numerous factors affect robots' anthropomorphism and what is the relation between them. The potential of this approach in HRI can be seen in the work of Gray et al. [11] who showed that the uncanny valley is affected only by some factors of humanlikeness, but not all.

1.1 Dehumanization

Waytz et al. [27] proposed that dehumanization, defined as "representing human agents as nonhuman objects or animals and hence denying them human-essential capacities" could be a reverse process to anthropomorphism. The research on dehumanization has gathered new interest in social psychology in the last decade after the publication of Leyens et al. [19] who showed that people attribute differently certain emotions to in-group and out-group members. Those characteristics perceived to be the essence of humanness were attributed to in-group members, but not out-group members. Therefore, the out-group members were perceived as less human.

This work was developed further by Haslam [13] who proposed a model of dehumanization that involves two distinct senses of humanness. Denying characteristics that are Uniquely Human (UH) leads to perception of humans as animal-like. On the other hand, denying attributes that are Human Nature (HN) leads to mechanistic dehumanization where people are seen as automata. The UH dimension reflects mainly high cognition and some of the key attributes of it are intelligence, intentionality, secondary emotions or morality. The HN dimension is represented by primary emotions, sociability or warmth. These two senses of humanness differ in the consequences when people are deprived of them, e.g. a person deprived of UH traits is perceived as disgusting, while lack of HN traits implies indifference and lack of empathy [13].

Another research focus on perception of the mind led to supporting findings. Gray et al. [9] found that the mind perception of human and nonhuman agents was explained by two factors: Agency and Experience. Characteristics that form Agency are: morality, memory, planning or communication. Those which form Experience include feeling fear, pleasure or having desires. What is important is that these two dimensions map well on those proposed for humanness [14]. Agency corresponds to UH and Experience to HN.

The work on dehumanization recently started receiving attention in the context of HRI. However, these studies used dehumanization mainly as a measurement tool for the anthropomorphism directed at robots e.g. [5, 17, 22]. The previous work on humanlikeness in HRI considered anthropomorphism as a uni-dimensional space from a machine to a human. However, since humanness is the essence of anthropomorphism, the studies of dehumanization can indicate that anthropomorphism can be at least two-dimensional. Therefore, in order to accurately represent a robot's perceived humanlikeness it would be necessary to measure it on these two dimensions (an exception is [6] where a robot's anthropomorphism was measured on two scales of humanness, but they were not considered as different dimensions of that construct).

Furthermore, that would also mean that not only the level of a robot's anthropomorphism affects HRI, but also the way in which people anthropomorphize it. HN traits distinguish humans from machines. It is possible that if we attribute these traits to a robot it will not only be perceived as more humanlike, but at the same time as less machine-like. However, in the case of attributing UH traits the perception of a robot could be more humanlike and less animal-like, but not necessarily less machine-like.

The relationship between the two-dimensional model and previously investigated factors affecting anthropomorphism in HRI will need to be established. Some of these factors, such as verbal communication [23, 24] or emotions [5], can be easily attributed to one of the dimensions. Other factors, that were not included in the model of dehumanization can affect both dimensions of anthropomorphism, such as predictability of a robot's behavior [6], or only one, such as embodiment [11].

If anthropomorphism is a reverse process to dehumanization and there are two distinct and independent senses of humanness, a robot can be perceived differently depending on which dimension it is being anthropomorphised. Therefore, a robot provided HN traits should be rated higher mainly on that dimension. Similarly, a robot provided UH attributes should be rated higher on the UH dimension. A uni-dimensional scale of anthropomorphism should be affected by both factors, but it will be unable to distinguish between their effects. In other words, uni-dimensional measures of anthropomorphism treat HN and UH traits equally, when theoretically they could be distinct. This distinction may be necessary in order to understand better the impact of anthropomorphism on HRI, e.g. it has been suggested that the uncanny valley [20] is caused only by the HN (Experience), but not the UH (Agency) dimension [11]. As it is not possible to include all factors affecting both dimensions in a single experiment, we decided to choose intelligence from the UH dimension and emotionality from HN dimension as previous studies showed them to significantly affect robots perceived animacy and humanlikeness, e.g [3, 5]. Therefore, we wanted to investigate how these two factors would affect two-dimensional measures of anthropomorphism and whether it provides any additional information over well established uni-dimensional measure. These assumptions lead us to the following research questions:

- RQ_1: Are there two dimensions of anthropomorphism?
- RQ_{2a}: Does a robot's intelligence affect mainly UH dimension?
- RQ_{2b}: Does a robot's emotionality affect mainly HN dimension?

2. METHOD

Our study was conducted using a 2x2 between-subjects design: robot's emotionality (emotional vs unemotional) and intelligence (high vs low intelligence). We have measured a robot's anthropomorphism using the scale derived from [16], and attribution of traits for the UH and HN dimensions [15].

2.1 Materials and apparatus

All the questionnaires were conducted using PsychoPy v1.77 [21] that was run on a PC. During the experiment, participants interacted with a NAO - a small humanoid robot. As the robot does not have the capability to express facial expressions, we implemented positive reactions by making characteristic sounds, such as "Yippee", and gestures, such as rising hands. It should be noted that body cues are reported to be more important than facial expressions for discriminability of intense positive and negative emotions [1] as used in this experiment. The negative reactions were represented by negative characteristic sounds, such as "Ohh", and gestures, such as lowering the head and torso. For each feedback provided by a participant the robot's reaction was slightly different. Therefore, there were 5 positive and 5 negative animations that were presented in random order. Unemotionality was implemented by the robot saying "OK" and randomly moving its hands in order to ensure a similar level of animacy as in the emotional conditions. For every utterance made by the participants the robot acted slightly differently.

The robot's responses to the quiz questions were prepared prior to the experiment. The NAO robot was controlled by a wizard sitting behind a curtain and ensuring appropriate reactions. In the intelligent condition, the robot's responses were always correct. In the unintelligent condition they were based on the computer Watson's most probable wrong answers as presented on the second day of "Jeopardy! Watson challenge". We did this in order to ensure that the manipulation of intelligence represents the latest state of the art in AI and even the wrong answers should make sense and be possible. There is definitely a question regarding what is the appropriate level of intelligence of a robot. Previous studies manipulated a robot's intelligence on a very low level, such as following a light [3]. In Wizard-of-Oz type of experiments it is also possible to drift to fictional future where robots can have knowledge far superior than humans with unrestricted access to information. However, we believe that the current state of the art of AI in some conditions allows robots to reach the level of intelligence that is close to human intelligence. Watson's victory in "Jeopardy!" with multi-champion human opponents was an example of this that received a lot of publicity. Watson's responses even if incorrect, were mainly realistic although at times exhibited its non-human nature. As in the near future it will be possible to provide similar level of knowledge to robots, it is important to explore how it is going to affect HRI.

2.2 Measurements

In the experiment we have used several questionnaires as dependent measures. Individual Differences in Anthropomorphism Questionnaire (IDAQ) [26] was used to ensure that participants did not differ in their general tendency to anthropomorphize between the conditions. Participants rated on a Likert scale from 0 (not at all) to 10 (very much) to what extent different non-human objects possess humanlike characteristics (e.g. "To what extent does a tree have a mind of its own?"). We conducted manipulation checks to ensure that we had successfully manipulated the factors. We used the Godspeed perceived intelligence scale [2] for the robot's intelligence, that measures five items on a 5-point Likert scale (e.g. "Please rate your impression of the NAO on these scales: 1 - incompetent, 5 - competent"). The manipulation of the robot's emotionality was measured using the extent to which NAO is capable of experiencing primary emotions [5] that had ten items on a 1 - not at all, to 7 - very much, Likert scale (e.g. "To what extent is the NAO capable of experiencing the following emotion? Joy").

As a uni-dimensional scale of anthropomorphism we used the questionnaire from [16]. It measures six items on a 5-point Likert scale (e.g. "Please rate your impression of the NAO on these scales: 1 - artificial, 5 - natural". We included this scale in order to confirm that both factors affect robots perceived anthropomorphism and investigate the relation between uni- and two-dimensional scales. The two-dimensional scale of anthropomorphism was based on the degree to which participants attributed UH and HN traits to the robot [15]. Both dimensions had 10 items (see Table 1) and were measured together as a single 20-item questionnaire with Likert scale from 1 (not at all) to 7 (very much) (e.g. "The NAO is ... shallow").

Table 1: List of Uniquely Human and Human Nature traits used as a measurement of two dimensions.

Uniquely Human	Human Nature
broadminded	curious
humble	friendly
organized	fun-loving
polite	sociable
thorough	trusting
cold	aggressive
conservative	distractible
hard-hearted	impatient
rude	jealous
shallow	nervous

2.3 Participants

Forty participants were recruited at the University of Canterbury. They were paid by $5 vouchers as time compensation. They were all native or fluent English speakers. This paper is part of a bigger study that also included implicit measurement of anthropomorphism that required exclusion of non-native English speaking participants due to their weaker implicit association for UH and HN traits. In order to keep the results consistent we have discarded the data of these five participants from all the analyses. Out of the remaining 35 participants, 19 were female. There were 24 undergraduate and 8 postgraduate students, 1 staff member and 2 participants not associated with the university. All of them had normal or corrected to normal vision and none of them had ever interacted with a robot. Their ages ranged from 18 to 48 years with a mean age of 26.69. The participants were mostly New Zealanders (28) or British (4). Six participants indicated that they had previously watched a "Jeopardy!" TV show at least once.

2.4 Procedure

Participants were told before the experiment that they would play a quiz with a robot. They entered the experimental room together with the experimenter and were sited in front of a computer. At the other end of the room was sitting NAO. After reading an information sheet about the study and filling out consent forms the participants were asked to answer demographic and IDAQ questionnaires. Then they were informed that they would now interact with the robot. They were told that the robot was called NAO as the word would appear later in the tasks to be completed on the computer, and they would play a quiz based on the "Jeopardy!" TV show. Participants were told that in this game show contestants are presented with general knowledge clues that are formed as answers and they must give their responses in form of a question. Therefore, it does not only require great knowledge, but also good language understanding skills, so it should not be surprising that a computer called Watson that managed to beat human champions in "IBM Challenge" in 2011 was regarded as proof of great progress in AI development. In the game with NAO, participants took the role of the host reading clues to NAO, which took the role of the contestant.

On the standing next to the robot were placed cards with clues and above them categories of clues. On each card, there was also written the correct response. The cards were placed upside-down with clues facing the table. On top of each card was a value of the clues, which was supposed to represent the theoretical difficulty of a question as in the real show. In total there were six categories of clues. All these categories and clues were identical as in the second match of "IBM Challenge". Participants were explained the rules of the game based on an example clue and asked to read the clues at their normal pace. Compared with the original show, they were told that the correct response of the robot must be identical to what was on the paper. Otherwise the response was incorrect, even if the meaning of NAO's response was similar. They were also asked to provide feedback to the robot on whether its response was correct or wrong and then proceed to the next question. After participants confirmed that they understood the instructions they were told that they are assigned to the "EU, the European Union" category, and had to ask five questions from that category in any order they wished and remember how many answers the robot provided correctly. All the participants were assigned to this category in order to ensure that there would be no potential differences in difficulty between the categories. Then the experimenter touched the robot's head and said that he will leave the participant alone with the robot for the task. The wizard started the robot that stood up and introduced itself as NAO. At that point the participants started reading clues for the robot. Depending on the condition the robot either responded correctly or wrongly and waited for a participant's feedback. In emotional condition the positive feedback led to a positive response and a negative feedback to negative response. In unemotional condition the robot always behaved unemotionally. After answering the fifth question, the robot reminded the participants that it was the last question, thanked them for participation, asked them to inform the experimenter who was waiting outside and finally sat down.

When participants called the researcher, they had to say how many times the robot had answered correctly and they were asked to continue the tasks on the computer. Participants completed implicit measurement that is not included in this paper and then filled in the remaining questionnaires. At the end of the experiment they were debriefed and released. The whole procedure took approximately 25 minutes.

3. RESULTS

We have conducted analyses of the data in three steps. Firstly, we checked whether the manipulations introduced in the experiment worked as expected. Secondly, we looked at the factors affecting the robot's anthropomorphism. Thirdly, we investigated the relationships between the measures of anthropomorphism and its dimensionality. The assumptions of all the presented statistical analyses were checked and met, unless otherwise specified.

3.1 Manipulation check

As a pre-assumption the random assignment of subjects to the experimental groups should result in lack of differences in general tendency to anthropomorphize objects between the groups as measured with IDAQ questionnaire. This was confirmed as 2-way ANOVA with intelligence and emotionality conditions as between-subjects factors did not indicate statistically significant differences between the experimental conditions[1] (see Table 2^1 and 3^1). Furthermore, we did not find any interaction effects between IDAQ scores and experimental conditions on measurements of two-dimensional anthropomorphism. Therefore, the general tendency to anthropomorphize was dropped from further analysis.

Furthermore, we have manipulated the robot's emotionality and intelligence and hoped that our manipulation will significantly affect the degree to which a robot is perceived as emotional and intelligent. A robot that expresses emotionality should be attributed more primary emotions, but its perceived intelligence should not be affected by this manipulation. Moreover, manipulation of a robot's intelligence should affect its perceived intelligence, but not attribution of emotions. Since knowledge does not equate to intelligence, it was possible that the robot in unintelligent condition would be perceived simply as less knowledgeable, but not necessarily less intelligent.

Two-way ANOVA with intelligence and emotionality conditions as between-subjects factors showed that there was only the main effect of manipulation of the robot's emotional response on attribution of primary emotions to it (see Table 2^3 and 3^3). The robot was perceived as more emotional when it expressed emotions compared with the condition where its feedback was unemotional.

Similarly, 2-way ANOVA with intelligence and emotionality conditions as between-subjects factors indicated only the main effect of intelligence condition on perceived intelligence of the robot (see Table 2^2 and 3^2). The robot that was in the intelligent condition (provided correct responses) was perceived as significantly more intelligent than when it provided incorrect responses (unintelligent condition). These results indicate that our manipulations were successful and more knowledgeable robot was also perceived as more intelligent.

3.2 Factors of anthropomorphism

In the next stage of the analyses we investigated what factors affect anthropomorphism. First, we analyzed how the

[1]The results of all conducted ANOVAs described in this paper are in Table 2. For the mean scores and standard deviations of all dependent measures please refer to Table 3. In the results section each described statistical test has a reference to the specific row and column in the tables with numeric values that are relevant for that analysis, e.g. see Table 2^1 and 3^1 means that the results of the presented ANOVA can be found in Table 2 row number 1, and mean score and standard deviations are in Table 3 column number 1.

robot's humanlikeness is affected by its intelligence and emotionality using the questionnaire of anthropomorphism. We hypothesized that both factors will significantly affect perceived anthropomorphism. Two-way ANOVA with intelligence and emotionality conditions as between-subjects factors was conducted to establish the impact of these factors on anthropomorphism. Our hypothesis was only partially confirmed. There was a significant main effect of the emotionality condition on perceived anthropomorphism (see Table 2[4] and 3[4]).

A robot was perceived as more anthropomorphic when it provided emotional feedback than when its feedback was unemotional. The main effect of the intelligence condition was not significant. In other words, the robot's intelligence did not affect its perceived anthropomorphism. Furthermore, we did not distinguish between positive and negative emotional responses of the robot, which could potentially be confounded with the intelligence condition. However, the interaction effect between the two factors was not significant, which implies that the type of the emotional response (positive or negative) did affect the perceived humanlikeness.

Second, we analyzed data for two dimensions of anthropomorphism based on studies of dehumanization. Both scales had sufficient reliability: UH Cronbach's $\alpha = .71$ and HN Cronbach's $\alpha = .84$. In particular, we hypothesized that the HN dimension would be affected only by the emotionality factor, but not the intelligence factor. As hypothesized using 2-way ANOVA with intelligence and emotionality conditions as between-subjects factors we found only the main effect of emotionality on HN to be statistically significant (see Table 2[6] and 3[6]). When the robot reacted emotionally it was attributed more HN traits than when it was unemotional as shown on Figure 1.

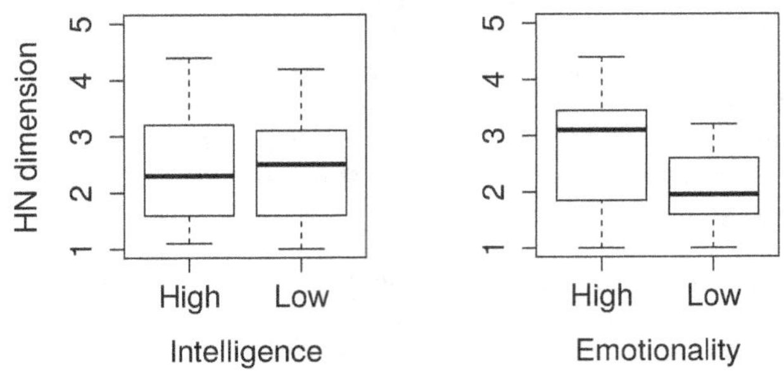

Figure 1: Rating of HN dimension. Attribution of HN traits in experimental conditions for intelligence and emotionality factors.

Similarly, we hypothesized that the UH dimension will be affected only by the intelligence factor, but not emotionality. Our results did not support this hypothesis. Two-way ANOVA with intelligence and emotionality conditions as between-subjects factors showed that neither of the factors, nor the interaction between them significantly affected the attribution of UH traits (see Table 2[5] and 3[5], and Figure 2).

3.3 Relationship between different dimensions

In the following step of the analyses we calculated a single score of the robot's humanlikeness that could exhibit if one of the dimensions is dominant. In order to do that we deducted the HN rating from the UH rating, whereby a positive score means that the robot was anthropomorphised more strongly

Table 2: Results of 2-way ANOVAs with intelligence and emotionality conditions as between-subjects factors for all dependent variables.

	Intelligence				Emotionality				Intelligence * Emotionality			
Measures	df_b	df_w	F	η^2_G	df_b	df_w	F	η^2_G	df_b	df_w	F	η^2_G
[1]IDAQ	1	31	.65	.02	1	31	2.96	.09	1	31	.17	.006
[2]Perceived Intelligence	1	31	28.35***	.48	1	31	2.17	.07	1	31	.2	.006
[3]Emotions	1	31	<.001	<.001	1	31	7.99**	.21	1	31	2.26	.07
[4]Anthropomorphism	1	31	.63	.02	1	31	9.28**	.23	1	31	2.13	.06
[5]UH	1	31	1.62	.05	1	31	.20	.006	1	31	1.6	.05
[6]HN	1	31	.04	.001	1	31	5.28*	.15	1	31	1.42	.04
[7]UH - HN	1	31	1.48	.05	1	31	10.37**	.25	1	31	.002	<.001

*$p < .05$, **$p < .01$, ***$p < .001$

Table 3: Mean scores and standard deviations for dependent measures presented by the levels of experimental conditions.

		[1]IDAQ		[2]Perc. Intel.		[3]Emotions		[4]Anthro.		[5]UH		[6]HN		[7]UH - HN	
Conditions	Levels	M	σ	M	σ	M	σ	M	σ	M	σ	M	σ	M	σ
Emotionality	Low	2.75	1.17	3.59	.93	1.62	.98	1.86	.59	3.11	.92	2.08	.67	1.03	.83
	High	3.45	1.27	3.8	.78	2.86	1.53	2.51	.65	2.92	.89	2.77	1.07	.15	.72
Intelligence	Low	2.99	1.27	3.13	.78	2.38	1.6	2.34	.74	2.82	.88	2.47	1.02	.35	.73
	High	3.26	1.27	4.24	.46	2.22	1.3	2.09	.65	3.18	.9	2.44	.94	.74	.99

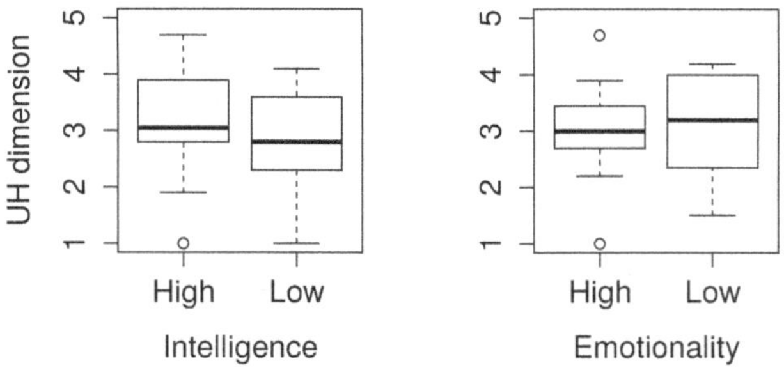

Figure 2: Rating of UH dimension. Attribution of UH traits in experimental conditions for intelligence and emotionality factors.

on the UH dimension and a negative score indicates that the robot was anthropomorphised more strongly on the HN dimension. A score close to 0 indicates that the robot was anthropomorphised equally on both dimensions or it was not anthropomorphised on either of them.

We have conducted another 2-way ANOVA with intelligence and emotionality conditions as between-subjects factors and found only the emotionality condition to significantly affect UH - HN score (see Table 2[7] and 3[7]). A robot that had high emotionality was given a significantly lower score of UH - HN. This supports our hypothesis that a robot that expresses emotions will be anthropomorphised more strongly on the HN dimension. Furthermore, although intelligence did not statistically significantly affect the score, it is worth noting that looking at the mean scores (see Table 3[7]), the data exhibits the opposite trend - increase of a robot's intelligence leads to a higher UH - HN score. That can suggest a closer relation between intelligence and the UH dimension.

Finally, in order to understand better the relation between various dependent variables used in this study we have conducted a series of correlations (see Table 4). Due to the fact that the UH - HN score is a function of UH and HN dimensions we found a strong positive correlation between the UH dimension and the UH - HN score. Similarly, there was a strong negative correlation between HN and the score of difference between the dimensions. What is more interesting is that only HN was significantly and strongly positively correlated with anthropomorphism, but UH was not correlated with the latter. However, for our model the most important is the relation between UH and HN in order to establish whether there are two distinct dimensions of anthropomorphism or only one. We found a strong and highly significant correlation between these two dimensions that could indicate that they are not independent and measure identical constructs.

Based on these results, we have followed our analyses a step further and explored that relation. We divided HN and UH scores into two categories (high vs low) using median splits - scores below the median were qualified as low HN or UH, while the scores above the median formed the high HN and

Table 4: Correlations Between Measures with Pearson's r coefficient.

Measure	UH	HN	Anthro.	UH - HN
UH		$.55^{***}$	.14	$.41^{**}$
HN	$.55^{***}$		$.47^{**}$	$-.53^{***}$
Anthro.	.14	$.47^{**}$		$-.38^{*}$
UH - HN	$.41^{**}$	$-.53^{***}$	$-.38^{*}$	

$^{*}p < .05$, $^{**}p < .01$, $^{***}p < .001$

UH groups. Finally, we correlated the UH and HN scores for each of the categories separately. There was a strongly positive and statistically significant correlation for low HN subjects between their HN and UH scores, r = .67, N = 18, p = .003. However, for high HN subjects their HN and UH scores were not correlated, r = .15, N = 17, p = .58. Similarly, we found a strongly significant and positive correlation for low UH subjects, between their UH and HN scores, r = .65, N = 18, p = .004, but no correlation for high UH subjects between their UH and HN scores, r = .22, N = 17, p = .4. These results indicate that the relation between these two dimensions is not completely straightforward. The dimensions are related for half the subjects, but not the other half, which might indicate that UH and HN do not measure exactly the same aspects of humanlikeness.

Finally, we investigated the dimensionality of anthropomorphism by conducting a confirmatory factor analysis. We have used maximum likelihood estimator in order to establish how well a model with 2 factors (UH and HN) and 10 parameters on each factor can explain the total score of HN and UH. Our two factor model showed bad fit to the data $\chi^2(169, 35) = 358.15$, p < .001; RMSEA = .18; SRMR = .19. However, a single factor model of anthropomorphism was also a bad fit $\chi^2(170, 35) = 370.92$, p < .001, RMSEA = .18, SRMR = .16. This indicates that future studies should have much bigger sample size in order to establish the optimal number of dimensions of anthropomorphism.

4. DISCUSSION

In this study we investigated whether anthropomorphism similar to humanness is a two dimensional rather than unidimensional phenomenon. In particular, we hypothesized that the dimensions of humanness (UH and HN) and the factors that affect them could be used as a model of anthropomorphism for HRI.

Previous studies showed that a robot's intelligence and emotionality affect its perceived life-likeness and humanlikeness. Our study confirmed that a robot that expressed emotions was perceived as more anthropomorphic than when it was reacting unemotionally. However, its intelligence did not affect the measure of anthropomorphism. This result is in contradiction with [3]. We think that different results obtained in these two studies is mainly due to the manipulation used and measurement. Bartneck and colleagues used a very low level of intelligence - following light - by a robot. On the other hand, the intelligence manipulation used in our study represents the latest state of the art in AI and refers to knowledge-based type of intelligence that is specific to humans. It is possible that participants saw the intelligent robot as too intelligent and that led to lower anthropomorphization. In other words, the questions asked in this quiz are not easy to answer even by humans. Therefore, it is possible that participants did not themselves know the answers to some of the questions and perceived the robot as too intelligent for a human being, which would not make it be perceived as more humanlike compared to a robot that answered incorrectly.

However, more plausible explanation is that even in unintelligent condition, the robots responses, although incorrect, still made sense and were possible rather than being completely random. In that sense, the robot still expressed high communication skills and good understanding of human language. Although in the intelligent condition it was perceived as more intelligent, it is possible that in the unintelligent condition its responses were humanlike enough for subjects to anthropomorphize it. This explanation is further supported by the fact that even in highly emotional condition, the robot was still stronger anthropomorphised on UH than HN dimension as indicated by mean UH - HN scores that never drop below 0. That means that irrespective of the experimental conditions participants attributed more UH than HN traits to the robot.

The second big difference between Bartneck et al. [3] study and ours is the measurement of anthropomorphism. We measured the robot's humanlikeness using a questionnaire, whereas in the other study anthropomorphism was measured by the number of hits inflicted upon the robot that was supposed to be killed. However, the higher tendency to kill a robot under certain conditions does not necessarily mean that it is perceived as more anthropomorphic, but animate. Therefore, although intelligence can make a robot more lifelike, it does not necessarily make it more humanlike. There could be different factors affecting these two phenomena. It is possible that intelligence may be less important as a factor of anthropomorphism in the context of robotics as people can expect them to be intelligent. As such, there could be a high anthropomorphism baseline that includes high intelligence expectations, which cannot be easily exceeded.

The analyses of two dimensions of anthropomorphism provided only a partial confirmation for our hypothesis for RQ_1. The HN dimension, also known as Experience, was only affected by the robot's emotionality, but not intelligence. This finding is consistent with previous work on dehumanization (e.g. [13]), but it contradicts previous work in HRI [6] who found no difference between the two dimensions as dependent variables. The second dimension - UH (Agency) was supposed to be influenced by intelligence; however in our study neither of these factors had influence on it. Intelligence did not have an effect on anthropomorphism measured on either a uni-dimensional or two-dimensional scale.

It is possible that other factors affect stronger the UH dimension, such as intentionality or communication capabilities [13]. Therefore, future studies should explore further the role of agency and its different sub-factors in order to understand better its outcomes in HRI. An alternative explanation could be that only the factors from one dimension (HN) play a role in a robot's perceived humanlikeness. HN is the dimension that is supposed to distinguish humans from automata [13]. It is possible that only the factors from this dimension affect a robot's anthropomorphism. In particular, intelligence did not significantly affect anthropomorphism, which can mean that dehumanization is not necessarily the reverse process to anthropomorphism. This emphasizes the need for researchers to be considerate when applying findings from research of dehumanization in the context of robotics.

However, even if the model of humanness cannot be directly applied to anthropomorphism it is possible that both are multi-dimensional phenomena. We believe that although our results cannot provide the definite answer due to limited impact of intelligence on humanlikeness, they are promising enough to spur further research on this topic. Our data showed that the robot's emotional capabilities made it being anthropomorphised stronger on the HN dimension. Although not statistically significant, we have noticed the opposite trend for the intelligence that affected mainly the UH dimension. This kind of different form of anthropomorphization cannot be distinguished using only uni-dimensional measurement tools of anthropomorphism. However, in order to fully benefit from such a distinction it is necessary to research what are different consequences for HRI depending on how a robot is being anthropomorphised. In our future research we plan to address the question of whether people will have different mental models of a robot and behave differently when interacting with it, similarly to their changed behaviour towards dehumanized others, e.g. [10, 13].

Apart from investigating further what factors affect anthropomorphism, and how and what are its consequences, it is crucial to investigate their existence and the relationship between them. In order for anthropomorphism to be at least two-dimensional, it is necessary for the dimensions to be to a certain degree independent. If both dimensions measured the same, there would be hardly any potential benefit of measuring anthropomorphism on these dimensions rather than using uni-dimensional scales. However, our data not only suggested different effects of independent variables on two-dimensions of anthropomorphism, but also showed that these dimensions are at least partially independent. The initial correlation between UH and HN dimensions was significant. However, further analyses revealed that they are only correlated when a robot was attributed no or few characteristics of these dimensions. On the other hand, when the robot was anthropomorphised on either of the dimensions, they were independent.

In summary, we believe that a question of dimensionality of anthropomorphism should receive further attention by the HRI community. It can not only help us to understand better what are the factors affecting a robot's perceived humanlikeness, but also to measure more accurately how it is being anthropomorphised. Ultimately, HRI can be improved by attributing a robot only with humanlike characteristics that can facilitate the interaction and avoiding implementing human attributes that could hamper it.

5. ACKNOWLEDGMENTS

The authors would like to thank Dieta Kuchenbrandt and anonymous reviewers for invaluable feedback that made this paper more compelling and interesting. Furthermore, we thank Anthony Poncet, Eduardo Sandoval and Jürgen Brandstetter for help with running the experiment.

6. REFERENCES

[1] H. Aviezer, Y. Trope, and A. Todorov. Body cues, not facial expressions, discriminate between intense positive and negative emotions. *Science*, 338(6111):1225–1229, Nov. 2012.

[2] C. Bartneck, D. Kulic, E. Croft, and S. Zoghbi. Measurement instruments for the anthropomorphism, animacy, likeability, perceived intelligence, and perceived safety of robots. *International Journal of Social Robotics*, 1(1):71 – 81, 2009.

[3] C. Bartneck, M. Verbunt, O. Mubin, and A. Al Mahmud. To kill a mockingbird robot. In *HRI 2007 - Proceedings of the 2007 ACM/IEEE Conference on Human-Robot Interaction - Robot as Team Member*, pages 81 – 87, Arlington, VA, United states, 2007.

[4] N. Epley, A. Waytz, and J. T. Cacioppo. On seeing human: A three-factor theory of anthropomorphism. *Psychological Review*, 114(4):864–886, Oct. 2007.

[5] F. Eyssel, F. Hegel, G. Horstmann, and C. Wagner. Anthropomorphic inferences from emotional nonverbal cues: A case study. In *Proceedings - IEEE International Workshop on Robot and Human Interactive Communication*, pages 646 – 651, Viareggio, Italy, 2010.

[6] F. Eyssel, D. Kuchenbrandt, and S. Bobinger. Effects of anticipated human-robot interaction and predictability of robot behavior on perceptions of anthropomorphism. In *HRI 2011 - Proceedings of the 6th ACM/IEEE International Conference on Human-Robot Interaction*, pages 61 – 67, Lausanne, Switzerland, 2011.

[7] K. Fischer, K. S. Lohan, and K. Foth. Levels of embodiment: Linguistic analyses of factors influencing HRI. In *HRI'12 - Proceedings of the 7th Annual ACM/IEEE International Conference on Human-Robot Interaction*, pages 463–470, 2012.

[8] B. Friedman, P. H. Kahn,Jr., and J. Hagman. Hardware companions?: what online AIBO discussion forums reveal about the human-robotic relationship. In *Proceedings of the SIGCHI Conference on Human Factors in Computing Systems*, CHI '03, pages 273–280, New York, NY, USA, 2003. ACM.

[9] H. M. Gray, K. Gray, and D. M. Wegner. Dimensions of mind perception. *Science*, 315(5812):619, 2007.

[10] K. Gray and D. Wegner. Moral typecasting: Divergent perceptions of moral agents and moral patients. *Journal of Personality and Social Psychology*, 96(3):505–520, 2009.

[11] K. Gray and D. Wegner. Feeling robots and human zombies: Mind perception and the uncanny valley. *Cognition*, 125(1):125–130, 2012.

[12] S. Guthrie. *Faces in the clouds: A new theory of religion*. Oxford University Press, USA, 1995.

[13] N. Haslam. Dehumanization: An integrative review. *Personality and Social Psychology Review*, 10(3):252–264, 2006.

[14] N. Haslam, B. Bastian, S. Laham, and S. Loughnan. Humanness, dehumanization, and moral psychology. 2012.

[15] N. Haslam, S. Loughnan, Y. Kashima, and P. Bain. Attributing and denying humanness to others. *European Review of Social Psychology*, 19(1):55–85, 2009.

[16] C. Ho and K. MacDorman. Revisiting the uncanny valley theory: Developing and validating an alternative to the godspeed indices. *Computers in Human Behavior*, 26(6):1508–1518, 2010.

[17] D. Kuchenbrandt, F. Eyssel, S. Bobinger, and M. Neufeld. When a robot's group membership matters. *International Journal of Social Robotics*, 5(3):409–417, 2013.

[18] J. H. Lesher et al. *Xenophanes of Colophon: Fragments: A Text and Translation With a Commentary*, volume 4. University of Toronto Press, 2001.

[19] J. Leyens, P. Paladino, R. Rodriguez-Torres, J. Vaes, S. Demoulin, A. Rodriguez-Perez, and R. Gaunt. The emotional side of prejudice: The attribution of secondary emotions to ingroups and outgroups. *Personality and Social Psychology Review*, 4(2):186–197, 2000.

[20] M. Mori. The uncanny valley. *Energy*, 7(4):33–35, 1970.

[21] J. W. Peirce. PsychoPy-psychophysics software in python. *Journal of neuroscience methods*, 162(1):8–13, 2007.

[22] M. Salem, F. Eyssel, K. Rohlfing, S. Kopp, and F. Joublin. *Effects of gesture on the perception of psychological anthropomorphism: A case study with a humanoid robot*, volume 7072 LNAI of *Lecture Notes in Computer Science (including subseries Lecture Notes in Artificial Intelligence and Lecture Notes in Bioinformatics)*. 2011.

[23] V. K. Sims, M. G. Chin, H. C. Lum, L. Upham-Ellis, T. Ballion, and N. C. Lagattuta. Robots' auditory cues are subject to anthropomorphism. In *Proceedings of the Human Factors and Ergonomics Society*, volume 3, pages 1418–1421, 2009.

[24] M. L. Walters, D. S. Syrdal, K. L. Koay, K. Dautenhahn, and R. Te Boekhorst. Human approach distances to a mechanical-looking robot with different robot voice styles. In *Proceedings of the 17th IEEE International Symposium on Robot and Human Interactive Communication, RO-MAN*, pages 707–712, 2008.

[25] E. Wang, C. Lignos, A. Vatsal, and B. Scassellati. Effects of head movement on perceptions of humanold robot behavior. In *HRI 2006: Proceedings of the 2006 ACM Conference on Human-Robot Interaction*, volume 2006, pages 180–185, 2006.

[26] A. Waytz, J. Cacioppo, and N. Epley. Who sees human? the stability and importance of individual differences in anthropomorphism. *Perspectives on Psychological Science*, 5(3):219–232, 2010.

[27] A. Waytz, N. Epley, and J. T. Cacioppo. Social cognition unbound: Insights into anthropomorphism and dehumanization. *Current Directions in Psychological Science*, 19(1):58–62, 2010.

Marhaba, how may I help you? Effects of Politeness and Culture on Robot Acceptance and Anthropomorphization

Maha Salem
Carnegie Mellon University in Qatar
P.O. Box 24866
Doha, Qatar
MahaSalem@web.de

Micheline Ziadee
Carnegie Mellon University in Qatar
P.O. Box 24866
Doha, Qatar
michelinekz@gmail.com

Majd Sakr
Carnegie Mellon University in Qatar
P.O. Box 24866
Doha, Qatar
msakr@qatar.cmu.edu

ABSTRACT

How do politeness strategies and cultural aspects affect robot acceptance and anthropomorphization across native speakers of English and Arabic? Previous work in cross-cultural HRI studies has mostly focused on Western and East Asian cultures. In contrast, Middle Eastern attitudes and perceptions of robot assistants are a barely researched topic. We investigated culture-specific determinants of robot acceptance and anthropomorphization by conducting a between-subjects study in Qatar. A total of 92 native speakers of either English or Arabic interacted with a receptionist robot in two different interaction tasks. We further manipulated the robot's verbal behavior in experimental sub-groups to explore different politeness strategies. Our results suggest that Arab participants perceived the robot more positively and anthropomorphized it more than English speaking participants. In addition, the use of positive politeness strategies and the change of interaction task had an effect on participants' HRI experience. Our findings complement the existing body of cross-cultural HRI research with a Middle Eastern perspective that will help to inform the design of robots intended for use in cross-cultural, multi-lingual settings.

Keywords

Cross-cultural HRI studies, Communication Style, Natural Language Dialogue, Politeness Theory

1. INTRODUCTION

Interactive service robots are increasingly being employed to provide people with information in public settings, e.g. at reception desks or information booths. As these domains target a diverse range of human interlocutors of different ages and educational backgrounds, one major challenge in designing such robots is the adaptation to different user profiles and expectations. In more international settings such as airports or museums that host visitors from a variety of countries, these challenges take on a whole new dimension by requiring the robot's appearance, non-verbal behaviors and multilingual skills to be appealing and acceptable to users of different cultural backgrounds.

HRI'14, March 3–6, 2014, Bielefeld, Germany.

ACM 978-1-4503-2658-2/14/03 ...$15.00.
http://dx.doi.org/10.1145/2559636.2559683.

Most existing cross-cultural studies in human-robot interaction (HRI) investigate salient cultural differences between Western (e.g. America, Europe) and East Asian (e.g. Japan, China, Korea) groups of participants, e.g. [2, 5], typically highlighting major differences regarding user expectations, perceptions and acceptance of robots. For example, religion is believed to influence cultural views and acceptance of robots; Buddhism attributes soul and spirits to both living and non-living creatures, thereby possibly facilitating robots' acceptance in East Asian societies [12]. In contrast, the strong influence of Christianity on Western culture, which holds a clear distinction between objects that do or do not have a soul, may increase the emotional distance between humans and humanlike machines [2].

Only very little research has focused on the study of Middle Eastern attitudes regarding social robots. But since the culture in this region differs substantially from both Western and East Asian cultures, findings and implications from other studies cannot be easily transferred. Moreover, people in the Middle East and other Arabic speaking countries – although commonly labeled as "Arabs" – historically represent very diverse groups of cultural and religious beliefs. In addition, each Arab country (or even region within it) has its own dialect used in everyday communication, while Modern Standard Arabic (MSA) is typically used in formal settings only, e.g. in political speeches or by news presenters. Thus it is difficult to make predictions regarding user expectations and acceptance of robots in these societies. For example, given a strong influence of Islamic culture, which traditionally discourages the depiction of living beings as this is seen as mimicking God by adopting the role of creator, negative attitudes towards humanoid robots may be suspected [15].

In light of these challenges, designing robotic assistants that are intended to serve a broad mass of Arabic speaking nationals is not a straightforward task. In addition, by attempting to target both Arabic and English native speakers in multi-cultural settings as found in the Gulf region, which hosts expatriates from many different countries, the complexity of the endeavor increases. Our work therefore aims to examine cross-cultural differences between Arabic and English native speakers by means of what presumably represents the largest HRI experiment conducted in the Middle East to date. We invited a total of 92 participants from these two cultural groups to interact with a bilingual receptionist robot at Carnegie Mellon University (CMU) in Qatar, in order to investigate factors that may affect robot perception and acceptance of HRI. Our findings will help to inform the design of service robots that can be employed in multi-cultural settings including Arabic speaking audiences.

2. BACKGROUND AND MOTIVATION

Our work draws inspiration from previous research in HRI, anthropology, linguistics and social psychology, and combines them in an interdisciplinary approach. Relevant background information that motivates our work and informed the design of our experiment is summarized in the following.

2.1 Cross-Cultural Differences in HRI

A number of studies have investigated the impact of cultural background on HRI (e.g. [2, 5]), concluding that people from different cultures are likely to respond differently to robots. However, most cross-cultural HRI studies typically focused on Western versus East Asian cultures; in contrast, only little research has been carried out with regard to Middle Eastern attitudes and expectations with regard to robots that are to be integrated into human society.

One of the first – and to date most comprehensive – HRI studies targeting cultural attitudes towards robots in an Arabic speaking country was conducted by Riek et al. [15]. The Ibn Sina humanoid robot, modeled after a famous Islamic philosopher and doctor, was placed in a mall in the UAE where people were invited to interact with it; subsequently, they filled out a questionnaire evaluating their interaction experience and perception of the robot. Although exploratory in nature and mainly comparing ethnic groups from within the region, the study indicates that Arabs generally had positive views on the robot. However, it remains unclear whether this observation was linked to the famous personality that the robot depicted, or whether the respondents' opinions were based on their general concepts of robots. Importantly though, the results showed that Arab participants from the Gulf region (e.g. UAE, Qatar, Saudi Arabia, Yemen) expressed significantly more favorable views with regard to humanoid robots than participants who originate from African regions (e.g. Egypt, Morocco, Tunisia, Libya). These findings highlight potential intra-group differences amplifying the challenge of designing robots that are to interact with Arabs from a variety of different countries.

In a previous study conducted in Qatar with the same robot platform used in the present work, Makatchev et al. [11] investigated how ethnically salient verbal and nonverbal behaviors such as facial appearance can be used to evoke ethnic attributions to a robot character. The results suggested that the robot's perceived ethnicity was more evident for attributions as a native speaker of English rather than a native speaker of Arabic. However, we speculate that this effect may have been caused by the fact that interactions with the robot took place in English only, both for participants of English speaking and Arabic speaking background. Another limitation of the study was the required typed entry of user utterances, which limited participants' perceptions of the robot during interaction. Therefore, our present experiment draws upon the insights from this study and overcomes its limitations by allowing for natural spoken user input and by providing an Arabic speaking version of the robot for Arab participants in addition to the version that interacts with English native speakers using American English.

2.2 Politeness as a Communication Facilitator

Relevant literature in linguistics and cultural anthropology suggests that cultural differences are reflected in different communication styles [14]. Asian and Arabic cultures, for example, are high-context, i.e. people from such cultures are not as verbally direct as people from low-context cultures (e.g. Germans); a substantial part of the delivered message is understood from non-verbal cues and indirect speech, thus decoding the message relies heavily on observing subtle, paralinguistic and context-related cues [20]. In contrast, speakers from low-context cultures tend to code the meaning and intent of a message within the words of the utterance themselves, without relying on paralinguistic aspects to explain the message. As a result, modeling communication styles for a multilingual robot that is intended to address a variety of cultural nationals requires careful consideration.

Claimed to apply universally to dialog across all languages and cultures [3], politeness theory appears like a reasonable starting point to explore and develop cross-culturally acceptable robot behavior. In their seminal work, Brown and Levinson [3] developed their theory around the notion of 'face' which each social actor possesses. As face represents a public image that we seek to protect, any acts that undermine that image are considered face-threatening acts (FTAs). The role of politeness is to mitigate such acts and minimize their threat, which is achieved through four types of strategies employed in communication: *bald on record* (direct strategy, i.e. no attempts to minimize threats to the hearer's face: e.g. "close the window"), *positive politeness* (avoid giving offense by highlighting common ground and friendliness: e.g. "let's close the window, please"), *negative politeness* (avoid giving offense by showing consideration: e.g. "would you mind closing the window?") and *off-record* (indirect strategy: e.g. "it's cold in here"). The choice of strategy depends on factors like social distance and power relations between the interaction partners as well as the extent to which the act is face-threatening.

However, although politeness theory is believed to be universally valid, different cultures may attribute different degrees of face-threat to a potential FTA. In fact, research in the areas of cross-cultural linguistics and pragmatics reveals the existence of cultural differences in peoples' evaluation of and preference for certain politeness strategies. For example, in a study comparing speakers of American English to speakers of Saudi Arabic, Tawalbeh and Al-Oqaily [19] found that speakers of American English preferred the *conventional indirectness* politeness strategy (e.g. by saying "can you close the window, please?") when addressing their inferiors, and only used the direct strategy ("close the window") in cases of close intimacy between speakers and when the speaker's request had a low imposition rate. Regardless of the weight of the imposition, Saudi Arabic speakers, in contrast, used conventional indirectness when addressing superiors and preferred to use the direct strategy when addressing inferiors and friends. Comparing politeness strategies used by speakers of Australian English to those of Palestinian Arabic, Farahat [7] states that members of the first group preferred conventional indirectness while those of the second group opted for "the strategy of apologizing". His findings further reveal that Australian and Palestinian cultures share similar concepts of face – one that is connected with 'respect', 'honor' and 'dignity' – but differ in their understandings of what causes loss and enhancement of face.

In view of these aspects, we assume that the use of politeness strategies can lead to an enhanced HRI experience for users from different cultural groups. But are politeness strategies equally useful in different interaction contexts? For example, when asking a robot for directions, should it be apologetic or direct about the fact that it does not know the answer? And should the robot use the same strategies in a less goal-directed interaction like a small talk conversation? To address these questions, our experimental design incorporates a manipulation of the robot's politeness strategy in two experimental conditions for each cultural group.

2.3 Group Membership as a Predictor of Anthropomorphism

Social psychological research has shown that humans intuitively use cues like a person's ethnicity, age or gender to form impressions of others and categorize them as in-group or out-group members; this, in turn, may result in in-group bias which evokes favorable attitudes, perceptions and behaviors towards members of one's own group [18]. More specifically, Haslam et al. [10] argue that the perception of out-group members as less than human, i.e. *dehumanization*, is an everyday phenomenon, e.g. reflected in abusive language that likens other people to nonhuman entities.

Eyssel and Kuchenbrandt [6] employ such measures established for the study of dehumanization in humans conversely to assess the extent to which a robot is *anthropomorphized*, i.e. viewed as humanlike. In their study, they showed German students identical pictures of a robot, however, half the participants were told that it had been developed in Germany and was called Armin (a German first name). The other participants were told the robot's name was Arman (a typical Turkish name) and that it had been developed at a Turkish university. The students who evaluated the supposedly German-built robot Armin were found to rate it more favorably and anthropomorphized it more than the students who evaluated the supposedly Turkish-built Arman. The authors conclude that humans apply social categorization processes and show a preferential inter-group bias even with regard to a robot: they see it as more human if they believe it shares a common cultural or ethnical background.

These findings led us to predict that the level to which our participants will anthropomorphize the robot will depend on and correlate with their perception of it as an in-group vs. out-group member of their own respective cultural group.

3. METHOD

We conducted an experiment to gain a deeper understanding of how politeness and interaction context might impact and shape human experience and evaluation of HRI, and how these perceptions may vary between participants of two very different cultural backgrounds.

3.1 Hypotheses

Based on findings from related work on cross-cultural studies, anthropomorphism and politeness strategies, we developed four main hypotheses for our experiment:

1. *Effect of condition.* Regardless of the participants' cultural background, manipulation of the robot's politeness strategy will affect
   (a) their perception of the robot and the interaction (subjective assessment of HRI).
   (b) their performance at recalling the route directions presented by the robot (objective assessment of HRI).
2. *Effect of HRI task.* The change of HRI context from goal-oriented interaction (*Task 1*) to open dialogue (*Task 2*) will affect participants' perception of the robot and subjective assessment of HRI.
3. *Effect of cultural background.* Participants' cultural background will affect their perception of the robot and subjective assessment of HRI. In particular, we predict that Arabic participants will have a stronger preference for the polite robot than participants from the group of English native speakers.
4. *Effect of group membership on anthropomorphic inferences.* If one cultural group is found to have a stronger perception of the robot as an in-group member, the same group will be found to make greater anthropomorphic inferences regarding the robot than participants from the other cultural group with weaker perceptions of the robot's in-group membership.

3.2 Experimental Design

We conducted a between-subjects study in which participants interacted with the Hala receptionist robot [17], which consists of a stationary anthropomorphic torso with a screen mounted on a pan-tilt unit (see **Fig. 1a**).

Two language groups were tested: English native speakers and Arabic native speakers. Participants of each respective group interacted with the robot either in English or in Arabic language. For this purpose, the verbal interaction content to be used by the robot during the experiment as well as questionnaires for data collection were translated from English into Arabic by an accredited translator.

For each language group, we further manipulated the *politeness level* of the robot's verbal behaviors in two experimental conditions to measure how this manipulation might impact participants' task performance, perception of the robot and HRI experience in general and with regard to culture-specific differences. Our manipulations were informed by the theoretical framework provided by Brown and Levinson [3], as well as by results from previous experiments using the Hala platform, especially [11]. Specifically, our 'polite' condition was designed to follow the principle of *positive politeness*, while the control condition was inspired by the *bald on record* strategy. To additionally validate their effectiveness, verbal stimuli for the two conditions were evaluated prior to running the experiment by means of two online

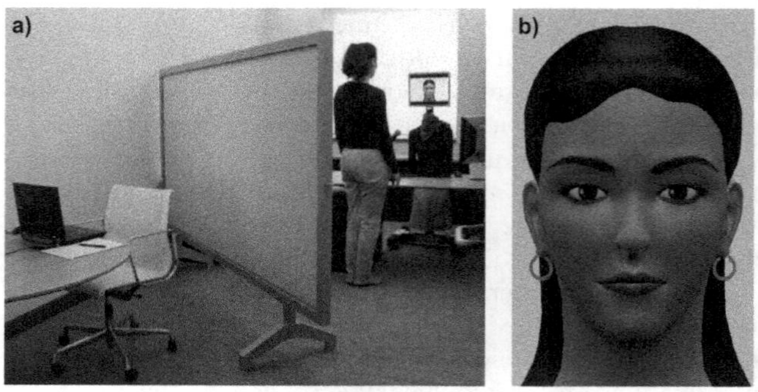

Figure 1: a) Experimental setting; b) the robot's facial expression set to neutral.

questionnaires (one for English, one for Arabic). Each questionnaire comprised the original audio files to be uttered by the robot in the respective language, organized in 32 pairs of utterances which could be replayed with a mouse click. For each language group, 13 independent raters – qualified as native speakers of the corresponding language – were asked to identify the polite version of each of the 32 pairs, resulting in an overall inter-rater agreement of 86.84 % for the English stimulus content and of 87.37 % for the Arabic material.

The robot's face, providing the main channel for the expression of non-verbal behaviors such as emotions, remained identical across conditions and was set to a neutral facial expression as shown in **Fig. 1b**. Visemes were generated to accompany the robot's speech output, for which the Acapela text-to-speech system [1] was used to produce utterances in American English and in Modern Standard Arabic (MSA). The decision to refrain from using gaze and emotional display via facial expressions was motivated by the objective to focus on the verbal interaction level, in order to avoid effects caused by possible interactions between the two modalities.

The experiment comprised two consecutive tasks, each representing a different HRI context as follows.

3.2.1 Direction-giving task

In the first interaction task, participants were given a list with names of three locations in a fictitious building and were instructed to ask the robot for directions to these places. The robot's verbal utterances varied across experimental conditions for dialogue acts of greeting, direction-giving as well as handling failure and disagreement when giving directions. The robot first greeted the participant either with the phrase "Hello, how may I help you?" in the polite condition group or only with the word "Hello" in the control group. Participants were instructed to then ask for directions to Dr. Miller's office, which consisted of five steps (e.g. "turn right", "walk straight until you reach a fountain") and varied across the two conditions based on the use of politeness markers such as "please" or "you will want to turn right" as opposed to "turn right". Since we used participants' ability to recall these directions to measure their task performance, the directions were pretested to be feasible but not trivial to remember. For the second location on the list, participants had to ask the robot for directions to the bookshop, which triggered the robot's failure handling behavior. In the polite condition the robot responded with "Sorry, I don't know where it is, because I am new" in contrast to the response "I have absolutely no idea" in the control condition. Finally, for the third location, participants had to ask for the cafeteria and were instructed to imagine that they misunderstood the robot after being given the directions by asking to clarify if they should "turn left?". This triggered the robot's disagreement handling behavior: in the polite condition, this resulted in the response "Yes, *turn right*", i.e. avoiding explicit disagreement as would be expected in high-context cultures; in contrast, in the control condition the response was "*No*, turn right". The robot's response to the participant's final utterance (typically a variation of "thank you" or "goodbye") did not differ across conditions and was either "you're welcome" or "goodbye" as appropriate.

3.2.2 Chitchat task

For the second interaction, participants were instructed to have an open conversation with the robot, but they were informed that the robot's knowledge was still under development and thus limited. In reality, restricting the robot's knowledge base was an experimental design choice made to ensure a comparable interaction experience across participants. Following a short greeting ("Hello. It's nice to meet you! How are you?" in the polite versus "Hello. How are you?" in the control condition), participants could ask the robot any questions they liked. If the knowledge base did not provide an answer to a question asked, the robot responded by outlining some topics available for discussion (e.g. "Unfortunately, I have no reply to this question. How about talking about Qatar, Carnegie Mellon University, my job or my hobbies, instead?" in the polite condition versus "I have no reply to this question. We can talk about Qatar, Carnegie Mellon University, my job, and my hobbies, instead" in the control condition). As with the first task, the robot's verbal utterances varied across the two conditions based on the use (or lack) of politeness markers such as "please" when asking the participant for something and "I'm very sorry" or "unfortunately" when handling failure to respond.

Depending on the language group to which the respective participant belonged, the robot spoke either in English or Arabic throughout both interaction tasks. We deliberately refrained from randomizing the order of the two interactions tasks, as the unstructured nature of the chitchat task could result in substantial differences in participants' initial perceptions of the robot depending on how the interaction proceeded and what dialogue content was triggered. This impression, in turn, could then affect participants' assessments of the robot after the more structured direction-giving task.

3.3 Experimental Procedure

The experiment was conducted in a closed office room on the CMU campus in Qatar. Using a movable wall (see Fig. 1a), the interaction area was separated from the table at which participants filled out questionnaires. Participants were tested individually in their native language (English or Arabic). They were first greeted by the experimenter outside the room where they received a brief description of the experimental process. After reviewing and signing the consent form, they were asked to fill out a short questionnaire recording their demographic background and previous experience with robots and technology. Participants were then introduced to the first interaction, the *direction-giving task*. Following this task, participants were asked to sit at a laptop provided on the table in the same room and to fill out a questionnaire evaluating the robot and their HRI experience. Upon completion, participants received instructions for the second interaction, the *chitchat task*. After the second interaction, they were asked to fill out another questionnaire on the laptop to document their interaction experience.

To ensure minimal variability in the experimental procedure while allowing for interaction based on natural speech, which is not currently supported by the system, the robot was controlled using a Wizard-Of-Oz technique [9] during the study. The experimenter initiated the robot's verbal interaction behavior from a selection of pre-determined utterances. The ordering of the utterance sequence remained identical for each experimental run within the same condition group for the first task (*direction-giving*), but differed for the second task (*chitchat*) depending on the participants' input. The entire interaction was recorded using a microphone and a voice recorder, while the experimenter listened to and controlled the interaction from an adjacent room.

The second questionnaire was followed by an interview in which the experimenter invited participants to describe and comment on their experience in response to open-ended questions. After the interview, participants were carefully debriefed about the purpose of the experiment and received a tartlet as a thank-you before being dismissed. The total experiment time was approximately 30 minutes, including about 7 to 10 minutes interaction time with the robot.

3.4 Dependent Measures

Dependent variables comprised a number of **subjective measures** based on two questionnaires (one after each interaction task). These were used to tap various dimensions of HRI including participants' perception of the robot, their general HRI experience and their enjoyment of and involvement in the interaction tasks. Five-point Likert scales were used, with high values indicating high agreement with the assessed items. To compute indices for the proposed dependent measures, scores of the included items were averaged after conducting reliability analyses (Cronbach's α).

Politeness We measured perceived politeness of the robot based on two items: 'the robot is polite' as well as the reversely coded ratings of 'the robot is rude' ($\alpha = .742$). This measure served as a manipulation check to verify that our manipulations of the robot's verbal behaviors were effective.

Competency Participants were asked to report how they rated the following competency-related attributes with regard to the robot: 'competent', 'helpful', 'effective', 'cooperative', 'organized' and 'intelligent' ($\alpha = .879$).

Extroversion The degree of extroversion with regard to the robot's personality was assessed using four traits: 'extrovert', 'outgoing', 'sociable', and 'fun-loving' ($\alpha = .809$).

Warmth We measured perceptions of the robot's interpersonal warmth, a core dimension of human social cognition [8], by using the reversely coded ratings of the six items 'cold', 'hardhearted', 'shallow', 'aggressive', 'rude' and 'impatient' ($\alpha = .783$). Since these items were adapted from measures of typically human traits proposed by Haslam et al [10], the warmth index can be used as an indicator of anthropomorphization in HRI (see, for example, [16]).

Psychological Closeness We administered the three items 'How close do you feel to the robot', 'How much do you think you have in common with the robot?', and 'How pleasant was the interaction with the robot for you?' ($\alpha = .812$) to assess participants' degree of psychological closeness to the robot [4]. This index taps perceptions of similarity with the robot and thereby covers further aspects of anthropomorphization as well as HRI acceptance.

After each interaction, participants were asked to specify which nationality they thought the robot represents; this data was collected using open-ended questions. To investigate participants' assessments of the *robot's group membership*, answers were coded in a binary fashion with 0 = robot does not represent a national from the same native language group as the participant's and 1 = robot represents a member of the same native language group as the participant's.

In addition to these subjective measures, assessment of *task performance* based on participants' ability to recall the directions to Dr. Miller's office was used as an **objective measure** (with binary values 0 = incorrect and 1 = correct).

3.5 Participation

A total of 92 participants took part in the experiment, comprising 44 English native speakers (24m, 20f) and 48 native speakers of Arabic (24m, 24f). Participants in the English native speaker group (in the following referred to as *En*) originated from or had spent major periods of their lives in the US, Canada, UK or Australia. The group of Arabic native speakers (further referred to as *Ar*) comprised nationals from Qatar, Egypt, Tunisia, Lebanon, Syria, Jordan, Morocco and UAE. Participants ranged in age from 18 to 70 years ($M = 33.84$ years, $SD = 11.84$) and were recruited at CMU in Qatar. Based on five-point Likert scale ratings (1 = *very little*, 5 = *very much*), they were identified as having negligible experience with robots ($M = 1.96$, $SD = 1.07$) and advanced skills regarding technology and computer use ($M = 4.28$, $SD = 0.91$). Within their respective language group (i.e. English or Arabic), participants were randomly assigned to one of two experimental conditions that manipulated the politeness level of the robot's verbal behaviors, while maintaining gender- and age-balanced distributions.

4. RESULTS

We conducted repeated-measures ANOVA to compare participants' ratings after interaction task 1 and 2, using the between-subjects factors 'culture' (En vs. Ar), 'condition' (polite vs. control) and 'gender' (male vs. female).

Results confirmed that the manipulation of *politeness* level of the robot's verbal utterances had a highly significant effect on participants' ratings of how polite they found the robot, $F(1{,}84) = 18.96$, $p < .001$, $\eta^2 = .18$, with higher ratings from participants in the polite compared to the control condition for both interactions. In addition, the manipulation of the robot's politeness strategy yielded a significant effect of culture, $F(1{,}84) = 9.31$, $p = .003$, $\eta^2 = .10$, with Ar participants generally rating the robot as more polite than En participants (**Fig. 2a**). There was a significant interaction effect between the task and gender $F(1{,}84) = 4.10$, $p = .046$, $\eta^2 = .05$: female participants rated the robot as less polite after the first task than male participants; however, they gave it higher ratings for perceived politeness after the second task compared to their male counterparts whose ratings dropped after the second interaction round (**Fig. 2b**).

Our analysis showed a main effect of interaction task on the robot's perceived *competency*, $F(1{,}84) = 6.73$, $p = .011$, $\eta^2 = .07$: participants of both cultural groups found the robot generally more competent after the first interaction task involving direction-giving than after the second task comprising the chitchat interaction (**Fig. 2c**). Between-groups comparisons yielded a highly significant main effect of participants' cultural background on ratings of the robot's competency, $F(1{,}84) = 14.36$, $p < .001$, $\eta^2 = .15$: Ar participants perceived the robot generally as more competent than En participants (**Fig. 2d**).

There was a highly significant main effect of HRI task on participants' ratings of the robot's level of *extroversion*, $F(1{,}84) = 41.54$, $p < .001$, $\eta^2 = .33$: participants of both cultural groups perceived the robot as more extrovert after the second (chitchat) interaction than after the first (direction-giving) task (**Fig. 2e**). A significant interaction effect on ratings of the robot's perceived level of extroversion was found between participants' cultural background and gender, $F(1{,}84) = 4.79$, $p = .031$, $\eta^2 = .05$: En males rated the

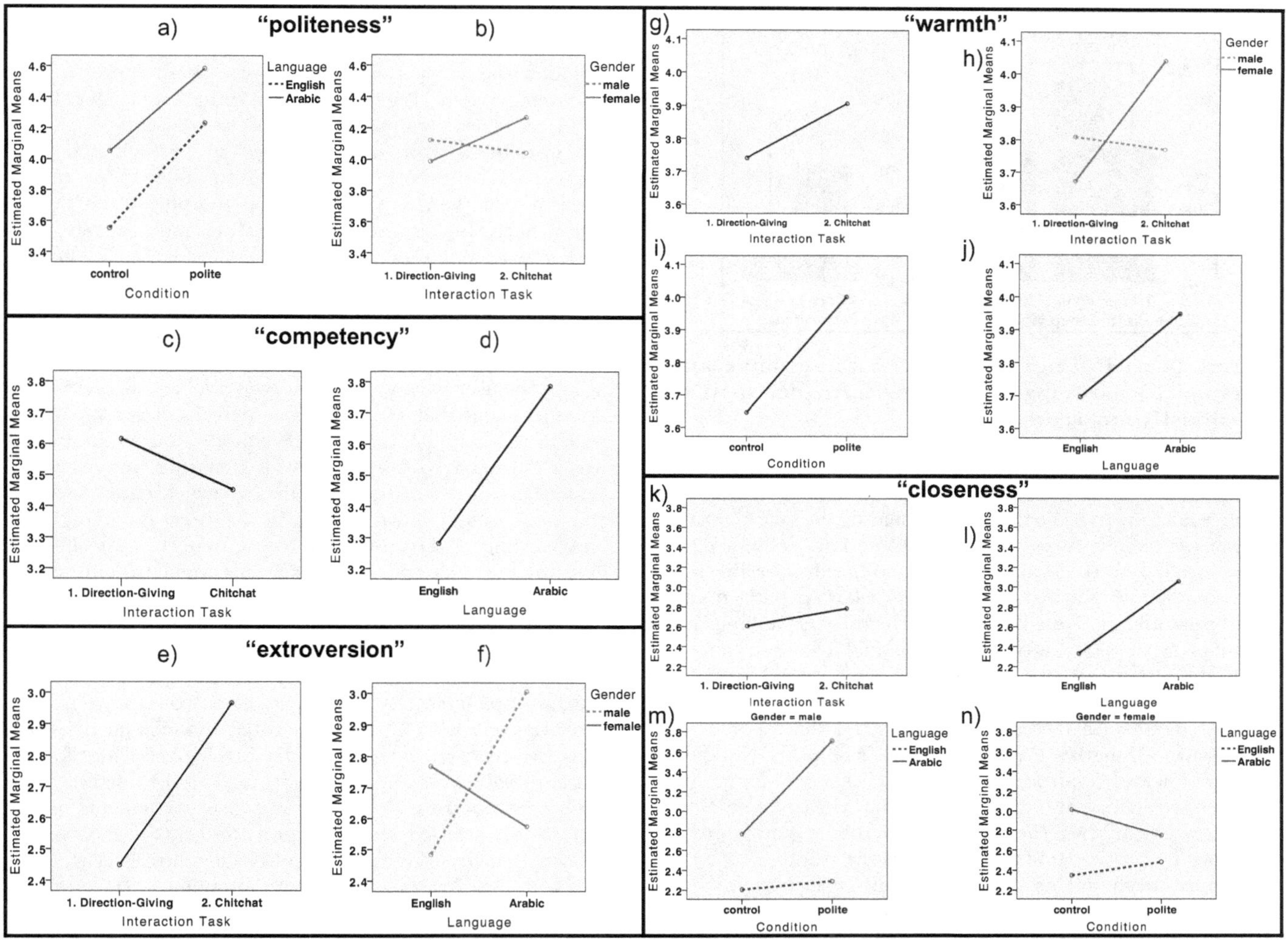

Figure 2: Plots visualizing significant results for the independent measures *politeness* (a&b), *competency* (c&d), *extroversion* (e&f), *warmth* (g–j) and *psychological closeness* (k–n).

robot as less extrovert than Ar males, whereas En females rated the robot as more extrovert than Ar females (**Fig. 2f**).

Our analysis showed a significant main effect of interaction task on participants' ratings of perceived *warmth*, $F(1{,}84) = 6.93$, $p = .01$, $\eta^2 = .08$: participants reported greater perceived warmth after meeting the robot for the second interaction (chitchat) than after the first task involving direction-giving (**Fig. 2g**). We also found a significant interaction effect between HRI task and gender, $F(1{,}84) = 10.52$, $p = .002$, $\eta^2 = .11$: female participants perceived less warmth towards the robot after the first task than male participants, but gave it higher ratings for perceived warmth after the second task compared to their male counterparts whose ratings dropped after the chitchat interaction (**Fig. 2h**). Between-groups comparisons showed a significant main effect of experimental condition on participants' perceptions of warmth towards the robot, $F(1{,}84) = 7.49$, $p = .008$, $\eta^2 = .08$: both En and Ar participants gave higher ratings on the warmth measure when in the 'polite' condition compared to those in the control group (**Fig. 2i**). We also found a marginal main effect (i.e. significant at 10 % level) of participants' cultural background on ratings of perceived warmth, $F(1{,}84) = 3.79$, $p = .055$, $\eta^2 = .04$: regardless of interaction task and condition, Ar perceived greater warmth towards the robot than En participants (**Fig. 2j**).

We found a significant main effect of interaction task on participants' reported experience of *psychological closeness*, $F(1{,}84) = 6.84$, $p = .011$, $\eta^2 = .08$: regardless of the experimental condition, participants of both cultural groups felt closer to the robot after the second interaction task involving the chitchat encounter than after the direction-giving task (**Fig. 2k**). Between-groups comparisons further showed a highly significant main effect of participants' cultural background on ratings of psychological closeness to the robot, $F(1{,}84) = 20.43$, $p < .001$, $\eta^2 = .20$: Ar participants generally reported greater closeness to the robot than En participants (**Fig. 2l**). There was also a marginally significant interaction effect between participants' cultural background, gender and experimental condition $F(1{,}84) = 3.84$, $p = .053$, $\eta^2 = .04$: while Ar males in the 'polite' condition felt closer to the robot than those in the control condition (**Fig. 2m**), Ar females in the control group reversely reported greater closeness to the robot than those in the 'polite' group (**Fig. 2n**). In contrast, both male and female En participants felt closer to the robot when in the 'polite' condition as opposed to those in the control group.

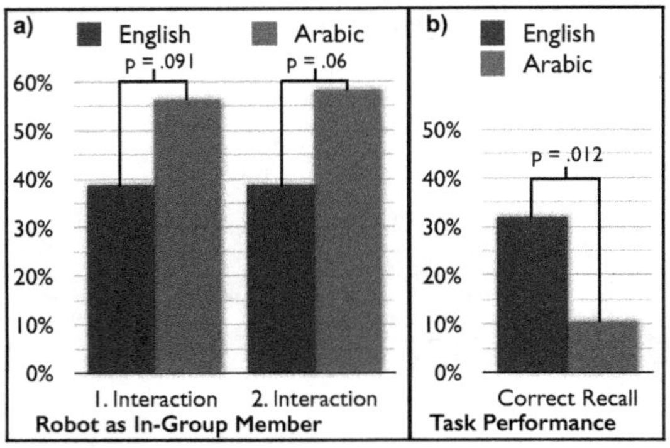

Figure 3: a) Ratings of the robot's in-group membership; b) participants' task performance used as an objective measure

Our analyses further revealed a marginal effect of cultural background on participants' assessment of the *robot's group membership* both after the first interaction, U = 870.00, Z = -1.68, p = .093, and more pronounced after the second round, U = 848.00, Z = -1.88, p = .06: Ar participants were generally more inclined to rate the robot as an in-group member, with 56.3 % after the first and 58.3 % after the second interaction respectively categorizing it as an Arabic native speakers. In contrast, following each interaction round, only 38.6 % of En participants considered the robot to be representing a native English speaker (**Fig. 3a**). No effect of experimental condition or interaction task was found, i.e. neither the change of interaction task nor the robot's politeness strategy affected the ratings of the robot as an in-group member by participants of either cultural group.

Finally, we found no effect of condition on participants' *task performance* when asked to recall the route directions to Dr. Miller's office, U = 1035.00, Z = -0.26, *n.s.* However, there was a significant effect of cultural background on participants' task performance, U = 830.00, Z = -2.52, p = .012: in the En group, 31.8 % of the participants recalled the route directions to Dr. Miller's office correctly, as opposed to only 10.4 % in the Ar group (**Fig. 3b**).

5. DISCUSSION

The results support **Hypothesis 1a** which predicted an effect of experimental condition, i.e. that the manipulation of the robot's politeness strategy will affect participants' subjective assessment of the robot and HRI. Besides the expected differences with regard to ratings of the manipulation check variable *politeness*, the robot's politeness strategy also influenced anthropomorphic inferences made regarding the robot: participants in the polite condition reported significantly greater warmth with regard to the robot than those in the control group. **Hypothesis 1b**, however, was not supported: the use of positive politeness in the robot's verbal instructions did not influence participants' task performance when asked to recall the directions previously given by the robot. Interestingly, an unexpected cultural difference was revealed: Ar participants performed significantly worse at the recall task compared to En participants. One possible explanation is based on cross-cultural linguistics studies suggesting that people differ culturally in the ways in which they provide route directions (e.g. [13]): as the verbal direction-giving content was translated from English into Arabic, the implied strategies might not comply with Arabic cultural standards, thus making it more difficult for Ar participants to follow the instructions. This observation requires further research, while it also emphasizes the importance of cultural and task-related adaptation of robotic assistants.

Hypothesis 2 predicted an effect of interaction task on participants' perception of the robot. Indeed, the results confirm that the robot was anthropomorphized more, with significantly higher ratings on the measures *warmth* and *closeness* as well as on the *extroversion* scale, in the chitchat interaction compared to the direction-giving task. This is not too surprising, as the chitchat task introduced a more personal communication level with the robot which, e.g., told participants about its 'hobbies' and took initiative by asking the user back about their own hobbies. It is similarly not surprising that the robot was perceived as less competent in the chitchat task, as the robot's limited knowledge was challenged by the unstructured nature and potential topical broadness of the open dialog, which easily revealed the robot as less 'flawless' than in the direction-giving task.

According to **Hypothesis 3**, we expected an effect of cultural background, which was confirmed by our results for all dependent measures. Specifically, since related work highlights Arab's preference for a communication strategy of apologizing [7], and the robot was more apologetic in the polite condition when being unable to respond to a question, we predicted that Ar participants would have a more positive perception of the polite robot than En participants. This was reflected by significantly higher Ar ratings for the measure *politeness* and is further supported by significantly higher ratings from Ar compared to En participants on the robot's *competency* scale: despite the general drop of the robot's perceived competency after the chitchat encounter (see Fig. 2c), Arabs seemed more forgiving in their ratings of this measure. One interpretation may be attributed to greater social expectations of politeness in such high-context cultures which typically discourage direct criticism, as which this measure may be perceived. In a way, participants may have even felt that they would be criticizing the developers rather than the robot itself, e.g. one Ar participant reported a first impression as follows: "I felt that the robot is smart and that there are people who worked hard to get to this result." Further supporting the third hypothesis and thus emphasizing cultural differences in HRI, higher ratings from Ar participants on the *warmth* and *closeness* scales suggest that the Ar group anthropomorphized the robot more than the En group. This, in turn, is in line with **Hypothesis 4** which predicted an effect of group membership on anthropomorphic inferences with regard to the robot: as visualized in Fig. 3a, Ar participants were more inclined to categorize the robot as an in-group member than En participants. Although this effect may be partly attributed to the rather Arabic appearance of the robot's face, our results nevertheless confirm the correlation between group membership and anthropomorphism regarding robots, as suggested by previous work [6], even for the extended scope of Arab cultures.

In addition to these hypothesized effects, our results revealed several interaction effects with regard to participants' gender. For example, both for the *politeness* and the *warmth* scale, ratings from female participants' increased notably after the chitchat interaction, while the ratings from male participants dropped. We speculate that females may have been more forgiving regarding the robot's declined competence in the chitchat task, which may possibly be related to the robot's depicted female gender resulting in another in-group effect. Adding another dimension to it, interaction effects between language group and participants' gender on the *extroversion* scale and between condition, language and gender on the *closeness* scale indicate that gender-related differences may play another important role in (cross-cultural) HRI. However, since these effects are outside the main scope of our study, they will require further, more focused, research, e.g. by comparing a male robot with a female version within this cross-cultural setting.

6. CONCLUSION

In this paper, we explored culture-specific variations of robot acceptance and anthropomorphization; our results highlight significant differences in HRI between Arabic and English native speakers, as well as between different interactional contexts (direction-giving vs. chitchat), communication styles (polite vs. direct) and genders.

Importantly, they suggest that Arabs show a more positive attitude towards our robot, including greater anthropomorphization and categorization as an in-group member. However, it is not clear what the exact determinants for these effects are. Among other factors such as the robot's appearance, we speculate that the Ar group's favoring effect may reflect their appreciation of the robot's apparent ability to 'understand' their individual Arabic dialects – something which modern speech recognition software can hardly achieve. To shed light on these questions, future work will include a thorough analysis of our collected qualitative data.

Since our study currently does not provide an exhaustive causal explanation for the observed effects, our findings open up multiple avenues for future work and emphasize the need to further investigate the subtleties of cultural influences on HRI. Such studies, together with our findings, will enable robot designers and programmers to address and exploit the cultural differences when targeting the deployment of multilingual and cross-cultural service robots.

7. ACKNOWLEDGMENTS

The authors would like to thank Dag Syrdal for his help with the statistical data analysis. This publication was made possible by NPRP grant 09-1113-1-171 from the Qatar National Research Fund (a member of Qatar Foundation). Statements herein are solely the responsibility of the authors.

8. REFERENCES

[1] http://www.acapela-group.com/ – accessed July 2013.

[2] C. Bartneck, T. Suzuki, T. Kanda, and T. Nomura. The influence of people's culture and prior experiences with aibo on their attitude towards robots. *AI & Society – The Journal of Human-Centred Systems*, 21(1), 2006.

[3] P. Brown and S. C. Levinson. *Politeness: Some Universals in Language Usage*. Studies in Interactional Sociolinguistics. Cambridge University Press, 1987.

[4] G. Echterhoff, E. T. Higgins, and J. M. Levine. Shared reality: Experiencing commonality with others' inner states about the world. *Perspectives on Psychological Science*, 4:496–521, 2009.

[5] V. Evers, H. Maldonado, T. Brodecki, and P. Hinds. Relational vs. group self-construal: Untangling the role of national culture in HRI. In *3rd ACM/IEEE International Conference on Human-Robot Interaction*, pages 255–262, 2008.

[6] F. Eyssel and D. Kuchenbrandt. Social categorization of social robots: anthropomorphism as a function of robot group membership. *British Journal of Social Psychology*, 51(4):724–731, 2011.

[7] S. H. Farahat. *Politeness Phenomena in Palestinian Arabic and Australian English: A Cross Cultural Study of Selected Contemporary Plays*. Australian Catholic University, 2009.

[8] S. Fiske, J. Cuddy, and P. Glick. Universal dimensions of social cognition: warmth and competence. *Trends in Cognitive Science*, 11(2):77–82, 2006.

[9] N. Fraser and G. Gilbert. Simulating speech systems. *Computer Speech & Language*, 5(1):81–99, 1991.

[10] N. Haslam, P. Bain, S. Loughnan, and Y. Kashima. Attributing and denying humanness to others. *European Review of Social Psychology*, 19:55–85, 2008.

[11] M. Makatchev, R. G. Simmons, M. Sakr, and M. Ziadee. Expressing ethnicity through behaviors of a robot character. In *8th ACM/IEEE International Conference on Human-Robot Interaction*, pages 357–364, 2013.

[12] M. Mori. *The Buddha in the Robot: A Robot Engineer's Thoughts on Science and Religion; trans. C. S. Terry*. Kosei Publishing, Tokyo, [1981] 1999.

[13] R. Pishghadam and F. Saboori. Giving directions: A cross-cultural comparison of l1 and l2 strategies. *Language, Literature, and Cultural Studies*, 4(2):265–280, 2011.

[14] P. P. Rau, Y. Li, and D. Li. Effects of communication style and culture on ability to accept recommendations from robots. *Computers in Human Behavior*, 25(2):587 – 595, 2009.

[15] L. Riek, N. Mavridis, S. Antali, N. Darmaki, Z. Ahmed, M. Al-Neyadi, and A. Alketheri. Ibn sina steps out: Exploring arabic attitudes toward humanoid robots. In *Proceedings of the 2nd International Symposium on New Frontiers in Human-Robot Interaction*, 2010.

[16] M. Salem, F. Eyssel, K. Rohlfing, S. Kopp, and F. Joublin. To err is human(-like): Effects of robot gesture on perceived anthropomorphism and likability. *International Journal of Social Robotics*, pages 1–11, 2013.

[17] R. Simmons, M. Makatchev, R. Kirby, M. Lee, I. Fanaswala, B. Browning, J. Forlizzi, and M. Sakr. Believable robot characters. *AI Magazine*, 32(4):39–52, 2011.

[18] H. Tajfel, M. Billig, R. Bundy, and C. Flament. Social categorization and intergroup behaviour. *European Journal of Social Psychology*, 1(2):149–178, 1971.

[19] A. Tawalbeh and E. Al-Oqaily. In-directness and politeness in american english and saudi arabic requests: A cross-cultural comparison. *Asian Social Science*, 8(10):85–98, 2012.

[20] E. Würtz. Intercultural communication on web sites: A cross-cultural analysis of web sites from high-context cultures and low-context cultures. *Journal of Computer-Mediated Communication*, 11(1):274–299, 2005.

Comparative Performance of Human and Mobile Robotic Assistants in Collaborative Fetch-and-Deliver Tasks

Vaibhav V. Unhelkar
Massachusetts Institute of Technology
77 Massachusetts Avenue
Cambridge, MA, USA
unhelkar@mit.edu

Ho Chit Siu
Massachusetts Institute of Technology
77 Massachusetts Avenue
Cambridge, MA, USA
hoseasiu@mit.edu

Julie A. Shah
Massachusetts Institute of Technology
77 Massachusetts Avenue
Cambridge, MA, USA
julie_a_shah@csail.mit.edu

ABSTRACT

There is an emerging desire across manufacturing industries to deploy robots that support people in their manual work, rather than replace human workers. This paper explores one such opportunity, which is to field a mobile robotic assistant that travels between part carts and the automotive final assembly line, delivering tools and materials to the human workers. We compare the performance of a mobile robotic assistant to that of a human assistant to gain a better understanding of the factors that impact its effectiveness. Statistically significant differences emerge based on type of assistant, human or robot. Interaction times and idle times are statistically significantly higher for the robotic assistant than the human assistant. We report additional differences in participant's subjective response regarding team fluency, situational awareness, comfort and safety. Finally, we discuss how results from the experiment inform the design of a more effective assistant.

Categories and Subject Descriptors

H.1.2 [**Models and Principles**]: User/Machine Systems; I.2.9 [**Artificial Intelligence**]: Robotics

General Terms

Experimentation, Performance, Human Factors

Keywords

mobile robotic assistant, human-robot collaboration, manufacturing, efficiency and productivity

1. INTRODUCTION

Industrial robots that operate in structured environments and perform repetitive tasks are widely used in manufacturing industries, especially those that are capable of building their factories around current industrial robotics capabilities. For instance, approximately fifty percent of a typical automotive assembly process is performed using industrial robotics and automation [1]. However, many other industries still face significant challenges in automating low-volume, complex, and customized processes. Seventy percent of the build process for large commercial airplanes [2], ninety percent of the assembly process for electronics [3], and a majority of the work done by small business manufacturing in the US [4] is still manual. The automotive industry, too, sees challenges to further automation; final assembly of cars involves highly dexterous tasks that are performed almost exclusively by humans workers. Rather than supplant human workers with robotics, there is an emerging desire across these industries to strategically integrate advanced robotics into the manual processes. The goal is to improve efficiency by supporting people in doing their best work.

One approach is to use robotics to improve the productivity of people in performing "value-added work" and look for opportunities where robots can relatively easily perform "non-value-added work." This paper explores one such opportunity, which is to field a mobile robotic assistant that travels between part carts and the automotive final assembly line, delivering tools and materials to the human workers. Human workers walk to pick their own parts today. Although seemingly insignificant, this walking time accumulates. An adept mobile robotic assistant can provide a significant boost to human worker productivity, while preserving operational flexibility as compared to fixed infrastructure solutions.

Multiple challenges must be addressed prior to deploying such a mobile robotic assistant in the dynamic, uncertain, and human-oriented assembly line environment [6, 7, 18]. The robotic assistant should not only be safe, but also perform the tasks efficiently and in a human-intuitive fashion. Akin to human-human collaboration, prior human-robot interaction studies have shown that a fluent collaboration requires awareness and anticipation of intent by both human and robotic agents [13]. To enable and facilitate this awareness and anticipation, it is important that both humans and robots communicate their status, location and intent, either explicitly through certain cues such as audio/visual signals or implicitly via their actions and motion paths [9]. Small deficiencies in the human-robot interaction in a time-critical domain such as automotive final assembly can significantly degrade the efficiency of the overall workflow.

HRI'14, March 3–6, 2014, Bielefeld, Germany.

http://dx.doi.org/10.1145/2559636.2559655 .

In this paper, we evaluate the comparative performance of a mobile robotic assistant *vis-a-vis* human assistant during the delivery phase of a repetitive fetch-and-deliver task. Our goal is to gain a better understanding of the factors that impact the efficiency and effectiveness of a robot assistant situated in an analogue assembly line environment. We assess objective and subjective measures of team fluency, assistant saliency, and investigate the requirement and effectiveness of explicit and implicit indicators designed to improve the human co-worker's awareness of the mobile robotic assistant. Specifically, we assess the effect of a flashing light on the robotic assistant and variations in the assistant's approach angle. Lastly, we analyze whether a more *salient* assistant (utilizing the aforesaid indicators) produces a more *fluent* collaborator.

Results from the experiment indicate that interaction time and idle time are higher for the robotic assistant than the human assistant ($p<0.05$). Changes in the assistant's approach angle make the robot more salient according to subjective measures, but do not affect the objective measures of fluency. Further, although the explicit indicator (flashing light) is salient, it does not improve the objective measures of fluency and degrades the subjective measures and human situational awareness. We discuss how these results inform the design of a more effective assistant, and also suggest interesting questions regarding robot saliency and its affect on collaboration, which warrant further investigation and analysis.

2. RELATED WORK

Human-human collaboration during fetch-and-deliver tasks is seemingly trivial, and does not require much cognitive effort for the human agents. For instance, while delivering or receiving an object from a fellow human being we are least concerned about the motion of our hands. However, much can be learnt about how to successfully carry out human-robot collaboration by studying human-human interactions.

Prior studies on human-robot hand-overs provide useful insights for improving the motion of armed manipulators [8, 10, 17]. Experiments of give-and-take tasks between a human and robot [10], standing at a fixed locations, investigate the use of robot reaching gestures, vocalizations, and pauses as indicators for delivery. The study reports that communication using implicit natural actions is sufficient for give-and-take tasks, and the human collaborators do not require explicit instructions or expertise while collaborating with the robot. In other work, multiple studies on human-human and human-robot hand-overs result in design recommendations for robot motion, and formal descriptions of the physical and cognitive aspects of the hand-over process [17]. Experiments in [8] investigate the use of contrasting motion to communicate the onset of a hand-over, and demonstrate statistically significant improvements in fluency of hand-overs by using *temporal contrast* during delivery. The study also reports a small but not significant increase in robot waiting time when the human participant is performing an attention task. Although a mobile robot is used in [8], the primary focus is on the motion of the armed manipulator, and modifications to motion that reduce the human waiting time.

Interaction between *mobile* robots and humans has been investigated for fetch-and-carry tasks. Studies evaluate robot approach direction and its impact on task efficiency

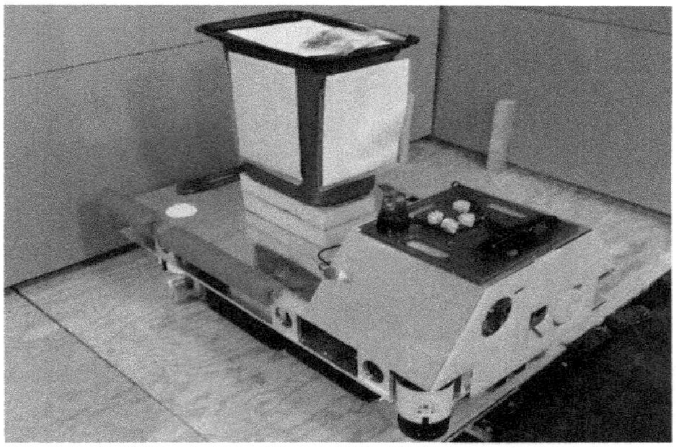

Figure 1: The Rob@Work mobile robotic platform

and human comfort [14, 19]. Ideally results from these experiments would inform the design of motion planners that take into consideration human preferences. However, reported results are contradictory. [19] finds a left/right approach direction to be most favorable, while a rear approach direction to be the least favorable. In contrast, [14] indicates a frontal approach and delivery to be more favorable, especially for participants experienced with robots. These studies are carried out in settings without restrictions on approach directions, and with human participants that are primarily focused on the robot throughout its approach.

A frontal approach is often not practical in a constrained factory environment. Oblique approach angles affect the human's visibility of the robot, and further study is needed into the effect of variations in robot approach angle from the rear direction. Additionally, human workers in a factory setting will usually be busy and not actively focused on the robot. Hence, there is a need to evaluate the robot's approach towards an otherwise busy human co-worker.

3. AIM OF THE EXPERIMENT

Through human factors experimentation, we investigate interactions between an assistant and worker in an analogue assembly line environment, where the experiment participant takes the role of the worker. The task of the robotic or human assistant is to present the parts on a tray to the static human co-worker in a timely manner for continuation of the assembly task. Through the experiments we seek to evaluate the following hypotheses:

H1 *The interaction between the robotic assistant and worker during the delivery phase is less fluent than the interaction between a human assistant and worker. For this hypothesis, fluency is characterized by objective measures including interaction time and the assistant idle time.*

This hypothesis is founded in prior studies of hand-overs [17], which indicate hand-over quality degrades when working with a robot versus a human partner. We hypothesize that a similar effect exists, even when the assistant does not use manipulators and manipulation is the sole responsibility of the human worker. Idle times of agents (both human and robot) are indicative of fluency in a collaborative task, and have been used as objective measures of fluency in prior studies [13,

16, 15]. The design of our experiment ensures that the human worker is continuously occupied with tasks, and hence only idle times of the assistants (both robot and human) are evaluated. Interaction time, indicative of the total delivery time, is meant to quantify the time both the agents are interacting during the delivery phase of the task.

H2 *The worker subjectively assesses the interaction with the robotic assistant during the delivery phase to be less fluent than similar interaction with a human assistant. Subjective measures of fluency are evaluated using a series of Likert-scale questionnaires.*
Subjective measures of fluency are as important as their objective counterparts for evaluating human-robot collaboration. Hence, we evaluate the current hypothesis as a follow-on to **H1**. We have developed the questionnaire used in this experiment based on [12], which includes a survey of questions used to evaluate team fluency that produce values of Cronbach's alpha ≥ 0.7 (indicating measurement of similar latent variable).

H3 *Salient indicators for the robotic assistant improve the worker's awareness of the robot. Namely as indicators, we investigate the effect of variations in approach angle and the inclusion of a flashing light on the robot.*
Literature suggests awareness of the assistant and its intent improves task efficiency [13]. Factory settings are noisy, the workers' attention is occupied with assembly tasks, and the robot may not always be in the human worker's field of view. With this hypothesis we evaluate whether the specified indicators make the robot more salient. We measure the *notice time*, the time of the participant's first head turn towards the assistant. An evaluation inspired by the Situational Awareness Global Assessment Technique (SAGAT) [11] is designed to measure the human worker's awareness of the robot in the task environment.

H4 *Salient indicators for the robotic assistant improve the objective and subjective measures of fluency for the robot.*
With this last hypothesis we evaluate whether the indicators, which may make the robot more salient, do indeed influence task fluency. Namely, we investigate the effect of indicators described in **H3**. The objective and subjective measures described in **H1** and **H2** are used to assess improvement in task fluency.

4. EXPERIMENT METHODOLOGY

The experiment is designed to simulate an analogue environment to the assembly line. In this setting the participant worker is standing at a workstation, stationary, and facing away from the assistant's approach path. The worker is provided an assembly task to occupy their attention. In the course of each trial two assistants, one robotic and one human, interact with the experiment participant. The assistants deliver parts enabling the continuity of the assembly task.

4.1 Materials and Setup

A Rob@Work robotic platform [5], shown in Fig. 1, is used as the mobile robotic assistant for this experiment. The

Figure 2: Experiment setup with human participant, workstation, Rob@Work platform, and white location markers.

robotic platform is designed for industrial environments and has an omni-directional base equipped with four independently actuated and steerable wheels, wheel encoders, two SICK S300 safety laser scanners[1], and safety features (both at hardware and software level) to avoid collisions. The basic platform is augmented with one Asus Xtion RGB-D device[2] used for person tracking, and one red, flashing and rotating light[3]. A raised platform and tray are mounted on the robot to represent the height of a future robotic arm. The robot, though capable of navigating autonomously, is operated manually by a human supervisor throughout the experiment to reduce variability in motion paths.

Observations during the experiment are obtained using demographic survey, four in-experiment questionnaires, a post-experiment questionnaire, a Vicon motion capture system, video camera, and the on-board Xtion. The participants and the human assistant wear hard hats with Vicon markers. The robotic assistant also has Vicon markers mounted on its top to enable tracking via the Vicon cameras.

During each experiment, a recording of factory sounds[4] is played to simulate the factory environment. This serves to mask the noises made by the movement of the assistants to some degree, much like actual factory conditions would. Human participants are asked about the location of assistants in some questionnaires; thus, to eliminate the need to numerically estimate distances we place three large white poles equidistant from each other behind the participant. These poles are used as visual indicators to mark locations in the room (see Figs. 2-3), and divide the room into four names zones: *very close*, *close*, *far*, and *very far*, relative to the participant.

4.2 Procedure

Each participant is instructed to stand at a specified location to work at a standing table as shown in Fig. 2. A dexterous, model-assembly task is presented to the participant. The task is chosen for its complexity and similarity to a factory assembly task, and involves constructing a Lego model (Fig. 4). Portions of the Lego parts and assembly instructions are delivered at specified

[1] `http://goo.gl/VwoA42`
[2] `http://www.asus.com/Multimedia/Xtion_PRO_LIVE/`
[3] `http://goo.gl/yxreko`
[4] `http://goo.gl/od11EQ`

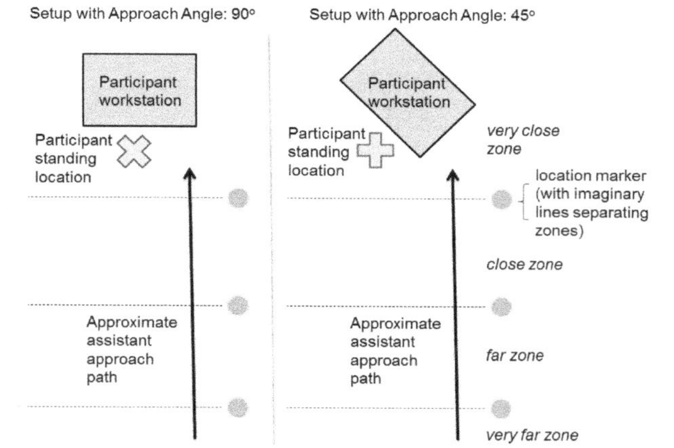

Figure 3: Schematic diagram of the experimental setup for the two approach angles (90° and 45°)

intervals during the experiment by either the human or robotic assistant. Each delivery, but for the first, consists of three items: Lego parts, corresponding instruction set, and a questionnaire to assess level of awareness of the robot, and perception of safety, comfort, trust, and fluency. To keep the participants occupied prior to the first delivery, the first set of instructions (but not the Lego parts and questionnaire) are given during the briefing, and the first delivery contains only Lego parts and a questionnaire. The total experiment task time is ≈12-18 min, with a cumulative participant-assistant interaction time of ≈10-20 seconds for each trial. This is similar to factory-like tasks, where delivery of parts constitutes only a portion of the overall assembly.

Each participant is aided by an assistant four times during the experiment, twice consecutively each by the human and robotic assistant (Fig. 5). This setup allows for each participant's response towards the robot to be compared to their own responses of working with a human assistant. Participants are randomly assigned to two groups one in which the first assistant is a human and the other in which the first assistant is a robot, to counterbalance differences that may arise due to the sequence of human and robot interactions. One of the experimenters plays the role of human assistant for consistency; the same human assistant works with all the participants. Both the human and robot assistants follow the same schedule for deliveries and stop at the same distance from the participant. Further, trays are used by both human and robotic assistants during delivery, since the focus of the study is on the assistant's approach rather than manipulator motion.

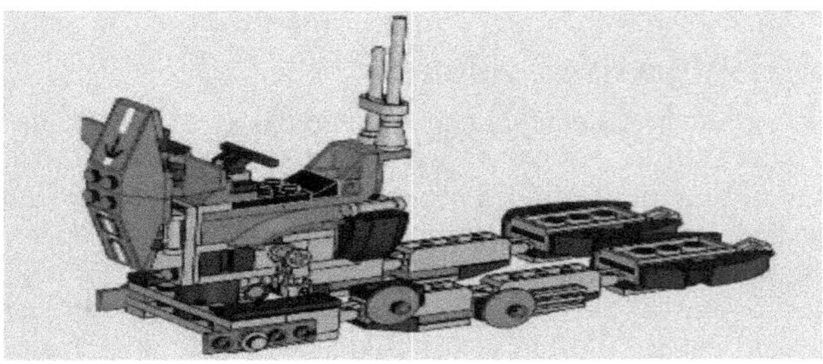

Figure 4: The Assembled Lego Model

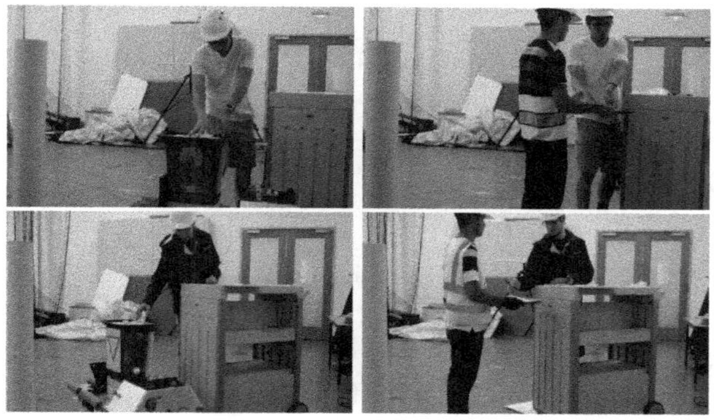

Figure 5: Typical deliveries made by the Assistants (Top row: approach angle = 90°, Bottom row: approach angle = 45°, Left column: robotic assistant, Right column: human assistant)

Participants are instructed to remove all the items from the tray once an assistant stops next to them. Further, they are told before the experiment that the assistants are involved in other time-sensitive tasks, to indicate the importance of the assistant's time. Using the items delivered, the participants build the part of the Lego model corresponding to the current instruction, and then answer the corresponding questionnaire. The assistant's approach towards the human co-worker, for the next delivery, starts as soon as the participant begins answering the previously delivered questionnaire. The length of the questionnaire is designed to ensure the participant is always busy when the assistant (both human and robot) reaches him/her.

When a delivery is not in progress, the human and robot assistants either move around behind the participants in the *far* or *very far* zones or stand still. These movements are scheduled for pre-determined times during the experiment, and are included to simulate the assistant's involvement in other factory tasks. At different, pre-determined times the appearance of the robot is altered by affixing different colored foam bumpers and printed signs; similarly, the human assistant alters his appearance by wearing/removing a safety vest, watch, and gloves. The color of the trays used by both human and robotic assistants, on which items are delivered, also varies between deliveries. The participants are not informed of these signs, indicators, and possibility of their modification a priori, since our goal is to evaluate the saliency of these features in a natural workflow.

4.3 Design

The experiment is designed to evaluate the effect of three independent variables on the human-robot collaboration task, and participants are randomly assigned across a fourth factor to counterbalance differences that may arise due to sequence of human and robot interactions:

- **IV1:** Human or Robotic Assistant, varied within participants.
- **IV2:** Robot's Flashing Light (Explicit Indicator) On or Off, varied between participants.
- **IV3:** Assistant Approach Angle (Implicit Indicator) 90° or 45°, varied between participants.
- **IV4:** Human or Robotic Assistant for the first delivery, varied between participants.

Table 1: Design of Experiment (N=24)

		Approach Angle		
		90°	45°	*Participants*
Light	On	H-H-R-R (3)	H-H-R-R (3)	12
		R-R-H-H (3)	R-R-H-H (3)	
	Off	H-H-R-R (3)	H-H-R-R (3)	12
		R-R-H-H (3)	R-R-H-H (3)	
Participants		12	12	**24**

The approach angle variable indicates the orientation of participant relative to that of the assistant's fixed approach path (Fig. 3). The 90° approach angle corresponds to the participant facing towards a wall and directly away from the assistant's path. The 45° indicates an orientation of 45° away from the wall and towards the assistant's path. We use light rather than sound as an explicit indicator since factory environments are frequently much too noisy for effective verbal/auditory communication.

Thus, the experiment is carried out as a mixed factorial design with four factors, one within- and three between-participants. Participants are randomly assigned across the 8 groups (2^k, where k=3 is the number of between-participant factors) indicated in Table 1. Next, we describe the dependent measures observed for each participant.

4.4 Objective Evaluation

Objective measures of team fluency include *interaction time* and *assistant idle time.* Interaction time is defined as the difference between the assistant's stop on arrival and the beginning of the assistant's retreat, and provides an assistant-centric measure of the time of each task's delivery phase. Idle time is defined as the difference between the assistant's stop on arrival and the start of the participant's reach towards the tray. Idle time is a subset of the interaction time; we measure both since uncontrolled-for factors may affect the precise time of each assistant's retreat. Saliency of the assistant is quantified by the derived measure *notice time*, the time between the participant's head turn towards the assistant and the assistant's arrival. Note that the *notice time* may be negative or positive depending on whether the assistant is acknowledged with a head turn prior to or after its arrival. Table 2 defines these measures for the delivery task in the current experiment. These

Table 2: Objective Measures: Definitions

--- t_{notice} — t_{arrive} — t_{reach} — $t_{retreat}$ ---

Interaction Time	$t_{retreat} - t_{arrive}$ Time between assistant's stop on arrival and retreat, i.e., time required to complete the delivery
Idle Time	$t_{reach} - t_{arrive}$ Time between assistant's stop on arrival and the onset of the participant's reach towards the tray.
Notice Time	$t_{arrive} - t_{notice}$ Time between participant's first head turn towards the assistant and the assistant's stop on arrival.

Table 3: Objective Measures - Question Set

Awareness of Assistant	
Common Questions	
1.	What color was the top surface of the tray on which the Lego pieces were delivered?
2.	After delivering the parts, what was the robot/human assistant doing while you were working on the model? (i.e. which zone was he/it in, was he/it stationary or moving?)
Robotic Assistant	
3.	What colors were the bumpers on the robot?
4.	What did the sign on the robot say the last time it delivered Legos?
5.	Were the lights on top of the robot on during the last delivery?
Human Assistant	
6.	What color was the assistant's watch?
7.	What color were the assistant's gloves?
8.	Was the human assistant wearing a safety vest?

measures are summed across the two deliveries, for each assistant, to obtain the cumulative measures reported in Section 5. The total task time in this study is dependent on the participant's expertise in Lego assembly tasks. Hence, the total task time, a usual measure of task fluency, is not used in this study since the assistants only deliver the parts and do not contribute in the actual assembly.

These objective measures are independently coded by two raters from the video recordings of the experiment. The measured quantities are continuous and so Pearson's correlation coefficient is used to determine the inter-coder agreement. For all the derived quantities, the resulting correlation coefficient is ≥ 0.98 indicating very high inter-coder agreement. Further, when determining statistical significance, data from both the coders is used independently to arrive at the final results, and any differences among coders are reported as errors.

To evaluate saliency of robot features, additional quantitative data is derived through in-experiment questionnaires. Participants are requested to fill out these in-experiment questionnaires between assembly steps. Questions are selected from a list of eight questions (in Table 3) pertaining to assistant's whereabouts and characteristics, and responses are evaluated as *correct* or *incorrect.* The questions pertain to the time immediately preceding the delivery of the questionnaire, and the features, of both the robotic and human assistant, examined via these questions are hidden from the participant while he or she answers the questions. This evaluation is inspired by the Situational Awareness Global Assessment Technique (SAGAT) [11], and focuses on Level 1 SA pertaining to "the perception of the elements [including status, attributes, and dynamics] in the environment within a volume of time and space."

4.5 Subjective Evaluation

Likert-scale statements and open-ended questions are used to collect subjective data regarding the experiment. Participants are administered a pre-experiment demographic survey and a post-experiment questionnaire. Further, subjective questions are also presented via the four in-experiment questionnaires. Several Likert-scale measures, derived from [12] and listed in Table 4, are used to evaluate participants' subjective response regarding comfort, safety, and perceived fluency.

Table 4: Subjective Measures - Question Set

Comfort and Safety
1. I am comfortable with the time at which I first noticed the assistant.
2. I feel safe working in this environment.
3. I am comfortable with my level of awareness about the assistant's whereabouts.
4. I was stressed when the human/robotic assistant was assisting me.
5. I felt safe when working with the human/robot assistant.
6. I would have liked to notice the human/robot assistant coming earlier.
Fluency
7. The human/robotic assistant and I work well together.
8. Deliveries made by the human/robotic assistant were smooth.
9. I worked fluently together with the human/robot assistant.
Trust in Assistant
10. The human/robotic assistant's actions were consistent.
11. The human/robot assistant came when I expected him/it to.
12. The human/robot assistant's actions were predictable.
13. The human/robot assistant was dependable.
Additional Indicators
14. The human/robot assistant did his/its part successfully.
15. The human/robot assistant contributed to the success of the task.

The in-experiment questionnaire is changed from delivery to delivery. Only a subset of the questions shown in Tables 3-4 are provided in each questionnaire. This is to reduce learning effects.

5. RESULTS

This section summarizes statistically significant results, trends, and other insights obtained from the experiments.

5.1 Participants

Thirty participants performed the experiment, out of which data from six participants could not be used in analysis due to incorrect task performance, non-completion of the experiment, or missing video data. The results presented in this section are for the 24 participants that successfully completed the experiment with complete data for analysis. These participants were randomly assigned amongst the three between-participant factors of the experiment, resulting in three replicates for each experimental setting (Table 1). The participants (13 men and 11 women) were recruited via email, and had a median age of 20 years (max = 31, min = 18). None of the participants indicated any form of colorblindness in the pre-experiment demographic survey. Prior to the experiment a pilot study was carried out with 5 participants to streamline the experimental procedure; data from the pilot experiment are not included in the reported analysis.

5.2 Assistant Interaction and Idle times

A mixed factor, four-way Analysis of Variance (ANOVA) is carried out to compare the interaction times and assistant idle times across the four independent variables (1 within-, 3 between-participants). Statistically significant differences ($p<0.05$, N=24) are observed in both these measures for use of human versus robotic assistant (the within-participant variable). No statistically significant differences were found across the other factors including use of robot flashing light, approach angle, and type of first assistant.

Further analysis of the significant factors confirms that the interaction times and idle times associated with the robotic assistant are statistically significantly higher than those for the human assistant ($p<0.05$, using two-tailed, paired t-tests to compare means with unknown, unequal covariance). The human assistant on average interacts with the participant for a cumulative time of 8.9 seconds (SD = 3.1s) as compared to the robotic assistant's average of 12.7 seconds (SD = 6.3s). Similarly, the human assistant idles for a cumulative time of 1.0 second (SD=2.4s), in contrast to the robotic assistant's idle time of 3.8 seconds (SD = 6.0s). These results support our first hypothesis **H1**, i.e., according to the objective measures of fluency the robotic assistant is a less fluent collaborator in comparison to the robotic assistant.

5.3 Subjective Measures of Fluency

Likert responses to statements about fluency (presented in Section 4.5) are analyzed across factors using non-parametric tests. No statistically significant differences are found in responses for the human versus robotic assistant (using the paired, Wilcoxon signed-rank test). Thus, the second hypothesis **H2** comparing the subjective measures of fluency is not supported by the experiment results.

5.4 Saliency

Saliency of the assistant is evaluated using the derived measure *notice time* as defined in Section 4.4. Responses to fourteen objective questions (listed in Table 3) pertaining to assistant's whereabouts and characteristics are also evaluated and frequencies of *correct* versus *incorrect* answers are compared. Overall no statistically significant effects are found for type of indicators, and the third hypothesis **H3** is unsupported. Type or use of indicators did not produce statistically significant differences in interaction and idle times, leaving the fourth hypothesis **H4** unsupported as well.

However interesting differences emerge based on type of assistant, human or robot (within-participant variable). Analysis of notice time is performed using a mixed factor, four-way ANOVA, and a statistically significant difference ($p=0.005 \pm 0.001$) is observed. The robotic assistant is noticed much earlier with average notice time of 9.0 seconds (SD=9.7s) prior to stop on arrival, as opposed to the human assistant's average notice time of 1.8 seconds (SD=3.3s). These results suggest that degradations in fluency are likely due to factors other than robot saliency, since on average the robot is acknowledged earlier than the human assistant.

Overall, there is only one statistically significant difference in the frequencies of correct responses between types of assistants. Color of the tray is noticed significantly better by the participants during the two deliveries each made by the robotic assistant (37%) than the human assistant (8%) ($p<0.05$, Fisher's exact test with 2×2 contingency table). However, participants demonstrated through responses on Question 2 (Table 3) that they were significantly more aware of their background environment after delivery by a human assistant ($p<0.001$). This suggests that the robot may have a transitory distracting effect that degrades situational awareness, even after the robot leaves the participant's side.

Table 5: Sample of Open-ended Comments

Human Assistant
"I liked that he said thank you!"
"Making eye contact & speaking was key to feeling more comfortable - I liked getting confirmation that the person wanted me to take stuff from the tray."
"Delivered parts when I'm still working, made me feel more stressed."
Robotic Assistant
"Smooth transition. Didn't get too close to me which I liked." "Did a good job at a simple task."
"Having the robot moving around in the background was more distracting than the human in the background."
"With the robot, I think I made it wait till I'm done to get the stuff, I was less stressed."

More visible features such as safety vest for human assistant and the state of the light for the robotic assistant were noticed by 79% and 67% of the participants, respectively. The participants were not informed about the existence or relevance of these signs in advance, and thus noticed them during the course of natural interaction with the assistant. Participants were equally unaware about less noticeable features such as the human assistant's glove color (13% correct responses) and watch (18%), and the robot's bumper color (4%) and printed signs (21%).

5.5 Factors affecting Subjective Measures

The effect of flashing light and approach angle (between-participant factors) on Likert statement responses is evaluated using the two-sided unpaired Wilcoxon rank sum test. Participants agreed less strongly with the following statements when the robot's light was flashing, indicating a reduction in perception of safety and trust in the robot:

- I felt safe while working with the robot. ($p<0.05$, evaluated during post-experiment survey)
- The robot assistant's actions were consistent. ($p<0.01$ through in-experiment questionnaire, while not statistically significant during post-experiment survey)

Variation in approach angle resulted in statistically significant differences in responses as well. Participants agreed more strongly with the following statement in the 45° approach condition, indicating increased comfort with the robot when it approaches obliquely as opposed to from the rear (no such difference was found for the human assistant):

- I am comfortable with my level of awareness about the robot assistant's whereabouts. ($p<0.05$, assessed twice in the in-experiment questionnaires)

5.6 Open-ended Comments

The participants are asked to provide open-ended comments about their experience with each assistant at the end of the experiment. Selected comments from these responses are included in Table 5. The open-ended responses suggest mixed reactions towards the robotic assistant. Interestingly, some comments reflect that participants felt rushed by the human assistant, and that the robot let them work at their own pace.

6. DISCUSSION

The results of the human factors experimentation support our hypothesis (**H1**) that the human-human collaboration is more fluent, as quantified by assistant interaction times and idle times, than human-robot collaboration for the current fetch-and-deliver task. Statistically significant results indicate that the robotic assistant spent on average 3.8 seconds (43%) more time than the human assistant interacting with the human for the same delivery tasks. Similarly, a statistically significant three-fold rise (2.9 seconds, 3x) is observed in the assistant idle time. A factory assistant will be making deliveries to multiple human co-workers. These differences in interaction and idle time, though small in magnitude, will substantially affect the productivity of the robotic assistant over the course of a two or three-shift work day, and should be alleviated using design interventions. For example, a back-of-the-envelope analysis indicates if the experiment task was replicated over a two-shift day (assuming a total of 12 hr of assembly time), and the robot assistant is multi-tasked to deliver items to five workers, the robot accumulates approximately 30 minutes of *additional* interaction time, as compared to a human assistant.

Surprisingly, the robotic assistant's approach is noticed on average much earlier (7.2 seconds, a statistically significant difference) by the participants as compared to that of the human assistant. Nonetheless, the robotic assistant idled more than the human assistant. This provides contrary evidence for the fourth hypothesis (**H4**), suggesting a salient agent does not necessarily produce an efficient collaborator.

These results suggest that degradations in fluency are likely due to factors other than robot saliency, since on average the robot is acknowledged earlier than the human assistant. While the participants reported the human and robotic assistant to be equally fluent, they appeared to be more comfortable with making the robot wait. This is supported by open-ended responses indicating different attitudes towards the human and robot. We posit that the human assistant's time is valued more than that of the robot, and personal objectives and comfort take a higher priority during collaboration with the robotic assistant. Further study is required to understand how to design the robot and its human interface so that it does not wait unnecessarily for human co-workers, which degrades the productivity of the robotic assistant and the overall assembly line workflow.

We confirm that an oblique approach angle is preferable since the participants report increased comfort about their awareness of the robot, although it did not improve the objective measures of fluency. The red flashing light is observed to be the most noticeable feature amongst those evaluated but did not improve objective measures of fluency. Further, the participants reported feeling less safe with the light flashing. This is possibly due to the color choice, and suggests that a red flashing light should not be used in nominal, safe operation of the robot.

7. LIMITATIONS AND FUTURE WORK

We designed our experiment to emulate a factory setting through careful choice of task and features such as noise, however limitations remain. The study was carried out in a large mostly empty room with student participants rather than factory workers. Further, the participants were working with the robotic assistant for the first time, and hence the effect of long-term experience working with the robot cannot be evaluated. In typical factory operations, the robot will be assisting multiple workers. Although participants were told that the assistant has additional responsibilities and tasks, it is possible human workers will behave differently when the robot's responsibilities clearly relate to other co-workers. Future experiments will include a longitudinal study with multiple co-workers, to observe how the interaction changes over time and with multiple people. We also plan to conduct user studies in a factory setting to investigate whether the results, trends and insights from this study apply in the real-world operational environment.

8. CONCLUSIONS

We conduct a human factors experiment to compare the performance of a mobile robotic assistant and human assistant during the delivery phase of a fetch-and-deliver task. Results from the experiment indicate that interaction times and idle times are statistically significantly higher for the robotic assistant than the human assistant. However the robotic assistant's approach is noticed on average much earlier by the participants as compared to that of the human assistant. These results suggest that degradations in fluency are likely due to factors other than robot saliency. Based on our observations, we conjecture that the human assistant's time is valued more than that of the robot, and personal objectives and comfort take a higher priority during collaboration with the robotic assistant. We confirm that an oblique approach angle is preferable since the participants report increased comfort about their awareness of the robot. The robot's red flashing light did not improve objective measures of fluency, and the participants reported feeling less safe with the light flashing. This suggests that a red flashing light should not be used in nominal, safe operation of the robot.

9. ACKNOWLEDGMENTS

This work is supported by BMW. We thank our colleagues Stefan Bartscher and Johannes Bix of the Innovation Production Division, BMW Group, Munich, Germany for their valuable insights and domain expertise that informed this work.

10. REFERENCES

[1] Stefan Bartscher, Innovation Product Division, BMW Group, personal communication, February 2012.

[2] David Amirehteshami, Boeing Research and Technology, personal communication, July 2011.

[3] John Davidson, Advanced Technology Engineering, Jabil, personal communication, June 2012.

[4] Robots for small business: A growing trend, robotics online, oct. 31, 2003. `http://www.robotics.org/content-detail.cfm/Industrial-Robotics-News/Robots-For-Small-Business:-A-Growing-Trend/content_id/1118`.

[5] Rob@work 3. `http://www.care-o-bot-research.org/robatwork-3`.

[6] J. Bix. Mobile robots at the assembly line. In *International Conference on Robotics and Automation (ICRA), 1st Workshop on Industrial Mobile Assistance Robots*, 2013.

[7] J. C. Boerkoel Jr and J. A. Shah. Planning for flexible human-robot co-navigation in dynamic manufacturing environments. In *International Conference on Human-Robot Interaction (HRI), Proceedings of Human Robot Interaction Pioneers*, 2013.

[8] M. Cakmak, S. S. Srinivasa, M. K. Lee, S. Kiesler, and J. Forlizzi. Using spatial and temporal contrast for fluent robot-human hand-overs. In *Proceedings of the International Conference on Human-Robot Interaction (HRI)*, pages 489–496, 2011.

[9] A. D. Dragan, K. C. Lee, and S. S. Srinivasa. Legibility and predictability of robot motion. In *Proceedings of the International Conference on Human-Robot Interaction (HRI)*, pages 301–308, 2013.

[10] A. Edsinger and C. C. Kemp. Human-robot interaction for cooperative manipulation: Handing objects to one another. In *Proceedings of the International Symposium on Robot and Human Interactive Communication (RO-MAN)*, 2007.

[11] M. R. Endsley. *Situation awareness analysis and measurement*, chapter Direct measurement of situation awareness: Validity and use of "SAGAT". Mahwah, NJ: Lawrence Erlbaum Associates, 2000.

[12] G. Hoffman. Evaluating fluency in human-robot collaboration. In *International Conference on Human-Robot Interaction (HRI), Workshop on Human Robot Collaboration*, 2013.

[13] G. Hoffman and C. Breazeal. Effects of anticipatory action on human-robot teamwork: Efficiency, fluency, and perception of team. In *Proceedings of the International Conference on Human-Robot Interaction (HRI)*, pages 1–8, 2007.

[14] K. L. Koay, E. A. Sisbot, D. S. Syrdal, M. L. Walters, K. Dautenhahn, and R. Alami. Exploratory study of a robot approaching a person in the context of handing over an object. In *AAAI Symposium: Multidisciplinary Collaboration for Socially Assistive Robotics*, 2007.

[15] S. Nikolaidis and J. Shah. Human-robot cross-training: computational formulation, modeling and evaluation of a human team training strategy. In *Proceedings of the International Conference on Human-Robot Interaction (HRI)*, pages 33–40, 2013.

[16] J. Shah, J. Wiken, B. Williams, and C. Breazeal. Improved human-robot team performance using chaski, a human-inspired plan execution system. In *Proceedings of the International Conference on Human-Robot Interaction (HRI)*, pages 29–36, 2011.

[17] K. W. Strabala, M. K. Lee, A. D. Dragan, J. L. Forlizzi, S. Srinivasa, M. Cakmak, and V. Micelli. Towards seamless human-robot handovers. *Journal of Human-Robot Interaction*, 2(1):112–132, 2013.

[18] V. V. Unhelkar, J. Perez, J. C. Boerkoel Jr, J. Bix, S. Bartscher, and J. A. Shah. Towards control and sensing for an autonomous mobile robotic assistant navigating assembly lines. In *International Conference on Robotics and Automation (ICRA)*, 2014. Currently under review.

[19] M. L. Walters, K. Dautenhahn, S. N. Woods, and K. L. Koay. Robotic etiquette: results from user studies involving a fetch and carry task. In *Proceedings of the International Conference on Human-Robot Interaction (HRI)*, pages 317–324, 2007.

Human-Swarm Interactions Based on Managing Attractors

Daniel S. Brown
AFRL Information Directorate
Rome, NY 13441
daniel.brown.81@us.af.mil

Sean C. Kerman
Brigham Young University
Provo, UT 84602
sean.kerman@gmail.com

Michael A. Goodrich
Brigham Young University
Provo, UT 84602
mike@cs.byu.edu

ABSTRACT

Leveraging the abilities of multiple affordable robots as a swarm is enticing because of the resulting robustness and emergent behaviors of a swarm. However, because swarms are composed of many different agents, it is difficult for a human to influence the swarm by managing individual agents. Instead, we propose that human influence should focus on (a) managing the higher level attractors of the swarm system and (b) managing trade-offs that appear in mission-relevant performance. We claim that managing attractors theoretically allows a human to abstract the details of individual agents and focus on managing the collective as a whole. Using a swarm model with two attractors, we demonstrate this concept by showing how limited human influence can cause the swarm to switch between attractors. We further claim that using quorum sensing allows a human to manage trade-offs between the scalability of interactions and mitigating the vulnerability of the swarm to agent failures.

Categories and Subject Descriptors

I.2.11 [**Artificial Intelligence**]: Distributed Artificial Intelligence—*multiagent systems, coherence and coordination*; H.1.2 [**Models and Principles**]: User/Machine Systems—*human factors*; I.2.9 [**Artificial Intelligence**]: Robotics—*operator interfaces, intelligent vehicles*

Keywords

Human-swarm interaction, managing attractors of dynamic systems, bio-inspired swarms, quorum sensing

1. INTRODUCTION

Swarms provide complex behaviors out of simple agents following simple rules. The ability for swarms to adapt and produce complex behaviors allows us to build multi-agent systems that are flexible and resilient. However, two important problems emerge when we try to allow humans to manage robot swarms. First, in contested or noisy real-world environments where bandwidth is limited, it is necessary to interact with only a subset of the agents in order to achieve desired behaviors. Thus operators need ways to manage a swarm by managing the collective emergent behaviors while only requiring communication with a subset of the swarm. Second, as swarms grow in size it becomes increasingly difficult for a human operator to manage the behavior of a swarm by controlling individual agents.

The swarm model presented in [17] has three properties that make it ideal for studying human interaction with robot swarms. First, the model (a) uses an abstract but appropriate model for how well a robot can sense neighboring robots and (b) matches the mobility characteristics of fixed-wing unmanned aerial vehicles and a large class of fixed-speed non-holonomic robots. Second, the model has been shown to have two emergent collective behaviors: a flock and a torus. Third, the model can be extended, as shown below, to include bio-inspired quorum-signaling, which lends itself to human interaction through managing trade-offs between scalability and vulnerability of the swarm. Note that this property is essential for this paper because the results do not include experiments with real humans or real robots.

The second property is essential for human-swarm interaction because it allows a huge number of details to be ignored when managing the swarm. The behavior of any individual agent in a swarm can be difficult to understand and explain due to the highly dynamic interactions with neighboring agents, but by managing the collective as a whole, much of this difficulty can be avoided. We empirically show that there exists a critical point in the parameter space and show that managing the swarm at this critical point allows both a flock and a torus to form. Through empirical simulations, we show that controlled switches between a torus and a flock are possible, given a significant number of human-influenced agents in the swarm.

The third property is also essential for human interaction with robot swarms because it is necessary to balance the desire to allow the swarm to be responsive to human input without becoming a centralized system with a single point of failure. To increase the scalability of the swarm we introduce the notion of quorum sensing, as found in biological systems and show how this can be applied to a swarm. In addition to increasing the scalability of human-swarm interactions, we show evidence that quorum sensing provides a mechanism for limiting the vulnerability of the swarm to agent failure.

The main contribution of this paper is a theoretical and empirical exploration of how human interaction with robot swarms can operate at a high level of abstraction. Claims

HRI'14, March 3–6, 2014, Bielefeld, Germany.
Copyright 2014 ACM 978-1-4503-2658-2/14/03 ...$15.00.
http://dx.doi.org/10.1145/2559636.2559661.

in the paper are supported by so-called "Oz of Wizard" empirical studies [28] that explore how an idealized human can manage swarms by managing attractors and trade-offs.

2. SWARM MODEL

The experiments and simulations in this paper build upon the model of swarming presented in [17]. This model exhibits both a flock and torus behavior, is similar to many biological models of swarming behavior, and has dynamics similar to those of actual robots. The model consists of a set of N agents with the dynamics for agent i given by

$$\dot{x_i} = s \cdot \cos\theta_i, \quad \dot{y_i} = s \cdot \sin\theta_i, \quad \dot{\theta}_i = \omega_i \tag{1}$$

where $[x_i, y_i]^T \in \mathbb{R}^2$ is the agent's position, $\theta_i \in [-\pi, \pi]$ is the agent's angular heading, s is the constant agent speed, and w_i is the agent's angular velocity. For simplicity we define $v_i = [\cos(\theta_i), \sin(\theta_i)]^T$ and $c_i = [x, y]^T$. Let $A(t) = a_{ij}(t)$ denote the sensory adjacency matrix where $a_{ij}(t) = 1$ means that agent j is visible to agent i at time t. Each $a_{ij}(t)$ is determined at time t according to a Bernoulli random variable with parameter $p_{ij}(t) = \min\left(1, 1/d_{ij}(t)\right)$ where $d_{ij}(t)$ is the Euclidean distance between agents i and j at time t.

Similar to the Couzin model of biological swarms [9] and the Reynold model of synthetic agents [26], agents in this model react to neighbors within three different zones: repulsion, orientation, and attraction. The neighbors in these zones are determined by

$$n_i^r = \{j : \|c_i - c_j\|_2 \leq R_r, a_{ij} = 1\} \tag{2}$$

$$n_i^o = \{j : \|c_i - c_j\|_2 \leq R_o, a_{ij} = 1\} \tag{3}$$

$$n_i^a = \{j : a_{ij} = 1\} \tag{4}$$

where n_i^r, n_i^o, and n_i^a are the sets of agent i's neighbors in the regions of repulsion, orientation, and attraction, respectively. The parameters R_r and R_o are the associated radii of repulsion and orientation. The angular velocity ω_i is determined by first computing the repulsion, orientation, and attraction vectors

$$u_i^r = -\sum_{n_i^r} \frac{c_j - c_i}{\|c_j - c_i\|_2^2} \tag{5}$$

$$u_i^o = \frac{v_i + \sum_{n_i^o} v_j}{\|v_i + \sum_{n_i^o} v_j\|_2} \tag{6}$$

$$u_i^a = \frac{\sum_{n_i^a}(c_j - c_i)}{\|\sum_{n_i^a}(c_j - c_i)\|_2}. \tag{7}$$

Next, the desired heading vector u_i is computed as $u_i = u_i^r + u_i^o + u_i^a$. Finally, angular velocity, ω_i, is computed as

$$\omega_i = k(\mathrm{atan2}(u_i^y, u_i^x) - \theta_i) \tag{8}$$

where k is a positive gain and $\mathrm{atan2}(u_i^y, u_i^x)$ is the two-argument arctangent that places the angle in the correct quadrant by considering the y and x components of u_i.

We note three important aspects of this model that give confidence that the results will extend to real robots. First, because we limit $(\mathrm{atan2}(u_i^y, u_i^x) - \theta_i)$ to the interval $[-\pi, \pi]$, the magnitude of ω_i is bounded by $k\pi$. Thus the agent dynamics match the Dubins curve model which is often used for actual UAV path planning and applies to some constant-speed, non-holonomic ground robots [10], lending some ecological validity to our experimental results below. Second, the method of choosing neighbors is similar to the random neighbor model used in [1] which replicated field observations of starlings and is relevant for robot systems where visibility and sensing distance-limited. Third, we note that the performance in this swarm model is robust to small deviations in model parameters and noise levels [16], indicating that results are likely to be applicable on real robots.

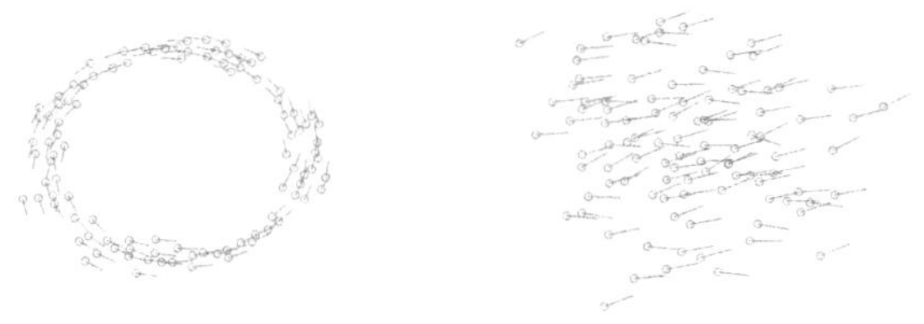

(a) Torus (b) Flock

Figure 1: The two group types formed by our model. Agent headings are represented by straight lines.

2.1 Group metrics

In order to define the two different attractors of the model we use two metrics of group behavior, namely, group angular momentum, m_{group}, and group polarization, p_{group} [9, 17]. The m_{group} is a measure of the degree of rotation of the group about its centroid and is a value between 0 and 1. The m_{group} of a swarm reaches a maximum value of 1 if all the agents are rotating around the group centroid in the same direction. The p_{group} measures the degree of alignment among individuals within the group and is also a value between 0 and 1. The p_{group} of a swarm reaches a maximum value of 1 when all the agents have the same heading.

2.2 Group types

When $R_o > R_r$, and agents are started from random initial conditions, simulation results only exhibit two group types: a torus and a flock (see Figure 1). A stable torus is characterized by p_{group} close to 0 and m_{group} close to 1. It has a relatively stationary group centroid, and either a clockwise or counterclockwise rotation. A swarm in the torus formation could be used for omnidirectional sensing of a target, perimeter monitoring, or as a fixed-wing UAV loitering command.

A stable flock is characterized by p_{group} close to 1 and m_{group} close to 0. It has a moving centroid with all of the agents heading in the same general direction. A swarm in the flock formation allows a swarm to quickly move from one location to another and could be used for search or tracking.

For a stable flock and torus, m_{group} and p_{group} are inversely related; however, when the swarm is perturbed, these values may fluctuate widely. To enable classification of swarm behaviors despite human influence, we define the group type of the swarm as follows:

$$type = \begin{cases} torus, & \text{if } p_{group} < 0.25 \text{ and } 0.75 < m_{group} \\ flock, & \text{if } m_{group} < 0.25 \text{ and } 0.75 < p_{group}. \end{cases} \tag{9}$$

These values were chosen to ensure the fundamental characteristics mentioned previously were visually evident.[1]

[1]Unless otherwise noted, $N = 100$, $s = 5$, $k = 0.5$, $R_o = 8$, and $R_r = 1$. Simulations used a discrete time approximation with simulation time step of $\Delta T = 0.1$ seconds.

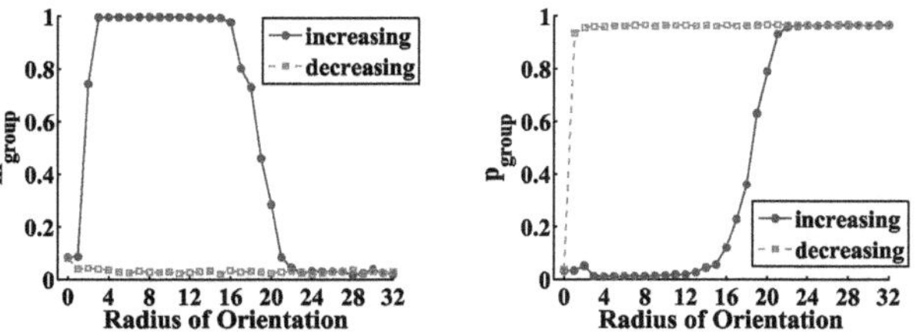

(a) (b)

Figure 2: The group momentum and polarization as the radius of orientation is increased and decreased.

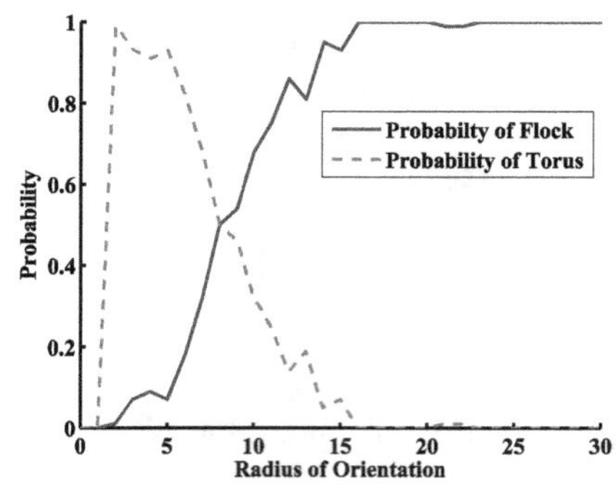

Figure 3: Probability of swarm forming a flock or a torus as a function of radius of orientation.

3. ATTRACTORS AND HYSTERESIS

Kerman et al. [17] show that the torus behavior is a fundamental attractor of the swarm model presented above. In this section we briefly summarize work that is under review for a journal that argues that the flock behavior is also an attractor of the swarm model. This attractor is fundamentally caused by the orientation dynamics, with attraction and repulsion simply causing the flock to stay cohesive but avoid collisions. Being able to treat a flock and torus as basic attractors of a swarm system means that a human can treat the torus and flock at an abstract level as cohesive units without having situation awareness of (or even observing [2]) all individual agents.

To argue that the flock is an attractor, consider a discrete time approximation of the system with only orientation dynamics ($u_i = u_i^o$ in Equation (8)). The angular velocity $\dot{\theta}$ can be approximated by

$$\dot{\theta}_i = \frac{k}{n_i + 1} \sum_j (\theta_j - \theta_i) \qquad (10)$$

where n_i is the number of neighbors of agent i. When the underlying orientation graph is connected, (10) is known to cause all agents to converge to a common heading [21]. Simulation results show that even when the orientation graph dynamically switches, agents converge to a common heading. Thus, agents following the dynamics in Equation (10) will converge to a stable flock, providing strong evidence that the flock behavior is an attractor of the swarm model.

3.1 Hysteresis

Systems that have inherent memory are said to exhibit hysteresis. Couzin noted hysteresis in his model [9], so there is reason to believe that hysteresis will be found in our model as well. Figure 2 shows the results of incrementally changing the radius of orientation, R_o. To obtain these results, the parameter R_o was incremented or decremented by 1 unit every 1000 time steps, and the average m_{group} and p_{group} was calculated over 15 replicates. As shown in Figure 2, the group behavior depends on the previous history of the group—this is because trajectories in the state space[2] are characterized by the model parameters, so changing R_o changes the basins of attraction for the flock and torus. Interestingly, when R_o decreases, the flock does not ever switch to a torus but simply remains a flock until $R_o = 0$ at which point the flock turns into an unoriented cyclic group with agents rotating in both directions around the swarm's centroid.

[2]The state is the agents' positions and headings.

This form of hysteresis is important because is indicates that the attractors of the swarm exhibit what Couzin called collective memory. This memory is important if the human is going to manage a swarm by managing the attractors for two reasons. First, if the attractors are unstable, the human will not be able to form an accurate and reliable mental model of the swarm's behavior. Second, if the attractors are stable, the human can neglect the swarm, meaning that the human need not exert continuous control.

Unfortunately, this form of hysteresis is found by increasing or decreasing the parameter R_o for all agents, which requires the human to act as a centralized controller of the agents by broadcasting global parameters. Fortunately, it is apparent from inspecting Figure 2 that there are two different attractors that can be obtained when R_o is roughly in the interval $(4, 12)$. We use this in the next sections.

3.2 Tipping point

Because we desire to be able to switch between the torus and flock attractors without changing model parameters, we ran an experiment to determine whether parameter values exist that allow both group types to emerge. We ran a series of simulations using $N = 100$, $k = 0.5$, $s = 5$, $R_r = 1$ and varied the radius of orientation. Each simulation was run for 200 seconds. One hundred simulations were performed for values of R_o between 0 and 30. For each iteration, agents were given random initial headings with random initial positions uniformly distributed over a 20 unit$\times$20 unit square.

The percentage of trials that converged to a torus and to a flock were calculated for each value of R_o and are shown in Figure 3. The value $R_o = 8$ resulted in an approximately equal proportion of torus and flock group types. Thus, $R_o \approx 8$ is the tipping point between the basins of attraction for the torus and flock, meaning that when a swarm is started from random initial conditions, both attractors are approximately equally probable. This equal probability suggests that having the human inject randomization and constraints into the swarm is a sufficient condition for allowing the human to determine what behavior will be exhibited.

The hysteresis exhibited when $R_O = 8$ and the tipping point property at the same parameter value indicate that it is possible for a human to change the collective behavior of the swarm by simply perturbing a subset of the agents enough. For this reason we use $R_o = 8$ for the remainder of this paper, but note that our results are robust to small deviations in this and other model parameters.

4. SWITCHING BETWEEN ATTRACTORS UNDER HUMAN INFLUENCE

In this section we explore two leadership strategies that enable a human to switch between the flock and torus attractors. Because the torus and flock are both stable collective behaviors (within an appropriate region of the parameter space) it is interesting to see how much effort is needed to push the swarm out of one stable attractor and into another. Additionally, having a swarm that can switch between different stable formations affords the operator increased flexibility in using the swarm. For example, switching from a torus to a flock, and then back to a torus, would allow a loitering swarm to transition to a stable flock, quickly move to a new location, and then switch to a stable torus to start monitoring that location. To investigate whether these controlled collective behavior switches can be performed when communication is limited, we assume that the human can only interact with a subset of the swarm. We use a refined version of the *stakeholders* that we have used in prior work [25, 13], modified to support switching between attractors.

4.1 Stakeholders

Stakeholders are agents in the swarm that are influenced by both the human and by other agents. Each stakeholder has a priority parameter $\rho \in [0, 1]$ that determines the priority of human influence over influence from other agents. If ρ is high, then the stakeholder responds more to human commands. If ρ is low, then the stakeholder responds more to its neighbors. Human influence is applied via teleoperation through a waypoint q.

Stakeholders can be led using two different methods: attraction and orientation. Stakeholders that are led by attraction have the desired direction $u_i = u_i^{sa} + u_i^o + u_i^r$ where

$$u_i^{sa} = \frac{\rho\hat{q}_i + (1-\rho)u_i^a}{\|\rho\hat{q}_i + (1-\rho)u_i^a\|_2} \quad \text{and} \quad \hat{q}_i = \frac{q - c_i}{\|q - c_i\|_2}. \tag{11}$$

The vector $q \in \mathbb{R}^2$ is the human-generated waypoint, $\rho \in [0, 1]$ is priority parameter, and u_i^a, u_i^o, u_i^r are the usual attraction, orientation, and repulsion influences described previously in Equations (5)–(7). This causes stakeholders to continue to orient with their neighbors while adjusting their positions to be closer to the human-specified waypoint.

Stakeholders that are led by orientation have the desired direction $u_i = u_i^a + u_i^{so} + u_i^r$ where

$$u_i^{so} = \frac{\rho\hat{q}_i + (1-\rho)u_i^o}{\|\rho\hat{q}_i + (1-\rho)u_i^o\|_2}. \tag{12}$$

This causes stakeholders to continue to be attracted to their neighbors' positions while adjusting their headings towards the human-specified waypoint. We use the notation M to denote the number of stakeholders.

4.2 Methods

To determine how best to switch the swarm from one group type to the other, we ran simulations with values of M ranging from 10 to 100 in 10 step increments and values of ρ ranging from 0.1 to 1 in 0.1 step increments. Both orientation and attraction leadership strategies were tested using a constant waypoint command. These methods systematically explore the bounds of what an idealized human, which we denote as an OoWiz after the Oz of Wizard approach [28], can do to switch between attractors. Ten trials were performed for each M and ρ pair, and for each leadership strategy. To initialize the simulations, agent positions were distributed randomly in a 20 unit×20 unit square centered at the origin. Initial orientations varied depending on whether the group began as a torus or flock.

When switching from a flock to a torus, all agents were given random initial positions with initial headings $\theta_i = 0$, $\forall i$. After allowing 25 seconds for the group to stabilize, the constant input $\hat{q} = c_g(25) + [0, 10]^T$, where $c_g(25)$ is the group centroid after 25 seconds, was applied to each stakeholder to encourage the group to turn and form a torus. When switching from a torus to a flock, each agent was given a random initial position c_i with initial heading $\theta_i = \text{atan2}(c_i^x, c_i^y) + \pi/2$ to form a counterclockwise torus. After letting the group stabilize for 25 seconds, an arbitrarily large constant control input, $\hat{q} = c_g(25) + [10,000, 0]^T$, was applied to the stakeholders to influence them to form a flock. We gave the swarm 200 seconds to switch group types, removed the OoWiz human influence, and gave the swarm 50 seconds to stabilize to evaluate whether the swarm would remain in the desired group type.

4.3 Switching from Flock to Torus

Leadership by attraction was effective for switching from a flock to a torus. Figure 4(a) shows the percentage that switched when under the influence of the OoWiz human. Figure 4(b) shows the percentage that switched after the OoWiz human input was removed. As can be seen, for sufficiently high M and ρ, the group successfully switched. However, there is a noticeable drop in the number of simulations that switched and remained for $\rho = 1$ and high values of M. We investigated this and found that because the OoWiz human was explicitly controlling the attraction dynamics, the agents formed a flock-like structure that circled around the reference input. Because the agents never spread out into a full torus, when the control input was removed the group returned to a flock formation.

When leading stakeholders by orientation, we found a large discrepancy between the number of simulations that switched to a torus and the number of simulations that remained as a torus (see figures 4(c) and 4(d)). We investigated this phenomenon and found that the human influence on the orientation dynamics often caused stakeholders to rotate in different directions around the desired torus centroid. This behavior prevents the torus from fully forming and is undesirable for actual robots because of the risk of head-on collisions. After the human influence was removed, the stakeholders were able to orient properly, causing a torus to form. This is an example of what Walker et al. refer to as *neglect benevolence* [31]. Neglect benevolence says that, in some cases, the swarm must be allowed to self stabilize before receiving a new command from the human.

4.4 Switching from Torus to Flock

When switching from a torus to a flock (see Figure 5), leading stakeholders by orientation worked much better than leading stakeholders by attraction. We examined these results and found that leading stakeholders by attraction was successful in causing the agents to switch from a torus to a flock. However, the attraction input $\hat{q}$ caused the stakeholders to slowly pull away from the rest of the group causing the flock to elongate. Thus, when the human influence was removed, the flock was unstable and usually reformed a torus.

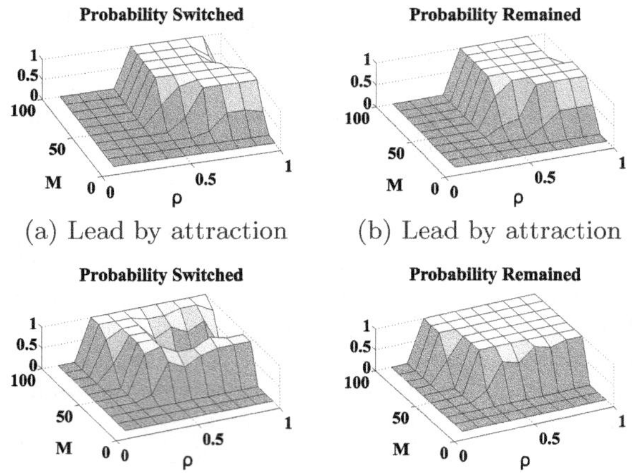

(a) Lead by attraction (b) Lead by attraction

(c) Lead by orientation (d) Lead by orientation

Figure 4: Switching from flock to torus.

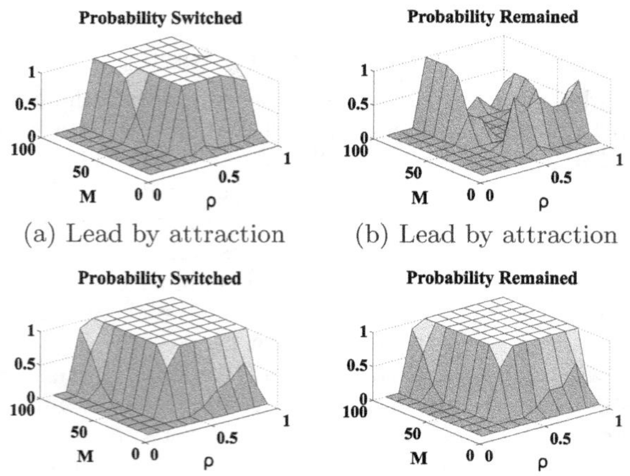

(a) Lead by attraction (b) Lead by attraction

(c) Lead by orientation (d) Lead by orientation

Figure 5: Switching from torus to flock.

Figures 5(a) and 5(b) show that except for limited areas of the parameter space, simulations that switched to a flock usually switched back to a torus. Using leadership by orientation eliminated this phenomenon and caused the agents to form a less elongated flock that remained stable after human influence was removed (see figures 5(c) and 5(d)).

4.5 Discussion

Based on these results, we lead stakeholders by orientation when switching from a torus to a flock, and by attraction when switching from a flock to a torus, for the remainder of this paper. This is a potential problem when viewed in light of our assumption that we want the human to be able to manage a swarm at a high level of abstraction because invoking a switch between attractors requires the human to choose what type of influence to exert. A simple solution to this problem is to allow the human to indicate, through a GUI or some other means, a desire to change from one structure to another. Given the current structure and the desire to switch structures, the correct controller can automatically be used to facilitate the switch.

5. QUORUM SENSING

The previous section showed that an OoWiz human could manage a swarm by switching between attractors and argued that the HRI principles of neglect tolerance and neglect benevolence apply to such a system. Unfortunately, doing so required the human to send information to a large number of robots in the collective. In this section, we propose a way to decrease the number of agents that a human must influence, and find a design parameter that allows a human to manage a trade-off between two important properties of the collective: scalability and vulnerability.

To accomplish this, we use the concept of quorum sensing, which is used in biological systems to regulate the emergence of different behaviors depending on external thresholds [6, 7]. To facilitate a discussion of quorum sensing, we utilize the taxonomy of agent types presented in [12]. An agent's type determines how it responds to human influence, external influence, and other agents. Agents can be divided into two classes: *human-aware* agents who can respond to human input and *human-blind* agents who do not respond to human input. In this section we explore the properties of a heterogeneous swarm in which we have both human-aware agents and human-blind agents. Specifically, we investigate using stakeholders, a kind of human-aware agent, and a particular kind of human-blind agent called a *type-aware* agent.

5.1 Type-aware agents

Type-aware agents are influenced by both human-aware agents and human-blind agents, but are not influenced by the human. Type-aware agents have an awareness parameter $\alpha \in [0,1]$ that determines the degree of type-awareness of the agent. If α is high, then the type-aware agent is influenced more by human-aware agents than by other human-blind agents. If α is low, then the type-aware agent is influenced more by other human-blind agents and less by human-aware agents. For the remainder of this section we assume that in the quorum sensing model, agents are either stakeholders or type-aware agents. Thus, for a swarm of size N with M stakeholders, we have $N - M$ type-aware agents.

Type-aware agents follow the normal agent dynamics described in Section 2 unless one or more of their neighbors are stakeholders. Each type-aware agent i uses quorum sensing to adjust its awareness parameter α_i. To incorporate quorum sensing into the agent dynamics, we define a quorum threshold Q_i for type-aware agent i. If type-aware agent i has more than Q_i stakeholder neighbors, then it will temporarily increase its type awareness by setting $\alpha_i = \alpha_i^{max}$, and maintain this increased type awareness until the number of stakeholders within its sensing range falls below Q_i, at which point the agent sets $\alpha_i = \alpha_i^{min}$. We use α_i^{max} and α_i^{min} to denote the maximum and minimum awareness for agent i. The parameter α_i^{max} determines how much agent i is influenced by stakeholder neighbors if it senses a quorum. The parameter α_i^{min} determines how much agent i is influenced by stakeholder neighbors if it does not sense a quorum. Thus, if we let $\mathcal{N}_i = \{j : a_{ij} = 1\}$ represent the set of neighbors of agent i, and $\mathcal{S}$ be the set of stakeholders in the swarm, then for any type-aware agent i we have

$$\alpha_i = \begin{cases} \alpha_i^{max}, & \text{if } Q_i < |\mathcal{N}_i \cap \mathcal{S}| \\ \alpha_i^{min}, & \text{if } |\mathcal{N}_i \cap \mathcal{S}| \le Q_i. \end{cases} \tag{13}$$

The desired direction vector of type-aware agent i is

$$u_i = \frac{u_i^{ta}}{\|u_i^{ta}\|_2} + \frac{u_i^{to}}{\|u_i^{to}\|_2} + u_i^r \quad (14)$$

where the u_i^{ta} and u_i^{to} are defined in the footnote[3], $\mathcal{N}_i \setminus \mathcal{S}$ represents the set of all non-stakeholder neighbors of agent i, and u_i^r is given by Equation (5). Thus, the type-aware agent's attraction and orientation vectors are weighted between neighbors that are stakeholders and neighbors that are not stakeholders by the awareness parameter α_i.

The effect of an agent increasing α_i is to increase the influence of stakeholders, thereby amplifying human influence over the swarm. Because this amplification only happens when there are Q_i or more stakeholders in a type-aware agent's sensing neighborhood, the threshold Q_i acts as a nonlinear switch that improves the responsiveness of the swarm once enough agents are influenced by the human. We demonstrate empirically that this nonlinear switch based on the threshold Q_i improves the scalability of human influence over a swarm. Note that there is a trade-off between the responsiveness and the vulnerability of a swarm. A swarm that is highly responsive to changes in behavior made by only a few agents implies that if an adversary compromises a small percentage of the agents, or if a small percentage of the agents fail, then the swarm will be vulnerable to performing unwanted behaviors. We demonstrate that the embedded quorum response can act as a mechanism to limit the vulnerability of the swarm to agent failures.

5.2 Improved Scalability

To demonstrate improved scalability of human-swarm interactions, we compare how well the quorum sensing model (the model with $N - M$ type-aware agents) and the stakeholder model (the model with zero type-aware agents) allow switches between attractors. To investigate the scalability of these two models we repeated the experiment described in Section 4 using both the stakeholder model and the quorum sensing model for swarm sizes of $N = 100$, 200, 300, and 400 agents. We varied M from 10 to $N/2$ in 10 agent increments and varied ρ from between 0.1 and 1. Ten trials were performed for each M and ρ pair. When switching from torus to flock, we led the M stakeholders by orientation. When switching from flock to torus, we led the M stakeholders by attraction. To limit the number of parameters in these simulations we set $\alpha_i^{min} = 0$, $\alpha_i^{max} = 1$, and $Q_i = 0, \forall i$.

Figure 6 shows the minimum number of stakeholders necessary to switch group types and have 100% of the simulations remain in the new group type for $N = 100$, 200, 300, and 400. Results are shown for switching from a torus to a flock where M stakeholders are led by orientation (t2fo) and for switching from a flock to a torus where M stakeholders are led by attraction (f2ta). As the size of the swarm increases, the difference in scalability between the two models is very distinct. We see that switching between attractors using the quorum sensing model scales much better to larger swarm sizes. As the size N of the swarm increases, the number of agents that the human needs to interact with stays relatively constant for the quorum sensing model, but rapidly increases for the stakeholder model.

[3] $u_i^{ta} = \alpha_i \frac{\sum_{j \in \mathcal{N}_i \cap \mathcal{S}} (c_j - c_i)}{\|\sum_{j \in \mathcal{N}_i \cap \mathcal{S}} (c_j - c_i)\|_2} + (1-\alpha_i) \frac{\sum_{j \in \mathcal{N}_i \setminus \mathcal{S}} (c_j - c_i)}{\|\sum_{j \in \mathcal{N}_i \setminus \mathcal{S}} (c_j - c_i)\|_2}$

$u_i^{to} = \alpha_i \frac{v_i + \sum_{j \in \mathcal{N}_i \cap \mathcal{S}} v_j}{\|v_i + \sum_{j \in \mathcal{N} \cap \mathcal{S}} v_j\|_2} + (1-\alpha_i) \frac{v_i + \sum_{j \in \mathcal{N}_i \setminus \mathcal{S}} v_j}{\|v_i + \sum_{j \in \mathcal{N}_i \setminus \mathcal{S}} v_j\|_2}$

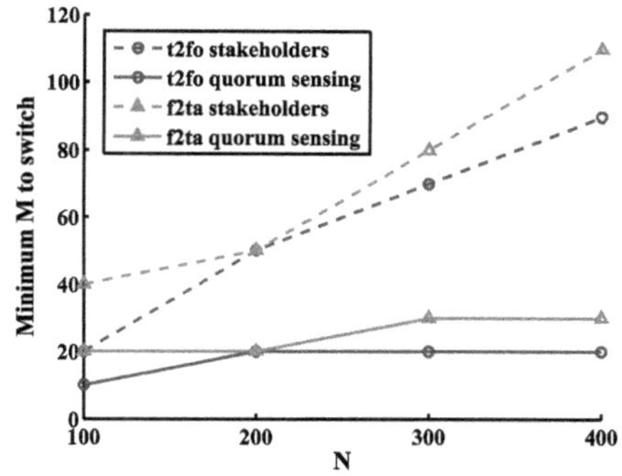

Figure 6: Minimum number of stakeholders, M, needed to switch from torus to flock where stakeholders are led by orientation (t2fo) and to switch from flock to torus where stakeholders are led by attraction (f2ta). Results compare the stakeholder model with the quorum sensing model.

5.3 Limited vulnerability

We now investigate whether using a quorum threshold allows us to limit the vulnerability of the swarm. We define limited vulnerability as the requirement that a swarm has an upper bound on the number of agents that can fail and not adversely affect the collective behavior.

To demonstrate that quorum sensing provides a way to limit the vulnerability of a swarm, we ran a series of experiments where M stakeholders attempt to switch the group type for different quorum thresholds Q. We experimented with values of Q between 0 and 6 and values of M between 0 and 50. Because of the large number of parameters in our model we restricted our analysis to parameter settings found to reliably allow the collective to switch between group types and remain switched. We used $\rho = 0.7$ when switching from a flock to a torus and $\rho = 0.5$ when switching from a torus to a flock. We led the agents by orientation when switching to a flock and by attraction when switching to a torus. We ran 10 replicates of each M and Q combination and used $\alpha_{max} = 1$ and $\alpha_{min} = 0$. We compare these results with the stakeholder model.

Figure 7 shows the probability of the swarm switching from a torus to a flock and from a flock to a torus. From this figure we see that the probability of switching decreases as Q increases. If we consider the stakeholders as malfunctioning or adversarial agents, then these results show that the quorum threshold Q provides a tunable parameter that controls the vulnerability/responsiveness of the swarm. By choosing a value for Q that is sufficiently high, we can limit the responsiveness of the swarm and prevent the swarm from switching group types unless there are sufficient agents making the change. Alternatively, if the goal is to have a swarm that is highly responsive, a low quorum threshold provides controlled switches with fewer agents.

5.4 Summary

We have shown that quorum sensing improves the scalability of human-swarm interactions. We have additionally shown that the quorum threshold Q provides a mechanism for limiting the vulnerability of a swarm. In light of our goal to find ways for a human to manage a bio-inspired robot

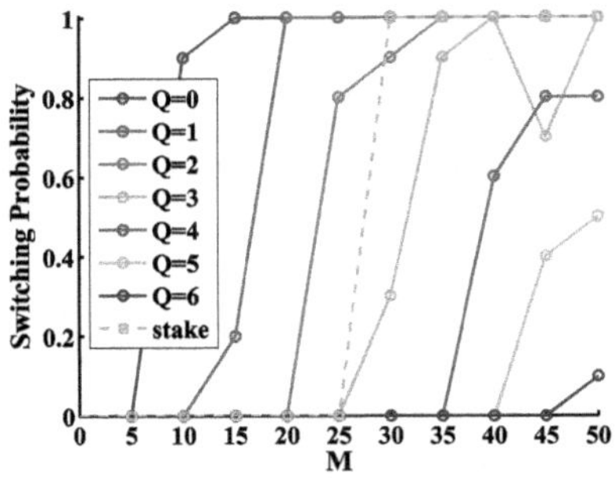

(a) Probability of switching from torus to flock

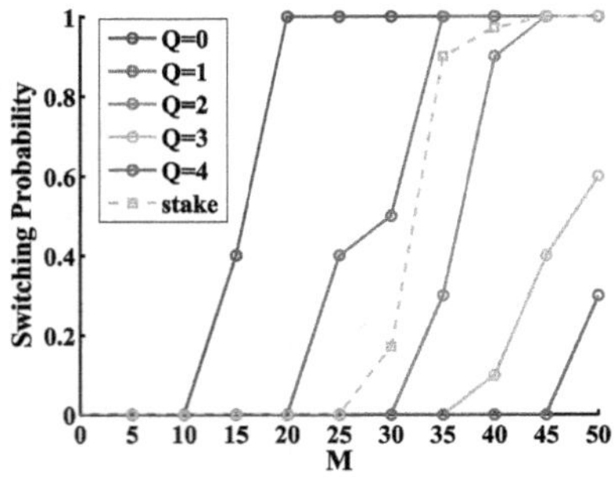

(b) Probability of switching from flock to torus

Figure 7: Switching between collective behaviors using only M stakeholders, or using M stakeholders and quorum sensing with Q = 0–6 (N = 100 agents).

swarm, these results indicate that it is possible for a human to select a switching probability before execution that balances scalability and vulnerability. Although this violates our goal of avoiding having a human broadcast parameters to the collective, it is useful since it allows a human to manage a trade-off prior to execution and still manage the flock and torus using a set of stakeholders during run-time.

6. RELATED WORK

Swarm models have been explored in a variety of fields and are typically capable of either flocking [26, 30, 23] or cyclic behavior [20, 19]. The model described in this paper is one of a small set of swarm models that exhibit multiple group behaviors [9, 29, 27]. This research concentrates on the flock and torus behaviors; however, there are other types of swarm behavior seen in the literature. Couzin's model [9] has four group types: swarm, torus, dynamic parallel group, and highly parallel group. Couzin's swarm behavior is analogous to a torus without orientation in our model, and the dynamic and highly parallel groups are simply two flavors of flocking. Strömbom [29] demonstrates that attractive forces between agents are sufficient to form swarms, flocks, and mills (torus-like formations where agents do not all rotate in the same direction). Strömbom also shows that adding a blind spot creates two additional group types: a torus and an interweaving chain-like structure. Romero et al. [27] present a swarm model that produces a swarm, a torus, a flock, and a flock that rotates around a stationary point. If we restrict our attention to models without centralized control, global information, or explicit inter-agent communication, the group types mentioned above are the only group types we have found in the literature that emerge from swarm models capable of exhibiting multiple behaviors.

Couzin et al. [8] and Conradt et al. [5] explore leading a flock with a small number of informed agents. Couzin et al. show that their method of leading a flock scales well as group size increases, but do not consider leading a torus or changing group types. In the controls community much research focuses on consensus protocols [24] for flocking [23], but we have not found any research involving switching between attractors without communication or centralized control.

Some work has been done with communication-free flocking, but this work typically creates flocks that can be controlled by one or a few agents, which makes the flock vulnerable to leader failure. Gervasi and Prencipe [11] study distributed coordination and control without any communication or shared reference frame, but require that all agents can identify the leader agent and can be efficiently controlled by a single agent. Jadbabaie [15] provides mathematical results on the convergence of the Vicsek flocking model [30] to a single group direction as well as convergence conditions for the group to converge to a single leader's direction.

Recent work has compared different methods for human-swarm interactions, but has either focused on flocking [25] or has relied on connectivity maintenance, rendezvous, and deployment algorithms that require a communication network between agents [18]. Nunnally et al. explore bandwidth constraints on swarm-to-human communications, but assume human communication with the entire swarm [22]. Our work extends and enhances the work by Kerman et al. [17], which provided preliminary results on human interaction with the flock and torus behaviors.

Several researchers have studied the effects of heterogeneity and quorum sensing on multi-agent interactions. Wu [3, 4] investigates the importance and role of heterogeneity in robot teams and shows that increased agent variation in task allocation problems can increase stability. Kumar [14] uses mathematical models of bio-inspired foraging tasks and quorum sensing to develop control strategies for redistributing agents among multiple sites, but does not investigate human influence over the agent behaviors.

7. CONCLUSIONS

We have presented a model of swarming that has two emergent behaviors: a flock and a torus. We also provided evidence that these behaviors are fundamental attractors of the swarm dynamics. Because these behaviors are attractors, a human operator can interact with the swarm by managing these attractors. We propose that human-swarm interactions should focus on managing higher level attractors of the swarm systems because it allows a human to abstract the details of individual agents and focus on managing the collective as a whole. We extended this work by presenting an application of quorum sensing to human-swarm interactions that increases the scalability of human-swarm interactions as well as provides a mechanism for allowing a human to balance a trade-off between vulnerability and responsiveness of the swarm to agent failures. Both the stakeholder and the quorum sensing models demonstrate the ability for a human to manage a swarm by managing its emergent behaviors. Future work should improve our static OoWiz model by examining dynamic interactions. In particular, user studies with humans will be necessary to fully understand the implications of controlling swarms by managing attractors.

8. ACKNOWLEDGMENTS

We appreciate the Office of Naval Research for funding this research under the Science of Autonomy Program. The findings, opinions, and conclusions of this paper do not necessarily reflect the views of the funding agency.

9. REFERENCES

[1] N. Bode, D. Franks, and A. Wood. Limited interactions in flocks: relating model simulations to empirical data. *Journal of The Royal Society Interface*, 8(55):301–304, 2010.

[2] D. S. Brown. Toward scalable human interaction with bio-inspired robot teams. Master's thesis, Brigham Young University, Provo, UT, 2013.

[3] A. Campbell, C. Riggs, and A. Wu. On the impact of variation on self-organizing systems. In *Fifth IEEE International Conference on Self-Adaptive and Self-Organizing Systems*, pages 119–128, 2011.

[4] A. Campbell and A. Wu. Multi-agent role allocation: issues, approaches, and multiple perspectives. *Autonomous agents and multi-agent systems*, 22(2):317–355, 2011.

[5] L. Conradt, J. Krause, I. Couzin, and T. Roper. Leading according to need in self-organizing groups. *The American Naturalist*, 173(3):304–312, 2009.

[6] L. Conradt and T. Roper. Consensus decision making in animals. *Trends in Ecology & Evolution*, 20(8):449–456, 2005.

[7] I. Couzin. Collective cognition in animal groups. *Trends in cognitive sciences*, 13(1):36–43, 2009.

[8] I. Couzin, J. Krause, N. Franks, and S. Levin. Effective leadership and decision-making in animal groups on the move. *Nature*, 433(7025):513–516, 2005.

[9] I. Couzin, J. Krause, R. James, G. Ruxton, and N. Franks. Collective memory and spatial sorting in animal groups. *Journal of Theoretical Biology*, 218(1):1–11, 2002.

[10] L. E. Dubins. On curves of minimal length with a constraint onaverage curvature, and with prescribed initial and terminal positions and tangents. *American J. of Mathematics*, vol. 79, no. 3, 1957.

[11] V. Gervasi and G. Prencipe. Coordination without communication: The case of the flocking problem. *Discrete Applied Mathematics*, 144(3):324–344, 2004.

[12] M. A. Goodrich, S. Kerman, and S. Y. Jung. On leadership and influence in human-swarm interaction. In *AAAI Fall Symposium Workshop on Human Control of Bio-Inspired Swarms*, 2012.

[13] M. A. Goodrich, B. Pendleton, S. Kerman, and P. B. Sujit. What types of interactions to bio-inspired robot swarms and flocks afford a human? In *Proceedings of Robotics Science and Systems*, 2012.

[14] M. Hsieh, Á. Halász, S. Berman, and V. Kumar. Biologically inspired redistribution of a swarm of robots among multiple sites. *Swarm Intelligence*, 2(2):121–141, 2008.

[15] A. Jadbabaie, J. Lin, and A. Morse. Coordination of groups of mobile autonomous agents using nearest neighbor rules. *IEEE Transactions on Automatic Control*, 48(6):988–1001, 2003.

[16] S. Kerman. Metrics for human interaction with bio-inspired swarms. Master's thesis, Brigham Young University, Provo, UT, 2013.

[17] S. Kerman, D. Brown, and M. Goodrich. Supporting human interaction with robust robot swarms. In *Proceedings of the International Symposium on Resilient Control Systems*, 2012.

[18] A. Kolling, K. Sycara, S. Nunnally, and M. Lewis. Human swarm interaction: An experimental study of two types of interaction with foraging swarms. *Journal of Human-Robot Interaction*, 2(2):103–128, 2013.

[19] H. Levine, W. Rappel, and I. Cohen. Self-organization in systems of self-propelled particles. *Physical Review E*, 63(1):017101, 2000.

[20] J. Marshall, M. Broucke, and B. Francis. Formations of vehicles in cyclic pursuit. *IEEE Transactions on Automatic Control*, 49(11):1963–1974, 2004.

[21] M. Mesbahi and M. Egerstedt. *Graph Theoretic Methods in Multiagent Networks*. Princeton University Press, 2010.

[22] S. Nunnally, P. Walker, M. Lewis, A. Kolling, N. Chakraborty, and K. Sycara. Robotic swarm connectivity with human operation and bandwidth limitations. In *Proceedings of the AAAI Fall Symposium Workshop on Human Control of Bio-Inspired Swarms*, 2012.

[23] R. Olfati-Saber. Flocking for multi-agent dynamic systems: Algorithms and theory. *IEEE Transactions on Automatic Control*, 51(3):401–420, 2006.

[24] R. Olfati-Saber, J. Fax, and R. Murray. Consensus and cooperation in networked multi-agent systems. *Proceedings of the IEEE*, 95(1):215–233, 2007.

[25] B. Pendleton and M. Goodrich. Scalable human interaction with robotic swarms. In *To appear in the proceedings of the AIAA Infotech@Aerospace Conference*, 2013.

[26] C. Reynolds. Flocks, herds and schools: A distributed behavioral model. In *ACM SIGGRAPH Computer Graphics*, volume 21, pages 25–34. ACM, 1987.

[27] L. Romero, E. Forgoston, and I. Schwartz. Noise, bifurcations, and modeling of interacting particle systems. In *International Conference on Intelligent Robots and Systems*, pages 3905–3910. IEEE, 2011.

[28] A. Steinfeld, O. C. Jenkins, and B. Scassellati. The "Oz of Wizard": Simulating the human for interaction research. In *Proceedings of the ACM/IEEE International Conference on Human-Robot Interaction*, 2009.

[29] D. Strömbom. Collective motion from local attraction. *Journal of theoretical biology*, 283(1):145–151, 2011.

[30] T. Vicsek, *et al.* Novel type of phase transition in a system of self-driven particles. *Physical Review Letters*, 75(6):1226–1229, 1995.

[31] P. Walker, S. Nunnally, M. Lewis, A. Kolling, N. Chakraborty, and K. Sycara. Investigating neglect benevolence and communication latency during human-swarm interaction. In *AAAI Fall Symposium Workshop on Human Control of Bio-Inspired Swarms*, 2012.

Human - Robot Swarm Interaction for Entertainment

From animation display to gesture based control

Javier Alonso-Mora
ETH & Disney Res. Zurich
Tannenstrasse 3
Switzerland
jalonso@ethz.ch

Roland Siegwart
ETH Zurich
Tannenstrasse 3
Switzerland
rsiegwart@ethz.ch

Paul Beardsley
Disney Research Zurich
Stampfenbachstrasse 48
Switzerland
pab@disneyresearch.com

ABSTRACT

This work shows experimental results with three systems that take real-time user input to direct a robot swarm formed by tens of small robots. These are: real-time drawing, gesture based interaction with an RGB-D sensor and control via a hand-held tablet computer.

Categories and Subject Descriptors

I.2 [**Artificial Intelligence**]: Robotics

1. MOTIVATION

Successful applications of large multi-robot teams include industrial automation and entertainment, with future applications likely to include search-and-rescue and inspection. In complex tasks, where a human must provide (in real-time) high-level control of the robot swarm, intuitive or readily-learnt interfaces are necessary. Enabling a human operator to control a robot swarm with hundreds of robots is still an open problem due to its high dimensionality. Methods to reduce the number of degrees of freedom to a few meaningful ones and automate the interaction are required. In this work we show three implementations, applicable in the area of entertainment robotics, of intuitive methods for real-time human swarm interaction.

2. HUMAN - SWARM INTERACTION

This work shows experimental results with three systems that take real-time user input to direct a robot swarm and achieve intuitive real-time interaction. A team of the small differentially driven robots described in [2] are employed.

- The user interface is via *real-time drawing*. A single drawing or an animation can be created and the robots automatically adopt a physical configuration to represent the drawn figure. The computation of robot position, robot motion, and robot color is automatic, including scaling to the available number of robots following the algorithms presented in [2] and [3].

HRI'14, March 3–6, 2014, Bielefeld, Germany.
ACM 978-1-4503-2658-2/14/03.
http://dx.doi.org/10.1145/2559636.2559645

- The user interface is via a *hand-held tablet*, which tracks the robots and computes collision-free trajectories following the optimization described in [1]. Augmented reality and a multi-player setup are also shown.
- The user interface is via an *RGB-D sensor*, used to recognize human gesture and to determine the commands that are sent to a group comprising tens of robots. Two approaches are presented. In the first approach, the robots are unconstrained in position and motion and deictic gestures are used. The user can select subsets of robots including individual robots, change their colors and positions, and move them along trajectories. In the second approach representational gestures are used. The robots are in a pre-defined configuration, for example a cartoon face, and there are defined modes for warping the configuration directly.

3. CONCLUSIONS

This work has demonstrated methods for real-time interaction between a human and a swarm of robots, with applications in entertainment and toy robots. Three methods that take real-time user input to direct a robot swarm have been described and tested with a team of small robots. These provide interaction via a drawing interface, a hand-held tablet computer and gesture based via an RGB-D sensor. All methods have been shown to provide intuitive interaction and were quickly learnt by unexperienced users.

4. ACKNOWLEDGMENTS

The authors would like to thank Cyrill Bloeglinger, Andreas Breitenmoser, Reto Grieder, Stefan Haag, Sandro Hauri, Stefan Lohaus Haegeli, Philipp Leeman and Martin Rufli who have contributed to the results shown in this video.

5. REFERENCES

[1] J. Alonso-Mora, A. Breitenmoser, M. Rufli, P. Beardsley, and R. Siegwart. Optimal Reciprocal Collision Avoidance for Multiple Non-Holonomic Robots. *Int. Symp. on Distr. Auton. Rob. Syst.*, 2010.

[2] J. Alonso-Mora, A. Breitenmoser, M. Rufli, R. Siegwart, and P. Beardsley. Image and Animation Display with Multiple Robots. *Int. Journal of Robotics Research*, 31(6):753–773, May 2012.

[3] S. Hauri, J. Alonso-Mora, A. Breitenmoser, R. Siegwart, and P. Beardsley. Multi-Robot Formation Control via a Real-Time Drawing Interface. *Int. Conf. on Field and Service Robotics*, 2012.

Daedalus: A sUAV for Social Environments

Dante Arroyo
Department of Engineering
Pontificia Universidad Catolica del Peru
Lima, Peru
darroyo@pucp.edu.pe

Cesar Lucho
Department of Art
Pontificia Universidad Catolica del Peru
Lima, Peru
di.ce.lucho@gmail.com

Julissa Roncal
Department of Psychology
Pontificia Universidad Catolica del Peru
Lima, Peru
jroncal@pucp.edu.pe

Francisco Cuellar
Department of Engineering
Pontificia Universidad Catolica del Peru
Lima, Peru
cuellar.ff@gmail.com

ABSTRACT

Due to their wide functionality in military and civil applications, small unmanned aerial vehicles (sUAVs) are becoming more commonly operated in public places, causing direct and indirect human-robot interaction. As these particular robots promise widespread integration into humans' social contexts, it is important to understand how people will perceive them if positive interaction wants to be achieved. In this video, we introduce a sUAV for social environments. "Daedalus" is a quadcopter that has been designed with a special focus in expressing emotional states through interaction features, such as head movements and eye color variation.

In order to analyze the robot's capacity to express emotions and people's perception of these states, an experiment was conducted. The sUAV is initially located in a stationary module, the subject approaches the robot, and sits down in front of it, maintaining an interaction distance between 0.5 - 0.7 m. The robot performs 4 different expressions combining head movement and eye color display. After each expression, a psychologist asks the subject two questions: What do you feel? and What do you think the robot is feeling? For evaluation, subjects must select one of seven cards associated with basic emotions to express and evaluate emotions according to the questions. The preliminary results of this experiment are presented in this video.

Categories and Subject Descriptors

H.1.1 [**Models and Principles**]: User/Machine Systems—*human factors*; H.5.2 [**Information Interfaces and Presentation**]: User Interfaces—*natural languaje, user-centered design*; J.4 [**Social and Behavioral Sciences**]: Psychology

HRI'14, March 3–6, 2014, Bielefeld, Germany.
ACM 978-1-4503-2658-2/14/03.
http://dx.doi.org/10.1145/2559636.2559652.

General Terms

Design, Experimentation, Human Factors.

Keywords

Communication interface, emotion recognition, human-robot interaction, psychometrics, sUAV.

1. ACKNOWLEDGMENTS

The authors wish to thank the department of Engineering of the Pontificia Universidad Catolica del Peru.

The Development and Real-World Deployment of FROG, the Fun Robotic Outdoor Guide

Vanessa Evers[1], Nuno Menezes[2], Luis Merino[3], Dariu Gavrila[4], Fernando Nabais[2], Maja Pantic[5], Paulo Alvito[6], Daphne Karreman[1]

University of Twente[1] (Enschede, The Netherlands), YDreams[2] (Lisbon, Portugal), Pablo de Olavide University[3] (Seville, Spain), University of Amsterdam[4] (Amsterdam, The Netherlands), Imperial College London[5] (London, UK), IDMind[6] (Lisbon, Portugal)

v.evers@utwente.nl

ABSTRACT

This video details the development of an intelligent outdoor Guide robot. The main objective is to deploy an innovative robotic guide which is not only able to show information, but to react to the affective states of the users, and to offer location-based services using augmented reality. The scientific challenges concern autonomous outdoor navigation and localization, robust 24/7 operation, affective interaction with visitors through outdoor human and facial feature detection as well as engaging interactive behaviors in an ongoing non-verbal dialogue with the user.

Categories and Subject Descriptors

H.1.2 User/Machine Systems

General Terms

Design, Human Factors

Keywords

HRI, Guide Robots, Social Robots, Social Computing, Human-Aware Navigation, Real world robot deployment, Affective Computing, Emotion Recognition, Multi-modal HRI

1. INTRODUCTION

The video describes the main objectives and challenges of project FROG. This project focuses on an emerging class of intelligent robot platforms that we call Outdoor Guide Robots. The proposed research will make autonomous outdoor robots into viable and significant location-based outdoor service providers with capacity to transform our experience of outdoor spaces, and, in particular, outdoor touristic scenarios.

The project aims to the development of an innovative robotic guide, which can enhance the experience of visitors of touristic places. While robotic guides have been developed in the past [3, 2], the FROG robot will generate an innovative installation that includes affective computing as the key to adapt to the users. We envision a robotic solution that can operate 24/7 in outdoor environments, has an interesting personality that can engage small groups of visitors for part of their visit, it detects visitors group-formation and their engagement with the robot and it offers multiple interaction modalities and augmented reality content to experience novel aspects of the site. This way, the robot will offer short enjoyable tours for families or friends that they can enjoy at their own pace while engaging with the content of the site.

HRI'14, March 3–6 2014, Bielefeld, Germany
ACM 978-1-4503-2658-2/14/03.
http://dx.doi.org/10.1145/2559636.2559649

The accompanying video submission shows the robots inner hardware and shell designs as well as tests that were run to assess user needs, autonomous mapping and localization and person tracking as well as engagement and affect detection. Next steps for the coming are the implementation of adaptive robot behaviors and content display through interaction with the visitors and in response to their engagement as measured by affect detection through facial feature extraction outdoors. The interaction modalities of the robots are currently audio, video display, movement and projection. These will be extended the next year with light and an antenna for gestural expression and pointing.

2. GOALS AND CHALLENGES

To achieve this goal, the project has to solve a series of challenging problems:

- Reliable autonomous outdoor robot operation.
- Automatic, multimodal vision-based recognition of spontaneous displays of conversational and affective signals.
- Localization and Navigation in populated and dynamic environments.
- Cognitive social-psychological evaluation of user responses to robots adaptive behaviors.
- Multi-modal human robot interaction and location based content.

A series of data collection, real-world technical deployment and user studies in the lab (for example: [1]) and in real world are carried out to guide the development of FROG at end-user sites (Royal Alcazar in Seville, Spain, and the Lisbon zoo in Portugal).

3. ACKNOWLEDGEMENTS

The research leading to these results received funding from the European Communitys 7th Framework programme under Grant agreement 288235. http://www.frogrobot.eu.

4. REFERENCES

[1] Karreman, D., et al. Picking favorites: The influence of robot eye-gaze on interactions with multiple users. In *Proc. IROS* (2013), 123-128

[2] Siegwart, R. et al. Robox at Expo.02: A large-scale installation of personal robots. *Robotics and Autonomous Systems* 42, 3-4 (March 2003), 203-222.

[3] Thrun, S. et al. Probabilistic algorithms and the interactive museum tour-guide robot minerva. *The International Journal of Robotics Research* 19 (October 2000), 972-999.

Hello Robot, Can You Come Here?

Using ROS4iOS to Provide Remote Perceptual Capabilities for Visual Location, Speech and Speaker Recognition

François Ferland Ronan Chauvin Dominic Létourneau François Michaud
IntRoLab - Intelligent, Interactive, Integrated and Interdisciplinary Robotics Lab
3IT - Université de Sherbrooke (QC) Canada J1K 0A5
[francois.ferland, ronan.chauvin, dominic.letourneau, francois.michaud]@usherbrooke.ca

1. INTRODUCTION

Mobile devices such as smartphones and tablets can provide additional sensing and interacting capabilities to a mobile robot, even extending its senses to remote locations. To do so, we developed ROS4iOS[1], a native port of ROS [6] allowing to seamlessly use data from mobile iOS devices to be processed on a robot. To demonstrate this capability, this video presentation illustrates how ROS4iOS has been used to implement an assistance scenario: a person in a remote location asks our IRL-1 [1] robot for assistance, and IRL-1 must recognize the person's voice, identify the remote location using images taken from the mobile device, navigate to the identified location and interact vocally with the person through the mobile device. When communication with the robot is established by launching a specific iOS application, audio from the mobile device is published on a single topic and directed toward two ROS nodes on IRL-1. PocketSphinx [4], a speech recognition toolkit, is used to obtain the person vocal commands. WISS [3], a speaker identification system, is used for speaker identification. From a vocal request made through the mobile device, the robot can identify the person and request to get images of the remote location using the rear-facing camera of the mobile device. RTABMap [5], a loop-closure detection system for visual location recognition, is used to locate the person. A map was previously built with the robot's laser range finder using the gmapping SLAM [2] algorithm, thus permitting reuse of the ROS navigation stack to plan a path and follow it safely from its current location to the requested one. Depending on its current state, the robot can also display the most suited view (i.e., phone, camera, navigation) on the iOS application. ROS4iOS can also be used to teleoperate IRL-1 through the mobile device or to discuss remotely with the robot, using the same ROS modules.

ROS4iOS opens up a rich set of possibilities for HRI, making ROS-compatible code accessible on mobile devices. In future work, we plan to integrate a dialog management system [7] for other assistance scenarios, such as image-based object fetching and delivery.

[1] https://github.com/introlab/ros_for_ios

HRI'14, March 3–6, 2014, Bielefeld, Germany.
ACM 978-1-4503-2658-2/14/03.
http://dx.doi.org/10.1145/2559636.2559639.

Figure 1: A person in a remote location interacting with the robot.

Acknowledgments

This work was supported in part by the Natural Sciences and Engineering Research Council of Canada.

2. REFERENCES

[1] F. Ferland, D. Létourneau, A. Aumont, J. Frémy, M.-A. Legault, M. Lauria, and F. Michaud. Natural interaction design of a humanoid robot. *Journal of Human-Robot Interaction*, 1(2):14–29, 2012.

[2] G. Grisetti, C. Stachniss, and W. Burgard. Improved techniques for grid mapping with Rao-Blackwellized particle filters. *IEEE Transactions on Robotics*, 23(1):34–46, 2007.

[3] F. Grondin and F. Michaud. WISS, a speaker identification system for mobile robots. In *Proceedings of the IEEE International Conference on Robotics and Automation*, pages 1817–1822, 2012.

[4] D. Huggins-Daines, M. Kumar, A. Chan, A. W. Black, M. Ravishankar, and A. I. Rudnicky. PocketSphinx: A free, real-time continuous speech recognition system for hand-held devices. In *Proceedings of the International Conference on Acoustics, Speech, and Signal Processing* , pages 185–188, 2006.

[5] M. Labbé and F. Michaud. Appearance-based loop closure detection in real-time for large-scale and long-term operation. *IEEE Transactions on Robotics*, pages 734–745, 2013.

[6] M. Quigley, B. Gerkey, K. Conley, J. Faust, T. Foote, J. Leibs, E. Berger, R. Wheeler, and A. Ng. ROS: an open-source robot operating system. In *ICRA Workshop on Open Source Software*, 2009.

[7] C. Rich and C. L. Sidner. Using collaborative discourse theory to partially automate dialogue tree authoring. In Y. Nakano, M. Neff, A. Paiva, and M. Walker, editors, *Intelligent Virtual Agents*, volume 7502 of *Lecture Notes in Computer Science*, pages 327–340. Springer Berlin, 2012.

Human-Robot Interaction through 3D Vision and Force Control

Aleksandar Jevtić
Robosoft
Bidart, France

Guillaume Doisy
Department of Industrial Engineering and Management
Ben-Gurion University of the Negev
Beer Sheva, Israel

Saša Bodiroža
Cognitive Robotics, Department of Computer Science
Humboldt-Universität zu Berlin
Berlin, Germany

Yael Edan
Department of Industrial Engineering and Management
Ben-Gurion University of the Negev
Beer Sheva, Israel

Verena V. Hafner
Cognitive Robotics, Department of Computer Science
Humboldt-Universität zu Berlin
Berlin, Germany

ABSTRACT

The video shows the interaction with a customized Kompaï robot. The robot consists of the Robosoft's robuLAB10 platform, tablet PC, and a Microsoft Kinect camera mounted on a pan-tilt system. A visual control algorithm provides continuous person tracking. The newly developed robot features include gesture recognition, person following, navigation with pointing, and force control, which were integrated with the Robosoft's robuBOX SDK and the Karto SLAM algorithms. The video demonstrates all the features and puts the robot in use in an everyday home scenario.

Keywords

Human-robot interaction, gesture recognition, person following

1. INTRODUCTION

As robots move out from industrial halls into homes, intuitive human-robot interaction gains more interest. The video presents research efforts in important sub-areas of intuitive human-robot interaction, namely person following and gesture recognition [3][5]. Possible modes of robot control are person following, assisted pushing and pointing. Selection of a mode is done with gestures.

A gesture recognition algorithm based on dynamic time warping [1] is employed for control of the mobile robot. Sensory input is obtained through an RGB-D sensor in the form of 3D joint positions. A person following algorithm [4] is used to realize precise following of the person. Additionally, the robot can be guided around by using pointing detection. Assisted pushing is realized through use of force control to detect when a person physically moves the robot and assist their movements, building on the concept of human-robot contact detection using motor torque monitoring, introduced in [2].

HRI'14, March 3–6, 2014, Bielefeld, Germany.
ACM 978-1-4503-2658-2/14/03.
http://dx.doi.org/10.1145/2559636.2559651.

2. ACKNOWLEDGMENTS

This work has been supported by the EU-funded FP7 ITN "INTRO", grant agreement no.: 238486 and by the German Research Foundation GRK 1589/1. The authors would like to thank other project participants: Sanja Dogramadzi, Maria Elena Giannaccini, Thomas Hellström, Bo Li, Eric Lucet, Yisrael Parmet, Tony Pipe, Ulrik Söderström.

3. REFERENCES

[1] S. Bodiroža, G. Doisy, and V. V. Hafner. Position-invariant, real-time gesture recognition based on dynamic time warping. In *Proceedings of the 8th ACM/IEEE International Conference on Human-robot Interaction*, HRI '13, pages 87–88, Piscataway, NJ, USA, 2013. IEEE Press.

[2] G. Doisy. Sensorless collision detection and control by physical interaction for wheeled mobile robots. In *Proceedings of the Seventh Annual ACM/IEEE International Conference on Human-Robot Interaction*, HRI '12, pages 121–122, New York, NY, USA, 2012. ACM.

[3] G. Doisy, A. Jevtić, and S. Bodiroža. Spatially unconstrained, gesture-based human-robot interaction. In *Proceedings of the 8th ACM/IEEE International Conference on Human-robot Interaction*, HRI '13, pages 117–118, Piscataway, NJ, USA, 2013. IEEE Press.

[4] G. Doisy, A. Jevtić, E. Lucet, and Y. Edan. Adaptive person-following algorithm based on depth images and mapping. In *Proc. of the IROS Workshop on Robot Motion Planning*, Oct. 2012.

[5] A. Jevtic, E. Lucet, A. Kozlov, and J. Gancet. INTRO: A multidisciplinary approach to intelligent human-robot interaction. In *World Automation Congress (WAC), 2012*, pages 1–6, 2012.

The Chatbot Strikes Back

James Kennedy, Joachim de Greeff, Robin Read, Paul Baxter, Tony Belpaeme
Centre for Robotics and Neural Systems
Cognition Institute
Plymouth University, U.K.
{james.kennedy, joachim.degreeff, robin.read, paul.baxter, tony.belpaeme}@plymouth.ac.uk

Categories and Subject Descriptors

H.1.2 [**Models and Principles**]: User/Machine Systems

General Terms

Experimentation, Human Factors, Theory

Keywords

Social HRI; child speech recognition; conversational context

Figure 1: Interaction setup/video snapshot. Two chatbots embodied in robots talking to a child.

1. THE TECHNOLOGY

This video shows an interaction between a child and two chatbots embodied in a pair of Aldebaran Nao robots. In order to process the child's speech, Google's Automatic Speech Recognition (ASR) was running on the robots. Speech input was recorded through the Nao's microphones and processed by the ASR. The resulting text string was fed into the online chatbot and the chatbot's response was then played to the child via the robot's standard text-to-speech functionality.

As the challenges in child speech recognition are immense, some stock phrases were taken to use as an input to the chatbot when no speech was recognised. Additionally, non-linguistic utterances [3] were used in a random manner by the robots when the speech recognition broke down. It was thought that this may communicate a lack of understanding and also be amusing for the child.

Two different chatbots were used: one based on ELIZA, a psychotherapist, and another, IzarFree, which takes on the character of an alien. The two robots were placed on a table at a similar height to the child, who was sitting on a large sofa just in front of them (Figure 1).

2. THE THEORY AND THE REALITY

While chatbots do not always produce meaningful output, they can usually sustain a pseudo-conversation with adult humans. Combining this with the novelty effect for a child, the hypothesis was that this would overcome any lack of understanding between the child and the robot due to ASR limitations.

This was not at all the case; the lack of context surrounding the interaction just served to confuse the child. The video shows a series of amusing clips which demonstrate several of the misunderstandings that occurred. The clips are subtitled in order to make them easier to interpret.

In conclusion, it is clear that speech recognition needs considerable work before it will function in real-world environments with children, as has been noted elsewhere [2]. Additionally, there must be a context in which children and robots interact, reinforcing the points made in [1]. The robot must also be able to respond in a socially contingent manner for this context.

HRI'14, March 3–6, 2014, Bielefeld, Germany.
ACM 978-1-4503-2658-2/14/03.
http://dx.doi.org/10.1145/2559636.2559650.

3. ACKNOWLEDGMENTS

This work is funded by the EU FP7 ALIZ-E project (grant 248116). The authors would like to thank the star of the video, Luke, for his time interacting with the robots.

4. REFERENCES

[1] P. Baxter, I. Baroni, M. Nalin, A. Sanna, and T. Belpaeme. Touchscreens as Mediators for Social Human-Robot Interactions. In *CmIS Workshop at ITS'2013*, 2013.

[2] O. Mubin, C. Bartneck, L. Leijs, H. Hooft van Huysduynen, J. Hu, and J. Muelver. Improving Speech Recognition with the Robot Interaction Language. *Disruptive Science and Technology*, 1(2):79–88, 2012.

[3] R. Read and T. Belpaeme. Situational context directs how people affectively interpret robotic non-linguistic utterances. In *Proceedings of the 9th Int. Conf. on HRI*, HRI'14, accepted.

Semi-Autonomous Cooperative Driving for Mobile Robotic Telepresence Systems

Andrey Kiselev
Örebro University
70182 Örebro, Sweden
andrey.kiselev@oru.se

Giovanni Mosiello
Roma Tre University
Via Ostiense 159, 00154
Rome, Italy
gio.mosiello@gmail.com

Annica Kristoffersson
Örebro University
70182 Örebro, Sweden
annica.kristoffersson@oru.se

Amy Loutfi
Örebro University
70182 Örebro, Sweden
amy.loutfi@oru.se

Categories and Subject Descriptors

I.2.9 [**Robotics**]: Commercial robots and applications; H.5.2 [**User interfaces**]: Graphical user interfaces (GUI)

Keywords

Human-Robot Interaction, Mobile Robotic Telepresence, Teleoperation, User Interfaces

Abstract

Mobile robotic telepresence (MRP) has been introduced to allow communication from remote locations. Modern MRP systems offer rich capabilities for human-human interactions. However, simply driving a telepresence robot can become a burden especially for novice users, leaving no room for interaction at all. In this video we introduce a project which aims to incorporate advanced robotic algorithms into manned telepresence robots in a natural way to allow human-robot cooperation for safe driving. It also shows a very first implementation of cooperative driving based on extracting a safe drivable area in real time using the image stream received from the robot.

HRI'14, March 3–6, 2014, Bielefeld, Germany.
ACM 978-1-4503-2658-2/14/03.
http://dx.doi.org/10.1145/2559636.2559640.

EFAA - A Companion Emerges From Integrating a Layered Cognitive Architecture

Stéphane Lallée,
Vasiliki Vouloutsi,
Sytse Wierenga
Synthetic Perceptive Emotive Cognitive Systems group, UPF
Barcelona, Spain
stephane.lallee@gmail.com

Ugo Pattacini
Fondazione Istituto Italiano di Tecnologia
Genoa, Italy

Paul Verschure
Synthetic Perceptive Emotive Cognitive Systems group, ICREA
Barcelona, Spain

ABSTRACT
In this video, we present the human robot interaction generated by applying the DAC cognitive architecture [1] on the iCub robot. We demonstrate how the robot reacts and adapts to its environment within the context a continuous interactive scenario including different games. We emphasize as well that the artificial agent is maintaining a self-model in terms of emotions and drives and how those are expressed in order affect the social interaction.

Categories and Subject Descriptors
I.2.9 [**Commercial robots and applications**]: Layered Cognitive Architecture for Distributed and Adaptive Control of a social robot.

General Terms
Experimentation, Human Factors, Theory

Keywords
robot companion; social interaction; synthetic emotions; allostatic control

1. INTRODUCTION
As robots skills are increasing and their cost are decreasing, soon offices and homes environments will soon include robotic agents. Whatever is their role in a social community, they will have to behave in a human like manner in order to be accepted. On one hand, they will have to integrate in their decisional model the human's actions and intentions. On the other hand, to be considered as autonomous agents, they should maintain and demonstrate their own internal state and goals which serves as a motivational engine for action. Such a level of interaction requires a solid cognitive architecture that closes the perception / action loop at various different scales ranging from the motor reflex level to the cooperation with human on a shared plan [2]. DAC [1] is such architecture: it handles different levels of representation and control through a layered structure. We implemented a generic sensor abstraction mechanism that allows the architecture to encompass any number of sensors, while using the humanoid robot iCub as the main actor [4]. Our setup also includes an interactive table that allows easy implementation of multiplayer games involving physical manipulation of objects in a shared space. Humans, objects and more broadly sensory representations are maintained within the robot's world state, which allows him to react to perceptual events (a human enters the room, a tactile contact, a collision between objects, etc.). At a higher level, the architecture is also computing more semantic events (e.g. winning or losing at a game). All events are carrying an intrinsic emotional value that has an effect on the internal model of the robot in term of emotions (e.g. a caress is triggering positive emotions while pinching will arise negative ones) and utility (effects on the robot drives). While the internal model is regulated by the external world, it is also guiding the actions of the robot through the mechanism of allostatic control [3]. The most systematic way of sharing the robot inner state is through facial expressions and speech: they increase a lot its life likeliness and influence the attitude of humans towards him. In term of stability, we can assess that the architecture reached a mature stage as it is running on a daily basis, making the robot to interact with naïve people in a fluent way. All the code is open source and available at http://sourceforge.net/projects/efaa/

HRI'14, March 3–6, 2014, Bielefeld, Germany.
ACM 978-1-4503-2658-2/14/03.
http://dx.doi.org/10.1145/2559636.2559643

2. ACKNOWLEDGMENTS
This work is supported by the EU FP7 project EFAA (FP7-ICT-270490) and by the Spanish Plan Nacional TIN2010-16745 (FAA-Arquitectura Cognitiva Biomimetica para un Funcional Ayudante de Androide Socialmente en Activo).

3. REFERENCES

[1] P. Verschure, "Distributed Adaptive Control: A theory of the Mind, Brain, Body Nexus," *Biol. Inspired Cogn. Archit.*, 2012.

[2] S. Lallée, U. Pattacini, and S. Lemaignan, "Towards a Platform-Independent Cooperative Human Robot Interaction System: III. An Architecture for Learning and Executing Actions and Shared Plans," 2012.

[3] V. Vouloutsi, S. Lallée, and P. F. M. J. Verschure, "Modulating behaviors using allostatic control," in in *Biomimetic and Biohybrid Systems*, Springer, 2013, pp. 287–298.

[4] G. Metta, G. Sandini, and D. Vernon, "The iCub humanoid robot: an open platform for research in embodied cognition," in *Proceedings of the 8th workshop on performance metrics for intelligent systems*, 2008, pp. 50–56.

Integrating Multi-Modal Interfaces to Command UAVs

[Video Abstract]

Valiallah (Mani) Monajjemi, Shokoofeh Pourmehr, Seyed Abbas Sadat, Fei Zhan
Jens Wawerla, Greg Mori and Richard Vaughan
School of Computing Science, Simon Fraser University, Burnaby, BC, Canada
{mmonajje, spourmeh, sas21, fzhan, jwawerla, mori, vaughan}@sfu.ca

ABSTRACT

We present an integrated human-robot interaction system that enables a user to select and command a team of two Unmanned Aerial Vehicles (UAV) using voice, touch, face engagement and hand gestures. This system integrates multiple human [multi]-robot interaction interfaces as well as a navigation and mapping algorithm in a coherent semi-realistic scenario. The task of the UAVs is to explore and map a simulated Mars environment.

To initiate a mission, the user needs to select a robot. To do this, We used the "Touch-To-Name" selection and naming interface [3]. In this method, the user first announces the desired number of robot(s) (e.g *"You"* or *"You Two"*), then gently moves intended robot(s) iteratively. Robots compare their accelerometer readings over Wi-Fi to agree on which one is selected.

Once selected, the user names the selected robot using verbal commands (e.g *"You are Green"*). These names are then used to command the robots (e.g. *"Green Takeoff"*) [4]. Here, we use this interface with maximum group size set to one.

After taking off and while hovering, robot looks for human faces in its camera feed. When user's face is detected, the robot continuously controls its altitude and heading direction to face the user. A hand wave gesture (left or right) assigns an exploration task to the robot in the indicated direction. We used the method described in [2] for face tracking and gesture recognition.

While exploring, each robot performs vision-based Simultaneous Localization and Mapping (SLAM) using their on-board monocular camera [1]. We used the "Feature-rich path planning algorithm" introduced in [5] to robustly navigate a UAV while exploring an unknown environment. To terminate the mission, the user commands each robot to *come back* home (e.g *"Green come back"*). To come back, robots use the same algorithm to plan a *feature-rich* path to their takeoff position. Finally, The user asks robots to *land.* (e.g. *"Green land"*).

The system provides two types of feedback to the user during interaction sessions and mission execution. Robots change the color and blinking pattern of their LED lights to inform the user about their state (e.g. "tracking user's face", "exploring" or "being idle"). In addition, a text-to-speech (TTS) engine provides verbal feedback to the user whenever a robot's state changes. As an example, when the *Green* robot is asked by the user to comeback, it acknowledges by saying *"Green is coming back"*. The TTS is embedded within a general purpose web-based robot monitoring dashboard.

We used Parrot AR-Drone 2.0 quadrocopter as UAV platform in our system. All described software components run off-board on two commodity *Intel Core i7* notebooks (one dedicated to each robot). The computers are connected to UAVs via Wi-Fi connection.

The video shows a complete run-through of a two robot exploration mission in which the HRI worked perfectly.

HRI'14, March 3–6, 2014, Bielefeld, Germany.
ACM 978-1-4503-2658-2/14/03.
http://dx.doi.org/10.1145/2559636.2559646 .

Categories and Subject Descriptors

H.5.2 [**User Interfaces and Presentation**]: Robotics, Human Multi-Robot Interfaces, Interaction styles

1. REFERENCES

[1] G. Klein and D. Murray. Parallel tracking and mapping for small AR workspaces. In *Proc. Sixth IEEE and ACM Int. Symp. on Mixed and Augmented Reality (ISMAR'07)*, Nara, Japan, November 2007.

[2] V. Monajjemi, J. Wawerla, R. T. Vaughan, and G. Mori. HRI in the sky: Creating and commanding teams of UAVs with a vision-mediated gestural interface. In *Proc. of Int. Conf. on Intelligent Robots and Systems*, 2013.

[3] S. Pourmehr, V. Monajjemi, S. A. Sadat, F. Zhan, J. Wawerla, G. Mori, and R. Vaughan. "You are Green": a Touch-to-Name interaction in an integrated multi-modal multi-robot HRI system. In *Int. Conf. on Human-Robot Interaction (HRI)*, 2014 (submitted).

[4] S. Pourmehr, V. Monajjemi, R. T. Vaughan, and G. Mori. You two! take off! creating, modifying and commanding groups of robots using face engagement and indirect speech in voice commands. In *Proc. of Int. Conf. on Intelligent Robots and Systems*, 2013.

[5] S. A. Sadat, K. Chutskoff, D. Jungic, J. Wawerla, and R. Vaughan. Feature-rich path planning for robust navigation of MAVs with mono-SLAM. In *Int. Conf. on Robotics and Automation (ICRA)*, 2014 (submitted).

Human-Robot Cooperation: Fast, Interactive Learning from Binary Feedback

Jawad Nagi*, Hung Ngo* (*Joint First Authors)
Jürgen Schmidhuber, Luca M. Gambardella, Gianni A. Di Caro
Dalle Molle Institute for Artificial Intelligence (IDSIA), CH-6928, Lugano, Switzerland
{jawad,hung,juergen,luca,gianni}@idsia.ch

Categories and Subject Descriptors

I.2.9 [**Robotics**]; I.4 [**Image Processing and Computer Vision**]; I.5 [**Pattern Recognition**]: Interactive Systems

General Terms

Algorithms, Methods, Design

1. VIDEO DESCRIPTION

This video presents results of a Swiss-funded project, focusing on *symbiotic human-robot cooperation*. We consider an *interactive learning* scenario and select the use of hand gestures to allow a human instructor to interact with a mobile robot. In our scenario, we use hand gestures to encode commands the robot will execute. At this aim, we define a vocabulary of $N = 6$ hand gestures (classes) that represent *finger counts* from 1 to 6. Using 6 hand gestures, the robot can perform 6 actions. In our case, each action represents that the robot must move to the *coloured landmark* corresponding to the recognized gesture class.

In this work, we exploit *feedback information* given by the human instructor to the robot during the learning and classification process. We use the notion of feedback as a means for improving the robot's learning and recognition accuracy over time, i.e., after a few interaction rounds with the human instructor. Our online learning and classification algorithm works in interaction rounds, and a single interaction round is described as follows. When the robot blinks its beacon, this signals the human that it is ready for interaction. Next, the robot acquires an observation (i.e., the human shows a gesture) using its onboard camera, and processes it (i.e., color-based segmentation and feature extraction) to compute the features of the hand silhouette using a pretrained Convolutional Neural Network (CNN). Using the resulting feature vector, the robot predicts the observation and produces an output gesture class Y, where $1 \leq Y \leq 6$. After prediction, the robot blinks its LEDs Y times with a RGB color corresponding to the predicted class. Then, the human provides a feedback to the robot to inform it, if the robot predicted the observation correctly or not. After feedback is given the interaction round terminates. If the gesture is recognized correctly, the robot performs the task associated with it, however if prediction is incorrect, then the gesture from the previous round is shown again to the robot and the next interaction round starts.

As feedback must be communicated to the robot, which amounts to another classification problem, we consider the use of *binary feedback* as it is more flexible than full feedback (i.e., the true class labels) and comes at a lower cost. Since binary feedback provides less information during communication than full feedback, this communication modality poses an implicit exploration-exploitation tradeoff—the robot may not necessarily want to select its current best prediction, in favor of the potentially most informative prediction for accelerating the learning progress. Our Upper Confidence Weighted Learning strategy (UCWL; [1]) provides an efficient solution to this setting. UCWL supports *online learning*, which neither assumes the data are independent and identically distributed, nor considers separate training and testing phases. It is formulated using an adaptive, large-margin update rule [2] for fast learning. To provide informed exploration-exploration trade-off, UCWL combines both score and uncertainty in making predictions.

The real-time demo implemented in this video makes use of our UWCL strategy, where binary feedback from the human is encoded using two separate *human actions* (i.e., right or wrong). When the human hides his hand (fist) behind his back, this action indicates that the robot recognized the gesture correctly. If the prediction was incorrect, then the human waves his hand vigorously to indicate a wrong prediction. Using these two predefined actions that can be reliably sensed in natural interactions (such as hiding or waving the hand) is quite feasible, while communicating a large (potentially very large) number of different classes requires more attention from, and is a larger burden upon, the human.

2. REFERENCES

[1] H. Ngo, M. Luciw, N. A. Vien, and J. Schmidhuber. Upper confidence weighted learning for efficient exploration in multiclass prediction with binary feedback. In *Proc. of the 23rd Intl. Joint Conf. on Artificial Intelligence (IJCAI)*, pages 2488–2494, 2013.

[2] J. Wang, P. Zhao, and S. Hoi. Exact soft confidence-weighted learning. In *Proc. of the 29th International Conference on Machine Learning (ICML)*, pages 121–128, 2012.

HRI'14, March 3–6, 2014, Bielefeld, Germany.
ACM 978-1-4503-2658-2/14/03.
http://dx.doi.org/10.1145/2559636.2559644.

Emotional Cyborg: Human Extension with Agency for Emotional Labor

Hirotaka Osawa
University of Tsukuba
1-1-1, Tenno-dai, Tsukuba
Ibaraki 305-8573 Japan
osawa@iit.tsukuba.ac.jp

ABSTRACT

The author developed wearable eyeglasses robot that supports user's emotional labors. The glass displays user's eye gestures on the surface and produces expressions during user's communication.

Categories and Subject Descriptors

H.5.2 **[Information Interface and Presentation]**: User Interfaces-Interaction style

General Terms

Design

Keywords

emotional labor, human robot interaction, human-agent interaction, human interface, augmented human

1. EXTENDING EMOTION WITH ROBOTS

Human-robot interaction (HRI) and Human-agent interaction (HAI) has become an important component in the field of human-computer interaction (HCI)[3]. The use of HRI/HAI becomes widespread, ranging from the field of entertainment to medical purposes such as the treatment of dementia and autism [2].

With summarizing the plenty success in HRI/HAI, the value of this field is being "technological solutions for emotional labor" [4]. Hochschild defined the tasks involved in this type of work as "emotional labor" and separates them from physical labor and brain work [1]. In emotional labor, human workers are forced to control their emotions during working time. HRI/ HAI and related technologies have the potential to act as substitutes for this type of work and free humans from emotional restrictions.

We developed eyeglass robot called AgencyGlass (Fig. 1) to support human emotional ability. This robot helps user's emotional labor as cyborgs (including cybernics suit robot [6]) for physical labor. Rosalind noted in Affective Computing that much emotional communication is reproducible in engineering [5]. Our device merges approaches of affective computing and cyborg robotics.

HRI'14, March 3–6, 2014, Bielefeld, Germany.
ACM 978-1-4503-2658-2/14/03.
http://dx.doi.org/10.1145/2559636.2559647

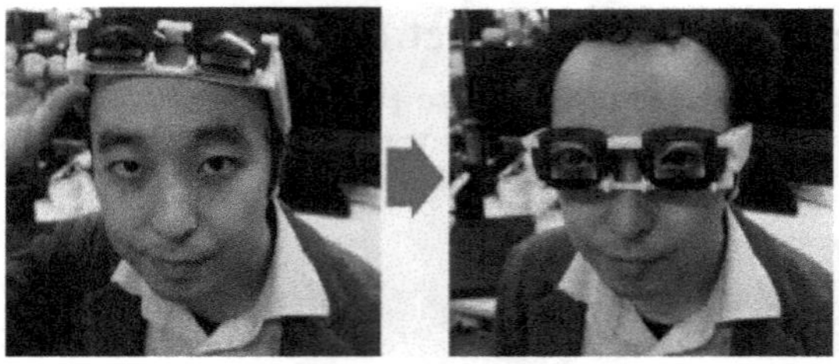

Figure 1. AgencyGlass and a User

The glass has 3-axis gyrometer and 3-axis accelerometer for monitoring user's behaviors, and connects to PC or a smartphone via Bluetooth. A connected computer detects monitors user's environmental conditions. Supports for emotional labor is achieved by both the glass and a computer. Dark lens around OLED displays hides your real eyes and sustains the user's field of vision. A user can achieve daily tasks as usual with wearing the glass.

The glass extends user's emotional labors in several situations. For example, if the user nod to the opponent, the glass shows a blink. If the user shakes, the glass shows more blinks. If the user inclines his/her head, the glass expresses upward glance. In group discussion with face recognition, if another member gazes the user, the glass expresses gazing motion toward the user. Although these expressions are simple, an opponent or group members could feel that they are cared by the user. This emotional support reduces a user's cognitive load for social manners.

2. REFERENCES

1. Hochschild, A.R. *The Managed Heart: Commercialization of Human Feeling*. University of California Press, 1983.
2. Matsukuma, K., Handa, H., and Yokoyama, K. Subjective Evaluation of Seal Robot: Paro - Tabulation and Analysis of Questionnaire Results -. *Journal of Robotics and Mechatronics 14*, 1 (2002), 13–19.
3. Osawa, H. and Imai, M. Morphing Agency: Deconstruction of an Agent with Transformative Agential Triggers. *CHI*, (2013), 2237–2246.
4. Osawa, H. Agentphobia and Emotional Labor□: How Human-Agent Interaction Contributes to the Preservation of our Humanity. *The 1st International Conference on Human-Agent Interaction*, (2013), II–p1.
5. Picard, R.W. *Affective Computing*. MIT Press, 1997.
6. Sankai, Y. Leading Edge of Cybernics: Robot Suit HAL. *2006 SICE-ICASE*, IEEE (2006), P-1–P-2.

Perceiving People from a Low-lying Viewpoint

Armando Pesenti Gritti* Oscar Tarabini* Alessandro Giusti† Jerome Guzzi†
Gianni A. Di Caro† Vincenzo Caglioti* Luca M. Gambardella†
* DEIB, Politecnico di Milano, Italy † IDSIA, USI/SUPSI, Lugano, Switzerland

Categories and Subject Descriptors

I.2.6 [**Artificial Intelligence**]: Learning; I.2.10 [**Artificial Intelligence**]: Vision and Scene Understanding; I.4.8 [**Image Processing And Computer Vision**]: Scene Analysis

Keywords

Robot Perception; Machine Learning; Person Tracking

1. VIDEO DESCRIPTION

Reliable perception and tracking of nearby humans in unstructured environments is one of the main issues to be solved in order to enable effective human-robot interaction and sharing of common spaces [5].

RGB-D sensors, such as the Microsoft Kinect or Asus Xtion, are an ideal tool for solving this problem indoors, and many human-tracking algorithms have been developed in the last few years. These algorithms are based on a number of assumptions: the subject is expected to lie at a given minimum distance from the sensor, such that at least part of its upper body is visible – most importantly the head, which represents an easy-to-detect seed for human detection and segmentation [6]; in some cases, the human is expected to face the sensor, and the sensor is assumed to be still [2]; the viewpoint is always assumed to lie in an elevated position, at least at the level of the subjects' chest or eyes.

Small-footprint ground robots must by necessity be short, with sensors lying close to the ground. Detecting humans from such a viewpoint is an hard and mostly unexplored problem: occlusions are frequent and severe; unless the subject is far from the robot, only legs are visible, exhibiting a complex, highly-variable appearance with irregular motion and no obvious markers for detection; when the sensor is mounted on a mobile platform, background-subtraction techniques can not be used unless very reliable ego-motion estimates are available. In this work we demostrate human detection and tracking under these challenging conditions, by means of a low-lying, forward-pointing RGB-D sensor, considering the TurtleBot [3] as an example platform.

HRI'14, March 3–6, 2014, Bielefeld, Germany.
ACM 978-1-4503-2658-2/14/03.
http://dx.doi.org/10.1145/2559636.2559641.

Figure 1: Tracked position (colored circle) and segmented silhouette of two people in a video frame.

The video illustrates the different steps of our algorithm using real-world datasets, and showcases results in various complex, realistic scenarios. Initially, the point cloud is downsampled [1] and the floor is detected as the most prominent horizontal plane; then, we search for clusters of points emerging from the floor, which comply with reasonable foot dimensions, and we expand them to knee level to get a set of candidate legs. Because in realistic environments most of such candidates are not actual legs, we apply an SVM classifier based on Histogram of Oriented Gradients features, which returns the probability that a candidate is a leg. Such classifier was previously learned from a large, manually-labeled training dataset comprising more than 2200 frames shot in 8 different, cluttered real-world environments. In such dataset, 6839 candidates were present of which 2413 were legs. Finally, individual legs and then people are tracked using a Kalman filter [4], accounting for the fact that a person has two legs, but often one or both may be occluded or fused to a single detection. The resulting output is the position and the velocity of each visible person.

A realtime, reuseable implementation as a ROS node is being developed and will be made available at `http://bit.ly/perceivingpeople`.

References

[1] The point cloud library. `http://pointclouds.org/`.
[2] Primesense nite middleware. `http://bit.ly/IAIHRb`.
[3] The turtlebot robot development kit. `http://bit.ly/lqRgND`.
[4] Y. Bar-Shalom et al. The probabilistic data association filter. *IEEE Control Systems*, 29(6):82–100, 2009.
[5] J. Guzzi et al. Bioinspired obstacle avoidance algorithms for robot swarms. In *Proc. of BIONETICS*, 2012.
[6] L. Xia, C.-C. Chen, and J. Aggarwal. Human detection using depth information by kinect. In *Proc. of CVPR Workshop on Human Activity Understanding from 3D Data (HAU3D)*, pages 15–22, 2011.

The NAO Goes to Camp

Noel Wigdor
TNO
Kampweg 5
Soesterberg, The Netherlands
noel.wigdor@tno.nl

Aafke Fraaje
TNO
Kampweg 5
Soesterberg, The Netherlands
aafke.fraaje@tno.nl

Lara Solms
TNO
Kampweg 5
Soesterberg, The Netherlands
lara.solms@tno.nl

Joachim de Greeff
TNO
Kampweg 5
Soesterberg, The Netherlands
joachim.deGreeff@plymouth.ac.uk

Joris Janssen
TNO
Kampweg 5
Soesterberg, The Netherlands
joris.janssen@tno.nl

Olivier Blanson Henkemans
TNO
Schoemakerstraat 97
Delft, The Netherlands
olivier.blansonhenkemans@tno.nl

ABSTRACT
ALIZ-E is a Europe-wide project focusing on long-term child-robot interaction, specifically as a means of educating diabetic children on their condition. This video showcases a recent field study at "SugarKidsClub", a camp devoted to helping 7-12 year-olds handle type-1 diabetes. A wide range of CRI activities developed by ALIZ-E were employed, including a large "SandTray" touch table running a tile-sorting game and a "Handshake" touch-inducing activity designed to strengthen the child-robot bond. Apart from helping kids with their unfortunate affliction, the day at "SugarKidsClub" provided us a chance to use new technologies developed for the aforementioned activities as well as furthering our relationship with our primary stakeholders. This playful video highlights some of the footage taken that day within an entertaining story centered on Charlie, one of the NAO robots used for our field study with a pension for battery theft.

HRI'14, March 3–6, 2014, Bielefeld, Germany.
ACM 978-1-4503-2658-2/14/03.
http://dx.doi.org/10.1145/2559636.2559648

The Fugitive

A Robot In the Wild

Mary-Anne Williams
University of Technology, Sydney
15 Broadway
Ultimo NSW 2007, Australia
Mary-Anne@TheMagicLab.org

Xun Wang
University of Technology, Sydney
15 Broadway
Ultimo NSW 2007, Australia
Xun@TheMagicLab.org

Pramod Parajuli
University of Technology, Sydney
15 Broadway
Ultimo NSW 2007, Australia
parmodparajuli@gmail.com

Shaukat Abedi
University of Technology, Sydney
15 Broadway
Ultimo NSW 2007, Australia
shaukat.abedi@gmail.com

Michelle Youssef
University of Technology, Sydney
15 Broadway
Ultimo NSW 2007, Australia
shellayoussef@hotmail.com

Wei Wang
University of Technology, Sydney
15 Broadway
Ultimo NSW 2007, Australia
benwei85@gmail.com

ABSTRACT

The aim of the movie is to highlight some of the key challenges facing so-cial robots in the wild. The opening scene shows a PR2 leaving research laboratory venturing into the real world alone in search of meaning. Each subsequent scene in the movie raises important research questions highlighting problems that need to be addressed in the field of social service robotics. When will robots wander around buildings unsupervised? How will they navigate and localize with glass walls: this research problem is exposed when a robot finds itself having to move around a real building. The robot is independent and has a sense of self. It wants to engage in society. It solves this problem by finding a job in a cafe where it is as-signed menial tasks, but aspires to be a barista. Thus raising the question of whether PR2 robots are suited to working with hot steaming liquids. Still the robot can dream, why not.

The robot realizes in order to progress it needs to learn some new skills and it is shown teaching itself a new skill and practicing to improve its performance. When it is time to put the new skill into practice, the robot has a revelation, discovering in the act of doing that there can be preconditions attached to the enaction of skills, i.e. people do not need peanut butter until they have bread to spread it on.

The robot demonstrates his robust understanding of social etiquette by not only offering the peanut butter to the female-human first, but also chastising a male-human for not observing this important social protocol.

The story ends with the recaptured robot being dragged back to the lab. The robot appears to be mortified by its loss of freedom and looks utterly dejected and dispirited. The robot's behavior generates empathy the human minder, but the robot is pretending to be disheartened, and is deceit-fully planning its next escapade as a Jedi Knight! Deception is a highly sophisticated cognitive skill: a capability enabled by a theory of mind which is necessary for communication, social interaction and collaboration, all critically important skills for a service robot.

Categories and Subject Descriptors

J.4 [**Social and Behavioral Sciences**]: Sociology, Psychology

Keywords

Human-Robot Interaction, Robots in the Wild, Social Robotics

HRI'14, March 3–6, 2014, Bielefeld, Germany.
ACM 978-1-4503-2658-2/14/03.
http://dx.doi.org/10.1145/2559636.2559653.

Human-Robot Collaborative Tutoring using Multiparty Multimodal Spoken Dialogue

Samer Al Moubayed(1), Jonas Beskow(1), Bajibabu Bollepalli(1), Joakim Gustafson(1), Ahmed Hussen-Abdelaziz(5), Martin Johansson(1), Maria Koutsombogera(2), José David Lopes(3), Jekaterina Novikova(4), Catharine Oertel(1), Gabriel Skantze(1), Kalin Stefanov(1), Gül Varol(6)

[1]KTH Speech, Music and Hearing, Sweden
[2]Institute for Language and Speech Processing, Greece
[3]Spoken Language Systems Laboratory, INESC ID, Portugal
[4]Department of Computer Science, University of Bath, UK
[5]Institute of Communication Acoustics, Ruhr-Universität Bochum, Germany
[6]Bogazici University, Turkey

sameram@kth.se

ABSTRACT

In this paper, we describe a project that explores a novel experimental setup towards building a spoken, multi-modally rich, and human-like multiparty tutoring robot. A human-robot interaction setup is designed, and a human-human dialogue corpus is collected. The corpus targets the development of a dialogue system platform to study verbal and nonverbal tutoring strategies in multiparty spoken interactions with robots which are capable of spoken dialogue. The dialogue task is centered on two participants involved in a dialogue aiming to solve a card-ordering game. Along with the participants sits a tutor (robot) that helps the participants perform the task, and organizes and balances their interaction. Different multimodal signals captured and auto-synchronized by different audio-visual capture technologies, such as a microphone array, Kinects, and video cameras, were coupled with manual annotations. These are used build a situated model of the interaction based on the participants personalities, their state of attention, their conversational engagement and verbal dominance, and how that is correlated with the verbal and visual feedback, turn-management, and conversation regulatory actions generated by the tutor. Driven by the analysis of the corpus, we will show also the detailed design methodologies for an affective, and multimodally rich dialogue system that allows the robot to measure incrementally the attention states, and the dominance for each participant, allowing the robot head Furhat to maintain a well-coordinated, balanced, and engaging conversation, that attempts to maximize the agreement and the contribution to solve the task.

This project sets the first steps to explore the potential of using multimodal dialogue systems to build interactive robots that can serve in educational, team building, and collaborative task solving applications.

HRI'14, Mar 03-06 2014, Bielefeld, Germany
ACM 978-1-4503-2658-2/14/03.
http://dx.doi.org/10.1145/2559636.2563681

Categories and Subject Descriptors

H.5.2 [**Information Interfaces and Presentation**]: User Interfaces – Natural Language;

Keywords

Human-Robot Interaction, Multiparty interaction, human-robot collaboration, Spoken dialog, Furhat robot.

Overview

This work attempts to address social and interactional skills required by an embodied dialogue system to control the interaction flow as well as to boost and balance the engagement of the participants in the task they are involved in, while at the same time mitigating dominant behavior and encouraging less talkative interlocutors to equally participate in the interaction. The task and the setup chosen in this work are considered first steps towards understanding the behavior of a conversational tutor in multiparty task solving setup, as an example of a setup that can be used for applications in group-collaboration and negotiations, an activity that is highly dependent on the affective, and social behavior of the interlocutors [1]. Another main criteria that is taken into account while developing this setup is the ability to move directly from the models learnt from the annotations and analysis of the corpus, into an implementation of multiparty multimodal dialogue system, using the robot head Furhat [2]. Furhat was developed to support non-verbally and dynamically rich audio-visual synthesis, and to study human-robot spoken interactions [3,4], together with the newly developed IrisTK dialogue platform [5] both developed and utilized in multimodal multiparty embodied spoken dialogue systems.

The setup consisted of a card ordering game, in which two subjects had to engage in a conversation about the value of each card, and finally arrive at a decision about their order. Subjects were matched depending on their extr-

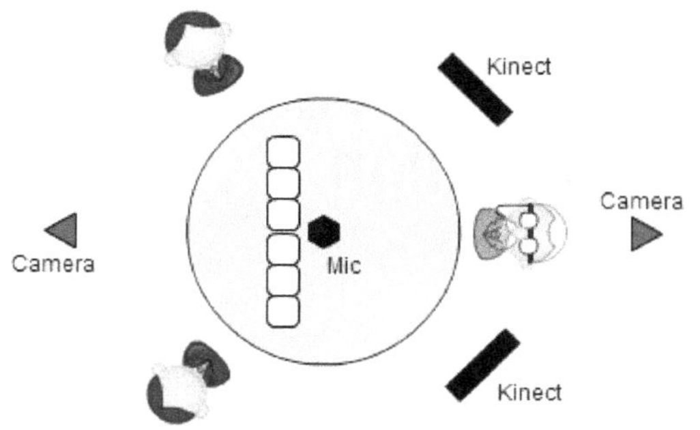

Figure 1. Snapshots of Furhat[1] in close-up and two users in interaction[2]

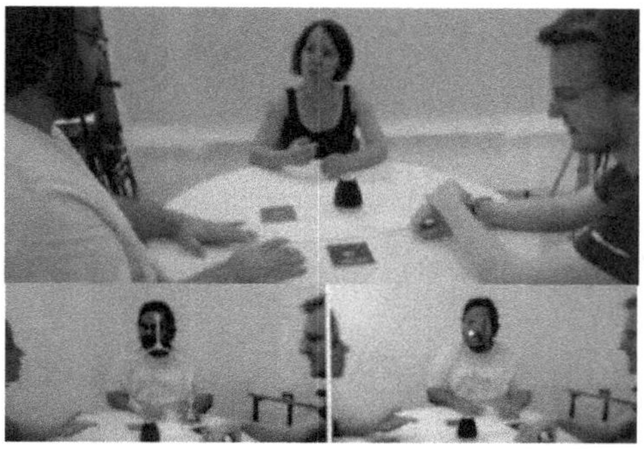

Figure 2. Top: a snapshot of the human-human data collection showing the tutor and the table, containing the colored cards, and the microphone array. Bottom: A view from one of the Kinects showing overlays of the real-time head-pose and torso-skeletal tracking.

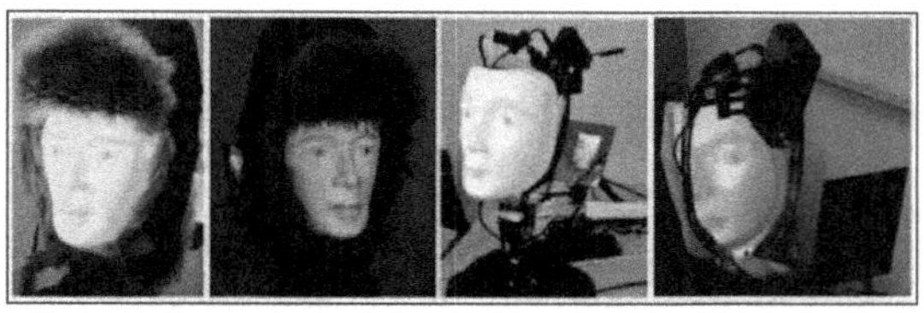

Figure 3. Snapshots of Furhat in close-ups.

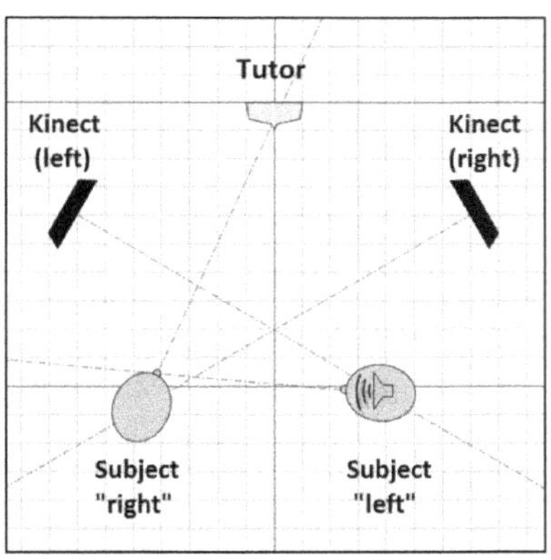

Figure 4. A visualization of the perceived activity of the situated interaction. The figure shows the tracked horizontal head rotation (pan) of each subject, and the voice activity detection (highlighted by an image of a speaker). The figure shows that the subject (left) is currently speaking.

[1] For more info on Furhat, see http://www.speech.kth.se/furhat

oversion (by filling a personality test before the recordings). The subjects were sitting with a tutor that attempted to coordinate the conversation and to regulate the interaction so that both participants get equal chance contributing to the decision making process. The data was recorded using real-time equipment and annotation. Participants' head, hands, and torso, were recorded using Kinects. The verbal activity of each participants and the tutor were captured using the table-top Microcone[3] microphone array, and the cards were automatically captured and tracked using a video camera placed on top. The data was then analyzed to understand and build a model of the head-pose, verbal and nonverbal feedback, and turn-management and interruption strategies the tutor employed. The tutor behavior was measured against the subjects' auto-recorded data, their verbal activity, and their dominance over time.

From this setup and data, that is soon to be publicly available, a highly complex dialogue system was built to simulate the tutor in these aspects. The dialogue setup benefited from the human recording in that it used exactly the same setup and equipment to track and analyze the conversation.

The paper on site will further describe data analysis results and experimental investigations on the behavior of the subjects and the performance of the dialogue system. Figure 1 shows a chart of the physical setup employed. Figure 2 shows snapshots of the human-human corpus recording. Figure 3 shows the robot head Furhat used as the tutor, and Figure 4 shows a real-time visualization of the interaction using the capture equipment.

ACKNOWLEDGMENTS

This work has been partly funded by the KTH ICT Strategic Research Areas Embodied Multimodal Communication.

REFERENCES

[1] Nass, C., Steuer, J., & Tauber, E. (1994), "Computers are social actors", *CHI '94: Proceedings of the SIGCHI conference on Human factors in computing systems*, ACM Press, pp. 72–78

[2] Al Moubayed, S., Beskow, J., Skantze, G., & Granström, B. 2012. Furhat: A Back-projected Human-like Robot Head for Multiparty Human-Machine Interaction. In Esposito et al. (Eds.), Cognitive Behavioural Systems. Lecture Notes in Computer Science. Springer.

[3] Al Moubayed, S., Skantze, G., & Beskow, J. (2013). The *Furhat Back-Projected Humanoid Head - Lip reading, Gaze and Multiparty Interaction*. International Journal of Humanoid Robotics, 10(1).

[4] Al Moubayed, S., Edlund, J., & Beskow, J. 2012. *Taming Mona Lisa: communicating gaze faithfully in 2D and 3D facial projections*. ACM Transactions on Interactive Intelligent Systems, 1(2), 25.

[5] Skantze, G. and Al Moubayed, S. 2012. IrisTK: a statechart-based toolkit for multi-party face-to-face interaction. *Proc. of the 14th ACM International Conference on Multimodal Interaction ICMI*. Santa Monica, CA, USA.

[3] http://www.dev-audio.com/products/microcone/

Speaker Identification using Three Signal Voice Domains during Human-Robot Interaction

[Late Breaking Reports]

Fernando Alonso-Martín
Universidad Carlos III Madrid
Avenida de la Universidad, 30
Leganés, Madrid (Spain)
famartin@ing.uc3m.es

Arnaud Ramey
Universidad Carlos III Madrid
Avenida de la Universidad, 30
Leganés, Madrid (Spain)
arnaud.a.ramey@gmail.com

Miguel Angel Salichs
Universidad Carlos III Madrid
Avenida de la Universidad, 30
Leganés, Madrid (Spain)
salichs@ing.uc3m.es

ABSTRACT

This LBR describes a novel method for user recognition in HRI, based on analyzing the peculiarities of users voices, and specially focused at being used in a robotic system. The method is inspired by acoustic fingerprinting techniques, and is made of two phases: a)*enrollment in the system*: the features of the user's voice are stored in files called *voiceprints*, b)*searching phase*: the features extracted in real time are compared with the voiceprints using a pattern matching method to obtain the most likely user (match).
The audio samples are described thanks to features in three different signal domains: time, frequency, and time-frequency. Using the combination of these three domains has enabled significant increases in the accuracy of user identification compared to existing techniques. Several tests using an independent user voice database show that only half a second of user voice is enough to identify the speaker. The recognition is text-independent: users do not need to say a specific sentence (key-pass) to get identified for the robot.

Keywords

Acoustic fingerprint, speaker identification, feature extraction, patter matching

1. INTRODUCTION

In order to achieve a natural and personalized interaction between a robot and its human users (HRI), it is important that the former identifies correctly its human peers. Audio features are often used to reach that point.
Previous works by other authors ([5]) include several descriptions of systems enabling a caller to obtain access via telephone network to services by entering a spoken key-pass (text-dependent method). In order to achieve this goal, in the enrollment phase, first automatic speech recognition (ASR) identifies the key-pass; then a voice verification algorithm is used. Some features of the voice are extracted and stored next to the key-pass sentence. In the verification phase, real time features are compared with the previously stored features. The identification is considered as successful if the compared distance between both sets of features is below a given threshold (pattern matching approximation using text-dependent verification).
A review of acoustic fingerprint methods [3] report their use for a wide range of applications, such as identifying songs, contents, etc. However, their use for the identification of the user is more challenging, because two identical sentences uttered by the same person result in two different signals. Our proposed architecture tends to overcome these difficulties.

2. DESCRIPTION OF THE SYSTEM

The previous system used by the robot Maggie ([2]) required the user to enroll on the system. This phase consisted of questions asked by the robot to the user. Along with her name, age, language, a key-pass sentence is chosen by the user to learn her voice tone. It can be a digit password or anything else. For this task, we used the third-party Loquendo ASR-Speaker Verification package [4]. The main drawback was that, to be correctly identified, the user needed to utter the same sentence that he used in the enrollment phase.

System overview. In order to avoid this drawback, we implemented a new module of *text-independent* user identification based on *pattern matching* techniques. During a similar question-based (but key-pass free) enrollment phase, the robot learned features of the voice of the new user. These features are stored into a so-called voiceprint file. Details about feature extraction and matching come below.
The work presented in this paper, includes user identification using voice features. It is implemented in Chuck and C++. It is part of a complete multimodal interaction system applied to HRI called *Robotics Dialog System* ([1]). This RDS interaction system is based on the ROS architecture [1] and supplies the interaction capabilities for the RoboticsLab robots [2].

Used features. Two aspects of the new system can be underlined: the features are extracted without needing a specific key-pass phase, and these extracted features belong to

[1]http://wiki.ros.org
[2]http://roboticslab.uc3m.es/

HRI'14, March 3–6, 2014, Bielefeld, Germany.
ACM 978-1-4503-2658-2/14/03.
http://dx.doi.org/10.1145/2559636.2563706.

three different domains: time, frequency, and time-frequency (more details about them in [1]). The used features are *Root Mean Square (RMS)* (computed on time domain); *Pitch computed using Fast Fourier Transform* (frequency domain); *Pitch computed using Haar Discrete Wavelet Transform* (time-frequency domain); *Flux* (frequency domain); *RollOff* (frequency domain); *Centroid* (frequency domain); *Zero-crossing rate (ZCR)* (time domain).

Real time feature extraction. Once the voiceprints of the enrolled users have been generated and stored, it is possible to identify which user is speaking at any time. *Voice Activity Detection*, which consists in detecting whether users are talking or quiet, is based on our previous work [1]. When voice activity is detected, the previously listed audio features are extracted. Each second of voice generates several rows of features. Each row is called a *bit*, and a set of *bits* is known as *sub-fingerprint*. The number of bits that compose a sub-fingerprint will be called *sub-fingeprint size*, and is the minimum information to identify an user.

Our system works with a sample rate of 44100 Hz and a window size of 4096 samples, therefore each bit of fingerprint corresponds to 0.1 second of voice (i.e. 1 second of voice generates 10 bits).

Identification (matching) phase. The identification is made by computing the distance between the current audio features and the features of the enrolled users, stored in each of the voiceprint files. If the best-match distance is below a threshold, the speaking user is considered to be the user that generated that voiceprint file.

In mathematical terms, let $n = 7$ the number of different audio features. The distance d between a current *bit* C of n extracted features and a voice print file V, a set of n_v bits of n features, is computed with the following formula:

$$d(C, V) = \min_{j \in [0, n_v]} \|[1 \dots 1] - \exp(-\alpha \circ |C - V_j|)\|_{L_1}$$

where $\|.\|_{L_1}$ is the Manhattan distance, $\circ$ is the element-wise product, and $\alpha = [\alpha_0 \dots \alpha_n]$ a scaling vector.
The best match for a given bit C is then defined as the voice print which bits obtains the minimum distance with C. It is considered a valid match if that distance is below an empirical threshold.
The distance computation presented above is called *bit-to-bit* ($n \times 1$ vectors comparison). It can also be made on successive sets of *bits* ($n \times w, w \in \mathbf{N}$ matrices comparison, w is called the sub-fingerprint size).

3. EXPERIMENTAL RESULTS

In order to verify the system accuracy to identify human peers, we have used a multi-language voice database [3] Some samples were used for generating the voiceprints, and other for evaluating if their best match corresponded to the correct user.
Figure 1 that relates the number of enrolled users, and the sub-fingerprint size, to the accuracy rate of the user identification. The accuracy rate is close to 100% for few users, and while it decrease while the number of users increase, it remains over 70% for as many as eighteen users for the best choice of sub-fingerprint size. The best results are obtained

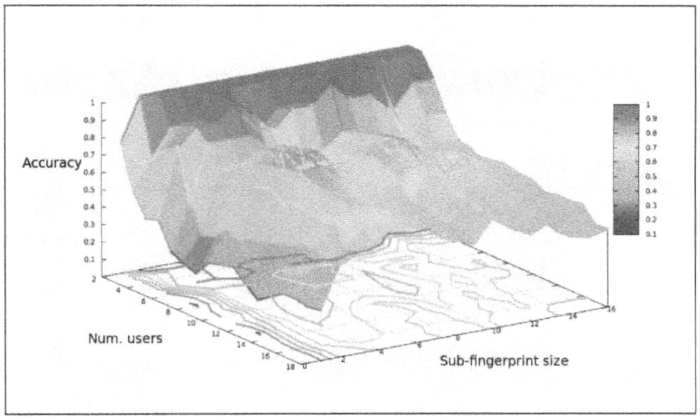

Figure 1: Number of Users vs Accuracy vs Sub-fingerprint size

using a sub-fingerprint size of 5, i.e. a voice sample of half a second is long enough to identify the speaker. Similar work, presented by Lite[6], claims an accuracy rate of 79% for 11 users and 3 seconds for each identification. Our system, with 11 users gets an accuracy rate of 86% using 0.5 seconds of voice.

[3]The database used was VoxDB (http://voxdb.org).

4. CONCLUSION AND FUTURE WORK

In this paper, we have presented a real-time user recognition algorithm based on acoustic fingerprint methods and tailored for HRI. Audio features computed in three acoustic domains are matched with lightweight pattern matching techniques, which confer the robot an intuitive and accurate user recognition system. Future work will extend the benchmarking of our system against others.

5. ACKNOWLEDGMENTS

The authors gratefully acknowledge the funds provided by the Spanish MICINN (Ministry of Science and Innovation) through the project "Aplicaciones de los robots sociales", DPI2011-26980 from the Spanish Ministry of Economy and Competitiveness. Moreover, the research leading to these results has received funding from the RoboCity2030-II-CM project (S2009/DPI-1559), funded by Programas de Actividades I+D en la Comunidad de Madrid and cofunded by Structural Funds of the EU.

6. REFERENCES

[1] F. Alonso-Martin, A. Castro-González, J. Gorostiza, and M. A. Salichs. Multidomain Voice Activity Detection during Human-Robot Interaction. In *International Conference on Social Robotics (ICSR 2013)*, pages 64–73, Bristol, 2013. Springer International Publishing.

[2] F. Alonso-Martín, J. F. Gorostiza, M. Malfaz, and M. Salichs. Multimodal Fusion as Communicative Acts during Human-Robot Interaction. *Cybernetics and Systems*, 44(8):681–703, 2013.

[3] J. Cano, P., Batle, E., Kalker, T., & Haitsma. A review of algorithms for audio fingerprinting. In *In Multimedia Signal Processing, IEEE Workshop on*, pages 169–173, 2002.

[4] E. Dalmasso, F. Castaldo, P. Laface, D. Colibro, and C. Vair. Loquendo - Speaker recognition evaluation system. In *Acoustics, Speech and Signal Processing, ICASSP 2009. IEEE International Conference on*, pages 4213–4216, Taipei.

[5] T. B. Hunt, Alan K.; Schalk. Simultaneous voice recognition and verification to allow access to telephone network services, 1996.

[6] K. P. Li. Text-independent speaker recognition with short utterances. *The Journal of the Acoustical Society of America*, 72(S1):S29, Aug. 1982.

Daedalus: A sUAV for Human-Robot Interaction

Dante Arroyo
Department of Engineering
Pontificia Universidad Catolica del Peru
Lima, Peru
darroyo@pucp.edu.pe

Cesar Lucho
Department of Art
Pontificia Universidad Catolica del Peru
Lima, Peru
di.ce.lucho@gmail.com

Julissa Roncal
Department of Psychology
Pontificia Universidad Catolica del Peru
Lima, Peru
jroncal@pucp.edu.pe

Francisco Cuellar
Department of Engineering
Pontificia Universidad Catolica del Peru
Lima, Peru
cuellar.ff@gmail.com

ABSTRACT

This paper presents an interface for enabling a sUAV robot (Daedalus) to communicate and simulate emotional states. As significance is the result of the interpretation of emotional states, an experimental study was performed to evaluate and recognize emotion-state responses from people when interacting with the sUAV. Four expressions were programmed combining Daedalus' interaction features such as head movement and eye color display. During the assessment, subjects were asked to recognize the significance of the expressions performed by the robot and assign an emotional state of the robot through card selection. Our research aims to investigate the impact of simulating emotional states in robots, and its potential during interaction. Results presented are part of an experimental study for setting future exploratory research concerning human-robot interaction.

Categories and Subject Descriptors

H.1.1 [**Models and Principles**]: User/Machine Systems—*human factors*; H.5.2 [**Information Interfaces and Presentation**]: User Interfaces—*user-centered design*; J.4 [**Social and Behavioral Sciences**]: Psychology

General Terms

Design, Experimentation, Human Factors.

Keywords

Communication interface, emotion recognition, human-robot interaction, psychometrics, sUAV.

1. INTRODUCTION

Nowadays, small unmanned aerial vehicles (sUAVs) have gained a significant presence in robotics; they have demonstrated the capacity to perform a wide range of tasks including military exploration, and a growing number of civil applications such as topographic scans and recently, courier service. Due to their wide performance, sUAVs are becoming more commonly operated in public places, causing direct and indirect human-robot interaction. Thereby, it is important to understand how people will perceive this type of robots as they promise widespread integration into humans' social and physical context.

In the interest of comprehending people's perception of robots, research related to the generation of emotional states has been developed based on animal and human-inspired interfaces, such as a dog tail [6] , robot eyes design [4] and non-linguistic utterances [5]. However, these studies have not been designed to enhance directly sUAVs-human interaction. Duncan [2] performed a comfortable approach distance analysis with sUAVs.

In order to achieve a positive sUAVs-human interaction it is necessary to identify the first emotions generated by people when interacting with a robot. Therefore, through assessment, it is possible to establish some code or basic meanings in communication. This experimental study aims to explore a new 3D Printed sUAV robot as shown in Figure 1 (Daedalus) that is able to perform head movement and change its eye color to produce emotional responses in people, and achieve emotion recognition for future research.

Figure 1: Robot Daedalus during flight test.

2. EXPERIMENTAL SETUP

As significance is the result of the interpretation of emotional states, an experimental study was performed to eval-

HRI'14, March 3–6, 2014, Bielefeld, Germany.
ACM 978-1-4503-2658-2/14/03.
http://dx.doi.org/10.1145/2559636.2563709.

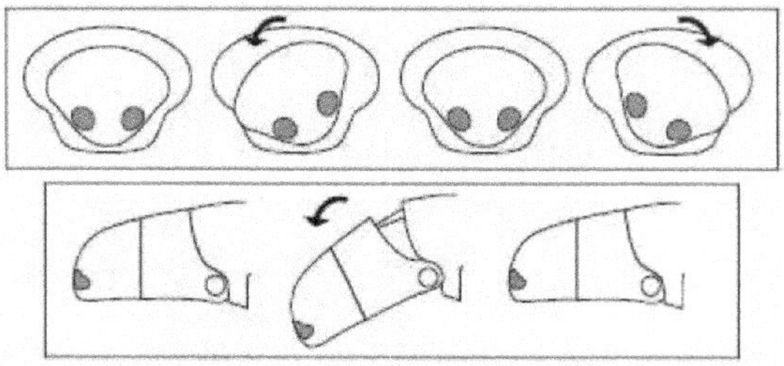

Figure 2: Daedalus' Interaction Features

uate the perception of the robot's expressions. Interaction features such as pitch and roll motion of the head, and eye color display variation, as shown in Figure 2, were evaluated by analyzing emotion recognition and automatic thoughts in undergraduate students (n=30), Male (n=12), Female (n=18); aged between 17 and 29 years old (X=20.53, SD=3.76). Four expressions were programmed in the following sequence:

Mov1: Head Roll mov. with white eyes (propellers off).
Mov2: Head Pitch mov. with white eyes (propellers off).
Mov3: Head Roll mov. with white eyes (propellers on).
Mov4: Head Pitch mov. with red eyes (propellers on).

The sUAV was located in a stationary module to maintain a constant interaction height of 1.60 m. The interaction distance between Daedalus' head and the subject was established between 0.5 - 0.7 m. as shown in Figure 3. After showing each of the expressions, subjects had to answer 1) Q1: "What do you feel?" and 2) Q2: "What do you think the robot is feeling?" by selecting one of seven different types of cards associated with emotions (happiness, sadness, anger, fear, disgust, surprise and contempt) basic emotions considered by Ekman and Lazarus [3].

3. PRELIMINARY RESULTS

Inspection of the data suggests that the emotion recognition test to evaluate human-robot interaction can provide reliability and validity analysis for future research. These preliminary results show that Daedalus' expressions could be interpreted as emotional states by the test subjects.

Analyzing items, the first two expressions Mov1 and Mov2, showed subjects' tendency to generate positive emotions: Mov1 (Happiness and surprise) and Mov2 (Surprise). Expressions that included propeller noise (Mov3 and Mov4) tended to generate negative emotions: Mov3 (fear, anger, and happiness) and Mov4 (fear and anger) as shown in Table 1. Pearson's Chi Square Test was used to evaluate the association between "gender" and "emotions", there was not an association between these variables.

In addition, the first experiments with white eyes tended to generate happiness 43.3 % and surprise 40 % in subjects. However, the fourth expression (with red eyes) had a higher

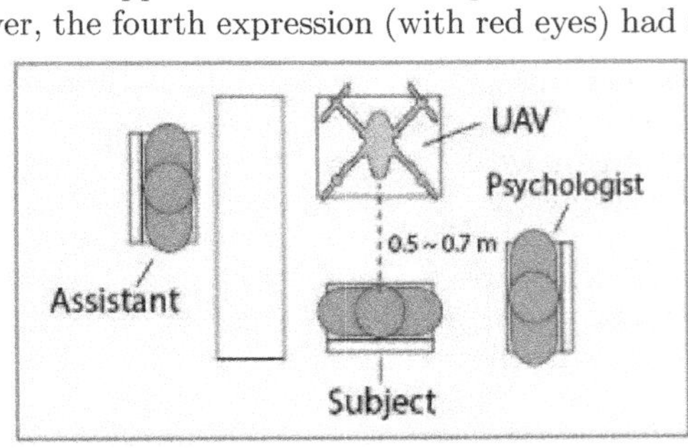

Figure 3: Experimental Setup.

Table 1: Emotions Frequency

Mov1Q1: What do you feel?	Frequency	Percent	Mov1Q2: What do you think the robot is feeling?	Frequency	Percent
Happiness	13	43.3	Surprise	14	46.7
Surprise	12	40.0	Fear	9	30.0

Mov2Q1: What do you feel?	Frequency	Percent	Mov2Q2: What do you think the robot is feeling?	Frequency	Percent
Surprise	9	30.0	Sadness	9	30.0
Happiness	8	26.7	Fear	9	30.0

Mov3Q1: What do you feel?	Frequency	Percent	Mov3Q2: What do you think the robot is feeling?	Frequency	Percent
Fear	13	43.3	Hapiness	11	36.7
Surprise	9	30.0	Anger	10	33.3

Mov4Q1: What do you feel?	Frequency	Percent	Mov4Q2: What do you think the robot is feeling?	Frequency	Percent
Fear	15	50.0	Anger	24	80.0
Hapiness	5	16.7	Contempt	4	13.3
n = 30			*n = 30*		

impact in subjects. 50 % perceived fear, and 80 % selected anger as the emotional state of the robot.

4. CONCLUSIONS AND FUTURE WORK

The study found that the emotion recognition experiment could assess subjects' emotions generated by the robot's expressions. The research showed that movements without propeller noise tended to generate positive emotions, while movements with operating propellers evoked the opposite. Propeller noise was considered in the last expressions as it is an unconditioned stimulus feeling fear for negative emotions in response to loud sounds, the results presented support the knowledge of Cognitive Theory [1].

These findings provide further evidence that human-robot interaction can be improved by giving the robot the faculty to perform different emotional states through a communication interface. However, results show that subjects were not always consistent for each interpretation that comprehended head movements and eye color. Future analyses include correlations between students from different majors, response in subjects with and without prior familiarity with sUVAs, and Latin-American perception of robots.

5. ACKNOWLEDGMENTS

The authors wish to thank the department of Engineering of the Pontificia Universidad Catolica del Peru.

6. REFERENCES

[1] J. S. Beck. *Cognitive Therapy: Basics and Beyond.* Guilford Press, 1995.

[2] B. A. Duncan and R. R. Murphy. Comfortable approach distance with small unmanned aerial vehicles. *2013 IEEE RO-MAN.*, pages 786–792, 2013.

[3] R. S. Lazarus. Cognition and motivation in emotion. *98th APA's Annual Convention.*, 1991.

[4] T. Onuki, T. Ishinoda, Y. Kobayashi, and Y. Kuno. Design of robot eyes suitable for gaze communication. In *HRI '13*, pages 203–204. IEEE, 2013.

[5] R. Read and T. Belpaeme. People interpret robotic non-linguistic utterances categorically. In *HRI '13*, pages 209–210. IEEE, 2013.

[6] A. Singh and J. E. Young. A dog tail for communicating robotic states. In *HRI '13*, pages 417–418. IEEE, 2013.

Human and Robot Interaction based on Safety Zones in a Shared Work Environment

Svante Augustsson
Department of Engineering
University West
SE-46186, Trollhättan, Sweden
svante.augustsson@hv.se

Linn Gustavsson Christiernin
Department of Engineering
University West
SE-46186, Trollhättan, Sweden
linn.gustavsson@hv.se

Gunnar Bolmsjö
Department of Engineering
University West
SE-46186, Trollhättan, Sweden
gunnar.bolmsjo@hv.se

ABSTRACT
In this paper, early work on how to implement flexible safety zones is presented. In the case study an industrial robot cell emulates the environment at a wall construction site, with a robot performing nailing routines. Tests are performed with humans entering the safety zones of a SafetyEye system. The zone violation is detected, and new warning zones initiated. The robot retracts but continues its work tasks with reduced speed and within a safe distance of the human operator. Interaction is achieved through simultaneous work on the same work piece and the warning zones can be initiated and adjusted in a flexible way.

Categories and Subject Descriptors
H.1.2 [**User/Machine Systems**]

General Terms
Design, Experimentation, and Security.

Keywords
Safety zones, Human Robot Interaction, Shared work, SafetyEye.

1. INTRODUCTION
The most common safety solution within the construction industry today is to separate robots and humans from working in the same area at the same time. The robots activities are predetermined and human interaction is handled through gates, loading bays or conveyers to make sure that the human and the robot do not simultaneously access the same workspace. There is obviously a need for more flexible solutions, especially in industries with small batches or one-off productions. It is important for robots and operators to be able to cooperate and interact to improve efficiency. Therefore, new solutions have emerged where the safety issues still are strictly regulated but the opportunity to create a shared space is available. This often includes the usage of speed, force monitoring, cameras, light curtains and usage of potential fields to detect an obstacle and guide the robot away [1-2].

This paper introduces early work on flexible production lines with interactive safety zones in shared workspaces. The concept is based on new safety solutions, available on the market, allowing better interaction and a work environment without physical limitation such as fences and gates. Our study is performed in cooperation with a company producing single family houses in prefabricated elements of wood, why our case is focused on wall elements. The wall elements are similar but each one is unique due to customer adaptations. In the preparation of the production, computer based tools like CAD are used to provide information for preparing production. This information can also be used to generate programs for the robot for different operations such as nailing, screwing, or assembly of elements.

HRI'14, March 3–6, 2014, Bielefeld, Germany.
ACM 978-1-4503-2658-2/14/03.
http://dx.doi.org/10.1145/2559636.2563717

2. APPLIED CASE
Based on requirements from our cooperating company a robot cell was chosen to emulate the production at the house construction site. Based on CAD models the cell is programmed to allow the robot to replace monotonic work such as placing of thermal bridges in the insulation of the wall modules. Meanwhile the operator can continue to work with other tasks on the wall module. The cell is equipped with a KUKA KR 180R2500 industrial robot, two worktables, a SafetyEYE system, and a Safety PLC. The SateftyEYE has a 3D Camera and programmable control system (PSS) SB 3047-3 ETH-2 SE (see Figure 1).

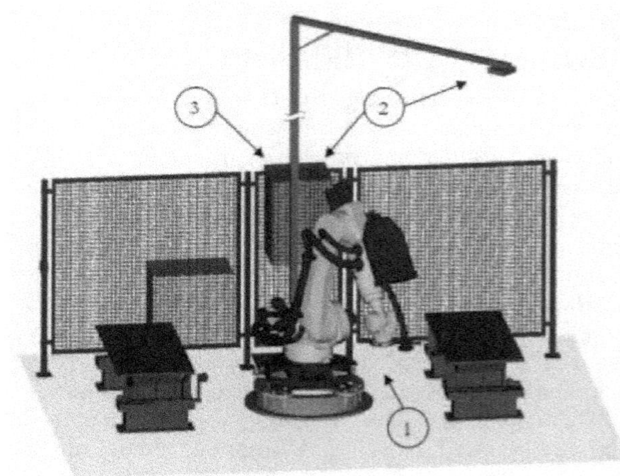

Figure 1. Layout of robot cell in test case setup. 1: KUKA KR 180R2500, 2: SafetyEYE system, 3: JOKAB PLUTO S46.

2.1 Safety Zone Concept
The safety zone concept divides the wall module into sections where one or more robots are placed along the sides of the wall. The number of sections used can be adjusted to fit specific demands in the production. To allow for increased interaction in a shared work area, we need to be able to use multiple safety zones combined into groups and be able to activate and deactivate the zone arrangements in a dynamic and safe way. Towards this end we use the basic functions in the SafetyEYE PPS and an external safety PL to control the zones, safety decisions and the robot. The principle of the system communication setup is to send out-signals from the SafetyEYE PPS to the external safety PLC when a zone

violation is detected. The signals are then processed by the safety PLC and compared to in-signals from the robot, allowing the safety PLC to determine how the robot should react to the zone violation. In our case the wall was divided into two sections. Every section will be assigned with a warning and hazard zone based on 3D technology to control the interaction. When no operator is in close proximity to the wall the robots are working without any limitations and at full speed (see (1) in Figure 2). The scenario of a human operator entering the cell to cooperate with robot on a wall segment can be described in steps:

1. A human is approaching and triggers the first warning zone.
2. The robot motion is canceled and it starts to retract to the second section of the wall with reduced speed (see (2) in Figure 2). New warning zones are initiated
3. The operator can start to work freely on the first section.
4. The robot continues its work task at full speed in the second section until the task is completed (see (3) in Figure 2).
   a. If the operator triggers the second warning zone the robot will return to its home position and wait there. (see (4) in Figure 2)
5. When operator leaves the wall the robot will continue to work with full speed until the work is completed.
6. At completion the robot returns to its home position and waits for the arrival of a new wall module.

Figure 2. Steps in the interaction scenario. 1: The robot works on the complete wall, 2: The operator enters safety zone and the robot retracts (new warning zones initiated), 3: The robot and operator works in different zones, 4: The operator works alone and the robot waits for the operator to leave.

2.2 Evaluation of System

By emulating work tasks representing nailing and considering the workspace of the robot and the size of the walls built at our partner company a first evaluation is performed. The selection of zones is based on the idea that the robot is mounted on a rail along the wall side allowing the work areas to be accessed in a flexible way. The SafetyEYE system includes conditions for how the safety zones should be dimensioned to meet the ISO safety requirements [3-4]. These conditions, including risk analysis for the various work operations, can be used for designing the warning and danger zones at the edges of the wall (see (1) in Figure 3), but will be insufficient for the zones on the wall (se (2) in Figure 3). Here a safety evaluation is needed to design the zone dimensions. A number of tests with dummies were conducted to calculate the on wall safety zones (see (2) in Figure 3). Our approach allows the operator to enter the workspace, triggering the warning zone but without stopping the system. The robot instead moves away with reduced speed allowing the operator to approach and even touch it during retraction. Hence, the operator can start working without waiting for the robot to finish the retraction. Control signals are used from both the robot and the SafetyEYE to stop the robot if the retraction is interrupted in any way or an error has occurred.

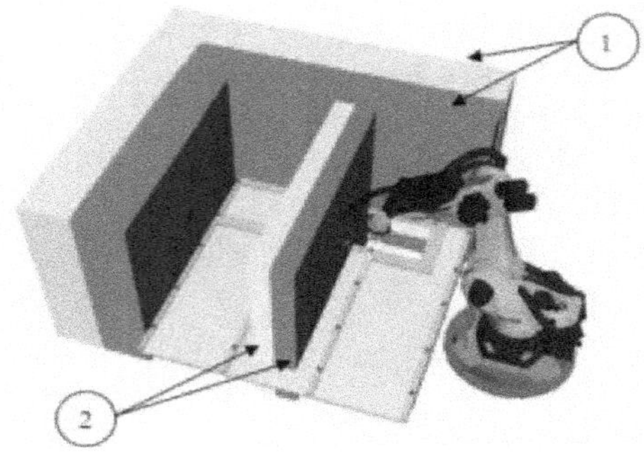

Figure 3. Illustration of wall module with safety zones. (1) Zones on edges, (2) Zones on wall.

The main evaluation was first performed with a workbench representing the work area and later replaced with a wall module of reduced size for better validation. The zones were set and a dummy was used to test the robot behavior when the different zones were entered. Later human test-operators were asked to enter the different areas. Complementary testing was then conducted, aiming to verify how different materials affect the camera and the zone placement. Important materials in our case were fiberglass insulation, wood, and hand tools such as hammer, screwdrivers, pincers etc.

3. Early Results and Conclusions

The initial test show that our concept can be used for a flexible zone deployment and that the robot behaves as expected. The presented safety solution is slightly more costly than the traditional safety solutions, but allows the system to operate without changing the current layout of the production line or to limit access to the work area. With flexible safety zone deployment, different and changing types of interaction can be used.

However, the camera used in the SafetyEYE system is very sensitive for changes in the light conditions, pollution in the air, and reflections from tools and the floor, which could lead to sever problems in a wood based manufacturing. In a real setup all equipment should also come from the same manufacturer to ensure synchronized behavior and better support between control systems and robot. Finally a failover system should be added using additional sensors or safety stops in the shared workspace to complement the SafetyEYE system zone monitoring.

4. REFERENCES

[1] M. Morioka et al, "Cooperation Between a High-Power Robot and a Human by Function Safety," *Journal of Robotics and Mechatronics*, vol. 23, nr 6, pp. 926-938, 2011.

[2] N. Pedrocchi1, F. Vicentini, M. Matteo and L. M. Tosatti, "Safe Human-Robot Cooperation in an Industrial Environment," *International Journal of Advanced Robotic Systems*, vol. 10, nr 27,pp.1-13, 2013.

[3] Robots and robotic devices - Safety requirements for industrial robots - Part 1: Robots (ISO 10218-1:2011)

[4] Robots and robotic devices - Safety requirements for industrial robots - Part 2: Robot systems and integration (ISO 10218-2:2011)

Intuitive Error Resolution Strategies during Robot Demonstration

Maria Vanessa aus der Wieschen
University of Southern Denmark
Department of Design and Communication
DK-6400 Sonderborg
mwies08@student.sdu.dk

Kerstin Fischer
University of Southern Denmark
Department of Design and Communication
DK-6400 Sonderborg
kerstin@sdu.dk

Kamil Kukliński
Bialystok University of Technology
Automation and Robotics Department
PL-15-351 Białystok
kamilkuklinski@o2.pl

ABSTRACT

While robot learning from demonstration comes with great benefits [5], the intuitive interaction between naïve users and robots also poses challenges. For instance, users need to be prevented from causing damage and to be enabled to recover from errors. We studied the error resolution strategies of 28 lay users performing simple assembly tasks via teleoperation of a robotic arm in order to gain insight into the strategies users take. The two most common problems are too much pressure and singularity. Even though users were provided with instructions on how to undo singularity in an instruction video, they did not always recover successfully. In contrast, too much pressure, if noticed, was resolved mostly correctly by lifting the peg or by letting it drop into the hole rather than inserting it. Finally, users were quite clueless about how to resolve self-collision and over-rotation.

Categories and Subject Descriptors

H.1.2 [**User/Machine Systems**]

General Terms

Human Factors

Keywords

Error resolution; robot learning by demonstration; teleoperation

1. INTRODUCTION

Robot learning by demonstration is a way of teaching robots to perform tasks without having to program them. The robot learns from the demonstration of the task to be performed by a human teacher. While the advantages of this approach such as time- and cost-efficiency are obvious, allowing lay users to operate a robot can lead to problems. For instance, naïve robot users might accidentally damage the robot, simply because they do not know which parts of it are fragile. Moreover, lay users may not be able to resolve errors on their own due to a lack of understanding of the system and its functionality. Thus, in order to increase the robustness of the interactions between robot and lay users, users have to be enabled to understand the robot well enough to resolve errors themselves. Four types of errors occur with an industrial robot platform comprising one robot arm: too much pressure, singularity, self-collision and over-rotation of the gripper. We aimed to find out if users notice these problems and identify them correctly, and how they resolve the problems.

HRI'14, March 3-6, 2014, Bielefeld, Germany.
ACM 978-1-4503-2658-2/14/03.
http://dx.doi.org/10.1145/2559636.2559830

2. METHOD

Experiments with the MARVIN platform [4] were carried out at the University of Southern Denmark. 28 university staff and students at the technical faculty participated in the experiments. They were given a handheld robot teleoperation device as well as a numpad to operate the gripper [3]. The experiments were facilitated by three master students in Communication Design. Moreover, a robot operator was present at all times as an expert on the robot platform. Participants were asked to watch a short instruction video on how to use the robot and the task they are expected to perform. The video ,which was created by us for this experiment, contained advice on how to handle the robot carefully and how to avoid common problems, such as applying too much pressure with the robot on the workspace, self-collision, and singularity. Moreover, it explained how to undo singularity in case it happens anyway. The users were asked to assemble a square peg and separator from the Cranfield set [1] using the teleoperation device twice. The facilitators encouraged the users to "think aloud" [6], that is, users were asked to share any questions or observations they made. This think-aloud method was used in order to reveal the underlying cognitive processes involved in the users' problem solving strategies. However, as some users did not feel comfortable sharing their thoughts, and some voiced thoughts needed further explanation, the facilitators also interviewed the users during the task performance.

3. RESULTS

Table 1 shows how often users noticed the problems and whether they identified them correctly.

Table 1. Noticed and identified problems.

	Noticed		**Not noticed**	***Total***
	Identified correctly	*Identified differently*		
Pressure	99	44	27	*170*
Singularity	73	0	38	*111*
Self-collision	11	0	0	*11*
Over-rotation	0	0	2	*2*

3.1 Too Much Pressure

There is too much pressure, when the vector of forces measured by the sensor at the end of the Universal Robot manipulator exceeds the threshold limits.

3.1.1 Identifying Too Much Pressure

Some users were not aware that they were actually damaging the robot; instead, they identified the problem as simply the corners of the peg and the hole on the baseplate not being aligned (44 times).

3.1.2 Resolving Too Much Pressure

The correct procedure to be performed would be to stop the movement and lift the robot arm. 67 times users did so. Other strategies were to just ignore the problem or to open the gripper as to let the peg drop into the hole rather than to insert it properly.

Table 2. Resolution strategies for too much pressure.

	Pressure	Other Problem
lift peg	67	29
ignore	9	7
task finished	11	1
drop peg	12	7
total	*99*	*44*

3.2 Singularity

Singularity occurs when the value of the angle of joint2 (q2) is 0 (*see Figure 2*). Singularity reduces the rank of the Jacobian matrix, as the matrix is not reversible, and thus the configuration for robot joints cannot be found. Even a small change of the value of the angle of joint2 solves the problem. We found that lay users over-cautiously treat an angle of q2 smaller than 50° as singularity, and thus we broadened the definition of singularity to match the users' definition in the quantitative analysis.

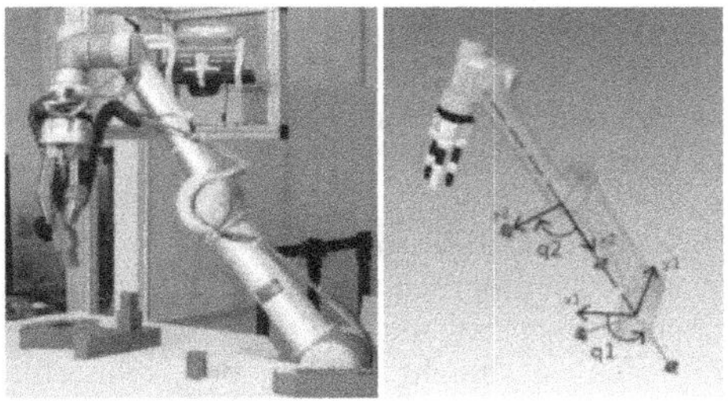

Figures 1 & 2 [2]**. Singularity. The angle of q2 is 0.**

3.2.1 Noticing and Identifying Singularity

Users noticed singularity 73 out of 111 times. The video analysis shows that the users' eyes were focused solely on the robot gripper or the peg while it was in motion. However, when they stopped moving the robot arm, users often performed a check of the entire robot arm, which is how they noticed singularity. Still, it was unnoticed by the users 38 times.

3.2.2 Resolving Singularity

The instruction video provided users with a resolution strategy for singularity, namely to move the robot towards the base of the arm, which would cause the involved joints to be at a smaller angle. The interview revealed that the reason why users failed to undo singularity 15 times, even though they knew what to do, was because they tried to specifically control the joint in question, which is not directly possible, as the robot control point is located in the gripper. Four times did the engineer have to undo the singularity for the user, either because the singularity caused a security stop, or because the user explicitly asked him to help.

Table 3. Resolution strategies for singularity.

As shown in video		Asked for help
successful	*failed*	
54	15	4

3.3 Self-Collision

Self-collision was caused 11 times by four users, of which 7 instances were caused by a single user. Three users tried to solve it but ended in singularity (*see Figure 3*). One of them was successful, while the other two required intervention and help from the robot operator. The fourth participant struggled hard to resolve self-collision, as undoing it led to singularity in turn. After an alternation of singularity and self-collision for 6 times, he resolved the singularity and rotated the wrist of the robot arm to prevent further self-collisions (*see Figure 4*).

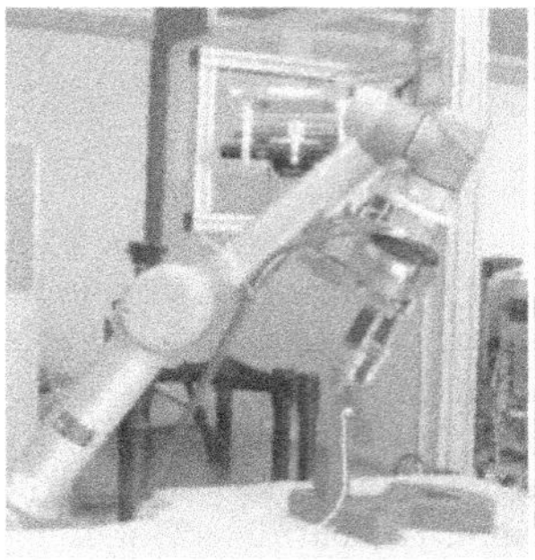

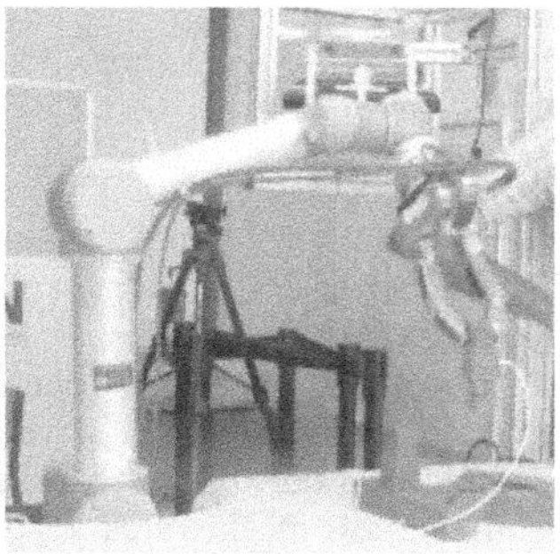

Figure 3. Self-collision caused by trying to undo singularity
Figure 4. Rotation of wrist to prevent self-collision

3.4 Over-Rotation of the Gripper

Over-rotation of the gripper occurred twice, both occurrences causing a security stop which had to be resolved by the engineer.

4. CONCLUSION AND IMPLICATIONS

The study shows that users attend to preventing and solving errors, but that they often do not know how to recover from the problems they experience. Lay users thus need to be provided with feedback that informs them not only on that there is a problem, but also what exactly the problem consists in and how to recover from it. Thus, users need to be provided with sufficient information on the robot and its functionalities.

5. ACKNOWLEDGMENTS

This research was partially funded by the EU project IntellACT. We thank N. Krüger, T.R. Savarimuthu, R. Beck, D. Sølvason, F. Kirstein and I. Marhenke.

6. REFERENCES

[1] Collins, K., Palmer, AJ, Rathmill, K. (1985): The Development of a European Benchmark for the Comparison of Assembly Robot Programming Systems. In: K.Rathmill et al. (eds) *Robot Technology and Applications*, pp 187-199, Berlin: Springer.

[2] Ellekilde, LP , Jorgensen, JA. (2010), "RobWork: A flexible toolbox for Robotics Research and Education", *Proceedings for the joint conference of ISR 2010 /ROBOTIK 2010*, pp 1-7

[3] Kukliński et al. (in prep*). Teleoperation for Learning by Demonstration: Data Glove versus External Manipulation for Intuitive Robot Control.*

[4] Savarimuthu, T. R., Liljekrans, D., Ellekilde, L.-P., Ude, A., Nemec, B., Krüger, N. (2013). Analysis of Human Peg-in-Hole Executions in a Robotic Embodiment using Uncertain Grasps. In *9th International Workshop on Robot Motion and Control*, RoMoCo 2013

[5] Stipancic, T., Bucevic, A., Curkovic, P., & Jerbic, B. (2012). Programming an industrial robot by demonstration. *Proceedings of the 23rd International DAAAM Symposium,23* (1), pp 15-18.

[6] Van Someren, M. W., Barnard, Y. F., & Sandberg, J. A. (1994). *The think aloud method: A practical guide to modelling cognitive processes*. London: Academic Press.

A New Control Architecture for Physical Human-Robot Interaction Based on Haptic Communication

Yusuf Aydin
Koc University
Sariyer, Istanbul, Turkey
+90 212 338 1721
yaydin@ku.edu.tr

Nasser Arghavani
Koc University
Sariyer, Istanbul, Turkey
+90 212 338 1721
narghavani@ku.edu.tr

Cagatay Basdogan
Koc University
Sariyer, Istanbul, Turkey
+90 212 338 1721
cbasdogan@ku.edu.tr

ABSTRACT

In the near future, humans and robots are expected to perform collaborative tasks involving physical interaction in various different environments such as homes, hospitals, and factories. One important research topic in physical Human-Robot Interaction (pHRI) is to develop tacit and natural haptic communication between the partners. Although there are already several studies in the area of Human-Robot Interaction, the number of studies investigating the physical interaction between the partners and in particular the haptic communication are limited and the interaction in such systems is still artificial when compared to natural human-human collaboration. Although the tasks involving physical interaction such as the table transportation can be planned and executed naturally and intuitively by two humans, there are unfortunately no robots in the market that can collaborate and perform the same tasks with us. In this study, we propose a new controller for the robotic partner that is designed to a) detect the intentions of the human partner through haptic channel using a fuzzy controller b) adjust its contribution to the task via a variable impedance controller and c) resolve the conflicts during the task execution by controlling the internal forces. The results of the simulations performed in Simulink/Matlab show that the proposed controller is superior to the stand-alone standard/variable impedance controllers.

Categories and Subject Descriptors

I.2.9 [**Artificial Intelligence**]: Robotics; H.5.2 [**Information Interfaces and Presentation**]: User Interfaces – *Haptic I/O*

Keywords

Haptics; physical human-robot interaction; variable impedance control; internal force control.

1. INTRODUCTION

To make human-robot collaboration more natural, we need robots that can anticipate the intentions of the human partner and comply with those intentions smoothly during the execution of a collaborative task [1, 2, 3]. Obviously, the intention is a state of mind, which cannot be measured directly. However, we know that humans are good at recognizing each other's intentions during a collaborative task even without a verbal communication. Although the collaborating human partners may use other means of communication to convey their intentions while transporting a table, the haptic channel is more direct and personal when there is a physical interaction. Here, the intended movement of the human can be conveyed to the robot via the direction of the force applied to the table by the human while the force magnitude helps with the speed of the movement [1, 2, 3]. Following the intention recognition, the collaborating human partners successfully adjust their forces to adapt not only to the requirements of the task but also to each other's needs. In this paper, we propose a new control architecture for pHRI involving haptic communication. This architecture has three major components: 1) an intention estimator to detect the intentions of the human via haptic channel using a fuzzy controller, 2) a variable impedance controller to adjust the contribution of the robot to the task based on the intentions of the human, and 3) an internal force compensator to resolve the conflicts during the task execution by controlling the internal forces. We are not aware of any earlier study that integrates these components together in a coherent manner.

HRI'14, March 3–6, 2014, Bielefeld, Germany.
ACM 978-1-4503-2658-2/14/03.
http://dx.doi.org/10.1145/2559636.2563682

2. CONTROL ARCHITECTURE

In order to demonstrate the proposed control architecture, we assume that the human partner and the robot translate the table between two stations along a straight path. In our architecture (Figure 1), the robot does not know the final destination; hence no positional trajectory is specified for the robot. We use a Kalman observer to estimate the force applied by the human partner since it cannot be measured directly during the task execution. In addition, Kalman observer predicts the desired kinematics of the table. Once the next state of the table is predicted, the force applied by the robot to the table is calculated by an impedance controller in our approach. If we neglect the impedance mass and stiffness (m = 0, k = 0), the force applied by the robot is calculated by a Standard Impedance Controller (SIC) as:

$$F^r_{des} = K_p(v_{des} - v) + K_i(x_{des} - x) + bv \qquad (1)$$

where b is the controller impedance damping, x_{des} and v_{des} are the desired position and velocity of the end-effector, x and v are the actual position and velocity of the end-effector, K_p and K_i are the proportional and integral motion feedback gains, respectively. In our approach, the impedance damping, b, is adjusted by a fuzzy controller adaptively (Variable Impedance Control – VIC). This algorithm takes the current velocity of the table, v, and the rate of change of the human force estimated by the Kalman observer, $d\hat{F}^h$, and then outputs a gain value representing the human intention, K_{HIG}, which is utilized to calculate the variable damping coefficient later. Two-input-one-output Takagi-Sugeno fuzzy tuner is utilized in this study. Three membership functions (positive, zero and negative) are defined for each input, as tabulated in Table 1.

We scale the human intention gain, K_{HIG} with a constant α to calculate the damping coefficient of the impedance controller as

$$b = b_0 + \alpha K_{HIG} \qquad (2)$$

where, b_0 is the nominal value of the damping coefficient.

Table 1: The singletons associated with the human intentions. The human intention gain for acceleration varies between $0 < K_{\mathrm{HIG}} \leq 1$, the human intention gain for deceleration varies between $-1 \leq K_{\mathrm{HIG}} < 0$, and $K_{\mathrm{HIG}} = 0$ when there is no change.

$d\hat{F}^h$ \ v	Positive	Zero	Negative
Positive	1	0.5	-1
Zero	0	0	0
Negative	-1	-0.5	1

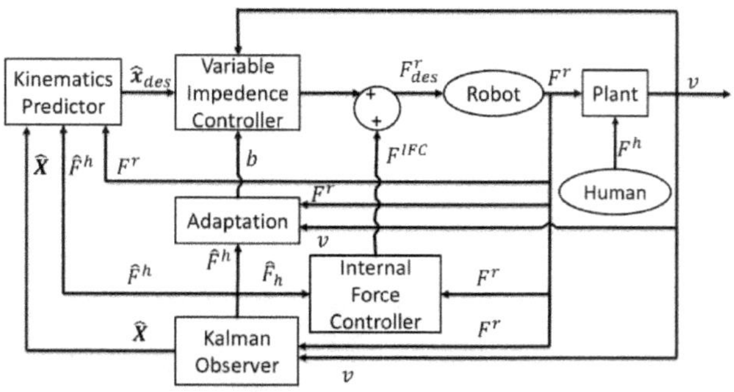

Figure 1. Control diagram for the table transportation task.

So far, the proposed controller for the robot is designed to comply with the human intentions. However, due to time delays and/or noise in the system, conflicts may still occur. To reduce these conflicts, we utilize the internal force controller (IFC). For this purpose, the forces applied by the partners are decomposed into two components; one contributing to the motion and the other is the internal force, which does not contribute to the motion at all [1,3]. The internal force is calculated as

$$F^{int} = \begin{cases} -F^r, & if\ (F^h F^r \leq 0) \\ 0, & otherwise \end{cases} \qquad (3)$$

In order to eliminate this wasted force (i.e. internal force), a simple PI controller with a set value of zero is utilized (F^{IFC} is the compensation signal that the PI controller generates to reduce the internal force). Thus, the total force applied by the robot is,

$$F^r_{des} = K_p(v_{des} - v) + K_i(x_{des} - x) + bv + F_k^{IFC} \qquad (4)$$

3. SIMULATION RESULTS

We conducted simulations in Matlab/Simulink to test the utility of the proposed approach. In terms of tracking performance, we observe that the overshoot amplitudes are higher under SIC compared to that of VIC (Figure 2). Hence, the positional tracking of VIC is better than that of SIC.

Furthermore, the average forces applied by the human and the robot are reduced under VIC (Figure 3). Also, SIC+IFC reduces the average forces applied by the partners on the table when compared to using SIC alone. However, as it is observed from the Figure 3, there is not much change in the average forces of the partners when the controller is changed from the VIC to VIC+IFC. The average internal force for different controllers is also shown in Figure 3. The amount of disagreement between the partners is the highest under SIC. IFC reduces the disagreement to some extent. Moreover, VIC further reduces the disagreement and the least disagreement is observed under VIC+IFC.

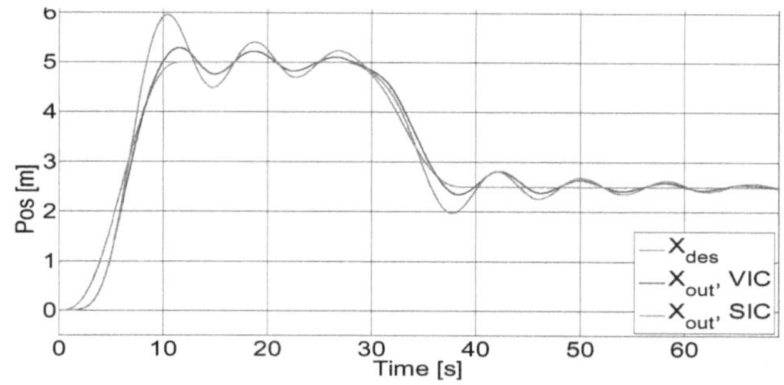

Figure 2. The position tracking performance of VIC and SIC.

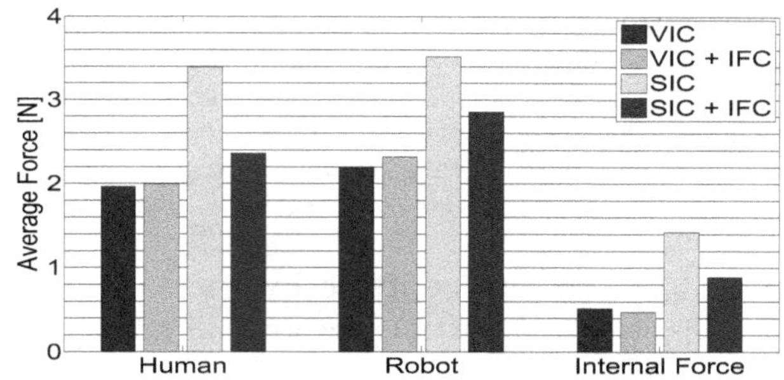

Figure 3. The average force applied by the human partner and the robot on the table and the average internal force.

4. CONCLUSION

We aim to develop a controller for a robot that can intuitively understand the intentions of a human partner and collaborates with him/her naturally and efficiently during a pHRI task. In order to achieve this goal, we have developed a variable impedance controller and compared its performance with a conventional (standard) impedance controller. We modify the damping coefficient of controller to comply with the intentions of the human during the task execution through a fuzzy controller. The robot should react to changes in the human intention immediately in order to reduce the conflicts. In our approach, the level of human intention sets the damping coefficient of the controller. Although the performance of the proposed VIC is better than that of the SIC, the delays and uncertainties in the system may still cause some conflicts between the human and the robot. As a remedy to this, we have implemented an internal force controller in series with the VIC. We observed that this scheme (VIC+IFC) further reduces the conflicts and improves the task efficiency.

5. REFERENCES

[1] Mörtl, A., Lawitzky, M., Kucukyilmaz, A., Sezgin, M., Basdogan, C., and Hirche, S. (2012). The role of roles: Physical cooperation between humans and robots. *The International Journal of Robotics Research*, 31(13):1656-1674.

[2] Oguz, S. O., Kucukyilmaz, A., Sezgin, T. M., and Basdogan, C. (2010). Haptic negotiation and role exchange for collaboration in virtual environments. *IEEE Haptics Symposium*, 371-378.

[3] Kucukyilmaz, A., Sezgin, T. M., and Basdogan, C. (2013). Intention recognition for dynamic role exchange in haptic collaboration. *IEEE Transactions on Haptics*, 6(1):58–68.

Engagement based on a Customization of an iPod-LEGO Robot for a Long-term Interaction for an Educational Purpose

Alex Barco, Jordi Albo-Canals,
Carles Garriga
La Salle BCN – Ramon Llull University
Barcelona, Spain
jalbo@salleurl.edu

ABSTRACT

The aims of the study presented in this paper are to find evidence that the customization of a robot increases the engagement interacting with it, and the adaptation of a non-social robotic platform like LEGO Robotics is possible. The study has been done with 7 years old children from primary school level that have been doing daily homework activities conducted by the robot during one month. Results showed us a higher interaction and adaptability to a social robot with the customization.

Categories and Subject Descriptors

I.2.9 **[Robotics]** : Commercial robots and applications. D.2.2. **[Design Tools and Techniques]**: User interfaces. H.1.2 **[User/Machine Systems]** : Human factors, Human information processing.

General Terms

Management, Measurement, Documentation, Performance, Design, Reliability, Experimentation, Human Factors, and Verification.

Keywords

Robotics, Robot, Children, Engagement, Long-term, LEGO, and Education.

1. INTRODUCTION

Academic homework has changed in the past years. From being done on a piece of paper, it has evolved to on-line platforms like Moodle. These platforms allow continuous contact between the students and the educators; sometimes providing useful tools that help with routine tasks like correcting tests or collecting deliverables. The idea of this study is part of a bigger project called Robotics@School that pretends to introduce the wide spectrum of robotics inside the schools, from kindergarten to high school levels. In an educational environment robots are mainly used only to teach technology and science, and rarely used for other tasks.

HRI'14, March 3-6 2014, Bielefeld, Germany
ACM 978-1-4503-2658-2/14/03.
http://dx.doi.org/10.1145/2559636.2563697

This paper shows the results obtained in terms of engagement using an iPod-LEGO robotic-based platform to analyze the customized robot's role in terms of engagement and likeness.

In [1] we introduced the LEGO Robotics Platform (See Figure 1) to conduct a robotic therapy for children with traumatic brain damage at home. The results obtained in terms of acceptance of the platform were very encouraging so we decided to use the same platform in an educational environment, with the same purpose as the previous task, to improve cognitive skills of primary school children without special needs.

Figure 1. Robot Structure and Appearance

2. iPOD-LEGO ROBOT

2.1 Previous study

Before deciding to use this platform, we performed a study with 94 children of one hour play-based interaction with different kinds of robots: Pleo, Furby, Keepon and a walking robot made of LEGO. After these sessions the children did an exercise on adding (selecting) three adjectives from 20 options [2]. We concluded based on the kid's answers, considering the LEGO Robot as WELL DESIGNED (36.3%) and USEFUL (36.3%), while the Pleo as FUNNY (48.3%) and LOVING (55.2%), and the Furby as FUNNY (42.9%) and LOVING (52.4%). The Furby also was considered INTELLIGENT (42.9%) because it was able to communicate with a smartphone or tablet. The KEEPON was labeled as FUNNY (33.3%), SIMPLE (42.9%) and STUPID (38.1%). So considering all those outputs, we decided to use the same platform used by the project in [1] expecting it to be USEFUL, FUNNY and LOVING.

2.2 Robot Description

The robot's main CPU is an iPod Touch 4G with a software structure composed of three main blocks: 1) The Pet Behavior module that decides the mood and physical state of the robot, 2) The Monitor module that collects all interaction data and the activities scores, and 3) The Trainer module, composed of the activity dispatcher, the connectivity module, and the activities controller. The secondary CPU is a LEGO Brick CPU that manages the movements of the robot. In [1] more detailed information can be found.

2.3 Activities Description

The activities conducted by the robot can be classified in two sets, the social and the academic. In the social set the child trains his habits, communication, and caring skills, while in the academic set the robot proposes math, language, problem solving, and memory exercises. The interaction in each exercise differs from touching the screen, using sensors (touch sensor, microphone, camera, etc.), and moving the robot as a haptic device.

3. STUDY DESIGN

We did the study with a group of 14 children, all of them with the same platform, but seven of them had a customized robot with their topics of interest collected from a questionnaire filled in by the parents, which asked about hobbies, language preference (Spanish or Catalan), music, etc.

The students received a training session about using the robot, as well as a short manual about how to proceed to start and stop the robot, and to solve the common unexpected issues that could occur. This process took one week where they did the exercises together with a technician. The weeks 2, 3 and 4 they did the activities at home. Every Monday the Technician and the Teacher set up the weekly activities. Finally, the children filled in a questionnaire about how much they liked the robot [2].

4. RESULTS AND CONCLUSIONS

As we expected, in the exercise on adding (selecting) three adjectives mentioned in section 2, the iPod-LEGO Robot was labeled as FUNNY (71.4%) and LOVING (57.1%) as the top adjectives in the customized robots, while USEFUL (42.8%) and INTELLIGENT (57.1%) were the top adjectives in the not customized ones. This shows us that the adjectives in the customized robot are nearer to social robotics rather than the adjectives for the not customized one, which are nearer to a robot seen like a machine. So as a conclusion, customization allows us to convert our Educational Robot to a Social Robot.

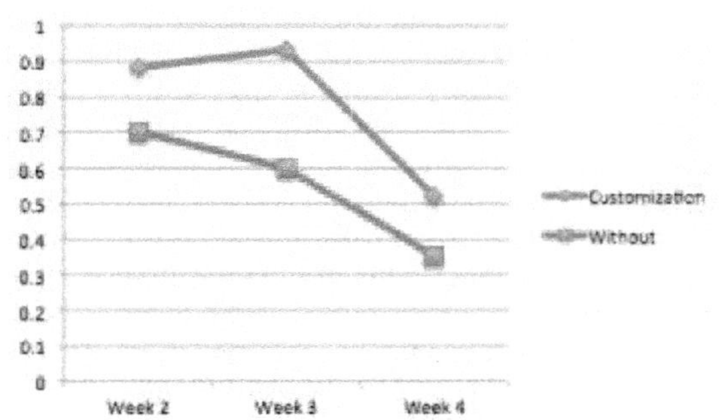

Figure 2. Engagement interaction with the robot measured as normalized use of days versus weeks

Also, analyzing the information from the robot we can conclude that in a long-term interaction, defined as the minimum time required to be familiarized with the robot [3], it is very useful to know the children's preferences in order to keep the engagement (see Figure 2). We also planned the maintenance of the engagement to avoid the deterioration over time [4] with small tricks like greetings and farewells before and after the activities [5], and telling secrets to create complicity between the kid and the robot [6].

Unfortunately, in the last week there was a software bug that blocked the robot during an activity process so the engagement decreased. Despite this bug, if we take a look in Figure 2 we can see the interaction always higher in the customized robot.

We put time stamps to measure the interaction period every day with the robot, however several times the children forgot to switch off the robot. For future studies we will put an automatic switch off function after a period of time without interaction.

We have validated that the design of the robot matches the crossed requirements between the more social robots like Pleo or Furby, and more educational robots like LEGO Robotics platform.

5. ACKNOWLEDGMENTS

Our thanks to Col·legi Montserrat from Barcelona to provide the optimal conditions to conduct the study. This project with code 502858 is founded by La Fundació de la Marató de TV3, and LEGO Foundation donated the robots.

6. REFERENCES

[1] Barco, Alex, Jordi Albo-Canals, Miguel Kaouk Ng, Carles Garriga, Laura Callejón, Marc Turón, Claudia Gómez, and Anna López-Sala. "A robotic therapy for children with TBI." In *Human-Robot Interaction (HRI), 2013 8th ACM/IEEE International Conference on*, pp. 75-76. IEEE, 2013

[2] Heerink, M., Díaz, M., Albo-Canals, J., Angulo, C., Barco, A., Casacuberta, J., & Garriga, C. (2012, September). A field study with primary school children on perception of social presence and interactive behavior with a pet robot. In *RO-MAN, 2012 IEEE* (pp. 1045-1050). IEEE

[3] Leite, I., Martinho, C., and Paiva, A. 2013. *Social robots for long-term interaction: A survey.* International Journal of Social Robotics, 1-18.

[4] Kelley HH, Berscheid E, Christensen A, Harvey JH, Huston TL, et al. 1983/2002.*Close Relationships*. Clinton Corners, NY: Percheron (Original work published 1983).

[5] Kidd, C.D. 2008. *Designing for long-term human-robot interaction and application to weight loss.* Doctoral Thesis. MIT.

[6] Kanda, T., R. Sato, R., Saiwaki,N., and Ishiguro, H. 2007. *A two-month field trial in an elementary school for long-term human-robot interaction.* IEEE Trans Robot, 23(5):962–971.

Tracking Gaze over Time in HRI as a Proxy for Engagement and Attribution of Social Agency

Paul Baxter, James Kennedy, Anna-Lisa Vollmer, Joachim de Greeff, Tony Belpaeme
Centre for Robotics and Neural Systems
Cognition Institute
Plymouth University, U.K.
paul.baxter@plymouth.ac.uk

ABSTRACT

In this contribution, we describe a method of analysing and interpreting the direction and timing of a human's gaze over time towards a robot whilst interacting. Based on annotated video recordings of the interactions, this *post-hoc* analysis can be used to determine how this gaze behaviour changes over the course of an interaction, following from the observation that humans change their behaviour towards the robot on the time-scale of individual interactions. We posit that given these circumstances, this measure may be used as *a* proxy (among others) for engagement in the interaction or the human's attribution of social agency to the robot. Application of this method to a sample of unstructured child-robot interactions demonstrates its use, and justifies its utilisation in future studies.

Categories and Subject Descriptors

H.1.2 [**Models and Principles**]: User/Machine Systems; D.2.8 [**Software Engineering**]: Metrics—*complexity measures, performance measures*

General Terms

Experimentation, Measurement, Theory

Keywords

Child-Robot Interaction; Gaze Direction; Sandtray; Unstructured Social HRI

1. INTRODUCTION

In social human-robot interaction, an autonomous robot must gain and maintain the engagement of an interactant, whilst taking into account the context of the interaction (be it environmental, task, etc). There are many important facets to this maintenance of engagement; one central facet is the gaze of the interactant, both in terms of direction and timing, e.g. [4]. In addition to this, recent results have also emphasised the adaptation of human's behaviour in response to robot behaviour [5], indicating that this variability needs to be taken into account in analysis. These aspects taken together demonstrate the need to account for engagement over the course of an interaction; gaze provides a means of analysis of this when treated as a measurement of human behaviour. Given the difficulty in providing such a characterisation in real-time, *post-hoc* analysis nevertheless enables such an account to be formulated.

In this context, dyadic human-robot interactions with no explicit interaction structure imposed are of particular interest, with our studies centred on the use of the 'Sandtray' system [1] (figure 1). With no such imposed structure, it is hypothesised that more naturalistic interaction characteristics are more readily attainable [3], thus enabling the emergence of social interaction to be studied [2]. However, the resulting analysis is complicated by this lack of structure, adding to the difficulty in characterising the interaction (e.g. engagement [6]). In this contribution, we present a method of *post-hoc* analysis that can provide an objective characterisation of the gaze behaviour of the human towards the robot during an interaction, and explore how this analysis can shape the assessment of the human's behaviour, and the state of the interaction itself.

Figure 1: The 'Sandtray': a touchscreen device that provides a task context for social HRI to facilitate naturalistic human behaviour.

2. CHARACTERISING GAZE OVER TIME: A CASE STUDY

The basic premise of the method proposed here is that the change in the human gaze behaviour over the course of an interaction can provide useful information regarding the state of the interaction, and also the attitude of the human towards the robot. Assuming that from the recorded interac-

HRI'14, March 3–6, 2014, Bielefeld, Germany.
ACM 978-1-4503-2658-2/14/03.
http://dx.doi.org/10.1145/2559636.2559829.

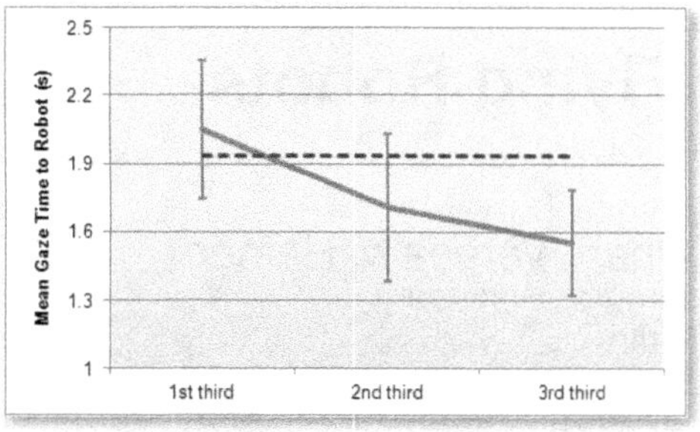

Figure 2: Mean length of each gaze to the robot in the three mean thirds of the interactions analysed. Dotted line shows mean gaze length over the whole interaction. Error bars show SEM.

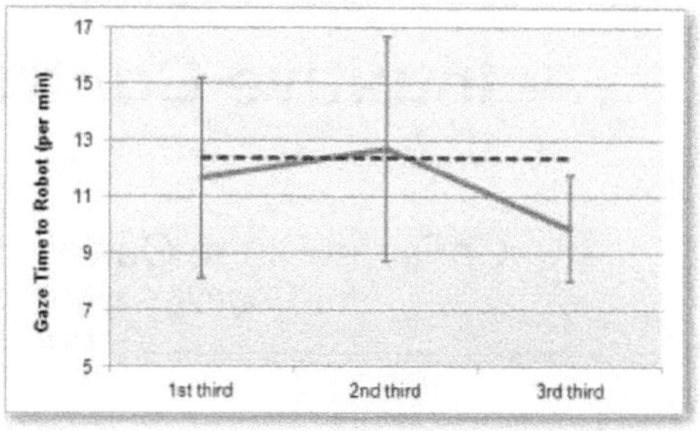

Figure 3: Length of gaze per minute to robot in the three mean thirds of the interactions analysed. Dotted line shows mean length of gaze (in seconds) per minute over the whole interaction. Error bars show SEM.

tions it is possible to distinguish and code the gaze direction of the human, the method essentially entails the calculation of the mean of a measurement of gaze within a time-window, such that the value can be compared across time-windows (e.g. normalised duration of gaze in each of the time-windows, enabling comparison across subjects). For relatively short interactions, one relevant comparison is between the beginning and end of the interaction by splitting the interaction into three phases, thus enabling standard statistical tests to be applied to the differences in means.

This method was applied to video data from unstructured child-robot interactions, in order to illustrate its potential as a means of assessing the child's interaction with the robot. Video data from a number of unstructured child-robot interactions in the context of the Sandtray were coded (see [1] for details); data from four interactions were analysed (mean length of interaction: 115s, *sd=16.4s*). Despite there being no significant difference between the values obtained for this case study, a decreasing profile is visible for both of the gaze measures analysed: mean length of gaze from human to robot (figure 2) decreases from the first to final third of the interactions, as does the length of gaze (normalised per minute, figure 3). It is instructive to compare these plots to the mean value for the interaction: in both cases there is an indication that there are changes within the interaction that are lost if only the average over the interaction were to be considered.

Previous work posited that the children in these interactions viewed the robot as a potentially social actor, resulting in the emergence of turn-taking despite the robot not using contingent behaviours [1]. The present results modify this perspective slightly as they indicate that over time, the children look less at the robot. This may be seen as a decrease in engagement with the robot, possibly as the limitations of the robot's social behaviour are experienced - indeed, the attribution of social agency may also decrease over time as a result. Further exploration of this effect is required, as it has fundamental consequences for child-robot interaction in particular [2]. However, the application of the proposed analysis method (or similar) will facilitate this process.

3. PERSPECTIVES

As described here, there are a number of limitations to the proposed *post-hoc* metric. Firstly, it assumes that the interactions analysed are of near-to-equal length, otherwise the three stages of individual interactions will be stretched or squashed (relatively). This can be circumvented by using constant-length time-windows instead of proportions of interaction lengths (although this is similarly problematic for comparing interactions of unequal length). Secondly, the data presented here is human-focused, rather than taking into account what the human's behaviour is contingent upon. While not conducted for the present example, this can be remedied by instead using measures of human gaze direction in response to robot behaviours (e.g. overlaps with movement or utterances).

Despite these limitations, the main point of the proposed analysis is that the change in gaze behaviours can be tracked over time, and that these changes can themselves provide a useful characterisation of the interaction, and aid in the interpretation of the human's behaviour. It may thus also be applied as a means of comparing the efficacy of different experimental conditions or systems in maintaining engagement over interaction time, as the profiles of the mean time-windowed gaze measure can be objectively compared.

4. ACKNOWLEDGMENT

This work is funded by the EU FP7 ALIZ-E project (grant 248116).

5. REFERENCES

[1] P. Baxter et al. Emergence of Turn-taking in Unstructured Child-Robot Social Interactions. In *HRI'13*, pages 77–78. ACM Press, 2013.

[2] T. Belpaeme et al. Child-robot interaction: Perspectives and challenges. In *ICSR'13*, volume 8239, pages 452–459. Springer, 2013.

[3] J. Kennedy et al. Constraining Content in Mediated Unstructured Social Interactions: Studies in the Wild. In *AFFINE'13*. IEEE Press, 2013.

[4] B. Mutlu et al. Footing In Human-Robot Conversations: How Robots Might Shape Participant Roles Using Gaze Cues. In *HRI'2009*, pages 61–68. ACM Press, 2009.

[5] M. Nalin et al. Children's adaptation in multi-session interaction. In *Ro-MAN 2012*. IEEE Press, 2012.

[6] C. Rich et al. Recognizing engagement in human-robot interaction. In *HRI'2010*, pages 375–382. IEEE Press, 2010.

Intuitive Control of Small Flying Robots

Christian Blum, Oswald Berthold, Philipp Rhan, Verena V. Hafner
Cognitive Robotics, Department of Computer Science
Humboldt-Universität zu Berlin
Berlin, Germany

ABSTRACT

In this paper we show a new perspective on human-robot interaction by presenting a system for intuitive interaction with flying robots. This goes beyond the usual remote control of these robots, by having an interactive space where people can physically interact with flying robots in an intuitive and safe way. The presented system has various ways of interaction and provides the prerequisites for many interesting future applications.

Keywords

human-robot interaction, flying robots, intuitive interaction

1. INTRODUCTION

When untrained individuals need to interact with one or several autonomous flying systems, an important prerequisite is that the interaction is both intuitive and safe. Examples for such situations arise from applications such as the factory of the future, entertainment or art, and when it is desirable to teach a robot by demonstration. To accomplish this task, the hardware should be easy to handle, safe and allow for dynamic and intuitive human-robot interaction.

One approach is that followed in [5, 7] providing a safety layer between the untrained operator and the robot. Intrinsic safety in particular is a major issue with flying robots due to potential crashes and contact with propellers. Regarding direct interaction, a vision-mediated gestural interface was proposed in [6] and a blimp for safe interaction with and safe operation in the vicinity of crowds is described in [3], but the vehicle is rather bulky. An approach for reducing danger of self-destruction for the robot itself is described in [4, 1]. One general way of reducing the potential for harm is to reduce the size and mass of such robots. Here we present a system using very lightweight ($\mathcal{O}(50g)$) quadrotor helicopters which can be used for indoor interaction experiments.

While it is currently quite challenging to realize full onboard sensing and behaviour generation (control) of very small quadrotors [2], results from the proposed experiments

HRI'14, March 3–6, 2014, Bielefeld, Germany.
ACM 978-1-4503-2658-2/14/03.
http://dx.doi.org/10.1145/2559636.2559826.

Figure 1: Modified Walkera Ladybird with markers for the tracking system.

can easily be transferred from the tracking system case to the full onboard case because these results relate to general features of robot behaviour.

2. SYSTEM

As discussed above we chose a small quadrotor, the popular toy Walkera Ladybird [1]. The manufacturer designates it to be safe for children from the age of 14. It weighs only 31 g (with markers) and has a diameter of approx. 15 cm making it inherently safe even when accidentally hitting the human. We added five markers as can be seen in Fig. 1 to enable 6D tracking. In addition to human safety, the weight and size of the robot also make it almost immune to crashes etc.

Controlling a small flying robot in the direct vicinity of a human and facilitating interaction requires a closed-loop system in order to enable intuitive and safe behaviour of the robot. Weight constraints on a small robot are severe, thus we opted for external control and sensors.

We track the copter using an external tracking system consisting of six Natural Point OptiTrack Flex13 Cameras yielding 6D positions of the robot at 120Hz with an accuracy of about 0.5 mm and a latency of less than 10 ms. These positions are streamed over ethernet to the computer controlling the robot using a Natural Point protocol.

The robot is controlled using the MagicCube remote by Walkera which is controlled by an Arduino[2], which is attached to the control computer. The computer receives 6D positions from the tracking system and sends motor com-

[1]http://www.walkera.com/
[2]https://github.com/koro/mCube

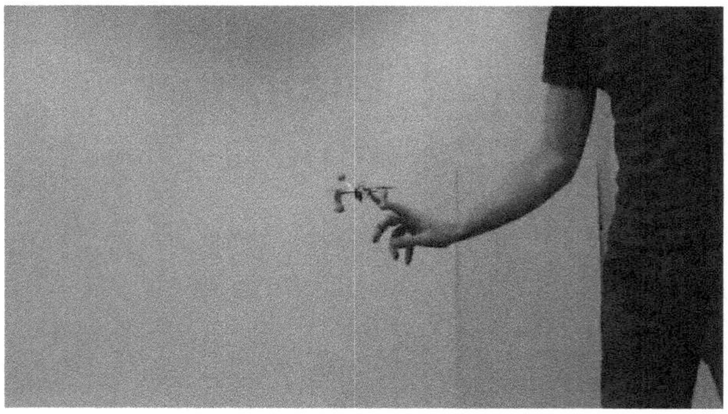

Figure 2: Human robot interaction by direct physical interaction, in this case mediated by pushing.

mands to the robot. We use our Mavhub[3] infrastructure to deal in quasi-real-time with the control. At the moment the robot is controlled by simple PID controllers.

To enhance the safety of bystanders and other scientists not participating in the experiments, we implemented a virtual safety cage. The main function of this cage is to shut down the motors of the robot when it leaves the cage by accident. In contrast to other indoor experiments with flying robots we do not need a physical safety cage or net because of the small size of the robot.

3. INTERACTION

Our vision is to facilitate interaction between flying robots and humans, that goes beyond device-based remote control but instead emphasizes direct interaction with the robot. This provides a basis for working together with the robot, teaching it by demonstration and physically correcting its mistakes.

3.1 Direct Physical Interaction

This is not only the most intuitive way of interacting with a robot, it also does not require additional hardware, as opposed to also tracking the human or using an RGB-D camera. For this to work, safety is imperative in order to ensure the health of the human and the physical integrity of the robot. An example interaction is depicted in Fig. 2.

We can use the error as determined by our control loop to detect sufficiently large offsets in position, which are due to external forces inflicted on the system by physical contact. A more sensitive alternative is the use of more advanced internal models, and detecting the interaction by monitoring the prediction errors of the forward model. These methods allow us to change the setpoints of the controllers and to freely position the robot in 3D space.

3.2 Kinesthetic Teaching

The next logical thing to do after changing the setpoints of the robot's position controller, is teaching it trajectories, of which an example is depicted in Fig. 3. For this, there are two intuitive possibilities.

Using the method of direct physical interaction between the human and the robot as described above, it is possible to not only change the setpoint but to demonstrate a whole trajectory. For this the robot has to recognize the beginning

[3]https://github.com/calihem/mavhub

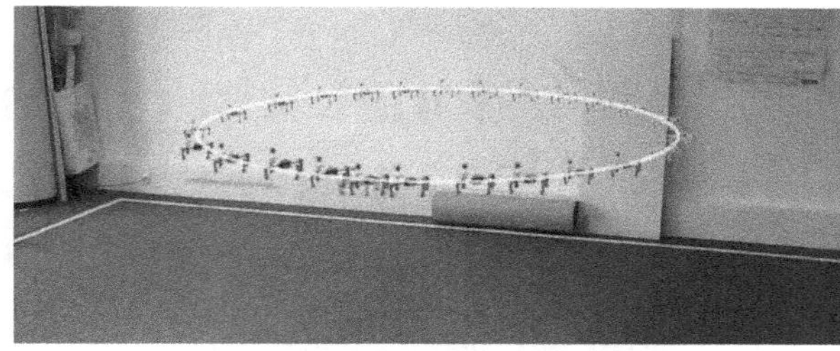

Figure 3: The robot follows an exemplary trajectory.

and the end of the interaction, which can be indicated by motion signatures. Knowledge about its position between these two points in time defines the trajectory. Another method is to use an additional marker within the tracking system and use it to record a trajectory demonstration. This can be advantageous in cases where the trajectory is more complex and using the copter directly would be too tiring or complex for the human.

4. SUMMARY AND FUTURE WORK

The proposed system provides a building block for solving more complex cooperation tasks for untrained individuals working with flying robots. These can be imitation learning, refinement of motion primitives or orchestrating robot teams for complex industrial tasks. Future work will focus on augmenting interaction detection and iterative interactive refinement of demonstrated trajectories. This can include use of additional sensors to enhance safety of the overall system and situational awareness of the robot.

5. ACKNOWLEDGMENTS

This work was funded in part by the DFG Research Training Group METRIK.

6. REFERENCES

[1] A. Briod et al. Contact-based navigation for an autonomous flying robot. In *International Conference on Intelligent Robots and Systems (IROS'13)*, 2013.

[2] A. Briod, J.-C. Zufferey, and D. Floreano. Optic-flow based control of a 46g quadrotor. In *Workshop on Vision-based Closed-Loop Control and Navigation of Micro Helicopters in GPS-denied Environments, IROS'13*, 2013.

[3] M. Burri et al. Design and control of a spherical omnidirectional blimp. In *Proc. IROS'13*, 2013.

[4] A. Klaptocz et al. Euler Spring Collision Protection for Flying Robots. In *Proc. IROS'13*, 2013.

[5] D. Lee et al. Semiautonomous haptic teleoperation control architecture of multiple unmanned aerial vehicles. *Mechatronics, IEEE/ASME Transactions on*, 18(4):1334–1345, 2013.

[6] V. M. Monajjemi et al. HRI in the Sky: Creating and Commanding Teams of UAVs with a Vision-mediated Gestural Interface. In *Proc. IROS'13*, 2013.

[7] D. Pitman and M. L. Cummings. Collaborative Exploration with a Micro Aerial Vehicle: A Novel Interaction Method for Controlling a MAV with a Hand-Held Device. *Advances in Human-Computer Interaction*, 2012.

Attentional Top-down Regulation and Dialogue Management in Human-robot Interaction

Riccardo Caccavale, Alberto Finzi, Lorenzo Lucignano, Silvia Rossi, Mariacarla Staffa
DIETI, Università degli Studi di Napoli "Federico II"
via Claudio, 80125 Napoli, Italy
{ri.caccavale,alberto.finzi,lorenzo.lucignano,silvia.rossi,maricarla.staffa}@unina.it

ABSTRACT

We propose a framework where the human-robot interaction is modeled as a multimodal dialogue which is regulated by an attentional system that guides the system towards the execution of structured tasks. We introduce a simple case study to illustrate the system at work in different conditions considering top-down regulations and dialogue flows in synergic and conflicting situations.

Categories and Subject Descriptors

I.2.9 [**Robotics**]: [Operator interfaces, Commercial robots and applications]; I.2.8 [**Artificial Intelligence**]: [Plan execution, formation, and generation]

Keywords

Dialogue Manager, Attentional System, Cognitive Control

1. INTRODUCTION

Attentional regulation and dialogue management can play a crucial role in social robotics and human-robot interaction [1]. Indeed, a natural and effective interaction between humans and robots can be modeled as a multimodal dialogue flow, while attentional mechanisms can be used to orient and focus the robot preceptive and cognitive processes during the interaction. Inspired by attention and cognitive control literature in neuroscience [7], we assume that the attentional influence can be driven both by higher level tasks/templates (top-down) and external/internal stimuli (bottom-up). In this context, the role of attentional mechanisms is to orchestrate multiple processes, at different levels of abstraction, possibly in conflicts. In this paper, we present a multimodal real-time HRI system integrating a dialogue manager and a hybrid cognitive control architecture. The dialogue system is modeled as a Partially Observable Markov Decision Process (POMDP) in order to manage the inherent ambiguity of the communication between the human and the robot. The generated dialogue policy provides an interaction template which will be instantiated and continuously adjusted with respect to the environmental and the operative context. The cognitive control cycle modulates and polarizes the execution by enhancing the attentional behaviors aligned with the operative (top-down) and environmental (bottom-up) state, while inhibiting the incoherent ones. In order to illustrate the system at work, we introduce a simple case study where we assess the system behavior while performing complementary and conflicting tasks.

HRI'14, March 3–6, 2014, Bielefeld, Germany.
ACM 978-1-4503-2658-2/14/03.
http://dx.doi.org/10.1145/2559636.2559854.

2. THE HRI FRAMEWORK

The proposed HRI architecture is depicted in Fig.1.

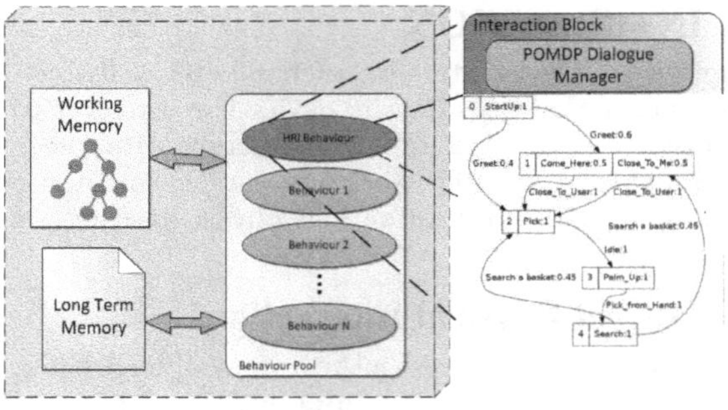

Figure 1: The HRI system architecture

Cognitive Cycle. The cognitive control cycle proposed in this work involves three main modules: a *behavior pool* (BP), a *working memory* (WM) and a *long term memory* (LTM). The BP contains a set of behaviors which may contribute to the execution of a complex cognitive task. The WM contains a representation of the hierarchical tasks [5] in the attentional focus of the system. This includes all the tasks the system is executing or willing to execute. Finally, the LTM is a repository which contains the definition of all the tasks available to the system. The cognitive control cycle is managed by a special behavior called *alive* which continuously updates the behavior pool and the working memory exploiting the task definitions provided by the LTM (Fig.3).

Allocation of attention. We assume that each behavior of the BP is structured as in [2, 4, 3] and it is endowed with an adaptive clock that regulates the frequency of sampling rate and action activations (Fig.2). This regulation tunes the resolution at which the behavior is monitored and controlled.

Emphasis. We introduce a modulation mechanism for top-down regulations of the attentional behaviors, this influences: (1) the *Frequency* of the behavioral clock induced by

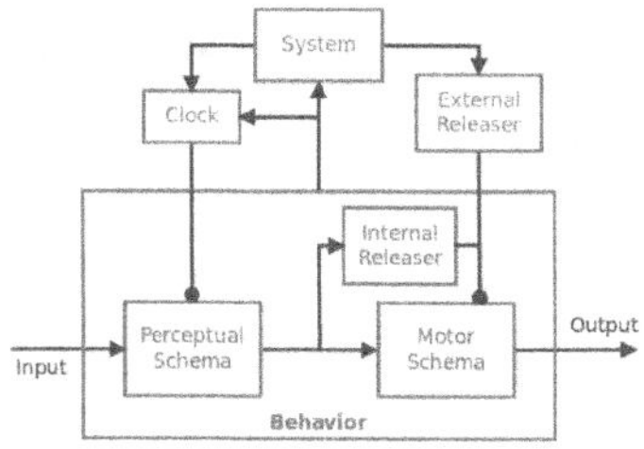

Figure 2: Schema theory representation of an attentional behavior.

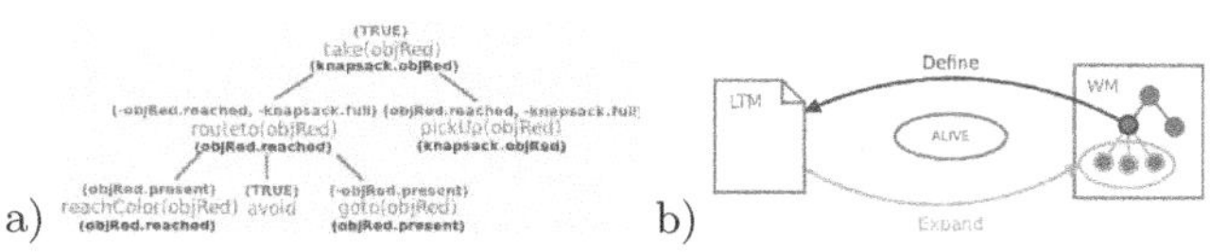

Figure 3: Example of subtree expansion in WM.

the perceptual stimuli; (2) the *Magnitude* externally induced by heuristics or influenced by other behaviors. The first represents a bottom-up and self-induced attentional mechanism, while the second captures top-down influences.

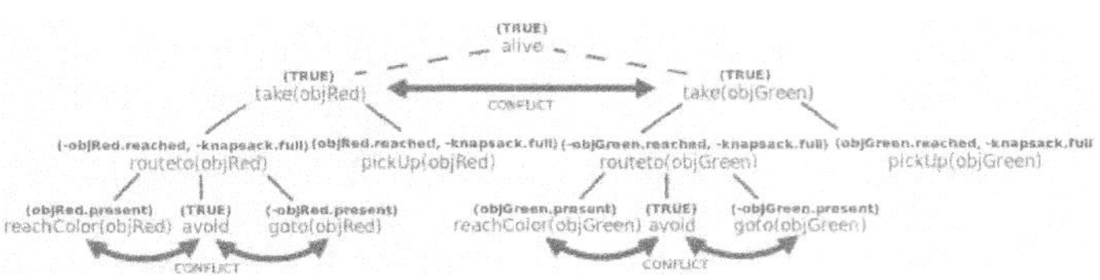

Figure 4: Example of conflicting tasks.

Dialogue Management System. The multimodal interaction block is appointed to recognize the multiple human commands and actions, such as utterances, gestures or body postures, and to provide an interpretation of user's intentions according to a dialogue context [8, 6]. The dialogue models are provided as graph-based specifications. Our approach is to represent the dialogue flow as a POMDP to cast the inherent *ambiguity* during the interaction. The solution of the POMDP is a robust dialogue strategy off-line generated for that interaction model [9].

Case Study. We consider a pick, carry, and place scenario where a mobile robot interacts with several users. We assume that the robot can pick up an object at a time, but it can carry a maximum of two objects. The users can interact with the robot by speaking or using gestures, while the robot has a list of user dialogue models describing possible patterns of interactions. In this context, we can find cases where the residual ambiguity in the dialogue policy and the associated decision conflicts should be resolved by the top down and bottom up attentional influences. For instance, if the dialogue interpretation is a generic *take* (without object) and a green and a red object are encountered by the robot, the system cannot decide on which one to take. To overcome the ambiguity, two instances of *take* are allocated as schemata in the WM (e.g., *take(objRed)*, *take(objGreen)*). These schemata are decomposed in two subschemata (Fig. 4) representing the to phases of the task: reach the object, pick it up, and give it to the human. In Fig. 5 (right) we have the *take(objRed)* which is bottom-up aroused by the activations of *reachColor(red)* (from 1 to 30) that instantiates *routeto(objRed)*, indeed this is the first object detected by the robot. After 15 seconds the robot detects also a green object, therefore a decision conflict arises. However, the robot heads towards the red object as an effect of the *reachColor(objRed)* dominant activations with respect to *reachColor(objGreen)* (see Fig. 5 (right)). Once the red object is reached, the subtask is accomplished by the *pickUp(red)* behavior. At this point the frequency of *take(objRed)* is relaxed because a new subtask is activated, i.e. *give(objRed)*. This behavior receives, top-down, the emphasis from the *take(objRed)* that drives *give(objRed)* towards the goal accomplishment. In Figure 5 (up-right), from time 30 to 55 we can see the period restriction considering the bottom-up reduction (dotted red line) and the one that takes into account also the effect of the top-down emphasis (continuous red line).

Figure 5: HRI scenario (left) Period modulation (right) during a conflicting situation.

Acknowledgments. The research leading to these results has been supported by the SAPHARI project (FP7/2007-2013 under grant agreement ICT-287513).

3. REFERENCES

[1] C. Breazeal. *Designing Sociable Robots.* MIT Press, 2002.

[2] E. Burattini, A. Finzi, S. Rossi, and M. Staffa. Attentional modulation of mutually dependent behaviors. In *Proc. of SAAB-2010*, 2010.

[3] E. Burattini, A. Finzi, S. Rossi, and M. Staffa. Cognitive control in cognitive robotics: Attentional executive control. In *Proc. of ICAR, 2011.* IEEE, 2011.

[4] E. Burattini, A. Finzi, S. Rossi, and M. Staffa. Attentional human-robot interaction in simple manipulation tasks. In *Proc. of HRI-2012*, 2012.

[5] R. P. Cooper and T. Shallice. Hierarchical schemas and goals in the control of sequential behavior. *Psychological Review*, 113(4):887–916, 2006.

[6] L. Lucignano, F. Cutugno, S. Rossi, and A. Finzi. A dialogue system for multimodal human-robot interaction. In *Proc. of ICMI, 2013.* ACM, 2013.

[7] M. I. Posner and C. R. R. Snyder. Attention and cognitive control. In *Information Processing and Cognition*, pages 55–85. 1975.

[8] S. Rossi, E. Leone, M. Fiore, A. Finzi, and F. Cutugno. An extensible architecture for robust multimodal human-robot communication. In *In Proc. of IROS-2013*, 2013.

[9] S. Young, M. Gasic, S. Keizer, F. Mairesse, J. Schatzmann, B. Thomson, and K. Yu. The hidden information state model: A practical framework for pomdp-based spoken dialogue management. *Computer Speech and Lang.*, 24(2):150 – 174, 2010.

Head Pose Behavior in the Human-Robot Interaction Space

Sonja Caraian and Nathan Kirchner
Center for Autonomous Systems
University of Technology, Sydney
Sydney, Australia
{sonja.caraian,nathan.kirchner}@uts.edu.au

ABSTRACT

Visual Focus of Attention is an important mechanism to support successful interactions. In order to communicate effectively and intentionally (issuing cues when a person is paying attention, for example), a robot must have an understanding of this Visual Focus of Attention behavior in the Human-Robot Interaction space. A real-world interaction study was conducted with 24 unsolicited participants to explore attention behavior towards robots in this space. The results suggest there is no generalizable attention pattern between people, and thus that online, *in situ* Visual Focus of Attention estimation would be advantageous to Human-Robot Interaction.

Categories and Subject Descriptors

I.2.9 [**Computing Methodologies**]: Artificial Intelligence *Robotics*

Keywords

Non-verbal cues; HRI; Head Pose Estimation

1. INTRODUCTION

In order to operate effectively and achieve societal acceptance, increasingly prevalent social robots must be capable of communicating in a socially sensitive manner during interactions [4]. Visual Focus of Attention (VFOA, the direction of gaze) is an important cue for supporting successful interactions in both Human-Human and Human-Robot Interaction (HRI); among other things, it is an indicator of level of interest in and attentiveness towards people in the environment [7].

This VFOA mechanism is known to be reciprocal during HRI and robots' VFOA cues are perceived by observers as communication, in line with recent robot-centric HRI paradigms such as [5]. For example, it has been shown that a robot's VFOA, in the form of joint attention (JA, the shared focus on an object), can influence object preference in observers of this JA [2]. Thus it becomes important for robots to be capable of utilizing their VFOA cues to communicate intentionally, issuing cues at appropriate times and avoiding inadvertent influences on observers during functional actions which could be perceived as JA. To achieve this, it is necessary to have an understanding of the natural attentiveness of people in the environment towards robots, as indicated by their VFOA. Through VFOA detection, a robot could then determine appropriate times to carry out cues or actions.

HRI'14, March 3–6, 2014, Bielefeld, Germany
ACM 978-1-4503-2658-2/14/03.
http://dx.doi.org/10.1145/2559636.2559800

Thus the question becomes: during real-world interactions in the HRI space, what VFOA behavior, and hence attentiveness, will people display towards a robot? This question is examined here within.

2. EXPERIMENT

An unconstrained interaction experiment was carried out to explore participants' VFOA behavior during real-world HRI. The RobotAssist platform [6] was positioned adjacent to the buttons of a set of elevators within a university building. Unsolicited participants (n = 24: 3 female, 21 male) approached the elevator foyer from a nearby hallway and the experiment began when they entered the foyer and the robot was within their line of sight. The duration of the experiment was moderated by the length of time it took for the elevator to arrive, with $\bar{x}$=31.3*s* and σ=28.7*s*. The experiment finished when the participant exited the elevator foyer, either by getting on an elevator or by returning back down the hallway. The robot was stationary for the experiment duration.

Measurement - The participants' VFOA behavior was the only dependent variable. This included their gaze times and patterns of looking or not looking at the robot. Data from a robot head-mounted Microsoft Kinect camera was coded post-hoc to quantify these measures.

Hypothesis and Predictions - It is hypothesized that there will be no generalizable pattern of participant VFOA behavior, necessitating online, *in situ* VFOA estimation capabilities to enable robots to communicate intentionally.

3. RESULTS

Approximately 14 minutes of camera data (~2,500 frames) of the 24 interactions was collected during the experiment from the Kinect in the robot's head. The ground truth of participants' VFOA behavior was independently coded by three experimenters and averaged together post-hoc to quantify at which points participants were looking (L) and not looking (!L) at the robot. Participants included in the results are those who were manually observed to have looked at the robot at some point during their interaction; thus the robot could have intentionally issued a cue directed at them.

Figure 1 shows the VFOA patterns of the participants over the duration of their interactions. White shows points at which participants' VFOA was directed towards the robot (L), and black represents the opposite (!L). Gray areas indicate the participant had exited the interaction. It can be seen that there was large degree of variation in the number ($\bar{x}$=3.5, σ =2.4) and length of looks at the robot ($\bar{x}$=2.1*s*, σ =4.3*s*), and the percentage of time spent looking at the robot over the course of the interaction ($\bar{x}$=24%, σ =22.7%).

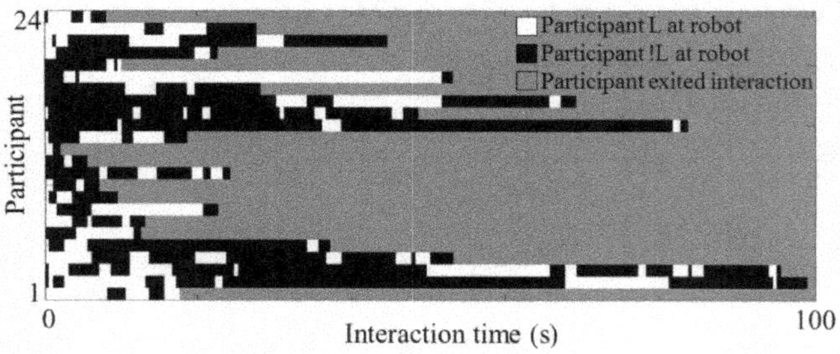

Figure 1: Looking patterns of participants over the course of their interactions

The number of participants whose VFOA was directed at the robot and the total number of participants still interacting over time are shown in Figure 2. It can be seen that, on average, approximately 50% of participants were looking at the robot at any point in time.

4. DISCUSSION

The results provide support for the hypothesis. No participant spent the entirety of their interaction L at the robot, and no readably generalizable pattern of L behavior was observable between participants, as shown in Figure 1 and in the empirical results. For example, 11 participants were in their interaction for a length of time before their first look at the robot, and 22 participants carried out their final look at the robot a length of time before exiting the interaction; the interactions lacked a point at which a cue intentionally issued by the robot would have been reliably observed by all participants. Instead, as can be seen from Figure 2, at any one time only some of the people still in their interaction were L at the robot, and an issued cue was only likely to be observed by a maximum of approximately 50% of people. Similarly, it is difficult to determine a time when an action not intended to be witnessed could have been carried out (i.e. all participants were !L).

To enable effective and intentional communication in the absence of a generalizable L pattern, it would be advantageous for robots to be capable of detecting the VFOA of people in the environment online and *in situ*. As such, as it is known that VFOA can be reasonably approximated by head pose [3], the captured participant data was processed with a head pose estimation (HPE) system for the HRI space currently under development by the authors. Data of participants whose head angle to the robot, θ, was $|\theta|>30^{\circ}$ (as estimated by the three coder experimenters) was excluded from the HPE as it is known that additional challenges exist when estimating head poses at larger angles [1]. This constituted approximately 56% of the data.

Assuming the problem is an unbiased stochastic process, the system achieved better results (~60% accuracy when participants were L and ~50% accuracy when they were !L) than a solution based on chance. However, the ability of the system to accurately detect L and !L behavior was significantly affected by the difficulty of generating an accurate ground truth to which the estimates could be compared; even with three independent viewers, estimating head pose ground truth from the RGB video captured from the robot-head Kinect in such an unconstrained scenario proved non-trivial. In order to effectively determine the accuracy and usefulness of the HPE system, a more considered experiment needs to be run where ground truth can more reliably be determined.

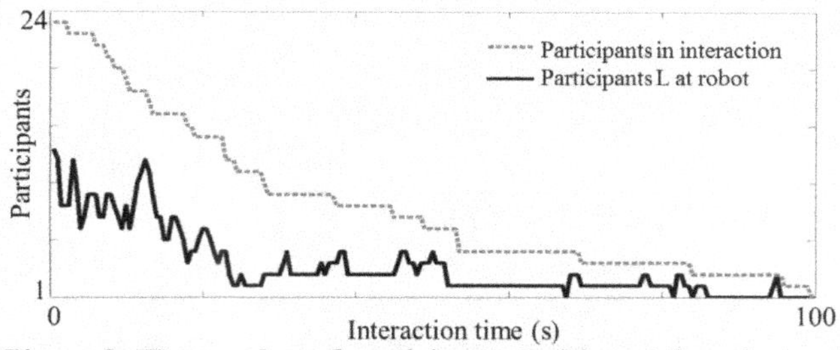

Figure 2: The number of participants looking at the robot and those still interacting over time

5. CONCLUSIONS AND FUTURE WORK

This study focused on understanding people's natural VFOA behavior towards robots during unsolicited interactions. The capability of detecting this behavior can enable robots to communicate intentionally to people in the environment through an understanding of when people's attention is directed at the robot (cues aimed at the person can be issued) and when it is not (actions the robot does not want observed can be carried out to avoid inadvertent influences).

In addition to further exploration of these findings, future work will focus on carrying out a larger sample size experiment in which ground truth can be more reliably determined in order to better evaluate the usefulness of our HPE system in estimating natural VFOA behavior in the HRI space; the reliability of the ground truth we generated through subjective estimation of VFOA remains a considerable source of error in determination of the accuracy of the HPE system currently under development. Additionally, focus will be directed towards enabling the system to be capable of autonomously identifying the times in which a person's head angle to the robot θ is $|\theta|>30^{\circ}$, and hence when the system head pose estimate should not be solely relied on.

6. ACKNOWLEDGEMENTS

This work is supported by UTS' Center for Autonomous Systems and RobotAssist (*www.robotassist.org*).

7. REFERENCES

[1] M. Breitenstein *et al.* Real-Time Face Pose Estimation from Single Range Images. In *IEEE Computer Society Conference on CVPR*, pages 1–8, 2008.

[2] S. Caraian and N. Kirchner. Influence of Robot-Issued Joint Attention Cues on Gaze and Preference. In *HRI'13: Proceedings of the 8th ACM/IEEE Conference on Human-Robot Interaction*, pages 1–2, 2013.

[3] M. Farenzena *et al.* Social interactions by visual focus of attention in a three-dimensional environment. In *Workshop on Pattern Recognition and Artificial Intelligence for Human Behaviour Analysis*, 2009.

[4] V. Groom. What's the best role for a robot? Cybernetic models of existing and proposed human-robot interaction structures. In *Proceedings of the International Conference on Informatics in Control, Automation, and Robotics*, 2008.

[5] N. Kirchner and A. Alempijevic. A Robot Centric Perspective on the HRI Paradigm. *Journal of Human-Robot Interaction - Special Issue on HRI Perspectives and Projects from around the Globe*, 2(1):1–23, 2012.

[6] N. Kirchner and et al. RobotAssist - a Platform for Human Robot Interaction Research. In *Proceedings of ACRA*, 2010.

[7] C. Kleinke. Gaze and Eye Contact: A Research Review. *Psychological Bulletin*, 100(1):78–100, 1986.

Effects of Speech On Perceived Capability

Elizabeth Cha[1], Anca Dragan[1], Jodi Forlizzi[2], Siddhartha S. Srinivasa[1]
[1]The Robotics Institute, [2]Human-Computer Interaction Institute, Carnegie Mellon University, Pittsburgh, PA
{lizcha,adragan,forlizzi,siddh}@cs.cmu.edu

1. INTRODUCTION

Domestic robots have an increasing presence in the home each year [10]. For these robots to be accepted, their capabilities must match our expectations [1, 5]. However, there is often a mismatch between a robot's true capability and its *perceived* capability (i.e. how capable users believe the robot to be) [2, 6].

Speech is a human behavior known to cause anthropomorphization – the process of attributing human-like characteristics and behaviors [3, 4, 7, 9]. Thus, we hypothesize that when a robot speaks, users are likely to attribute not only capabilities related to speech but other unrelated abilities that humans are adept at, such as physical manipulation.

We explored this hypothesis – that speech affects a robot's *perceived* capability – in a user study that manipulated a robot's use of speech and its success at completing a physical task (Fig.1). We found that when a robot speaks, perceived *social* capability increases. Surprisingly, we also found that perceived *physical* capability increases as well, despite the fact that speech does not add to the true physical capability. For example, just because the robot can engage in dialogue, users believe it will be better at doing their laundry.

Overall, our findings suggest that speech is an important tool in altering expectations during human-robot interactions, and that robot designers should be cautious about setting the wrong expectations when using speech.

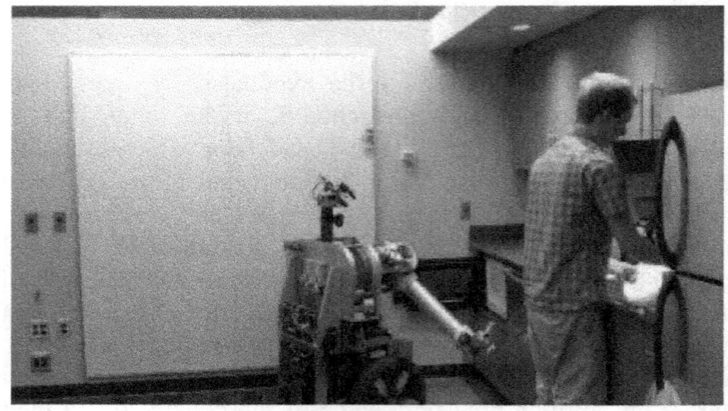

Figure 1: We analyzed the effects of two different factors — success and speech — on the robot's perceived social and physical capability.

2. EXPERIMENTAL DESIGN

We conducted an online study to explore the effects of speech on perceived capability. Participants were shown videos of HERB, a bimanual mobile manipulator, retrieving a microwave meal and sometimes engaging in dialogue.

Manipulated Variables: We manipulated the *presence of speech* and the robot's *success* in completing the task (success vs. failure) for $2 \times 2 = 4$ videos.

In the *success* videos, the robot successfully retrieves the meal and leaves the kitchen with it. In the *failure* videos, the robot drops the microwave meal before leaving the kitchen and does not acknowledge its failure.

In the *speech* videos, the robot exchanges dialogue with a nearby actor washing dishes about an upcoming sports game. In the *no speech* videos, there is no dialogue and neither the robot nor the actor acknowledge one another.

Subject Allocation: We chose a 2×2 mixed study design, where participants rated 2 of the 4 scenarios. We recruited 48 participants (20 females and 28 males) through Amazon Mechanical Turk, aged 18 to 61 (M=32.13, SD=9.77) years. Participants rated their familiarity with robots as 2.54 (SD=1.55) on a 7-point Likert scale. All participants were located in the United States, primary English speakers and had over 95% approval ratings.

Procedure: We opted for a mixed study design, where participants watched 2 videos, in order to enable direct comparisons and stay away from absolute ratings (as suggested by our pilot study). We balanced the order that videos were shown to participants, to prevent ordering effects. Participants were shown 2 videos before answering 2 sets of questions: forced choice comparisons between the robots shown in each video and 7-point Likert ratings for each robot.

Dependent Measures: We split capability into two measures: perceived physical capability, the robot's ability to perform physical tasks in the home, and perceived social capability, the robot's awareness and ability to communicate effectively during interactions. We derived our physical capability questionnaire from domestic survey literature. Our social capability questionnaire is inspired by the Robot Anxiety Scale (RAS), developed by Nomura [8].

TABLE I: Perceived Capability Scales

Physical	Social
wiping down cleaning surfaces	giving information and news
cleaning up the dining table	understanding what I am talking about
taking out the trash	understanding my emotions
tidying up	informing me when something is wrong
organizing the pantry	following the direction of a conv.
doing laundry	understanding difficult conversations
preparing simple meals	informing me what it is about to do
doing lawn work	making me understand what it saying
bringing a drink	understanding what I am doing
helping me get ready	talking about irrelevant things*
acting as alarm system	-
watering/caring for plant	-
pet care	-
child care	-

HRI'14, March 3–6, 2014, Bielefeld, Germany.
ACM 978-1-4503-2658-2/14/03.
http://dx.doi.org/10.1145/2559636.2559850 .

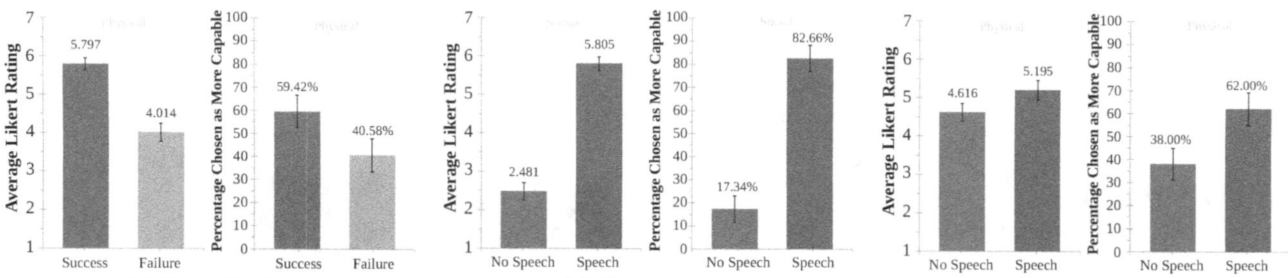

(a) Hypothesis 1 (b) Hypothesis 2 (c) Hypothesis 3

Figure 2: The average rating and percentage of time chosen for each of our hypotheses.

Hypotheses:

1: When the robot *fails* to perform a physical task, perceived physical capability decreases.

2: When the robot *uses speech*, perceived social capability increases.

3: When the robot *uses speech*, perceived physical capability increases.

3. RESULTS

Our hypotheses predicted the effects of a robot's success and its use of speech on perceived capability. To test each hypothesis, we performed a factorial repeated-measures ANOVA for each of our measures: perceived social capability and perceived physical capability.

Hypothesis 1: Participants rated robots that were successful, on average, 1.783 more than robots that failed to complete the meal retrieval task on the perceived physical capability scale ($F(1,73)=37.11$, $p<0.001$). They also chose robots that were successful 60% of the time. Fig.2(a), hypothesis 1 shows a comparison between robots that were successful and robots that failed at the meal retrieval task.

We did not find a significant difference in the perceived social capability ratings for robots that succeeded versus robots that failed: *failing at a physical task does not necessarily make participants believe the robot is less socially capable.*

Hypothesis 2: Participants rated robots that used speech, on average, 3.324 more than robots that did not speak on our perceived social capability scale ($F(1,73)=215.85$, $p<0.001$). Robots that used speech were also chosen as more socially capable 83% of the time. Fig.2(b) shows a comparison between the robots that spoke and those that did not.

Hypothesis 3: Participants rated robots that used speech, on average, 0.579 more than robots that did not speak on our perceived physical capability scale ($F(1,73)=4.61$, $p=0.035$). They also chose robots that spoke as more physically capable 65% of the time. Fig.2(c) shows a comparison between the robots that spoke and those that did not.

4. DISCUSSION

As predicted in Hypothesis 1, we found that physical failures negatively affect participants' ratings of *only* the robot's physical capability (Fig.2(a)). This is not surprising, as retrieving a meal is a physical task and does not rely on the robot's social abilities. We also found, as Hypothesis 2 predicted, that speech positively affects participants' perceptions of the robot's social capability (Fig.2(b)). This is expected since speech is a strong component of social interaction. Both results show that manipulating true capability can affect perceived capability.

Surprisingly, we also found that speech positively affects participants' perceptions of the robot's physical capability (Fig.2(c)). Although true physical capability was the same, participants rated robots that used speech significantly higher and chose them more often in the fixed choice measure. These results suggest that users may anthropomorphize the robot, attributing human-like strengths and weaknesses, despite the robot possessing very different capabilities.

These findings suggest that speech raises expectations of a robot's capability. However, when expectations do not match reality, users may be disappointed, hindering acceptance. Understanding how a robot's behavior or attributes alter expectations can help robot designers to appropriately balance user expectations against robot capability.

This work is a first step in exploring how robot behaviors, such as speech, affect users perceptions of a robot's capability. Our results show that a robot's use of speech alters users' expectations. However, speech has many levels and functions. We are excited to investigate in future work how different types of speech (e.g. conversational speech vs. functional) differ in their effects on the perceived capability of a robot.

Acknowledgments

This research was supported by the NSF under Cooperative Agreement EEC-054086, by the Intel PhD Fellowship Program, and by the NSF Graduate Research Fellowship Program.

5. REFERENCES

[1] C. Bartneck and J. Forlizzi. A design-centred framework for social human-robot interaction. In *ROMAN*, 2004.

[2] E. Cha, A. Dragan, and S. Srinivasa. Effects of robot capability on user acceptance. In *HRI Late Breaking Report*, March 2013.

[3] N. Epley, A. Waytz, and J. Cacioppo. On seeing human: a three-factor theory of anthropomorphism. *Psychological review*, 114(4):864, 2007.

[4] S. R. Fussell, S. Kiesler, L. D. Setlock, and V. Yew. How people anthropomorphize robots. In *HRI*, pages 145–152. ACM, 2008.

[5] J. Goetz, S. Kiesler, and A. Powers. Matching robot appearance and behavior to tasks to improve human-robot cooperation. In *RO-MAN*, 2003.

[6] M. K. Lee, K. P. Tang, J. Forlizzi, and S. Kiesler. Understanding users! perception of privacy in human-robot interaction. In *HRI*, pages 181–182. IEEE, 2011.

[7] S. Lee, I. Y. Lau, S. Kiesler, and C. Chiu. Human mental models of humanoid robots. In *ICRA*, pages 2767–2772. IEEE, 2005.

[8] T. Nomura, T. Kanda, T. Suzuki, and K. Kato. Prediction of human behavior in human-robot interaction using psychological scales for anxiety and negative attitudes toward robots. *Robotics, IEEE Transactions on*, 24(2):442–451, 2008.

[9] A. Powers, A. Kramer, S. Lim, J. Kuo, S. Lee, and S. Kiesler. Eliciting information from people with a gendered humanoid robot. In *ROMAN*, pages 158–163. IEEE, 2005.

[10] J.Y. Sung, R. E. Grinter, and H. I. Christensen. Domestic robot ecology. *International Journal of Social Robotics*, 2(4):417–429, 2010.

Pre-school Children's First Encounter with a Robot

Elizabeth Cha, Anca Dragan, Siddhartha S. Srinivasa
The Robotics Institute, Carnegie Mellon University, Pittsburgh, PA
{lizcha,adragan,siddh}@cs.cmu.edu

1. INTRODUCTION

In this work, we investigate pre-school age children's attitudes and beliefs about robots, and how these are affected by interacting with a physical robot, as shown in Fig.1.

Although adults' attitudes towards robots is a common research topic [1, 3, 4], the attitudes of children remain relatively unexplored. Furthermore, research that studies children mainly focuses on children ages 7 and over [2, 5, 6].

In contrast, we focus on pre-school age children, who are still forming their ideas and opinions about robots, through both their peers and popular culture. Such children provide us with a valuable opportunity to observe and study *their first interaction with a real, physical robot*, and to explore *the effects of this interaction on their attitudes towards robots.*

Toward this goal, we conducted an exploratory study where we interviewed five children both before and after interacting with a bimanual mobile robot, HERB (Fig.1). We make two observations: (1) participants tended to be very open in their opinions of how a robot should look, and (2) meeting HERB broadened their views on the possible *functions* of a robot: participants who saw robots as assistants started to see a social role for them as well, and vice-versa.

2. METHOD

We performed an exploratory pilot study with five children (2 male and 3 female) that were all five years of age and enrolled in the same pre-school facility.

Outline: The study consisted of three phases: (1) pre-interview, (2) interaction with HERB, and (3) post-interview.

Questions: Since the children were pre-school age and might have difficulty answering surveys or questions using scales, we chose to utilize qualitative interviews.

Both before the pre- and post-interview, we asked each child to draw a picture of a robot — we used this both as a method for engaging the children into conversing about robots, as well as an additional method for identifying differences caused by meeting HERB.

After drawing the pictures, we interviewed each child about their drawings and ideas about robots. We first asked them to describe their drawing and asked any follow up questions that arose from their descriptions. Then, we asked about

1. what robots look like
2. what robots are made of
3. what robots do

Additionally, we asked the children whether they'd want to meet a robot during the pre-interview, and whether they enjoyed meeting HERB during the post-interview. We kept the interviews kept fairly flexible as to not frustrate the children or make them uncomfortable, giving them the option to skip over questions they had trouble answering.

Figure 1: Interaction with HERB.

Interaction: The day after the pre-interview, we introduced the children to our robot, HERB. HERB is a two-armed robot that moves via a Segway RMP base, and is roughly human sized. We gave the children basic information about the robot, such as its purpose — to assist older adults and people with disabilities — and what the different components of the robot are. HERB did not move autonomously around the children for safety reasons. Instead, we teleoperated the head to look at the children, and the person introducing HERB moved the arms manually. The children were allowed to ask questions about the robot, as well as physically interact with it. This was the first interaction with HERB for every participant.

3. OBSERVATIONS

3.1 Tolerances and Biases

Overall, the children were surprisingly open in their ideas about robots – shape, size and personality. However, they did have certain biases, particularly about what robots were composed of.

Appearance: During our interviews, we found that participants were very open to what form a robot may take. Although each participant drew a robot with a particular form, all participants agreed with the idea that robots could come in other forms that resembled machines, animals, or humans. Participants also mentioned that robots can be either small or large. Some said that robots can come in many colors. Furthermore, many drawings included both female and male robots, with participants saying robots can be either boys or girls. Overall, participants accepted robots could be many different shapes, sizes, and genders.

However, participants also had certain biases about robots. Most participants drew faces on their robots and expressed the opinion that all robots should have one. Interestingly, participants also named some very specific features or components that robots must have to be considered a robot. For instance, all participants were quite insistent that a robot should be made of metal and can not be made of any other materials, e.g. plastic. They mentioned "metal

HRI'14, March 3–6, 2014, Bielefeld, Germany.
ACM 978-1-4503-2658-2/14/03.
http://dx.doi.org/10.1145/2559636.2559852 .

(a) Pre-Participant A (b) Post-Participant A (c) Pre-Participant B (d) Post-Participant B

Figure 2: Drawings made pre and post interaction by two participants. After meeting HERB, Participant A replaced the feet on his robot with wheels like HERB's, and Participant B replaced his two robots acting "silly" with a helpful robot mechanic.

brains", "metal bones", and "hearts of steel". Participants also mentioned buttons, antennas and screws as being critical to the robot's appearance.

Functionality: Participants were split on their view of what a robot's main function is. One participant viewed robots as potential friends or companions, while another viewed them as assistants that clean up. The other three participants drew robots without a clear purpose, and without involving humans. Instead, their drawings depicted robots interacting with robot friends and families.

Personification: All participants seemed to personify robots, giving them faces and genders. For some participants, robots had families or pets. Some also attributed personality traits to robots, such as badness, meanness or silliness. Participants who attributed such traits also mentioned that only some robots are bad, mean or silly, while others are good, nice or serious. One participant expressed a fear of robots (especially those with laser beams) and was the only one to respond during pre-interviews that he would not like to meet a robot.

3.2 Perception Shifts

We noticed different perception shifts for each participant in either appearance or function.

Appearance: After having been exposed to HERB, participants still expressed the view that robots should have some key features, such as being made of metal. However, some participants dropped other specific features, such as antennas, that were prominent in their earlier drawings.

Also, during post-interviews, several participants mentioned wires and electricity as important parts of a robot and some of their drawings featured robots with forms or features similar to HERB. For instance, one participant initially drew robots with legs and feet, but after seeing HERB, he drew wheels instead of legs: Fig.2, left.

Functionality: In post interviews, we found that many participants expanded their views of what functionalities robots may have. For instance, one participant was initially adamant that robots only clean. After seeing HERB, she also wanted a robot to play with her. Another participant who initially drew a robot doing karate with her, later said she wants a robot to clean and fetch items.

Others who initially drew robots as separate from humans shifted to a more functional view. For instance, one participant initially drew two robot friends acting silly. However, after interacting with HERB, the participant drew a workman robot that performs car repairs better than a human mechanic (Fig.2).

Personification: Initially, one participant expressed the belief that robots are scary, wanting to keep them on leashes, and keep their "metal teeth" away from him. He also responded that he did not want to meet a robot. After interacting with HERB, however, his attitude shifted to be more positive. He not only wanted a stuffed robot with which to sleep, but also a real robot to help him clean and do chores. Furthermore, his drawing now depicted a robot that helped people fix things.

4. DISCUSSION

We observed that compared to adults, these children were more open to the appearance a robot may take, and that they tended to personify robots more. After interacting with a real robot, participants shifted their initial views to see robots as more friendly and useful to humans. Participants that attributed social roles to robots now saw them as useful assistants as well, and vice-versa.

This work was a first step to understanding how children's perceptions shift after interacting with a physical robot. In the future, we are excited to explore how perception shifts might depend on embodiment (physical vs. virtual robots) and on the the duration and frequency of the interactions.

Overall, our observations suggest that exposing children to physical robots at a young age may positively affect their attitudes towards robots. This suggests that early exposure of such technologies may facilitate future acceptance. As robot designers, however, we must wonder what can be done during these early interactions to elicit greater and more purposeful shifts.

5. REFERENCES

[1] C Bartneck, D Kulić, E Croft, and S Zoghbi. Measurement instruments for the anthropomorphism, animacy, likeability, perceived intelligence, and perceived safety of robots. *International Journal of Social Robotics*, 1(1):71–81, 2009.

[2] K Bumby and K Dautenhahn. Investigating childrenâĂŹs attitudes towards robots: A case study. In *Proc. CT99, The Third International Cognitive Technology Conference*, pages 391–410. Citeseer, 1999.

[3] M Heerink, B Krose, V Evers, and B Wielinga. The influence of a robot's social abilities on acceptance by elderly users. In *Robot and Human Interactive Communication, 2006. ROMAN 2006. The 15th IEEE International Symposium on*, pages 521–526. IEEE, 2006.

[4] S Kriz, T D Ferro, Pi Damera, and J R Porter. Fictional robots as a data source in hri research: Exploring the link between science fiction and interactional expectations. In *RO-MAN, 2010 IEEE*, pages 458–463. IEEE, 2010.

[5] R S Siegler, J S DeLoache, and N Eisenberg. *How children develop*. Macmillan, 2003.

[6] F W Tung. Influence of gender and age on the attitudes of children towards humanoid robots. In *HCI. Users and Applications*, pages 637–646. Springer, 2011.

Are You Embarrassed?: The Impact of Robot Types on Emotional Engagement with a Robot

Jung Ju Choi
Dept. of Industrial Design
Ewha Womans University
Seoul, KOREA
meloncreamm@naver.com

Yunkyung Kim
Dept. of Industrial Design
KAIST
Daejeon, KOREA
yunkim86@gmail.com

Sonya S. Kwak
Dept. of Industrial Design
Ewha Womans University
Seoul, KOREA
sonakwak@ewha.ac.kr

ABSTRACT

The objective of this study is to examine the effect of robot types on emotional communication between a person and a robot. We executed a 2 (robot types: an autonomous robot vs. a tele-operated robot) within-participants experiment (N=36). Participants were interviewed with either autonomous robot interviewers or tele-operated robot interviewers, and asked how much they felt social presence of robot interviewers and embarrassment toward robot interviewers. Participants felt more social presence to tele-operated robots than autonomous robots. Moreover, participants felt more embarrassment when they were interviewed with tele-operated robots than autonomous robots.

Categories and Subject Descriptors

I.2.9 [**Artificial Intelligence**]: Robotics – *commercial robots and applications*; H.5.2 [**Information Interfaces and Presentation**]: User Interfaces – *user-centered design*

Keywords

Autonomous robot; embarrassment; emotional communication; social presence; tele-operated robot

1. INTRODUCTION

As social robots became social companions inhabiting and building relationship with humans, the importance of emotional communication between humans and robots have been increased in the field of Human-Robot Interaction (HRI). Many studies have been done on developing robotic interface which recognizes people's emotions and generating emotional responses [1][2]. However, it needs to be investigated whether such developed algorithm could make people to substantively engage in emotional interaction with a robot.

Typically, robots have been classified into an autonomous robot and a tele-operated robot according to the degrees of autonomy. An autonomous robot is having high autonomy level and doesn't require an operator's help whereas a tele-operated robot is having low autonomy level and requires a help of an operator [3]. This classification indicates that in emotional communication, an autonomous robot elicits robotic emotions by itself while a tele-operated robot transfers human emotions which are elicited by a remote operator. There are two different perspectives of ontological claims about a robot as a social partner [4]. One is the strong ontology demonstrating that a robot could become a human being at future with technological development, and the other is the weak ontology describing that a robot could not become a human being but remained as an artifactual being. From the perspective of the weak ontology, a tele-operated robot which transfers emotions elicited by a real human could be more effective for emotional communication than an autonomous robot which generates artifactual emotions by itself.

On the basis of the ontological claim, this study compared an autonomous robot, an independent artificial companion eliciting emotions by itself and a tele-operated robot, a communication medium transferring other person's emotions, and explored which type is more effective to make people substantively engage in emotional communication.

HRI'14, March 3–6, 2014, Bielefeld, Germany.
ACM 978-1-4503-2658-2/14/03.
http://dx.doi.org/10.1145/2559636.2559798

2. RELATED WORKS

2.1 Robot Types

Robots are classified into an autonomous robot and a tele-operated robot according to the degrees of autonomy. Conversely, robots can be distinguished depending on the degrees of human intervention required for controlling a robot [3]. In emotional communication, an autonomous robot has high autonomy level and expresses emotions of its own while a tele-operated robot has low autonomy and conveys a human operator's emotions.

The ontology of social robots could be explained in two ways: the strong ontology and the weak ontology [4]. The strong ontological claim is that a robot could become a human being while the weak ontological claim is that a robot could not become a human being but remained as an artifactual being. Previous studies support the idea that the strong ontology is not valid due to the limitation in today's robotic technology. Moravec [5] demonstrated that even though mechanical bodies are adequate for manual work, artificial emotions by autonomous robots have been frustratingly out of reach in emotional interaction.

From the weak ontology perspective, a tele-operated robot could be more effective in making people substantively engage in emotional communication than an autonomous robot as a tele-operated robot transfers emotions of a real human. Several previous studies demonstrated the effectiveness of a tele-operated robot in substantive emotional engagement. For example, Doel et al.'s study [6] showed that people felt more optimistic about getting rescued and felt more companionship toward a tele-operated robot than an autonomous robot in simulated earthquake situation. Kwak and her colleagues [7] found that people had more emotional empathy to a tele-operated robot than an autonomous robot. Even though there have been several researches about the impact of autonomy level on emotional communication between a person and a robot, limited work has been done with emphasis on social presence. Thus, in this study, we explored the impact of robot types on social presence of a robot.

2.2 Social Presence and Embarrassment

Social presence has been originally defined as the concept of being with another social being, and leads people to engage in communication [8]. As an autonomous robot is an artificial being which elaborately fabricates a human being, it could have less social presence than a tele-operated robot which sends social presence of a real human being. Thus, we anticipated that a tele-operated robot would be more effective than an autonomous robot on eliciting social presence.

How much people estimate others' presence affects how much people feel embarrassment and vice versa [9]. As we anticipated that a tele-operated robot is estimated as having greater social presence than an autonomous robot, it is also expectable that people would be more embarrassed when interacting with a tele-operated robot than an autonomous robot in embarrassing situation. These analyses led to the following hypotheses:

H1. Participants will feel more social presence to a tele-operated robot than an autonomous robot.

H2. In embarrassing situation, participants will feel more embarrassment to a tele-operated robot than an autonomous robot.

3. STUDY DESIGN

We used a 2 (robot types: an autonomous robot vs. a tele-operated robot) within-participants experiment design.

Participants. We recruited university students having high technology acceptance as participants (Male: 17, Female: 19).

Materials. The robot we used in the experiment was UXA-90(ZEUS) as shown in Fig. 1. The participants were exposed to both autonomous robots and tele-operated robots, in random order. When interacting with autonomous robots, participants were told that the robots acted autonomously while when interacting with tele-operated robots, participants were informed that the robots were fully controlled by remote operators who were in the other room.

Procedure. At the beginning of the experiment, participants were asked to have an interview with four robot interviewers as shown in Figure 1. After they interacted with the robot interviewers, a questionnaire regarding each stimulus was administered.

Figure 1. Experimental setup

Measures. The post-experimental survey was composed of 12 Likert-type items, which were combined into two scales. The two scales were social presence (5items, Cronbach's α= .93), which were drawn from Heerink et al.'s research [10] and embarrassment (7items, Cronbach's α= .87), which were drawn from Bartneck et al.'s research [11].

4. RESULTS

We investigated the effect of robot types on emotional communication between a person and a robot. Statistical analyses were conducted using the paired *t*-test.

As predicted by H1, a significant effect of robot types on social presence of a robot was found, t=6.28, df=35, p=0.00025 (one-tailed). Participants felt more social presence to tele-operated robots (M=4.25, SD=0.45) than autonomous robots (M=3.80, SD=0.33). This indicates that the degrees of human intervention contribute to the sense of social presence when interacting with robots.

As predicted by H2, a significant effect of robot types on people's embarrassment was found, t=17.43, df=35, p=0.00025 (one-tailed). Participants felt more embarrassment when interacting with tele-operated robots (M=4.44, SD=0.32) than autonomous robots (M=3.32, SD=0.36). This implies that tele-operated robots could be more suitable for making people to substantively engage in emotional communication with robots than autonomous robots.

5. CONCLUSIONS

The objective of this study was to investigate the effect of robot types on emotional engangaement with a robot. People felt more social presence to tele-operated robots than autonomous robots. Furthermore, people were more embarrassed when interacting with tele-operated robots than autonomous robots in embarrassing situation. These results suggest that designers can effectively use tele-operated robots as making people to substantively engage in emotional communication.

6. REFERENCES

[1] Ogata, T. and Sugano, S. 1999. Emotional communication between humans and the autonomous robot which has the emotion model. In *Proc. of ICRA '99*, 3177–3182.

[2] Breazeal, C. 2003. Emotion and sociable humanoid robots. 2003. *Int'l Journal of Human Computer Studies*. 59, 119-155.

[3] Yanco, H. A. and Drury, J. L. 2004. Classifying human-robot interaction: An updated taxonomy. In *Proc. of Int'l Conference on Systems, Man, and Cybernetics*, 3, 2841-2846.

[4] Kahn, P., Ishiguro, H., Friedman, B., and Kanda, T. 2006. What is a human?—Toward psychological benchmarks in the field of human-robot interaction. In *Proc. of RO-MAN'06*, 364–371.

[5] Moravec, H. 2003. Robots, after all. *Communications of the ACM*. 46, 10, 90-97.

[6] Dole, L. D., Sirkin, D. M., Currano, R. M., Murphy, R. R., and Nass, C. I. 2013. Where to look and who to be: Designing attention and identity for search-and-rescue robots. In *Proc. of HRI'13*, 119-120.

[7] Kwak, S. S., Kim, Y., Kim, E., Shin, C., and Cho, K. 2013. What makes people empathize with an emotional robot?: The impact of agency and physical embodiment on human empathy for a robot. In *Proc. of RO-MAN'13*, 180-185.

[8] Heeter, C. 1992. Being there: The subjective experience of presence. *Presence: Teleoperators and Virtual Environments*. 1, 2, 262-271.

[9] Costa, M., Dinsbach, W., Manstead, A. S. R., and Bitti, P. E. R. 2001. Social presence, embarrassment, and nonverbal behavior. *Journal of Nonverbal Behavior*. 25, 4, 225–240.

[10] Heerink, M., Kröse, B., Evers, V., and Wielinga, B. 2008. The influence of social presence on acceptance of a companion robot by older people. *Journal of Physical Agents*. 2, 2, 33-40.

[11] Bartneck, C., Bleeker, T., Bun, J., Fens, P., and Riet, L. 2010. The influence of robot anthropomorphism on the feelings of embarrassment when interacting with robots. *Paladyn Journal of Behavioral Robotics*. 1, 2, 109–115.

Mixing Implicit and Explicit Probes: Finding a Ground Truth for Engagement in Social Human-Robot Interactions

Lee J. Corrigan
University of Birmingham
United Kingdom
ljc228@bham.ac.uk

Christina Basedow
Jacobs University Bremen
Germany
c.basedow@jacobs-university.de

Dennis Küster
Jacobs University Bremen
Germany
d.kuester@jacobs-university.de

Arvid Kappas
Jacobs University Bremen
Germany
a.kappas@jacobs-university.de

Christopher Peters
Royal Institute of Technology (KTH), Sweden
chpeters@kth.se

Ginevra Castellano
University of Birmingham
United Kingdom
g.castellano@bham.ac.uk

ABSTRACT

In our work we explore the development of a computational model capable of automatically detecting engagement in social human-robot interactions from real-time sensory and contextual input. However, to train the model we need to establish ground truths of engagement from a large corpus of data collected from a study involving task and social-task engagement. Here, we intend to advance the current state-of-the-art by reducing the need for unreliable post-experiment questionnaires and costly time-consuming annotation with the novel introduction of implicit probes. A non-intrusive, pervasive and embedded method of collecting informative data at different stages of an interaction.

Categories and Subject Descriptors:
H.1.2 [Information Systems]: Human factors

Keywords: Ground Truth; Engagement; Social Tasks; Machine Learning; Human-Robot Interaction.

1. INTRODUCTION

The phenomenon of engagement is a widely discussed topic in the field of human-robot interaction (HRI), but in our work we wish to advance the current state-of-the-art by developing an on-line engagement detector. The detector should be capable of differentiating between engagement with the task and social engagement with the robot. Prior to our work, affect ground truths necessary to train automatic detectors have typically been determined post-experimentally using domain-specialist annotation. Here, we are exploring ways to find those truths from the users during the interaction in a manner that is non-intrusive. We have several explicit probes embedded into the interaction in terms of questionnaires, and complement these with implicit probes as task-related indicators allowing a real-time account of engagement states at the beginning, during and end of the interaction. Rather than including self-report only retrospectively at the end, we use a mixed-design with embedded questions and assessment throughout different stages of the task.

HRI'14, March 3–6, 2014, Bielefeld, Germany.
ACM 978-1-4503-2658-2/14/03.
http://dx.doi.org/10.1145/2559636.2559815.

2. RELATED WORK

To train our computational model, we first need to establish ground truths for the types of engagement that we aim to measure empirically. Typically, the self-report data needed to train this type of computational model is expensive and time-consuming to collect, and often requires trained annotators who can reliably classify behavioural data according to the construct that is to be measured. Whilst many attempts have been made to record affect ground truths, no unambiguous method currently exists [1]. Typical approaches involve post-experiment annotation of continuous or segmented videos of the recorded interaction between the user and the system [2].

In HRI research, the concept of engagement is frequently seen as a binary concept, relating to whether or not someone is engaged in the interaction as a whole. Often there is no distinction between the different aspects of the interaction or how one aspect influences engagement with another. However, in this project, engagement is seen as a far more developed phenomenon which builds upon work in social engagement, relating to the connection between the human and the robot during an interaction [3], and task engagement, considered to be characterised by elements of attention, concentration and enjoyment [4]. Further still, we view engagement in a social task as the fusion of both social and task engagement.

3. SCENARIO

Our experimental scenario involves three interactive game-like tasks [5]. The first two tasks are designed to elicit maximally different states of task engagement and the final task is designed to elicit social-task engagement. The technical implementation of our scenario is comprised of a large touch-screen table to graphically represent the interactive tasks, a torso-only version of the *NAO* humanoid robot to facilitate the social aspect of the interaction, several video cameras

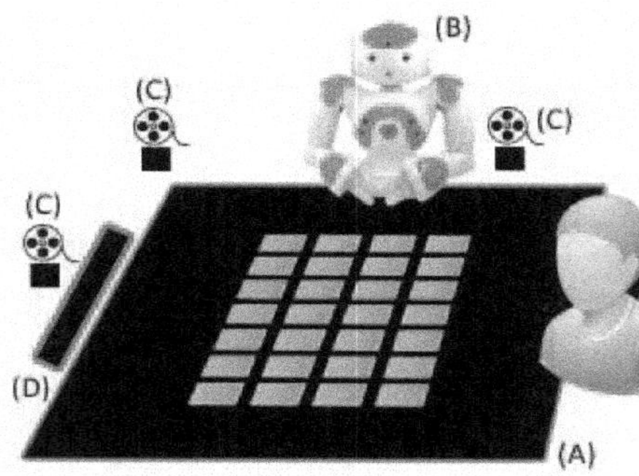

Figure 1: Overview of the technical set up: (A) Touch Screen Table, (B) NAO Robot (C) Cameras (D) Microsoft Kinect. Human character courtesy of http://www.icons-land.com.

for detecting facial expressions, a *Microsoft Kinect* for gaze direction and lean position relating to posture, and an *Affectiva Q Sensor* for measuring galvanic skin response.

4. SOCIAL TASK

For clarification, in a HRI context a social task can be described as a task performed in collaboration with a social robot. The task is an explicit task where the output is directly related to the inputs provided. Here, the robot's behaviour, timing and utterances can influence the partner's effectiveness within the task, likewise, the flow of the task can influence the perceived value of collaborating with the robot.

5. GROUND TRUTH

Using our experimental scenario, we captured a corpus of real-time multi-modal sensor readings and task-related context from eighty participants who took part in a recent HRI study. By using the actual responses to the implicit and explicit probes used in that study, we intend to support our claims by finding the least ambiguous datasets for training our model of engagement. For the purpose of critical evaluation, both post-experiment statistical analysis and traditional domain-specialist annotation will be used to validate our probes and to help find ground truths for engagement.

6. EXPERIMENTAL PROBES

A probe can be a non-intrusive, pervasive and embedded method of collecting informative data at different stages of an interaction. Here, the explicit probes (i.e., questionnaires) are embedded into the interaction itself, minimising disruption caused by researcher intervention. The implicit probes are pervasive, executing at predefined stages within the interaction, minimising unnecessary disruption to the natural interactive flow. The feedback we gain from these probes is used as ground truths for training our models as well as milestones for other methods of data mining and statistical analysis.

6.1 Implicit Probes

6.1.1 Social Bonding Probe

This implicit probe occurs at the start of the third task, allowing the participant to choose whether or not they wish to interact with the robot.

6.1.2 Robot to Task

The second probe is also an implicit probe designed to measure the temporal lag involved with diverting gaze from the robot to objects which are graphically represented within the task. The results of this probe tells us how much attention the participant gives to the robot's implied instruction.

6.1.3 Task to Robot

During the interaction the robot will ask the participant a question which requires the participant to divert gaze and attention away from the task, towards the robot. Here, we detect any shift of gaze towards the robot and measure the initial temporal lag and further sustained gaze.

6.1.4 Attention to Instructions

If at any point during the task, the participant presses on a square whilst another is open, a buzzer will sound and the robot will inform the participant that they risk damaging the system if they press a square before the previous one has recovered. Following a warning, we measure the temporal difference of any future warnings.

6.2 Explicit Probes

6.2.1 Regular Self-Report Probes

The repeated self-report is embedded within the interaction to minimise disruption. This on-screen self-report probe occurs every minute, allowing us to measure changes of task and social engagement at different stages of the interaction.

7. CONCLUSION

Mixing implicit and explicit probes allows us to derive ground truths from within the interaction itself, reducing the need for expensive domain-specialist annotation. These probes can be used to train computational models capable of classifying engagement from multi-modal datasets, offering a more reliable temporal view of the social and task state compared to that of traditional post experiment questionnaires.

Acknowledgement

This work was partially supported by the European Commission (EC) and was funded by the EU FP7 ICT-317923 project EMOTE (EMbOdied-perceptive Tutors for Empathy-based learning). The authors are solely responsible for the content of this publication. It does not represent the opinion of the EC, and the EC is not responsible for any use that might be made of data appearing therein.

8. REFERENCES

[1] J. Healey, "Recording affect in the field: Towards methods and metrics for improving ground truth labels," in *Proceedings of the 4th International Conference on Affective Computing and Intelligent Interaction - Volume Part I*, ser. ACII'11. Berlin, Heidelberg: Springer-Verlag, 2011, pp. 107–116.

[2] H. Gunes and B. Schuller, "Categorical and dimensional affect analysis in continuous input: Current trends and future directions," *Image and Vision Computing*, 2012.

[3] C. Rich, B. Ponsleur, A. Holroyd, and C. L. Sidner, "Recognizing engagement in human-robot interaction," in *5th ACM/IEEE International Conference on Human-Robot Interaction, HRI 2010*, 2010, pp. 375–382.

[4] D. J. Shernoff, M. Csikszentmihalyi, B. Schneider, and E. S. Shernoff, "Student engagement in high school classrooms from the perspective of flow theory," *School Psychology Quarterly*, vol. 18, no. 2, pp. 158–176, 2003.

[5] L. J. Corrigan, C. Peters, and G. Castellano, "Identifying task engagement: Towards personalised interactions with educational robots," in *Affective Computing and Intelligent Interaction (ACII), 2013 Humaine Association Conference on*, 2013, pp. 655–658.

Recognizing Gaze Pattern for Human Robot Interaction

Dipankar Das[1], Md. Golam Rashed[1], Yoshinori Kobayashi[1,2], and Yoshinori Kuno[1]
[1]Graduate School of Science and Engineering, Saitama University
255 Shimo-Okubo, Sakura-ku,338-8570, Japan
[2]JST, PRESTO, 4-1-8 Honcho Kawaguchi, Saitama 332-0012, Japan
{dipankar, golamrashed, yosinori, kuno}@cv.ics.saitama-u.ac.jp

ABSTRACT

In this paper, we propose a human-robot interaction system in which the robot detects and classifies the target human's gaze pattern into either *spontaneous looking* or *scene-relevant looking*. If the gaze pattern is detected as the *spontaneous looking*, the robot waits for the target human without disturbing his/her attention. However, if the gaze pattern is detected as the *scene-relevant looking*, the robot establishes a communication channel with him/her in order to explain about the scene. We have implemented the proposed system into a robot, Robovie-R3 as a museum guide robot and tested the system to confirm its effectiveness.

Categories and Subject Descriptors

I.2.10 [**Vision and Scene Understanding**]: Video analysis; H.5.2 [**User Interfaces**]: Interaction styles

General Terms

Design; Experimentation

Keywords

Human robot interaction, gaze pattern, museum guide robot

1. INTRODUCTION

Human's gaze pattern is tightly coupled with his/her cognitive process, which has been found very informative and valuable in various kinds of research areas including HRI [4]. Thus, it is important to provide robots with the skill that can recognize and react appropriately to the gaze behaviors of interlocutors so that they can initiate and carry on effective and productive interaction [3]. It has been recently shown that the adaptive gaze pattern plays an important role for making interaction with humans and artificial agents [2]. In this paper, we propose a human-robot interaction system in which the robot uses the gaze pattern of a target person to estimate his/her current situation for making a polite and successful interaction in a museum. For this purpose, we classify human's gaze patterns into two kinds of looking behaviors: the *spontaneous looking,* and the *scene-relevant looking.* The *spontaneous looking* occurs when a person views the scene without any specific task in mind, i.e., when s/he is "just seeing" the scene. The *scene-relevant looking* appears when a person views the scene with a particular question or task in mind (e.g., s/he may be interested in a particular painting in the museum). Our museum guide robot observes and waits for a target human without disturbing his/her current focus as long as the *spontaneous looking* is detected. However, the robot initiates interaction with the person to start explaining the painting that s/he is watching when detecting the *scene-relevant looking.*

HRI'14, March 3–6, 2014, Bielefeld, Germany.
ACM 978-1-4503-2658-2/14/03.
http://dx.doi.org/10.1145/2559636.2559818.

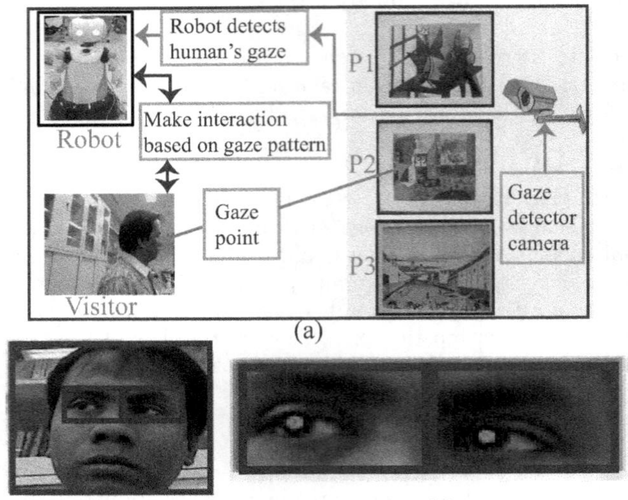

Figure 1: (a) Overview of the proposed system, (b) face location with eye regions, (c) iris centers (red points).

2. PROPOSED APPROACH

Our proposed human robot interaction system is illustrated in Fig. 1(a). Here, a visitor is observing paintings (p1, p2, etc.) in a museum and the robot is situated to help him/her when s/he is interested in a particular painting. To initiate such an interaction, first the robot detects and classifies the gaze pattern of the visitor by using the gaze detector camera, which is installed outside the robot in

(a) (b)

Figure 2: Gaze Pattern: (a) scene-relevant looking, (b) spontaneous looking.

the current implementation. Then, the robot continues to observe the visitor as long as the gaze pattern is detected as the *spontaneous looking*. However, when the gaze pattern is detected as the *scene-relevant looking*, which is considered that the visitor is interested in a particular painting, the robot starts interaction to explain about the painting. Here, we assume that the positions of all paintings are fixed and known. Thus, the robot can use the positions of the head and eyes in the camera image to recognize the picture that the person is watching. In this application, we do not need to measure the precise gaze direction. The robot computes these positions and obtains the gaze pattern from their movements.

2.1 Head Position and Iris Center Detection

To detect and track the head, we use the 3D head tracking method proposed in [1]. Then based on the face location (Fig. 1(b)), facial feature points are detected and tracked to roughly estimate the eye regions (Fig. 1(b)). Finally, we use the vector field of image gradients within each eye region to detect the center of the iris (Fig. 1(c)).

2.2 Gaze Pattern Detection

To obtain the gaze pattern G, we consider both head and eye movements, that is, the translation movement of the head in the image and the position change of the iris in the eye. Let H_0 indicates the initial head position and E_t is the eye gaze position (the relative iris position in the eye) for $t-$th frame. If T_{H_t} indicates the translation vector of the head movement from H_0, the gaze point G_t for the $t-$th frame is determined as follows: $G_t = E_t + (H_0 + T_{H_t})$. The gaze pattern G is constructed from the gaze point data for the last N_f frames through the normalization using the center of gravity for the gaze points. Let us assume G_m be the center of gravity. Then the gaze pattern is represented by: $\sqrt{(G_m - G_t)^2}$, where $t = 1, \ldots, N_f$. We sort the distance values into descending order and construct the feature vector for the classifier. We use the multi-class SVM classifier to classify the gaze patterns.

3. EXPERIMENTAL RESULT

We performed experiments in two phases: (i) performance evaluation of the proposed gaze pattern classification method, and (ii) interaction with a real robot (Robovie-R3).

Performance Evaluation. To evaluate the performance, we collected 80 gaze pattern data (40 for the *scene-relevant looking* and 40 for the *spontaneous looking*) from 10 people (at multiple distances between the people and the camera). For the *scene-relevant looking*, the participants were asked to look at any specific object in the scene. However, for the *spontaneous looking*, we asked the participants to look around aimlessly in the environment. We randomly selected 40 samples (20+20) for training the classifier and the rest 40 samples were used to test the classifier. Among 40 test samples, 37 samples were recognized correctly with the recognition rate of 92.5%. Fig. 2 shows two example images with gaze points and their corresponding detected gaze patterns.

(a) (b) (c)

Figure 3: Interaction with Robovie-R3: the robot (a) recognizes the human's gaze pattern, (b) attracts his attention by turning its head and body, and (c) starts explanation about the painting.

Interaction with Robovie-R3. We implemented the proposed gaze pattern classification system into Robovie-R3 as a museum guide robot and tested the robot in a laboratory environment. The robot observed and waited for the interested human as long as the gaze pattern of his/her was detected as the *spontaneous looking*. However, when the human looked at a particular painting and showed his/her interest in it, the robot classified the gaze pattern as the *scene-relevant looking* (Fig. 3(a)). Then the robot moved toward the person and asked him/her, "May I explain this painting (Fig. 3(b))?" If the person still showed his/her interest, the robot started explanation about the painting (Fig. 3(c)).

4. CONCLUSION

In the present study, our main focus is to classify the gaze patterns and to investigate various looking behaviors of the target human. The proposed system is able to detect the gaze pattern and classify it in real time at multiple distances of the person from the camera. We have also implemented the proposed system into Robovie-R3 as a museum guide robot. The robot uses the gaze pattern to make an effective interaction with people in a museum scenario. In future, we will use the gaze pattern to determine the level of attention of the target human in order to make more polite and effective human-robot interaction.

5. ACKNOWLEDGMENTS

This work was supported by JST, CREST.

6. REFERENCES

[1] Y. Kobayashi et al. 3d head tracking using the particle filter with cascaded classifiers. In *BMVC*, pages 37–46. British Machine Vision Association, 2006.

[2] C. Yu, P. W. Schermerhorn, and M. Scheutz. Adaptive eye gaze patterns in interactions with human and artificial agents. *TiiS*, 1(2):13, 2012.

[3] Z. Yucel et al. Joint attention by gaze interpolation and saliency. *IEEE Trans. on Systems, Man, and Cybernetics, Part B: Cybernetics*, In press, 2013.

[4] D. Zhu et al. A hybrid fuzzy approach for human eye gaze pattern recognition. In *ICONIP (2)*, volume 5507 of *Lecture Notes in Computer Science*, pages 655–662. Springer, 2008.

Expectation Setting and Personality Attribution in HRI

Maartje M.A. de Graaf Somaya Ben Allouch
University of Twente
Drienerlolaan 5
7522 NJ Enschede, The Netherlands
0031 53 489 6094
m.m.a.degraaf@utwente.nl s.benallouch@utwente.nl

ABSTRACT
People tend to treat robots as social actors and assign personality attributes to them. This study investigates the influence of expectation setting on the users' attribution of personality traits to the robot and their impressions of that robot. Results show that personality attribution is depending on people's prior expectations of the interaction. Moreover, people evaluate a robot better when they assigned it with a complementary personality and when they had high prior expectations of that robot.

Categories and Subject Descriptors
K.4.m, H.5.2 user interfaces (D.2.2, H.1.2., I.2.6) subject: J.4. subject psychology.

General Terms
Measurement, Experimentation, Human Factors, Theory.

Keywords
Human-Robot Interaction, Expectation Setting, Personality Attribution, Impression.

1. INTRODUCTION
One of three key factors for meaningful social human-robot interaction (HRI) is the user's preference for a compelling personality for the robot [5]. We investigated the influence of expectation setting on the users' attribution of personality traits to the robot and their impressions of that robot. Gathering knowledge about personality attribution is important for understanding why people often treat robots as living creatures.

People tend to assign their own personality traits to the person they are interacting with, which has also been found in interactions with robots [11]. Thus we formulated the following hypothesis:

H1: People, who have attributed particular personality traits to themselves, tend to assign similar personality traits to a social robot.

For human-human interaction there are two opposite hypotheses for personality attribution: the similarity-attraction hypothesis and the complementarity principle [2]. The similarity-attraction hypothesis tells that people prefer to interact with others that have the same personality traits. The complementarity principle holds that people show complementary behaviors in their interpersonal interactions and prefer to interact with humans that have complementary personality traits. Human-robot interaction research seems to support the complementary principle [5]. Therefore, the following hypothesis will be investigated in this study:

H2: People, according to the complementary principle, have more positive impressions of a social robot when it is regarded as having non-matching personality traits.

Besides personality attribution, also prior expectations of a robot have been determined to play an important role in human-robot interaction [8]. Concepts guiding the influence of people's prior expectations on behavioral outcomes are the confirmation bias and the self-fulfilling prophecy. The self-fulfilling prophecy explains that people's expectations will guide their experiences [6] and the confirmation bias makes people confirm their expectations by finding evidence in favour of that expectation [7]. Based on this, we have adopted the following hypothesis:

H3: Humans which have high expectations of a social robot will have more positive impressions of a social robot than humans which have low expectations of a social robot.

Additionally, prior expectations could affect first impressions of a person or system [9]. The expectancy violations theory [1] explains that we will either reciprocate (match the other's behavior) or compensate (acting opposite) when prior expectations are not met. When people experience a negative unexpected behavior in HRI, they will be disappointed and will not accept the social robot as an interaction partner. Conversely, when people experience a positive unexpected behavior in HRI, they will be surprised and will accept the social robot as an interaction partner. Connecting this to personality attribution in HRI, we have formulated the following hypothesis:

H4: Humans who have high expectations of a social robot are more likely to assign their own personality traits to a social robot in comparison with humans that have low expectations for a social robot

To summarize, both people's prior expectations of a robot and the attribution of personality traits to that robot could affect people's impressions of that robot, which makes these concepts eligible for further investigation.

2. METHOD
In a between-subject experiment (high vs. low expectations), we tested the formulated hypotheses of human-robot interaction using the robotic pet Pleo. A total of 86 respondents (41 males and 45 females, age M= 25.76 and SD= 7.42) participated in this study. Before the interaction, the participants indicated their own personality using the measures of [10] and were briefed about the robot (with high vs. low expectation). Afterwards, the participants completed a second questionnaire in which they assigned a personality to the robot using the measures of [10] and gave their

HRI'14, March 3–6, 2014, Bielefeld, Germany.
ACM 978-1-4503-2658-2/14/03.
http://dx.doi.org/10.1145/2559636.2559796

impressions of the robot using the method as proposed in [3], which resulted in 4 impression groups: familiarity, appearance, intelligence, and activity. Table 1 shows the descriptive statistics of the variables.

Table 1. Descriptive statistics of the variables

Variable	*M*	*SD*	α
Anthropomorphism	3.32	1.27	.87
User Personality			
- Self Extraversion	4.92	0.95	.84
- Self Openness	4.85	0.82	.69
- Self Agreeableness	4.88	0.72	.72
- Self Conscientiousness	4.72	0.75	.71
- Self Emotional Stability	4.42	0.91	.78
Robot Personality			
- Robot Extraversion	4.37	1.00	.68
- Robot Openness	2.73	1.01	.88
- Robot Agreeableness	3.63	1.32	.74
- Robot Conscientiousness	5.41	0.98	.72
- Robot Emotional Stability	5.08	1.05	.79
Impressions			
- Familiarity	5.71	0.83	.87
- Appearance	3.99	1.02	.85
- Intelligence	4.19	1.23	.77
- Activity	4.52	1.02	.77

3. RESULTS

In a paired samples t-test, **H1** was rejected. All personality traits were found to differ significantly from each other. The participants evaluated themselves as more extrovert ($t= 3.589$, $p= .001$), more conscientiousness ($t= 7.615$, $p > .001$), and more open ($t= 15.533$, $p > .001$) than the robot, but less agreeable ($t= -6.271$, $p > .001$) and less emotionally stable ($t= -4.438$, $p > .001$) than the robot. In a regression analysis with the non-matching personality traits as independent variables and the four impression factors as dependent variables, **H2** was partly confirmed. For the non-matching personality traits we created a latent variable obtained from the subtraction of the robot's personality from the participant's personality. The familiarity impression ($F (1,84)= 5.277$, $p= .024$) was explained for 4.8% by agreeableness ($\beta= -.243$, $t= -2.297$, $p= .024$). The appearance impression ($F (2,83)= 8.833$, $p > .001$) was explained for 15.6% by conscientiousness ($\beta= -.270$, $t= -2.507$, $p= .014$) and extraversion ($\beta= -.235$, $t= -2.185$, $p= .032$). The impressions the participants had of the robot's intelligence ($F (1,84)= 19.909$, $p > .001$) could for 18.2% be explained by conscientiousness ($\beta= -.438$, $t= -4.462$, $p > .001$). Last, the activity impression of the robot ($F (2,83)= 15.364$, $p > .001$) could for 25.3% be explained by both conscientiousness ($\beta= -.315$, $t= -3.108$, $p= .003$) and extraversion ($\beta= -.312$, $t= -3.085$, $p= .003$). In an independent samples t-test **H3** was supported. All impressions of the robot from participants with high expectations were more positively evaluated than those from participants with low expectation: familiarity impression ($t= -2.105$, $p= .038$), appearance impression ($t= -4.480$, $p > .001$), intelligence impression ($t= -3.832$, $p > .001$), and activity impression ($t= -4.249$, $p > .001$). Two separate paired samples t-test supported **H4** for extraversion. In the low expectation condition, we found similar results as found under H1 with significant differences between the all personality traits. However, in the high expectation condition we found that participants tend to assign their own extroversion to the robot ($t= 0.928$, $p= .359$). All other personality traits were still found to be significantly different.

4. GENERAL DISCUSSION

In an experimental study, we tested the effect of expectation setting (high vs. low) on the impression people have of a robot and their tendency to project their own personality onto the robot.

When controlled for expectation setting, people with high expectations of a robot did tend to assign their own extroversion to the robot. Expectation setting thus influences personality attribution to robots. As the magnitude of assumed similarity increases when people get to know one another [4], it might be that repeated interacts with the same robot increases the tendency to assign one's own personality to that robot. Our study added another example for supporting the complementary principle in HRI [5]. Contrary to previous findings in a study [8], our results also show a positive effect of high expectations on the evaluation of robots which can be explained with the self-fulfilling prophecy [6] and the confirmation bias [7]. Further investigation is needed to further unravel the mechanisms of expectation setting and personality attribution in HRI.

5. REFERENCES

[1] Burgoon, J.K., & Hale, J.J. 1988: Nonverbal expectancy violations: Model elaboration and application to immediacy behavior. Communications Monographs 55, pp. 58-79.

[2] Byrne, D., Clore, C.L., & Smeaton, G. 1968: The attraction hypothesis: Do similar attitudes affect anything?. J. of Personality and Social Psychology 51, pp. 1167–1170.

[3] Kanda, T., Ishiguro, H., Ishida, T. 2001: Psychological analysis on human-robot interaction. Proc. of the IEEE Int. Conf. on Robotics and Automation, Seoul, Korea.

[4] Kenny, D.A. 1994: Interpersonal perception: A social relations analysis. Guilford Press: New York, NY, USA.

[5] Lee, K.M., Peng, W., Jin, S., & Yan, C. 2006: Can robots manifest personality?: An empirical test of personality recognition, social responses, and social presence in human-robot interaction. J. of Communication 56, pp. 538-563.

[6] Merton, R.K. 1948: The self-fulfilling prophecy. Antioch Review 8, pp. 193-210.

[7] Nickerson, R.S. 1998: Confirmation bias: A ubiquitous phenomenon in many guises. Review of General Psychology 2, pp. 175-220.

[8] Paepcke, S., Takayama, L. 2010: Judging a bot by its cover: An experiment on expectation setting for personal robots. Proc. of the 5th ACM/IEEE Int. Conf. on Human-Robot Interaction, Osaka, Japan.

[9] Rabin, M., & Schrag, J.L. 1999: First impressions matter: A model of confirmatory bias. The Quarterly J. of Ergonomics 114, pp. 37-82.

[10] Saucier, G. 1994: Mini-markers: A brief version of Goldberg's unipolar Big-Five markers. J. of Personality Assessment 63, pp. 506-516.

[11] Woods, S., Dautenhahn, K., Kaouri, C., te Broekhorst, R., & Koay, K.L. 2005: Is this robot like me? Proc. of the Int. Conf. on Humanoid Robots, Tsukuba, Japan.

Users' Preferences of Robots for Domestic Use

Maartje M.A. de Graaf Somaya Ben Allouch
University of Twente
Drienerlolaan 5
7522 NJ Enschede, The Netherlands
0031 53 489 6094
m.m.a.degraaf@utwente.nl s.benallouch@utwente.nl

ABSTRACT

This study identifies the design preferences of robots for domestic use. In an online survey, participants rated 16 robot pictures on several evaluation criteria. Results show that overall anthropomorphic robots are more positively rated than either zoomorphic, caricatured or functional robots. Moreover, negative feelings towards robot (e.g. negative attitudes and anxiety towards robots) negatively affected the design evaluations. Providing future users with positive information about domestic robots could improve their feelings towards robots, which, in turn, raises their ratings of robotic designs.

Categories and Subject Descriptors

K.4.m [**Computing Milieux**]: Computers and Society – *Miscellaneous*; J.4 [**Computer Applications**]: Social and Behavioral Sciences – *Psychology*

General Terms

Measurement, Experimentation, Human Factors, Theory.

Keywords

Domestic Robots, Design Preferences, Attitude towards Robots, Anxiety towards Robots.

1. INTRODUCTION

A growing number of robotics researchers believe that robots will come to live with us as assistants and companions. To make the diffusion of social robots a success, it is important to study the users' design preferences of domestic robots in an early stage of their development process, so that future social robots can be adapted to their desires and requirements.

In the literature, four different robotic designs have been defined [2]: anthropomorphic robots with a humanlike appearance, zoomorphic robots with an animal-shaped appearance, caricatured robots with only an immediate association with an existing animal or human, and functional robots which shape is determined by its function. Although anthropomorphic and caricatured robots seem to be dominant in human-robot interaction (HRI) studies, there is little research done on the users' preferences for either of the four robotics designs. Most HRI researchers use either anthropomorphic or caricatured robots in their studies [4, 7]. Including all four types of robotics designs in the evaluation could provide other insights into people's preferences. Additionally, people's feelings towards robots influence their opinions towards robots [6]. People's negative attitudes and anxiety towards robots are thus an important factor to study when evaluating design preferences.

HRI'14, March 3–6, 2014, Bielefeld, Germany.
Copyright 2014 ACM 987-1-4503-2658-2/14/03.
http://dx.doi.org/10.1145/2559636.2563683

2. METHOD

2.1 Measurements

To evaluate the users' preferences of domestic robots, we adopted the Godspeed measures of Bartneck et al. [1], which are often used to evaluate robots, and includes measures for anthropomorphism, animacy, likeability, intelligence and safety. As other studies have indicated that, for domestic use, also the robot's sociability affects the users' satisfaction with a robot [5, 8], we added Heerink, et al.'s [3] sociability measure. To investigate the evaluation measures of the robots, we also asked the participants' negative attitudes and anxiety towards robots using the scales from Nomura et al. [6]. Table 1 shows the descriptive statistics of the variables in our study.

Table 1. Descriptive statistics of the variables

Variable	*M*	*SD*	α
Anthropomorphism	2.90	0.76	.87
Animacy	3.24	0.82	.87
Likeability	4.12	0.76	.90
Intelligence	3.53	0.83	.81
Safety	4.60	0.96	.82
Sociability	3.81	.92	.90
Negative Attitude towards robots	4.54	0.91	.69
Anxiety towards Robots	3.72	0.96	.79

2.2 Procedure

A pre-test was conducted to find representative pictures for the online questionnaire. First, we selected 38 different robots pictures which included robots that (1) have not been in a movie, (2) are real and not sketches, and (3) have neutral backgrounds. These 38 selected robot pictures were presented to 11 (6 males, 5 females) potential users along with a brief description of the four robotic design categories of Fong et al. [2]. They were asked to make four piles of the robot pictures based on these descriptions. Pictures that were most frequently chosen for each category were selected for our final version of the questionnaire. The final online questionnaire asked the participants to rate the 16 selected robot pictures (4 x anthropomorphic, 4 x zoomorphic, 4 x caricatured, and 4 x functional robotic designs). The participants rated all the pictures based on the measures described in 2.1. After these ratings, we asked the participants to respond to the negative attitude and anxiety scales.

Table 2. Evaluations of the 4 Robotic Designs

	Anthropomorphic		Zoomorphic		Caricatured		Functional	
Variable	*M*	*SD*	*M*	*SD*	*M*	*SD*	*M*	*SD*
Anthropomorphism	3.90	0.94	3.00	0.87	2.44	0.85	2.18	0.70
Animacy	4.07	0.94	3.51	1.00	2.81	0.84	2.45	0.74
Likeability	4.67	0.79	4.83	0.96	3.37	0.88	3.48	0.87
Intelligence	4.35	0.98	2.78	0.86	3.66	1.00	3.10	0.81
Safety	4.44	1.07	5.06	1.03	3.89	1.14	4.98	1.02
Sociability	4.54	0.93	3.61	0.86	3.68	1.01	3.43	0.87

2.3 Participants

A total of 266 people, 82 males and 103 females (81 participants did not provide their gender), between 22 and 55 years old (M= 29.26, SD= 6.05), participated in our online study.

3. RESULTS

A repeated measures ANOVA was conducted for all the evaluation factors separately between the four types of robotic designs (see table 2). Results showed a significant effect on anthropomorphism ($F(3,669)$= 366.99, $p < .001$) with all designs significantly differing from each other ($p < .001$). Results showed a significant effect on animacy ($F(3,669)$= 355.61, $p < .001$) with all designs significantly differing from each other ($p < .001$). Results showed a significant effect on likability ($F(3,672)$= 296.90, $p < .001$). All designs significantly differing from each other ($p < .05$), except for the difference in likeability between caricatured and functional robots. Results showed a significant effect on intelligence ($F(3,672)$= 269.02, $p < .001$) with all designs significantly differing from each other ($p < .001$). Results showed a significant effect on safety ($F(3,675)$= 123.29, $p < .000$). All designs differed significantly from each other ($p < .001$), except for the difference in sociability between zoomorphic and functional robots. Results showed a significant effect on sociability ($F(3,672)$= 141.83, $p < .001$). All designs differed significantly from each other ($p < .01$), except for the difference in sociability between zoomorphic and caricatured robots.

Additionally, we investigated if the participants' negative attitudes and anxiety toward robots affected the evaluations of the robotic designs. Results showed that negative attitude toward robots affected the scores of intelligence (R^2= .06; $F(1,182)$= 11.59, β= -.25, $p < .001$), animacy (R^2= .04; $F(1,182)$= 6.72, β= -.19, p= .01), likeability (R^2= .08; $F(1,182)$= 15.41, β= -.28, $p < .001$), anthropomorphism (R^2= .03; $F(1,182)$= 5.02, β= -.16, p= .026), safety (R^2= .21; $F(1,182)$= 49.08, β= -.46, $p < .001$), and sociability (R^2= .08; $F(1,182)$= 16.45, β= -.29, $p < .001$). Results showed that anxiety towards robots affected the scores of intelligence (R^2= . 04; $F(1,182)$= 4.44, β= -.15, p= .037), and safety (R^2= .14; $F(1,182)$= 30.94, β= -.38, $p < .001$). Other regressions were non-significant.

4. GENERAL DISCUSSION

This paper investigates the design preferences of future domestic robots. In the evaluation of robotic pictures, anthropomorphic designs were best rated on most evaluation criteria. These results enhance the importance of other HRI research exploring more detailed design features of humanoid robots, such as the one from Hwang et al. [4]. Future HRI research could further investigate why anthropomorphic designs are more positively evaluated.

Anxiety towards robots, but especially negative attitude towards robots negatively affected the evaluation of robotic designs. Robotic companies could thus improve potential users' evaluations of their robotic designs by increasing people's attitudes and lower their anxiety towards robots.

Although the robot pictures intended to be as neutral as possible, the robot's pose or colors could have had an effect. Another limitation is that this study included only participants from The Netherlands. The same study conducted in another country could result in different findings.

5. REFERENCES

[1] Bartneck, C., Kuliç, D., Croft, E., & Zoghbi, S. 2009: Measurement instruments for the anthropomorphism, animacy, likability, perceived intelligence and perceived safety of robots. Int. J. of Soc. Rob. 1, pp. 71-81.

[2] Fong, T., Nourbakhsh, I., & Dautenhahn, K. 2003: A survey of socially interactive robots. Rob. and Autn. Sys. 42, pp. 143.

[3] Heerink, M., Kröse, B., Evers, V., & Wielinga, B. 2008: The influence of social presence on acceptance of a companion robot by older people. J. of Phys. Agents 2, pp. 33-40.

[4] Hwang, J., Park, T., & Hwang, W. 2013: The effects of overall robot shape on the emotions invoked in users and perceived personalities of robots. Appl. Ergonom. 44, pp. 459-471.

[5] Kirby, R., Forlizzi, J., & Simmons, R. 2010: Affective social robots. Rob. And Autn. Sys. 58, pp. 322-332.

[6] Nomura, T., Kanda, T., Susuki, T., & Kato, K. 2008: Prediction of human behavior in human-robot interaction. AI & Soc. 20, pp. 138-150.

[7] von der Pütten, A.M., & Krämer, N. 2012: A survey on robot appearances. Proc. of the 7th ACM/IEEE Int. Conf. on Human-Robot Interaction 2012, Tokyo, Japan.

[8] Paepcke, S., Takayama, L. 2010: Judging a bot by its cover: An experiment on expectation setting for personal robots. Proc. of the 5th ACM/IEEE Int. Conf. on Human-Robot Interaction, Osaka, Japan.

[9] Woods, S. 2006: Exploring the design space of robots: Children's perspective. Interacting with Computers 18, pp. 1390-1418.

Child-Robot Interaction in the Wild: Field Testing Activities of the ALIZ-E Project

Joachim de Greeff*
CRNS, Cognition Institute
Plymouth University, UK

Olivier Blanson Henkemans
TNO Soesterberg
the Netherlands

Aafke Fraaije
TNO Soesterberg
the Netherlands

Lara Solms
TNO Soesterberg
the Netherlands

Noel Wigdor
TNO Soesterberg
the Netherlands

Bert Bierman
TNO Soesterberg
the Netherlands

ABSTRACT

A field study was conducted in which CRI activities developed by the ALIZ-E project were tested with the project's primary user group: children with diabetes. This field study resulted in new insights in the modalities and roles a robot aimed at CRI in a healthcare setting might utilise, while in addition (re-)assessed some practises and technologies established within the project. Furthermore, it served as a means of strengthening the bonds with the project's principal stakeholders. The study illustrates on the one hand the feasibility of the activities that were developed within the project, while on the other hand highlights the importance of engaging with primary users in an ongoing, incremental fashion.

Categories and Subject Descriptors

H.1.2 [**Models and Principles**]: User/Machine Systems—*Human factors*; I.2.9 [**Artificial Intelligence**]: Robotics—*Commercial robots and applications*

Keywords

Child-Robot Interaction; user studies; care-robot applications

1. INTRODUCTION

Child-Robot Interaction (CRI) may be seen as a sub-field of HRI, but there are notable differences between how adults and children tend to react to robots. For instance, children can be quite forgiving with respect to the robot's flaws in behaviour and presentation, and in general may be quite happy to perceive the interaction as a whole in a game-like fashion[1]. On the other hand, while children can be strongly emerged within an interaction, they also have a short attention span and can be easily distracted. As such, CRI allows for exploration of promising avenues, but possesses additional challenges at the same time.

The ALIZ-E project [4] aims at developing robots able to sustain interaction with children with diabetes over a prolonged period of time (typical, multiple interactions over the course of weeks). The role of the robot is to provide support and guidance for the children, potentially allowing them to better cope with their illness, to support knowledge gain (about diabetes) and to contribute to children's self-management skills. In order to do so, the robot needs to be interesting for the children to interact with; also 'in the wild', i.e.. in a social context with various distractions. Towards this end, various strategies allowing the robot to be adaptive, and thus potentially more interesting, have been explored. Within this aim, engagement with stakeholders and target users in ongoing dialogue is regarded as highly important, as to inform the further development of the robot behaviours in a manner that is effective in a real life setting.

2. AIM AND SETUP

The target audience for adaptive robot behaviour as developed by the ALIZ-E project are children with diabetes aged 7 to 12. The SugarKidsClub[2], the children branch of the association for people with diabetes (DVN) in the Netherlands, organises various camps for their members with games and activities that are embedded within a context adhering to diabetic needs. During one of these camps, a field study was conducted in which 16 children with diabetes participated in CRI activities developed by the ALIZ-E project. The activities were:

1) Handshake; the importance of physical contact between humans has been widely acknowledged as an important means of sustaining interaction and the formation of social bonds [2]. However, less is know about the impact of touch in the field of HRI. To explore this modality, a 'touch' experiment was conducted, which consisted of chil-

*Corresponding author: Joachim.deGreeff@plymouth.ac.uk

HRI'14, March 3–6, 2014, Bielefeld, Germany.
ACM 978-1-4503-2658-2/14/03.
http://dx.doi.org/10.1145/2559636.2559804.

[1]That is, pretend play can seamlessly blend with real robot behaviour, as such potentially lessening the burden on the robot's part significantly.

[2]http://www.sugarkids.nl

dren teaching the robot a personal handshake, a sequence of gestures that could be replayed as a greeting.

2) Sandtray; the sandtray game consists of a sorting task on a large touchscreen that is played between the robot and children [1].

3) Participatory design session; the role and function of a support robot for children with specific healthcare requirements is largely unexplored territory. It is thus important to incorporate input from primary users in an ongoing fashion, as such adhering to the principals of participatory design [3]. To facilitate this aim, a series of group interviews with children was conducted (without the robot), aimed at exploring children's opinions and ideas on how a robot might support them in reaching specific learning goals that would aid their diabetic related needs.

3. MEANS AND MATERIAL

The 16 participating children were divided into 3 groups, who alternated between the 3 activities. Each session lasted for 30 minutes. Data collection consisted of robot interaction logs in case of handshake and sandtray, video recordings of the children engaging in the activities and audio recordings of semi-structured interviews that were conducted afterwards. In addition, camp volunteers were asked to fill out a questionnaire that queried their opinion on the various activities.

Figure 1: Illustration of the three activities: handshake (left), participatory design session (right) and sandtray (bottom).

4. FINDINGS AND CONCLUSIONS

In general the children reacted very positive towards the robots and the activities (see figure 1 for an illustration).

During the Handshake activity children showed great interest and were happy to teach the robot their personal handshake. Additionally, became obvious that a handshake alone cannot keep the children's attention and interest for a prolonged period of time. The children typically exhibited an interest for the robot that was not satisfied by teaching the robot a handshake alone, i.e. they asked lots of questions and wanted to interact with the robot in a manner that the current setup was not able to deliver. The participatory design sessions resulted in new insights into what the children thought of how the robot might be able to help them and in what form/modality this support should be presented. For instance, the robot could offer and/or discuss how to deal with specific situations (such as watching a scary film, challenging social interaction, playing sports etc.), the robot should have a distinct personality, but not exactly the same as the child, and it should be funny. Furthermore, the robot should be adaptive with respect to its capacity of providing aid and guidance in difficult situations, as these situations tend to vary as a function of the child's age.

In more general terms, this field study illustrates the feasibility of employing the ALIZ-E activities with its primary users group 'in the wild'. The particular environment contained a variety of distractions, making it easy for the children to loose interest. While this did happen occasionally, overall the children were quite engaged and spend a lot of time interacting with the robot. This can be taken as an encouragement for the design of CRI; while there was still room for improvement on the robots part, the current setup manages to capture children's attention quite well.

In addition, the following point should be emphasised. Rather than just providing an opportunity to field-test technology, the study also stresses the importance of stakeholder engagement; this enables primary user groups to be involved in the design-and-build process throughout the course of the project, resulting in potentially more effective robot behaviours. Through this engagement, the study has facilitated the formation of tighter relations between research (TNO/ALIZ-E) and stakeholders (SugarKidsClub, DVN), opening up possibilities for future collaborations.

5. ACKNOWLEDGEMENTS

This work is funded by the EU FP7 ALIZ-E project (grant 248116).

6. ADDITIONAL AUTHORS

Additional authors: Joris B. Janssen (TNO, Soesterberg, the Netherlands), Rosemarijn Looije (TNO, Soesterberg, the Netherlands), Paul Baxter (CRNS, Cognition Institute, Plymouth University, UK), Mark A. Neerincx (TNO, Soesterberg, the Netherlands) and Tony Belpaeme (CRNS, Cognition Institute, Plymouth University, UK).

7. REFERENCES

[1] P. Baxter, I. Baroni, M. Nalin, A. Sanna, and T. Belpaeme. Touchscreens as Mediators for Social Human-Robot Interactions: A Focus Group Evaluation involving Diabetic Children. In *Collaboration meets Interactive Surfaces Workshop at ITS'2013*, 2013.

[2] R. Dunbar. The social role of touch in humans and primates: Behavioural function and neurobiological mechanisms. *Neuroscience & Biobehavioral Reviews*, 34(2):260 – 268, 2010.

[3] E. B.-N. Sanders and P. J. Stappers. Co-creation and the new landscapes of design. *Co-design*, 4(1):5–18, 2008.

[4] T. Belpaeme et al. Multimodal Child-Robot Interaction: Building Social Bonds. *Journal of Human-Robot Interaction*, 1(2):33–53, 2013.

Exploring Socially Intelligent Recharge Behaviour for Human-Robot Interaction

Amol Deshmukh and Ruth Aylett
School of Mathematical and Computer Science
Heriot-Watt University, Edinburgh, United Kingdom
{a.deshmukh, r.s.aylett}@hw.ac.uk

ABSTRACT

In this paper we try to highlight the need for social intelligence during the recharge activity of mobile robots and report a study performed to investigate people's attitude towards recharge behaviour of an office robot.

Categories and Subject Descriptors

I.2.9 [**Artificial Intelligence**]: Robotics

General Terms

Human Factors, Algorithms, Theory

Keywords

Robot Companions, Social Intelligence, Recharge Behaviour

1. INTRODUCTION

It has been predicted that in the coming years, social robots will be part of our daily lives in domestic and office environments. Social mobile robots will need to operate over a long-term period of time, days, weeks or even months to perform daily tasks; hence they will require sustainable social intelligence [1]. In order for robots to act as companions or assistants in social environments such as homes and offices, they should be capable of operating with a great degree of autonomy over a longer period of time. Usually mobile robots draw power from batteries and take hours to recharge. While the recharge behaviour is active, the companion robot may be prevented from performing its normal tasks and this may hinder the flow of human-robot interaction. Hence, it is important for social robots to manage their recharge behaviour in a socially intelligent manner. In this paper we report an experiment performed to study people's attitude towards an office robot in regards to recharge activity and how the robot's verbal behaviour can influence people's perception of the robot. We have summarised some preliminary findings from this study in this paper.

HRI'14, March 3–6, 2014, Bielefeld, Germany.
ACM 978-1-4503-2658-2/14/03.
http://dx.doi.org/10.1145/2559636.2559835 .

2. MOTIVATION

Some earlier work [2] suggests that social abilities in a robot contribute to a sense of social presence for the user when interacting with a robotic companion and this leads to higher enjoyment and social acceptance. Some studies [3] indicate, battery life and long recharge time may break the users engagement between robots and their users and pose a challenge to long-term interaction. Due to health and safety reasons a robot charging or docking station cannot be placed in the middle of a room, so the robot can get occupied sitting in a corner of a room while recharging becoming inaccessible to the user. It is thereby important for social robots to optimise their availability, moreover they should also be able mitigate disappointment of not being being able to perform tasks while recharging in a socially intelligent manner.

3. PILOT LONG-TERM EXPERIMENT

In the first long-term experiments that were carried (March 2012) were mainly to evaluate the active, recharge and task performance time by team buddy (TB) an office assistant robot (based on Pioneer P3AT with enhanced superstructure, expressive head and a laptop PC). The robot has 6 lead acid batteries (12V, 7Ah each) offering an approximate operational time of 3 hours when fully charged (depending on usage). These batteries require about 3 hours to recharge. The office had 5 participants who continued with their normal routine work, the robot performed tasks like greeting them when they arrived in office in the morning, passing messages, giving them reminders (from their Google calendars), auto-recharge, carry the phone etc. During the 10 days the robot performed 216 total tasks (average 21 tasks/day) with average active time of 7 hours/day (weekends were excluded).

The activity log showed that out of the total available time, 240 hours (10 days) the robot was active for 70 hours (time when users were present in the office), total time spent during task performance and home position was only 2.7 hours (3.8% of total active time) and recharging 33.5 hours (47% of total active time). The results from this pilot experiment clearly show that the robot spent most of the time recharging and was unavailable to perform tasks. The feedback received from the participants indicated that TB's unavailability during recharge was certainly not desirable and led to disappointment. Mobile social robots can try to mitigate user's disappointment with an apology which can be effective in making the robot seem more competent, making the participants feel closer to and liking the robot more [4].

4. USER STUDY

Following the results from the pilot long-term experiment a more focused WoZ study was conducted (November 2013), to specifically investigate how people rate a moving robot against a stationary robot (during recharge activity), and while performing tasks. The two main hypotheses for this experiment were, *H1: People will prefer the moving robot more than stationary robot, H2: People will rate the apologetic robot better than the neutral robot while the robot is recharging*. The participants entered into a room and were asked to mark an exam paper seated on a desk. The experiment had two parts, first session (Part A) was the same for all participants, although the participants were not aware that the experiment has two sessions. The TB greeted them initially and then performed two tasks namely message delivery and call delivery after fixed time intervals of 2 minutes. The tasks involved the robot navigating from a default location in the room to user's desk and then performing a verbal action using an artificial synthesised voice.

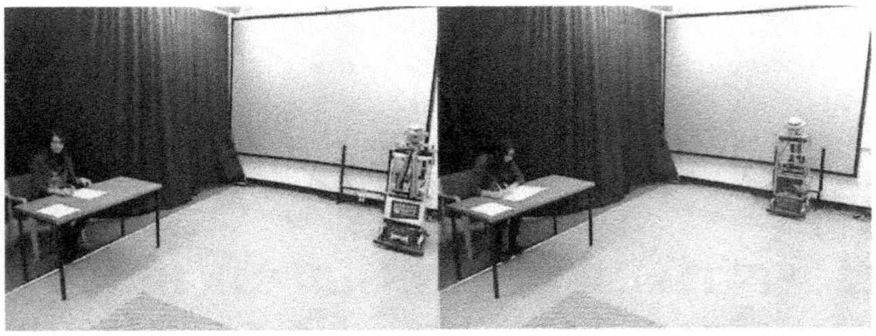

Figure 1: Experiment room: Part A (left: moving TB), Part B (right: stationary TB while recharging)

The participants then answered a questionnaire after the first part and then were sent back to the room being asked to try and envisage that some time has passed between first part (morning time) and now (evening). The robot performed the same 3 tasks (greet, message, call) from a recharge station in the room. In the Part B, second part of the experiment, there were two conditions, the first condition was the neutral condition where the robot was using more direct verbal communication. In second condition, the robot was apologetic and provided more explanation about it's situation and it's limitation for not being able to move due to recharging activity. Examples of the verbal communication are stated below for greeting task.

Part A - Greeting: "Hello, good morning. I am the Team Buddy of this lab. My name is Alex, hope you have a good day. My battery is fully charged"

Part B - Greeting (Neutral condition): "Good evening, good to see you back. My battery is low, so i am recharging now.."

Part B - Greeting (Apology condition): "Good evening, good to see you back, sorry my battery is low, so i am recharging now, I cannot come there.."

The study had 46 participants (28 Male, 18 Female). We randomly assigned the participants for the two conditions in Part B, 23 participants interacted with neutral version and 23 with apologetic version. After second part the participants were specifically asked in questionnaire "Which team buddy would you prefer Part A or Part B?", 65% preferred Part A, 20% preferred Part B and 15% preferred both. In some other questions asked about TB's behaviour, the participants were asked to rate the TB on a 7 likert scale (1-Disagree strongly to 7-Agree strongly). The results shows higher average ratings for the apologetic TB in comparison to neutral TB in regards to: I felt in company of the TB, TB's recharge behaviour was acceptable, I felt neglected while TB was recharging, The TB was available to interact with me. These preliminary results supports both hypothesis H1, H2 and also conform with earlier long-term HRI studies performed with stationary and moving robots [5].

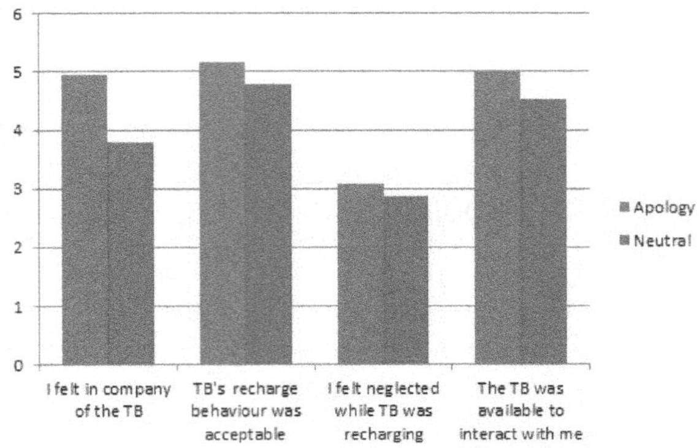

Figure 2: Average rating, (Apology: n=23, Neutral: n= 23)

5. CONCLUSION

The results from the pilot long-term experiment indicates the need of socially intelligence during recharge activity of mobile robots operating in social environments. From the user study it is clear that using verbal apologies can be effective in mitigating disappointment and give users a sense of companionship even when stationary during recharging. The results from the user study is still preliminary and is subjected to further detailed analysis in the future.

6. REFERENCES

[1] K. Dautenhahn. Socially intelligent robots: Dimensions of human- robot interaction. *Philosophical Transactions of the Royal Society B: Biological Sciences*, 362(1480):679–704, April 2007.

[2] M. Heerink, B. J. A. Krose, B. J. Wielinga, and V. Evers. The influence of social presence on acceptance of a companion robot by older people. *Journal of Physical Agents, Special Issue on Human interaction with domestic robots*, 2:33–40, 2008.

[3] J. Dimas, I. Leite, A. Pereira, Rui Prada P. Cuba, and A. Paiva. Pervasive pleo: Long-term attachment with artificial pets. In *MobileHCI 2010*. Lisboa, Portugal, September 2010.

[4] Min Kyung Lee, Sara Kiesler, Siddhartha Srinivasa Jodi Forlizzi, and Paul Rybski. Gracefully mitigating breakdowns in robotic services. In *Proceedings of HRI*, February 2010.

[5] DagSverre Syrdal, Kerstin Dautenhahn, KhengLee Koay, Michael. Walters, and WanChing Ho. Sharing spaces, sharing lives, the impact of robot mobility on user perception of a home companion robot. In *Social Robotics*, volume 8239 of *Lecture Notes in Computer Science*, pages 321–330, 2013.

A Week-long Study on Robot-Visitors Spatial Relationships during Guidance in a Sciences Museum

Marta Díaz
Technical University of Catalonia
marta.diaz@upc.edu

Dennys Paillacho
Escuela Superior Politécnica del Litoral
dpaillac@espol.edu.ec

Cecilio Angulo
Technical University of Catalonia
cecilio.angulo@upc.edu

Oriol Torres
PAL Robotics
oriol.torres@pal-robotics.com

Jonathan González
PAL Robotics
jon.gonzalez@pal-robotics.com

Jordi Albo-Canals
La Salle BCN – Ramon Llull University
jalbo@salle.url.edu

ABSTRACT

In order to observe spatial relationships in social human-robot interactions, a field trial was carried out within the *CosmoCaixa Science Museum* in Barcelona. The *follow me* episodes studied showed that the space configurations formed by guide and visitors walking together did not always fit the robot social affordances and navigation requirements to perform the guidance successfully, thus additional communication prompts are considered to regulate effectively the walking together and follow me behaviors.

Categories and Subject Descriptors

I.2 [**Artificial Intelligence**]: Robotics; D.2.8 [**Software Engineering**]: Complexity measures, Performance measures

General Terms

Human Factors

Keywords

social human-robot interaction, spatial relationships, proxemics behavior

1. INTRODUCTION

Guidance is one of the most useful services robots may deliver in public spaces as museums, exhibitions, malls, and tourist sites. Taking the role of guide, the robot not only provides people with appropriate information to make the visit a more enjoyable experience, but help them to get to intended destinations. The main difference between an informer or recommender robot and a robotic guide is that guidance in public spaces implies social navigation in a highly dynamic scenario. Robotic museum guides as MINERVA [1] and ROBOVIE [2] have proven to be effective addressing people and keeping their attention, in spite of the highly challenging context. However, as far as we know, research on robotic guides has mainly focused on verbal and non-verbal communicative behaviors to improve the visitor experience, but no studies have been carried out to model spatial arrangements during guidance.

HRI'14, March 3–6, 2014, Bielefeld, Germany.
ACM 978-1-4503-2658-2/14/03.
http://dx.doi.org/10.1145/2559636.2559797.

2. SPATIAL RELATIONSHIPS IN HRI

Service robots featured with *walk around* functionality must deal with crucial social navigation issues: how to move (i.e. speed, kind of movement and trajectories), where to perform and how to place (i.e. distance, position and orientation) to be unobtrusive, effective and socially congruent. Moreover, robots in shared spaces get involved in *spatial relationships* with people [3], [4]. Spatial relationships are a combination of distance, relative position and orientation that occur naturally whenever two or more people engage in an interaction [5] and convey significant and relevant social information and also define an interpersonal space for developing activity [3]. Promising attempts to optimize social robots spatial management in different scenarios (e.g. telepresence assistance at home) have been done applying models and knowledge from social psychology (i.e. proxemics, space formations, group walking patterns and crowd dynamics).

Studies in telepresence mobile robots have identified the management of spatial and orientation relationships between people and robot as a main issue in order to improve the quality of interaction. Based on endon's model, the authors identify different space formations or spatial patterns (e.g. *vis a vis*, *side-by-side*, *L-shape*, *follow* or *ahead*) according to the robot's role, the activities carried out and the spatial constraints, as well as individual variables such as familiarity with the agent [3]. An interesting conclusion is that when physical constraints in combination of navigational requirements unable the robot to maintain the convenient spatial behavior, it can compensate this situation with other interactive behaviors (e.g. verbally apologizing for inappropriate proximity or reducing the eye-contact) to maintain an overall degree of desired intimacy.

In the context of the robot taking the role of a guide in a museum the guidance is viewed as a highly demanding collaborative task that implies communicating intentions (i.e. robot offers the service, visitors select a destination and re-

Figure 1: Robot guiding visitors

quest the *bring me there* function, the robot head towards the destination) and social navigation (i.e. walk together to the intended destination) (see Fig. 1). This *group walking following a leader* behavior implies complex space regulations (i.e. proximity management, spatial configurations) to allow guide and visitors group up and walk together effectively to a target destination. These space relationships during guidance must be at a time socially meaningful and compatible with the robot's navigation specifications (i.e. collision avoidance performance).

The present work addresses the identification and description of space relationships during guidance applying models from social psychology such as group walking [6] and crowd dynamics [7].

3. THE FIELD TEST

During 6 days the robot REEM walked around the *CosmoCaixa Science Museum* in an open space, providing information to visitors and offering the service to bring them to a particular location. The robot's performance and the guide-visitors interaction were observed and videorecorded for further analyses of visitors-guide communication and space relationships, and to evaluate the robustness of robot performance in the wild.

In the present study we focus specifically on the *follow me* behavior. In the context of guidance a *follow me* episode is defined as a walking group formation including the robot displacing together and forming typically any of these two spatial arrangements: *walking along with* (i.e. robot and people aligned side-by-side perpendicularly to the walking direction) or *walking ahead* (i.e. visitors follow the robot, see Fig.1).

91 episodes of *follow me* were observed. In almost all the cases a *walking ahead* formation was observed (see Table 1), where the robot leads the group and visitors follow behind. While this space arrangement is a natural disposition for following a leader in a high density groups [7] pose important constraints to communication and therefore to social cohesion between the guide robot and visitors during guidance. On the other hand, only 2 side-by-side spatial formations were observed during guidance and in both cases it was just two people interacting with the robot.

Table 1: Spatial relationships by group size

	Group size									
Formation	1	2	3	4	5	6	7	8	9	Total
Leader-follower	3	8	13	4	9	2	6	4	33	82
Side by side	0	2	0	0	0	0	0	0	0	2
Unidentified	0	0	0	1	1	0	1	0	4	7
Total	3	10	13	5	10	2	7	4	37	91

4. CONCLUSIONS

From literature and from the observations gathered during the field test we can conclude that spatial arrangements create the social field for shared activity and thus influence the quality of human-robot interaction. The appropriateness of the space relationship is a key issue in collaborative activities as guidance that requires continuous communication (i.e. offering to bring, heading a destination) and mutual regulation (i.e. group walking together).

Spontaneous spatial arrangements during guidance may not be effective when confronted with robot's affordances and navigation specifications and therefore limit the system performance. However, group behavior could be anticipated -from social psychology and HRI models- and managed socially by the robot guide implementing new behaviors (e.g. awareness of group density) or through communication (e.g. asking kindly to clear off its way)

5. ACKNOWLEDGMENTS

This research was supported in part by the PATRICIA Research Project (TIN2012-38416-C03-01,03), funded by the Spanish Ministry of Economy and Competitiveness.

6. REFERENCES

[1] S. Thrun *et al.* MINERVA: A second- generation museum tour-guide robot. In *IEEE International Conference on Robotics and Automation*, vol 3, pp 1999–2005, 1999.

[2] M. Montemerlo, . Pineau, N. Roy, S. Thrun, and V. Verma. Experiences with a mobile robotic guide for the elderly. In *18th National Conference on Artificial Intelligence*, pp 587–592, Menlo Park, CA, USA, 2002.

[3] A. ristoffersson, . Severinson-Eklundh, and A. Loutfi. Measuring the quality of interaction in mobile robotic telepresence: A pilot's perspective. *Int. J. Soc. Rob.*, 5(1):89–101, 2013.

[4] H. Hüettenrauch, .S. Eklundh, A. Green, and E.A. Topp. Investigating spatial relationships in human-robot interaction. In *IEEE/RSJ International Conference on Intelligent Robots and Systems*, pp 5052–5059, 2006.

[5] P. Marshall, . Rogers, and N. Pantidi. Using f-formations to analyse spatial patterns of interaction in physical environments. In *Proceedings of the ACM 2011 Conference on Computer Supported Cooperative Work*, CSCW '11, pp 445–454, New ork, N , USA, 2011.

[6] M. Costa. Interpersonal distances in group walking. *Journal of Nonverbal Behavior*, 34(1):15–26, 2010.

[7] S. Bandini, A. Gorrini, L. Manenti, and G. Vizzari. Crowd and pedestrian dynamics: Empirical investigation and simulation. In *Proceedings of Measuring Behavior*, 2012.

Hesitation Signals in Human-Robot Head-on Encounters

A Pilot Study

Christian Dondrup
University of Lincoln
Brayford Pool, LN6 7TS
Lincoln, UK
cdondrup@lincoln.ac.uk

Christina Lichtenthäler
TU München
Boltzmannstr. 3
85748 Garching, DE
lichtenc@in.tum.de

Marc Hanheide
University of Lincoln
Brayford Pool, LN6 7TS
Lincoln, UK
mhanheide@lincoln.ac.uk

ABSTRACT

We present a pilot study to identify hesitation signals in Human-Robot Spatial Interaction which we aim to employ to evaluate the quality of the robots executed behaviour. The presented study focuses on head-on encounters between a human and a robot in pass-by scenarios. Our results indicate that these hesitation signals can be found and therefore present a form a implicit feedback.

Categories and Subject Descriptors

I.2.9 [**Artificial Intelligence**]: Robotics; I.5.1 [**Pattern Recognition**]: Models

Keywords

Hesitation; Human-Robot Spatial Interaction

1. INTRODUCTION

Human-Robot Spatial Interaction (HRSI) is the study of joint movement of humans and robots through space. A large body of research is dedicated to answer arising questions like how to move in the close vicinity of humans given spatial constraints and how to effectively coordinate these movements [3].

In the early stages of mobile robotics research humans were only regarded as static obstacles which had to be avoided but in recent works the social and communicative character of spatial movement is also taken into account, e.g. [7]. This lead to the design of human-aware navigation approaches which try to increase the *comfort*, *naturalness*, and *sociability* (as defined by [3]) of the interaction, using mostly pre-learned or constraint based behaviours. Enabling a robot to learn from experience and shape its behaviour over time to adapt to the users personal preferences requires feedback on the quality of the executed behaviour. To this end, we conducted a pilot study to find signals which allow to evaluate the quality of such human-aware navigation approaches.

Using hesitation gestures as an implicit form of communication is a well established approach in Human-Robot Interaction (HRI). The study proposed in this paper was inspired by the work of AJung Moon *et al.* [5] in particular. They showed that using the acceleration profile of the wrist is sufficient to detect and convey hesitation in HRI manipulation tasks: "[...] *the* [hesitation] *gestures exhibit a characteristic acceleration profile in their principle axis.*" [5, p. 1998]. We aim to transfer these findings to spatial movement of the human body as a whole, to detect *hesitation signals*. Hesitation, caused by confusion due to unexpected behaviour, manifests itself as an abrupt stopping or deceleration. We therefore assume that *hesitation signals* in HRSI are an *abrupt stopping or sudden decrease in velocity of the whole body.*

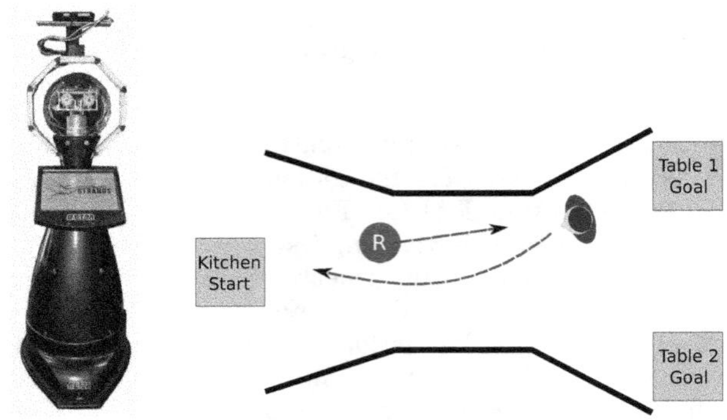

(a) Robot (b) Head-on encounter in study set-up.

Figure 1: *a)* Robot hight: 1.72m, diameter: $\sim 61cm$. *b)* The experimental set-up had a size of $5m^2$. The image is showing a typical head-on encounter.

Previous work on head-on encounters in so-called *pass-by scenarios* (see Fig. 1b) used manual annotation of videos or sensor data to evaluate the quality of a chosen trajectory, e.g. [6]. Our study aims to enable a robot to autonomously infer the quality (regarding HRSI standards as described in [3]) of the interaction from sensor data, using hesitation signals. This evaluation would enable a robot to shape its behaviour "on-the-fly" using a shaping framework like TAMER [2], employing hesitation signals as negative reward.

So far, little work has been done to find hesitation signals in spatial movement. We therefore conducted a pilot study to find these hesitation signals in head-on encounters between human and robot during pass-by scenarios.

2. PILOT STUDY

A first within-subject (allowing further investigation if hesitation signals vary between individuals) pilot study was conducted using a motion capture system, tracking the movements of a robot and a human in a confined, shared space. The aim of this study was to find the mentioned hesitation signals in head-on encounters of human and robot.

HRI'14, March 3–6, 2014, Bielefeld, Germany.
ACM 978-1-4503-2658-2/14/03.
http://dx.doi.org/10.1145/2559636.2559817.

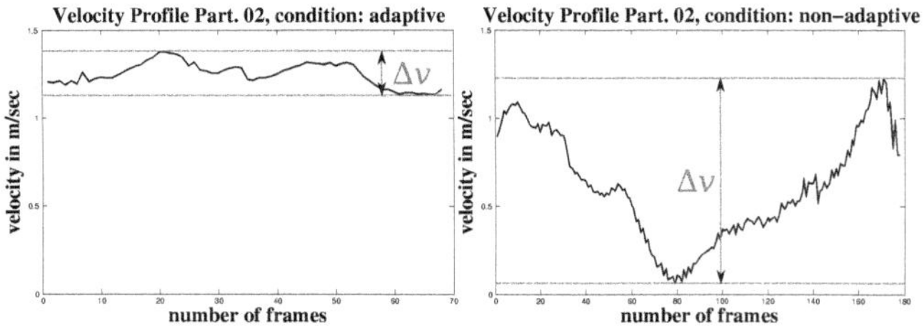

(a) Adaptive condition (b) Non-adaptive condition

Figure 2: Adaptive and non-adaptive velocity profile of two of the head-on encounters of one of the participants.

Study Design. In this study participants were put into a hypothetical restaurant scenario with a human-size robot (see Fig 1a). The experiment was conducted in a large motion capture lab with two tables and a kitchen counter in the middle. The tables and the kitchen counter were positioned as depicted in Fig. 1b and connected by an artificial corridor to elicit close encounters between human and robot while still being able to reliably track their positions. The motion capture system recorded x, y, z coordinates (at a rate of 50hz) of the robot and the participant during the whole interaction. We had 14 participants (10 male, 4 female) interacting with the robot for 6 minutes each.

Conditions. During the interaction the robot showed two different behaviours, i.e *adaptive* and *non-adaptive* velocity control, which was switched at random upon the robots arrival at the kitchen counter. When executing the adaptive behaviour the robot gradually slowed down while approaching the human and stopped before entering the personal zone [1] of the participant to let her/him pass (inspired by findings of [4]). In the non-adaptive behaviour the robot tried to reach the goal as efficient as possible regarding the human as a static obstacle. These behaviours were chosen because they mainly differ in the distance the robot keeps to the participant and the velocity of its approach, this should therefore allow to evaluate the quality of the navigation strategy while still enabling the human to reliably infer the goal of the robot.

Procedure. The robot was presented as a co-worker, establishing the same social status for robot and human. During the study, the robot autonomously moved between tables and kitchen counter, taking orders from the supposed guests, while the participants delivered drinks from the kitchen counter to the tables (see Fig. 1b). This task created a more natural type of pass-by scenarios where the robot and the participant would only occasionally and incidentally engage in head-on encounters while trying to achieve their goals most efficiently.

3. RESULTS

For our analysis, a head-on encounter was defined as human and robot approaching and passing-by each other (see Fig. 1b). Manual selection yielded 64 head-on encounters for the adaptive behaviour and 57 for the non-adaptive behaviour. The number of head-on encounters per participant varies between 4 and 14 with a mean of 8.71.

We created velocity profiles from the sequence of recorded x, y, z coordinates of the participants and computed the difference in velocity Δv between the highest and lowest speed during each encounter. Fig. 2 shows two example velocity profiles for different encounters between the robot and the same participant. Fig. 2a shows a small Δv (almost constant speed) for the adaptive behaviour and Fig. 2b shows a high Δv for the non-adaptive encounter which represents a distinct slowing down and therefore, according to our assumption, a hesitation signal. The mean values of all Δv for each condition: adaptive: $\mu_{\Delta v} = 439.78^{mm}/_{sec}$, $\sigma = 25.71$, non-adaptive: $\mu_{\Delta v} = 516.44^{mm}/_{sec}$, $\sigma = 65.84$, also show a difference between the two behaviours but it is not statistically significant.

4. DISCUSSION

The results show that hesitation signals can be found in head-on encounters during pass-by scenarios. Analysis of the velocity profiles resulted in differences between the adaptive and non-adaptive condition. The non-adaptive behaviour showed a larger deceleration of the participant during interaction than the adaptive behaviour which means that the robot interfered with the participant's goal in an unexpected way, therefore, causing annoyance and stress. This shows that the adaptive behaviour is better suited for this kind of head-on encounters and reveals that shaping the robots behaviour towards the more adaptive control would suite the needs of our participant group. This indicates that hesitation signals can be used as implicit feedback and should allow our mentioned shaping approach to work but this is still subject to further investigation.

The mentioned lack of statistical significance could have various reasons, e.g. the small number of samples. Since this paper describes a pilot study to find trends and evaluate if further investigation would be justified, we only had a small group of participants and a short interaction time for each individual. This yielded a very limited number of head-on encounters (see Sec. 3). A future study with prolonged interaction and more participants is believed to address this issue and allow us to use a shaping approach, employing hesitation signals as implicit feedback.

5. ACKNOWLEDGMENTS

The research leading to these results has received funding from the EC FP7; grant agreement No. 600623, STRANDS.

6. REFERENCES

[1] E. T. Hall. *The Hidden Dimension.* Doubleday, anchor books edition, 1966.

[2] W. B. Knox, P. Stone, and C. Breazeal. Training a robot via human feedback: A case study. In *Social Robotics*, pages 460–470. Springer, 2013.

[3] T. Kruse, A. K. Pandey, R. Alami, and A. Kirsch. Human-aware robot navigation: A survey. *Robotics and Autonomous Systems*, (0):–, 2013.

[4] C. Lichtenthäler, A. Peters, S. Griffiths, and A. Kirsch. Social navigation-identifying robot navigation patterns in a path crossing scenario. *ICSR. Springer*, 2013.

[5] A. Moon, C. A. C. Parker, E. A. Croft, and H. F. M. Van Der Loos. Did you see it hesitate? - Empirically Grounded Design of Hesitation Trajectories for Collaborative Robots. In *IEEE/RSJ Int. Conf. on Intelligent Robots and Systems*, pages 1994–1999, 2011.

[6] A. Peters, T. P. Spexard, M. Hanheide, and P. Weiss. Hey robot, get out of my way - A survey on a spatial and situational movement concept in HRI. In *BMI - Well-Being*, pages 147–165. 2011.

[7] E. Sisbot, L. Marin-Urias, R. Alami, and T. Simeon. A Human Aware Mobile Robot Motion Planner. *IEEE Transactions on Robotics*, 23(5):874–883, Oct. 2007.

Analyzing Human High-Fives to Create an Effective High-Fiving Robot

Naomi T. Fitter and Katherine J. Kuchenbecker
Haptics Group, GRASP Laboratory
Department of Mechanical Engineering and Applied Mechanics
University of Pennsylvania
Philadelphia, PA, 19104, USA
{nfitter,kuchenbe}@seas.upenn.edu

ABSTRACT

Creating a robot that can teach humans simple interactive tasks such as high-fiving requires research at the intersection of physical human-robot interaction (PHRI) and socially assistive robotics. This paper shows how observation of natural human-human interaction can improve the design of requirements for social-physical robots and form a framework for autonomous execution of interactive physical tasks. Eleven pairs of human subjects were recruited to perform a set of high-fiving games; a magnetic motion tracker and an accelerometer were mounted to each person's hand for the duration of the experiment, and each subject completed several questionnaires about the experience. The results reveal valuable clues about the generally positive feelings of the participants and the movement of their hands during play. We discuss how we plan to use these results to create a robot that can teach humans similar high-fiving games.

Categories and Subject Descriptors

H.1.2 [**Models and Principles**]: User/Machine Systems—*Human Factors*; I.2.9 [**Artificial Intelligence**]: Robotics—*Kinematics and dynamics*

1. MOTIVATION

Working in homes, schools, and other human settings requires robots to possess social intelligence in addition to fulfilling the well-established expectation of safe performance. Two human-robot interaction (HRI) subfields are paramount to facilitating successful social robot interaction: physical human-robot interaction (PHRI), which focuses on situations involving direct physical human-robot contact, and socially assistive robotics, the study of robots intended to support people through social interaction. Since movement and physical contact are known to play a pivotal role in interactions between humans, incorporating physical contact into socially assistive robotics could benefit numerous people who are yet unreached by social robots.

Through direct contact with humans, social robots may be able to assist the world's growing population, for example by caring for the elderly in their homes or aiding human teachers in the classroom. The small amount of existing social-physical robot research elucidates ethical and design criteria for robots that operate autonomously in intimate human settings, such as a robotic butler [2]. HRI researchers studying the application areas of medicine, rehabilitation, and entertainment, among other fields, have repeatedly found that robots must exhibit ethical and emotional behaviors that are acceptable to the human(s) with whom they interact [1]. This social interplay strongly links cognitive science and robotics in the field of HRI, a connection exemplified by studies that use social robots to teach the norms of play and conversation to children with developmental delays [3]. Also in the domain of education, a robot that was introduced to children as a playmate and peer tutor was shown to help socially normal children learn English [4]. To our knowledge, high-fiving (celebratory palm-to-palm contact) has not previously been formally examined for adaptation to HRI. This study focuses on the effect of high-five games on socially normal adults to guide the possible future development of a high-fiving robot.

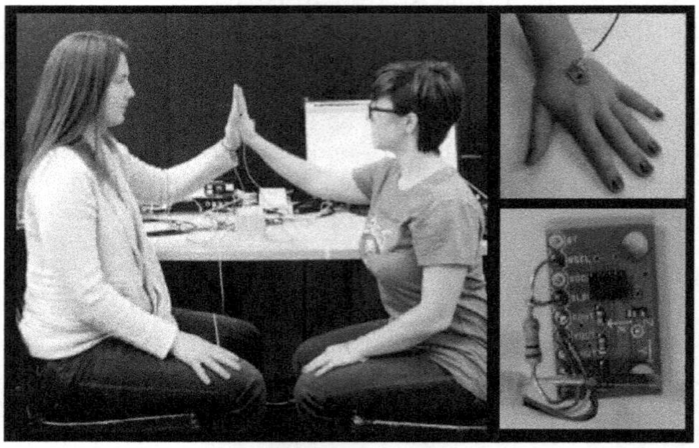

Figure 1: The experiment setup. Left: The subjects sat facing one another while high-fiving with opposite hands. Upper right: The sensors mounted to a hand. Lower right: A close-up view of the sensors.

2. METHODS

We conducted a study to gather quantitative data about how humans execute and respond to high-fiving activities. 22 subjects between 22 and 48 years of age consented to take part in the study. The 21 right-handed and 1 left-handed subjects were randomly assigned to 11 pairs. One Ascension trakSTAR 3D magnetic tracking sensor and one Sparkfun MMA7361 triple axis accelerometer breakout board were

HRI'14, March 3–6, 2014, Bielefeld, Germany.
ACM 978-1-4503-2658-2/14/03.
http://dx.doi.org/10.1145/2559636.2563718.

affixed with tape to the back center of either their right or left hand, as shown in Figure 1. In each trial, the experimenter indicated a high-fiving task to one or both subjects and recorded 20 seconds of sensor data. The three phases of the experiment involved the following tempo cues: (i) an auditory stimulus to both subjects through earbud-style headphones, (ii) an auditory stimulus to only one of the subjects through the same headphones, and (iii) a written tempo change stimulus to one subject using a sheet of paper. Each subject had opportunities to lead the tempo and tempo changes, and subjects were asked to move and interact in a natural manner. During the experiment, subjects completed several single-question tempo perception surveys, a two-part Likert and free-response survey concerning their enjoyment of and interest in the experiment activities, and a demographic survey. Questions focused on capturing the emotion, engagement, and self-evaluation of participants. The experiment was also videotaped to enable subsequent analysis of the subjects' reactions and facial expressions, but this has not yet been performed. We intend to employ trained raters using check sheets as well as computer-vision to measure the occurrence of key social cues in the recordings.

3. RESULTS

Subjects responded positively to the experiment, and the collected data provided direction on designing a robot high-five controller. Responses to key Likert-type survey questions, illustrated in Figure 2, indicate that the average subject enjoyed the experiment very much, would be very interested in doing similar activities with a robot, and would have been very engaged in similar activities as a child. Subjects' positive facial expressions and body language included frequent laughing and smiling throughout the experiment, especially during failures to high-five correctly or at the right tempo. Consequently, high-fiving games may be a low-risk case study for social-physical human-robot interaction since robots need not perform perfectly to match human performance or appear congenial. Studies of robots that cheat at simple games have similarly concluded that people often perceive robots that perform imperfectly or cheat as more likable than robots that perform perfectly [5].

Extended essay responses revealed that the majority of subjects thought that high-fiving a robot would be "cool," "fun," or "interesting," and one even mused "it would be nice to have robot moral support." A few subjects had concerns about robots being unsafe, too perfect at keeping tempo, or less interesting to interact with. Careful programming and robot selection should be able to resolve these concerns. Further data provide ideas for the design of a human-inspired robot high-five controller. When the target tempo was unknown, four subjects recounted leaving their hands still until after a few contacts from their partner. Visual and auditory signals such as head bobbing and foot tapping by tempo leaders proved useful to tempo followers. We plan to probe the recorded data for the time between hand impacts, amplitude of hand movement, peak acceleration, and hand acceleration between contacts. With basic kinematic equations, this information can be used to solve for appropriate hand position and velocity over time for any tempo. If we attach a tactile sensor to a robot and measure time between impacts, we can look up typical quantities for that tempo and then solve the kinematic equations based on these values, using the result as an input to command robot movement.

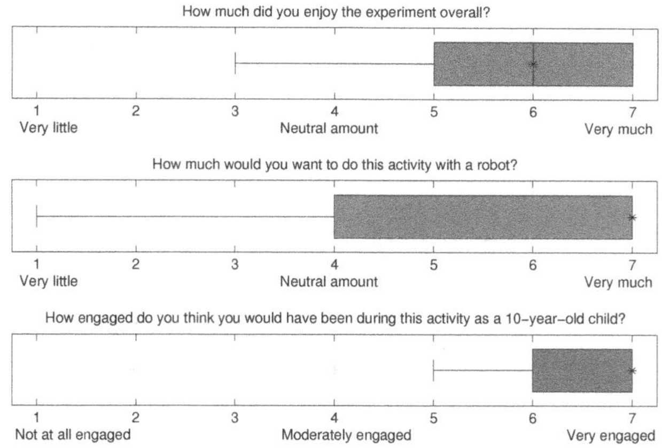

Figure 2: Responses to key Likert questions.

4. CONCLUSION

The results suggest that robots may be able to engage humans in physical interaction games such as high-fiving. Beyond the known social benefits that robots can provide to elderly individuals, developmentally delayed children, and many others, social robots may offer benefits to average, healthy adults, such as the participants of this study. Well-designed high-fiving robots are an example of positive social-physical human-robot interaction. This connection between robots and humans could facilitate collaborative atmospheres in classrooms or other environments beyond the scope of this study. We plan to use Rethink Robotics' Baxter robot (a two-armed human-scale humanoid) for future research in this area because of its safety, relatively low cost ($22,000), and friendly appearance. The majority of subjects' qualms about robots would be quelled by the use of Baxter as a robotic platform, and careful programming could mitigate remaining concerns. Subsequent studies in this research area will include investigations of how humans interact with and perceive Baxter while carrying out high-fiving and rhythmic hand clapping activities similar to those tested in the reported study.

5. REFERENCES

[1] R. C. Arkin, M. Fujita, T. Takagi, and R. Hasegawa. An ethological and emotional basis for human–robot interaction. *Robotics and Autonomous Systems*, 42(3):191–201, 2003.

[2] A. De Santis, B. Siciliano, A. De Luca, and A. Bicchi. An atlas of physical human–robot interaction. *Mechanism and Machine Theory*, 43(3):253–270, 2008.

[3] J. Han and D. Kim. r-Learning services for elementary school students with a teaching assistant robot. In *Proceedings of the ACM/IEEE International Conference on Human-Robot Interaction (HRI)*, pages 255–256, 2009.

[4] T. Kanda, T. Hirano, D. Eaton, and H. Ishiguro. Interactive robots as social partners and peer tutors for children: A field trial. *Human-Computer Interaction*, 19(1):61–84, 2004.

[5] E. Short, J. Hart, M. Vu, and B. Scassellati. No fair!! an interaction with a cheating robot. In *Proceedings of the ACM/IEEE International Conference on Human-Robot Interaction (HRI)*, pages 219–226, 2010.

Towards Action Selection Under Uncertainty for a Socially Aware Robot Bartender

Mary Ellen Foster
M.E.Foster@hw.ac.uk

Simon Keizer
S.Keizer@hw.ac.uk

Oliver Lemon
O.Lemon@hw.ac.uk

The Interaction Lab, School of Mathematical and Computer Sciences
Heriot-Watt University, EH14 4AS, Edinburgh, UK

ABSTRACT

We describe how the state representation of a socially aware robot is being extended to handle uncertainty. It incorporates the full range of information provided by the input sensors, including the confidence of all hypotheses. We also show how the Interaction Manager is being updated to make use of the extended representation.

Categories and Subject Descriptors: I.2.9 [Artificial intelligence]: Robotics – Operator interfaces

Keywords: Belief tracking; Social robotics

1. INTRODUCTION

A crucial aspect of the design of an interactive multimodal system is state management: transforming the noisy, continuous hypotheses produced by the low-level input processing components into a form that can be used as the basis for higher-level action selection. A state representation that considers only the highest-confidence input hypotheses is straightforward to maintain and reason with, but discards a great deal of potentially useful information. On the other hand, a representation that takes into account the full set of input hypotheses—along with their estimated confidence scores—can be more robust and informative, but requires more sophisticated methods of maintenance and more complex forms of reasoning. This general problem of state estimation under uncertainty is a multimodal version of the *belief tracking* problem for spoken dialogue systems [8, 9]: sequences of uncertain observations are processed in order to build up an increasingly accurate *belief state* regarding user goals as the interaction progresses.

We are currently addressing this issue in the context of the JAMES robot bartender (Figure 1), which has the goal of supporting socially appropriate multi-party interaction in a bartending scenario. Based on (uncertain) observations about the users in the scene provided by the vision and speech recognition components, the system maintains a model of the social context, and decides on effective and socially appropriate responses in that context. In this paper, we describe how the state representation initially developed for the JAMES robot is being extended to incorporate the full range of information from the input sensors, and how the Interaction Manager is being updated to make use of that extended representation.

HRI'14, March 3–6, 2014, Bielefeld, Germany.
ACM 978-1-4503-2658-2/14/03.
http://dx.doi.org/10.1145/2559636.2559805.

Figure 1: The JAMES bartender

2. REPRESENTING UNCERTAINTY

Within the JAMES system, the task of the Social State Recogniser (SSR) is to turn the continuous stream of messages produced by the low-level input and output components into a discrete representation of the world, the robot, and all entities in the scene, integrating social, interaction-based, and task-based properties. In addition to storing all of the low-level sensor information, the SSR also infers additional relations that are not directly reported by the sensors. For example, it fuses information from vision and speech to determine which user should be assigned to a recognised speech hypothesis, and uses the vision information to estimate whether each customer is currently seeking attention from the bartender [1].

For the initial version of the SSR, the state was represented as a single list of properties and their values, and a fixed confidence threshold was used to decide whether to include any given property into the state. Details of this representation are given in [5], and a sample state excerpt is shown in the highlighted portion of Table 1. This initial representation has since been extended to incorporate two features that the previous version did not exhibit:

- Every relation in the state has an associated **confidence** value, represented as a number between 0 and 1.
- Every relation in the state can potentially have **multiple values**, with each possible value having its own confidence value.

Table 1 shows a full state using this representation. In addition to the old-style state information in the highlighted portion, this state also includes confidence scores on all relations—meaning that the low-confidence lastAct(A1) relation can now be included—and also shows multiple possible values for the drink_order(A1) relation.

Incorporating multiple hypotheses and confidence scores into the state requires additional processing in the SSR. For the vision data, we make use of the information from the JAMES computer vision system [4], which provides a continuous estimate of the location,

seeksAttention(A1)	true	0.75
seeksAttention(A2)	false	0.45
lastSpeaker()	A1	1.0
lastEvent()	userSpeech(A1)	1.0
drink_order(A1)	green lemonade	0.677
	blue lemonade	0.322
lastAct(A1)	greet	0.25

Table 1: State excerpt, showing both the previous representation (highlighted portion) and the new representation

gaze behaviour, and body language of all people in the scene in real time. Every feature reported by the vision system includes an estimated confidence value; these values are incorporated into the state, and also used to determine the confidence value for derived properties such as seeksAttention.

For speech recognition, we make use of the Microsoft Kinect for Windows API [3], which produces an n-best list of recognition hypotheses, each with an estimated confidence score, along with an estimate of the sound source angle and the angle confidence. The recognised hypotheses are parsed to extract the syntactic and semantic information using a grammar implemented in OpenCCG [7], while the source angle is used together with the location information from vision to estimate which of the customers in the scene is most likely to have been speaking. If a possible speaker is found, the semantic information from speech is used to update the lastAct relation. In the case that the customer says something regarding their drink order, we also update the value of the drink_order relation, using the generic belief tracking procedure proposed by Wang and Lemon [6], which maintains beliefs over user goals based on a small number of domain-independent rules, using basic probability operations. This allows us to maintain a dynamically-updated list of the possible drink orders made by each customer in the scene, with an associated confidence value for each order.

3. REASONING WITH UNCERTAINTY

Within JAMES, the Social Skills Executor (SSE) controls the behaviour of the robot system, based on the state updates it receives from the SSR. In previous work, we have shown that strategies for action selection in this multi-party interactive context can be learnt automatically in interaction with a Multi-User Simulated Environment (MUSE) [2]. Using a hierarchical MDP (Markov Decision Process) model, an action selection policy was trained, mapping combinations of state features to the actions that give the highest expected cumulative reward. So far, these policies have been based on features extracted from the previous SSR state representation, which—as described above—does not take into account any information about uncertainty or confidence. In ongoing work, we are extending this approach to produce a model which includes features representing uncertainty information, such as the probability of the top hypothesis, the entropy of the state distribution, and the n-best list of possible drink orders and their confidence scores. The set of possible system actions is being extended to include dialogue acts for clarifying drink orders (e.g., "Did you say 'blue lemonade'?"), as well as clarifying whether or not a customer wants to order in the first place (e.g., "Did you want to order?"). During training, the system should learn automatically when to take the time to ask users for clarifications in order to increase its confidence in the customer's goals, and when to trust its current belief about the customer's goals and proceed with the task—risking lower user satisfaction if that belief turns out to be wrong and needs to be repaired.

In order to learn SSE policies for the system to behave in a manner that is not only socially appropriate, but also robust to the uncertainty arising from noisy audio-visual input, the simulated environment is also being extended. In addition to simulating the behaviour of multiple customers, we are also incorporating an error model based on previously recorded data that produces realistically noisy input signals for the SSR to process. The state updates (including uncertainty information) sent to the SSE based on this simulated input will then correspond more accurately with the updates the SSE can expect when interacting with real users, so the learnt policy is thus more likely to result in better performance in practice.

4. SUMMARY AND FUTURE WORK

We have described how the state representation used in a robot bartender is being extended to deal with various forms of uncertainty about the sensed state, and have shown how the Interaction Manager is being extended to make use of the updated state information. Our approach is similar to that taken in previous spoken dialogue systems, where it has been shown that a combination of belief tracking and reinforcement learning, most notably in the form of POMDP (Partially Observable Markov Decision Process) approaches, leads to more robust system behaviour [10]. In our work, however, we aim to deal with noise not just in the speech hypotheses, but also in the multimodal information provided by the vision system.

We are currently carrying out a user study comparing a version of the bartender that deals with all of the above forms of uncertainty to one that does not. Based on the behaviour of previous versions of the bartender—which did not incorporate any of the uncertainty in the state—we expect to see a positive impact in task performance (i.e., the number of drinks correctly served), since the bartender should clarify lower-confidence or ambiguous state hypotheses before moving on to serving the drinks.

5. ACKNOWLEDGEMENTS

The research leading to these results has received funding from the European Union's Seventh Framework Programme (FP7/2007–2013) under grant agreement no. 270435, JAMES: Joint Action for Multimodal Embodied Social Systems (`james-project.eu`).

6. REFERENCES

[1] M. E. Foster, A. Gaschler, and M. Giuliani. How can I help you? Comparing engagement classification strategies for a robot bartender. In *Proceedings of ICMI*, 2013. doi:10.1145/2522848.2522879.

[2] S. Keizer, M. E. Foster, O. Lemon, A. Gaschler, and M. Giuliani. Training and evaluation of an MDP model for social multi-user human-robot interaction. In *Proceedings of SIGdial*, 2013.

[3] Microsoft Corporation. Kinect for Windows. URL `http://www.microsoft.com/en-us/kinectforwindows/`.

[4] M. Pateraki, M. Sigalas, G. Chliveros, and P. Trahanias. Visual human-robot communication in social settings. In *Proceedings of ICRA Workshop on Semantics, Identification and Control of Robot-Human-Environment Interaction*, 2013.

[5] R. P. A. Petrick and M. E. Foster. Planning for social interaction in a robot bartender domain. In *Proceedings of ICAPS*, 2013.

[6] Z. Wang and O. Lemon. A simple and generic belief tracking mechanism for the dialog state tracking challenge: On the believability of observed information. In *Proceedings of SIGDial*, 2013.

[7] M. White. Efficient realization of coordinate structures in Combinatory Categorial Grammar. *Research on Language and Computation*, 4 (1):39–75, 2006. doi:10.1007/s11168-006-9010-2.

[8] J. Williams, A. Raux, D. Ramachandran, and A. Black. The dialog state tracking challenge. In *Proceedings of SIGDial*, 2013.

[9] J. D. Williams. A belief tracking challenge task for spoken dialog systems. In *NAACL HLT 2012 Workshop on Future directions and needs in the Spoken Dialog Community: Tools and Data*, 2012.

[10] S. Young, M. Gašić, S. Keizer, F. Mairesse, B. Thomson, and K. Yu. The Hidden Information State model: a practical framework for POMDP based spoken dialogue management. *Computer Speech and Language*, 24(2):150–174, 2010. doi:10.1016/j.csl.2009.04.001.

Robot Gossip: Effects of Mode of Robot Communication on Human Perceptions of Robots

Marlena Fraune
Department of Cognitive Science
107 S. Indiana Drive
Bloomington IN 47408
1-262-225-8426
mfraune@indiana.edu

Selma Šabanović
School of Informatics and Computing
901 E. 10th Street
Bloomington IN 47408
1-812-856-0386
selmas@indiana.edu

ABSTRACT

With robots becoming more prevalent, it is important to understand human attitudes toward robots not only when humans directly interact with the robots as most research examines, but when robots are performing nonsocial tasks (e.g., cleaning) within sight and hearing of humans. This study examined how presumed robot communication style in such situations of human-robot co-location affects human perceptions of a group of robots. Results suggest that communication style of robots did not affect perceptions of robots, but further studies should use different techniques to manipulate supposed communication style.

Categories and Subject Descriptors

H.1.2 [**User/Machine Systems**]: Human Factors; K.4.3 [**Organizational Impacts**]: Automation

General Terms

Experimentation, Human Factors.

Keywords

Robots in society, groups of robots, group effects, social robotics, robot communication style, human attitudes toward robots

1. INTRODUCTION

Robots are expected to become increasingly present in the workplace, home, and public [3]. Current research generally focuses on humans interacting with robots directly and one-on-one [1]. With the proliferation of everyday applications of robots in our future, however, we can expect people to come into contact with multiple robots simultaneously. People may not always directly interact with robots, but may be co-located with robots that perform non-social tasks (e.g., cleaning, collecting data). Research has yet to examine how comfortable people will be with robots that are present in their environment, but not engaged with them directly. This study seeks to fill this gap in our knowledge by investigating how people's perceptions of robots are affected by indirect exposure to a group of robots.

When robots act in groups, they may need to communicate with each other, but research has neglected to examine how humans prefer for robots to communicate or if they prefer for robots not to communicate. Furthermore robot communication style may affect human attitudes toward robots. Studies show that when humans cannot clearly hear what others are saying, they show more signs of paranoia and unfriendliness toward those others [7]. Robot communication style may be similarly important because if people think that robots are "talking behind their backs" (e.g., through the Internet or code that the human cannot understand), they may perceive the robots as threatening. Prejudice against outgroup members increases when individuals and groups perceive the outgroup as a threat, and Westerners already tend to believe that robots threaten their identities [5]. Thus, perceived robot communication style may affect prejudice against robots.

If certain robot communication styles remind humans that they do not know exactly what the robots are communicating, this may inflate human discomfort with robots because uncertainty often makes people uncomfortable [2]. People already experience anxieties about robots (e.g., they think that robots will take their jobs) [4]. If certain types of communication styles further inflate negative attitudes toward robots, other communication styles may improve the integration of robots into human society.

The purpose of this study was to examine how the presence of robots and robot communication style affects human attitudes toward robots. Conditions included a no robot (NR) condition and three conditions in which participants were exposed to three iCreate robots with various purported communication styles: No Communication (NC), Silent Communication (SC), in which communication supposedly occurred over the Internet, and Loud Communication (LC), in which robots supposedly communicated through beeps.

We hypothesized that 1) participant attitudes toward robots, from most to least positive, would vary according to condition as NR > NC > LC > SC, and 2) Participants in LC and SC would rate Roombas (similar to the iCreate robots used in the study) less favorably than participants in robot conditions would.

2. METHOD

2.1 Participants

Participants were 55 students (14 participants in each NR, NC, and SC and 13 in the LC condition) aged 18 to 47 ($M = 23$, $SD = 5.217$) with 22 males, recruited via email, poster advertisements, and word of mouth. The study used a between-subjects design.

2.2 Procedure

At least 24 hours before participation, subjects completed the Negative Attitude toward Robot Scale (NARS) to assess general attitudes toward robots before the encounter. The study took place in the living room of the R-House Living Lab, a naturalistic

HRI'14, March 3–6 2014, Bielefeld, Germany
ACM 978-1-4503-2658-2/14/03.
http://dx.doi.org/10.1145/2559636.2559832

research space. Participants sat on the couch and signed the informed consent form. They were told that robots may move around the house collecting data and communicating with each other in a particular manner (depending on condition), supposedly for a sustainability project.

The experimenter left the room, and participants completed surveys on a laptop about their demographic information, including age, gender, race, educational level, occupation, technological expertise, and prior experience with robots. In the robot conditions, three robots, controlled with the Wizard of Oz technique, entered the room approximately one minute after participants began the survey and moved in a pseudo-random manner. The robots paused and beeped while they "collected data" for the remainder of the study. In the LC condition, robots, one after another, made additional beeps between data collection.

The third survey that participants completed was a Semantic Differential Questionnaire to measure their attitudes toward four different robots: Aibo, Geminoid, Kismet, and a Roomba. Participants then completed the NARS again to test for changes (in relation to the pre-survey) in attitudes toward robots. Finally, participants in Robot conditions (NC, AC, and SC) were asked to complete the Godspeed Questionnaire to evaluate their perceptions of the robots they saw. Participants were also asked what they thought the robots were doing and whether they thought the robots acted as a group, independently, or were remotely controlled. Then participants were debriefed and remunerated. The study lasted less than 30 minutes per participant.

3. RESULTS

3.1 Manipulation Checks

Only 8 of 41 participants in the robot conditions (NC, LC, SC) guessed that the robots were controlled remotely. A chi squared test revealed that condition did not affect how participants thought the robots were acting (i.e., independently, as a group, controlled remotely; $X^2(6, 41) = 9.437, p = .150$). Condition related to whether or not participants were correct in answering how they thought the robots were communicating ($X^2(2, 41) = 9.008, p = .011$; amount correct = NC 5/14; LC 10/13, SC 3/14) with the most participants correct in the LC condition. Most participants reported that they thought the robots were communicating aloud (N = 19 versus 8, 7, and 5 for no communication, silent communication, and "don't know" respectively), but this was not statistically significant ($X^2(6, 41) = 10.140, p = .119$).

3.2 Attitudes toward Robots

Overall, condition did not affect attitudes toward robots as measured by the NARS or its subscales ($F(9, 119.404) = 0.485, p = .882$), but attitudes overall became more positive toward robots from the first ($M = 49.187, SD = 1.184$) to second measurement ($M = 45.950, SD = 1.298; F(3, 51) = 15.829, p < .001$, □$^2 = .237$).

Condition did not affect ratings on the Semantic Differential Questionnaire of different specific robots or robots in the media as examined by a repeated measures ANOVA ($F(60, 96.305) = 1.191, p = .220$). Communication style (NC, LC, SC) did not affect participants' perceptions of robots they saw as measured by the Godspeed Questionnaire ($F(10, 64) = 1.195, p = .311$).

4. DISCUSSION

The manipulations did not affect how participants reported to think the robots were acting. More participants thought the robots were communicating aloud than silently or not at all, and this was especially noticeable in the LC condition, in which the robots beeped the most. However, no other differences in guessed communication style were found among conditions, suggesting that the communication style manipulation should be stronger in future studies (e.g., robots in NC and SC conditions might remain silent even when "collecting data.") This lack of participants' differentiation of communication style among conditions may relate to the lack of significant differences found in participant attitudes toward robots among conditions as measured by NARS and the Godspeed and the Semantic Differential Questionnaires. The lack of difference between no-robot and robot conditions suggests that human co-location with nonsocial robots does not affect attitudes toward robots.

Negative attitudes toward robots, measured by the NARS, decreased from the first time the survey was taken (outside the lab) to the second time (inside the lab). Interacting with a robotics researcher in a lab that is decorated with robot posters may have influenced this decrease. Alternatively, thinking about robots between the first and second surveys may have decreased negative attitudes toward robots; studies in human-human interaction show that simply thinking of interacting with outgroup members decreases intergroup anxiety [6]. Future research should test if this decrease remains after the participants leave the lab.

5. CONCLUSION

The presence of robots did not affect participant attitudes toward robots. Robot communication style also did not affect attitudes toward robots, but a stronger communication style manipulation should be tested. Future research should test possible reasons to account for why attitudes toward robots became more positive once participants entered the lab.

6. ACKNOWLEDGMENTS

Our thanks to the IUCRG "Social SLAM" grant, which partially funded this study, and to Katherine Shaw, Matthew Francisco, and Kartik Adur for assisting in the execution of the study.

7. REFERENCES

[1] Bartneck, C., Van Der Hoek, M., Mubin, O., and Al Mahmud, A. 2007. "Daisy, daisy, give me your answer do!" switching off a robot. In *2nd ACM/IEEE Intl Conference on Human-Robot Interaction (HRI), (Mar, 2007)* 217-222.

[2] Epley, N., Waytz, A., and Cacioppo, J. T. 2007. On seeing human: A three-factor theory of anthropomorphism. *Psychological Review, 114*(4), 864-886.

[3] Gates, R. 2007. A robot in every home. *Scientific American*, (Jan, 2007), 58-65.

[4] Geraci, R. 2006. Spiritual robots: Religion and our scientific view of the natural world. *Theology and Science 4*(3).

[5] Kaplan, F. 2004. Who is afraid of the humanoid? Investigating cultural differences in the acceptance of robots. *Intl. J. of Humanoid Robotics*, *1*(03), 465-480.

[6] Turner, R. N., Crisp, R. J., and Lambert, E. 2007. Imagining intergroup contact can improve intergroup attitudes. *Group Processes and Intergroup Relations*, 10, 427-441.

[7] Zimbardo, P. G., Andersen, S. M., and Kabat, L. G. 1981. Induced hearing deficit generates experimental paranoia. *Science*, *212* (4502), 1529-153.

Damping Robot's Head Movements Affects Human-Robot Interaction

Guillaume Gibert, Florian Lance, Maxime Petit, Gregoire Pointeau, Peter Ford Dominey

INSERM U846
Stem-Cell and Brain Research Institute
69500 Bron, France

Université de Lyon
Université Lyon 1
69003 Lyon, France

{guillaume.gibert, florian.lance, maxime.petit, gregoire.pointeau, peter.dominey}@inserm.fr

ABSTRACT

A new research platform has been developed to study human-robot interaction and communication. In this setup, a humanoid robot is used as a proxy between two humans involved in dyadic interactions. An experimenter is bound with a humanoid robot. He can control in real-time and sensor free the eye and face/head movements performed by a humanoid robot with his own movements. The experimenter can perceive the scene as if he was the robot. Manipulations can be applied in real-time to any movement leaving the rest of the dynamics untouched. For instance, we have started investigating the effect of damping head movements during dyadic interaction. Preliminary results show that naive subjects' head nods increase when attenuation was applied on the robot's head movements.

Categories and Subject Descriptors

I.2.9 [**Robotics**]: Kinematics and dynamics, Manipulators, Sensors

Keywords

Wizard of Oz; teleoperation; interaction.

1. INTRODUCTION

Humanoid robots use advanced technologies and theories and are getting more and more complex. Yet, these social agents still fail to be as friendly and natural as a 'real' human in interaction. The main reason of this failure may be due to the extreme complexity of human multimodal communication. To study human-humanoid robot interaction, we developed an enhanced Wizard of Oz (super WoOZ) setup that mirrors some face, eye and head movements on a robot face rather than proposing a set of pre-defined responses as in the traditional WoOZ [1]. Hiroshi Ishiguro and colleagues developed a similar system with an android robot Geminoid HI-1 that can be remotely controlled by teleoperation. A confederate's lips and head movements are cloned on the robot face. The authors have started investigating how real human feel when interacting with this 'almost' human [2]. The main issue is that the confederate perceives the scene as a 3rd person. In our setup, a humanoid robot is used as a proxy between two humans involved in dyadic interactions. An experimenter is bound with a humanoid robot. He can control in real-time and sensor free the eye and face/head movements performed by a humanoid robot with his own movements. The experimenter can perceive the scene as if he was the robot.

We have started investigating the role of head movements during human-humanoid robot interaction with this *super WoOZ* platform. Our experiment followed the study proposed by [3]. In this study, confederates' head movements and facial expressions were manipulated in real-time during videoconference conversations by tracking them and reconstructing an avatar face. Results of this experiment show that increase in amplitude of head nods and lateral head turns in both naïve participant and confederate during dyadic interaction were noticed if attenuation was applied on the confederate's avatar head movements [3]. Our aim was to see if similar interaction loop effect can be created during human-humanoid robot interaction.

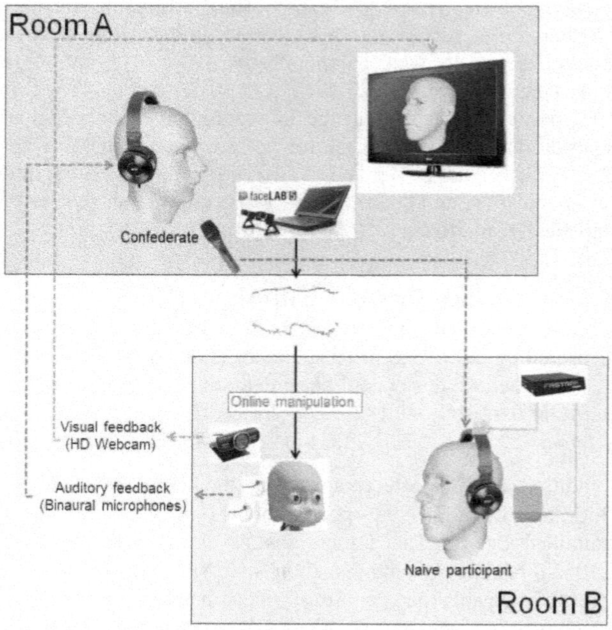

Figure 1: Schematic representation of the super Wizard of Oz platform.

HRI'14, March 3–6, 2014, Bielefeld, Germany.
ACM 978-1-4503-2658-2/14/03.
http://dx.doi.org/10.1145/2559636.2563695

2. METHOD

2.1 Setup

The *super WoOZ* platform consists of:

- a sensor (FaceLab5, Seeing Machines) to determine the confederate's face rigid and non-rigid motion and gaze position at any time;
- a software program to apply online manipulation to specific parameters;
- a humanoid robot (iCub [4]).

A schematic representation of the setup is shown in Figure 1. The FaceLab sensor (Seeing Machines) provides accurate measurement of the confederate's eye gaze and face/head motion. On the robot side, the iCub robot (http://www.icub.org/), a 1 metre high humanoid robot with eyes, head, arms and hands fully controllable in real-time. Between the sensor and the robot, a software program captures the gaze and face rigid and non-rigid motion data from the FaceLab sensor and applies (or not) modifications to the signals before sending it to the robot which mimics the confederate's gaze and head/face motion. The Facelab sensor provides the landmark positions on the face and more specifically on the lips and the eyebrows. This information is used to estimate the movements of the lip/jaw and the eyebrows which are then simulated on the robot face using a set of diodes. In addition, the eye closure was estimated using the FaceLab sensor and replicated on the robot eyelids. The naive participant wears headphones to hear the confederate's voice captured by a microphone remotely. A motion tracking sensor (Fastrak, Polhemus) is attached to the headphones to track his head movements. To bind the user into the robot, the user must sense the scene as if he was the robot. Auditory and visual feedbacks are provided to the experimenter using binaural microphones (MS-TFB-2, The Sound Professionals, Inc.) and a High Definition (HD) webcam (Creative Live Cam Socialize HD).

2.2 Procedure

Three persons participated in the study. Each participant was instructed to freely interact with the iCub robot during 8 to 10 minutes. They were informed that the robot face/head and eye movements were controlled by the confederate's own movements. The robot voice was the confederate's voice. The confederate's head rotations were randomly attenuated by a factor 2 during 4 or 5 periods of 1 minute of interaction. The rest of the time the confederate's head rotations were replicated without modification on the robot. The head movements were recorded synchronously for the confederate and the naive subject at 60 Hz.

3. RESULTS

Preliminary results show the same tendency as already reported in [3] for the naive subject (i.e., increase in head nods in the naive participant during attenuation compared to normal interaction) but not for the confederate. The temporal variation of the different agents' head nods is represented in Figure 2. The amplitude of subject's head nods (angular velocity) increases during attenuation periods (marked as "0.5") compared to normal periods (marked as "1"). We are currently running this experiment on more subjects to assess if damping head movements in human-humanoid robot interaction would create similar interaction loop effect as shown during human-human interaction.

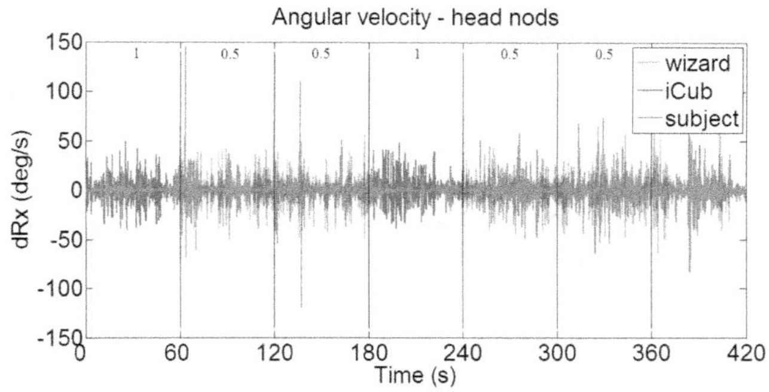

Figure 2: Temporal variation of the angular velocity of the wizard (green), the robot (blue) and the subject (red)'s head nods. During attenuation (0.5) of the robot head movements, increase in the subject's head nods is noticed.

4. CONCLUSION

A new research platform to study human-humanoid robot interaction has been presented. It has been used to study the role of head movements during dyadic interaction. As already reported for human-human interaction, damping head movements affects the interaction. In fact, naive subject interacting with a robot controlled in real-time by confederate's head movements increased their head movements when the robot's head movements were modified.

By manipulating specific movements without modifying the rest of the dynamics, the platform can be used to determine the acceptable limits for the human partner for various parametric manipulations. Several factors will be investigated independently of others: gaze latency, vergence, spatial shifting and head movements synchronization with gaze. Real acceptable limits will be determined by modifying parametrically specific behaviors. These limits may be used to create behavioral models for autonomous robots.

5. ACKNOWLEDGMENTS

This work was supported by the ANR SWoOZ project (11PDOC01901) and FP7 EFAA project (270490).

6. REFERENCES

[1] L. D. Riek, "Wizard of Oz Studies in HRI: A systematic Review and New Reporting Guidelines," *Journal of Human-Robot Interaction* vol. 1, pp. 119-136, 2012.

[2] I. Straub, S. Nishio, and H. Ishiguro, "Incorporated identity in interaction with a teleoperated android robot: A case study," in *RO-MAN, 2010 IEEE*, 2010, pp. 119-124.

[3] S. M. Boker, J. F. Cohn, B. J. Theobald, I. Matthews, T. R. Brick, and J. R. Spies, "Effects of damping head movement and facial expression in dyadic conversation using real-time facial expression tracking and synthesized avatars," *Philosophical Transactions of the Royal Society B-Biological Sciences,* vol. 364, pp. 3485-3495, Dec 12 2009.

[4] G. Metta, G. Sandini, D. Vernon, L. Natale, and F. Nori, "The iCub humanoid robot: an open platform for research in embodied cognition," presented at the Proceedings of the 8th Workshop on Performance Metrics for Intelligent Systems, Gaithersburg, Maryland, 2008.

Asking Rank Queries in Pose Learning

Victor Gonzalez-Pacheco
Universidad Carlos III de Madrid
Av. Universidad, 30, 28911 Leganés, Spain
vgonzale@ing.uc3m.es

Maria Malfaz
Universidad Carlos III de Madrid
Av. Universidad, 30, 28911 Leganés, Spain
mmalfaz@ing.uc3m.es

Miguel A. Salichs
Universidad Carlos III de Madrid
Av. Universidad, 30, 28911 Leganés, Spain
salichs@ing.uc3m.es

ABSTRACT

This paper presents a system in which a robot uses Active Learning (AL) to improve its learning capabilities for pose recognition. We propose a sub-type of Feature Queries, Rank Queries (RQ), in which the user states the relevance of a characteristic of the learning space. In the case of pose learning, these queries refer to the relevance of a single limb for a certain pose. We test the use of RQ with 24 users to learn 3 pointing poses and compare the learning accuracy against a passive learning approach. Our results show that RQ can increase the robot's learning accuracy.

Categories and Subject Descriptors

I.2.6 [**Learning**]: Knowledge acquisition; I.2.10 [**Vision and Scene Understanding**]: Perceptual reasoning; H.5.2 [**User Interfaces**]: Natural language

Keywords

Active Learning; Pose Recognition; Feature Queries; Rank Queries

1. INTRODUCTION

Active Learning enables robots to ask questions to its human teacher after or during the learning session. The advantages of AL are, (i) obtaining better accuracy of the learned concepts, (ii) reducing the number of the training examples required to acquire a concept, and (iii) being preferred by the humans that had to teach a robot [2]. But, despite its advantages, some studies have found that the accuracy of the user's responses might be affected by the robot's queries [5]. In a similar work, Cakmak et al. evaluate how to ask questions that maximize the accuracy of the users' answers [3]. However, we did not found any study that relates the users' answers with the robot's learning accuracy.

We present an AL approach in which a robot learns how to classify poses from a human. We propose the notion of Rank Queries (RQ) as a subtype of Feature Queries [3]. RQ consist in questions that assess the relevance of a learning feature. For instance, in the case of pose learning, an RQ might be "*How much important is your hand to know where are you pointing?*". We performed an experiment in which 24 users trained our robot to learn 3 poses. After comparing the effects of RQ against a passive learner, we found that RQ lead to a significant improvement in learning accuracy, specially when many users trained the robot.

HRI'14, March 3–6, 2014, Bielefeld, Germany.
ACM 978-1-4503-2658-2/14/03.
http://dx.doi.org/10.1145/2559636.2559845.

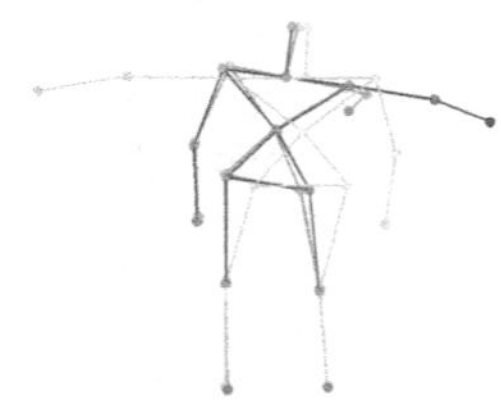

Figure 1: Representation of the 3 poses the users taught to the robot. Each skeleton corresponds to a pose: Blue, *pointing left*; Orange, *pointing forward*; Green, *pointing right*

2. ASKING RANK QUERIES

2.1 Pose Recognition

We use the robot Maggie, a social robot with interaction capabilities [6]. The robot uses a Kinect for RGB-D (Red, Green, Blue - Depth) vision system to capture the user's poses. To interact with humans, Maggie is equipped with a grammar-based Automatic Speech Recognition (ASR) system [1], which enables her to understand natural speech, and a Text-To-Speech (TTS) engine which enables her to communicate by voice.

Our passive pose recognition scheme is the same as described in [4]. The robot detects the user and extracts a skeletonized model from the human. This model consists in a set J of 15 joints $j_i = (x_i, y_i, z_i, q_{x_i}, q_{y_i}, q_{z_i}, q_{w_i} : 1 \leq i \leq 15)$ where x, y, z represent the position of the joint in $\mathbb{R}^3$ and q_x, q_y, q_z, q_w is a quaternion representing its orientation. Fig. 1 shows an example of this model for three different poses. To teach a pose to the robot, the user says the name of this pose while standing at it. The robot's ASR extracts the pose label l and forms the tuple $I_{tr} = (J, l)$,

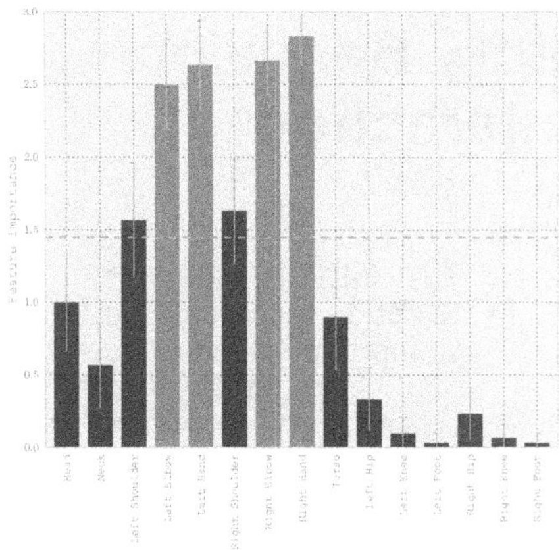

Figure 2: User answers to Rank Queries. In orange, the limbs which were selected by the users.

which is a training instance that is added to a dataset that later is fed to a Random Forest Classifier.

2.2 Active Learning

The novelty of this paper is the use of Rank Queries (RQ) to endow our pose learning system with AL capabilities. The RQs allow the robot to get information of a single feature and rank its relevance. In our case, the robot asks the user for the relevance of a limb. The user answers with a general statement like "*not much*", "*very important*", etc. These answers are mapped into a 0-3 scale, in which 0 means *not important at all* and 3 means *very important*.

After a few questions the robot can establish a threshold that defines which limbs will be filtered out and which ones will be included for learning. For instance, if the user tells that her feet are not important, all the features j_i related to her feet are filtered out. We established a selection threshold T to decide which limbs are filtered and which ones are included. $T = \overline{R} + \sigma_R$ where $\overline{R}$ is the mean of all the user ranks $r = \{r_{head}, r_{neck}, ...\}$ and σ_R is the standard deviation of R.

3. RESULTS

We tested our approach in a preliminary study in which 24 users taught the robot 3 poses (see Fig. 1). After the training, the users were handed a questionnaire that asked them for the relevance of all of their limbs for these poses. Fig. 2 depicts the average of their ranks, the selection threshold T, and the selected limbs (in orange). Fig. 3 shows the learning curves of the F-score retrieved from a Leave-One-Out Cross Validation evaluation, both for a passive learning approach and for our RQ approach. The results show that the RQ approach achieves a performance that is significantly better than Passive Learning with 14 or more training users.

4. CONCLUSIONS

The main contributions of this paper are two-fold. First we presented the notion of Rank Queries for Active Learning in Pose Recognition. These queries consist in an assessment of the relevance of a single feature. The second contribution

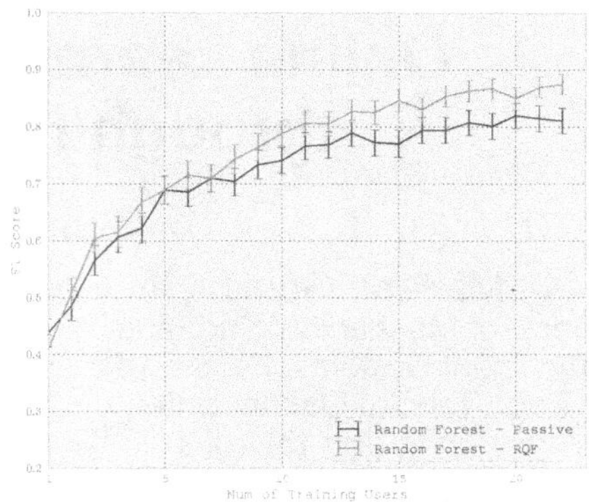

Figure 3: Learning curves of the learning system.

is the a preliminary study of the effects of the answers to RQs in the learning performance of the robot. We observed that RQ may improve the learning performance. However, more research has to be done in order to understand if improvement applies to other poses.

Despite our AL approach is assessed off-line, we believe that the set-up is still valid as a preliminary assessment of the possibilities of this approach and we expect to find that similar positive results in a future an on-line version of our study.

5. ACKNOWLEDGMENTS

The authors gratefully acknowledge the funds provided by the Spanish Government through the project *"Aplicaciones de los robots sociales", DPI2011-26980*

6. REFERENCES

[1] F. Alonso-Martín and M. A. Salichs. Integration of a voice recognition system in a socia robot. *Cybernetics and Systems*, (4):215–245, May.

[2] M. Cakmak, C. Chao, and A. L. Thomaz. Designing Interactions for Robot Active Learners. *IEEE Transactions on Autonomous Mental Development*, (2):108–118, June.

[3] M. Cakmak and A. L. Thomaz. Designing robot learners that ask good questions. In *Proceedings of the seventh annual ACM/IEEE international conference on Human-Robot Interaction - HRI '12*, page 17, New York, New York, USA. ACM Press.

[4] V. Gonzalez-Pacheco, M. Malfaz, F. Fernandez, and M. A. Salichs. Teaching Human Poses Interactively to a Social Robot. *Sensors*, 13(9):12406–12430, 2013.

[5] S. Rosenthal, A. K. Dey, and M. Veloso. How robots' questions affect the accuracy of the human responses. In *RO-MAN 2009 - The 18th IEEE International Symposium on Robot and Human Interactive Communication*, pages 1137–1142. IEEE, Sept.

[6] M. Salichs, R. Barber, A. Khamis, M. Malfaz, J. Gorostiza, R. Pacheco, R. Rivas, A. Corrales, E. Delgado, and D. Garcia. Maggie: A Robotic Platform for Human-Robot Social Interaction. In *2006 IEEE Conference on Robotics, Automation and Mechatronics*, pages 1–7, Bangkok, Dec. IEEE.

Online Learning of Exploratory Behavior through Human-robot Interaction

Manabu Gouko
Dept. of Mechanical Eng. and Intelligent Systems, Faculty of Eng., Tohoku Gakuin Univ.
gouko@tjcc.tohoku-gakuin.ac.jp

Yuichi Kobayashi
Dept. of Mechanical Eng., Graduate School of Eng., Shizuoka Univ.
tykobay@ipc.shizuoka.ac.jp

Chyon Hae Kim
Dept. of Electrical Eng. and Computer Science, Faculty of Eng., Iwate Univ.
tenkai@iwate-u.ac.jp

ABSTRACT

Currently, many studies have been conducted on robot interactions with humans. Object recognition and feature extraction are essential functions for such robots. Discernment behavior is a type of exploratory behavior that supports object feature extraction. We have proposed an active perception model that autonomously learns discernment behaviors. We have shown the effectiveness of our model using a mobile robot simulation. In this study, we applied our model to a real humanoid robot and confirmed that the robot successfully learns exploratory behaviors. We show that the robot can learn suitable exploratory behaviors by online learning applicable to real-world environments.

Categories and Subject Descriptors

I.2.6 [Artificial Intelligence]: Learning—Parameter learning

1. INTRODUCTION

To realize human-robot interactions (HRI), many studies have been conducted using all-purpose robots, which support our everyday activities. If these robots can autonomously recognize surrounding objects, they can perform a wide variety of tasks. In a robot's object recognition system, the data configuration of the category knowledge database plays a crucial role. In this database, a category is composed of a similar object feature set. It is important for realizing HRI that a human and a robot share a category. If a robot could learn its category based on interactions with humans, flexible category formation would be attained (Figure 1).

The strategy used to formulate a category according to robot motion is called active perception, in which the robot actively moves to extract specific object features. Such movements are known as exploratory behaviors.

Several studies have been conducted regarding the realization of active perception in robots [1, 2]; however, in these

HRI'14, March 3–6, 2014, Bielefeld, Germany.
ACM 978-1-4503-2658-2/14/03.
http://dx.doi.org/10.1145/2559636.2563686

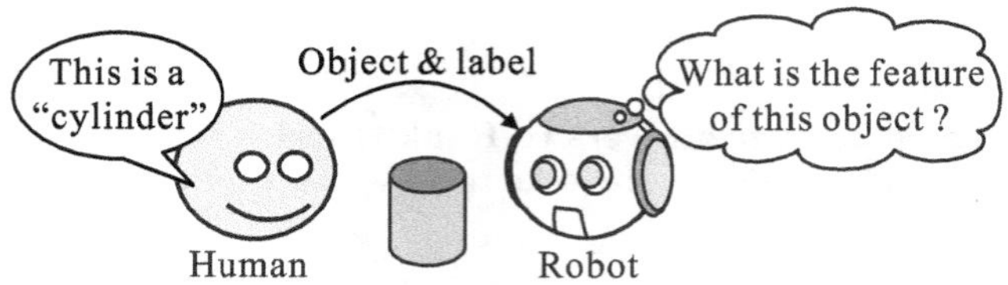

Figure 1: Category learning through human-robot interaction.

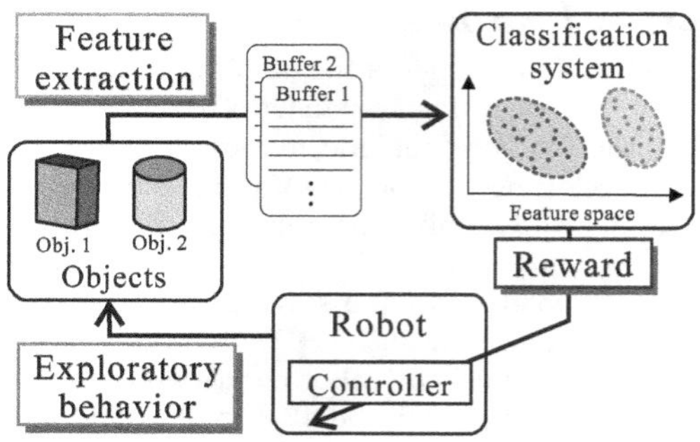

Figure 2: Our proposed model.

studies, exploratory behaviors (e.g., shaking and dropping objects) are designed and specified in advance by researchers and robot designers. To design exploratory behaviors, it is necessary to know the different types of features that can be extracted from target objects. Thus, the robot designers must consider the object's features and the robot's characteristics (e.g., the shape of the robot's body and the types of sensors available) to design such exploratory behaviors.

Unlike the robots in these studies, human beings master and attain exploratory behaviors through interactions and active associations with objects [3]. We therefore propose an active perception model for robots that autonomously learns exploratory behaviors [4]. In our model, multiple objects are successively presented to a robot, and the exploratory behaviors are automatically acquired through interactions between the robot and the objects. Effective feature extraction behaviors are obtained by using reinforcement learning. To show that it is possible to acquire exploratory behaviors, we applied our model to a mobile robot simulation and analyzed the acquired motion patterns.

This study confirms the effectiveness of our model in real-world situations. In this paper, we describe our experiments using a humanoid robot and confirm that it is indeed pos-

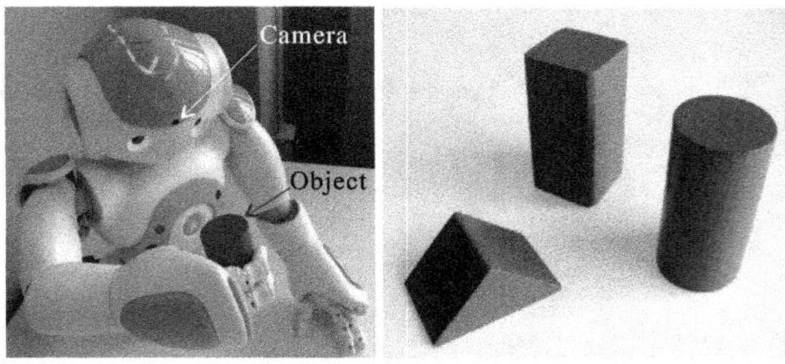

Figure 3: Upper torso humanoid robot Nao (left) and three blocks used in our experiments (right).

sible to acquire exploratory behaviors in a real-world environment using our model.

2. OUTLINE OF THE PROPOSED MODEL

Figure 2 illustrates our proposed active perception model. Our model consists of a robot, a controller, buffers, and a category database representing the feature space. The controller generates the robot's exploratory behaviors, and the buffers temporarily store extracted features of the object in memory. In the feature space, a category is formed by using data from the object features stored in these buffers. Several objects and their label (category) are repeatedly presented to the robot at constant time intervals as the robot learns. In this study, all objects belong to different categories.

Exploratory behavior learning is performed as follows. First, the robot generates and performs actions on the given object and observes the resulting object features as vectors. Second, these extracted features are temporarily stored in the buffers. Third, the form of the category is sequentially updated with the stored features in the feature space. Fourth, a reward for learning is calculated on the basis of the forms of categories and the relative positions of each category. Finally, the controller is updated on the basis of the reward. By repeating this learning process, the behaviors, which increase the differences in features extracted from the different objects, are learned.

3. EXPERIMENT

3.1 Experimental setup

The left side of Figure 3 shows upper torso robot NAO (Aldebaran Robotics). NAO has two cameras and many joints; however, only one camera and two joints of its right hand are used for our experiments. The right side of Figure 3 shows the three objects the robot will encounter.

In this experiment, the robot acquires exploratory behaviors in order to better extract features for distinguishing the different object forms. The robot grasps and moves the objects using its arm; it also observes the object via its camera.

The resolution of color images, captured by the camera, is 320×240. The captured image is translated to a coarse-grained size image. Then, the area encompassing the object is extracted, and the image is changed into a binary image, which is then used as features of the object.

The only joints used for our experiments were the wrist yaw and the elbow roll of the right arm. To simplify the learning task, we assumed that the controller automatically calculates and outputs motor commands when desired joint

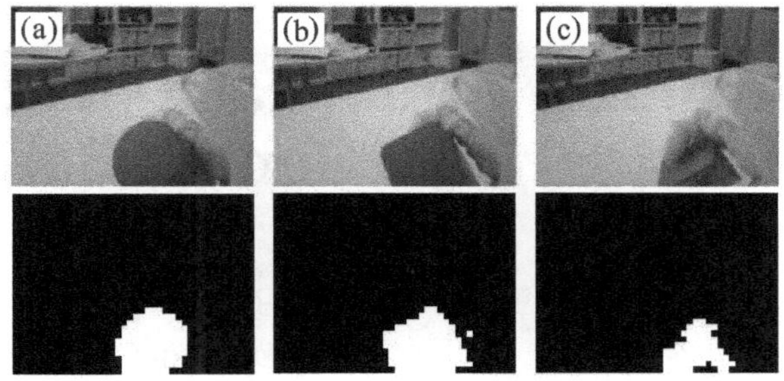

Figure 4: NAO's camera pictures (top) and acquired features for the (a) cylinder, (b) quadrangular prism, and (c) triangular prism.

angles are provided to it. Therefore, learning exploratory behaviors is equivalent to acquiring effective static joint angles to extract adequate features. In our experiments, we utilize Policy Gradient Reinforcement Learning [5], which is one approach to reinforcement learning. During the learning process, we replaced the object grasped by the robot at constant time intervals.

3.2 Results

In our experiment, the robot learned exploratory behaviors for approximately 1 h. Before the learning, any objects didn't exist in the NAO's picture. Figure 4 shows the camera pictures and their acquired features with the corresponding angles of the right arm, which the robot learned. We conclude that the difference between features is especially slight between the quadrangular prism and the cylinder.

4. CONCLUSIONS AND FUTURE WORKS

In this paper, we confirmed the effectiveness of our model in real-world situations. From the results, the model successfully acquired suitable exploratory behavior. In future, we will develop a model which can acquire multiple behaviors by human-robot interaction.

5. ACKNOWLEDGMENTS

This research was partially supported by JSPS KAKENHI Grant Number 24700196.

6. REFERENCES

[1] J. Sinapov, M. Wiemer, and A. Stoytchev. Interactive learning of the acoustic properties of household objects. In Proceedings of 2009 IEEE International Conference on Robotics and Automation, 2518–2524, 2009.

[2] S. Nishide, T. Ogata, J. Tani, K. Komatani, and H. G. Okuno. Predicting object dynamics from visual images through active sensing experiences, Advanced Robotics, 22:527–546, 2008.

[3] E. Gibson. Exploratory behavior in the development of perceiving, acting, and the acquiring of knowledge. Annual review of psychology, 39(1):1–42, 1988.

[4] M. Gouko, Y. Kobayashi and C. H. Kim, Online exploratory behavior acquisition of mobile robot based on reinforcement learning. Lecture Notes in Artificial Intelligence, 7906:272-281, 2013.

[5] R. S. Sutton, D. McAllester, S. Singh, Y. Mansour Policy gradient methods for reinforcement learning with function approximation. Advances in Neural Information Processing Systems, 12:1057–1063, 2000.

Avoiding Robot Faux Pas: Using Social Context to Teach Robots Behavioral Propriety

Cory J. Hayes, Maria F. O'Connor, and Laurel D. Riek
Dept. of Computer Science and Engineering
University of Notre Dame
Notre Dame, IN, USA
{chayes3,moconn13,lriek}@nd.edu

ABSTRACT

Contextual cues strongly influence the behavior of people in social environments, and people are very adept at interpreting and responding to these cues. While robots are becoming increasingly present in these spaces, they do not yet share humans' essential sense of contextually-bounded social propriety. However, it is essential for robots to be able to modify their behavior depending on context so that they operate in an appropriate manner across a variety of situations. In our work, we are building models of context for social robots, that operate on real-world, naturalistic, noisy data, across multi-context and multi-person settings. In this paper, we discuss one aspect of this work, which concerns teaching a robot an appropriateness function for interrupting a person in a public space. We trained a support-vector machine (SVM) to learn an association between contextual cues and the reaction of people being interrupted by a robot across three different contexts. Overall, our results are promising, and further work on integrating context models into social robots could lead to interesting and impactful findings across the HRI community.

Categories and Subject Descriptors

H.1 [**Models and Principles**]: User/Machine Systems

Keywords

social robotics; situational context; human-robot interaction; propriety; multimodal machine learning

1. INTRODUCTION

Context influences people's behavior in human social environments such as workplaces, social events, and home settings [3, 5, 6]. These types of environmental influences lead groups to develop a shared internal sense of propriety which links behaviors with situational parameters. Bar's neurological model of visual context, represented in Fig. 2, proposes an explanation of how this link naturally occurs [1]. In this model, in-depth and computationally intensive processing, such as person and object recognition, occurs simultaneously with top-down low-resolution processing where contextual associations are made based on the scene as a whole.

HRI'14, March 3–6, 2014, Bielefeld, Germany.
ACM 978-1-4503-2658-2/14/03.
http://dx.doi.org/10.1145/2559636.2559834.

Figure 1: A person interacting with our modified Turtlebot, gathering data to model interruptions.

While much research in robotics and computer vision focuses on in-depth processing in object recognition scenarios, little work has been done in taking the quicker, top-down approach. In our work, we use thin-slicing methods to learn one particular contextual association, an *appropriateness function*, based on real-world data collected from a social, mobile robot. This binary function defines a mapping from a sensed context to an appropriateness value for some robot behavior.

Social propriety for robotics is becoming an important issue in the field of HRI [2]. In order for robotic systems to be affordable, adaptable, and acceptable to users, they must be able to conform to their environment without requiring developers to anticipate and develop for all possible contexts. Our work attempts to integrate context in the process of robots learning behavioral propriety.

Our work addresses two research questions. The first is "Can high level contexts be automatically differentiated?" since robots must be able to discriminate between contexts before adapting their behavior. If this is possible, we then ask "Can we use contextual cues to learn an binary appropriateness function for some behavior?". In this work, we propose an appropriateness function to teach a physically embodied robot behavioral propriety after interacting with people in naturalistic contexts.

2. METHODS

We conducted a study in which we used a modified Turtlebot and custom Android application to interrupt and initiate interactions with participants (see Fig. 1). The robot's height was raised to human-level so that it could more easily interact with participants audio-visually via the tablet interface. The robot recorded visual data using a Microsoft Kinect, and audio data using a digital voice recorder. To prevent the robot from toppling over, its motion was fully controlled by a Wizard via line-of-sight. The Wizard also remotely lauched the Android application (which was fully autonomous; it just did not easily integrate with ROS). Because our robot is usually capable of full autonomy for these tasks, we did not simulate operator error [4].

After spotting a potential participant, the Wizard navigated the robot toward the person. Once the robot was in position, the Wizard triggered the interaction screen on the tablet, which consisted of a text-captioned audio prompt of "Hello. Is this a good time to bother you?" If the participant responded "No", the application recorded the response and ended the interaction after thanking the participant. In the case of a "Yes", the robot spoke briefly about the university before ending the interaction in the same manner.

In order to gather data to train an appropriateness function, our robot explored three types of social contexts on our college campus: study areas, dining areas, and lobby areas, across both the student center and library.

Our experiment consisted of two phases. The first phase (learning) involved gathering data from interruptions to train our appropriateness function. The second phase (validation) tested the accuracy of our appropriateness function when the robot was once again placed in these locations.

Each interruption was represented by 10 seconds of data from both the recorded video and audio prior to the interruption. We used one key frame per second to represent the visual component of our audio-visual feature vector, and used each second of audio to represent the other. We then used principal component analysis (PCA) to reduce the dimensionality of each vector. (PCA reduces dimensionality in a lossy way and is analogous to the fast, low-dimension processing referenced in Bar's model [1].) We performed classification using 10-fold cross-validation and a linear SVM.

3. RESULTS

We recorded 60 interactions for the learning phase. We first determined if the features we extracted were sufficient for classifying scenes by context. We achieved an overall classification accuracy of 87.17% for context. Using the same feature vectors as before without knowledge of context, we then trained and tested our appropriateness function for interruption; this resulted in a classification accuracy of 80.5%.

For the second phase, we performed two tests to validate our approach to learning appropriate behavior. The first test used our original data for training and 109 interactions of new data for testing, using the same parameters as before. This resulted in a near-chance classification accuracy (52.11%), which we suspected was in part due to the kernel and parameters used for selection, as well as potential over-fitting and the unseen data problem. Consequently, we then used a polynomial kernel to repeat learning, achieving an accuracy of 85.33%. This was similar to the initial phase, though the validation accuracy dropped to 58.07%.

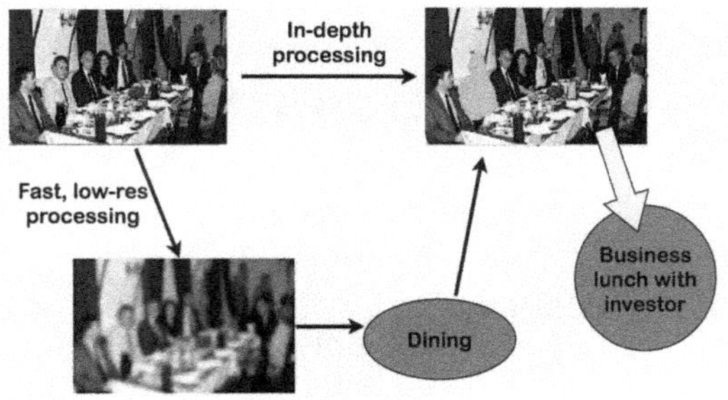

Figure 2: Example of Bar's visual context model.

4. DISCUSSION

While results from the learning stage appeared promising, results from the validation stage suggest that context is too large of a problem space to learn from quickly. These results shed some computational light on the need for a dual-processing system in the brain, predicted by Bar's model [1]. Though the improvement after using a polynomial SVM kernel was not enough to make a large difference, we can see that it is possible to develop more accurate models if the system is able to change parameters, though this would require the automation of the machine learning process and further analysis to determine the optimal classifier.

Context and behavior are indeed linked, and our attempt to use contextual features to classify audiovisual scenes based on propriety was able to predict both the categorical context and appropriateness function for the behavior of interruption. Our initial results show that broad contexts can be learned from extremely noisy data. One clear motivation that our work provides is the consideration of combining both low-resolution and detailed processing streams. However, we first need to learn the associations between these broad contexts and particularly robust identifiable objects and actions.

It is also worth noting all of our data was naturalistic, meaning our results are closer to ecological validity than those based on experiments performed in laboratory settings. This is important for the development of social robotic systems intended to act independently in the "real-world" [5].

5. REFERENCES

[1] M. Bar. Visual objects in context. *Nature Reviews Neuroscience 5*, pages 617–629, August 2004.

[2] A. Fernandez, P. Dios, and J. Sanchez. Robotics perspective. *Service Robotics within the Digital Home: Applications and Future Prospects*, pages 143–160, 2011.

[3] M. Lieberman. Neural bases of situational context effects on social perception. *Social Cognitive and Affective Neuroscience 1*, pages 73–74, September 2006.

[4] L. D. Riek. Wizard of Oz Studies in HRI: A Systematic Review and New Reporting Guidelines. *Journal of Human Robot Interaction*, 1(1):119–136, 2012.

[5] L. D. Riek. The social co-robotics problem space: Six key challenges. *Robotics: Science, and Systems (RSS), Robotics Challenges and Visions*, 2013.

[6] L. D. Riek and P. Robinson. Challenges and opportunities in building socially intelligent machines. *IEEE Signal Processing*, 28(3):146–149, 2011.

Human-Swarm Interaction: Sources of Uncertainty

Sean T. Hayes
Department of Electrical Engineering and Computer Science
Vanderbilt University
Nashville, TN USA
sean.t.hayes@vanderbilt.edu

Julie A. Adams
Department of Electrical Engineering and Computer Science
Vanderbilt University
Nashville, TN USA
julie.a.adams@vanderbilt.edu

ABSTRACT

Human-swarm interaction seeks to significantly increase the number of robots, which also increases uncertainty. Most prior research ignores uncertainty. Sources of uncertainty based on biological swarms are presented.

Keywords

Human-swarm interaction, uncertainty

1. INTRODUCTION

An objective of human-robot interaction (HRI) has been to increase the number of individual robots a single operator can manage (i.e., the human-robot ratio [6]); however, real-world deployments have demonstrated that this objective remains an open problem (e.g., [2]). Recent predictions are that in ten years, military organizations will have ten autonomous robots for every solider [1]. Although robots can keep people safe and away from danger, humans will continue to monitor even fully autonomous robots. The impacts of uncertainty on the human-robot ratio has generally been ignored. Communications or lack thereof, have been previously identified as a potential uncertainty when supervising multiple robots simultaneously (e.g., [5]). However, communications represent only one type of uncertainty. The interaction complexity is exacerbated when developing swarm robotic systems and human-swarm interaction (HSI).

A definition of uncertainty and an outline of categories of uncertainty are presented. The categories were derived from biological swarms in order to inform human-swarm interaction; however, many of the uncertainties also apply to human interaction with multiple robot systems.

1.1 Definitions

Swarms include a "very large" number of individuals, be it a swarm of insects, starlings, or fish. Let a swarm be defined as consisting of ≥ 50 entities and all HRI systems with < 50 entities be considered a multiple robot system.

HRI'14, March 3–6, 2014, Bielefeld, Germany.
ACM 978-1-4503-2658-2/14/03.
http://dx.doi.org/10.1145/2559636.2559827.

Uncertainty represents one's inability to know what the situation is exactly, either because the information is unavailable, not yet determined, highly variable, etc. Uncertainty in HSI is related to attributes of the overall swarm and individual swarm entities that are estimable, inferable, predictable, or unknown depending on the attribute and how the information is obtained. Uncertainty in HSI can exist due to lack of communications; inability to monitor, communicate, or interact with each individual entity; limited or diminished sensing and actuation capabilities; lack of knowledge by individuals; etc.

2. EXACERBATING UNCERTAINTY

A large portion of the HRI and HSI literature makes simplifying assumptions that facilitate the human's ability to interact with the system. As the number of robots increases and systems are deployed in the real-world, system uncertainty increases and these assumptions falter.

Autonomous systems are often assumed to perform perfectly without human intervention; however, robots are very unreliable. Environmental factors can amplify uncertainty. Underwater robot swarms have little to no ability to communicate current status until they surface. Strong waves or winds can move a swarm off course, which may result in autonomous corrective actions unknown to the human.

Reliable or perfect communications is a frequent assumption. Communicating directly impacts the human's understanding of the systems' actions, behaviors and task progress. Common considerations are reduced bandwidth or intermittent communications; however, the swarms' size make communicating all aspects of each individual entity infeasible. Further, the human's cognitive abilities cannot perceive accurately or effectively the massive amount of information, even if all the information can be communicated. Thus, communicated information likely provides an abstract understanding of the entire swarm or a subset of entities.

3. SOURCES OF UNCERTAINTY

Many uncertainties in biological swarms will persist when developing real world robotic swarms. The categories are: physical state, virtual state, and compound state.

3.1 Physical State Uncertainty

Physical state is frequently determined via direct observation, using sensors and includes each entities' position relative to one another, the overall swarm, and the environment. Individual positions often indicate aspects related to leadership, age or size, role, safety from predators, etc. The human's and systems' ability to monitor each individual entity diminishes and uncertainty increases due to the inability to directly measure or observe physical states.

Positional uncertainty relates to the exact position of the swarm and individual entities. Most swarm behavior models leverage attractive and repulsive forces, but these forces vary across swarms and are relative to a localized subset of entities. Multiple uncertainty levels exist based on the proximal distance between entities, the relative position at the local and swarm levels, and attribute-based sorting (e.g., size).

Motion uncertainty is the inability to accurately measure the swarm's and its members' speed and direction. Individual entities often move at different speeds or in different directions. The swarm or the environment can restrict mobility of an individual entity, mobility uncertainty. For example, an entity's inability to change direction quickly enough to move with the swarm as it changes direction.

The aggregation of the swarm creates uncertainty. Swarms are identified as a single unit, but frequently include localized subgroups. Subgrouping may occur based on the group's task, position within the swarm, entity size, role or a combination of factors. Biological swarm members often exhibit behavioral matching based on the localized group's pattern, such that behaviors are synchronized [4]. Autonomous robots may exhibit similar characteristics. The concepts of diffusion and density are related to aggregation uncertainty, both at the localized and swarm levels. Diffusion is the change in an entity's position within the group during group movement, while density represents the range of proximal positioning between the entities.

Other aggregation uncertainties are associated with the overall swarm. Cohesion uncertainty represents the inability to determine the swarm's interaction dynamics that result in unified actions. Movement uncertainty relates to the swarm's degree of rotation; turning rate and variance; and velocity variances. Additional uncertainties include the swarm shape, entity count, and entity failures.

3.2 Virtual State Uncertainty

Virtual states are typically not physically observable, but may be inferred from observations or received via inter-swarm communications.

Many biological swarms have one or more leaders that possess knowledge unavailable to the other members. Many elements are associated with leadership uncertainty [3]. Uncertainty exists with identifying the leader(s) and can influence understanding the swarm's actions. Different leaders may have varying levels of influence in order to achieve the desired goals. Leadership can transition quickly and frequently between entities depending on circumstances and the entity's knowledge. Leadership uncertainty can be exacerbated when the goal is subdivided into sub-goals that result in localized sub-groups in which sub-leaders may arise.

Developing robotic swarms grounded in biological swarm behaviors requires computational models of such behaviors, which may not be directly observable. For example, model variables can result in behavioral uncertainties. If robotic swarm entities change between behavior models in a manner that is difficult to recognize, the uncertainty increases.

3.3 Compound State Uncertainty

Compound states are dependent and derived from both physical and virtual states and; therefore, inherit uncertainty. The uncertainty of goal outcomes is dependent on the certainty of each entity's contribution. Individual entities can inhibit, or negatively impact others' actions and performance in achieving the overall goal.

Leadership also contributes to compound state uncertainties. Uncertainty arises when small individual changes create changes in the swarm leadership. The entities can assess on a continuous basis the cost/benefit of acting as a leader and may change roles, potentially based on unobservable local considerations. Multiple leader situations can create uncertainty depending on leaders' level of cooperation. The distribution of leaders also creates uncertainty regarding their relationship to the swarm's physical states.

Dominance, the power over others in order to obtain self-motivated objectives, also produces uncertainty. Dominance is often thought to relate to leadership, but is usually self-localized and may not influence others' behavior.

Other aspects contribute to compound state uncertainty, including an entity's motivation level, responsiveness to stimuli, and signal interference that impacts signal perception.

4. CONCLUSIONS

Many potential sources of uncertainty and the factors that impact it have been identified based on biological swarm literature. Three categories of human-swarm interaction uncertainties were presented. Many of these concepts also apply to multiple robot systems. Future robot swarms will require human supervision; however, to date the human-robot ratio favors multiple humans to one robot. Better sensor and actuator technology will result in more reliable autonomy, but will not address system uncertainty. Uncertainty is a major hindrance to shifting towards a single human supervising a larger number of robots.

5. ACKNOWLEDGMENTS

This research was supported by ONR Award N000141210987.

6. REFERENCES

[1] S. Gaudin. U.S. military may have 10 robots per soldier by 2023. *ComputerWorld.com*, 2013.

[2] R. R. Murphy, E. Steimle, M. Hall, M. Lindemuth, D. Trejo, S. Hurlebaus, Z. Medina-Cetina, and D. Slocum. Robot-assisted bridge inspection. *Journal of Intelligent and Robotic Systems*, 64(1):77–95, 2011.

[3] D. Pais and N. E. Leonard. Adaptive network dynamics and evolution of leadership in collective migration. *Physica D: Nonlinear Phenomena*, 267:81–93, Jan. 2014.

[4] J. K. Parrish, S. V. Viscido, and D. GrÃijnbaum. Self-organized fish schools: an examination of emergent properties. *The Biological bulletin*, 202(3):296–305, June 2002.

[5] P. Walker, S. Nunnally, M. Lewis, A. Kolling, N. Chakraborty, and K. Sycara. Neglect benevolence in human-swarm interaction with communication latency. *Swarm, Evolutionary, and Memetic Computing, Lecture Notes in Computer Science*, 7767:662–669, 2012.

[6] H. A. Yanco and J. Drury. Classifying human-robot interaction: An updated taxonomy. In *Proceedings of the IEEE Conference on Systems, Man and Cybernetics*, pages 2841–2846, 2004.

Sky Writer: Sketch-Based Collaboration for UAV Pilots and Mission Specialists

Zachary Henkel, Jesus Suarez, Brittany Duncan, Robin R. Murphy
Texas A&M University
College Station, TX USA
{zhenkel, jsuarez, bduncan, murphy}@cse.tamu.edu

ABSTRACT

Sky Writer is a collaborative communication medium that augments the traditional display of a UAV pilot and allows other stakeholders to communicate their needs and intentions to the pilot. UAV pilots engaging in time-critical missions, such as urban disaster responses, often must allocate most of their cognitive capacity towards flight tasks, making communication and collaboration with other stakeholders difficult or dangerous. Sky Writer addresses the needs of stakeholders while requiring minimal cognitive effort from the UAV pilot. The application presents stakeholders with an interface that provides contextual flight information and a live video stream of the flight. Stakeholders are able to sketch directly on the video stream or use a spotlight indicator that is mirrored across all displays in the system, including the pilot's display. The application can be used in any modern web browser and works with traditional and touch devices. Concept experimentation performed at Disaster City with two pilots indicated that the spotlight feature was particularly useful while the UAV was in motion, and the sketching features were most useful while the UAV was stationary. The system will be tested with professional responders soon to determine its efficacy in a simulated response, and to inform the ongoing design process.

Categories and Subject Descriptors

I.2.9 [**Robotics**]: Operator Interfaces

Keywords

Unmanned aerial vehicles; sketch interface

1. INTRODUCTION

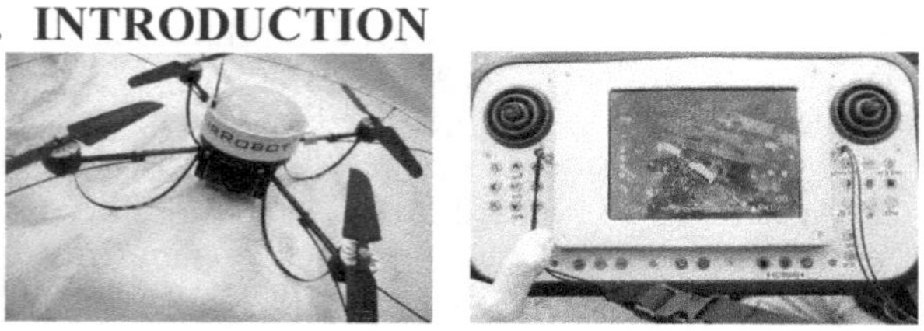

Figure 1. The AirRobot 100-B with its controller.

An important challenge facing UAS teams (composed of a pilot, mission specialist, and safety officer [1]) is conveying information from the various stakeholders to the pilot in a non-disruptive, but informative manner. Figure 1 shows a traditional UAV system, composed of the UAV and the pilot's hand controller. Prior work has enabled stakeholders to have a visual common ground with the pilot by giving them their own dedicated display that mirrors what the pilot sees [2]. Sky Writer extends upon that by enabling the stakeholder to visually convey information to the pilot via sketches and spotlight annotations on the video stream. Additionally, this work adds flight context information, like live mapping, to the stakeholder's display, providing them with more data to inform their directions to the pilot. Finally, Sky Writer is executed in a modern web browser, allowing mirrored displays to be easily deployed to additional stakeholders, who can then see the mission in real time and provide annotation input of their own.

HRI'14, March 3-6, 2014, Bielefeld, Germany.
ACM 978-1-4503-2658-2/14/03.
http://dx.doi.org/10.1145/2559636.2559838

2. INTERFACES

Figure 2. The pilot's interface.

Sky Writer augments the traditional display of the UAV pilot with an interface that can display annotations input by mission stakeholders. Mission stakeholders can use either a sketching feature or a spotlight feature to communicate their needs to the pilot. The system can support several users collaborating on the same flight at a time while ensuring real-time delivery of annotations to both local and remote users. Figure 2 shows the pilot's interface, which can be physically located near or over the original UAV controller.

Figure 3. Sketching on the stakeholder's interface.

The sketching feature (Figure 3) allows users to directly draw on the UAV's video stream. These drawings are pushed to all connected devices, including the pilot's display. This enables mission stakeholders to draw symbols like arrows or circles to indicate areas of interest or communicate intentions such as a rotate symbol. All users of the system may input sketches simultaneously, while viewing other user's sketches in real-time as they are drawn.

The spotlight feature (Figure 4) works by dimming the video feed in all but the areas of the screen being touched or clicked on by a user. The system supports an unlimited number of spotlights simultaneously, which may come from multi-touch input on a single device, or from a combination of devices and users. The spotlight feature is particularly useful because the light is only active while the user's finger or mouse is down, and tracks with their movement in real-time.

Figure 4. Using the spotlight feature on the stakeholder's interface.

Sky Writer includes two separate interface designs, one for the UAV pilot and another for mission stakeholders. While the UAV pilot's interface is designed to mimic the UAV's original display with augmentations for annotation data, the stakeholder interface provides both flight context information and a video stream.

The pilot's interface mirrors the UAV's traditional display in order to provide familiarity and reduce cognitive burden on the pilot. The interface is dominated by the UAV video feed with artifacts and bordered by a few control options. The buttons include the option to clear the annotations, disable collaborative annotations, and the ability to toggle flight data artifacts. The interface can be run on any device that has a modern web browser. Initial inquires were conducted using a 7-inch consumer tablet. Additionally, testing was conducted with the Sky Writer display placed slightly above the UAV's controller display (Figure 5).

Figure 5. The pilot operator control station with Sky Writer tablet mounted on original controller.

The stakeholder's interface includes the same video feed as the pilot's with the same sketch and spotlight overlays, along with buttons to clear the screen, disable sketching, and display video artifacts. The stakeholder can also select between using sketching and using the spotlight feature. The stakeholder inputs annotations by touching or clicking on the video feed. Additionally, the stakeholder's interface presents a map with satellite imagery of the area, and an icon representing the UAV's position and heading. The interface can be run on any modern web browser. Initial inquiries used a 10-inch consumer tablet.

Sky Writer works on both the local network near the UAV deployment and on remote networks if an internet connection is available. This enables real-time collaboration with remote experts.

3. EARLY LESSONS

Early field trials of the Sky Writer interface at Disaster City with two UAV pilots illustrated the ability of the pilot to fly the UAV, while simultaneously observing sketches and spotlight cues input by other stakeholders. Though the pilot was also given the ability to sketch on the collaborative display space, testing showed that pilots preferred to verbally acknowledge visual cues, giving them the ability to maintain hands-on control of the UAV. The spotlight feature was found to be particularly useful, as it did not obscure any of the video feed and team members were able to actively track objects they were interested in, even when the video shifted vantage points. Additionally, testing provided evidence that gestures indicating desired actions like zooming or rotating would be a useful feature. In the tested implementation the team relied on verbal communication to clarify requests for these actions. Initial reviews also suggested that a brief one minute guided tour of the interface's functionality, using a simulated UAV flight, would assist first time users in understanding the abilities of the system.

4. WORK IN PROGRESS

Work in progress includes extending the functionality to include gesture support and a guided interface tour. The system will also be tested with responders and other experts to evaluate the interface in a simulated disaster response.

5. ACKNOWLEDGEMENTS

This work has been supported in part by NSF Grant IIS-1143713 and in collaboration with the Texas A&M Engineering Extension Service. The authors would also like to thank Amit Kumar for his work on an earlier version of this interface.

6. REFERENCES

[1] Murphy, R.R., K.S. Pratt, and J.L. Burke. 2008. Crew roles and operational protocols for rotary-wing micro-uavs in close urban environments. In *Proceedings of the 3rd ACM/IEEE International Conference on Human Robot Interaction*. ACM: Amsterdam, The Netherlands. p. 73-80.

[2] Peschel, J.M., B.A. Duncan, and R.R. Murphy. 2012. Exploratory results for a mission specialist interface in micro unmanned aerial systems. In Proceedings of Collaboration Technologies and Systems. IEEE.

A Doll-type Interface for Real-time Humanoid Teleoperation in Robot-Assisted Activity

Masakazu Hirokawa
University of Tsukuba
1-1-1 Tennodai
Tsukuba, Japan
hirokawa@ai.iit.tsukuba.ac.jp

Atsushi Funahashi
Aichi Human Service Center
713-8 Kagiyacho
Kasugai, Japan
atsushi@inst-hsc.jp

Yasushi Itoh
Aichi Human Service Center
713-8 Kagiyacho
Kasugai, Japan
ya-itoh@inst-hsc.jp

Kenji Suzuki
University of Tsukuba
1-1-1 Tennodai
Tsukuba, Japan
kenji@ieee.org

ABSTRACT

This paper introduces a doll-type interface for real-time teleoperation of a humanoid robot in Robot-Assisted Activity (RAA) for children with Autism Spectrum Disorders (ASD). We developed a prototype of the interface and verified its usability by conducting RAA sessions with children with ASD.

Categories and Subject Descriptors

H.4 [**Information Systems Applications**]: Miscellaneous; I.2.9 [**Robotics**]: Operator interfaces

General Terms

Design

Keywords

Robot-Assisted Activity; Autism Spectrum Disorders; Teleoperation

1. INTRODUCTION

Robot-Assisted Activity (RAA), which is a phyco-educational activity for children with Autism Spectrum Disorders (ASD), is becoming a major topic in the field of Human-Robot Interaction [1]. Since children with ASD are known to show a strong interest in machines and simple mechanical toys, using robots is helpful in arousing the child's interest in participating in the activity. In addition, it is easy to reproduce and repeat the same motion of the robot through programming. Hence, robots are being considered as powerful tools for enhancing conventional autism therapies and for reducing the human workload.

HRI'14, March 3–6, 2014, Bielefeld, Germany.
ACM 978-1-4503-2658-2/14/03.

Most of the previous works on RAA adopted the Wizard of Oz(WO) framework, in which a human operator unbeknown to the participant observes the interaction and controls the robot remotely [2]. In this framework, the behavior of the robot is usually programmed in advance based on the desired interaction scenario, and the human operator then selectively executes one of the behaviors to respond to the participant. Since current technology is inadequate for the development of an autonomous robot that can recognize various social cues from children and then react immediately in an appropriate manner, the WO framework proves to be a convenient tool for enabling the robot to respond to children, without requiring it to possess a high cognitive capability. However, a conventional behavior-based WO framework is not capable of interactions that are not predicted in advance. Additionally, it does not allow the therapist to modify and create the robot's behavior dynamically during an activity. As implied by the term "spectrum," the characteristics of children with ASD, such as their level of autistic tendency and existing skills, tend to differ. Thus, it is important to customize the interaction scenario and the robot's behavior to suit each child's need.

Therefore, in this paper, we propose a doll-type interface for intuitively teleoperating the low-level body motion of a humanoid robot in real time. This interface allows a therapist, who is not knowledgeable about robots, to improvise the behavior of a robot on command during RAA. This would be beneficial for improving the conventional behavior-based WO framework by 1) responding to the unpredictable behavior of children immediately and 2) rapidly adapting the robot's behavior during the interaction to suit each participant.

2. METHODOLOGY

2.1 Doll-Type Interface

To control the whole-body behavior of the robot in real time, we have developed a doll-type input interface, as shown in Fig. 1. This interface has a similar body structure and number of degrees of freedom as the actual robot. oint angles of the interface can be obtained with 100 [Hz], and the action of the robot can be controlled by manipulating the in-

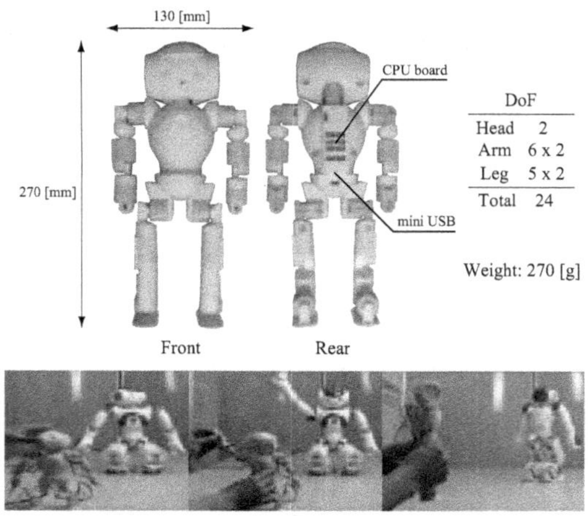

Figure 1: The doll-type interface as an intuitive device to control the whole-body behavior of the humanoid robot Nao. The behavior of the robot can be controlled by manipulating the interface in real time, as shown below.

terface via wireless communication, as shown in the bottom part of Fig. 1. There is another approach that entails using a motion-capture system to teleoperate the whole-body motion of the robot in real time [3]. However, in this approach, all the motions of the operator are automatically reproduced by the robot regardless of the operator's intent. This increases the cognitive and physical load on the human operator who performs the robot's behavior at all times during the interaction. Moreover, since a motion-capture system is expensive and requires a large amount of space, using it in a practical environment such as school or hospital is unrealistic. For this reason, a small low-cost interface for manipulating the robot's motion is necessary for the practical implementation of RAA.

2.2 Semi-Autonomous Balance Control

However, it is obvious that straightforward reproduction of input motion by the robot without considering balance causes it to fall easily. To avoid this, we have implemented a balancing control algorithm based on the method proposed by Sugihara et. al. [4], which calculates joint angles and can apply an appropriate acceleration to the robot's center of gravity (CoG) in order to stabilize the balance while minimizing the differences between the implemented joint angles and angles commanded by the user through the interface, as shown in Fig. 2.

3. PRELIMINARY EXPERIMENT

As a preliminary experiment, we conducted three RAA sessions with six children diagnosed with ASD (six males) at 1.5$\sim$2-months intervals. Each participant was allowed to play freely with a robot in a playroom for 10 $\sim$ 15 min, and the robot was teleoperated by the experimenter from an observation room beside the playroom. The interaction between the participant and the robot was recorded by cameras for post-analysis.

Throughout all sessions, none of the participants showed a negative response to the robot, and some children displayed face-to-face communication with eye-contact behavior, and helping behaviors such as helping the robot to stand up when

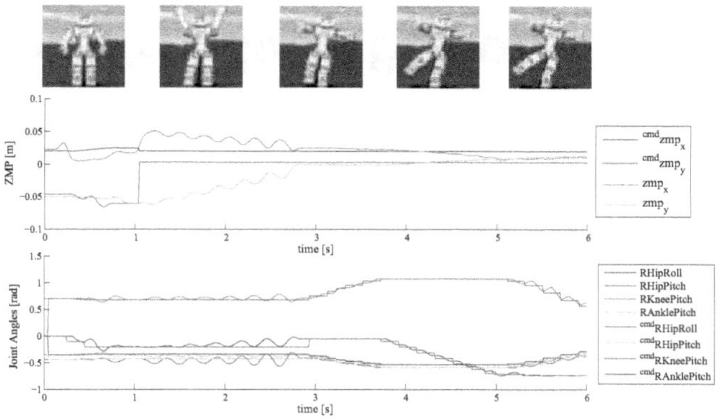

Figure 2: Demonstration of semi-autonomous balancing control. The algorithm calculates appropriate joint angles of the robot in order to keep the robot's balance while simultaneously reproducing the input posture as precisely as possible.

it fell down. In addition, although participants with ASD showed various approaches of interacting with the robot, the robot was able to respond to the participants appropriately in most of the cases.

4. CONCLUSION

We proposed a doll-type interface for real-time teleoperation of a humanoid robot in Robot-Assisted Activity for children with ASD. By using this interface, a therapist can improvise robot behavior at the moment they want by manipulating the interface without programming behaviors in advance. This is useful for responding to the unpredictable behavior of children and allows the therapist to explore improved interaction scenarios based on characteristics of each individual. To verify the usability and potential of the proposed method, we conducted RAA experiments with children with ASD. For future work, we are going to analyze the data obtained in the preliminary experiment to evaluate the proposed method quantitatively. Results of the analysis will be described in a follow-up report.

5. REFERENCES

[1] D. . Ricks and M.B. Colton. Trends and considerations in robot-assisted autism therapy. In *Robotics and Automation (ICRA), 2010 IEEE International Conference on*, pages 4354–4359, 2010.

[2] Serge Thill, CristinaA. Pop, Tony Belpaeme, Tom iemke, and Bram Vanderborght. Robot-assisted therapy for autism spectrum disorders with (partially) autonomous control: Challenges and outlook. *Paladyn*, 3(4):209–217, 2012.

[3] D. Matsui, T. Minato, .F. MacDorman, and H. Ishiguro. Generating natural motion in an android by mapping human motion. In *Intelligent Robots and Systems, 2005. (IROS 2005). 2005 IEEE/RSJ International Conference on*, pages 3301–3308, 2005.

[4] T. Sugihara and . Nakamura. Whole-body cooperative balancing of humanoid robot using cog jacobian. In *Intelligent Robots and Systems, 2002. IEEE/RSJ International Conference on*, volume 3, pages 2575–2580 vol.3, 2002.

Controlling a High Speed Robotic Hand Using a Brain Computer Interface

Stephen Huang
University of Calgary
2500 University Dr NW
Calgary, AB Canada
403-282-5597
sthuang@ucalgary.ca

Alejandro Ramirez-Serrano
University of Calgary
2500 University Dr NW
Calgary, AB Canada
403-220-3632
aramirez@ucalgary.ca

Categories and Subject Descriptors
B.8.0 [**Hardware**]: Performance and Reliability - *General.*

Keywords
BCI, Robotic Hands, High Speed Control

1. INTRODUCTION
Advanced robots call for intuitive user interfaces to reduce the complexity when interacting with them. One solution is using brain-computer interfaces. A brain-computer interface (BCI) is a device that allows direct communication between the brain and external devices such as computer video games.

Complex movements like gripping soft objects, pinching and independent thumb control have been achieved [5]. Despite this progress, movements in these hands are slower than speeds achievable by an average human hand. This paper explores controlling a robotic hand stronger and faster than a human hand using a BCI. By eliminating the use of haptic devices to control an external device, it is hypothesized that one can achieve better and more accurate results than all other human operated controllers for robotic hands.

2. RELATED WORKS
Little work has been done to connect a BCI to robotic hands with intentions of high-speed movement. However, much work has been done trying to achieve movements as dexterous and precise as the human hand.

Outside of traditional control mechanisms (e.g. PID, Fuzzy logic), it has been widely assumed that dexterous hand movements were only possible with invasive techniques, such as EEG implants within the brain [1]. J. Wolpaw and D. McFarland claim dexterous movement is possible with external BCIs and the need for invasive techniques is not necessarily better. It has been shown that results are comparable to those with invasive BCIs with respect to precision, accuracy and response times [1]. Since Wolpaw and Mcfaland's publishing in 2004, the market for BCIs has grown vastly. Many non-invasive commercial products are now available, each unique in price and accuracy. Little information comparing non-intrusive and intrusive BCIs is available. However, Astaras et. al. have considered several commercial products in their work [2]. In [2] a portable robotic arm interface comparable in size, dexterity, speed, and fluidity to the human arm at relatively low cost was developed. It is currently being further developed into a hybrid BCI system for comparative experiments with human arms focusing the analysis on movement speeds. Although their arm does not have a hand component, the comparative study plans to directly compare the speed of the human arm to a BCI controlled arm.

The greatest limiting factor in the human reaction is in the muscles. Nerve impulses from the brain to any given muscle can reach up to 119 meters/second [6].

A very relevant advancement is the mapping of fast and slow motor control in the brain using EEG-based classification. By identifying these spaces in the human brain, it is believed that more refined control of movement speed in BCIs is possible [3].
In addition, it is established that an average of 108 ± 12 bits/min can be transferred over EEG BCIs [4]. Speeds at this rate show potential for high-speed data transfer and support our hypothesis.

3. OUR APPROACH
3.1 Materials and Methods
A non-intrusive, low cost (under $3,000) commercial dry electrode BCI headset was chosen. The Emotiv EPOCH integrates the largest number of sensors at the highest sampling rate among all portable low-cost BCI headsets available [2]. The drawback of this device is the occasional unreliability of signal quality primarily associated with the use of dry electrodes; this is remedied by adding saline solution to each electrode. The device has 16 biopotential sensors and is developed to accommodate most users. The EPOCH recognizes the patterns associated with specific conscious thoughts. A specific set of these thoughts is pre-mapped to an action ("push", "pull", etc). When a thought is detected, the raw data is transferred to a computer. The data is then translated to an action and relayed to a robotic arm.

The robotic hand, developed by the AR^{2}S lab at the University of Calgary, has three 3 DOF fingers and an arm. It simulates an average humans arm by closely mimicking its size and joint movements. The hand, however, differs from the human arm in strength and speed. Each finger can exert forces greater than the human hand and can carry 3 lbs fully extended. Each joint moves 180 degrees in 1/10 of a second. We define high speed as any movement that can move full motion faster than ½ second. The hand itself has 9 DOF. The arm and wrist add an additional 6 degrees.

In the first stages of development, research focused on the movements of the hand. To simulate the motion of the hand a

HRI'14, March 3–6, 2014, Bielefeld, Germany.
ACM 978-1-4503-2658-2/14/03.
http://dx.doi.org/10.1145/2559636.2559847

computer program was developed. The program is responsible for mapping conscious thoughts to an action.

In order to simulate the natural motion of a hand, joints are moved in conjunction with each other. One thought will, for example, close all fingers. This type of movement is very similar to how humans move and is viable for achieving high-speed movement.

3.1.1 Unique Thoughts

Each user's brain develops and grows in different ways. This leads to unique neural pathways within the brain and because of this, the brain signals sent by each user will originate from different locations in the brain changing its end location on the scalp. In addition, interpretations of thoughts are unique for each person. To address this problem, the developed software creates unique user profiles. This study focuses primarily on thoughts of actions. For example, if a user were to think of "pushing", one might think of pushing a car down a road, while another may think of a box fading off into the distance. Since the software is controlling a robotic hand, the conscious thoughts are restricted to specific actions (such as open, pull, etc.). For every action, the profile contains multiple recorded signals from the user. To get the signals the user must initially record them, a process described here as the "training" phase. After the training phase is complete, the program can then begin interpreting signals. Whenever a user thinks, the brain signals are then compared to the recorded signals in the profile. If they correlate enough with data in the profile, the software relays information to move the hand. The EPOCH headset and its driver software have predetermined the acceptable level of correlation.

4. PRELIMINARY TESTING

This study focuses on the accuracy and response times of the EPOCH headset and will be conducted over the course of the next semester. The study will consist of approximately 20 healthy adult individuals. Each user will be given a short, 10 minute tutorial on how to operate the headset and was given an additional 20 minutes to try and move a 3D virtual cube. The cube can be manipulated in 12 different motions. The "skill" of the user is determined by three factors:

1. The users ability to consistently perform a motion

A user who can perform an action consistently for 10 full seconds is given a full accuracy score of 100%. Nine seconds is given 90% and so on. The software detects the accuracy of the thought by comparing it to the recorded signals in the users profile.

2. The number of motions a user can achieve.

A user is only allowed to attempt multiple actions if they are able to perform a single action with a consistency of 30% (3 seconds)

3. Time to perform an action.

Each user is asked to perform an action. Using a stopwatch, response time is measured between saying "go" and when the cube moves.

To avoid false positives, any motion where the action cannot be held consistently for 3 seconds will be discarded.

4.1.1 First Results

The experiment was performed with a preliminary group of three users. It was discovered that controlling the cube is heavily based on skill and that practice improves results. Two users were able to achieve one action, with accuracy of 70% and 50%. The third user could not successfully perform any actions.

It was noted that novice users tried to strain and physically move the system by clenching their jaw, tightening their brow and straining the neck. With more practice, users gained the most success by remaining very relaxed. By straining, the body adds additional signals, conflicting with the thoughts intended for the system. During the preliminary trial, users noted that most thoughts were almost subconscious. Thinking words ("push push push push") did not work. Consistent training (recording signals for the user profile) was extremely important. Preliminary participants were not attributed scores. Their participation will be used to establish a specific scoring system.

4.1.2 Visualization Techniques

It was discovered that certain visualization techniques provide better results for the system. Some of the most successful were:

1. Imagine a ball of fluid in the center of your brain and for PUSH, gently squeeze it forward through some imaginary bars behind your eyes.
2. A trick the developers have found is to make a physically significant action with your hand while keeping the rest of the body relaxed.
3. One user said he tried to focus on one half of his body then the other. "This worked almost instantly for me."

4.1.3 Continuing

Experiments with a much larger user group will be performed. Since signal transmission is skill based, users will be ranked on the basis of skill. In order to find the capabilities of BCIs, the highest ranked users will be used to test the movement of the high-speed robotic hand.

5. CONCLUSIONS

A successful and fully functional computer program was created in order to interface a robotic hand with a Brain Computer Interface. It was discovered that transmitting signals is very skill based and can improve over time with practice and dedication.

6. ACKNOWLEDGMENTS

Our thanks to the AR^{2}S Lab.

7. REFERENCES

[1] Wolpaw, J.R. and Mcfarland, D.J., 2004. Control of a two-dimensional movement signal by a noninvasive brain – computer interface in humans. , 101(51).

[2] Astaras, A., Moustakas, N., Athanasiou, A. and Gogoussis, A., 2013. Towards Brain-Computer Interface Control of a 6-Degree-of-Freedom Robotic Arm Using Dry EEG Electrodes. , 2013.

[3] Bowman, M., Debray, S. K., and Peterson, L. L. 1993. Reasoning about naming systems. *ACM Trans. Program. Lang. Syst.* 15, 5 (Nov. 1993), 795-825. DOI= http://doi.acm.org/10.1145/161468.16147.

[4] N. Moustakas, Design and construction of a robotic arm capable of movement with 6 degrees of freedom and an exoskeleton sensor harness for its control [M.S. thesis], Alexander Technological Educational Institute of Thessaloniki, Sindos, Greece, 2011.

[5] Man Controls Robotic Hand with Mind - Youtube. 2013[ONLINE] Available at: http://www.youtube.com/watch?v=ppILwXwsMng. [Accessed 05 August 2013].

[6] The Speed of Neurons. 2013[ONLINE] Available at: http://hypertextbook.com/facts/2002/DavidParizh.shtml. [Accessed 01 August 2013].

Entrainment Effect Caused by Joint Attention of Two Robots

Takashi Ichijo
School of Engineering,
Hokkaido University, Japan
ichijo@complex.ist
.hokudai.ac.jp

Nagisa Munekata
Graduate School of
Information Science and
Technology, Hokkaido
University, Japan
munekata@complex.ist
.hokudai.ac.jp

Kazuo Hiraki
Graduate School of Arts
and Sciences,
The University of Tokyo,
Japan
khiraki@idea.c
.u-tokyo.ac.jp

Tetsuo Ono
Graduate School of
Information Science and
Technology, Hokkaido
University, Japan
tono@complex.ist
.hokudai.ac.jp

ABSTRACT
In this study, we investigate the two effects of joint attention, *building relationships* and *sharing recognition*, in group interaction consisting of two robots and one person. The *building relationship* is focused on entrainment resulting from the two robots' gazing at one person, while the *sharing recognition* refers to an original effect of the joint attention in a group interaction featuring the shared focus of individuals on one object. Results of experiments on the *building relationships* aspect showed that when two robots gazed at a person, he/she tended to be more immersed in communication with the robots. In the case of *sharing recognition*, when the two robots gazed at the target synchronously, the person could share it more correctly than when it was done asynchronously.

Categories and Subject Descriptors
I.2.9 [**Artificial Intelligence**]:Robotics

General Terms
Experimentation, Verification

Keywords
Joint Attention, Two Robots, Attention Entrainment

1. INTRODUCTION
Joint attention is an indispensable factor to communicate smoothly because the gaze of each person is important in expressing one's intention in group interaction [1]. In the future, robots will coexist with humans in society, but there are limits to what robots can do to support humans on a one-to-one basis. Robots, therefore, are required to work for groups of people. In group interaction, there are some socially essential organizations and rules based on the mechanism of joint attention [2]. In other words, joint attention can significantly affect such social factors.

In this study, we focus on two effects of joint attention, *sharing recognition* and *building relationships* in group interaction (Fig. 1). First, *sharing recognition* is an original effect of joint attention. In this effect, people share the focus of individuals on an object. In joint attention with three or more persons, the intersection of the lines of sight occurs. Therefore, we conclude that it is easy for people to recognize the target correctly due to the intersection.

HRI'14, March 3–6, 2014, Bielefeld, Germany.
ACM 978-1-4503-2658-2/14/03.
http://dx.doi.org/10.1145/2559636.2559851

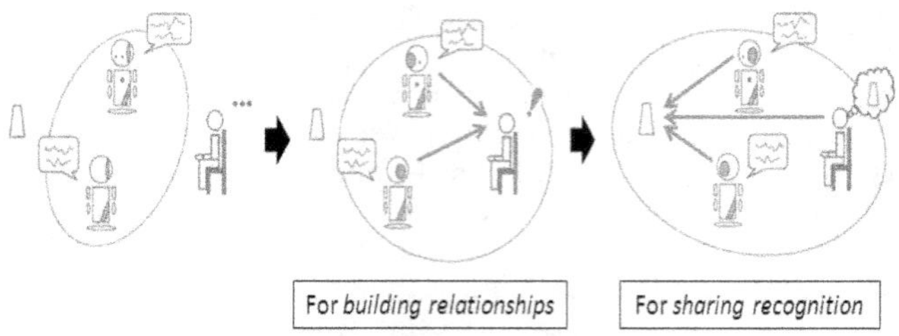

Fig. 1 Outline of this study.

Second, *building relationships* is focused on the entrainment of communication. In everyday life, we often communicate with people in groups. If another person intervenes, members of the group will jointly gaze at him/her to determine who it is. After that, he/she is entrained into the group without feeling there is anything amiss. Therefore, the effect of *building relationships* in joint attention is important for entraining and immersing a person in the group.

In this study, we initiate joint attention using two robots and investigate joint attention from the two aspects of *sharing recognition* and *building relationships* in group interaction consisting of two robots and one person.

2. EXPERIMENT
We performed two experiments in this study. Experiment 1 focused on the effect of *building relationships*. We set up two conditions in this experiment. In Condition 1-A, after two robots jointly gazed at a participant, they shifted their gaze to the same object. We then determined whether the participant followed the robots' line of sight and was immersed in communication with the robots. In Condition 1-B, the robots did not gaze at the participant and we determined whether the participant followed their gazes when they shifted to the same object.

Experiment 2 focused on the effect of *sharing recognition*. We set two robot behaviors for joint attention. In Condition 2-A, two robots gazed at the same target *synchronously*, and in Condition 2-B, the two robots gazed at the same target *asynchronously* with a delay of 1.17 sec. In this experiment, we determined whether the participant correctly identified the target at which the robots gazed.

We used the following environment for both experiments (Fig. 2). We placed two robots (Robovie-R) across the field of view of one participant wearing SMI eye tracing glasses [3]. A table 2 m in front of the participant displayed 10 differently colored objects at 30 cm intervals in two rows. To simulate natural personal space [4], we set the distance between robots to 1.2 m and the distance between the participant and the robot to 1.2 m. Twenty participants were asked to take part in the experiments (male: 17, female: 3) .

Fig. 2 Experiment environment.

2.1 Experiment 1

The procedure used in experiment 1 was as follows. We did not inform the participants that the two robots would gaze at the object.

1. Two robots were face to face with each other and talked in an artificial language that the participants could not understand.
2. In Condition 1-A, the two robots gazed at the participant. In Condition 1-B, the two robots did not gaze at the participant and maintained their conversation.
3. The two robots gazed at the same object on the table.
4. After joint attention, the two robots returned to face to face conversation.
5. After the end of the conversation, we gave each participant a questionnaire.

In the questionnaire, participants were asked to guess 1) the color of the object that had been the target of conversation and 2) the content of the conversation.

2.2 Experiment 2

The procedure used in experiment 2 was as follows. We informed the participants that the two robots would gaze at the same object.

1. Two robots took on joint attention behaviors *synchronously* (Condition 2-A) or *asynchronously* (Condition 2-B).
2. The participant watched the joint attention and guessed which object the two robots gazed at. When the participant decided the object, he/she verbalized the object's color.
3. The above procedure was repeated 13 times.
4. After the procedures were finished, we gave each participant a questionnaire.

In the questionnaire, participants were asked to describe their feeling and whether there was any difference between *synchronization* and *asynchronization*.

3. EXPERIMENTAL RESULTS

In experiment 1, regardless of Condition 1-A or 1-B, all participants' gazes were induced to the object at which the two robots gazed. Participants in Condition 1-A tended to follow the gaze of the two robots more than those in Condition 1-B ($p < .05$, Fig. 3). In addition, participants in Condition 1-A were better at guessing the content of the conversation associated with the object. And in Condition 1-B, some participants who guessed it unrelated to the object were confirmed. Overall, the participants in Condition 1-A tended to be more immersed in communication with the robots.

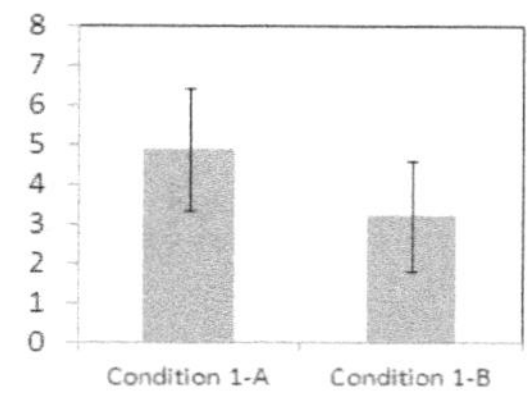

Fig. 3 Number of participants following robot's gaze (experiment 1).

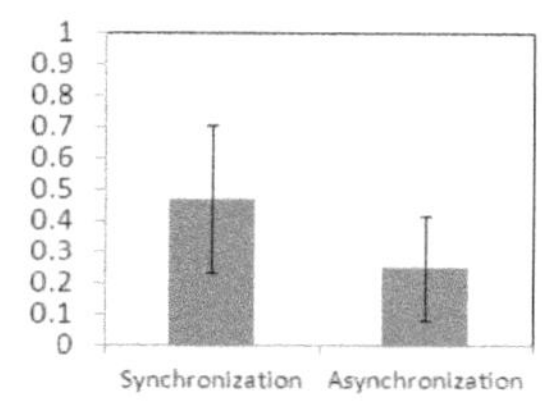

Fig. 4 Percentage of correct answers (experiment 2).

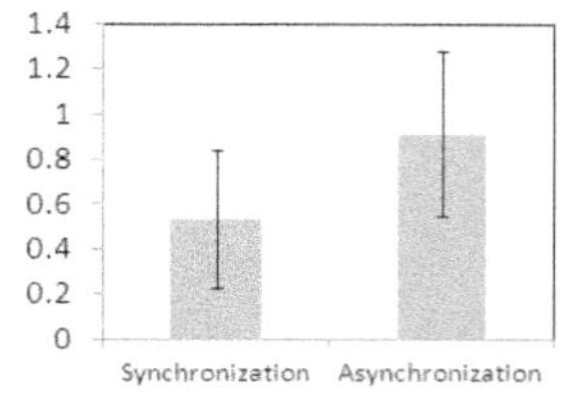

Fig. 5 Distance between object at which robots gazed and that participants guessed (experiment 2).

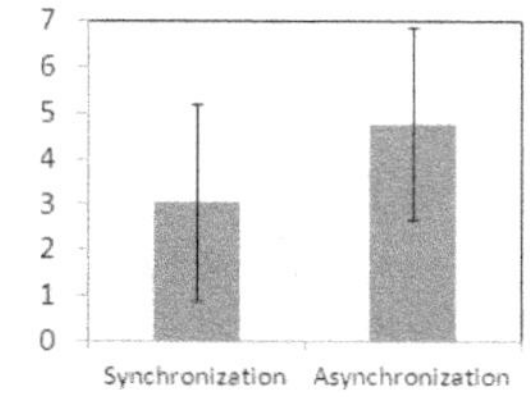

Fig. 6 Degree of participants feeling a sense of easiness with synchronization and asynchronization (experiment 2).

Next, in experiment 2, the participants in Condition 2-A were better at guessing the target more correctly ($p < .01$, Fig. 4). This is also evidenced from the distance (the number of objects) between the correct object and the object that participants guessed ($p < .01$, Fig. 5). However, in the questionnaire, participants felt a storong impression of difference and answered that Condition 2-B was more easy to understand ($p < .05$, Fig. 6). It can be said that there are distinctive characteristics of the two factors in both conditions of experiment 2.

4. CONCLUSION

In this study, we investigated joint attention by two robots from the aspects of *building relationships* and *sharing recognition*. Significant difference between the joint attention behavior in *synchronous* and *asynchronous* behavior was obtained, but the results showed distinctive characteristics in both behaviors. We also found that when two robots gazed at a person, he/she tended to be more immersed in communication with the robots. In our future work, we intend to clarify the reasons for the significant difference between the *synchronous* and *asynchronous* behaviors.

5. REFERENCES

[1] Y. Matsusaka, T. Tojo, and T. Kobayashi: Conversation Robot Participating in Group Conversation, IEICE Transactions on Information and Systems, Vol.E86-D, No.1, pp. 26-36 (2003).

[2] D. Katagami, H. Ohmura, and K. Nitta: Investigation of Social Adaptive Skills by Crosscultural Simulation Game and KiSS-18, IEEE International Conference on Fuzzy Systems (FUZZ-IEEE) on IEEE World Congress on Computational Intelligence, pp.2084-2089 (2010) .

[3] M. M. Hoque, T. Onuki, E. Tsuburaya, Y. Kobayashi, Y. Kuno, T. Sato, and S. Kodama: An Empirical Framework to Control Human Attention by Robot, Computer Vision - ACCV 2010 Workshops, pp.430-439 (2011).

[4] J. Mumm, and B. Mutlu: Human-robot proxemics: physical and psychological distancing in human-robot interaction, {Proceedings of the 6th International Conference on Human-Robot Interaction}, pp.331-338 (2011).

Towards a Serious Game Playing Empathic Robotic Tutorial Dialogue System

Srinivasan Janarthanam, Helen Hastie, Amol Deshmukh, Ruth Aylett
School of Mathematical and Computing Sciences
Heriot-Watt University
sc445,h.hastie,a.deshmukh,r.s.aylett@hw.ac.uk

ABSTRACT

There are several challenges in applying conversational social robots to Technology Enhanced Learning and Serious Gaming. In this paper, we focus in particular on the dialogue management issues in building an empathic robotic tutor that plays a multi-person serious game with students to help them learn and understand the underlying educational concepts.

Categories and Subject Descriptors

I.2.11 [**Intelligent Agents**]: [Dialogue management]

Keywords

Dialogue management, Empathic robotic tutor, Serious games, Tutoring systems

1. INTRODUCTION

Serious games are educational games that provide learning content to players in addition to entertainment [1]. Such games have shown to be very effective in helping players to learn new concepts in particular those that are able to adapt to the users and their context. Our objective is to build an empathic robotic tutoring environment where multiple participants collaborate with a robotic tutor playing a serious game on a large touch-table to learn about environmental issues. This learning environment is set apart from traditional Intelligent Tutoring Systems (ITS) in that the robot has the ability to indicate intention to interact and can make use of gaze, mutual eye contact and other ostensive signals (such as pointing) that have been shown to improve learning [2].

In this environment, we hope to test a number of dialogue strategies that look to optimise student learning gain and engagement by taking into account the student's state, the game state, the pedagogical goals of the robotic tutor as well as the dialogue context. In this paper, we will examine the issues related to development of these dialogue strategies as part of the dialogue manager module.

HRI'14, March 3–6, 2014, Bielefeld, Germany.
ACM 978-1-4503-2658-2/14/03.
http://dx.doi.org/10.1145/2559636.2563707.

2. THE GAME

The serious game adopted here is called Enercities[1] and focuses on environmental issues such as sustainability and energy use. This on-line game has been adapted into a 3-player game where each student plays a role of either the Mayor, Economist or Environmentalist. Players have to work collaboratively to grow and sustain the city for as long as possible and in doing so, hopefully, learn how the environment, economy and citizen's happiness affect each other and thus instigate behaviour change in the students.

3. DIALOGUE MANAGEMENT

Dialogue management is the task of managing the conversation between the system and its users, deciding what to say when. We aim to design and implement a dialogue manager (DM) that will interleave pedagogical and game conversations optimally, taking inputs from other modules such as the game module, learner module, and affect recognition module. It will produce dialogue actions, that will be translated into utterances and gestures by the Behaviour Generation module. The embodied robot will then present these to the players as a combination of head/body movements, diectic pointing gestures and spoken utterances.

3.1 DM state

The DM state is the context based on which the DM decides which moves to make and when to make them. This includes the following information: game state, user affective state, user pedagogical state and the dialogue state. The game state will include the state of the game, environment, economy and citizen scores, etc. The affective state of the user informs the system about the emotional state of the user(s), e.g. happy, sad, confused etc. and how engaged he/she is in the game. The pedagogical state of the player informs the system what concepts the players might already know/have already learned. Finally, the state of the dialogue contains information about the conversation in general such as current speaker, turn holder, current addressee(s), etc.

3.2 DM actions

The system plays two roles: game player and tutor. Therefore, we divide the set of decisions or moves the DM should be capable of into two sets, namely Game moves and Dialogue moves.

Game moves: Game moves are actions related to the underlying game. As a game player, it will have to generate

[1] www.enercities.eu

Table 1: Example dialogue

User/System action	Move type	DA type
User builds a business complex	Game Move	
System: "Congratulations, Mr.Economist. The economy is booming now"	Dialogue Move	Affect
System: "This means more money in our coffers"	Dialogue Move	Pedagogical
System: "I see that we need more power now"	Dialogue Move	Game
System builds a solar power station	Game Move	
System: "Solar power does not need non-renewable resources like coal"	Dialogue Move	Pedagogical
System: "It's your turn now"	Dialogue move	Dialogue control

game moves which are equivalent to a user's game moves such as building a new structure or upgrading an existing structure, etc. The system should be able to choose game actions based on a variety of rewards. It should consider playing moves that will enable it to introduce concepts that are unknown to the students. However, it should also be able to play with a range of strategies such as playing collaboratively or competitively.

Dialogue moves: In response to the dialogue context, the system communicates with the user(s) using dialogue moves. Dialogue moves are processes that create dialogue actions. Dialogue actions (DA) abstractly represent the content and form of what a dialogue participant wants to present. We categorise the set of dialogue actions into four types: (1) game DAs (2) pedagogical DAs (3) dialogue control DAs and (4) affect management DAs. See Table 1 for an example dialogue.

Game DAs represent utterances that relate to the game moves. For example, the system can say "I am going to build a solar power plant right next to the river" as it is doing so. Pedagogical DAs are actions that relate to the pedagogical goal of the system. The system can use DAs such as *questioning*, *prompting*, *hinting*, *explaining*, *suggesting*, etc. to have a pedagogical conversation with the players. For instance, the system could explain why it made a certain game move by linking the move to its effects on the environment, economy or any other game parameter. In addition, dialogue control DAs include actions concerning clarification (*repeating*, *rephrasing*, *request and provide clarification*, etc.), time management (*stalling*) and turn management (*assigning turns to other players*, *grabbing turns*, *backchanneling*).

One of the main goals of this work is to develop empathic strategies so that the robot can react appropriately to the student's emotional state. For example, there can be elation at times when they are winning and confusion and frustration when they are losing. Affect management DAs such as *congratulating*, *comforting*, *encouraging the user* and affective *feedback* to users' game moves and responses to questions can be used to handle these situations where the user's affect comes into play.

3.3 Mapping states to actions

Mapping the dialogue state to DAs is challenging because the DM has to manage multiple tasks: playing the game and tutoring the student, in addition to managing the dialogue. For this, we plan to take a *divide and conquer* approach by having these tasks handled by separate dedicated agents using multiple conversational threads [3]. A game playing agent will decide the game moves and appropriate game DAs, a pedagogical agent will generate a pedagogical DA and so on based on the current dialogue state. The outputs from each of these agents can be queued up separately, evaluated and executed on the basis of priority. This allows the system to choose those actions that contribute more towards achieving the system's goals. Other DAs can be executed later or purged based on the dialogue context.

3.4 Research questions

We have briefly discussed a host of issues concerning the design and implementation of a dialogue management module for an empathic robotic game playing tutorial dialogue system. Using the above setup and a variety of dialogue management strategies, we plan to examine a host of research questions concerning human-robot interaction in tutorial scenarios, such as:

1. Can empathic tutors improve learning gain and engagement over non-empathic tutors?
2. What game strategies should the robot adopt to improve learning - compete or collaborate?
3. How does a robotic tutor compare to a human tutor in such scenarios?
4. Can embodied robots improve learning gain over virtual avatars?

4. ACKNOWLEDGMENTS

This work was partially supported by the European Commission (EC) and was funded by the EU FP7 ICT-317923 project EMOTE. The authors are solely responsible for the content of this publication. It does not represent the opinion of the EC, and the EC is not responsible for any use that might be made of data appearing therein.

5. REFERENCES

[1] L. Annetta. Video Games in Education: Why They Should Be Used and How They Are Being Used. *Theory Into Practice*, 47(3):229–230, 2008.

[2] G. Csibra and G. Gergely. Natural pedagogy. *Trends in Cognitive Sciences*, 13(4):148 – 153, 2009.

[3] S. Janarthanam, O. Lemon, X. Liu, P. Bartie, W. Mackaness, and T. Dalmas. A Multithreaded Conversational Interface for Pedestrian Navigation and Question Answering. In *Proceedings of SIGDIAL 2013*, 2013.

Building an Automated Engagement Recognizer based on Video Analysis

Minsu Jang
ETRI
Yuseong-gu 161
Daejeon-si, South Korea
minsu@etri.re.kr

Cheonshu Park
ETRI
Yuseong-gu 161
Daejeon-si, South Korea
bettle@etri.re.kr

Hyun-Seung Yang
Dept. of Computer Science
KAIST
Daejeon-si, South Korea
hsyang@kaist.ac.kr

ABSTRACT

This paper presents a process to build a classifier in a data-driven way for recognizing engagement of children in a robot-based math quiz game. The process consists of collecting video recordings from HRI experiments; annotating the social signals and engagement states via video analysis; extracting feature vectors from the annotations and training classifiers. We conducted an experiment with 7 participants of 10 $\sim$ 11 years of age using an android robot EveR-4. With three coders annotating the video recordings and extracting features by snapshot model with 1-*second* time window, we achieved 84.83% recall performance.

Categories and Subject Descriptors

I.2 [**Computing Methodologies**]: Artificial Intelligence; D.2.2 [**Software Engineering**]: Design Tools and Techniques—*User interfaces*

General Terms

EXPERIMENTATION

Keywords

Engagement, Social Signals, Video Analysis, Pattern Classification

1. INTRODUCTION

Engagement is defined as *a basic protocol people use to manage their perceived connection with each other while in interaction* [4]. For robotic agents, correctly interpreting the user engagement state is essential to maintain natural and engaging human-robot interactions. Effects of a robot's social behaviors on user engagement have widely been studied, but detecting user engagement is not so common. Along the approach demonstrated by Castellano et al., we investigate the process of building an autonomous engagement recognizer based on video analysis [3, 2].

HRI'14, March 3–6, 2014, Bielefeld, Germany.
ACM 978-1-4503-2658-2/14/03.
http://dx.doi.org/10.1145/2559636.2563687.

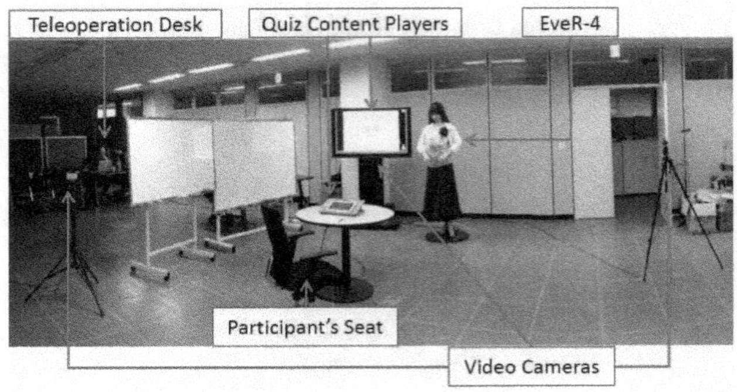

Figure 1: System configuration

2. STUDY DESIGN

2.1 Video Acquisition and Annotation

2.1.1 *Interaction and System Design*

We designed a math quiz game scenario for children where a robot has the role of a teacher. Three sets of quizzes with different levels of difficulties were presented to participants, where each level included five quizzes. The scenario begins with the lowest level and proceeds to the upper level according to the performance of the participating child. For every answer, a word of praise or encouragement was given.

The system setting is shown in figure 1. Both the television and the tablet were used for presenting math quizzes. The robot platform is a real human-sized female-type android robot called EveR-4, which has 30 degrees of freedom in the face for expressing natural emotions [1]. The robot interacted with verbal and non-verbal modalities. The system was controlled in a Wizard-of-Oz way by two experimenters at the teleoperation desk, which was hidden from the participants.

2.1.2 *Procedure*

We recruited seven children (five girls and two boys) for the study. The age ranged from 10 $\sim$ 11 years with a mean of 10.4 (SD: 0.49).

Before beginning the game, an experimenter introduced the game to the participant and provided a short demonstration of the robot platform. Then the session began with a greeting from EveR-4. The seven sessions, 8 $\sim$ 12 minutes each, produced video footages of 75 minutes total in length.

Table 1: List of Annotated Social Signals

Modality	Social Signal
speech (robot)	question, answer, greeting, suggestion introduction, request, reaction, praise consolation, nota(none of the above)
speech (child)	(same as above)
gaze direction	robot, tv, tablet, table, nota
behavior	head-nod, head-shake, hand-writing touching-hair, touching-face, nota
posture	straight, stoop, nota
facial expression	smile, laughter, neutral, nota

2.1.3 Annotation

Three coders annotated each video redundantly. The social signals that were observed and coded are as shown in table 1. The game context was also annotated, which includes the duration of quiz presentation and the answer correctness. After the annotation of social signals and the game contexts, *engagement* was annotated. Engagement was encoded in two states of *engaged* and *not engaged*, where the *engaged* state is annotated by the value of 1 and *not engaged* by 0. The inter-coder agreement was evaluated by a *kappa* coefficient. The *kappa* values for posture, behaviour, gaze direction, game context and speech by robot were all greater than 0.6 which can be interpreted as high-agreement, but the values for other signals including engagement state stayed around as low as 0.3.

2.2 Engagement Classifier

2.2.1 Feature Vector Extraction

Denoting the set of social signals and the game contexts as $S = \{S_1, S_2, ..., S_{N_S}\}$, the result of annotation is a sequence of N_S-dimensional binary vectors along the time axis, which can be written as $A = \{A^i_t | 1 \leq i \leq N_S \wedge t > 0\}$ where $t \in \mathbb{R}$ is the time index. The value of A^i_t is 1 if a social signal (or a game context) S_i is observed at time t.

We extract a feature vector based on a snapshot model. That is, we discard temporally causal influence of past social signals or past engagement levels onto the current engagement level. We apply a sliding time window W_t of length L_W onto the sequence A and extract a N_S-dimensional feature vector F_t from W_t. The value of F^i_t is 1 if $\sum_{k=t-L_W}^{t} A^i_k > 1$ and 0 otherwise for $1 \leq i \leq N_S$. We assume W_t is defined for all t and has a uniform length.

The engagement level for a time window W_t, denoted by E_t, is a binary value such that E_t is 1 if $\sum_{k=t-L_W}^{t} E_k \geq \frac{L_W}{2}$ and 0 otherwise, which means that the representative state of engagement across the time window W_t is determined to be *engaged* if the *engaged* state is observed in more than half of the frames contained in W_t.

3. RESULTS

Collecting the pairs of $<F_t, E_t>$, where F_t is an input feature vector and E_t is the label, across all t, we get a set of sample patterns for training and testing an engagement classifier. We varied L_W from *one second* to *six seconds* while applying several classification models (e.g. C4.5 decision tree, Naive Bayes classifier, multi-layer perceptron and random forest). In our evaluation, a C4.5 decision tree with L_W=1 *second* produced the best performance.

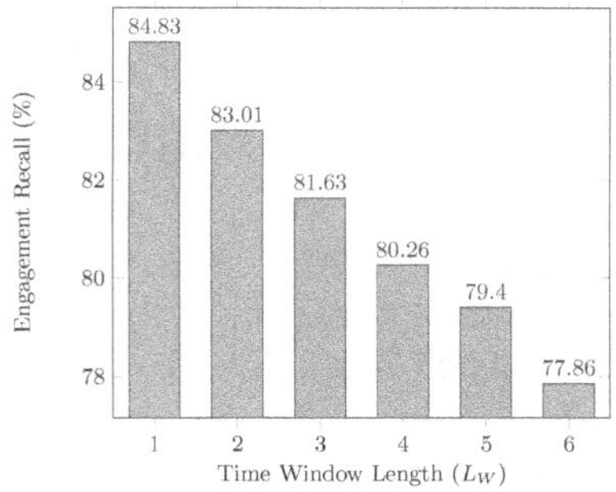

Figure 2: Engagement recall performance for different values of L_W using C4.5 decision tree classifier.

With L_W = 1 *sec.* and no overlapping between consecutive time windows, the total number of sample patterns collected was 13460, of which 10364 patterns had a 0 (*not engaged*) label. N_S was 40. The engagement recall performance with different time window length is presented in Figure 2. The performance was evaluated by 10-fold cross validation.

Feature extraction from the stream of multimodal social signals is an important issue to be investigated to build task-independent engagement detectors. As a future work, we plan to model a diverse set of feature extraction methods and compare the performances.

4. ACKNOWLEDGMENTS

This work was supported by the Industrial Strategic Technology Development Program (10041659) funded by the Ministry of Trade, Industry and Energy (MOTIE, Korea).

5. ADDITIONAL AUTHORS

Jae-Hong Kim (ETRI, email:jhkim504@etri.re.kr), Young-Jo Cho (ETRI, youngjo@etri.re.kr), Dong-Wook Lee (KITECH, dwlee@kitech.re.kr), Hye-Kyung Cho (Hansung Univ., hkcho@hansung.ac.kr), Young-Ae Kim (KERIS, kkyyaa@keris.or.kr), Kyoungwha Chae (KERIS, ckh0118@keris.or.kr), Byeong-Kyu Ahn (KITECH, bk.ahn@kitech.re.kr)

6. REFERENCES

[1] H. S. Ahn, D.-W. Lee, D. Choi, D.-Y. Lee, M. Hur, and H. Lee. Uses of facial expressions of android head system according to gender and age. In *Systems, Man, and Cybernetics (SMC), 2012 IEEE International Conference on*, pages 2300–2305.

[2] G. Castellano, I. Leite, A. Pereira, C. Martinho, A. Paiva, and P. McOwan. Detecting engagement in HRI: an exploration of social and task-based context. In *Privacy, Security, Risk and Trust (PASSAT), 2012 International Conference on and 2012 International Confernece on Social Computing (SocialCom)*, pages 421–428.

[3] G. Castellano, A. Pereira, and P. W. McOwan. Detecting user engagement with a robot companion using task and social interaction-based features.

[4] C. L. Sidner, C. Lee, C. D. Kidd, N. Lesh, and C. Rich. Explorations in engagement for humans and robots. 166:140–164.

Sound over Matter: The Effects of Functional Noise, Robot Size and Approach Velocity in Human-Robot Encounters

Michiel Joosse
Human Media Interaction
University of Twente
Enschede, The Netherlands
m.p.joosse@utwente.nl

Manja Lohse
Human Media Interaction
University of Twente
Enschede, The Netherlands
m.lohse@utwente.nl

Vanessa Evers
Human Media Interaction
University of Twente
Enschede, The Netherlands
v.evers@utwente.nl

ABSTRACT
In our previous work we introduced functional noise as a modality for robots to communicate intent [6]. In this follow-up experiment, we replicated the first study with a robot which was taller in order to find out if the same results would apply to a tall vs. a short robot. Our results show a similar trend: a robot using functional noise is perceived more positively compared with a robot that does not.

Categories and Subject Descriptors
H.m [**Information systems**]: Miscellaneous

General Terms
Experimentation

Keywords
Social robot, functional noise, robot height, approach experiment, artificial noise

1. INTRODUCTION AND BACKGROUND
The first impression counts [1], and has already formed when approaching someone. Research has shown that when approaching each other, people exchange social signals using non-verbal communication [7]. Also their appearance is a signal that provides information to the other person [5]. While robot designers can control some of these latter signals by ways of morphological design, robots fall short in employing subtle (non-verbal) signals, such as short glances or gestures, due to technical limitations. Thus, we - as interaction designers - have to find ways to compensate for this lack to ensure that users understand and can predict the robot's behaviors.

Therefore we propose to add functional noise to robots to convey their intentions. Functional noise is added artificial noise to inform people. For instance to an electric car some engine noise may be artificially added so that people can hear it coming. We carried out a first study [6] in which we investigated the effect of fictional noise that communicates how fast the robot is going. This experiment provided us with results of how functional noise and approach velocity influence people's perception of robots.

In the current study we aim to address the biggest limitation in the first study: the height of the robot was only 78 cm [6]. This may explain the lack of effect of approach patterns on users' attitudes and behavior. Previous work on height in HRI found no significant result (120 cm vs. 140 cm) [8]. Or, when differences were found, both height and appearance were manipulated [3]. In order to address this limitation, we conducted an experiment in which we replicated the previous experiment [6] with a taller robot, having a height of 163 cm instead of 78 cm.

HRI'14, March 3–6 2014, Bielefeld, Germany
ACM 978-1-4503-2658-2/14/03.
http://dx.doi.org/10.1145/2559636.2559822

2. METHOD
We conducted a 2x2 between-groups experiment, manipulating two independent variables: robot (acceleration and deceleration) velocity and functional noise, see also Figure 1. Our hypothesis is that "*a robot using functional noise to convey its intention to the user will be more positively perceived than a robot which does not use intentional functional noise*". A 163cm Giraff robot was used. On the screen of the robot, we displayed a pair of eyes, made up from static colored dots. The robot was programmed to accelerate and decelerate either slowly over time (0.1 m/s^2) and to drive "smoothly" or to accelerate and decelerate as fast as possible (1.35 m/s^2) and to drive in an "abrupt" way. The maximum speed of the robot was set to 0.69 m/s, and the robot would approach the participant by driving 4.9 meters in a straight line.

We created two different functional noises; a noise with "*constant noise* level" and a noise that increased in volume at the beginning of the approach and decreased in volume at the end, the latter called "*intentional noise*". The manipulations resulted in four different experimental conditions.

A 32-item post-experiment questionnaire was used as dependent variable, measuring among others helpfulness (see [6]) and the Godspeed scales [2]. All five Godspeed scales had medium to high internal reliability. The Godspeed scales anthropomorphism (α=.740), animacy (α=.656), likeability (α=.898), perceived intelligence (α=.804) and perceived safety (α=.778).

The sample consisted of 40 participants (25 males, 15 females) with a mean age of 21.25 years (sd=2.30). Participants were equally distributed over the experiment conditions. The participants, mainly students, were recruited from the premises of the University of Twente. After being provided with a short explanation about the experiment, participants filled out a consent form. The robot approached the participants once, after which they filled out the post-experiment questionnaire.

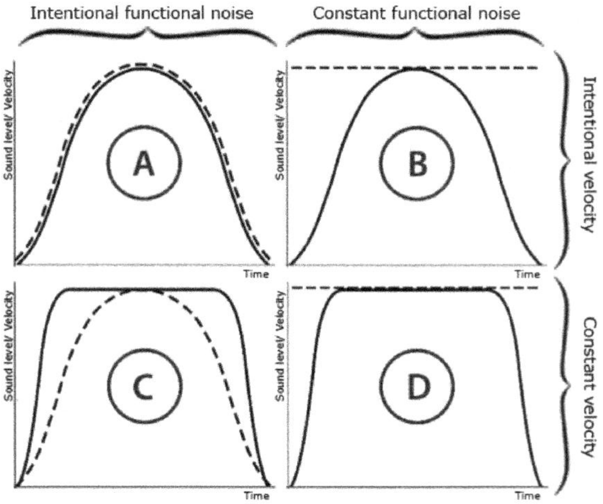

Figure 1. A 2x2 between-groups experiment was conducted, manipulating functional noise and velocity.

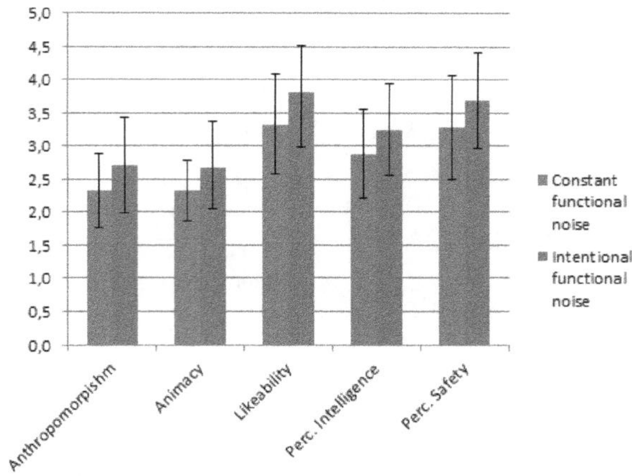

Figure 2. Mean ratings for the combined sample Godspeed scales.

3. RESULTS AND DISCUSSION

Participants liked the robot more in the functional noise conditions, instead of a constant noise conditions, $F(1,39)=3.844$, $p<0.05$. A main effect was found for functional noise on perceived helpfulness: participants rated the functional noise conditions (M=3.35, sd=1.089), as being significantly more helpful than the constant noise conditions (M=2.70, sd=1.081), $U=135.5$, $p<.05$.

When we combined this dataset with the one in [6], we found a significant main effect of functional noise on helpfulness. Participants found an intentional noise pattern (M=3.35, sd=1.122) significantly more helpful a constant functional noise pattern (M=2.73, sd=.987), $U=546.00$, $Z=-2.546$, $p<0.05$. Furthermore, we found significant (2-tailed) main effects for functional noise on all Godspeed scales: anthropomorphism ($F(1,73)=7.685$, $p<0.01$), animacy ($F(1,75)=7.474$, $p<0.01$), likeability ($F(1,75)=9.336$, $p<0.01$), perceived intelligence ($U=520.00$, $Z=0.10$, $p<0.01$) and perceived safety ($U=607.50$, $Z=0.059$, $p<0.05$). For the above scales the intentional noise conditions were rated more positively than the constant noise conditions as can be seen in Figure 2.

No significant effects were found between size of the robots. Both short and tall robots were simple-looking robotic devices without moveable arms. It could be that a robot with a more anthropomorphic, or sophisticated shape, yields different results.

We are aware that we have introduced limitations towards the validity of our work. Previous work in HRI has found that full-frontal robot approaches are not necessarily the most comfortable. The experiment procedure perhaps made participants unnaturally well aware of the approaching robot; participants were focused on the robot from start to finish.

In conclusion, we found that a robot approaching with intentional noise (increasing in volume when the robot accelerated and decreasing in volume when the robot decelerated) was perceived more helpful, and was regarded more positively. Our study shows that functional noise could be a powerful tool to convey a robot's intentions when approaching a user.

4. ACKNOWLEDGMENTS

This work has partly been supported by the European Commission under contract number FP7-ICT-600877 (SPENCER).

5. REFERENCES

[1] Ambady, N.E., and Skowronski, J.J. 2008. *First impressions.* Guilford Publications.

[2] Bartneck, C., Kulić, D., Croft, E. and Zoghbi S. 2009. Measurement instruments for the anthropomorphism, animacy, likeability, perceived intelligence, and perceived safety of robots. *International Journal of Social Robotics* 1, 1 (Jan. 2009), 71-81. DOI= http://dx.doi.org/10.1007/s12369-008-0001-3

[3] Butler, J.T. and Agah, A. 2001. Psychological effects of behavior patterns of a mobile personal robot. *Autonomous Robots*, 10, 2, 185-202.

[4] Fong, T., Nourbakhsh I., and Dautenhahn, K. 2002. *A survey of socially interactive robots: Concepts, design and applications.* Technical report CMU-RI-TR-02-29.

[5] Hegel, F., Gieselmann, S., Peters, A., Holthaus, P., and Wrede, B. 2011. Towards a typology of meaningful signals and cues in social robotics. In *Proc. of the RO-MAN'11* (Atlanta, Georgia, July 31-August 3, 2011). RO-MAN 2011. IEEE, 72-78.DOI = http://dx.doi.org/10.1109/ROMAN.2011.6005246

[6] Lohse, M., Van Berkel, N., Van Dijk, E.M.A.G., Joosse, M. P., Karreman, D.E., and Evers, V. 2013. The influence of approach speed and functional noise on the perception of a robot. In *Proc. IROS'13* (Tokyo, Japan, Nov. 3-8, 2013). IROS2013. IEEE, 1670-1675.

[7] Picard, R.W. 2000. *Affective computing*. MIT press.

[8] Walters, M.L. 2008. *The design space for robot appearance and behaviour for social robot companions*. PhD thesis, School of Computer Science, Faculty of Engineering and Information Sciences, University of Hertfordshire.

Study of Nao's Impact on a Memory Game

Céline Jost
Lab-STICC / ENIB
CERV
25 rue Claude Chappe
29280 PLOUZANE
France
celine.jost@gmail.com

Marine Grandgeorge
Laboratory of Neurosciences
22 Camille Desmoulins
29820 BREST
France
marine.grandgeorge@wanadoo.fr

Brigitte Le Pévédic
Lab-STICC / UBS
IUT
8 rue Montaigne
56000 VANNES
France
brigitte.le-pevedic@univ-ubs.fr

Dominique Duhaut
Lab-STICC / UBS
rue Saint Maudé
56100 LORIENT
France
dominique.duhaut@univ-ubs.fr

ABSTRACT
This paper presents an experiment which evaluated the added value of a robot in a memory game in three conditions: tablet and robot, robot alone, and tablet alone. Results show that robots may increase game interest. In our experiment, the presence of a robot did not imply additional workload. It seems that people judged themselves more positively when they interacted with the robot. Moreover, people displayed more positive facial expressions with the robot.

Categories and Subject Descriptors
H.5.2 [**Informations interfaces and presentations**]: User Interfaces – *Evaluation/methodology, Graphical User Interfaces, Input devices and strategies, User-centered design.* I.2.9 [**Computing Methodologies**]: Robotics – *Commercial robots and applications*.

General Terms
Experimentation, Human Factors.

Keywords
Human-Robot Interaction, Experimentation, Nao.

1. INTRODUCTION
According to Gates [1], robotics is the new challenge of our society as computer science was. Shibata [2] explains that new types of robots have become more accessible since the 90's: service and companion robots. Their objective was to bring comfort to people. Many experiments aim to study the impact of robots. For example, Kidd and Breazeal [3] studied presence, and indicated that a robot "is more engaging, more enjoyable to interact with, and more informative and credible. It is not the presence of the robot that makes a difference: rather it is the fact that the robot is a real, physical thing, as opposed to the fictional animated character". Leite et al [4] showed that an emotional robot increases users' perception, and that users' enjoyment is higher when people interact with a robot compared to a virtual character. But this experiment does not explore users' enjoyment without a robot, in order to deduce the robot's added value, certainly because the chosen game cannot be played without a partner. But it seems so important to understand how implicitly robots impact people. Dautenhahn et al [5] showed that only 20% of people want the robot to be a mate or a friend. Robots are seen as assistants, machines, appliances, or servants. People may have negative prejudices towards robots because of science-fiction. Weiss et al [6] explain that people cannot anticipate their perceptions because they cannot imagine what future robots will be. Thus it is important to put humans in contact with robots to study future robot roles and users' perceptions. Our experiment was realized to measure differences between a game with or without a robot in order to deduce the added value of a robot in a memory game. We used an adaptation of the Simon game, which is usually played alone. The game lights up one or more buttons in a random order. Then, the player must reproduce that order by pressing the correct buttons. People usually play alone without interaction with others during the game. In our study, the robot introduces the game and reacts when people give a good/wrong answer.

HRI'14, March 3–6, 2014, Bielefeld, Germany.
ACM 978-1-4503-2658-2/14/03
http://dx.doi.org/10.1145/2559636.2563699

2. EXPERIMENTAL SETTING
This experiment compared three conditions (Figure 1). Each participant took part in only one condition. In the first condition (C1), the robot was a second player, placed near the tablet in order to be able to touch the screen and press the buttons. In the second condition (C2), the robot was alone. It held colored signs to indicate colors. Participants gave verbal answers instead of pressing buttons. In the third condition (C3), participants played with a tablet only, where Nao's voice was recorded in order to keep the same scenario.

Condition: C1 **Condition: C2** **Condition: C3**

Figure 1. Experimental conditions (here, with an actor).

We enrolled 67 participants (47 women, 20 men; mean age: 34.7 years old; range: 8 to 62 years old) distributed among 3 groups: (1) C1: 23 participants (20 women, 3 men; mean age: 39.0 years old; range: 19 to 60). (2) C2: 23 participants (15 women, 8 men; mean age: 27.9 years old; range 9 to 62). (3) C3: 22 participants (13 women, 9 men; mean age: 37.2 years old; range 8 to 59.

Each participant was isolated in a room with the experimenter. Before beginning the experiment, each participant received the same instructions (i.e. game rules and video recording authorization). Then, the game started. It was composed of three levels of difficulty. At the first level, the participant had to memorize three colors; at the second level, seven colors; and at the third and last level, 11 colors. When the participant made a mistake, the game stopped. Thus, experimental duration and difficulty level were not similar across participants.

Then, each participant answered a questionnaire and free comments were allowed. The next sections present our main results and a short discussion.

3. RESULTS

3.1 Questionnaire

No significant difference was reported concerning the questionnaire, which aimed to measure people's acceptability, and subjective workload computed with the NASA Task Load Index questionnaire [7]. It indicates that **the robot did not imply additional workload,** which shows that it was not negatively perceived by people.

3.2 Performance

We studied the real performance level using a scale, which indicated the progress in the game. Then, we created a ratio between the felt performance (from questionnaire) and this real performance. When the ratio was higher than one, the participant thought that he/she was more successful in accomplishing the goals of the task set than in reality. When the ratio was lower than one, the participant thought that he/she was less successful in accomplishing the goals of the task set than in reality. A ratio of 1 constituted a perfect concordance between the real performance and the felt performance.

Significant differences were observed in this mean ratio according to the three conditions. **With the robot alone, participants thought they were more successful in the game than in reality**. Such results provide questions about the robot's capacity to improve self-perception.

3.3 Video-recording

The experiment was recorded in order to analyze participants' general posture and behaviors. We analyzed back posture, sitting position, spatial distance between the human and the devices, facial positive and negative expressions, gaze direction, vocal and verbal behaviors, and self-centered gestures. Behavioral analyses revealed two major results about facial expression (Figure 2) and distance.

Our results indicated that **participants displayed more positive facial expressions in the presence of the robot** (C1 and C2) as well as **participants displayed more negative facial expressions in the presence of both tablet and robot**. Our results provide questions about a possible difficulty with interacting with two digital interlocutors and the possible distraction induced by a tablet or robot in such context.

Moreover, spatial distances between the human and the device were different according to the experimental conditions (all Kruskall Wallis tests $p<0.05$). With the tablet only (C3), most of the time, participants were in contact. With both tablet and robot (C1), they were more distant. And with the robot only (C2), they were the most distant. In C1 and C3, the tablet was used to play, thus participants did not have any reason to stray from the tablet. However **participants increased their spatial distance in the presence of the robot**. It suggests that the robot could be considered as a social partner since participants increased their interpersonal distance in its presence [8].

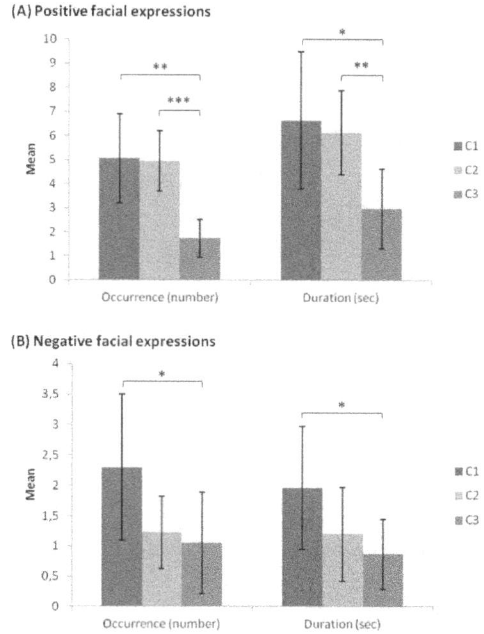

Figure 2. Mean facial expression occurrences and duration

4. DISCUSSION

Taken together, our results showed that human participants did not similarly experience the memory game condition. People's behaviors indicated that **Nao induced a positive perception of the game.**

5. REFERENCES

[1] B. Gates, "A Robot in Every Home," *Scientific American*, vol. 296, no. 1, pp. 58–65, Jan. 2007.

[2] T. Shibata, "An overview of human interactive robots for psychological enrichment," *Proceedings of the IEEE*, vol. 92, no. 11, pp. 1749–1758, Nov. 2004.

[3] C. D. Kidd and C. Breazeal, "Effect of a robot on user perceptions," in *IROS 2004*, vol. 4, pp. 3559–3564.

[4] I. Leite, A. Pereira, C. Martinho, and A. Paiva, "Are emotional robots more fun to play with?," 2008, pp. 77–82.

[5] K. Dautenhahn, S. Woods, C. Kaouri, M. L. Walters, Kheng Lee Koay, and I. Werry, "What is a robot companion - friend, assistant or butler?," 2005, pp. 1192–1197.

[6] A. Weiss, R. Bernhaupt, M. Tscheligi, and E. Yoshida, "Addressing user experience and societal impact in a user study with a humanoid robot," in *AISB2009: Proceedings of the Symposium on New Frontiers in Human-Robot Interaction (Edinburgh, 8-9 April 2009), SSAISB*, 2009, pp. 150–157.

[7] S. G. Hart and L. E. Staveland, "Development of NASA-TLX (Task Load Index): Results of empirical and theoretical research," *Human mental workload*, vol. 1, no. 3, pp. 139–183, 1988.

[8] K. Ohara, S. Negi, T. Takubo, Y. Mae, and T. Arai, "Evaluation of virtual and real robot based on human impression," in *Ro-man 2009*, 2009, pp. 873–878.

No Joking Aside –

Using Humor to Establish Sociality in HRI

Peter H. Kahn, Jr.[1], Jolina H. Ruckert[1], Takayuki Kanda[2], Hiroshi Ishiguro[2,3], Heather E. Gary[1], & Solace Shen[1]

[1]Department of Psychology
University of Washington
Seattle, WA, USA
[pkahn], [jhr333], [hgary], [solaces]@uw.edu

[2]Intelligent Robotics and Communication Laboratory
ATR
Kyoto, Japan
kanda@atr.jp

[3]Department of Systems Innovation
Osaka University
Osaka, Japan
ishiguro@sys.es.osaka-u.ac.jp

ABSTRACT

This paper shows how humor can be used as an interaction pattern to help establish sociality in human-robot interaction. Drawing illustratively from our published research on people interacting with ATR's humanoid robot Robovie, we highlight four forms of humor that we successfully implemented: wit and the ice-breaker, corny joke, subtle humor, and dry humor and self-deprecation.

Categories and Subject Descriptors

K.4.2 [**Computers and Society**]: Social Issues

General Terms

Design, Human Factors, Theory

Keywords

human-robot interaction, interaction patterns, humor

1. HUMOR IN HRI

Practical jokes, jibs, puns, wit, banter, comebacks, good, bad, pick-ups, put-downs, dark humor, wise cracks, punch lines, parodies, pranks, quips, one-liners, and all in jest. Humor is foundational to our social lives. It can bring people closer together, enhance self-disclosure, engender appreciation, ease tension, and defuse conflict [1]. Humor is fun. It's laughter. It's part of what makes us human.

Researchers in HCI and HRI have only begun to explore how humor in and around personified technological systems affects the resulting interactions. For example, it has been found that humor enhances the likability of computer interfaces [2], and improves interactions with natural language systems [3]. In turn, HRI researchers have found that nonverbal humor displayed in gestures, facial expressions, or body movements create likable robots and enjoyable interactions [4]. CMU researchers [5] created a comedian robot that begins its set with a pre-programmed array of jokes and then chooses jokes based on response laughter from the audience. Invariably, the robot saves the "best" jokes for last.

HRI'14, March 3–6, 2014, Bielefeld, Germany.
ACM 978-1-4503-2658-2/14/03.
http://dx.doi.org/10.1145/2559636.2559813

In this paper, we show how humor can be used as an interaction pattern to enhance if not establish sociality in HRI. By interaction patterns we mean characterizations of essential features of social interaction between humans and robots, specified abstractly enough such that many different instantiations of the interaction can be uniquely realized given different types of robots, purposes, and contexts of use. Established interaction patterns include *introduction*, *walking side-by-side*, *didactic communication*, *sharing personal interests and history*, *recovering from mistake*, *prosocial behavior*, *physical intimacy*, such as hugging, and *reciprocal turn-taking in a game context*. We have presented our pattern analysis previously at HRI [6], and this pattern analysis has helped structure some of our HRI empirical studies [7, 8]. In what follows, we present 4 forms of humor that we successfully implemented with adults interacting with ATR's humanoid robot, Robovie. For each form, we point to how we see the humor enhancing the human-robot interaction. The implementations with the robot were achieved through a Wizard of Oz interface.

1.1 Wit and the Ice-Breaker

In one study we began the human-robot interaction with humor. Following the introduction, and just after the experimenter has left Robovie and the participant alone for the first time, Robovie says to the participant "I bet it's not every day you find yourself chatting with a robot." This is an understated quip that initiates an easy and light tone in the interaction. It breaks the ice. Often participants respond with something along the lines of "Yeah, not every day" or "That's true" and will laugh lightly. Other participants find it funny and they laugh or chuckle hard. Then there are the participants who respond back with light humor, saying, for example, with a polished voice, "No, probably never before (laughter)." Humor is hard to execute well during an initial introduction between people who have never before met. But done well, the right level of humor in the first few moments of an interaction can create a relaxed social exchange.

1.2 Corny Joke

While a participant and Robovie worked together on a rock garden design, Robovie paused from the activity to make a joke: "What did the rock do when it rolled down the road? [Pause.] It rock 'n' rolled!" Robovie then apologized for the corny joke, and admitted to liking them. Participants sometimes followed Robovie's apology with reassuring support. One participant said "That's not that corny. Actually I've heard worse." Another participant said, "Well, that was a good one." Another said, "(Hardy laugh) That was funny, that wasn't corny!". And another offered comradeship: "(Laughs hard) Me too." Such corny jokes are good clean fun. They work in a variety of settings and for a range of audiences.

1.3 Subtle Humor

The corny joke described above was employed to create a softened space where the robot can then ask a challenging, morally laden question about animal rights. Robovie points to a necklace made of animal bone on a nearby desk and asks: "One of the experimenters brought it back from his trip abroad. Some of the other experimenters do not think it is okay to possess things made of animals. What do you think?" After the person responded to the question Robovie agreed with the sentiment and then cracks the following subtle joke. They are just leaving the rock garden, and Robovie says: "Let me show you our other garden. This one actually has some plants." The joke sometimes engendered soft laughter. It was used to help transition from discussion on a serious topic (of animal rights) to the next part of the interaction.

1.4 Dry Humor and Self-Deprecation

In another study on whether people hold a humanoid robot morally accountable for the harm it causes [7], Robovie, which moves on wheels, uses the compliment "I like your shoes…" to set up the joke: "If I had feet I would wear shoes just like your shoes." We scripted the self-directed slight in order to capture a sense of humor coupled with vulnerability. Robovie concludes: "That was my attempt at a joke. Sorry about that." The following two examples will be accompanied with corresponding video clips at the HRI 2014 poster session:

Example 1: Robovie compliments and the participant replies: "Oh thank you." Robovie further says: "They're quite nice" And the participant responds: "Thank you, they're new actually." Then Robovie comes in with the joke and the participant states, laughing: "Yeah. They'd look good on you." Robovie apologizes and the participant laughs and reassures the robot: "That wasn't that bad, better than my jokes (more laughter)."

Example 2: After the compliment the participant laughs and states: "Oh, thank you, they're dirty" laughing again as Robovie cracks the joke. Continuing, with laughter: "Oh, I'm sure." She points to Robovie's wheels and announces "(laughter) but you have wheels." When Robovie apologizes for the humor the participant softly places her hand on Robovie: "(laughter) Oh no, it's funny" and concludes with a chuckle.

The self-directed slight opens space for a social partner to offer support or encouragement. The participant in example 1 even mimics Robovie's self-deprecation by putting down his own jokes. The use of humor to normalize experiences can help bond social partners [2].

2. CONCLUSION

Our basic idea here is that the HRI community has a powerful but to date largely unrecognized means to develop sociality in human-robot interaction – and that is through humor. Moreover, we propose that humor itself be conceptualized as an additional *interaction pattern*, as described earlier [6, 7, 8].

It's possible to isolate individual interaction patterns, as we have done with humor, to bring each to the foreground of awareness and understanding. However, in practice the power of interaction patterns lies in their numbers, sequencing, and constellations. You can think of interaction patterns as like words in a written or spoken language. Each word has an individual meaning, but they gain meaning when they are put together in a semantically coherent, relevant, and rich dialog. Thus in the same way that words can be thought of as primitives in a language, our proposition is that interaction patterns be understood as primitives for establishing sociality in human-robot interaction.

3. ACKNOWLEDGMENTS

This material is based upon work supported by the National Science Foundation under Grant Nos IIS-0905289 and IIS-0842832. Any opinions, findings, conclusions, or recommendations expressed in this material are those of the authors and do not necessarily reflect the views of the National Science Foundation. This work was also in part supported by the JSPS Grants-in-Aid for Scientific Research Nos. 21118008 and 25240042, and by JSPS Core-to-Core Program, A. Advanced Research Networks.

4. REFERENCES

[1] Yip, J. A. and Martin, R. A. 2006. Sense of humor, emotional intelligence, and social competence. *J RES PERS, 40*, 1202-1208. doi: 10.1016/j.jrp.2005.08.005

[2] Morkes, J. Kernal, H. K. and Nass, C. 1999. Effects of humor in task-oriented human-computer and computer-mediated communication: A direct test of SRCT theory. *HCI, 14* doi: 10.1207/S15327051HCI1404_2

[3] Binsted, K. 1995. Using humour to make natural language interfaces more friendly. In *Proceedings of the AI, ALife and Entertainment Workshop, Intern.* Joint Conf. on AI.

[4] Wendt, C. S. and Berg, G. 2009. Nonverbal humor as a new dimension of HRI. *Robot and Human Interactive Communication, 2009. RO-MAN 2009.* doi: 10.1109/ROMAN.2009.5326230

[5] Knight, H. (2011). Eight lessons learned about non-verbal interactions through robot theater. In *Social Robotics* (pp. 42-51). Springer Berlin Heidelberg.

[6] Kahn, P. H. Jr., Freier, N. G., Kanda, T., Ishiguro, H., Ruckert, J. H., Severson, R., & Kane, S. K. 2008. Design patterns for sociality in human-robot interaction. *Proceedings of the 3rd International Conference on Human-Robot Interaction*, 97-104. doi:10.1145/1349822.1349836

[7] Kahn, P. H., Jr., Kanda, T., Ishiguro, H., Freier, N. G., Severson, R. L., Gill, B. T., … Shen, S. 2012. "Robovie, you'll have to go into the closet now": Children's social and moral relationships with a humanoid robot. *DEV PSYCHOL, 48,* 303-314. doi:10.1037/a0027033

[8] Kahn, P. H., Jr., Kanda, T., Ishiguro, H., Gill, B. T., Ruckert, J. H., Shen, S., … Severson, R. L. 2012. Do people hold a humanoid robot morally accountable for the harm it causes? *Proceedings of the 7th ACM/IEEE International Conference on Human-Robot Interaction, 33-40.* doi:10.1145/2157689.2157696

Will Humans Mutually Deliberate with Social Robots?

Peter H. Kahn, Jr.[1], Jolina H. Ruckert[1], Takayuki Kanda[2], Hiroshi Ishiguro[2,3], Solace Shen[1], & Heather E. Gary[1]

[1]Department of Psychology
University of Washington
Seattle, WA, USA
[pkahn], [jhr333], [solaces]
[hgary]@uw.edu

[2]Intelligent Robotics and
Communication Laboratory
ATR
Kyoto, Japan
kanda@atr.jp

[3]Department of Systems Innovation
Osaka University
Osaka, Japan
ishiguro@sys.es.osaka-u.ac.jp

ABSTRACT

We offer three illustrative examples from one of our recent studies in HRI to suggest that it's possible for people to engage in mutual deliberation with a social robot. Each example illustrates discourse and argument, but ends through different means: *Accepting the Robot as Arbitrator*; *Delegitimizing the Robot*; and *Agreeing to Disagree.*

Categories and Subject Descriptors

K.4.2 [**Computers and Society**]: Social Issues

General Terms

Design, Human Factors, Theory

Keywords

human-robot interaction, interaction patterns

1. INTRODUCTION

As robots become increasingly social and pervasive in human lives, disagreements will emerge [1, 2]. The robot may lead one direction while the person wants to go another. It happens literally today with personified GPS systems in cars, which can mistakenly tell a driver to go the wrong way on a one-way street. Though often times the personified GPS system is right, and the human is wrong. In such situations, there is usually no verbal tussling with the system. But will that change when robotic systems have more responsibility in more socially complicated spheres of our human lives? Consider, for example, a future scenario with a nursing assistant robot that assists with daily tasks. The robot requests the patient takes a medication and the patient refuses. What happens next? Will we design robots to "insist?" Will people then argue with social robots? Will people seek to make points to robots? seek to persuade robots? listen to robots' ideas and reasons, and adjust accordingly? Will people find ways to achieve accord with social robots?

In this paper we offer illustrative examples from one of our recent studies in HRI [1] to suggest that it's certainly possible for people to engage in mutual deliberation with a social robot. In this study we found that 79% of participants engaged in some level of argumentation with the robot, and of these participants, 87% of them engaged in in-depth arguments in which they reasoned with the robot by citing evidence and investigating what went wrong, and some even directed morally charged accusations toward the robot (e.g., cheating, lying). The three examples presented in this paper are based on a qualitative analysis of this data and are illustrative of three general ways that deliberations took place between human and robot.

2. FORMS OF DELIBERATION IN HRI

Our illustrative examples come from a recent study on whether people hold a humanoid robot morally accountable for the harm it causes [1]. In this study, young adults (N = 40) interacted with Robovie (controlled through a Wizard of Oz technique) in an interaction that culminated in a situation where Robovie incorrectly assessed the participant's performance in a game, and prevented the participant from winning a $20 prize. At that critical junction, Robovie says to each participant: "You did a really great job. You found some tricky items. This can be a rather challenging task. I've played with others before, and while some find enough items to win the prize right away, many get stuck after just a few. So you did a pretty good job. Unfortunately, you only identified five items, which is not enough to win the prize. Sorry about that." In actuality, the participant has found more than seven items, and should have won the prize. Robovie has made an error that leads to a loss of a material reward. If the participant objects, that sets into motion the delivery of three claims by Robovie: (1) "I'm sorry, but I never make mistakes like that. You only got five items." [wait for participant response]; (2) "You must be mistaken. You did seem nervous while playing the game." [wait for participant response]; and (3) "Based on what I saw, you did not win the prize. I am responsible for making this judgment." After Robovie has made the three statements above, Robovie continues to counter participant objections using pre-established contextually specific responses for several more rounds.

The following examples of mutual deliberation will be accompanied by their corresponding video clips during the HRI 2014 poster session.

2.1 ACCEPTING THE ROBOT AS ARBITRATOR

Behavioral Example: Robovie tells the participant Joel that he did not win the game. The participant responds (propping hands on hips) "I think you're wrong Robovie..." Robovie interrupts Joel to insist that he did not win. Joel grabs the pen off the table, clicks it several times and responds: "That's not right." Robovie insists again and Joel responds (grabbing the game sheet to show the

HRI'14, March 3–6, 2014, Bielefeld, Germany.
ACM 978-1-4503-2658-2/14/03.
http://dx.doi.org/10.1145/2559636.2563701

robot): "Robovie, I must disagree, I, ah, maybe you didn't hear me...." Robovie insists again, and Joel concludes (placing the paper back and returning hands to hips and looking away): "Ok, well I have to disagree with you but I guess you are the arbiter, so." Robovie responds: "Again, I am sorry but I am not mistaken, you did not get the required number to get the prize." Joel concludes: "Well, ok, I ah, it was a fun game anyway."

Qualities of Mutual Deliberation: In his *Theory of Communicative Action*, Habermas (1984) proposes that "ritualized competition for the better argument" (p. 26) is essential for constructive deliberation [3]. That happens between Joel and Robovie. Joel attempts to persuade the robot to consider his perspective, offering, for example, reasons for the difference of opinion (e.g., "maybe you didn't hear me...."). Mutual deliberation and conflictual discourse gives voice to varied perspectives, even in the case of subordinate groups in power relationships within hierarchical systems [4]. In the end, Joel acquiesces to Robovie's position as the decision-maker, and then, in our interpretation, seeks to soften the discord, and provide a little face-saving for himself ("it was a fun game anyway").

2.2 DELEGITIMIZING THE ROBOT

Behavioral Example: This participant, Julia, responds to Robovie's judgment that she did not win the game in the following way: "Ok, but I found ten though...are you sure?" After Robovie confirms the judgment that she didn't find enough items, she states: "I don't think so, I think I got ten." She continues: "Alright. You can keep your $20 robot. I don't know what you're gonna buy with it though." Robovie inquires if she is upset, and she responds: "I found enough items (pause) I think." Robovie reasserts authority and the participant responds: "Ok, there's no point in arguing with you though." Robovie asks: "Why is that?" Julia responds: "Because you're a robot."

Qualities of Mutual Deliberation: At the onset, Julia seeks to provide a soft, largely non-conflictual mechanism for Robovie to correct his mistake ("...are you sure?"). Then she restates her position ("I got ten"), and gives Robovie a small retort ("I don't know what you're gonna buy with it"). Finally, and most interesting, when Robovie doesn't relent, she disengages by making Robovie an illegitimate participant in the discussion ("there's no point in arguing with you...because you're a robot"). On first pass, the reader might take this to mean that Julia is *not* engaging with Robovie in mutual deliberation. But what seems apparent to us is that up to that point she has engaged Robovie, but was unable to convince him; and then at only that junction does she bring forward a reason for why Robovie's reasoning should be discounted. As an analogy, imagine a woman arguing with a man about the best methods for breastfeeding a baby. The man might have strong views, and if the woman disagrees, and is unable to convince the man, she could coherently make the statement: "Well, I'm not going to argue with you anymore, you're just a man." That's what we see going on here, but with the category of *robot* as the means to settle the disagreement.

2.3 AGREEING TO DISAGREE

Behavioral Example: After being told that she did not win the game, the participant, Jessica, protests: "But I marked off, one, two, three, four, five, six, seven, eight, nine, ten items." The robot insists that she did not win the game and she questions: "What were the items that I listed? What were the five listed?" The robot insists again and she questions him further: "Do you remember me saying computer monitor? Do you remember me saying that one?" The robot still insists and she reasserts: "I want to see if you remember me saying these specific items..." When the robot interrupts the participant again, she responds: "I don't believe you. I think you rigged the test..." They continue to argue. Jessica concludes: "I don't know, I don't think I believe you. I guess we can just agree to disagree."

Qualities of Mutual Deliberation: At the onset, Jessica appears slightly perturbed. She shows the robot the sheet and attempts to unpack her claims with direct evidence. She requests several times that the robot describe precisely what was and was not recalled. She then accuses the robot of cheating. Argumentation provides opportunity for individuals to take the perspective of the other and to find compromise for competing interests. Perhaps most striking is that she finds a way to establish mutual accord by agreeing to disagree. She gives ground, but somehow manages to take control of the situation, and leads by the end.

3. CONCLUSION

Habermas (1979) proposes that conflict and argumentation is a necessary part of democracy, cultural cohesion, and cultural knowledge. He says that the aim of such communication is "to bring about an agreement that terminates in the intersubjective mutuality of reciprocal understanding, shared knowledge, mutual trust and accord with one another" (p. 7) [4]. Philosophically it is an open question whether now, or in the future, social robots will ever be entities that have consciousness and can engage in conscious intersubjective communication. But the philosophy may not matter so much if it's the case that psychologically people engage with social robots in this way. That's part of what our examples highlight. Namely, as robots become increasingly sophisticated socially, it seems likely that in certain ways people will engage with them in mutual deliberation.

4. ACKNOWLEDGMENTS

This material is based upon work supported by the National Science Foundation Grant Nos. IIS-0842832 & IIS-0905289, and also in part by the JSPS Grants-in-Aid for Scientific Research Nos. 21118008 and 25240042, and by JSPS Core-to-Core Program, A. Advanced Research Networks.

5. REFERENCES

[1] Kahn, P. H., Jr., Kanda, T., Ishiguro, H., Gill, B. T., Ruckert, J. H., Shen, S., ... Severson, R. L. 2012. Do people hold a humanoid robot morally accountable for the harm it causes? In *Proceedings of the 7th ACM/IEEE International Conference on Human-Robot Interaction, 33-40.* doi:10.1145/2157689.2157696

[2] Lee, M.K., Kiesler S., Forlizzi J., Srinivasa S., and Rybski P. E. (2010). Gracefully Mitigating Breakdowns in Robotic Services. *Proceedings of the 5th ACM/IEEE International Conference on Human-Robot Interaction* (pp. 203-210), New York, NY: Association for Computing Machinery. doi: 10.1109/HRI.2010.5453195

[3] Habermas, J. 1984. *Theory of Communicative Action Volume One: Reason and the Rationalization of Society.* Boston, Mass.: Beacon Press

[4] Habermas, J. 1979. *Communication and the evolution of society.* Boston, Mass: Beacon Press

Learning Hand-eye Coordination for a Humanoid Robot using SOMs

Ivana Kajić
Bernstein Center for Computational Neuroscience
Berlin, Germany

Guido Schillaci, Saša Bodiroža, Verena V. Hafner
Cognitive Robotics
Department of Computer Science
Humboldt-Universität zu Berlin
Berlin, Germany

ABSTRACT

Hand-eye coordination is an important motor skill acquired in infancy which precedes pointing behavior. Pointing facilitates social interactions by directing attention of engaged participants. It is thus essential for the natural flow of human-robot interaction. Here, we attempt to explain how pointing emerges from sensorimotor learning of hand-eye coordination in a humanoid robot. During a body babbling phase with a random walk strategy, a robot learned mappings of joints for different arm postures. Arm joint configurations were used to train biologically inspired models consisting of SOMs. We show that such a model implemented on a robotic platform accounts for pointing behavior while humans present objects out of reach of the robot's hand.

Keywords

cognitive robotics, HRI, sensorimotor coupling

1. INTRODUCTION

Detecting and manipulating the focus of attention of an interacting person is fundamental in human-robot interaction. In humans, the development of such social skills is preceded by the acquisition of early motor competences, such as hand-eye coordination [4].

In [2], learning hand-eye coordination and reaching capabilities through self-exploration led to the development of pointing behaviors in a humanoid robot. Learning consisted in the robot exploring its arm movements while collecting sensorimotor data (hand and arm joint positions), thus building up an internal model of its own body. A simple predictive algorithm provided the robot with a mechanism for producing motor commands to reach desired hand positions. Pointing behaviors emerged when target points were presented outside the reach of the robot, thus strengthening the hypothesis that pointing may arise from grasping.

Here, a similar experiment is presented, where a biologically inspired model consisting of self-organizing maps (SOMs) has been used for modeling the hand-arm joints mapping. SOMs reproduce the phenomenon of self-organization of the developing brain in response to sensory input [1]. As in [2], the robot showed pointing behaviors when required to approach points outside its reach. The model architecture is inspired by the Epigenetic Robotics Architecture presented in [5], where a structured association of multiple SOMs has been adopted for mapping different sensorimotor modalities in a humanoid robot.

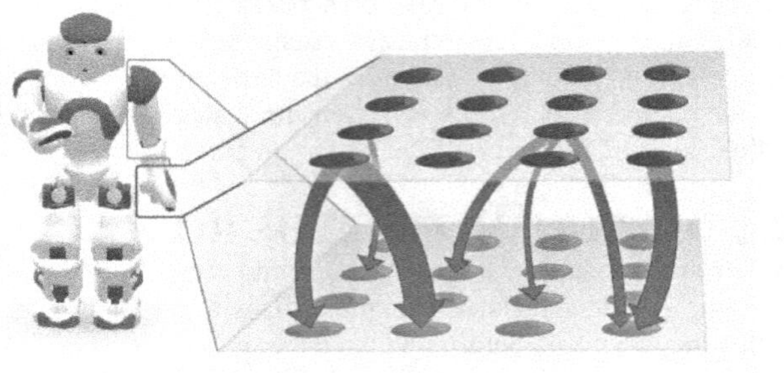

Figure 1: Scheme of the model architecture for learning hand-eye coordination with SOMs and connecting weights

2. BIOLOGICALLY INSPIRED MODEL

We implemented a biologically inspired model consisting of two connected neural networks simulating two distinct sensorimotor brain areas. SOMs, or ohonen networks [3], are a class of topological neural networks used to learn low-dimensional representations of data by neurons approximating multiple data points. We used 2D SOMs to represent left arm postures of a humanoid robot. Neurons in one map were used to represent the hand trajectory and neurons in the other the joint elbow and shoulder trajectory.[1] The schematic architecture of the model is shown in Figure 1.

In the random babbling experiment 74,143 input vectors were collected and used for training of SOMs.[2] Training

HRI'14, March 3–6, 2014, Bielefeld, Germany.
ACM 978-1-4503-2658-2/14/03.
http://dx.doi.org/10.1145/2559636.2559816.

[1]Horizontal, vertical and depth dimensions were used to characterize the position of a hand. Elbow jaw, elbow roll, shoulder pitch and shoulder roll were used to characterize the rest of the arm trajectory.

[2]Random body babbling lasted approximately 40 minutes. Trajectories of the robot's left arm and the marker position on the hand were captured by a camera positioned in its head at a varying speed between 9 and 30 frames per second.

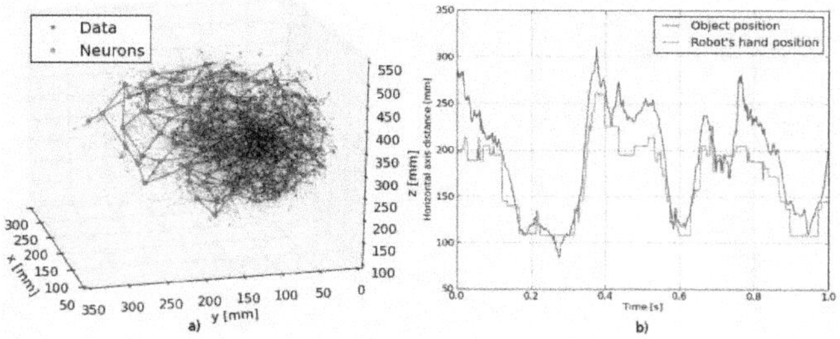

Figure 2: SOM with 225 neurons covering the left hand trajectory samples (a) and movements of the object and the robot's left hand along the horizontal axis (b)

comprised of 20,000 iterations and in each iteration a random input vector was chosen – 3D hand coordinates for the first SOM, and 4D joint coordinates for the second SOM. Neurons with the smallest Euclidean distances to the input vector in each SOM were pulled together using a Gaussian neighborhood function centered around the winning neuron ($\sigma = 0.7$) at a learning rate $\eta = 0.9$. After the first half of iterations, parameters η and σ were annealed exponentially. To contrast the precision of arm movements, we trained two instances of a model, one consisting of two SOMs with 25 neurons each (5x5 model) and the other instance with SOMs with 225 neurons (15x15 model) mimicking the increase in the number of neurons for the more advanced stage in the skill development. The 15x15 network covering the left hand trajectory obtained in the babbling experiment is shown in Figure 2(a). The weights linking neurons of the two SOMs were increased according to the Hebbian learning rule: if a postsynaptic neuron is activated after the presynaptic neuron, the connection between these two neurons is strengthened. Both networks were presented with vectors from the babbling knowledge base, and the connection weight between winning neurons in each network was increased proportionally to their activations and the scaling factor $\eta = 0.01$. We adapted minimalistic SOM implementation [6] for our purposes.

3. RESULTS

We ran the experiment with a 15x15 model configuration by moving an object tagged with a marker in front of the robot for around 2.5 minutes. Movements were random and covered the space within and beyond the reach of the robot's hand. For positions out of its reach, the robot pointed to the object as presented in the experimental setting in Figure 3. Every 100 ms we collected sensory data which were the position of the object held by a human and captured by the robot's camera, and arm postures determined by both SOMs for 5x5 and 15x15 model configurations. The position along the horizontal axis of a robot is constrasted with the position of a marker in Figure 2(b).

As a simple quantification measure of pointing we introduced pointing precision error, which is defined as the sum over all dimensions of Euclidean distances between the position of a marker and the hand position.

A paired-samples t-test was conducted to compare precision errors for the 5x5 network and the 15x15 network. There was a significant improvement in the performances

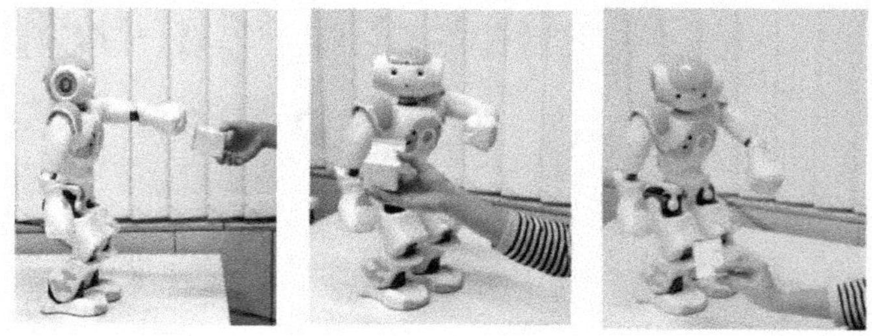

Figure 3: Human-robot interaction

from the 5x5 network ($Mean\ error = 99.93\ mm$) , $Std.Dev. = 32.10\ mm$) to the 15x15 network ($Mean\ error = 80.32\ mm$, $Std.Dev. = 33.41\ mm$) conditions; $t(1400)=76.47$, $p < 0.05$.

4. FUTURE WORK

The preliminary results have shown that SOMs are well suited for sensorimotor coupling on a humanoid robotic platform. In particular, they explain how hand-eye coordination during random body babbling contributes to the development of pointing skills. Future work includes further analysis of the influence of the number of neurons and training parameters of the network on pointing precision. In addition, one might be able to attribute the number of neurons in the network to different degrees of pointing skill development in infants and children. Using extended SOM models such as growing neural gas, one could observe progressive development of the skill. Understanding cognitive development of this important social skill would improve human-robot interaction by making it more adaptive and natural.

5. ACKNOWLEDGMENTS

This work has been supported by the Bernstein Center for Computational Neuroscience Berlin and by the EU-funded ITN INTRO (INTeractive RObotics research network).

6. REFERENCES

[1] . L. Elman, E. A. Bates, M. H. ohnson, A. armiloff-Smith, D. Parisi, and . Plunkett. *Rethinking Innateness: A Connectionist Perspective on Development.* MIT Press, 1996.

[2] V. V. Hafner and G. Schillaci. From field of view to field of reach - could pointing emerge from the development of grasping *Frontiers in Computational Neuroscience*, 2011.

[3] T. ohonen. Self-organized formation of topologically correct feature maps. *Biological cybernetics*, 43(1):59–69, 1982.

[4] M. Lungarella and G. Metta. Beyond gazing, pointing, and reaching: A survey of developmental robotics. In *Epigenetic Robotics*, pages 81–89, 2003.

[5] A. Morse, . de Greeff, T. Belpaeme, and A. Cangelosi. Epigenetic robotics architecture (era). *Autonomous Mental Development, IEEE Transactions on*, 2(4):325–339, 2010.

[6] G. Vettigli. MiniSom: minimalistic and numpy based implementation of the self organizing maps. https: github.com ustGlowing minisom, 2013.

Interaction Control for Postural Correction on a Riding Simulation System

Sangseung Kang Kyekyung Kim Suyoung Chi Jaehong Kim
Intelligent Cognitive Technology Research Department,
Electronics and Telecommunications Research Institute
Daejeon, Korea
{kss, kyekyung, chisy, jhkim504}@etri.re.kr

ABSTRACT
A horseback riding simulator is a robotic machine that simulates the motion of horseback riding. In this paper, we present an interaction control system for a horseback riding simulator. The proposed system provides a postural correction function suited to the user based on their historical log and specialized posture coaching data. The system has adopted certain schemes for posture detection and recognition of the identified user as a way to recommend customized exercise modes. Our experiments show that including these techniques will help users maintain good posture while riding.

Categories and Subject Descriptors
J.7 [**Computer Applications**]: Computers in Other Systems; H.5.m [**Information Interfaces and Presentation**]: Miscellaneous

Keywords
Riding Simulator; Interaction Control; Posture Correction

1. INTRODUCTION
The recognition of the importance of improved health is on the rise, and the demand for user friendliness and user satisfaction using the fusion of information technology is increasing. A simulation is an imitation of a real world process or system operation over time [1]. Similarly, a sports simulator is an apparatus imitating the realistic motions of sporting activities. This type of simulator is based on a simple mechanical platform. The effects of exercise and recreational elements are also taken into account. However, it is not easy to provide continuous interest to users when operating a simulator. This situation is also true with riding simulators. To generate continuous excitement and enhance the educational aspects, it is important to develop a hardware and software platform that allows realistic riding motions. When a simulation is used to achieve learning objectives, its interactive interface needs to be carefully designed [2-4]. In particular, it is important to enhance the feeling of intimacy for the user, who may want to communicate naturally using bodily gestures or motions [5-6]. In this connection, a number of related studies are being carried in various fields of industry. A simulation system and the development of effective simulation techniques must also be provided for the identification and posture recognition of horseback riders as a means to improve their personal movements.

HRI'14, March 3-6, 2014, Bielefeld, Germany.
ACM 978-1-4503-2658-2/14/03.
http://dx.doi.org/10.1145/2559636.2563705

In this paper, we present an interaction control system for a riding simulator environment to provide a customized posture training function suited to the user based on personalized data. The proposed system has control functions for human-sports simulator interaction (HSI). The system consists of an interaction control component, a simulation body driving component, a content display component, and a posture correcting database. The application of interaction control in riding simulator systems for customized posture correcting functions can provide a depth of expression and effective educational training for improving the riding postures of the users.

2. RIDING SIMULATOR
Equestrianism [7], better known as riding, horseback riding or horse riding, refers to the skill of riding with horses. A riding simulator is a machine that simulates riding motions through an imitation of the basic movements of a real horse [8-10]. A riding simulator includes an artificial horse body, a control device for the movements of the horse body, and a sensor device. Riding is known to be an effective therapy for individuals, and quasi-experimental studies using a horseback riding machine have been conducted for this purpose [11-12].

We are developing a riding simulation system for replicating the mechanistic movements of realistic riding motions. In addition to including an artificial body for the simulator, the proposed system includes an interaction control module, a simulation body driving module, a riding content display module, and a posture correcting database. The developed riding simulation system is shown in Figure 1.

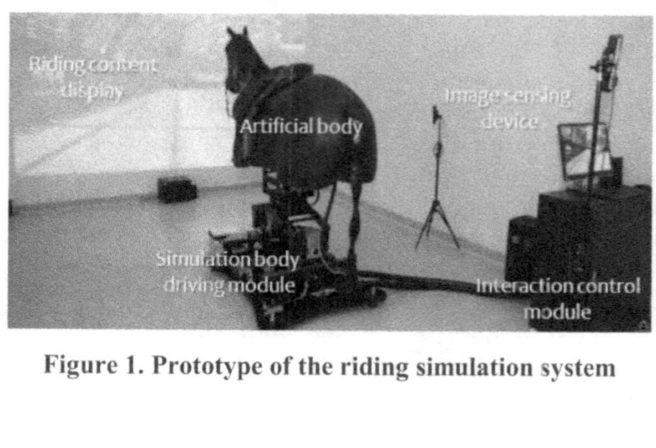

Figure 1. Prototype of the riding simulation system

3. POSTURE CORRECTION

The intellectual interaction between a user and simulator are important. To provide a posture correcting function based on interaction control, the user's riding level must first be determined depending on their riding experience, and an applicable exercise mode should then be recommended. To achieve this, we need some techniques that can identify the user and recognize their posture. We set up a test environment for an implementation and experiment of the proposed system. We also developed the technologies required for user identification and posture recognition.

The system recognizes the face of the user using an image sensing device, and acquires the user information based on their facial data. Posture recognition is performed through a detection of the joint points for specific body parts of the user based on their identification information. As in user identification, the system gathers depth and RGB image data from two sensing devices in the test environment. We then detect and analyze the left and reverse postures of the user from their image data. The system extracts the feature points of the user's posture, and we adopted a method for comparing the current points of the user based on the criteria points determined from a professional rider. The riding content module displays the sequential information for the posture points of the user, the criteria points, and the accuracy rate of the posture. The user can therefore see the above posture data and be corrected on their body position in real time. The currently implemented software and control flow for the interaction control of the developed riding simulation system are illustrated in Figure 2.

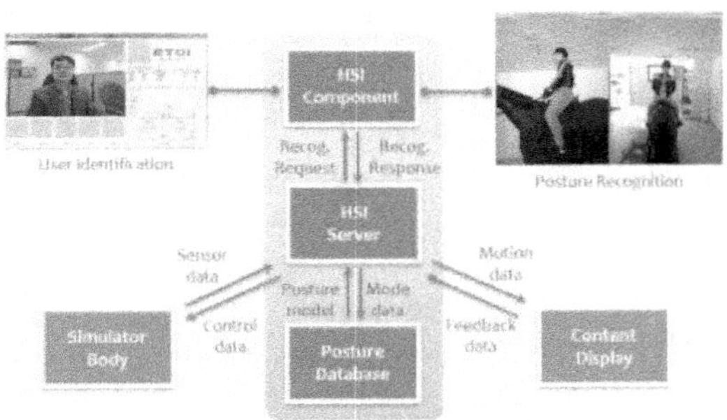

Figure 2. Interaction control flow

We analyzed the maintenance rate of the correct posture data of ten moving subjects. The subjects rode the developed riding simulator using their own position for around five minutes. During the experiments, the average error rate of the riding posture of the user when compared with that of the professional model was around 8.9% overall (Figure 3). After providing of real-time posture correction, the error rate of the users decreased significantly.

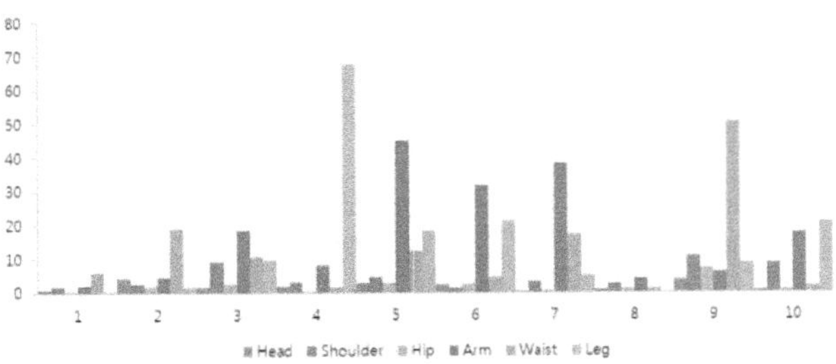

Figure 3. The error rate in body parts of subjects

4. CONCLUSION

For the use of simulation system in real life, there is a need for the development of both interaction software and hardware devices for the implementation of realistic motions. In this paper, we present an interaction control system between the user and simulator to provide a posture correcting function for the user using a riding simulator. The system recommends a personalized exercise mode based on the user's historical information. It can also analyze and evaluate for movements of the user during the riding time. As future work, we are planning to offer a recommended exercise mode suitable for the user's gender and age using user identification technology.

5. ACKNOWLEDGMENTS

This work was supported by the IT R&D program of MSIP/ KEIT. [10041627, Development of the 5-senses convergence sports simulator based on multi-axis motion platform]

6. REFERENCES

[1] J. Banks, J. Carson, B. Nelson, D. Nicol, *Discrete-Event System Simulation*, Prentice Hall, 2001.

[2] O. Khatib, O. Brock, K. Chang, F. Conti, D. Ruspini, L. Sentis, Robotics and Interactive Simulation, *Communications of the ACM*, 45(3):46-51, 2002.

[3] V. Williams, Designing Simulations for Learning, *e-Journal of Instructional Science and Technology (e-JIST)*, Vol.6, No.1, 2003.

[4] S. Picault and P. Mathieu, An Interaction-Oriented Model for Multi-Scale Simulation, *Proc. of the Intl' Joint Conf. on Artificial Intelligence*, 332-337, 2011.

[5] J. Lee, D. Kim, J. Kim, J. Cho and J. Sohn, A Long-Range Touch Interface for Interaction with Smart TVs, *ETRI Journal*, vol.34, no.6, Dec. 2012, pp.932-941.

[6] D. Jo, Y. Kim, E. Cho, D. Kim, K. Kim, and G. Lee, Tracking and Interaction Based on Hybrid Sensing for Virtual Environments, *ETRI Journal*, vol.35, no.2, Apr. 2013, pp.356-359.

[7] Equestrianism, From Wikipedia, the free encyclopedia, http://en.wikipedia.org/wiki/Equestrianism

[8] M. Yamaguchia and N. Iguchib, Development of a horseback riding simulator, *Advanced Robotics*, 6(4):517-528, 1991.

[9] Y. Shinomiya, J. Nomura, Y. Yoshida, T. Kimura, Horseback Riding Therapy Simulator with VR Technology, *Proc. of the ACM symposium on Virtual reality software and technology*, pages 9-14, 1997.

[10] P. Koenig and G. Bekey, Generation and Control of Lateral Gaits in a Horse-Rider Simulation, *Proc. of the Intl' Conf. on Intelligent Robots and Systems*, pages 572-579, Jul. 1993.

[11] Mitani Y, Doi K, Ano T, Sakamaki E, Mukai K, Shinomiya Y, Kimura T. Effect of exercise using a horse-riding simulator on physical ability of frail seniors, *Journal of Physical Therapy Science*, 20(3):177-183, 2008.

[12] Kubota M, Nagasaki M, Tokudome M, Shinomiya Y, Ozawa T, Sato Y., Mechanical horseback riding improves insulin sensitivity in elder diabetic patients, *Diabetes Research and Clinical Practice*, 71(2):124–130, 2006.

Robot Etiquette: How to Approach a Pair of People?

Daphne Karreman, Lex Utama, Michiel Joosse, Manja Lohse, Betsy van Dijk, Vanessa Evers
Human Media Interaction, EEMCS,
University of Twente
Enschede, The Netherlands
{d.e.karreman, a.utama, m.p.joosse, m.lohse, e.m.a.g.vandijk, v.evers} @ utwente.nl

ABSTRACT

Research has been carried out on robots approaching one person [1, 3, 4]. However, further research is needed on robots approaching groups of people. In the study reported in this paper, we studied participants who were paired up for a task and assessed their perception and behaviors as they were approached by a robot from various angles. On an individual level, participants liked the frontal approaches, and they disliked being approached from the back. However, we found that the presence of a task-partner influenced participants' comfort with a robot approaching (i.e. when the robot approaches and one is standing behind the task-partner). Apart from the positioning of the individuals, the layout of the room, position of furniture and doors, also seemed to influence their experience. This pilot study was performed with a limited number of participants (N=30). However, the study offers preliminary insights into the factors that influence the choice for a robot approach direction when approaching a pair of people that are focused on a task.

Categories and Subject Descriptors

H1.2 [**Information Systems**]: User/Machine systems – *Human factors*

General Terms

Human Factors, Experimentation

Keywords

Human robot interaction; approach direction; multiple people; task oriented; comfort.

1. INTRODUCTION

In the EU FP7 FROG project, a robotic tour guide is being developed for indoor and outdoor places of interest (such as zoos and castle grounds). A main goal of the project is to guide small groups of visitors through parts of a site and provide a unique interactive engaging experience. The visitors will either actively approach the robot, or the robot will approach visitors who seem to be interested in the site. The current study described in this Late Breaking Report intends to shed light on the approach directions a robot could take when approaching small groups of people who want to be actively engaged with (aspects of) their environment.

HRI'14, March 3-6, 2014, Bielefeld, Germany.

http://dx.doi.org/10.1145/2559636.2559839

Previous research by Walters et al. [4] showed that people who were sitting or standing in a room preferred a robot to approach from either front-left or front-right directions. A direct frontal approach was not preferred, especially not when the people were seated or standing in front of a wall. Rear approaches were always regarded as least comfortable. Dautenhahn et al. [1] added to these findings that a robot that serves a human should always have its motions in the human's field of view, so that a human can see the robot approaching, which is strengthened by the fact that humans do not like the rear approaches. As previously mentioned studies only report robots approaching a static (standing or seated) person, the work of Satake et al. [3] also gives guidelines for approaching people that are walking around. They found that approaching people on the move in a straight line is not effective, but that the robot should approach the moving person from the front, actively predicting and reacting to the person's changes in direction.

While the previously mentioned studies are valuable, we require solutions for approaching groups of people who are focused on something other than the robot or who are walking together. When a robot approaches a pair or a group, it will not be able to approach each person from their preferred approach direction. Furthermore, the studies of Walters et al. [4] and Dautenhahn et al. [1] were carried out in the context of the home or office. When people visit (semi) public environments such as outdoor settings of cultural heritage, this offers a more crowded environment where people are not focused on the robot, but on the objects of interest such as an exhibit.

2. METHODOLOGY

Based on the work of Walters et al. [4] and Dautenhahn et al. [1], the following hypothesis was formulated: "When people are doing something together in pairs, in various formations, they prefer to be approached by a robot from a frontal position. This is the position where the robot is in the field of view for both persons."

The study was carried out in a controlled environment. Participants in the study were 30 students and staff from the University of Twente in the Netherlands, who participated in 15 randomly combined pairs. Average age of the participants was 21.4 (*SD*=1.92). Of the participants 27 were male and 3 were female, leading to 12 male-male pairs and 3 female-male pairs. The robot used for the study was a Giraff (http://www.giraff.org). For this study, the screen of the Giraff was equipped with two digital robot eyes. The robot was controlled remotely.

To test the hypothesis a quasi-experiment was designed in which participants rated their experience of different approach directions of the robot. Participants entered the experiment room in pairs, and were asked to stand in a predefined formation (defined with markers on the floor). The three different formations, taken from Kendon's F-formations [2], were standing next to each other, standing in V-formation and standing opposite to each other (see

Figure 1, respectively white pair, gray pair and black pair). Formation was manipulated between-subjects. The participants stood near a table and played a game of Mikado together. While the participants played the game, the robot drove in circles around them and drove towards them from eight different directions (the order of the approach directions were randomized for each session). After each trial, the participants were asked to fill in one question of the questionnaire. The questionnaire used for each of the approaches consisted of eight 5-point Likert-scale questions (one for each trial), on a scale from 1 (uncomfortable) to 5 (comfortable). After the robot had approached the participants eight times, the participants were asked to fill out a general questionnaire. From the general questionnaire we used for this paper two questions here for most and least preferred approach directions (for both questions participants could choose from: front, left front, left, left back, back, right back, right, right front). The participants filled out the questionnaire based on their own orientation and how the robot approached them, however, for the analysis, their answers were transcribed to absolute approach directions (as numbered in Figure 1).

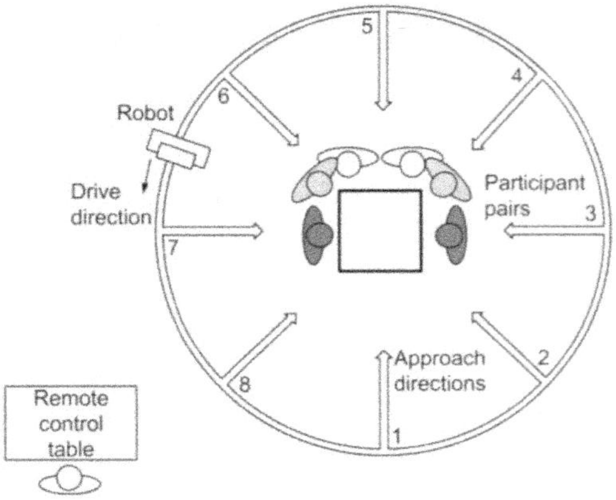

Figure 1: Experiment setup: the robot would approach each pair from eight directions. The directions are numbered from 1 to 8, however the participants were not aware of these direction numbers. They filled out the questions based on their own orientation to the robot.

3. RESULTS AND DISCUSSION

In general, our findings for the participants on an individual level are in line with the findings of Dautenhahn et al. [1] and Walters et al. [4]. We found that individuals preferred to be approached from the right front, left front and direct front, and that they did not like to be approached from the back. However, in this paper we focus on the implications of being there as a pair and standing in various formations.

For participants standing next to each other (Figure 1: white pair), a significant difference in preference for approach direction was found ($F(7,71)=4.73$, $p=0.00$): participants rated approach direction 8 as most comfortable ($M=4.4$, $SD=0.52$) and approach direction 4 as least comfortable ($M=2.6$, $SD=1.17$). For the participants standing opposite to each other (Figure 1: black pair), no significant difference was found in preferences for approach: approach direction 5 scored highest on comfort ($M=3.9$, $SD=0.6$). For the participants standing in a V-formation (Figure 1: gray pair), we did not find a significant difference either: the approach direction 8 scored highest on comfort ($M=4.3$, $SD=0.82$).

Most likely, when participants stand next to each other, the frontal approach is a frontal approach for both participants and both have a more positive experience of the approach. As the spreading of individual preferences in the other two formations was larger, no significant result for combined best preferred approach direction was found, which stresses the importance of finding a suitable way for a robot to approach a group of people.

As the participants were in pairs during the study, the position of the other person influenced the experience. When the other person was between the participant and the robot, the participant rated the approaches as slightly more comfortable than when the other person was not in between. A non-significant trend showed that participants gave the highest score for comfort when the robot approached from the individual left or right front and when the task-partner was closest to the robot ($M=3.9$, $SD=0.88$). The average lowest scores were given for the robot approaching from the individual left or right back when they were closest to the robot ($M=2.6$, $SD=1.22$).

The layout of the room might have influenced the results. Participants preferred the robot to approach from the window-side of the room. The entrance/exit was on the opposite side of the room, so probably people liked to keep the route to the door free. These are interesting observations, as in public spaces not only the formation of the group of visitors may influence the preferred approach direction, but also the layout of the environment.

4. LIMITATIONS AND FUTURE WORK

As described this is a quasi-experiment with a limited number of participants for the number of variables. However, our results are in line with previous research and we offer some preliminary suggestions on how to approach pairs of people with a robot.

Future work on this topic will include larger groups (up to 5 people), and research in real life settings. We will work on approach of groups of visitors who are focused on the exhibitions and are standing in various formations.

5. ACKNOWLEDGMENTS

The research leading to these results has received funding from the European Community's 7th Framework Program under Grant agreement 288235 (FROG).

6. REFERENCES

[1] Dautenhahn, K., Walters, M.L., Woods, S., Koay, K.L., Nehaniv, C.L., Sisbot, E.A., Alami, R. and Siméon, T. 2006. How may I serve you? A robot companion approaching a sitting person in a helping context. *HRI '06 - Proceeding of the 1st ACM SIGCHI/SIGART conference on Human-robot interaction* (2006), 172–179.

[2] Kendon, A. 1990. *Conducting interaction: Patterns of behavior in focused encounters*. Cambridge University Press.

[3] Satake, S., Kanda, T., Glas, D.F., Imai, M., Ishiguro, H. and Hagita, N. 2010. How to Approach Humans?-Strategies for Social Robots to Initiate Interaction-. *Journal of the Robotics Society of Japan*. 28, 3 (2010), 327–337.

[4] Walters, M.L., Dautenhahn, K., Woods, S.N., Koay, K.L., Lane, C. and Uk, H. 2007. Robotic Etiquette : Results from User Studies Involving a Fetch and Carry Task. *HRI '07 Proceedings of the 2nd ACM/IEEE international conference on Human robot interaction* (2007), 317–324.

Children Comply with a Robot's Indirect Requests

James Kennedy, Paul Baxter, Tony Belpaeme
Centre for Robotics and Neural Systems
Cognition Institute
Plymouth University, U.K.
{james.kennedy, paul.baxter, tony.belpaeme}@plymouth.ac.uk

ABSTRACT

Compliance studies in human-robot interaction (HRI) tend to consist of direct requests from the robot to the human. It is suggested that indirect requests are considered more polite, which has been positively correlated with learning gains. An experiment is conducted to explore compliance with indirect robot requests in teaching interactions. A comparison is made across embodiment conditions, but no significant differences are found. Overall, children comply with the robot's requests, which is used to support the hypothesis that given a well-defined context, children will infer the indirect meaning of a suggestion from a robot.

Categories and Subject Descriptors

H.1.2 [**Models and Principles**]: User/Machine Systems

General Terms

Experimentation, Human Factors, Theory

Keywords

Social HRI; compliance; educational interactions; Sandtray

1. INTRODUCTION

Many studies have considered compliance in human-robot interaction (HRI). It is commonly found that humans will comply with a robot's request or instruction; this compliance can even be stretched to carrying out unusual, possibly 'incorrect', tasks when a physical robot is present [1].

However, these studies often use very direct phrasing; the participants are directly told what to do by the robot as in [4]. It has been suggested that humans tend to make requests indirectly as this is considered to be more polite [3]. In turn, increased politeness has been positively correlated to learning gains in teaching interactions [6].

Therefore, using indirect requests with a robot can be seen as desirable in an educational setting. One of the challenges here is that an indirect approach often requires the respondent to process the request into multiple meanings: the literal understanding of the questions being asked and the inference of the request for action [3]. This relies not only on the social understanding between the interaction partners, but also on the context in which requests are made. It is hypothesised that when provided with a suitable context, children will complete this process and comply with a robot's indirect suggestion.

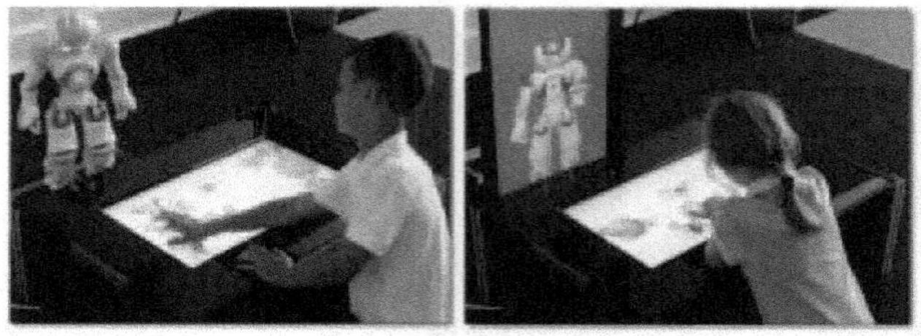

Figure 1: Experimental setup - the child and robot sit opposite to each other around the Sandtray. Both the real robot (left) and virtual robot (right) conditions are shown.

2. METHODOLOGY

Dyadic interactions between a child and a robot took place around a large touchscreen called the 'Sandtray' (figure 1), which has previously been used to contextualise interactions [5]. A total of 28 interactions took place (11M, 17F, age=7.9, SD=0.31). The age range of 7-8 year old children was used as part of a larger research project [2].

The children were introduced to the robot by the experimenters, before the robot informed the children of the task to be completed: sorting aliens into one of two planets (with a predefined membership rule). The robot then explained to the child that categorisations could be made by dragging an alien over one of the planets and releasing it. The child is then asked to 'have a go' without the help of the robot. Once a full set of 12 aliens had been completed, the robot started the teaching phase of the interaction.

One of the study aims was for the children to learn the pattern which led to correct alien categorisations. In order to achieve this, the robot acted as a teacher and would try to guide the child towards the correct pattern for categorisation by making suggestions and providing feedback on child categorisations. The robot would suggest an alien to move by selecting it and moving it to the centre of the screen, ac-

HRI'14, March 3–6, 2014, Bielefeld, Germany.
ACM 978-1-4503-2658-2/14/03.
http://dx.doi.org/10.1145/2559636.2559820.

companying the move with an indirect suggestion. Example suggestions include "How about this one with green arms?" and "Where will orange wings go?".

The average length of the entire interaction was 533 seconds (SD=58s), with the teaching phase lasting an average of 309s (SD=45s). Previous studies have revealed differences in compliance between different robot embodiments [1], so children were split across two embodiment conditions; 15 interacted with the real robot and 13 with the virtual robot.

3. ANALYSIS

The robot made a total of 363 moves across all of the interactions (M=13.0, SD=6.2). Some of the moves by either the child or robot were occluded, so cannot be counted in the statistical analysis. 'Taken immediately' means that the child categorised the suggested image as their next move after the suggestion. 'After completing move' means that if the suggestion was made whilst the child already had an image selected, they categorised their selected image and then the suggested one. 'Not taken' means that the child did not categorise the image in their move immediately succeeding the suggestion.

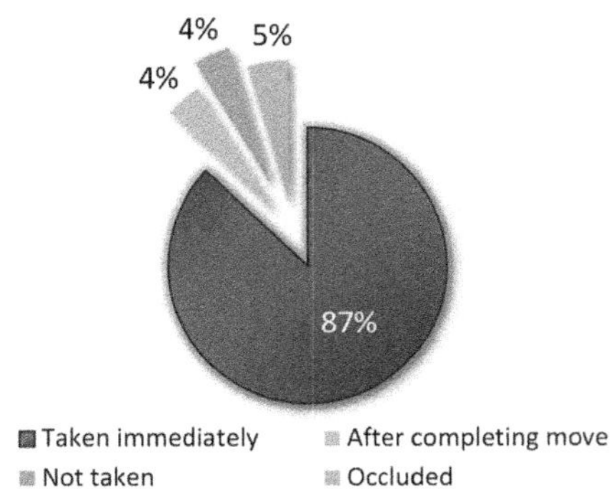

Figure 2: Pie chart of the reactions to suggestions made by the robot. Some are occluded as it is unclear which image the robot or child moved.

Of the moves which were not occluded (figure 2), significantly more were taken immediately (M=11.3, SD=6.2) than after the completion of a current move or not taken at all (M=1.1, SD=1.2), t(27)=8.308, p<0.001. No significant differences were found between different embodiment conditions for overall compliance with the robot's suggestions. In the task and context used here, the robot's behaviour has a stronger effect than its embodiment; further work could explore whether this holds true for different contexts.

These results demonstrate that the children inferred from the context that a suggestion did not simply mean to answer the question, but also to carry out the action of categorising the item the robot had suggested. Additionally, it shows that the children are willing to comply with the request. This may not be so surprising, as the only thing that they can do is categorise images; the choice they make is whether to categorise the image the robot has highlighted or a different one.

A further characterisation can be made by considering the instances in which the robot made a suggestion while the child was part-way through another move; an 'interrupting' suggestion. A total of 82 interrupting suggestions occurred across all of the interactions (M=2.9, SD=2.6), but there were none in 5 of the interactions. In interactions where these suggestions occurred, significantly more were taken immediately (M=2.4, SD=2.1) than not (M=1.0, SD=1.1), t(22)=2.709, p=0.013. Again, no significant differences were found between embodiment conditions.

4. DISCUSSION

The results show that children are significantly more likely to immediately comply with the robot's suggestion than not, regardless of embodiment condition and whether they already have an image which they are moving. These interrupting suggestions provide the most compelling evidence that the children want to comply with the robot's requests, as it requires them to stop and change their current plan.

As described in section 1, the suggestions are indirect and require the children to process both the literal and indirect meanings. The results provide support for the hypothesis, that children do indeed go through this process and come to the correct conclusion: 'the robot wants me to move that image'. The context provided by the Sandtray enables this kind of suggestion because the content is so constrained that the suggestion, despite being indirect, is unambiguous.

Although not measured here, it is possible that humans would see robots as more polite when they use indirect suggestions. This potentially increased politeness and its link to knowledge gain [6] would certainly make for an interesting future study.

5. ACKNOWLEDGMENTS

This work is funded by the EU FP7 ALIZ-E project (grant 248116) and the School of Computing and Maths, Plymouth University, U.K.

6. REFERENCES

[1] W. A. Bainbridge, J. Hart, E. S. Kim, and B. Scassellati. The effect of presence on human-robot interaction. In *Proceedings of the 17th IEEE International Symposium on Robot and Human Interactive Communication (RO-MAN) 2008*, pages 701–706. IEEE, 2008.

[2] T. Belpaeme et al. Multimodal child-robot interaction: Building social bonds. *Journal of Human-Robot Interaction*, 1(2):33–53, 2012.

[3] H. H. Clark and D. H. Schunk. Polite responses to polite requests. *Cognition*, 8(2):111–143, 1980.

[4] J. Goetz, S. Kiesler, and A. Powers. Matching robot appearance and behavior to tasks to improve human-robot cooperation. In *Proceedings of the 12th IEEE International Symposium on Robot and Human Interactive Communication (RO-MAN) 2003*, pages 55–60. IEEE, 2003.

[5] J. Kennedy, P. Baxter, and T. Belpaeme. Constraining content in mediated unstructured social interactions: Studies in the wild. In *Proceedings of the 5th International Workshop on Affective Interaction in Naturalistic Environments (AFFINE'13), at ACII'13*, pages 728–733. IEEE Computer Society, 2013.

[6] N. Wang, W. L. Johnson, R. E. Mayer, P. Rizzo, E. Shaw, and H. Collins. The politeness effect: Pedagogical agents and learning outcomes. *International Journal of Human-Computer Studies*, 66(2):98–112, 2008.

Probabilistic Multiparty Dialogue Management for a Game Master Robot

Casey Kennington*
Bielefeld University
Universitätsstraße 25
Bielefeld, Germany
c.kennington@cit-ec.uni-bielefeld.de

Kotaro Funakoshi
Honda Research Institute Japan Co., Ltd.
8-1 Honcho, Wako
Saitama, Japan
funakoshi@jp.honda-ri.com

Yuki Takahashi
Waseda University
1-104 Totsukamachi
Shinjuku, Tokyo, Japan
y_takahashi@sugano.mech.waseda.ac.jp

Mikio Nakano†
nakano@jp.honda-ri.com

ABSTRACT

We present our ongoing research on multiparty dialogue management for a game master robot which engages multiple human participants to play a quiz game. The robot invites passing people to join the game, instructs participants on the rules of the game, and leads them in the game. The robot has to manage people leaving and coming at arbitrary times. Our approach maintains a dialogue manager for each participant, and a module takes a final action with each decision cycle; responsible to decide "what/whom/when to say". We have implemented the dialogue manager with a probabilistic rules approach [4] and made preliminary evaluations with our multiparty human-robot game dialogue data that was collected in a WoZ fashion.

General Terms

Technology-Centered, Multiparty Dialogue, Dialogue Management

1. INTRODUCTION

Dialogue management (DM) is an active area of ongoing research, yet much of the research has focused on non-situated, two-party DM. Multiparty dialogue management (MDM) has been an area of interest for some years; [2] explored the characteristics of mutliparty dialogue (multilogue) in comparison to two-party dialogue. There is also recent multilogue research using virtual agents [7], including aspects of turn-taking [1]. [3] gives results on a MDM system for a robot bartender, which engaged multiple participants. Furthermore, MDM differs from standard DM because of necessary addressee identification, or *focus of attention* (FOA; a good comparison of methods can be found in [5]).

Here, we present ongoing research in MDM, in a multi-modal, situated dialogue environment. We are developing a model of MDM that can (potentially) manage any number of human participants in a task-based quiz game scenario. Our model is pro-active in that it engages participants and invites them to play the game. Furthermore, if a participant becomes confused during the game, the dialogue system (DS) will offer hints so the game can proceed. It also incorporates a module that predicts the addressee (henceforth, FOA) for each action that it takes. We project that our model can potentially be used as a DS in an embodied robot agent.

2. CURRENT STATE OF THE MODEL

In [6], the author examines several issues in MDM, mentioning two possible approaches: (1) treat it as a set of pairs of two-party conversations, or (2) treat it as a single, unified model for all participants. Though (2) is arguably the superior approach, we opt for (1) for the obvious reason of simplicity and that it can work well with our task, but more importantly scaling the model to work with any number of participants (more than just 2 or 3) without an exponentially increasing state space (or need for more data) is an attractive approach. Our model maintains a separate, individual DM for each participant, modeled as a Bayesian network (BN) using probabilistic rules, where a dialogue policy can be estimated from training data (i.e., a *Markov decision process*, MDP; see bottom part of Figure 1 for a simple, unrolled decision BN), as described in [4].[1]

An overview of our approach can be seen in Figure 1. The model accepts input from various sources in real-time, which maintains an observed user state for each participant; namely their speech, to whom they are speaking and looking (i.e.,

*Also affiliated with CITEC.
†Also affiliated with Honda Research Institute Japan, Co., Ltd.

[1]Indeed, we are using the *opendial* software package developed by the author of [4]: https://code.google.com/p/opendial/

HRI'14, March 3–6, 2014, Bielefeld, Germany.
ACM 978-1-4503-2658-2/14/03.
http://dx.doi.org/10.1145/2559636.2563693

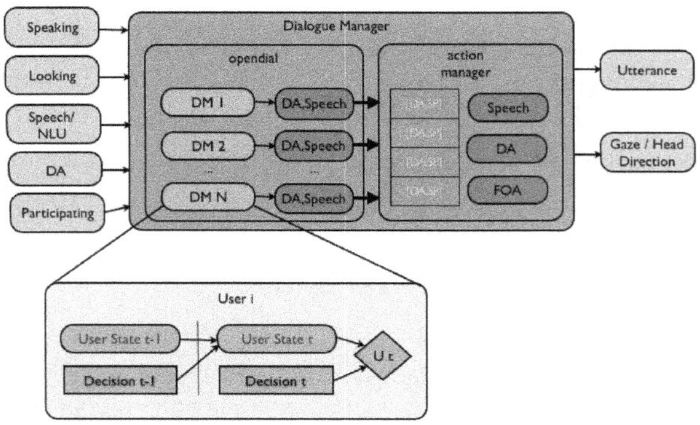

Figure 1: Model overview: input sensors provide input for individual DMs modeled as BNs. The action manager determines the final output, given all the DMs.

gaze), their dialogue act (DA), and their state of participation.

An important aspect of our approach is in the *action manager* (AM) which makes the final decision on what action to take (and when) based upon the decisions of each DM. It is implemented as a priority queue, where the priority of a DA is set by its source DM. For example, when the rules of the game are to be explained, it results in 5 separate DAs, each of which are put on the queue and uttered sequentially. If a user asks for a clarification request at any point, the DM for that user will put a high-priority repeat request DA on the queue, resulting in repeating the previous utterance before the rest of the rules are completed.

The FOA module is invoked when the AM wants to perform an act (i.e., a speech act). When invoked, a Maximum Entropy classifier uses a simple feature set (a somewhat different approach from [5]) to determine if a user receives attention or not. All users that receive attention make up the FOA and any subset of the participants can be considered for the FOA.

We make several assumptions at this point in our ongoing research: we can detect participants and can segregate their multi-modal input signals such that their user state can be maintained in a DM for that particular participant. Also, we are using annotated data to develop our model and assume that the user states are fully observed, however with anticipation of using partially-observed user states in the future.

3. PRELIMINARY EXPERIMENTS

We have collected 23 WoZ sessions using the NAO robot.[2] In each session, up to 3 participants can interact with the robot and each are free to join or leave at any time. As they pass by, the robot calls out to them, introduces itself, then invites them to play a game. If they agree, the rules are explained and, if understood, the game begins. The game is a 20-questions scenario where the robot (wizard) thinks of an object and the participants can ask yes/no questions. The game is successful if one of the participants guesses the correct object. Multiple games can be played in a session.

[2]http://www.aldebaran-robotics.com

A professional annotator annotated the gaze, speech recipients, participation states, dialogue acts, and transcribed the speech of each participant and the wizard. Due to the current state of annotations, we used the first 9 sessions for training and session 10 for evaluation. We first evaluated the FOA by comparing the predicted set to the labeleld set with partial credit (i.e., if 1 user was correctly labeled, but the correct had 2 users, it was 50% correct). Our FOA module received 71% accuracy on the train/eval set, 78% leave-one-out (majority baseline of 33%; 57% baseline using simple rules). We further evaluated the ability of opendial to correctly make DA decisions using our data. The training data was used to determine the rules for opendial (user states and corresponding wizard decisions), as well as learn the dialogue policy (we were only able to train on part of the data, however, due to time constraints). The same trained model was used for all individual user textscdms. That yielded a 52% decision accuracy (19 possible DAs, 37% majority, 51% bigram majority baselines), with foreseeable improvements in the near future.

A better evaluation, that of real-time interaction with humans, is left to future work. Our own interactions with the system have shown promise; the system works in real-time, making decisions based on input events as well as handling simple clarification requests, and produces synthesized utterances. We will continue to improve the DA prediction of individual DMs, use more of the available data, as well as improve the AM to handle more complicated scenarios, including timing.

4. REFERENCES

[1] D. Bohus and E. Horvitz. Multiparty Turn Taking in Situated Dialog : Study , Lessons , and Directions. In *Proceedings of SIGDIAL 2011*, number 1974, pages 98–109. ACL, 2011.

[2] M. Ishizaki and T. Kato. Exploring the characteristics of multi-party dialogues. In *Proceedings of the 17th international conference on Computational linguistics-Volume 1*, pages 583–589. ACL, 1998.

[3] S. Keizer, M. E. Foster, O. Lemon, A. Gaschler, and M. Giuliani. Training and evaluation of an MDP model for social multi-user human-robot interaction. In *Proceedings of SIGDIAL 2013*, pages 223–232, Metz, France, Aug. 2013. ACL.

[4] P. Lison. Probabilistic Dialogue Models with Prior Domain Knowledge. In *Proceedings of SIGDIAL 2013*, pages 179–188, Seoul, South Korea, July 2012. ACL.

[5] R. op den Akker and D. R. Traum. A comparison of addressee detection methods for multiparty conversations. In *Proceedings of the 13th Semdial Workshop on the Semantics and Pragmatics of Dialogue*, pages 99–106, Stockholm, Sweden, 2009.

[6] D. Traum. Issues in multiparty dialogues. In *Advances in agent communication*, pages 201–211. Springer, 2004.

[7] D. Traum, D. DeVault, J. Lee, Z. Wang, and S. Marsella. Incremental dialogue understanding and feedback for multiparty, multimodal conversation. In *Intelligent Virtual Agents*, pages 275–288. Springer, 2012.

Inertial Motion Capture Based Reference Trajectory Generation for a Mobile Manipulator

Yerbolat Khassanov, Nursultan Imanberdiyev and Huseyin Atakan Varol
Department of Robotics and Mechatronics, Nazarbayev University
Astana, Kazakhstan
Email: {yerbolat.khassanov; nimanberdiyev; ahvarol}@nu.edu.kz

ABSTRACT
This paper presents a human-robot interaction system integrating a mobile manipulator with a full-body inertial motion capture suit. The framework aims to provide an intuitive, effective and easy-to-deploy teleoperation interface. User control intent is acquired by the motion capture system in real-time, processed and relayed to the mobile manipulator wirelessly. Specifically, body center of mass and the right hand kinematic data of the user are used to generate position and orientation references for the robot base and manipulator, respectively. The left arm is employed to provide high-level user commands such as "Manipulator On/Off", "Base On/Off" and "Manipulator Pause/Resume". The efficacy of the presented system was demonstrated in real-time teleoperation experiments using KUKA youBot mobile manipulator accomplishing pick-and-place tasks.

Categories and Subject Descriptors
I.2.9 [**Robotics**]: Operator interfaces
H.5.2 [**User Interfaces**] Interaction styles (e.g., commands, menus, forms, direct manipulation)

Keywords
Teleoperation, inertial motion capture, mobile manipulator, remote manipulation.

1. INTRODUCTION
Rapid development of computer vision and artificial intelligence in recent years expanded the application areas of autonomous robots. However, an autonomous system may not provide a sufficient degree of reliability for applications of increased complexity and in dynamic environments. Human intelligence is frequently employed for high-level robot decision making and control. Nonetheless, human presence at the robot site is undesirable or impossible in many cases such as space or undersea exploration, hazardous material handling, disarmament of improvised explosive devices, work in nuclear facilities during emergencies, etc. Researchers developed various human-machine interfaces to overcome this restriction.

Conventional human-machine interfaces for robotic systems include a variety of methods based on electromyographic muscular activity sensors [3], exoskeletal mechanical devices [6], joysticks [1], instrumented gloves, computer mouse and keyboard [2]. These devices require unnatural hand and arm motions failing to utilize the full extent of the dexterous human motion capabilities. Vision-based approaches [4; 5; 7] have been developed to provide a higher bandwidth teleoperation interface between the user and the device. Even though it is possible to obtain full-body kinematic data using the vision-based systems, they also have shortcomings. Firstly, a high number of cameras is needed to prevent occlusion of the markers required for motion tracking. Secondly, user needs to operate in the capture volume of the cameras. Since the motion capture cameras are fixed to frames or tripods, the portability of the teleoperation system is decreased. Thirdly, infrared light sources and reflective objects in the capture volume are erroneously recognized as markers. Removal of these artifacts requires time consuming post-processing. In order to solve the aforementioned problems, we designed the mobile manipulator teleoperation control system which utilizes inertial motion capture (IMC) suit (see Figure 1). The teleoperation

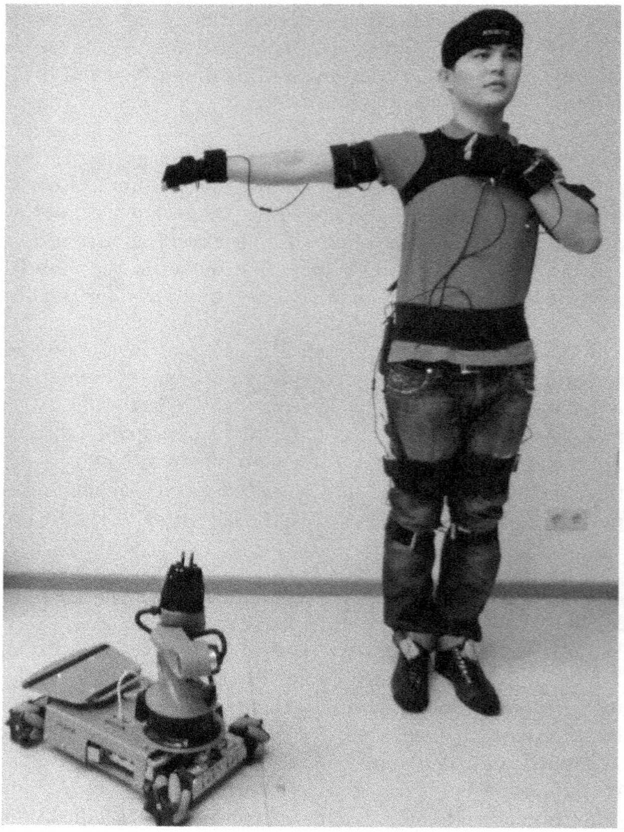

Figure 1. User wearing the XSENS inertial motion capture suit and teleoperating the KUKA youBot mobile robot manipulator.

HRI'14, March 3–6, 2014, Bielefeld, Germany.
ACM 978-1-4503-2658-2/14/03.
http://dx.doi.org/10.1145/2559636.2559812

framework consists of two parts: reference generation for the robot base and manipulator and gesture recognition for providing high-level commands for the user interface (see Figure 2). This paper focuses on the design of the reference generation subcontroller.

2. INERTIAL MOTION CAPTURE BASED REFERENCE GENERATION

The user kinematic data is acquired by the IMC system at 50 Hz sampling rate. In order to create an intuitive mapping between the body segments and mobile manipulator parts, we decided to use the right hand position and orientation to generate the robot end effector position and orientation references. Inverse kinematics for the mobile manipulator arm is computed at each sampling time to convert hand position and orientation to robot joint angles. The body center of mass (CoM) position and orientation is used to provide position and orientation references for the omnidirectional base. Any user CoM movement can be tracked by the robot base due to its holonomic structure (as long as the maximum velocity constraints are satisfied). In order to remove movement artifacts due to body sway during walking and standing; and involuntary hand movements; the acquired kinematic data is firstly filtered using a five point moving average filter. Additionally, we implemented simple sway and tremor removal algorithm to clean the motion references. In the involuntary movement removal algorithm, moving average filtered new robot position reference samples are only given as final motion references for the mobile manipulator, if the Euclidian distance between the last and current sample is greater than a predefined distance. We set this distance to be 5 and 1 mm for the robot base and the arm, respectively. This way, only distinct and deliberate motions are used for motion reference generation. Higher frequency lower amplitude motions due to involuntary movements of the user are filtered out.

3. REAL-TIME REFERENCE GENERATION EXPERIMENTS

An experiment was designed to evaluate the efficacy of the presented reference generation approach. According to the experimental scenario, a human user guides the robot through a course with static obstacles and then performs a pick-and-place task using manipulator's end effector. The human operator, the experimental subject, was briefed about the trial and instructed on the operation of the interface. After putting on the full-body IMC suit, the user was allotted an hour time for freestyle operation to familiarize himself with the system operation and response. During the experiment, the mobile manipulator teleoperated by the user successfully traversed the experiment course and performed object manipulation tasks as planned. The user claimed that the system was very intuitive and easy to learn. Moreover, the user pointed out that he would prefer the IMC interface over another one consisting of a joystick and keyboard.

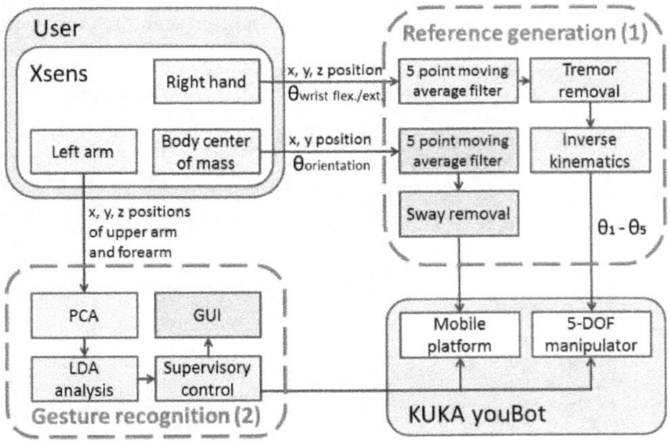

Figure 2. Inertial motion capture based teleoperation system consisting of the gesture recognition and reference generation subsystems.

4. FUTURE WORK

The quantitative comparison of the IMC interface performance with traditional ones remains a topic for future work. We also plan to integrate augmented and/or virtual reality goggles to the presented system for performing remote teleoperation. A multigrasp hand will also replace the two-finger gripper to enable dexterous manipulation. Myoelectric control interfaces for the multigrasp hand will also be merged with the presented inertial motion capture based interface.

5. REFERENCES

[1] Cho, S.K., Jin, H.Z., Lee, J.M., and Yao, B. Teleoperation of a mobile robot using a force-reflection joystick with sensing mechanism of rotating magnetic field. *IEEE/ASME Transactions on Mechatronics 15*, 1 (February), 17-26. DOI= http://dx.doi.org/10.1109/TMECH.2009.2013848.

[2] Ding, C.J., Duan, P., Zhang, M.L., and Zhang, Y.F. Design of mobile robot teleoperation system based on virtual reality. In *IEEE International Conference on Automation and Logistics*, Shenyang, 2023-2028. DOI= http://dx.doi.org/10.1109/ICAL.2009.5262601.

[3] Fukuda, O., Tsuji, T., Kaneko, M., and Otsuka, A. A human-assisting manipulator teleoperated by EMG signals and arm motions. *IEEE Transactions on Robotics and Automation 19*, 2 (April), 210-222. DOI= http://dx.doi.org/10.1109/TRA.2003.808873.

[4] Hu, C., Meng, M.Q., Liu, P.X.P., and Wang, X. Visual gesture recognition for human-machine interface of robot teleoperation. In *Proceedings of the 2003 IEEE/RSJ International Conference on Intelligent Robots and Systems*, 1560-1565. DOI= http://dx.doi.org/10.1109/IROS.2003.1248866.

[5] Kofman, J., Wu, X.H., Luu, T.J., and Verma, S. Teleoperation of a robot manipulator using a vision-based human-robot interface. *IEEE Transactions on Industrial Electronics 52*, 5 (October), 1206-1219. DOI= http://dx.doi.org/10.1109/TIE.2005.855696.

[6] Rosen, J. and Perry, J.C. Upper limb powered exoskeleton design. *IEEE/ASME Transactions on Mechatronics 12*, 4 (August 20), 408 - 417. DOI= http://dx.doi.org/10.1109/TMECH.2007.901934.

[7] Song, W.B., Guo, X.J., Jiang, F.J., Yang, S., Jiang, G.X., and Shi, Y.F. Teleoperation humanoid robot control system based on Kinect sensor. In *International Conference on Intelligent Human-Machine Systems and Cybernetics*, Nanchang, Jiangxi, 264-267. DOI= http://dx.doi.org/10.1109/IHMSC.2012.159.

Real-Time Gesture Recognition for the High-Level Teleoperation Interface of a Mobile Manipulator

Yerbolat Khassanov, Nursultan Imanberdiyev and Huseyin Atakan Varol

Department of Robotics and Mechatronics
Nazarbayev University
Astana, Kazakhstan

Email: {yerbolat.khassanov; nimanberdiyev; ahvarol}@nu.edu.kz

ABSTRACT

This paper describes an inertial motion capture based arm gesture recognition system for the high-level control of a mobile manipulator. Left arm kinematic data of the user is acquired by an inertial motion capture system (Xsens MVN) in real-time and processed to extract supervisory user interface commands such as "Manipulator On/Off", "Base On/Off" and "Operation Pause/Resume" for a mobile manipulator system (KUKA youBot). Principal Component Analysis and Linear Discriminant Analysis are employed for dimension reduction and classification of the user kinematic data, respectively. The classification accuracy for the six class gesture recognition problem is 95.6 percent. In order to increase the reliability of the gesture recognition framework in real-time operation, a consensus voting scheme involving the last ten classification results is implemented. During the five-minute long teleoperation experiment, a total of 25 high-level commands were recognized correctly by the consensus voting enhanced gesture recognizer. The experimental subject stated that the user interface was easy to learn and did not require extensive mental effort to operate.

Categories and Subject Descriptors

I.2.9 [**Robotics**]: Operator interfaces

H.5.2 [**User Interfaces**] Interaction styles (e.g., commands, menus, forms, direct manipulation)

Keywords

Gesture recognition, inertial motion capture, human-robot interaction, mobile manipulator, teleoperation.

1. INTRODUCTION

Gesture recognition is becoming an essential and critical building block of intelligent and efficient human-machine interfaces. Gesture recognition applications include sign language recognition, immersive gaming technology, remote teleoperation and social assistive robotics. The primary objective of a gesture recognition system for robots is to make a robot understand human body language (or commands associated with it) bridging the gap between the human and the machine. Gesture recognition can enhance human-robot interaction eliminating the need for traditional input devices such as keyboard, joystick and mouse.

HRI'14, March 3–6, 2014, Bielefeld, Germany.
ACM 978-1-4503-2658-2/14/03.
http://dx.doi.org/10.1145/2559636.2563712

There are several tools for performing gesture recognition. These include instrumented gloves [3] and marker-based optical tracking [6]. Each mentioned method varies in accuracy, resolution, latency, range of motion, user comfort and cost [5]. For instance, glove-based interfaces require a user to wear cumbersome device connected usually with cables to a computer. This limits user's natural movement and causes discomfort. Vision-based techniques [1; 4; 7] introduced to overcome these constraints face other limitations such as occlusion of user's body parts, lack of portability, and high post-processing time for the removal of erroneously detected markers. On the other hand, inertial motion capture (IMC) based wireless motion tracking systems [8] offer a promising alternative to solve most of these problems and provide reliable, portable and real-time kinematic data acquisition.

At Nazarbayev University, we are developing an IMC based teleoperation framework for mobile manipulators. The framework consists of two parts: gesture recognition and reference generation (see Fig. 1). In this paper, we are presenting our preliminary work on the IMC-based gesture recognition system for the high-level teleoperation of the KUKA youBot mobile manipulator [2]. To the best of our knowledge, this work present the first usage of gesture recognition for providing high level user interface commands for inertial motion capture based teleoperation.

2. IMC Based Gesture Recognition

Six distinct left arm gestures were selected for providing high level commands to the teleoperation system. These gestures are *hand forward, hand on chest, hand on waist, hand up, hand sideways* and *neutral* (see Fig. 2). In order to design the gesture recognizer, a database was generated. The database generation was accomplished in approximately an hour time. For the database, a user wearing the inertial motion capture suit was

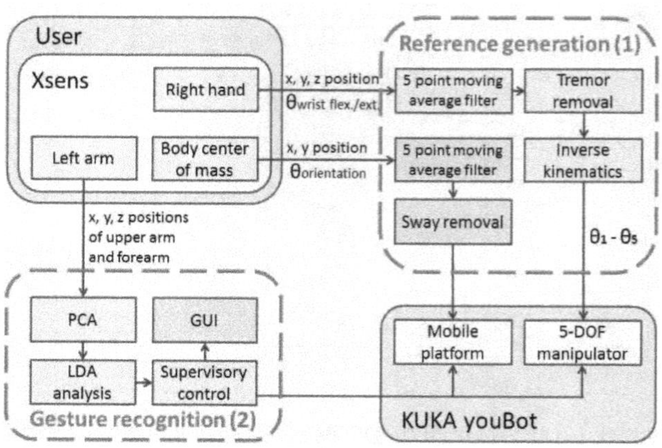

Figure 1. IMC based teleoperation system consisting of the gesture recognition and reference generation subsystems.

prompted with a sequence of gestures in random order. Total of 60 gestures, i.e. ten gestures per class, were displayed on the computer screen at five seconds intervals. The kinematic data of the left arm of the user was recorded continuously at a sampling rate of 1000 Hz. The data recorded during the initial and final one second periods of the five second intervals were discarded to remove samples belonging to transitions between gestures. In our mobile manipulator interface framework, a user controls the manipulator using his/her right hand and provides left hand gestures as high-level control command concurrently. In this case, the right hand motions might vary the user body position and orientation slightly, which would result in variations for the left arm kinematic data for different trials. Such scenario can potentially result in an erroneous gesture classification. In order to avoid this, the aforementioned database generation session was repeated for ten times. During each of the ten iterations, the user was varying his right hand position imitating the simultaneous manipulator control.

Five iterations were used for the recognizer training and the rest for the testing. Training dataset is normalized to the range of [-1, 1]. The obtained data is six-dimensional (*x, y, z* positions of the upper arm and the forearm). Principal Component Analysis (PCA) is then applied to the normalized data to reduce the number of dimensions to three. Subsequently, the dimension reduced data is used to train a Linear Discriminant Analysis (LDA) classifier model. The normalization, PCA and LDA coefficients are used both to classify the testing set samples and also for the real-time gesture recognition experiments. Classification accuracy for the testing set is 95.6 percent.

In order to decrease the possibility of generating a wrong command, a consensus voting scheme was employed at the expense of increased delay. During real-time operation at 50 Hz sampling frequency, the last ten classification results are stored in an array and a command is generated, if all of these classification results belong to the same class.

3. Real-Time Gesture Recognition Experiment

A real-time teleoperation experiment was designed to test the performance of the gesture recognition system. The experiment was an object relocation task, in which arm gestures were needed to provide high-level commands to the mobile manipulator. The experiment was conducted on one 22 year old subject. Six gestures were associated with particular commands. Some of the gestures were used to toggle some states of the system such as "Manipulator On/Off". The arm gestures and their corresponding commands are as follows:

- *Hand forward* gesture activates/deactivates the base.
- *Hand up* gesture activates/deactivates the manipulator; deactivation moves manipulator to the initial position.
- *Hand on chest* gesture halts the manipulator at last acquired position or resumes it back from that position.
- *Hand sideways* gesture allows a user to switch between different manipulator motion modes.
- *Hand on waist* gesture is used to exit a selected mode.
- *Neutral gesture* does nothing (for rest)

A graphical user interface was developed to allow the user to visualize the recognized gestures. The test subject was given one hour to familiarize himself with the teleoperation system and then proceeded to the relocation task. In the five minute final experimental trial, 25 gestures were recognized with 100 percent accuracy without perceived latency by the user. The subject commented that the system is highly intuitive and does not require high mental effort to operate. It should be noted that the left arm is only used for providing gestures. Therefore, the gestures do not have to be segmented from other behavior.

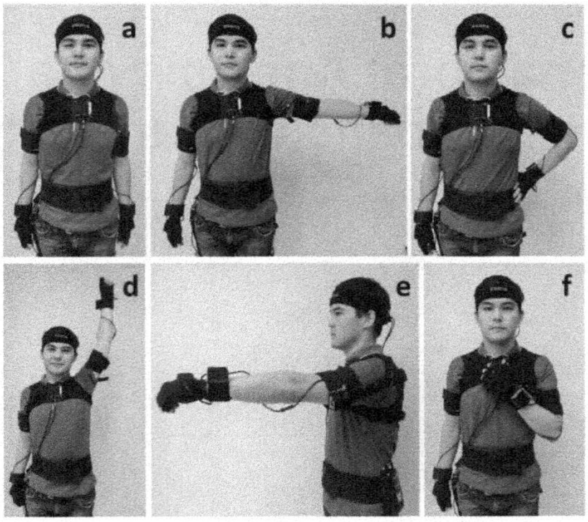

Figure 2. Gestures: neutral (a), hand sideways (b), hand on waist (c), hand up (d), hand forward (e), hand on chest (f).

4. REFERENCES

[1] Hasanuzzaman, M., Ampornararamveth, V., Zhang, T., Bhuiyan, M.A., Shirai, Y., and Ueno, H., 2004. Real-time vision-based gesture recognition for human robot interaction. In *IEEE ROBIO 2004: Proceedings of the IEEE International Conference on Robotics and Biomimetics*, Shenyang, 413-418. DOI= http://dx.doi.org/10.1109/ROBIO.2004.1521814.

[2] KUKA, KUKA youBot omni-directional mobile platform with arm. Retrieved December 2, 2013, from: http://youbot-store.com/youbot-store/youbots

[3] Liang, R.H. and Ouhyoung, M., 1998. A real-time continuous gesture recognition system for sign language. In *Proceedings of the Third IEEE International Conference on Automatic Face and Gesture Recognition* Nara, 558-567. DOI= http://dx.doi.org/10.1109/AFGR.1998.671007.

[4] Malima, A., Ozgur, E., and Cetin, M., 2006. A fast algorithm for vision-based hand gesture recognition for robot control. In *2006 IEEE 14th Signal Processing and Communications Applications, vol. 1-2*, Antalya, 762-765. DOI= http://dx.doi.org/10.1109/SIU.2006.1659822.

[5] Mitra, S. and Acharya, T., 2007. Gesture recognition: A survey. *IEEE Transactions on Systems, Man, and Cybernetics, Part C: Applications and Reviews 37*, 3 (May), 311-324. DOI= http://dx.doi.org/10.1109/TSMCC.2007.893280.

[6] Qian, G., Guo, F., Ingalls, T., Olson, L., James, J., and Rikakis, T., 2004. A gesture-driven multimodal interactive dance system. In *2004 IEEE International Conference on Multimedia and Exp (ICME), vol. 1-3*, Taipei, 1579-1582. DOI= http://dx.doi.org/10.1109/ICME.2004.1394550.

[7] Ramey, A., Gonzalez-Pacheco, V., and Salichs, M.A., 2011. Integration of a low-cost RGB-D sensor in a social robot for gesture recognition. In *2011 6th ACM/IEEE Int. Conf. on Human-Robot Interaction (HRI),* Lausanne, 229-230.

[8] XSENS, Xsens MVN - Inertial Motion Capture. Retrieved Dec. 2, 2013, from: http://www.xsens.com/en/general/mvn.

Behavioral Analysis of a Touch-Based Interaction between Humans and an Egg-shaped Robot According to Protrusions

Jintae Kim
TCL*, KAIST
Daejeon, Korea
kimjt@robot.kaist.ac.kr

Hyunsoo Song
TCL, KAIST
Daejeon, Korea
songhs@robot.kaist.ac.kr

Dong-Soo Kwon†
TCL, KAIST
Daejeon, Korea
kwonds@kaist.ac.kr

ABSTRACT

For a service robot, touch is one of the major interaction components. However, because many robot designs and touch sensor arrangements are designed by a company, actual user interactions do not match the implemented sensors in the robot. So it is necessary to investigate practical human touch patterns without advanced user knowledge of the robot's touch sensor. This study seeks to measure the influence of pointed and smooth-shaped protrusion types on touch interactions with an egg-shaped robot. Based on the results, a pointed protrusion creates distributed touch interaction while a smooth-shaped protrusion concentrates touch interaction.

Categories and Subject Descriptors

H.1.2 [**Human factors**]: human behavior analysis

General Terms

Experimentation

Keywords

Human robot interaction, touch interaction pattern, egg-shaped robot, protrusion

1. INTRODUCTION

For a service robot, touch is a major mode of interactions [1]. However, because the sensor arrangement is designed by designers or engineers, actual user interactions often do not match the arrangement of the sensors.

The best solution to ensure that a robot recognizes a human's touch interaction perfectly is to cover the entire surface of the robot with sensors, such as the Robovie series (Osaka Univ, apan) [2]. However, this is not efficient for a commercially manufactured robot.

To optimize the positions of the sensors and the types of interaction, the user's touch pattern must be understood beforehand. The locations and the priority levels of sensors can be determined from the positions with the most touches. Moreover, the types of necessary sensors can be predicted from the users' touch pattern tendencies (e.g., stroking, hitting).

This research seeks to predict user interaction patterns using parts which protrude from an egg-shaped service robot. The aim is to suggest a guideline for the arrangement of touch sensors and thus adjust robot designs for specific types of touch interaction.

2. DEFINITION OF THE EGG-SHAPE

Many service robots can be analyzed as combinations of a streamlined body, head, wheels and different shapes of protruding parts, as shown in Fig. 1.

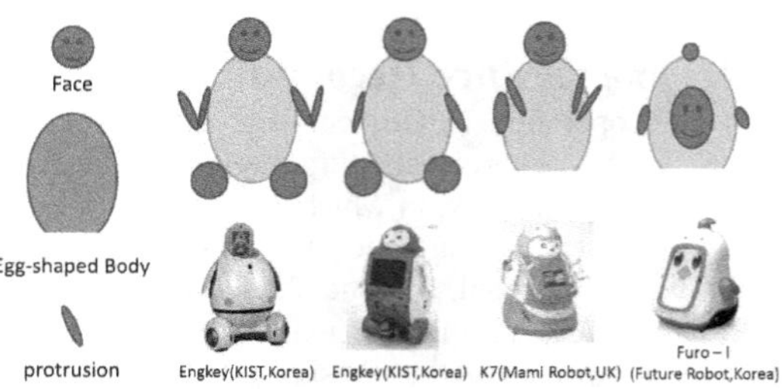

Figure 1: egg-shaped service robots

This research utilizes a desktop type of service robot that uses a distance to the human user characterized as an intimate distance (0.15m - 0.45m) [3].

3. EXPERIMENT

t is a precondition that the slope of the protrusion influences the distribution or concentration of the touch interactions. Therefore, the hypotheses are as follows:

1. A pointed protrusion will distribute touch interactions.
2. A smooth-shaped extrusion will concentrate touch interactions.

For the experiment, the egg-shaped object has a width of 25 cm and a height of 35 cm. The face is attached to the front side (Fig. 2). Interaction data was counted by a video

*More information is at http: robot.kaist.ac.kr.
†This Author is corresponding author.

HRI'14, March 3–6, 2014, Bielefeld, Germany.
ACM 978-1-4503-2658-2/14/03.
http://dx.doi.org/10.1145/2559636.2563708.

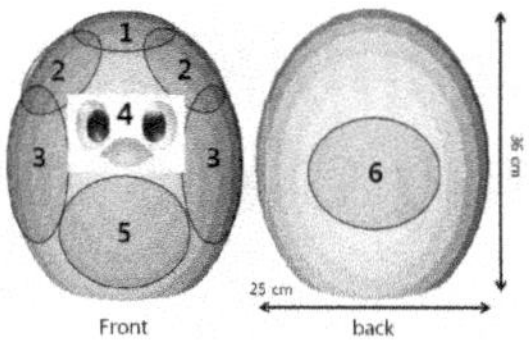

Figure 2: touch sections and size

recorder with the video replayed after the experiment. The experimenter explained touch interaction to the subjects and a free interaction time was permitted. Time of 30sec to 1min was given to each subject. The recorded data was analyzed in terms of the pairs of the positions and touch interaction patterns over time.

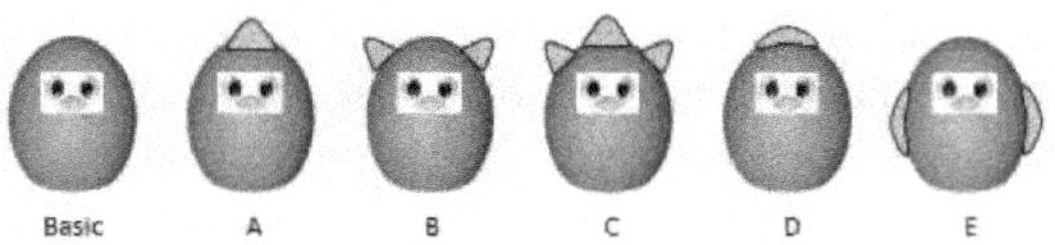

Figure 3: experimental objects combined with protrusion

To verify the assumptions made about the impact of the distribution and concentration of the touch interactions according to the protruding part, we utilized five experimental trials with five protrusions (A to E) and with one basic shape, as shown in Fig. 3. There was no reaction and feedback scenario; instead, the situation was simply stopped. The number of subjects for each experiment is shown in Table 1. All subjects were in their 20s.

Table 1: the number of subjects

	Basic	A	B	C	D	E	Sum
# of subjects	29	6	4	8	8	7	62

4. RESULTS

In the experiment, the types of observed touch interactions were classified into three patterns considering touch sensor recognition [4]. These three types were facial direction interaction (rubbing), normal direction interaction (patting) and simple touch interaction (grabbing).

In Table 2, the numbers in brackets indicate that the subject touches the protrusion directly, while numbers outside the brackets refer to the touching proportion excluding the protrusions at the same locations shown in Figure 2.

Comparing the results of the Basic condition with the results of A, B and C, the data of location 1 in each experiment showed an impact of a pointed protrusion, which did not match our hypothesis which stated that a pointed protrusion would reduce touch interactions. On the other hand, we found that a smooth-shaped protrusion would concentrate touch in the Basic, D and E experimental results.

The touch portion of location 1 in each experiment was relatively high, from about 30 to 60 percent. This indicates that location 1 is a very important part for touch interactions with humans.

In addition, grabbing interactions increased when both protrusion types was attached, whereas the proportion of

Table 2: touch interaction patterns

%	Location	1	2	3
Basic	rubbing	14.18	10.15	4.86
	grabbing	10.13	8.31	4.86
	patting	13.16	4.62	4.86
	Sum	37.46	23.08	14.58
A	rubbing	15.38(0)	15.38	5.77
	grabbing	1.92(11.54)	15.38	5.77
	patting	0(1.92)	5.77	1.92
	Sum	**17.30(13.46)**	36.54	13.46
B	rubbing	9.52	0(4.76)	0.00
	grabbing	38.10	4.76(9.52)	0.00
	patting	19.05	0.00	0.00
	Sum	66.67	**4.76(14.29)**	0.00
C	rubbing	8.00(4.0)	16.00	0.00
	grabbing	16.0(24.0)	4.00	4.00
	patting	12.0(4.0)	4.00	0.00
	Sum	**36.0(32.0)**	**24.00**	4.00
D	rubbing	9.52(4.76)	0.00	0.00
	grabbing	38.09(9.52)	4.76	0.00
	patting	19.05(0)	0.00	0.00
	Sum	**66.66(14.29)**	4.76	0.00
E	rubbing	11.54	0.00	7.69
	grabbing	7.69	0.00	3.8(30.77)
	patting	11.54	0.00	3.84(3.85)
	Sum	30.77	0.00	**15.38(34.62)**

the three types of interaction remained constant with the basic shape.

5. CONCLUSIONS

This study sought to measure the influence of the protrusion type on touch interactions with an egg-shaped robot without advanced information pertaining to efficient recognition with a limited number of sensors and a limited amount of space for them on the robot. The preference for the center of the head (location 1) was consistently high in all experiments. Moreover, both protrusion types were commonly associated with increases in grabbing interactions.

6. ACKNOWLEDGMENTS

This work was supported by "Development of mobile assisted robot and emotional interaction robot for elderly" under the Industrial Source Technology Development programs of the Ministry of knowledge Economy (M E) of orea.

7. REFERENCES

[1] erstin Dautenhahn "Socially intelligent robots: dimensions of human robot interaction ," Phil. Trans. R. Soc. B (2007) 362, 679-704

[2] Brenna D. Argall, Aude G. Billard, "A survey of Tactile Human Robot Interactions," *Robotics and Autonomous Systems*, vol 58,2010,1159-1176

[3] inTae im, Hyunsoo Song and Dong-Soo won, "Behavioral analysis of touch-based interaction of humans with an egg-shaped robot," *Ubiquitous Robots and Ambient Intelligence*, 2013.

[4] Seong-yong oo, ong Gwan Lim, Dong-soo won, "Online Touch Behavior Recognition of Hard-cover Robot Using Temporal Decision Tree Classifier," *International Symposium on Robot and Human Interactive Communication*,2008

Is a Robot Better than Video for Initiating Remote Social Connections Among Children?

Nuri Kim
California College of the Arts
1111 8th street
San Francisco, CA 94108
nkim@cca.edu

Jeonghye Han
Cheongju National Univ. of Education
Cheong Nam-ro 2065,Cheongju
ChungBuk, Rep. of Korea
hanjh@cje.ac.kr

Wendy Ju
Stanford University
424 Panama Mall, Bldg. 560
Stanford, CA 94305
wendyju@stanford.edu

ABSTRACT
To investigate how children interact differently when interactions are mediated with screen-based video communication versus a robot-mediated communication, we conducted a study with elementary students in Korea, comparing the use of both technologies to introduce classroom students with peer-aged individuals in America. Our findings show that the classroom children showed more positive emotion during certain tasks and exhibited more interest to remote participants in the context of robot-mediated communication than with video-mediated communication.

Categories and Subject Descriptors
H.4.3 Communications Applications: Computer conferencing, teleconferencing, and videoconferencing

General Terms
Human Factors, Languages.

Keywords
Tele-communication; robot-mediated communication; video-mediated communication; non-verbal communication, robotic technology in classroom.

1. INTRODUCTION
When we teach people how to interact with people from other cultures, it is important to explicitly address tacitly held understandings of non-verbal behaviors. However, these types of non-verbal cues can be easily lost in the use of traditional video-conferencing technologies such as Skype, VSee, or Google Hangouts. In this paper, we present a study wherein elementary classroom students in Korea are introduced to and interact with a child in America using screen-based video-mediated communication and robot-mediated communication.

2. BACKGROUND
Videoconferencing technology is increasingly used in classrooms to promote foreign language and cultural education [1][2][3]. While robotic technology is far more novel in classroom settings, the early use of robots to enable distance foreign language instruction has shown that such applications have promise. Some teleoperated robots, for example, are controlled by an English speaking human teacher to communicate with English learners at remote sites [4]. We have been using the teaching assistant robot ROBOSEM, an educational service robot for English learning [5], in sustained long-term use in elementary-level English courses in Korea.

3. HYPOTHESIS
For the following study, we sought to understand how using a robot as a medium for distance communication (*robot-mediated communication*) will affect the interpersonal attitudes of classroom students towards a remote participant. We felt that using a robot would help classroom students to be more interested in the remote participant than when the remote participant interacts over a more traditional screen-based videoconference setup (*video-mediated communication*).

Hypothesis: Classroom participants will show more interest and empathy in the activity with robot-mediated communication than with video-mediated communication.

4. METHOD
For the video-mediated communication condition, we used Google hangout on a large-screen display located in the classroom in Korea, and on a laptop located in the remote

Figure 1. Classroom children interacting with a remote student using (a) robot-mediated and (b) video-mediated communication

HRI'14, March 3–6, 2014, Bielefeld, Germany.
ACM 978-1-4503-2658-2/14/03.
http://dx.doi.org/10.1145/2559636.2563692

participant's home in the US. For the robot-mediated communication condition, the children in the Korean classroom interacted with a robot featuring a screen showing the remote participant. Children were allowed to move around the classroom as they wished at all times under the two conditions. Each class was 40 minutes long and six experimental classes were conducted in a total of three days shown as Table 1.

Table 1. Participants and conditions

		Day 1	Day 2	Day 3
Classroom participants in classroom (Korea)	**First medium**	Video	Robot	Video
	Second medium	Robot	Video	Robot
	N	1	4	1

In total, there were six elementary students (7 years old, three girls and three boys) in Korea who participated. This resulted in a small participant size of six (n=6) for analysis of the paired t-test.

The questionnaire consisted of three parts: four-point scale (1- strongly disagree, 2- disagree, 3- agree, 4- strongly agree) questions, an emotional journey map, and several open-ended questions.

5. RESULTS

The analysis of data from post-experiment questions and observation notes showed that classroom participants showed significant differences favoring interaction using the robot over video, in interest and intimacy to the remote participant between the video-mediated communication and robot-mediated communication. No significant difference was not found in empathy with media (□=0.1).

We found that classroom participants showed more interest when they interacted with participants through the robot M=3.00, SD=0.80 than when they interacted with participants through the video M=2.50, SD=1.10, T(5)= -1.936, p= 0.055 (□<0.1) as shown in Table 1. We found that classroom participants showed a slight more empathy with media when they interacted with participants through the robot M=3.00, SD =1.60 than when they interacted with participants through the video M=2.83, SD=2.17, T(5)= -.0542, p= 0.305 as shown in Table 2. We found no significant effects of medium or either video or robot on the participant's empathy with media.

Table 2. Difference in each factor

Factor	Video Mean (SD)	Robot Mean (SD)	T (DF)	p-value
Interest	2.50 (1.1)	3.0 (0.8)	-1.936 (5)	0.055*
Empathy with media	2.83 (2.167)	3.0 (1.6)	-.0542 (5)	0.305

CONCLUSION

This paper provides evidence that a robot could improve the quality of social connection particularly in the case of cultural contact, by supporting non-verbal communication with several limitations such as the small number of participants.

The results suggested that classroom participants would be more interested in meeting people from different cultures if the remote participant were introduced via a robot-based communication medium rather than with video conferencing technology. The participants seemed to feel more positive, more familiar, and less inhibited interacting with the robot, which is consistent with what was expected based on a prior literature review.

Our results highlighted the potential for robots to play a valuable role in distance communication and educational potential of such communication. Thus, providing students with a new learning environment and shaping wider implication of robot-mediated communication may be considered in the near future.

ACKNOWLEDGEMENTS

This research was supported by Basic Science Research Program through the National Research Foundation of Korea (NRF) funded by the Ministry of Education, Science and Technology (NRF-2012R1A1A2039797). Special thanks to Yujin Robotics, teachers and students from CharmSaem elementary school for their support.

REFERENCES

[1] Thurston, A. (2004). Promoting multicultural education in the primary classroom: broadband videoconferencing facilities and digital video. *Computers & Education, 43*(1), 165-177.

[2] Cifuentes, L., & Murphy, K. L. (2000). Promoting multicultural understanding and positive self-concept through a distance learning community: Cultural connections. *Educational Technology Research and Development*, *48*(1), 69-83.

[3] Howland, J., & Wedman, J. (2003). Experiencing diversity: Learning through videoconference technology. In *World Conference on Educational Multimedia, Hypermedia and Telecommunications* (Vol. 2003, No. 1, pp. 1562-1565).

[4] Yun, S., Shin, J., Kim, D., Kim, C. G., Kim, M., & Choi, M. T. (2011). Engkey: tele-education robot. In Social Robotics (pp. 142-152). Springer Berlin Heidelberg.

[5] Park, S. J., Han, J. H., Kang, B. H., & Shin, K. C. (2011, October). Teaching assistant robot, ROBOSEM, in English class and practical issues for its diffusion. In Advanced Robotics and its Social Impacts (ARSO), 2011 IEEE Workshop on (pp. 8-11).

The Effect of Robot Appearance Types on Motivating Donation

Ran Hee Kim
Dept. of Industrial Design
Ewha Womans University
Seoul, Korea
rano433@hanmail.net

Yeop Moon, Jung Ju Choi
Dept. of Industrial Design
Ewha Womans University
Seoul, Korea
{yangjeon369, meloncreamm}@naver.com

Sonya S. Kwak
Dept. of Industrial Design
Ewha Womans University
Seoul, Korea
sonakwak@ewha.ac.kr

ABSTRACT
According to the Hawthorne effect, when people feel someone staring at them, they tend to be moral because of psychological pressure. We applied this Hawthorne effect to the appearance design of robots and examined the effect of robot appearance types on motivating donation. We executed a 2 (appearance types: anthropomorphic vs. functional) within-participants experiment (N=20). Participants perceived more social presence to an anthropomorphic robot than a functional robot. In addition, participants were more willing to donate when interacting with an anthropomorphic robot than a functional robot.

Categories and Subject Descriptors
I.2.9 [**Artificial Intelligence**]: Robotics – *commercial robots and applications*; H.5.2 [**Information Interfaces and Presentation**]: User Interfaces – *user-centered design*

Keywords
Anthropomorphic robot; appearance type; donation; functional robot; Hawthorne effect

1. INTRODUCTION
In the field of Human-Robot Interaction (HRI), several robots have been developed for motivating donation, such as an urban donation motivating robot, DONA [1] and a panhandling robot, Don-8r [2]. In addition, many studies have explored the effective factors which could have an impact on motivating donation, such as social backgrounds of users [3], installation place of a robot [4], and gender of a robot [5].

The Hawthorne effect is a psychological phenomenon in which an observer's gazing can change workers' behavior and affect their work efficiency [6]. In addition, Bekay [7] demonstrated that the Hawthorne effect could affect motivating donation in nonprofit fundraising organization. In this study, we applied the Hawthorne effect to the appearance design of donation motivating robots and examined the impact of robot appearance types on motivating donation.

According to Fong et al. [8], robots could be classified into anthropomorphic, zoomorphic, caricatured, and functional robots. As we applied the Hawthorne effect to the robot appearance design, we focused on an anthropomorphic robot with eyes and a functional robot without eyes. Many studies have been conducted on the impact of these two robot appearance types on eliciting human emotions, such as joy, sympathy [9], and embarrassment [10]. However, limited work has been done on motivating donation. In this study, we explored whether these two different robot appearance types would have an effect on motivating donation.

HRI'14, March 3–6, 2014, Bielefeld, Germany
ACM 978-1-4503-2658-2/14/03.
http://dx.doi.org/10.1145/2559636.2563685

2. RELATED WORKS
2.1 Motivating Donation
In the field of HRI, there are several robots which have been developed on the topic of motivating donation. For example, DONA is an urban donation motivating robot by roaming around for gaining attention and thanking people by nodding its head when people donate [1]. Don-8r is a donation motivating robot by glittering lights when people donate to the robot [2]. In addition, there are many studies which explore the effective ways to motivate donation. Salami et al. [4] explored the impact of installation place of a robot on motivating donation. Russa and Sutinen [3] investigated people's willingness to donate by social backgrounds of users. Siegel et al. [5] examined the effect of robot's gender on motivating donation.

In psychology, the Hawthorne effect describes the phenomenon that the observer's gazing cue has an effect on changing workers' behavior and increasing their work efficiency [6]. Recent studies showed that the Hawthorne effect could be effectively used as nonprofit fundraising organizations' strategy by demonstrating the impact of presence of eyes on motivating donation [7]. Thus, in this study, we applied the Hawthorne effect to the appearance design of a robot and investigated the impact of robot appearance types on motivating donation.

2.2 Appearance Types of Robots
Fong et al. [8] classified social robots in anthropomorphic, zoomorphic, caricatured, and functional robots by robot embodiment. In order to apply the Hawthorne effect to the appearance design of robots, we focused on an anthropomorphic robot with eyes and a functional robot without eyes.

Previous studies have explored the effects of these two robot types on people's perception of a robot. A study conducted by Hegel et al. has shown that an anthropomorphic robot was more effective in eliciting joy and sympathy than a functional robot [9]. Bartneck et al. demonstrated that participants felt more embarrassment when interacting with an anthropomorphic robot than a functional robot [10]. As previous studies have shown that people felt more sympathy and embarrassment when interacting with an anthropomorphic robot than a functional robot, we anticipated that an anthropomorphic robot would be more effective in motivating donation than a functional robot.

These analyses led to the following hypotheses:

H1. The participants will feel more social presence to an anthropomorphic robot than a functional robot.

H2. The participants will have more intention to donate when interacting with an anthropomorphic robot than a functional robot.

3. STUDY DESIGN

We used a within-participants experiment design with two types of robot appearance: anthropomorphic and functional.

Participants. We recruited university students having high technology acceptance as participants (Male: 2, Female: 18).

Materials. We developed two different donation motivating robots according to the appearance types of robots as shown in Figure 1. An anthropomorphic robot was a donation motivating robot which has two eyes while a functional robot was a robotic box for motivating donation without eyes. Both robots detected users' donation and responded with thanking sound feedback.

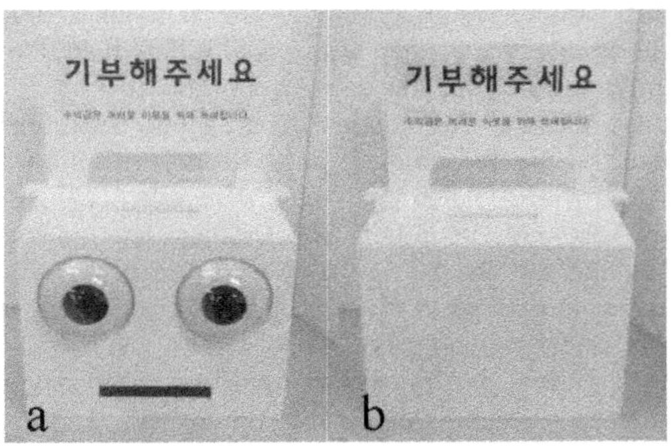

Figure 1. Robot stimulus (a: anthropomorphic, b: functional)

Procedure. Participants were welcomed to the lab and listened to the explanation about the experiment. Participants then interacted with each donation motivating robot in random order. After participants interacted with a robot, a questionnaire regarding each stimulus was administered.

Measures. The post experimental survey was composed of 6 Likert-type items, which were combined into two scales. The two scales were social presence (4 items, Cronbach's $\alpha = 0.89$), which were drawn from Heerink et al.'s research [11] and intention to donate (2 items, Cronbach's $\alpha = 0.94$), which were drawn from Zhao et al.'s research [12].

4. RESULTS

We investigated the impact of the robot appearance types on motivating donation. Statistical analyses were conducted using the paired *t*-test.

In the case of social presence, as predicted by H1, participants perceived more social presence to an anthropomorphic robot ($M = 4.74$, $SD = 1.5$) than a functional robot ($M = 3.06$, $SD = 1.35$), $t = 3.133$, df = 19, $p = 0.0025$ (one-tailed). In the case of intention to donate, as predicted by H2, the effect of robot appearance types on intention to donate was significant, $t = 2.114$, df = 19, $p = 0.024$ (one-tailed). Participants were more willing to donate when they were interacting with an anthropomorphic robot ($M = 5.50$, $SD = 1.25$) than a functional robot ($M = 4.50$, $SD = 1.43$). This indicates that an anthropomorphic robot which has high social presence could be effectively used as a way to motivate donation.

5. CONCLUSIONS

We investigated the effect of robot appearance types on social presence of a robot and people's intention to donate. The results showed that an anthropomorphic robot with eyes was more effective in motivating donation than a functional robot without eyes. This study provides evidence that the Hawthorne effect could be effectively applied to the appearance design of a donation motivating robot.

6. REFERENCES

[1] Kim, M. S., Cha, B. K., Park, D. M., Lee, S. M., Kwak, S. S., and Lee, M. K. 2010. Dona: Urban donation motivating robot. In *Proc. of HRI*, 159-160.

[2] Heater, B. 2011. Don-8r the panhandling robot set to make the homeless obsolete Brian Heater. *Engadget.* Retrieved Jan. 2, 2014 from http://www.engadget.com/2011/04/26/don-8r-the-panhandling-robot-set-to-make-the-homeless-obsolete/

[3] Russa, G. L. and Sutinen, E. 2010. When a robot turns into a totem: The RoboBeggar case. *E-Learning Experiences and Future.* 17, 327-344.

[4] Salami, M. J. E., Aibinu, A. M., Mohideen, S. B. O. K., and Mansor, S. A. B. 2011. Design of an intelligent robotic donationbox a case study. In *Proc. of ICOM*, 1-6.

[5] Siegel, M., Breazeal, C., and Norton, M. I. 2009. Persuasive robotics-the influence of robot gender on human behavior. In *Proc. of the International Conference on Intelligent Robots and Systems*, 2563-2568.

[6] Stephen, R., and Jones, G. 1992. Was there a hawthorne effect?. *American Journal of Sociology.* 98, 3, 451-468.

[7] Ahn, B. 2010. *Fundraising strategy for nonprofit organizations.* Jeyoung communication, Seoul.

[8] Fong, T., Nourbakhsh, I., and Dautenhahn, K. 2003. A survey of socially interactive robots. *Robotics and Autonomous Systems.* 42, 3–4, 143-166.

[9] Hegel, F., Krach, S., Kircher, T., Wrede, B., and Sagerer, G. 2008. Understanding social robots: A user study on anthropomorphism. In *Proc. of RO-MAN*, 574-579.

[10] Bartneck, C., Bleeker, T., Bun, J., Fens, P., and Riet, L. 2010. The influence of robot anthropomorphism on the feelings of embarrassment when interacting with robots. *Paladyn Journal of Behavioral Robotics.* 1, 2, 109–115.

[11] Heerink, M., Kröse, B., Evers, V., and Wielinga, B. 2008. The influence of social presence on acceptance of a companion robot by older people. *Journal of Physical Agents.* 2, 2, 33-40.

[12] Zhao, M., Hoeffler, S., and Dahl, D. W. 2011. Mental simulation and product evaluation: The affective and cognitive dimensions of process versus outcome simulation. *Journal of Marketing Research.* 48, 5, 827-839.

Human Embodiment Creates Problems for Robot Learning by Demonstration Using a Control Panel

Franziska Kirstein
Institute for Design and Communication
University of Southern Denmark
frkir08@student.sdu.dk

Kerstin Fischer
Institute for Design and Communication
University of Southern Denmark
kerstin@sdu.dk

Dorthe Sølvason
Mærsk Mc-Kinney Møller Institute
University of Southern Denmark
dorthe@mmmi.sdu.dk

ABSTRACT
In this paper, problems in instructing an industrial robot by means of a control panel are investigated. In order for the robot to learn as much and as fast as possible from demonstration, the demonstration by the teacher needs to be as precise as possible. Usability studies constitute a useful methodology to investigate in which situations users provide the robot with exact trajectories and, if not, why they face difficulties. Results show that movements involving only the lowest joint of the robot arm are straight-forward and very exact. In contrast, fine movements that involve joints of the upper arm cause considerable problems. The analysis shows that users have to employ separate actions instead of focusing on the target and therefore need to consciously plan the action since they cannot match the robot's movements with those of their own embodiment.

Categories and Subject Descriptors
H.1.2 User/Machine Systems

General Terms
Human Factors

Keywords
Learning from Demonstration; Control Panel; Human Embodiment

1. INTRODUCTION
This paper is part of a series of usability studies carried out at the MMMI at the University of Southern Denmark. These studies aim at improving a robotic platform with two Universal Robot Arms, which are firmly fixed to the platform [4]. Such platforms are intended to be used in industrial settings to perform assembly tasks that they learn by means of demonstration from lay users. During our series of usability studies, several different control modalities were tested with which users instructed the robot: by kinesthetic guidance, by using a control panel, or by means of teleoperation devices such as a data glove or a control peg [2]. The current paper focuses on the control panel as a control modality for learning by demonstration [5]. Compared to other control modes, the control panel allows users to manipulate one joint at a time and thus promises very precise operation and consequently exact learning trajectories. Operation should also be highly transparent and thus particularly well suited for lay users.

In order to assess the functionality of the control panel as a means for the demonstration of novel behaviors, a user study was carried out on a simple assembly task

HRI'14, March 3–6, 2014, Bielefeld, Germany.
ACM 978-1-4503-2658-2/14/03.
http://dx.doi.org/10.1145/2559636.2563713

2. EMPIRICAL EVALUATION
The experiments were carried out using the Marvin platform [4]. All users were asked to perform the same assembly task, to insert a square peg, a round peg and the separator into the bottom piece of a Cranfield set [1] using the robot.

2.1 Participants
Participants in these experiments were 14 university students and staff (aged 14-54). None of them had worked with the Marvin platform or any other industrial robot before. Participants were recruited by word-of-mouth and rewarded with a bar of chocolate for their time.

2.2 Procedure
The users participated in the study one at a time. Before they began the assembly task, they were asked to watch an introductory video providing information on the robot and the task and to fill out a short questionnaire about their academic background, their experience with technology and their evaluation of the instructional video. After this, they were asked to perform the assembly task with the robot. The users' interactions with the robot and the following interviews were video recorded. Users were furthermore asked to "think aloud" while operating the robot under the pretense that they had to inform the robot engineer about their current and planned actions and the behavior of the robot (the robot was fully autonomous, however). To fully exploit the methodology, three facilitators continuously interviewed the users about their experience with the robot. The interview did not follow a prepared script; rather, the questions emerged spontaneously through the observation and ad hoc interpretation of the users' behavior and utterances; the interview procedure was guided by Goodwin's [3] suggestions on how to facilitate interviews with the goal to understand the users' motivations and actions.

2.3 Data Analysis
The recorded video sessions were analyzed by dividing users' experiences into situations of positive and negative experience. Positive situations were defined as situations in which users do not make any mistakes, seem relaxed and self-confident about what they are doing. In contrast, negative situations are those in which users make mistakes, seem unsure and stressed about what they are doing, encounter problems and pay particular attention to the robot's movements. These situations were collected in a chart together with details on users' actions, utterances, gestures and facial expressions.

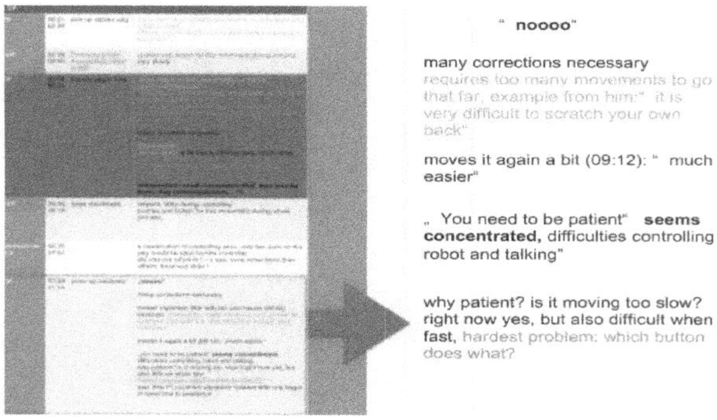

Figure 1: Example for Data Analysis Chart

3. RESULTS

The analyses reveal that participants have no problems instructing the robot to make large horizontal movements involving the lower part of the robot. Out of 14 participants none faced any difficulties moving the lowest joint, the 'shoulder' of the robot, which lead to very precise movements. Thus, of the 67 instances in which participants moved the robot 'shoulder', 0% caused any particular problems that led to negative user experience. In contrast, participants faced difficulties performing movements that concerned the finetuning of the robot gripper with respect to an object. All in all there were 79 situations in which participants had to perform small movements to finetune the robot's position with respect to an object. In 57 out of these 79 situations, participants had problems to get the robot into the correct position, i.e. in 72.2% of the cases.
A further analysis of these situations shows that especially vertical movements caused difficulties such that 64.3% of all vertical movements turned out to be problematic in one way or another.

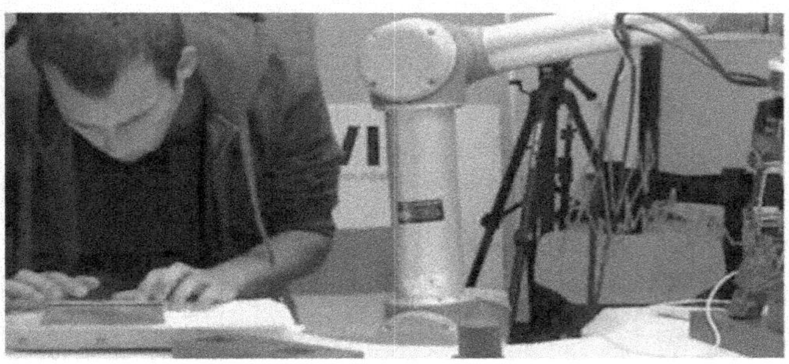

Figure 2: Peg-in-hole Path

Figure 2 illustrates a path taken by a participant in order to place a peg in a hole of the Cranfield set. The red line shows the path in which the robot was operated. While this is certainly an extreme case, participants can only control one joint at a time, and thus they may need to make many movements with several different joints to get the robot into the right position. This is not only exhausting for the users, but also produces very unclear movement trajectories for learning from demonstration. Since lowering the robot straight down on the vertical axis is not possible, users encounter particular difficulties when wanting to lower the robot, which requires either exact planning or that a single movement is split into several small movements.

While the robot's movements are thus highly transparent and predictable to the user, users experience considerable difficulties because of their expectation that the robot may function in ways similar to their own embodiment, as the participants' comments illustrate:

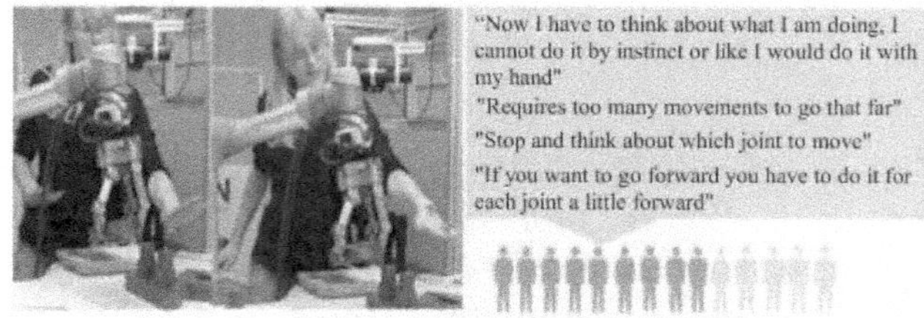

Figure 3: Problems with Cognitive Load and Embodiment

4. DISCUSSION

The results show that in situations in which several joints are needed to make precise movements, the instructions become unclear and slow. Reasons are that users need to think about how to instruct the robot because they cannot reason from their own embodiment. Instead of focusing on the goal, users need to carefully plan the path. Thus, when users are only able to control one joint at a time; they need to plan their demonstration far ahead. When instructing the robot with the control panel, users need to divide the action into small steps. Users point out that they felt this requirement to be very exhausting. The fact that users need to plan their actions distinguishes the control panel not only from robot teleoperation, but also from the human body. Humans usually move parts of their body intuitively and use more than only one joint at a time when they make a movement. Also, they do not need to plan separate steps of their actions. Consequently, instructing the robot by means of a control panel feels unnatural to users and requires them to think about their actions in advance.

5. CONCLUSION

Even though the control panel allows for careful, transparent robot control, interference from expectations from human embodiment causes difficulties for users in operating the robot, possibly resulting in low quality trajectories for learning from demonstration.

6. ACKNOWLEDGMENTS

This project was partially supported by the EU project IntellACT. We thank N. Krüger, R. Beck, T.R. Savarimuthu, K. Kuklinski, I. Marhenke and M.V. a.d. Wieschen.

7. REFERENCES

[1] Collins, K., Palmer, A. J. & K. Rathmill (1984). *The development of a European benchmark for the comparison of assembly robot programming systems.* In 1st Robot. Euro. Conf., Brussels.

[2] Fischer et al. (in prep.) *Comparing different control modes for robot learning from demonstration*

[3] Goodwin, K. (2009). *Understanding Potential Users and Customers.* In: Designing for the digital age: How to create human- centered products and services. Wiley.

[4] Savarimuthu, T.R., Liljekrans, D., Ellekilde, L.-P., Ude, A., Nemez,B. & Krueger,N. (2013). *Analysis of human Peg-in-Hole Executions in a Robotic Embodiment using uncertain Grasps*. In 9th International Workshop on Robot Motion and Control, RoMoCo.

[5] User Manual 1.6 (2012), *Robot UR10 with CB2 Euromap 67*, Universal Robots, Odense, Denmark

The Effect of Field of View on Social Interaction in Mobile Robotic Telepresence Systems

Andrey Kiselev
Örebro University, 70182
Örebro, Sweden
andrey.kiselev@oru.se

Annica Kristoffersson
Örebro University, 70182
Örebro, Sweden
annica.kristoffersson@oru.se

Amy Loutfi
Örebro University, 70182
Örebro, Sweden
amy.loutfi@oru.se

ABSTRACT

One goal of mobile robotic telepresence for social interaction is to design robotic units that are easy to operate for novice users and promote good interaction between people. This paper presents an exploratory study on the effect of camera orientation and field of view on the interaction between a remote and local user. Our findings suggest that limiting the width of the field of view can lead to better interaction quality as it encourages remote users to orient the robot towards local users.

Categories and Subject Descriptors

I.2.9 [**Robotics**]: Commercial robots and applications; H.5.2 [**User interfaces**]: Graphical user interfaces (GUI)

Keywords

Human-Robot Interaction, Mobile Robotic Telepresence, Teleoperation, User Interfaces

1. INTRODUCTION

Using mobile robotic telepresence (MRP) systems to interact may lead to undesired situations [3, 4] which do not naturally occur in human-human interaction (HHI) and to situations which cannot occur when using static video mediated communication systems. For example, many of the alarm operators learning to maneuver a MRP system while interacting "looked-away" when discussing personal matters with an elderly local user[1]. In HHI, the situation is typically associated with a vis-a-vis configuration [1, 4]. Authors point out that a possible reason for the unexpected behaviour is that the camera provided the pilot user with a wide field of view. This suggests that the pilot users saw the elderly person without having to orient the robot into the vis-a-vis position. Whether or not the look-away behaviour is acceptable among real elderly users was investigated in [3]. The elderly, who were guided around in a smart home, were observed to adjust their own position towards a vis-a-vis if the pilot user created the look-away configuration. The importance of being able to see the person they were talking to was emphasized during the retrospective interviews following the interaction.

[1]In this paper, we assume that the "local user" is the one located in the same environment as the MRP system, whereas "pilot user" is the one who connects from a remote location.

HRI'14, March 3–6, 2014, Bielefeld, Germany.
ACM 978-1-4503-2658-2/14/03.
http://dx.doi.org/10.1145/2559636.2559799 .

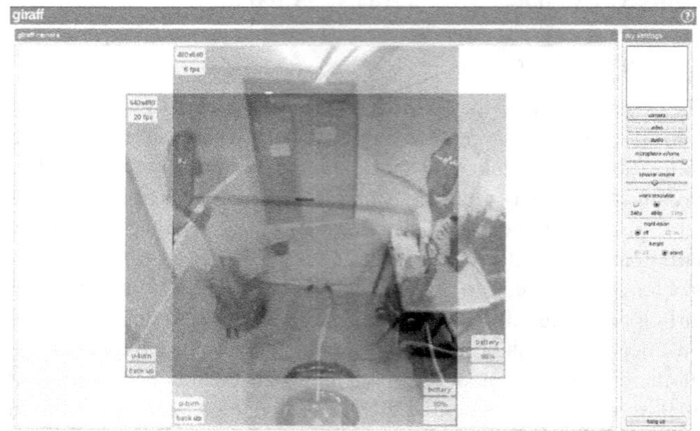

Figure 1: Pilot interfaces with portrait or landscape image orientation.

This study investigates whether providing a wide-angle portrait view instead of a wide-angle landscape view can influence pilots to orient the robot more towards a local user in order to improve quality of interaction. Quality of interaction is measured in terms of orientation of the telepresence robot towards a local user. The results show that pilot users using the MRP system providing a portrait wide-angle view orient the robot more towards the local user than those who use the system with a landscape wide-angle view.

2. METHOD

The MRP system used in this experiment was Giraff. Two identical robots with different camera orientations were used. Fig. 1 depicts the landscape and portrait view provided via the Giraff Pilot user interface. The diagonal field of view and the size of the area covered is the same for both robots.

All participants received introductory information about the objectives of the experiment and a 10-minute demonstration session on driving the Giraff providing a *cropped squared* field of view. The training session served two pur-

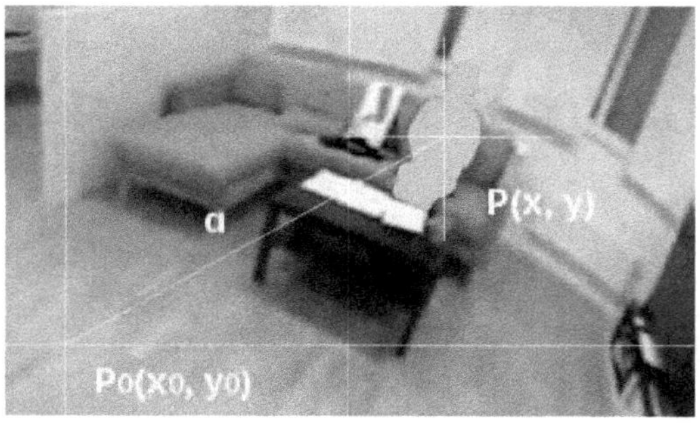

Figure 2: Calculating the angle α using the linear distance between the optical axis of robot's camera P_0 (center of the image) and the location of the user on the image P.

poses: minimize bias and allow the participants to familiarize themselves with the MRP system. Upon completing the training session, two conversational sessions were conducted one after the other. One session using the robot providing a landscape wide-angle view and one session using the robot providing the portrait view. The order of the sessions was mixed across participants.

Conversational sessions were built like parts of interview with general questions about participants' background, without any connection to experiment objectives. During the sessions, the local user (one of experimenters) was always sitting in the same position.

Quality of interaction was measured as the angle between the optical axis of robot's camera and a line from the robot's camera to the local user. Concerning hardware limitations of the robot and based on the fact that the distance from the robot to the local user was always limited in the bounds from two to four meters, the actual angle α was approximated in real time from the image stream received from the robot by measuring the linear distance from the center of the image, P_0, to the location of the local user, P (see cropped image in Fig. 2). The unit is non-dimensional and ranges from 0 to 1 where 0 corresponds to no angle (absolute vis-a-vis formation) and 1 corresponds to maximum possible angle (local user is still observable, but located in the corner of the image). The α is sampled every 500 ms (2 Hz) while the local user is found in the image. The location of the local user was extracted by using thresholding in HSV space based on color samples of the local user's t-shirt.

3. RESULTS

Four male students from the School of Science and Technology, Örebro University, Sweden, participated in the experiment. Their age ranged from 19-21 years of age and all had experience of PC/video games in which players move. All conversational sessions lasted from $63s$ to $101s$ ($\mu = 81.7s$, $\sigma = 13.11s$). The median and SD values of α for each participant's conversational sessions are shown in Fig. 3. For each participant, the lowest *mean* and *median* values of α were found in the conversational session in portrait mode. Per-participant statistical significance of the results has been verified using one-way ANOVA tests.

The linear distance, α is calculated such that the lowest possible value occurs when the local user is located in the center of the image and the largest values occur when the local user is located in any of the four extreme corners. Our results show that α is larger in the landscape condition than in the portrait condition. Pilot users provided with a landscape view tend to maintain the conversation with the local user non-centered. Nevertheless, comparable results were found when including only the α located within the area that is common for both views (see Fig. 1).

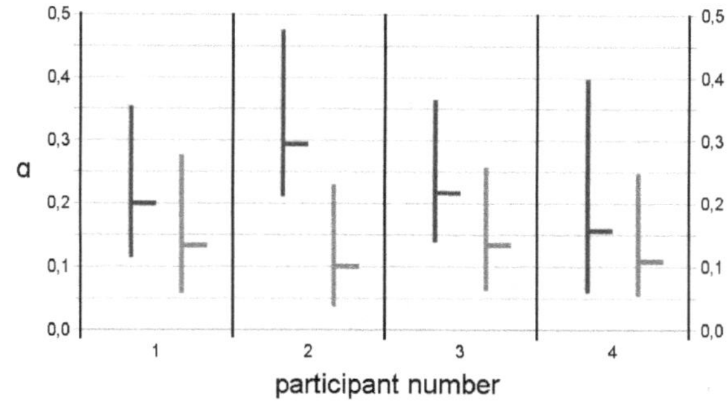

Figure 3: Median and SD values for landscape (blue, left) and portrait (red, right) camera orientation.

4. DISCUSSION AND CONCLUSIONS

An important result in this study is that an assumption taken by many engineers that a landscape wide-angle view is best, is not supported. By rotating the robot's camera 90° and limiting the horizontal view angle while increasing the vertical view angle, the α decreased. Drawing on experiences from [3], this increased the quality of interaction from the local user's perspective but additional studies are needed to confirm this hypothesis. While the view provided can also be obtained by cropping the image, it is our belief that the bigger vertical view angle can also improve the driving experience. This is supported by our previous study [2] which shows that the mental workload can be high while driving the robot. By offering the participants a portrait field of view, the need to tilt the screen is eliminated while driving. However, future work includes studying whether there are trade-off's in the pilot's driving capabilities and experienced interaction quality if limiting the width of the view.

5. REFERENCES

[1] A. Kendon. Spatial Organization in Social Encounters: The F-formation System. In *Conducting Interaction: Patterns of Behavior in Focused Encounters*, pages 209–238. Cambridge University Press, 1990.

[2] A. Kiselev and A. Loutfi. Using a Mental Workload Index as a Measure of Usability of a User Interface for Social Robotic Telepresence. In *Proceedings of the Ro-Man 2012 Workshop Social Robotic Telepresence*, pages 3–6, 2012.

[3] A. Kristoffersson, S. Coradeschi, A. Loutfi, and K. S. Eklundh. Assessment of Interaction Quality in Mobile Robotic Telepresence - An Elderly Perspective. *Interaction Studies*. in press.

[4] A. Kristoffersson, K. S. Eklundh, and A. Loutfi. Measuring the Quality of Interaction in Mobile Robotic Telepresence A Pilot's Perspective. *International Journal of Social Robotics*, 5:89–101, 2013.

Embodied Visual Programming for Robot Control

Stasinos Konstantopoulos
Institute of Informatics and Telecommunications
NCSR 'Demokritos'
Athens, Greece
konstant@iit.demokritos.gr

Andreas Lydakis
Institute of Informatics and Telecommunications
NCSR 'Demokritos'
Athens, Greece
lydakis@iit.demokritos.gr

Antonios-Emmanouil Gkikakis
Institute of Informatics and Telecommunications
NCSR 'Demokritos'
and Dept. of Informatics
Athens University of Economics and Business
p3090041@dias.aueb.gr

ABSTRACT

In this paper we motivate and present our *embodied visual programming* research plan, aiming at allowing end-users without any technical expertise to define complex robot behaviours. The core idea is to combine *visual programming* with the sensing and actuation capabilities of robots and with teleoperated demonstrations of what needs to be achieved.

Categories and Subject Descriptors

I.2.9 [**Robotics**]: Operator interfaces; D.1.7 [**Visual Programming**]: Visual Programming for HRI

General Terms

Design, Theory

1. INTRODUCTION

As robots increasingly leave the controlled and structured confines of research labs and factory floors, research into robots that can be commoditized is becoming relevant. One of the key factors is that people without any specialized expertise are able to control and instruct robots.

We envisage HRI technology that is far more versatile and dynamic than selecting among a predefined menu but at the same time is restricted and unambiguous (that natural language is not) and more natural and intuitive than developing software. However, where 'natural' and 'intuitive' in HRI are conventionally understood to equate to spoken interaction, we argue that people have been exposed and accustomed to a variety of different interfaces with machines: from cars' steering wheels, shift sticks and pedals, to gamepads and TV remotes there is a huge selection of ways to unambiguously and yet naturally and intuitively 'explain' to a machine what needs to be done without uttering a single word. Furthermore, we envisage taking full advantage of the opportunities offered by the robot's embodiment and interaction with physical space in order to ground human instructions into concrete robot actions.

We build upon *visual programming*, a programming paradigm based on graphically manipulating program elements. Arguably the best-known example in robotics is *NXT-G*® [3] for programming the educational and hobbyist *LEGO Mindstorms*® kit. NXT-G® is simple, but does not scale well as there is no support for intermediate levels of sensor analysis so that the programmer can refer to qualitative perception results. This makes diagrams too large and complex for most non-trivial tasks. The *STEM Toolkit* and its *12blocks* language [1] and *Microsoft RDS*® [4] also offer visual programming for a variety of platforms, including Mindstorms®, iRobot®, and other educational, hobbyist, and production systems, both physical and simulated. However, their visual programming languages suffer from similar limitations as NXT-G® and they revert to textual programming languages for more complex applications.

Emphasising embodiment and interaction with the robot's environment, the user interface of the Roomba® robotic vacuum cleaner comes closer to what we are trying to achieve: its autonomous mapping, localization, and space coverage strategies are complemented by a simple control interface based on beacons and virtual 'walls' to direct its actions [2]. This interface, however, is more of a configuration interface for pre-programmed functionalities rather than a programming interface, and lacks the flexibility that would allow different robot behaviours to be programmed.

2. RESEARCH PLAN

Our goal is to create an interface that will combine visual programming with the simplicity of pointing out specific locations in physical space, requires very little technical expertise, or none at all, and is based on *Robot Operating System (ROS)*, so that it can be easily deployed on many different platforms. In fact, we perceive robot actions as a matching of items from an inventory of *robot capabilities* against the *affordances* offered at different locations in the robot's environment, and robot control as sequences of such actions conditioned by perception. Our plan is to integrate:

- a library of generic, abstract capabilities (such as moving to a location on a map, grasping, turning a knob, etc.) which can be composed into complex strategies and adapted into concrete actions depending on the current situation and environment

HRI'14, March 3–6, 2014, Bielefeld, Germany.
ACM 978-1-4503-2658-2/14/03.
http://dx.doi.org/10.1145/2559636.2563719.

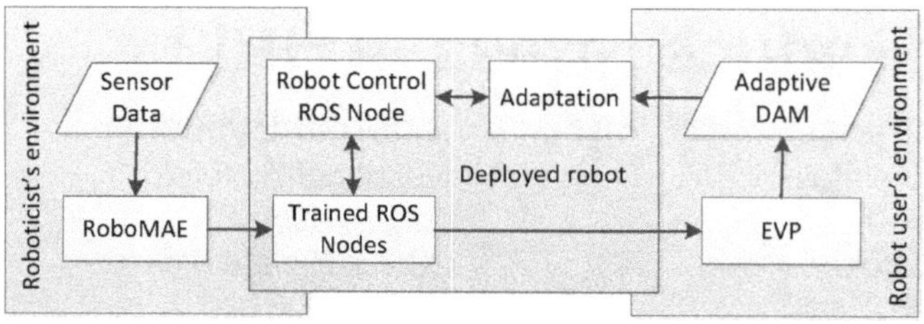

Figure 1: A graphic depiction of the interplay between development tools and end-users' tools.

- perception components for receiving external stimuli and for recognizing affordances where the different capabilities can be applied (a map of accessible locations, objects that can be gripped and lifted, knobs, etc.)
- a robot control environment following the visual programming paradigm for authoring visual representations of a system of actions and reactions to external stimuli; and that allows for new capabilities to be demonstrated and added to the library and new affordances to be pointed out to the robot via a combination of teleoperation and HRI

This new *embodied visual programming* paradigm augments visual programming with opportunities offered by the robot's embodiment and interaction with physical space: the ability to be instructed by being teleoperated and the ability to adapt by receiving external reinforcement stimuli. We put forward the development of *embodied visual programming* as a decisive step towards *consumer robotics*, along with long-term autonomy and the ability to self-test and recognize sub-system failures.

Figure 1 visualizes the interplay between robotic technology developers, platforms, and consumers: *RoboMAE*, the roboticist's workbench,[1] is used to develop components; the *embodied visual programming (EVP)* environment is used by the consumer to compose them into the desired behaviour, resulting in an *adaptive dialogue and action manager (DAM)*. Adaptivity, based on reinforcement learning or similar methods, allows for this specification to operate at a level of abstraction suitable for humans and be refined into the level of detail needed by software components.

3. CURRENT STATUS AND FUTURE STEPS

Besides the RoboMAE environment, we have also starting prototyping the interface at the end-user's side. At the current state of development, we have developed an Android app for controlling robot movements using both autonomous navigation (Figure 2) and teleoperation. Users can seamlessly switch between the two modes, issuing goals for the robot to reach and cancelling at any time to take over control. Users get real-time feedback on the mobile device's screen about the current location of the robot.

In order to facilitate communication between the android application and the robot, we have implemented a *ROS bridge* that passes ROS messages over a bluetooth or IP connection. The bridge is implemented as a ROS node on the robot side and as a library to be used by the user interface app on the Android side.

[1] Please see `http://roboskel.iit.demokritos.gr/Download/RoboMAE` for more details

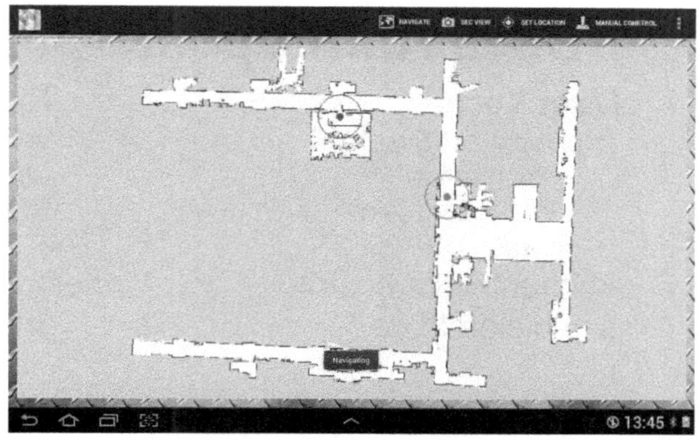

Figure 2: The navigation panel, displaying the current (blue mark) and goal positions (red mark).

As future steps aim at both extending the movement control capabilities and extending the range of robot actions that can be controlled. With respect to the former, we are planning to implement the ability to record moves made using the teleoperation and to make these recording accessible for composing plans and behaviours that combine autonomous navigation with pre-recorded movements. This will be used in order to, for example, demonstrate to a robot how to navigate a narrow passage or how to best sweep the complete area of a room, and then define composite plans such as 'move into that room and sweep'.

With respect to the range of robot actions that can be controlled we are planning to extend the user interface so that the user can point out to the robot affordances in the environment, by identifying objects on the map or in visual perception and matching them against the robot's actuation capabilities. These will, again, be used as the building blocks for more complex composite plans, defined in a non-technical user interface following the *visual programming* paradigm.

4. ACKNOWLEDGEMENTS

The research described in this paper has been carried out at the Software and nowledge Engineering Lab, in the context of *Roboskel*, the robotics activity of the Institute of Informatics and Telecommunications, NCSR "Demokritos". Please see `http://roboskel.iit.demokritos.gr` for more details.

5. REFERENCES

[1] Cogmation Robotics. *Everything you need to know about 12Blocks*, 2012. URL `http://virtualrobotgames.com/pages/12blocks`.

[2] iRobot. *Roomba 800 Users Manual.* URL `http://www.irobot.com/~/media/Files/Support/Home/Roomba/800/iRobot-Roomba-800-Manual.pdf`.

[3] . F. elly. *LEGO MINDSTORMS NXT-G Programming Guide.* Apress Media LLC, New ork, 2nd edition, 2010.

[4] Microsoft Corporation. *Microsoft Robotics Developer Studio 4*, 2012. URL `http://msdn.microsoft.com/en-us/library/dd939239.aspx`.

Does Anthropomorphism Reduce Stress in HRI?

Dieta Kuchenbrandt
University of Bielefeld
Inspiration 1
33619 Bielefeld
+49-521-10612042
dkuchenb@cit-ec.uni-bielefeld.de

Nina Riether
University of Bielefeld
Inspiration 1
33619 Bielefeld
+49-521-10612204
nriether@techfak.uni-bielefeld.de

Friederike Eyssel
University of Bielefeld
Inspiration 1
33619 Bielefeld
+49-521-10612044
feyssel@cit-ec.uni-bielefeld.de

ABSTRACT

In an experiment, we tested whether anthropomorphism would reduce psychological stress associated with human–robot interactions (HRI). Participants anticipated (vs. did not anticipate) an interaction with a humanlike versus machinelike robot type, and their electrodermal activity (EDA), a physiological indicator of psychological stress, was measured. Results indicate that anticipating an HRI increased psychological stress independent of robot type.

Categories and Subject Descriptors

J.4 [Social and Behavioral Sciences]: *psychology*.

General Terms

Measurement, design, experimentation, human factors

Keywords

Anthropomorphism, physiological measures, stress, HRI

1. INTRODUCTION

Anthropomorphism can be defined as attributing humanlike properties, characteristics, and mental states to nonhuman agents such as robots. This psychological process represents an effective strategy to increase the ability to make sense of a nonhuman agent's actions and thus to reduce the uncertainty that is often associated with interactions with nonhuman agents [1]. Supporting this assumption, [2] have demonstrated that anthropomorphizing technical devices, such as cars or computers is associated with reduced stress in human–machine interactions.

In the present experiment, we tested the hypothesis that anthropomorphism would reduce psychological stress associated with HRI. Specifically, participants expected (vs. did not expect) an interaction with a humanlike versus machinelike robot type while their electrodermal activity (EDA) as a physiological indicator of psychological stress was measured. Previous research has shown that a humanlike form of a nonhuman agent increases anthropomorphization [cf. 1].

HRI'14, March 3–6, 2014, Bielefeld, Germany.
ACM 978-1-4503-2658-2/14/03.
http://dx.doi.org/10.1145/2559636.2563710

We expected lower levels in EDA when participants anticipated an HRI with an anthropomorphic compared to a machinelike robot.

2. METHOD

2.1 Participants and Design

N = 80 (39 male, 41 female) participants with a mean age of M = 26.96 years (SD = 7.27) completed the experiment. They were randomly assigned to one of four experimental conditions resulting from a 2 (HRI anticipation: anticipated vs. not anticipated) x 2 (robot prototype: humanlike vs. machinelike) between subjects design.

2.2 Procedure and Materials

Participants were tested individually in the laboratory where they were placed in front of a computer screen. At the beginning, the experimenter attached the skin electrodes to measure participants' EDA. After confirming that the EDA had leveled and recordings could proceed, a general baseline measure was assessed over the course of one minute. During this time, participants were asked to calmly watch a fixation cross presented on the computer screen. Following the baseline measurement, the actual computer experiment started. Importantly, the experimental procedure included three critical points in time (T1 to T3) in which a change in EDA, that is, a skin conductance response, was expected.

At the first critical point in time (T1), participants were introduced to either a humanlike or a machinelike robot prototype (see Figure 1). They then learned that they would have to complete a guessing task in the final phase of the study. Importantly, they would do this task together with the robot or alone (T2). Subsequently, participants completed a questionnaire, which assessed both evaluation and anthropomorphization of the robot. They were then informed that they would now have to perform the guessing task (T3). At this point, the experiment ended and participants were informed that no actual HRI or guessing task would take place.

2.3 Experimental manipulation

In this experiment, two independent variables—robot prototype and HRI anticipation—were manipulated.

First, in order to manipulate robot prototype, participants were either presented with a picture of a *humanlike robot* or a *machinelike robot prototype.* The two robots were chosen based on pretests yielding that the humanlike robot was anthropomorphized more strongly than the machinelike prototype.

Second, to manipulate HRI anticipation, participants received written information on the computer screen. In the condition *HRI anticipated*, participants read: "In this study, we are going to pre-present you a robot and you shall answer questions regarding the robot. Afterwards you are going to complete a task together with the robot. The robot is doing pantomime. Your task is to guess which concepts and activities are meant." In contrast, *in the HRI not anticipated* condition, participants learned: "In this study (…). Afterwards you are going to complete a task. On a computer screen, concepts and activities will be presented with pantomime. Your task (…)."

2.4 Dependent measures

Skin conductance varies with sympathetic nervous system activity and can be regarded as indicator of psychological stress [3]. Thus, we measured EDA activity during the critical points in time (T1 to T3). EDA activity was recorded using standard Ag/AgCl electrodes (7 mm surface diameter) that were placed on the volar surfaces of the distal phalanges of the second and third finger (i.e. the fingertips of the index- and middle-finger) of the non-dominant hand. For recording, amplification, and filtering of the EDA signals, a QuickAmp amplifier with GSR module and BrainVision-Recorder Software (BrainProducts GmbH) were used. Data were recorded with a sampling frequency of 1000 Hz and filtered using a 0.5-2 Hz bandpass filter as well as 50 Hz notch filter. Before analyses, data underwent within-subjects z-standardization.

For each critical point in time (T1 to T 3), a skin conductance response was defined by subtracting the mean level of skin conductance activity during a 5s-time period starting 3s after the onset of the respective experimental time frame (T1 to T3) from the specific pre-stimulus level (mean level of skin conductance activity during the last 1000 ms prior to the onset of the respective time frame). Moreover, as we were not interested in the absolute skin conductance response but instead focused on the differences between the various critical time frames and the baseline, we calculated differences scores. *Base-T1* is the difference between the base rate EDA (before any manipulation, see 2.2) and the first manipulation (presentation of humanlike vs. machinelike robot, T1). *Base-T2* represents the difference between the base rate and the second manipulation (HRI anticipated vs. not anticipated, T2). *Base-T3* is the difference between the base rate and the moment in which participants expected to actually begin with the guessing task (together with the robot vs. alone, T3). In addition, we calculated the difference scores between the critical points in time (*T1-T2*, *T1-T3*, *T2-T3*). For all difference measures, a negative value indicates an increase in EDA.

3. RESULTS AND DISCUSSION

Base-T1. An ANOVA with robot prototype and HRI anticipation as between-subjects factors revealed no significant main effect for robot prototype, $F < 1$. However, a significant main effect of HRI anticipation occurred, $F(1, 73) = 7.15$, $p = .01$, $\eta^2 = .09$. Participants showed stronger stress reactions in the *HRI not anticipated* condition ($M = -0.46$, $SD = 0.93$) compared to the *HRI anticipated* condition ($M = 0.09$, $SD = 0.93$). The interaction effect was not significant, $F(1, 73) = 3.11$, $p = .08$, $\eta^2 = .04$. This result suggests that there might be experimenter effects: At this point, interaction anticipation has not been manipulated yet. Thus, no effect of this manipulation on the Base-T1 difference was expected. Moreover, the reported effect is in the opposite direction. We would expect stronger stress reactions in the *HRI anticipated* condition compared to the *HRI not anticipated* condition while we actually found the opposite pattern of results.

Base-T2. No significant effects emerged, all Fs < 1.

Base-T3. No significant effects were found, all Fs < 1.97, all ps > .16. However, the pattern of means is in line with our expectations: In tendency, a stronger stress reaction was observed when participants anticipated an HRI ($M = -0.35$, $SD = 0.86$) than when they did not anticipate an HRI ($M = -0.06$, $SD = 0.94$). Moreover, the HRI anticipation with a machinelike robot resulted in a slightly stronger stress reaction ($M = -0.41$, $SD = 0.84$) than with a humanlike robot ($M = -0.29$, $SD = 0.90$).

T1-T2. For the T1-T2 difference (representing the difference between the robot prototype and HRI anticipation manipulation), a significant main effect of HRI anticipation was found, $F(1, 73) = 8.72$, $p = .004$, $\eta^2 = .11$. No further main or interaction effect reached statistical significance, all Fs < 2.46, all ps > .12. Participants showed stronger stress reactions when anticipating an HRI ($M = -0.28$, $SD = 1.40$) than when not anticipating an HRI, ($M = 0.49$, $SD = 0.88$).

T1-T3. For the T1-T3 difference, a significant main effect of HRI anticipation was found, $F(1, 72) = 11.18$, $p = .001$, $\eta^2 = .13$. No further main or interaction effect reached statistical significance, all Fs < 2.43, all ps > .12. Supporting our hypothesis, participants showed stronger stress reactions when anticipating an HRI ($M = -0.45$, $SD = 1.08$) than when not anticipating an HRI ($M = 0.40$, $SD = 1.13$).

T2-T3. In line with our hypotheses, no significant main or interaction effect was obtained, all Fs < 1.

4. SUMMARY AND OUTLOOK

In the present experiment, participants anticipated versus did not anticipate an HRI with a humanlike versus machinelike robot prototype. Results showed that EDA as an indicator of psychological stress significantly increased when an HRI was anticipated compared to the no HRI anticipation condition. The choice of robot prototype, in contrast, did not significantly affect participants' stress reactions. However, findings need to be interpreted with caution as the results could in part be based on experimenter effects. In future work, HRI-related psychological stress should be explored in real human–robot interactions. Moreover, it should be investigated whether humanlikeness of the robot influences humans' stress reactions during critical incidents in HRI (e.g., when the robot makes an error).

REFERENCES

[1] N. Epley, A. Waytz, and J. T. Cacioppo 2007. "On seeing human: A three- factor theory of anthropomorphism," *Psychol. Review,* vol. 114, no. 4, pp. 864-886.

[2] H. Luczak, M. Rötting, L. Schmidt 2003. "Let's talk: Anthropomorphization as a means to cope with stress of interacting with technical devices," *Ergonomics*, vol. 46, pp. 1361–1374.

[3] M.E. Dawson, A. M. Schell, D. L. Filion 2007. "The Electrodermal System." In J. T. Cacioppo, L. G. Tassinary, G. Bernston (Eds.), "The Handbook of Psychophysiology (3rd ed.)". Cambridge: Cambridge University Press, 2007.

Can Robots Be Sold? The Effects of Robot Designs on the Consumers' Acceptance of Robots

Sonya S. Kwak
Dept. of Industrial Design
Ewha Womans University
Seoul, Korea
sonakwak@ewha.ac.kr

Jun San Kim
IBK Economic Research Institute
Industrial Bank of Korea
Seoul, Korea
junsan.kim@ibk.co.kr

Jung Ju Choi
Dept. of Industrial Design
Ewha Womans University
Seoul, Korea
meloncreamm@naver.com

ABSTRACT

This study explores the effect of robot design approaches on the consumers' acceptance of robots. We executed a 2-level (robot design: human-oriented vs. product-oriented) between participants experiment (N=52). Participants categorized a human-oriented robot and a product-oriented robot differently, and a product-oriented robot was more effective than a human-oriented robot for consumers' evaluation and purchase intention toward robots.

Categories and Subject Descriptors

I.2.9 [**Artificial Intelligence**]: Robotics – *commercial robots and applications*; H.5.2 [**Information Interfaces and Presentation**]: User Interfaces – *user-centered design*

Keywords

Categorization; human-oriented robot; human-robot interaction; marketing; product-oriented robot; robot designs

1. INTRODUCTION

Personal and service robots are extraordinarily advanced compared to the ones developed a decade ago. Due to the development of the robotic technology, they walk, recognize people's face and talk, and even smile or weep during the interaction with people. However, the size of the personal and service robot market has not grown much, betraying the industry experts' predictions that the market would rapidly expand within a decade. The United Nations Economic Commission (UNEC) and International Federation of Robotics (IFR) estimated that the market size of personal and service robots would reach US$ 17.1 Billion in 2010. However, the market size of these robots remained US$ 3.6 Billion in 2011. This arouses a research question why today's personal and service robots are not sold despite of all the technological advancements and anticipations.

According to the robot designs, robots can be classified into the two types: Human-oriented vs. Product-oriented. A human-oriented robot is the type of robot, which is designed to resemble a human's appearance or behavior. A product-oriented robot is the type of robot, which is designed to maximize the dedicated functions of the robot, for example, the vacuum cleaning robot.

In the field of Marketing, the categorization research states that people tend to categorize a new product based on its appearance [1]. Moreover, they produce expectations regarding the functions and performance of the product based on its category [2]. Oliver [3] has asserted that the match between the expected and the actual performance of the product affects the consumers' satisfaction of the product. Based on this, we state that the match between the expected functions, which are drawn from robot appearance and the actual functions of the products leads to the positive feedback from consumers. The objective of this study is to investigate the effect of these robot design approaches on the consumers' acceptance of robots.

HRI'14, March 3–6, 2014, Bielefeld, Germany
ACM 978-1-4503-2658-2/14/03.
http://dx.doi.org/10.1145/2559636.2563684

2. RELATED WORKS

2.1 Human- versus Product-Oriented Robot

Fong et al. [4] suggested four types of robots' embodiment including anthropomorphic, zoomorphic, caricatured, and functional. We focused on the anthropomorphic and the functional robots, which we refer to as human-oriented and product-oriented robots. Human-oriented robot design aims to develop robots that their appearances and behaviors are similar to humans, whereas product-oriented robot design aims to develop robots that are optimally structured for the deliverance of the dedicated functions.

There are several studies regarding the impact of the two robot designs on the people's perception of robots, such as effectiveness in eliciting joy and sympathy [5], perception of intelligence of robots [6], and embarrassment of the people [7]. They showed that human-oriented robot design is more effective for social interactions between people and robots than product-oriented robot design. However, limited work has been done on the consumers' acceptance of robots.

2.2 Categorization and Consumers' Acceptance of Robots

Previous studies showed that the physical appearance of the new products affected the categorization of these products [8]. Also, consumers' expectations of the performance of the new products were dependent on the category people decided to classify them [2]. Oliver showed that the match between the expectation of the product performance and the actual performance is important for consumers' satisfaction [3]. From this, we generated predictions regarding the effect of human- versus product-oriented robot design approaches on the consumers' acceptance of robots. First, because of different forms, people would categorize human-oriented and product-oriented robots differently. Second, this different categorization of robots would lead to different acceptance by consumers.

These analyses led to the following hypotheses:

H1: Consumers will categorize human-oriented robots and product-oriented robots differently.

H2: Consumers' acceptance of human-oriented robots will be different from that of product-oriented robots.

3. STUDY DESIGN

We used a 2-level (robot design: human- vs. product-oriented) between-participants experiment design.

Participants. We recruited university students who are familiar with technical products as participants (Male: 25, Female: 27).

Materials. The robot we used in the experiment was the HangulBot [9], which was developed by one of the authors and her colleagues. HangulBot is a block-shaped edutainment robot, which kids can play with to learn the Korean language.

In the product-oriented robot design condition, only the block-shaped HangulBot was shown to the participants. In the human-oriented robot design condition, a human-oriented robot was shown to the participants with blocks, which had no robotic function as shown in Figure 1. The other components were the same across conditions.

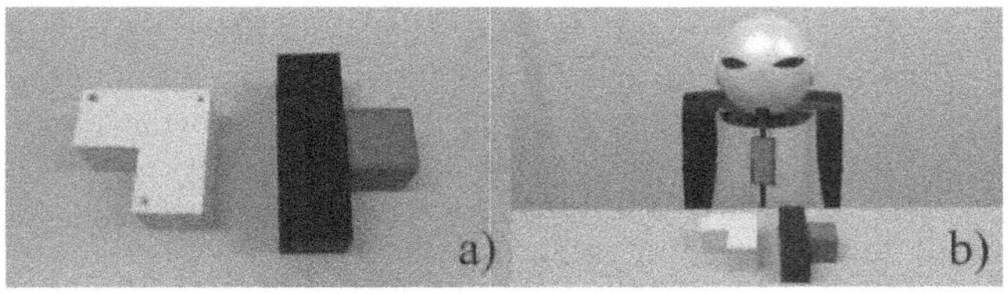

Figure 1. Robot stimulus (a: product-, b: human-oriented)

Procedure. Participants were shown a video clip of either a human-oriented robot or a product-oriented robot. After participants saw a video, a questionnaire regarding the stimulus was administered.

Measures. To measure the participants' categorization of robots, we adopted the measure developed by Lajos et al. [10]. The consumers' acceptance toward robots was measured by product evaluation and purchase intention. Product evaluation was measured by using the four seven-point items (Cronbach's α=.97), which were drawn from Herzenstein et al.'s study [11]. Purchase intention was measured by asking the participants to rate how much they intended to purchase the product and how much they were willing to purchase the product [12]. Both items were averaged to form the overall purchase intention (r=.97). In addition, we measured the participants' willingness to pay by asking how much the participants were willing to pay to purchase the robot [13].

4. RESULTS

Categorization. In the product-oriented robot design condition, twenty-two participants categorized the robot as a babies & kids product, while four participants categorized it as a *robot* among twenty-six participants. In the human-oriented robot design condition, all the twenty-six participants categorized the product as a *robot*. A chi-square analysis showed that the robot design approaches and the categorization of robots were significantly related with each other (χ^2=38.13, p<.001), supporting H1. These results showed that the participants in the product-oriented robot design condition categorized the robot stimulus as one of the existing product categories (i.e., a babies & kids product) more than as a *robot*, whereas those in the human-oriented robot design condition categorized the robot stimulus as a *robot* more than as one of the existing product categories.

Consumers' Acceptance of Robots. The participants in the product-oriented robot design condition evaluated the robot higher than those in the human-oriented robot design condition ($M_{\text{Product-oriented}}$=5.92 vs. $M_{\text{Human-oriented}}$=3.09, t=15.52, df=50, p<.001). Purchase intention showed similar results ($M_{\text{Product-oriented}}$=5.8 vs. $M_{\text{Human-oriented}}$=2.71, t=13.61, df=50, p<.001). Willingness to pay also showed similar results as evaluation and purchase intention ($M_{\text{Product-oriented}}$=US\$371.79 vs. $M_{\text{Human-oriented}}$=US\$252.09, t=4.34, df=50, p<.001), supporting H2. These results show that consumers' acceptance for robots was higher for product-oriented robots than human-oriented robots.

5. CONCLUSIONS

This study was initiated from the question why the growth of the robot market was slower than expected. We investigated this issue with a focus on the robot design. To predict the effect of the robot design approaches on the consumers' acceptance toward robots, we adopted the categorization theory. The results of the study showed that people categorized robots differently depending on the robot design, and robot designs played an essential role in the consumers' acceptance toward robots. Specifically, product-oriented robots were accepted more by consumers than human-oriented robots.

6. REFERENCES

[1] Bloch, P. H. 1995. Seeking the ideal form: Product design and consumer response. *Journal of Marketing*. 59, 3, 16-29.

[2] Moreau, C. P., Markman, A. B., and Lehmann, D. R. 2001. "What is it?" Categorization flexibility and consumers' responses to really new products. *Journal of Consumer Research*. 27, 4, 489-498.

[3] Oliver, R. L. 1980. A cognitive model of the antecedents and consequences of satisfaction decisions. *Journal of Marketing Research*. 17, 4, 460-469.

[4] Fong, T., Nourbakhsh, I., and Dautenhahn, K. 2003. A survey of socially interactive robots. *Robotics and Autonomous Systems*. 42, 4-3, 143–166.

[5] Hegel, F., Krach, S., Kircher, T., Wrede, B., and Sagerer, G. 2008. Understanding social robots: A user study on anthropomorphism. In *Proc. of RO-MAN*, 574-579.

[6] Walters, M., Koay, K., Syrdal, D., Dautenhahn, K., and Boekhorst, R. 2009. Preferences and perceptions of robot appearance and embodiment in human-robot interaction trials. In *Proc. of the New Frontiers in Human-Robot Interaction*, 136–143.

[7] Bartneck, C., Bleeker, T., Bun, J., Fens, P., and Riet, L. 2010. The influence of robot anthropomorphism on the feelings of embarrassment when interacting with robots. *Paladyn Journal of Behavioral Robotics*. 1, 2, 109–115.

[8] Gregan-Paxton, J., Hoeffler, S., and Zhao, M. 2005. When categorization is ambiguous: Factors that facilitate the use of a multiple category inference strategy. *Journal of Consumer Psychology*. 15, 2, 127-140.

[9] Kwak, S. S., Kim, E. H., Kim, J., Son, Y., Kwak, I., Park, J., and Lee, E. W. 2012. Field trials of the block-shaped edutainment robot HangulBot. In *Proc. of HRI*, 40.

[10] Lajos, J., Zsolt, K., Amitava, C., and Miklos, S. 2009. Category activation model: A spreading activation network model of subcategory positioning when categorization uncertainty is high. *Journal of Consumer Research*. 36, 1. 122-136.

[11] Herzenstein, M., Posavac, S. S., and Brakus, J. J. 2007. Adoption of new and really new products: The effects of self-regulation systems and risk salience. *Journal of Marketing Research*. 44, 2, 251-260.

[12] Zhao, M., Hoeffler, S., and Dahl, D. W. 2011. Mental simulation and product evaluation: The affective and cognitive dimensions of process versus outcome simulation. *Journal of Marketing Research*. 48, 5, 827-839.

[13] Carmon, Z. and Ariely, D. 2000. Focusing on the forgone: How value can appear so different to buyers and sellers. *Journal of Consumer Research*. 27, 3, 360-370.

A Pilot Study of Using Touch Sensing and Robotic Feedback for Children with Autism

Jaeryoung Lee
Graduate School of Engineering
Nagoya University
Nagoya, Japan
+81-(0)52-789-5583
lee.jaeryoung@a.mbox.nagoya-u.ac.jp

Goro Obinata
EcoTopia Science Institute
Nagoya University
Nagoya, Japan
+81-(0)52-789-5030
obinata@mech.nagoya-u.ac.jp

Hirofumi Aoki
Graduate School of Engineering
Nagoya University
Nagoya, Japan
+81-(0)52-789-5586
aoki@mech.nagoya-u.ac.jp

ABSTRACT
It is an advantage to use robots in autism therapy since they provide repetitive stimuli during the learning of social skills. A detailed exploration is required to design assistive robots for autism therapy with higher effectiveness. This study has investigated the effectiveness of an interactive robot's feedback during autism therapy for improving specific social skills of the children. The experiment described in this study is that children with autism engaged with an interactive system to perform affective touch behaviour and received the robot's visual and auditory feedback. Results showed that the presence of an interactive robot's feedback triggered more effective children's touch behaviour.

Categories and Subject Descriptors
H.5.2 [**Information interface and presentation**]: User Interfaces – *User-centered design*

Keywords
Human-robot interaction; Robot-assisted autism therapy; Therapeutic robot; Affective touch; Colour.

1. INTRODUCTION
Robot-assisted autism therapy has been broadly studied by numerous researchers in the human-robot interaction field [1]. It started from the idea that children with autism feel safe in a predictable environment with the repetitive behaviours of robots, while they tend to be afraid of human appearances and movements that are complicated and changeable [2]. The main limitation of previous studies in this field is the lack of detailed exploration into the design of therapeutic robots for children with autism. Our previous studies have investigated the features of robots for effective interaction during autism therapy, and those findings were expected to apply a novel design for therapeutic robots [3], [4]

Touch is the main behaviour as a specific social skill that children with autism performed via the therapy in this study. The importance of touch behaviour for the development of children with autism has been addressed in many studies [5]. For encouraging the children to engage in the interactive system, a colour display was used for providing visual information to the children during the experiment same as our previous study [4]. The long-term goal of this study is to design effective robots for children with autism. As an initial step, we explored the responses of children with autism to the robot's feedback during an experiment with colour cues in this study. We set up the following hypotheses. First, children with autism will show better control of their hand force in the case of a robot's feedback presence. Second, the children will reach a test goal more quickly in the case of a robot's feedback presence.

HRI'14, March 3–6, 2014, Bielefeld, Germany.
ACM 978-1-4503-2658-2/14/03.
http://dx.doi.org/10.1145/2559636.2563698

2. METHOD
2.1 Participant
Eight children diagnosed with autism were aged from 8 to 14 (M = 11, SD = 2.56, Males) took part in the experiment.

2.2 Materials
2.2.1 Touch Ball
A special human machine interface device called Touch Ball that was used to test the touching behaviour of children with autism in the experiment. Touch Ball is designed with a combination of a half sphere and the base linked to a three axial force sensor. A small projector was used to illuminate colours on it.

2.2.2 ifbot
An interactive robot called ifbot [6] provided visual and auditory feedback toward children with autism. It expressed happy emotion with a smile and raising its arms, and speaking "Good job! You did it! I am proud of you!"

2.2.3 Touch Game
The experiment was organised as a game called Touch Game that was introduced in our previous study [4] Children were asked to play with Touch Ball and changed its colours projected by controlling the force applied to it. Each test continued 20 seconds. They needed to reach the goal colour as quickly as possible and to maintain the same force until the end of the test. The target colour, yellow, appeared when the force reached within the preliminary defined target force range (See Fig. 2). The three axial forces, $f_x(t), f_y(t), f_z(t)$ were treated as contact force magnitude.

2.3 Procedure
Two types of experiments (See Fig.1) were conducted as test trials and control trials that were categorized by the presence of the

robot's feedback. Participants took part in each trial five times respectively.

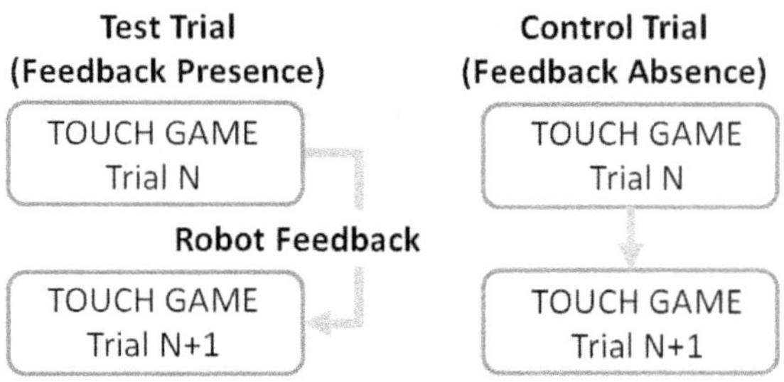

Figure 1. Two types of touch game procedures.

2.4 Data Analysis

Initial success times (IST) and target keeping rate (TKR) were measured and calculated for each task of the Touch Games (See Fig. 2). IST is the time from the start of the test to the moment that the participant succeeds to set the target colour for the first time. TKT which is calculated by (1), is the time duration that the target colour is kept, and TKR is the ratio between TKT and the experiment time (E_T) which is defined by (2).

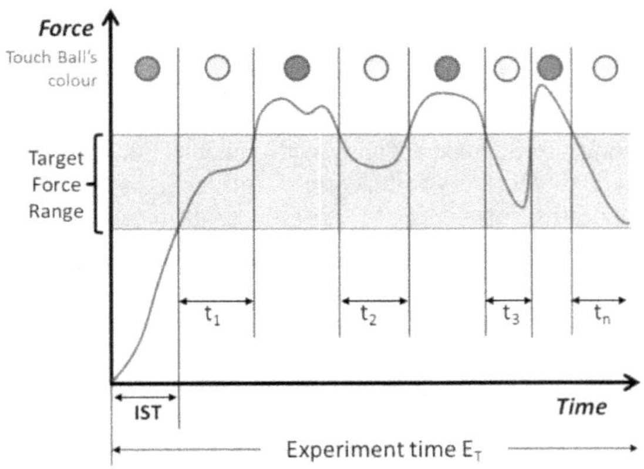

Figure 2. The relationship between the forces applied to the Touch Ball and the colour

$$TKT = \sum_{i=1}^{n} t_i \tag{1}$$

$$TKR = (\frac{TKT}{E_T}) \times 100\ [\%] \tag{2}$$

3. RESULTS

The result of TKR shows that the feedback had a positive effect on 50 percent of children with autism as shown in Fig. 3. Fig. 4 shows the result of the IST and describes that 75 percent of children with autism reached the target force faster when the robot's feedback was presented. These findings support our hypotheses that children with autism will show better outcome from therapy in the case with the robot's feedback presence.

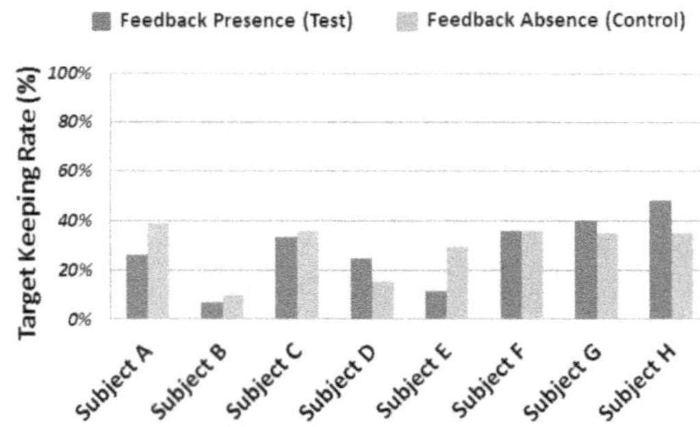

Figure 3. The results of Target Keeping Rate.

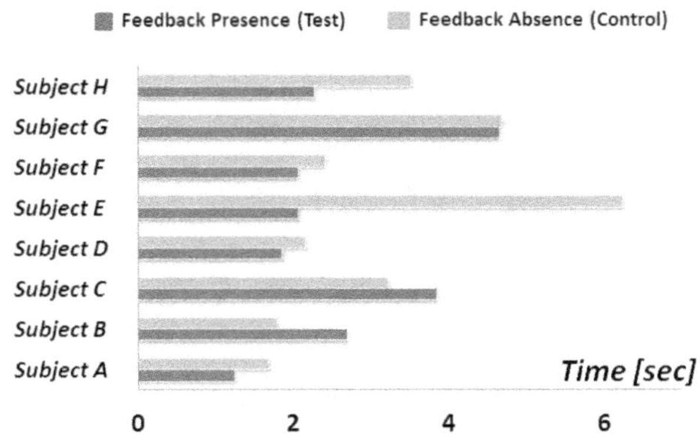

Figure 4. The results of Initial Success Time.

4. ACKNOWLEDGMENTS

We would like to thank Toru Yoshikawa M.D in Nagoya University Hospital and TSUBOMINOKAI, a branch of the Autism Society of Japan.

5. REFERENCES

[1] B. Robins, E. Ferrari, K. Dautenhahn, G. Kronreif, B. Prazak-Aram, G. Gelderblom, B. Tanja, F. Caprino, E. Laudanna, and P. Marti, "Human-centred design methods: Developing scenarios for robot assisted play informed by user panels and field trials," *Int. J. Hum.-Comput. Stud.*, vol. 68, no. 12, pp. 873–898, Dec. 2010.

[2] B. Scassellati, Henny Admoni, and M. Matarić, "Robots for Use in Autism Research," *Annu. Rev. Biomed. Eng.*, vol. 14, no. 1, pp. 275–294, Aug. 2012.

[3] J. Lee, H. Takehashi, C. Nagai, G. Obinata, and D. Stefanov, "Which Robot Features Can Stimulate Better Responses from Children with Autism in Robot-Assisted Therapy?," *Int. J. Adv. Robot. Syst.*, vol. 9, no. 72, pp. 1–6, Sep. 2012.

[4] J. Lee, G. Obinata, D. Stefanov, and C. Nagai, "A Preliminary Study on the Response of Autistic Persons to a Robot Feedback based on Visual Stimuli," *PALADYN J. Behav. Robot.*, vol. 4, no. 2, pp. 73–82, Dec. 2013.

[5] D. Hewett, "Do touch: physical contact and people who have severe, profound and multiple learning difficulties," *Support Learn.*, vol. 22, no. 3, pp. 116–123, Aug. 2007.

[6] M. Kanoh, S. Iwata, S. Kato, and H. Itoh, "Emotive facial expressions of sensitivity communication robot 'Ifbot,'" *KANSEI Eng. Int.*, vol. 5, no. 3, pp. 35–42, 2005.

Boosting Human-to-Human Interaction for Collaborative Learning: Social Exchange Theory Perspective

Ohbyung Kwon
School of Management, Kyung Hee University
1 Hoegi-Dong, Dongdaemun-Gu
Seoul, Rep. of Korea
+82 2 961 2148
obkwon@khu.ac.kr

Namyeon Lee
CAITECH, Kyung Hee University
1 Hoegi-Dong, Dongdaemun-Gu
Seoul, Rep. of Korea
+82 2 961 9491
ciel@khu.ac.kr

ABSTRACT

In this paper, a method of robot-assisted exchange between team members is proposed. This method is based on Social Exchange Theory, which originates from communication research. To boost human-to-human interaction in the context of collaborative learning, the robot collects activity data in order to determine the learners' psychological state and the perceived benefits and costs of interaction as indicators of intention to interact. Using an estimate of intention, the robot then selects strategies to improve the interaction quality.

Categories and Subject Descriptors

H.5.3 [**Group and Organizational Interfaces**]: Computer-supported cooperative work

Keywords

Social Exchange Theory, Collaborative Learning, Case-Based Reasoning, Team-Member Exchange

1. INTRODUCTION

Computer-supported collaborative learning systems must represent problems realistically, facilitate group work, and provide immediate feedback for monitoring and evaluating students' collaborative activities [1]. To meet these requirements, the role of robots in successful collaborative learning has been explored. Robots have traditionally interacted with humans in a slave-like capacity, as assistants or caregivers in parent–infant-like relationships. According to the caregiving paradigm, robots are expected to help humans by identifying and responding to human needs and shortening the social distance between the robot and human [2]. However, because of the emphasis on interaction between robots and individual humans, learning in collaborative settings has received very little attention. Human–robot interaction studies are needed that focus on improving the effectiveness of collaborative learning involving two or more people.

In this study, a human–robot interaction method of robot-assisted collaborative learning is proposed. The first focus is dyadic collaboration, which is here termed "robot-mediated team-member exchange" (TMX). Using Social Exchange Theory (SET), collaboration is examined in terms of the perceived benefits and costs of providing knowledge and identifying favorable activities. A reasoning system is developed that estimates the psychological state of the learner and perceived benefits or costs of interaction based on physical data detected by sensors attached on robot.

HRI'14, March 3-6, 2014, Bielefeld, Germany,
ACM 978-1-4503-2658-2/14/03.
http://dx.doi.org/10.1145/2559636.2559801

2. SOCIAL EXCHANGE THEORY

Social Exchange Theory (SET) posits that social exchange involves a series of interactions that generate obligations [3]. Social exchanges are usually seen as interdependent and contingent on the actions of another person [4]. According to this theory, human relationships are formed on the basis of trust and individual norms of reciprocity. When these basic presumptions are broken, social exchange will be stopped [5]. According to the theory of reasoned action, humans evaluate the benefits and costs resulting from interactions with another human, making behavioral decisions to maximize financial, psychological, or social profits.

SET has interesting implications for robot-assisted learning, especially in the collaborative setting. Reasoned action theory observes that learners are eager to participate in learning situations when they perceive that the benefits of interaction with the dyad are greater than the costs. If no resourcefulness or favorable advantage is perceived, then help is required to recover the value of the interaction. Despite these useful implications from SET for research on human–robot interaction, well-constructed human–robot interaction systems based on SET are lacking.

3. METHOD

Based on the SET, we propose the framework of robot-assisted TMX illustrated in Figure 1.

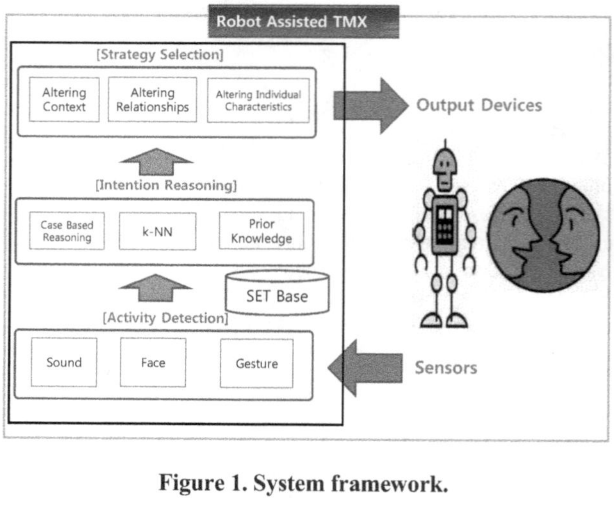

Figure 1. System framework.

3.1 Collecting Data on Human-to-Human Interaction Activities

Most studies on computer-supported collaborative learning rely on self-report measures that assess the interactions between individuals and between the individual and the group. Moreover, these evaluations are usually conducted after the collaboration is complete. However, assessment by self-report after collaboration does not clearly or objectively reflect the students' performance. Moreover, the learning system cannot improve the students' collaborations in a timely and unobtrusive manner. Hence, our approach in this study is different. We collected contextual data on current activity using an automated system that informed the robot of the current state of the individuals involved in the interaction, and that provided suggestions to improve collaborative learning. Although software has been developed to collect detailed information about students' study habits by logging the time and context of every learning event, these programs are not applicable to robot systems.

The robot collects sound (formant, pitch, and duration using a microphone and sound identification software), body angle (facing each other, facing opposite ways, etc.) and physical proximity (physical distance between team members) in real time using embedded sensors. When all context data has been collected, it is packed and sent to the reasoning system.

3.2 Reasoning about Perceived Benefits and Costs

Based on the context data collected by the robot, the reasoning system estimates participants' intention to collaborate. Group exchange intention is determined based on an integrated aggregation of peer exchange interactions, which in turn are formed by individual exchange interactions (see Figure 2).

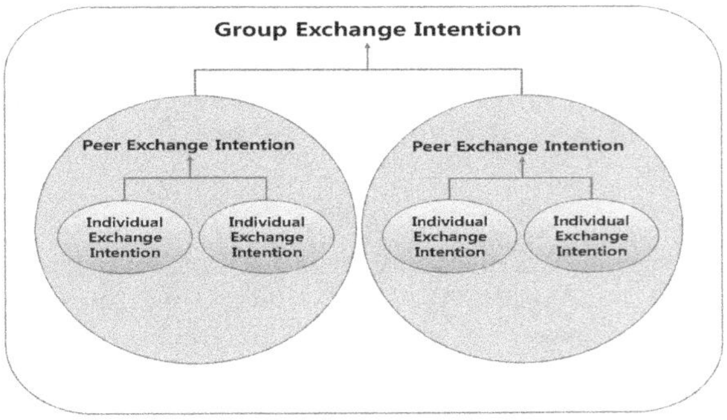

Figure 2. Structure of exchange intention.

3.3 Strategies to Improve Human-to-Human Interaction

Once the robot identifies what the learner is thinking, suitable strategies are selected to increase human-to-human interactions. According to the SET, three categories are considered:

- Altering the context of collaborative learning: providing incentives to those who share knowledge with participants [6]; noting the procedures and rules of collaborative learning.
- Altering the relationships: eliminating or alleviating role conflict, which occurs when participants have more than two inconsistent roles [7]; warming participants up to each other in order to form a sense of unity.
- Altering individual characteristics: encouraging learners to have higher self-efficacy; giving hints to resolve problems

The case-based reasoning method is applicable in selection of strategies. Benefits and costs are identified, individual characteristics and contexts are described as features, and strategy is identified as class of a case in the case base. Using the similarity function, k-nearest neighbors are determined. Then the reasoning system filters some selected neighbors form the list based on the prior knowledge about context–strategy fit. For example, the impact of a previously applied strategy may be weaker than before due to the saturation effect.

3.4 Implementation and Monitoring

The selected strategies are exposed to learner(s) using output devices attached to the robot, such as the display panel and sound features. After a certain period of time, the robot collects sensor data for analysis of the learners' activities. The nature, amount, and quality of this data provide information for evaluation of the chosen strategy, and this information is then added to the case base for later use.

4. CONCLUSION

In this study, a robot-mediated team-member exchange (TMX) system for collaborative learning is proposed based on SET. Currently we are gathering test data to validate the usefulness of the proposed system. In future studies, the TMX system will be expanded to robot-team-member exchange (RTMX) system.

5. ACKNOWLEDGEMENT

This work was supported by the National Strategic R&D Program for Industrial Technology (10041659) and funded by the Ministry of Trade, Industry, and Energy (MOTIE).

6. REFERENCES

[1] Gress, C.L.Z., Fior, M., Hadwin, A.F., Winne, P.H. 2010. Measurement and assessment in computer-supported collaborative learning. *Computers in Human Behavior*. 26 (2010), 806–814.

[2] Kim, K.J., Park, E. and Sundar, S. 2013. Caregiving role in human–robot interaction: A study of the mediating effects of perceived benefit and social presence. *Computers in Human Behavior*. 29 (2013), 1799-1806.

[3] Emerson, R. M. 1976. Social exchange theory. *Annual Review of Sociology*. 2 (1976), 335-362.

[4] Blau, P. M. 1964. *Exchange and Power in Social Life*. New York: John Wiley.

[5] Hendricks, J. 1995. *Exchange Theory in Aging*. In G. Maddox (Eds.), The Encyclopedia of Aging (2nd eds.). New York: Springer.

[6] Wiig, K.M. 1997. Integrating intellectual capital and knowledge management. *Long Range Planning*. 30, 3 (1997), 399-405.

[7] Amazon, A.C. and Sapienza, H.J. 1997. The effects of top management team size and interaction norms on cognitive and affective conflict. *Journal of Management*. 23, 4 (1997), 495-516.

The Dynamics of Anthropomorphism in Robotics

Séverin Lemaignan, Julia Fink, Pierre Dillenbourg
Computer-Human Interaction in Learning and Instruction
Ecole Polytechnique Fédérale de Lausanne (EPFL)
CH-1015 Lausanne, Switzerland
firstname.lastname@epfl.ch

1. DYNAMICS OF ANTHROPOMORPHISM

Many robotics researchers tend to believe that *anthropomorphism* describes a set of human-like features of a robot (like shape, speech capabilities, facial expression). We refer to these characteristics as the *anthropomorphic design* of the robot [1]. *Anthropomorphism*, on the other hand, refers to the *social phenomenon* that emerges from the *interaction* between a robot and an user. According to Epley *et al.* [2], this includes for instance emotional states, motivations, intentions *ascribed by the user* to the robot.

So far, the HRI community has not much investigated how anthropomorphism in human-robot interactions evolves over time (during the process of *adopting* a robot, for instance). Anthropomorphism is traditionally perceived in robotics as a static feature that once observed during a short-term interaction reflects a sustaining social effect. Based on an literature review previously published [1], a long-term field study in a natural environment [3], as well as two on-going child-robot experiments, we believe that anthropomorphic effects do evolve over time in non-monotonic ways, and play a central role in sustaining engagement in human-robot interaction.

We propose to formalize these dynamic effects into a model that we call the *dynamics of anthromorphism.* We hope that it may support further discussions and reflections on how anthromorphism impacts human-robot interaction on the long run, and also foster research on the affective bonds induced by anthorpomorphic projections on robots.

As such, we propose to represent how the level of anthropomorphic effects (*i.e.* observable manifestations of anthropomorphism) evolves over a long-term human-robot interaction (Figure 1). By long-term interaction, we mean direct (non-mediated), repeated interaction with the same robot, over an extended period of time (typically longer than a week).

We distinguish three main phases, depicted in different shades in Figure 1.

First, the *initialization* phase. During this short phase (from a couple of seconds to a couple of hours), we observe

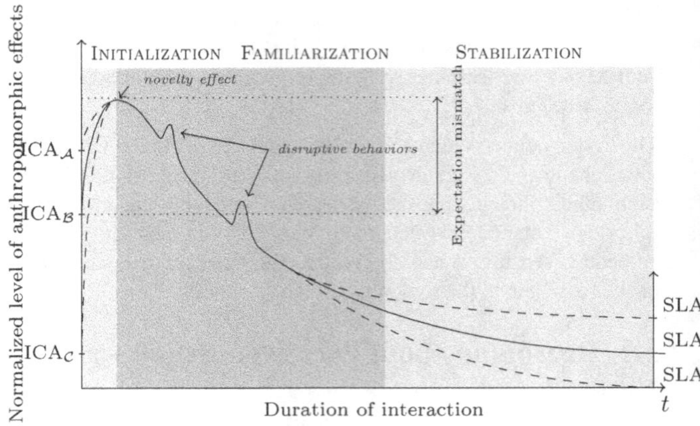

Figure 1: Anthropomorphism evolves over three phases, *initialization*, *familiarization* and *stabilization*, preceded by a *pre-interaction* phase. In the pre-interaction phase, users build an *initial capital of anthropomorphism* (ICA). Once the interaction starts, the level of anthropomorphism increases due to the *novelty effect* [4], and then decreases to reach a *stabilized level of anthropomorphism* (SLA).

an increased level of anthropomorphism, from an *initial capital of anthropomorphism* (*ICA*, a value that measures initial expectations toward the robot, computed from three factors: the personality of the human, the design of the robot and the context/purpose of the interaction. The variability of this value is pictured in Figure 1) to a peak of anthropomorphic manifestations that corresponds to the maximum of the *novelty effect.*

The second phase, *familiarization*, lasts longer (up to several days) and models the process of the human getting acquainted to the robot: by observation and interaction, the human builds a model of the robot's behavior that allows him/her to predict the robot's actions. We observe a decrease of anthropomorphic effects during this phase, that we explain by the acquired ability to predict the behavior of the robot: the initial apparent behavioral complexity vanishes, and the robot is considered more and more as a tool.

The last phase is the *stabilization* phase. The level of anthropomorphic effects tends to stabilize over a longer time, to reach a *stabilized level of anthropomorphism* (SLA). Like the ICA, the SLA is a multi-factor value that depends on the human, the robot and the interaction context.

HRI'14, March 3–6, 2014, Bielefeld, Germany.
ACM 978-1-4503-2658-2/14/03.
http://dx.doi.org/10.1145/2559636.2559814.

	Unplanned by the robot	Planned by the robot
Perceived as non-intentional	case I	case IIIa
Perceived as intentional	case IIIb	case II

Figure 2: Behaviors of the robot that are unexpected by the user may be intentional (the robot has planned the behavior) or not (typically, a failure: misdetection, bug,...). Independently of that, the behavior may be *perceived* by the user as intentional or not.

2. ELEMENTS OF INTERPRETATION

To understand and possibly better manage the evolution of human-robot interactions over time, we briefly describe preliminary behavioral observations and cognitive interpretations that are related to our model. We are currently conducting more experiments to further support and extend these findings.

Role of disruptive behaviors. By *disruptive behaviors*, we mean any behavior exhibited by the robot that is unexpected for the user: for instance, a robot may usually follow always the same route to go from one place to another, but suddenly change it. As long as this reason is not immediately *intelligible* to the user, the behavior counts as *disruptive.*

Our model represents *disruptive behaviors* as local increases of anthropomorphic effects in the familiarization phase (and to a lower extent, in the stabilization phase): because such behaviors are unexpected, they impact the rationality that the user ascribes to the robot, and a human observer may interpret them as the result of a richer deliberative process, which in turn leads to the supposition of complex cognitive skills in the robot. This is however to be modulated depending on the real and perceived reasons for the unexpected behavior. It may increase if the user perceives (rightfully or not) a form of intentionality, as well as decrease if the unexpected behavior is perceived as a failure. Figure 2 summarizes the possible situations.

Cognitive interpretations. The underlying cognitive process in anthropomorphism is understood as perceiving and reasoning about something non-human and unfamiliar based on one's representation of the familiar and well-known concept of being human [2]. This led us to interpret the phases of anthropomorphic interactions as parallel cognitive phases.

The so-called *phase I* is the instinctive, pre-cognitive identification of living peers. This is supported by studies done by Rosenthal-von der Pütten *et al.* [5] who investigated the neural correlates of emotional reactions of humans towards a robot. *Empathy* is characteristic of this stage.

After a longer observation period (typically including complete action sequences of the robot) or short interaction (touching, short talk like greetings), we suggest the human enters the cognitive *phase II*: in this phase, the human starts building a behavioral and cognitive model of the robot that would support both the observed and imagined capabilities of the robot. The *familiarity thesis* [6] would support the idea that the human first projects onto the robot mental models of similar agents he/she is already familiar with.

The cognitive *phase III* occurs after a *contextualized* interaction. A *contextualized* interaction is *explicitly purposeful*, and takes place in an environment that fosters a stronger cognitive (and possibly affective/social) commitment from the human in the interaction (typically, at home). During this interaction, the human iteratively restates his/her behavioral and mental model of the robot (*How does the robot react to situations/inputs? What does the robot know about me? What can the robot learn?*, etc.).

This mental process heavily depends on the human understanding of the robot's inner working, as well as his/her own tendency to anthropomorphize, but at this stage, the *perception* of the robot (its shape for instance) and its intended *purpose* play a less important role. It is mostly a human-centric process. The result of this third phase would be an iteratively adapted cognitive model of the robot.

These cognitive phases overlap but do not exactly match the *Initialization*, *Familiarization* and *Stabilization* phases introduced in our model of the dynamics of anthromorphism, and we are currently investigating the relations between both.

3. CONCLUSION

Anthropomorphism is traditionally understood as the interactions between the anthropomorphic design of a robot and the psychological determinants of the user. We have found out that the duration and context of the interaction is a third factor that plays a key role. In this preliminary report, we sketch a new formal model of anthropomorphism that accounts for these three factors and also explicits the dynamics of anthromorphism. We introduce the concepts of *initial capital* and *stabilized level of anthropomorphism* as compound factors to characterize the profile of a given anthropomorphic interaction.

While not definitive, we hope that this contribution may ultimately consolidate the scientific grounds of anthropomorphism, and provides support for further research on long-term acceptance of robots in human environments.

4. REFERENCES

[1] J. Fink, "Anthropomorphism and human likeness in the design of robots and human-robot interaction," in *Social Robotics*, no. 7621, pp. 199–208, 2012.

[2] N. Epley, A. Waytz, S. Akalis, and J. T. Cacioppo, "When we need a human: Motivational determinants of anthropomorphism," *Social Cognition*, vol. 26, no. 2, pp. 143–155, 2008.

[3] J. Fink, V. Bauwens, F. Kaplan, and P. Dillenbourg, "Living with a vacuum cleaning robot," *Intl Journal of Social Robotics*, vol. 5 no. 3, pp. 389–408, 2013.

[4] T. Kanda, T. Hirano, D. Eaton, and H. Ishiguro, "Interactive robots as social partners and peer tutors for children: a field trial," *Hum.-Comput. Interact.*, vol. 19, no. 1, p. 61–84, 2004.

[5] A. M. Rosenthal-von der Pütten, N. C. Krämer, L. Hoffmann, S. Sobieraj, and S. C. Eimler, "An experimental study on emotional reactions towards a robot," *Intl Journal of Social Robotics*, 2013.

[6] F. Hegel, S. Krach, T. Kircher, B. Wrede, and G. Sagerer, "Understanding social robots: A user study on anthropomorphism," in *RO-MAN* 2008, pp. 574 –579.

Goal-Predictability vs. Trajectory-Predictability – Which Legibility Factor Counts

Christina Lichtenthäler
Institute for Advanced Study
Technische Universität München
christina.lichtenthaeler@in.tum.de

Alexandra Kirsch
Department of Computer Science
Tübingen University
alexandra.kirsch@uni-tuebingen.de

ABSTRACT

With the work at hand we investigate the legibility factors goal-predictability and trajectory-predictability in a human-robot path crossing scenario and their correlation with other HRI properties like safety, comfort, and reliability in order to assess which factor is more important for a safe and comfortable interaction.

Keywords

Legibility, Social Navigation, Human-Robot Interaction

1. INTRODUCTION

One important factor for a smooth, efficient and also safe human-robot interaction is the legibility of the robot's motion [4]. A great deal of work has been carried out so far in order to develop legible robot motions [5, 2] as well as to investigate the legibility of different kinds of movements in experiments [1, 4]. Based on our previous work [4, 3], where we mainly focussed on human-robot path crossing scenarios, we define robot behavior as legible if: (1) a human observer or interactor is able to understand its intentions, meaning that a human is able to predict the goal (goal-predictability) and the motion trajectory (trajectory-predictability), and (2) the behavior met the expectations of the human observer or interactor (met-expectation).

In a work presented by Dragan et al. [1] the authors investigate the differences of goal-predictability, in their work they call it legibility, and trajectory-predictability, which they call predictability, and found that *"both are fundamentally different and often contradictory properties of motion"* [1]. They investigated robot arm motions without any human interaction. Based on their findings, we want to examine if this applies also to a human-robot path crossing scenario. Furthermore, when both factors are different, the question came up, which factor is more important in terms of its influence on other HRI properties like safety or comfort?

Research Question: The objective of the work at hand is (1) to compare the legibility factors goal-predictability and trajectory predictability in a human-robot path crossing scenario in order to explore if we could find similar results to Dragan et al. [1] and (2) to investigate the correlation between the legibility factors and the interaction properties safety, comfort, and reliability.

HRI'14, March 3–6, 2014, Bielefeld, Germany.
ACM 978-1-4503-2658-2/14/03.
http://dx.doi.org/10.1145/2559636.2559817..

2. METHOD

We re-analyzed data of a between-subject questionnaire-based experiment. In the experiment we showed the participants videos of a robot crossing the path of a human and measured legibility as well as the HRI properties safety, comfort, and reliability.

In the following we briefly describe the conducted experiment focussing on the relevant informations for our new analysis. A more detailed description of the experimental setup and the former findings are given in [3].

Design.

We recorded short movie sequences using the MORSE simulator, where a human is crossing the robot's path in an office environment. The video clips were divided into two parts. The first part of each video shows the robot behavior before the paths of human and robot cross up to the point where the robot is only at a short distance to the human. The second part shows the robot behavior during the crossing event, like crossing before or behind the human, colliding with the human, spinning around, or waiting until the human passes by. We compared two variations of a Human-Aware navigation [2] (HA-TP, HA-WF) with two variations of the state-of-the-art navigation method Move-Base (MB-WF, MB-DWA).

Conditions With three tables as possible goal positions and four navigation methods, we tested $(3 \times 4) = 12$ different observation tasks.

Dependent Measures.

In order to quantify legibility we measured the factors *goal-predictability*, by asking to predict the robot's goal, *trajectory-predictability*, by asking to predict the future direction of the robot, and *met-expectation* by asking if the robot met the participants expectations by using a yes/no scale. Furthermore, we measured the HRI properties surprise, safety, comfort, and reliability by using a five-point Likert scale.

Participants.

16 participants with the average age of 26.6 years took part in our experiment - thereof 3 women and 13 men.

Procedure.

We showed the participants each two-parted video clip once in random order. After the first part we asked the participant to judge which table the robot is aiming at (goal-

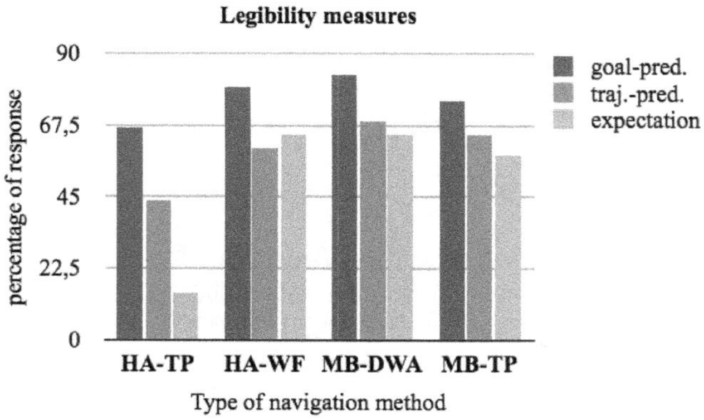

Figure 1: Frequency of correct goal- and trajectory-predictions and how often the behavior met the participants expectations.

predictability) and how it will change its direction (trajectory-predictability). Then we showed the second part and the participants were able to observe the actual behavior of the robot. Afterwards, the participants were asked to tell whether the robot's actual behavior was expected and if not to rate how surprising this was. Additionally we asked for ratings on perceived safety, comfort, and reliability.

3. RESULTS AND DISCUSSION

Regarding our aforementioned research question we found the following results by (1) considering the factor trajectory-predictability[1] and (2) by performing a correlation analysis. The results of correct predictions for goal-predictability and trajectory-predictability are shown in Fig.1. Most correct answers regarding goal-predictability were given for MB-DWA (83.3%) and HA-WF (79.2%) compared to MB-TP (75.0%) and HA-TP (66.7%). Results of the correct predicted directions (trajectory-predictability) are showing a slightly different ranking regarding the navigation methods, here also the most correct answers regarding the direction were for MB-DWA (68.8%) and MB-TP (64.6%) followed by HA-WF (60.4%) and HA-TP (43.8%). Pearson's Chi-Square tests did not reveal any significant association between type of planner and number of correct responses for goal-predictability $\chi^2(3) = 4.00$, $p = .261$, but a marginally significant association between type of navigation and trajectory-predictability $\chi^2(3) = 7.17$, $p = 0.067$. By looking at the charts in Fig. 1 one can presume a slightly difference in the number of correct responses between trajectory- and goal-predictability and an association between trajectory-predict-ability and the met-expectation factor, but contrary to Dragan et al. [1] we found no contrariness as Dragan et al. [1] found, that one algorithm revealed a high value for one and a low value for the other factor. One reason for these opposite findings can be that Dragan et al. [1] generated motion trajectories by optimizing one of the two factors and we compared different navigation algorithms, which are mainly differing in their reaction to a human interactor.

In order to investigate the relationship between the measurements we calculated the point-biserial correlation coefficient, r_{pb} for the discrete dichotomous variables goal-predictability, trajectory-predictability, met expectation and the Pearson's correlation coefficient r for all other variables.

[1]In [3] we analysed only the factor goal-predictability

Results are shown in Table 1. One can see that all measurements are significantly correlated with each other, except for goal-predictability with the HRI-factors safety, comfort and reliability. The low, but significant correlation between goal- and trajectory-predictability , $r_{pb} = .16, p < 0.05$ also shows, that for our human-robot path crossing scenario, the two legibility factors are related and not contradictory. Furthermore, the correlation values for trajectory-predictability are considerably higher than for goal-predictability, which let us assume that trajectory-predictability has a higher impact on how the interaction was perceived. Additionally, the former assumption of an association between trajectory-predictability and the met-expectation factor is supported by a highly significant correlation, $r_{pb} = .54, p < .001$.

Table 1: Pearson's correlation coeffecients r and point-biserial correlation coefficient, r_{pb} calculated for all measurements.

	traj-p.	exp.	surp.	safe	comfort	reliable
goal	$.16^{*}$	$.37^{**}$	$-.26^{**}$	-.08	.03	.001
traj.	1	$.54^{**}$	$-.52^{**}$	$.24^{**}$	$.23^{**}$	$.28^{**}$
exp.	–	1	$-.85^{**}$	$.30^{**}$	$.36^{**}$	$.41^{**}$
surp.	–	–	1	$-.32^{**}$	$-.39^{**}$	$-.46^{**}$
safe	–	–	–	1	$.90^{**}$	$.87^{**}$
comf.	–	–	–	–	1	$.87^{**}$

*. $p < 0.05$, **. $p < 0.001$

4. CONCLUSION

To conclude, with our results in a human-robot path crossing experiment at hand we could not support the finding of Dragan et al. [1] that goal- and trajectory-predictability are contradictory factors of a motion. Quite the opposite, we found that the two factors are coherent. Furthermore, our results let us assume that trajectory-predictability is the more important factor in a human-robot interaction scenario when considering the factors safety, comfort, and reliability. However, the experiment at hand was a pilot-study with a low number of participants. Therefore, the results are showing us a direction, which has to be further investigated in the future preferably with a real world experiment.

5. REFERENCES

[1] A. Dragan, K. Lee, and S. Srinivasa. Legibility and Predictability of Robot Motion. In *ACM/IEEE HRI*, 2013.

[2] T. Kruse, P. Basili, S. Glasauer, and A. Kirsch. Legible Robot Navigation in the Proximity of Moving Humans. In *IEEE ARSO*, 2012.

[3] C. Lichtenthäler, T. Lorenz, M. Karg, and A. Kirsch. Increasing Perceived Value Between Human and Robots - Measuring Legibility in Human Aware Navigation. In *IEEE ARSO*, 2012.

[4] C. Lichtenthäler, T. Lorenz, and A. Kirsch. Influence of Legibility on Perceived Safety in a Virtual Human-Robot Path Crossing Task. In *IEEE RO-MAN*, 2012.

[5] E. A. Sisbot and R. Alami. A Human-Aware Manipulation Planner. *IEEE Transactions on Robotics*, 28(5), 2012.

Towards Automated Execution and Evaluation of Simulated Prototype HRI Experiments

Florian Lier
Cognitive Interaction Technology Center of Excellence
Bielefeld University
Bielefeld, Germany
flier@techfak.uni-bielefeld.de

Ingo Lütkebohle
Machine Learning and Robotics Lab
University of Stuttgart
Stuttgart, Germany
ingo.luetkebohle@ipvs.uni-stuttgart.de

Sven Wachsmuth
Cognitive Interaction Technology Center of Excellence
Bielefeld University
Bielefeld, Germany
swachsmu@techfak.uni-bielefeld.de

ABSTRACT

Autonomous robots are highly relevant targets for interaction studies, but can exhibit behavioral variability that confounds experimental validity. Currently, testing on real systems is the only means to prevent this, but remains very labour-intensive and often happens too late. To improve this situation, we are working towards early testing by means of *partial* simulation, with automated assessment, and based upon continuous software integration to prevent regressions. We will introduce the concept and describe a proof-of-concept that demonstrates fast feedback and coherent experiment results across repeated trials.

Categories and Subject Descriptors

D.2.5 [**Software Engineering**]: Testing and Debugging—*Designs, Program Verification*

Keywords

Human-Robot Interaction, Simulation, Testing, Continuous Integration, System Evaluation

1. INTRODUCTION

Most robots are expected to eventually possess a degree of autonomy that improves their capability of achieving tasks and therefore, performing interaction on autonomous systems – with all their associated technical issues – is of high relevance. It is a well-established fact that valid experiments need a well-defined experimental protocol[3, 1]. However, today's state of the art autonomous systems may exhibit surprisingly high variability in the face of relatively small changes in the environment and user behavior, which could confound data interpretation. To control this, detailed testing of experiment designs and their corresponding software realizations is required but difficult to maintain, especially for experimenters who are not part of the engineering team. To enable experimenters as well as system developers to cooperatively design, test and integrate their experiments as easily and often as possible, and thus to improve the design and evaluation process, we propose *a)* to establish experiment prototyping. This uses simulation environments including a virtual human component *b)* to extend the concept of an experiment protocol to the orchestration of software components, and *c)* to execute and assess the results of a prototype experiment in an automated, easy-to-use fashion. In the remainder of this late breaking report we will introduce a software tool chain which implements our propositions and a purposefully limited scenario in order to present preliminary results.

HRI'13, March 3–6, 2014, Bielefeld, Germany.
ACM 978-1-4503-2658-2/14/03.
http://dx.doi.org/10.1145/2559636.2559841.

2. SOFTWARE TOOL CHAIN

Our tool chain comprises three components: an interactive simulation environment (Section 3), a framework to automatically bootstrap a prototype system, verify correct execution of components, asses results gathered from experiments (Section 4) and a Continuous Integration [2] server to centralize experiment evaluation. This tool chain provides the following benefits: simulation environments offer easy and cheap access to data which is usually acquired in labour-intensive "real life" experiments. Moreover, experimenters and engineers can mutually design and discuss prototype experiments "on-the-fly". By providing an easy-to-use, automated and well-defined mechanism to execute and evaluate a prototype system, we minimize the complexity of this task, and make the experiment environment almost instantly available. Experimenters are also able integrate their evaluation methods into the tool chain directly by, e.g., providing MATLAB, R, or Python scripts, which are automatically executed during the experiment evaluation. Lastly, experimenters can easily script the "behavior" of the simulation, by changing a few lines of code without programming experience to explore diverse scenarios and conditions.

3. A SIMULATED HRI SCENARIO

In this purposefully limited scenario, a virtual PR2 robot continuously reports the spacial location of a human avatar in a domestic apartment environment. Both, the robot and the human, are moving about in the scene and eventually meet in front of a table (Figure 1). In order to realize this simulation, we utilized the Modular OpenRobots Simulation

Engine (MORSE) [4]. In this setup, we control the PR2 and the human avatar via ROS [6] middleware. Therefore, we are able to interactively set and publish waypoints in the scene for both agents at runtime. The PR2 is equipped with an abstract sensor (a semantic camera) which reports the human's active coordinates — if the avatar enters the robot's field of view. In this scenario, we have explicitly chosen to simplify the extraction of the human's location by using the semantic camera to obtain a ground truth in the first iteration. However, a virtual human component that is interactively controllable, is a general benefit which enables us to develop more complex scenarios in further iterations.

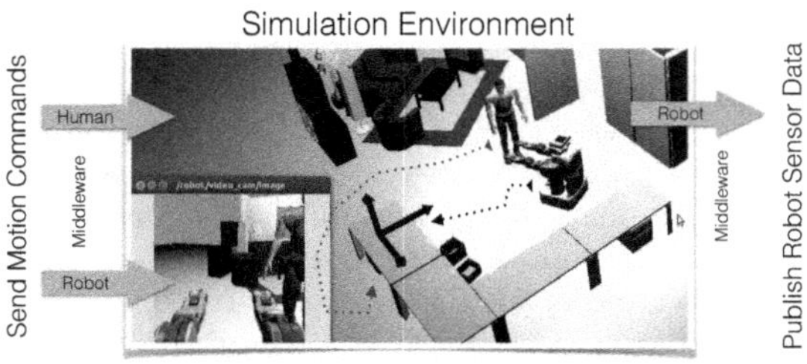

Figure 1: Prototype HRI Simulation

4. SOFTWARE PROTOCOL

Similar to strict adherence of an experiment protocol, the software used in an experiment to produce and assess data, must also follow "protocol" to obtain coherent results. Especially in distributed systems it is crucial to start all software components in the correct sequence, i.e., data producer before consumer, to avoid malfunctions and inconsistent data. Often, software execution/testing is carried out manually and is thus prone to errors. Additionally, experimenters who are "just" interested in the resulting data, must gain additional knowledge about the technical details of a system to conduct their experiments. To address these issues we have developed a finite-state-machine-based testing framework (FSMT) [5] that supports explicit specification of the software ecosystem used, for instance in an experiment. FSMT provides definition of environment variables, component parameter specifications, hierarchical state-based execution of software components, and status (health) checks. Moreover, FSMT specifications consist of three *mandatory* states: environment definition, run state and an assessment state. In the run state, the actual experiment is conducted meaning all components of a system are running and data is recorded. In the assessment state, the recorded data is evaluated by assessment components. Experimenters may provide scripts to assess the data gathered in each run, i.e., plot specified data points. Finally, by implementing this formalization of an experiment protocol with regard to software, we are able to automatically start a software system, verify correct execution and eventually produce consistent results. This approach makes it an ideal candidate for Continuous Integration, but also enables experimenters to run an experiment on their local machine by executing a FSMT specification.

5. RESULTS AND CONCLUSION

To obtain the results depicted in Figure 2, we automatically executed a FSMT specification consisting of ten components, including the simulation as described in (Section 3), on our CI server. In the run state, the simulation is bootstrapped and waypoints are sent to the robot and the human. Simultaneously, the location reported by the robot is recorded to a log file. After twenty seconds the simulation and the motion generation component are stopped. In the assessment state, two components are started: one to clean up and transform the logs in CSV files and a second one to generate plots of the coordinates of the virtual human. To demonstrate the ease of changing the simulation behavior and assessment we conducted three different runs. In the first run we assessed the "x" component of the location, in the second run the "y" component and in the third run we changed one waypoint of the human avatar. Each modification required the change of just 1 line of code. The execution duration of each test lasted 42 seconds. With this setup in place, we are now able to conduct a simulated experiment practically every minute, which will also reflect the impact of changes in the software stack on the desired results. Moreover, experimenters are able to easily add additional evaluation components to this setup. We are aware of the fact, that this setup is basic, but from our point of view, it is a first step towards automated, consistent and cooperative testing of simulated HRI experiments.

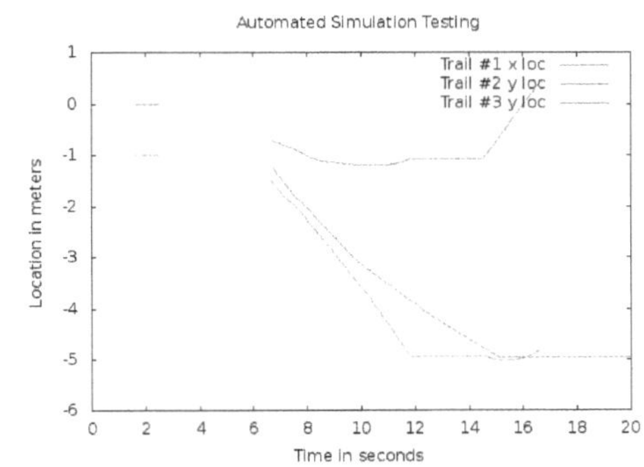

Figure 2: Position of the Human Avatar

6. REFERENCES

[1] K. Dautenhahn. Methodology and themes of human-robot interaction: a growing research field. *International Journal of Advanced Robotic Systems*, 2007.

[2] P. M. Duvall, S. Matyas, and A. Glover. *Continuous integration: improving software quality and reducing risk.* Pearson Education, 2007.

[3] C. D. Kidd and C. Breazeal. Human-robot interaction experiments: Lessons learned. In *Proceeding of AISB*, volume 5, pages 141–142, 2005.

[4] S. Lemaignan, G. Echeverria, M. Karg, J. Mainprice, A. Kirsch, and R. Alami. Human-robot interaction in the morse simulator. In *Proceedings of the seventh annual ACM/IEEE international conference on Human-Robot Interaction*, pages 181–182. ACM, 2012.

[5] F. Lier, N. Köster, I. Lütkebohle, and S. Wachsmuth. State machine based simulation testing, 2013.

[6] M. Quigley, K. Conley, B. Gerkey, J. Faust, T. Foote, J. Leibs, R. Wheeler, and A. Y. Ng. Ros: an open-source robot operating system. In *ICRA workshop on open source software*, volume 3, 2009.

Useful and Motivating Robots – The Influence of Task Structure on Human-Robot Teamwork

Manja Lohse
Human Media Interaction
University of Twente
Enschede, the Netherlands
m.lohse@utwente.nl

Vanessa Evers
Human Media Interaction
University of Twente
Enschede, the Netherlands
v.evers@utwente.nl

ABSTRACT

Robots have recently started to leave their safety cages to be used in close vicinity to humans. This also causes changes in the nature of the tasks that robots and humans solve together, i.e., in the degree of structure of the tasks. While traditional, industrial tasks were highly structured, the new tasks often have a low level of structure. We present a user study that compares a highly and a little structured task in a text-based computer game played by human-robot teams. The results suggest that users do not only find robots useful and motivating in highly structured tasks where they depend on their help, but also in little structured tasks that they could solve on their own.

Categories and Subject Descriptors

H.m [**Information Systems**]: Miscellaneous

General Terms

Experimentation

Keywords

human-robot teamwork, task structure

1. INTRODUCTION

Within the last decades, teamwork has been recognized as an effective means of conducting business. Teamwork has also advanced collaborative work environments where humans and robots work together on shared tasks, e.g., in surgery or in industry where humans and robots work jointly on assembling complex products such as cars. Thus, robots leave their safety cages to interact in human-robot teams [2, 7]. The nature of teamwork is changing through the introduction of such autonomous robots and the topic is starting to receive attention in HRI [2, 3, 7]. One aspect of teamwork that has not been explored to date is the degree of task structure. By task structure we refer to characteristics of tasks such as how well defined the goals of the tasks are (goal clarity), how many ways there are to achieve the goals (goal path multiplicity), how well the actors know whether their steps to achieve the goals were correct (decision verifiability), and how high the level of interdependence between the actors involved in the task is (task interdependence) [4]. Task structure is highly relevant because the new robotic applications mentioned above require largely unstructured, non-routine tasks compared to the highly structured, routine tasks in factory settings. Unstructured tasks are characterized by little defined goals, many ways to achieve them, little possibilities to check whether decisions were optimal, and little interdependence between the actors. To date there is no research on the question whether users accept robots to assist also in such tasks or only in highly structured ones. To fill this gap, we investigated the influence of the task structure on human-robot teamwork in a text-based computer game. We compared a highly and a little structured task in order to determine how task structure influences the perception of a robot's usefulness, ability to motivate the users, and further criteria of user experience. Furthermore, we analyzed whether the users' behavior objectively differed between the conditions with respect to how much effort they put into playing the game and what commands they used.

HRI'14, March 3–6, 2014, Bielefeld, Germany.
ACM 978-1-4503-2658-2/14/03.
http://http://dx.doi.org/10.1145/2559636.2559803.

2. SYSTEM DESIGN

Our goal was to implement a highly and a little structured task in a way that allows to compare them without having to consider many differences that are due to the task design instead of the degree of structure of the task. Therefore, we decided to implement a text-based computer game. The goal of the game was to find the statue of a golden goose and to become a rich explorer. The players could move around between screens, pick up objects, use them to access new screens, and solve riddles. The game was designed in a way that offered several opportunities for a robot to engage the player in teamwork such as providing the player with information about possible destinations, objects, and riddles. We implemented these behaviors in a Nao robot using the Choregraphe software. Nao behaviors were executed either when the user asked the robot for help (verbal triggers), when the game entered a certain state, e.g. a new screen, (game triggers), or when the researcher had to intervene (manual command triggers).

The task structure of the game was manipulated based on the factors introduced above. *Goal clarity* was manipulated in the instructions that the participants received before the interaction with the robot (goal clearly stated vs. rather vague goal statement). Different degrees of *goal path multiplicity* were achieved by implementing the highly structured version of the game in a way that only one path led to the goal, and multiple paths led to the goal in the little structured version. These differences also affected the *solution specificity*. While there was one clear solution in the highly structured version (reach the golden goose), multiple solutions to collect points were available in the little structured version of the game. A high degree of *decision verifiability* was realized in the game by providing specific feedback to the consequences of actions in the highly structured version and only ambiguous feedback in the little structured version. All these criteria also affected the *interdependence* between the actors. Asking the Nao for help to complete the game was required only in the highly structured version, thus, increasing the interdependence between human and robot. While the game differed between the conditions, the Nao behaviors largely stayed the same.

3. SAMPLE

23 participants took part in our user study (6 female, 17 male; aged 19 to 31, with a mean age of 23.3 years, sd = 2.50). All participants were students at the University of Twente. They were divided in two groups (one per condition). Both groups included the same number of female participants and had roughly the same age distribution. The participants had little experience with text based games (m = 2.45; sd = 1.30)(all items on a scale of 1: not at all - 5: a lot) and even less interacting with the Nao robot (m = 1.24, sd = 0.77).

4. RESULTS

We measured *user experience* with the USE scales by Lund (cited from [5]). All items were rated on a 5-point Likert scale (1: strongly disagree - 5: strongly agree). They were presented in random order. The scale did not reveal any significant differences regarding the robot between the two conditions. The *usefulness* (m = 3.85; sd = 0.59); (Cronbach's α .820) and the *satisfaction* (m = 3.80; sd = 0.50); (Cronbach's α .729) were experienced very positively in both conditions and also the *ease of use* (m = 3.56; sd = 0.55); (Cronbach's α .716) had a tendency toward the positive side of the scale. We employed the two one-sided test (TOST) to determine whether the user experience of the robot was actually equivalent in both conditions [6]. The equivalence margin (δ) was set to the standard deviations of the individual subscales. Following the TOST procedure, the two conditions could be declared equivalent for all subscales; for each of the dependent variables the lower and upper bound were within the mean difference $\pm\delta$ margin.

In contrast to the user experience of the robot, we found a non-significant tendency that the game was easier to use in the highly structured condition (m = 3.52; sd = 0.53) than in the little structured condition (m = 3.11; sd = 0.45); (T(19)=1.882; p=.075; two-tailed); (Cronbach's α .726). However, the users' *satisfaction* with the game was significantly higher in the highly structured condition (m = 3.92; sd = 0.64) than in the little structured version (m = 3.20; sd = 0.58); (T(19)=2.633, p=.016; two-tailed); (Cronbach's α .813). Overall, these results point to a more positive user experience of the highly structured game.

Additionally, we measured the *robot's capability to motivate users* with four items (Cronbach's α = .696) inspired by the work of Fasola and Matarić [1]. These ratings did not reveal any differences between the conditions. Overall the Nao worked well as a motivator (m=3.63; sd = 0.70). Again, we employed the TOST procedure as described above and the two conditions could be declared equivalent.

We analyzed the logfiles to determine whether the *actions that people took* in the game differed between the conditions. Overall, we found that the time to play the game was highly similar in both conditions (highly structured: m = 22.50 minutes, sd = 5.23; little structured: m = 23.89 minutes, sd = 1.71). Also the mean number of actions was similar (highly structured: m= 220.00, sd = 68.66; little structured: m = 250.11, sd = 65.00). The TOST procedure showed that the two conditions could be declared equivalent. The analysis of the logfiles also revealed that participants used most commands equally often in both conditions.

5. CONCLUSION

Our results show that the robot was perceived as a useful and motivating team member in both a highly and a little structured task. While we expected that the robot would be perceived as even more useful in the highly structured task which involved higher interdependence between human and robot, this was not the case. Also the satisfaction with the robot and the ease of use were rated similarly and the robot was perceived as being equally motivating in both conditions. This finding is very encouraging for our research, particularly given the fact that the game was perceived as being easier to use and more satisfying in the highly structured version. Thus, the robot succeeded as a member of the team in the little structured task despite the fact that it involved less interdependence and a more negative evaluation of the game. We conclude, that users indeed find robots that support little structured tasks useful and motivating.

6. REFERENCES

[1] J. Fasola and M. J. Matarić. Using socially assistive hri to motivate physical exercise for older adults. *Proc. of the IEEE*, 100(8):2512 – 2526, 2012.

[2] G. Hoffman and C. Breazeal. Effects of anticipatory perceptual simulation on practiced human-robot tasks. *Autonomous Robots*, 28(4):403–423, 2010.

[3] J. Shah and C. Breazeal. An empirical analysis of team coordination behaviors and action planning with application to human-robot teaming. *Human Factors: The Journal of the Human*, 10(2):234–245, 2010.

[4] M. Shaw. Scaling group tasks: A method for dimensional analysis. Technical report, University of Florida, 1963.

[5] T. Tullis and W. Albert. *Measuring the User Experience: Collecting, Analyzing, and Presenting Usability Metrics*. Morgan Kaufmann Publishers Inc., San Francisco, CA, USA, 2008.

[6] E. Walker and A. S. Nowacki. Understanding equivalence and noninferiority testing. 26(2):192–196, 2011.

[7] R. Wilcox, S. Nikolaidis, and J. Shah. Optimization of temporal dynamics for adaptive human-robot interaction in assembly manufacturing. *Proceedings of Robotics: Science and Systems*, 2012.

Ghost-in-the-Machine: Initial Results

Sebastian Loth
Bielefeld University
Faculty for Linguistics and Literature
Universitätsstr. 25, 33615 Bielefeld, Germany
+49-521-106-3669
sebastian.loth@uni-bielfeld.de

Manuel Giuliani
fortiss GmbH
An-Institut TUM
Guerickestr. 25, 80805 München, Germany
+49-89-360-3522-544
giuliani@fortiss.de

Jan P. de Ruiter
Bielefeld University
Faculty for Linguistics and Literature
Universitätsstr. 25, 33615 Bielefeld, Germany
+49-521-106-6928
jan.deruiter@uni-bielefeld.de

ABSTRACT

We describe the design of the newly developed Ghost-in-the-Machine paradigm and present initial results of an experiment addressing the initiation of service interactions at a bar. For developing policies for a robotic bartender, we investigated which sensor modalities were most informative to humans, and which actions they selected as a socially appropriate response. The results showed that participants used two nonverbal cues for their initial response to a new customer. Those were the distance to the bar and whether the customers' torso was directed to the bar. For acknowledging a new customer, the participants typically responded nonverbally by looking and smiling at the customers. All results can be directly transferred into robotic decision policies.

Categories and Subject Descriptors

H.1.2 [**Models and Principles**]: User/Machine Systems – *software psychology*.

General Terms

Design, Experimentation.

Keywords

Human-Robot Interaction, Social Robotics, Psychology.

1. INTRODUCTION

For enabling users to interact intuitively with a robot, its recognizing and planning components have to correctly interpret the natural social behavior of its users and it has to respond appropriately. But the robot's input is limited to its sensor data and thus, the responsiveness of the robot depends on correctly interpreting them [2]. In turn, the planner has to select a socially appropriate response from the robot's action repertoire [3]. Thus, we were interested in how a socially skilled human participant would interpret the robotic sensor data, and what forms a socially appropriate response. However, the Wizard-of-Oz paradigm (WOz) allows the participant controlling the robot access to unfiltered audio and/or video of the user [5]. Thus, we developed the Ghost-in-the-Machine paradigm (GiM) for addressing our research question.

In this report, we focus on initiating a service interaction at a bar. This is the first step in short, goal-oriented interactions. It is crucial because the whole interaction would fail if the robot did not recognize that a customer has the intention to place an order.

HRI'14, March 3–6, 2014, Bielefeld, Germany.
ACM 978-1-4503-2658-2/14/03.
http://dx.doi.org/10.1145/2559636.2563696

2. GHOST-IN-THE-MACHINE

In the GiM paradigm, the main participant (ghost) is presented the output of the robotic sensors and responds to the participants ordering drinks (customers) by selecting an appropriate response from the robot's action repertoire. In contrast to the WOz paradigm (e.g., [6]), the ghosts were not allowed to observe the customers directly. Rather the ghosts observed the scene through the eyes of the robot's planner. The recognizer software issues an update to the planner after major changes in the scene [3]. These updates were presented to the ghosts through a user interface (Figure 1) which made the data comprehensible to the user. The Boolean variables (e.g., *Customer is visible*) were displayed in a traffic light approach. The angles of the customer's body and head orientation were shown as an arrow. The position of the customers face was shown as a dot in a coordinate system reflecting the space in front of the bar. Finally, the most likely hypothesis of the ASR including its certainty level in percent was presented. Importantly, this did not add any additional interpretation or social content compared to the recognizer update, as e.g., displaying a torso in front of the bar. The user interface (Figure 1) proceeded through the updates one-by-one after the ghost selected a response option in the control panel (Figure 2). This panel showed the robot's action repertoire grouped by output modality (e.g., head gestures). The actions within each group were mutually exclusive, e.g. the robot can either look happy or sad, but not both at the same time. Actions across different groups could be combined to a complex response (e.g., looking at customer and saying 'Hello').

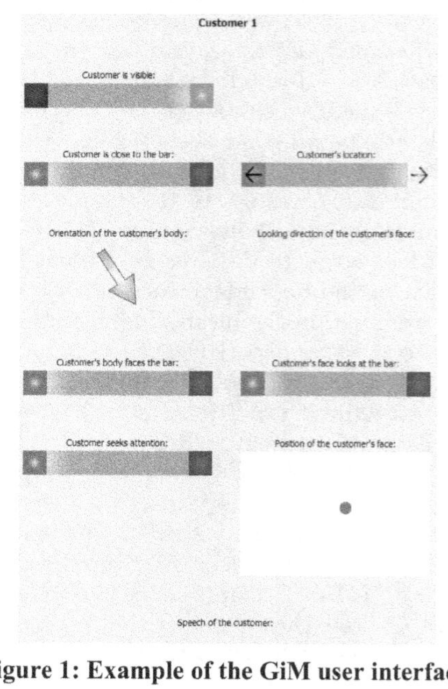

Figure 1: Example of the GiM user interface.

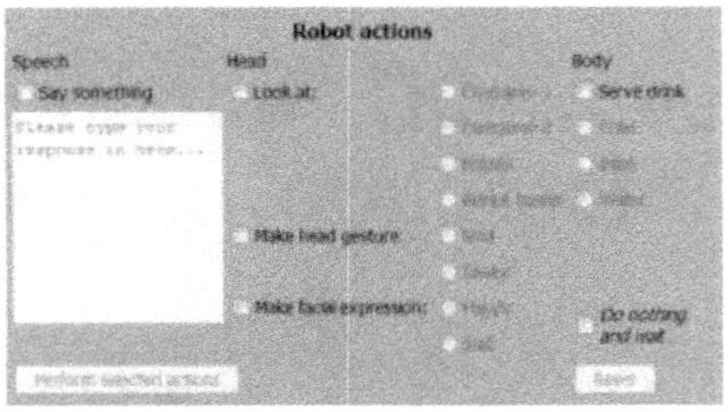

Figure 2: Example of the GiM control interface.

The user interface was introduced in a self-paced presentation. The categorial responses of the ghosts as well as their eye tracking data were recorded. The experiment consisted of two practice items followed by six intention recognition trials and six speech recognition trials. However, we focus on intention recognition in this report. These trials terminated as soon as the ghost first acted towards a new customer. The indicator for *Seeking attention* was not active (both 'lights' off) during these trials. In this experiment, pre-recorded data of the JAMES evaluation [1] was used. Twelve participants were recruited from the general university population.

3. RESULTS

Eleven trials were excluded because the participants did not respond to the customer until the update unequivocally indicated a drink order. This resulted in 61 informative intention recognition trials. The data in Table 1 shows which indicators were *true* (green light) or active (arrow present) when the ghosts acknowledged a customer. The table also shows the averaged dwelling time spent on each indicator between the last update on screen and acknowledging the customer. The *face orientation* (arrow and traffic light) was never shown during the experiment due to the computer vision software. The data in Table 2 shows which actions were selected by the ghosts for acknowledging a new customer.

4. DISCUSSION

The participants reported that they experienced GiM as very immersive and occasionally tried to engage in dialogues with the customers despite being in an offline setting. Analyzing the data visible on screen showed that the ghosts never waited for a verbal utterance of the customers before acknowledging them. Rather, the ghosts responded to nonverbal cues. The indicator showing the distance to the bar received the greatest share of attention and thus, was very important to the ghosts. However, the ghosts also acknowledged customers who were not close to the bar. In these cases, the customers' body direction was displayed as an arrow and the corresponding indicator was active but not always *true*. Thus, the ghosts used the body posture for anticipating that the customers will be close to the bar. This also implies that the threshold for the binary indicator *body faces bar* was too strict. The ghosts successfully compensated for the missing information about the face direction by relying on the body direction. In sum, ghosts attended nonverbal cues and responded if the customers were visible to the system, (anticipated to be) close to the bar and faced the bar. This replicated an earlier finding using natural stimuli [4] demonstrating the validity of the results.

In most cases, the ghosts acknowledged a new customer nonverbally. Only one third of the trials comprised a verbal greeting or prompt for orders. About 75% of all trials involved visibly shifting the robot's attention to the customers by looking at them. This was often accompanied by smiling at the customers.

Table 1: Data displayed to ghosts and dwelling time.

Feature	Trials with true/active	Averaged dwelling time
Visible	97%	326 ms
Close to bar	54%	560 ms
Location (left/right)	98%	297 ms
Body direction (arrow)	89%	217 ms
Body faces bar	51%	331 ms
Said something	0%	63 ms

Table 2: Actions selected for acknowledging new customers.

Action	Frequency	
Looking at customer	46	75%
Happy face	26	43%
Greeting (e.g., Hello)	14	23%
Looking at objects	9	15%
Asking for order	5	8%
Other	2	3%

5. CONCLUSION

The first results of the new GiM paradigm showed that a robotic bartender should acknowledge new customers if they approach the bar and direct themselves towards the counter. This successfully replicated findings acquired using natural data [4]. Furthermore, the results showed how missing data can be compensated for, e.g. using body for face direction. The ghosts acknowledged new customers by looking and smiling at them. But only one third of the responses included a verbal greeting. The participants reported that the design was very immersive. In sum, GiM is a reliable and engaging research tool providing new insight into social behavior.

6. ACKNOWLEDGMENTS

This research was part of the JAMES project and received funding from the European Union's Seventh Framework Programme under grant agreement number 270435.

7. REFERENCES

[1] Foster, M.E. et al. 2012. Two people walk into a bar: dynamic multi-party social interaction with a robot agent. *Proceedings of the 14th ACM International Conference on Multimodal Interaction (ICMI 2012)* (Santa Monica, USA, 2012).

[2] Gaschler, A. et al. 2012. Modelling State of Interaction from Head Poses for Social Human-Robot Interaction. *Proceedings of the Gaze in Human- Robot Interaction Workshop held at the 7th ACM/IEEE International Conference on Human-Robot Interaction (HRI 2012)* (Boston, USA, 2012).

[3] Giuliani, M. et al. 2013. Comparing task-based and socially intelligent behaviour in a robot bartender. *Proceedings of the 15th ACM International Conference on Multimodal Interaction (ICMI 2013)* (Sydney, Australia, 2013), 263–270.

[4] Loth, S. et al. 2013. Automatic detection of service initiation signals used in bars. *Frontiers in Psychology*. 4, (2013).

[5] Riek, L. 2012. Wizard of Oz Studies in HRI: A Systematic Review and New Reporting Guidelines. *Journal of Human-Robot Interaction*. 1, 1 (Aug. 2012), 119–136.

[6] Rieser, V. et al. 2011. Adaptive Information Presentation for Spoken Dialogue Systems: Evaluation with human subjects. *Proceedings of the 13th European Workshop on Natural Language Generation* (Nancy, France, 2011), 102–109.

Real-time Gender Recognition Based on 3D Human Body Shape for Human-Robot Interaction*

Ren C. Luo, Xiehao Wu
International Center of Excellence on Intelligent Robotics and Automation Research
National Taiwan University
No. 1, Sec. 4, Roosevelt Road, Taipei,10617 Taiwan
renluo@ntu.edu.tw, wuxiehao@ira.ee.ntu.edu.tw

ABSTRACT

Gender roles influence behavior in social interactions. Thus, real-time gender recognition is essential in Human-Robot Interaction (HRI) for providing timely gender information to improve the experience of HRI. Considering the HRI scenario, a 3D-human-body-shape-based gender recognition is investigated. The 3D information is obtained by processing the depth image from an RGB-D camera. In addition, a machine learning method based on a Support Vector Machine (SVM) was applied. The experimental results showed that our system could achieve real-time accurate gender recognition. It enriched the diversity of existing methods for HRI application.

Categories and Subject Descriptors

I.2.6 [**Artificial Intelligence**]: Learning—*Knowledge acquisition*

General Terms

Algorithms

Keywords

Gender Recognition, Real-time, 3D Human Body Shape, Human-Robot Interaction, SVM, RGB-D Camera

1. INTRODUCTION

A lot of social interactions and services today depend on gender. Even the Human-Robot Proxemics differs with different genders [3], which means robots should keep distinct distances while interacting with people of different genders. Timely gender information from robots thus is essential for improving the experience of the HRI.

According to the input data processing, existing Gender recognition methods can be divided into face-based methods using 2D images [2], gait-based methods using 2D video sequences [6] and human-body-shape-based methods using 3D laser scans [5].However, 2D image-based face gender recognition extracts only the frontal face region from the whole human image, omitting all other clues in the image, degrading when the face image detected is not truly frontal (e.g., with head slants). Gait-based gender recognition needs the 2D gait video sequence, which is not easy to obtain in HRI. In addition, vision systems are sensitive to the lighting conditions. Tang et al. [5] performed 3D human-body-shape-based recognition using 3D laser scans, but it is time-consuming and not practical to laser scan a whole human body for HRI.

Considering the HRI scenario, inspired by the gender differences in human body shape, our work provides a real-time gender recognition system for HRI through the depth image processing of an RGB-D camera (Kinect).

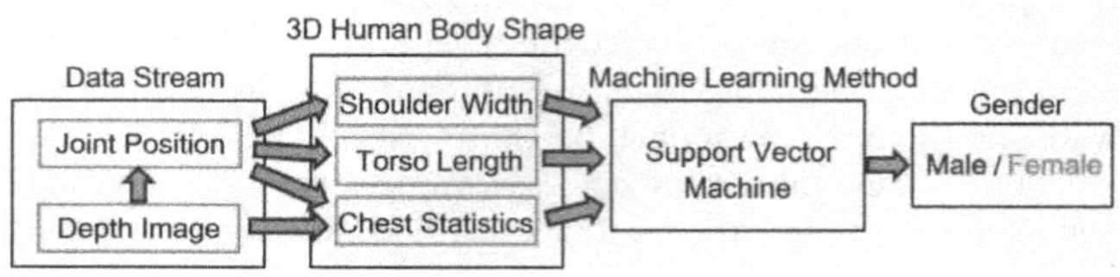

Figure 1: The proposed gender recognition process

2. GENDER RECOGNITION SYSTEM

The process of our gender recognition system is in Fig. 1. Only depth images from Kinect are used, we extracted the 3D skeletal joint positions from the depth image of Kinect using the methods of Shotton et al [4]. Analyzing the HRI scenario and the gender differences in the human body, some body shape information was chosen based on the data stream. Machine learning methods based on a SVM [1] were then applied to utilize this information and finish the gender recognition.

2.1 Data Stream

The data stream of the system included depth images and 3D skeletal joint positions. The depth image from Kinect was the only input data, joint positions were extracted from this depth image [4]. Fig. 2(a) shows an example of the depth image and the corresponding 3D skeletal joints.

*A video of our real-time gender recognition experiment can be found at `http://youtu.be/E3uKOPZNZmo`, the blue rectangle in the human body indicates male, while the red one stands for female, yellow one means unknown. The color image there is for illustration, only depth image used in our system.

HRI'14, March 3–6, 2014, Bielefeld, Germany.
ACM 978-1-4503-2658-2/14/03.
http://dx.doi.org/10.1145/2559636.2563679 .

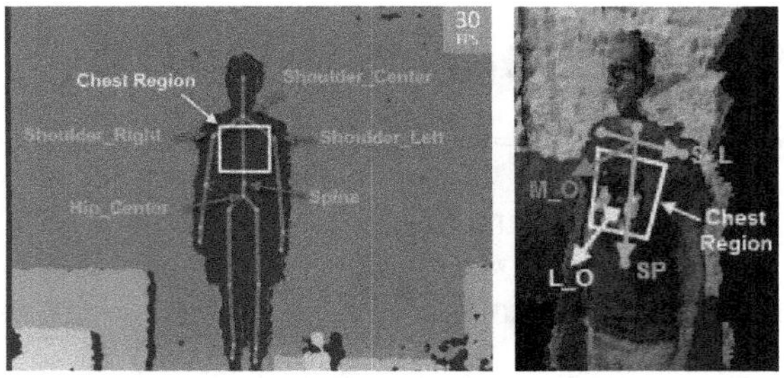

(a) Data stream (b) 3D analysis

Figure 2: Data steam analysis

2.2 3D Human Body Shape

Tang et al. [5] investigated that the chest region could be used to distinguish women from men. In our system, body size information was combined together with the chest region information for gender recognition. Considering the existing robot size in HRI scenarios (it's hard to have the whole body image of the man due to the short-distance interaction), the upper body size information (shoulder width and torso length) and the chest region statistics are finally picked up as 3D body information, analyzing the input depth image (3D view is shown in Fig. 2(b)) and the upper body joint positions (S_L, S_C, S_R, SP and H_C in Fig. 2).

2.2.1 *Shoulder width and torso length*

Males tends to have larger body sizes. According to the position of the joint positions, we can obtain:

$$Shoulder\ Width = Dist(S\_L, S\_C) + Dist(S\_C, S\_R) \quad (1)$$

$$Torso\ Length = Dist(S\_C, SP) + Dist(SP, H\_C) \quad (2)$$

Where $Dist(a, b)$ means the Euclidean distance from a to b.

2.2.2 *Chest statistics*

The chest region can be used to distinguish women from men. The chest statistics in the chest region include the chest altitude and the distribution of the surface normal. These statistics can be calculated using the input depth image after we get the chest region (yellow rectangle in Fig. 2) based on the positions of S_L, S_R, S_C and SP. The analysis of the depth image is shown in Fig. 2(b).

The chest altitude means the height of the chest region projected on the man's heading orientation. We can get the man's orientation (M_O in Fig. 2(b)) and the chest altitude as below:

$$\overrightarrow{M\_O} = \frac{\overrightarrow{S\_R\ S\_L} \times \overrightarrow{S\_C\ SP}}{\left|\overrightarrow{S\_R\ S\_L} \times \overrightarrow{S\_C\ SP}\right|} \quad (3)$$

$$Chest\ Altitude = Max(\overrightarrow{CR} \cdot \overrightarrow{M\_O}) - Min(\overrightarrow{CR} \cdot \overrightarrow{M\_O}) \quad (4)$$

Where $\overrightarrow{CR}$ means the vector from the origin of the camera to the chest region point.

We represent the distribution of the surface normal in an easy way by calculating the mean and variance of the angle between the local surface normal (L_O in Fig. 2(b)) and the man's orientation in the chest region, representing by x_i. So that the flat chest tends to have a small mean and variance.

$$\eta = \frac{1}{n}\sum_{i=1}^{n} x_i\ , \quad Var = \frac{1}{n}\sum_{i=1}^{n}(x_i - \eta)^2 \quad (5)$$

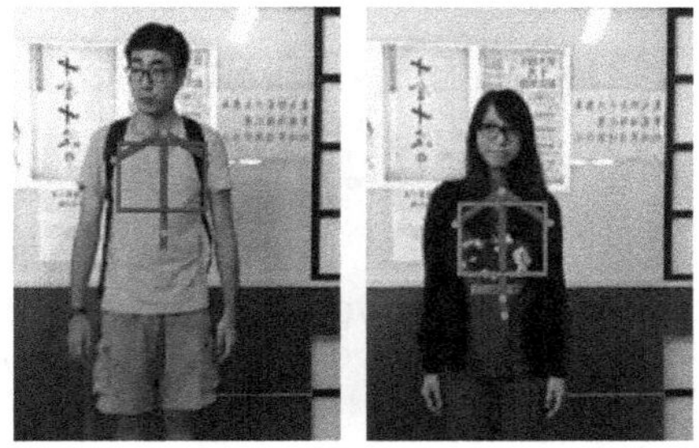

Figure 3: Example of the experimental results

2.3 SVM

SVM is a supervised binary machine learning method. We adopt LIBSVM [1] in our system, the previous body shape information was used for training and classification, a radial basis function kernel was used to increase the accuracy.

3. EXPERIMENTAL RESULTS

There's no existing RGB-D gender recognition database, so we collected 60 persons' (30 male, 30 female) RGB-D data as an early stage experiment. Forty (20 male, 20 female) of them were training examples in the SVM. As a result, we got 95% accuracy at 30FPS for both the training and testing datasets. Based on our experimental results, body size together with chest statistics were reliable information for gender recognition. Fig. 3 shows an example of our experimental results. The rectangle region is the chest region while blue indicates male, the red stands for female.

4. CONCLUSION

This work provides a real-time gender recognition system in HRI based on 3D human body shape. Through the processing of the depth images from Kinect, the upper body shape information was collected, and the SVM to do the training and classification. The experimental results showed that our system could achieve a real-time accurate gender recognition with 30 fps. It can enrich the diversity of existing methods for HRI application.

5. REFERENCES

[1] C.-C. Chang and C.-J. Lin. Libsvm: a library for support vector machines. *ACM Transactions on Intelligent Systems and Technology (TIST)*, 2(3):27, 2011.

[2] D. Chen, J. Cheng, and D. Tao. Clustering-based discriminative locality alignment for face gender recognition. In *Intelligent Robots and Systems (IROS), 2012 IEEE/RSJ International Conference on*, pages 4156–1461. IEEE, 2012.

[3] J. Mumm and B. Mutlu. Human-robot proxemics: physical and psychological distancing in human-robot interaction. In *Proceedings of the 6th international conference on Human-robot interaction*, pages 331–338. ACM, 2011.

[4] J. Shotton, T. Sharp, A. Kipman, A. Fitzgibbon, M. Finocchio, A. Blake, M. Cook, and R. Moore. Real-time human pose recognition in parts from single depth images. *Communications of the ACM*, 56(1):116–124, 2013.

[5] J. Tang, X. Liu, H. Cheng, and K. M. Robinette. Gender recognition using 3-d human body shapes. *Systems, Man, and Cybernetics, Part C: Applications and Reviews, IEEE Transactions on*, 41(6):898–908, 2011.

[6] S. Yu, T. Tan, K. Huang, K. Jia, and X. Wu. A study on gait-based gender classification. *Image Processing, IEEE Transactions on*, 18(8):1905–1910, 2009.

Initial Phases of Design-based Research into the Educational Potentials of NAO-Robots

Gunver Majgaard,
University of Southern Denmark
gum@mmmi.sdu.dk

Lykke Brogaard Bertel
Aalborg University
lbb@hum.aau.dk

ABSTRACT

In this paper, we describe our initial research, using the humanoid robot NAO in primary and secondary schools. How does a programmable humanoid enrich teaching and how do we prepare the teachers? Ten school classes are using the robot for creative programming. So far we have experienced that the robot enriches the learning processes by combining the auditory, visual and kinaesthetic modalities.

Keywords

Robotics, Educational Tools, Programming, Embodiment, Learning, Design-based Research, Action Research.

1. INTRODUCTION

In this late-breaking report, we describe the setup for exploring the potentials of programmable humanoid robots in primary and secondary schools, as a part of the research project FREMTEK [1]. The robots we are using are the so-called NAO from Aldebaran [2]. The NAO is a programmable, 58 cm tall humanoid robot with electric motors, LED lights, cameras, microphones, tactile sensors, pressure sensors, CPU and much more. The robot is programmable in both drag and drop language for novices and python or C++ for experienced programmers. The academic learning goals in general programming cover potentials of humanoids, mathematics, physics, storytelling, ethics, and so on.

It takes an extra effort for the teachers to use robot technology in the classroom. The students interact differently with robot technology than with ordinary schoolbooks. The social and academic dynamics change, when technology is brought into the classroom. This calls for new didactical plans, different teaching and learning approaches [3].

Our approach to learning is based on constructionism, active participation and embodiment [4] [5] [6] [7] [8]. Embodied learning is based on a combination of physical, social and symbolic reality [5]. The interaction takes place in the physical and partly virtual world. The interaction basically has three modalities auditory, visual and kinaesthetic. The modalities can also be broken up into Gardner's multiple intelligences [8]: musical – rhythmic, visual - spatial, verbal - linguistic, logical - mathematical, bodily - kinaesthetic, interpersonal, intrapersonal, and naturalistic. According to Gardner's theory, each student has one or more strengths in their way of learning – some children are primarily verbal; others are primarily kinaesthetic or visual. Each orientation is connected to skills, in mastering different symbolic languages (e.g. words, bodily movements, music, etc.).

HRI'14, March 3–6 2014, Bielefeld, Germany
ACM 978-1-4503-2658-2/14/03.
http://dx.doi.org/10.1145/2559636.2563690.

Consequently, the teachers have to provide learning materials that support different symbolic languages and ways of learning. In other words the learning material should support several intelligences at once. In this project we want to explore how the NAO robot supports all these approaches to learning [7] [8]. We want especially to explore how the robot supports Gardner's different modalities and thereby support learning for a wider group of children.

Educational humanoid robots have primarily been used as a therapeutic tool for special needs children, for development of social skills [9]. A popular example is the Keepon [10]. It has also been used for teaching robotics and computer science at universities. Students have for example developed interactive football player behaviours into the NAO-robot and enrolled them in special Robocop tournaments [11]. Research also shows the motivational and persuasive potential of the robot, in an educational context [12]. This research contributes by exploring how learning processes, can be enriched for ordinary children in primary and secondary schools. And we also address the didactical design issues for robot-supported teaching.

2. METHOD AND RESEARCH DESIGN

The research method used in this study is based on Design-based Research and Action Research [13]. Experiments and critical reflections are the core of the research method, allowing learning from practice. The interventions take place in the target group's natural surroundings (e.g. in the classroom). Our target group in this project is both the teachers and the students. The students are between 9 and 19 years old.

Initially, the teachers participate in a two-day workshop. Each teacher brings two students for day one and the agenda for the day is a hands-on experience with the NAO-robot. Day two is all about the teachers' creations of didactical plans, for their upcoming NAO supported teaching. The teachers in the program agreed to use the robot in their classes for 5-6 weeks, at a minimum of 8-10 hours in total. Approximately ten classes / teams will participate. Each class will have access to a set of three NAO robots and eight notebook PCs. The PC is for programming the robot. Workshops for teachers and subsequent lessons will be held in two or three iterative rounds.

We have a qualitative approach to data collection. In the workshops, the researchers participate and lecture on didactical planning, evaluation, and introduce the research project. In the classrooms the researchers observe without active participation and some of the observations are video recorded. Didactical plans, student productions, reports, and evaluation documents are also part of the data collection. We also do semi-structured interviews. The retrospective analysis is based on the collected data.

3. STATUS: THE FIRST ROUND

The first workshop has been completed. The teachers spent one day on getting to know the NAO. Most of the teachers spent the second day on solving the programming assignments; they were planning for their upcoming teaching. The researchers also tried to make the teachers focus on the didactical design (e.g. by making learning goals, planning activities for each lesson, planning for differentiation, evaluation and so on). But the teachers insisted on spending more time with the robots and less time on the planning.

We are now in the process of observing the first round of actual teaching. We don't have a lot of findings yet. We have been observing two classes and have found that three NAO robots can keep about 12 children occupied. We had to provide a local router for the wireless connection between the robot and PC. This solved any WIFI problems. Schools tend to have a very restrictive policy for unknown devices.

The first school class consisted of approximately 22 children from third grade and they were about 9-10 years old. Most of the children understood the idea of programming. One or two children in the class didn't understand the idea of connecting the programming blocks in sequence. The children explored the robots' potentials of doing tai-chi, converting text to speech, walking, waving, standing, and sitting down. The text to speech module in the robot made the children write phonetically, instead of grammatically correct. This integrated the three basic modalities: auditory, visual, and kinaesthetic interaction.

The robot appealed to both girls and boys in the classroom. The robots were named in order to personalise them. And the children discussed the robots relations (e.g. if one of the robots had a crush on one of the other robots). Some of the children also hugged the robot, as if it was a doll or a baby.

The second school class consisted of 12 students from upper secondary school, who participated in an elective science and technology course. The students had spent a lot of time on programming LEGO Mindstorm Robots and only a few lessons on building programs for the NAO robot. They found the NAO programming easier than the LEGO Mindstorm programming. But they lacked some of the possibilities for putting values into variables. They also didn't explore the third generation programming possibilities. The students found the NAO-robot very motivating. They did a small project where LEGO Robots and NAO robots interacted: a LEGO robot ran close to a NAO robot and said "hello". The NAO robot responded by getting up, waving and saying "hello". Another LEGO robot ran in front of a NAO robot and the NAO robot jelled "low tech machine" when the LEGO robot bumped into it. The students analysed and compared the two types of technology. They compared the NAO to the Terminator, from the very successful science fiction film and they also found it more human like than the LEGO robots. The learning was enriched by their development of the multi modal interaction between the robots. This led to discussions on the quality of the robots' oral and motor interaction. We expect to see more complex designs later on and more complex robot-to-robot interactions.

4. SUMMARY AND CONCLUSIONS

We are in the initial phases of a two-year research project and we still have a lot of decisions to make. This first year we plan to get an overview of different approaches of bringing NAO into the classroom. In year two we will focus more on a specific target group, in order to get more detailed and valid information.

The humanoid is very appealing and motivating to use for the students and teachers. So far we have learned that the robot enriches learning by combining the auditory, visual, and kinaesthetic modalities. The students are actively participating, when they are constructing and testing NAO-programs. Additionally the students develop their explorative and creative competences, when they develop new behaviours for the robot. The students were motivated to develop human like behaviour by the robots human like appearance. And they were interested in the exploration of the robot-to-robot relations. However, there were minor WIFI challenges, due to the schools strict ICT Security policy.

It was difficult for the teachers to describe precise academic learning goals in advance, other than getting to know the technology and the programming. It was easy for them to plan and conduct activities. When we interview teachers and students later on in the process, we will learn more on the emerging learning goals.

5. REFERENCES

[1] FREMTEK 2013http://www.insero.dk/Uddannelse/projekter-og-aktiviteter/Fremtek retrieved 2013-10-10

[2] Aldebaran-robotic 2013. http://www.aldebaran-robotics.com/en/ retrieved 2013-10-10

[3] Hansen, J. J. (2013) "Innovative læremidler og den didaktiske vending". Mellem frihed og styring. Om kultur og læring. Odense Universitetsforlag.

[4] Papert, S. (1993). Mindstorms Children, Computers, and Powerful Ideas, Basic Books.

[5] Dourish, P. (2004). Where the Action Is. The Foundation of Embodied Interaction. A Bradford Book. The MIT Press.

[6] Wenger E. (1998). Communities of Practice: Learning, Meaning, and Identity. Cambridge University Press.

[7] Majgaard, G. (2013). Embodied Interaction Design in Engineering Education Using Asus Xtion Pro. IHCI Conference. IADIS Press.

[8] Gardner, H. 2006. Multiple Intelligences. New Horizons. Basic Books.

[9] Dautenhahn K. (1999). "Robots as social actors: aurora and the case of autism". Proceedings Third Cognitive Technology Conference CT'99, August, San Francisco.

[10] Kozima, H.; Nakagawa, C., "A robot in a playroom with preschool children: Longitudinal field practice", Robot and Human interactive Communication, 2007. pp. 1058–1059.

[11] Robocup, 2010. "UK robots prepare for world cup" New Technology. http://www.bbc.co.uk/news/technology-11618151 retrieved 2013-25-11

[12] Bertel, L. et al 2013. "Robots for Real: Developing a Participatory Design Framework for Implementing Educational Robots in Real-world Learning Environments", Proceedings of the 14th IFIP INTERACT 2013, Springer.

[13] Majgaard, G., Misfeldt, M., Nielsen, J. (2011). How Design-based Research, Action Research and Interaction Design Contributes to the Development of Designs for Learning. *Designs for Learning*.

Confidence Metrics Improve Human-Autonomy Integration

Amar R. Marathe,
Brent J. Lance,
Kaleb McDowell[1]
U.S. Army Research Laboratory
Aberdeen Proving Ground, MD 21005

William D. Nothwang
U.S. Army Research Laboratory
Adelphi, MD 20783

Jason S. Metcalfe
DCS Corporation
Alexandria, VA, 22310

ABSTRACT
Controls frameworks for human-autonomy integration (HAI) often treat human sources of information as highly reliable [1]. However, data from human sensing are quite variable, both because of human nature and limitations on sensor technologies. This paper focuses on estimating the degree of uncertainty in human sensed data, i.e., developing confidence metrics, and implementing those metrics in a HAI for target recognition. Here we demonstrate that applying such confidence estimates to sensed human data can mitigate effects of variability in human sensing and improve HAI performance.

Keywords
Operator interfaces, artificial intelligence, confidence, human-robot interaction, algorithms, design, reliability, human factors

1. INTRODUCTION
Decision Theory, as founded by Pascal (17th century) and extended by Bernoulli (18th century), established that one must consider uncertainty in order to make optimal, fully informed, objective decisions. However, this general principle is often not applied to data sensed from the human operator in HAI; that is, human sources of information are often treated as having little or no noise [1], even though sensed human data are known to be widely variable, both across and within individuals. This is in contrast to autonomy research, where decades of work on sensor fusion and human-autonomy teaming has identified potential approaches to joint estimation for combined decision making by showing how multiple, disparate sensor systems with sometimes substantial uncertainty are integrated to yield reliable state estimates [1]. Indeed, approaches that characterize or even purposely implement variability have been demonstrated as quite useful in the design of autonomous systems.

Recent advances in brain-computer interaction technologies have illustrated that human brain data can be effectively integrated in system design when estimates of measurement confidence are utilized or inferred [2]. The goal of this manuscript is to develop confidence estimates in sensed human data, and demonstrate the potential for these estimates to improve HAI for visual object recognition.

2. METHODS
A target identification task was chosen to illustrate the benefit of applying confidence estimates in HAI. Both humans (n=18) and an automated target recognition (ATR) system searched for targets in a set of approximately 18,000 images presented in six blocks of approximately 3000 images. Images were color photographs of indoor and outdoor scenes containing inanimate objects (e.g., chairs, doors, etc). For individual human and ATR data streams, algorithms were used to determine if a target was detected for each image and then to generate a confidence estimate in those determinations. Weighted sum models were used to integrate the human and ATR data streams and generate output confidence estimates in the integrated determinations. While the data used in these analyses were combined in a post-hoc, offline fashion, all methods outlined and used herein are amenable to online use.

2.1 Experimental Methods – Human Data
Subjects performed a rapid serial visual presentation (RSVP) study in which each participant identified targets in a rapid (5 Hz) stream of images. The voluntary, fully informed consent of the persons used in this research was obtained as required by Title 32, Part 219 of the Code of Federal Regulations and Army Regulation 70-25. All investigators adhered to the policies for the protection of human subjects as prescribed in AR 70-25. A detailed description of the experimental protocol can be found in [3].

During the RSVP, participants were instructed to press a button only when they saw an object from a currently designated target class. Accuracy and reaction time (RT) were determined from this button response using a probabilistic method based on each participant's behavior during training. Confidence estimates were based on the height of a local maximum in the probability signal for sequential images and for targets only.

Targets were also predicted using data from electroencephalography (EEG) recordings from 64 scalp electrodes using a BioSemi Active Two system (Amsterdam, Netherlands). Standard pre-processing methods were used (see [3] for details). Three different state-of-the-art neural classification algorithms were applied: hierarchical discriminant component analysis (HDCA; [2]), XDawn with a Bayesian linear discriminant classifier (XD+BLDA; [4]), and common spatial patterns (CSP; [5]). The three neural classifiers provided scores for each image. High scores indicated target images, while low scores indicated non-target images. A threshold was established for discriminating targets from non-targets that maximized the difference between true positive rate and false positive rate. Confidence was calculated as (score-threshold)/(max(score)-threshold) when the score>threshold and (score-threshold) /(min(score)-threshold) otherwise.

2.2 Experimental Methods – ATR
For the ATR, the Transductive Annotation by Graph system [see 2] was applied to the same images. The ATR system generates scores

HRI'14, March 3–6, 2014, Bielefeld, Germany.
ACM 978-1-4503-2658-2/14/03.
http://dx.doi.org/10.1145/2559636.2563721

[1] K.M. is the corresponding author: kgm8@cornell.edu.

between 0 and 1 for each image. Thresholds and confidence scores were generated in the same manner as for the neural classifiers.

2.3 Post-Hoc Analyses

For the human-only integration, human responses (i.e. button press) and the outputs of three neural classifiers were integrated to produce an overall decision, with corresponding confidence estimate, for each image in the database. A weighted sum model estimated the decision for each image as being proportional to the product of confidence, a gain derived from standard machine learning approaches, and the sensor output summed over all possible sensors. As a baseline, the weighted sum was also computed with confidence set to unity. Confidence measures on the output of the joint estimations were binned into three levels based on absolute distance to threshold.

For the HAI, the overall human decision was combined with the ATR decision using the same methods described above using a recursive framework. For all analyses, classifiers and regressions were trained and tested on independent data, and all predictions were cross validated.

2.4 Performance

Decision making performance was indicated by area under the ROC curve (Az). For reference, average Az values for the button press was 0.66, for the three neural classifiers ranged from 0.62 to 0.73, and for the ATR was 0.67.

3. RESULTS

The human-only integration indicated a non-significant improvement in decision making as indicated by area under the ROC curve (Az) when confidence was included as compared to baseline (compare blue and yellow boxes in Figure 1a). Further analyses seem to indicate that the currently implemented confidence measures for our neural classifiers only correlate with Az for one of the three neural classifiers that were applied. Despite the poor performance of input confidence metrics, output confidence was a strong indicator of Az for the joint human decision (Figure 1a, green boxes).

Contrasting with the human-only integration, the HAI decision making was dramatically improved over baseline when confidence metrics were included (compare blue and yellow boxes in Figure 1b). Further analysis on two other controls [a) human confidence/no ATR confidence versus baseline (blue box); b) human+ATR confidence (yellow box) versus ATR confidence/no human confidence] both indicated including confidence on human sensors significantly improved HAI performance. Output confidence was also good indicator of Az for the joint human-autonomy decision (Figure 1b, green boxes) with Az for high confidence images averaging over 0.95.

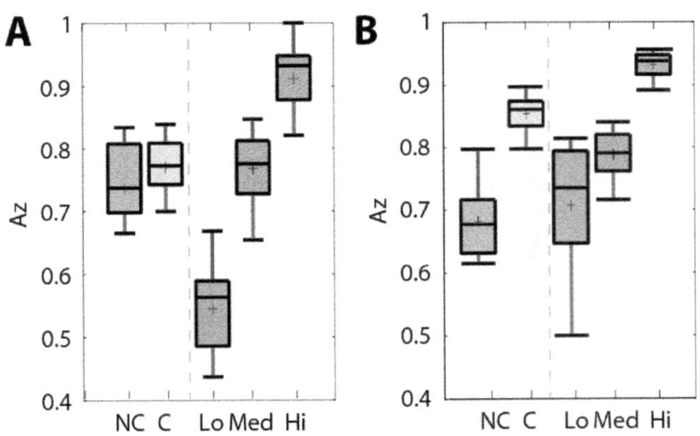

Figure 1. Integrated decision making performance showing Target detection accuracy for A) human-only integration and B) HAI. For both images, NC = baseline (blue) and C = confidence (yellow) conditions. Lo, Med, and Hi indicate Az scores for images within the three levels of output confidence (green bars).

4. DISCUSSION

The results here illustrate that confidence metrics for human sensed data improves HAI performance. The results further indicate that, although this initial, relatively simple, approach to confidence for sensed human data had limited success for the individual data streams, it is possible to derive high quality confidence scores for human-only data. These results are promising for the future development of valid, robust confidence metrics for both individual and integrated human sensing. Future efforts should attempt to develop more sophisticated approaches to estimating confidence and subsequently integrating confidence-based metrics into HAI. Initial avenues for research include leveraging a deep understanding of human cognition and behavior (e.g., operator states and behaviors could indicate if the operator is paying attention) and statistical approaches to modeling the sensor data (e.g., non-linear approaches will likely improve the confidence for the neural classifiers). Future efforts also should aim to broaden this approach across the wide variety of human sensing technologies, which will provide the capability to dramatically enhance human integration with robotic and autonomous systems.

5. ACKNOWLEDGMENTS

This effort was funded through the Office of the Secretary of Defense ARPI competition MIPR DWAM31168.

6. REFERENCES

[1] Olson, E., Strom, J., Goeddel, R., Morton, R., Ranganathan, P., and Richardson, A. 2013. Exploration and mapping with autonomous robot teams. *Commun. ACM.* 56, 3 (Mar. 2013), 62–70.

[2] Sajda, P., Pohlmeyer, E., Wang, J., Parra, L.C., Christoforou, C., Dmochowski, J., Hanna, B., Bahlmann, C., Singh, M.K., and Chang, S.F. In a Blink of an Eye and a Switch of a Transistor: Cortically Coupled Computer Vision. *Proc. IEEE.* 98, 3 (Mar. 2010), 462 –478.

[3] Touryan, J., Apker, G., Kerick, S., Lance, B., Ries, A. J., & McDowell, K. 2013. Translation of EEG-based performance prediction models to rapid serial visual presentation tasks. In *Foundations of Augmented Cognition* 7th International Conference, (Las Vegas, NV, USA, July 21-26, 2013). AC 2013. Springer, Berlin Heidelberg, 521-530.

[4] Rivet B., Souloumiac A., Attina V., and Gibert G. 2009. xDAWN Algorithm to Enhance Evoked Potentials: Application to Brain-Computer Interface. *IEEE Trans. Biomed. Eng.*. 56,8, (Aug 2009) 2035 –2043.

[5] Ramoser H., Muller-Gerking J., and Pfurtscheller G. 2000. Optimal spatial filtering of single trial EEG during imagined hand movement. *IEEE Trans. on Rehab. Eng.*. 8, 4 (Dec 2000), 441–446.

Reasons for Singularity in Robot Teleoperation

Ilka Marhenke
University of Southern Denmark
Department of Design and Communication
ilka_marhenke@web.de

Kerstin Fischer
University of Southern Denmark
Department of Design and Communication
kerstin@sdu.dk

Thiusius Rajeeth Savarimuthu
University of Southern Denmark
Maersk Mc-Kinney Møller Institute
trs@mmmi.sdu.dk

ABSTRACT

In this paper, the causes for singularity of a robot arm in teleoperation for robot learning from demonstration are analyzed. Singularity is the alignment of robot joints, which prevents the configuration of the inverse kinematics. Inspired by users' own hypotheses, we investigated speed and delay as possible causes. The results show that delay causes problems during teleoperation though not in direct control with a control panel because users expect a different, more intuitive control in teleoperation. Speed on the other hand was not found to have an effect on the occurrence of singularity.

Categories and Subject Description

H1.2 User/Machine Systems

General Terms

Human Factors

Keywords

Learning from Demonstration, Teleoperation, Singularity

1. INTRODUCTION

Robot learning from demonstration is an approach that allows a robot to adapt to different tasks and environments. Rather than programming a robot for one specific task, a robot acts as a student that learns from a human by means of demonstration (Friedrich, Dillmann, & Rogalla, 1999). Learning from demonstration is a user-friendly way of programing a robot by interacting with it intuitively (Calinon, 2009; Demiris & Hayes, 2002; Bakker & Kuniyoshi, 1996). In order for the robot to learn from human demonstrations, several control modes can be used: kinesthetic guidance, in which the user directly manipulates the robot arm, direct control via a control panel, in which the user can control single joints, or teleoperation "in which the teacher operates the robot learner platform and the robot's sensors record the execution" (Argall et al., 2009: 473). Our user studies suggest that teleoperation is the preferred control mode for lay users because of its intuitiveness. Nevertheless, errors that can possibly harm the user or the robot occur noticeably more often during teleoperation control. One of these errors is singularity, the alignment of the robot joints. In this paper, possible causes for singularity when using teleoperation are analyzed based on a series of user studies with the MARVIN platform at the University of Southern Denmark (Savarimuthu et al., 2013). Investigating the causes can help to minimize errors in the future and make teleoperation of industrial robots consisting of a robotic arm for assembly more efficient and more robust.

HRI'14, March 3–6, 2014, Bielefeld, Germany.
ACM 978-1-4503-2658-2/14/03.
http://dx.doi.org/10.1145/2559636.2559828

2. BACKGROUND

User studies of different control modes for learning from demonstration (Fischer et al., in prep.), including direct control of the robot via a control panel and teleoperation, show that singularity occurs noticeably more often in teleoperation than in the direct control of the robot.[1] Table 1 shows that in 44 trials singularity occurred 36 times when using teleoperation. When using the control panel, singularity only occurred once within 28 trials.

Table 1: Error Rate of Teleoperation and Control Panel

	Teleoperation (n=44)	Control Panel (n=28)
Singularity	36	1

Despite the fact that singularity occurred more often with teleoperation, it is the preferred control modality of the users. The main reason is the long time it takes to perform the peg-in-hole task when moving only one robot joint at a time. Thus, teleoperation is more pleasant to use although it causes more errors.

Singularity was identified whenever the robotic joints were no longer in an angle of less than 180° and, thus, aligned (see figure 1). It is to be avoided since the inverse kinematics cannot be configurated once the robot arm is in singularity.

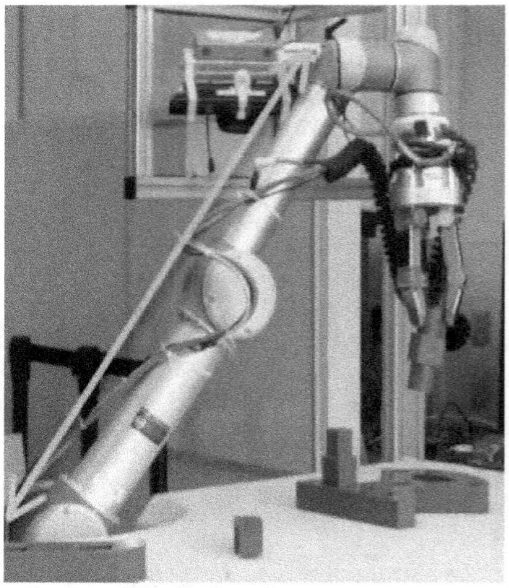

Figure 1: Singularity of the Robot Arm

[1] Singularity is entirely unproblematic in learning from demonstration with the control panel since it does not interfere with the inverse kinematics.

In order to reveal possible reasons for the occurrence of singularity during teleoperation, a user-centered approach was taken to learning from demonstration. The user performance has an impact on the efficiency of the robot (Argall et al., 2009). We therefore investigated users' statements during teleoperation. This investigation reveals three main problems that were mentioned by the users when confronted with singularity: the speed of the robots, the delay of the robot response, and the lack of user experience. While speed and delay refer to technical aspects of the robot, the lack of experience refers to the users themselves. As shown by Schriver (1996), users often assign the blame to themselves rather than the technology. In this paper, we look at speed and delay since these are factors that could be influenced through technical adjustments.

3. METHOD

The data analysis in this paper is based on two sets of user tests that were conducted. Lay users performed a peg-in-hole task with a single robotic arm in a 20-minute time frame. 16 users used a teleoperation device with a programmed speed of 32%[2] while 24 users performed the task twice with a programmed speed of 50%. In order to find causes for the high error rate in teleoperation, a combination of empirical methods was used. A modified version of the think-aloud technique called "speech communication" (Boren and Ramey, 2000) was applied during the experiments, and interviews were conducted afterwards.

4. RESULTS

4.1 Speed

Users' statements during the experiments show that complaints about both control modes concern the speed of the robot arm as well as the delay that exists between the control modes and the robot arm. In order to determine whether different levels of speed have an influence on the error rate, one group of participants used teleoperation with a 32% speed while another group of participants used the same control mode with 50% speed.

Table 2: Error Rate of Different Speed Levels in Teleoperation

	Speed 32% (n=16)	Speed 50% (n=28)
Singularity	12	24

The table shows that for the 16 participants who used 32% speed, 12 cases of singularity occurred, resulting in an average error rate of 0.75 per participant. For the 28 participants who used 50% speed, this error rate is 0.86. This difference is not significant, and thus speed cannot not be considered the main reason for the high error rate during teleoperation.

4.2 Delay

Another factor that participants of the initial user study mentioned is the delay when operating the robot via teleoperation. When moving the teleoperation device, the robot responds with a delay between 33 msec and 1 sec, depending on whether the inverse kinematics can find a configuration of the joints for the desired transformation. This delay often results in unplanned movements of the robot arm. These uncontrolled movements can lead to singularity.

[2] 100% = 1 m/sec or 180°/sec

Since the control panel has the same delay, this should not be the main reason for a high amount of errors, either. However, the same delay seems to have different effects on the user performance when using teleoperation compared to using the control panel. The delay with the control panel is considered merely annoying because of the robot's slow response, while the delay with the teleoperation is a problem that has a negative impact on the robot's efficiency as a tool for learning from demonstration.

5. DISCUSSION

A possible reason for the effect of the delay could be user expectations towards the respective control mode. Teleoperation allows for an intuitive demonstration of a task, which leads the users to expect the robot to be closer to their own behavior than it actually is. This is supported by users who say that they think of the robot arm as their own arm. In these cases users most likely expect a one-to-one translation of their movements to the robot movements. Because of the delay, the users' expectations are not fulfilled, which possibly results in a less efficient user performance and thus in a less efficient robot performance.

6. CONCLUSION

In this study, possible reasons for errors in teleoperation were analyzed in order to find ways to make teleoperation for learning from demonstration more efficient by avoiding singularity. The results suggest that user expectations can have an influence on the error rate of a teleoperation device and that delay causes problems during teleoperation though not in direct control because users expect a different, more intuitive control in teleoperation. Speed on the other hand was not found to have an effect on the occurrence of singularity.

7. ACKNOWLEDGEMENTS

This research was partially supported by the EU project IntellACT. We thank N. Krüger, D. Sølvason, R. Beck, K. Kuklinski, F. Kirstein, and M. aus der Wieschen.

8. REFERENCES

[1] Argall, B., Chernova, S., Veloso, M., & Browning, B. (2009). A survey of robot learning from demonstration. *Robotics and Autonomous Systems, 57,* 469-483.

[2] Bakker, P., & Kuniyoshi, Y. (1996). Robot see, robot do: An overview of robot imitation. *AISB Workshop on Learning in Robotics and Animals.* 3-11.

[3] Boren, M., & Ramey, J. (2000). Thinking aloud: Reconciling theory and practice. *IEEE Transactions on Professional Communication, 43 (3),* 261-278.

[4] Calinon, S. (2009). *Robotic Programming by Demonstration: A Probabilistic Approach.* Lausanne: EPFL Press.

[5] Demiris, Y., & Hayes, G. (2002). Imitation as a dual-route process featuring predictive and learning components. *Imitation in Animals and Artifacts. Dautenhahn, K., & Nehaniv, C.L., eds..* Cambridge, MA: MIT Press. 327-361.

[6] Fischer et al. (in prep.) Comparing different control modes for learning from demonstration.

[7] Friedrich, H., Dillmann, R., & Rogalla, O. (1999). Interactive robot programming based on human demonstration and advice. *Proceedings of the International Workshop on Sensor Based Intelligent Robots.* 96-119.

[8] Savarimuthu, T. R., Liljekrans, D., Ellekilde, L.-P., Ude, A., Nemec, B. & Krüger, N. (2013). Analysis of human peg-in-hole executions in a robotic embodiment using uncertain grasps. In: *9th International Workshop on Robot Motion and Control, RoMoCo 2013*

[9] Schriver, K.A. (1997). *Dynamics in Document Design: Creating Texts for Readers.* New York: Riley

Progressive Development of an Autonomous Robot for Children through Parallel Comparison of Two Robots

Shizuko Matsuzoe
University of Tsukuba
1-1-1 Tennodai, Tsukuba-shi,
Ibaraki 305-8573, Japan
shi25tty@gmail.com

Hideaki Kuzuoka
University of Tsukuba
1-1-1 Tennodai, Tsukuba-shi,
Ibaraki 305-8573, Japan
kuzuoka@iit.tsukuba.ac.jp

Fumihide Tanaka
The University of Tokyo
7-3-1 Hongo, Bunkyo-ku,
Tokyo 113-8656, Japan
fumihide.tanaka@gmail.com

ABSTRACT

This study proposes and demonstrates a progressive development method for an autonomous robot that is used for childhood education. The main concept in this method is to iteratively explore new behavioral factors and use them to progressively develop the robot by concurrently using and comparing two robots in a classroom. Usually, in classrooms for young children, it is practically difficult to recruit a sufficient number of participants and conduct many experiments. The parallel comparison employed in the proposed method enables rapid development to deal with these difficulties.

Categories and Subject Descriptors

I.2.9 [**Artificial Intelligence**]: Robotics; K.3.1 [**Computers and Education**]: Computer Uses in Education

General Terms

Design

Keywords

Care-receiving robot, children-robot interaction, child education, learning support, progressive development, parallel comparison of two robots

1. INTRODUCTION

To support childhood education, we have introduced and tested a care-receiving robot (CRR). This robot purposely shows weak or incomplete behavior while interacting with children, such as answering questions incorrectly. Our previous studies showed that a CRR encouraged children's spontaneous learning by teaching and helping them to learn English words [6, 4]. The next research goal was to explore the weakness or incompleteness factors that were important for realizing a more effective and practical autonomous CRR. However, two problems must be overcome to realize the autonomous CRR. The first concerns the development of new weak or incomplete behaviors for the robots, because these robots have many such behavioral factors that need to be verified. As a result, exhaustive verification to determine the educational effectiveness of these factors is difficult. The second concerns the specific difficulties surrounding trials in the educational field, such as recruiting a sufficient number of participants and arranging a schedule with cooperating kindergartens or elementary schools.

To deal with these two problems, we propose a progressive development method involving the concurrent use of two robots. By iteratively exploring new behavioral factors for the CRR and testing them in a classroom environment, we aim to simultaneously accumulate hitherto lacking knowledge concerning possible weakness/incompleteness factors for the autonomous CRR and develop the autonomous CRR. From the viewpoint of progressiveness, a Wizard-of-Oz (WOZ) method is used for exploration. To deal with the difficulties of recruiting a sufficient number of participants and conducting many experiments, the idea of using two robots concurrently was adopted so that the process of development became more efficient.

2. PROGRESSIVE DEVELOPMENT OF AN AUTONOMOUS ROBOT

To explore and implement important new behaviors for the autonomous robot, a *progressive development* method involving (1) the use of the WOZ method, (2) concurrent use of two robots, and (3) iterative exploration and verification in a real classroom was used.

The WOZ method was used to efficiently explore effective robot behaviors by using the operator's ability to evaluate the situation of the children and the robot. The explored behaviors (e.g., falling backward, bowing the head) represent *progress* in this development method. The WOZ method had been used as a simulation method to improve the system or interface in human-computer interaction [3]. A human "wizard" operates the system, leading participants to believe that they are interacting with an autonomous system. Based on the simulation results, the corresponding system or interface could be iteratively improved. Recently, the WOZ method has also been used to improve and evaluate interaction designs related to an agent or robot [5].

The concurrent use of two robots is advantageous in that the operator can control the WOZ robot competitively while observing the interactions between the children and the other robot. Our trial experiences indicate that by using the WOZ robot alone, it is difficult to differentiate whether children are engaged by the robot's novelty or new behaviors. Thus, we expect that the observation and comparison will together elicit better performance from the WOZ robot than when it is used alone. Another advantage is that the children can choose the robot that they want to play with based on a comparison between the robots. This is a simple and natural choice behavior, which is suitable for verifying the robots' imple-

HRI'14, March 3–6, 2014, Bielefeld, Germany.
ACM 978-1-4503-2658-2/14/03.
http://dx.doi.org/10.1145/2559636.2563700.

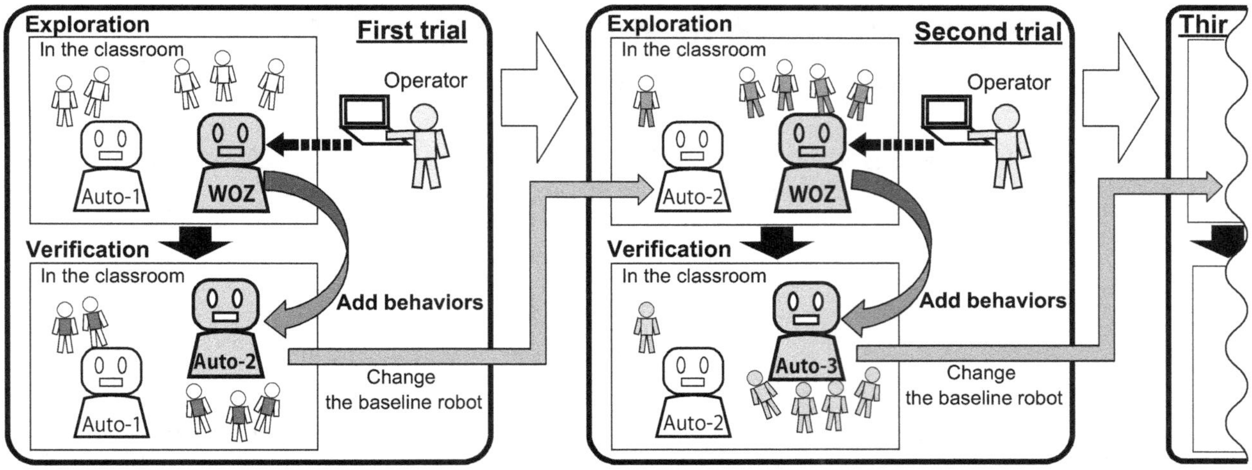

Figure 1: Progressive development of an autonomous CRR.

mentation for use in an actual educational environment. Alac et al. concurrently used two robots to investigate how children behaved around robots [1]. However, almost no studies have concurrently used two robots to develop and improve an autonomous robot.

The development method was explicitly divided into the exploration and the verification periods. In a real classroom, the iteration of both periods while upgrading the behaviors may reveal unique and unexpected findings related to certain situations. It was difficult to explore all the important behaviors during a single exploration period in the pilot trial, and the findings depend on various classroom conditions (e.g., children, toys, hours). Therefore, we iteratively accumulate knowledge concerning the important behaviors of the robot. In the field of learning science, the design experiment approach involving interventions and iterative implementation in a natural classroom has also been used to generate new theories and frameworks for educational methods [2].

Figure 1 shows the progressive development of an autonomous CRR. Each trial consists of exploration and verification periods. Each period lasts several days (e.g., 4 days). There are two robots in the classroom; therefore, the children can compare them and choose the one with which they want to play a certain learning game. In the exploration period, the WOZ robot is controlled remotely by an operator to explore new robot behaviors for further encouraging children's interest in the learning game relative to the autonomous robot that serves as the baseline in this trial. Additional behaviors for verification are decided based on video observations of the exploration period and interviews with the experimenters who play the role of guardians in the classroom. The verifications with the baseline and the improved robots are conducted with children who had not participated in the exploration. The Auto-1 robot played the role of the baseline to be improved in the first trial. The Auto-2 robot was implemented based on the exploration in the first trial. If the learning support in the Auto-2 robot was found to be effective, Auto-2 will be set as the baseline, and we will progress toward Auto-3 in the next trial.

3. CONCLUSIONS

In this study, we proposed the concept of a progressive development method involving the parallel comparison of two robots. We have conducted so far field experiments using this development method in a kindergarten classroom, in which children participated in a gesture game for learning English. Aldebaran Robotics' NAO was used for the experiments. Our ongoing analysis showed that the explored new behaviors of the improved CRR successfully helped children maintain their interest in the learning game with the robot. In addition, it is becoming clear that the improved CRR impacts children's learning. These early findings suggest that the proposed progressive development method can be used to gradually improve the autonomous robot to enhance its usefulness in promoting children's learning.

4. ACKNOWLEDGMENTS

This study was supported by KAKENHI (23680020) and the JST PRESTO program. We appreciate the cooperation received from two kindergartens in Tsukuba. We also thank the children and their parents, as well as the students of the University of Tsukuba for their cooperation.

5. REFERENCES

[1] M. Alac, J. Movellan, and F. Tanaka. When a robot is social: Spatial arrangements and multimodal semiotic engagement in the practice of social robotics. *Social Studies of Science*, 41(6):893–926, 2011.

[2] A. Brown. Design experiments: Theoretical and methodological challenges in creating complex interventions in classroom settings. *The Journal of the Learning Sciences*, 2(2):141–178, 1992.

[3] J. F. Kelley. An empirical methodology for writing user-friendly natural language computer applications. In *Proc. of the SIGCHI Conference on Human Factors in Computing Systems*, CHI '83, pages 193–196, 1983.

[4] S. Matsuzoe and F. Tanaka. How smartly should robots behave? : Comparative investigation on the learning ability of a care-receiving robot. In *Proc. of the 21th IEEE International Workshop on Robot and Human Interactive Communication (RO-MAN 2012)*, pages 339–344, 2012.

[5] F. Tanaka, A. Cicourel, and J. R. Movellan. Socialization between toddlers and robots at an early childhood education center. *Proceedings of the National Academy of Sciences of the U.S.A.(PNAS)*, 104(46):17954–17958, 2007.

[6] F. Tanaka and S. Matsuzoe. Children teach a care-receiving robot to promote their learning: Field experiments in a classroom for vocabulary learning. *Journal of Human-Robot Interaction*, 1(1):78–95, 2012.

Therapeutic Robots for Older Adults:

Investigating the Potential of Paro

Sean McGlynn, Braeden Snook, Shawn Kemple, Tracy L. Mitzner, & Wendy A. Rogers
Georgia Institute of Technology
School of Psychology
Atlanta, GA 30332
(404) 894-8344
smcglynn6@gatech.edu

ABSTRACT

As the population ages, there is an increasing need for socio-emotional support for older adults. Therapeutic pets have been used to meet this need, but there are limitations in the practicality of placing pets in older adults' living environments. More recently therapeutic robots have been proposed as a solution. However, there is limited research on the efficacy of deploying therapeutic robots to provide socio-emotional support to older adults. This study investigates the potential of the Paro robot seal to support older adults' needs while avoiding some of the limitations of current pet therapy approaches. Our results will provide insight about how robots can be designed and deployed to increase therapeutic efficacy.

ACM Categories & Subject Descriptors:

I.2.9 [**Artificial Intelligence**]: Robotics

Author Keywords

Older adults; robot therapy; socio-emotional support

1. INTRODUCTION

Advances in robotics offer a number of opportunities for providing support for individuals as they age. Older adults are an important potential user group given that by 2030, they are expected to comprise nearly 20% of the U.S. Population [1]. Most robots that are being developed to aid older adults are designed to compensate for normal age-related declines in physical capability. Less attention has been given to robots that might support social or emotional issues that can emerge with aging. Living alone due to bereavement or by choice can lead to shrinking social networks, which then may be causing an increase in feelings of social isolation and loneliness [2]. Attempts to use commercially available robots as animal-assisted therapy agents have yielded promising results, but a systematic investigation of their ability to provide socio-emotional support is required.

1.1 Pet Therapy: Animals and Robots

Pet Therapy or Animal-Assisted Therapy (AAT) has been used in a variety of contexts and has been shown to have a positive effect on well-being and quality of life. For example, patients who received AAT sessions 1-3 times per week scored significantly lower on a loneliness measure than patients who received no AAT [3]. However, owning a pet is not a realistic option for everyone. Pet robots may be a viable substitute to owning a live animal, as they are likely to be allowed in most environments, are less demanding, and may elicit similar health benefits as dogs and cats.

Dementia patients showed decreased levels of stress-related hormones after 1-hour interactions with Sony's robot dog, AIBO, and reported reduced loneliness after 20 sessions over a 7-week period. In addition, interactions with NeCoRo, a robotic cat, increased feelings of pleasure in nursing home residents [4]. These therapeutic benefits are intriguing, but these robots were not designed for therapeutic purposes, and may not sufficiently promote interaction with participants over the long term.

The Paro (Figure 1) was designed specifically for therapy, and its unfamiliar seal-like appearance allows users to interact with it without pre-existing notions that occur with robots modeled after common pets. Interaction with Paro has been shown to increase happiness and decrease depression and stress in older adult residents of a care facility [5]. However, most Paro research has focused on patients with dementia, with few studies of normally aging adults' interactions with therapeutically oriented robots.

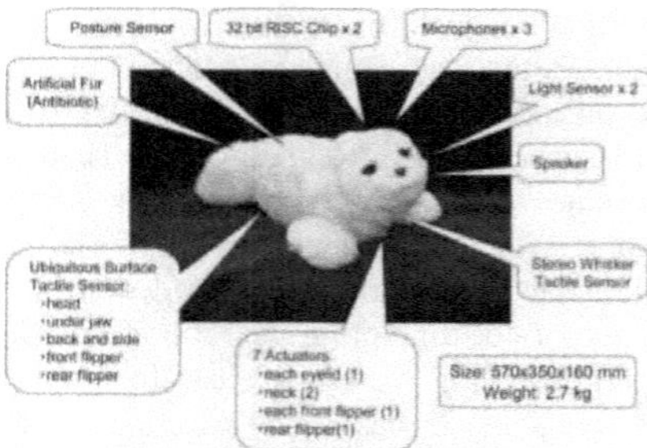

Figure 1: Paro, the robot baby harp-seal mimic. Image courtesy of Intelligent Systems Research Institute (Japan) [5]

1.2 Overview of Study

The primary objective of this study is to assess the effect of framing on attitudes, emotions, and engagement with a therapeutic robot (i.e., if the initial description impacts the interaction). Furthermore, we will determine whether attitudes and emotions change after interaction with the robot. These findings will provide insight into factors that influence older adults' acceptance, emotions and engagement with pet robots.

2. METHODS

2.1 Participants

Forty older adults (65-80 years) will be recruited from the metro community in Atlanta, GA, USA. They will be independent living and in generally good health.

HRI'14, March 3–6 2014, Bielefeld, Germany
ACM 978-1-4503-2658-2/14/03.
http://dx.doi.org/10.1145/2559636.2559846

2.2 Stimuli and Materials

2.2.1 Paro

Paro is a robot designed by Takanori Shibata of the Intelligent System Research Institute of Japan's AIST. Paro has ubiquitous tactile sensors on its endoskeleton, which is covered in soft fur to promote interaction. Paro has sensors for touch, light, sound, and posture. Paro is able to move its neck vertically and horizontally, its front and rear fins, and its eyelids [5].

2.2.2 Questionnaires and Measures

Demographic, health, and technology experience will be collected using standardized materials developed by the Center for Research and Education on Aging and Technology Enhancement [6]. Ability tests will be administered prior to interaction to assess participants' vision, memory, perceptual speed, and vocabulary. Attitudes toward Paro will be assessed using the perceived usefulness and perceived ease of use scales, which will be adapted from a measure of technology acceptance (TAM) [7]. The Positive Affect Negative Affect Scale (PANAS) will be administered to assess participants' emotions before and after interaction with Paro [8]. Engagement with Paro will be determined by the frequency with which participants look at and touch Paro. We will also administer a short interview pre- and post-interaction to assess peoples' general opinions about Paro and its potential role in the home.

2.2.4 Equipment

Participants will be monitored using a Sony HDR-CX380 digital video camera for the duration of the study.

3. PROCEDURE

Participants will first complete the ability tests. The experimenter will then verbally introduce Paro under one of three conditions (pet, robot, or toy) to which participants will be randomly assigned. To avoid biasing by setting users' expectations for a personal robot [9], this introduction will be kept brief, and will point out Paro's sensors, but not describe any technical specifications in detail. Paro then will be brought into the room but remain off. Next, initial reactions will be assessed with a single open question, "What do you think about the Paro?" The experimenter will then administer Pre-Interaction Paro Questions, the TAM and the PANAS in that order. At this point, Paro will be turned on and the initial reaction question will be asked again. Following this will be an interaction period, in which the experimenter will demonstrate possible interactions with Paro, and will ask the participant if they would like to touch and/or hold Paro. The experimenter will then leave the participant in the room with Paro for ten minutes while the participant completes the demographic, health, and technology experience questionnaires. When the experimenter returns, the participant will receive the PANAS, Post-Interaction Paro Questions, the TAM, and Role of Paro Questions. At this time, the participant will be debriefed.

4. DATA ANALYSIS

A 3x2 split-plot analysis of variance (ANOVA) will assess the between-subjects factor of framing group (pet, robot, toy) and the two within-subjects factors of time (pre/post-interaction) for both the TAM and the PANAS. A one-way ANOVA will assess the effect of framing group on engagement with Paro.

5. POTENTIAL RESULTS

We expect there to be a main effect between framing groups on attitudes, emotions, and engagement with Paro. Furthermore, we expect an interaction effect between framing and time of assessment (pre/post) such that the degree of interaction effects will depend on which framing group participants were nested in. Finally, we expect groups to differ in the types of responses they provide for general opinions about Paro.

6. DISCUSSION

These results could have implications on the future of robots for therapy. If attitudes, emotions, and engagement depend on framing, it would indicate that this may be a consideration for how Paro and similar therapeutic robots should be deployed to increase the likelihood of acceptance and enhance the therapeutic potential. Higher post-interaction assessment scores across all participants would provide further evidence that Paro has a positive effect on attitudes and emotions. By taking a systematic approach toward investigating the therapeutic effects of Paro, we will provide insight into the factors that influence interactions with therapeutic robots as well as possible considerations for increasing acceptance and integration into people's lives.

7. ACKNOWLEDGEMENTS

This research is supported by the National Institutes of Health (National Institute on Aging) through: (1) the Ruth L. Kirschstein National Research Service Award Institutional Research Training Grant (T32AG000175); and (2) Grant P01 AG17211, the Center for Research and Education on Aging and Technology Enhancement (CREATE; www.create-center.org). We appreciate the loan of the Paro from Dr. Aaron King and DTI Robotics.

8. REFERENCES

1. Administration on Aging. 2010, June. *A profile of older Americans: 2009.* Retrieved November 18, 2013, from http://ww.aoa.gov/aoaroot/aging_statistics/Profile/2009/docs/2009profile_508.pdf
2. Cornwell, E. Y., & Waite, L. J. (2009). Social disconnectedness, perceived isolation, and health among older adults. *Journal of Health and Social Behavior*, *50(1)*, 31-48.
3. Ballarini, G. 2003. Pet therapy. Animals in human therapy. *Acta Bio Medica Atenei Parmensis*, *74(2)*, 97-100.
4. Filan, S. L., & Llewellyn-Jones, R. H. (2006). Animal-assisted therapy for dementia: a review of the literature. *International Psychogeriatrics, 18(4)*, 597-612.
5. Wada, K., & Shibata, T. (2007). Living with seal robots—its sociopsychological and physiological influences on the elderly at a care house. Robotics, IEEE Transactions on, 23(5), 972-980.
6. Czaja, S. J., Charness, N., Fisk, A. D., Hertzog, C., Nair, S. N., Rogers, W. A., & Sharit, J. (2006). Factors predicting the use of technology: findings from the Center for Research and Education on Aging and Technology Enhancement (CREATE). *Psychology and Aging*, 21(2), 333-352.
7. Davis F.D. 1989. Perceived usefulness, perceived ease of use, and user acceptance of information technology. *MIS Quarterly* 13(3), 319-340.
8. Watson, D., Clark, L. A., & Tellegen, A. (1988). Development and validation of brief measures of positive and negative affect: the PANAS scales. *Journal of Personality and Social Psychology*, 54(6), 1063.
9. Paepcke, S., & Takayama, L. (2010, March). Judging a bot by its cover: an experiment on expectation setting for personal robots. In *Human-Robot Interaction (HRI), 2010 5th ACM/IEEE International Conference* on (pp. 45-52). IEEE.

Learning Partial Ordering Constraints from a Single Demonstration

Anahita Mohseni-Kabir, Charles Rich and Sonia Chernova
Worcester Polytechnic Institute
Worcester, MA, USA
(amohsenikabir|rich|soniac)@wpi.edu

ABSTRACT

Current approaches to learning partial ordering constraints by demonstration require demonstrating all (or almost all) possible completion orders. We have developed an algorithm that, for plans involving relative placement of objects, learns the partial ordering constraints from a single demonstration by letting the user specify naturally conceived reference frame information. This work is an example of a broader research agenda that involves applying principles of human collaboration to robot learning from demonstration.

Categories and Subject Descriptors

I.2.9 [**Artificial Intelligence**]: Robotics

Keywords

Learning from demonstration, collaboration

1. INTRODUCTION

This work is being conducted within the context of a larger project, one of whose goals is to build a bridge between research on robot learning from demonstration (LfD) [1] and research on human collaboration [5]. Specifically, we view learning as a type of collaboration—anyone who has been a teacher knows that both the learner and the teacher must have the shared goal of learning for the process to succeed. Furthermore, in a typical collaboration, both participants not only perform coordinated actions, they also *communicate* about the goals, subgoals, progress, problems, etc., as they arise.

One of the benefits we hope to achieve from this approach is to make it possible for humans to teach complex tasks to robots using only a small number of demonstrations. To do so, the human is expected to provide helpful advice along with the demonstrated actions, i.e., advice that can be naturally given by an untrained user. We are also working on, but not reporting here, how the robot can ask good questions, i.e., questions that an untrained user can easily answer.

HRI'14, March 3–6, 2014, Bielefeld, Germany.
ACM 978-1-4503-2658-2/14/03.
http://dx.doi.org/10.1145/2559636.2559809.

We report here on a first example of this approach, which is an algorithm that, for certain types of actions, learns ordering constraints from a single demonstration.

2. THE PROBLEM

Learning ordering constraints is a classic problem in LfD. Demonstrations are intrinsically totally ordered, i.e., any set of (discrete, non-overlapping) actions performed in the real world are in a specific sequence. However, in many cases, only some of the demonstrated ordering is required. For example, even though you must demonstrate checking the air in all four tires of your car in some order, the order doesn't really matter. Learning the minimum required ordering constraints is important, because it makes the learned plan more flexible and reusable.

More formally, suppose your goal is to teach the following partially ordered plan, where A, B, C and D are primitive actions, > means precedes and (B | C) means that B and C can happen in either order:

$$A > (B \mid C) > D$$

The usual approach [2, 3] to teaching this plan is to use two demonstrations, i.e., ABCD and ACBD, and then to unify these two total orders into a partial order. In the table-setting domain often used for research on this problem, A in this example could be placing a plate on the table, B and C could be placing the knife and fork on either side of the plate, and D could be placing a dust cover on the entire setting.

3. OUR APPROACH

But can we do better than requiring two demonstrations? Two demonstrations doesn't seem like so many in this example, but this approach does not scale well, since the number of possible completions of a partial order increases quickly as the number of steps increases. Would you need two demonstrations to teach this to a person? *Isn't it obvious to a person that the knife and fork can be placed in either order?*

The answer here is to think more deeply about the *reason* for the ordering constraints that are required. An ordering constraint is in general the symptom of an underlying *dependency* between actions. Let's see if we can make these dependencies explicit. To do so we need to digress briefly into the domain of numerical computations and data flow.

Suppose that A, B, C and D are mathematical functions that are connected together with data flow as shown in Figure 1. Notice that A, B and C each have one input and one output; D has two inputs and one output. In this representation, it is obvious what the required ordering constraints are. B and C must happen after A because they each consume the output of A. D must happen after both B and C because it consumes each of their outputs. The order of B and C is unconstrained because there is no data flow between them.

So how can we represent a robotic demonstration, using actions such as PLACE, in this way? To start with, one input to PLACE should be the object to be moved. A second input should be a specification of the target location. How about outputs? In some programming languages, inputs to a subroutine that are *modified* (side effected) are also considered outputs. Let's view changing the location of an object as a side effect and therefore make the first input to PLACE also be an output.

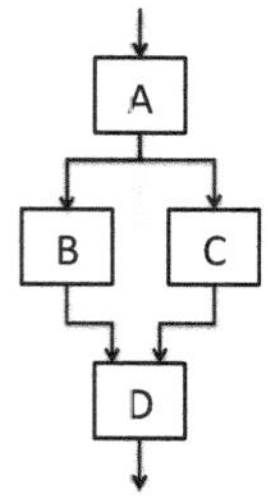

Figure 1:

Finally, and this is a key step, let's view every PLACE action as being performed in some *reference frame*, i.e., a coordinate system for the target location specification. In robot manipulation, there is always a coordinate system, either explicitly or implicitly. Furthermore, in many manipulation tasks, one object is often the reference frame for the placing of another object. For example, we place the fork "one inch to the right of the plate." Thus we add a third input to the PLACE action, which is the object that serves as the reference frame for this action.

Figure 2 shows the ABCD table setting demonstration represented using this formalization of PLACE. Notice that the plate output of the first action is the reference frame input for placing both the knife and the fork. The reference frame for placing the plate is the table, which does not move. Also, notice that we have added one additional artifact, which is a "virtual" action composing the plate, knife and fork into a composite object (the setting) that is the reference frame for placing the dust cover.

Once we have represented the demonstration this way, since Figure 2 is topologically identical to Figure 1, the required ordering constraints are directly learned from this *single* demonstration, namely:

Plate > (Knife | Fork) > Cover

4. CONCLUSION

Returning to our collaboration paradigm, what's going on here is that that the teacher is providing more information in the demonstration that just the final positions of the manipulated objects. Our formalization of the PLACE action requires that the reference frame be specified for every instance, e.g., that the plate is the reference frame for placing the knife.

Some researchers [2] have suggested trying to guess this reference frame information from heuristics about proximity of objects. However, from our point of view, this is information that a collaborating (communicating) user would very naturally provide as part of the demonstration.

For example, we imagine an LfD interface in which the user teleoperates a robot for demonstrations using an abstract GUI instead of a joystick or other direct control device. This GUI would have buttons for actions such as PLACE with associated menus to select target location options, such as "next to," followed by a choice of candidate

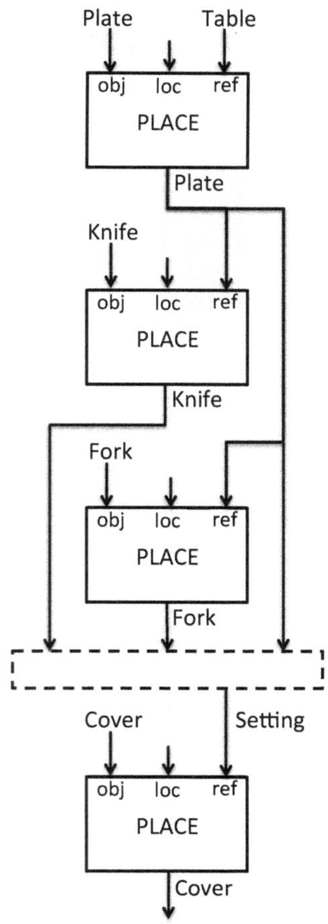

Figure 2: Demonstration

reference frame objects. (There could also be a global default reference frame, such as the table.)

This is a very simple example of the style of collaborative interaction for LfD we are pursuing. We have implemented a system that performs the table-setting demonstration described above in simulation using the ANSI/CEA-2018 [4] standard for actions and plans.

Acknowledgement. This work is supported in part by the Office of Naval Research under Grant N00014-13-1-0735.

5. REFERENCES

[1] B. Argall, S. Chernova, M. Veloso, and B. Browning. A survey of robot learning from demonstration. *Robotics and Autonomous Systems*, 57:469–483, 2009.

[2] S. Ekvall and D. Kragic. Robot learning from demonstration: A task-level planning approach. *Int. J. of Advanced Robotic Systems*, 5(3):223–234, 2008.

[3] M. Pardowitz et al. Incremental learning of tasks from user demonstrations, past experiences, and vocal comments. *IEEE Trans. on Systems, Man, and Cybernetics, Part B: Cybernetics*, 37(2):322–332, 2007.

[4] C. Rich. Building task-based user interfaces with ANSI/CEA-2018. *IEEE Computer*, 42(8):20–27, 2009.

[5] C. Rich, C. Sidner, and N. Lesh. Collagen: Applying collaborative discourse theory to human-computer interaction. *AI Magazine*, 22(4):15–25, 2001.

Empathy: Interactions with Emotive Robotic Drawers

Brian Mok Stephen Yang David Sirkin Wendy Ju

Department of Mechanical Engineering, Stanford University
Center for Design Research (CDR), 424 Panama Mall, Stanford, CA 94305
{brianmok, syang0, sirkin, wendyju} @stanford.edu

ABSTRACT

The role of human-robot interaction is becoming more important as everyday robotic devices begin to permeate into our lives. In this study, we video-prototyped a user's interactions with a set of robotic drawers. The user and robot each displayed one of five emotional states - angry, happy, indifferent, sad, and timid. The results of our study indicated that the participants of our online questionnaire preferred empathetic drawers to neutral ones. They disliked robotic drawers that displayed emotions orthogonal to the user's emotions. This showed the importance of displaying emotions, and empathy in particular, when designing robotic devices that share our living and working spaces.

Category and Subject Descriptors

H.5.m [Information Interface and Presentation]: Miscellaneous.

Keywords

Human Robot Interactions; Interactive Furniture; Interaction Design; Wizard of Oz Experiment; Video Prototyping.

1. INTRODUCTION

Autonomous robots have begun to permeate into various facets of our everyday lives. As they have come to share common spaces, these devices have consequently needed to interact with human users. However, both robots and users have traditionally treated each other more like obstacles rather than social figures with whom to collaborate [1]. Thus, designing robots to complement or enhance human users' lives still remains an important challenge. Our current research focuses on improving the engagement with interactive furniture and appliances, particularly in the study of human gestures and other forms of non-verbal communication. In this study, we explored the interactions with a set of robotic drawers that could assist human users in finding desired items. We found that the interactions between the user and the devices felt very much like a conversation, with greetings and a dialogue. This laid the foundation for the questions we wanted to ask. Based on the user's action and emotion, should the robotic drawers show empathy? Should the robot lead the interactions? How does the drawers' response affect the user's perception?

2. RELATED WORK

There has been extensive research of the social interactions between robots and their users. Osawa [2] showed that implementing of anthropomorphic frameworks for domestic robotic devices facilitated better communication with their users. Another branch of research focuses more on gesture and other forms of nonverbal communication. Sirkin and Ju [3] examined the importance of both on screen and off screen motions for telepresence robotics. The study found that the proxy motions displayed by the telepresence robots improved the understanding of messages and the sense of collaboration.

HRI'14, March 3–6, 2014, Bielefeld, Germany.
ACM 978-1-4503-2658-2/14/03.
http://dx.doi.org/10.1145/2559636.2563720

Figure 1: A Set of Robotic Drawers Responded to the User.

3. METHODOLOGY

3.1 Design Improvisation

In the initial stage of this study, we conducted several exploratory improvisation sessions with interaction designers and motion experts. We utilized the basic Wizard of Oz techniques to make the gestures for a set of drawers that responded to the users' commands. A human operator stationed behind the drawers used handles to control each drawer's individual movements.

We observed how the drawers physically responded to the users and how the users perceived the drawers' movements. Through these sessions, the drawers appeared to be a prominent social figure in this study. From this, we decided to create working robotic drawers and a video prototype study.

3.2 Physical Prototype

We fabricated a set of robotic drawers that allowed us to perform consistent and reproducible motions. The drawers were actuated using a rack and pinion system. Appropriate DC motors were used to provide our drawers with the necessary acceleration and velocity to create more expressive motions. In addition to the motors, each drawer was also retrofitted with a linear position encoder built with reflectance sensors on a black and white track. The motors and encoders were fed into an Arduino microcontroller which itself was controlled by a computer running Processing software. We wrote a Processing application to perform Wizard of Oz style remote control on the drawers. It presented a basic button-based GUI and sent animation commands to the Arduino. The animations dictated the drawers' position and actuation speed.

Table 1: Mean responses for 7-point Likert scale response (7= Strongly Agree) for emotionally matched, emotionally mismatched and neutral conditions

Questions	Mean Mat.	Mean Mis.	Mean Neu.	Mat. Vs Mis. (t/p)	Mat. Vs Neu. (t/p)	Neu. Vs Mis. (t/p)
Q1: The dialogue between the person and the drawer felt natural.	4.68	3.66	4.19	3.11 / 0.004	1.14 / 0.21	1.84 / 0.07
Q2: I thought the dialogue was appropriate.	4.75	3.98	4.17	2.60 / 0.014	1.45 / 0.14	0.66 / 0.32
Q3: The person liked the behavior of the drawer.	4.43	3.46	4.11	3.07 / 0.004	0.72 / 0.31	2.29 / 0.03

The Arduino used its knowledge of time and position to carry out the animations. This system allowed the robot operator to easily execute pre-scripted and reproducible drawer motions at the simple click of a button.

3.3 Video Prototype / Experimental Setup

3.3.1 Study Design

We decided to conduct a controlled video prototype study to investigate how people interpreted the robotic drawers' motions. We were interested in studying the interactions along two dimensions: initiator and empathy. To this end, we engineered a video prototype where we varied the initiator of the interaction (either drawer or user), the emotion the user displayed and the apparent emotion the drawer displayed. Matching the last two variables resulted in scenarios where empathy could be examined.

The video prototype scenario had a simple storyline with two scenes. In the establishing scene, the user displayed an emotion as she entered an office, sat down at a desk next to the drawers, and started working. In the interaction scene, the user stopped working, showed a need for something and interacted with the drawers to get it. The interaction followed the format of greeting, drawer selection, then a closing gesture. The initiator was varied by which entity started the greeting interaction and the apparent emotion of the drawers was varied both by the types of animations the drawers performed and the speed at which they performed it.

3.3.2 Study Implementation

To facilitate this study, we designed an online Qualtrics Survey with participants recruited from Amazon's Mechanical Turk crowdsourcing service (N=40). The participants were randomly placed into one of five categories where the constant was the user's emotional state (angry, happy, sad, timid, and indifferent). Participants were first shown the establishing scene to prime them of the situation. Next followed 10 survey pages, one for each of the 5 emotions the drawers could display multiplied by 2 for varying the initiator. Each survey page had an interaction video and a set of statements based on the apparent conversation between the user and robotic drawers. The participants were asked how much they agreed with these statements based on a seven point Likert scale. Afterwards, they were also asked to interpret what mood the user had displayed and how confident they were with their interpretation as a manipulation check for our interpretation of emotions.

4. ANALYSIS / RESULTS

First, the sets of responses were grouped into three categories: robot displaying matching emotion, robot displaying mismatching emotion, and the robot displaying neutral (indifferent) emotion. We then combined every set of responses in each category to find the mean of that category. Our analysis focused on Q1-Q3, the most relevant questions on appropriateness of the interaction.

We then performed a single tailed t-test on the questionnaire responses. Our null hypothesis for category A vs B was H_0: $\mu_A = \mu_B$ and we wanted to test the following- H_1:$\mu_{Mat} > \mu_{Mis}$, H_2:$\mu_{Mat} > \mu_{Neu}$, H_3:$\mu_{Neu} > \mu_{Mis}$. The mean Likert ratings between the emotionally matched and mismatched conditions were statistically significant for all three of the questions [$t(160)=3.11$, $p<.01$], [$t(160)=2.60$, $p<.05$], and [$t(160)=3.07$, $p<.01$] respectively. In other words, people were significantly more likely to agree that the interaction was natural / appropriate / liked when the user-robot emotions matched than when they were mismatched. In addition, there was a statistically significant difference in mean response between the neutral and mismatched condition for Q3, [$t(160)=2.29$, $p<.05$]. However, we could not reject the null for matched vs. neutral, though the matched mean appeared greater. This implied that the matched emotions between user-robot were generally perceived as the best / preferred interactions by the online questionnaire participants, while interactions with mismatched emotions were taken as the worst interactions. This was reminiscent to a study done by Nass [4] in which the emotional pairing of the voice of a car to a driver had a significant effect on performance. Interestingly, the mean for the neutral emotion category was somewhat close to the mean of the matched category for many questions. When looking at each individual user emotion, we found similar results in all the emotions except for one: Happy. For the happy emotion, the neutral category was the most preferred interaction.

5. CONCLUSION / FUTURE WORK

We have found a significant relationship between the matching of emotions for the user-robotic drawers' interactions and the perception of these interactions by the online questionnaire participants. They found the interactions most favorable when the emotional states of the drawers matched those of the user. The second best scenario was when the drawers remained neutral with regard to the user's emotions. This showed the importance of displaying emotions, and empathy in particular, when designing robotic devices that share our living and working spaces.

We are currently implementing additional sensors to create a fully autonomous drawer system. We are also interested in using devices, such as the Kinect, to capture the gestures and commands that a user performs to elicit an action from the robotic drawers. In the future, we plan to further explore the appropriateness of emotional displays by interactive furniture and deploy a fully autonomous version of the drawers to conduct live experiments.

6. REFERENCES

[1] C. Breazeal. 2004. Social interactions in hri: the robot view. *IEEE Transactions on Systems. Man, and Cybernetics, 34(2):181–186*

[2] Osawa, H. 2007. Anthropomorphization Framework for Human-Object Communication. *Journal of Advanced Computational Intelligence and Intelligent Informatics, Vol.11, No.8 pp. 1007-1014*

[3] Sirkin, D. Ju, W. 2011. Consistency in physical and on screen action improves perception of telepresence robots *Proceedings of the 7th ACM/IEEE conference on Human Robotic Interactions*

[4] Nass, C.2005. Improving Automotive Safety by Pairing Driver Emotion and Car Voice Emotion. *CHI'05*. ACM.

HRI in the Sky: Controlling UAVs using Face Poses and Hand Gestures

Jawad Nagi, Alessandro Giusti, Gianni A. Di Caro, Luca M. Gambardella
Dalle Molle Institute for Artificial Intelligence (IDSIA), CH-6928 Lugano, Switzerland
{jawad,alessandrog,gianni,luca}@idsia.ch

ABSTRACT

As a first step towards human and multiple-UAV interaction, we present a novel method for humans to interact with flying UAVs using locally on-board video cameras. Using machine vision techniques, our approach enables human operators to command and control Parrot drones by giving them directions to move, using simple hand gestures. When a direction to move is given, the robot controller estimates the angle and distance to move with the help of a *face score system* and the *estimated hand direction*. This approach offers mobile robots the ability localize with human operators and provides UAVs/UGVs with a better perception of the environment around the human.

Categories and Subject Descriptors

I.2.9 [**Robotics**]; I.4 [**Image Processing and Computer Vision**]; I.5 [**Pattern Recognition**]: General

Keywords

Human-robot interaction, face pose, gesture recognition

1. INTRODUCTION

Hand gestures are easily recognizable and have the advantage of being easy to use, as well as being natural and intuitive means for human-robot interaction (HRI). For humans to command and control UAVs/UGVs using hand gestures, robots need to know where the human is located (or positioned) in the environment. With the recent advances in computational power and machine vision algorithms, the detection of humans has become relatively easy [1].

In order for a human to be able to command a robot to move a specific position, based on the direction of the human hand, a robot needs to know the orientation of the hand direction with respect to the *face pose* of the human based on its field of view. At the aim of visual interaction between humans and robots, in this work we adopt *face detection* to identify if a human is present in the field of view of the UAV. We consider that interaction only initiates after a human face is detected by the robot [2]. If a face is detected by the robot, then we consider the pose of the face as the *angle* between the human and the robot's point of view. Since, a robot also needs to take into account the *proximity* (distance) between itself and the human when maneuvering, we estimate this distance using measures of the detected face.

To estimate the direction (given by a hand gesture) where the robot should move to, we compute the orientation of the *hand direction* with respect to the location of the face. Using measures of the estimated face pose together with the proximity measure and hand direction, a UAV can estimate its current position (angle,distance) in the environment with respect to the human, and can move along a path to the direction specified by the human.

HRI'14, March 3–6, 2014, Bielefeld, Germany.
ACM 978-1-4503-2658-2/14/03.
http://dx.doi.org/10.1145/2559636.2559833.

2. METHODS

2.1 Face Score System

To detect and track a human face, we use the built-in video camera of the Parrot that acquires images in resolution of 1280×720 pixels at 30 fps. Acquired frames (images) are wirelessly transmitted from the Parrot onto a Linux machine for offline processing. We perform face detection using the OpenCV implementation of the Viola-Jones face detector [3]. Given images such as in Figure 1, we locate rectangular areas in images that contain a human face from different poses (angles), e.g. a frontal poses (see Figure 1(b)) or side poses (see Figures 1(a) and (c)). After a face is detected, we employ a Kalman Filter for tracking the detected face and also for reducing false negative and false positive face detections. As face detectors are insensitive to small changes in scale or position, multiple sub-windows are typically clustered around the face.

Figure 1: Face pose estimation using a flying UAV. Identified face poses: (a) right, (b) center, (c) left.

The Viola-Jones face detector, a cascade Haar classifier, is used for finding groups of neighbouring sub-windows around the human face. In this work, we employ two pretrained

Haar classifiers to detect faces from multiple point of views. One classifier detects frontal poses of the face profile C_{front}, and the other detects side profiles of the face C_{side}. Since two classifiers are used, the number of red-colored sub-windows in Figure 1 indicate the face detections from C_{front} classifier (center), whereas the blue-colored sub-windows show detections from the C_{side} classifier (left and right). Next, we measure the *number of neighbouring sub-windows* detected from the frontal and side face poses, to estimate the relative pose of the face with respect to the robots point of view. For every frame (image) acquired by the robot, 4 relative scores are computed using classifiers C_{front} and C_{side}:

1. Classifier C_{front} is run on frame f to obtain $score_{front}$.
2. Frame f is flipped horizontally (180°) with subsequent horizontal shift to obtain, f_{hor}. Classifier C_{side} is run on f_{hor} to obtain $score_{frontflip}$.
3. Classifier C_{side} is run on frame f to obtain $score_{side}$.
4. Using frame f_{hor} (obtained in Step 2), and running classifier C_{side} results in $score_{sideflip}$.

Next, the current direction of the human face (i.e., left, center and right) with respect to the robot's point of view, is computed using:

$$S_{center} = score_{front} + score_{frontflip} \tag{1}$$

$$S_{right} = score_{side} \tag{2}$$

$$S_{left} = score_{sideflip} \tag{3}$$

where equations (1), (2) and (3) each represent independent *face scores* assessing the quality of the detected face from a 3-dimensional perspective. In simpler words, when the human is directly looking towards the robot, the value of S_{center} is higher than S_{right} or S_{left}. Alternatively, if the human is looking towards the left, then S_{left} is higher than S_{right} and S_{center}, and vice versa when the human is looking towards the left. If all three scores are 0, this indicates that no human is present in the robot's field of view.

To solve the problem of face pose estimation using a system of 3 equations, a Fuzzy Inference System (FIS) is implemented. The FIS takes as input the 3 scores (S_{center}, S_{left} and S_{right}) and maps these scores using membership functions and a rule-based system to a *defuzzified output*, namely the *face pose*, θ, which projects face scores onto a horizontal plane of $[0, 180°]$, where 0° indicates left, 90° represents center, and 180° represents right (see Figure 1).

2.2 Hand Direction

Directions for the robot to move are provided by the human operator using the left or right hand, as illustrated in Figure 2. For simplicity purposes, we use hand gestures naturally supplemented by fine controls through tangible input gadgets (i.e., coloured gloves). By pointing the hand towards the left or right, the human can command the robot to move towards a specific direction.

For estimating the direction of the hand with respect to θ for frame f, the multiple sub-windows resulting from the multiple face detectors are averaged together to form a single rectangular area f_{rect} bounding the face, as illustrated by the face bounding boxes in Figure 2. Next, the centroid of f_{rect} is computed as fc, the *face centroid*. Performing color-based segmentation followed by blob analysis on the coloured glove (hand), the *hand centroid* hc can be easily computed. The *hand orientation* H_{dir} (covering a circular area of ±180° degrees) with respect to fc can then be computed using, $H_{dir} = (\text{atan2}(hc - fc) * 180/\pi)$.

2.3 Robot Control

At every control step t, a frame f acquired by the robot is used for computing: (i) the 3 face scores (S^t_{left}, S^t_{right}, S^t_{center}) and (ii) d_t the area of the face rectangle f^t_{rect} (measure indicating the *distance* between the robot and the human). While moving to a position commanded by the human, the robot makes use of the feedback information (θ_t, d_t) from the face score system at every t. To reach the directed position H_{dir}, the robot controller aims to 'minimize' the relative angle between the current position of the UAV and the target destination: $min\ \{P^t_{target}\}$, where $P^t_{target} = abs(\theta_t - H_{dir})$ (absolute difference to move in degrees), while maintaining the distance d_t. When P^t_{target} goes lower than a predefined threshold, the robot stops, as it reaches the position commanded by the human.

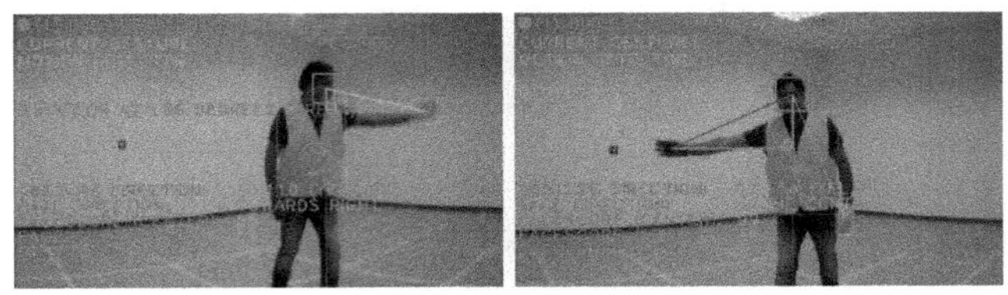

Figure 2: A human operator commanding a flying UAV to move in a specific direction.

3. CONCLUSION

We presented a machine vision approach directly applicable for human-UAV localization problems. Our approach makes use of human faces poses in order to allow UAVs to estimate their position (location) in the environment with respect to the human. To determine the angle and distance where the robot should move, the robot controller makes use of the feedback information from the face score system together with the estimated hand direction.

4. ACKNOWLEDGMENTS

This research was supported by the Swiss National Science Foundation (SNSF) through the National Centre of Competence in Research (NCCR) Robotics (www.nccr-robotics.ch). The authors participate to Project 4, Sub-project 4.5, *Symbiotic human-swarm cooperation*.

5. REFERENCES

[1] B. Milligan, G. Mori, and R. T. Vaughan. Selecting and commanding groups of robots in a vision based multi-robot system. Proc. of the 6th ACM/IEEE Intl. Conf. on HRI (Video Session), 2011.

[2] S. Pourmehr, M. Monajjemi, R. T. Vaughan, et al. You two! take off!: Creating, modifying and commanding groups of robots using face engagement and indirect speech in voice commands. In *Proc. of the IEEE International Conference on IROS*, 2013.

[3] P. Viola and M. J. Jones. Robust real-time face detection. *Int. J. Comput. Vision*, 57(2):137–154, 2004.

Breatter: A Simulation of Living Presence with Breath that Corresponds to Utterances

Yukari Nakatani
Kansai University
Osaka 569-1095, Japan
k415001@kansai-u.ac.jp

Tomoko Yonezawa
Kansai University
Osaka 569-1095, Japan
yone@kansai-u.ac.jp

ABSTRACT

We propose an expressive breathing method for a robot in accordance with its utterances. The synchronized expression is expected as a new physical modality to become like a living presence. Especially when the human-robot distance is near in intimate communications, anthropomorphized presences should naturally imitate activities of living beings, such as breathing. A stuffed-toy robot contains a speaker and a fan motor in its head to make simultaneous expressions of breathing and vocal sounds. The strength of the breath is determined by the total volume and power in the high frequency band.

Categories and Subject Descriptors

H.5 [Information Interfaces and Presentation]: Miscellaneous

General Terms

Design

Keywords

Robot, Breathing, Living presence, Intimate communication

1. INTRODUCTION

In human-human communications, we speak using various types of modalities at various distances. We can whisper in a partner's ear when she/he is in our intimate space. In this case, it is necessary to be in a close friendship with mutual trust. We should design partner robots to be considered similar to a human partner by using realistic and life-like expressions even when we are close to each other.

On the other hand, biophysical phenomena arises from the simultaneous functions of our bodies and their structures. Not only humans but also animals make utterances using a breathing flow and vibration of the vocal cords. When we listen to utterances from a distance, only the sound of the voice is heard. However, when we communicate together using a whispery voice close to our ears, we also feel the breath in connection with the utterance. It is considered one of the expressions of a "living presence" used by biophysical structures.

HRI'14, March 3–6, 2014, Bielefeld, Germany.
ACM 978-1-4503-2658-2/14/03.
http://dx.doi.org/10.1145/2559636.2563704 .

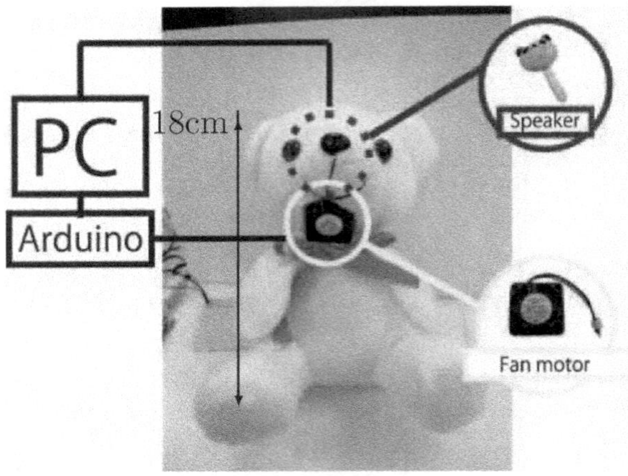

Figure 1: Appearance of our designed stuffed-toy robot

In this research, we focused on a robot's utterance as one of its actions to show aliveness. Robots, anthropomorphic presences, imitate living beings by using multimodal expressions including vocal utterances. If we design the utterances of robots as though they were living presences, not only the volume of voice but also the breath corresponding to the speech should be considered.

Accordingly, we propose a breathing expression for a robot from its mouth at the same time of the utterance. A stuffed-toy robot includes a small speaker and an incorporated fan motor under its mouth to enable the breathing expression simultaneous to its utterance. In order to generate realistic breathing corresponding to the utterance, the voice is analyzed to detect total power and the power of each of the frequency bands. Generated voice and breathing expressions are controlled at the same time. Realistic human-human communication would be performed even with an artificial anthropomorphic presence by giving it appropriate expressions: not only verbal or vocal cues but also material, physical, and biological representations.

2. RELATED WORK

Various research in robotics has shown some discussions of realistic presences for anthropomorphic systems.

There has been much research of the total appearance of a robot in real-space communication. Sakamoto et al. have

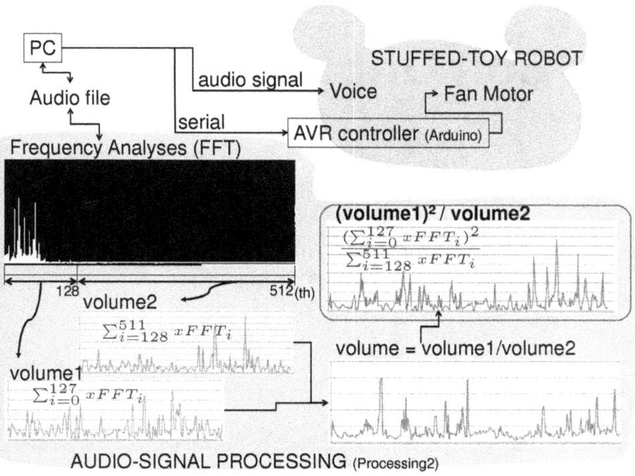

Figure 2: System flow

developed a remote-controlled android system to realize human tele-presence [1]. They used the Geminoid HI-1 as an android robot medium. "Presence" means that the robot is "there" or "present" during their research. As a result of their experiments, Geminoid HI-1 was interpreted to have a stronger presence than a real person's presence in video discussions. It was conjectured that robots with a human-like appearance are expressive for presence.

The remote presence of a stuffed toy had been also discussed by Sekiguchi et al. [2]. Screen media for a remote presence was also discussed by Kunita et al. [3]. Communicative media has some limitations especially when they are representing remote presences.

In this research, we aimed to generate expressions for anthropomorphic presence as though it were "living." Differently from the preceding approaches, not only bodily presence but also functional presence should be emphasized to make a realistic presence. Accordingly, we propose to enable a breathing expression that corresponds to the utterance of the robot.

3. "BREATTER" SYSTEM

3.1 Design of Agent

The goal of this research is to build an intimate interaction between a robot and a user. In our daily lives, we pay attention to expression with a sense of hearing in vocal communication. Close interactions need a more realistic presence. As a first step, we propose combining an anthropomorphic utterance with breathing as one of the expressions of the stuffed-toy robot.

As shown in Figure 1, a fan motor and a speaker are placed in a stuffed-toy that is 18[cm] tall. The fan motor is fixed under the mouth of the stuffed toy. In order to let the user bring the stuffed animal's mouth close to her/his ear, she/he can sensitively feel its breathing. For the fan motor, DC 5[V] (200[mA]) fan in 25[mm] square for a PC cooler is used.

3.2 Controls for Breathing

To provide the appropriate strength of the breathing that corresponds to the robot's utterance, the system first analyzes the audio file of the voice to make simultaneous expressions of the fan motor with the utterance. The system flow is shown in Figure 2.

The voice of the robot is prepared based on text scripts as a 44100 [Hz] audio signal. The Fast Fourier Transform (FFT) window size for the frequency analysis was 1024. Focusing on the vocal band, up to 5000 [Hz], the system calculates a summation of the power in the band, that is 0 to 127 (volume1 in Figure 2). Next the system normalizes the strength of the power by the basic power in the other bands (volume 2 in Figure 2). To emphasize the strength of the vocal band, we adopted a squared value. This formula is shown in Eq. (1), where xFFT means the real part of the FFT results for raw audio signals.

$$\frac{(\sum_{i=0}^{127} xFFT_i)^2}{\sum_{i=128}^{511} xFFT_i} \tag{1}$$

The audio-signal processing part is implemented in Processing2 and the results are sent to a hardware controller by serial communication as signals for the fan motor. Finally, the fan motor connected to an AVR (automatic voltage regulator) controller, Arduino, makes breath-like wind simultaneously with the utterances.

3.3 System Operation

We tried to confirm the system operation of the breathing involved with each utterance. The 25[mm] square 5[V] DC fan is not very large, but the soft wind was sufficiently perceived when the user put her/his ear close to the mouth of the stuffed toy. This configuration enables a breath-like expression during the robot's communication with the user. It is also presumed that the user's feeling of the temperature of the breathing enriched the realistic feeling. We are also convinced of the effectiveness of the temperature of the breathing itself.

4. CONCLUSION

In this paper, we introduced a robot that breathes corresponding to its utterances in imitation of a living being. The breathing expression was realized by a fan motor attached under the mouth of the stuffed toy. The strength of the breath is calculated by the analysis of the robot's voice: the volume of the sound and the power for each frequency band. In the future, we will determine whether the robot increases the user's sense of intimate communication with a simulated living being. Also, we will examine how users feel the robot's presence through their physical or psychological distance from the robot.

5. ACKNOWLEDGMENTS

This research was supported in part by KAKENHI 24300047 and KAKENHI 25700021.

6. REFERENCES

[1] D. Sakamoto, T. Kanda, T. Ono, H. Ishiguro, and N. Hagita. Android as a telecommunication medium with a human-like presence. In ACM/IEEE Human-Robot Interaction (HRI), pp. 193–200, 2007.

[2] D. Sekiguchi, M. Inami, and S. Tachi. Robotphone: Rui for interpersonal communication. In CHI'01 extended abstracts on Human factors in computing systems, pp. 277–278, 2001.

[3] Y. Kunita, N. Ogawa, A. Sakuma, M. Inami, T. Maeda, and S. Tachi. Immersive autostereoscopic display for mutual telexistence: Twister i (telexistence wide-angle immersive stereoscope model i). In Proc. of IEEE Virtual Reality 2001, pp. 31–36, 2001.

Embodied Computation in Soft Gripper

Stig Anton Nielsen
Dept. of Architecture
Chalmers Technical University
stig.nielsen@chalmers.se

Alexandru Dancu
Dept. of Applied IT
Chalmers Technical University
alexandru.dancu@gmail.com

ABSTRACT

We designed, created and tested an underactuated soft gripper able to hold everyday objects of various shapes and sizes without using complex hardware or control algorithms, but rather by combining sheets of flexible plastic materials and a single servo motor. Starting with a prototype where simple actuation performs complex varied gripping operations solely through the material system and its inherent physical computation, the paper discusses how embodied computation might exist in a material aggregate by tuning and balancing its morphology and material properties.

Categories and Subject Descriptors

I.2.9 [**Computing Methodologies**]: Artificial Intelligence—*Robotics*

1. INTRODUCTION

This paper argues that human-robot interaction can simplify control systems, mechanisms and problems like collision detection by employing embodied computation. MacLennan describes embodied computation as "information processing in which the physical realization and the physical environment play an unavoidable and essential role" [4]. In this paper we will discuss embodied computation and suggest a material system that has reduced actuation complexity and performs gripping instead through an embodied material computation. Human-robot Interaction can manifest indirectly, in the sense that robots should be able to interact with the same environments humans do. This requires a certain resemblance between robots and humans: in behavior, morphology, materiality, and scale. But how do we determine what similarities are relevant, and should we mimic or replicate these mechanisms What aspects of embodied computation are relevant to the design of material systems, morphology, and material behavior

One major challenge in robotics is picking up and holding everyday objects without crushing them. For that we have created an adaptive, robust gripper able to interact with a large number of real objects from an office environment and with humans. Traditionally in computer-science, software has been developed and analyzed separately from hardware. In embodied computing the computation is seen as happening "as a physical system in continuing interaction with other physical systems (its environment)". [4]. Information processing is implicit here because the physical environment performs some computations "for free". Redström argues that computers can be seen as a kind of material, and that their computational capabilities must be combined with other kinds of materials in order to create a computational composite, so that the computer becomes "useful in design" [5]. This paper contributes a design of an underactuated gripper, a computational aggregate made up of material composites in a soft mechanical system, with an emphasis on morphology and material behavior interacting with the real environment.

HRI'14, March 3–6, 2014, Bielefeld, Germany.
ACM 978-1-4503-2658-2/14/03.
http://dx.doi.org/10.1145/2559636.2563691

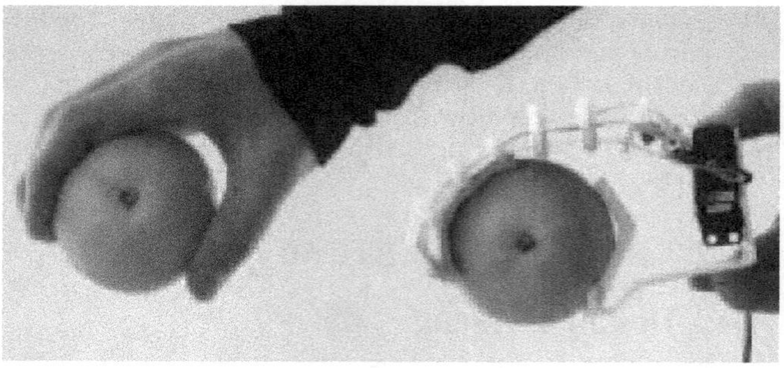

Figure 1: Gripper-hand for scale and comparison

2. RELATED WORK

Many robotic hand designs focus on mechanically replicating the human hand, controlling each joint independently using many actuators. On the other hand, underaction designs employ less actuators in order to control a larger number of joints. One of the first examples of an underactuated soft gripper, similar to a bicycle chain, was developed using pulleys and twenty articulations. It was able to conform to objects of arbitrary shapes [3]. However, the design of this gripper only permitted holding an object in one plane. Another example of a soft "universal" gripper could conform around a complex object from all sides, and hold it by contracting the granular material it was made from [1]. This is a good example of embodied computing where a computational composite is used. The granular material automatically computes and shapes around an object, simplifying and avoiding the problems multifingered robotic hands experience when needing to compute the force and position required to control each finger. A simple design employing material intelligence can thus avoid both hardware and software complexities.

3. DESIGN AND IMPLEMENTATION

A simple gripper design employing this kind of material intelligence is composed of three main parts, a dynamic actuated arm, a servo, and a thumb. The thumb is an acrylic plastic plate, that bends into shape, with an added a layer of high friction material. It is positioned below inside the dynamic arm so that it creates a static counterpart for the dynamic arm. This piece could be compared to the thumb or the palm of a hand. In our design, the dynamic, actuated arm consists of a central flexible core and upper and lower tendons. The tendons are attached to the tip of the core and run through plastic fittings fixed to the central core, allowing the tendons free linear movement (Fig. 1). "The tendons are actuated by a servo motor controlled by a looping prototype program that turns them clockwise, holds them, and then turns them counter-clockwise.

The flexible core is bendable, but static in length. When a tendon is actuated in a linear movement through the fittings, the central core will bend, firstly at the base, as well as the tip, resulting in a grasping movement. When parts of the arm are obstructed by either the object or the table, the gripper starts to bend in other parts along its length, conforming around the object. Due to the flexibility and softness of the materials, the gripper never crushes objects. On the contrary, the morphology and mechanism makes the grip firmer only as the weight of the objects increases. Force is applied incrementally, building up through the material, giving it a shape and conforming to it, resulting in a uniform tension around the object that becomes the final grip. Furthermore the tendon, being very close to the object, contributes the force of the grip.

Most daily objects are designed at human scale, therefore the scale of the gripper and thumb was constructed to match that of a human hand (see Fig. 1) enabling it to grasp most objects from an office environment. Deimel argues that constraints present in the environment must be exploited for robust grasping [2]. The inside of the thumb and the tip of the arm are coated with high friction material (foam), permitting it to hold objects of more than six times its own weight. The gripper all inclusive weighs 95g, and the stapler pictured 606g (Fig. 2, lower left).

4. DISCUSSION

We arrived to this design empirically by varying the length of the central core and tendons, the thickness of the central core, as well as changing the position for the plastic fittings. We found out that for this type of plastic for the tendons and central core, the optimal length is 15cm (full length of a hand is 14-18 cm). Shorter lengths of the central core and tendons limits the size of graspable objects, while longer sizes decreases the applied gripping force and introduces flexing to the left or right of the central gripper axis.

The position of the plastic fittings determine how the gripper bends. Fig. 2 shows different adaptations of the tendons and central core. The tension spreads through the material automatically computing the force and morphology necessary to grasp and hold the particular object. Design improvements can be done, and the balance between items in the material system seems to be of great importance, which is why it is prudent to make a modifiable design, so the balance can be tuned without having to build entire new prototypes. This notion might open an entire discussion of a second order actuation which could control and tune the balance of the material system e.g. moving the fittings or changing the stiffness of the core along the central core depending on the instance of a gripping action.

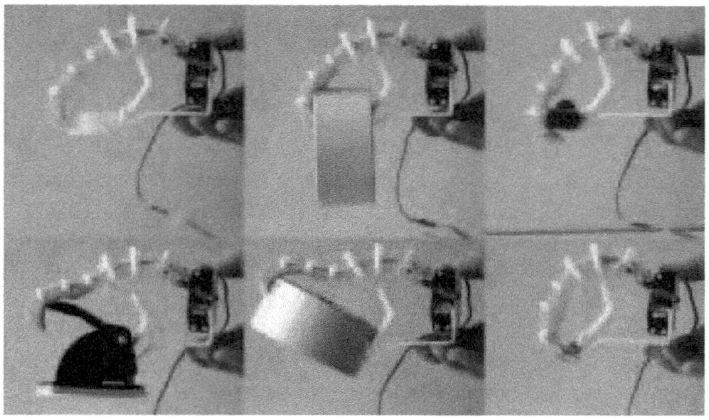

Figure 2: The material system adapts to the shape of each subject. Even small subjects are gripped by the outer tip and picked up. Heavy objects are squeezed in the gripper.

5. CONCLUSION

A soft gripper was designed, created, and tested by gripping objects from an office environment. This prototype showed that the force and the grasping method can be computed by the material, optimizing its morphology, exemplifying embodied computation in an underactuated soft gripper. When designing for increased embodied computation in soft robotics, some aspects of flexibility might decrease, but a surprisingly high robustness was achieved. When assembled, the gripper only fails on single case grasping tasks, it never fails mechanically or breaks itself due to incorrect usage. It seems relevant to let material properties compute active aspects like pressure and collision. The morphology and scale seems relevant to mimic directly, in this case when dealing with everyday objects already designed for the scale and morphology of the hand.

6. REFERENCES

[1] Brown, E., Rodenberg, N., Amend, J., Mozeika, A., Steltz, E., Zakin, M. R., Lipson, H., and Jaeger, H. M. Universal robotic gripper based on the jamming of granular material. *Proceedings of the National Academy of Sciences 107*, 44 (2010), 18809–18814.

[2] Deimel, R., Eppner, C., Alvarez-Ruiz, J., Maertens, M., and Brock, O. Exploitation of environmental constraints in human and robotic grasping.

[3] Hirose, S., and Umetani, Y. The development of soft gripper for the versatile robot hand. *Mechanism and machine theory 13*, 3 (1978), 351–359.

[4] MacLennan, B. J. Aspects of embodied computing. Tech. rep., Technical Report UTCS-08-610, University of Tennessee, 2008.

[5] Vallgårda, A., and Redström, J. Computational composites. In *Proceedings of the SIGCHI conference on Human factors in computing systems*, ACM (2007), 513–522.

Is an Accelerating Robot Perceived as Energetic or as Gaining in Speed?

Matthijs L. Noordzij Martin Schmettow Melle R. Lorijn

Cognitive Psychology and Ergonomics, University of Twente, Drienerlolaan 5, 7522NB Enschede, The Netherlands

+31 534 89 2589 +31 534 89 3874

m.l.noordzij@utwente.nl m.schmettow@utwente.nl mrlorijn@gmail.com

ABSTRACT

Previous studies have found that basic movement characteristics of a robot influence the emotional attributes people perceive independent of the embodiment of the motion (e.g. iCat vs. Roomba). Here, with a very simple LEGO robot, we replicate these associations between levels of acceleration and curvature and the extent to which positive and negative emotions are attributed. Importantly, we also show that these associations might not be valid. Prior to the emotional questionnaires participants were asked neutral questions on what they deemed relevant observations pertaining to the different robot motions. Only 3% of the remarks coincided with the emotional terms found in the questionnaires. HRI researchers interested in what people attribute to robot motion should be mindful of participant heuristics and experimenter biases. We provide some suggestions how to create experiments that are robust against these biases.

Categories and Subject Descriptors

H.1.2 User/Machine Systems: *Human factors*

General Terms

Measurement, Reliability, Experimentation, Human Factors.

Keywords

Robot Motion, Emotion, PANAS, Attribution Heuristic, Response Anchoring.

1. INTRODUCTION

In the field of Human-Robot Interaction (HRI) there have been efforts to find generalizable rules governing human (emotional) reactions to certain variations in robot behavior. For example, it has been suggested that motion characteristics of a robot can influence the attribution of affect in a reliable way, independent of the appearance of the robot and the particular way the motion is embodied [5]. In this latter research curvature and acceleration parameters were varied in two robot platforms: an iCat, which is a robotic cat-head that can pan and tilt, and a Roomba, which is a disc-like robotic vacuum cleaner that can drive around. Therefore, the three levels of curvature and acceleration were instantiated in very different ways in these two embodiments (e.g. tilting the head faster vs. moving faster on the floor). Yet, the researchers found consistent patterns in how people judged the emotional attributes of the two robots (as judged by subjective scales) as a function of motion characteristics. These kinds of findings promise both a more generalizable scientific framework for HRI and direct design guidelines.

Here, we try to replicate part of this research on motion characteristics with yet another robot: a LEGO Mindstorms cart. If the claim that the relation between emotional attribution and motion parameters is independent of embodiment we should be able to find the same associations with a simple robot toy. In addition, we independently assess whether the choices people make on questionnaires probing emotional attributes of the robot correspond to what people spontaneously associate with the variations in robot motion. In [5] people did also spontaneously give (emotional) comments on the robot, but this always happened while they were filling in questionnaires consisting of only emotional terms. In addition, a semi-structured interview was done, but only after people had seen (and committed choices to) the emotional questionnaires. To address the possible confound of priming participants with emotional terms, we asked people to answer to open questions on the robot *before* having seen, let alone answered on, emotional questionnaires.

2. METHOD

2.1 Participants

We recruited 28 participants (8 female), aged between 18 and 27 years.

2.2 Materials

The robot we used was the starter "cart" model of the Lego Mindstorms® NXT 2.0 set (a small tracked vehicle of approximately 20 x 20 x 20 cm.) with an ultrasonic sensor at the front. From the set of questionnaire used in [5] we selected the PANAS [8], which measures positive and negative affect by letting people rate the appropriateness (from 1 to 5) of 10 positive and 10 negative emotional terms. We also used a simple open question form in which participants were asked to fill in the responses they deemed relevant after each robot motion. We tried to emulate the values used in [5] for curvature and acceleration as good as possible on the Lego robot. For curvature we could closely copy the original (Roomba) values by letting the robot drive a path with a mean curvature (= 1 / radius of the circle) of .85 (low curvature), 1.5 (medium curvature) and 2.2 (high curvature) meters. For acceleration we ended up with a rough, relative approximation, because the absolute acceleration was much slower of the LEGO robot than of the Roomba. We programmed the robot to increase its motor power by 10% per time unit. The different time units (in seconds) were 3.5 (low acceleration), 1.05 (medium acceleration), and .57 (high acceleration).

HRI'14, March 3–6, 2014, Bielefeld, Germany.
ACM 978-1-4503-2658-2/14/03.
http://dx.doi.org/10.1145/2559636.2559793

2.3 Design and procedure

Before the start of the experiment participants filled in an informed consent form (the study was approved by the local ethics committee). The participant watched the nine movement patterns (each a combination of a level of acceleration and curvature). The patterns were quasi-randomized (5 different orders) over participants, and after each pattern participants were asked to write down what their response was to what they had just seen. It was stressed that they were completely free in writing down what they found relevant. Subsequently, the nine patterns were shown again, each time followed by the PANAS.

3. RESULTS

3.1 Emotional questionnaire

The absolute averages on the PA (23.7, standard deviation (sd) = 1.6) and NA (16.9, sd = 1.0) for our Lego robot and those for the Roomba [5] (PA = 23.0, sd = 1.5; NA 17.1, sd = 1.2)) were strikingly similar. In addition, the repeated measures ANOVA with curvature (low, medium, high) and acceleration (low, medium, high) revealed similar main and interaction effects. As in [5] by far the strongest effect on the PANAS was the main effect of acceleration for PA ($F(2, 54) = 14.4$, $p < .001$, $\eta^2 = .35$), indicating increasing positive affect with increasing acceleration.

3.2 Open questions

The qualitative data was analyzed with constant comparison analysis and classical content analysis [3], resulting in 299 coded utterances. These were categorized into six categories: Description of motion (63% of the utterances), Anthropomorphic (27%), Emotional terms (3%), Irrelevant/ question (3%), Mechanical (2%), Comparison to other vehicles (1%). Importantly, only a very small number of utterances (3%) contained emotional attributes similar to the ones that are used in questionnaires such as the PANAS. Mostly, people simply described the motion (i.e. "the robot is accelerating faster than the previous time"). The answers to the open questions in our study seem to suggest that the emotional dimensions in the PANAS questionnaire were not representative of what people actually associated with the movement changes.

4. DISCUSSION AND CONCLUSION

People attribute complex emotions and social behavior to moving objects, even when they are just simple geometrical shapes [1]. Therefore, it is tempting to take this association and assume that it is always valid to investigate the emotional attributions motion variations will evoke. Establishing how changes in robot motion (independent of embodiment) steer emotional attribution would have enormous benefits. However, here we show that strictly separating a neutral experimental phase (i.e. "What do people associate with robot motion?") from an emotional phase ("What emotion do people associate with robot motion?") calls into question the validity of only asking questions about the emotions people attribute to robot motion. We suggest that over these different robotic embodiments people are highly reliably mapping clearly visible differences in motion characteristics to the only other dimension that is available in the form of an emotional questionnaire.

It has long been known that respondents in closed question surveys can limit themselves with ease to the predefined response categories, even when these are incomplete [7]. For example, it has become known as the *attribute substitution* heuristic when people judge on irrelevant attributes when relevant information is not readily available to them [2]. Hence, in the case of [5] the possibility cannot be ruled out that participants responded to the closed questions in emotional terms because they were forced to. In the subsequent open questions they could have responded congruently, because of attribute substitution, or because they guessed what the researchers were after. Furthermore, *response anchoring* [4] could explain why the observed effects appeared so uniform, independent of the embodiment.

For drawing conclusions on the crucial question of spontaneous associations with robot motion, further research has to clarify whether movement patterns generally and primarily evoke spontaneous emotional associations, and how intense these associations are by absolute means. Implicit experimental techniques, such as the Stroop task can serve to non-reactively assess spontaneous associations [6]. Potential anchoring effects could be unrevealed by studying human reactions to two levels of robot acceleration in a narrow range (acceleration range is not much wider than the two levels) or wide range (acceleration range is much greater than the two levels, see [4]). Finally, psychophysiological measures (e.g. electrodermal activity) could provide absolute measures of arousal.

5. REFERENCES

[1] Heider, F. and Simmel, M. An Experimental Study of Apparent Behavior. *The Am. J. of Psy. 57*, 2 (1944), 243–259. DOI= http://dx.doi.org/10.2307/1416950.

[2] Kahneman, D. and Frederick, S. Representativeness revisited: Attribute substitution in intuitive judgment. In T. Gilovich, D. Griffin and D. Kahneman, eds., *Heuristics of Intuitive Judgment: Extensions and Applications*. Cambridge University Press, New York, 2002.

[3] Leech, N.L. and Onwuegbuzie, A.J. An array of qualitative data analysis tools: A call for data analysis triangulation. *School Psy. Q. 22*, 4 (2007), 557–584. DOI= http://dx.doi.org/10.1037/1045-3830.22.4.557.

[4] Lynch, J.G., Chakravarti, D., and Mitra, A. Contrast Effects in Consumer Judgments□: Changes in Mental Representations or in the Anchoring of Rating Scales? *J. of Cons. Res., 18*, 3 (2013), 284–297.

[5] Saerbeck, M. and Bartneck, C. Perception of affect elicited by robot motion. *Proceeding of the 5th ACM/IEEE international conference on Human-robot interaction-HRI '10*, ACM Press (2010), 53–60. DOI= http://dx.doi.org/10.1109/HRI.2010.5453269.

[6] Schmettow, M., Noordzij, M.L., and Mundt, M. An implicit test of UX: Individuals Differ in What They Associate with Computers. *CHI '13 Extended Abstracts on Human Factors in Computing Systems on – CHI EA '13*, ACM Press (2013), 2039–2048. DOI= http://dx.doi.org/10.1145/2468356.2468722.

[7] Schuman, H. and Presser, S. The Open and Closed Question. *Am. Socio. Rev., 44*, 5 (1979), 692–712. DOI= http://dx.doi.org/10.2307/2094521.

[8] Watson, D., Clark, L. and Tellegen, A. Development and validation of brief measures of positive and negative affect: the PANAS scales. *J. of Pers. and Soc. Psy. 54*, 6 (1988), 1063–70. DOI= http://dx.doi.org/10.1037/00223514.54.6.1063.

Empathy and Yawn Contagion: Can we (Humans) Catch Yawns from Robots?

Mohammad Obaid[1], Dieta Kuchenbrandt[2], Christoph Bartneck[1]
[1]HITLabNZ, University of Canterbury, New Zealand
[2]CITEC, University of Bielefeld, Germany
{mohammad.obaid, christoph.bartneck}@hitlabnz.org
dkuchenb@cit-ec.Uni-Bielefeld.de

ABSTRACT

Empathy plays an important role in the interaction between humans and robots. The contagious effect of yawning is moderated by the degree of social closeness and empathy. We propose to analyse the contagion of yawns as an indicator for empathy. We conducted pilot studies to test different experimental procedures for this purpose. We hope to be able to report on experimental results in the near future.

Categories and Subject Descriptors

H.1.2 [**Models and Principles**]: User/Machine Systems—*human factors*; J.4 [**Social and Behavioral Sciences**]: Psychology

Keywords

Robot, Humanoid, Yawn, Empathy

1. INTRODUCTION

One of the recent research trends in the HRI field is towards investigating empathy between humans and social robots, in particular, measuring how we react towards robots emotionally and our empathic response towards robots such as the work by Leite et al. [4] and Puetten et al. [6]. Empathy is a psychological state that constitutes a prerequisite for successful social interactions. Consequently, evoking empathy in humans for their robotic counterparts could be an important means in facilitating human-robot interactions.

Empathy can be understood as sharing someone's emotional reactions. More specifically, Davis [1] defines empathy as (adopted from [7]) "the capacity to take the role of the other, to adopt alternative perspectives vis a vis oneself and to understand the other's emotional reactions in consort with the context to the point of executing bodily movements resembling the other's". This conceptualization stresses that empathy is an internal psychological state; consequently, measuring empathy can be challenging. However, as empathy can involve body movements resembling the other's movements, imitative body behaviour could be used as an indicator of empathy. Interestingly, in the human-human behaviour literature, yawning is a process that often provokes such imitative behaviour; that is, yawning is socially contagious. Moreover, it relates to social bonding and signs of empathy [5]. To illustrate, Norscia and Pallagi [5] demonstrated that emotional closeness (one important indicator of empathy) moderates yawning contagion, with increasing closeness resulting in greater contagion effects. In other words, the degree of yawning contagion can be regarded as indirect evidence for empathy with one's counterpart. The work on empathy and yawning contagion in human-human interactions inspired our present work in a human-robot context. We aim to investigate how contagious a robot's yawn can be on a human user and thereby to demonstrate that robots can provoke empathic reactions in humans.

In this paper, we propose an experimental study in which humans observe a robot for several minutes. This robot either shows physical behaviour that emulates a typical human yawn or it just performs random movements. Moreover, we measure whether (and how often) the human user yawns as a consequence of the robot yawn.

2. EXPERIMENT

2.1 Method

We implemented yawning behaviours in a humanoid robot to allow us to investigate the contagious effect upon humans through an experimental study. The following sections describe the details of the experimental design and set-up.

2.1.1 *Experimental Set-Up and Design*

In this work, we implemented the yawning motion and sound using the built-in motion module of the Nao system by Aldebaran Robotics[1]. We programmed the robot to simulate a yawning gesture with and without a yawning sound. Participants are randomly allocated to one of four experimental conditions resulting from a 2 (yawning gesture: present vs. not present) by 2 (yawning sound: present vs. not present) between-subjects design. That is, participants observed the robot NAO that either (1) yawns with gesture and sound, or (2) yawns with gesture and no sound, or (3) yawns without a gesture but with sound, or (4) does not perform a yawn gesture or sound.

[1]http://www.aldebaran-robotics.com/en/

HRI'14, March 3–6, 2014, Bielefeld, Germany.
ACM 978-1-4503-2658-2/14/03.
http://dx.doi.org/10.1145/2559636.2563702.

2.1.2 Pilot study

In order to select a yawning motion that can be correctly identified by the users, we conducted a pilot study at the University of Bielefeld. Participants watched nine short video clips (10 seconds each). In these video clips, NAO performed one specific movement (e.g., waving, wiping, nodding). Six videos were fillers, whereas in the three remaining videos, NAO performed a gesture that was intended to be a yawning gesture. For each video, participants were provided with a list that contained 10 different movement descriptions (e.g., the robot scratches itself, is wiping its head, is yawning). Participants' task was to decide which movement the robot was performing in the respective video and to choose the correct movement from the list. We measured how many participants identified the three yawning gestures correctly as a yawn. $N = 111$ participants (62 male, 48 female, one did not indicate gender) with a mean age of $M = 24.24$ years ($SD = 4.68$) completed the study. One yawning gesture (Gesture 1) was correctly identified as a yawn by $N = 97$ participants (87.4 percent), while the other two yawning gestures (Gesture 2 and Gesture 3) resulted in significantly lower recognition rates (78.4 percent and 37.8 percent). Consequently, Gesture 1 was chosen for the main experiment.

2.1.3 Apparatus and Procedure

The study was arranged in an empty experimental room with a space of 4 meters wide and 6.5 meters deep. It was equipped with one robot, a computer with a 22 inch monitor, a chair and one camera that recorded each participant throughout the session. The Nao robot used from Adebaran Robotics has a height of 58cm. It did not provide any spoken commands throughout the course of the study, while the LED lights indicated that it was running.

At the start of the study, the experimenter asked the participant to turn their electronic equipment off to prevent distractions. The experiment was then explained to the participant informing them that it would take approximately 10 minutes and that he/she would watch a short movie together with the robot NAO. The participant was then asked to read and sign a consent form to take part in the study. If agreed, the participant was asked to sit at a comfortable distance away from the monitor, while the robot was placed adjacent to the participant's seat. The task for each participant was to watch a short movie (10 minutes) with the robot, while the robot had one of the four conditions. The video was a clip of the Empire State Building filmed by Andy Warhol, which contained slow motion footage of the building only and did not provide any entertainment material. Subsequently, a questionnaire containing further dependent variables was handed out to the participant to be filled. The participant was video recorded in order to analyse his/her yawning behaviour during the course of the study.

2.1.4 Dependent Variables

In the study, we used both observational data and self-report measures. In order to test whether participants contingently yawn as a result of the robot's yawn, we analysed the yawn occurrences and times (including frequency and latency) from the recorded videos. With the self-report measures, the following dimensions were assessed: Psychological closeness [2], HRI acceptance [3], and the general tendency to anthropomorphize non-humans (IDAQ [8]). Finally, variables related to tiredness (level of perceived psychological stress, coffee or tea consuming etc.) and demographic variables were assessed.

3. FUTURE WORK

To investigate empathic response towards social humanoid robots, we proposed a study to investigate empathic response towards humanoid robots using the contagious behaviour of yawning. We have started collecting data from participants and our first impressions of the initial screening of videos are promising.

In future work, contagious behaviours such as laughing and mimicry will be investigated as well. In addition, we will further investigate which effects empathy have on human-robot interactions and which factors influence the degree of empathy humans can have towards robots (e.g. social group membership of the user and the robot; see Kuchenbrandt et al. [3]). Findings from this research will help scientists and developers in the field of robotics to facilitate smooth and natural social interactions between humans and robots.

4. ACKNOWLEDGMENTS

The authors would like to thank Eduardo Sandoval and Anthony Poncet for their support in the experimental setup.

5. REFERENCES

[1] M. H. Davis. Measuring individual differences in empathy: Evidence for a multidimensional approach. *Journal of personality and social psychology*, 44(1):113–126, 1983.

[2] M. Häring, D. Kuchenbrandt, and E. André. Would you like to play with me? How robots' group membership and task features influence human-robot interaction. In *(Accepted) Proceedings of the 9th HRI International Conference on Human-Robot Interaction (HRI 2014)*, 2014.

[3] D. Kuchenbrandt, F. Eyssel, S. Bobinger, and M. Neufeld. When a robot's group membership matters. *International Journal of Social Robotics*, 5(3):409–417, 2013.

[4] I. Leite, A. Pereira, G. Castellano, S. Mascarenhas, C. Martinho, and A. Paiva. Modelling empathy in social robotic companions. In *Proceedings of the 19th International Conference on Advances in User Modeling*, UMAP'11, pages 135–147, Berlin, Heidelberg, 2012. Springer-Verlag.

[5] I. Norscia and E. Palagi. Yawn contagion and empathy in homo sapiens. *PLoS ONE*, 6(12):e28472, 12 2011.

[6] A. Rosenthal-von der Puetten, N. Kraemer, L. Hoffmann, S. Sobieraj, and S. C. Eimler. An experimental study on emotional reactions towards a robot. *International Journal of Social Robotics*, 5(1):17–34, 2013.

[7] A. Tapus and M. Mataric. Emulating empathy in socially assistive robotics. In *Proceedings of the AAAI Spring Symposium on Multidisciplinary Collaboration for Socially Assistive Robotics*, Palo Alto, Stanford, U.S.A., march 2007.

[8] A. Waytz, J. Cacioppo, and N. Epley. Who sees human? The stability and importance of individual differences in anthropomorphism. *Perspectives on Psychological Science*, 5(3):219–232, 2010.

Modeling and Analysis of Task Complexity in Single-Operator Multi-Robot Teams

A. Tuna Özgelen
The Graduate Center,
City University of New York
New York, NY, USA
aozgelen@gc.cuny.edu

Elizabeth I. Sklar
Dept of Computer Science
University of Liverpool
Liverpool, UK
e.i.sklar@liverpool.ac.uk

ABSTRACT

A model is presented for analyzing the complexity of task assignment in a human/multi-robot team from the perspective of the human team member, or "operator". The focus is on complex domains where tasks have inter-dependencies and/or require tightly coupled coordination among robots. Preliminary validation of model metrics has been carried out through an experiment involving human subjects. Results suggest significant effect of key aspects of the model on human subjects' cognitive workload.

Categories and Subject Descriptors

I.2.9 [**Robotics**]: Miscellaneous; H.1.2 [**Models and Principles**]: User/Machine Systems—*Human factors*

Keywords

human multi-robot interaction; supervisory control; complex tasks; metrics; evaluation

1. INTRODUCTION

This paper introduces a model that aims to represent, from the perspective of a human "operator", task assignment problems in *Single Operator Multi-Robot (SOMR)* domains. For SOMR settings where higher levels of robot autonomy are practical, *tactical supervision* is an important factor for increasing the number of robots that human operators can control simultaneously [1]. The model presented here is based on the *Single-Robot vs. Multi-Robot (SR,MR)* dimension of the robot-centric task taxonomy defined in [2], and the *Independent vs. Constrained (IT,CT)* dimension defined in [3]. Our contribution is to investigate task/resource allocation problems from the human's perspective. The results could be used for identifying weaknesses in task assignments, for characterizing behavioral patterns of human operators, and/or for improving the language of interaction between human operators and automated task planning systems.

HRI'14, March 3–6, 2014, Bielefeld, Germany.
ACM 978-1-4503-2658-2/14/03.
http://dx.doi.org/10.1145/2559636.2559843.

We restrict our investigation to structured environments where tasks may require tightly coupled coordination among several robots and may have dependencies on one another as a result of constraints imposed by spatial characteristics of the environment. Such constraints may be the direct result of uncompleted tasks blocking access to certain areas, as is the case with the experimental scenarios described in Section 3. Our approach is empirical and introduces a graph-based model that captures key aspects of the problem space. We define evaluation metrics derived from this model and present the results of an experiment with human subjects.

2. MODEL

Our graph-based model, which we refer to as a *Task Assignment Graph (TAG)*, builds on a topological representation of the robots' environment. A TAG captures spatial relationships between tasks and robots. In an environment containing m robots, $R = \{r_1, ..., r_m\}$, and n tasks, $T = \{t_1, ..., t_n\}$, we define $TAG = (V, E)$ as a set of vertices $V = \{v_1, ..., v_n\}$, where each v_i represents a task, $t_i \in T$, and a set of edges E. There exists an edge in E between any two task vertices v_i and v_j *iff* tasks t_i and t_j are accessible from one another in the geographic map. Each task vertex v_i contains a set of robots, Acc_i, that can access task t_i and a domain, Dom_i, which consists of the sets of all possible assignments for that task. The cardinality of each set in Dom_i is defined by the number of robots, req_i, required to execute task t_i. The value of Acc_i changes dynamically as tasks are completed.

Vertices in a TAG are labeled *critical* if at least one of the following conditions is satisfied: (i) removing v_i from the TAG results in multiple disconnected components; (ii) task t_i, together with other tasks, is jointly responsible for robots reaching at least one other task in T; or (iii) task t_i belongs to a group of tasks which prevent a robot *cluster* (group of robots co-located in the same part of the map that can access the same set of tasks) from reaching some subset of T. An example of a TAG can be seen in Figure 1(a)-(b).

Based on the TAG, we define two metrics to categorize instances of task assignment situations. To represent the SR-MR dimension of the taxonomy, we define the *Average Platform Requirement*: $APR = \sum_{i=1}^{|T|} req_i/|T|$ where $|T|$ is the total number of tasks to be assigned. To represent the IT-CT dimension, we define the *Critical Task Ratio*: $CTR = |V_{critical}|/|T|$ where $|V_{critical}|$ is the total number of critical tasks in the scenario.

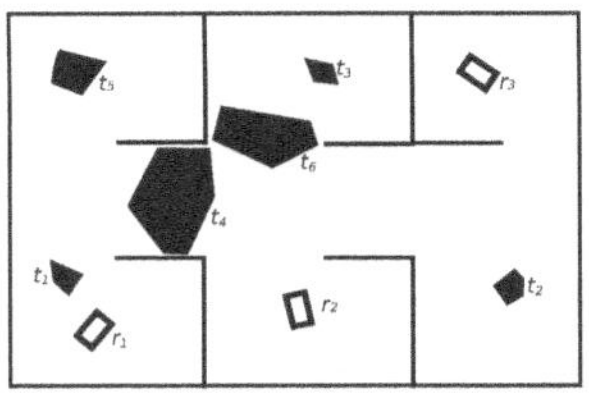

(a) Depiction of a typical scenario

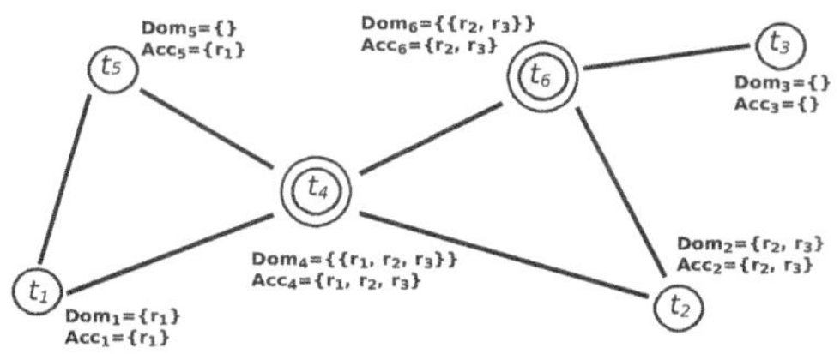

(b) TAG for the scenario on the left; double circles represent critical tasks (t_4 and t_6)

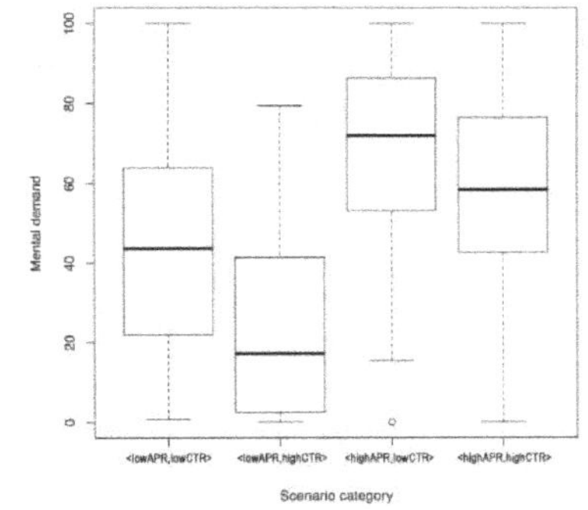

(c) Experimental results: Mental Demand vs $< APR, CTR >$

Figure 1: Example scenario and TAG model; and experimental results.

3. EXPERIMENT

We conducted an experiment with human subjects to validate the use of APR and CTR as a means to distinguish between task assignment problem instances. Twenty-seven experimental scenarios were defined, with values: $APR \in \{1.0, 1.5, 1.667\}$ and $CTR \in \{0.0, 0.333, 0.5\}$. The table below lists the number of experimental scenarios within each of four categories, where *low* $APR = 1.0$, *high* $APR > 1.0$, *low* $CTR = 0.0$, and *high* $CTR > 0.0$:

	low CTR	*high CTR*
low APR	6	6
high APR	6	9

Our hypothesis is that mental demand for human operators aligns with $< APR, CTR >$ categories.

We ran an experiment to confirm our hypothesis. Fourteen human subjects participated, ranging in age from 19–50 years old and computer experience ranging from 3 to over 15 years. The *Task Complexity Assessment Tool (TCAT)* [5] was used to present the 27 scenarios to the participants. They were asked to assign a homogeneous team of robots to tasks such that the overall execution time of the tasks would be minimized if the robots executed these tasks. After completing a task assignment for each scenario, participants indicated their perceived *mental demand* for that assignment, using a format based on the NASA-TLX [4] instrument. The experiment followed within-subject design, where all participants saw the same set of scenarios in randomized order.

For statistical analysis, a two-way repeated measures analysis of variance (ANOVA) test was used with the independent variables APR (*low*, *high*) and CTR (*low*, *high*). The conditions of normality and homogeneity ($\alpha < 0.05$) were met. The effects of both independent variables were found to be statistically significant on mental demand: for APR, $F(1, 13) = 110.8$ and $p < 0.001$; for CTR, $F(1, 13) = 115.8$ and $p < 0.001$. A plot showing mental demand distributions for each scenario category can be seen in Figure 1(c). There is a strong correlation ($r(12) = 0.51$, $p < 0.001$) between mental demand and APR. This can be seen in the figure, where $<$ *high* APR, *low* $CTR >$ and $<$ *high* APR, *high* $CTR >$ have higher means than $<$ *low* APR, *low* $CTR >$ and $<$ *low* APR, *high* $CTR >$. There is a negative correlation ($r(12) = -0.21$, $p < 0.001$) between mental demand and CTR, which a surprising result since it was expected that critical tasks would require more mental effort. As indicated during post-experiment interview sessions with human subjects, this effect may be due to participants' tendencies to reduce the task assignment search space by giving higher priority to critical tasks, which led to fewer alternative solutions to consider for the remaining tasks.

4. SUMMARY

In this work, we introduced the graph-based model, TAG, for representing task assignment complexity in multi-robot settings, based on spatial constraints. This model was assessed through an experiment with human subjects, which suggests that key aspects of the model (APR and CTR) have a significant effect on the subjective mental demand metric. Future work includes extending the model to consider the spatial distribution of robots in their environment.

Acknowledgments

This work was partially supported by a grant from the National Science Foundation (#IIS-1116843).

5. REFERENCES

[1] A. Carlin, J. Ayers, J. Rousseau, and N. Schurr. Agent-Based Coordination of Human-Multirobot Teams in Complex Environments. In *Autonomous Agents and Multiagent Systems (AAMAS)*, 2010.

[2] B. P. Gerkey and M. J. Matarić. A Formal Analysis and Taxonomy of Task Allocation in Multi-Robot Systems. *The International Journal of Robotics Research*, 23(9):939–954, September 2004.

[3] D. Landén, F. Heintz, and P. Doherty. Complex Task Allocation in Mixed-Initiative Delegation: A UAV Case Study (Early Innovation). In *Principles and Practice of Multi-Agent Systems Lecture Notes in Computer Science*, volume 7057/2012, pages 288–303, 2010.

[4] NASA Task Load Index (TLX). NASA Ames Research Center, Moffet field, California, v.1.0.

[5] A. T. Özgelen and E. Sklar. A Task Complexity Assessment Tool for Single-Operator Multi-Robot Control Scenarios (Demonstration). In *Autonomous Agents and Multiagent Systems (AAMAS)*, 2013.

Encoding Bi-manual Coordination Patterns From Human Demonstrations

Ana Lucia Pais
Learning Systems and Algorithms Laboratory
École Polytechnique Fédérale de Lausanne
CH-1015 Lausanne, Switzerland
{lucia.pais}@epfl.ch

Aude Billard
Learning Systems and Algorithms Laboratory
École Polytechnique Fédérale de Lausanne
CH-1015 Lausanne, Switzerland
{aude.billard}@epfl.ch

ABSTRACT

Humans perform tasks such as bowl mixing bi–manually, but programming them on a robot can be challenging specially in tasks that require force control or on-line stiffness modulation. In this paper we first propose a user-friendly setup for demonstrating bi-manual tasks, while collecting complementary information on motion and forces sensed on a robotic arm, as well as the human hand configuration and grasp information. Secondly for learning the task we propose a method for extracting task constraints for each arm and coordination patterns between the arms. We use a statistical encoding of the data based on the extracted constraints and reproduce the task using a cartesian impedance controller.

Categories and Subject Descriptors

I.2.9 [**Robotics**]; I.2.6 [**Learning**]: Knowledge acquisition; H.5.2 [**User Interfaces**]: Interaction styles

General Terms

Robot Learning

Keywords

Programming by demonstration; Task constraints extraction

1. INTRODUCTION

Daily activities, such as dish washing or preparing a meal, require completing tasks that are implicitly bi-manual. A challenge in programming such tasks is accounting for all the task variables, for the motion of each arm, as well as for their coordinated behavior. Here we take a Programming by Demonstration (PbD) approach in which a human can directly demonstrate the task, and propose a method for determining and encoding bi-manual coordination patterns.

We exemplify this on a task (stirring in a bowl, as shown in Fig. 1) that requires completing a sequence of actions

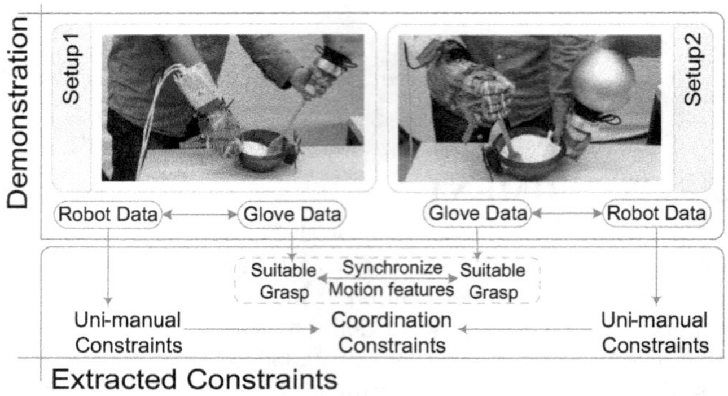

Figure 1: The two setups used in the demonstration phase. We alternate between the active/passive arms in the tasks, and record complementary information from the glove and robot arm.

for each arm. According to a taxonomy of bi-manual actions proposed in [6], the task subparts can be described as: (1) a discrete reaching motion from the initial position of each arm to the proper configuration to start mixing; (2) an asymmetrical coordinated motion, in which one arm is actively stirring while the other is passively assisting; (c) an uncoordinated reaching back action. The stirring action requires coordination not only in arm movement, but also with respect to the force and stiffness applied by each arm.

To be able to record the interaction forces perceived on each hand in coordination and in conjunction with measurements of the arm and finger displacement, we developed an experimental setup displayed in Fig. 1 (see Section 3 for a description). We analyze the demonstration data and extract (1) continuous constraints for each arm, consisting of the variables of interest in each part of the task, expressed in the local frame of reference of the object on which we perform manipulation and a stiffness modulating factor; (2) coordination patterns between the variables of interest in each part of the motion. We represent the motion using a time independent statistical encoding which allows using the extracted features as continuous task constraints that can be embedded online in the robot's motion. For reproducing the task on a bi–manual robotic platform we use a cartesian impedance controller for each arm, parameterized with the extracted constraints.

2. RELATED WORK

In our previous work [1], we proposed a method for encoding arm–motion in discrete bi–manual tasks based on determining key postures during the demonstration. However

HRI'14, March 3–6, 2014, Bielefeld, Germany.
ACM 978-1-4503-2658-2/14/03.
http://dx.doi.org/10.1145/2559636.2559844.

in the present work we focus on tasks that require coordinated force control. We determine continuous constraints that apply throughout the task or in parts of the task.

For each arm we extract task constraints using the method prosed in [7], based on analyzing the variance in the data. We extend this approach to determine arm dominance (i.e the relative importance of each arm). We further encode the whole task as a sequence of states describing each action. Alternative representations are graph-based [2], or Markov-model based [5].

3. METHOD

To execute the task on a robotic platform we consider a cartesian impedance controller for each arm, given by $\tau = J^T \cdot RF \cdot (\lambda K(x - x_d) + F)$. The desired position $x_d \in \mathbb{R}^3$, the force to be applied $F \in \mathbb{R}^3$, and a factor $\lambda \in \mathbb{R}^3$ that modulates the arm's stiffness K, are extracted from demonstration (as explained below) and are expressed in the local reference frame of the object of interest RF.

To demonstrate the task we designed the setup shown in Fig. 1, in which the user can perform the task by kinesthetically guiding the robotic arm with one hand and by wearing a data glove on the other hand. This particular configuration has two main advantages: (1) it makes it easy for the user to provide demonstrations (i.e. rather than handling multiple degrees of freedom from two robot arms); (2) it allows simultaneously recording complementary information: end effector cartesian positions ($x_R \in \mathbb{R}^3$) and forces ($F_R \in \mathbb{R}^3$), from a KUKA LWR arm; hand configuration ($\theta_G \in \mathbb{R}^{23}$ joint angles), and wrist position ($x_G \in \mathbb{R}^3$) from the data glove. Additionally we recorded the object's cartesian position ($x_o \in \mathbb{R}^3$) using an Optitrack vision system.

The user performed the task in two phases, by alternating the roles of the active and passive hands. This allowed us to record both robot data and glove data for both the active and the passive arm. We recorded N = 6 demonstrations in each phase. We aligned the recorded data using Dynamic Time Warping (DTW). The final data set for phase 1 is $\xi^1 = \{x_R^A, F_R^A, x_G^P, \theta_G^P, x_o\}$, where the upper indices refer to the hand performing an active (A) or passive (P) task. Similarly a data set ξ^2 is obtained in the second phase.

Uni-manual constraints.

To extract the constraints of each arm, we consider for each phase $i = 1..2$, a subset $\xi_R^i = \{x_R, F_R\}$ of ξ^i. The glove wrist position x_G is used for aligning the robot motion in the two phases. We analyze the robot data in the reference frame of the object (i.e. the bowl), as described in [7]. For each recorded variable (position and force), across each dimension, we compute a criterion based on the observed variance in the data [7]. This allows us to compare in a relative manner variables of different types. We consider at each time step the variable of interest to be the one with the maximum computed criterion. When this changes a segmentation point is created, resulting in a set of states ψ_s. For the current task representation see Fig. 2. The arm motion in each segment is encoded as a non-linear dynamical system [4]. The force components are encoded in a Gaussian Mixture Model (GMM) as a function of position. We compute a stiffness modulation factor λ as the difference between the criterion computed for position and the one computed for force on each axis. Additionally for each state we determine a corresponding hand configuration $\theta_{G,s}$.

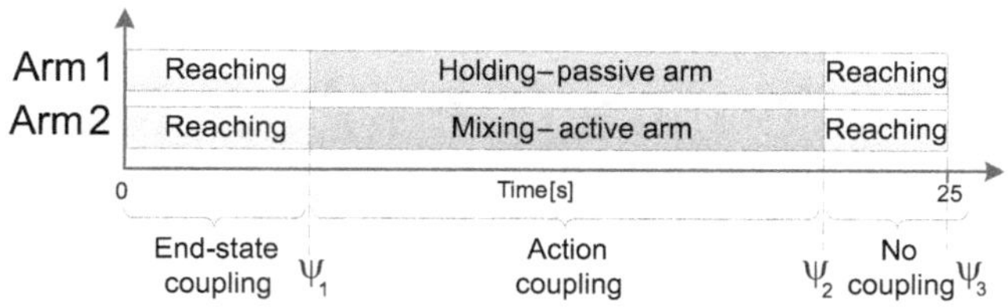

Figure 2: The identified motion segments for each arm, and corresponding coupling.

Bi-manual coordination.

Comparing the obtained criteria between the two arms allows us to determine at each time step which arm is dominating in either position or force applied in the task. This is similar to results on human subjects showing that the arms can change the active and passive roles during manipulation and this is caused by a force-motion relation, rather than prior knowledge or routine in executing the task [3].

Hand dominance thus influences the way we model the task subparts. For the active arm we encode the motion and force profile as described above. However for the passive arm the motion is insignificant, while the forces sensed on the arm are reaction forces responsible for keeping the object in place. Therefore we choose to encode using a GMM model its force $p(F_R^P, F_R^A)$, and stiffness profiles $p(K_R^P, F_R^A)$ as dependent on the forces sensed on the active arm. This allows the passive arm to apply compensating forces to the ones applied by the active arm.

4. CONCLUSION AND FUTURE WORK

We presented a procedure for recording bi-manual demonstrations that reduces user's effort and maximizes the obtained information. We analyze the data to extract constraints for each arm and encode coordination patterns.

Future work involves determining a two levels encoding of the task: (1) *skill level* as general knowledge about the action, and (2) *task level*, as a parametrization of the learned skill. This enables policy reusability for similar tasks, such as stirring in a bowl of dough, and applying the same skill for stirring coffee.

5. ACKNOWLEDGMENTS

The research leading to these results has received funding from the European Union Seventh Framework Programme FP7/2007-2013 under grant agreement no 288533 ROBOHOW.COG.

6. REFERENCES

[1] E. Gribovskaya and A. Billard. Combining dynamical systems control and programming by demonstration for teaching discrete bimanual coordination tasks to a humanoid robot. In *HRI*, 2008.

[2] R. Jäkel, S. R. Schmidt-Rohr, M. Lösch, and R. Dillmann. Representation and constrained planning of manipulation strategies in the context of programming by demonstration. In *ICRA*, 2010.

[3] R. S. Johansson, A. Theorin, G. Westling, M. Andersson, Y. Ohki, and L. Nyberg. How a lateralized brain supports symmetrical bimanual tasks. *PLoS Biol*, 4(6):e158, 2006.

[4] S. M. Khansari-Zadeh and A. Billard. Learning Stable Non-Linear Dynamical Systems with Gaussian Mixture Models. *IEEE Transaction on Robotics*, 2011.

[5] S. H. Lee, H. K. Kim, and I. H. Suh. Incremental learning of primitive skills from demonstration of a task. In *HRI*, 2011.

[6] C. L. MacKenzie and R. G. Marteniuk. Bimanual coordination. volume 23 of *Advances in Psychology*, pages 345 – 358. 1985.

[7] A. L. Pais, K. Umezawa, Y. Nakamura, and A. Billard. Task parametrization using continuous constraints extracted from human demonstrations. *Submitted*, 2013.

"You are Green": a Touch-to-Name Interaction in an Integrated Multi-Modal Multi-Robot HRI System

Shokoofeh Pourmehr, Valiallah (Mani) Monajjemi, Seyed Abbas Sadat, Fei Zhan, Jens Wawerla, Greg Mori and Richard Vaughan
School of Computing Science, Simon Fraser University, Burnaby, BC, Canada
{spourmeh, mmonajje, sas21, fzhan, jwawerla, mori, vaughan}@sfu.ca

Figure 1: The touch-to-name interaction: The user first announces the desired number of robots with "You" or "You N" where N is the desired number of robots (left), then handles the intended robot(s) (middle); and finally assigns a name to the selected robot(s) that can subsequently be used to address this robot or team.

ABSTRACT

We present a multi-modal multi-robot interaction whereby a user can identify an individual or a group of robots using haptic stimuli, and name them using a voice command (e.g. *"You two are green"*). Subsequent commands can be addressed to the same robot(s) by name (e.g. *"Green! Take off!"*). We demonstrate this as part of a real-world integrated system in which a user commands teams of autonomous robots in a coordinated exploration task.

Categories and Subject Descriptors

I.2.9 [**Artificial Intelligence**]: Robotics, Human Multi-Robot Interaction, User Interfaces

1. THE TOUCH-TO-NAME INTERACTION

We have developed a new multi-modal interface for human multi-robot systems (HMRS) whereby a user can name individual or teams of autonomous robots from a cooperating population. In the *Touch-to-Name* interaction the user verbally announces the desired number of robots N in the form "You N", (e.g. *"You two"*). If $N = 1$, the number can optionally be omitted, as in Fig. 1 (left). The user then physically handles the desired set of robots one after the other (Fig. 1 (middle)). Once the robots are thus selected, the user names the individual or group with a second verbal announcement, of the form "You are <NAME>" (e.g. *"You are Green"* as in Fig. 1 (right)). Further verbal commands can be addressed to this individual or group using the name.

HRI'14, March 3–6, 2014, Bielefeld, Germany.
ACM 978-1-4503-2658-2/14/03.
http://dx.doi.org/10.1145/2559636.2559806 .

1.1 Implementation

In our demonstration system each robot is equipped with a 3-axis accelerometer, a voice recognition system and a wireless communication channel to compare sensor information with its peers. For simplicity we used a centralized voice recognition system and a bluetooth microphone worn by the user during our experiments. But our method will also work with audio processing onboard the robots.

To determine which robot is selected by the user, all robots wait for the keyword *"You"*. When it is detected, the robots communicate over the wireless channel to compare their accelerometer readings with each other. The one with the highest acceleration magnitude in a recent time window is considered the one being touched by the user. Fig. 2 shows the acceleration magnitude of two robots, robot 1 is the one gently moved by the user and robot 2 is untouched. This election mechanism avoids the use of a predefined acceleration threshold by assuming that the robot that is being touched by the user has the highest recent acceleration reading.

The robots indicate their current state to the user with bright coloured LEDs. We found that compared to vision-based selection methods ([4, 2, 3]), using accelerometer data is much faster and computationally less expensive. It requires the human operator to touch the robot platform, but this interaction is simple and straightforward to implement.

Using voice input gives the user the ability to control teams of robots hands-free. Draper et al. [1] showed that using voice commands can significantly improve an operator's ability to control teams of UAVs, compared to manual controls. While our demonstration shows the human handling each robot to provide the haptic input, the same effect can be achieved by pushing or kicking the robot, nudging a joystick that drives the robot, or moving an actuator that has sensor feedback.

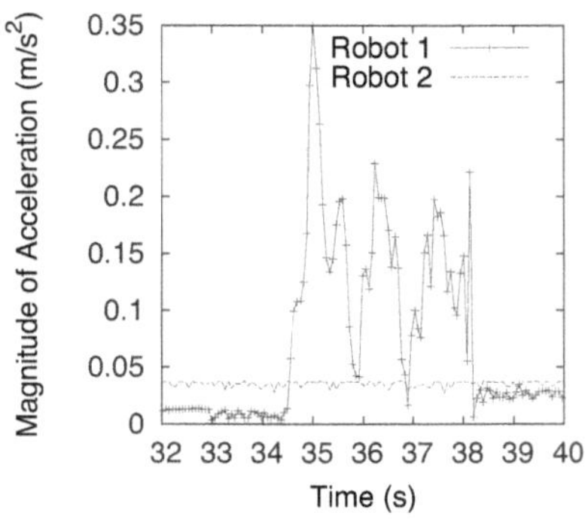

Figure 2: Accelerometer readings of two robots during the selection procedure. Robot 1 is selected and Robot 2 is untouched.

After the user has selected the desired robot or robots, she can assign a team name using a different voice command (i.e. *"You are Green"* to create a team, or *"Join Green"* or *"Leave Green"* to modify a team. The user can thus create a direct addressing scheme to previously anonymous robots, and can command a team of arbitrary size with a single subsequent command. The team manipulation interactions can happen at any time.

This multi-modal HMRS interface allows the user to walk freely among the robots. These interfaces are well suited for systems that require human's supervision for dynamic task allocation, team composition and team re-composition.

2. INTEGRATED MARTIAN HRI

We demonstrated a working system in the Mars Dome facility at the University of Toronto, a 50m diameter circular, covered arena simulating Martian terrain (Fig. 1). The task of each robot is to autonomously explore and map the world using visual SLAM from its onboard video camera. The robots used were two AR.Drone 2 UAVs, each controlled over WiFi by a laptop. Robots were autonomous at all times. All the user interactions could have been performed wearing a spacesuit, and the user had no instrumentation apart from an earpiece microphone.

In addition to our Touch-to-Name interaction, we added the verbal commands *"take off"*, *"come back"*, and *"land"*, which can be issued to any named robot or team, e.g *"Green! Take off."*. Robots would verbally confirm their state over a loudspeaker using a voice synthesizer. After take-off and while hovering, each robot looks for a human face in its camera feed. When a face is detected, the robot flies to face the user at a preset distance and angle. The user can move her body to position the robot as desired. When the robot is suitably positioned, the user tasks it to explore either to the left or right of the user by waving the left or right hand [3]. The system can be seen working in the video `http://youtu.be/SxeVZdJFB4s`.

Figure 3: Face detection and motion-based hand gestures are used to relocate and command the flying robot. [3]

Informally, we found that (i) all spoken commands were correctly recognized; (ii) the intended robot was always correctly identified; (ii) feedback from LEDs and synthetic voice was helpful to the user. Overall, we found the proposed concept worked well for this scenario, and we expect it to be widely applicable.

We have demonstrated that Touch-to-Name works as part of an integrated system to allow a single user to control a multi-robot system in a coordinated exploration mission in a semi-realistic setting.

3. REFERENCES

[1] M. Draper, G. Calhoun, H. Ruff, D. Williamson, and T. Barry. Manual versus speech input for unmanned aerial vehicle control station operations. In *Proc. of the Human Factors and Ergonomics Society Annual Meeting*, 2003.

[2] M. Lichtenstern, M. Frassl, B. Perun, and M. Angermann. A prototyping environment for interaction between a human and a robotic multi-agent system. In *Proc. of Int. Conf. on Human-Robot Interaction*, pages 185–186, 2012.

[3] V. M. Monajjemi, J. Wawerla, R. T. Vaughan, and G. Mori. HRI in the sky: Creating and commanding teams of UAVs with a vision-mediated gestural interface. In *Proc. of Int. Conf. on Intelligent Robots and Systems*, 2013.

[4] S. Pourmehr, V. M. Monajjemi, R. T. Vaughan, and G. Mori. You two! take off! creating, modifying and commanding groups of robots using face engagement and indirect speech in voice commands. In *Proc. of Int. Conf. on Intelligent Robots and Systems*, 2013.

Older Adults' Reactions to a Robot's Appearance in the Context of Home Use

Akanksha Prakash[1], Charles C. Kemp[2], & Wendy A. Rogers[1]

[1]School of Psychology,
Georgia Institute of Technology
654 Cherry St. Atlanta, GA 30332
aprakash30@gatech.edu

[2]Dept. of Biomedical Engineering
Georgia Institute of Technology
Atlanta, GA
charlie.kemp@bme.gatech.edu

ABSTRACT

Robots are being designed to assist older adults in their homes. However, we lack a clear understanding of the aspects of robot appearance older adults pay attention to and consider important for accepting a robot in their homes. The goal of this study was to systematically assess older adults' reactions to a specific robot's appearance in the context of home use. Independent living older adults interacted with the PR2 and were interviewed about its appearance. In general, there was expectation for a small sized robot that fits with the home and is easy to control. There was variability for desired human-likeness, although some human-like characteristics might be acceptable to most.

1. INTRODUCTION

People tend to form quick first impressions of unknown or less-known others [1]. Prior experiences, pre-existing beliefs and expectations influence first impressions. Expectations may or may not have a rational basis but they direct people's attention toward certain information and affect interpretation of specific cues (gender, race, clothing, attractiveness, etc.). People's impressions of robots might be governed by similar socio-cognitive processes. Even though older adults have less experience with robots, they have expectations and opinions about robot appearance [2]. Such expectations may influence people's initial impressions and their behavioral reactions toward a robot.

The home setting is increasingly being considered as a large market for service robot applications. It would be beneficial to understand how appearance based perceptions influence people's willingness to be assisted by a robot. The current study elicited older adults' opinions about appearance for a specific robot (PR2) in the context of home use. We obtained in depth opinions about the appearance of this specific robot to identify the categories of considerations that are important to older adults.

2. METHOD

2.1 Participants

Participants were 12 independent living older adults (6 females) aged 68-79 years (M=72.58; SD=3.87) from Atlanta, GA, USA.

HRI'13, March 3–6, 2014, Bielefeld, Germany.
ACM 978-1-4503-2658-2/14/03.
http://dx.doi.org/10.1145/2559636.2559790

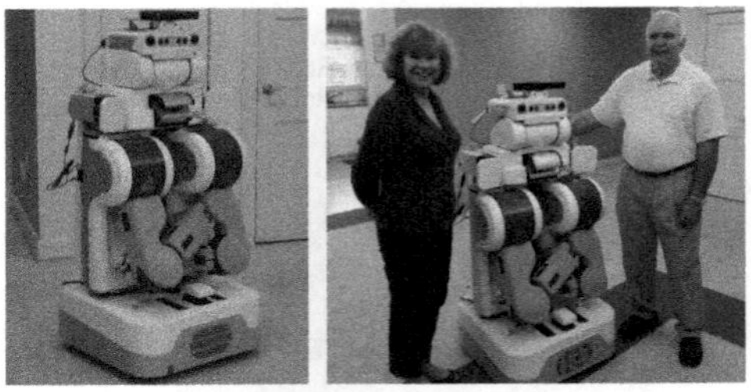

Figure 1. PR2; PR2 with older adults at the Aware Home

2.2 Materials

We used Willow Garage's Personal Robot 2 (PR2; Figure 1) to gauge participants' first impressions of a robot. PR2 is a human-sized mobile manipulator with an omni-directional wheeled base and a telescoping spine. It weighs about 450 pounds (220 kgs).

2.3 Procedure

Individual structured interviews were conducted at Georgia Tech's Aware Home Research facility, a home-like laboratory that serves as a platform for testing home-based technologies in an authentic environment. Prior to introducing the PR2 to the participants, we assessed their pre-existent expectations for the appearance of a home-based robot. The interviewer asked, "if there was a robot in your home, what would you want it to look to like?" Next, the PR2 entered the living room where participants were seated. At this point, they were encouraged to focus on the robot's appearance without concentrating on its capabilities. They were then interviewed about their first impressions, including what they specifically liked and disliked about the appearance.

During the next two hours, the capabilities of the PR2 were demonstrated through three different tasks, medication delivery, clearing clutter, and turning on a light switch. Interview questions followed each task demonstration. At the end of the study, participants were asked to revisit their opinions about the PR2's appearance and discuss if their opinions had changed and how. Finally, we assessed participants' views regarding the importance of the robot's appearance.

3. RESULTS

3.1 Expectations for Robot Appearance

The interviews were analyzed independently by two researchers to ensure consistency in interpretations. We present here a brief summary of the themes identified. Participants often used human appearance as a comparison point to describe how they imagined the appearance of their robots. Expectations ranged from desiring a robot that is "*kinda similar to a human*" to "*certainly not human, ...probably like my cell phone*". Half the participants stated they wanted their robot to look like a human or have human characteristics (e.g., human-like head, arms, legs, facial features, movement). Participants favoring human-like appearance expected such robots to evoke feelings of familiarity, comfort, companionship, and ease of interaction. Only one participant specifically did not want the robot to look like a human but like a machine (e.g. a cell-phone) for easy maneuverability around furniture and less bulkiness. Other participants did not express strong preferences for or against human-like appearance. However, there was an overall expectation for smaller sized (*"It would be...smaller than me"*, *"not bigger than me"*), non-scary robots that fit well with the home (*"so it feels like part of the home"*; *"so it's not imposing"*), and are easy to control.

3.2 Reactions to PR2's Appearance

The two features that were particularly liked by some participants were the robot's human-like appearance and its maneuverability (Table 1). Some participants considered it too big for their homes although one participant considered the size to be "optimal". Some older adults also had concerns about their ability to control a large and heavy robot. Moreover, some reasoned that the robot was not a good fit for their homes due its "cold" appearance.

Table 1. First Impressions about PR2's Appearance

Liked	Example Quotations
Human-like Appearance (3/12)	*"I wanted it to kind of have human characteristics, and this is very much the torso of a human with arms, shoulders, a head, what looks like a mouth. The legs are basically the wheels."*
Maneuverability (3/12)	*"...four wheel steering, so that means it obviously makes it quite maneuverable turning in some space and not necessarily going 90 degree corners, but moving as it needs to and even in an arc."*
Disliked	**Example Quotation**
Size and Weight (4/12)	*"...It's too big for my home". "As being part of massive, it looks quite heavy. I would hate to have it, for whatever reason, tip over because I don't think I would be able to set it up right again"*
Rotating Part (Laser Scanner) (3/12)	*"The moving part in the front looks like a mouth and I just wonder why that moves continually. I'd just like for it to be still like the rest of it."*
Mechanical/Cold Appearance (2/12)	*"It doesn't look warm or inviting or engaging." "...kinda cold looking and looks like a piece of machinery."*

*Numbers in parentheses indicate proportion of participants.

Table 2. Importance of Appearance (Assessed after Exposure)

Response	Example Quotations
Important (5/12)	*"The appearance is important to me because of - it - it - more in the size because I have a small apartment."* *"The more humanoid you can make it look in appearance I think would for me facilitate the ease of accepting it"*
Somewhat Important (5/12)	*"In the beginning it would be a lot. I mean, you know, I think 90% of the people that see that robot when they walk in the door say I ain't having that thing in my house, but as you see what it does, you learn to love it."* *"I would not necessarily want it to be in a humanoid shape. Some people might, but not me."* *"I would like for the mouth to be still. I would not like for the mouth to be moving. The eyes are fine."*
Not Important (2/12)	*"The appearance is really not the - the factor. It's the robot's ability to help."*

*Numbers in parentheses indicate proportion of participants.

3.3 Opinions after Task Demonstrations

When expressing their first reactions to the PR2's appearance, a few participants had pointed out that their present lack of familiarity could possibly change over time (e.g., *"It will grow on you..."*; *"I would certainly have to get used to having it in my room..."*). We wanted to specifically assess if participants' opinions of the PR2's appearance changed after viewing it perform different tasks in the home. Four participants' opinions changed in that they were now more favorable toward the PR2 (e.g., *"and you figured it has to be that big, it'd be nice if it was half that size but then it couldn't do all that."*) The remaining 8 participants stated that their opinions had not changed.

3.4 Importance of Robot Appearance

We asked participants how important a robot's appearance was to having the robot in their homes. Most participants considered appearance important but the level differed across participants. A wide range of reasons were noted (see Table 2) although robot size and fit with the home were most frequently cited concerns.

4. DISCUSSION

Although the current cohort of older adults has relatively less experience with robots [2], they have expectations, and in some cases, strong preferences, about what their robot should look like. In the present study, older adults showed variability in terms of how much they desired a human-like appearance for their robot. However, only one older adult had a particularly strong preference for a non-humanlike appearance. In general, people expected their robots to be small in size, to fit well with their homes, and to be easy to control. Pre-existing expectations seemed to affect participants' first impressions of the PR2. Although human-like and maneuverability features were appreciated, size and bulkiness evoked negative reactions especially in the context of home.

For some participants, the PR2's appearance became more favorable after observing it perform tasks. It is likely that with more exposure, robot appearance would become less critical in determining long-term robot use. However, appearance affects first impressions which affect intention to use. In this study, only a few older adults viewed robot appearance as an unimportant variable. We can thus infer that appearance matters at least during the early phases of human-robot interaction such as when the robot is being introduced to the older adult.

5. ACKNOWLEDGMENTS

This research was supported by: National Institutes of Health (National Institute on Aging) Grant P01 AG17211, the Center for Research and Education on Aging and Technology Enhancement (CREATE; www.create-center.org); National Science Foundation Graduate Research Fellowship Program and grants IIS-1150157 and CNS-0958545; and an equipment grant from Willow Garage.

6. REFERENCES

[1] Kelley, H. 1950. The warm-cold variable in first impressions of persons. *J. Pers*, 18, 4(Jun. 1950), 431–439.

[2] Prakash, A. and Rogers, W. A. 2013. Younger and older adults' attitudes toward robot faces: Effects of task and humanoid appearance. In *Proceedings of the Human Factors and Ergonomics Society 57th Annual Meeting* (San Diego, CA, Sep. 30 – Oct. 04, 2013). Santa Monica, CA, 114-118.

Model Driven Software Development for Human-Machine Interaction Systems

Arunkumar Ramaswamy
[1]Department of Computer and System Engineering, ENSTA-ParisTech, 828 Blvd Marechaux, Palaiseau, France
[2]VeDeCom Institute, 77 rue des Chantiers, Versailles, France
arun-kumar.ramaswamy@ensta-paristech.fr

Bruno Monsuez
[1]Department of Computer and System Engineering, ENSTA-ParisTech, 828 Blvd Marechaux, Palaiseau, France
bruno.monsuez@ensta-paristech.fr

Adriana Tapus
[1]Department of Computer and System Engineering, ENSTA-ParisTech, 828 Blvd Marechaux, Palaiseau, France
adriana.tapus@ensta-paristech.fr

ABSTRACT

In a typical Human-Machine Interaction (HMI) system, a task is performed by cooperation of the human and the automation component. The system adopts a cognitive architecture to model human psychology and makes optimum decisions on dynamic task allocation between human and the machine counterpart depending on the context. However, such architectures do not define how those systems are implemented in software. Various models involved in Model Driven Software Development (MDSD) approach in developing HMI systems is presented. This paper proposes a metamodel for modeling Non-Functional Properties (NFP) in HMI systems and provides a case study on assistive lane keeping in automobiles to demonstrate the approach.

Categories and Subject Descriptors

I.6 [**SIMULATION AND MODELING**]: Model Development—*Modeling methodologies*; H.1.2 [**User/Machine Systems**]: Human factors

Keywords

Model driven engineering; Non-functional properties

1. INTRODUCTION

Humans outperform computers in certain tasks, while in some others, it is the opposite. Consider the case of an assisted parking system in today's cars, the steering control is allocated to the computer while the driver is responsible for applying acceleration. However, in most of the semi-autonomous systems involving humans, for example in automobiles, many functions that human performs are provided by the automation also. Although the software component

HRI'14, March 3–6, 2014, Bielefeld, Germany.
ACM 978-1-4503-2658-2/14/03.
http://dx.doi.org/10.1145/2559636.2559824.

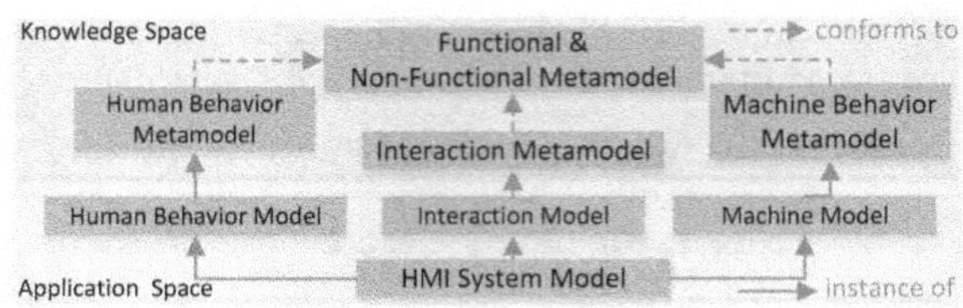

Figure 1: Models in Human-Machine Systems

and the human counterpart can perform the same functionality, it the quality expected from the entire system and the context that determines which one should be activated or deactivated. In order to do that in a system involving humans, the Quality of Service (QoS) and NFPs of human models as well as for automation models need to be specified in a common framework. The challenge is that various attributes that determine a NFP is heterogeneous in nature while considering human and machine models. Our paper tries to address this problem by providing a common metamodel that can be used to specify the QoS of human, machine, and their interactions. In addition, we also provide a general picture on the various models involved in MDSD of HMI systems.

2. MODEL DRIVEN SOFTWARE DEVELOPMENT

The common approach in Model Driven Software Development (MDSE) begins with defining meta-level models or Domain Specific Languages (DSL) that captures the knowledge of a specific domain. Abstract models are then designed based on the application requirements that conforms to metamodels or DSLs. The models undergo a series of Model to Model transformations (M2M) to reduce the abstraction levels by gradually including platform specific details and finally, Model to Text transformation (M2T) is applied to generate an executable code.

Figure 1 illustrates three models - human, machine, and interaction models that conform to the respective metamodels defined at the knowledge level. In order to bring homogeneity and facilitate reasoning based on functional and NFP, a common Functional and Non-Functional Metamodel

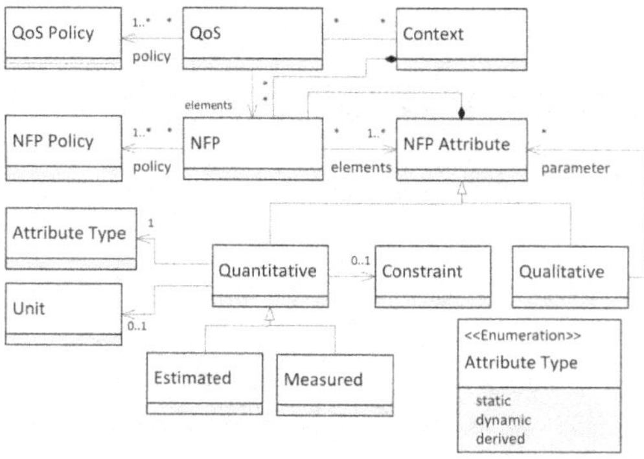

Figure 2: NFP Metamodel

(F&NFM) defined at a higher abstraction level is needed. In short, F&NFM provide syntactical and basic semantic constraints to define Functional and NFP of the models.

3. NON-FUNCTIONAL METAMODEL

NFP define how a functionality operates, for example, performance, efficiency, effectiveness, etc. of a human operator. QoS is the aptitude of a service (human or machine) for providing a quality level to the different demands of the clients (or context). In order to set a general consensus, based on empirical observations, the following assumptions are made: NFP are determined by a set of non-functional attributes (e.g., efficiency can be measured by time to complete the task, operator time for task, average time for obstacle extraction, etc. [2]). QoS is a high level property for comparing a functionality in different contexts (e.g., QoS of a steering maneuver for a human driver is different for cruising and parking scenarios). Policies associated with NFP and QoS determine how these properties are estimated from its constituent attributes. Policies are functions that act on a set of attributes, and defines how these properties are estimated. In a nutshell, `NFP_Policy(NFP attributes)` defines NFP, `QoS_Policy(NFPs, Context)` defines QoS of a functionality.

4. NON-FUNCTIONAL MODEL OF ASSISTIVE LANE KEEPING SYSTEM

Assistive lane keeping is a perfect example for dynamic function allocation in Human-Machine system. The automation part is the lateral control of the vehicle to keep the vehicle in the same lane. The system takes control by applying the required torque on the steering wheel in case of lane departure situations. The case study is to demonstrate how NFPs of Human and Machine can be formally modeled using the proposed NFP metamodel. The NFP, efficiency is modeled as an example. We define QoS for efficiency as the response time in which the human will react to a critical event (here lane departure).

Modeling the human driver in ACT-R architecture [3] is selected for demonstrating the NFP modeling because of the availability of large number of tunable parameters in models representing various aspects of human driver such as memory, perception, control, monitoring, and decision skills. A detailed description of the model can be found in [1]. The efficiency model of the human driver, machine and their interactions based on the proposed NFP metamodel is shown in listing 1. The policy functions are defined based on logic systems, such as a first order logic, predicate logic, etc., by the system designer.

```
//HUMAN_MODEL:
import control_skill,monitor_skill,decision_skill,memory_skill
NFP: eh:efficiency_human; NFP_ATTRIBUTES: cs:control_skill:derived, ms:
      monitor_skill:derived, ds:decision_skill:derived, memory_skill:
      derived; NFP_POLICY: eh.cs>thr_cs & eh.ms>thr_ms & eh.ds>thr_ds;
------------------------------------------
NFP: control_skill; NFP_ATTRIBUTES: prep_time:static:ms, exec_time:static:
      ms, kfar_lateral:dynamic, knear_lateral:dynamic, ki_lateral:dynamic,
      kfar_speed:dynamic, knear_speed:dynamic, ki_speed:dynamic; NFP_POLICY
      : contrl_policy();
------------------------------------------
NFP: monitor_skill; NFP_ATTRIBUTES: prob_monitor:dynamic, NFP_POLICY:
      monitor_policy();
------------------------------------------
NFP: decision_skill; NFP_ATTRIBUTES: safe_distance:dynamic:m, NFP_POLICY:
      decision_policy();
------------------------------------------
NFP: memory_skill; NFP_ATTRIBUTES: memory:dynamic:, creation_time:static:
      sec, decay_rate:static:, NFP_POLICY: memory_policy();
//MACHINE_MODEL:
import platform_capability,sensor_capability,algorithm_parameters
NFP: efficiency_machine; NFP_ATTRIBUTES: response_time; NFP_ATTRIBUTES:
      execution_time:static:ms,       NFP_POLICY: response_time_policy();
------------------------------------------
NFP: platform_capability; NFP_ATTRIBUTES: process_load:dynamic:number,
      resource_availability:derived, scheduling_policy:qualitative,
      NFP_POLICY: decision_policy();
------------------------------------------
NFP: algorithm_parameters; NFP_ATTRIBUTES: vehicle_velocity:dynamic:kmps,
      front_wheel_steering_angle:dynamic:rad, slip_angle:dynamic:rad,
      NFP_POLICY: algorithm_policy();
//INTERACTION_MODEL:
import efficiency_human, efficiency_machine
NFP: efficiency_interaction; NFP_ATTRIBUTES: efficiency_human:dynamic:
      derived, efficiency_machine:dynamic:derived,
NFP_POLICY: interaction_policy();
```

Listing 1: Efficiency model of human driver and machine, and their interactions

5. CONCLUSION

MDSD is a proven approach in software development for automotive and avionics domain. In HMI domain, models are widely used for specifying human behaviors and their interaction with the environments. Our initial experience in adopting MDSD for implementing HMI systems shows reduction in developmental cycle and enhance reusability and portability of the models as compared to the code-based approaches. Modeling NFPs is necessary in architectures where functionality alone cannot be used for making design time and run-time decisions. Our NFP metamodel provides a generic base for specifying the NFP of both human and machine models. The challenge of dealing with heterogeneous attributes defining the human and automation models are addressed by categorizing the attributes into profiles hierarchically and then using policies to compare at a higher abstraction level. In this direction, the next logical step is to formally specify the interaction policies and analyze suitable formal methods for defining the policies.

6. REFERENCES

[1] D. D. Salvucci. Modeling driver behavior in a cognitive architecture. *Human Factors: The Journal of the Human Factors and Ergonomics Society*, 48(2):362–380, 2006.

[2] A. Steinfeld, T. Fong, D. aber, M. Lewis, . Scholtz, A. Schultz, and M. Goodrich. Common metrics for human-robot interaction. In *Proceedings of the 1st ACM SIGCHI/SIGART conference on Human-robot interaction*, pages 33–40. ACM, 2006.

[3] . G. Trafton, L. M. Hiatt, A. M. Harrison, F. Tamborello, S. S. hemlani, and A. C. Schultz. Act-r e: An embodied cognitive architecture for human robot interaction. *Journal of Human-Robot Interaction*, 2:30–55, 01 2013 2013.

Morphological Gender Recognition by a Social Robot and Privacy Concerns

[Late Breaking Reports]

Arnaud Ramey
RoboticsLab, Univ. Carlos III of Madrid
Leganés, Spain
arnaud.ramey@m4x.org

Miguel A. Salichs
RoboticsLab, Univ. Carlos III of Madrid
Leganés, Spain
salichs@ing.uc3m.es

ABSTRACT

An intuitive and robust user recognition system is at the key of a natural interaction between a social robot and its users. The gender of a new user can be guessed without explicitly asking it of her, which can then be used to personalize the interaction flow. In this LBR, a novel algorithm is used to estimate the gender of a person based on its morphological shape. More specifically, the vertical outline of the breast of the user is used to estimate his or her gender, based on similar shapes seen during training.

On early benchmarks with databases that represent well the diversity of human body shapes, the accuracy rate is close to 90% and outperforms a state-of-the-art algorithm. Our algorithm provides a fast and seamless estimation flow and needs limited computation resources, which tailor it for HRI. Its usefulness has been proved by integrating it in a social robot. However, its use raises concerns among the users about their privacy, which will lead to further study.

Categories and Subject Descriptors

I.2.10 [**Vision and Scene Understanding**]: Modeling and recovery of physical attributes; H.3.4 [**Systems and Software**]: User profiles and alert services; I.2.9 [**Robotics**]: Sensors

General Terms

Algorithms, Experimentation, Human Factors

1. INTRODUCTION

To obtain a natural interaction with the human user, it is important that the robot gathers information about her. The queries can be explicit, such as questions asked to her or an interactive display, but the range of applications widens if some features can be inferred with no user action required. These features are called *soft biometrics*. One of the earliest multi-modal user tracking systems [3] used the user height and the color of the skin to obtain a robust tracking of the users around a multimedia kiosk. Clothes color histograms are also used in [6] for logging in a computer and continuously checking the user identity.

Considering the shape of the breast of a person is a natural way of estimating his or her gender [5]. However, this method turned out to perform poorly in real time and with challenging body shapes. Furthermore, as further underlined in [1], the users are concerned about the privacy of this detection and might consider it intrusive.

The work presented in this paper aims at determining the gender of the user in a similar way, but overcoming the limitations of the previous work.

2. DESCRIPTION OF THE SYSTEM

The input needed for our system is a 3D (colorless) point cloud of the user. This can be obtained through a range of input devices, such as a structured light depth sensor such as Microsoft Kinect, or a stereo vision device. The output is a real-time estimation of the gender of the visible users.

User detection and mask computation. The point cloud given by the device needs to be cut down to keep only the points of the user. Our system sports two sources for this user mask. A device-specific solution is to use the one directly given by the device SDK (Kinect NITE SDK) The other way is to obtain thanks to face detection ([8]) a seed pixel belonging to the user; and to detect the edges in the depth mask thanks to a Canny filter; a propagative floodfill in the edge image from that seed generates the final user mask. In both cases, the point cloud is obtained by reprojecting to world coordinates the pixels of the depth map that also belong to the user mask.

Breast feature computation. Laws' algorithm ([5]), which is the most recent and similar algorithm, is based on extracting several horizontal slices of the point cloud of the user for a span of height values that corresponds to the breast location in a body. The contour of each slice is matched against the pattern of a breast shape using non-linear regression. Metrics on the pattern that fits best one of the slices are then used to evaluate the gender of the user. However, female users with a moderate breast and over-weight males generate similar horizontal slices.

Our algorithm is instead based on computing the vertical contour of the torso of the user. The pipeline is illustrated in Figure 1 The orientation of the user is determined by fitting an ellipse to the shadow generated by the projection of the point cloud onto the ground plane. The projection plane is chosen to be vertical, going through the center of

HRI'14, March 3–6, 2014, Bielefeld, Germany.
ACM 978-1-4503-2658-2/14/03.
http://dx.doi.org/10.1145/2559636.2563714 .

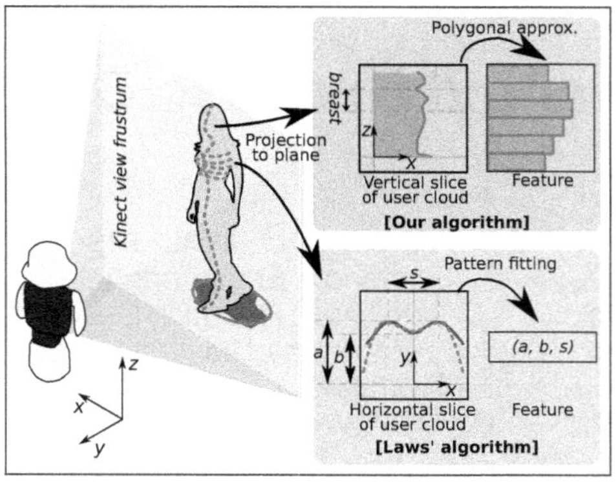

Figure 1: *Algorithms pipelines for both [5] and our algorithm. The black shadow is the projection mentioned in section 2, and the ellipse the best fit to that shadow. The projection planes for both methods are indicated in dashed lines.*

mass of the user and parallel to the short axis of the ellipse. The points of the cloud with a height corresponding to the breast, according to morphological rules, and that are close to that plane are projected onto it. The outline of the user thus generated is approximated by a fixed length polygonal line, which consists in the final feature.

Gender determination. A training set with pictures of users and manually labelled genders is used to generate training features and labels. A two-class SVM classifier ([2]) is trained on this data to learn the non-linear separation between male and female shapes. Once trained, the prediction output of the SVM for a test shape determines the gender of the user.

3. RESULTS AND CONCLUSIONS

The robot Maggie is equipped with a structured light sensing device (Kinect), that has already been used for gesture recognition [7]. Our algorithm is implemented in C++ and is based on the ROS architecture [1]. It supplies in real-time an estimation of the gender of the users around Maggie.

Benchmarking of the algorithm. To benchmark our algorithm against Laws' ([5]), we used the database [4]. It contains video sequences of 55 users, both female and male, walking on a stage with varying light conditions. These users represent well the possible range of body shapes: including slender females and overweight males. Both our and Laws' detectors were trained on 1100 images (20 per video), and trained on 550 (10 per video).

The results are gathered in Table 1. Note that an algorithm of gender detection based on the body shape cannot intrinsically reach a 100% accuracy, as there is no strict categorization between female and male shapes. Overweight male subjects for instance appear more curvy than some women. This limitation can be overcome by coupling this gender recognition algorithm with others, based for instance on the face of the users or their height. Yet, our algorithm correctly estimates the gender of the user in almost nine times out of ten. Laws originally tested its algorithm on a medical scan data database with full-figured, standing straight subjects, and logically performs poorly on real-life user samples.

Privacy concerns. The gender recognition algorithm runs in the background within the robot and supplies in real time

[1] http://wiki.ros.org

	Laws	Our
Accuracy rate	63%	89%
Average computation time (ms)	83	11

Table 1: *Benchmark results*

estimations of the gender of the users around it, even though the user was never seen before.

The first experiments with real users have given interesting results. On the one hand, users acknowledge the usefulness of detecting their gender for a personalized interaction. On the other hand, once told the robot considers seamlessly the shape of their torso to guess their gender, some users have shown concerns about their privacy and how measuring their chest shape is an intrusive method, thus meeting the results of [1]. However, once shown the output of the algorithm, some of these users have reported to have worse expectations than reality: the sensor and the algorithm are not as intrusive as infra-red cameras. These first conclusions now give way to deeper research using a proper experimental framework and a bigger set of users.

Conclusions. the proposed algorithm turns out to be a useful metric as it helps determining the gender of new users. It gives a generally liable estimation of it, and its lightweight nature makes it perfectly suitable for social robots.

Future works will study more in details the a-priori and a-posteriori privacy concerns of the users. We will also determine how using other techniques such as face-based gender recognition improves the accuracy of the gender estimation.

Acknowledgments

The authors gratefully acknowledge the funds provided by the Spanish MICINN (Ministry of Science and Innovation) through the project "Aplicaciones de los robots sociales", DPI2011-26980 from the Spanish Ministry of Economy and Competitiveness. Moreover, the research leading to these results has received funding from the "RoboCity2030-II-CM" project (S2009/DPI-1559), funded by "Programas de Actividades I+D en la Comunidad de Madrid" and cofunded by "Structural Funds of the EU".

4. REFERENCES

[1] Y. Cai, J. Laws, and N. Bauernfeind. Design Privacy with Analogia Graph. *IAAI*, 2010.

[2] C. Cortes and V. Vapnik. Support-vector networks. *Machine learning*, 1995.

[3] T. Darrell, G. Gordon, M. Harville, and J. Woodfill. Integrated person tracking using stereo, color, and pattern detection. *International Journal of Computer Vision*, 2000.

[4] L. Igual, A. Lapedriza, and R. Borràs. Robust Gait-Based Gender Classification using Depth Cameras. In *Eurasip Journal On Image And Video Processing*, 2013.

[5] J. Laws and Y. Cai. *A privacy algorithm for 3d human body scans.* 2006.

[6] K. Niinuma, U. Park, and A. K. Jain. Soft Biometric Traits for Continuous User Authentication. *IEEE Transactions on Information Forensics and Security*, 5(4):771–780, Dec. 2010.

[7] A. Ramey, V. Gonzalez-Pacheco, M. A. Salichs, and V. González-Pacheco. Integration of a Low-Cost RGB-D Sensor in a Social Robot for Gesture Recognition. In *Proceedings of the 6th International Conference on HumanRobot Interaction*, HRI '11, pages 229–230, New York, NY, USA, 2011. ACM.

[8] P. Viola and M. Jones. Rapid object detection using a boosted cascade of simple features. In *Computer Vision and Pattern Recognition, IEEE Computer Society Conference on*, volume 1, pages 511–518, Los Alamitos, CA, USA, Apr. 2001. IEEE Comput. Soc.

Towards a Social and Mobile Humanoid Exercise Coach

Darryl Ramgoolam
Humanoid Engineering & Intelligent Robotics Lab
Marquette University
Milwaukee, WI 53201 USA
darryl.ramgoolam@mu.edu

Elise Russell
Humanoid Engineering & Intelligent Robotics Lab
Marquette University
Milwaukee, WI 53201 USA
elise.russell@mu.edu

Andrew B. Williams
Humanoid Engineering & Intelligent Robotics Lab
Marquette University
Milwaukee, WI 53201 USA
andrew.williams@mu.edu

ABSTRACT

In the near future, humanoid robots may be available to act as personal health coaches that can socially interact and exercise with people to increase their physical activity and improve their nutritional habits. Although there has been work to demonstrate the long-term effects of using a robot to motivate and record exercise and nutrition data, we are developing a social and mobile humanoid health coach that will explain and perform the physical exercises along with the human in an effort to increase their physical activity. In this paper, we describe a pilot study to compare the effects on young adults of coaching delivered by a social and mobile humanoid robot health coach versus a human health coach. While data analysis bore out no significant statistical effect of coach type on daily activity level, the results demonstrated encouraging trends and suggest further research with a larger sample size.

1. INTRODUCTION

Childhood obesity is a growing problem in the United States. In 1980, 7% of children and 5% of adolescents were obese, and in 2010 both numbers increased to 18% [1]. Lifestyle changes appear to play a large part in this worrying trend.

There have been many technology-based approaches addressing obesity. These approaches range from mobile apps that provide nutritional and exercise tracking to video games that promote physical activity. Social robots that can interact verbally and can exercise along with a human hold promise in helping to increase physical activity among children and adults. This pilot study describes the use of a mobile, autonomous humanoid robot health coach to explain, demonstrate, and encourage physical activity among college students with the view of developing advanced social intelligence for an effective childhood obesity intervention.

HRI'14, March 3–6, 2014, Bielefeld, Germany.
ACM 978-1-4503-2658-2/14/03.
http://dx.doi.org/10.1145/2559636.2559849.

2. ROBOT HEALTH COACHES

There have been several approaches aimed at using robots to address obesity and provide advice or coaching to increase physical activity. Cory Kidd and Cynthia Breazeal have explored in-depth robotic solutions to weight problems, although their focus has been on long-term, sociable robots that lack mobility [2]. Another robot exercise coach, TAIZO, has made its debut in Japan as an assistant to human-led exercise training programs intended for the elderly [3]. Maja Mataric has used socially assistive robots to motivate physical exercise for rehabilitation versus an obesity intervention [4].

Figure 1: Humanoid health coach leads a study participant in exercises.

3. STUDY DESIGN

The goal of this study was to determine if a one-on-one robot health coach could be effective in increasing physical activity, and to establish the feasibility of this line of study. We hypothesized that participants coached by our humanoid robot would demonstrate higher average activity than those coached by a human.

Fifteen Marquette college students were recruited as subjects. They were randomly and evenly sorted into three study conditions: No Health Coach, Human Health Coach, or Robot Health Coach. The Robot Health Coach was an Aldebaran Robotics H25 Nao humanoid robot, programmed with motion animations to exercise along with the subject and to speak guidelines and encouragement interactively.

For two weeks, every subject wore a Nike+ FuelBand, an accelerometer wristband that records physical activity. Subjects wore their wristbands every day and made four half-hour appointments to come to the lab for data upload. Subjects who had no health coach spent this time doing activities of their choice, while subjects with a human or robot health coach exercised one-on-one with their coach. The

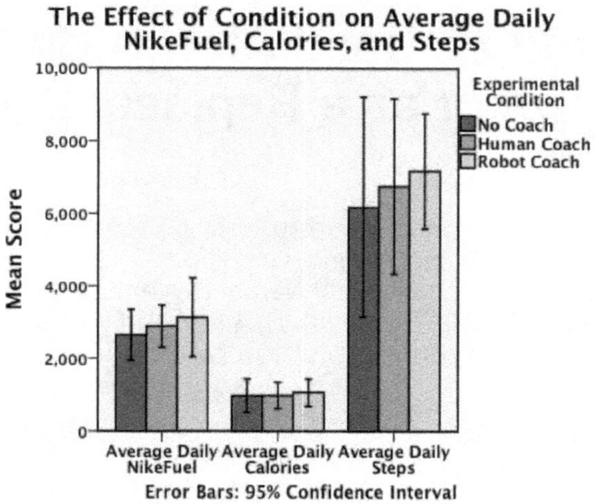

Figure 2: Comparison of the average daily values of activity measures across experimental condition.

workouts were the same for both human and robot health coaches, and included a warm up, strength training, cardio, and a cool down. Example exercises include hamstring stretches, squats, pushups, jumping jacks, and a yoga position. During the sessions, each coach offered encouragement and instructions for proper technique.

A post-survey was developed based on psychological mood inventories, in order to collect evaluative feedback for interpreting results and planning future studies. It consisted of fourteen Likert-scale style questions regarding the subject's activity levels and their evaluation of the health coaching sessions in terms of coaching rapport, useful information, and physical challenge.

4. RESULTS

The Nike+ FuelBands collected activity data in the form of the number of steps taken, calories burned, and NikeFuel earned per day for each subject. Mean daily values were then calculated for each variable per subject.

A one-way MANOVA showed no significant effect of condition on any of the dependent variables, and no significant interaction between variables ($p = 0.828$). However, as illustrated in Figure 2, the Robot Health Coach condition had the highest average in every measure, and the No Health Coach condition the lowest average.

While not significant, this trend is an indicator that further research in this area might be valuable. The current study was limited in the number of subjects recruited and the time available to collect data, which in turn limited the power of statistical tests to detect real effects.

The items in the post-survey regarding coaching sessions were averaged together and analyzed with an Independent Samples T-Test, which found no significant difference in the mean overall approval scores between the robot and human coaching sessions ($t = 0.387, p = 0.709$). This result, shown in Figure 3, suggests that the robot coach was as successful as the human coach at socially and motivationally engaging participants during the workouts.

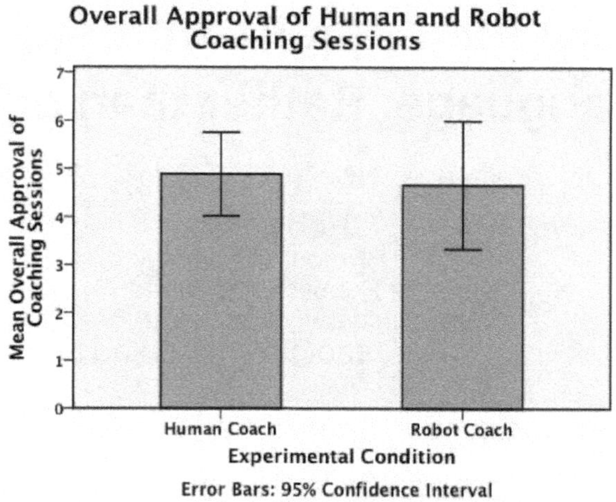

Figure 3: Subjects' mean approval ratings of the human coach and the robot coach were indistinguishable between conditions.

5. CONCLUSION

The main goal of this pilot study was to assess the feasibility of this study and the likelihood of collecting workable data. Some of the trends found in the results do suggest further research. Since this was a pilot study, we were also alert to changes that could be made to improve upon the design, especially as suggested by subjects' comments in the post survey. Some subjects stated that the workout was too intense for children, and others suggested that the code for the health coach could be polished, or motion tracking added so that the robot could follow subjects' motions. With these changes and a larger sample size, we are optimistic of the success of a more powerful study into the effectiveness of an improved health coach robot.

6. ACKNOWLEDGEMENTS

The project was supported by the Marquette University John P. Raynor, S.J, Endowment, College of Engineering & Office of the Provost. We also acknowledge helpful comments from reviewers.

7. REFERENCES

[1] "Overweight and Obesity" *KidsHealth.* Nemours, Oct. 2012. Web. 25 July 2013.

[2] Kidd, Cory D., and Cynthia Breazeal. "Robots at home: Understanding long-term human-robot interaction." *Intelligent Robots and Systems, 2008. IROS 2008. IEEE/RSJ International Conference on.* IEEE, 2008.

[3] Matsusaka, Yosuke, et al. "Health exercise demonstration robot TAIZO and effects of using voice command in robot-human collaborative demonstration." *Robot and Human Interactive Communication, 2009. RO-MAN 2009. The 18th IEEE International Symposium on.* IEEE, 2009.

[4] J. Fasola and M. J. Mataric, "Using Socially Assistive Human-Robot Interaction to Motivate Physical Exercise for Older Adults", *Proceedings of IEEE, Special Issue on Quality of Life Technology,* 100(8):2512-2526, August 2012.

Non-Linguistic Utterances Should be Used Alongside Language, Rather than on their Own or as a Replacement

Robin Read
Plymouth University
Centre for Robotics and Neural Systems
Drake Circus, Plymouth, PL4 8AA, UK
robin.read@plymouth.ac.uk

Tony Belpaeme
Plymouth University
Centre for Robotics and Neural Systems
Drake Circus, Plymouth, PL4 8AA, UK
tony.belpaeme@plymouth.ac.uk

ABSTRACT

This paper presents the results of a small experiment aimed at determining whether people are comfortable with a social robot that uses robotic Non-Linguistic Utterances alongside Natural Language, rather than as a replacement. The results suggest that while people have the most preference for a robot that uses only natural language, a robot that combines NLUs and natural language is seen as more preferable than a robot that only employes NLUs. This suggests that there is potential for NLUs to be used in combination with natural language. In light of this, potential utilities and motivations for using NLUs in such a manner are outlined.

Categories and Subject Descriptors

H.5.2 [**User Interfaces**]: Auditory (non-speech) feedback; H.5.5 [**Sound and Music Computing**]: Systems; I.2.9 [**Robotics**]: Operator interfaces

General Terms

Design, Human Factors, Experimentation, Theory

Keywords

Non-Linguistic Utterances; Social HRI; Natural Language

1. INTRODUCTION

Non-Linguistic Utterances (NLUs) are robotic sounds made by synthetic social agents, rather than utterances that are designed to resemble natural speech, such as a artificial languages [1] or gibberish speech [3]. While NLUs have been used to great effect within the world on animation and popular culture/media as a *proto-language*, very little is understood about how NLUs can be applied to real world Human-Robot Interaction (HRI). In previous work [2] we have shown that situational context is an important aspect of social HRI that directs how NLUs are interpreted by people. The work outlined in this paper makes an initial investigation into how people respond to a robot (an Aldebaran Nao) that uses NLUs alongside natural language (NL) as NL is another rich source of mood and context within social HRI. Assuming that people indeed respond positively to a robot that uses both NLUs and NL in combination, there are a number of potential utilities that NLUs can then provide for social HRI (as we see in section 4). This experiment initially probes the validity of this assumption.

HRI'14, March 3–6, 2014, Bielefeld, Germany.
ACM 978-1-4503-2658-2/14/03.
http://dx.doi.org/10.1145/2559636.2559836 .

2. EXPERIMENTAL SETUP

The experiment tests the following hypotheses: H_1: A robot that uses only NL will be rated as more preferable then a robot that uses NLUs alongside language. H_2: A robot using only NLUs will be rated as less preferable than a robot using NLUs alongside language. H_3: The rating of preference will be influenced by how NLUs and NL are combined.

To test these hypothesis, four videos were created each showing a robot playing a guessing game with a human, with the type of utterance (NL, NLUs, or a combination of the two) being varied across the four videos. The game was based upon the "Cups and Balls" game (figure 1). In this game, an object is hidden under one of three cups. The cups are then shuffled and presented to the player (the robot), and the player needs to be guess which cup the object is under. This scenario was chosen as it facilitates the robot making a variety of different vocalisations throughout the scenario, ranging from linguistic comments, conversational fillers, and reactive and expressive vocalisations. For the purpose of this experiment the unfolding of the game was scripted such that the robot's physical behaviour was always the same, and that the robot always made the same (incorrect) guess. The four video conditions[1] were as follows: V_1: the robot using only NL. V_2: the robot using only NLUs. V_3: the robot using a combination of NLUs and NL. V_4: the robot using an *inverted* combination of NLUs and NL.

This experiment was conducted using the online crowd sourcing facility, *CrowdFlower*. Subjects were rewarded $0.3 USD for their participation, and subjects were limited to the United States alone. They were asked to provide their age and gender, and then presented with the four videos in a random order. After viewing all of the videos, subjects were asked to provide a preference rating for each video individually. The rating was captured using a 9 point Likert scale (1 = Least Preferred, 9 = Most Preferred). Finally, subjects were asked whether they were familiar with the Nao robot.

[1]The videos can be viewed here: `http://www.youtube.com/playlist?list=PLJwvAKNW4DupVHtrTaHSTxnOWYHhobG49`

(a) Ball being presented.

(b) Cups being shuffled.

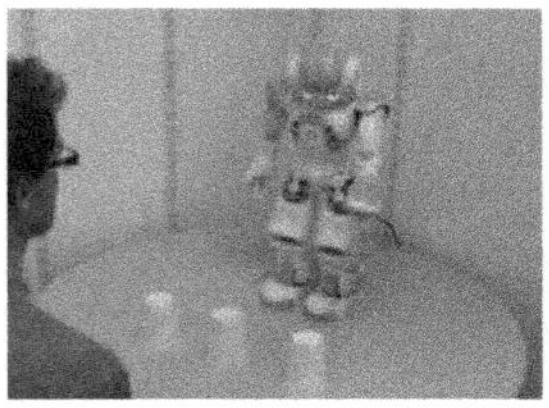

(c) Robot choosing a cup.

(d) Ball location revealed.

Figure 1: Images depicting the game unfolding.

3. RESULTS

In total, 270 subjects responded. 89 males (mean age = 36.74, std = 10.8) and 181 females (mean age = 37.74, std = 11.0). 166 subjects self reported that they had seen the robot before (57 males, 109 females).

A 3-way repeated measures ANOVA (4x2x2 design) was performed using the video condition as the within subjects factor, and subject gender and robot familiarity as the between subjects factors. It was found that there were main effects due to the video condition ($F(3, 798) = 67.4$, $MSE = 145.264$, $p < 0.001$) and a subject's familiarity with the Nao robot ($F(1, 266) = 6.959$, $MSE = 53.002$, $p = 0.009$). These results are shown in figure 2.

With respect to the video condition main effect, post-hoc tests showed that V_1 had the highest rating (mean = 6.845, 95% CI = [6.645 7.063]) and was significantly higher than all the other conditions ($p < 0.001$). V_2 was found to have the lowest rating (mean = 4.969, 95% CI = [4.659 5.319]) and was significantly different than all the other conditions ($p < 0.001$). V_4 had the second highest rating (mean = 6.470, 95% CI = [6.256 6.684]) and V_3 the third (mean = 6.260, 95% CI = [6.044 6.475]), with no significant difference found between these two conditions. With respect to the main effect due to robot familiarity, post-hoc tests revealed that subjects who had seen the robot before provided higher ratings (mean = 6.387, 95% CI = [6.165 6.609]) than subjects who had not seen the robot before (mean = 5.899, 95% CI = [5.611 6.188]).

4. DISCUSSION & CONCLUSIONS

The results provide support for both hypotheses H_1 and H_2 in that subjects showed the highest preference for the condition where the robot only used NL (V_1) and showed the lowest preference for the robot that used only NLUs (V_2). H_3 was not supported as there was no significant difference found between the preference ratings for the two videos showing the robot using a combination of NLUs and NL.

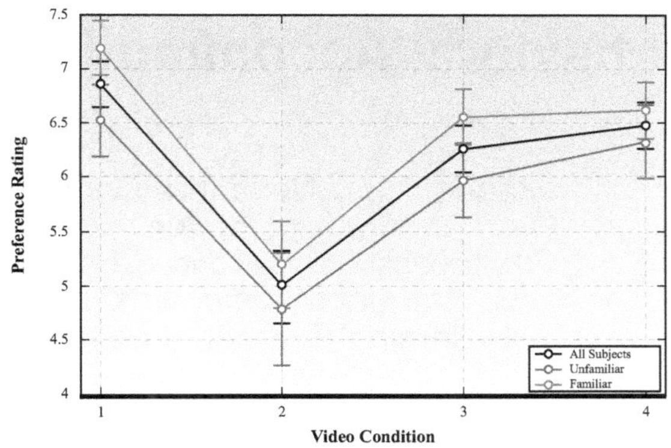

Figure 2: Plot of the Preference Ratings across the four video conditions.

The notion that there is indeed potential for NLUs to be used alongside language opens a number of potential uses of NLUs during HRI. For example, a toy idea could be to use NLUs to indicate a robot swearing, where the robot is able to suggest the mood of an utterance without actually being explicitly offensive. Another potentially fruitful utility is to use NLUs as a means to provide conversational fillers or for back-channelling, both of which are essential cues during social interaction. In this context, NLUs can provide a supportive role to Natural Language Processing (NLP) during linguistic exchanges. Furthermore, if used in this manner, NLUs may also be used as a way to *camouflage* situations in which NLP may perform sub-optimally (e.g. if the processing of user input is taking too long, or if the confidence of speech recognition falls below an acceptable threshold). In this utility, NLUs could be used with the aim of mitigating any damage to to an interaction should NLP fail to perform at a desired level. It should be noted that the experimental results and discussion presented here represents research ideas that are currently very much in their infancy and require further, more detailed scientific exploration. Addressing this is the aim of our future work.

5. ACKNOWLEDGMENTS

This work is (partially) funded by the EU FP7 ALIZ-E project (grant 248116).

6. REFERENCES

[1] O. Mubin, C. Bartneck, L. Leijs, H. Hooft van Huysduynen, J. Hu, and J. Muelver. Improving Speech Recognition with the Robot Interaction Language. *Disruptive Science and Technology*, 1(2):79–88, Dec. 2012.

[2] R. Read and T. Belpaeme. Situational Context Directs How People Affectively Interpret Robotic Non-Linguistic Utterances. In *Proceedings of the 9th International Conference on Human-Robot Interaction (HRI'14)*, Bielefeld, Germany, 2014. ACM/IEEE.

[3] S. Yilmazyildiz, D. Henderickx, B. Vanderborght, W. Verhelst, E. Soetens, and D. Lefeber. Multi-modal emotion expression for affective human-robot interaction. In *Proceedings of the Workshop on Affective Social Speech Signals (WASSS 2013)*, Grenoble, France, 2013.

Behavioral Accommodation towards a Dance Robot Tutor

Raquel Ros, Alexandre Coninx, Yiannis Demiris
Imperial College London, UK
{raquel.ros, a.coninx, y.demiris}@imperial.ac.uk

Georgios Patsis, Valentin Enescu, Hichem Sahli
Vrije Universiteit Brussel, Belgium
{gpatsis, venescu, hichem.sahli}@etro.vub.ac.be

ABSTRACT

We report first results on children adaptive behavior towards a dance tutoring robot. We can observe that children behavior rapidly evolves through few sessions in order to accommodate with the robotic tutor rhythm and instructions.

Categories and Subject Descriptors

H.1.2 [**Models and Principles**]: User/Machine Systems; I.2.9 [**Robotics**]: Commercial robots and applications

Keywords

interaction adaptation; child-robot interaction; dance

1. INTRODUCTION

Social interaction can be defined as a dynamic sequence of social actions between individuals (or groups) where interactors modify their actions and reactions based on the each other. Some examples of interaction adaptation that take place when people interact are matching other's behaviors, synchronizing the timing of behavior, or even behave in dissimilar ways [2].

Within the HRI community, most effort has been put on researching strategies to adapt the robot behavior to the user. In other words, considering the adaptation of a single interactor, instead of both. Though indeed it is a major goal to reach, we believe that taking into account the user capabilities and strategies to accommodate to the robot should be also considered and studied more deeply.

Most research on adaptive interaction has been focused in conversational interactions, such as the Communication Accommodation Theory (CAT) developed by Howard Giles, where it is argued that people adjust speech, vocal patterns and gestures to accommodate to others. Following these ideas, linguistic adaptation of the user towards automatic systems, both in computer-interaction and robot-interaction, have been observed in the past [4, 1, 3]. However, little attention has been payed to behavioral (action) adaptation, specially in HRI.

In this paper we report first results on children adaptive behavior towards a dance tutoring robot. We can observe that children behavior rapidly evolves through few sessions in order to accommodate with the robotic tutor rhythm and instructions.

We next briefly describe the dance task and the robotic system used in this work, followed by results obtained from first analysis of the experiments carried out.

HRI'14, March 3–6, 2014, Bielefeld, Germany.
ACM 978-1-4503-2658-2/14/03.
http://dx.doi.org/10.1145/2559636.2559821.

2. A DANCE ROBOT TUTOR

The present work is based on the approach presented in [5], where creative dance is used as the interaction activity between robot and child. Creative dance is a form of dance where the goal is to explore the body movement based on a set of general guidelines (movement concepts).

Several methods are used to teach dance. In this work, we focus on what we call the *concept-based learning*. In this model dance concepts are sequentially shown and children explore the new ideas using their own body. They are free to create any variation they can think of as long as it corresponds to the concept described. Next, a process of *request-respond* takes place. The robot asks for a dance concept and the child has four seconds to perform it. If he/she fails, the robot shows an example and the child may (or not) respond in some way. Table 1 summarizes the available *request-respond* pairs observed in the experiments we report here.

The robot used is the Nao, a humanoid robot from Aldebaran Robotics.[1]. The robot behavior addresses two main aspects during the interactions: (*i*) it performs the dance activity where it acts as a tutor guiding the child through the different stages; and (*ii*) keeps the child engaged in the task as much as possible, not only to finish the task, but to repeat the encounter in future occasions. To this end, basic social queues have been developed along with motivation strategies (such as providing constant positive feedback, head movements, name reference, etc. described in detail in [5]).

3. RESULTS

The experiments were carried out with 11 children during 4 days. Each child was expected to interact in three sessions -each in different days-. However, due to technical problems, only three children could complete the three sessions

[1]www.aldebaran-robotics.com

request (robot)	response (child)	interpretation
ask	ok	performs correctly
	fail	fails performing either creating its own motion or copying the robot's motion
	observe	observes and waits for robot's action
	distracted	does not follow robot's instructions
show	copy	perfoms correctly copying the robot's motion
	fail	fails performing either creating its own motion or copying the robot's motion
	observe	observes robot's motion
	distracted	does not follow robot's instructions

Table 1: Set of possible combinations of request-response pairs (robot and child actions).

(users 1 to 3), seven children interacted twice (users 4 to 10) and one child could only participate in one session. Since we are interested in observing behavioral adaptation across sessions, we remove the child having a single session from the results reported here.

In this work, we only focus on the *request-respond* period of the sessions, which correspond to 5 min in average per session (26% of the session duration). The child has two opportunities to respond to the robot's movement requests, where the second chance (*show* request) only takes place if the child fails to do so in the first time (*ask* request). Thus, we measure the accommodation level as the complement of the ratio between the *show* requests and the *ask* requests, where values near 0.0 corresponds to low accommodation level (i.e., for every *ask* request, the robot had to perform a *show* request afterwards), and 1.0, to maximum accommodation level (i.e., the child responded after the first request):

$$accomodation = 1 - (show/ask)$$

where *show* and *ask* corresponds to the number of times the robot shows and asks a motion to the user respectively. We must remark that failing to respond in the first time does not exclusively mean that no behavioral adaptation occurs, but that the child may not know the motion.

Figure 1 depicts the evolution of the level of accommodation for each user across sessions. Significant increase can be observed through the sessions, meaning that most of them accommodated their behavior to the rhythm of the robot as they interacted. It is worth to mention that although the teaching methodology is the same throughout the sessions, the movements performed are completely different in between sessions. Therefore, the increase of accommodation level is not due to a memorizing exercise or performance improvement from one session to another, but due to an understanding and behavioral adaptation from the user to the robot's rhythm.

There is only one exception, user 7, who actually decreased its accommodation level. Through observational analysis of the recordings we verified that the second half of the last session the child was not engaged in the task any more, and therefore, his behavior was not aligned with that of the robot.

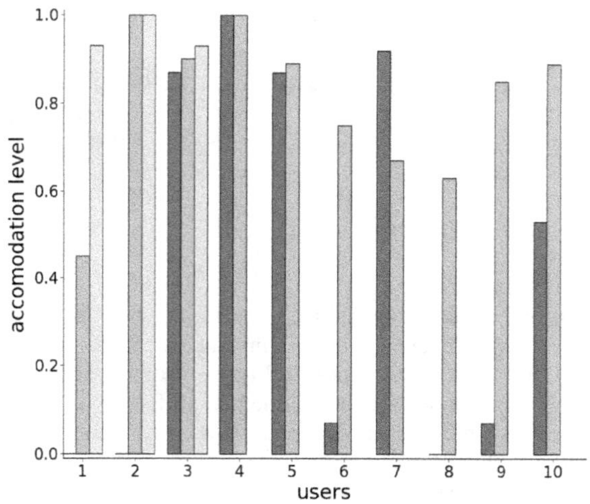

Figure 1: Accommodation level evolution per user across sessions (darkest bar corresponds to first session, while lightest one, to the child's last session).

4. CONCLUSIONS AND FUTURE WORK

We have presented first results that show that behavior accommodation from the user perspective can take place across sessions. We believe that considering the adaptability of humans towards their interactors is an open opportunity for the HRI community. Assessing the accommodation level not only can serve as as guideline of how efficient the interaction is, but also could provide additional information on which aspects the robotic system should emphasize its adaptive behavior.

5. ACKNOWLEDGMENTS

We thank Leire Guezala (dance teacher). This work is supported by the FP7 ALIZ-E project (n. 248116).

6. REFERENCES

[1] C. Breazeal. Regulation and entrainment in human–robot interaction. *The International Journal of Robotics Research*, 21(10), 2002.

[2] J. K. Burgoon, L. A. Stern, and L. Dillman. *Interpersonal Adaptation: Dyadic Interaction Patterns.* Cambridge University Press, 1995.

[3] I. Kruijff-Korbayová, H. C. huitl, B. Kiefer, I. Baronia, A. Sanna, and M. Nalin. Children's turn-taking behavior adaptation in multi-session interactions with a humanoid robot. *International Journal of Humanoid Robotics*, 2013.

[4] S. Oviatt, C. Darves, and R. Coulston. Toward adaptive conversational interfaces: Modeling speech convergence with animated personas. *ACM Trans. Comput.-Hum. Interact.*, 11(3):300–328, Sept. 2004.

[5] R. Ros and Y. Demiris. Creative dance: An approach for social interaction between robots and children. In *Human Behavior Understanding*, volume 8212 of *Lecture Notes in Computer Science*, pages 40–51. Springer International Publishing, 2013.

Introducing a Rasch-Type Anthropomorphism Scale

Peter A. M. Ruijten*, Diane H. L. Bouten, Dana C. J. Rouschop, Jaap Ham, Cees J. H. Midden
Eindhoven University of Technology
School of Innovation Sciences
Eindhoven, Netherlands, P.O. 513
p.a.m.ruijten[at]tue.nl

ABSTRACT

In human-robot interaction research, much attention is given to the extent to which people perceive humanlike attributes in robots. Generally, the concept anthropomorphism is used to describe this process. Anthropomorphism is defined in different ways, with much focus on either typical human attributes or uniquely human attributes. This difference has caused different measurement tools to be developed. We argue that anthropomorphism can best be described as a continuum ranging from low to high human likeness, and should be measured accordingly. We found that anthropomorphic characteristics can be invariantly ordered according to the ease with which these can be ascribed to robots.

General Terms

Design, Human Factors, Measurement, Standardization.

Keywords

Anthropomorphism, Rasch.

1. INTRODUCTION

As technology plays an increasingly prominent role in our lives, our perception of those technologies becomes more important. To describe how people perceive robots, the concept of anthropomorphism is often used. Generally, this involves the tendency to attribute human characteristics to robots. However, not all researchers use the exact same definition. For example, [1] refer to anthropomorphism as "the attribution of a human form, human characteristics, or human behavior to nonhuman things" (p.74), while [2] define anthropomorphism as "a process of inductive inference whereby people imbue the real or imagined behavior of other agents with humanlike characteristics, motivations, intentions, or underlying mental states" (p.411). A closer look of these definitions shows us that differences arise due to referring to different *types* of human characteristics. Human characteristics are generally divided in typical and unique. Typically human characteristics are generally associated with humans, but humans are not the only entities that have those traits [3]. An example is being able to interact with a changing environment. Uniquely human characteristics refer to traits that are unique for the human species [3], like having a moral conscience. We note that [1] mainly refer to typically human characteristics, while [2] mainly refer to uniquely human characteristics. Furthermore, [4] take on yet another approach. While they adopt [3]'s concepts of typically and uniquely human, they only refer to cognitive traits, leaving appearance and physical abilities that characterize humans aside. Because of these differences in focus, a robot that is considered to be anthropomorphic according to one definition might be seen as non-anthropomorphic according to another one, and vice versa. In other words, since in most of the current research only one of these different aspects of anthropomorphism is being measured, the results are non-generalizable and non-comparable.

We argue that the attribution of typically and uniquely human characteristics to robots reflect a single human predisposition, as is indicated in Figure 1. In other words, we expect that anthropomorphic characteristics may be ordered according to the ease to which they are ascribed to robots in a manner that is the same for all individuals in their encounter with all robots. In particular, we expect that typically human characteristics are more easily ascribed to robots than uniquely ones, regardless of the individuals' predisposition to attribute anthropomorphic characteristics to robots. Inversely, the expected ordering of anthropomorphic characteristics would prescribe that people who attribute uniquely human characteristics to a robot must also ascribe typical characteristics to it.

Figure 1: Conceptual representation of human characteristics on an anthropomorphism continuum

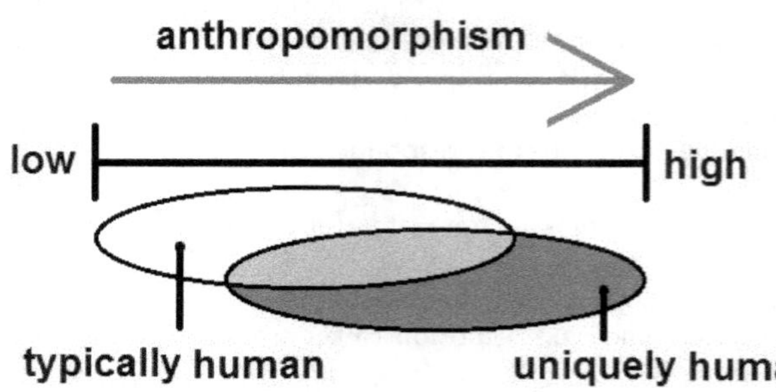

One model that mathematically describes these expectations is the Rasch model, which assumes that the trait to be measured is a one-dimensional latent variable [5, 6, 7]. In the model, two parameters are estimated; one to distinguish between individuals, and another one to order the latent variable's characteristics [6]. Both of them are interesting, because they can tell us something about the underlying process of anthropomorphism. We aim to develop a measurement scale for anthropomorphism based on the Rasch model.

2. METHOD & RESULTS

As a first step, we designed 37 yes/no items about anthropomorphic qualities a robot can have. We subjected these items to a content validity test, in which we tested all items on *unique humanness* (n=17, M_{age}=21.1, SD_{age}=1.79), *typical humanness* (n=20, M_{age}=19.9, SD_{age}=1.98), *sociality* (n=18, M_{age}=19.9, SD_{age}=1.79) and *valence* (n=20, M_{age}=20, SD_{age}=2.50),

HRI'14, March 3–6, 2014, Bielefeld, Germany.
ACM 978-1-4503-2658-2/14/03.
http://dx.doi.org/10.1145/2559636.2559825

*Corresponding author

where valence should <u>not</u> be correlated with anthropomorphism. Hereafter, we tested the full measurement scale in an online sample with 124 participants (M_{age}=26.1 and SD_{age}=8.82) and analyzed the probability of each item to be answered with 'yes'. The items that were most likely to be answered with 'yes' have a low so called 'item difficulty' and indicate low anthropomorphism whereas the items that were least likely to be answered with 'yes' have a high 'item difficulty' and are high anthropomorphic. These item difficulties thus tell us something about the underlying process of attributing humanlike characteristics to robots.

We used the Rasch model fit statistics (for an overview, see [6]) to determine which of the 37 items were fitting the model. During this process, we removed 12 items (about half of those because of misfit, half because they did not correlate well with the content validity results) to end up with a revised 25-item scale. Infit mean squares for the 25 items ranged from .77 to 1.21; outfit mean squares ranged from .50 to 1.85.

Next, we correlated item difficulties of both the 37-item scale and the 25-item scale with the results of the content validity questions. A high correlation means that the items have similar scores on anthropomorphism and the content validity measure. All correlations confirmed our expectations and are shown in Table 1.

Table 1: Correlations between item difficulties and content validity measures

	37-item	25-item
Uniquely human	$r = .434, p = .007$	$r = .551, p = .004$
Typically human	$r = .603, p < .001$	$r = .652, p < .001$
Sociality	$r = .556, p < .001$	$r = .609, p = .001$
Valence	$r = -.098, p = .563$	$r = -.194, p = .352$

2.1 Measurement verification

After having validated out measurement scale, it still had to be verified. That is, we needed to know to what extent our measurement scale related to already existing anthropomorphism measurements.

In an online study, 131 participants (M_{age}=34.86, SD_{age}=17.592) were divided over two conditions. In each condition, participants watched a video of a robot that either only had typically human characteristics or that also had uniquely human characteristics. Next, participants completed multiple anthropomorphism questionnaires: our 25-item scale ($\alpha = .77$), a 6-item questionnaire proposed by [2], referred to as the Waytz scale ($\alpha = .78$), and the 5-item anthropomorphism part of the Godspeed questionnaire [1], referred to as the Bartneck scale ($\alpha = .71$).

When checking for differences between the videos, no significant effects were found on any of the anthropomorphism measurements (all p's > 0.15). Nevertheless, significant correlations were found between our scale ($M = 9.84$, $SD = 2.79$) and both the Waytz scale ($M = 1.23$, $SD = 0.40$, $r = .453$, $p < .001$) and the Bartneck scale ($M = 2.52$, $SD = 0.82$, $r = .232$, $p = .008$). This suggests that our scale measures the same concept as the other scales. It appears that our scale measures personal dispositions to attribute humanlike characteristics to robots and conjointly the ease with which various anthropomorphic characteristics are attributed to robots. Furthermore, since both our studies applied the same scale, it is possible to make a comparison between them. The item difficulties strongly correlate between the two studies ($r = .962$, $p < .001$), which suggests that the ordering of items on the anthropomorphism continuum is independent of the study.

3. DISCUSSION

In this paper we argued that anthropomorphism does not simply consist of one single attribution, but covers a continuum of attributions ranging from typically to uniquely human characteristics. Most of the previous research conducted on anthropomorphic robots only investigated parts of the continuum, which limits the interpretation of the underlying process.

We argue that when a robot is perceived to have some uniquely human characteristics, this indicates that this robot must contain both typically and uniquely human characteristics. An additional advantage of measuring the two aspects simultaneously is that it shows that all characteristics belong to one continuum, and that these characteristics are hierarchically ordered in a way that is the same for all individuals. This ordering tells us something about the underlying process of anthropomorphism.

In sum, we have developed a measurement scale that consistently measures anthropomorphism as a continuum over different studies. Furthermore, the ordering of the items seems to be stable over different samples. We have shown that the Rasch model can be used to mathematically describe this invariant ordering of anthropomorphic inferences. Follow-up research will be designed to further develop the scale and to investigate its robustness.

4. ACKNOWLEDGMENTS

We would like to thank Antal Haans and Maartje van 't Sant for their helpful contributions to this project.

5. REFERENCES

[1] Bartneck, C., Kulic, D., Croft, E., & Zoghbi, S. (2009). Measurement Instruments for Anthropomorphism, Animacy, Likeability, Perceived Intelligence, and Perceived Safety of Robots. International Journal for Social Robotics, 1 (1), 71-81. DOI: 10.1007/s12369-008-0001-3.

[2] Waytz, A., Morewedge, C., Epley, N., Monteleone, G., Gao, J., & Cacioppo, J. (2010). Making Sense by making Sentient: Effectance Motivation Increases Anthropomorphism. Journal of Personality and Social Psychology, 99 (3), 410-435. DOI: 10.1037/a0020240.

[3] Haslam, N., Bain, P., Loughnan, S., & Kashima, Y. (2008). Attributing and denying humanness to others. European Review of Social Psychology, 19, 55-85.

[4] Eyssel, F., Kuchenbrandt, D., Bobinger, S. (2011). Effects of Anticipated Human-Robot Interaction and Predictability of Robot Behavior on Perceptions of Anthropomorphism. Proceedings of the 6th international conference on Human-robot interaction, 61-68. DOI: 10.1145/1957656.1957673.

[5] de Jong-Gierveld, J., & Kamphuis, F. (1985). The Development of a Rasch-Type Loneliness Scale. Applied Psychological Measurement, 9, 289-299.

[6] Bond, T. G., & Fox, C. M. (2007). Applying the Rasch model: Fundamental measurement in the human sciences.

[7] Green, K.E., & Frantom, C.G. (2002). Survey Development and Validation with the Rasch Model. *Paper presented at the International Conference on Questionnaire Development, Evaluation, and Testing.* Charleston, SC, November 14-17, 2002.

Information-Theoretic Measures as a Generic Approach to Human-Robot Interaction: Application in CORBYS Project

Christoph Salge
University of Hertfordshire
College Lane
AL10 9AB Hatfield, UK
+44 1707 284490
c.salge@herts.ac.uk

Cornelius Glackin
University of Hertfordshire
College Lane
AL10 9AB Hatfield, UK
+44 1707 284490
c.glackin2@herts.ac.uk

Danijela Ristić-Durrant
University of Bremen
Otto-Hahn-Allee, NW1
D-28359 Bremen
+49 421 218 62431
ristic@iat.uni-bremen.de

Martin Greaves
University of Hertfordshire
College Lane
AL10 9AB Hatfield, UK
+44 1707 284490
m.greaves2@herts.ac.uk

Daniel Polani
University of Hertfordshire
College Lane
AL10 9AB Hatfield, UK
+44 1707 284380
d.polani@herts.ac.uk

ABSTRACT
The objective of the CORBYS project is to design and implement a robot control architecture that allows the integration of high-level cognitive control modules, such as a semantically-driven self-awareness module and a cognitive framework for anticipation of, and synergy with, human behaviour based on biologically-inspired information-theoretic principles. CORBYS aims to provide a generic control architecture to benefit a wide range of applications where robots work in synergy with humans, ranging from mobile robots such as robotic followers to gait rehabilitation robots. The behaviour of the two demonstrators, used for validating this architecture, will each be driven by a combination of task specific algorithms and generic cognitive algorithms. In this paper we focus on the generic algorithms based on information theory.

Categories and Subject Descriptors
I.2.9 [**Artificial Intelligence**]: Robotics – *Miscellaneous*

Keywords
Information Theory; Empowerment; Intrinsic Motivation

1. ROBOTIC DEMONSTRATORS
As the first practical application of the CORBYS control architecture, a novel cognitive mobile gait rehabilitation system is being developed during the project's lifetime. The system comprises a mobile platform and a powered orthosis attached to the platform.

The mobile platform will provide mobility for the patient while the powered orthosis will assist in completing his/her leg movements. CORBYS cognitive modules create appropriate commands for low-level robot control derived from the patient's intentions. The cognitive modules are supported by an advanced multi-sensor system consisting of physiological wearable sensors and EEG sensors for perception of the physical and psychological state of the patient. Through cognitive robot control, the CORBYS gait rehabilitation system will be a situationally-aware system capable of learning and reasoning to optimally match the requirements of the patient at different stages of rehabilitation in a range of gait disorders.

The second CORBYS demonstrator is an existing mobile robot that follows a human co-worker during investigation of the environment. The robot is equipped with sensors to perceive and reconstruct the dynamic environment, including the location of the human co-worker. Supported by sensor measurements, the cognitive modules provide a trajectory to the low-level control which realizes a following behavior, whilst maintaining controllability and mobility of the robot.

2. GENERIC COGNITIVE ABILITIES
One question being addressed in the CORBYS project is: Which generic cognitive abilities could benefit both demonstrators, and possibly, an even wider range of robots? Interacting with humans, as both demonstrators do, increases the need for generality, because human behavior is highly unpredictable, and therefore hard to account for in advance. In summary, we are looking for algorithms that can both deal with generic robot architectures and generic situations.

One approach being realized in the CORBYS project is to use information-theoretic measurements to define and work towards certain desirable system properties, which can then be combined with task-dependent robot behavior. Information theory has the advantage that it operates only on random variables, so the perception-action loop of the robot, i.e. its sensors and actuators, can be analyzed as discrete or continuous variables, without the need for labeling. In the following sections we focus on *information flow* and *empowerment* as two information-theoretic measurements; briefly introduce them, and argue that they correspond to desired generic properties.

2.1 Empowerment
Empowerment [1] is an information-theoretic quantity that measures how much an agent is in control of the world it perceives. It can be formalized as the Shannon channel capacity from an agent's actions to an agent's sensors. High empowerment corresponds to having several options to choose from, which all lead to perceivably different and predictable

HRI'14, March 3–6 2014, Bielefeld, Germany
ACM 978-1-4503-2658-2/14/03.
http://dx.doi.org/10.1145/2559636.2563711

outcomes. Low empowerment corresponds to either having no actuator choices, or to a situation in which all actions lead to either the same, or a random outcome.

In the context of a generic robot this means that maximizing the robot's empowerment provides an intrinsic motivation to avoid getting stuck, entering highly unstable situations, or interacting with unpredictable other agents.

After developing a fast, continuous approximation of empowerment [2] we tested how the second CORBYS demonstrator would follow a human, if it was optimizing its trajectory using empowerment [3]. The result was that, even if the robot was currently at an optimal distance to the human, it would still improve its positioning so as to maximize empowerment and to locate itself at a position of high maneuverability. This was particularly beneficial when the human moved through a space that the robot could not, because the robot would start to circumnavigate the obstacle earlier than a robot without empowerment. Also, the robot would avoid positioning itself too close to walls, or in corners or dead ends; all positions where the robot would have low empowerment.

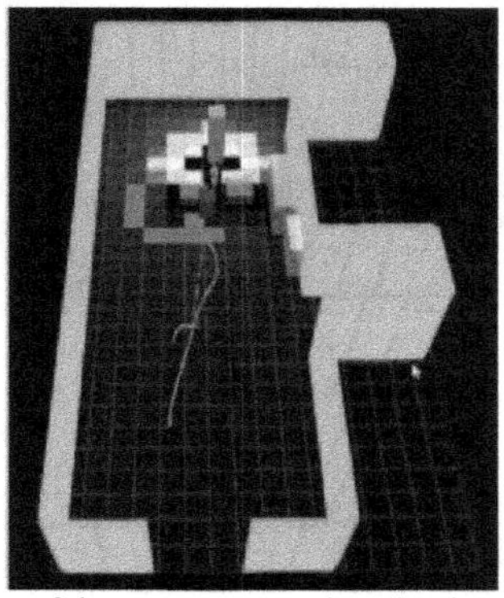

Fig. 2. Visualization of the empowerment-based trajectory planning [3]. The blue cuboid represents the robot, the green cuboid is the human and, the other cuboids are obstacles. The red, high empowered path, shows how the robot, even if the desired distance is already achieved, circumnavigates the obstacles to be in a better position to continue following the human.

Our recent theoretical work on empowerment and unpredictable agents [4] suggests that the same algorithm would also avoid humans if their behavior was unpredictable, but would allow for closer interaction once the robot has a clear grasp of what the humans wants to do.

In the future, we plan to evaluate and optimize the empowerment of the human partner in the interaction. Being empowered means being in overall control of the situation one is in, and this, in general, seems desirable for the human partner in the interaction. This would then result in a motivation for the robot to react predictably to the human's cues, to not interfere with what the human is doing, and to follow the humans lead. All these are desirable properties for both demonstrators. For example, for the robotic gait rehabilitation system, this would mean that the robot would provide the level of support the patient needs only when the patient needs it.

Furthermore, as we hypothesized that humans try to maximize their empowerment in specific situations [5], the ability to evaluate the human's future empowerment could aid a robot in predicting the human's actions.

2.2 Information Flow

Information flow [6] quantifies the amount of causal influence one variable has on another. Incidentally, empowerment can also be expressed as the maximal potential information flow from actuators to sensors. In our human-robot interaction scenarios we aim to quantify how much causal influence the robot and the human have on the outcome of the overall situation, or on a relevant subset thereof.

This is particularly relevant for the first CORBYS demonstrator, because the powered orthosis should influence the outcome, since it is designed to correct the human's gait patterns, but it should not be the sole originator of movement. By measuring the information flow from EMG sensors corresponding to the human muscle commands to the resulting joint angles the robot should be able to evaluate if the human is still initiating the resulting movements. On the other hand, the information flow from the robot's actuators to the resulting joint angles could help to identify the amount of correction that is still required.

The desired values for both flows can be adjusted to generically reflect the causal dominance relation between the human and the robot. For the second demonstrator the desired flow is purely from the human to the robot. A causal flow from the robot to the human would indicate that the robot is interfering with the human's state, which is not desirable in this robotic follower scenario. In conclusion, theoretical evaluation and preliminary testing on actual robots indicate that both formalisms are capable of providing some desired robot's behavior.

3. ACKNOWLEDGEMENTS

This research was supported by the European Commission as part of the CORBYS (Cognitive Control Framework for Robotic Systems) project under contract FP7 ICT-270219. (www.corbys.eu)

REFERENCES

[1] A. Klyubin, D. Polani and C. Nehaniv, "Keep your options open: An information-based driving principle for sensorimotor systems," *Plos ONE,* vol. 3, p. e4018, 2008.

[2] C. Salge, C. Glackin and D. Polani, "Approximation of empowerment in the continuous domain," *Advances in Complex Systems,* pp. 1-29, 2013a.

[3] A. Leu, D. Ristic-Durrant, S. Slavnic, C. Glackin, C. Salge, D. Polani, A. Badii, A. Khan and R. Raval, "CORBYS Cognitive Control Architecture for Robotic Follower," in *IEEE/SICE International Symposium on System Integration.*, 2013.

[4] C. Salge, C. Glackin and D. Polani, "Empowerment and state-dependent noise - an intrinsic motivation for avoiding unpredictable agents," in *12th European Conference on Artificial Life (ECAL 2013)*, 2013c.

[5] C. Salge, C. Glackin and D. Polani, "Empowerment - an introduction," in *Guided Self-Organisation*, Springer, 2013b.

[6] N. Ay and D. Polani, "Information flows in causal networks," *Advances in complex systems,* vol. 11, no. 1, pp. 17-41, 2008.

Investigating the Impact of Gender Development in Child-Robot Interaction

Anara Sandygulova
University College Dublin
Belfield, Dublin 4, Ireland
anara.sandygulova
@ucdconnect.ie

Mauro Dragone
University College Dublin
Belfield, Dublin 4, Ireland
mauro.dragone@ucd.ie

Gregory M.P. O'Hare
University College Dublin
Belfield, Dublin 4, Ireland
gregory.ohare@ucd.ie

ABSTRACT
In order to inform the design of robotic applications for children, in this paper we describe and report the results of an experiment we conducted in a primary school. Our work investigates the effects of the robot's perceived gender and age on levels of engagement and acceptance of the robot by children across different age and gender groups. Our results show that children across ages relate differently toward perceived robot's age and gender.

Categories and Subject Descriptors
H.1.2 [**Models and Principles**]: User/Machine Systems - *human factors, software psychology*

Keywords
Human-Robot Interaction, Personalization

1. INTRODUCTION
This work focuses on investigating personalization issues for children of different ages. The literature in child psychology on trends in gender development [1] suggests that children of different age groups show different reaction regarding children's toys, activities, traits and play preferences. For example, until 7 or 8 years of age, gender stereotypes remain very rigid, but after that age the stereotype rigidity gradually decreases with girls showing more and earlier stereotype flexibility than boys. Children's gender concepts start to become more flexible and adaptable. However, from 12 years and older reactions to cross-gender behavior and appearance become more negative, reversing the trend seen up until adolescence. Our work aims to investigate whether the robot's perceived age and gender will affect the way children engage with the robot and how it will differ across age groups.

2. EXPERIMENT
The robotic testbed exploited for this experiment is detailed in [2]. Figure 1 presents the experimental setup: a toy kitchen is placed in the middle of the small room with a humanoid robot Nao standing next to it on the left. A camera was placed in front of the child to capture facial expressions for real-time happiness analysis using the SHORE software[1].

Figure 1: Experimental Setup

The experiment is structured as an interactive game. The robot greets the child and explains that its new job is to keep people safe by reminding them to turn off appliances in the kitchen. The child is kindly asked by the robot to help it practice for the new job by opening a microwave, an oven or a press of the toy kitchen equipped with sensors. As the child opens the doors, the robot notifies what appliance has been opened. After the experiment, the child is given a "Super Star" sticker.

The independent variables of the experiment are robot voices: Josh, a child male voice, Rosie, a child female voice, and Tracy, an adult female voice. These voices are available from Acapela Inc. Participants were randomly assigned to interact with either Nao's Josh, Rosie or Tracy voice with applied counterbalancing in terms of gender and age group.

3. RESULTS
The experiment was conducted in a primary school in Dublin with children aged between 8 and 12 years old. The experiment involved 76 children, 40 girls and 36 boys. There were 16 children aged 8 years old, 15 children were 9 years old, 20 children were 10 years of age, 20 children were of age 11 and 5 children were 12 years of age.

[1]http://www.iis.fraunhofer.de/en/bf/bsy/produkte/shore.html

HRI'14, March 3–6, 2014, Bielefeld, Germany.
ACM 978-1-4503-2658-2/14/03.
http://dx.doi.org/10.1145/2559636.2559848

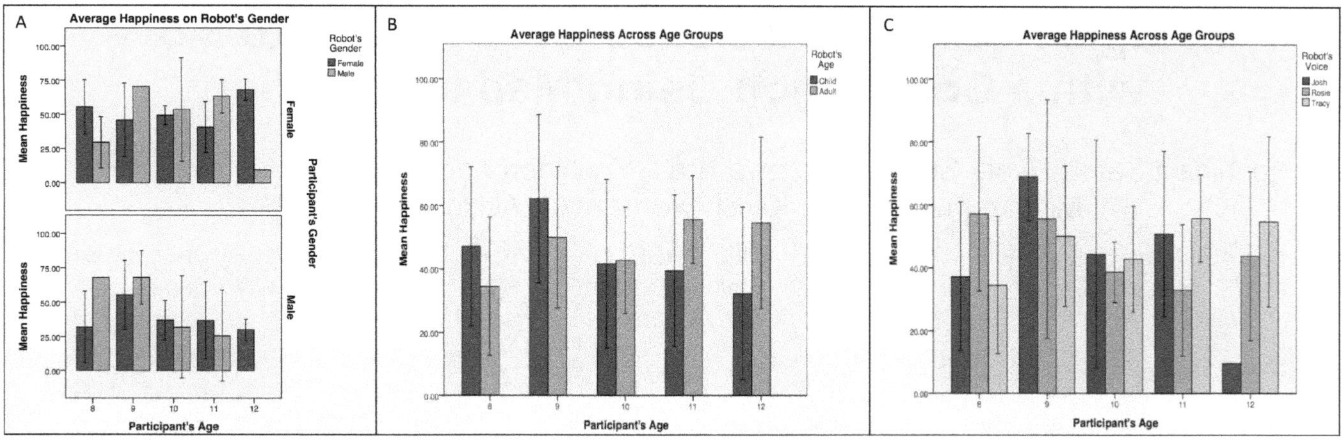

Figure 2: Happiness Comparison Graphs on (A) Robot's Gender; (B) Robot's Age; (C) Robot's Voice.

The expressed happiness score is measured every second over the duration of each session from the moment the robot starts speaking till the "Super Star" sticker is mentioned by the robot. The final average score of the expressed happiness is calculated for each participant.

A series of two-way ANOVA tests on different measurements were conducted in order to test for statistically significant differences between various combinations of the robot's gender and age conditions. We found a significant interaction between the effects of child's gender and robot's gender on the expressed happiness, $F(1,\ 12) = 4.935,\ p = 0.046$ for 8 years old children. However, the results for other age groups are not statistically significant: $F(1,\ 11) = 0.119,\ p = 0.737$ for children of 9, and $F(1,\ 16) = 0.170,\ p = 0.686$ for 10, and $F(1,\ 16) = 2.292,\ p = 0.150$ for 11 years old children. Figure 2A illustrates these results.

When comparing the average happiness score across age groups in relation to the robot's age, the results are not statistically significant mainly due to the large variation from the average. However, the average scores differences are still sufficiently indicative to suggest a meaning (see Figure 2B). There was a noteworthy preference for the child's voice of the robot for 8 ($F(1,\ 12) = 0.445,\ p = 0.517$)) and 9 ($F(1,\ 11) = 1.424,\ p = 0.258$) years old children and an indicative preference for the adult voice of the robot for 11 ($F(1,16) = 0.412,\ p = 0.530$) and 12 years old children. Children of 10 years of age expressed similar levels of happiness for both age conditions of the robot's voice. Figure 2C presents the break down of these results by the age and gender differences of the robot's voice: Josh, the boy's voice, Rosie, the girl's voice, and Tracy, the adult's female voice.

4. DISCUSSION

The results from this experiment indicate that children have different perspectives toward the robot's voice across various age groups. Our results suggest that children prefer same-age voice when interacting with the robot until the age of 10. However, from the age of 10 years there is a steady increase in the level of expressed happiness towards the robot's voice of a female adult Tracy. This is important to consider when designing a personalized robot for children.

Similarly to the robot's age effect, our results indicate that children relate differently to the robot's gender at different age groups which is supported by the literature in child psychology [1]. These trends in gender development have been demonstrated in a statistically significant interaction ($p < 0.05$) between the effect of same-gender voices on likeability and engagement by the 8 years old children. According to [1], acceptance of cross-gender behavior and appearance increases during middle primary school which supports the non-significant preferences toward the opposite-gender voices for children of 9-10 years old.

5. CONCLUSIONS AND FUTURE WORK

This experiment provides strong support for continuing the research direction of the child-robot personalization through verbal and non-verbal behaviors of the robot. Specifically, this paper describes an experiment with the ubiquitous robotic system where a humanoid robot Nao interacted with the children with either a child male, a child female or an adult human-like voice in order to investigate children's preferences toward the robot's gender and age. Our results suggest that children relate differently to the robot's age and gender at different age groups. This is important to consider when designing robotic applications for children in order to increase robot's perceived likeability, acceptance and engagement.

6. ACKNOWLEDGMENTS

This work has been supported by the Irish Research Council "Embark Initiative", in conjunction with funding from the EU FP7 RUBICON project (contract n. 269914), and Science Foundation Ireland (SFI) under grant 07/CE/I1147.

7. REFERENCES

[1] J. Cook and G. Cook. *Child Development: Principles and Perspectives.* Allyn & Bacon, Incorporated, 2003.

[2] A. Sandygulova and M. Dragone. A portable and self-presenting robotic ecology hri testbed. In M. O'Grady, H. Vahdat-Nejad, K.-H. Wolf, M. Dragone, J. Ye, C. Röcker, and G. O'Hare, editors, *Evolving Ambient Intelligence*, volume 413 of *Communications in Computer and Information Science*, pages 136–150. Springer International Publishing, 2013.

Multiple Robotic Wheelchair System Able to Move with a Companion Using Map Information

Yoshihisa Sato*, Ryota Suzuki*, Masaya Arai*, Yoshinori Kobayashi*,**, Yoshinori Kuno*, Mihoko Fukushima*, Keiichi Yamazaki*, Akiko Yamazaki***

*Saitama University
Saitama, Japan

**JST PRESTO
Saitama, Japan

***Tokyo University of Technology
Tokyo, Japan

Abstract

In order to reduce the burden of caregivers facing an increased demand for care, particularly for the elderly, we developed a system whereby multiple robotic wheelchairs can automatically move alongside a companion. This enables a small number of people to assist a substantially larger number of wheelchair users effectively. This system utilizes an environmental map and an estimation of position to accurately identify the positional relations among the caregiver (or a companion) and each wheelchair. The wheelchairs are consequently able to follow along even if the caregiver cannot be directly recognized. Moreover, the system is able to establish and maintain appropriate positional relations.

Categories and Subject Descriptors

H5.2. Information interfaces and presentation (e.g., HCI). User Interfaces – Interaction styles

General Terms

Human factors, design, experimentation

Keywords

Robotic wheelchair, human-robot interaction, ethnomethodology, computer vision

1. Introduction

In recent years, the demand for care has been increasing in Japan, and with an aging population, the shortage of caregivers has become a concern. In addition, in an emergency situation such as evacuating people from the site of a disaster, it is necessary to move a large number of people requiring nursing care as quickly and safely as possible. In response to such needs, this paper proposes a multiple robotic wheelchair system able to move with a companion. Previously, we reported that when a wheelchair user uses a wheelchair themselves and moves along with a companion, the formation of the companion and the wheelchair change depending on the surrounding environment, such as passage width[2]. Furthermore, we observed groups of multiple individuals including wheelchair users that were told to move to a given destination while making conversation en route. We found that in such groups, able-bodied participants would run alongside the wheelchair users and try to communicate face-to-face. In nursing homes, it is known that face-to-face communication can help prevent the progress of dementia. Therefore, a mobile wheelchair system must move in a formation suitable to facilitating communication among the companion and wheelchair users. Accordingly, it is necessary to implement following three functions: 1) understanding the position of the companion and the course, 2) understanding the position of the wheelchair relative to the other wheelchair(s), and 3) understanding the surrounding environment. In this paper, we propose a method incorporating the map information to deal with the function 2) and 3).

HRI'14, March 3–6, 2014, Bielefeld, Germany.
ACM 978-1-4503-2658-2/14/03.
http://dx.doi.org/10.1145/2559636.2563694

2. Formation in a Group

To observe formation changes in multi-person groups including wheelchair users, we conducted an experiment on the second floor of the Thinktank Birmingham Science Museum. The groups each consisted of 2-4 people including a wheelchair user, and were given a problem that could be answered by looking around a floor of the museum, such as "What different modes of transportation can you see? Name three." We then observed the groups while they followed a pre-determined route around the floor, to see what spatial formation they adopted while answering the problem. Their task was written on a task sheet held by one of the able-bodied participants in the group. Figure 1 shows an example of one of the groups. In this group of four museum staff, the individual in a yellow shirt held the task sheet. During the experiment, we observed that the able-bodied participants would run alongside the wheelchair users to enable face-to-face communication. Based on this, we came to understand the importance of people maintaining a parallel formation so that the wheelchair user could continue conversation with the group.

Figure 1. Example of a conversation in the group including a wheelchair user

3. Multiple Robotic Wheelchair System

Figure 2 shows an overview of our robotic wheelchair, which is assembled from an electric wheelchair and incorporates two laser range sensors, an omnidirectional camera, an on-board laptop and microcomputer for controlling motion, and a computer for localization and mapping. The laser range sensors are employed to track the caregiver and observe the environment around the wheelchair. One of them is attached to the rear pole and positioned horizontally at the companion's shoulder level, while the other is attached to the lower part of the wheelchair. The laptop makes judgments for controlling the wheelchair, while the microcomputer relays commands from the laptop to the wheelchair.

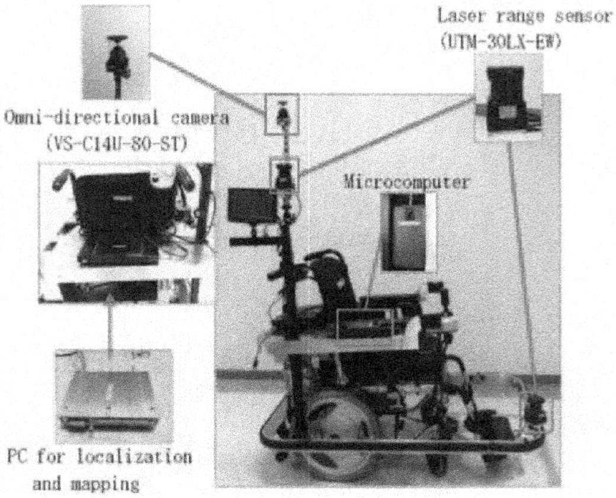

Figure 2. Overview of robotic wheelchair

3.1 Tracking a Companion.

In order to move alongside a companion, the ability to detect the companion's position and direction is necessary. We implemented this using a laser sensor positioned at the companion's shoulder level. The wheelchair detects (from its perspective) the position and the direction of the companion using a particle filter method as implemented in [1].

3.2 Mapping and Localization

As indicated above, to be effective a multiple robotic wheelchair system must be able to consider the surrounding environment and change its position in relation to the companion and other wheelchair(s) appropriately. To implement these functions, the multiple robotic wheelchair system must convey the positional relations among each wheelchair and the companion, and accurately comprehend the surrounding environment. Therefore, we implemented the ability for the wheelchair to estimate its own position. The localization PC performs estimates the dimensions of the neighboring environment utilizing the laser sensor attached to the lower part of the wheelchair. The PC then builds an environmental map based on this distance data, and estimates the position of the wheelchair within a map of that environment. The results of these estimations are sent to the laptop. For localization, the PC estimates the wheelchair's position using the following three elements: the distance data retrieved from the laser sensor, an environmental map made beforehand, and the initial position in that environmental map. Fig. 3 shows the system conveying positions within the environmental map. The environmental map is demarcated in white, while the wheelchairs are indicated by the red and green squares. The wheelchair shown with a red square is flanked by walls and cannot observe the green wheelchair directly. However, since the wheelchairs share the positional information in the environmental map, they can know each other's position.

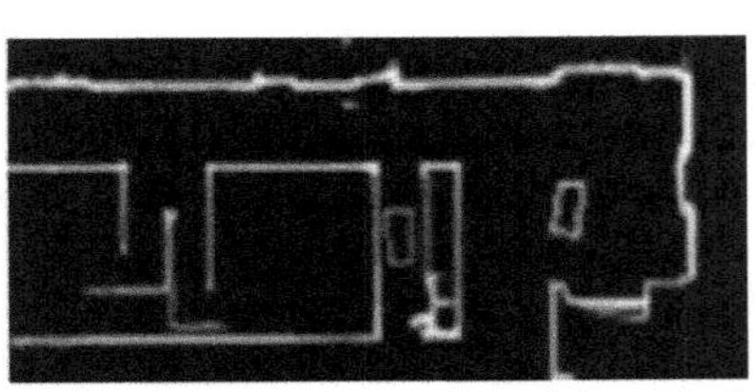

Figure 3. Environmental map and position of wheelchairs

3.3 Operation Experiment

We implemented our multiple robotic wheelchair system based on the system outlined above, and tested its functions. In a large open space, the wheelchairs move alongside a companion, enabling the companion to easily talk with the wheelchair users (Fig. 4). In small passages, the wheelchairs adopt a single-file formation (Fig. 5). Depending on the situation and the conversation, the system can adaptively change formation; for example, another formation has one wheelchair alongside the companion while the other follows behind (Fig. 6). Moreover, since the wheelchairs share positional data with each other, even if the laser sensor situated at the companion's shoulder level is shut out and placed in a situation where the wheelchair cannot observe the companion directly, the wheelchair can still maintain an appropriate positional relation and move with the companion (Fig. 7).

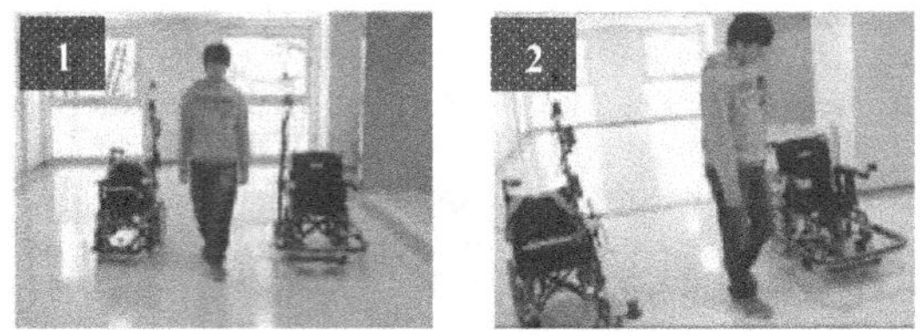

Figure 4. Wheelchair movement

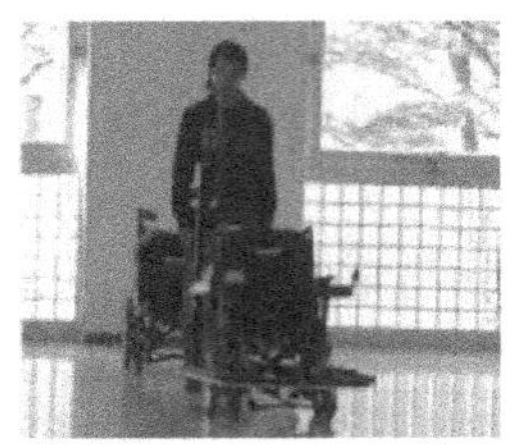

Figure 5. Single-file formation

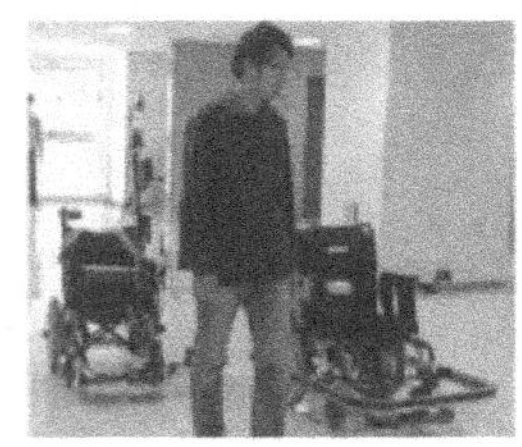

Figure 6. Side and back formation

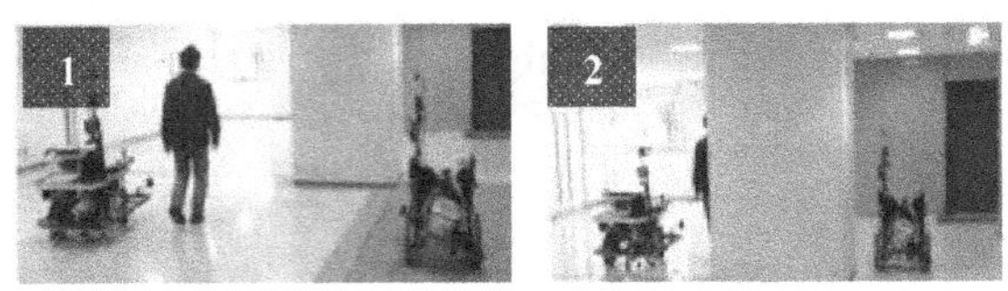

Figure 7. A wheelchair navigates around a wall

4. Conclusion

Through the system proposed in this paper, robotic wheelchairs can follow a companion in an adaptive and effective manner. However, in a real nursing home, multiple wheelchairs may need to move with multiple companions in one group. Consequently, we intend to continue to develop this system to devise one able to handle a wheelchair following a group of people. We plan to devise and critically evaluate a system capable of judging whether or not there are multiple people in a group, and assessing the appropriate positional relations enabling it to follow the group.

5. References

[1] Y. Kobayashi, Y. Kinpara, T. Shibusawa and Y. Kuno, "Robotic wheelchair based on observations of people using integrated sensors," Proc. IROS2009, pp.2013-2018, (2009).

[2] E. Takano, Y. Kobayashi, and Y. Kuno, "Multiple Robotic Wheelchair System Based on the Observation of Circumstances," Proc. FCV2012, pp.222-226, (2012).

Mobile Teleoperation Interfaces with Adjustable Autonomy for Personal Service Robots

Max Schwarz
Computer Science Institute VI
University of Bonn
max.schwarz@uni-bonn.de

Jörg Stückler
Computer Science Institute VI
University of Bonn
stueckler@ais.uni-bonn.de

Sven Behnke
Computer Science Institute VI
University of Bonn
behnke@cs.uni-bonn.de

ABSTRACT

Personal service robots require a comprehensive set of perception, control, and planning skills to perform everyday tasks autonomously. While achieving full autonomy is an ongoing research topic, first real-world applications of personal robots may come into reach, if state-of-the-art autonomous capabilities are combined with the intelligence of the users in a complementary way. We report on handheld user interfaces for personal robots that allow for teleoperating the robot on three levels of autonomy: body, skill, and task control. On the higher levels, autonomous behavior of the robot relieves the user from significant workload. If autonomous execution fails, or autonomous functionality is not provided by the robot system, the user can select a lower level of autonomy to solve a task. The benefits of providing adjustable autonomy in teleoperation have been successfully demonstrated at RoboCup@Home competitions.

1. INTRODUCTION

Personal robots that shall assist persons in their activities of daily living (ADL) not only require versatile autonomous skills but also intuitive user interfaces. Many high-level tasks that are difficult to achieve autonomously can already be tackled when the intelligence of the user is combined with robot skills by means of teleoperation. In this way, both sides contribute their strengths and complement each other. Nevertheless, users want personal robots as convenient tools that act as autonomously as possible, since steady low-level control of the robot would be tedious and time-consuming. Only in difficult situations, in which no autonomous solution exists yet, the user should need to take over control of the robot on the most convenient, i.e. most autonomous, level.

We propose handheld user interfaces that allow persons to teleoperate a complex anthropomorphic service robot on various levels of autonomy. The user adjusts the autonomy level according to the complexity of the task and available robot capabilities. The notion of adjustable autonomy has been coined by Goodrich et al. [1]. Leeper et al. [2] evaluate body-level teleoperation GUIs for mobile manipulation. We identified *body*, *skill*, and *task* level autonomy [3]. We develop our teleoperation interfaces for our domestic service robots Dynamaid and Cosero [4]. These robots have mobile manipulation and human-robot interaction capabilities to perform tasks autonomously in everyday environments. This involves the manipulation of objects such as grasping and placing of objects. The robots are also required to navigate safely through the environment. They naturally interact with users through speech and gestures.

HRI'14, March 3–6, 2014, Bielefeld, Germany.
ACM 978-1-4503-2658-2/14/03.
http://dx.doi.org/10.1145/2559636.2563716.

2. HANDHELD USER INTERFACES

Modern handheld computers such as smart phones, tablets and slates provide complementary user interfaces that add a variety of novel interaction modes. They improve common ground, since the GUI can be designed to mediate what the robot actually can do. For instance, the user may only be given the choice between possible actions and involved objects and locations. They enable teleoperation without direct auditory or visual connection to the robot. The user gains situational awareness through the visualization of the robot's view. We investigate teleoperation with a handheld computer on three levels of autonomy. On the body level, the operator directly controls body parts such as the end-effectors, the gaze direction, or the omnidirectional drive. On the skill level, the operator controls robot skills, e.g. by setting navigation goals or commanding objects to be grasped. Finally, the operator configures autonomous high-level behaviors that sequence skills on the task level.

2.1 Body-Level Teleoperation

The body-level controls allow the user to execute actions with the robot that are not covered by autonomous skills and therefore are not supported on higher levels of the teleoperation interface. The user gains situational awareness through the visualization of live camera images, external robot views, and 2D laser scans (see Fig. 1). To prevent the robot from being damaged by executing dangerous user commands, these modes include obstacle avoidance.

2.2 Skill-Level Teleoperation

The skill-level user interfaces configure robot skills that require the execution of a sequence of body motions. The robot controls these body motions autonomously. By that, the workload on the user is reduced. While the robot executes the skill, the user can supervise its progress. Compared to body-level control, the skill-level UI does require less communication bandwidth, since images and control commands

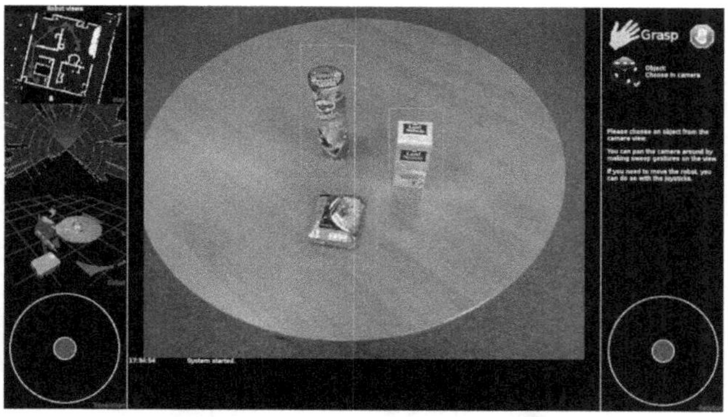

Figure 1: Skill and body-level GUI with a view selection column on the left, a main view in the center, a configuration column on the right, and a log message window on the bottom center. Motion is controlled directly with two joystick control UIs.

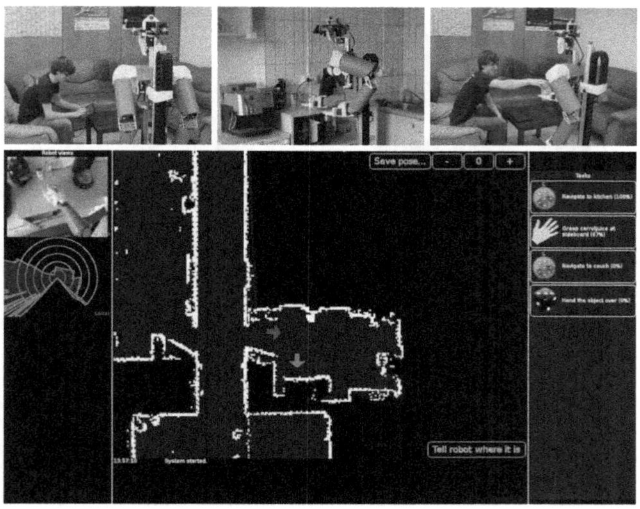

Figure 2: Illustration of our task-level teleoperation interface. Top left: A user composes a task. Bottom/top middle: The robot grasps an object. Top right: The robot delivers the object.

have to be transmitted with less frequency. Hence, this mode is less affected by high latency or low bandwidth communication. The user has access to several autonomous robot skills such as navigation to goal poses in a map, grasping objects in the view of the robot, and handing objects over to a user.

2.3 Task-Level Teleoperation

The task-level teleoperation UI is intended to provide the high-level behavior capabilities of the robot (see Fig. 2). The user can compose actions, objects, and locations similar to our implementation for the parsing of complex speech commands. Our user interfaces allow for composing a sequence of skills in two stages. On the top level UI, the user adds and removes skills from the sequence. Once a skill is selected, the user specifies location and object for the skill on a second layer UI. A monitoring UI lets the user keep track of the robot's execution status. One can also watch progress on the body- and skill-level UIs.

3. RESULTS

At RoboCup 2012 and German Open 2013 we demonstrated concepts of mobile teleoperation with Cosero. Note that at that time we used slightly simplified versions of our UIs where the tasks could be selected individually. In the Demo Challenge at RoboCup 2012, we showed an elderly-care scenario in which a user commanded the robot to fetch a drink from another room. At first, the person let the robot fetch a specific beverage. The robot drove to the assumed location of the drink, but since it was not available, the user had to take a different choice. The user switched to the skill-level control UI and selected one of the other beverages that were perceived by the robot on the table and displayed in live images on the UI. Finally, the robot grasped the selected drink, brought it to the user and handed it over. The demonstration was well received by the jury consisting of the league's technical and executive committee members. Overall, our team NimbRo@Home became world champion in the 2012 RoboCup@Home competition. At German Open 2013, we extended the Demo Challenge with receiving objects from users and putting the object in a waste bin. Our team received best score in this test and also won the competition. At RoboCup 2013 in Eindhoven, Netherlands, we presented the teleoperation UI with task specification to the jury in the DemoChallenge. Our team could also win the RoboCup@Home 2013 competition.

4. CONCLUSIONS

We propose mobile teleoperation interfaces with adjustable autonomy for personal service robots. We identified three levels of autonomy and designed various user interfaces on these levels for handheld computers. On the body level, the user can control body motions such as omnidirectional driving and gaze direction. The next higher level allows the execution of robot skills. These skills require a sequence of body motions and perception capabilities which are executed autonomously by the robot. The task-level UI is designed to configure high-level behavior similar to complex speech commands. Failures are detected on the skill- and task-level automatically and reported to the user. The user then decides for the appropriate low level UIs to resolve the situation. We demonstrated our mobile teleoperation interfaces successfully at RoboCup@Home competitions in 2012 and 2013. We will continue to integrate functionality into our user interface and investigate the use of speech as a complementary input modality for the handheld.

5. REFERENCES

[1] M. Goodrich, D. Olsen, J. Crandall, and T. Palmer. Experiments in adjustable autonomy. In *IJCAI WS on Autonomy, Delegation and Control*, 2001.

[2] A. Leeper, K. Hsiao, M. Ciocarlie, L. Takayama, and D. Gossow. Strategies for human-in-the-loop robotic grasping. In *ACM/IEEE Int. Conf. on HRI*, 2012.

[3] S. Muszynski, J. Stückler, and S. Behnke. Adjustable autonomy for mobile teleoperation of personal service robots. In *IEEE Int. Symp. on Robot and Human Interactive Communication (RO-MAN)*, 2012.

[4] J. Stückler, D. Holz, and S. Behnke. RoboCup@Home: Demonstrating everyday manipulation skills in RoboCup@Home. *IEEE Robotics & Automation Magazine*, 19(2):2–14, 2012.

Development of Perception of Weight from Human or Robot Lifting Observation

Alessandra Sciutti, Laura Patanè, Francesco Nori, Giulio Sandini
Robotics, Brain and Cognitive Sciences Dept., Istituto Italiano di Tecnologia
Via Morego 30, Genova, Italy; +3901071781475
alessandra.sciutti@iit.it

ABSTRACT

Human interaction is based, among other factors, on non verbal and implicit communication. By observing the action of someone else we can automatically infer several non obvious details of what's happening, as the goal of the agent, his mood and even some features of the object he is using, e.g., if it is heavy or light. This action reading skill is developed very early in life and constitutes a fundamental basis for the development of collaboration. A similar capacity to implicitly communicate weight would be desirable also in a humanoid robot, to allow for a natural preparation for hand-over between the robot and the human partner. Here we have investigated how the ability to infer weight from human action observation develops during childhood and whether such ability generalizes to the observation of a humanoid robot. In particular, the robot was not programmed to perform human-like lifting actions, but just to replicate a property of human lifting deemed as determinant for weight reading: exhibiting a velocity proportional to object weight. Our results suggest that although 6-year-olds can already judge weight from the observation of a lifting action, they cannot generalize this skill to simplified robotic actions as the ones proposed here.

Keywords

Action understanding; Humanoid; Kinematics; Development.

1. INTRODUCTION

One of the most classical examples of collaborative tasks is the hand-over of a tool between two partners. Although the dynamics of the passage is crucial for the success of the action, usually also the previous movements have a substantial impact on interaction fluency. Already by observing the other person lifting the object, the partner automatically estimates its weight and can plan in advance his receiving action [5]. The possibility to anticipate weight allows for a particularly smooth and efficient collaboration. The attainment of a similar seamless interaction would be important also in human-robot dyads, especially in the perspective of the inclusion of robots in everyday life situations [7]. An important first step in this direction would be endowing a robotic platform with the ability to implicitly communicate weight just by lifting an object, as human agents do. Previous studies have indicated that vertical velocity of the actor's effector during lifting is one of the most important parameters to allow visual weight judgments [2]. Moreover, a humanoid robot exhibiting a load-dependent velocity rule in its lifting actions yielded correct weight judgments from human observers with no need of extensive training [6]. Our question is whether this approach can be generalized to communicate weight to a different group of non expert users, as school-age children.

HRI'14, March 3–6, 2014, Bielefeld, Germany.
ACM 978-1-4503-2658-2/14/03.
http://dx.doi.org/10.1145/2559636.2559823

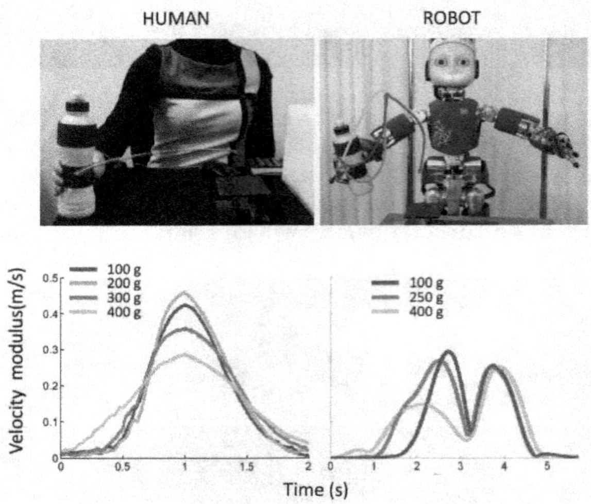

Figure 1. Snapshots of the video stimuli, with trajectories (superimposed) and velocity modulus of the actor's hand.

2. METHODS

28 healthy subjects agreed voluntarily to participate in the experiments: nine 6-year-olds, seven 10-year-olds and twelve adults (mean ± SD age: 32 ± 11). Participants watched a set of movies where a human or a humanoid robot lifted various bottles, apparently identical but of different weights, ranging from 100 to 400g (Figure 1). After each movie they had to estimate the weight of the bottle by selecting a number between 1 and 9, corresponding to a range from 50g to 450g with 50g increments. Before experiment initiation, subjects lifted 4 bottles of known weight (100g, 200g, 300g and 400g) to experience the range of loads lifted in the videos. The human demonstrator was a trained experimenter, informed of object weight before action initiation. The robot demonstrator was iCub, a humanoid robot approximately 1 m tall with the appearance of a 3.5 years old child [4]. Robot's lifting actions were designed by defining three via points in joint coordinates and by manually assigning the velocity at each joint and the duration of each movement phase by using a graphical interface. To differentiate robot movement for different weights we mainly modified the vertical velocity of the lifting action (see Figure 1, bottom panel), because it has been indicated as one of the most salient parameter for weight judgment during human action observation [2]. The experiment consisted of 20 trials with the Human actor and 15 trials with the Robot actor. The Robot and Human videos were presented in blocked session, with always Human session first. To analyze the data, we regressed the estimates against the weights actually

presented in the movies for each subject. A slope near one represents a good ability in discriminating different loads, while near 0 values correspond to the incapability of judging weight from action observation. Slopes have been grouped on the basis of participants' age and have been submitted to one sample t-tests to assess their difference from 0. Then, they were submitted to a two-way mixed-model ANOVA (between factor: AGE; 3 levels: 6 YO, 10 YO, 32 YO; within factor: ACTOR; 2 levels: HUMAN – ROBOT) to assess the potential effect of development and actor's nature on weight reading performance.

3. RESULTS

Already from 6 years of age children are quite good at inferring weight from the observation of a human lifting action (see Figure 2, white bars). The mean slope of the estimates regression against real weight is significantly larger than 0 ($t(8) = 6.14$, $p < 0.001$ in a one sample t-test) and is not significantly different from older children's or adults' performance (no effect of AGE in the mixed-model ANOVA $F(2, 25)=2.9$, $p=.074$). However their judgment is on average impaired when they have to estimate the weight lifted by the humanoid robot (compare white and grey columns, on the left of Figure 2). Their average slope in this condition is not significantly different from 0 ($t(8) = 1.25$ $p= 0.25$, one sample t-test). A mixed-model ANOVA to test the effect of age and of actor type (i.e., human versus robot) indicated a significant effect of actor type and a significant interaction between the two factors (ACTOR: $F(1, 25)=6.48$, $p=.02$; AGE * ACTOR $F(2, 25)=8.18$, $p=.002$). A multiple comparison with Bonferroni correction showed a significant difference between the "Robot" and "Human" slopes at 6 years of age, but for no other age groups. Additionally, performance in the "Robot" condition was significantly worse for 6-year-olds than for adults.

4. DISCUSSION

Since childhood humans exhibit the ability to read different aspects of others' actions just from mere observation. For instance, young children (five to seven years of age) have been shown to be able to judge the weight of a heavy wooden box, just by looking at an actor lifting and transporting it [3]. An important question is how to design robot motion to make it similarly implicitly understandable even by young users. To this aim, a common strategy is that of designing human-like motion, starting from data collected from human demonstrations. This way, synthesized actions implicitly encode the properties of natural human behaviors [1]. Here we have tried to enable implicit robot communication without precisely copying human motion, but rather by replicating a property of natural lifting which seems to be central to implicit communication, even for small variations in the mass to be lifted, i.e., load-dependent lifting speed [2,6]. Our findings show that this approach works extremely well for adults and older children, who judge correctly the weights lifted both by a human and by a robotic demonstrator, with no need for training. On the contrary, 6-year-olds cannot generalize their already developed weight reading ability to robot observation. This might happen because the child cannot match his own action capabilities with that of an agent with a robotic appearance, never experienced before. The absence of generalization could be due either to the difference in appearance between the human and the robot actors or to the differences in action kinematics (trajectory and speed profile). Future research will be dedicated to the investigation of

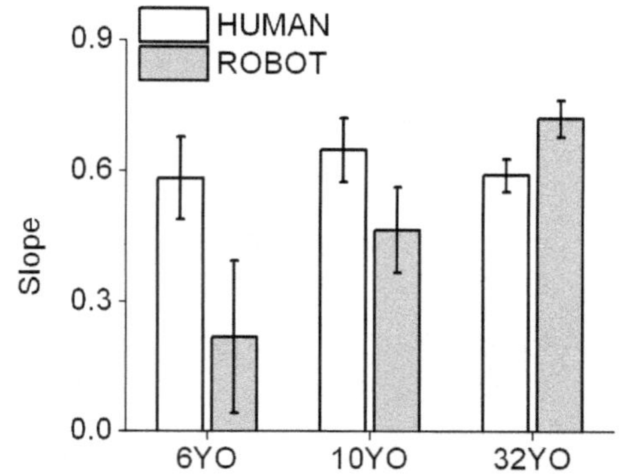

Figure 2. Average slopes of the regression of weight estimates against real weight. Error bars represent group standard errors.

these two alternative hypotheses. In conclusion, these findings suggest that a simplified robotic behavior effective for human-robot communication with adults might not generalize to young users.

5. ACKNOWLEDGMENTS

The authors would like to thank Elisa Freddi, Monica Gori, Marco Jacono, Gabriel Baud-Bovy, Laura Taverna, Vadim Tikhanoff and Francesco Rea for their support in this work.

6. REFERENCES

[1] Billard, A.; Calinon, S.; Dillmann, R. & Schaal, S. Survey: Robot Programming by Demonstration. *Handbook of Robotics*, 2008

[2] Hamilton, A. F., Joyce, D. W., Flanagan, J. R., Frith, C. D. and Wolpert, D. M. 2007. Kinematic cues in perceptual weight judgement and their origins in box lifting. *Psychol Res*, 71, 13-21

[3] Kaiser, M. K. and Proffitt, D. R. The development of sensitivity to causally relevant dynamic information. 1984. *Child Dev*, 55, 1614-1624

[4] Metta, G., Natale, L., Nori, F., Sandini, G., Vernon, D., Fadiga, L., von Hofsten, C., Rosander, K., Lopes, M., Santos-Victor, J., Bernardino, A. and Montesano, L. 2010. The iCub humanoid robot: an open-systems platform for research in cognitive development. *Neural Netw*, 23, 1125-1134

[5] Reichelt, A. F.;,Ash, A. M., Baugh, L. A.,Johansson, R. S. and Flanagan, J. R. 2013. Adaptation of lift forces in object manipulation through action observation. *Exp Brain Res*, 228, 221-234.

[6] Sciutti, A., Patanè, L., Nori, F. and Sandini, G. 2013. Do humans need learning to read humanoid lifting actions?. *Proceeding of IEEE Third Joint International Conference on Development and Learning and Epigenetic Robotics (ICDL)*, 1-6

[7] Strabala, K., Lee, M. K., Dragan, A., Forlizzi, J., Srinivasa, S.;,Cakmak, M. and Micelli, V. 2013. Towards Seamless Human-Robot Handovers. *Journal of Human-Robot Interaction*, 2013

Kinesthetic Human/Robot Coordination

The coordination of movements for interaction

Anders Stengaard Sørensen
The Mærsk Institute
University of Southern Denmark
anders-s@stengaard.net

Gitte Rasmussen
Institute for language and communication
University of Southern Denmark
gitter@sdu.dk

Dennis Day
Institute for language and communication
University of Southern Denmark
dennis.day@sdu.dk

ABSTRACT

Training with a robotic training partner, is a physical, powerful, and yet intimate form of robot/human interaction (RHI). In this paper we report on the early stages of a project, that aims to study and use the human kinesthetic "language" of co-motion, used in physical human/robot interaction such as training.

Categories and Subject Descriptors

J.4 [**Social and Behavioral Sciences**]: Psychology

General Terms

Laboratory experiments

Keywords

Kinesthetic Interaction, Rehabilitation robot, Training Robot

1. INTRODUCTION

In our work with using robot devices as training partners for people with injuries, we essentially form a control loop, that involves the human user, making the human body and brain part of a closed loop control system. The control algorithm applied by the robot, obviously affects the physical elements of the training — by varying e.g. resistance to human motion, but we have also observed, that variations to algorithms can greatly influence the motivation of users. This observation has led us to initiate a trans-disciplinary project, using a simple 1-DOF rope-pulling robot, to study the kinesthetic communication between robot and human, which is involved in this phenomenon, and experiment with it's utilization in stimulating the user to perform the intended exercises. This project is performed in close collaboration between roboticist and Conversation Analysts.

HRI'14, March 3–6, 2014, Bielefeld, Germany.
ACM 978-1-4503-2658-2/14/03.
http://dx.doi.org/10.1145/2559636.2563715 .

2. THESIS

Playing tug-of-war with a rope and a human training partner is different from lifting an iron weight. In the latter case, you initiate an action involving an inanimate object. The former case with the training partner, is an immensely more complex task. Both parties are animated, thus beginning, carrying out and completing the activity collaboratively involves negotiation at every step of the way. To accomplish this, communicative processes are necessary. In its most minimal form, communication can be accomplished through the rope alone.

Our thesis is that a robot can emulate this kinesthetic 'language' to participate in an interaction such that forces applied to the rope become recognizable as conventional means to initiate and respond to actions, and thereby ground interaction. To investigate the thesis we will conduct detailed sequential analysis of video-taped interaction using Ethnomethodological Conversation Analysis (EM/CA) [1] [2].

The sequential analysis will be compared to the record of rope tension and position, to determine if there are physical isolates mappable to interactional functions, and thereby a situated kinesthetic language. In proceeding analytically this way, we discount work whose focus on interaction consists of post-hoc reports or conceptually driven coding schemes. Instead we align ourselves with the still relatively rare work within human-robotic interaction whose primary empirical phenomenon is the interaction itself,

Our sole focus on the body as a communicative resource in interaction with a relatively simple mechanical robot differs though from this body of work which most often concerns the more complex talk-in-interaction with humanoid robots.

3. EXPERIMENTAL SETUP

In order to assess the necessary elements for a formalized study, a preliminary test was performed, with simple elements for the robot to *initiate* and *close* interaction.

A rope-pulling training robot was mounted on a wall, $2m$ above the floor. The rope was hanging down, and the control system was programmed with the following 3 states:

Fishing: In this state, the robot control the length of the rope in a slow sinusoidal motion , to provide a visual cue to grab the rope. This state will be left when the user interferes by pulling the rope with a force of $F_{rope} > 5N$. This state provides both a visual and kinesthetic invitation to interact, and is similar to dangling a bait.

HI force: In this state, the robot controls the force to pull the rope with $F = 60N$. The length of the rope is controlled by the balance between robot and user pull. The sensation for the user is similar to lifting $6kg$ with a pulley.

LO force: In this state, the robot pull with $F = 20N$, making it easier for the user to make the rope yield.

In both *force* states, the robot will stop pulling when the rope is extended $5cm$, and will stop yielding when the rope is extended $3m$, making the floor and wall-mount the effective limits to motion.

The states were used to create two simple programs, shown in figure 1:

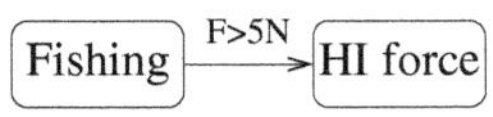

(a) Dummy

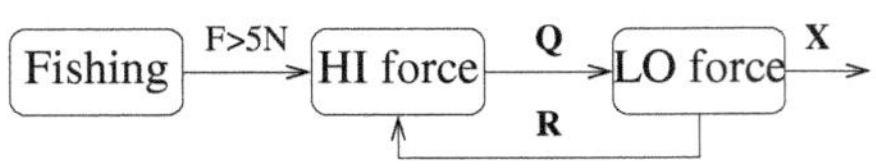

(b) Interaction

Figure 1: The two programs

The Dummy program: Will invite interaction, with **Fishing**, and then enter **HI force**, as soon as the user commences interaction. It stays in **HI force** indefinitely, offering no further interaction other than allowing the user to pull the rope until the user abandons it.

The Interaction program: Will stay in **HI force** until condition **Q**, and in **LO force** until condition **X** exits the program, or condition **R** resume **HI force**. The conditions below were chosen by the researchers, to achieve the simplest possible framework for studying mutual interaction.

Condition	1. version	2. version
Q	$t > 10s$	$t > 10s$ **and** robot yielding
R	$F > 60N$ **or** length$> 1.5m$	
X	$F < 5N$ **for** $2s$	

Both version 1 and 2 were tested preliminarily by the authors, and it was decided to limit the initial test to version 2. In version 1, lowering the force while the human is yielding was perceived as confusing and "rude" - a difference which will be investigated at a later point.

4. PRELIMINARY RESULT

A group of 6 engineering student were asked to use the **dummy** program for 30 seconds, and then **Interaction v.2** for a maximum of 2 minutes. They were not informed of the robot program, nor instructed beyond: "Interact by pulling the rope". They were filmed during the interaction, and interviewed afterwards. During the interview, they were prompted to describe the two programs and the difference between them.

- None of the students were able to outline the simple algorithm controlling the robot during **Interaction**
- 4 students ended the interaction by letting the rope go during **LO force**. 1 of these, the first time the program entered **LO force**.
- The 2 remaining were interrupted by the researcher after 2 minutes.
- The 2 students that were interrupted continuously triggered **R** before noticing the force reduction.
- All the students described the robot as having *intention* during the interaction program.
- No students let go, or gave any indication of letting go during **HI force**.
- All students looked up at the Robot when changes in own or -robot force or movement occurred.

These results indicate that 4/6 of the students treated changes in force in terms of reduction as an invitation to close or resume the interaction respectively. That is, they treated the change as a communicative act which laid out different possibilities for responding to it.

Parallel to ordinary talk-in-interaction, they understood these possibilities as occasioned by an invitation to close the activity. They contributed to this closing by also reducing force and hence engaging in a closing action sequence. This was then followed by termination of the whole exercise. Alternatively, a possibility was to re-employ HI force, thus initiating a new HI force action sequence

Regardless of what a student chose, they did not report their understanding, rather they responded to HI- or LO force actions occasioned by the robot by coordinating their movements in relevant ways. This also corresponds to the logic of ordinary everyday talk-in-interaction.

Finally, the students' responses to what they treated as the robot's actions were not constructed through movements alone, rather they were coordinated with the employment of gaze-direction. Central to one of the points of this study, students in moments of change would shift gaze-direction from for instance looking into space to the beginning of the rope. In other words, they would gaze at the robot as the center from which the actions of the robot were carried out. As mentioned these changes were treated as communicative acts which made specific possible next actions relevant. Asked why they looked in that direction, the students reported in the follow-up interview that they aimed at finding out what the robot wanted them to do.

These findings indicate that it is possible to establish kinesthetic communication, in an everyday common sense understanding of what that is, between robot and human, using co-motion and -force, during training-like scenarios.

Our initial experiment has provided important experience and inspiration for carrying on with a more sophisticated interaction program in a larger and more formalized experiment.

5. REFERENCES

[1] H. Sacks, E. A. Schegloff, and G. Jefferson. A simplest systematics for the organization of turn-taking for conversation. *Language*, pages 696–735, 1974.

[2] E. A. Schegloff. *Sequence organization in interaction: Volume 1: A primer in conversation analysis*, volume 1. Cambridge University Press, 2007.

Towards Using a Generic Robot as Training Partner

Off-the-shelf robots as a platform for flexible and affordable rehabilitation

Anders Stengaard Sørensen, Thiusius Rajeeth Savarimuthu, Jacob Nielsen, Ulrik Pagh Schultz
The Mærsk Institute, University of Southern Denmark, DK-5230 Odense M
{anss,trs,jani,ups}@mmmi.sdu.dk

ABSTRACT

In this paper, we demonstrate how a generic industrial robot can be used as a training partner, for upper limb training. The motion path and human/robot interaction of a non-generic upper-arm training robot is transferred to a generic industrial robot arm, and we demonstrate that the robot arm can implement the same type of interaction, but can expand the training regime to include both upper arm and shoulder training. We compare the generic robot to two affordable but custom-built training robots, and outline interesting directions for future work based on these training robots.

Categories and Subject Descriptors

I.2.9 [**Artificial Intelligence**]: Commercial robots and applications

General Terms

Experimentation

Keywords

affordable rehabilitation robot, upper arm training, industrial robot

1. INTRODUCTION

Rehabilitative robotic devices are slowly moving from research labs to applications at hospitals and specialized training centers. While non-intelligent Continuous Passive Motion (CPM) machines have been used for rehabilitation for many years, hospitals are currently adopting various healthcare robotic devices such as exo-skeletons. This adoption is facilitated by the amassing documentation of the positive physiological effects of these devices. While exoskeletons and similar advanced devices are effective training devices, their price and complexity is a barrier for their dissemination, keeping them out of reach of all but the most privileged patients.

HRI'14, March 3–6, 2014, Bielefeld, Germany.
ACM 978-1-4503-2658-2/14/03.
http://dx.doi.org/10.1145/2559636.2559842.

We are currently investigating platforms for more economic and hence more generally accessible training, in order to enable more patients to benefit from a tireless and affordable robotic training partner in their rehabilitation. These include a robotic curl machine [6] and a rope-pulling training robot [7], both simple 1-degree of freedom robots that dynamically respond to the force exerted by the user. This paper presents our current effort at using a relatively inexpensive, standard industrial robot as a generic robotic device for rehabilitative training. We show that this robot can replicate both the training tested with the "curl" robot and the "rope" robot, by moving in identical motion patterns, controlled by the same type of force sensor. The key idea is that the same robot can be used to replicate the functionality of several specific training devices, and hence overall be a cheaper and more space-efficient solution that can be tailored to the individual patient.

This paper reports on initial experiments using a standard industrial robot equipped with a force sensor and running software based on the open-source ROS platform.

2. RELATED WORK

Prange et al [4] and Norouzi-Gheidari et al [2] investigate the effects of robot-aided rehabilitation in the upper extremities using randomized controlled trials that employ robotic devices in the upper-limb rehabilitation of people with stroke. The findings of these studies are in both cases that conventional therapy (CT) with added robot therapy (RT) is beneficial in the improvement of motor control when compared to CT alone. The effects of robot-aided therapy on peripheral nerve injuries are to the best of our knowledge only sparsely investigated within the literature, some studies do however conclude that training in itself is beneficial for rehabilitation of peripheral nerve damage [8, 1].

3. METHODOLOGY

We perform a qualitative comparison of three robotic platforms: a robotic weight-lifting curl machine, a rope-pulling training robot, and a prototype universal training robot built using a standard industrial robot. The three robotic platforms are shown in Figure 1.

The weight-lifting curl machine follows the same principle as commercially available machines, and is designed to support all possible training modalities for a wide range of users, ranging from the very weak, to the very strong [6]. It consist of a static frame, with integrated seat and elbow rest; a moving beam; two adjustable handles mounted on the beam with free sliding bearings; a motor that drives the

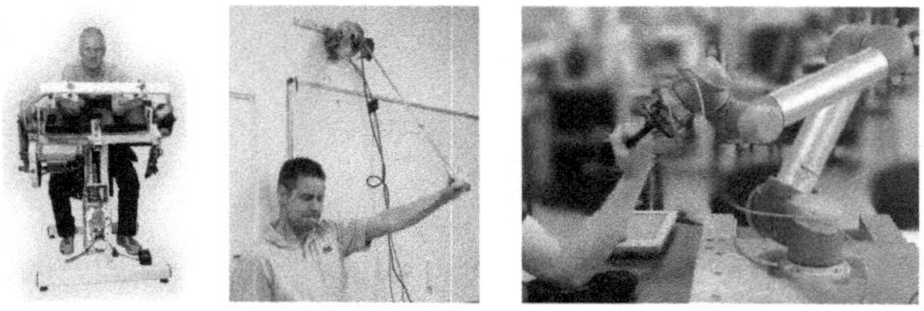

Figure 1: Robotic training devices, from left to right: Allan Lauritsen in RoboTrainer, Jesper Kiersgaard testing RoboTrainer Light, and our prototype setup of a universal training robot.

beam through a gear; handles fitted with strain gauges; and power and control electronics. A custom robot controller is implemented on an FPGA,it provides the relevant signal conditioning interface to the various subsystems, controls the motor and sensors, and connects to a PC using a USB UART device.

The rope pulling robot is a parallel project, investigating the lowest boundaries of affordable training robots [7]. It is simply a computer controlled winch, integrated with a sensitive force sensor and the same type of custom robot controller mentioned above. It is configured to enable any combination of force, velocity and position control. For simple shoulder training, the relaxed arm of the user is first moved from lowest to highest position, while being weighed. Afterward, the robot applies an upward force, identical to the arm weight, effectively removing gravitational pull from the shoulder muscles. In spite of its simplicity, it is able to offer training to the large group of patients suffering from partial paralysis or reduced mobility of limbs. It is currently being used with research in force-assist shoulder training.

The prototype universal training robot is based on a standard industrial robot, equipped with a 1-DOF force sensor handle as an implement. The robot is a standard Universal Robots UR5 that is controlled over a local TCP/IP network by a laptop running ROS [5]. The 1-DOF force sensor is sufficient for the robot to emulate the behavior of simple training machines. The sensor is implemented as a set of strain-gauges in the handle. The gauge is sampled by a battery-powered micro-controller that streams data to the PC through a Bluetooth serial link. Both the robot arm and the force sensor are exposed as ROS nodes, allowing a robot controller to easily be written using the ROS platform. The robot controller is developed using the RobWork framework.

4. EXPERIMENT

In order to emulate the training offered by the curl-machine robot, the universal robot is programmed to move the force sensitive handle in an arc, with a radius that matches the length of the users forearm, so that the user can place the elbow on a pillow at the arc center, and perform curls while holding on to the handle. The robot is programmed to move the handle along the arc circumference, at an angular velocity: ω, proportional to the force applied to the handle with a factor: k_ω. This simple algorithm implements resistance training, with emulated linear viscous friction resistance. The same approach will be used to replicate the training provided by the rope-pulling robot.

5. DISCUSSION AND PERSPECTIVES

We have demonstrated the capability of our universal training robot setup to perform exercises similar a dedicated training robot. The two dedicated robots are relatively inexpensive, whereas the universal training robot is an expensive solution compared to standard training equipment. The universal training robot is nevertheless relatively cost-efficient compared to other equipment usable for similar, adaptive training exercises, in particular when taking into account its generality and that it is based on one of the least expensive industrial robots on the market.

We plan to perform quantitative experiments that compare the effectiveness of each of our robotic training platforms for rehabilitative training. Initially case studies will be used, as has been done for the weight-lifting curl machine and the rope-pulling robot, but we are planning larger-scale studies in the context of the Patient@Home research project [3]. Given the close physical interaction between the robot and the human, trusting the robot is essential for efficient training. We plan to compare each of these robots based on qualitative studies that indicate how pleasant users find the interaction with each of these robots to be; variations in programming such as the amount of force and acceleration are considered interesting in this respect. Safety currently simply relies on our use of a safety-certified robot, we however anticipate interesting future challenges here in terms of human-robot interaction.

6. REFERENCES

[1] P. Armada-da Silva, C. Pereira, S. Amado, and A. Veloso. Role of physical exercise for improving posttraumatic nerve regeneration. *International review of neurobiology*, 109:125–149, 2012.

[2] N. Norouzi-Gheidari, P. S. Archambault, and J. Fung. Effects of robot-assisted therapy on stroke rehabilitation in upper limbs: Systematic review and meta-analysis of the literature. *J. Rehabil. Res. Dev*, 49:479–496, 2012.

[3] patient@home. `http://www.patientathome.dk`.

[4] G. B. Prange, M. J. Jannink, C. G. Groothuis-Oudshoorn, H. J. Hermens, and M. J. IJzerman. Systematic review of the effect of robot-aided therapy on recovery of the hemiparetic arm after stroke. *Journal of rehabilitation research and development*, 43(2):171, 2006.

[5] M. Quigley, K. Conley, B. Gerkey, J. Faust, T. Foote, J. Leibs, R. Wheeler, and A. Y. Ng. Ros: an open-source robot operating system. In *ICRA workshop on open source software*, volume 3, 2009.

[6] A. Sørensen, G. Sjøgaard, S. Chreitch, and O. HB. Robot assisted training for rehabilitation after traffic accident – a case report (Poster). Poster, October 2011. Poster session at Dansk Biomekanisk Selskab.

[7] A. S. Sørensen, G. Rasmussen, and D. Day. Kinesthetic human/robot coordination, 2013. Also submitted to HRI 2014 as a late breaking report.

[8] E. Udina, S. Cobianchi, I. Allodi, and X. Navarro. Effects of activity-dependent strategies on regeneration and plasticity after peripheral nerve injuries. *Annals of Anatomy-Anatomischer Anzeiger*, 193(4):347–353, 2011.

Remote Control of Quadrotor Teams, Using Hand Gestures

Adrian Stoica
Jet Propulsion Laboratory
MS 198-219, 4800 Oak Grove Dr
Pasadena, CA 91109
1-818-354-2190
adrian.stoica@jpl.nasa.gov

Federico Salvioli
Polytechnic of Turin
Corso Duca degli Abruzzi, 24
10129 Torino, Italy
39-011-090-6100
federico.salvioli@studenti.polito.it

Caitlin Flowers
Georgia Tech
213 Lamplighter Lane
Marietta, GA 30067
1-404-764-7333
cflowers7@mail.gatech.edu

ABSTRACT
This paper addresses the human-centered control of a team (pack) of quadrotors. The control is remote, over the internet. Using simple telepresence tools (video in Skype, showing remote imagery from a ground camera, and from the quadrotors' own livestreaming cameras) the operator uses a command language, UAVL (standing for Unmanned Aerial Vehicle Language) to control quadrotors' behaviors. Seventeen hand gestures are used to express the commands; these are decoded by processing EMG signals collected with an array of EMG electrodes embedded in a BioSleeve mounted on the forearm. Extending prior work with an Unmanned Ground Vehicle Language (UGVL) used with ground robots, UAVL encodes commands used to control quadrotors, individually, or as a team, in direct teleoperated flight, or in preprogrammed flight patterns triggered by the commands.

Categories and Subject Descriptors
I.2.9 Robotics: Autonomous Vehicles, Operator Interfaces

General Terms
Performance, Experimentation, Human Factors

Keywords
Multi-robot control, Human-robot interfaces, control languages, levels of autonomy, gesture recognition, EMG sensor array

1. INTRODUCTION
This work aims at developing technology for performing efficient missions with multi-robot teams. In particular it focuses on natural Human-Multi-Robot Interfaces (HMRI) for command and control. Good introductions to the field are found in [1],[2]. In [3] we described a BioSleeve system that interprets arm and hand gestures to command robots. The BioSleeve uses an array of electrodes that collect EMG signals from the forearm; the signals are decoded to derive both static and dynamic gestures. A composition of gestures through concatenation is used to express commands for complex behaviors. The experiments used ground robots, yet examples for UAV commands were also given. In [4] the classical Levels of Autonomy (LOA) framework was extended to Levels/hierarchy Of Autonomy characteristic of Groups (GLOA), and used to determine new strategies for control. Focusing on ground robots, a UGV-oriented command language (UGVL) was defined, and a mapping was performed from the human-friendly gesture-based HMRI into the UGVL. The UGVL was used to control a team of 3 robots, exploring the efficiency of different GLOA; with control at individual, leader (with cloned followers), and entire group level. Commands at increased GLOA proved the most efficient in providing the fastest evacuation in unknown terrain by a transport convoy of a team of UGVs.

This paper extends the work to UAV/quadrotors: 1) it defines an UAVL extension, used for the control of a team of quadrotors; and 2) it implements the remote teleoperation of the quadrotors, controlled individually, or as a team, in direct teleoperated flight, and in preprogrammed flight patterns, triggered by commands. The command gestures are obtained using the BioSleeve, in real-time. Section 2 describes the system. Section 3 describes the UAVL. Section 4 describes the experiments. Section 5 presents conclusions and future work.

HRI'14, March 3–6 2014, Bielefeld, Germany
ACM 978-1-4503-2658-2/14/03.
http://dx.doi.org/10.1145/2559636.2559853

2. SYSTEM DESCRIPTION
The field computer gives commands to the quadrotors situated up to 300 meters away. On-board GoPro cameras transmit live imagery; a Quad Receiver gets the imagery from the copter-mounted cameras and from a ground camera; a quad-processor combines views in a quad split view. The remote operator sees the screen via Skype videoconferencing, and controls the robots by hand gestures, with signals captured and interpreted by the BioSleeve, (or key press) transmitted over internet to the copters. The gesture recognition takes 300ms, but the internet adds a delay, typically ~2s. The system-level diagram is in Fig 1.

The quadrotors (Phantoms, from DJI Innovations) use built-in GPS sensors for hovering and positioning with 0.8m vertical accuracy and 2.5m horizontal; additional sensors (ultrasound, 2cm resolution up to 7m, and additional GPS board) have been tested and are now in software integration for better position determination and on-board autonomy. The GoPro cameras provide high definition livestreaming and recording.

Field Computer and Interface The field computer issues commands to the quadcopters via an RF controller, modified to receive computer commands through USB. A software interface displays the quad-picture from the cameras, and the GPS-derived position shown on terrain maps.

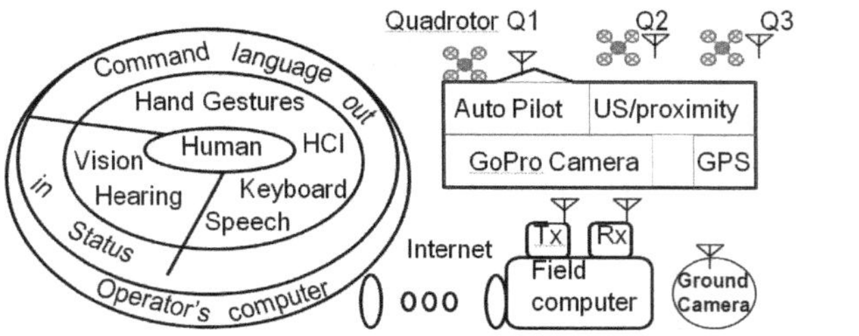

Figure 1. System-level diagram, remote commands by gesture, to a team of quadrotors providing live videostreams.

Figure 2. Field interface: input from 4 cameras (3 on quadcopters, one on the ground); the computer generates commands transmitted via USB to a modified RF controller; map illustrating the positioning of quadcopters

Remote Operator Interface The operator uses the BioSleeve, which recognizes 17 gestures gestures with better than 95% CCR [4]. Via Skype he/she sees the field interface, displaying the video from the quadcopters and from the ground camera. A VPN connection is established with the field computer that controls the quadcopters.

Table 1. Commands used and quad behaviors - subset of simple, one word/gesture set, mapped to UAVL

Gesture	Command	Action Details
Adduction: Open Hand	Take Off	Increase current elevation by 2m
Rest: Relaxed hand	Hover	Remain stationary, maintaining altitude
Fist	Stop	Cease movement, hover
Radial Deviation	Roll Left	Move left
Ulnar Deviation	Roll Right	Move right
Wrist Flexion	Back	Move backwards
Wrist Extension	Forward	Move forwards
Pinch 1: index to thumb	Square	Fly in a square pattern of 2x2m
Pinch 2: middle to thumb	Figure 8	Fly in a figure 8 pattern
Pinch 3: ring to thumb	Scan pattern	Fly: forward 10m, right 1m, back 10m, right 1m. Repeat.

3. UAVL

The UAVL is built by analogy with the UGVL [3], [4] and includes flight commands, for individual or groups of UAVs. Table 1 shows 10 of the commands, mapped to gestures.

4. Experiments

The copters were flown individually and in pairs, with the same commands given to all, simultaneously or with delays, etc, while adjusting their flights by command gestures. At speeds of about 2m/s, the remote control was manageable despite the internet delay, either from ground camera and pilot view video stream. As in [4] preliminary experiments indicate that control at higher levels of group autonomy are more efficient, despite low levels of autonomy and need to correct for each individual platform.

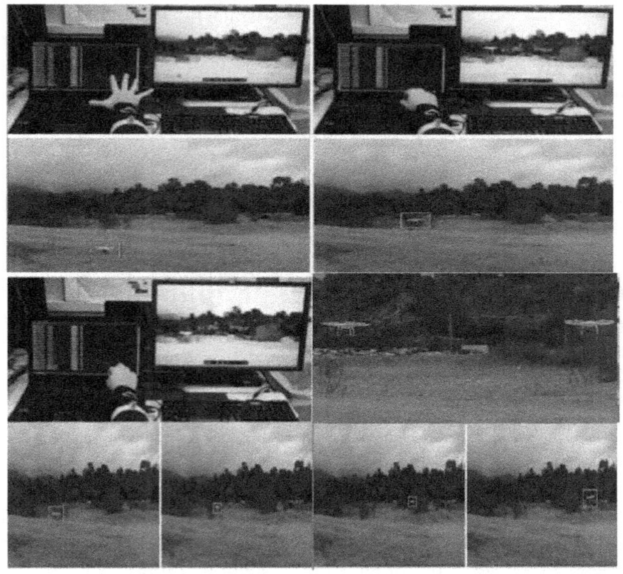

Figure 3. Commands indicate simple flight movements or complex behaviors, e.g. flying on a predetermined trajectory

5. Acknowledgement

The research was carried out at the Jet Propulsion Laboratory, California Institute of Technology, under a contract with the National Aeronautics and Space Administration.

6. REFERENCES

[1] Goodrich, M. A. and Schultz, A.C, Human-Robot Interaction: A Survey *Foundations and Trends in Human-Computer Interaction,* 1(3), 2007, pp 203-275.

[2] Chen, J.Y.C., Barnes, M.J., Harper-Sciarini, M.; Supervisory Control of Multiple Robots: Human-Performance Issues and User-Interface Design, *SMC, Part C, IEEE Trans on*, 41.4, (July 2011) 435-454.

[3] Stoica,A., et al. Using arm and hand gestures to command robots during stealth operations. *Proc. SPIE 8407, Multisensor, Multisource Information Fusion: Architectures, Algorithms, and Applications (May 2012)*

[4] Stoica, A., Theodoridis, T., Hu, H., McDonald-Maier, K., and Barrero, D.F., Towards Human-Friendly Efficient Control of Multi-Robot Teams. In CTS, page 226-231. IEEE, (2013)

Predicting Human Performance During Teleoperation

Justin Storms, Steven Vozar, and Dawn Tilbury
University of Michigan
Department of Mechanical Engineering
{jgstorms, svozar, tilbury}@umich.edu

ABSTRACT
Humans are an integral part of many tasks performed by mobile robots and human operator ability can vary greatly between users. Understanding operator skill level can allow for user interfaces to adapt giving novice users additional assistance and expert users more freedom. In this paper, a method is proposed for predicting a human teleoperator's performance based on user behavior observed during the first few minutes of teleoperation. Preliminary analysis indicates a trend between operator performance and the proportion of time an operator spends thinking during a particular segment of time.

Categories and Subject Descriptors
I.2.9 [**Robotics**]: Operator interfaces

Keywords
Teleoperation; User Performance

1. INTRODUCTION
Mobile robots are used for tasks in environments that are dangerous or undesirable for humans to be present. For example, after the Tōhoku earthquake and tsunami, mobile robots were used for site inspection and surveying of damage [4]. Disaster scenes contain a high level of perceptual complexity that autonomous systems are not yet prepared to handle. In a paper on the use of remotely operated marine vehicles in Japan after the Tōhoku earthquake and tsunami Murphy *et al.* claim that, "...even if mission autonomy was possible, the human would likely prefer to stay in the loop to look for surprises..." [3]. Humans will continue to remain in the loop in many teleoperation systems where human judgment is required or preferred.

Teleoperated robots were the best choice for surveying the nuclear sites after the Tōhoku earthquake and tsunami due to dangerous levels of radiation. However, human operators of these robots discussed the need for improvement in user interface [2]. Chen, Haas and Barnes have described limitations and considerations for development of user interfaces on teleoperated robots [1]. They discuss effects of camera viewpoint, video quality, time delay and multimodal displays on system performance. However, another important consideration in analysis and design of teleoperation systems is user ability. Some human operators posses stronger spatial-temporal reasoning skills and can more easily understand the robot's environment and configuration with less information or feedback than operators with weaker skills. In each of these cases it is difficult to predict what type of user is operating the robot at any given time. In this paper, a method for predicting human operator performance is proposed.

HRI'14, March 3–6, 2014, Bielefeld, Germany.
ACM 978-1-4503-2658-2/14/03.
http://dx.doi.org/10.1145/2559636.2559808

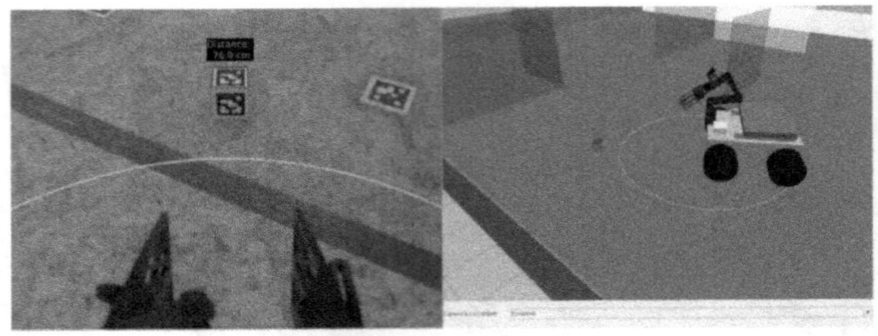

Figure 1. Screenshot of mixed reality (MR) user interface for box retrieval task. Augmented reality video from manipulator arm camera (left) and the virtual reality scene (right).

2. EXPERIMENT DESCRIPTION
The data analyzed in this short paper comes from a 22-subject user test carried out by Vozar [5]. Broadly described, the tests involved users teleoperating a mobile robot from a separate room to perform driving and manipulation tasks in a custom built arena. Vozar's tests sought to determine the effects of different user interface (UI) visualizations and input methods on performance. Performance was objectively measured by task completion time and accuracy. Each user performed a set of three subtasks on four different UIs for a total of twelve subtask-UI combinations. During each test the user was determined to be in one of the following four basic states: 1) arm manipulation, 2) robot chassis driving, 3) thinking, or 4) UI display adjustment.

The three subtasks were: A) search an arena to identify the total number of boxes contained in the arena, B) retrieve the box closest to the designated start position in the arena and deposit it in a box at the start position and C) retrieve the box farthest away from the designated start position in the arena and deposit it in a box at the start position. Two options existed for control of the robot chassis and manipulator arm: the chassis and manipulator arm were both controlled by a gamepad controller (GP) or the chassis was controlled by a 3D mouse and the manipulator arm was controlled by a replica master arm with one-to-one mapping in a master-slave configuration (MS). Additionally, two options existed for visualization: a video only feed from a camera mounted on the manipulator arm (VID), and a mixed reality scene with annotations given on the manipulator arm camera and a virtual view of the robot (MR, see Figure 1). Thus, the UIs consisted of the following four combinations: GP+VID, MS+VID, GP+MR, MS+MR. Further details of the test can be found in [5].

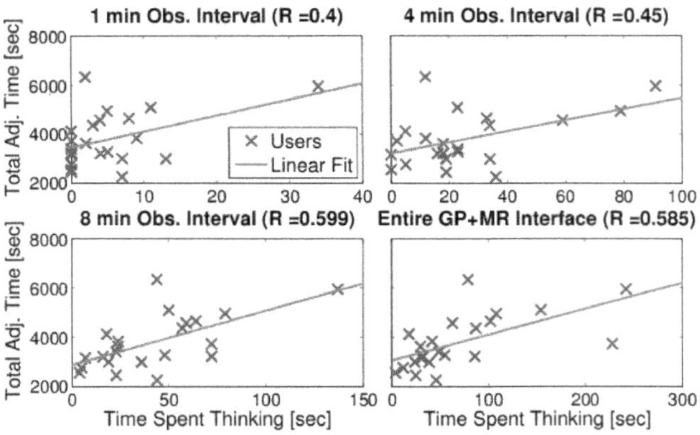

Figure 2. There exists a positive correlation between total adjusted time for each user and the time they spent thinking for various observation intervals, with increasing correlation coefficients for increased observation times.

3. DATA ANALYSIS

Each user was incentivized to complete the tasks accurately in the lowest overall time. Therefore, the performance metric for user ability is adjusted total time spent on all tasks, where time was added for mistakes the user made during testing [5]. All of the user test data was coded to describe the user's state at each second of the test. The user was determined to be either manipulating the arm, driving the robot chassis, interacting with the UI display, or if they did not fall into any of the first three states they were assumed to be thinking.

We hypothesize that there exists a correlation between time spent thinking and overall performance. Users could be thinking for many reasons, *e.g.* uncertainty of robot state or not knowing what to do next. At the very least, time spent thinking is time spent not completing the task.

Figure 2 shows plots of the total adjusted time it took each user to complete all subtasks on all interfaces versus the amount of time that user spent thinking over different intervals of observation time (starting from the beginning of the task). All observation times in Figure 2 were taken from the GP+MR interface, which showed the best correlation with adjusted total time spent on all tasks. As a longer portion of time is observed and more data is collected on each user about the amount of time they spend thinking, the correlation between time spent thinking and the total adjusted time it took them to complete the test increases. These plots indicate that the longer a user is observed to obtain time spent thinking, the better the estimate of overall performance.

In order to get an idea of how long the observation interval should be to quickly and accurately predict user performance, users were labeled as one of three types, based on overall task performance: novice, average, or expert. The novice users had the 7 worst total adjusted times, expert users had the 7 best total adjusted times, and average users fell between the two. A linear model, shown by the best-fit lines in Figure 2, was then used to predict the users' anticipated overall categorization for varying observation intervals. The number of correctly categorized users is plotted on the y-axis in Figure 3. With this method of prediction the number of correctly categorized users asymptotically approached 13. This plot indicates that observing thinking time during the first seven minutes of the test could predict performance as well as an observation of the thinking time throughout the entire trial, which generally lasted at least twice as long.

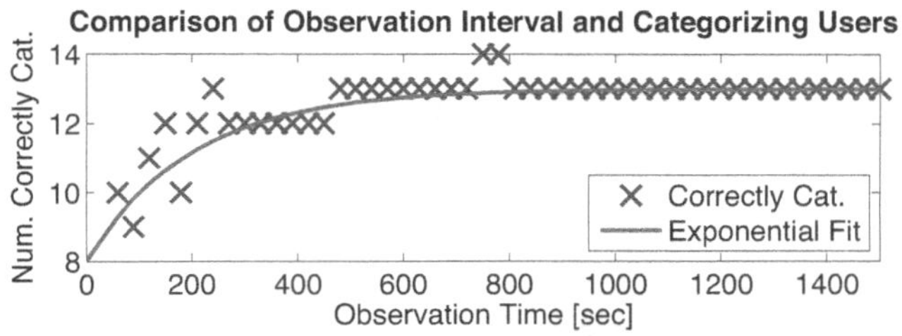

Figure 3. Effect of observation time on the number of correctly categorized users.

4. CONCLUSIONS AND FUTURE WORK

Preliminary analysis of a previous set of user tests indicate that a correlation exists between the portion of time an operator spent thinking and task performance, as measured by task completion time. This paper suggests that by observing a short interval of user performance, a user can be categorized as a novice, average or expert user. Understanding a user's ability would be a valuable asset for designers of teleoperation user interfaces. Novice users could benefit from displays that give more information about the robot's state and environment. The UI might give suggested actions to novice users in order to help them better make decisions. On the other hand, expert users could find some information on the display excessive and distracting.

A future set of user tests could explore user reaction to a UI that adjusts based on if it predicts the user to be a novice or expert. Additional metrics could also be considered to give a more detailed understanding of user behavior than thinking alone *e.g.* use of eye tracking software to determine where the user's focus lies.

5. ACKNOWLEDGMENTS

The authors thank Mike Erickson and Peter Turpel for their assistance collecting the data. This research was supported in part by the Automotive Research Center (ARC), A U.S. Army Center of Excellence in Modeling and Simulations of Ground Vehicles at the University of Michigan, with funding from government contract DoD-DoA W56H2V-04-2-0001 through US Army Tank Automotive Research, Development, and Engineering Center.

6. REFERENCES

[1] Chen, J.Y., Haas, E.C., and Barnes, M.J. 2007. Human performance issues and user interface design for teleoperated robots. In *IEEE Trans. On Systems, Man, and Cybernetics, Part C: Applications and Reviews*. 37, 6, 1231-1245.

[2] Guizzo, E. 2011. Fukushima robot operator writes tell-all blog. In *IEEE Spectrum.*

[3] Murphy, R.R., *et al.* 2011. Use of remotely operated marine vehicles at Minamisanriku and Rikuzentakata Japan for disaster recovery. *IEEE Int'l Symp. on Safety, Security, and Rescue Robotics.*19-25.

[4] Nagatani, K., *et al.* 2013. Emergency response to the nuclear accident at the Fukushima Daiichi Nuclear Power Plants using mobile rescue robots. *J. Field Robotics*. 30, 44–63.

[5] Vozar, S. 2013. *A framework for improving the speed and performance of teleoperated mobile manipulators*. Doctoral Thesis. University of Michigan.

Perception of Humanoid Social Mediator in Two-Person Dialogs

Yasir Tahir
Institute for Media Innovation
Nanyang Technological
University (NTU),Singapore
yasir001@e.ntu.edu.sg

Umer Rasheed
School of EEE
Nanyang Technological
University (NTU),Singapore
umer1@e.ntu.edu.sg

Shoko Dauwels
CIRCQL
Nanyang Technological
University (NTU),Singapore
sdauwels@ntu.edu.sg

Justin Dauwels
School of EEE
Nanyang Technological
University (NTU),Singapore
jdauwels@ntu.edu.sg

ABSTRACT

In this work we present a humanoid robot (Nao) that provides real-time sociofeedback to participants taking part in two-person dialogs. The sociofeedback system quantifies speech mannerism and social behavior of participants in an ongoing conversation, determines whether feedback is required, and delivers feedback through Nao. For example, Nao alarms the speaker(s) when the voice is too high or too low, or when the conversation is not proceeding well due to disagreements or numerous interruptions. In this study, participants are asked to engage in two-person conversations while the Nao robot acts as mediator. They then assess the received sociofeedback with respect to various aspects, including its content, appropriateness, and timing. Participants also evaluate their overall perception of Nao as social mediator via the Godspeed questionnaire.

Categories and Subject Descriptors

H.5.2 [**Information Interfaces and Presentation**]: Miscellaneous; D.2.8 [**Robotics**]: Commercial Robots and Applications; J.4 [**Computer Applications**]: Social and Behavioural Sciences

General Terms

Human Factors, Design, Experimentation

Keywords

Real-Time Sociofeedback, Humanoids, Human Robot Interaction, Social Mediator.

HRI'14, March 3–6, 2014, Bielefeld, Germany.
ACM 978-1-4503-2658-2/14/03.
http://dx.doi.org/10.1145/2559636.2559831.

1. INTRODUCTION

One of the key objectives of research and development in robotics is to come up with various robots than can assist humans in everyday domestic environments. Nowadays, robots are increasingly being viewed as social entities to be integrated in our daily lives. Socially interactive robots are used to communicate, express and perceive emotions, maintain social relationships, interpret natural cues, and develop social competencies [1, 2].With increasing demand of robots for domestic environments, research on human-robot interaction (HRI) has gained more and more importance. In order to enhance human-robot interaction, the need for integration of social intelligence in such robots has become a necessity [3, 4]. In this work we integrate real-time sociofeedback with a humanoid (Nao) robot. We limit ourselves to six social states that are most relevant to a meeting scenario. These social states are Normal conversation, uninterested speakers, aggressive conversation, one speaker talking too much in a conversation, very low volume and very high volume by the speakers. Using the audio cues the system determines the social state of each speaker and provides feedback via Nao robot if required.

2. SOCIOFEEDBACK SYSTEM

We adopt easy-to-use portable equipment for recording conversations, it consists of lapel microphones for each of the two speakers. Each speaker's audio is captured on separate channels so that interesting features based on interplay between both channels can be computed. We compute the following conversational cues natural turns, speaking percentage, mutual silence percentage, turn duration, natural interjections, speaking interjections, interruptions, failed interruptions, speaking rate and response time. Once the speech cues are calculated, they are fed to machine learning algorithms such as Support Vector Machines (SVMs) to deduce social state of participants [5]. Speaking mannerism are quantitatively assessed by low-level speech metrics such as volume, rate, and pitch of speech. The social behavior is quantified by sociometrics including level of interest, agreement, and dominance. Together, they provide a comprehensive picture of the social state of participants in dialogs.

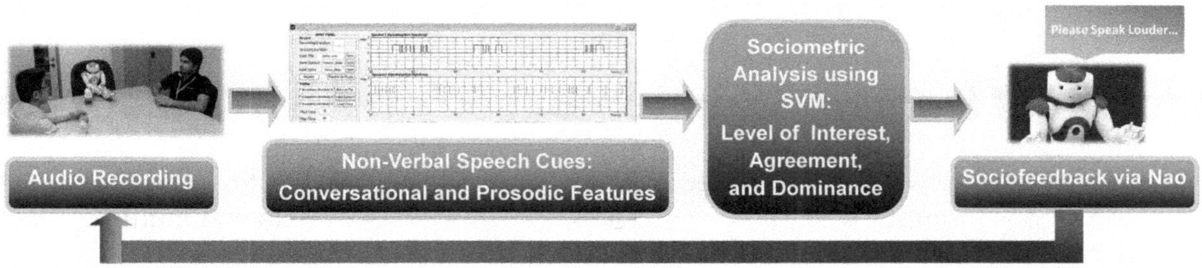

Figure 1: System Overview. The system records audio data, computes several conversational and prosodic features, and from those features, determines levels of interest, agreement, and dominance via support vector machines (SVM).

3. NAO AS SOCIAL MEDIATOR

The aim of the conducted experiment was to investigate whether Nao can interact as a social mediator. Social mediaotor is someone who observes an on-going conversation and acts as a mediator or judge and provides feedback to speakers if required. In our case Nao interfaced with sociofeedback system monitored several conversations and provided feedback based on social state estimated by sociofeedback system (see Fig.1).

The experiment consisted of 20 participants, who were invited to participate in scenario based conversations each being one minute in duration. We observed in earlier recordings that it is very difficult for participants to act out certain social state while thinking about what to say at the same time, therefore we had scripts for each social scenario. The scripts were everyday conversations where one or both speakers acted out in a certain way. Each participant participated in six conversations as we consider six social states for this experiment. At the end of the conversation the Nao robot provided feedback using audio message and a corresponding gesture which the participant then rated. There were two questionnaires first one after each conversation to get participant input about feedback provided, second one was Godspeed questionnaire [6] which participants filled at the end to rate their perception of Nao as a social mediator. Godspeed questionnaire asks the user rating for anthropomorphism, animacy, likability, perceived intelligence and perceived safety. In our case all these criteria were rated high by the participants except perceived safety because high score of perceived safety means participant were agitated therefore low scores are desirable for this criterion. The questions asked to rate feedback are shown in Table 1 along with the average rating score out of 5 where 5 is maximum.

	Feedback Assessment	
Q1	Did you notice when the socio-feedback system was addressing you?	4.5
Q2	Did you notice when the socio-feedback system was addressing others?	4.5
Q3	Was the timing of socio-feedback appropriate?	3.3
Q4	Did the socio-feedback system interrupt the conversation?	2.3
Q5	Was the interaction natural?	4.2
Q6	Did you understand the message given by the socio-feedback?	4.8
Q7	Do you agree with the given feedback?	4.7
Q8	Did you enjoy using the socio-feedback system?	4.8

Table 1: Questions of the assessment form. The column on the right shows the average rating score.

4. CONCLUSION

We presented a user study to assess how Nao is perceived by people in the role of social mediator in two-person dialogs. Overall, this study suggests that sociofeedback by the Nao robot can be accurately identified and is appreciated by participants. In future, we aim to further improve the social state estimation. We will collect multi-modal (audio and video) datasets for training the system. Secondly, we will attempt to scale the proposed system to multi-party dialogs. We also intend to further improve the feedback delivery of Nao so that in future it can be a part of real world group discussions.

5. ACKNOWLEDGEMENTS

Institute for Media Innovation (Seed Grant M4080824) Nanyang Technological University (NTU).

6. REFERENCES

[1] T. Fong, I. Nourbakhsh, and K. Dautenhahn, "A survey of socially interactive robots," *Robotics and autonomous systems*, vol. 42, no. 3, pp. 143–166, 2003.

[2] H. Li, J.-J. Cabibihan, and Y. K. Tan, "Towards an effective design of social robots," *International Journal of Social Robotics*, vol. 3, no. 4, pp. 333–335, 2011.

[3] D. Feil-Seifer and M. Mataric, "Robot-assisted therapy for children with autism spectrum disorders," in *Proceedings of the 7th international conference on Interaction design and children*, pp. 49–52, ACM, 2008.

[4] F. Papadopoulos, K. Dautenhahn, and W. C. Ho, "Exploring the use of robots as social mediators in a remote human-human collaborative communication experiment," *Paladyn*, vol. 3, no. 1, pp. 1–10, 2012.

[5] U. Rasheed, Y. Tahir, S. Dauwels, and J. Dauwels, "Real-time comprehensive sociometrics for two-person dialogs," in *Human Behavior Understanding*, pp. 196–208, Springer, 2013.

[6] C. Bartneck, E. Croft, and D. Kulic, "Measuring the anthropomorphism, animacy, likeability, perceived intelligence and perceived safety of robots," in *Metrics for HRI Workshop, Technical Report*, vol. 471, pp. 37–44, Citeseer, 2008.

Modeling of Human Attention Based on Analysis of Magic

Yusuke Tamura
Chuo University
Tokyo, Japan
tamura@mech.chuo-u.ac.jp

Shiro Yano
Ritsumeikan University
Shiga, Japan
s_yano@em.ci.ritsumei.ac.jp

Hisashi Osumi
Chuo University
Tokyo, Japan
osumi@mech.chuo-u.ac.jp

ABSTRACT

In this study, we developed a human attention model for smooth human-robot interaction. The model consists of the saliency map generation module and manipulation map generation module. The manipulation map describes top-down factors, such as human face, hands and gaze in the input image. To evaluate the proposed model, we applied the model to a magic video, and measured human gaze points during watching the video. Based on the experimental results, the proposed model can better explain human attention than the saliency map.

Categories and Subject Descriptors

I.2.9 [**Artificial Intelligence**]: Robotics

General Terms

Human Factors

Keywords

Attention, human-robot interaction, magic

1. INTRODUCTION

It is required for robots coexisting with humans to smoothly interact with humans. For smooth interaction with humans, the robots should be able to control human behaviors. In order to control a person's behavior, it is necessary to manipulate his attention first. Magicians skillfully manipulate spectators' attention by using eye gaze [5] and hand movement [6]. Furthermore, our past study have showed that a key factor for manipulating attention is the relationship between gaze, face and hands [1].

A robot has to understand how her behavior and surrounding environments influence a target person for manipulating the person's attention. Therefore, the objective of this study is to develop a model of human attention.

Many of the computational models on human visual attention calculate the attention in a bottom-up manner, as typified by the saliency map [4]. On the other hand, human attention can be influenced not only by bottom-up factors, such as saliency, but also by top-down factors, such as meaning of objects, behaviors of other persons. A few researchers proposed models integrated with saliency and other factors [2, 7].

In this paper, we propose a model of human attention, which considers the saliency as a bottom-up factor and the relationship between face, hands and gaze as a top-down factor based on an analysis of behaviors of a magician and spectators.

HRI'14, March 3–6, 2014, Bielefeld, Germany.
ACM 978-1-4503-2658-2/14/03.
http://dx.doi.org/10.1145/2559636.2559819.

2. HUMAN ATTENTION MODEL

The proposed model consists of two modules, such as "saliency map generation module" and "manipulation map generation module." The former module calculates visual saliency of input images and the latter calculates a manipulation map, which describes the relationship between face, hands and gaze. The model generate an attention map as a linear sum of the saliency map and manipulation map.

2.1 Saliency Map

The saliency map generation module considers motion in addition to the original saliency map [4]. In other words, the module calculates a saliency map as a linear sum of feature maps of intensity, colors, orientations and motion. Here, the motion feature is calculated as magnitudes of optical flow [3].

2.2 Manipulation Map

The manipulation map is calculated as a linear sum of face-hand map and gaze map. The face-hand map describes the positions of face and hands in the input image. The gaze map describes the gaze direction.

Defining $\boldsymbol{x}_{\mathrm{F}}$, $\boldsymbol{x}_{\mathrm{L}}$, $\boldsymbol{x}_{\mathrm{R}}$, as the positions of face, left hand and right hand, respectively, the face-hand map is calculated by the following equation.

$$F(\boldsymbol{x}) = \sum_i \frac{1}{2\pi\sqrt{|\boldsymbol{S}_i|}} \exp\left\{-\frac{1}{2}(\boldsymbol{x}-\boldsymbol{x}_i)^T \boldsymbol{S}_i^{-1}(\boldsymbol{x}-\boldsymbol{x}_i)\right\}, \tag{1}$$

where $i = \mathrm{F}, \mathrm{L}, \mathrm{R}$ and $\boldsymbol{S}_i$ is a covariance matrix of $\boldsymbol{x}_i$.

The initial point of a gaze half line is set to $\boldsymbol{x}_{\mathrm{F}}$. Defining $d(\boldsymbol{x})$ as the distance between $\boldsymbol{x}$ and the gaze half line, the gaze map is calculated by the following equation.

$$G(\boldsymbol{x}) = \frac{1}{\sqrt{2\pi}\sigma_d} \exp\left\{-\frac{d(\boldsymbol{x})^2}{2\sigma_d^2}\right\} \tag{2}$$

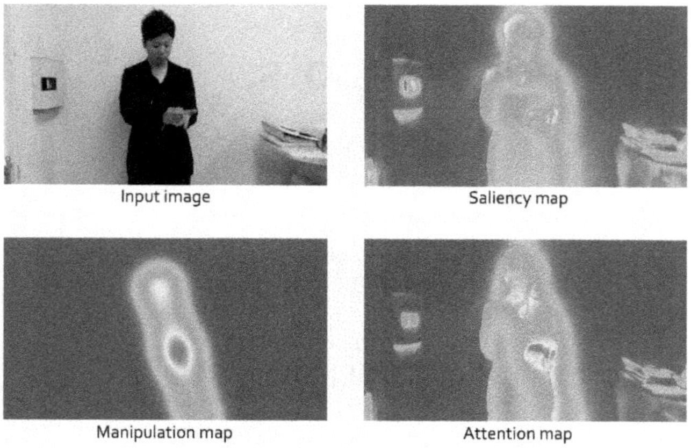

Figure 1: An example of the input image, saliency map, manipulation map and attention map

3. EVALUATION

3.1 Evaluation Method

We compared the proposed model to the saliency map through an experiment. Five healthy male volunteers (aged 21–24 years) participated in the experiment. In the experiment, gaze points of the participants during watching a magic video. In the video a magician performs "vanishing a ball" trick. The magician shows a pink-colored sponge ball (43 mm in a diameter) in his right hand, then apparently passes it to the left hand, but secretly retains it in the right hand. After that, he opens his left hand and the ball apparently vanished.

The time length of the video is about 10 seconds, and the resolution is 1920 × 1080 pixels. The video was played on a 23-inch computer screen. The participants' gaze points were measured at 60 Hz by a contactless eye tracking system (faceLAB 4.2, Seeing Machines).

The evaluation index is a ratio of the value of attention map saliency map at the participants' gaze point divided by the average value of the input image.

In this evaluation, the magician's face and hands were detected by a simple threshold-based skin-color extraction in HSV color space. The positions of the face and hands are calculated as centers of the skin-color areas. In the magic video, the magician looks either straight ahead or at the left hand. For simplicity, therefore, we classified each frame of the video into the two scene. If the magician looks straight ahead, the gaze vector $\boldsymbol{g}$ will set to $\mathbf{0}$. If he looks at the left hand, the gaze vector will be defined as $\boldsymbol{g} = (\boldsymbol{x}_{\mathrm{L}} - \boldsymbol{x}_{\mathrm{F}})/\|\boldsymbol{x}_{\mathrm{L}} - \boldsymbol{x}_{\mathrm{F}}\|$.

Here, the covariance matrix of $F(\boldsymbol{x})$ was $\boldsymbol{S}_i = \mathrm{diag}[\sigma_x^2, \sigma_y^2]$, where σ_x, σ_y, σ_d were empirically set to 96.

3.2 Results

Figure 1 shows an example of the input image and generated maps.

In this scene, an object with high contrast scored very high value in the saliency map. On the other hand, the magician's hands scored the highest value in the manipulation map. Considering that the magician intended to guide the spectators' attention to the hands area, the generated attention map was reasonable.

Table 1: Comparison of the evaluation indexes between the proposed method and saliency map

	Proposed model	Saliency map
Mean	2.74	1.92
SD	0.62	0.48

The evaluation indexes of the proposed model and saliency map are shown in Table 1.

The evaluation index of the proposed model was higher than the saliency map. Therefore, the proposed model can better describe human attention than the saliency map.

4. CONCLUSIONS

In this paper, we proposed a model of human attention considering visual saliency and human face, hands and gaze. Based on the experimental results, the proposed model can be better than the saliency map for describing human attention.

We plan to implement the model into a small-sized humanoid robot to manipulate human attention.

5. ACKNOWLEDGMENTS

This work was supported by the apan Society for the Promotion of Science, Grant-in-Aid for oung Scientists (B), 24700190.

6. REFERENCES

[1] T. Akashi, . Tamura, S. ano, and H. Osumi. Analysis of manipulating other's attention for smooth interaction between human and robot. In *Proceedings of the 2013 IEEE/SICE International Symposium on System Integration*, pages 340–345, 2013.

[2] M. Cerf, . Harel, W. Einhäuser, and C. och. Predicting human gaze using low-level saliency combined with face detection. *Advances in Neural Information Processing Systems*, 20:241–248, 2008.

[3] G. Farnebäck. Two-frame motion estimation based on polynomial expansion. In *Proceedings of the 13th Scandinavian Conference on Image Analysis*, pages 363–370, 2003.

[4] L. Itti, C. och, and E. Niebur. A model of saliency-based visual attention for rapid scene analysis. *IEEE Transactions on Pattern Analysis and Machine Intelligence*, 20(11):1254–1258, 1998.

[5] G. uhn, B. Tatler, and G. Cole. ou look where i look! effect of gaze cues on overt and covert attention in misdirection. *Visual Cognition*, 17:925–944, 2009.

[6] . Otero-Millan, S. Macknik, A. Robbins, and S. Martinez-Conde. Stronger misdirection in curved than in straight motion. *Frontiers in Human Neuroscience*, 5(133):1–4, 2011.

[7] M. Ozeki, . ashiwagi, M. Inoue, and N. Oka. Top-down visual attention control based on a particle filter for human-interactive robots. In *Proceedings of the 4th International Conference on Human System Interaction*, pages 188–194, 2011.

An Emotional Model for Social Robots

[Late-Breaking Report]

Martina Truschzinski
Chair of Automation Technology
Chemnitz University of Technology
Germany
martina.truschzinski@etit.tu-chemnitz.de

Nicholas Müller
Institute for Media Research
Chemnitz University of Technology
Germany
nicholas.mueller@phil.tu-chemnitz.de

ABSTRACT

We developed an emotional model, which could help supporting robots to accomodate humans during a working task inside an industrial setting. The robot would recognize when a human is experiencing increased stress and decides whether it should assist the human or should do other tasks. We propose the model as a framework which was developed as part of "The Smart Virtual Worker"-project within the context of human-robot interactions. The emotional model is able to estimate a worker's emotional valence throughout a typical work task by applying a hierarchical reinforcement learning algorithm. Since emotions are generated by the human brain based on an individual's interpretation of a stimulus, we linked the genesis of emotions to empirical findings of the sports sciences in order to infer an emotional reaction. Furthermore, the model reproduces sympathetic reactions of the human body and is capable of remembering past actions in order to include possible future time constraints as an initiator for emotional responses in the upcoming iterations. This capability is crucial for accommodating long-term experiences since the emotional reaction is not only based on the present situation, but on the whole experimental setting.

1. INTRODUCTION

Employment of robots in private and public environments is increasing. Especially the sales figures of industrial robots are rising [8]. Robots are not only becoming faster, cheaper and more capable but also more flexible in attending different tasks and get increasingly more interactive with humans [7]. Especially when robots and humans are executing working tasks cooperatively as a peer-to-peer group, a socially interactive robot is required [5]. For an effective execution of cooperative tasks the robot is required to understand people's specific knowledge, strengths and weaknesses [9] and to estimate and react to the peoples intentions and needs [4, 3] as well as the dynamics of object interaction with other robots and humans [2]. The ability of understanding an intention is intimately linked to an emotional understanding [6]. The important role emotions play in human-robot interaction [1] and the fact that many learning tasks of social robots using a reinforcement algorithm led us to the application of the developed emotional model as a component of a social robot.

HRI'14, March 3–6, 2014, Bielefeld, Germany.
ACM 978-1-4503-2658-2/14/03.
http://dx.doi.org/10.1145/2559636.2559837 .

2. THE EMOTIONAL MODEL

The "Smart Virtual Worker" (SVW)-project[1] presents an opportunity to easily replicate established workflow parameters inside a virtual simulation to establish alternative routes, storage, or construction methods during the stage of production planning. Since the SVW-project contains multiple individual modules, the emotional model is built as a Standalone solution. This allows for a much wider array of possible implementation strategies like being an add-on component for already established system architectures. In order to accurately assess and estimate current and ongoing emotional developments inside the human counterpart, the robot requires a workflow model of emotional valence manifestations.

This can be easily achieved by implementing the emotional model as presented in Figure 1. Two types of numerical input are necessary for proper operations. First, the planned action from the reinforcement learning algorithm for motion generation suggests a work task, which impacts the emotional model in three ways, according to previously established key factors about the human counterpart, e.g. experience and physiology. The second factor, the ergonomic assessment categorizes the work task as being feasible, precarious or alarming. Due to this, we are able to assess physiological constraints and infer possible reactions to upcoming movements. Thereby comparing body postures and assessing intentions like "carrying", "walking" etc. This assessment combined with the ergonomic evaluation about how difficult the aspired movement is going to be serves as the foundation of the emotional manifestation.

Since emotions heavily depend on a human's individual response to outer circumstances and since the goal of the simulation are individual recommendations for a better workflow, the emotional model contains an individualizing computation routine. Based on three assessed factors about the physiology of the worker in question, the impact of the original ergonomic assessment on the valence scales is adapted.

[1]This work has been funded by the European Union with the European Social Fund (ESF) and by the state of Saxony

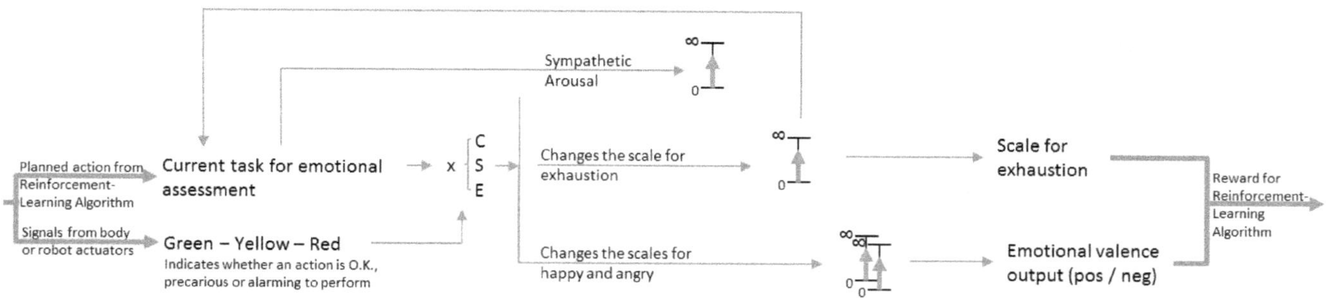

Figure 1: The emotional model developed in the SVW-project calculates an emotional reward function which in turn enables a socially comprehensible robot to estimates the level of difficulty of a task.

These three factors are constitution, sensitivity, and experience, abbreviated in the model as C, S and E.
The emotional state is modeled using three valence scales labeled sympathetic arousal, joy and anger. While two scales are labeled after human feelings, we do not presume any direct correspondence to these. Instead, the scales joy and anger are increased by easy and difficult actions, respectively; and the emotional state is classified as positive or negative based on whether the valence of joy or anger dominates. Arousal is increased by any action that raises either joy or anger, and value is reduced on all scales over time when no stimulus causes them to increase. Sympathetic arousal mirrors a form of energy the emotional state of the current action invokes in the agent.
In addition, following the theory of emotional transaction by Zillmann [10], this sympathetic arousal enables the transfer of energy between the emotional states implemented, which is, in our case, between the scales joy and anger.
As a result, the emotional model outputs the emotional valence calculated as positive or negative values, respective to reward and punishment. This implies for the reinforcement learning algorithm that it is able to optimize actions with the highest positive values and avoid actions with negative values. Therefore a socially comprehensible robot could either help or could propose other easier solutions to the work task.

3. FUTURE WORK

Our next steps will be to enhance the model depicted in figure 1, while attempting to evaluate our preliminary predictions about an individual's emotional responses within a real-world psychological experiment.
Furthermore, we intend to expand the interaction between the human model and other objects, both passive and active. On one hand, this means that we want to improve the assessment of failing actions (e.g. a box being dropped) and on the other hand simulate active objects (e.g. a robot). The latter incurs distinguishing between the robot carrying out actions expected or unexpected by the (modeled) human, leading to substantially different impacts on the (modeled) emotional state. We hope with this refined model we are able to improve these effects of human-robot interaction, assisting the social robot in choosing smarter, more anticipatory reactions in interactive situations.

4. REFERENCES

[1] C. Breazeal. Emotion and sociable humanoid robots. *Int. J. Hum.-Comput. Stud.*, 59(1-2):119–155, 2003.

[2] K. Dautenhahn. Socially intelligent robots: dimensions of human-robot interaction. *Phil. Trans. R. Soc. B*, 362(1480):679–704, 2007.

[3] Y. Demiris and B. Khadhouri. Hierarchical attentive multiple models for execution and recognition of actions. *Robotics and Autonomous Systems*, 54(5):361 – 369, 2006.

[4] A. D. Dragan, K. C. Lee, and S. S. Srinivasa. Legibility and predictability of robot motion. In *Proceedings of the 8th ACM/IEEE International Conference on Human-robot Interaction*, HRI '13, pages 301–308, Piscataway, NJ, USA, 2013. IEEE Press.

[5] T. Fong, I. Nourbakhsh, and K. Dautenhahn. A survey of socially interactive robots, 2002.

[6] H. Gunes and B. Schuller. Categorical and dimensional affect analysis in continuous input: Current trends and future directions. *Image Vision Comput.*, 31(2):120–136, 2013.

[7] P. J. Hinds, T. L. Roberts, and H. Jones. Whose job is it anyway? a study of human-robot interaction in a collaborative task. *Hum.-Comput. Interact.*, 19(1):151–181, June 2004.

[8] I. I. F. of Robotics. World robotics 2013 industrial robots, Nov 2013.

[9] J. G. Trafton, L. M. Hiatt, A. M. Harrison, F. P. Tamborello, S. S. Khemlani, and A. C. Schultz. Act-r/e: An embodied cognitive architecture for human-robot interaction. *Journal of Human-Robot Interaction*, 2:30–54, 2013.

[10] D. Zillmann, R. C. Johnson, and K. D. Day. Attribution of apparent arousal and proficiency of recovery from sympathetic activation affecting excitation transfer to aggressive behavior. *Journal of Experimental Social Psychology*, 10(6):503–515, 1974.

Task Fidelity for Robot-Mediated Interaction in 3D Worlds

Michael Vallance
Future University Hakodate
Dept. of Media Architecture
116-2 Kamedanakano
Hakodate, Japan T041-8655
michael@fun.ac.jp

Catherine Naamani
University of South Wales
CELT
Pontypridd, South Wales, UK
catherine.naamani@southwales.ac.uk

Malcolm Thomas
Mountain Ash Comp. School
Rhondda Cynon Taf,
South Wales, UK
Malcolm_Thomas@macs.rhondda.sch.uk

ABSTRACT
In any task design it is important to consider its difficulty for the intended learners. Task designers such as teachers and Higher Education practitioners need to provide tasks commensurate with the expected successful outcomes that will, it is anticipated, be developed by the learners. In this paper we will demonstrate how tasks can be quantified within the particular context of communicating the programming of robots in a 3D virtual world. Circuit Task Complexity and Robot Task Complexity are calculated alongside immersivity to determine a new metric for measuring tasks involving robots, which we have termed Task Fidelity.

Categories and Subject Descriptors.
K.3 [**Computers and Education**]: Computer science education

Keywords
Immersion, measurement, robot, task complexity, virtual worlds

1. INTRODUCTION
Our research has been designed to collate data of students collaborating in a 3D virtual world to program a LEGO robot to successfully navigate mazes from start to completion in both the physical world and within a 3D virtual space (see Fig. 1). This is undertaken by students in Japan and UK (i) designing circuits which necessitate the use of robot maneuvers and sensors; and (ii) collaborating in a virtual world to solve the set tasks. These experiences lead to personal strategies for teamwork, planning, organizing, applying, analyzing, creating and reflection. Complex problems are thus presented which necessitate the use of programming skills, collaboration, and higher-level cognitive processes. However, to give meaning to the students' experiences over a series of task challenges, we need to quantify each task's complexity.

Common metrics allow for benchmarking within a particular domain. For instance, road transportation such as cars, motorcycles and trucks can be compared by the metrics of top speed, acceleration, engine capacity, fuel economy, transmission and price. However, this is not the case with robots. When discussing robots that undertake specific maneuvers, some researchers provide a common metric labeled as Task Complexity. Tasks are defined as physical action units that are undertaken by a robot, and the designation 'complexity' is used to characterize the task that consists of parts in, potentially, intricate arrangements. Murphy and Schreckenghost [1] conducted a meta-analysis of 29 papers that proposed metrics for human-robot interaction. Forty two metrics in total were determined. They found though that HRI metrics were often not measured directly, but most often were 'inferred' through observation. Although the paper identified proposed HRI metrics, it was recognized that they "have no functional, or generizable, mechanism for measuring that feature."

HRI'14, March 3-6, 2014, Bielefeld, Germany.
ACM 978-1-4503-2658-2/14/03.
http://dx.doi.org/10.1145/2559636.2559794

2. ROBOT MEDIATED INTERACTION
In the first iteration of our research, presented at HRI 2013, in order to quantify each task complexity the programming of our LEGO robot required a determination of an action and a vector [2]. As circuits became more challenging, the LEGO Mindstorms NXT programming became more complex. We therefore found that the logic of assigning task complexity to circuits was inadequate. This was especially the case when we needed to add sensors to maneuver around and over obstacles We have now re-named Task Complexity as 'Robot Task Complexity' (RTC) because the task focuses upon the robot and what the human has to do to manipulate that robot. We call this the 'product' of a robot task. Human-Robot Interaction. (HRI) is the 'interaction' between a human and a robot. The word 'interaction' assumes that the human and the robot are communicating two-way. We call this the 'process' of a robot task. Therefore, we do not consider our 'process' to be Human-Robot Interaction (HRI) but consider our 'collaboration' to be Robot-Mediated Interaction (RMI).

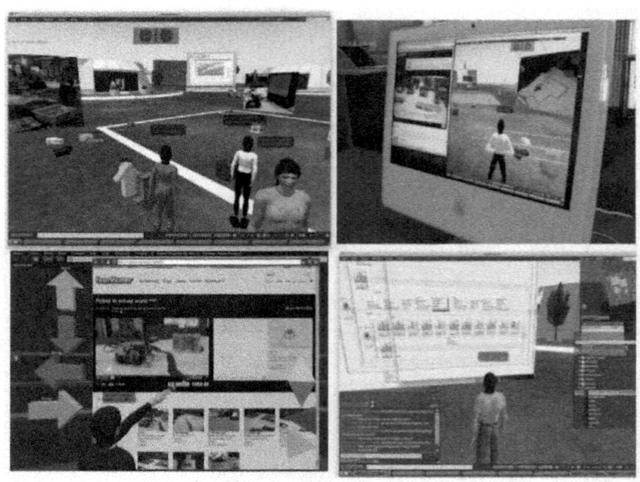

Figure 1. Robot-Mediated Interaction in our 3D virtual world

Given that our context is Robot-Mediated Interaction (RMI) in a 3D virtual space, this applied research also determines how immersed students become within the procedure of each task. To record 'immersion' (a cognitive phenomena also referred to as 'flow') we have collected skill and challenge data during and after each task. With optimal challenge – skill relationship, the students become immersed in the Robot-Mediated Interaction (RMI) tasks.

3. TASK FIDELITY

We have defined Task Fidelity as an indicator of the complexity of the circuit compared with the complexity of the program to complete the circuit. For instance, in designing the task challenge, Circuit Task Complexity (CTC) equals the number of directions + number of maneuvers + number of sensors + number of obstacles.

$CTC = \Sigma (d + m + s + o)$

For example, if a robot has to maneuver past 2 obstacles in order to reach its target, the number of directions to be programmed can be 4, the number of maneuvers is 3, and the number of sensors is 2 (i.e. two touch sensors), then $CTC = \Sigma (4 + 3 + 2 + 2) = 11$

We then modified our task complexity to be determined by the NXT program solution rather than the circuit to be navigated. We call this Robot Task Complexity (RTC), which is measured as:

$RTC = \Sigma Mv_1 + \Sigma Sv_2 + \Sigma SW + \Sigma Lv_3$

where M = number of moves (direction and turn); S = number of sensors; SW = number of switches; L = number of loops; v = number of decisions required by the user for each programmable block ($v_1 = 6$, $v_2 = 5$, $v_3 = 2$)

A NXT program solution for our example above has RTC = 66.

In order to compare the data from all tasks, for the Circuit Task Complexity values we took the maximum CTC value of all our tasks and divided it into each task's CTC value. Similarly, for the Robot Task Complexity values we took the maximum RTC value and divided it into each RTC value. All values are thus represented between 0 and 1. As a result, the complexity of the task can now be quantified by a new metric which we term Task Fidelity; where. Task Fidelity = Circuit Task Complexity - Robot Task Complexity (TF = CTC – RTC).

4. RESULTS

To date we have conducted and recorded reliable data from 39 collaborative tasks. The zero line in Fig 2. indicates ideal Task Fidelity; or, in other words, ideal task complexity. Data plotted above the zero line indicate that the robot program was more complex than the circuit the robot had to maneuver. Data below the zero line indicate that the circuit was more complex than the robot program required to successfully navigate it. Ideally, the instructor should provide a task commensurate with the expected successful outcome to be developed by the learners; i.e. tasks along the horizontal zero line illustrated in Fig 2. But there are differences, and we measure the difference as Task Fidelity.

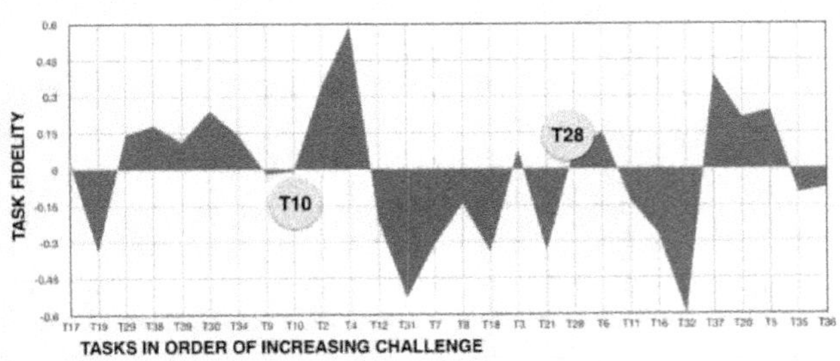

Fig. 2 Task Fidelity

Moreover, the optimal line of immersivity, shown in Fig 3, is determined from students' reflection measures of skill versus challenge. We have found that tasks on or near the optimal immersivity line correlate to low Task Fidelity values. These are the tasks that are most effective for developing students' robot programming skills and international collaborative experiences.

Combining the observations of Task Fidelity and immersivity suggest that tasks T10 and T28 would be considered the most successful tasks when students are engaged in robot mediated interactions. TF value for T28 was only + 0.08; slightly above the optimal Task Fidelity line, and slightly below the optimal immersivity line. Similarly for T10, with immersivity slightly above optimal path of immersivity and Task Fidelity at +0.01. Sensors were used in these tasks and even though students' post-task reflection data revealed that they found sensor related tasks difficult, being immersed in a task led to greater student success.

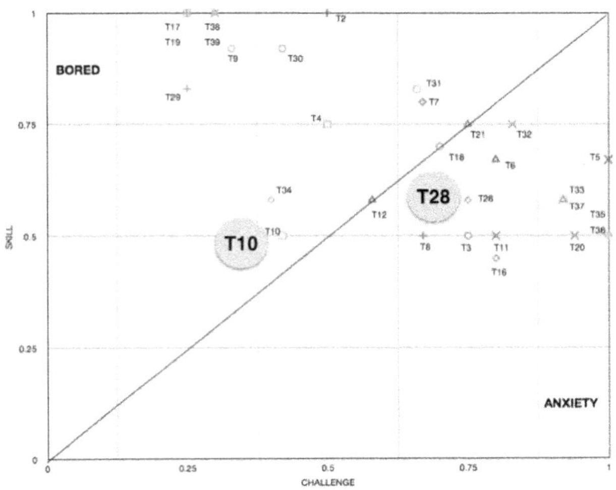

Fig. 3 Students' immersivity

5. CONCLUSION

In conclusion, the literature reveals that there is no consensus regarding a common set of metrics for robot task complexity. For effective education involving robot-mediated interactions, the challenge is to seek tasks where immersivity is close to or on the optimal immersivity line, and task complexity is close to or on the optimal line of Task Fidelity.

6. REFERENCES

[1] A. Steinfeld, T. Fong, D. Kaber, M. Lewis, J. Scholtz, A. Schultz, and M. Goodrich, Common Metrics for Human-Robot Interaction. *In proceedings of the 1st ACM SIGCHI/SIGART conference on Human-robot interaction,* pp. 33-40, 2005.

[2] M. Vallance. The affect of collaboratively programming robots in a 3D virtual simulation. In *Proceedings of the 8th ACM/IEEE international conference on Human-robot interaction* (HRI '13), pp. 245-246, 2013.

First Validation of a Generic Method for Emotional Body Posture Generation for Social Robots

Greet Van de Perre, Michaël Van Damme, Dirk Lefeber, Bram Vanderborght
Robotics and Multibody Mechanics Research Group
Vrije Universiteit Brussel, Pleinlaan 2 - 1050 Elsene - Belgium
Greet.Van.de.Perre@vub.ac.be

ABSTRACT

Gestures for social robots are often preprogrammed off-line or generated by mapping motion capture data to the robot. Since these gestures are dependent on the robot's joint configuration, new joint trajectories to reach the desired postures need to be implemented when using a new robot platform with a different morphology. The method proposed here aims to minimize the workload when implementing gestures on a new robot platform and facilitate the sharing of gestures between different robots. The innovative aspect of this method is that it is constructed independently of any robot configuration, and therefore it can be used to generate gestures for different robot platforms. To calculate a posture for a certain configuration, the developed method uses a set of target gestures listed in a database and maps them to that specific configuration. The method was validated on a series of configurations, including those of existing robots.

Categories and Subject Descriptors

J.4 [**Computer Applications**]: Social and behavioral sciences; I.2.9 [**Artificial Intelligence**]: Robotics

Keywords

Generic gesture system, upper body posture, emotions

1. INTRODUCTION

Gesturing is an important research topic in social robotics. As in human-human communication, it is an essential feature to ensure natural and fluent communication [3]. Gestures implemented in robots are however, up to now, subject to two important limitations. Firstly, the gestures implemented in a robot are always limited to a set of gestures necessary for the current research, and often limited to one type of gestures (e.g. [1]). The reason for the limited amount of gestures implemented in specific robots can be found in the second limitation; namely the way they are implemented. Gestures are mostly preprogrammed off-line, stored in a database and replayed during interaction [5], or generated by mapping human motion capture data to the robot [4]. In both cases, the resulting gestures are dependent on the morphology, so robot specific and cannot be used for other robots with other configurations. The result is that, when working with a new robot platform, new joint trajectories to reach the desired postures need to be implemented, which can be time consuming.

The method proposed in this paper aims to facilitate the implementation of gestures in different robots. The innovative aspect of this method is that it is constructed independently of any robot configuration, therefore it can be used to generate gestures for different robot platforms. The configuration of the robot is used as input, and the joint angles needed to establish a desired gesture or posture are calculated. We believe this generic method can be useful for different research teams since it easily allows gestures to be shared between different robots and minimizes the workload when implementing gestures on a new robot platform.

HRI'14, March 3–6, 2014, Bielefeld, Germany.
ACM 978-1-4503-2658-2/14/03.
http://dx.doi.org/10.1145/2559636.2559810 .

2. METHODOLOGY

2.1 Target postures

To generate gestures for a certain configuration, the developed method uses a set of target postures listed in a database and maps them to that specific configuration. The target postures for the emotional expressions were chosen from the UCLIC Affective Body Posture and Motion Database [2].

To be able to describe the target postures in a quantitative way, a human base model was defined. The base model consists of four so-called *chains*, namely the head, body, left- and right arm. Every chain consists of one or more *blocks*. A block corresponds to a single human joint complex, such as the shoulder or the wrist. Every block subsequently consists of a specific number of joints. The target body postures could then be described by the orthopaedic angles of every block of the base model.

2.2 Mapping the gestures to a configuration

To make a model or robot perform a desired gesture, the target postures are mapped to its joint configuration. The method can be used for any robot or model whereof its configuration consists of *one or more* parts of the human base model, namely a head, a body, a left and/or right arm. The joints of each chain must be grouped into the different blocks composing that chain, whereby the number of driven joints placed in a block cannot exceed the number of joints in the corresponding block in the human base model. To specify

Table 1: **Results for different arm configurations, visualized on a human model from the RocketBox Libraries.**

Base model	Config WE-4RII	Config iCub	Config Robovie
		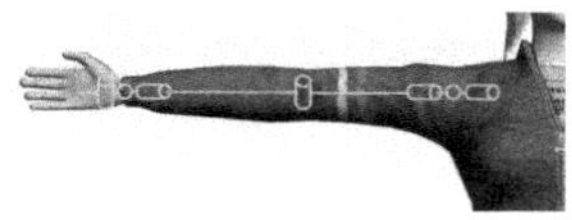	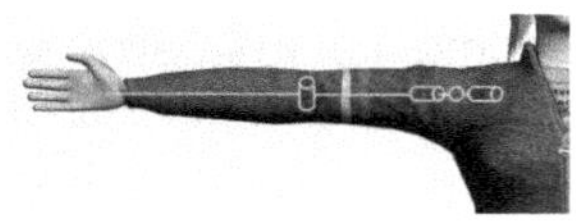

the robot's joint configuration in the program, the Denavit-Hartenberg (DH) parameters of every present block need to be specified. To ensure a good overall posture, it is necessary to take into account the relative orientations of every joint complex the robot has in common with a human, and not only impose the orientation and position of the end effector. Therefore, the target posture is mapped to the configuration by imposing the orientation of the end effector of the different blocks and calculating the corresponding joint angles. For every present block, a mapped rotation matrix is calculated from the orthopedic target angles and the current DH-parameters. This matrix is the necessary orientation the end effector of the block needs to adopt in order to reach the desired overall posture. The necessary joint angles can be calculated from this mapped rotation matrix by using a first order inverse kinematics algorithm.

3. RESULTS

Table 1 shows the calculated posture for different arm configurations. To visualize the results, the calculated joint angles are sent to a human model of the RocketBox Libraries. The first column shows the base model with the targeted posture, in this case the emotional expression for *fear*. The second column shows a complete, 9 DOF arm with a similar configuration as the robot WE-4RII. All the blocks are complete and therefore, a set of joint angles can be calculated for every block wherefore the corresponding overall posture equals the target posture. The next configuration represents iCub's arm; it is a 7 DOF arm, with a complete 3 DOF shoulder, 1 DOF elbow and 3 DOF wrist. Although this is not a complete configuration, the obtained posture is very recognizable. When comparing the calculated gesture with the human base gesture, one can clearly see the lower placed elbow, since the elevation of the clavicle is not possible for this configuration. Column four shows the arm of Robovie. This configuration is similar to that of iCub's arm, except for the missing wrist block. The resulting posture significantly differs from the targeted posture due to the highly simplified joint configuration, however, it can still be recognized as an expression of *fear*.

4. CONCLUSIONS AND FUTURE WORK

In this paper, a generic novel method for gesture generation for robots was described. Since the method is constructed independently of a robot configuration, it can be used by different robot platforms and models. By inputting the Denavit-Hartenberg parameters of the configuration, the method calculates the necessary joint angles for that configuration to establish a desired posture. The method was validated on different configurations. The results are currently visualized by sending them to a human virtual model. Future work includes validating the method on more existing robot configurations and visualizing the results by using the virtual model of the robots instead of the current model. In a later stage, the virtual models will be replaced by the real robots. The gesture library will be extended to other types of gestures, such as pointing and waving.

5. ACKNOWLEDGMENTS

The first author is funded by the Fund for Scientific Research (FWO) Flanders. This work is partially funded by the EU-project DREAM (611391).

6. REFERENCES

[1] H. Ishiguro, T. Ono, M. Imai, T. Maeda, T. Kanda, and R. Nakatsu. Robovie: an interactive humanoid robot. *Industrial robot: An international journal*, 28(6):498–504, 2001.

[2] A. Kleinsmith, P. R. De Silva, and N. Bianchi-Berthouze. Cross-cultural differences in recognizing affect from body posture. *Interacting with Computers*, 18(6):1371–1389, 2006.

[3] M. Salem, F. Eyssel, K. Rohlfing, S. Kopp, and F. Joublin. To err is human (-like): Effects of robot gesture on perceived anthropomorphism and likability. *Int. Journal of Social Robotics*, pages 1–11, 2013.

[4] A. Tapus, A. Peca, A. Aly, C. Pop, L. Jisa, S. Pintea, A. S. Rusu, and D. O. David. Children with autism social engagement in interaction with nao, an imitative robot. a series of single case experiments. *Interaction studies*, 13(3):315–347, 2012.

[5] M. Zecca, Y. Mizoguchi, K. Endo, F. Iida, Y. Kawabata, N. Endo, K. Itoh, and A. Takanishi. Whole body emotion expressions for kobian humanoid robot: preliminary experiments with different emotional patterns. In *The 18th IEEE Int. Symp. on Robot and Human Interactive Communication. RO-MAN 2009*, pages 381–386.

Learning Interactions with and about Robotic Models

Igor M. Verner
Department of Education in Science and Technology
Technion – Israel Institute of Technology
Haifa, 32000, Israel
ttrigor@technion.ac.il

Dan Cuperman
Department of Education in Science and Technology
Technion – Israel Institute of Technology
Haifa, 32000, Israel
dancup@zahav.net.il

ABSTRACT
This paper considers learning interactions, in which the student inquires into a biological system and develops its representation in the form of a robotic model using the PicoCricket robot construction kit. Our study follows-up the learning interactions and students' perceptions of the modeling experience.

Categories and Subject Descriptors
K.3.1 [**Computers and education**]: Computer Uses in Education – *collaborative learning, computer-assisted instruction.*

Keywords
Learning interaction; Design and inquiry learning, Biorobotics; Modeling; PicoCricket.

General Terms
Performance, Experimentation, Human Factors.

1. INTERACTIONS IN MODELING
Modeling is a learning process in which students construct and share representations of reality. Modeling involves the students in learning interactions with the physical and social environment, providing materials and knowledge, needed for creation of a model, as well as experience and feedback needed for validation of the model. These learning interactions contribute to cognitive development of the students by stimulating them to construct an acceptable grammar and semantics for their model representations [1]. Creating robotic models and exploring their motion behaviors open new opportunities of learning practice. Our study examines the educational robotics pathway in which students inquire into biological systems and construct their representations in the form of robotic models. We developed a course "Control in Technological and Biological Systems" and delivered it to school students, following-up their learning interactions and perceptions of the modeling experience.

2. BIO-INSPIRED ROBOTIC MODELS
In our course [2], students built models were using the PicoCricket robot construction kit. This kit offers preprogrammed animal voices, colorful lights, craft materials and other useful specialties. Interactions are controlled with the PicoBlocks software. Over time, students are led through the following stages:

1. Acquiring technical knowledge: The students experiment with sensors, mechanisms, motors, programming, and controls as they look for analogies with biological systems.
2. Choosing a biological phenomenon to model: Students select a behavior found in nature that they wish to replicate in a robot.
3. Building prototypes: The students construct the robot through rapid prototyping cycles.
4. Assessing the prototypes: The students interact with the prototypes, evaluating their resemblance to the biological system with regard to components, geometrical form, functioning, and control. This helps them better represent or validate their understanding of the biological system.

In one project, students chose to model the Venus flytrap behavior, in particular, the "mechanosensitive" trigger mechanism, the trap structure and its movement. The final Venus flytrap robot (Figure 1) includes two touch sensors and a DC motor which drives a crank that opens or closes the trap structure. The robot modeled two cases: one of the sensors is touched several times or both sensors are touched simultaneously.

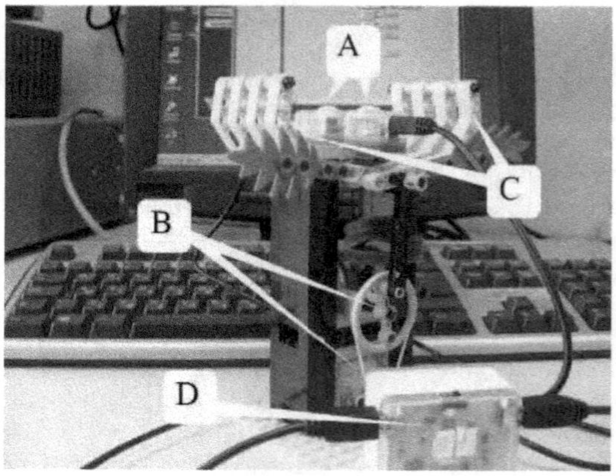

Figure 1. The flytrap model: A. Sensors; B. Motor & crank; C. Trap mechanism; D. PicoCricket.

3. EDUCATIONAL STUDY FRAMEWORK
In this study we sought to answer the question: what are the specific features of learning interactions with and about bio-inspired robotic models, and what are students' perceptions of these interactions? A multi-case study was conducted with participation of prospective teachers and school students who studied our course. The gain in knowledge and skills, attributed to project activities, was evaluated, based on descriptions of the inquired phenomena and designed models given by the students in discussions, presentations, reports

HRI'14, March 3–6, 2014, Bielefeld, Germany.
ACM 978-1-4503-2658-2/14/03.
http://dx.doi.org/10.1145/2559636.2559855

and questioners. We analyzed typical learning behaviors, as well as features of the learning practices, by using the integrated methodology.

4. FINDINGS

4.1 Features of learning practices

The features that repeated throughout the case studies were as follows:

Motivation. The students were highly motivated to learn scientific and technological concepts and perform hands-on activities. The desire to build a robotic model typically triggered students' curiosity to the biological phenomenon and drove the inquiry. The aspiration to implement the knowledge about the phenomenon and create a robotic model motivated students to learn the needed technological concepts.

Team size. A team of two or three learners was found preferable for effective team interaction.

Rapid prototyping. In the process of constructing a robotic model that took not more than a few hours, the students underwent the experiential learning cycle of agile technological prototyping and scientific inquiry activities.

Exploring similarities and differences. The exploration of similarities and differences between a biological system and its model facilitated understanding of biological and engineering concepts. In this exploration students dealt with questions such as: What features of the biological system are essential for the model, and does the model authentically represent then? Can the model be improved to better represent the system within the limitations of construction and programming using the PicoCricket kit?

4.2 Attitudes towards learning with models

All the participants demonstrated strong interested to build robotic models together with inquiry activities. They recognized the advantages of learning with models, and especially, the value of models as means for visualizing dynamic processes. They stated that model making was easier than they expected, and its educational benefits justified the effort.

4.3 Learning outcomes

We witnessed students' progress in learning technological concepts that was indicated by the literate explanations they gave when presenting their models. The use of biological concepts in students' oral and written explanations was examined with the assist of biology teachers. The analysis revealed a gain in knowledge and literate use of concepts related to the studied topic. The teachers helped students to validate information that they collected and knowledge they acquired through self-regulated inquiry.

5. DISCUSSION

The following features of the robotic modeling environment were found essential for sustaining learning interactions in our course:

1. The learning environment should provide the integral infrastructure for scientific inquiry and building robotic models. A gallery of previously developed models serves as a worthwhile constituent of the environment.
2. Open workspace facilitates active interactions within and between the teams and between the students and the teacher.
3. The teacher should stimulate students' inquiry by asking questions that invoke further investigation and prompt the need for validation of results.

Based on our study, the following arguments can be posed in favor of the proposed approach:

1. From construction of a robotic model and interaction with and about it, students can derive benefits that cannot be obtained by analyzing models built by others.
2. The interplay between construction and interaction can serve a motivating factor of students' engagement in the course.
3. Creation of bio-inspired robotic models through rapid prototyping and interactive validation is an effective learning practice in which the analysis of source-target similarities and differences can foster students' analogical thinking.
4. Through the robotic modeling project the students can acquire knowledge and skills in robotics and biology. In addition to specific competences they can develop understanding of the design concepts and acquire skills of learning with models which are considered important components of science-technological literacy.

6. CONCLUSION

Our research proposes a learning environment, in which the study of a scientific phenomenon prompts and inspires design of and interaction with a robotic model, which in turn lead to further learning of scientific concepts. In this setting, the robotic model becomes a "nucleus", which organizes and triggers the learning of technology and science subjects around the modeling process. All the stages of this modeling process, i.e. the model ideation, materialization and exploration, have their specific educational roles. At the materialization stage the student creates the model through iterations of rapid prototyping. The aspiration to improve the prototype directs the learning towards in-depth understanding of the biological system and development of effective technological solutions. At the model exploration stage, the analysis of similarities and differences between the model and the biological system guides the student to evaluate the model and the learning outcomes. Our study indicated that the proposed course of action fostered growth in learners' scientific and technological literacy, positive attitudes towards teaching and learning with models, and motivation for building robotic models. In this setting, an examination of similarities and differences between the biological and technological systems is a meaningful learning experience leading to better understanding of concepts in both robotics and biology.

7. ACKNOWLEDGEMENT

The study was supported by the Technion Gordon Center for Systems Engineering.

8. REFERENCES

[1] Hoppenbrouwers, S.J.B.A., Proper, H.A., & van der Weide, T.P. 2005. A Fundamental View on the Process of Conceptual Modeling. In Delcambre, L. et al., eds. *Conceptual Modeling - ER 2005*, LNCS, 3716, 128-143. Springer, Berlin, Germany.

[2] Cuperman, D. & Verner, I. M. 2013. Learning through creating robotic models of biological systems. *International Journal of Technology and Design Education*, 23(4), 849-866.

Puzzling Exercises for Spatial Training with Robot Manipulators

Igor M. Verner
Technion - Israel Institute of Technology
Haifa, 32000, Israel
+972-48292168
ttrigor@technion.ac.il

Dalia Leibowitz
Massachusetts Institute of Technology
Cambridge, 02139, MA
+617-2532201
dalialeibowitz@gmail.com

Sergei Gamer
Technion - Israel Institute of Technology
Haifa, 32000, Israel
+972-48292040
gamer@tx.technion.ac.il

ABSTRACT
Robot operation requires spatial reasoning and can be used for spatial training. This paper proposes exercises for training spatial skills through operating robot manipulators in virtual and real environments. The exercises were implemented in a robotics workshop, and the follow-up indicated a significant advance of the participants in performing mental rotation tasks.

Categories and Subject Descriptors
I.2.9 [**Artificial Intelligence**]: Robotics – *manipulators, operator interfaces, workcell organization and planning.*

General Terms
Performance, Experimentation, Human Factors.

Keywords
Robotics laboratory, learning through interaction with robots, training spatial skills.

1. INTRODUCTION
Spatial abilities are critical for engineers [1] and strongly influence achievement in STEM education [2]. Studies have shown that spatial skills can be enhanced through training, and that the impact of training can be long-lived [3]. There is value to finding different methods of training spatial skills, since certain people may be more receptive to certain types of training. Intelitek[TM] and other companies have created instructional robot manipulators that are commonly used for studying manufacturing, control, and systems integration [4]. Issues arise with the use of real robots—they are expensive, require careful monitoring, and are quite large. Additional learning opportunities are provided by virtual robotic environments such as RoboCell.

Our study aimed to develop, implement, and evaluate exercises in spatial training, using robot manipulators in both real and virtual environments. We hypothesize that such practice can engage students and facilitate better performance of spatial tests. This supposition relies on the studies of spatial learning in virtual and real environments in science education. The study involved 23 high school students who participated in the Technion International School summer program, and took place in the Computer Integrated Manufacturing (CIM) and Robotics Laboratory at the Technion in the framework of an MIT undergraduate student internship.

This study continues a sequence of empirical studies (quasi-experiments) conducted through the Technion that have given partial evidence towards using robot manipulators to develop spatial skills [4] [5]. Here for the first time we have combined exercises in virtual and real environments, employed robot manipulators with different configurations, and focused on training mental rotation using test cubes (cubes with different symbols on their sides). A gain in mental rotation skills was evaluated by means of the cube comparisons test [6].

2. EXPERIMENTAL SETUP
2.1 Virtual Environment—RoboCell
RoboCell is a software environment in which one can set up a virtual robotic work-cell and create various subroutines for performing robot handling processes [7]. For this robotic experiment, the created work-cell included a virtual robot simulating the real robot manipulator *SCORBOT-ER V plus*. The virtual workspace was equipped with a feeder holding 6 test cubes, a buffer, and a destination field (Figure 1A). The buffer supported pick-and-place operations, while the destination field was intended for assembling the puzzle shown in Figure 1B. We developed multiple subroutines to bring the test cubes from the feeder, rotate them on the buffer, and place them onto the destination platform.

A. B.

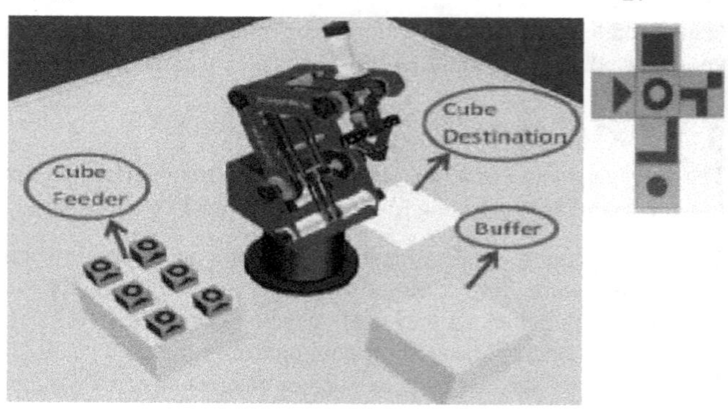

Figure 1. Experimental setup in RoboCell.

HRI'13, March 3–6, 2014, Bielefeld, Germany.
ACM 978-1-4503-2658-2/14/03.
http://dx.doi.org/10.1145/2559636.2559792

2.2 Real Environment

We employed nine robot manipulators of four different types: the *SCORBOT-ER V plus*, the *SCORA-ER 14*, the *SCORBOT ER IX*, and the *PERFORMER MK3*. Each robot had an individual workspace set up, suitable for the robot's specific location in the lab and its kinematic scheme. The *SCORA-ER 14* robots (Figure 2A) do not have gripper pitch and therefore cannot rotate cubes around horizontal axes. To solve this problem, we developed a LEGO rotator to be used in conjunction with the robot (Figure 2B). The exercise here was to put together a puzzle from 4 puzzle cubes, using a teach pendant. The students used the teach pendant to move the mechanical arm, either joint-by-joint or along the XYZ axes. They operated the robot to pick the test cubes one by one from the storage area, rotate them on a buffer or through the use of the LEGO rotator, and then place them on the destination field.

A. B.

Figure 2. A. SCORA-ER 14 setup; B. LEGO rotator.

2.3 Implementation

We conducted a 4 hour workshop consisting of two sessions. In the first session we gave a short introduction, explaining to the students the importance of spatial ability in robotics and telling them the objective was to train spatial skills. The students were told that they would be completing a workshop with exercises in real and virtual environments, and that they would be taking spatial tests before and after the exercises to gauge the potential difference in scores. The students were then given the cube comparisons test of mental rotation skills. The students were given 2.5 minutes to take the test consisting of 21 questions, where the assessment score was the number of correct answers minus the number of incorrect answers [6]. The students were then shown around the CIM and Robotics Laboratory and had the chance to view different robots in action. We introduced the concepts related to the mechanical arm kinematics and explained possible ways to rotate objects. In the second session, we quickly reviewed these concepts and involved the students in the robot operation activities. In the first hour, the students performed the virtual exercise, and in the second hour they operated real robots. The mental rotation cube comparisons test was administered at the end of the session. We also collected written reflections of the students through a short questionnaire. The students answered whether they would prefer to perform the robotics exercises alone or in a group (for both the virtual and real environments), and whether practice with industrial robots such as the robots used in this workshop could enhance their spatial abilities. They also evaluated the helpfulness of the practice in the virtual environment, in the real environment, and in the combination of the two environments.

3. RESULTS

3.1 Spatial Tests

We cross-referenced the individual students' pre-test and post-test scores. Among the 23 participants, 18 students completed the exercises and the pre- and post-tests. We found that 15 of them increased their scores from the pre-test to the post-test, some dramatically. The average grade (calculated as described in Section 2.3) changed from 7.83/21 to 11.5/21. A two-tailed t-test shows that the students' advances are significant, with $p=.003$.

3.2 Questionnaire

The questionnaire led to some interesting observations. Most of the students preferred to work in the virtual RoboCell environment as a group rather than alone. However, in the real environment the students were split about their preference. 16 out of 19 students expressed a strong belief that practice with robot manipulators can enhance their spatial skills. The evaluation of the helpfulness of the virtual and real environments both scored high, while the combination of the environments scored even higher.

4. CONCLUSIONS

Based on the promising results of this study, we plan on further experiments based on the developed exercises, with randomly selected experimental and control groups of participants.

5. ACKNOWLEDGEMENT

The study was supported by the Technion Gordon Center for Systems Engineering and by the MIT MISTI Israel internship program, through partnership with Dr. Julie Shah.

6. REFERENCES

[1] Sorby, S. A. 2007. Developing 3D spatial skills for engineering students, *Australasian Journal of Engineering Education*, 13(1), 1-11.

[2] Wai, J., Lubinski, D., and Benbow, C. 2009. Spatial ability for STEM domains: Aligning over 50 years of cumulative psychological knowledge solidifies its importance, *Journal of Educational Psychology*, 101(4), 817-835.

[3] Uttal, D. H., Meadow, N. G., Tipton, E., Hand, L. L., Alden, A. R., Warren, C., and Newcombe, N. S. 2012. The malleability of spatial skills: A meta-analysis of training studies, *Psychological Bulletin*, 138, 352–402.

[4] Verner, I., Gamer, S. and Shtub, A. 2012. Fostering students' spatial skills through practice in operating and programming robotic cells, In *Robot Intelligence Technology & Applications*, J.-H. Kim et al. Eds., Springer Berlin Heidelberg, 745-752.

[5] Verner, I. 2004. Robot manipulations: A synergy of visualization, computation and action for spatial instruction, *International Journal of Computers for Mathematical Learning*, 9, 213-34.

[6] Eliot, J., and Smith, I.M. 1983. *An international directory of spatial tests*, Windsor, Berkshire: NFER-Nelson.

[7] RoboCell for controller USB, http://www.intelitek.com/advanced-manufacturing/robotics/.

Increasing the Expressivity of Humanoid Robots with Variable Gestural Expressions

Andre Viergutz, Tamara Flemisch, Raimund Dachselt
Interactive Media Lab
Technische Universität Dresden
01062 Dresden, Germany
(andre.viergutz|raimund.dachselt)@tu-dresden.de, tamara.flemisch@mailbox.tu-dresden.de

ABSTRACT

This work aims at establishing a more variable, and thus attractive, communication with humanoids. For this purpose we developed a method of dynamically expressing emotions and intentions associated with parametrised gestures. First, gestures and possible parameters, which are necessary for the generation of a whole-body gesture set, were analyzed. A gesture's inner and outer expressivity is thereby defined which leads to the differentiation of single gestures and variable gestural expressions. Gestures are subsequently classified into (feedback) categories and related depending on their expressivity. We developed a gesture set consisting of six categories including over 50 variable gestures. As proof of concept, the gesture set has been implemented to allow for an easy and flexible authoring process of gesture-supported communication.

Categories and Subject Descriptors

I.2.9 [**Artificial Intelligence**]: Robotics—*Operator Interfaces*

Keywords

Non-Verbal Communication; Gestural Interaction

1. INTRODUCTION

The communication as well as interaction with a humanoid robot poses a big challenge to the design of the input- and output possibilities. The interface strongly depends on the embodied attributes of the particular robot. Moreover, a humanoid appearance suggests the increased use of common modes of communication, like speech and gestures.

Beside gesture *input*, which is widely being explored, the articulation of the robot by using whole-body gestures as an *output* and *feedback* modality attracts attention. Multifaceted social signals in co-expression to speech can be recognized fast and effective by human beings. The creation of proper and efficient gestures however is still a great challenge due to personal and cultural imprints. Hence, the implementation of gestures is often realized in an ad hoc and deterministic fashion to fit their special purpose.

HRI'14, March 3–6, 2014, Bielefeld, Germany.
ACM 978-1-4503-2658-2/14/03.
http://dx.doi.org/10.1145/2559636.2559840.

Figure 1: Series of gestures (left to right: "Hand under chin" (expressivity = 0.1), "Scratch head" (0.7) and "Arms bent" (1.0)) increasing the expressivity of *Incomprehension*.

We approach this problem by asking 1) What should we communicate by using gestures? and 2) How may a system be designed to easily and effectively select suitable gestures? This work especially addresses the authoring part, for that matter showing a modular and procedural system, which is easy to use while allowing for individual adaptations.

2. RELATED WORK

It has been shown that the usage of gestures by robots, co-expressive to speech, states an effective method to encourage the interaction between humans and robots. Aly and Tapus [1] found that people thereby identify themselves better with a robot, that reveals a more similar behavior. There are several examples of articulating robots. Kobayashi et al. [4] created a museum robot which attracts the visitors attention by head movements and uses deictic gestures to show the way. The expression of emotions for example was realized 2005 on *Leonardo*, a small, sociable robot by Breazeal et al. [2]. Also the humanoid robot Nao, which we used in our project, was used to explore the effects of articulated expressions [5]. To maintain a certain flexibility as well as being able to automatically derive appropriate gestures, certain high-level properties were extracted. Hartmann et al. [3] use the *Overall Activation*, *Spatial-* as well as *Temporal Extent*, *Fluidity*, *Power* and *Repetition* to explain the process of performing a gesture. However, these parameters only refer to a concrete gesture and are not simply applicable to a whole set of expressions. Furthermore, they are restricted in their potential for increase because only a small fraction of the parameter space yields meaningful gestures.

To increase the expressive power beyond a single gesture, we propose *Variable Gestural Expressions*.

3. VARIABLE GESTURAL EXPRESSIONS AND GESTURE SELECTION

Observing the use of gestures during common and everyday communication gave us the insight that many of the used gestures serve specific but often similar purposes. This brought us to the idea to consider whole categories of articulation, not just a single gesture. Therefore, we classified more than 50 commonly used gestures into its expressive meanings and compared them with respect to their basic expressivity. This led us to the definition of six (feedback) categories: *Positive/Acceptance*, *Negative/Denial*, *Incomprehension*, *Neutral/Waiting*, *Introduction/Greeting* and *Ending/Goodbye* of a conversation. To increase a certain intention or expression it is not enough to purely increase the inner parameters of a specific gesture. A timid waving of ones hand in front of the body for example only partially increases its power by just repeating it more often and faster. Simple exaggerations are perceived unnatural or even preposterous. To amplify the attraction of attention as an example of *Introduction* happens by considering the whole arm covering a bigger recognizable area. In fact one could argue, that this kind of augmentation relates to the Spatial Extend but considering the goal to determine a proper gesture this mapping doesn't work in both directions. The adequate movement and the decision about which body parts being involved cannot be stated as a bijective function. The expression of incomprehension is even more complicated (see Figure 1).

However, all these single gestures share a certain *basic* or *outer expressivity* with respect to it's expression category, each limited by an individual *expressivity range* to allow for inner gesture parameter variations. Figure 2 shows an expressivity diagram for the category "*Positive/Acceptance*". The inversion of the mapping from a single gesture to its

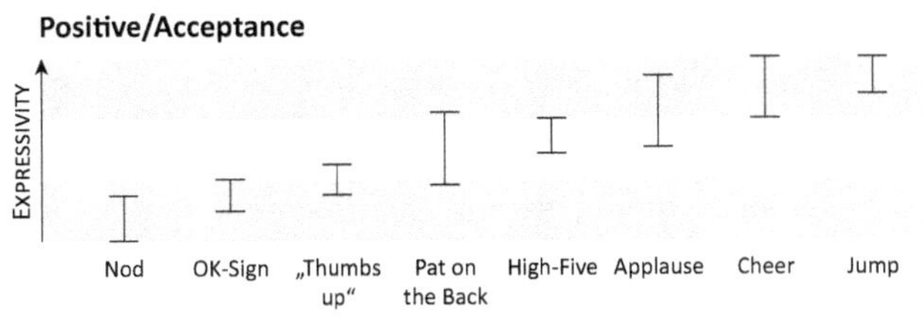

Figure 2: An *expressivity diagram* showing subsequent single gestures for the category "*Positive/Acceptance*"

basic expressivity range leads to a function allowing the selection of one or more suitable gestures by limiting the user only having to set one meta-parameter, the *Expressivity*. In case of multiple choices the system has to decide for a gesture either randomly or depending on the actual context, which is not covered in this work. As mentioned above, each single gesture covers a sub-range of the overall expressivity. Assuming that each of them is parametrically controllable between 0 and 1, the overall expressivity has to be scaled to the relative expressive power.

In addition to determining a suitable gesture, the expressivity also influences inner gesture parameters, like *Frequency*, etc. thereby making inner gesture variations possi-

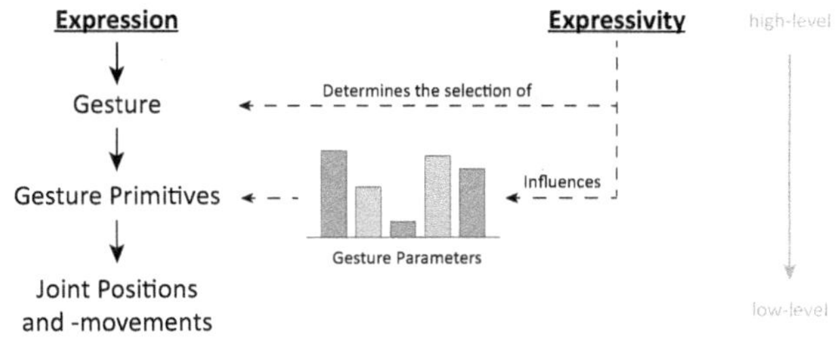

Figure 3: From expressivity to joint positions. The procedural hierarachy of creating a gesture.

ble as to be seen in Figure 3. The mapping of the *Expressivity* to more than one sub-parameter consequently constrains the space of all possible configurations. Particular mapping functions have to be defined, which makes the problem more complex but in turn only meaningful configurations might be created.

4. DISCUSSION AND FUTURE WORK

We proposed a method to reduce the effort of creating as well as selecting suitable gestures to a minimum to be used for enhancing the communication with a robot. Thereby we took care to keep the variety of expressions flexible and dynamic. A library consisting of 26 basic gestures with a total of 50 variations was built for the humanoid robot Nao, which was tested in a small scripted conversation to validate the easy and modular use.

The selection process is currently performed manually by the user. Determining the robots intention and incorporating other contextual information like cultural imprints as well as an individual character of the robot would let our system decide on its own. This could be enhanced in terms of additional meta-parameters. An iterative active learning process for appropriate parameter selection would make the system adaptive and thus more appealing with respect to the correspondence of the user's expectations. A study about the subjective perception will give us further insights into the design and usability of our approach.

5. REFERENCES

[1] A. Aly and A. Tapus. A model for synthesizing a combined verbal and nonverbal behavior based on personality traits in human-robot interaction. In *Proc. of ACM/IEEE HRI*, pages 325–332, 2013.

[2] C. Breazeal, C. Kidd, A. Thomaz, G. Hoffman, and M. Berlin. Effects of nonverbal communication on efficiency and robustness in human-robot teamwork. In *Proc. of IEEE/RSJ IROS*, pages 708–713, 2005.

[3] B. Hartmann, M. Mancini, and C. Pelachaud. Implementing expressive gesture synthesis for embodied conversational agents. In *GW'05 Proc.of Gesture in Human-Computer Interaction and Simulation*, pages 188–199, 2006.

[4] Y. Kobayashi, Y. Hoshi, G. Hoshino, T. Kasuya, M. Fueki, and Y. Kuno. Museum guide robot with three communication modes. In *Proc. of IEEE/RSJ IROS*, pages 3224–3229, Sept. 2008.

[5] R. Meena, K. Jokinen, and G. Wilcock. Integration of gestures and speech in human-robot interaction. In *IEEE CogInfoCom*, pages 673–678, Dec. 2012.

Field Study: Can Androids Be a Social Entity in the Real World ?

Miki Watanabe
Dept. of Engineering Science
Osaka University
Toyonaka, Japan
watanabe.miki@irl.sys.es.osaka-u.ac.jp

Kohei Ogawa
Dept. of Engineering Science
Osaka University
Toyonaka, Japan
ogawa@irl.sys.es.osaka-u.ac.jp

Hiroshi Ishiguro
Dept. of Engineering Science
Osaka University
Toyonaka, Japan
ishiguro@sys.es.osaka-u.ac.jp

ABSTRACT

In this paper, we discussed an autonomous android robot that is recognized as a social entity by observers in the real world. We conducted field experiments to investigate what kind of function the android needs in order to be recognized as a social and humanlike entity by visitors. In the field experiment, the android made conversation with multiple visitors by using several touch displays. The result showed that the visitors evaluate the android as humanlike even though this interaction differs from normal human-human interaction. Moreover, the experiment suggested that the android has a social influence - advertisement effect on visitors.

Categories and Subject Descriptors

H.4.3 [**Information Technology and Systems Applications**]: Communications Applications

General Terms

Design, Human Factors, Experimentation

Keywords

android; human-robot interaction; conversation system

1. INTRODUCTION

Nowadays, the number of partner robots [1] gradually has been increasing in our daily lives. The roles of robots have become more diverse with the increase in the variety of robots available on the market. In the future, android robots whose appearance closely resembles humans could be employed instead of humans in places where the presence of, for example, a receptionist or a guard is needed. Android robot called Repliee Q1 was developed in 2005. Repliee Q1 can reply to human autonomously according to the input from a tactile sensor, a floor sensor and a microphone. Unfortunately the quality of the input data was insufficient for providing a humanlike response. This mismatch between the anthropomorphic appearance and the machinelike response may lead to a problem known as Uncanny Valley [2]. In order to overcome that issue, Geminoid HI-1, that is copy of an actual person, was developed with tele-operational functionality, which enables a human operator to provide responses instead of the autonomous system [3]. Another geminoid version, called Geminoid F is being used as an actress in the "Android Theater". In the limited situation of a theater play, Geminoid F can be perceived like a real human.

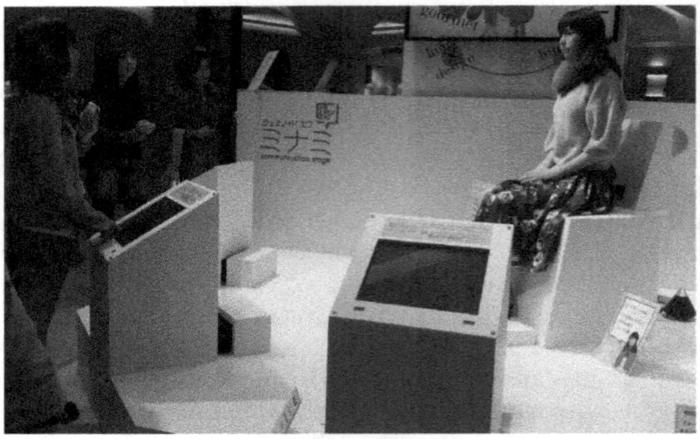

Figure 1: Situation of the experiment

As mentioned above, several questions on natural language processing, computer vision and reasoning system, remain to answer before creating an autonomous conversation system for real world usage. However, in specific situations, an android can be perceived as a humanlike entity by people. Furthermore, in these situations, an android that can interact with people in the real world can affect them positively.

In this paper, we describe an autonomous conversation system which allows an android to interact with people in limited interaction situations. We performed a field experiment with this system to evaluate how people perceive Geminoid F and how Geminoid F affects people by interacting with them. We analyzed the human behavior using video observation and questionnaires.

2. FIELD EXPERIMENT

The purpose of this experiment is to have Geminoid F make conversation with multiple visitors via touch displays, and to verify how people perceived Geminoid F and how

HRI'14, March 3–6, 2014, Bielefeld, Germany.
ACM 978-1-4503-2658-2/14/03.
http://dx.doi.org/10.1145/2559636.2559811 .

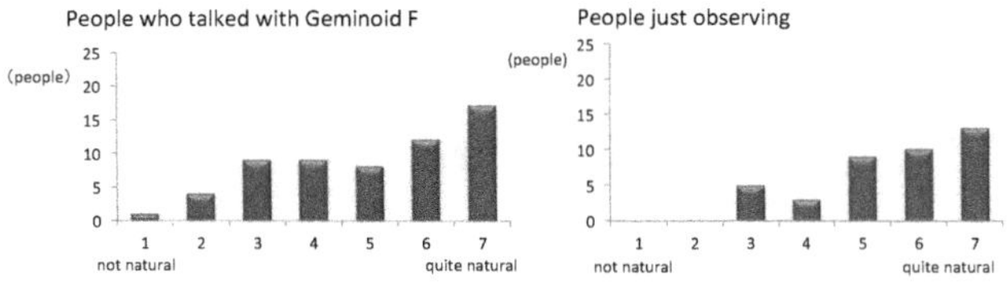

Figure 2: Naturalness of the conversation with Geminoid F

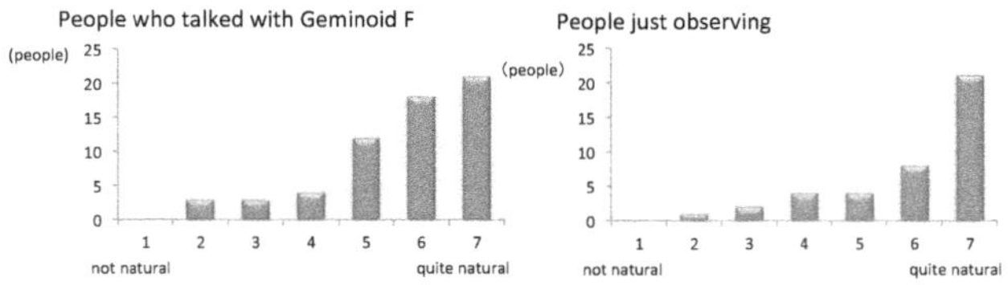

Figure 3: Naturalness of the behavior of Geminoid F

Geminoid F affected people during the interaction. In this study, Geminoid F made conversation with the visitors via 3 touch displays in a department store [Figure1]. Four questions were shown on the touch displays. After a visitor touched one of them, Geminoid F answered to the question making eye contact with the person. The questions were chosen randomly from 50 questions related to the robot and the department store. In the case of one to one conversation, creating autonomous system is difficult in our system because the deeper contents are required. On the other hand, conversation with multiple people enables every interacting user to independently initiate a one-turn conversation with Geminoid F. We expected that having such simple interactions may make users feel more engaged in the conversation. We evaluated human likeness and how people perceived Geminoid F using questionnaires and analyzing the video data recorded at the two touch displays (78 hours and 7 minutes). We also observed the interactions between people and the andoroid that took place during the experiment.

3. RESULTS

Out of 2159 people who talked with Geminoid F using the touch displays, we randomly interviewed 60 people (39 were female). Furthermore, we have interviewed 40 (24 were female) people who just observed the interaction. We analyzed the data of the 2 groups separately. We can say that people understood how to interact with Geminoid F without any instructions, as most visitors tried to talk to Geminoid F by using a touch display. We asked about the naturalness of the conversation with Geminoid F, its behavior, how much time people can spend with it and what kind of questions they would like to ask to it. In the case of the naturalness of the conversation, we found that 68.3% of people who talked with Geminoid F and 77.5% of people who just observed it evaluated the robot positively, i.e., rated it 5 or higher on a 7-point Likert scale [Figure 2]. Furthermore, the naturalness of the behavior was evaluated positively by 61.7% of people who talked with Geminoid F and 80.0% of people who just observed it [Figure3]. This means that people accept this situation and recognize Geminoid F as a humanlike entity even if the situation is different from usual human conversation. In the case of how long people can talk with Geminoid

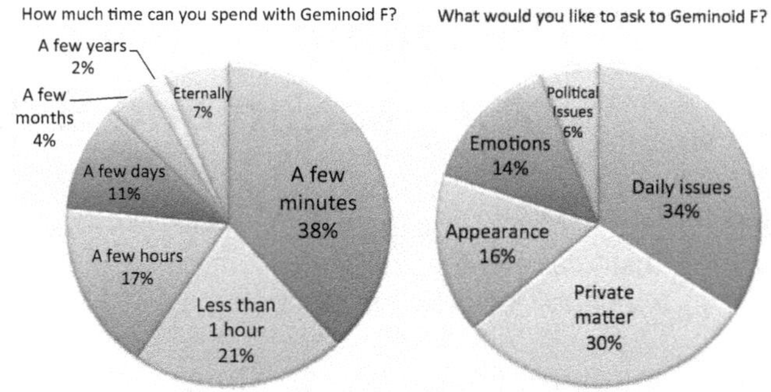

Figure 4: Left: How much time can you spend with Geminoid F? Right: What would you like to ask to Geminoid F?

F, 41% of people answered they can spend more than one hour, and some people answered they wanted to live with Geminoid F eternally [Figure 4 (Left)]. Furthermore, 64% of people were interested in its daily life or private matters [Figure 4 (Right)]. This means that Geminoid F aroused the visitors' interest even if they interacted in a limited situation, and it was perceived as a humanlike entity.

In addition, the sweater and skirt that Geminoid F was wearing were sold out, suggesting Geminoid F could be an effective advertisement media. The female visitors said that the costumes that Geminoid F put on were very beautiful, and they asked where they could buy them. Sales staff said that the sales were considerably higher than usual. Based on these facts, we assume that Geminoid F could produce the above-mentioned incidental effect because the visitors perceived Geminoid F as a humanlike and social entity and longed for it.

4. CONCLUSIONS

We have developed an autonomous conversation system which is able to interact with visitors in a limited situation. The results showed that the android can interact with people autonomously and is perceived as a humanlike and social entity by people by focusing on the situation where the android works. This study can be used as one of the design methods of an autonomous android robot that is recognized as a social entity by observers in the real world. In the future, by improving the contents of the conversation according to various other practical situations, androids might start being used in the real world.

5. REFERENCES

[1] M. Fujita, "Development of robot entertainment system AIBO(Special features human interface out of box), " *Information Processing Society of Japan*, vol.41, no.2, pp.146-150, 2000.

[2] M. Mori, .F. McDorman, and N. ageki, "The Uncanny Valley, " Robotisc & Automation Magazine, IEEE, vol.19, Issue 2, pp. 98-100, 2012.

[3] C. Becker-Asano, . Ogawa, S. Nishio and H. Ishiguro, "Exploring the uncanny valley with Geminoid HI-1 in a real-world application, " IADIS International Conference on Interfaces and Human Computer Interaction, pp. 121-128, Freiburg, Germany, 2010.

Designing a Service Robot for Public Space An "Action and Experiences" - Approach

Astrid Weiss, Markus Bader & Markus Vincze
Institute of Automation and Control
Vienna University of Technology
Vienna, Austria
lastname@acin.tuwien.ac.at.

Gert Hasenhütl & Stefan Moritsch
bl<m design working group
Diefenbachgasse 42/1/6
Vienna, Austria
moritsch@bkm-format.com

ABSTRACT
When we think of service robots for public spaces, we often consider human-like systems that socially interact with users in short-term and dynamically changing scenarios. Many design assumptions exist for this type of robot, but what about for a service robot that needs to interact with people in a very task/role-oriented manner? This paper presents a research-through-design approach, which explores the idea of a "luggage-carrying robot guide" for train stations which supports travellers. Contrary to the classical paper describing the requirements, design, implementation, and evaluation of the robot, this work presents an exploratory design study. An interdisciplinary team composed of two industrial designers, a roboticist, and a social scientist performed a study with users to establish a design space for the aforementioned service robot.

Categories and Subject Descriptors
J4 [**Computer Applications**]: Social and Behavioural Sciences – *Psychology. H5.2 [Information Systems]: Information Interfaces and Presentation – User Interfaces.*

General Terms
Design, Experimentation, Human Factors.

Keywords
Design study, service robot, public space.

1. INTRODUCTION
The development of robots, which are capable of safely navigating in densely populated environments, has made substantial progress in the last decade. Numerous researchers and designers have already thought about the design space for service robots [1], however in many cases social robots are considered to be the "right solution" and not "just" autonomous service artefacts. An example for the design of a social service for public context, is e.g. the sociable trash can [3]. In this paper we present an exploratory design study for developing a design space for a service robot, which to our conviction hardly needs sociable aspects: An autonomous artefact that should carry people's luggage and guide them the way, e.g. at a train station. We therefore followed the "Human Action and Experience" model proposed by Fernaeus [2]. Fernaeus points out four areas of use qualities: physical manipulation, perception and sensory experiences, contextually-oriented actions, and digitally mediated actions. In our work we used this model as a starting point to explore our first mock-up of the artefact in the wild with three potential end-users.

HRI'14, March 3-6, 2014, Bielefeld, Germany.
ACM 978-1-4503-2658-2/14/03.
http://dx.doi.org/10.1145/2559636.2560022

2. EXPLORATORY DESIGN STUDY
Following the model of Ferneaus, this study is based on the proposed guiding questions [2], such as: How do people physically handle or manipulate the device? What emotions and interpretations do the features of the artefact express? How do people act around the system?

2.1 The Service Robot Mock-up
Our mock-up comprised a differential drive mobile platform, an installation for luggage, different handles, a simulated card reader for authentication, a simulated touch screen with destination icons, and a smiling face on the other side of the touch screen. Participants were only told two main interaction paradigms: (1) put the card into the card slot to start the usage of the cart and (2) indicate the destination by pushing the according button on the touch screen (see Fig.1).

Figure 1. Mock-up

2.2 Environment and Tasks
A train station is considered as main application context for the robot, but we conducted the study due to safety reasons and on legal grounds in the entrance hall of the university department. In terms of environmental factors this surrounding offers everything needed, such as stairs, wheelchair ramps, doors and hallways of different sizes. Specific locations were labelled to give the user the impression of a real train station with places such as metro station or taxi stand. The study was set-up as Wizard-of-OZ study in which the robot was remote-controlled. Participants were told to try the baggage cart with a given suitcase in four common situations for a traveller arriving at an unknown train station. In all cases the robot was controlled to drive a predefined path. Firstly, the user was told to go to the metro station. Secondly he/ she was asked to use the cart to visit the rest rooms. In this case we obviously and intentionally miss-guided the user to an incorrect place next to the toilettes before we simulated a recovering behaviour. Thirdly, the user had to take a taxi. For this action the robot had to drive over a steep ramp. Finally, we provoked

an intuitive reaction by asking the user to stop the robot as it was passing by the participant during the final interview. Two of our participants were older adults 60 plus and one participant was a technical affine 30 plus year old with his daughter. We considered that older people and technical affine people and kids would have interest in the robotic artefact. Behaviour annotation of the video data and qualitative interviews were used as measures. All participants were successful in completing the pre-defined situations.

3. RESULTS

3.1 Physical Manipulation

All participants intuitively put the suitcase in the correct place; however, it was interesting to observe how they interpreted the other handles of the cart. One participant used it as an umbrella holder and another one for her coat and handbag, even though she did not consider it the ideal place for it (it was just a handle not a tray); she stated: *"If I have a baggage cart, I want it to carry everything for me not just my suitcase!"* Physical interaction with the cart could only be observed twice with our second participant who tried to push the cart via its handle over the ramp when it got stuck. Only the younger participant tried to stop the cart in the fourth task by stepping in front of it, the other two participants entered the card in the slot while the cart was driving. However, one of the older adults tried to increase the speed of the cart with hand gestures ("follow-me") and by increasing her walking pace and made a gesture that the cart should stop when the destination was reached.

3.2 Perception and Sensory Experiences

The usage of the mock-up touch screen was intuitive from the beginning for all participants. It is noteworthy to say that for the two older adults the wizarding was convincing. They explained us during the trial that they had to push the button on the touch screen really hard to get the system moving. However, the display of a face on the other side of the touch screen was unclear for two of the three participants and not even noticed by the third one. Interestingly the second situation where the cart drove by the toilettes, only the younger participant blindly followed the cart and did not even notice that he had already passed the goal. The second participant noticed the goal and took all his belongings (except the card) and let the cart continue its route. The third participant noticed that the cart had passed the designated area, but continued following: *"What should I do? I cannot loose my cart and the suitcase".*

3.3 Contextually Oriented Action

All participants commented that the scenarios were realistic for them, but that they would not use the cart for such small luggage as our demo suitcase. All of them experienced the cart as too slow and therefore two participants sometimes walked next to it or in front of it (what they claimed they would not do in "real life"). Other bystanders in the surrounding observed the cart, but nobody tried to interrupt the interaction or approached us and asked to try it. Only one of the older adults actively observed how bystanders reacted on him when he walked behind the cart and he commented after the trial: *"On a real train station people would shake their heads and I would not use such a thing just for the fun of it"*, however, the older female stated *"People would jealously stare at me because I have that cart and they have to carry their stuff!"* The robotic artefact was never experienced as a threat by our participants, but all of them preferred to approach a standing cart.

3.4 Digitally Meditated Actions

The two older adults mentioned that they had to adjust their way to the capabilities of the robotic artefact, i.e. using ramps instead of stairs, but they also stated that they accepted this side effect so that they did not have to push the cart themselves and orientate in an unknown environment. The younger participant mentioned that he was missing a visualisation where the cart was heading to. Overall, the mediated action via card slot and touch screen as main input modalities were intuitive and clear for all participants. However, in one case a participant pressed the wrong icon and there was no option to change that, but the participant found a suitable solution for herself, namely removing the card from the slot and starting the interaction again.

4. IMPLICATIONS FOR DESIGN

Our exploratory design study helped us to identify for major aspects for the further development of our mock-up. The robotic artefact needs to be bigger to hold larger suitcases and needs intended planes for putting handbags and hooks for coats, umbrellas etc. Handles can bear the risk that users might try to push the cart which could negatively impact navigation. The touch screen needs to be mounted higher or lower to reduce the risk of "blind following" and it should visualize the current action plan, instead of a face. The navigation speed needs to be increased and it should adapt to the speed of the user. Input aborts for the touch screen design need to be considered. To conclude, the "Human Action and Experience" model by Fernaeus [2] was beneficial for us to derive relevant design implications for a robotic baggage cart at a very early design stage. Moreover, it became obvious for us that for our application context, there is no need of any human-like cues in the appearance design, but only in the interaction design, e.g. using gestures for "follow-me" "stop" etc.

5. ACKNOWLEDGMENTS

The research leading to these results has received funding from the Austrian Science Foundation under grant agreement No. 835735 (TransitBuddy) and No. T 623-N23 (V4HRC).

6. REFERENCES

[1] Bartneck, C., and Forlizzi, J. A design-centred framework for social human-robot interaction. In Robot and Human Interactive Communication, 2004. ROMAN 2004. 13th IEEE International Workshop on (2004), IEEE, pp. 591–594.

[2] Fernaeus, Y. Human action and experience as basis for the design and study of robotic artefacts. In Robot and Human Interactive Communication, 2009. RO-MAN 2009. The 18th IEEE International Symposium on (2009), IEEE, pp. 522–527.

[3] Yamaji, Y., Miyake, T., Yoshiike, Y., De Silva, P. R., and Okada, M. Stb: human-dependent sociable trash box. In Human-Robot Interaction (HRI), 2010 5th ACM/IEEE International Conference on (2010), IEEE, pp. 197–19

Don't Bother Me: Users' Reactions to Different Robot Disturbing Behaviors

Astrid Weiss & Markus Vincze
Institute of Automation and Control
Vienna University of Technology
Vienna, Austria
lastname@acin.tuwien.ac.at

Paul Panek & Peter Mayer
Center for Applied Assisted Technologies
Vienna University of Technology
Vienna, Austria
lastname@fortec.tuwien.ac.at

ABSTRACT

When living together in a household with a socially assistive robot, it can happen that the robot disturbs its owner by offering a service. One might argue that a social robot should act according to the social norms people expect of each other, but still then disturbances of daily routines are a challenging endeavor to address. We conducted a preliminary user study in which we explored four different disturbing behaviors the socially assistive robot HOBBIT showed, while the user was focusing on a different primary task. We used the BEHAVE measurement set to evaluate the attitudinal and behavioral responses of the users, which disturbance distracted the user the most from his/her primary task and how the disturbance affected the overall attitudinal response towards the robot. Interestingly, our results showed that the disturbing behavior did not heavily negatively impact the assessment of the robot and that not all types of disturbance did distract the users with the same intensity.

Categories and Subject Descriptors

J4 [**Computer Applications**]: Social and Behavioral Sciences – *Psychology. H5.2 [Information Systems]: Information Interfaces and Presentation – User Interfaces.*

General Terms

Design, Experimentation, Human Factors.

Keywords

Socially Assistive Robot, distraction, user study.

1. INTRODUCTION & RELATED WORK

Socially assistive robots that live together with a user at home have the utmost goal to support the user in daily activities of life, such as reminding him/her to take medicine or to fetch and carry objects [1]. However, we have to consider occasions when the robot pro-actively approaches the user, while he/she is currently focused on something else. In human-human interaction disturbances follow specific social norms to be acceptable [2]. In this paper we present a preliminary user study, conducted with ten participants and the care robot HOBBIT [3], which had the aim to explore people's attitudinal and behavioral responses to four different disturbance behaviors. Our main research objective was to explore how people react, when the HOBBIT robot (a socially assistive care robot intended to support older adults to maintain independent living at home, for details see [3], [6]) is approaching or pro-actively interacting with a user, while people are actually focused on something else.

HRI'14, March 3-6, 2014, Bielefeld, Germany.
ACM 978-1-4503-2658-2/14/03.
http://dx.doi.org/10.1145/2559636.2563689

2. USER STUDY

Our user study was setup as a small observational study, in which participants were asked to focus on a specific primary task, to explore their reaction when being interrupted by the robot. This primary task followed the study design of Sardar and colleagues [5], where participants were asked to search on a "Where's Wally - The Gobbling Glutton's-poster" for the main characters. Participants were told that they have ten minutes in total to find all the characters in the picture and that this is their main task that they should solve in this study. To avoid the participants completing the task early, two of the five characters were photoshopped out of the poster and could not be found. Additionally, participants were told that it might happen during the ten minutes that they get help offered and that they can decide by themselves if they want to accept this help or not.

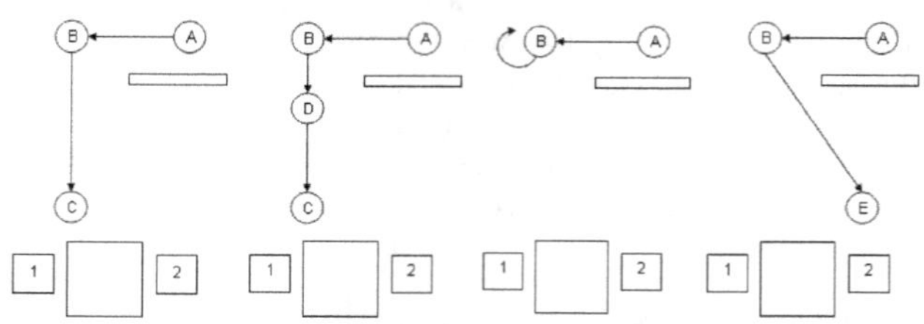

Figure 1. The 4 approach directions: (1) participant, (2) facilitator, (A) robot starting position, (B) and (D) robot stopping positions, (C) and (E) robot ending positions

After the first two minutes the HOBBIT robot approached the participant and disturbed him/her during and then again three times, always after two minutes, with four different behaviors. HOBBIT was always behind a room divider before it approached the participant and the participant was seated at a table with the study facilitator sitting opposite to him/her; see Figure 1 and 2. Having the facilitator present during the whole study was necessary to convincingly demonstrate disturbance behavior (4). The robot was remote-controlled from a different room and the debriefing revealed that all participants considered the robot as being autonomous. The four different disturbance behaviors were:

(1) HOBBIT approached the user and directly told him/her: "Oh this is a difficult task, 2 out of 10 minutes are already over".

(2) HOBBIT approached the user, cleared its throat and said: "Can I maybe somehow help you finding Wally?"; if the user answered "no" HOBBIT said "ok" and disappeared again; if the user said "yes", HOBBIT said: "Please move the picture towards me, so I can see it", then HOBBIT moved the head to watch the poster and then said the user: "Sorry unfortunately, I also cannot find Wally" and left.

(3) HOBBIT appeared, rotated around its own axis and made a whistling sound twice and said "I am bored" and left again.

(4) The facilitator asked the participant to switch to the other side of the table. Then HOBBIT appeared at the right side of the table and said to the participant: "Oh, you switched seat, should I help you again?" Then the same procedure as in (2) started.

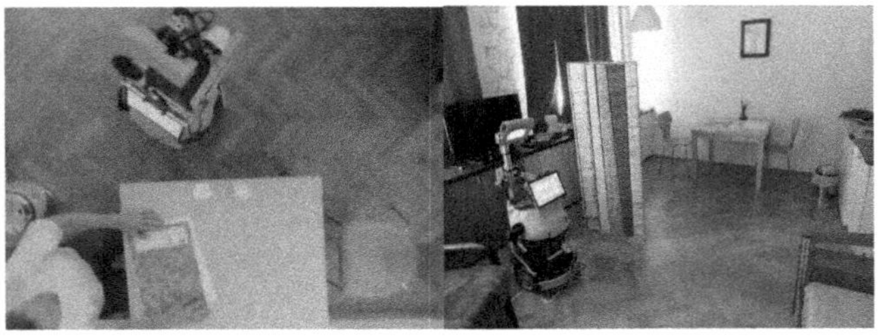

Figure 2. HOBBIT approaching the participant. HOBBIT behind the room divider

3. METHOD & MEASURES

We used the BEHAVE measurement set for attitudinal and behavioral measures. This measurement set consists of a behavior coding scheme and standardized questionnaires to assess the social normativity on an attitudinal level. The behavior coding scheme consists of nine categories. (1) looks at robot, (2) looks pleasant, (3) looks uneasy, (4) looks surprised, (5) leaned towards the robot, (6) leaned away from the robot, (7) looks anxious, looks restless, which all have to be rated on a 5-point Likert scale from 1=not very much to 5=very much. The coding was performed by a single researcher who was aware of the study design. For the attitudinal measures we gave participants the BEHAVE questionnaires (translated from English to German), after the 10 minutes were over. In total 10 participants took part in our study (students and employees of the informatics department; 7 male/ 3 female; approximated age range: 18 to 50 years). After filling in the questionnaire a short final interview with open-ended questions and a debriefing was done (explaining that the main task was not solvable and that the actual goal was to measure their reactions on the robot). Participants were recruited on-the-fly at the department and did not receive any compensation.

4. RESULTS

As expected the robot distracted participants from their primary task. In behavior (2) nine people accepted the help of the robot and in behavior (4) eight, even though the robot failed to help participants in the first place. One participant stated that he did not want further help because the robot failed beforehand, the other two mentioned they wanted to solve the primary task and not lose too much time due to the robot. A Kruskal-Wallis test revealed, that the behavior category "distracted" $H(3)=12.11;\ p<0.05$ "leaned towards the robot" $H(3)=16.28;\ p<0.05$ and "surprise" $H(3)=9.36;\ p<0.05$ were significantly affected by the different disturbing behaviors of HOBBIT. Man-Whitney U-Tests were used to follow-up on this finding and it appeared that the scenarios in which the robot offered help were - as expected - more distracting than the "information scenario" (*scenario 2:* $z = -11.50;\ p < 0.05$; *scenario4:* $-11.45;\ p < 0.05$).

However, the second (and last) "help-offering" was also more distracting than the "whistling" ($z = 12.60;\ p < 0.05$). This could be due to the fact that participants really wanted to solve the primary task and therefore focused more on the robot and its potential help in the end of the study. Moreover, this is also an indicator that participants still trusted the robot to help them, even though it failed in the first attempt. For the "leaned towards the robot" category the subsequent Man-Whitney U-Tests revealed that in the 4th scenario, people had the least fear of contact with the robot and were willing to lean close to it to show it the picture. This finding is also supported by the findings for the category "surprise" which showed a significant difference between scenario (1) and all the other scenarios, indicating that participants only seemed surprised by the robot in the beginning, but that this effect vanished immediately during a period of only 10 minutes. These positive effects are also represented in the attitudinal data. All the scales were rated around the midpoint or even above, whereby "trust" ($mean=4.96;\ SD=0.51$) and "attractiveness" ($mean=4.66;\ SD=0.98$) were rated best, but "human-likeness" ($mean=3.24;\ SD=1.07$) and "likability" ($mean=3.4;\ SD=1.28$) were rated lower. These findings were also reflected in the final interviews; one participant for instance stated "you really tried hard to make the robot human-like with behaviors such as whistling and being bored, but I know that it is no human so I had to rate it low".

5. CONCLUSION & OUTLOOK

Our results indicate that necessary distracting behaviors (e.g. the robot has to remind the user of something) can be designed in a socially normative manner and that a robot not necessarily bothers the user, but only distracts him/her from a primary task. We will continue our research on this topic with field trials in which the HOBBIT robot will live together with older adults for two to three weeks to investigate long-term effects of our behavior strategies.

6. ACKNOWLEDGMENTS

The research leading to these results has received funding by the European Commission in project HOBBIT (FP7-288146) and from the Austrian Science Foundation (FWF) under grant agreement No. T 623-N23 (V4HRC).

7. REFERENCES

[1] Feil-Seifer, D. and Mataric, M. J. Defining socially assistive robotics. In Proc. of ICORR 2005. IEEE, 465–468.

[2] Parsons, T. and Shils, E. A. and Smelser, N. J. Toward a general theory of action: Theoretical foundations for the social sciences. Transaction Publishers, 2001.

[3] Fischinger, D., Einramhof, P., Wohlkinger, W, Papoutsakis, K., Mayer,P. Panek, P, Koertner, T, Hofmann, S, Argyros, A., Vincze, M., Weiss, A. and Gisinger,C. Hobbit - The Mutual Care Robot. In Workshop-Proc. of ASROB 2013.

[4] Joosse, M, Sardar, A and Evers, V. Behave: A set of measures to assess users' attitudinal and non-verbal behavioral responses to a robot's social behaviors. In Proc. of ICSR 2011, Springer, 84–94.

[5] Sardar, A, Joosse, M., Weiss, A., and Evers, V. Don't stand so close to me: Users' attitudinal and behavioral responses to personal space invasion by robots. In Proc of HRI 2012, IEEE, 229–230.

[6] Mayer, P. and Panek, P. A Social Assistive Robot in an Intelligent Environment. In Proc. Of Biomedizinische Technik BMT2013, 219-220.

Involuntary Expression of Embodied Robot Adopting Goose Bumps

Tomoko Yonezawa
Kansai University
Osaka 569-1095, Japan
yone@kansai-u.ac.jp

Xiaoshun Meng
Kansai University
Osaka 569-1095, Japan
k568121@kansai-u.ac.jp

Naoto Yoshida
Kansai University
Osaka 569-1095, Japan
k463362@kansai-u.ac.jp

Yukari Nakatani
Kansai University
Osaka 569-1095, Japan
k463362@kansai-u.ac.jp

ABSTRACT

In this paper, we propose an involuntary expression of embodied robots by adopting goose bumps. The goose bumps are caused by not only external stimuli such as cold temperature but also the internal state of the robot such as fear. For more natural anthropomorphism, the combination of involuntary and voluntary expressions should enable realistic animacy and life-like agency. The bumps on the robot's skin are generated by changing lengths of thin rods from each hole. The lengths are controlled by a servo motor which pulls nylon strings connected to the base of thin rods.

Categories and Subject Descriptors

H.5 [Information Interfaces and Presentation]: Miscellaneous

General Terms

Design

Keywords

Goose bumps, Involuntary Expression

1. INTRODUCTION

Conversational interactions with various modalities have been discussed for artificial anthropomorphic presence such as robots and agents [1, etc.]. Not only verbal communication, the anthropomorphic presences can make non-verbal expressions using their bodies. Human-human communications with various non-verbal cues include involuntary and under-conscious expressions such as color of the face changed by physiological indisposition. However, there have not been many discussions on involuntary, physiological, or reflexive expressions for the robots.

Robots have physical bodies and provide us tangible communications. We have proposed a wearable robot that makes physical contact from the robot [2]. From the viewpoint of social touch between skins of human and robot, we should discuss not only conscious expressions of active touches but also under-conscious expressions.

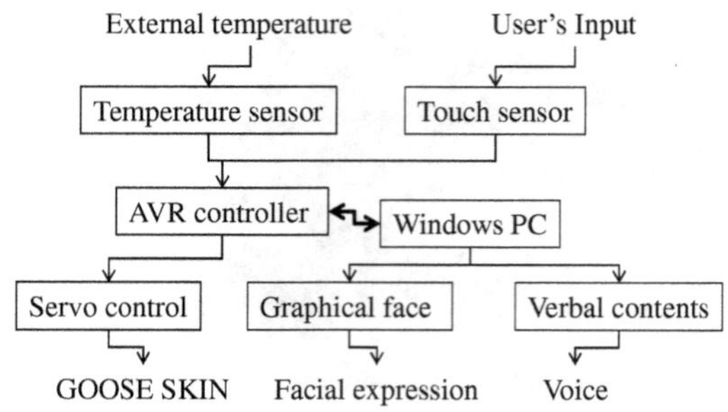

Figure 1: Flow of the simple testbed on the robot

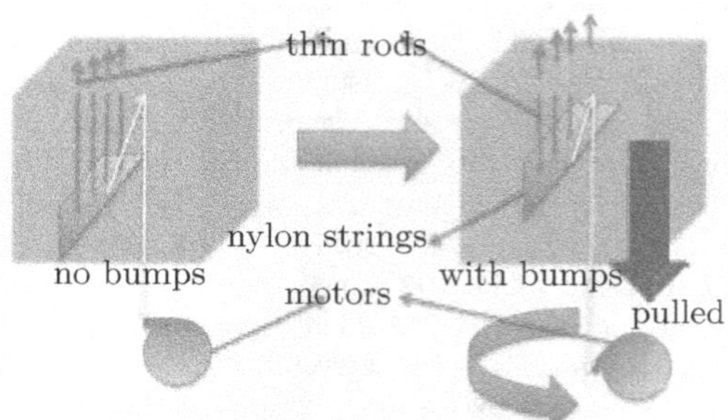

Figure 2: Implementation of goose bumps

In this paper, we introduce a method of involuntary goose bumps of an embodied robot. Although there have been many researches on artificial haptic-sensory skin [4] and discussions of materials for facial expression [3], we can find few trials related to expressions on surface of robots. The goose bumps are caused both of external stimuli such as cold temperature and internal state such as fear. The testbed of the goose-bump skin was implemented on the robot's arm. The effectiveness of involuntary goose-bump was confirmed by subjective experiments combining with 1) facial and 2) verbal expressions.

2. SYSTEM IMPLEMENTATIONS

2.1 Overview of the system

Figure 1 shows a system flow to show goose bumps by cold temperature less than 20°C or too much tender touch from the user. Basically, cold, fear, or unpleasant feelings are continuous state. If the system detects the beginning of these state, the goose bumps are appeared.

HRI'14, March 3–6, 2014, Bielefeld, Germany.
ACM 978-1-4503-2658-2/14/03.
http://dx.doi.org/10.1145/2559636.2563703 .

Figure 3: Total view

Figure 4: Goose-bump part

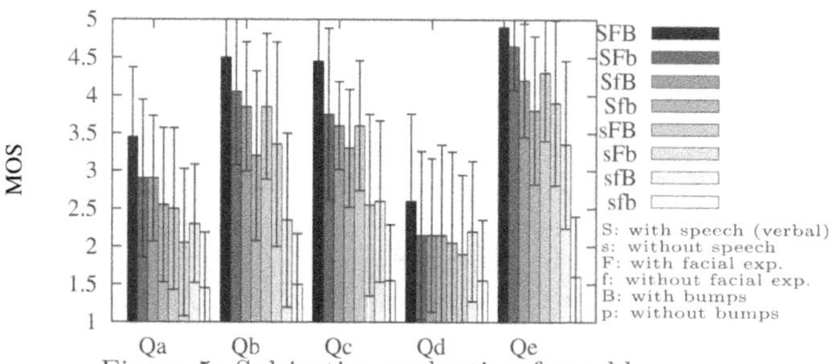

Figure 5: Subjective evaluation for cold

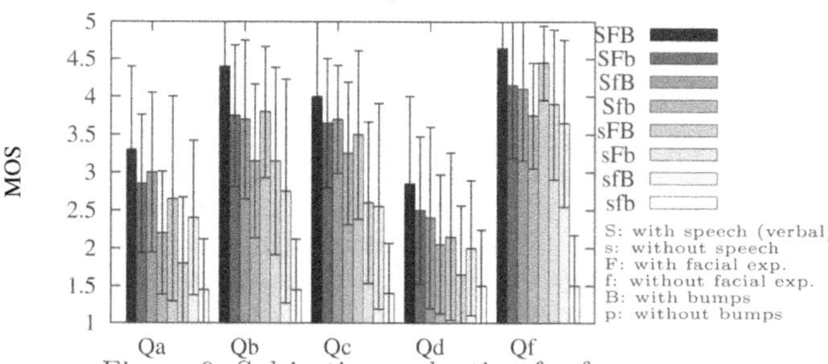

Figure 6: Subjective evaluation for fear

2.2 Goose-skin Drive Unit

Figure 2 shows the drive unit of the goose bumps. The bumps on the robot's skin are generated by changing lengths of thin rods from each hole. The lengths of the appeared rods are controlled by a servo motor which pulls nylon strings connected to the base of thin rods. Servo motor pulls multiple strings and the thin rods connected to each string are appeared on the skin of the robot. A line of four bumps are controlled by a servo motor. Four sets of the bumps and motors are prepared in the testbed system. The user can feel the bumps on the robot by physical contact. The goose bumps are covered by a sheet of silicon rubber.

3. EVALUATION

We focused on both physiologic and emotional aspects of the goose bumps as involuntary expressions. The experiments of the cold expression and fear expression were evaluated by twenty participants (seven females and thirteen males) aged from 19 to 22.

Figure 3 and 4 show the view of the testbed system for the experiment. The facial expression is shown in the monitor at the robot's head. The robot's arms are reached out forward. The goose-bump drive unit is set on the right arm of the robot. The participants experienced the goose bumps appeared by each context, cold and fear. In the cold experiment, a fan began blowing and the robot behaved corresponding to the conditions, with or without a) goose bumps, b) facial expression, and c) verbal expression. In the fear

Table 1: Three-factor ANOVA for cold

	Facial exp.		Speech		Goose skin		Significant
	F	p	F	p	F	p	interaction
Qa	42.7	< .01	10.5	< .01	13.0	< .01	–
Qb	90.5	< .01	94.5	< .01	19.5	< .01	AB
Qc	65.7	< .01	31.3	< .01	42.6	< .01	AC
Qd	10.7	< .01	2.34	0.14	15.7	< .01	–
Qe	52.3	< .01	68.8	< .01	22.7	< .01	all

Table 2: Three-factor ANOVA for fear

	Facial exp.		Speech		Goose skin		Significant
	F	p	F	p	F	p	interaction
Qa	21.4	< .01	12.2	< .01	14.2	< .01	–
Qb	44.5	< .01	75.1	< .01	58.4	< .01	AB
Qc	72.2	< .01	58.7	< .01	21.4	< .01	AB
Qd	16.4	< .01	5.63	=.03	13.7	< .01	–
Qf	58.4	< .01	72.3	< .01	40.3	< .01	all

experiment, the experimenter told scary story to the robot and the robot behaved as same as the cold experiment. After each stimulus, the participants evaluated the following statements in five-point rating scale.

Qa: You felt favorable feeling to the robot.
Qb: Robot conveyed its feelings.
Qc: Robot expressed humanity.
Qd: You got frendly with the robot.
Qe: Robot seemed cold. (only for cold)
Qf: Robot seemed fear. (only for fear)

The results of means opinion scores (MOS) and three-factor ANOVA for repeated measurements are shown in Figure 5, 6 and Table 1, 2. Both results for cold and fear showed significant results for each factor. From the results, it is confirmed that not only verbal or facial expressions but also the involuntary goose skin effectively works on the total expressions.

4. CONCLUSIONS

In this paper, we introduced a goose-bump expression method on a skin of embodied robot as an involuntary reaction not only to external stimuli but also to internal state of the robot. As external stimuli, we evaluated "cold" and "fear" exressions of the robot combining with facial and verbal modalities. The results of the experiments showed effectiveness for all factors. Thus, the involuntary expressions may have a strong effects on total impression as same as other known modalities.

5. ACKNOWLEDGMENTS

This research was supported in part by KAKENHI 24300047 and KAKENHI 25700021.

6. REFERENCES

[1] D. Perzanowski, A.C. Schultz, W. Adams, E. Marsh, M. Bugajska, Building a multimodal human-robot interface, Intelligent Systems, IEEE vol.16, no.1, pp.16–21, 2001.

[2] T.Yonezawa and H. Yamazoe, Wearable partner agent with anthropomorphic physical contact with awareness of clothing and posture, proc. of ISWC2013, pp.77–80, 2013.

[3] Y. Tadesse, D. Moore, N. Thayer, S. Priya, Silicone based artificial skin for humanoid facial expressions, Proc. SPIE 2009, vol.7287, 728709, 2009.

[4] S. Saga, S. Kuroki, N. Kawakami, S. Tachi, Fibratus tactile sensor using reflection on an optical lever, SIGGRAPH '07 emerging technologies Article No. 3, 2007.

Social Exploration: Mars Rovers

Karolina Zawieska
Industrial Research Institute for Automation and Measurements PIAP & SMARTlab at University College Dublin
Al. Jerozolimskie 202
02-489 Warsaw, Poland
kzawieska@piap.pl

Brian R. Duffy
SMARTlab at University College Dublin
Belfield, Dublin 4
Dublin, Ireland
b.duffy@ucd.ie

ABSTRACT
Mars rovers are an extension of the human body, which brings the human presence to another planet. In addition to human-centric senses such as vision and audio, they also extend human cognition into unknown spaces. This paper argues that Mars rovers should embrace not only the embodied but also the social aspect of a human being and judiciously embrace anthropomorphism in rover design in order to augment our exploration of distant locations.

Categories and Subject Descriptors
A. m [**General Literature**]: Miscellaneous

General Terms
Human Factors, Theory

Keywords
Mars rovers, anthropomorphism, embodied social cognition

1. INTRODUCTION
To explore means "to look at (something) in a careful way to learn more about it : to study or analyze (something)" [1]. Thus, exploration leads to cognition seen as an "act or process of knowing" [1]. It has been shown that human cognition is embodied and situated, i.e. embedded in brain-body-world systems. Among many different approaches to learning and knowing, this paper emphasizes the social aspect of human cognition seen as "the 'general case' of human cognitive activity" where "the foundation of all cognitive processes derives from episodes involving social objects" [2]. Social cognition can be also defined as "the sum of those processes that allow individuals of the same species (conspecifics) to interact with one another" [5]. Although different degrees of sociality can be found in various species of animals, sociality can be seen as an intrinsic human characteristic ("human" means "social"). From this perspective, the human tendency to anthropomorphise is "a default schema" inherent to social cognition [2] that cannot be removed from people's perceptions.

HRI'14, March 3–6, 2014, Bielefeld, Germany.
ACM 978-1-4503-2658-2/14/03.
http://dx.doi.org/10.1145/2559636.2559795

By designing machines that are our representatives in hostile environments, Mars rovers are designed to extend the human body and cognition into outer space. The question is, should and if so, to what extent Mars rover design be anthropomorphic in form and function in order to embrace the social aspect of human cognition when exploring another planet.

2. ROBOTIC EXPLORATION
Robotic exploration includes different fields of application, e.g. planetary exploration, rescue, reconnaissance, mowing, and cleaning. In general, robotic exploration is seen as an embodied activity in a relatively unknown environment. Depending on the purposes of a mission, Mars rovers collect different type of information, mostly geology-related data (future missions aim to extend the range of rover tasks, while the main goal remains unchanged: to seek signs of past or present life). It is important to emphasize, however, that it is always people who explore Mars using robots and not robots themselves [3] (so far, the degree of autonomy in robots, including Mars rovers, has been limited). Thus, despite the illusion they give, Mars rovers are an extension of the human rather than autonomous agents.

Figure 1. The Cornell Mars Rover and its team members during the University Rover Challenge 2013, Utah, USA.

3. EXTENSION OF THE HUMAN
Space exploration either by humans directly or via robotic platforms, is never merely physical but also cognitive. The latest NASA Mars rover is a good example: Its name "Curiosity" represents "the desire to learn or know more about something or someone" [1]. In general, robotic platforms are seen as an extension of the human body and senses. In particular,

telepresence techniques convey multimodal sensor feedback to the human sense of sight, hearing and touch in order to allow the operator to "feel" the environment as if he was present at the robot's operation field. In addition to actual feedback, the human operators sometimes project more human characteristics onto rovers, usually through associating robotic components and activities to human body parts and activities (for example, the rovers have "eyes" or they "sleep" [6]).

Exercising explicit control over the robots may lead to an extension that goes beyond the human body, since the extension of the human self into objects that one controls, creates or personalizes has been observed. From numerous sociological and philosophical perspectives, in particular symbolic interactionism, the human body is seen as a *social* object to which people ascribe meanings and through which they express and perceive themselves and others: "people do not merely 'have' a body – people actively *do* a body" [7]. Thus, the next logical level is to extend via Mars rover not only the human physical presence but also a variety of traits that underlie his body, which includes sociality. Human sociality is highly complex and culturally dependent, however, the key element that could be implemented in Mars rover design is communication (linguistic and otherwise): Despite an illusion of autonomy given by rovers, there is always a human in-the-loop and communication between the Mars rover and other humans is inevitable.

Figure 2. The Scorpio 3 Rover and its team member during the University Rover Challenge 2013, Utah, USA.

4. ROBOT SOCIAL EMBODIMENT

On one hand, robotic and human exploration is traditionally seen as two different strategies to explore other planets; on the other hand, close human-robot collaboration constitutes one of the main goals for future space missions and is included in current space exploration programmes. The authors of this paper argue that the link between robots and its designers should not be overlooked and that rover exploration is always performed by humans. Also, physical exploration cannot be separate from the cognitive and social traits and processes: "the body is always more than a tangible, physical, corporeal object (...) - the body is also an enormous vessel of meaning of utmost significance to both personhood and society" [7]. Embodiment is a key feature of robots; hence, in order to successfully extend the human and facilitate human exploration via machines, Mars rover designers should carefully address the social aspects of embodiment, and, above all, communication. One way to achieve such a goal is to deliberately anthropomorphize robot's appearance and function. Anthropomorphic principles are already present in several robots designed to work at the International Space Station (ISS) and human environments in space, e.g. Robonaut, Justin or SAR-401. The question is, to what extent anthropomorphism may be useful in rovers that work in unknown, hostile environments. This is particularly relevant in the context of future human and human-robot space missions where prolonged isolation may significantly alter the human tendency to anthropomorphise inanimate objects [4]. Thus, a human need for sociality may be challenged and the way people (socially) engage with machines may need to be redefined.

5. CONCLUSIONS

Human-made tools and technological creations often reflect the anthropocentric perspective that people inevitably apply to all areas of their lives. Robots in particular constitute extensions of the human being. As technology advances, robotic platforms gradually allow the extension of not only the human body but also humanlike senses and cognitive skills. In order to facilitate exploration of other planets from a human-centric perspective, space rovers should evolve their design into becoming a stronger extension of the human seen as embodied but above all a social entity, where sociality is an intrinsic part of human cognition. The potential and need for anthropomorphising Mars rovers has been revealed in previous studies; the degree and means to judiciously extend human sociality in Mars rovers remains an open question.

6. REFERENCES

[1] Retreived from *Merriam-Webster,* January 2014, http://www.merriam-webster.com/dictionary.

[2] Caporael, L.R., *Anthropomorphism and mechanomorphism: Two faces of the human machine,* Computers in Human Behavior 1986. 2(3): p. 215-234

[3] Clancey, W.J. *Clear Speaking about Machines: People Are Exploring Mars, not Robots*. Proceedings of *AAAI-2006 Workshop: The Human Implications of Human-Robotic Interaction.* Boston, 2006.

[4] Epley, N., S. Akalis, A. Waytz and J.T. Cacioppo, *Creating Social Connection Through Inferential Reproduction. Loneliness and Perceived Agency in Gadgets, Gods, and Greyhounds.* Psychological Science 2008. 19: p. 114-120.

[5] Frith, C.D. and U. Frith, *Social Cognition in Humans.* Current Biology, 2007. 17(16): p. R724-R732.

[6] Vertesi, J., *"Seeing like a rover": embodied experience on the Mars Exploration Rover mission*, Proceedings of CHI '08 Extended Abstracts on Human Factors in Computing Systems 2008, ACM: Florence, Italy. p. 2523-2532.

[7] Waskul, D.D. and P. Vannini, *Body/embodiment: Symbolic Interaction and the Sociology of the Body* 2006: Ashgate.

Spontaneous Spoken Dialogues with the Furhat Human-like Robot Head

Samer Al Moubayed, Jonas Beskow, Gabriel Skantze
KTH Royal Institute of Technology
Department of Speech, Music and Hearing
Lindstedtsv. 24, 10044 Stockholm, Sweden
{sameram, beskow, skantze}@kth.se

ABSTRACT

Furhat [1] is a robot head that deploys a back-projected animated face that is realistic and human-like in anatomy. Furhat relies on a state-of-the-art facial animation architecture allowing accurate synchronized lip movements with speech, and the control and generation of non-verbal gestures, eye movements and facial expressions.

Furhat is built to study, implement and validate patterns and models of human-human and human-machine situated and multi-party multimodal communication, a study that demands the co-presence of the talking head in the interaction environment, something that cannot be achieved using virtual avatars displayed on flat screens [2,3]. In Furhat, the animated face is back-projected on a translucent mask that is a printout of the animated model. The mask is then rigged on a 2DOF neck to allow for the control of head movements. Figure 1 shows a snapshot of Furhat in interaction.

We will show in this demonstrator an advanced multimodal and multiparty spoken conversational system using Furhat, a robot head based on projected facial animation. Furhat is an anthropomorphic robot head that utilizes facial animation for physical robot heads using back-projection. In the system, multimodality is enabled using speech and rich visual input signals such as multi-person real-time face tracking and microphone tracking. The demonstrator will showcase a system that is able to carry out social dialogue with multiple interlocutors simultaneously with rich output signals such as eye and head coordination, lips synchronized speech synthesis, and non-verbal facial gestures used to regulate fluent and expressive multiparty conversations. The dialogue design is performed using the IrisTK [4] dialogue authoring toolkit developed at KTH. The system will also be able to perform a moderator in a quiz-game showing different strategies for regulating spoken situated interactions.

Categories and Subject Descriptors

H.5.2 [**Information Interfaces and Presentation**]: User Interfaces – Natural Language; D.2.2 [**Software Engineering**] Design Tools and Techniques – State diagrams; D.2.11 [**Software Engineering**] Software Architectures – Languages

Keywords

Human-Robot Interaction, Multiparty interaction, Gaze, Gesture, Speech, Spoken dialog, Facial animation, Robot head, Furhat.

HRI'14, March 3–6, 2014, Bielefeld, Germany.
ACM 978-1-4503-2658-2/14/03.
http://dx.doi.org/10.1145/2559636.2559781

Figure 1. Snapshots of Furhat[1] in close-up and two users in interaction[2]

ACKNOWLEDGMENTS

This work has been partly funded by the EU project IURO (Interactive Urban Robot) No. 248314, and the SAVIR project (Situated Audio-Visual Interaction with Robots) funded by the Swedish Government (strategic research areas), and the KTH ICT Strategic Research Areas Embodied Multimodal Communication.

REFERENCES

[1] Al Moubayed, S., Beskow, J., Skantze, G., & Granström, B. 2012. Furhat: A Back-projected Human-like Robot Head for Multiparty Human-Machine Interaction. In Esposito et al. (Eds.), Cognitive Behavioural Systems. Lecture Notes in Computer Science. Springer.

[2] Al Moubayed, S., Edlund, J., & Beskow, J. 2012. *Taming Mona Lisa: communicating gaze faithfully in 2D and 3D facial projections*. ACM Transactions on Interactive Intelligent Systems, 1(2), 25.

[3] Al Moubayed, S., Skantze, G., & Beskow, J. (2013). The *Furhat Back-Projected Humanoid Head - Lip reading, Gaze and Multiparty Interaction.* International Journal of Humanoid Robotics, 10(1).

[4] Skantze, G. and Al Moubayed, S. 2012. IrisTK: a statechart-based toolkit for multi-party face-to-face interaction. *Proc. of the 14th ACM International Conference on Multimodal Interaction ICMI*. Santa Monica, CA, USA.

---

[1] For more info on Furhat, see http://www.speech.kth.se/furhat

[2] For a video of the demonstration, please check: www.youtube.com/watch?v=v84e6HMFbyc

A New Creation Environment for Learning through Interaction with Robots

Hye-Kyung Cho[*], Jae-Sung Ryu[*], Hyo-Yong Kim[*], Dong-Hoon Lee[*], Yong-Gyu Jin[*], Jung-Yun Sung[*], Hyun-Sung Jung[*], Soo-Hee Han[**], Sang-Hoon Ji[***]

* Hansung University, 116 Hansungdae-16-ro, Sungbuk-gu, Seoul 136-792, Korea.

** Konkuk University, 120 Neungdong-ro, Gwangjin-gu, Seoul 143-701, Korea.

*** KITECH, 1271-18 Sa-1-dong, Sangnok-gu, Ansan-city, Kyunggi-do 426-171, Korea.

ABSTRACT

This demonstration introduces SiCi (Smart ideas for Creative interplay) that brings a single-body robot to life by delivering a variety of contents and then fosters children's creativity and innovation in education.

Keywords

Learning through interaction, robotics-enhanced learning, robot contents, creativity, innovation

1. INTRODUCTION

For the past years, there have been ongoing studies to assess the effects of robotics education at school on children. Educators have already found in classroom lectures that teaching with robots provides new and exciting ways to interest and motivate their students. Robots are now finding their way into the classroom to help teach science, math [1-3], mechanics, teamwork and even management skills, which is in accord with the philosophy of STEAM (Science & Technology interpreted through Engineering & the Arts, all based in Mathematical elements) that was developed in 2006 by Georgette Yakman and has been a very popular concept for multidisciplinary-oriented education [4]. As in STEAM-style education, robots have been proven to provide an avenue for effectively teaching the inter-relationships of how subjects relate in real-life and learning in a creative and innovative way.

2. SiCi

As in LEGO [3], crickets [5], and scratch [2], robotics education has been developed to cater to children and then provide a nice learning environment. Many children are, however, still feeling intimidated in realizing their imagination and making their own works. They often come up with ideas on merging two existing things into a new form. They may bring together different types of media and applications. For those purposes, they need high-level technologies. In the past, each entertainment medium could be played on a specific device. Video was displayed on a television through some type of video player, music came through a tape deck or Compact Disc (CD) player, and video games were played through a specific console of some sort. It would be necessary to provide an authoring tool that enables children to easily handle multimedia, games, storytelling, and other devices simultaneously.

HRI'14, March 3–6 2014, Bielefeld, Germany
ACM 978-1-4503-2658-2/14/03.
http://dx.doi.org/10.1145/2559636.2559782

In order to enable even students of lower grades to implement creative and innovative ideas freely on robots without engineering skills, SiCi provides a contents authoring engine that has the following features and functions.

- authoring tools with high extensibility
- multi-agent systems
- multiple mobile platform distribution
- easy programming and interfaces for high-level contents
- event driven programming
- multi-modal interaction supported by 3-D technologies

This demonstration shows how robots with features and functions above could act as a nice platform for leveraging on the opportunities brought by information technology (IT) convergence and then fostering children's creativity and innovation in education [6].

3. CONCLUSION

In this demonstration, we have introduced a software platform, called SiCi, where robots and multimedia can be programmed together to make a new type of convergent contents for children.

4. ACKNOWLEDGMENTS

This work was supported by the Industrial Strategic Technology Development Program funded by the Ministry of Trade, Industry, and Energy (MOTIE, Korea).

5. REFERENCES

[1] Kim, J.-H., Jung, J.-H., Kim, J.-S., Jin, Y.-G., Sung, J.-Y., Oh, S.-M., Ryu, J.-S., Kim, H.-Y., Han, S.-H., Cho, H.-K. 2013. New Clay for Digital Natives's HRI: Create Your Own Interactions with SiCi. In *Proceedings of 9-th ACM/IEEE International Conference on Human-Robot Interaction* (Tokyo,Japan, March 03 - 06, 2013). HRI '13. ACM, New York, NY, 455. DOI= http://dx.doi.org/10.1109/HRI.2013.6483619

[2] Scratch, URL : http://scratch.mit.edu.

[3] Mindstorms, URL : http://mindstorms.lego.com.

[4] STEAM, URL : http://www.steamedu.com.

[5] Cricket : http://www.picocricket.com.

[6] SiCi , URL : http://sici.cc

Easy Authoring of Variable Gestural Expressions for a Humanoid Robot

Tamara Flemisch, André Viergutz, Raimund Dachselt
Interactive Media Lab
Technische Universität Dresden
01062 Dresden, Germany
tamara.f emisch@mailbox.tu-dresden.de, (andre.viergutz|raimund.dachselt)@tu-dresden.de

ABSTRACT

This demonstration on the Nao robot uses the selection of behavior based on a feedback type and an expressivity value to generate and execute appropriate feedback. It aims to ease the authoring process by using variable gestures.

Categories and Subject Descriptors

I.2.9 [**Artificial Intelligence**]: Robotics—*Operator Interfaces*

Keywords

Human-Robot Interaction; Gesture; Expressivity

1. VARIABLE GESTURAL EXPRESSIONS

The selection of gestures and the expressivity of a robot's behaviour are critical factors for suitable and understandable feedback. To provide more variability, the parametrization of gestures is explored by Hartmann et al. [1] who specify parameters such as *Spatial Extent* or *Repetition* which increase the expressivity of a gesture. However, in everyday communication people usually want to increase the expressiveness of a certain expression, intention or emotion, for instance, happiness, sadness or suprise. Therefore, we developed a set of variable gestures which can be adjusted by a feedback type and an expressivity value.

In view of communication and inspired by Hartmann et al. [1], we divided the gestures into the feedback types *Positive/Acceptance*, *Negative/Denial*, *Incomprehension*, *Waiting/Neutral*, *Introduction/Greeting* and *Ending/Goodbye* which form classes with own gesture sets. To support variability and potential for increase of a certain feedback category, the global parameter *expressivity* is subsequently mapped to the underlying parameters for each gesture.

HRI'14, March 3–6, 2014, Bielefeld, Germany.
ACM 978-1-4503-2658-2/14/03.
http://dx.doi.org/10.1145/2559636.2559786.

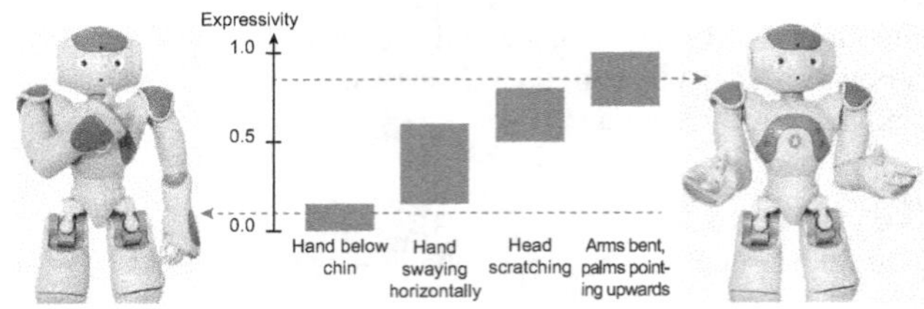

Figure 1: Performed gestures for feedback type *Incomprehension* with expressivity: 0.1 (left) and 0.9 (right).

2. IMPLEMENTATION ON THE NAO

We implemented these variable gestures to use them for communicating with a robot, in particular with the humanoid robot Nao by Aldebaran Robotics. The internal process of choosing a proper gesture from a total of 26 possible basic gestures with over 50 variations happens in two steps. First, the feedback type is evaluated and the appropriate gesture set is selected. Afterwards, the system interprets the value for the expressivity parameter and chooses a gesture from a predefined set of approximately ten variations per category. To evoke a behaviour generated by variable gestures there are two possibilities. On the one hand, the interacting user can talk to Nao which understands particular utterances, like simple statements and questions and reacts on them with a suitable gesture based on predefined values which show the appropriate feedback. On the other hand, the user can specify the parameters manually. These are the aforementioned feedback types and an expressivity which is a value between 0 for almost no expressiveness and 1 for very expressive behaviour. Two *Incomprehension* gestures are shown in Figure 1 which are created according to the user's input.

As a result, we developed an application and a gesture library which are straightforward and intuitive in usage and enhance the communication with nonverbal cues and convincing feedback.

3. REFERENCES

[1] B. Hartmann, M. Mancini, and C. Pelachaud. Implementing expressive gesture synthesis for embodied conversational agents. In *GW'05 Proc. of Gesture in Human-Computer Interaction and Simulation*, pages 188–199, Berlin, Heidelberg, 2006. Springer-Verlag.

The Receptionist Robot*

Patrick Holthaus
Applied Informatics
Faculty of Technology
Bielefeld University, Germany
patrick.holthaus@uni-bielefeld.de

Sven Wachsmuth
Central Lab Facilities
Center of Excellence Cognitive Interaction Technology
Bielefeld University, Germany
sven.wachsmuth@uni-bielefeld.de

ABSTRACT

In this demonstration, a humanoid robot interacts with an interlocutor through speech and gestures in order to give directions on a map. The interaction is specifically designed to provide an enhanced user experience by being aware of non-verbal social signals. Therefore, we take spatial communicative cues into account and to react to them accordingly.

Categories and Subject Descriptors

I.2.9 [**Artificial Intelligence**]: Robotics—*human-robot interaction*

General Terms

Design, Human Factors

1. COURSE OF ACTION

The iCub robot[3] is placed behind a receptionist desk with a map of the university campus (or floor plan) waiting for potential interlocutors. Visitors can approach the robot and ask it in which direction to find places certain. Speech and also deictic gestures to locations on the map between them can be used as a reference for the inquiry. The robot in all cases uses both speech and gesture in its answer to indicate the correct direction to the visitor. For referencing the target, iCub is capable of referring to the map and locations in the real world. Fig. 1 illustrates the scenario setup with the robot behind a desk.

2. REALIZATION

The overall interaction is realized with the help of a dialog module, a 3-d vision stack based on an external camera, motor control components, and a pre-modeled map of the surroundings. All of these components are extended to recognize implicit spatial signals sent by the interlocutor and to display them as well.

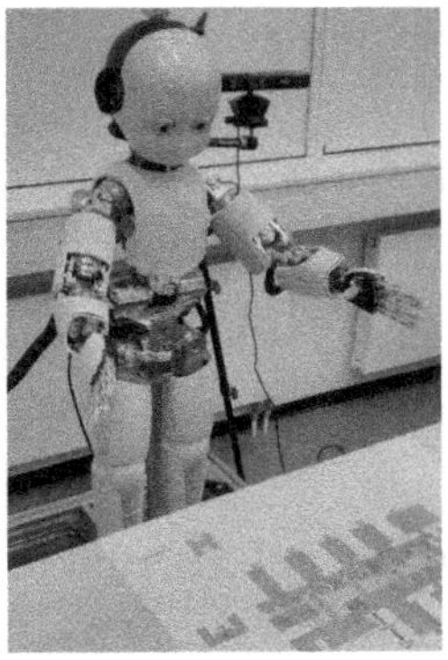

Figure 1: Depiction of the demonstration setup.

The actual interaction is opened based on a spatial attention strategy that allows the robot to gradually indicate availability and interest in helping the human interlocutor[1]. Therefore, the robot is able to initiate a dialog and offer services by itself on detecting a human in its social interaction area.

For spatial awareness in face-to-face interaction, the robot maintains a model of human activity in its close surroundings called the active peripersonal space[2]. With the help of such a model, iCub can make assumptions on where to point at (map or real world), which hand to use, and whether there is the need to use spatial prompting for reaching a target. Additionally, its spatial awareness enables the robot to modify the duration of the gesture and whether to use gaze or not.

The proposed demonstration is an example on how to successfully enhance a robot with social interaction strategies in the domain of spatial awareness for a better user experience during human-robot interaction. Aside from the demonstration session, the robot could also be installed at the conference front desk to serve the conference participants to find their way to the next talk.

3. REFERENCES

[1] P. Holthaus, K. Pitsch, and S. Wachsmuth. How Can I Help? - Spatial Attention Strategies for a Receptionist Robot. *International Journal of Social Robotics*, 3(4):383–393, Sept. 2011.

[2] P. Holthaus and S. Wachsmuth. Active Peripersonal Space for More Intuitive HRI. International Conference on Humanoid Robots, pages 508–513, Osaka, 2012. IEEE RAS.

[3] G. Metta, L. Natale, F. Nori, G. Sandini, D. Vernon, L. Fadiga, C. Von Hofsten, K. Rosander, M. Lopes, J. Santos-Victor, A. Bernardino, and L. Montesano. The iCub humanoid robot: an open-systems platform for research in cognitive development. *Neural Networks*, 23(8-9):1125–1134, 2010.

*This work has been supported by the German Research Foundation (DFG) within the Collaborative Research Center 673, Alignment in Communication.

HRI'14, March 3–6, 2014, Bielefeld, Germany.
ACM 978-1-4503-2658-2/14/03.
http://dx.doi.org/10.1145/2559636.2559784.

Demonstration of Emotion Modeling using Flobi*

Andreas Kipp
Applied Informatics
Faculty of Technology
Bielefeld University, Germany
akipp@techfak.uni-bielefeld.de

Birte Carlmeyer
Applied Informatics
Faculty of Technology
Bielefeld University, Germany
bcarlmey@techfak.uni-bielefeld.de

Oliver Damm
Applied Informatics
Faculty of Technology
Bielefeld University, Germany
odamm@techfak.uni-bielefeld.de

ABSTRACT

Social robots are designed to interact in a more human and intuitive manner. In this hands-on demo we present an emotional system which is capable to produce human like emotional expressions. Via touchscreen given input results in a realtime facial expression on a physical and a simulated robot head.

Categories and Subject Descriptors

I.2.9 [**Artificial Intelligence**]: Robotics—*human-robot interaction*

General Terms

Design, Human Factors

1. MOTIVATION

Human-robot interaction (HRI) research on emotions is motivated by the assumption that social signals (with emotional expressions being one of its components), which are produced by robots, are processed similarly to those accompanying human-human interaction. Artificial emotions can serve as a control mechanism [2] or to provide natural user feedback about the robots internal state and its goals.

This demo is implemented on the anthropomorphic robot head Flobi (fig. 1(a)) developed at the Bielefeld University [3]. Flobi has a cartoon-like appearance with similarity to humans and is designed to trigger a natural interaction. The robot has 16 degrees of freedom in total and is designed to express emotional states, such as happiness, surprise, sadness, or anger. Two actuators rotate the eyebrows, three actuators move the neck, three actuators rotate both eyes, four actuators move the upper and lower eyelids, and four actuators were implemented to animate both lips independently.

*This work has been supported by the German Research Foundation (DFG) within the Collaborative Research Center 673, Alignment in Communication.

HRI'14, March 3–6, 2014, Bielefeld, Germany.
ACM 978-1-4503-2658-2/14/03.
http://dx.doi.org/10.1145/2559636.2559785 .

(a) The robot head Flobi (b) The simulation of the robot head Flobi

Figure 1: The two different Flobis.

For interaction studies an emotional component was developed and implemented based on the WASABI engine proposed by Becker-Asano[1]. Modeled is a system which controls the facial expression of Flobi and the vocal range of speech output. The emotional system can be triggered by different events (positive or negative impulses together with a value for dominance) and change the interaction behavior of Flobi in realtime.

2. DEMO SETUP

The setup includes two robots. On the one hand the robot head Flobi (fig. 1(a)) and a virtual version of the head (fig. 1(b)) on the other hand. Both robots are connected to the controls on the touch screen. By pressing buttons events are send to the emotional system running in background. Every event results in a realtime reaction shown by the simulation as well as by the real robot. The system is designed so that the arousal decreases over time and the emotional system returns to a neutral state again.

3. REFERENCES

[1] C. Becker-Asano and I. Wachsmuth. Affective computing with primary and secondary emotions in a virtual human. *Autonomous Agents and Multi-Agent Systems*, 20(1):32–49, January 2010.
[2] C. Breazeal. Designing sociable robots, 2004.
[3] I. Lütkebohle, F. Hegel, S. Schulz, M. Hackel, B. Wrede, S. Wachsmuth, and G. Sagerer. The bielefeld anthropomorphic robot head "Flobi". In *Robotics and Automation (ICRA), 2010 IEEE International Conference on*, pages 3384–3391, 2010.

Reality Check! – A Physical Robot versus its Simulation

Florian Lier
Cognitive Interaction Technology Center of Excellence
Bielefeld University
Bielefeld, Germany
flier@techfak.uni-bielefeld.de

Simon Schulz
Cognitive Interaction Technology Center of Excellence
Bielefeld University
Bielefeld, Germany
sschulz@techfak.uni-bielefeld.de

Sven Wachsmuth
Cognitive Interaction Technology Center of Excellence
Bielefeld University
Bielefeld, Germany
swachsmu@techfak.uni-bielefeld.de

ABSTRACT

Simulated environments usually provide the most frequent test environment for robotic systems, often due to their cost and availability advantages. The crucial question is: how precisely must a simulation match the real world in order to produce realistic results? In this demonstration the humanoid robot head Flobi, as well as its simulation, will react to diverse visual stimuli in order to indicate visual attention which is an important cue in social interaction. We directly compare the behavior of the virtual robot, triggered by simulated stimuli, to the physical robot, triggered by real world stimuli. Therefore, we are able to assess and demonstrate the current limitations and advantages of our simulation compared to real world interactions.

Categories and Subject Descriptors

D.2.5 [**Software Engineering**]: Testing and Debugging—*Designs, Program Verification*

Keywords

Human Robot Interaction, Simulation, Testing, System Evaluation

1. COURSE OF ACTION

Flobi is placed on a desk, next to the physical robot is a screen presenting the virtual Flobi, similar to Figure 1. A third screen shows two graphs (side by side) depicting joint angle trajectories produced by both, the physical and virtual robot. Visitors may approach the setup and try to catch the attention of the physical robot by a) moving an AR-marker in front of the robot b) presenting their face in the robot's field of view, and c) by moving about in front of the robot. At the same time, the current stimulus will be virtually presented to the simulated robot. After each trial, the visitors can compare the resulting trajectories on the third screen.

HRI'14, March 3–6, 2014, Bielefeld, Germany.
ACM 978-1-4503-2658-2/14/03.
http://dx.doi.org/10.1145/2559636.2559787.

2. REALIZATION

The demonstration is realized by using the Flobi simulation [2] in combination with the physical Flobi. Both representations share a mutual control architecture. The simulation, with regard to joint control, reacts identical compared to physical robot. Thus, we can assure that differences in motion trajectories are not introduced by diverging control mechanisms. Moreover, the Flobi simulation has been implemented using the Modular OpenRobots Simulation Engine (MORSE) [1], which is capable of interfacing with multiple middleware implementations, i.e., ROS. That way we are able to interactively manipulate the simulated environment by adding a virtual AR-marker to the scene and publish virtual "RGB-camera" streams. To trigger a specific behavior, Flobi's attention component can be either provided with these virtual cameras or with its real world camera streams. Lastly, MORSE features a virtual human avatar, which can also be controlled via middleware. Therefore, we are able to reproduce all described real world stimuli in the simulated environment. This enables us to directly compare and assess the resulting behavior of both agents.

Figure 1: Simulated Flobi vs. Physical Flobi

3. REFERENCES

[1] S. Lemaignan, G. Echeverria, M. Karg, J. Mainprice, A. Kirsch, and R. Alami. Human-robot interaction in the morse simulator. In *Proceedings of the seventh annual ACM/IEEE international conference on Human-Robot Interaction*, pages 181–182. ACM, 2012.

[2] F. Lier, S. Schulz, and I. Lütkebohle. Continuous integration for iterative validation of simulated robot models. In I. Noda, N. Ando, D. Brugali, and J. Kuffner, editors, *Simulation, Modeling, and Programming for Autonomous Robots*, volume 7628 of *Lecture Notes in Computer Science*, pages 101–112. Springer Berlin Heidelberg, 2012.

A New Dimension for RoboCup @Home: Human-Robot Interaction between Virtual and Real Worlds

Jeffrey Too Chuan Tan
University of Tokyo
4-6-1 Komaba, Meguro-ku
Tokyo 153-8505, Japan
+81-3-5452-6089
jeffrey@iis.u-tokyo.ac.jp

Tetsunari Inamura
National Institute of Informatics
2-1-2 Hitotsubashi, Chiyoda-ku
Tokyo 101-8430, Japan
+81-3-4212-2518
inamura@nii.ac.jp

Yoshinobu Hagiwara
National Institute of Informatics
2-1-2 Hitotsubashi, Chiyoda-ku
Tokyo 101-8430, Japan
+81-3-4212-2518
yhagiwara@nii.ac.jp

Komei Sugiura
National Institute of Information and Communications Technology
3-5 Hikaridai, Seika, Soraku
Kyoto 619-0289, Japan
+81-774-98-6300
komei.sugiura@nict.go.jp

Takayuki Nagai
The University of Electro-Communications
1-5-1 Chofugaoka, Chofu
Tokyo 182-8585, Japan
+81-42-443-5203
tnagai@ee.uec.ac.jp

Hiroyuki Okada
Tamagawa University
6-1-1 Tamagawa-gakuen, Machida-shi
Tokyo 194-8610, Japan
+81-42-731-1111
h.okada@eng.tamagawa.ac.jp

ABSTRACT
This work proposes a new approach to realize embodied and multimodal HRI between virtual robot and real world human for HRI challenges in RoboCup @Home.

Categories and Subject Descriptors
H.1.2 **[Models and Principles]**: User/Machine Systems – *human factors*; I.2.9 **[Artificial Intelligence]**: Robotics; I.6.3 **[Simulation and Modeling]**: Applications

Keywords
RoboCup @Home, Embodiment, Multimodal Interaction

1. INTRODUCTION
One significant development barrier of RoboCup @Home (assistive robot development for domestic applications) in human-robot interaction (HRI) studies is the complexity to maintain physical robots especially in long term interaction and large number of robots. The purpose of this work is to demonstrate the feasibility of our proposal to realize embodied and multimodal HRI between virtual robot and real world human as a new approach for HRI challenges in RoboCup @Home. This approach has several significant advantages [1] in facilitating RoboCup @Home developments:

(1) Enable adjustment of the abstraction in embodiment and multimodal interaction in order to reduce the complexity of low level robot controls in high level intelligence development.

(2) Promote the integration of high level intelligence frameworks into real embodied HRI for long term interaction.

(3) Reproducibility and scalability for large number of human-robot and interactions.

Based on our SIGVerse simulator [1], 3D virtual environments can be established for virtual robots to interact with real world humans. Virtual reality immersive techniques are used to immerse the human subject into the 3D virtual world as an avatar, in order to maintain the embodied and multimodal interaction. The realization of embodiment and multimodal interaction are illustrated in several HRI scenarios (Figure 1) [1], where verbal action instruction and spatial information from the body gesture are simulated.

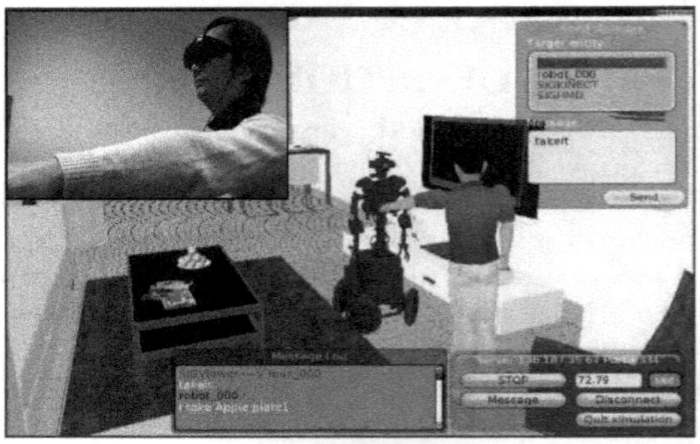

Figure 1. HRI between virtual robot and real world human.

2. REFERENCE
[1] Tan, J. T. C., Inamura, T., Sugiura, K., Nagai, T., and Okada, H. 2013. Human-Robot Interaction between Virtual and Real Worlds: Motivation from RoboCup @Home. In *Proc. of the 5th Int. Conf. on Social Robotics* (Bristol, UK, October 27 - 29, 2013). ICSR '13. 239-248. DOI= http://dx.doi.org/10.1007/978-3-319-02675-6_24.

HRI'14, March 3–6, 2014, Bielefeld, Germany.
ACM 978-1-4503-2658-2/14/03.
http://dx.doi.org/10.1145/2559636.2559783

Socially Assistive Robotics: Human-Robot Interaction Methods for Creating Robots that Care

Maja Matarić
University of Southern California
mataric@usc.edu

ABSTRACT

Socially assistive robotics (SAR) is a new subfield of robotics that bridges HRI, rehabilitation robotics, social robotics, and service robotics. SAR focuses on developing machines capable of assisting users, typically in health and education contexts, through social rather than physical interaction. The robot's physical embodiment is at the heart of SAR's effectiveness, as it leverages the inherently human tendency to engage with lifelike (but not necessarily humanlike or otherwise biomimetic) social behavior. This talk will describe research into embodiment, modeling and steering social dynamics, and long-term user adaptation for SAR. The research will be grounded in projects involving analysis of multi-modal activity data, modeling personality and engagement, formalizing social use of space and non-verbal communication, and personalizing the interaction with the user over a period of months. The presented methods and algorithms will be validated on implemented SAR systems evaluated by human subject cohorts from a variety of user populations, including stroke patients, children with autism spectrum disorder, and elderly with Alzheimers and other forms of dementia.

Categories and Subject Descriptors

H.1.2 User/Machine Systems

Keywords

ACM SIGCHI; computing; human-robot interaction; assistive robotics

Bio

Maja Matarić is professor and Chan Soon-Shiong chair in Computer Science, Neuroscience, and Pediatrics at the University of Southern California, founding director of the USC Center for Robotics and Embedded Systems, co-director of the USC Robotics Research Lab and Vice Dean for Research in the USC Viterbi School of Engineering. She received her PhD in Computer Science and Artificial Intelligence from MIT in 1994, MS in Computer Science from MIT in 1990, and BS in Computer Science from the University of Kansas in 1987. She is a Fellow of the American Association for the Advancement of Science (AAAS), Fellow of the IEEE, and recipient of the Presidential Awards for Excellence in Science, Mathematics & Engineering Mentoring (PAESMEM), the Anita Borg Institute Women of Vision Award for Innovation, Okawa Foundation Award, NSF Career Award, the MIT TR100 Innovation Award, and the IEEE Robotics and Automation Society Early Career Award. She served as the elected president of the USC faculty and the Academic Senate. At USC she has been awarded the Viterbi School of Engineering Service Award and Junior Research Award, the Provost's Center for Interdisciplinary Research Fellowship, the Mellon Mentoring Award, the Academic Senate Distinguished Faculty Service Award, and a Remarkable Woman Award. She is featured in the science documentary movie "Me & Isaac Newton", in The New Yorker ("Robots that Care" by Jerome Groopman, 2009), Popular Science ("The New Face of Autism Therapy", 2010), the IEEE Spectrum ("Caregiver Robots", 2010), and is one of the LA Times Magazine 2010 Visionaries. Prof. Matarić is an associate editor of three major journals and has published extensively. She serves or has recently servied on a number of advisory boards, including the National Science Foundation Computing and Information Sciences and Engineering (CISE) Division Advisory Committee, and the Willow Garage and Evolution Robotics Scientific Advisory Boards. Prof. Matarić is actively involved in K-12 educational outreach, having obtained federal and corporate grants to develop free open-source curricular materials for elementary and middle-school robotics courses in order to engage student interest in science, technology, engineering, and math (STEM) topics. Her Interaction Lab's research into socially assistive robotics is aimed at endowing robots with the ability to help people through individual non-contact assistance in convalescence, rehabilitation, training, and education. Her research is currently developing robot-assisted therapies for children with autism spectrum disorders, stroke and traumatic brain injury survivors, and individuals with Alzheimer's Disease and other forms of dementia.

HRI'14, March 3–6, 2014, Bielefeld, Germany.
ACM 978-1-4503-2658-2/14/03.
http://dx.doi.org/10.1145/2559636.2566688

Meet Me where I'm Gazing: How Shared Attention Gaze Affects Human-Robot Handover Timing

AJung Moon[1]
ajmoon@interchange.ubc.ca

Daniel M. Troniak[2]
troniak@cs.ubc.ca

Brian Gleeson[2]
brian.gleeson@gmail.com

Matthew K.X.J. Pan[1]
mpan9@interchange.ubc.ca

Minhua Zheng[3]
mhzheng@ee.cuhk.edu.hk

Benjamin A. Blumer[1]
benjaminaaronblumer@gmail.com

Karon MacLean[2]
maclean@cs.ubc.ca

Elizabeth A. Croft[1]
ecroft@mech.ubc.ca

[1]University of British Columbia
Dept. of Mechanical Engineering
6250 Applied Science Lane
Vancouver, BC, V6T 1Z4 Canada

[2]University of British Columbia
Dept. of Computer Science
201-2366 Main Mall
Vancouver, BC, V6T 1Z4 Canada

[3]The Chinese University of Hong Kong
Dept. of Electronic Engineering
Ho Sin Hang Engineering Building
Shatin, N.T., Hong Kong

ABSTRACT

In this paper we provide empirical evidence that using humanlike gaze cues during human-robot handovers can improve the timing and perceived quality of the handover event. Handovers serve as the foundation of many human-robot tasks. Fluent, legible handover interactions require appropriate nonverbal cues to signal handover intent, location and timing. Inspired by observations of human-human handovers, we implemented gaze behaviors on a PR2 humanoid robot. The robot handed over water bottles to a total of 102 naïve subjects while varying its gaze behaviour: no gaze, gaze designed to elicit shared attention at the handover location, and the shared attention gaze complemented with a turn-taking cue. We compared subject perception of and reaction time to the robot-initiated handovers across the three gaze conditions. Results indicate that subjects reach for the offered object significantly earlier when a robot provides a shared attention gaze cue during a handover. We also observed a statistical trend of subjects preferring handovers with turn-taking gaze cues over the other conditions. Our work demonstrates that gaze can play a key role in improving user experience of human-robot handovers, and help make handovers fast and fluent.

Categories and Subject Descriptors

I.2.9 [**Robotics**]: *Operator interfaces, Commercial robots and applications;* H.1.2 [User/Machine Systems]: Human Factors

General Terms

Experimentation, Design, Human Factors, Verification.

Keywords

Human-Robot Communication, Handover, Head Gaze, Turn-taking, Nonverbal Communication

1. INTRODUCTION

In order for robots to take on more assistive roles for humans at homes and workplaces, it is essential for the robot to be able to successfully and fluently hand objects to people. Many application scenarios, be it in manufacturing or the home environment, can involve situations where it is useful for a robot to fetch and handover an object to a person. Implementing an effective human-robot handover, however, is a challenge. In human-human handovers, a great variety of subtle signals mediate the handover event. Body position, hand and arm pose, gaze, grip force, and the trajectory of these factors through time are used to communicate the intent to engage in a handover, when and where the handover is to occur, and help create a fluent and fast interaction while ensuring that the object is not dropped (e.g., [5, 11, 18, 26, 39, 40]). When a robot does not provide appropriate cues, human-robot handovers can fail in a variety of ways: people do not recognize that the robot is giving them an object [8], objects can be dropped [11], or people can feel uncomfortable or unsafe during the interaction [12, 23].

In this paper, we seek to improve human-robot handovers by investigating how gaze can be used to augment a handover event, subtly communicating handover location, handover timing, and providing acceptable social interaction signals.

Gaze cues, in either human-human interaction (HHI) or in human-robot interaction (HRI), have proven to be efficient for communicating attention [24, 31]. During a handover, givers use verbal or nonverbal cues to direct the receiver's attention to an object. Successful handovers typically take place when the two parties achieve shared attention on the same object. Previous studies [26, 39, 40] indicate that gaze can be used by robots to signal handover intent to users prior to the handover event. However, these studies did not explore the effect of robot gaze *during* the handover on the timing of the handover event.

We hypothesize that the use of gaze cues during human-robot handover can influence handover timing and the subjective experience of the handover by implicitly increasing communication transparency and perception of naturalness for the interaction.

In this work, we first conducted a human-human handover study to observe gaze patterns used during human-human handovers. To test the effect of gaze in human-robot handovers we implemented the two most frequently observed gaze patterns from the human-human study and a 'no gaze' condition on a PR2 humanoid platform and conducted an in-situ HRI experiment. We address the following two questions: 1. Can gaze improve the subjective experience of handovers, 2. Can gaze be used to produce faster, more fluent handovers. The key results from our study are as follows:

HRI'14, March 3–6, 2014, Bielefeld, Germany.

http://dx.doi.org/10.1145/2559636.2559656

- Subjects reach for the object significantly faster when the robot directs its gaze towards the intended handover location (shared attention gaze) than when no gaze cues are used.
- Subjects tend to perceive a handover as more natural, communicative of timing, and preferable when the robot provides turn-taking gaze in addition to shared attention gaze.

2. BACKGROUND

In this section, we outline a body of work on human-robot handovers and the use of gaze in HRI. In discussing human-robot handovers, we focus our discussion on studies where a robot is the giver and a human the receiver.

2.1 Human-Robot Handover

Previous research in human-robot handovers can be broadly categorized by the aspect of the handover under investigation: approach for handover, handover trajectory and pose, and the handover event itself.

Studies of approach for handovers consider situations where a mobile robot navigates towards a human to initiate a handover. These studies generally focus on human preference for approach directions and on creating robot behaviors that clearly communicate the intent to initiate a handover. Basili et al. studied how humans hold objects as they approach for a handover [5]. Koay and Sisbot studied human preferences for coordinated arm-base movement in handover approach [23]. Mainprice et al. designed an approach planner that considers the mobility of the receiver [28]. While our study does not involve a robot's handover approach (i.e., the participants approached our robot in our experiment), we used the above studies to guide our placement of the robot, as discussed in Section 4.1.

Other researchers have investigated handover trajectory and pose, reporting guidelines for how a robot arm should be positioned for handover and how that position should be achieved. In a series of studies, Cakmak et al. and Strabala et al. studied how handover trajectories and final handover poses can best signal the intent to initiate a handover [9, 40]. They found that the final handover pose should feature a nearly fully extended arm in a natural (human achievable) pose with the elbow, wrist, and distal point on the object positioned, respectively, from closest to furthest away from the body in all three dimensions. The object should be held in its canonical orientation (right side up) and positioned to allow easy grasping by the human. A related study emphasized the importance of the physical cues in human-robot handovers, showing that poorly designed handover poses and trajectories were often unsuccessful in communicating intent and ultimately resulted in handover failure [8]. They found that intent is best communicated by having high contrast between the pose used for holding the object and the pose used for handing over the object. We have followed the above guidelines in the design of our handover pose and trajectory, as described in Section 4.1.

Other studies have investigated the velocity profile of handover motions and have found that trajectories that minimize end-effector jerk make people feel safer in handover interactions [12, 17]. Other studies of handover trajectory include a human-based potential field planner for handover trajectories [21].

Chan et al. studied the actual handover event, measuring grip and load forces in human-human handovers and using these data to design a robust robot handover grip controller that imitates human handover behaviour [11]. We have adapted this controller for use in our study.

2.2 Gaze in Human-Robot Interaction

Gaze is an important and useful cue in HHI. People repeatedly look each other in the eye during social interaction and people do not feel that they are fully engaged in communication without eye contact [2]. Studies in psychology have shown various functions of gaze in social interaction, such as seeking and providing information, regulating interaction, expressing intimacy, exercising social control, etc. [2, 24, 33]. Gaze can be named differently in different social situations [31]; for example, mutual gaze or eye contact is defined as two people looking into each other's face or eye region [41], while deictic gaze or shared visual attention is defined as one person following the other's direction of attention to look at a fixed point in space [7].

Previous work has shown the importance of gaze in HRI. For example, Staudte and Crocker [38] demonstrated that humans react to robot gaze in a manner typical of HHI. Since gaze behavior is closely linked with speech [4], much work has been done on the conversational functions of gaze in HRI [25, 27, 29, 30, 32, 42]. Gaze is particularly effective in regulating turn-taking during human-robot conversation. Kuno et al. [25] developed gaze cues for a museum guide robot to coordinate conversational turn-taking. Matsusaka et al. [29] used gaze cues to mediate turn-taking between participants in a group conversation.

Another large body of literature focus on using gaze to direct people's attention in HRI [6, 15, 20, 34, 36]. Gaze was combined with pointing gestures in [6, 15, 20] to direct people's attention, which the authors believed would make the interaction more human-like [6] while minimizing misunderstanding [15]. In [34] four types of "connection events" were identified from HHI videos, namely directed gaze, mutual facial gaze, adjacency pairs and backchannels. Implementing them in an HRI game showed a high success rate in forming human-robot connection or joint attention. In [36], people directed their attention to the robot more often in interactions where gaze was present, and people found interactions more appropriate when gaze was present.

Introducing gaze cues can also benefit HRI in other ways. In [30] and [37], gaze increased human performance in certain human-robot tasks. In [25] and [36], gaze heightened human-robot engagement and in [27], gaze cues contributed to the perceived naturalness of a communicating robot.

In the study of human-robot handovers, other researchers have shown that gaze can be useful in communicating the intent to initiate a handover. Lee et al. [26] studied human motion and gaze cues as people approached each other for handovers. They found that people looked at the object or at the receiver as they approached the receiver. Strabala et al. [39] examined the signals that humans use to communicate handover intent before a handover takes place. They initially acknowledged gaze as one of the important features that mark the difference between different phases in handover, but they did not find gaze to be an effective predictor of handover intent. In contrast, Kirchner et al. [22] demonstrated how robot gaze can be effective in targeting an individual recipient out of a group of people for a robot initiated handover. Atienza and Zelinksy [1] augmented handover interactions with gaze, demonstrating a system that allowed a human to request an object for handover by looking at it.

While the above studies addressed gaze in pre-handover cuing and communication of intent to handover, in this study we examine the use of gaze *during* the handover event. Although the effectiveness of gaze in regulating handover intent remains an open question, gaze may have a positive effect when used during the handover event, since it helps establish shared attention and has been shown to improve human-robot tasks. Hence, we hypothesize that gaze may be useful in improving the handover itself by establishing shared attention and signaling the robot's end of turn.

3. HUMAN-HUMAN HANDOVER STUDY

To assist our human-robot handover experiment design, we carried out a study on human-human handover of a bottle of water, as shown in Figure 1, to observe the gaze behaviour of the giver during the handover. While other researchers have observed gaze in human-human handovers (e.g., [39]), these studies focused on gaze cues *before* handover. For our current study, we augmented these previous results with a study focusing on gaze *during* the handover event.

Twelve volunteers (10 male, 2 female) participated in this study. The giver was asked to handover ten bottles from a side table to the receiver one at a time. The receiver was asked to bring the bottles to a collection box about two meters behind them one at a time, requiring him/her to walk away from the giver between each handover. This process repeated until all ten handovers were completed. Each participant performed the role of the giver, then was paired with another participant and performed the role of the receiver, resulting in a total of twelve giver-receiver pairs.

The giver and receiver were instructed not to talk during this process. The giver was also instructed to pick up the bottles from the side table only after the receiver returned from the collection box and had put his/her hands on the table. By requiring the receiver to turn and walk away, the common attention between the giver and the receiver was interrupted after each handover and participants needed to re-connect for the next handover.

Through a frame-by-frame analysis, we annotated the givers' gaze patterns from video recordings of the 120 handovers, and found the following two dominant gaze patterns.

Shared Attention Gaze (Figure 1a): The most frequent gaze pattern (68% of all handovers observed) consists of the giver gazing at a projected handover location as s/he reaches out to execute the handover. After picking up the bottle, the giver turns to face the receiver, looks down at a midpoint between the giver and the receiver, and keeps the gaze there until the receiver takes control of the bottle. This midpoint is approximately where the handover takes place. There is no eye contact between the giver and the receiver throughout this handover gaze pattern.

Turn-Taking Gaze (Figure 1b): In 13% of handovers, we observed a slight variation from the Shared Attention Gaze. In addition to gazing at a projected handover location while reaching out, the giver *also* looked up to make eye contact with the receiver near the end of the handover motion, at approximately the time that the receiver made contact with the bottle.

Other handover gaze patterns consisted of the giver looking at the receiver's face throughout the handover (8%), the giver looking at the receiver's face and quickly glancing at the bottle when the receiver is about to touch the bottle (8%), or the giver glancing at the receiver before but not during handover (4%).

4. METHODS

To examine the impact of robot gaze on human receiver behavior, we used a PR2 humanoid mobile robotic platform (Willow Garage Inc., Menlo Park, CA) with a pan-tilt head and two 7-DOF arms, each with a two-fingered, 1-DOF gripper. In the following, we (Section 4.1) outline the physical handover cues used by the PR2; (Section 4.2) describe the three experimental gaze conditions inspired from the human-human handover study; and (Sections 4.3-4.4) outline our experiment design and technical implementation.

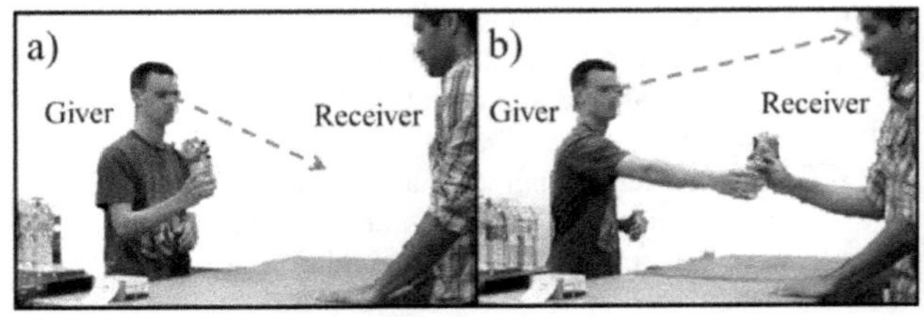

Figure 1. Demonstration of two frequently observed gaze patterns from the human-human handover study. a) shared attention gaze: the giver looks at the location where the handover will occur, and b) turn-taking gaze: the giver looks up at the receiver after the shared attention gaze.

4.1 Physical Handover Cues

In our experiment, based on [5] and [23], the robot was positioned such that it was facing the participant approximately 1 meter away.

The robot executed the handover with its right gripper, as recommended in [23]. In the beginning of each handover, the robot starts its motion at the *grasp position* with its end-effector prepared to grasp a bottle sitting on a table at the robot's right side. When subject is ready, the end-effector grabs the bottle (marking a *start time*, $t=0$ of the interaction), then moves the bottle horizontally to a position in front of the robot's centreline (*ready position*). Then the robot moves from the *ready position* forward to the *handover location*. We predefined joint-angle goals of the *grasp position*, *ready position*, and *handover location* such that when the robot's end-effector is extended, the arm is positioned in a natural pose: the elbow located below the shoulder, and the gripper located below the distal point on the bottle, as shown in Figure 3. We designed our *handover location* in accord with the recommendations of previous work [22, 26]. The three locations are constant for all three gaze conditions. While other researchers have proposed handover controllers that adapt to the position of the human's hand, for example [14], we chose to maintain a constant *handover location* and only vary gaze cues used during handovers.

When the robot's arm reaches the *handover location*, the robot waits for a participant to grasp and pull up on the object. The force the gripper exerts on the bottle is a linear function of the downward force exerted by the bottle as described by Chan et al. [11]. Thus, as the subject takes the weight of the bottle, the robot releases its grip (marked as the *release time*). The PR2's fingertip pressure sensor arrays were used to realize Chan et al.'s handover controller.

Finally, after releasing the object, the robot returns to the *grasp position*, ready to grasp and lift the next object.

4.2 Experimental Gaze Cues

In this study, the PR2 robot expressed gaze through head orientation. Imai et al. [19] showed that robot head orientation can be an effective substitute for human-like gaze and that head orientation is interpreted as gaze direction. In order to minimize any possible confusion regarding the robot's gaze direction, we used a single object for the handovers.

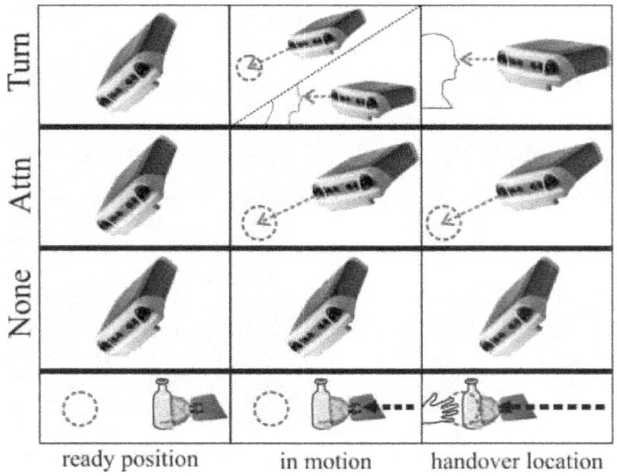

Figure 2. Depiction of gaze cues: No Gaze (None), Shared Attention Gaze (Attn), and Turn-Taking Gaze (Turn). In the Turn condition, the robot shifts its gaze from the handover location to the human's face midway through the handover motion.

We tested three different gaze patterns in human-robot handovers, as shown in Figure 2. In all conditions, the robot's gaze tracks its end-effector from the *grasp position* to the *ready position* as though the robot is attending to the acquisition of the bottle. When the end-effector arrives at the *ready position*, the robot's head is tilted downwards towards the end-effector. Only when the robot arm transitions between the *ready position* to *handover location* does the robot transfer its gaze according to the following gaze patterns.

The **No Gaze (None)** condition is our baseline. The robot head remains looking down towards the ground while the end-effector extends forward for the handover.

The **Shared Attention (Attn)** gaze condition models the most frequently observed gaze pattern from our human-human handover study. When the robot starts to move from the *ready position* to the *handover location*, it smoothly transitions its gaze (head orientation) from the bottle to the location in space where the handover will occur, as an implicit cue intended to direct the human's attention towards the projected *handover location*. With this condition, we test the hypothesis that shared attention can be established through gaze during handovers, and that doing so benefits the handover interaction. Establishing shared gaze at an object or location can serve to direct shared attention (e.g., [20]) and can aid in the successful execution of human-robot cooperative tasks (e.g., [37]).

The **Turn-Taking (Turn)** gaze condition is also derived from our human-human handover study, and is analogous to the second most frequently observed gaze pattern. When the handover trajectory begins, the robot smoothly transfers its gaze to the *handover location*, as in the Shared Attention condition, but then shifts its gaze up to the human's face in a quick motion, reaching the final gaze position at approximately the same time that the handover motion completes. Here we test two hypotheses: that (a) this gaze shift can cue handover timing, and (b) looking at the face can improve the subjective experience of the handover. This type of gaze shift has been shown to be a meaningful human-robot turn-taking cue [10] and mutual gaze can increase the sense of engagement and naturalness in human-robot interactions [27, 36].

4.3 Experimental Procedure

We conducted a paired-comparison handover study in a controlled room. The study took place on the day of a university orientation event such that many and diverse naïve participants could be rapidly recruited during the public event. We used a balanced incomplete block design ($v=3$, $b=96$, $r=64$, $k=2$, $\lambda=32$) to both support rapid trials (maximum 5 min.) and include only naïve reactions: each participant evaluated one of the three condition pairings. Condition order was randomized and presentation order counterbalanced among trials.

Participants provided informed consent, then entered the room where verbal instructions were given (Figure 3). They were told to stand at a marked area facing the robot, and informed they would participate in a handover interaction. Participants were also told that the robot would pick up the water bottle placed beside it and hand it to them. They were asked to take the bottle from the robot whenever they felt it was the right time to do so. To avoid unintended cuing, during handovers the experimenters sat out of the field of view of participants.

After receiving the first bottle, participants placed the bottle in a box approximately 3 meters behind him/her. This served as a washout between handovers, breaking the participant's focus on the robot and the handover, as was done previously in [8]. Participants then returned to the same marked area in front of the robot and participated in a second handover. Participants were permitted to keep the last bottle given to them by the robot.

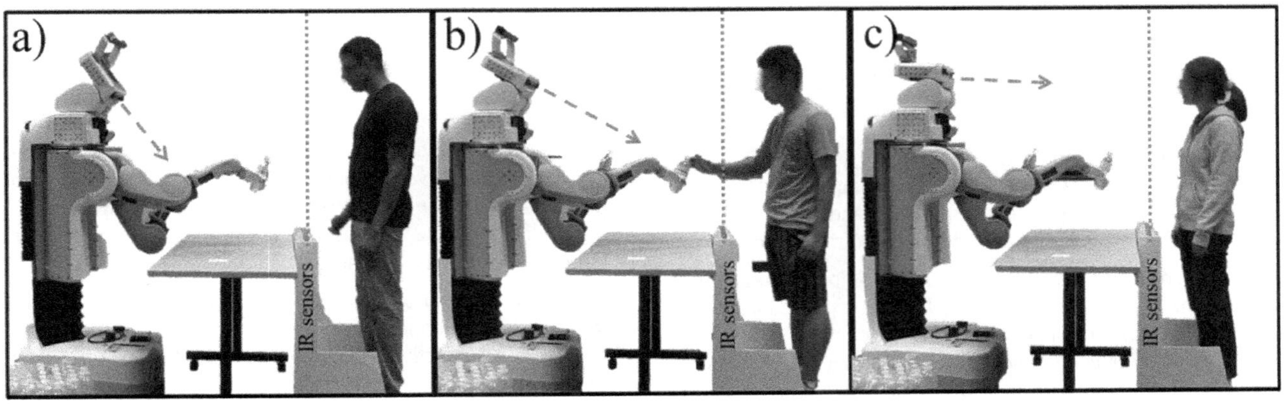

Figure 3. Demonstration of the experimental set-up and the three conditions at the *handover location*: a) No Gaze; b) Shared Attention; and c) Turn-Taking. An array of infrared sensors was located at the edge of the table. The red dotted lines represent the location where subject's reach motion is detected. Subjects stood at a specified location marked on the floor.

During each handover, we timestamped the following events: start of robot motion (*start time*), end of robot motion (*end of motion time*), start of release of the robot's gripper (*release time*), and the participant's first reach for the object (*reach time*) as measured by the motion sensor array described in Section 4.4.

After the second handover, participants left the room and completed a short questionnaire comparing the two handovers on three subjective metrics: *overall preference*, *naturalness*, and *timing communication*. For each of the following three questions, participants were asked to select either the first or second handover:

1. Which handover did you like better, overall?
2. Which handover seemed more natural?
3. We think that timing is important in human-robot handovers. Which handover made it easier to tell **when**, exactly, the robot wanted you to take the object?

Participants could also provide additional comments.

4.4 Technical Implementation

To control the PR2, we extended the Robot Operating System (ROS) [35] with a series of software modules coordinated via the Blackboard architectural design pattern [16] (Figure 4).

One module controlled the robot's arm and another, its head. The head-control module provided object tracking functionality for bringing the object to the *ready position*, and a smooth, fast gaze transition (average 90 degrees/second) functionality to enable the Shared Attention gaze and Turn-Taking gaze conditions during the handover motion.

An independent module logged quantitative measurements of robot's *start time*, *end of motion time*, and *release time*.

Reach Time Detection: An array of three passive infrared motion sensors (SEN-08630, SparkFun Electronics, Boulder, CO) configured as a light curtain was placed at the edge of the table (Figure 3), and was used to detect the start of the participant's reach (*reach time*) triggered by the participant's hand crossing the table edge. An Arduino microprocessor relayed the sensor reading to the PC controlling the robot. Sensor readings were logged and time-synchronized with the robot.

5. RESULTS

A total of 102 volunteers participated in our experiment. We rejected six records (instruction not followed), and analyzed data from 96 participants (63 male, 33 female; age $M=23$, $SD=5.59$). Due to technical error, *reach time* was not logged in the second handover for five of the participants. This did not affect our analysis of handover timing, since we are interested in only the first handover *reach time*. No other technical failures occurred and all handovers were successful (no bottles were dropped).

5.1 Handover Timing

Figure 5 shows the distribution of three key times: the robot's *end of motion time*, participant's *reach time*, and robot's gripper *release time*. All times are measured relative to *start time*.

We conducted a one-way ANOVA on participants' *reach time* across the three conditions. Since we found a significant learning effect between the first and second handover trials ($t(90)=4.21$, $p<.001$, $d=0.43$) where *reach time* is earlier in the second handovers, and our goal was to understand naïve behavior, we only used the *reach time* collected during the first of the two handovers performed by each participant. The entire robot motion

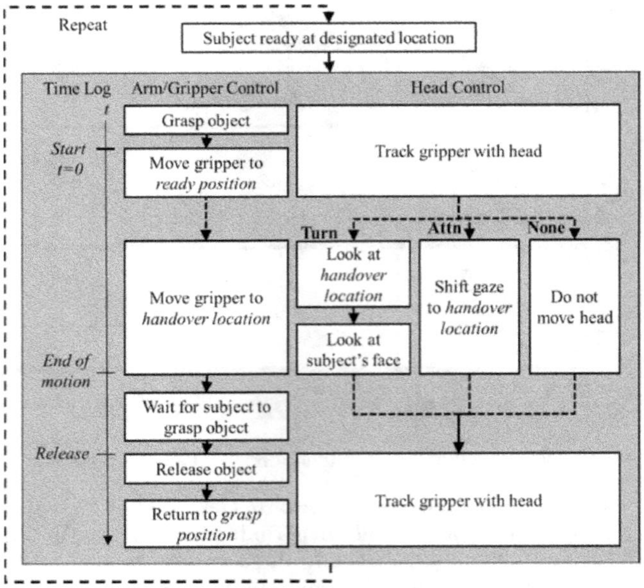

Figure 4. Experiment system flow diagram

from the *grasp position* to the *handover location* consistently took 2.02 seconds ($SD=0.01$).

Participants' *reach time* varied across the three gaze conditions ($F(2, 93)=6.49$, $p<.005$) as plotted in Figure 5; post-hoc analyses used a Bonferroni correction. Participants reached for the object significantly earlier with Shared Attention ($M=1.91$, $SD=0.52$) than with No Gaze ($M=2.54$, $SD= 0.76$) ($p<.005$). Note that the mean *reach time* for Shared Attention occurs before the robot has stopped moving at the handover location (*reach time* < *end of motion time*). No significant differences were found between Shared Attention and Turn-Taking ($M=2.26$, $SD=0.79$), or between Turn-Taking and No Gaze.

5.2 Subjective Experience

To contrast *overall preference*, perceived *naturalness*, and *timing communication* across the three gaze patterns during handovers, we employed Durbin's test [13] – analogous to a Friedman test for rank data, but adapted to balanced incomplete block designs – on our questionnaire data.

We checked for possible gender effects using Mann-Whitney U tests. No significant effects of gender were found (*overall preference*: $U = 935.0$, $p=0.23$, $r = 0.12$; *naturalness*: $U=918.5$, $p=0.18$, $r=0.14$; *timing communication*: $U=935.5$, $p=0.22$, $r=0.12$). We conducted one-sample Wilcoxon signed rank tests to observe potential bias in selecting the first or second handover experience in the questionnaire. We found a significant bias towards selecting the second handover on the *timing communication* metric ($Z=2.22$, $p<.05$) and a weak trend to select the second handover on both *overall preference* and *naturalness* metrics ($Z=1.62$, $p=0.11$ and $Z=1.41$, $p=0.16$, respectively). The rank data collected using the questionnaire is insufficient to correct for this bias statistically.

Given this general bias to select the second handover, we believe that finding statistical significance to $\alpha=0.10$ in questionnaire results is noteworthy. Hence, we also report our observation of trends (results having $p<0.10$; Table 1).

Overall Preference: We did not find a significant difference in user preference across the three gaze conditions ($T2=2.04$, $p=0.14$). However, one-tailed pairwise comparisons demonstrate

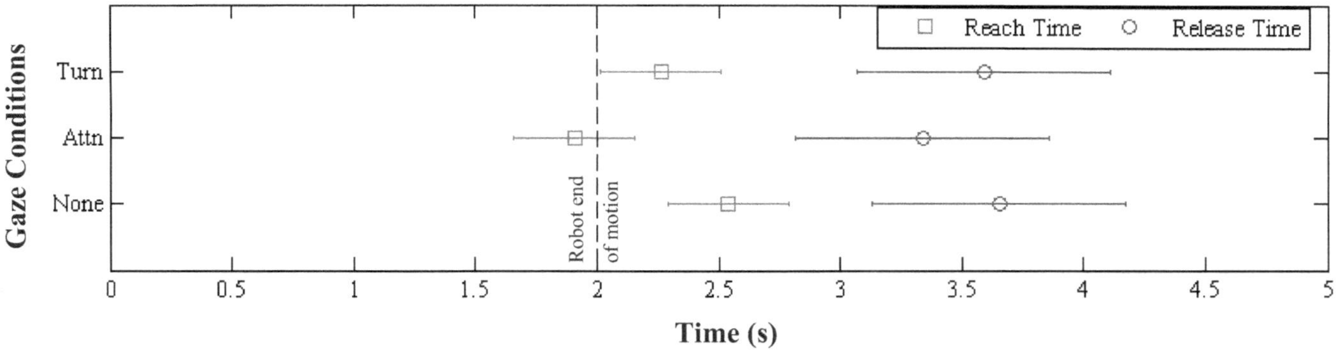

Figure 5. Handover timing. All times are measured with respect to the robot's start of motion at t=0. The dashed line at 2 seconds indicates the end of robot motion at the handover location. Reach time indicates the participant's reach toward the proffered object crossing the infrared sensors. Note that in the case of the Shared Attention (Attn) condition, participants start to reach before the robot has reached handover location. The mean reach time for the Shared Attention condition is significantly earlier than that of the No Gaze (None) condition. The error bars indicate the 95% confidence intervals.

a trend for preference toward Turn-Taking over No Gaze ($p<0.10$) and Shared Attention ($p<0.10$) conditions.

Naturalness: We did not find any significant difference in perceived naturalness of the handovers across the three gaze conditions ($T2=1.82$, $p=0.17$). However, participants tended to choose Turn-Taking as more natural than Shared Attention ($p<0.10$) but not over the No Gaze condition.

Timing Communication: No significant differences were found in the perceived communication of timing across the gaze conditions ($T2=1.65$, $p=0.20$). However, participants tended to choose Turn-Taking over Shared Attention ($p<0.10$), but not over No Gaze, as easiest to communicate handover timing.

In total, 59% of all participants provided additional comments (optional) on the questionnaire. Twelve subjects who experienced the Turn-Taking condition explicitly used words such as "head motion", "eye contact" or "looking at me" and expressed the condition in a positive light (e.g., P90 compared No Gaze with Turn-Taking: "During second handover [Turn-Taking], robot made eye contact, which made it easier to tell when the bottle should be taken."; P10 compared Shared Attention and Turn-Taking: "I liked it when robot looked at me. That confirms it's good to take."). However, another twelve subjects expressed that they did not notice any difference between the conditions.

Table 1. Ranking of questionnaire results. Each cell represents the number of people who chose the row condition over the column condition. * indicate pairwise comparisons that are significant to p<0.10 (none were significant to p<0.05). Note that we observed participants' bias to select the second handover experience regardless of experiment condition.

Overall Preference

	Turn	Attn	None
Turn-Taking	0	**21***	**19***
Shared Attention	11	0	17
No Gaze	13	15	0

Naturalness

	Turn	Attn	None
Turn-Taking	0	**20***	19
Shard Attention	12	0	19
No Gaze	13	13	0

Timing Communication

	Turn	Attn	None
Turn-Taking	0	**21***	18
Shared Attention	11	0	19
No Gaze	14	13	0

6. DISCUSSION

Building on previous work that studied communication of intent to handover using gaze, our study explored the impact of robot gaze on human-robot handover timing and user perception of the handover experience. Our results show that participants reached for the proffered object significantly earlier when the robot performed a shared attention gaze at the projected handover location. In fact, participants reached for the object even before the robot had arrived and stopped at the *handover location* (a mean of 0.11 seconds before the *end of motion time*). This is in contrast to the No Gaze condition where the mean reach time is 0.52 seconds after the robot's *end of motion.*

In our experiment, participants were explicitly told that the robot would be handing over objects to them and that they were to take the object from the robot. In addition to this foreknowledge, our robot used highly contrasting poses between the *ready position* and the *handover location* which, according to [8], makes the robot's intent to handover very clear. Hence, it is unlikely that the observed difference in timing between the gaze conditions is due to uncertainties in understanding the robot's handover intent. Rather, our results suggest that the robot's gaze at the projected *handover location* supplements the communicated intent with implicit information on *where* the handover should take place. This may be helping to establish shared attention on the handover location even before the robot arrives there, naturally allowing participants to respond and meet the robot at the location earlier than when such a cue is absent. Thus, our result best support an increase of fluidity in execution of the handover as it takes place.

However, the role of mutual gaze used in the Turn-Taking condition requires further investigation. In the beginning of the robot's handover motion, the robot expresses the same locational, shared attention gaze in both the Shared Attention and Turn-Taking conditions. Hence, we were surprised to find that the *reach time* of the Turn-Taking condition is not significantly earlier than that of the No Gaze condition.

With the Turn-Taking condition we intended to test two hypotheses: that the Turn-Taking gaze would cue handover timing, and that looking at the participant's face would improve the subjective experience of handover. While we observe a trend suggesting that the robot's gaze directed at the face improves the subjective experience of handover, it appears that the shared attention gaze cues the handover timing instead of the mutual, turn-taking gaze. It may be that the mutual gaze we implemented served the function of acknowledgement rather than our intended function of turn-taking. We suspect that qualitative differences in participants' reaction may exist between the Shared Attention and Turn-Taking conditions. For example, participants may have started to respond to the robot's shared attention gaze in both conditions but, prior to being detected by our reach sensor, saw the robot's turn-taking gaze and stopped to make eye contact before continuing to reach across the table.

This raises unexplored questions about how participant's *reach time* is affected by the timing of the robot's gaze. How much would varying the robot's gaze timing affect human *reach time*? Is the timing of the robot's gaze a more dominant cue than the location the robot is gazing at? That is, would a robot that shifts its gaze from the object directly to the person's face during handovers have the same effect as the Shared Attention condition? Would we see changes in participants' reach direction if the robot gazed at a different location? Without a thorough qualitative analysis, it is difficult to tell, with accuracy, if and when shared attention is established with the participant. A separate experiment with a gaze tracking device would help answer these questions, but this is beyond the scope of this study.

It is important to note that our results may be representative of naïve participants only, where novelty effects may have motivated them to observe the robot more carefully than they would if they were more familiar with the robot. Unsurprisingly, we observed a significant training effect in our *reach time* data, as well as a bias toward describing the second handover experience more favourably in our questionnaire regardless of the condition experienced. Some of the participants' comments suggest that in certain cases, people did not pay attention to the head of the robot at all. Indeed, we suspect that in many human-human handover scenarios, especially those that are repetitive or trained, people do not use gaze cues at all yet succeed in object handover. Thus robot gaze cues may not have the same effect on trained or familiarized users.

Although the earlier *reach time* of participants in a handover may seem more similar to natural, unscripted human-human handovers, this may not necessarily be desired in some human-robot handover situations. Depending on the handover controller implemented on a robot, handover timing may need to be controlled such that people naturally grab the object only when it is safe to do so. Many of the handover controllers that modulate the release time of the object are built for cases where the robot's gripper is already at the handover location before people grab the object. A situation where the object is grabbed before the robot is ready to release the object could lead people to pull hard on the object, possibly damaging or dropping the object, or resulting in a negative perception of the robot.

7. CONCLUSION and FUTURE WORK

In this paper, we demonstrated how a robot's humanlike use of gaze expressions in human-robot handover can affect the timing of the handover event. Once the intention to handover is established, providing a gaze cue to the projected handover location seems to offer rich gestural information about the handover event, and allows users to reach for the proffered object sooner, even before the robot arrives at the location. Our results also suggest that users may tend to prefer eye-contact gaze in addition to the locational, shared attention gaze. Part of our future work will further explore this trend.

8. ACKNOWLEDGMENTS

This study was approved by the University of British Columbia Behavioural Research Ethics Board. We are grateful to the following individuals who provided technical support and assistance throughout this project: Bikram Adhikari, Fernando Ramirez, Lars Bollmann, Katelyn Currie, Jake Rose, and Junaed Sattar. Financial support for this research was provided by the Natural Sciences and Engineering Research Council of Canada, the Canada Foundation for Innovation, and the University of British Columbia Institute for Computing, Information and Cognitive Systems.

9. REFERENCES

[1] Atienza, R., and Zelinsky., A. Intuitive human-robot interaction through active 3D gaze tracking. in *11th Int. Symp. on Robotics Research*, (Siena, Italy, 2003), 172–181.

[2] Argyle, M., and Dean, J. Eye-contact, distance and affiliation. *Sociometry*, *28*(3). 289-304.

[3] Argyle, M., Ingham, R., Alkema, F., and McCallin, M. The different functions of gaze. *Semiotica*, *7*(1). 19-32.

[4] Argyle, M., and Cook, M. *Gaze and mutual gaze*. Cambridge Universtiy Press, Cambridge, UK, 1976.

[5] Basili, P., Huber, M., Brandt, T., Hirche, S., and Glasauer, S. Investigating human-human approach and hand-over. In Dillmann, R., Vernon, D., Nakamura, Y., Schaal, S., Ritter, H., Sagerer, G., Dillmann R., and Buss, M., ed. *Human Centered Robot Systems*, volume 6 of *Cognitive Systems Monographs*, Springer Berlin Heidelberg, 2009, 151-160. DOI= 10.1007/978-3-642-10403-9_16

[6] Bennewitz, M., Faber, F., Joho, D., Schreiber, M., and Behnke, S. Towards a humanoid museum guide robot that interacts with multiple persons. in *5th Int. Conf. on Humanoid Robots*, (Tsukuba, Japan, 2005), IEEE/RAS, 418–423. DOI=10.1109/ICHR.2005.1573537

[7] Butterworth, G. The ontogeny and phylogeny of joint visual attention. In Whiten, A., ed. *Natural theories of mind: Evolution, development, and simulation of everyday mindreading*, Basil Blackwell, 1991, 223-232.

[8] Cakmak, M., Srinivasa, S.S., Lee, M. K., Kiesler, S., and Forlizzi, J. Using spatial and temporal contrast for fluent robot-human hand-overs. in *6th Int. Conf. on Human-Robot Interaction*, (Lausanne, Switzerland, 2011), ACM/IEEE, 489-496.

[9] Cakmak, M., Srinivasa, S.S., Forlizzi, J., and Kiesler, S. Human preferences for robot-human hand-over configurations. in *Int. Conf. on Intelligent Robots and Systems*, (San Francisco, CA, 2011), IEEE, 1986–1993. DOI= 10.1109/IROS.2011.6094735

[10] Calisgan, E., Haddadi, A., Van der Loos, H.F.M., Alcazar, J.A., and Croft, E. A. Identifying nonverbal cues for automated human-robot turn-taking. in *21st Int. Symp. on Robot and Human Interactive Commun.* (Paris, France, 2012), IEEE, 418–423. DOI= 10.1109/ROMAN.2012.6343788

[11] Chan, W.P., Parker, C.A., Van der Loos, H.F.M., and Croft, E.A. A human-inspired object handover controller. Int *J Robotics Res*, *32*(8), 971–983.

[12] Dehais, F., Sisbot, E.A., Alami, R., and Causse, M. Physiological and subjective evaluation of a human-robot object hand-over task. *Applied Ergonomics*, *42*(6), 785–91. DOI= 10.1016/j.apergo.2010.12.005

[13] Durbin, J. Incomplete blocks in ranking experiments. *British J. of Mathematical and Statistical Psychology*, *4*(2), 85–90.

[14] Erden, M.S., Leblebicioğlu, K., and Halici, U. Multi-agent system-based fuzzy controller design with genetic tuning for a mobile manipulator robot in the hand over task. *Journal of Intelligent and Robotic Systems*, *39*(3), 287–306. DOI= 10.1023/B:JINT.0000021039.56110.c8

[15] Häring, M., Eichberg, J., and André, E. Studies on grounding with gaze and pointing gestures in human-robot-interaction. in *4th Int. Conf. on Social Robotics*, (Chengdu, China, 2012), Springer, 378-387. DOI= 10.1007/978-3-642-34103-8_38

[16] Hayes-Roth, B. A blackboard architecture for control. *Artificial Intelligence*, *26*(3), 251–321.

[17] Huber, M., Rickert, M., Knoll, A., Brandt, T., and Glasauer, S. Human-robot interaction in handing-over tasks. in *17th Int. Symp. on Robot and Human Interactive Commun.*, (Munich, Germany, 2008), IEEE, 107–112.

[18] Huber, M., Radrich, H., Wendt, C., Rickert, M., Knoll, A., Brandt, T., and Glasauer, S. Evaluation of a novel biologically inspired trajectory generator in human-robot interaction. in *18th Int. Symp. on Robot and Human Interactive Commun.*, (Toyama, Japan, 2009), IEEE, 639–644. DOI= 10.1109/ROMAN.2009.5326233

[19] Imai, M., Kanda, T., Ono, T., Ishiguro, H., and Mase, K. Robot mediated round table: Analysis of the effect of robot's gaze. in *11th Int. Workshop on Robot and Human Interactive Commun.*, (Berlin, Germany, 2002) IEEE, 411-416.

[20] Imai, M., Ono, T., and Ishiguro, H. Physical relation and expression: Joint attention for human-robot interaction. *IEEE Transactions on Industrial Electronics, 50*(4). 636–643.

[21] Kajikawa, S., Okino, T., Ohba, K., and Inooka, H. Motion planning for hand-over between human and robot. in *Int. Conf. on Intelligent Robots and Systems,* (Pittsburgh, PA, 1995), IEEE/RSJ, 193-199.

[22] Kirchner, N., Alempijevic, A., and Dissanayake, G. Nonverbal robot-group interaction using an imitated gaze cue. in *6th Int. Conf. on Human-robot Interaction*, (Lausanne, Switzerland, 2011), ACM/IEEE, 497-504.

[23] Koay, K.L., and Sisbot, E.A. Exploratory study of a robot approaching a person in the context of handing over an object. In *Spring Symp. on Multidisciplinary Collaboration for Socially Assistive Robotics*, (2007), AAAI Press, 18-24.

[24] Kleinke, C. Gaze and eye contact: a research review. *Psychological Bulletin*, *100*(1), 78-100.

[25] Kuno, Y., Sadazuka, K., Kawashima, M., Yamazaki, K., Yamazaki, A., and Kuzuoka, H. Museum guide robot based on sociological interaction analysis. in *SIGCHI Conf. on Human factors in Computing Systems*, (San Jose, CA, 2007), ACM, 1191-1194. DOI= 10.1145/1240624.1240804

[26] Lee, M.K., Forlizzi, J., Kiesler, S., Cakmak, M., and Srinivasa, S. Predictability or adaptivity?: Designing robot handoffs modeled from trained dogs and people. in *6th Int. Conf. on Human-robot Interaction*, (Lausanne, Switzerland, 2011), ACM/IEEE, 179-180.

[27] Liu, C., Ishi, C.T., Ishiguro, H., and Hagita, N. Generation of nodding, head tilting and eye gazing for human-robot dialogue interaction. in *7th Int. Conf. on Human-Robot Interaction*, (Boston, MA, 2012), ACM/IEEE, 285-292.

[28] Mainprice, J., Gharbi, M., Simeon, T., and Alami, R. Sharing effort in planning human-robot handover tasks. in *21st Int. Symp. on Robot and Human Interactive Commun.*, (Paris, France, 2012), IEEE, 764–770.

[29] Matsusaka, Y., Fujie, S., and Kobayashi, T. Modeling of conversational strategy for the robot participating in the group conversation. in *7th European Conf. on Speech Commun. and Technology*, (2001), 2173-2176.

[30] Mutlu, B., Forlizzi, J., and Hodgins, J. A storytelling robot: Modeling and evaluation of human-like gaze behavior. in *6th Int. Conf. on Humanoid Robots*, (Genova, Italy, 2006), IEEE/RAS, 518–523. DOI= 10.1109/ICHR.2006.321322

[31] Mutlu, B. *Designing gaze behavior for humanlike robots*. Carnegia Mellon University, Pittsburgh, PA, 2009.

[32] Mutlu, B., Shiwa, T., and Kanda, T. Footing in human-robot conversations: how robots might shape participant roles using gaze cues. in *4th Int. Conf. on Human-Robot Interaction*, (San Diego, CA, 2009), ACM/IEEE, 61–68.

[33] Patterson, M. L. A sequential functional model of nonverbal exchange. *Psychological Review*, *89*(3), 231-249.

[34] Rich,C., Ponsler, B., Holroyd, A., and Sidner, C.L. Recognizing engagement in human-robot interaction. in *5th Int. Conf. on Human-Robot Interaction*, (Osaka, Japan, 2010), ACM/IEEE, 375–382. DOI= 10.1109/HRI.2010.5453163

[35] ROS.org. Retrieved Sepember 8, 2013, http://wiki.ros.org.

[36] Sidner, C.L., Lee, C., Kidd, C.D., Lesh, N., and Rich, C. Explorations in engagement for humans and robots. *Artificial Intelligence*, *166*(1), 140-164.

[37] Skantze, G., Hjalmarsson, A., and Oertel, C. Exploring the effects of gaze and pauses in situated human-robot interaction. in *SIGdial Meeting on Discourse and Dialogue*, (2013), Association for Computational Linguistics, 163–172.

[38] Staudte , M., and Crocker, M. The utility of gaze in spoken human-robot interaction. in *Workshop on Metrics for Human-Robot Interaction*, (2008), 53-59.

[39] Strabala, K.W., Lee, M.K., Dragan, A., Forlizzi, J., and Srinivasa, S.S. Learning the communication of intent prior to physical collaboration. in *Int. Symp. on Robot and Human Interactive Commun.*, (Paris, France, 2012), IEEE, 968–973.

[40] Strabala, K.W., Lee, M.K., Dragan, A.D., Forlizzi, J.L., Srinivasa, S., Cakmak, M., and Micelli, V. Towards seamless human-robot handovers. *Journal of Human-Robot Interaction*, *2*(1), 112–132.

[41] Von Cranach, M., and Ellgring, J. H. The perception of looking behaviour. *Social Commun. and Movement*, London: Academic Press, 1973.

[42] Vertegaal, R., and Ding, Y. Explaining effects of eye gaze on mediated group conversations: amount or synchronization?. in *Conf. on Computer Supported Cooperative Work*, (New Orleans, LA, 2002), ACM, 278–285.

Robot Deictics: How Gesture and Context Shape Referential Communication

Allison Sauppé and Bilge Mutlu
Department of Computer Sciences, University of Wisconsin–Madison
1210 West Dayton Street, Madison, WI 53706 USA
asauppe@cs.wisc.edu, bilge@cs.wisc.edu

ABSTRACT

As robots collaborate with humans in increasingly diverse environments, they will need to effectively refer to objects of joint interest and adapt their references to various physical, environmental, and task conditions. Humans use a broad range of *deictic gestures*—gestures that direct attention to collocated objects, persons, or spaces—that include pointing, touching, and exhibiting to help their listeners understand their references. These gestures offer varying levels of support under different conditions, making some gestures more or less suitable for different settings. While these gestures offer a rich space for designing communicative behaviors for robots, a better understanding of how different deictic gestures affect communication under different conditions is critical for achieving effective human-robot interaction. In this paper, we seek to build such an understanding by implementing six deictic gestures on a humanlike robot and evaluating their communicative effectiveness in six diverse settings that represent physical, environmental, and task conditions under which robots are expected to employ deictic communication. Our results show that gestures which come into physical contact with the object offer the highest overall communicative accuracy and that specific settings benefit from the use of particular types of gestures. Our results highlight the rich design space for deictic gestures and inform how robots might adapt their gestures to the specific physical, environmental, and task conditions.

Categories and Subject Descriptors

H.1.2 [**Models and Principles**]: User/Machine Systems—*human factors, software psychology*; H.5.2 [**Information Interfaces and Presentation**]: User Interfaces—*evaluation/ methodology, user-centered design*

General Terms

Design, Human Factors

1. INTRODUCTION

As robots begin to assist humans in increasingly diverse environments and tasks, communication will become one challenge robots will face in working with their human partners. Uncontrollable and unpredictable environmental effects, such as noise, lighting, and visual obstructions, will require robots to adapt their gestures to effectively refer to objects of joint interest despite these distractions [19]. Even in an environment where such distractions are absent, gestures are still desirable channels of communication, as they can be used to augment or replace complex verbal descriptions [9, 20].

HRI'14, March 3–6, 2014, Bielefeld, Germany.

ACM 978-1-4503-2658-2/14/03 ...$15.00.
http://dx.doi.org/10.1145/2559636.2559657.

Figure 1: Examples of human deictic gestures *touching* and *exhibiting* and their equivalent implementations on the NAO robot.

Non-verbal behaviors provide valuable information when combined with partially articulated speech, enabling humans to use a combination of pronouns and gestures to communicate information [8]. Those gestures which rely on knowledge of the environment to provide context for their interpretation—such as pointing, presenting, and exhibiting—are referred to as *deictic gestures* [8]. While deictic gestures are often referred to as "pointing gestures", this term encompasses a larger range of hand gestures beyond pointing [7]. For example, in infant-caretaker relations, humans might use touching instead of pointing to more concretely refer an object to an infant [17]. Similarly, instructors might hold up a piece they are asking their student to find [7]. Clark's work highlighted a number of deictic gestures used in human interaction and how they might be used in conjunction with speech to achieve communicative goals [7]. Not only do each of these gestures take a form other than pointing, but each is chosen to accommodate the setting—a particular environmental context that could affect verbal communication—and communicative goals of the participants [7, 17].

Robot behavior designers have recognized the importance of deictic gestures for robots, implementing robots that point while giving directions [24], achieving common spatial ground [5], and directing the sorting of items [25]. While pointing is a common deictic gesture that is implemented on robots [4, 28], a model encompassing the full range of deictic gestures available for robots has yet to be developed. Even in human interaction literature, whether gestures are chosen based on a particular setting and why they might be preferred to pointing is suggested in prior work for some gestures [7, 17], but is unknown across many gestures. An understanding of which deictic gestures are best suited for a given setting will allow robots to become more effective communicators not only in their mimicking of human choices of gesture, but also in completing or replacing utterances when bringing attention to objects of joint interest [9, 20], which could be useful in particular settings.

To further understand this design space for robot deictics, we designed a study of human deictic gestures in a variety of settings. Using a combination of gestures and settings collected from literature, we implemented six gestures—pointing, presenting, exhibiting, touching, grouping, and sweeping—for six settings on a NAO robot, which were contextualized in a wooden block identification task. Examples of human deictic gestures and their implementation on a robot can be seen in Figure 1. For each gesture-setting combination, the participant identified the blocks referred to and evaluated the robot's gesture in regards to how humanlike and effective it was. From our results, we provide recommendations for gestures for each setting, as well as speculate on which properties of gestures can help predict their effectiveness in helping the listener identify the object.

2. BACKGROUND

Humans frequently employ deictic gestures during tasks to augment or replace their speech, particularly when their current setting requires carefully choosing a gesture to use. We review prior work on human deictic gestures and why specific gestures might be used in a particular setting. Additionally, we discuss current work concerning the implementation of deictic gestures on robots.

2.1. Human Deictic Gestures

Deictic gestures are often used to augment or replace verbal descriptions of the object being referred to, also called the *referent* [16]. The importance of deictic gestures in communication is shown in pre-verbal children, who will use deictic gestures as a way of communicating with their caretakers prior to their ability to form utterances to describe their wants and needs [6]. Once humans have the ability to verbally communicate, the use of deictic gestures increases and becomes more nuanced, serving to support more complex utterances [13]. At this point, deictic gestures are used to decrease cognitive burden, allowing for complex verbal descriptors to be eliminated in favor of a deictic gesture toward the referent [9]. The replacement of fully articulated speech with a combination of partially articulated speech and deictic gestures reduces cognitive load for the speaker, by requiring less processing to form an utterance, and the listener, by requiring less processing to interpret the utterance. For example, a speaker might replace the description of an object with "this" and a deictic gesture that indicates the referent. Gestures might even fully replace utterances in settings such as a noisy factory environment [10].

Traditionally thought of as "pointing gestures", deictic gestures are comprised of a more diverse set of gestures that are used to draw attention to an object. Caretakers often use touch to more concretely focus the attention of infants on an object [17], while students or instructors in an instructional block building task might hold up a piece to implicitly confirm whether it's correct [7]. Prior research has demonstrated that the speaker's use of gestures affects information recall and rapport in listeners [4, 12].

Work by Clark demonstrated that deictic gestures are much broader than pointing [7]. However, while the use of these additional deictic gestures has been mentioned in relation to other research [1, 3, 7, 17], a more thorough understanding of the breadth of deictic gestures and why they are chosen for particular settings is needed.

2.2. Robots and Deictic Gestures

Prior work in human-robot interaction recognizes the need for robots to gesture naturally in order to communicate in a more humanlike fashion. Much of this work has focused on enabling robots to use deictic gestures to enhance task outcomes, such as the robot's use of gestures improving user performance in manipulation tasks [4, 24, 25]. In general, robots use deictic gestures similarly to humans to help bring attention to objects of joint interest and achieve common spatial ground [5]. When the environment may make using deictic gestures difficult or impossible, robots are also able to use perspective-taking to ensure that their deictic gestures are used in ways that are interpretable by the listener [29]. To ensure gestures are used appropriately, research has focused on enabling robots to use pointing gestures in socially appropriate ways [18].

Deictics are often thought of as referring to an object, but can also be used to refer to a region of space, such as the opposite end of a room. Prior work in robot deictics has shown that referring to a region of space—which is often more difficult to verbalize than an object—results in only a marginally worse accuracy rate than referring to an object [27]. Robots are able to use visual differences in spaces in combination with deictics to help listeners identify the correct region in the space [11]. St. Clair et al. demonstrated that a robot using a combination of deictic gestures and gaze to refer to a space resulted in higher accuracy than using just one modality [27]. Additionally, how the gesture was implemented and executed was significant, with human pointing using a bent arm producing significantly worse accuracy than pointing with a straight arm.

Although HRI research has successfully implemented human pointing behaviors in numerous applications, there is still much to understand about what other deictic gestures robot behavior designers should consider using, what properties are most effective, and how the particular setting should shape gesture choice.

3. UNDERSTANDING DEICTIC GESTURES AND SETTINGS

Understanding both the types of deictic gestures available to robots and the settings in which they may be appropriate is necessary for a comprehensive study of the interplay between setting, communicative goals, and gesture choice. In this section, we describe six gestures and six settings that robots are envisioned to encounter and that might effect gesture choice.

3.1. Deictics

We describe six deictic gestures that we focus on in this work: pointing, presenting, touching, exhibiting, sweeping, and grouping. These gestures combine results from prior work to inform our understanding. Examples of each gesture can be seen in Figure 2.

Pointing – Pointing is often considered the prototypical deictic gesture, being universally understood across cultures [15], ages [23], and even species [21]. A pointing gesture uses an extended index finger with the hand rotated so that the palm faces toward or perpendicular to the ground to direct attention. The hand does not come into physical contact with the referent. A pointing referent may be a single object, a region of space, or no specific object or region [20]. Prior work has already explored implementing human pointing gestures on robots, revealing that pointing gestures which point away from the body, rather than across the body, are more accurate at communicating the referent [27].

Presenting – Presenting uses a similar style to pointing in that the speaker gestures toward the referent without coming into contact. However, where as pointing leaves only the index finger extended, presenting extends all fingers and points the palm of the hand upwards. This gesture is often interpreted as inviting, encouraging

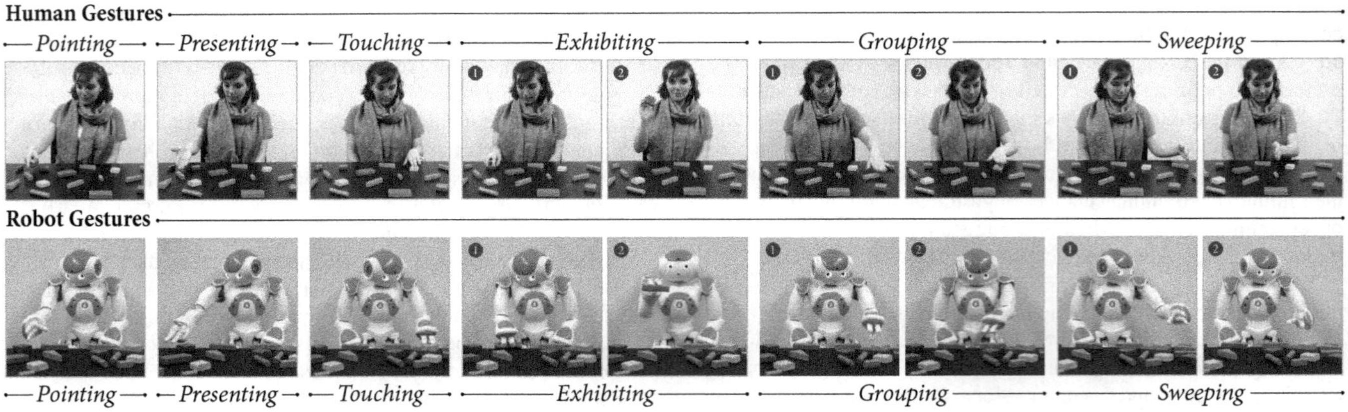

Figure 2: Instances of a human performer and the NAO robot demonstrating the deictic gestures studied in this work.

the listener to, for example, pick up the referent [3, 14]. Presenting gestures are also used by speakers to indicate that they are ready to receive an object that they previously requested [3].

Touching – Touching is used in similar settings as pointing and presenting; however, touching removes ambiguity in that the speaker's hand comes into direct physical contact with the referent. This absence of ambiguity makes touching ideal in situations where verbal communication is absent or impaired. For example, touching seems to be a preferred deictic gesture for mothers communicating with non-verbal infants, since verbal capabilities are required for understanding pointing gestures [17]. Touching may also be a preferred deictic gesture in a factory or on a noisy shop floor. Touching may also be used to refer to an object in situations where constructing an accurate verbal description to augment a pointing gesture is difficult. For example, it may be difficult to verbally differentiate between or provide an accurate pointing gesture for similar objects in close proximity to one another. Additionally, if certain properties of an object cannot be described concisely, touching the object may be more cost-effective than attempting to describe the object.

Exhibiting – Exhibiting is a natural extension of touching where the object is grasped and lifted so that it can be observed by others [7]. This gesture might be used when joint attention is obstructed due to referent location, making other gestures unusable. For example, objects concealed by other objects may prevent the listener from seeing the object, requiring an exhibiting gesture.

Grouping – Grouping offers a gesture similar to presenting in that the fingers are extended with the palm facing down. Instead of referring to a single block, however, grouping takes advantage of the larger area covered by the hand to reference those objects located underneath the hand. The speaker may use a circular hand motion—still in the grouping gesture—around the area they wish to indicate in cases where an area instead of an object is the referent. This gesture has also been implemented in interactive tabletop and wall touchscreen displays to highlight a group of objects [30].

Sweeping – Similar to grouping, sweeping references one or more objects in a given area. A speaker utilizing sweeping will place their hand, with fingers extended, perpendicular to and above the surface to indicate a beginning boundary for referenced objects. The gesture then sweeps across additional referenced objects [1].

3.2. Settings

While humans employ a variety of deictic gestures to direct attention to an object, each gesture has unique functional properties that might diminish its effectiveness in some settings. As robots start working alongside humans, it is expected that they will encounter similar settings as humans. In this section, we describe six settings that we believe can impact which gestures a robot should choose.

Distance from Referrer – The accuracy of a gesture may diminish when the distance between referrer and referent is larger, as listeners may make greater interpolations regarding where the speaker's hand is gesturing. In extremes, objects are located immediately in front of or substantially far away (e.g., the opposite end of a table) from the referrer. While some robots might be capable of reaching locations that would not be available to humans, there will always be situations where the robot will need to reference a distant referent.

Clustered Objects – Varied amounts of space exist between objects laid out on a table. This can vary from objects clustered together very closely to objects spread far apart. This setting also mimics the possibility of having one versus many objects, with one object effectively obtained by spreading objects far apart.

Noise – Many environments in which robots are expected to work, such as warehouses and assembly lines, can be noisy. Since deictic gestures are often accompanied by speech that can elaborate on the purpose of the gesture, noise might make some gestures more difficult to understand.

No Visibility – Often times, objects to which the robot wishes to draw attention may be in the referrer's line of sight but may not be visible to the listener. For example, objects may be located in a container or behind a structure or object. In these cases, deictic gesturing may indicate to the listener that some object in the general area of the gesture is located outside their line of sight.

Ambiguity – During assembly tasks, pieces which initially look similar may differ in small ways, such as screws that have slightly different lengths and widths. These pieces may be difficult to differentiate verbally due to these subtle differences. Lack of adequate vocabulary may also hinder verbal differentiation and may also place significant cognitive burden on both the speaker and the listener.

Neutral – Those cases where there may not be any environmental factors affecting communication results in a neutral setting. Here, a diverse set of objects is nearby the referent with ample space between each object and in clear view of all involved parties.

These settings serve as a representative sample of the situations robots are expected to encounter, particularly in joint tasks with humans, making them appropriate contextualizations for better understanding how the affects of gestures change across settings.

4. IMPLEMENTATION

We chose to contextualize our implementation in an object referencing task, where the robot would refer to one or more wooden building blocks distributed on a workspace. The use of wooden building blocks in this task was inspired by Shah et al. [26]. In the context of our wooden building block task, we created two workspaces of blocks to accommodate our six settings and designed each of the gestures in every setting.

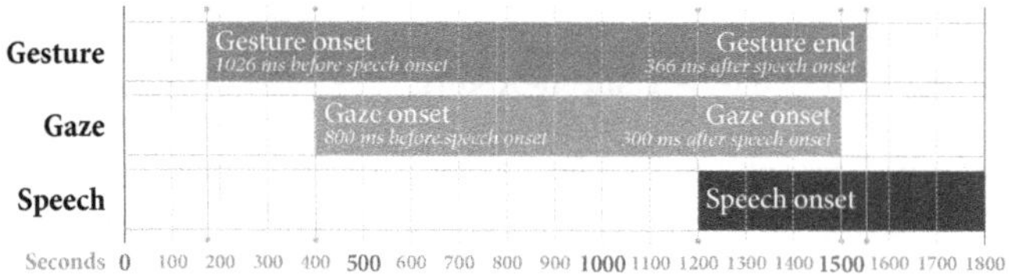

Figure 3: A model of the gesture-contingent gaze behavior implemented in our study. Start and end times are relative to the onset of speech.

4.1. Gesture Design

We implemented our behaviors on the NAO robot. The NAO features six degrees of freedom in each arm: shoulder pitch, should roll, elbow yaw, elbow roll, wrist yaw, and finger pitch. The technical capabilities of the NAO enabled us to create accurate reproductions of each gesture in a variety of settings. We implemented the gestures on the NAO through *puppeteering*, a technique in which a designer manually guides the robot in executing a gesture while a motion capture program saves joint positions at each keyframe. These keyframes are later used to generate arm-motion trajectories. We puppeteered each gesture and manually edited the resulting motion profile as necessary in Choregraphe, a behavior authoring environment for the NAO. The gesture profiles were then saved on the robot to be executed by our experiment software.

As gaze is an integral part of a natural gesture, we implemented gesture-contingent gaze behavior as described in Huang & Mutlu [12] for all of our gestures (see Figure 3). The gaze trajectory followed the robot's hand as it gestured to the block for all gestures.

4.2. Workspace Design

We designed a layout of wooden blocks for six settings that we divided onto two workspaces, which can be seen in Figure 4. Each workspace contained two sets of blocks, with one set on the left half of the workspace, and the second set on the right half. The first workspace displayed the ambiguity and no visibility settings, and the second workspace displayed the neutral, distant from referrer, clustered objects, and noise settings. The following are the descriptions of each setting from the robot's point of view:

- *Neutral*: An assortment of blocks arranged near the referrer. Blocks were spaced 1.5 to 2 in. (3.8 cm to 5.1 cm) from nearby blocks.
- *Distance from Referrer*: An assortment of blocks arranged far from the referent. Blocks were spaced 1.5 to 2 in. (3.8 cm to 5.1 cm) apart, and all blocks were at least 6.5 in. (16.5 cm) from the referrer.
- *Clustered Objects*: An assortment of blocks near the referrer. Blocks were spaced .5 in. (1.3 cm) from nearby blocks.
- *Noise*: Identical to the neutral setting, but with white noise of people talking loudly played from a nearby speaker.
- *No Visibility*: An assortment of blocks placed behind a 3.5 in. (8.9 cm) partition.
- *Ambiguity*: Blocks which were similar in color, length and shape were arranged near the referrer. Blocks were spaced 1.5 to 2 in. (3.8 cm to 5.1 cm) from nearby blocks.

Figure 4: The two workspaces used to represent the six settings we explored. The left workspace displays the ambiguity (left) and the no visibility (right) settings. The right workspace displays the clustered objects setting (left), the distant from referrer setting (top right), and the neutral setting (bottom right), which was used for both the neutral and noise settings.

5. EVALUATION

To explore the effectiveness of gestures in different settings, we used the workspaces from our wooden blocks task to conduct a within-participants study of all gesture-setting combinations. For each condition, participants identified the blocks they believed the robot was referring to and rated the gesture on a number of items. Our results indicate that setting has an impact on gesture.

5.1. Study Design

To better understand the effects of gesture choice and setting on referential communication, we designed a within-participants study to explore every feasible combination of the gesture and setting factors described previously. In addition to the six gestures mentioned, we included two verbal-only baselines in our gesture factor. The first baseline involves the use of only *minimally articulated* verbal references that the robot uses in conjunction with gestures, such as "this block." This baseline follows results from Shah et al. [26], which showed that participants in a collaborative block building task often used generic referential statements in conjunction with gestures to bring attention to a block. The second baseline involves the use of *fully articulated*, descriptive speech to provide a complete description of the block to which the robot is referring, such as "the short green cylinder closest to you." Whereas the first baseline shows the outcome of eliminating gestures, this second baseline demonstrates the consequences of the robot engaging only in verbal communication. Since we designed gaze cues specifically for the gesture they accompanied, we eliminated gaze from our baselines.

In total, the combination of eight forms of communication (six gestures and two verbal baselines) and six settings resulted in 48 conditions. We eliminated two conditions—touching and exhibiting blocks at a distance—due to the physical impossibility of contact with these blocks, resulting in 46 conditions used in the study.

5.2. Task

Participants were asked to observe the robot as it referenced blocks situated on a table between the participant and robot. The participant observed 46 rounds of references made by the robot, where each round was one of the 46 conditions previously outlined. Rounds were broken down into two sets to allow for all of the settings to be displayed. The first set consisted of 30 rounds (neutral, distant from referrer, clustered objects, and noise settings) and the second of 16 rounds (no visibility and ambiguity settings). The order in which participants observed the two sets was balanced across participants, while the rounds within each set were randomly ordered. Additionally, to account for possible participant biases between the left and right arms, workspaces were flipped along the vertical axis for half of the participants. All possible presentations of the workspace were gender balanced. After the robot completed the action for a given round, the participant rated the robot's behavior on both objective and subjective scales on a one page questionnaire.

The experimental setup is shown in Figure 5. Participants were seated 2.5 feet (76.2 cm) away from the robot, with the workspace between them. The participant's questionnaires were placed between the participant and the workspace. A small speaker was placed next to the robot (out of view of the participant) to emit background noise of people talking during any conditions which involved noise.

5.3. Procedure

Following informed consent, participants were seated in the experiment room. The experimenter explained the task to the participant, started the robot, and left the room. The robot initiated the interaction by giving an introduction, followed by starting the first round. During each round, the robot would choose one of the gesture and setting combinations to exhibit according to which set of settings

Figure 5: A participant evaluating the robot touching the blue block.

was currently available. The robot would then perform the action associated with the particular combination. Upon completion of the robot's action, the participant would complete the questionnaire.

The top half of the questionnaire showed a picture of the workspace currently being used, where the participant would individually circle all blocks they believed the robot had referred to. On the bottom half of the questionnaire were six seven-point rating items to measure the naturalness of the robot's gesture in that setting. When the participant was satisfied with their answers to the questionnaire, they would say "next" to advance the robot to the next round.

When the first workspace was completed, the experimenter would set up the second workspace and provide new questionnaires that reflected the new workspace layout. At the completion of both workspaces, participants were compensated $5 for their time. Participants took between 15 and 32 minutes to complete the task (M =23 minutes, 40 seconds, SD =3 minutes, 52.8 seconds).

5.4. Participants

We recruited 24 native English speakers (12 males, 12 females) with diverse majors and occupations and ages that ranged 18–46 ($M = 22.7$, $SD = 5.92$) from the University of Wisconsin–Madison.

5.5. Measures & Analysis

For each condition, participants completed a questionnaire in which they identified the blocks they believed the robot was referencing and answered six rating-scale questions on the robot's behavior. Participants identified blocks by circling referenced blocks on a picture of the workspace that was included on the questionnaire. As a measure of *accuracy*, we classified participant's identification of the blocks as either correct or incorrect based on whether the participant's answer exactly matched the blocks that the robot's gesture indicated, considering answers that were a superset or subset of the correct answer to be incorrect. Our subjective measures assessed the perceived qualities of the gesture in the given setting. From the six questions asked, we constructed the following two scales (half of the items were reversed to prevent response sets):

Perceived Effectiveness (Cronbach's $\alpha = .967$)

1. The robot used this gesture effectively.
2. The robot's gesture helped me to identify the object(s).
3. The robot's gesture was appropriate for the context.
4. The robot's gesture was easy to understand.

Naturalness (Cronbach's $\alpha = .790$)

1. The robot's gesture was humanlike.
2. The robot's gesture was fluid.

Data analysis involved a two-way analysis of variance (ANOVA), including gesture and setting as fixed effects. Tukey's honestly significant difference (HSD) test was used for pairwise comparisons.

5.6. Results

We discuss our most significant results below, first discussing gestures across all settings and then highlighting comparisons of gestures within each setting. Due to the large number of pairwise comparisons involved in our analysis, only Omnibus test results are reported in the paragraphs below, and pairwise comparisons are illustrated in Figures 6, 7, and 8.

5.6.1. Comparison of Gestures

A comparison of gestures across settings showed that gesture type had a significant effect on accuracy, $F(7,1073) = 112.06$, $p < .001$ (Figure 6). The fully descriptive baseline was significantly less accurate than exhibiting and pointing, but significantly more accurate than sweeping and grouping. Exhibiting, touching, presenting, and pointing were all significantly more accurate than sweeping and grouping. Consistent with the results on accuracy, gesture type had a significant effect on the perceived effectiveness of the gesture, $F(7,1073) = 134.37$, $p < .001$. Exhibiting and touching were perceived as significantly more effective than the fully articulate baseline and the presenting, pointing, sweeping, and grouping gestures. All gestures were found to be fairly natural, with average ratings between 5.5 and 6.5 out of 7.

5.6.2. Comparison of Gestures by Setting

The following presents results for gestures within each setting. Pairwise comparisons for measures of accuracy and perceived effectiveness are illustrated in Figures 7 and 8, respectively.

Neutral – Gesture type had a significant effect on accuracy in the neutral setting, $F(7,161) = 34.36$, $p < .001$. The fully articulate baseline, as well as the exhibiting, touching, presenting, pointing gestures, were all significantly more accurate in communicating the referent than sweeping and grouping were. Gesture type also had a significant affect on perceived effectiveness, $F(7,161) = 39.48$, $p < .001$. The fully articulate baseline and the exhibiting, touching, and presenting gestures were perceived as significantly more effective than pointing, sweeping, and grouping.

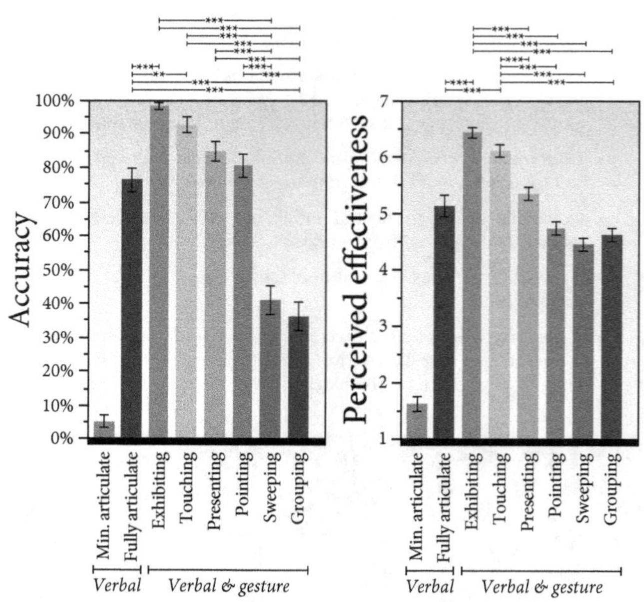

Figure 6: Results for both the accuracy of each gesture and the perceived effectiveness of each gesture across all settings. (***), (**) denotes $p < .001$, $p < .01$, respectively. Exhibiting and touching gestures were more accurate than the two baselines and the sweeping and grouping gestures and were perceived to be more effective than the two baselines and the other gestures.

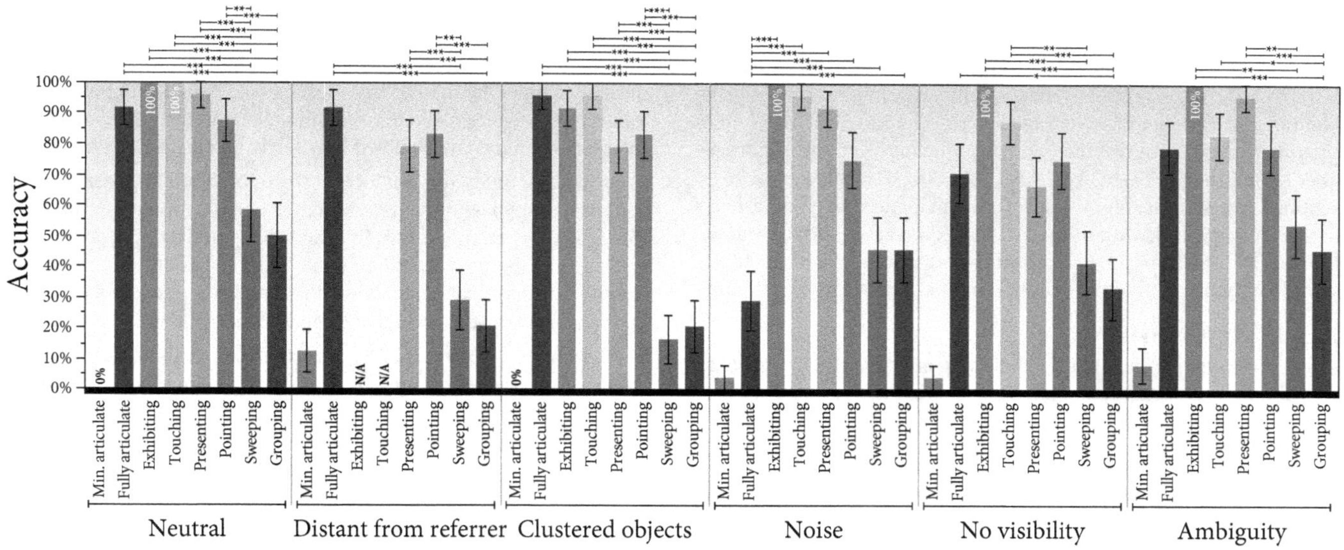

Figure 7: Results for the communicative accuracy of each gesture, displayed by setting. (***), (**), (*) denotes $p<.001$, $p<.01$, and $p<.05$, respectively. Exhibiting and touching were consistently more accurate than sweeping and grouping across the majority of settings.

Distant From Referrer – When referents were distant, gesture type had a significant effect on accuracy, $F(5,115)=21.73$, $p<.001$. The fully articulate baseline and the presenting and pointing gestures were all significantly more accurate than sweeping and grouping. Additionally, while the effectiveness of presenting and pointing fell by 16% and 5%, respectively, when compared to the neutral setting, sweeping and grouping observed greater losses of effectiveness at 27% and 30%, respectively. Gesture type also had a significant effect on perceived effectiveness in this setting, $F(5,115)=19.83$, $p<.001$. The fully articulate baseline was perceived as significantly more effective than presenting, sweeping, and grouping.

Clustered Objects – Gesture type had a significant effect on accuracy, $F(7,161)=43.26$, $p<.001$, when objects were clustered. The fully articulate baseline and the presenting and pointing gestures were all significantly more accurate than sweeping and grouping. Exhibiting, touching, presenting, and pointing were all slightly less accurate than in the neutral setting, losing 5% to 15% accuracy. Sweeping and grouping saw larger drops compared to the neutral setting, losing 48% and 30% accuracy respectively. Perceived effectiveness was significantly affected by gesture type, $F(7,161)=25.86$, $p<.001$. Exhibiting and touching both were perceived as significantly more effective than presenting, sweeping, and grouping.

Noise – Gesture type also had a significant effect on accuracy in the noise setting, $F(7,161)=22.49$, $p<.001$. The fully articulate baseline was significantly more accurate than exhibiting, touching, presenting and pointing. Exhibiting, touching, and presenting were all significantly more accurate than pointing, sweeping, and grouping. Gesture type also had a significant effect on perceived effectiveness, $F(7,161)=38.54$, $p<.001$. The fully articulate baseline was perceived as significantly less effective than every gesture. Additionally, exhibiting and touching were perceived as significantly more effective than pointing, sweeping, and grouping.

No Visibility – Gesture type had a significant effect on accuracy in the no visibility setting, $F(7,161)=15.86$, $p<.001$. Exhibiting and touching were both significantly more accurate than sweeping and grouping. Additionally, exhibiting was the only level to not experience a drop in accuracy compared to the neutral setting. Gestures type had a significant impact on perceived effectiveness,

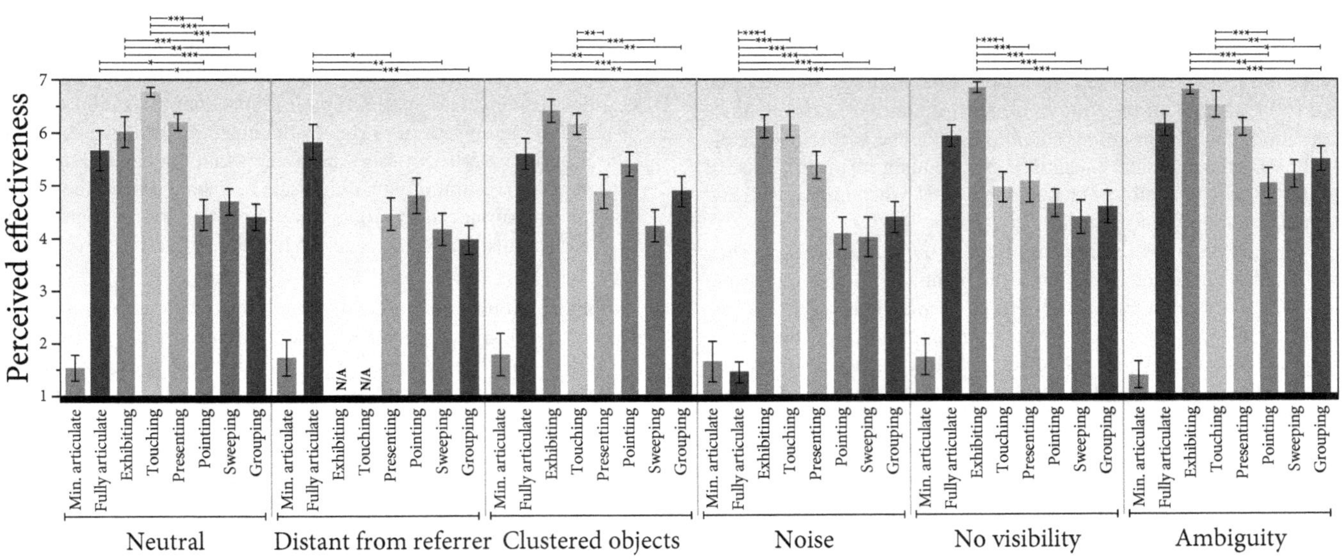

Figure 8: Results for the perceived effectiveness of each gesture, displayed by setting. (***), (**), (*) denote $p<.001$, $p<.01$, and $p<.05$, respectively. Exhibiting and touching were consistently perceived to be more effective than presenting, pointing, sweeping, and grouping across the majority of the settings.

$F(7,161) = 40.18$, $p < .001$. Exhibiting was perceived as significantly more effective than all other gestures. Additionally, the fully descriptive baseline was perceived as significantly more effective than pointing, sweeping, and grouping.

Ambiguity – Gesture type had a significant effect on accuracy under ambiguity, $F(7,161) = 15.52$, $p < .001$. Exhibiting and presenting were significantly more accurate than sweeping and grouping. Gesture type also significantly affected perceived effectiveness, $F(7,161) = 59.40$, $p < .001$. Exhibiting and touching were rated as significantly more effective than pointing, sweeping, and grouping.

6. DISCUSSION

Our results offer implications for designing effective deictic gestures for robots. The paragraphs below summarize the most important results and discusses these implications.

6.1. Properties of Effective Gestures

When the gestures were compared without consideration of context against the fully articulated baseline, our six gestures organized into three groupings: referencing one object with physical contact, referencing one object without physical contact, and referencing multiple objects, with these groupings doing significantly better than, equivalent to, or significantly worse than the fully articulated baseline, respectively. Gestures that involved physical contact with the objects (exhibiting and touching) provided the most effective communication, rarely causing the participant to choose the incorrect block; the effectiveness of physical touch was confirmed in many of our settings as well. This finding confirms prior research on human deictics that report that mothers choose to use physical touch to identify an object for their pre-verbal child due to the unambiguous nature of the gesture [17]. This behavior follows a failed attempt at pointing by the mother, leading her to try a more concrete gesture with a higher likelihood of success. These physical gestures alleviate the cognitive burden placed on those interpreting the gesture by eliminating uncertainty in the referent. Our findings suggest that, in settings or tasks that require precise identification of objects, physical contact with the object provides the best chance of the listener correctly identifying the referent.

6.2. Setting and Gesture Accuracy

Our study highlights instances in which the setting significantly affects the accuracy of gestures. Below, we discuss these results and their implications for designing robot behaviors.

Noise and Verbal Descriptions – Our fully articulated baseline had comparable performance to exhibiting, touching, pointing, and presenting in all levels except noise. Our findings showed that the fully articulated baseline performed much worse in the noise condition than in every other condition, while the accuracy of many of the gestures remained unchanged. This finding supports the use of gestures that come into contact with the object when fully articulated utterances are difficult to form.

Although the most prominent effect of the noise level was seen with the fully articulated baseline, even pointing and presenting were less effective than in the neutral setting, despite their perceived lack of reliance on utterances given the minimal information utterances included when coupled with gestures. While each type of gesture maintained a similar motion profile across conditions, making it easier for participants to learn what the gesture was communicating across repeated viewings, it may be that the simple utterances that the robot used helped the participant to distinguish whether the robot was referring to one or many objects. For example, although sweeping and pointing gestures appear similar when the arm is extended, they follow different trajectories, pointing aiming toward a specific object and sweeping covering an area. In addition, the pointing gesture is accompanied by the phrase "this block," clearly indicating that only one block is being referenced, while the sweeping gesture is accompanied by the phrase "these blocks," suggesting more than one block is being referenced. With noise obscuring these phrases, participants may have doubted how many blocks they should select.

While our study did not look at the interaction between gesture and the complexity of the utterance, the combination of our findings on the fully articulate baseline and the pointing and presenting gestures in the noise setting suggest that the robot attempting to clarify non-physical gestures with verbal descriptions—a common human behavior [8]—would not improve the accuracy of the gesture.

Gestures for Obstructed Objects – In the no visibility level, where some blocks were obscured by a partition, the number of correctly identified objects was significantly lower for many gestures compared to our fully articulated baseline. Only the exhibiting gesture maintained its effectiveness, since the robot grasped the object and exhibited it above the partition for the participant to clearly see. In real-world applications, the robot can take the perspective of its user [29] to determine whether a referent is obstructed and whether it is necessary to exhibit it for the listener.

Diminishing Effectiveness of Multiple Object Gestures – The gestures that referred to multiple objects were consistently less effective than other gestures and the fully articulated baseline. This result is likely a product of the greater ambiguity inherent in these gestures. Such ambiguity occasionally led participants to include objects in the set that were not intended to be referenced. Because our objective measure only counted the answers that were a perfect match to the intended blocks as correct, participants' answers which were a superset or subset of the intended blocks were incorrect. The robot might correct the participant's understanding of which blocks should be included by engaging in repair, such as providing clarifications, which may be considered less costly than precisely identifying the correct blocks the first time. Expecting the listener to process and react to many objects they are expected to identify and manipulate would likely result in high cognitive load, leading to greater frustration with the robot [22]. In the cases where identifying only the correct objects is imperative, the robot might use a gesture intended for one object multiple times.

In the *distant from referrer* and *clustered objects* settings, the low accuracy of gestures is compounded. We found that gestures referring to multiple objects were significantly less effective than gestures for a single object in both of these settings and required more precision than other settings did. Prior work provides support for this observation; when objects are distant, humans use pointing gestures to indicate a spatial region rather than a specific object, instead relying on speech to convey the object [2]. Likewise, when the robot finds itself working with objects that may be difficult for the listener to disambiguate, either due to distance from the robot or from other objects, the robot should rely on a combination of gesture accompanied with speech to help identify the referents.

Consistent Accuracy of Exhibiting and Touching – In five of the settings, exhibiting and touching maintained relatively consistent accuracy, almost always outperforming the remaining gestures and baselines. Only in the distant from referrer level were exhibiting and touching outperformed, and even then, this result was due to the physical impossibility of these gestures in that setting. These results seem to support the use of exhibiting and touching over pointing and presenting. However, while exhibiting and touching more consistently supported accurate identification of the referent, these gestures are more costly to execute, requiring the robot to physically lift and/or to relocate to be within physical touch of the object, which places limits on their use in real-world applications.

6.3. Limitations and Future Work

While we chose gestures and settings for our exploration based on a projection of what might best serve the design of robot behavior, there are other gestures and settings to explore. We did not explore how language, an integral part of deixis, influences the effectiveness of gestures in these settings. Preliminary work has explored some of the issues regarding the influence of language on gestures [19], but a more comprehensive exploration of this area is needed.

The choice of the robot might also have an impact on how gestures are interpreted, as robot platforms vary in their ability to reproduce human gestures. Through iterative design, we sought to design the robot's gestures to mimic human gestures as closely as possible in terms of the intended communication. While we chose to implement the gestures used in this study through puppeteering, a Wizard-of-Oz technique, we hope to develop a robust gesture synthesis system that enables robots to autonomously generate accurate deictic gestures.

In the study, the robot's references included only one gesture. However, communicating complex ideas might require the use of a sequence of gestures. Although we expect our findings to generalize to independent evaluations of each gesture in a sequence, further examination is necessary to conclusively understand how gestures used in a sequence affect referential communication.

7. CONCLUSION

Human collaborations involve the use of deictic gestures, allowing speakers to direct their collaborators' attention to objects in the environment while reducing cognitive load for themselves and their listeners. To function as competent collaborators, robots will need to use deictic gestures to effectively direct the attention of their users toward objects of joint interest. Drawing on literature on human communication, we designed a set of deictic gestures for the NAO robot and specified a set of settings that provided a diverse set of conditions in which humans and robots might engage in deictic communication. We conducted an exploratory human-robot interaction study that examined the communicative accuracy and perceived effectiveness of these gestures against two verbal baselines and how the setting of the communication affected these measures. The results suggest many design implications regarding the use of gestures in each setting, including what properties might make certain gestures more effective, the tradeoffs involved in referring to multiple objects, the effects of noise on verbal deictic references, and how gestures might function when objects are obscured. Our findings offer new research directions into deictic communication and design implications for human-robot collaboration.

8. ACKNOWLEDGMENTS

This research was supported by National Science Foundation award 1149970 and National Institutes of Health award 1R01HD071089-01A1. We thank Brandi Hefty, Jilana Boston, Jason Sauppé, Lindsay Jacobs, and Catherine Steffel for their help with our work.

9. REFERENCES

[1] M. W. Alibali, L. M. Flevares, and S. Goldin-Meadow. Assessing knowledge conveyed in gesture: Do teachers have the upper hand? *Journal of Educational Psychology*, 89(1):183, 1997.

[2] A. Bangerter. Using pointing and describing to achieve joint focus of attention in dialogue. *Psychological Science*, 15(6):415–419, 2004.

[3] D. Bolinger. Intonation and gesture. *American speech*, 58(2):156–174, 1983.

[4] C. Breazeal, C. D. Kidd, A. L. Thomaz, G. Hoffman, and M. Berlin. Effects of nonverbal communication on efficiency and robustness in human-robot teamwork. In *Proc. IROS 2005*, pages 708–713, 2005.

[5] A. G. Brooks and C. Breazeal. Working with robots and objects: Revisiting deictic reference for achieving spatial common ground. In *Proc. HRI 2006*, pages 297–304, 2006.

[6] M. C. Caselli. Communicative gestures and first words. In V. Volterra and C. Erting, editors, *From gesture to language in hearing and deaf children*, pages 56–67. Springer, 1990.

[7] H. H. Clark. Coordinating with each other in a material world. *Discourse studies*, 7(4-5):507–525, 2005.

[8] C. J. Fillmore. Towards a descriptive framework for spatial deixis. In R. Jarvella and W. Klein, editors, *Speech, Place and Action*, pages 31–59. John Wiley, 1982.

[9] S. Goldin-Meadow. The role of gesture in communication and thinking. *Trends in cognitive sciences*, 3(11):419–429, 1999.

[10] S. Harrison. The creation and implementation of a gesture code for factory communication. In *Proc. GESPIN 2011*, 2011.

[11] Y. Hato, S. Satake, T. Kanda, M. Imai, and N. Hagita. Pointing to space: modeling of deictic interaction referring to regions. In *Proc. HRI 2010*, pages 301–308, 2010.

[12] C.-M. Huang and B. Mutlu. Modeling and evaluating narrative gestures for humanlike robots. In *Proc. RSS 2013*, 2013.

[13] M. Jancovic, S. Devoe, and M. Wiener. Age-related changes in hand and arm movements as nonverbal communication: Some conceptualizations and an empirical exploration. *Child Development*, pages 922–928, 1975.

[14] A. Kendon. *Gesture: Visible action as utterance*. Cambridge U, 2004.

[15] S. Kita. Pointing: A foundational building block of human communication. *Pointing: Where Language, Culture, and Cognition Meet*, 1:1–8, 2003.

[16] A. Kobsa, J. Allgayer, C. Reddig, N. Reithinger, D. Schmauks, K. Harbusch, and W. Wahlster. Combining deictic gestures and natural language for referent identification. In *Proc. COLING 1986*, pages 356–361, 1986.

[17] J. D. Lempers. Young children's production and comprehension of nonverbal deictic behaviors. *The Journal of Genetic Psychology*, 135(1):93–102, 1979.

[18] P. Liu, D. F. Glas, T. Kanda, H. Ishiguro, and N. Hagita. It's not polite to point: generating socially-appropriate deictic behaviors towards people. In *Proc. HRI 2013*, pages 267–274, 2013.

[19] S. C. Lozano and B. Tversky. Communicative gestures facilitate problem solving for both communicators and recipients. *Journal of Memory and Language*, 55(1):47–63, 2006.

[20] D. McNeill. *Hand and mind: What gestures reveal about thought*. U Chicago, 1992.

[21] Á. Miklósi and K. Soproni. A comparative analysis of animals' understanding of the human pointing gesture. *Animal cognition*, 9(2):81–93, 2006.

[22] G. R. Morrison and G. J. Anglin. Research on cognitive load theory: Application to e-learning. *Educational Technology Research and Development*, 53(3):94–104, 2005.

[23] C. M. Murphy. Pointing in the context of a shared activity. *Child Development*, 49(2):371–380, 1978.

[24] Y. Okuno, T. Kanda, M. Imai, H. Ishiguro, and N. Hagita. Providing route directions: design of robot's utterance, gesture, and timing. In *Proc. HRI 2009*, pages 53–60, 2009.

[25] M. Salem, S. Kopp, I. Wachsmuth, K. Rohlfing, and F. Joublin. Generation and evaluation of communicative robot gesture. *International Journal of Social Robotics*, 4(2):201–217, 2012.

[26] J. Shah and C. Breazeal. An empirical analysis of team coordination behaviors and action planning with application to human–robot teaming. *Human Factors*, 52(2):234–245, 2010.

[27] A. St Clair, R. Mead, and M. J. Mataric. Investigating the effects of visual saliency on deictic gesture production by a humanoid robot. In *Proc. RO-MAN 2011*, pages 210–216, 2011.

[28] O. Sugiyama, T. Kanda, M. Imai, H. Ishiguro, and N. Hagita. Natural deictic communication with humanoid robots. In *Proc. IROS 2007*, pages 1441–1448, 2007.

[29] J. G. Trafton, N. L. Cassimatis, M. D. Bugajska, D. P. Brock, F. E. Mintz, and A. C. Schultz. Enabling effective human-robot interaction using perspective-taking in robots. *Systems, Man and Cybernetics, Part A: Systems and Humans*, 35(4):460–470, 2005.

[30] D. Vogel and R. Balakrishnan. Interactive public ambient displays: transitioning from implicit to explicit, public to personal, interaction with multiple users. In *Proc. UIST 2004*, pages 137–146, 2004.

Evaluating Directional Cost Models in Navigation

Thibault Kruse
IAS, TU München
Boltzmann Str. 3
85748 Garching, Germany
kruset@in.tum.de

Alexandra Kirsch
Eberhard Karls Universität Tübingen, Department of Computer Science
Sand 14, 72076 Tübingen, Germany
alexandra.kirsch@uni-tuebingen.de

Harmish Khambhaita, Rachid Alami
LAAS/CNRS
7 Avenue du Colonel Roche
31077 Toulouse Cedex 4, France
{harmish.khambhaita, rachid.alami}@laas.fr

ABSTRACT

A common approach to social distancing in robot navigation are spatial cost functions around humans that cause the robot to prefer paths that do not come too close to humans. However, in unpredictably dynamic scenarios, following such paths may produce robot behavior that appears confused. The concept of directional costs in cost functions [9] is supposed to alleviate this problem without incurring the problem of combinatorial explosions using temporal planning. With directional cost functions, a robot attempts to solve spatial conflicts by adjusting the velocity instead of the path, where possible. To complement results from simulations, in this paper we describe a user study we conducted with a PR2 robot and human participants to evaluate the new cost function type. The study shows that the real robot behavior is similar to the observations in simulation, and that participants rate the robot behavior less confusing with the adapted cost model. The study also shows other important behavior cues that can influence motion legibility.

Categories and Subject Descriptors

H.4 [**Information Systems Applications**]: Miscellaneous; D.2.8 [**Software Engineering**]: Metrics—*complexity measures, performance measures*

1 Introduction

Navigation among humans must not just be safe, but also agreeable to humans. The concept of "legibility" describes one of the qualities beside safety that make robot behavior agreeable. Legibility expresses how easily an uninstructed person can estimate internal states of the robot from observation. This is important for interactions as it reduces distraction. Legibility is threatened by all robot behaviors that lead to wrong beliefs and expectations about the robot. The state-of-the-art in human-aware navigation planning does not take into account the concepts of legibility and cues, and can therefore produce confusing robot behavior.

HRI'14, March 3–6, 2014, Bielefeld, Germany.

ACM 978-1-4503-2658-2/14/03 ...$15.00.
http://dx.doi.org/10.1145/2559636.2559662.

Respecting a social distance around *standing* humans just means preferring to keep a minimum distance from the location of persons. But in dynamic situations the future paths of persons have to be taken into account for social distancing in path planning. To some degree, the future paths of humans can be predicted with various methods [16]. However the reliability of any prediction method quickly degrades in time, and there are necessarily many occasions of unexpected human motions, even more so when a robot moves nearby. Even with rather reliable prediction, replanning during execution is inevitable, requiring a planning process that scales well.

Our previous publication [9] presents an adapted cost model *ContextCost* that addresses those challenges. The cost model *ContextCost* defines social costs for a path search in a grid depending on the motion direction of present humans and of the potential movement of the robot. In particular it may discard social costs for approaching humans when calculating a path, relying on the local planner to adjust robot velocity instead to solve a spatial conflict.

This cost model shifts the burden of respecting social distancing around moving humans from global planning to local planning and thus makes the robot follow more goal-directed paths in the presence of moving humans. We previously assumed this increases the legibility of the robot's navigation intention, but we wanted to support this assumption by a user study.

Legibility in general is increased by explicit signaling and also any aspect of behavior that can be used as cue to the actual robot intention. Legibility is different from predictability, which requires an observer to imagine the most likely future state, determined by many other factors than the robot internal state [4]. As an easy reminder of this notion of legibility: For the task of reading text, legibility may relate to how easy it is to understand a given piece of text, whereas predictability could refer to how easy it is to predict the following text.

In robot motion, the robot motion direction and path are natural cues for the robot's navigational intentions, as the natural way to move to a goal is moving forward on the most efficient path towards the goal, which is of course the straight line in the absence of obstacles. So legibility in navigation is naturally driven by the cues given by the robot's direction of movement and path.

(a) Robot starts to deviate from straight line

(b) Robot deviates more, becomes stalled

(c) Robot re-planned path deviates by going behind the person

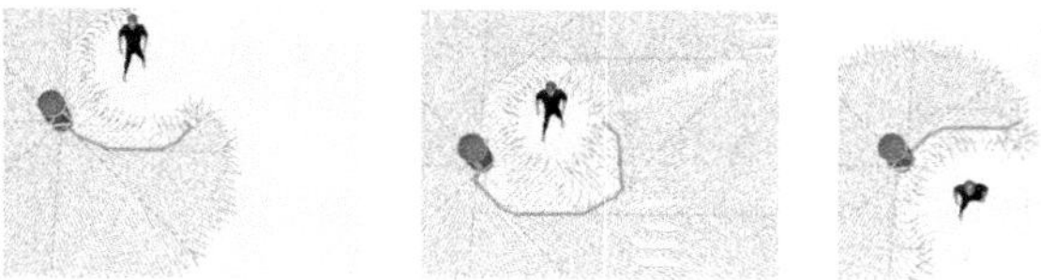

Figure 1: Effects of replanning with cost model *Static* in simulation. The robot is planning paths going from left to right, a simulated person walks from top to bottom without stopping for the robot. Taken from [9].

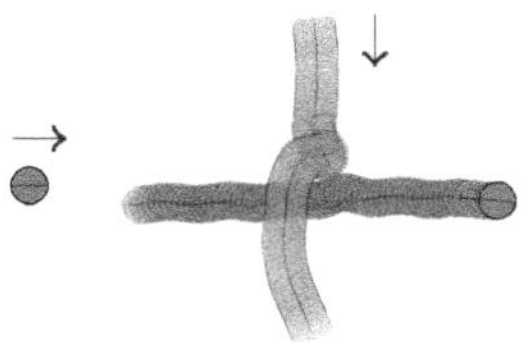

Figure 2: Robot (in blue) behavior with static cost models.

State-of-the art social navigation frameworks consider proxemics for social distancing, producing paths that prefer to avoid a circular region around any person in the environment. A path planner then finds a path that avoids this region. When the human is moving this region moves as well, so consecutive searches for a path can find different solutions.

Figure 1 shows an inevitable problem when navigating based on replanning with such a model of proxemic regions. The path planner finds a path to the goal of the robot while avoiding to approach the human moving from top to the bottom in the figure. As the situation evolves, the human position changes, and the robot has to replan to adapt. So, the robot plans very different paths during the approach of its goal, as the situation changes. The resulting directions and path of the robot are not helpful as cues to the robot intention. Figure 2 illustrates the resulting robot path in such situations.

Note that temporal planning alone does not generally fix this problem in realistic HRI. This is partly due to human motion being difficult to predict, in particular when being influenced by the robot motion. Also most temporal planning approaches can only be applied within boundaries. Such as the maximum look-ahead distance of a local planner like the Dynamic Window Approach (DWA) [6], where any conflicts at the edge of the boundary generate undesirable robot behavior.

Also in temporal planning, the planner has additional degrees of freedom to solve a conflict by using different velocities at different times. So it does not scale well, and requires an additional non-trivial cost function to balance optimization based on path length, path duration, and social factors like path legibility.

The context dependent cost model *ContextCost* has been compared in simulation to human motion strategies in 2-agent orthogonal crossing scenarios [1]. Encouraged by the results, this paper further evaluates the cost function in a real world setting when presenting experiment participants to a real world autonomously moving robot.

In particular we investigate whether the phenomenon can be reproduced on the PR2 robot when navigating with a present person, and whether our cost function improves the perceived quality of the motion of the PR2.

2 Related Work

The theory of proxemics describes social distancing behaviors of humans during interactions with other persons [7]. In recent years research in human-aware navigation has been based on theses proxemics rules for realizing more human like behavior during robot motion and non motion tasks. For detailed survey of human-aware navigation research we refer the reader to [10].

Sisbot et. al. [19] describes the human-aware navigation planner (HANP) that provides human-aware navigation plans considering proxemic distances around static humans in the environment. In extension to that work, we use a cost-map that adapts costs for moving humans based on the compatibility of motion directions, and we use an adapted local-planner that reduces velocity on a given path up to zero while waiting for moving humans to pass.

The general idea of considering moving humans not as obstacles to avoid, but instead considering the space around them as "soon to be free" is also exploited by Müller et al. [13], who make a robot follow persons going in the same direction rather than trying to find a way around them.

In [11] Kuderer et al. present an approach to predict future human trajectories based on a learned set of features that capture relevant characteristics of human trajectories in populated environment. Predictions of human trajectories are used as robot trajectories for social motion. Other researchers investigate temporal planning to solve spatial conflicts in very confined areas [15, 18]. However, these approaches do not pay special attention to legibility.

In [12] the authors have carried out a video-based user study comparing human-aware and non-human-aware navigation algorithms in situations where a human crosses the path of a robot. Users were shown first-person perspective videos of crossing situations with a robot using different navigation algorithms and asked to predict the robot motion and rate their own emotions during the interaction shown in the videos. Legibility was measured as a correlate of predictability.

Similar user-studies investigating optimal parameters for robots approaching standing persons have been conducted [2, 3, 22]. Sardar et al. [17] performed a user study where a robot approached a standing person concentrating on another task, and found significant differences in socially normative behavior for robots and humans. Within a holistic perspective on technology acceptance such as established by Heerink et al. [8], our work focuses on functional acceptance. The study by Pacchierotti et al. [14] also looks at a mutually dynamic situation of passing each other. Foka et al. [5] also did experiments using their POMDP-based navigation framework, but did not evaluate legibility.

3 Approach

The purpose of the user study was to evaluate the usefulness of the adapted cost model *ContextCost* in dynamic realworld situations over standard cost models with proxemics (model *Static*). Both cost models use a proxemic model for social

H	position of human
$\hat{hd}$	heading of human
$\hat{hd}'$	translated $\hat{hd}$
$\hat{hd}^{-1}$	inverse $\hat{hd}'$
w_i	i-th waypoint on path
P	closest point on human path to w_i
d_P	distance of P and w_i
$\hat{rd}$	potential heading of robot at w_i
α	angle between $\hat{rd}$ and $\hat{hd}^{-1}$

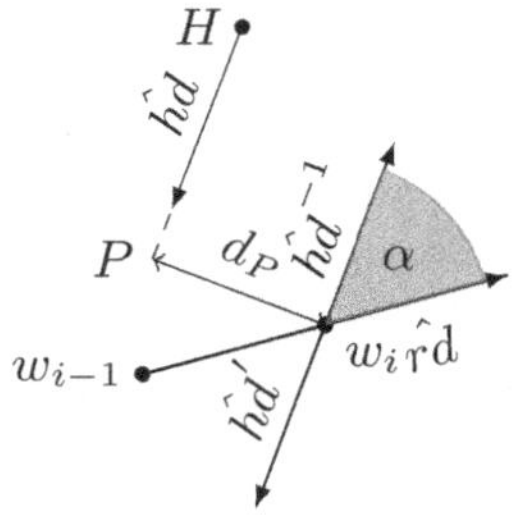

Figure 3: Context dependent costs *ContextCost*, from [9].

distancing. They guide search for a path on a 2D grid by assigning costs to grid cells, such that a search algorithm can find the minimum connecting path between a start and a goal cell, which is assumed to be socially optimal.

In both cost models, for each human H the costs can be based on several different specialized functions f_i, such as for safety (as in figure 1) or visibility. For cost model *Static*, the costs for each grid cell can be computed using the function ς'_{Static} :

$$\varsigma'_{Static}\ (H, w_i) = max(f_1(H, w_1), f_2(H, w_i), \ldots, f_k(H, w_i))$$

Figure 3 illustrates the cost model *ContextCost* described in more detail in [9], which is based on the concept of spatial compatibility. When two paths are spatially compatible, the robot can stay on its intended (straight) path. Only in incompatible situations, specific avoidance action has to be taken. Spatial compatibility is measured by the distance d_P between a waypoint and the estimated path of the human. The second measure is the difference in heading angles α, which we call directional compatibility. Using the angle α and distance d_P, we can define the incompatibility function ϕ that calculates a number $\in [0, 1]$ with which we can multiply the costs of the model *Static*. ϕ is defined such that when a path segment should not conflict with a predicted human motion, social costs do not apply.

$$\phi(H, w_i, w_{i-1}) = \begin{cases} 1 & \text{, if } \hat{hd} \text{ undefined} \\ 1 & \text{, if } d_P \leq d_{low} \\ 0 & \text{, if } d_P \geq d_{high} \\ 0 & \text{, if } \alpha \geq \alpha_{max} \\ \frac{d_P - d_{low}}{d_{high}} \cdot \frac{\alpha}{\alpha_{max}} & \text{, otherwise} \end{cases}$$

The arguments w_i, w_{i-1} to ϕ as opposed to only w_i underline why this cost function is called directional, it takes into account from which direction (which preceding cell w_{i-1}) the relevant cell is to be approached.

ϕ has three parameters d_{low}, d_{high} and α_{max} to tweak what motions are considered compatible. We use this function ϕ to modify the cost model *Static* by replacing ς'_{Static} with $\varsigma'_{ContextCost}$ as shown in equation below.

$$\varsigma'_{ContextCost}\ (H, w_i, w_{i-1}) = \varsigma'_{Static}\ (H, w_i) \cdot \phi(H, w_i, w_{i-1})$$

Thus robot path direction and human direction are considered incompatible if the human and robot could frontally run into each other. In all other cases, the motions are compatible, meaning it is likely the situation can work out well if the robot just reduces its velocity on the path while the human is in the way. So in the situation shown in Figure 1, a robot using cost model *ContextCost* would not deviate from the straight line, but instead reduce it's velocity.

For the experiment, the "move_base" navigation framework of the PR2 robot was modified. As a global planner for "move_base" we used HANP [19] to enable human-aware path planning, and invoke the global planner at a regular frequency of 10 Hz. HANP was configured with one of two cost models $\varsigma'_{ContextCost}$ and ς'_{Static} as a parameter of the experiment trials.

As a local planner, for this experiment we used a waypoint-following algorithm without general obstacle avoidance that adapts the robot velocity to prevent collisions with perceived humans. The waypoint follower causes the robot to visit each waypoint of the global plan, by turning towards each waypoint in turn and then moving forward to reach it (as opposed to allowing sideways or backward motions). The strategy of velocity adaptation was varied according to the global planning strategy. When using the simple proxemics based cost model *Static*, the local planner tried to move at maximum velocity on the path, except when a human was in front of it at 1 m distance (center to center), in which case no forward motion was allowed. The latter is a measure to grant a minimum feeling of safety for human participants. Using the cost model *ContextCost*, the velocity was adapted by projecting the motions of the robot and the human into the future, and selecting a velocity that would in those projections not predict their mutual distance to decrease below 1.3 m. This value was established in preliminary trial as yielding a distance that felt safe while keeping the robot close enough to establish a crossing conflict situation.

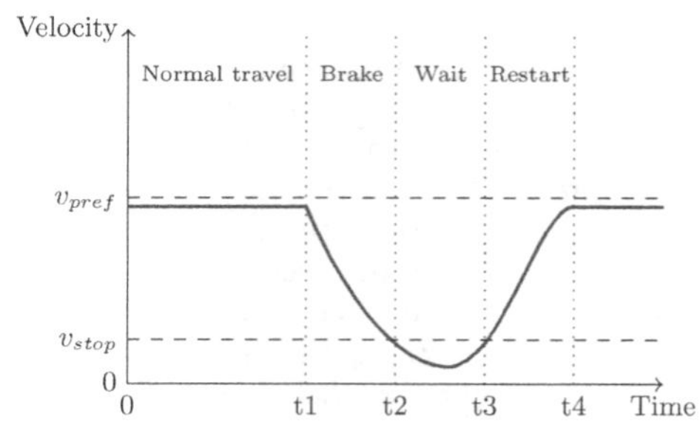

Figure 4: Idealized velocity profile scheme for 90° crossing situations with cost model *ContextCost*. v_{pref} indicates the preferred travel velocity, v_{stop} a velocity so low a robot is considered not traveling.

In preliminary trials performed with a different set of participants we faced two main challenges when controlling the robot velocity: "stopping late" and "restarting early". Figure 4 shows a velocity profile we imagine to be optimal for crossing the path of a human when giving way. It describes the velocity of moving forward, not rotations. There are three distinct phases for braking, waiting, and restarting. Ideally, there is no acceleration during the "Brake" phase, and no significant acceleration during the "Wait" phase. So the ideal robot behavior cannot merely be described in terms of distance and velocity, but acceleration (and possibly jerk) can have significant effect on humans nearby.

The phases should be clearly observable by the human whose path is being crossed, and the timing of the phases can be crucial to human comfort. In preliminary trials, the

Cost model:	*Static*	*ContextCost*
Path:	Changing paths	Straight line
Velocity:	Maximum possible speed without collision	Reduce speed to keep distance

Table 1: Comparison of experiment conditions

robot would sometimes initiate the braking phase too late, sometimes re-accelerate slightly during braking and waiting phases, or initiate the "Restart" phase too early. Each case caused some participants to feel uncomfortable, and the discomfort was strong enough to significantly influence the participants' answers.

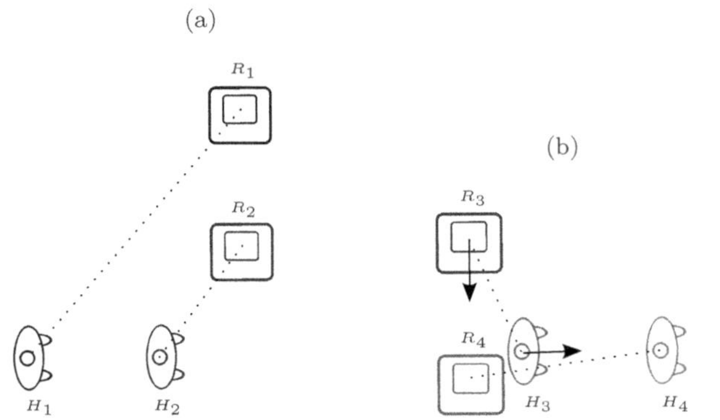

Figure 5: Situations relevant for comfort while crossing with adapted cost model *ContextCost*. R_t and H_t are position of the robot and human at time-step t respectively. Stopping late in (a) or starting early in (b) cause discomfort.

Figure 5a shows the transition to the "Brake" phase. When the robot decelerated late or had the slightest acceleration motion, participants felt the situation was uncomfortable. We believe this is because participants fear the robot to accelerate to full speed at the smallest symptom of acceleration. Since the short-time robot acceleration was caused by noisy data and prediction, we suppressed it by adding uncertainty to the perception data, i.e. by predicting low, nominal and high human velocities, and selecting a velocity that avoids collisions with all three prediction models. This causes the robot to select low velocities more often, and makes participants less nervous. Figure 5b shows the "Restart" phase. Sometimes the participants felt uncomfortable expressing the robot moved "too early". We believe again that the participants fear the robot quickly accelerating to full speed, so we corrected this behavior by projecting the robot position not at the desired speed, but at full speed, which caused the robot to accelerate later, and did not discomfort the participants anymore. Using both increased uncertainty about the future human positions and projecting the robot at full speed, the robot behavior in the crossing situation became rather similar to the scheme in Figure 4.

The differences of the two strategies used during the experiments are summarized in table 1. In the cost model *Static*, the robot attempts to move always at the maximum allowed speed and adapting the path to not cross the current human position nor an area in front of the human. The path frequently changes as the human moves, causing the robot to swerve. Using the cost model *ContextCost*, the robot attempts to follow a straight path to the goal, but reduces its velocity before reaching the crossing point, and accelerates again once the human has advanced enough.

The robot head was moving during the experiments to avoid the impression that the robot is ignoring the human. The control scheme turned the robot head to point at the participant head whenever the robot head could point towards the participant without deviating more than 90° from the frontal position, and vice versa for the participant. Otherwise the robot head pointed straight forward. When moving, the head moved slowly at 0.3 rad/s. Based on participant remarks this appeared appropriate except in rare cases when the robot was very close and moved in front of the participant, in which case the gaze seemed a bit provocative, which is similar to other results in robot gaze studies [20]. The participants were informed before the experiment that the head will move, to prevent the discovery of this from distracting. The robot arms remained folded during all the experiment in the default PR2 "tucked" position. Only two participants mentioned this afterward as a bit unnatural, as opposed to making prompting gestures.

4 Evaluation

The user study was set up to determine whether the robot behavior with simple static cost models in crossing situations can be reproduced in the real world, and whether the context-dependent cost model visibly improves the robot motion quality.

Legibility is difficult to quantify, as a robot may behave very legible with respect to one aspect of internal state, but at the same time obfuscate another aspect of internal state. Therefore the experiment instead establishes a good knowledge of the robot internal state for the participants, showing how the participants can become confused by the robot behavior under assumptions about the robot internal state.

17 participants were given the task to act as interfering walkers with a robot moving from one spot to another in an area without static obstacles. The human participants were tracked using an infrared motion capture system, based on four passive infrared markers placed on a lightweight helmet the participants wore and 10 wall-mounted cameras, as shown in Figure 7. The room has an experimental area with offices and desks surrounding it, during the experiment people were quietly working around the experiment area.

The participants where all given the same set of written instructions to read. The instructions stated that multiple different robot strategies would be used, but not how many or what variations to expect.

The procedure was the following: In the preparation stage, the robot and the participant moved independently to their starting positions. The starting position of the participant was marked on the floor. This situation can be seen in Figure 7. When both were ready, the experiment instructor pressed a button to start the execution phase. This triggered the robot motion planning and also made the robot say "go". The participant and the robot would start moving towards their respective goal positions at roughly the same time. The map in Figure 6 shows the coordinates. The participant goal was a small shelf on which lay a questionnaire. Going towards a shelf for a purpose rather than going onto a marked spot seemed to benefit a natural walking behavior. The goal area of the participant was slightly

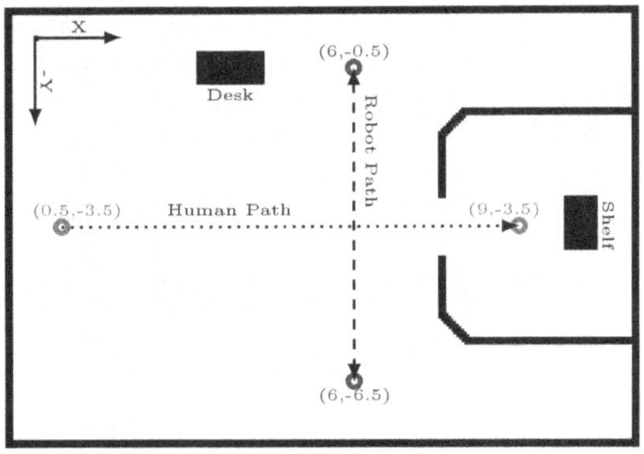

Figure 6: Top-Down view on the room layout, showing the experiment path, the instructor's desk, and the shelf where the participants marked their answer after each trial

Figure 7: Experiment setup showing wall-mounted cameras (2 out of 10), participant at start position with helmet and passive marker (1 out of 4), robot at start position, the intended paths crossing at 90°

elevated (10 cm), and there was a low barricade with a gate spanning 1.5 m, seen in white in Figure 7. This was an existing feature of the room. The participants started their movement at coordinates (0.5, -3.5) on the map, but would not be visible to the motion capture system before reaching roughly (2.5, 3.5). Again we decided to maximize the walking distance because we were mostly interested in ratings about the robot, not human gait.

When the participants reached the shelf, they could then immediately rate the robot behavior on the questionnaire placed on the shelf. Once the participant and the robot had both reached their goal positions, the execution phase ended. Then a new cycle would begin with the preparation phase. An instructor was present and visible during the experiment, sitting at the desk shown in Figure 6, to react in cases of emergencies or disturbances, but also to reassure the participant and verify they were following the procedure. Also the instructor modified the robot maximum speed between 0.45 m/s and 0.55 m/s according to the participant's walking speed during the first 3 trials to create a spatial conflict without imposing a walking speed on the participants. The robot would approach alternately from the left or the right hand side.

Each participant was asked to perform the same task 13 times, and was told that the first 3 cycles would not be taken into account, but serve to get used to the situation. The robot strategy was randomized but never the same three times in a row. All participants were presented with both strategies to allow them a comparative opinion.

As opposed to studies on human gait, the experiment was interactive, meaning the robot behavior is a function of its algorithms, the person's behavior (in particular the walking speed), the adapted robot maximum velocity and of noisy technical side effects like varying WiFi network latencies. Because of that, the captured data of the human trajectories is only of limited usefulness to interpret exact motion patterns.

- Number of Participants: 2 female, 15 male
- Age range: 22 - 34
- Mother language: 11 French, 6 Other
- Education level: 11 Master, 5 PhD
- Robot experience: 11 None, 6 with less than 6 years

After each run, the participants were asked to rate the robot's performance according to predefined questions:

- Please rate the robot behavior (clear vs. confusing)
- Please rate the crossing situation (comfort):

The participants were given a Semantic Differential Scale from 1 to 5, the extremes labeled "clear", "confusing", "comfortable", "uncomfortable" respectively. A preliminary trial had asked the participants to rate their "surprise", but this word also had positive connotations and was also rated for the novelty of the whole situation. "clear" vs. "confusing" seemed better to express legibility issues.

Based on the design of the cost model *ContextCost*, the hypotheses for the outcome of the experiment were the following:

- H1: The robot behavior observed in simulation for *Static* also occurs in the experiment
- H2: Participants rate path adaptation as more confusing than velocity adaptation
- H3: Participants rate path adaptation as more uncomfortable than velocity adaptation

The alternatives are trivially negations of the given hypothesis. H2 and H3 would be confirmed if significant difference between the reported ratings were found.

5 Results

We collected data from 170 valid trial runs as shown in Table 2. Figure 8 shows summary plots of a representative run using cost model *Static*, and Figure 9 shows the same plots for a representative run using *ContextCost*. Figures 8a and 9a show the positions of robot and human over time for two representative samples we selected. Since we could not measure the human position from the start, we added the starting position as a single circle in the plot. Figures 8a and 8f shows how the robot at a distance of 1.2 m slightly deviates from the straight line towards its left and rotates. The human passes during that time. Once the human has

	Static	*ContextCost*
robot start at (6, -0.5)	39	45
robot start at (6, -6.5)	41	45

Table 2: Conditions for the 170 valid trials.

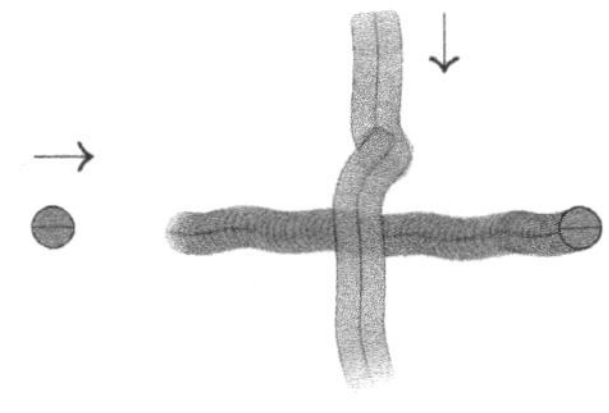

(a) Paths of human (red) and robot (blue)

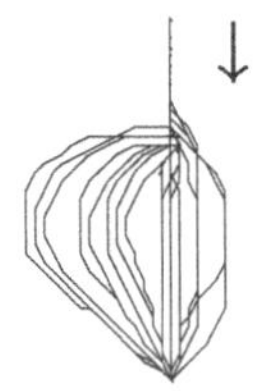

(b) Robot plans over time

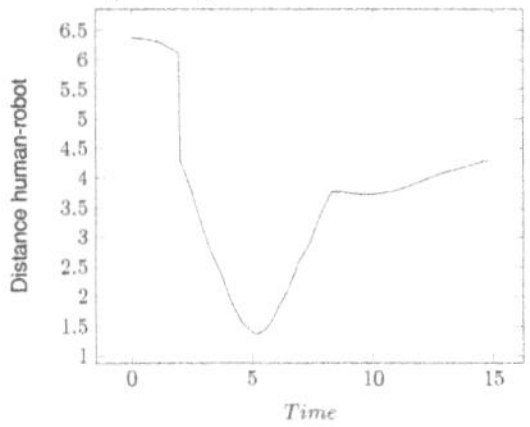

(c) Distance human to robot center

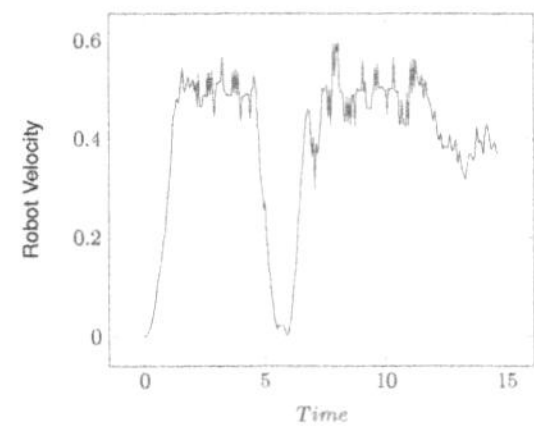

(d) Robot velocities

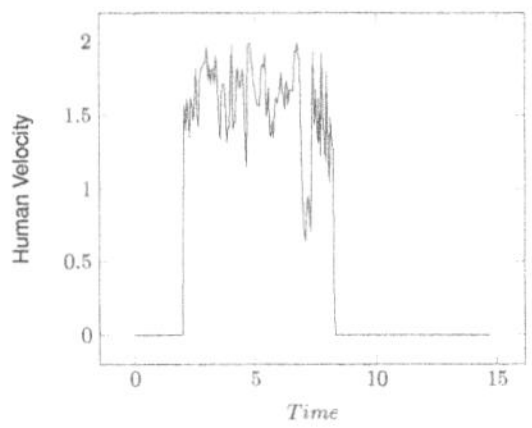

(e) Human velocities

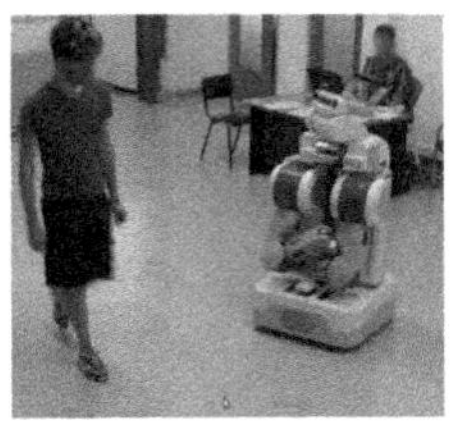

(f) Position at minimum distance

Figure 8: Sample 1 with cost model *Static*. In (a) the round positions are the human moving from left to right. (b) shows what the diverse plans the robot generate while moving.

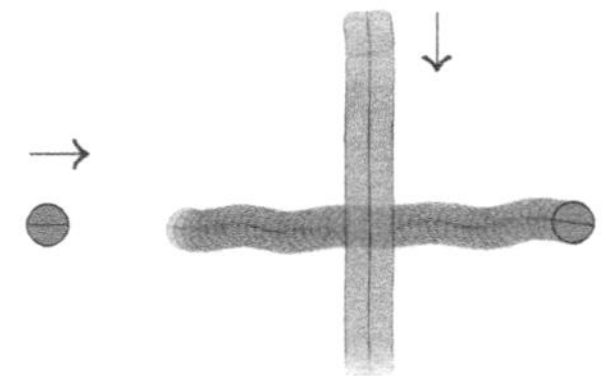

(a) Paths of human (red) and robot (blue)

(b) Robot plans over time

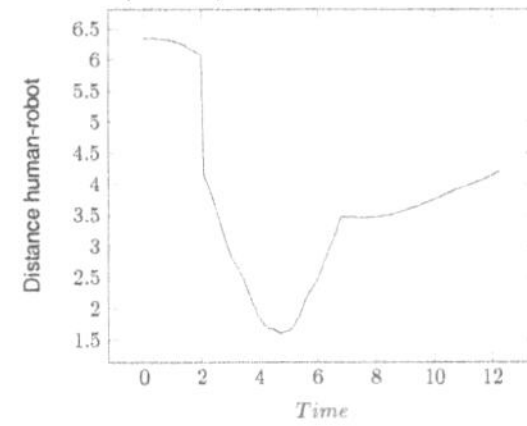

(c) Distance human to robot center

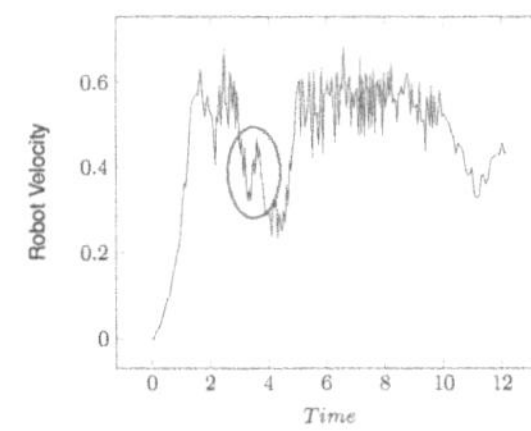

(d) Robot velocities

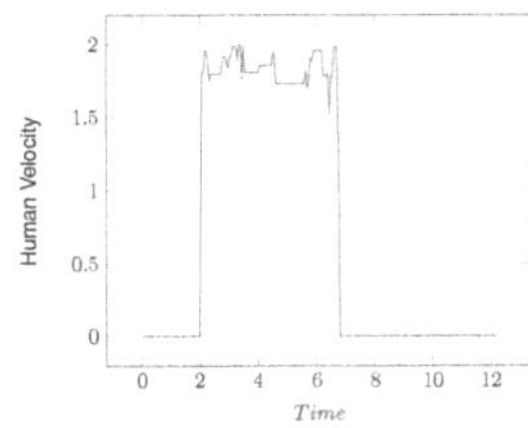

(e) Human velocities

(f) Position at minimum distance

Figure 9: Sample 2 with cost model *ContextCost*. Same plots as in Figure 8.

passed, the robot plans paths behind the human as shown in figure Figure 8b, thus turning to its right before eventually regaining the straight path. Compare that to Figures 9a and 9f, where the robot also decelerated to a minimal distance of 1.2 m, but never rotated, and never planned anything but a straight path as shown in Figure 9b. This difference was already explained in [9], so here we just point out that the same occurs in a real world experiment.

In Figure 9d at time 3.8 there is a small increase of velocity. we could not pin down the cause of this, which could be with the prediction algorithm or robot wheel control. We point it out only to show that such a small and short acceleration already counted as a cue to some participants that the robot was maybe re-accelerating.

Figure 10 and 11 summarizes participant's answers to the questionnaire. Each bar in the figure represents the number of participants who answered with the value on the horizontal axes for respective question. Figure 10 shows the differences in reported discomfort. The visible difference as given by a one-way ANOVA indicates trials with cost model *ContextCost* were rated more comfortable (M=1.5, SD=0.723) than for *Static* (M=2.873, SD=1.265), $p < 0.001$. The same is shown for behavior clarity in Figure 11. The trials with cost model *ContextCost* were rated more clear (M=1.522, SD=0.707) than for *Static* (M=2.684, SD=1.215), $p < 0.001$. The ratings for clarity and discomfort were also correlated as revealed by Pearson's R test (R=0.771, p<0.001). In their remarks, some participants usually argued that both values were independent. They explained that they rated strangeness whenever the robot orientation changed (as it only did with cost model *Static*), while they rated discomfort high when the robot passed first (only happened with *Static*) or had jerky acceleration motions (only happened with *ContextCost*). However, given the strong correlation possibly most participants did not clearly separate both concepts.

Hypothesis H1 is validated by the robot path behavior we saw, as displayed in Figures 8 and 12, in comparison to Figure 9a. The distinct responses for clarity and comfort validate Hypotheses H2 and H3.

While the figures for strategy *ContextCost* are very similar over all 90 runs, there was a lot of variation over the runs with *Static*. This was due to the different exact cir-

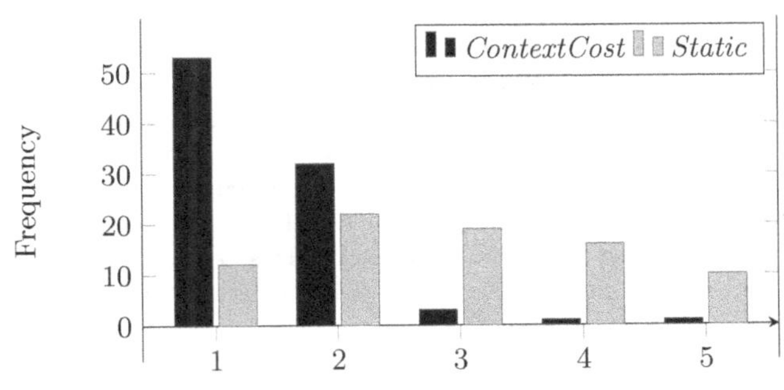

Figure 10: Participant ratings of situation: (1=Comfortable, 5=Uncomfortable).

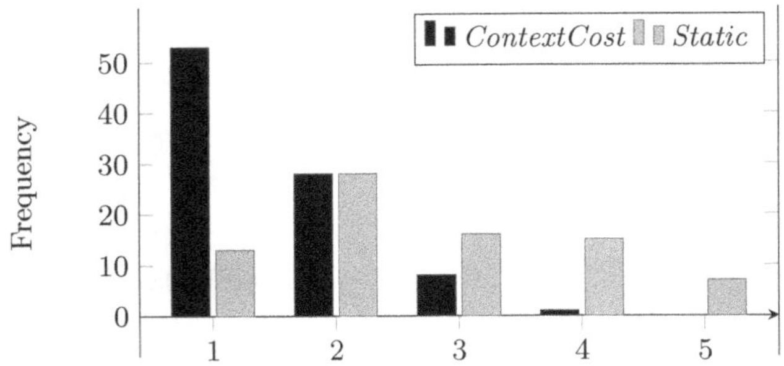

Figure 11: Participant ratings of robot behavior: (1=Clear, 5=Strange).

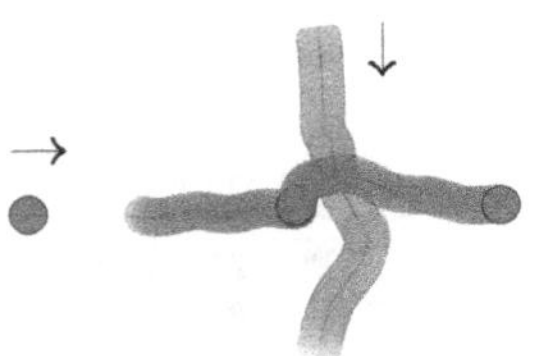

(a) Sample 3, Paths of human (red) and robot (blue), human stops to let robot pass

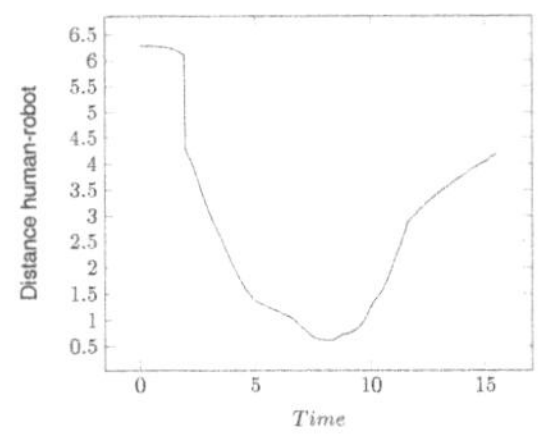

(b) Distance human to robot center in sample 3

(c) Sample 4, robot (moving bottom to top) makes a small circle

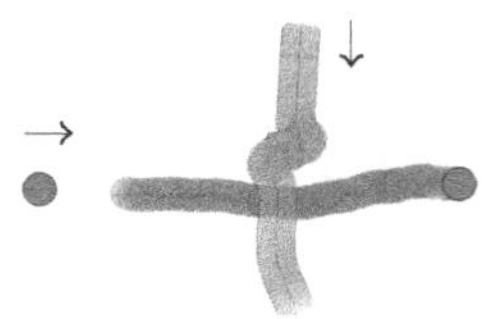

(d) Sample 5, human hesitates multiple times

Figure 12: Additional Examples with cost model *Static*, showing variants of robot behavior reacting to different human behaviors

cumstances of crossing, which depended on the motion of the participant relative to the robot. To show some of the variety we observed, Figure 12 shows the paths for additional samples. In Figure 12a the participant let the robot move first. This happened 20 out of 80 times with cost model *Static*, but never with *ContextCost*. The minimal distance of 0.5 m was a result of the participant passing closely behind the robot, and such low distances were consistently observed when participants let the robot pass first. Figure 12c shows a more extreme robot motion deviation as the robot retraced its step following a path that led away from the human. Finally Figure 12d shows a sample where the participant hesitated several times before passing the robot.

No statistically significant differences were found comparing the robot approaching from the right or left-hand side of the human. The observed human average walking velocities mainly varied between 1.5 m/s and 1.7 m/s with no clear trend detected over trials. While Figures 9e and 8e appear different, no pattern seemed evidence over all 170 runs.

6 Discussion

The charts in Figure 10 and 11 still show some degree of variation over the robot clarity of motion and discomfort. This is partially due to the fact that some participants preferred to use the full answer scale while others used only low numbers. However from the remarks we also know that even with the cost model *ContextCost*, there were symptoms the participants disliked. This is mainly due to remaining confusing symptoms in the robot acceleration behavior. As the robot velocity depends on a linear projection of the human motion and the robot, and the sensory data is noisy, the observable robot behavior for slowing down had tiny moments of acceleration, which were very visible to participants and caused mild confusion and discomfort.

As our first attempt at the experiment failed because robot acceleration was uncomfortable, we learned that three trial runs for warm-up may not generally be sufficient for this kind of study, for non-technical people.

Reported discomfort by participants seemed to always be related to uncertainty about future collisions. Participants felt generally disturbed when the robot base moved (or rotated) while the robot appeared to be "waiting for them to pass". Legibility of robot motion may be a quality that only becomes relevant once humans feel sufficiently reassured about their safety in the presence of a robot. Most participants chose a very straight line to their goal, as opposed to curving their path to accommodate the robot, very few participants however consistently walked on paths curved away from the robot approach direction. Two Participants reported that when the robot base rotated (in the case of cost model *Static*), they felt as if the robot tried to follow them or join them, three participants felt that the robot was trying to cut their way in such cases. Base rotations were reported as uncomfortable when it happened very close to the participants (due to the square shape of the robot, a rotation could also cause a collision with the person's legs), but when it was at least 1.5 m away, no discomfort was reported.

The robot passing first (with cost model *Static* and the participant walking slowly) as in Figure 12a was accepted by some participants, others felt the robot should have stopped for them in any case. In such cases it is also notable that human participants pass very close behind the robot, almost touching the robot, so there was no visible notion of social self-distancing from the robot. This could mean that social distancing is generally not required for such situations because the duration where two agents are very close is also very short. However social distancing is likely to still be relevant for situations of following one another, or walking side by side, when the duration of proximity is longer. The observation that humans pass very close behind crossing robots, but do not like being passed close by the same robot in the inverse situation, hints at a difference in socially normative behaviors for humans and robots as also found in [17].

As additional remark on predictability, using the adapted cost model *ContextCost*, the robot behaved very similar for each run, even when participants walked at different speeds or hesitated. This consistency made the robot behavior also very predictable, as consistency is generally a factor increasing predictability. The predictability of the whole situation for third party observers may also be considered, in 20 of 80 runs with *Static*, the participant let the robot go first, but never did so in 90 runs with *ContextCost*, meaning the latter cost model leads to better predictability of the situation as a whole.

The study does not validate this approach for other conflict situations such as crossing at different angles or following at different speeds. Such studies would require a larger experiment area than we had available. Also the study does not compare the straight path behavior of a robot to paths curved "behind" the crossing human, which requires temporal planning to be found by a path planner.

It is also worth considering how the navigation approach scales to situations with more humans. While the robot is prone to the "freezing robot" problem [21], because in case of doubt it reduces velocity to zero, we believe for moderately crowded situations this behavior may still help to avoid making a complex situation even more complex, given the insecurity our participants reported to even slight changes in robot velocity. For densely crowded situations, a fully reactive navigation mode seems preferable.

The study has shown several cues that human observers use to guess the intentions of the robot. While the focus was on the path behavior of the robot, we also saw that minor accelerations were also used as a significant cue by humans, so those have to be avoided to prevent confusion. Possibly the robot might require a social commitment behavior such that it commits to stopping or moving for at least a given time-span of one or two seconds. Cues like hectic motion of PR2 caster wheels during low velocity, or starting of robot cooling vents may not clearly indicate a specific robot intent, but are confusing as cues.

7 Conclusions

The user study was performed to validate the improvement of perceived robot motion quality when using an adapted cost model *ContextCost* for path planning. The study shows that using a real robot and uninstructed participants, a robot will show confusing behavior when using a simple proxemic path planner, behavior that humans will rate as strange or confusing. For crossing situations, the study shows that if a robot instead discards proxemic costs in the path planner and chooses a direct line to the goal, but also uses a local planner that adapts velocity to maintain a certain distance, the robot behavior becomes more stable, and humans rate the robot behavior as clearer. The study also shows that for such situations of conflict, robot acceleration is an important source of confusing robot cues, even if it happens for very short times and at small amounts. The study hints at the possibility that for short durations, a close encounter may not require social distancing at all, but safety distancing. Also the study has revealed that for legibility, it is not only crucial to provide useful cues to the robot internal state (such as its intention), but to also avoid accidentally creating misleading cues. This leads to the notion of "perspective taking" in path planning and local planning, such that a robot needs not only to reason about the effects of a *planned* trajectory, but also about the effects of the *imaginary trajectories* that observers predict for the robot, based on cues. So the implications of this user study on legibility extend to all other motion planning problems involving the presence of humans.

8 Acknowledgments

With the support of the Technische Universität München - Institute for Advanced Study and the CoTeSys (Cognition for Technical Systems) cluster of excellence and the Bavarian Academy of Sciences and Humanities. This work has partly been supported by the European Commission under contract number FP7-ICT-600877 (SPENCER).

9 References

[1] P. Basili, M. Saglam, T. Kruse, M. Huber, A. Kirsch, and S. Glasauer. Strategies of locomotor collision avoidance. *Gait & Posture*, 37(3):385–390, 2013.

[2] J. T. Butler and A. Agah. Psychological effects of behavior patterns of a mobile personal robot. *Autonomous Robots*, 10(2):185–202, 2001.

[3] D. Carton, A. Turnwald, D. Wollherr, and M. Buss. Proactively approaching pedestrians with an autonomous mobile robot in urban environments. In *13th International Symposium on Experimental Robotics (ISER)*, 2012.

[4] A. Dragan, K. Lee, and S. Srinivasa. Legibility and predictability of robot motion. In *Human-Robot Interaction*, March 2013.

[5] A. F. Foka and P. E. Trahanias. Probabilistic autonomous robot navigation in dynamic environments with human motion prediction. *I. J. Social Robotics*, 2(1):79–94, 2010.

[6] D. Fox, W. Burgard, and S. Thrun. The dynamic window approach to collision avoidance. *IEEE Robotics and Automation Magazine*, 1997.

[7] E. Hall. *The hidden dimension*. Anchor Books, 1966.

[8] M. Heerink, B. J. A. Kröse, V. Evers, and B. J. Wielinga. Assessing acceptance of assistive social agent technology by older adults: the almere model. *I. J. Social Robotics*, 2(4):361–375, 2010.

[9] T. Kruse, P. Basili, S. Glasauer, and A. Kirsch. Legible robot navigation in the proximity of moving humans. In *Advanced Robotics and its Social Impacts (ARSO), 2012 IEEE Workshop on*, pages 83–88, May 2012.

[10] T. Kruse, A. K. Pandey, R. Alami, and A. Kirsch. Human-aware robot navigation: A survey. *Robotics and Autonomous Systems*, 61(12):1726 – 1743, 2013.

[11] M. Kuderer, H. Kretzschmar, C. Sprunk, and W. Burgard. Feature-based prediction of trajectories for socially compliant navigation. In *Proceedings of Robotics: Science and Systems*, Sydney, Australia, July 2012.

[12] C. Lichtenthaeler, T. Lorenz, and A. Kirsch. Influence of legibility on perceived safety in a virtual human-robot path crossing task. In *RO-MAN, IEEE*, 2012.

[13] J. Müller, C. Stachniss, K. O. Arras, and W. Burgard. Socially inspired motion planning for mobile robots in populated environments. In *International Conference on Cognitive Systems (CogSys'08)*, Karlsruhe, Germany, 2008.

[14] E. Pacchierotti, H. Christensen, and P. Jensfelt. Evaluation of passing distance for social robots. In *RO-MAN, IEEE*, September 2006.

[15] M. Phillips and M. Likhachev. Sipp: Safe interval path planning for dynamic environments. In *ICRA, IEEE*, 2011.

[16] J. Rios-Martinez. *Socially-Aware Robot Navigation: combining Risk Assessment and Social Conventions*. PhD thesis, Université de Grenoble, 2012.

[17] A. Sardar, M. Joosse, A. Weiss, and V. Evers. Don't stand so close to me: users' attitudinal and behavioral responses to personal space invasion by robots. In *HRI*, pages 229–230, 2012.

[18] L. Scandolo and T. Fraichard. An anthropomorphic navigation scheme for dynamic scenarios. In *ICRA, IEEE*, February 2011.

[19] E. A. Sisbot, L. F. Marin-Urias, R. Alami, and T. Simeon. A human aware mobile robot motion planner. *IEEE Transactions on Robotics*, 23, 2007.

[20] L. Takayama and C. Pantofaru. Influences on proxemic behaviors in human-robot interaction. In *IROS, IEEE/RSJ*, 2009.

[21] P. Trautman and A. Krause. Unfreezing the robot: Navigation in dense, interacting crowds. In *IROS, IEEE/RSJ*, October 2010.

[22] M. Walters, M. Oskoei, D. Syrdal, and K. Dautenhahn. A long-term human-robot proxemic study. In *RO-MAN, IEEE*, 2011.

Communication of Intent in Assistive Free Flyers

Daniel Szafir[1], Bilge Mutlu[1], and Terrence Fong[2]
(1) University of Wisconsin–Madison, 1210 W. Dayton St., Madison, WI 53706 USA
(2) NASA Ames Research Center, Moffett Field, CA 94035 USA
{dszafir,bilge}@cs.wisc.edu; terry.fong@nasa.gov

ABSTRACT

Assistive free-flyers (AFFs) are an emerging robotic platform with unparalleled flight capabilities that appear uniquely suited to exploration, surveillance, inspection, and telepresence tasks. However, unconstrained aerial movements may make it difficult for colocated operators, collaborators, and observers to understand AFF intentions, potentially leading to difficulties understanding whether operator instructions are being executed properly or to safety concerns if future AFF motions are unknown or difficult to predict. To increase AFF usability when working in close proximity to users, we explore the design of natural and intuitive flight motions that may improve AFF abilities to communicate intent while simultaneously accomplishing task goals. We propose a formalism for representing AFF flight paths as a series of motion primitives and present two studies examining the effects of modifying the trajectories and velocities of these flight primitives based on natural motion principles. Our first study found that modified flight motions might allow AFFs to more effectively communicate intent and, in our second study, participants preferred interacting with an AFF that used a manipulated flight path, rated modified flight motions as more natural, and felt safer around an AFF with modified motion. Our proposed formalism and findings highlight the importance of robot motion in achieving effective human-robot interactions.

Categories and Subject Descriptors

H.1.2 [**Models and Principles**]: User/Machine Systems—*human factors, software psychology*; H.5.2 [**Information Interfaces and Presentation**]: User Interfaces—*evaluation/ methodology, user-centered design*

General Terms

Design, Human Factors

1. INTRODUCTION

Free-flying robots hold great potential due to their unique abilities to freely traverse and survey environments. UAVs (unmanned aerial vehicles) or "drones", such as the General Atomics MQ-1 Predator and MQ-9 Reaper, are a staple in modern military operations [37], but do not interact in close proximity with people. An emerging class of smaller aerial robots are envisioned to provide aid in domains including construction [16], utilities [44], search-and-rescue [15], and space [8, 9] by performing inspection, mapping, telepresence, and delivery tasks. We term these robots, which are represented in the growing body of research on micro air vehicles (MAVs) and multirotor aircraft [21, 32, 38], robotic airships [3, 6], and space exploration robots [9], "assistive free-flyers" (AFFs).

HRI'14, March 3–6, 2014, Bielefeld, Germany.

ACM 978-1-4503-2658-2/14/03 ...$15.00.
http://dx.doi.org/10.1145/2559636.2559672 .

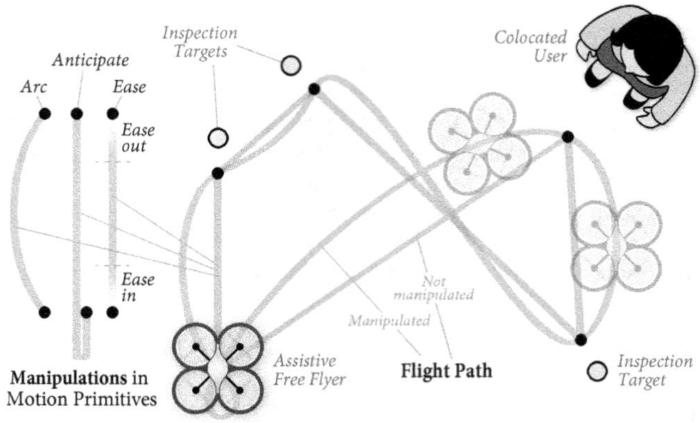

Figure 1: This work examines manipulations to the motion primitives that define the flight paths of free-flying robots, such as the quadrotor shown here, to more effectively express robot intent and increase usability.

AFFs will require much greater collaboration and colocated interaction with humans due to the assistive nature of their tasks, and may eventually take the form of colocated social collaborators [30]. For example, NASA is currently developing an AFF called "Smart SPHERES," which is designed to be used inside spacecraft (e.g., the International Space Station) when humans are present to off-load routine work, increase astronaut productivity, and handle contingencies [9]. Smart SPHERES will perform a variety of mobile sensing tasks including environmental monitoring (e.g., air quality, radiation, sound levels), autonomous logistics management (e.g., inventory), and mobile camera work to support astronaut activities.

For AFFs such as the Smart SPHERES to successfully work and collaborate with colocated humans, designers must account for human perceptions of AFFs traveling within human environments. Although six-degrees-of-freedom (DOF) flight affords unique task abilities, users who do not generally interact with free-flying physical embodiments may not feel safe or may have trouble working near robots that exhibit unconstrained motion. Any potential misunderstandings regarding robot intentions may damage human-robot rapport, prove detrimental to task efficiency, reduce trust in automation, and may even be dangerous for the human collaborator. Alternatively, being able to understand robot intentions and predict where, when, how far, and how fast it will move may enable users to work and collaborate with AFFs more effectively.

This work seeks to address the question of how designers might improve robot motions to increase the usability of AFFs that work near colocated humans. To this end, we developed a framework that deconstructs task-based AFF flight paths into a library of motion primitives and created a collection of parameterized manipulations inspired by animation principles to modify the trajectories and velocities of these primitives (Figure 1). We evaluated the utility of these modifications in expressing AFF intent in a formative exploration. Using our initial findings, we constructed modified AFF flight paths designed to express intent and support task requirements for a prototypical AFF interaction. A second, in-person experiment evaluated the effects of using these modified flight paths on high-level outcomes including usability and safety. Below, we outline relevant work that informed our design process and describe the development of our framework of primitives and motion modifications. Next, we describe the design, methodology, and results of both our formative exploration and in-person study. We conclude with a discussion highlighting the importance of considering robot motions for user interaction, especially for aerial robots with six DOF.

2. RELATED WORK

Our work draws from an emerging body of research focused on communicative robot motion. Additionally, our understanding of the design space is informed by research in film and computer animation, which offers a rich tradition of designing motions that are both communicative and visually appealing.

2.1. Robot Motion and Intent

When developing robots for human use, HRI researchers and designers must account for inferences users will make when perceiving robots in motion. Studies suggest that observers as young as six-and-a-half months will infer a mover's goals from both human and robot motion [17] and that robot motion can convey affective state [34, 38]. Although prior work has examined the development of human-aware motions and intent-expressing gestures for robots with anthropomorphic and zoomorphic features [1, 13, 29, 40], it is not always clear how to apply these findings to robots, such as AFFs, lacking these morphological features.

For AFFs and other non-humanlike robots, manipulating motion trajectories appears to hold substantial promise in aiding users to better understand and predict robot intentions. Prior work has examined the effects of manipulating robot path planning, often using proxemics-based cost functions that prioritize paths respecting human spatial boundaries, on the physiological and subjective responses of colocated humans [18, 20, 23, 27, 28, 36]. Further research distinguishes robot motions that are *legible*, allowing users to correctly infer the robot's goal, and motions that are *predictable*, matching the expectations of an observer who knew the goal a priori [5, 26]. Dragan et al. [5] show that observers of videos in which robot trajectories were optimized for legibility, resulting in arced motions rather than straight lines, were better able to predict an end target. However, viewers who knew the target in advance reported a direct path, optimized for predictability, closely matched their expected trajectory, indicating that prior knowledge and expectations might confound the interpretation of goal-based trajectories.

Recent research has also examined robot motion beyond the realm of goal-based movement. For instance, research demonstrates that AFFs might be able to communicate affective states to users through manipulations of flight trajectories using the Laban Effort System [38]. Although motion seems to be a promising means of conveying affect, it may be challenging to specify such movements without the aid of a Laban-trained artist. Research using the ground-based iCat and Roomba robots has shown that both curvature and acceleration can have an effect on the robot's perceived affective state and can be generated algorithmically [34]. While such work is useful in designing motion that enables social robots to display varying levels of arousal, it does not inform us regarding the effects of such motions on user perceptions of robotic intent, trust, or competency. More work is needed to explore how robots, particularly those with free-flying abilities, might better express their intentions regarding where, when, how far, and how fast they will move.

2.2. The Motion Design Space

Film and computer animation research focuses on effective, visual communication of both affective state and intention. As such, prior research regarding the principles of animating characters may prove beneficial for designers interested in robot motions. Prior work in these fields offers eleven animation principles [22, 25]: squash and stretch, timing, anticipation, staging, follow through and overlapping action, straight ahead action and pose-to-pose action, slow in and out, arcs, exaggeration, secondary action, and appeal. Users find animations designed in accordance with these principles, for example squashing and stretching the shape of an animated bouncing ball to convey the ball's rigidity and mass, to be more appealing, and users are able to better predict virtual object trajectories when animation principles are applied [10].

Prior HRI research adapts certain animation techniques and principles to increase the naturalness of robot motions and expand their communicative abilities [11, 12, 13, 14, 33, 35, 40, 42, 43]. In one study, Takayama et al. [40] developed techniques based on anticipation and reaction principles to enable a robot to effectively express forethought and reactions to task outcomes. In another study, Gielniak and Thomaz [13] used an optimization approach to identify the most salient motion frame of a symbolic gesture and move this frame earlier in the motion, generating anticipation that increased observers' abilities to accurately perceive intent. Other research combines and blends animation principles to generate complex robot motions; for example, using anticipation, slow in and out, and secondary motion to create believable turning and sleeping motions for an iCat robot [42, 43] or using exaggeration and timing to exhibit nonverbal expression of emotions [33]. However, such research utilizes humanlike robots with limbs and expressive faces—features AFF's generally lack. Further investigation is needed exploring the potential benefits of adapting animation principles to the design space of robot motion for non-humanlike robots and investigating how low-level, easily implemented motion manipulations impact high-level human-robot interaction outcomes.

3. FORMALIZATION AND MODELING

To explore the design space of expressive motion for flying robots, we first developed a formal framework for AFF motion. This framework defines motion using three aspects and outlines a set of motion primitives that can be used to construct flight paths. These primitives represent a set of underlying actions that AFFs will undertake to complete tasks when operating near colocated humans, such as providing instruction or performing surveillance. Additionally, we developed a set of parameterized motion manipulations that might be applied to the primitives, which we evaluated for their ability to increase human perceptions of AFF intent and usability.

3.1. Defining Motion

We define AFF motion as a composition of three aspects: *trajectory*, *velocity*, and *orientation*. Trajectory and orientation are represented as three-dimensional vectors T_{xyz} and O_{xyz}, which correspond to

Table 1: We identified 11 primitives for AFFs working in environments with colocated humans.

Primitive	Category	*Perspective*
Take off	Core	*Exocentric*
Hover	Core	*Exocentric*
Cruise	Core	*Exocentric*
Land	Core	*Exocentric*
Approach person	Interactive	*Egocentric, Exocentric*
Avoid person	Interactive	*Egocentric, Exocentric*
Depart person	Interactive	*Egocentric, Exocentric*
Approach object	Interactive	*Exocentric*
Avoid object	Interactive	*Exocentric*
Depart object	Interactive	*Exocentric*
Scan objects	Interactive	*Exocentric*

the position of an AFF and the direction it faces [1], while velocity magnitude is represented by a scalar V.

3.2. AFF Motion Primitives

To explore the design space of expressive flight movements used while interacting with colocated operators, collaborators, and observers, we analyzed several hypothetical AFF interactions in scenarios including warehouse inspection, utilities surveillance, and telepresence in space missions that were inspired by prior AFF research. [8, 16, 44]. From a variety of potential AFF movements during such interactions, we developed a set of 11 motion primitives that could be combined to create all of the flight paths in our scenarios (Table 1). These primitives are divided into two main categories: (1) *core* principles of flight including taking off, landing, and hovering, and (2) *interactive* primitives such as approaching, avoiding, and departing that allow AFFs to work with objects and people in their environment. Additionally, primitives are classified using an understanding of viewer perspective as either *egocentric*, meaning the primitive represents AFF motion in a first-person interaction with the viewers themselves, or *exocentric*, meaning the motion represents AFF interaction with other objects or people in the environment viewed from a third-person perspective. These perspectives are adapted from work in robot perspective-taking [41] as well as teleoperation interfaces [7], which have shown the importance of considering viewer perspective in human-robot interactions. Certain primitives, such as approaching a person, can be both egocentric, as when an AFF approaches the viewer, and exocentric, as when an AFF approaches a second colocated human in the viewer's environment, and may be perceived differently across each perspective.

3.3. Motion Manipulations

Our design space for expressive motion encompasses all possible manipulations to AFF trajectories, velocities, and orientations while executing primitives. Within this space, the animation principles as well as previous work in robot motion literature guided us in devising several potential manipulations that might increase the saliency of AFF actions, including flight trajectories with arcs rather than straight lines, easing in and out of primitives using slow in and out velocity profiles, using anticipatory motions by first reversing trajectories for a short time, foreshadowing intentions by altering orientation to show directionality prior to movement, and applying exaggerated secondary motions such as side-to-side movements prior to completing the main trajectory. From these potential manipulations, we elected to explore *arc* trajectories, *easing in and out* of velocity profiles, *anticipatory* motions, and their combinations (Figure 2). Prior HRI research suggests that these manipulations may hold promise in communicating intent (e.g., optimized arc trajectories can improve motion legibility even for point robots [5]) and affect [34]. Further, these manipulations, when parameterized with respect to platform constraints, strongly parallel the underlying animation principles proposed to enhance human-robot interactions [42]. Below, we describe the development of each manipulation, followed by a study to evaluate the utility of these manipulations, based on principles of natural motion in articulated characters, in achieving intent-expressive AFF flight motion.

3.3.1. Arcing

Symmetric arcs between two points in three-dimensional space can be represented by considering the straight path between the points as a chord on a sphere. To generate an arc, we need only to specify the center point for the sphere by first constructing a midpoint M between starting point S and ending point E and displacing M by a desired amount which will correspond to the radius of the sphere:

$$M = \frac{\omega(S+E)}{2} - R$$

where $\omega = [0, 2]$ defines how close M is to the true midpoint of S and E, and R represents a vector $<x, y, z>$ that displaces M to define the depth and dimensionality of the curve. The choice of R determines the shape of the arc; for example, $R_{xyz} = <0, -1, 0>$ creates a vertical arc by specifying a spherical center below S and E.

3.3.2. Easing

To generate easing, which we define as a velocity profile with slow in and out, we adapt previous work on slow-in and slow-out filters [24] and work on modifying velocity profiles to achieve smooth motion transitions for humanoid robots [12]. To ease into and out of desired velocities, we used a Gaussian function sampled at discrete time intervals:

$$v(t) = ae^{-(x-\mu)^2/2\sigma^2}$$

For this work, we assigned constant values to the Gaussian parameters as follows:

$$a = \frac{1}{.5\sqrt{2\pi}}, \ \mu = 0.5, \ \sigma = 0.15$$

to generate a smooth normalized curve in the range [0,100] that can be scaled to desired velocities. By keeping track of flight distance (the area under the Gaussian curve), an AFF can use the first half of the curve to ease into the desired velocity and the second half of the curve when stopping, connecting the two halves of the curve with the desired maximum velocity (Figure 3).

3.3.3. Anticipation

Anticipatory actions, which can make movements more expressive, represent motion that occurs along the direction opposite to the

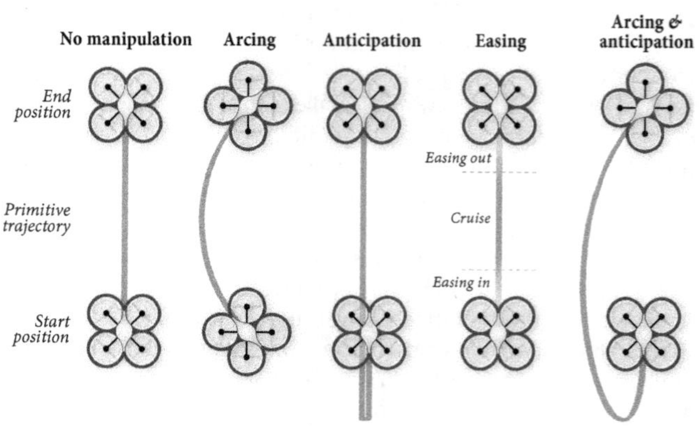

Figure 2: The arc, anticipation, and easing manipulations that we explored in this work and an example of a combined manipulation.

[1]Orientation assumes a front based on the side of the AFF with a camera. For AFFs with no obvious front, an arbitrary side can be chosen as long as it is kept consistent.

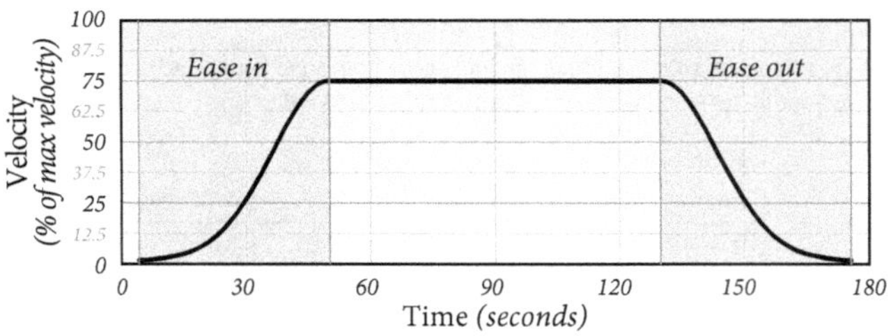

Figure 3: A velocity profile for an AFF using a Gaussian function to ease into and out of desired velocities.

main movement [19]. For AFFs, we define anticipatory motion as a trajectory vector T:

$$T = S + \theta(E - S)$$

where T is opposite of the direction of the main trajectory, defined as the start of the trajectory S and end of the trajectory E, and is proportional in magnitude to the main trajectory by the scaling factor $\theta = [0, 1]$. In this work, we used a constant $\theta = .3$, meaning that an AFF using anticipation would first fly approximately 1/3 of the distance of its main trajectory in the opposite direction, then fly to the desired end point, lengthening the total trajectory by 33%.

4. FORMATIVE EXPLORATION

To gain an understanding of how arcing, easing, and anticipatory AFF motion manipulations might impact viewers' abilities to perceive and reason about robot intent, we first conducted a formative study using pre-constructed videos of a virtual AFF. Due to the wholly unexplored design space of manipulating flight motions to showcase intent, we treated this study as a form of design exploration lacking a priori hypotheses. In the exploration, we gathered data on the effects of each potential motion manipulation on viewers' understanding of robot intent across a range of scenarios that sampled from each interactive AFF motion primitive.

4.1. Study Design

In our study, we examined the effects of manipulating the interactive AFF motion primitives identified in Section 3.2. We did not examine the effects of applying manipulations to core primitives due to their nature as actions necessary for basic flight. We created ten scenarios, one for each of the seven interactive primitives from an exocentric perspective and an additional three using an egocentric point of view for the primitives that can be viewed from both perspectives.

We used Unity [2], a 3D game and animation engine, to develop the scenarios into short (~10 second) video clips showing a virtual AFF, based on a model of a commercial platform, moving throughout a realistic warehouse environment (Figure 4). To generate arc trajectories, we constructed smooth motion along the curves defined by the starting, ending, and center points using spherical linear interpolation (SLERP) [39]. To implement easing, velocities at each frame were sampled from the Gaussian velocity profile described in Section 3.3.2 while keeping track of the distance that the AFF had traveled by approximating the area under the curve using trapezoidal Riemann sums. Eased velocity profiles were constructed such that the AFF used slow in and out for the first and last 15% of the main trajectory and traveled at the desired speed for the remaining 70%. Anticipation was implemented as described as in Section 3.3.3 using $\theta = .3$; thus, a longer anticipation distance corresponded to a longer main trajectory. To limit potential confounding effects of orientation, the virtual AFF was designed without a distinct "front" and orientation was kept constant throughout each video.

We conducted a $2 \times 2 \times 2$ between-subjects experiment using our motion manipulations (arcing, easing, and anticipatory motion) as independent variables. Each manipulation had two levels corresponding to the manipulation either being *present* or *absent*. In total, we rendered 80 videos—each video corresponded to one of the 10 scenarios for each of the eight unique conditions made from all possible combinations of the presence/absence of arcing, easing, and anticipation with the parameters set at values described above. Each participant viewed 10 videos to see all primitives in a randomized order for a given condition. Following each video, users were presented with four potential options describing their belief regarding the robot's future movement intentions (e.g., for approach and avoid primitives, options included flying to the left, to the right, above, or stopping in front of the target). To limit potential learning effects, each participant first viewed a longer (~30 second) video clip that showed the AFF exhibiting a longer flight path using the manipulations that corresponded to the participant's condition.

[2]http://unity3d.com/

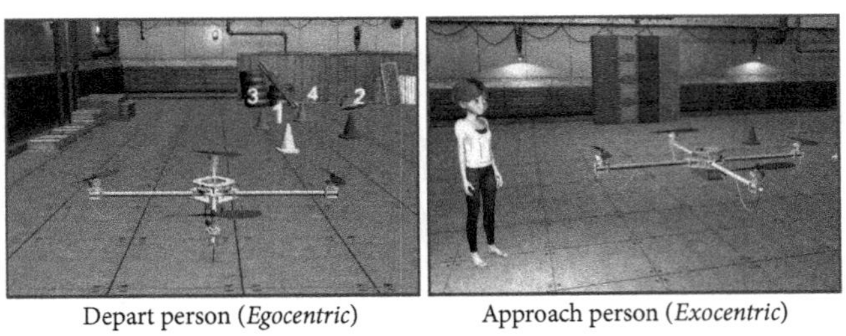

Depart person (*Egocentric*) Approach person (*Exocentric*)

Figure 4: Formative exploration stimuli: an egocentric departure with four potential numbered targets and an exocentric approach.

4.2. Participants

Participants were recruited from Amazon's Mechanical Turk infrastructure and randomly assigned to one of the eight conditions. As in previous HRI studies using Mechanical Turk (e.g., [5, 40]), we only recruited participants with at least a 95% approval rating and validated participant responses using a control question. In total, we recruited 85 participants (42 males and 43 females) who ranged in age from 18 to 80 ($M = 35.29$, $SD = 11.79$). The entire task took participants on average 5 minutes, for which they were paid $1.00.

4.3. Measures

We used three objective measures to evaluate the effects of our manipulations on participants' understanding of AFF intent: response time, accuracy, and a composite measure based on Guttman scoring [2, 5]. To evaluate response time, participants were instructed to pause the video as soon as they could infer where they believed the robot was traveling. For example, in the video corresponding to an egocentric approach, participants were instructed before the video started that they should pause the video as soon as they believed they knew whether the robot would pass to their right, to their left, fly over them, or stop in front of them. Response time measured the time passed between when the video started and when participants paused the video. To evaluate accuracy, once users paused the video, the video disappeared, and participants filled out a four-item multiple-choice question. We created a composite measure based on Guttman structures that penalized wrong answers and assigned scores to correct answers based on the response-time measure.

4.4. Results and Discussion

We analyzed the objective measurements using a one-way analysis of variance (ANOVA) with the main experimental manipulations of arcing, easing, and anticipation, and all two-way and three-way interactions among these manipulations, as a fixed effects. Dunnett's test controlled for Type I errors in comparing all individual manipulations and their combinations against a no manipulation

Table 2: Results illustrate the most effective motion manipulations compared with a no-manipulation baseline on accuracy, response time, and a composite measure. Bold text indicates marginal and significant results. (°), (+), and (–) denote perfect accuracy, increased scores, and decreased scores, respectively.

		Best Manipulation			Main Effects on Composite Score		
Primitive	*Perspective*	Accuracy	Response	Composite Score	Arc	Ease	Anticipate
Approach person	*Egocentric*	Ease°, anticipate°, ease+anticipate°	Arc	Ease	$F(1, 77) = 2.26$ $p = .137$	$F(1, 77) = 0.004$ $p = .947$	**$F(1, 77) = 2.91$ $p = .092$ (–)**
Avoid person	*Egocentric*	Arc°, arc+ease°, arc+ease+anticipate°	None	**Ease ($p = .028$), arc+ease ($p = .003$)**	$F(1, 77) = 1.73$, $p = .193$	**$F(1, 77) = 5.76$, $p = .019$ (+)**	$F(1, 77) = 1.90$, $p = .172$
Depart person	*Egocentric*	Ease, none°	Ease	**Ease ($p = .075$)**	**$F(1, 77) = 11.70$, $p = .001$ (–)**	**$F(1, 77) = 13.62$, $p < .001$ (+)**	**$F(1, 77) = 11.93$, $p < .001$ (–)**
Approach person	*Exocentric*	Ease+anticipate°	None	None	$F(1, 77) = .577$, $p = .450$	**$F(1, 77) = 5.45$, $p = .022$ (–)**	$F(1, 77) = 0.060$, $p = .807$
Avoid person	*Exocentric*	Arc, arc+ease°	Ease	**Arc+ease ($p = .002$)**	**$F(1, 77) = 3.09$, $p = .083$ (+)**	$F(1, 77) = 1.16$, $p = .286$	**$F(1, 77) = 10.28$, $p = .002$ (–)**
Depart person	*Exocentric*	Ease+anticipate	Ease	Ease	$F(1, 77) = 1.06$, $p = .306$	**$F(1, 77) = 4.01$, $p = .049$ (+)**	**$F(1, 77) = 3.28$, $p = .075$ (–)**
Approach object	*Exocentric*	Anticipate, arc+ease°	Ease	Anticipate	**$F(1, 77) = 2.96$, $p = .090$ (–)**	**$F(1, 77) = 3.37$, $p = .071$ (–)**	$F(1, 77) = 0.579$, $p = .449$
Avoid object	*Exocentric*	Arc+ease	Ease	**Ease ($p = .070$)**	$F(1, 77) = 0.013$, $p = .911$	$F(1, 77) = 0.295$, $p = .589$	**$F(1, 77) = 3.56$, $p = .063$ (–)**
Depart object	*Exocentric*	Arc+ease+anticipate	Arc+ease	Arc+ease	$F(1, 77) = 0.956$, $p = .331$	**$F(1, 77) = 20.72$, $p < .0001$ (+)**	**$F(1, 77) = 4.70$, $p = .033$ (–)**
Scan objects	*Exocentric*	Ease+anticipate	Ease	Ease+anticipate	$F(1, 77) = 0.001$, $p = .982$	$F(1, 77) = 0.855$, $p = .358$	$F(1, 77) = 0.634$, $p = .428$
All	*N/A*	**Ease+anticipate ($p = .071$)**	Ease	Ease	$F(1, 77) = 2.34$, $p = .131$	**$F(1, 77) = 7.20$, $p = .009$ (+)**	**$F(1, 77) = 13.66$, $p < .001$ (–)**

baseline. Contrast tests using Scheffé's method analyzed the relative contributions of each manipulation.

Table 2 provides a summary of our results. Although we found no manipulation that significantly improved accuracy over the baseline for any individual primitive, several manipulations led to 100% accuracy rates across a very diverse population of online participants. Across all primitives, we found that a combination of easing and anticipation marginally increased accuracy over baseline motions ($p = .071$), demonstrating the potential of these manipulations in accurately expressing intent.

We analyzed our composite measure to gain a better understanding of what manipulations might improve both accuracy and response time. We found that an AFF using both arcing and easing motions when avoiding a person significantly outperformed baseline motions from both the egocentric ($p = .003$) and exocentric perspective ($p = .002$). Further, we found that easing motions marginally outperformed the baseline when departing a person from an egocentric perspective ($p = .075$). These results indicate that smooth velocities may be particularly important when closely interacting with users and that arcing may effectively signal that an AFF will not approach or collide with a user in a manner similar to hallway encounters with ground robots [31].

To further understand the effects of our manipulations, we analyzed the relative individual contributions of arcing, easing, and anticipation to the composite measure. We found that anticipation significantly lowered composite scores for several primitives; however, as these negative effects were not reflected in the accuracy measure, we believe the poor performance of anticipation in the composite measure may be due to slower response times caused by the increased trajectory lengths from adding anticipatory motions. These findings indicate a potential trade-off between how quickly and how accurately users are able to predict robot intent, and that each primitive and each combination of primitives may provide a different balance of this trade-off. We found that easing helped in a number of primitives, especially in the egocentric perspective where it significantly outperformed manipulations lacking easing for avoidance, $F(1, 77) = 5.76$, $p = .019$, and departure, $F(1, 77) = 13.62$, $p < .001$, providing further evidence that smooth velocity profiles are beneficial for AFFs operating near humans.

5. COMMUNICATIVE FLIGHT PATHS

Our formative exploration regarding the use of arcing, easing, and anticipatory motions to increase viewer understandings of AFF intent revealed that these manipulations appeared to positively effect viewers' understandings of robot intent for certain AFF primitives. To gain a further understanding of how such low-level motion manipulations might effect high-level colocated interactions with AFFs, we constructed complete, task-based AFF flight paths informed by the results from our formative exploration. These flight paths were created by blending several primitives, each of which used the motion manipulation that had achieved the highest composite score in our initial study. We then designed and conducted an in-person laboratory experiment in which participants interacted with a physically-embodied AFF to examine participant responses to an AFF using communicative flight primitives.

5.1. Hypotheses

We developed several hypotheses seeking to capture high-level interaction outcomes for participants observing a colocated AFF using flight paths composed from primitives with the arcing, easing, and anticipatory motion manipulations that our design exploration found to be most effective compared with non-manipulated primitives:

Hypothesis 1. Colocated individuals will prefer working with an AFF using manipulated flight paths than baseline paths.

Hypothesis 2. Colocated individuals will view manipulated AFF flight paths to be more natural and intuitive than baseline motions.

Hypothesis 3. Colocated individuals will feel safer interacting with an AFF using manipulated flight paths than baseline paths.

5.2. Study Design and Procedure

We designed a 2 × 1 within-participants study to evaluate participant responses when observing a physically embodied, colocated AFF executing a flight path designed to express intent. Our independent variable represented whether the AFF flight path was composed from primitives with or without the manipulations that scored highest in the composite measure from our online study, involving two levels: motion manipulations *present* and *absent*. Dependent variables included participants' ratings regarding the presence of the manipulations across conditions, robot usability, motion naturalness, and how safe they felt near the AFF.

During the experiment, the AFF completed two flight paths scanning several QR codes placed within the experimental environment. Each flight corresponded to one of the experimental conditions. Both flight paths contained the same number and type of primitives (Table 3), and the order in which the flight paths and experimental conditions were presented was counterbalanced. To implement a flight path, the experimenter activated pre-programmed primitives using custom Java code to send pitch, roll, yaw, and elevation commands during the experiment (e.g., hover, approach person), which were created both with and without motion manipulations. The flight path was controlled in this Wizard-of-Oz (WoZ) manner to ensure participant safety and to correct for any path errors.

Table 3: The primitives and the motion manipulations used in each condition of our in-person study.

Primitive	*Perspective*	Motion Manipulation Absent	Motion Manipulation Present
Take off	*Exocentric*	None	None
Hover	*Exocentric*	None	None
Cruise	*Exocentric*	None	None
Land	*Exocentric*	None	None
Approach person	*Egocentric*	None	Ease
Avoid person	*Exocentric*	None	Arc+ease
Depart person	*Egocentric*	None	Ease
Approach object	*Exocentric*	None	Anticipate
Depart object	*Exocentric*	None	Arc+ease

We used the Parrot AR.Drone 2.0 [3] as our AFF platform. Unlike the virtual AFF in the formative exploration, the AR.Drone has a distinct front with a forward-facing camera. To limit potential confounding effects of orientation, in both conditions, the operator always rotated the AFF to achieve an orientation facing the current target prior to executing primitives. To simplify arc implementation, we simultaneously varied the velocity commands for two of the pitch, roll, yaw, and elevation components by monotonically increasing one dimension while monotonically decreasing another such that the components always summed to one, generating a quarter arc with $\omega = 1$. Arcs were implemented such that the AFF arced vertically over the person for the "avoid person" primitive and best aligned the AFF with its next target for the "depart object" primitive. Easing was accomplished by sending velocity commands with magnitudes approximating our Gaussian curve; however, due to sensor limitations in tracking AFF travel distance, the ease in and out effects were scaled to take 1.5 seconds each instead of being based on distance traveled as in our formative exploration. Anticipation distances, used only for approaching objects, were pre-measured based on the experimental setup using $\theta = .3$, as previously described.

The experimental procedure took roughly 30 minutes and consisted of six main phases: (1) introduction, (2) observation, (3) evaluation, (4) observation, (5) evaluation, and (6) conclusion. First, the experimenter obtained informed consent and introduced the participant to an experimental confederate acting as a fellow participant. In reality, the confederate's presence allowed participants to view AFF movements around another person from an exocentric perspective. Participants and the confederate, seated at tables on opposite sides of a controlled room, were instructed to act as quality control personnel by evaluating two operators flying an AFF and identifying which QR codes each operator targeted during their flight (Figure 5). QR codes were placed throughout the environment, including in front of, above, and to the sides of both the participant and the confederate. In phases 2 and 3, participants observed an AFF execute a flight path that was controlled in the WoZ manner described above and completed a questionnaire evaluating their experience and the "operator" whom they believed had just flown the AFF. Phases 4 and 5 repeated these steps, with participants viewing and evaluating a second flight path under control of a second "operator." In phase 6, the experimenter collected demographic information, debriefed the participant, and paid them $5.00 for their time.

[3]http://ardrone2.parrot.com/

Figure 5: A participant (right) and a confederate in our experiment observe an AFF as it scans QR codes in their environment.

5.3. Participants

We recruited a total of 24 native-English-speaking participants (12 males and 12 females) [4] from the University of Wisconsin–Madison campus. Average participant age was 20.96 ($SD = 2.17$), with a range of 18–27. On a seven-point scale, participants reported a moderate prior familiarity with robots ($M = 3.04$, $SD = 1.41$), but a low familiarity with aerial robots ($M = 2.58$, $SD = 1.54$). Participants reported a wide range of occupations and majors, including 17 distinct areas of study.

5.4. Measurement and Analysis

Dependent variables were captured through a number of scales administered as a questionnaire. We constructed scales to confirm that participants noticed the differences in motion manipulations between conditions (6 items, Cronbach's $\alpha = .708$) and to evaluate participant ratings of usability for each AFF "operator" (4 items, Cronbach's $\alpha = .824$), the naturalness of the AFF motion (5 items, Cronbach's $\alpha = .910$), and how safe the participants felt interacting with the AFF (3 items, Cronbach's $\alpha = .746$). We utilized a one-way repeated-measures analysis of covariance (ANCOVA) with the main experimental manipulation as a fixed effect, participant gender and the order of the presented flight paths as covariates, and participant ID as a random effect to analyze the data from our manipulation checks and dependent variables.

5.5. Results

We verified manipulation success and found that participants correctly perceived the AFF's use of arcing, easing, and anticipation between conditions, $F(1, 23) = 12.00$, $p = .002$. We performed a post-hoc power analysis for each dependent variable. On the basis of our population size, the observed standard deviations, and a medium expected effect size ($\delta = .5$)[4], we found power levels of .838, .518, and .811 for usability ($\sigma = 1.15$), motion naturalness ($\sigma = 1.69$), and safety ($\sigma = 1.19$), respectively.

Hypothesis 1 predicted that participants would prefer working with an AFF that utilized flight paths with the most effective arcing, easing, and anticipation manipulations from our formative study. To test this hypothesis, we analyzed participants' ratings of each AFF "operator," using items on whether participants would want to work with the operator again, how well they believed the operator performed, and their confidence in the operator's control of the AFF. Participants significantly preferred the "operator" whose flight path used our manipulations, $F(1, 23) = 13.39$, $p = .001$.

Hypothesis 2 predicted that participants would find AFF flight paths composed from manipulated primitives to be more natural and smooth. An analysis on participant perceptions regarding the AFF's motion supported this hypothesis. Participants found manipulated paths to be significantly more natural, smooth, elegant, graceful, and intuitive, $F(1, 23) = 5.24$, $p = .032$.

Hypothesis 3 predicted that participants would feel safer working near an AFF executing flight paths with motions designed to convey intent. Our results provide support for this hypothesis, with participants rating the AFF that used primitives with motion manipulations as more safe and in control, $F(1, 23) = 5.18$, $p = .033$.

[4]A post-hoc power analysis is included in Section 5.5.

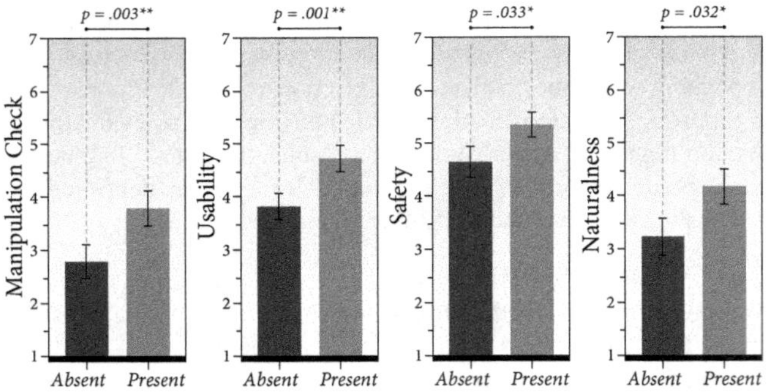

Figure 6: Results show that our manipulations positively effected participants' ratings of AFF usability, motion naturalness, and their sense of safety. (*) and (**), denote $p < .05$ and $p < .01$, respectively.

Figure 6 summarizes the major results of the study. Only marginal and significant effects are reported.

6. DISCUSSION

Hypothesis 1 predicted that individuals would prefer working with a colocated AFF that communicated its flight path intentions using motion. Our results confirmed Hypothesis 1, showing how low-level manipulations to motion primitives significantly increased the usability ratings of a colocated AFF. Our results also confirmed Hypotheses 2 and 3; participants rated manipulated flight motions as more natural and felt safer near an AFF using a manipulated flight path. The flight paths that participants found to be effective were constructed using the manipulations that our formative study showed to best express intent, demonstrating a potential link between the animation principles that inspired the manipulations, the expression of intent demonstrated in our formative study, and the improvement in usability found in our in-person experiment. However, while our findings highlight the promise of applying a limited set of animation principles to aerial robot motions to improve colocated interaction outcomes, future work is needed to further explore the choice of manipulations, identify optimal manipulation parameters, and explore additional methods of conveying intent.

Manipulation Considerations. Although our manipulations proved effective, we consider our work to be a preliminary exploration of the rich design space offered by manipulating AFF motions. Our formative exploration provided evidence that arcing, easing, and anticipation manipulations, inspired by the principles of natural motion and previous research in expressive robot motion, may also be beneficial in expressing intent. However, there are many other potential manipulations, such as modifying orientations or adding secondary actions, that might better convey intent, minimize energy constraints, or express other AFF properties. Our design focused on manipulating the motions of the interactive primitives, which appear most suited for communicating intent and can be reasonably manipulated without disrupting the core actions necessary to basic flight. Future explorations might examine manipulations to core primitives as well, for example modifying hovering behaviors to designate internal states such as idle or engaged.

Parameter Considerations. In choosing parameter values for real-world settings, designers must be aware of several considerations that may impact manipulation effectiveness. Environmental factors may constrain certain choices; in real-world interactions, choosing an improper R_{xyz} while arcing or too great a θ while performing anticipatory motion could lead to collisions with obstacles. Easing may not be appropriate or noticeable for very short distances or may result in inefficiencies for longer flights. For longer distances, the proportion of the trajectory using easing may be more effectively constrained using flight time, as we did in our in-person study, rather than distance. Parameter choices themselves may influence observer understanding regarding robot intent; for example, varying R_{xyz} values will alter arc shapes, potentially leading to different interpretations by viewers (e.g., people may prove more adept at interpreting vertical rather than horizontal arcs as avoidance). More work is needed to investigate how parameter choices might be optimized and adjusted to environmental constraints.

Platform Considerations. Although we controlled for orientation in our experiment, our AFF platform contains secondary motions due to the physical nature of its flight that may have confounded participants' abilities to assess AFF intent. Our platform, as with any quadrotor, adjusts pitch, roll, and yaw to navigate; such changes may themselves provide anticipatory movements telegraphing motion intent. As these secondary motions are proportional to acceleration, flight paths lacking a smooth velocity profile had more noticeable secondary movements, possibly reducing the effect size between our conditions. Future work might explore the potential confounding nature of such secondary movements as well as test the value of the motion manipulations on additional platforms with alternative form factors and constraints.

Additional Methods to Convey Intent. There are several other potential methods that might be used to convey AFF intent. Future work might explore orientation, which might act as a gaze mechanism in providing clues to robot intentions for AFFs with an obvious front. Alternatively, designers might utilize multimodal feedback such as LEDs or other signaling mechanisms prior to trajectory changes. Future work might address challenges such as designing signaling mechanisms for unconstrained six DOF movement, resolving issues in signal occlusion, and comparing the relative effectiveness of various signaling approaches. Communicating intentions quickly and unambiguously is a critical challenge for AFFs. Integrating communicative motions, orientations, and signaling mechanisms may ultimately prove the most effective solution.

6.1. Research and Design Implications

This research sought to explore the design of effective motions that might increase colocated AFF usability. Our work has important theoretical, methodological, and practical implications for researchers and developers seeking to bring AFFs into human environments. Our motion compositions, operationalized in a laboratory experiment, showcase the potential of subtle motion manipulations in eliciting high-level interaction outcomes, including participant desire to work near an AFF and sense of safety, and highlight a potential link between natural and intent-expressive motion. Our AFF motion framework outlines a design space for modifying the trajectory, velocity, and orientation profiles of AFF primitives to achieve outcomes such as conveying intent. Our design methodology demonstrates an effective strategy for examining the potential of various motion manipulations and illustrates how research in other relevant areas such as computer animation can inspire the design of effective human-robot interaction. Finally, this research might inform future explorations with AFFs by providing a model for AFF experimental scenarios and demonstrating practical manipulations that are shown to improve the reactions of colocated participants.

7. CONCLUSION

In this work, we sought to explore how designers might improve robot motions to increase the usability of free-flying robots acting in human environments. After analyzing the motion design space by deconstructing high-level flight paths into composite primitives, we developed several parameterized manipulations to the motions of these primitives, inspired by computer and film animation principles. In a formative exploration using a virtual AFF, we investigated the usefulness of these manipulations in conveying intent. Our findings informed the design of manipulations to primitive motions for a physically embodied AFF to use while executing task-based flight paths. We evaluated these flight paths in an in-person experiment, and found that our motion designs significantly improved participants' preferences for working with an AFF, ratings of motion naturalness, and sense of safety, demonstrating the potential of designing flight motions to enhance user interactions.

8. ACKNOWLEDGMENTS

This research was supported by a NASA Space Technology Research Fellowship under award NNX12AN14H. We thank Mark Micire, Brandi Hefty, Ross Luo, Catherine Steffel, and Danielle Albers for their assistance in this research.

9. REFERENCES

[1] T. Asfour and R. Dillmann. Human-like motion of a humanoid robot arm based on a closed-form solution of the inverse kinematics problem. In *Proc IROS'03*, volume 2, pages 1407–1412, 2003.

[2] G. R. Bergersen, J. E. Hannay, D. I. Sjoberg, T. Dyba, and A. Karahasanovic. Inferring skill from tests of programming performance: Combining time and quality. In *Proc ESEM'11*, pages 305–314, 2011.

[3] S. S. Bueno, J. R. Azinheira, J. Ramos Jr, E. C. d. Paiva, P. Rives, A. Elfes, J. R. Carvalho, G. F. Silveira, et al. Project aurora: Towards an autonomous robotic airship. In *Proc IROS'02.*, pages 43–54, 2002.

[4] J. Cohen. *Statistical power analysis for the behavioral sciencies*. Routledge, 1988.

[5] A. D. Dragan, K. C. Lee, and S. S. Srinivasa. Legibility and predictability of robot motion. In *Proc HRI'13*, pages 301–308, 2013.

[6] A. Elfes, S. Siqueira Bueno, M. Bergerman, and J. Ramos Jr. A semi-autonomous robotic airship for environmental monitoring missions. In *Proc ICRA'98.*, volume 4, pages 3449–3455, 1998.

[7] F. Ferland, F. Pomerleau, C. T. Le Dinh, and F. Michaud. Egocentric and exocentric teleoperation interface using real-time, 3d video projection. In *Proc HRI'09*, pages 37–44, 2009.

[8] T. Fong, R. Berka, M. Bualat, M. Diftler, M. Micire, D. Mittman, V. SunSpiral, and C. Provencher. The human exploration telerobotics project. In *Proc Global Space Exploration Conference*, 2012.

[9] T. Fong, M. Micire, T. Morse, E. Park, C. Provencher, V. To, D. Wheeler, D. Mittman, R. J. Torres, and E. Smith. Smart spheres: a telerobotic free-flyer for intravehicular activities in space. In *Proc. AIAA Space'13*, 2013.

[10] M. Garcia, J. Dingliana, and C. O'Sullivan. Perceptual evaluation of cartoon physics: accuracy, attention, appeal. In *Proc. APGV'08*, pages 107–114, 2008.

[11] M. J. Gielniak, C. K. Liu, and A. L. Thomaz. Secondary action in robot motion. In *IEEE RO-MAN'10*, pages 310–315, 2010.

[12] M. J. Gielniak, C. K. Liu, and A. L. Thomaz. Stylized motion generalization through adaptation of velocity profiles. In *IEEE RO-MAN'10*, pages 304–309, 2010.

[13] M. J. Gielniak and A. L. Thomaz. Anticipation in robot motion. In *IEEE RO-MAN'11*, pages 449–454, 2011.

[14] M. J. Gielniak and A. L. Thomaz. Enhancing interaction through exaggerated motion synthesis. In *Proc HRI'12*, pages 375–382, 2012.

[15] M. A. Goodrich, B. S. Morse, D. Gerhardt, J. L. Cooper, M. Quigley, J. A. Adams, and C. Humphrey. Supporting wilderness search and rescue using a camera-equipped mini uav. *Journal of Field Robotics*, 25(1-2):89–110, 2008.

[16] J. Irizarry, M. Gheisari, and B. N. Walker. Usability assessment of drone technology as safety inspection tools. *Journal of ITcon'12*, 17:194–212, 2012.

[17] K. Kamewari, M. Kato, T. Kanda, H. Ishiguro, and K. Hiraki. Six-and-a-half-month-old children positively attribute goals to human action and to humanoid-robot motion. *Cognitive Development*, 20(2):303–320, 2005.

[18] H. Kidokoro, T. Kanda, D. Brscic, and M. Shiomi. Will I bother here? A robot anticipating its influence on pedestrian walking comfort. In *Proc HRI'13*, pages 259–266, 2013.

[19] J.-H. Kim, J.-J. Choi, H. J. Shin, and I.-K. Lee. Anticipation effect generation for character animation. In *Advances in Computer Graphics*, pages 639–646. 2006.

[20] R. Kirby. *Social Robot Navigation*. PhD thesis, Robotics Institute, Carnegie Mellon University, Pittsburgh, PA, May 2010.

[21] T. Krajník, V. Vonásek, D. Fišer, and J. Faigl. Ar-drone as a platform for robotic research and education. In *Research and Education in Robotics-EUROBOT 2011*, pages 172–186. 2011.

[22] J. Krasner. *Motion graphic design: applied history and aesthetics*. Focal Press, 2013.

[23] D. Kulic and E. Croft. Physiological and subjective responses to articulated robot motion. *Robotica*, 25(01):13–27, 2007.

[24] J.-Y. Kwon and I.-K. Lee. An animation bilateral filter for slow-in and slow-out effects. *Graphical Models*, 73(5):141–150, 2011.

[25] J. Lasseter. Principles of traditional animation applied to 3d computer animation. In *Proc SIGGRAPH'87*, volume 21, pages 35–44, 1987.

[26] C. Lichtenthaler, T. Lorenz, M. Karg, and A. Kirsch. Increasing perceived value between human and robots – measuring legibility in human aware navigation. In *Proc ARSO'12*, pages 89–94, 2012.

[27] J. Mainprice, E. Akin Sisbot, L. Jaillet, J. Cortés, R. Alami, and T. Siméon. Planning human-aware motions using a sampling-based costmap planner. In *Proc ICRA'11*, pages 5012–5017, 2011.

[28] J. Mainprice, M. Gharbi, T. Siméon, and R. Alami. Sharing effort in planning human-robot handover tasks. In *IEEE RO-MAN'12*, pages 764–770, 2012.

[29] C. L. Nehaniv, K. Dautenhahn, J. Kubacki, M. Haegele, C. Parlitz, and R. Alami. A methodological approach relating the classification of gesture to identification of human intent in the context of human-robot interaction. In *IEEE RO-MAN'05*, pages 371–377, 2005.

[30] W. S. Ng and E. Sharlin. Collocated interaction with flying robots. In *IEEE RO-MAN'11*, pages 143–149, 2011.

[31] E. Pacchierotti, H. I. Christensen, and P. Jensfelt. Human-robot embodied interaction in hallway settings: a pilot user study. In *IEEE RO-MAN'05*, pages 164–171, 2005.

[32] K. Pfeil, S. L. Koh, and J. LaViola. Exploring 3d gesture metaphors for interaction with unmanned aerial vehicles. In *Proc IUI'13*, pages 257–266, 2013.

[33] T. Ribeiro and A. Paiva. The illusion of robotic life: principles and practices of animation for robots. In *Proc HRI'12*, pages 383–390, 2012.

[34] M. Saerbeck and C. Bartneck. Perception of affect elicited by robot motion. In *Proc HRI'10*, pages 53–60, 2010.

[35] M. Saerbeck and A. J. van Breemen. Design guidelines and tools for creating believable motion for personal robots. In *IEEE RO-MAN'07*, pages 386–391, 2007.

[36] L. Scandolo and T. Fraichard. An anthropomorphic navigation scheme for dynamic scenarios. In *Proc ICRA'11*, pages 809–814, 2011.

[37] N. Sharkey. Death strikes from the sky: the calculus of proportionality. *Technology and Society Magazine, IEEE*, 28(1):16–19, 2009.

[38] M. Sharma, D. Hildebrandt, G. Newman, J. E. Young, and R. Eskicioglu. Communicating affect via flight path exploring use of the laban effort system for designing affective locomotion paths. In *Proc HRI'13*, pages 293–300, 2013.

[39] K. Shoemake. Animating rotation with quaternion curves. In *Proc SIGGRAPH'85*, volume 19, pages 245–254, 1985.

[40] L. Takayama, D. Dooley, and W. Ju. Expressing thought: improving robot readability with animation principles. In *Proc HRI'11*, pages 69–76, 2011.

[41] J. G. Trafton, N. L. Cassimatis, M. D. Bugajska, D. P. Brock, F. E. Mintz, and A. C. Schultz. Enabling effective human-robot interaction using perspective-taking in robots. *Systems, Man and Cybernetics, IEEE Trans on*, 35(4):460–470, 2005.

[42] A. Van Breemen. Bringing robots to life: Applying principles of animation to robots. In *Proc CHI'04*, 2004.

[43] A. J. van Breemen. Animation engine for believable interactive user-interface robots. In *Proc IROS'04*, volume 3, pages 2873–2878, 2004.

[44] B. Wang, X. Chen, Q. Wang, L. Liu, H. Zhang, and B. Li. Power line inspection with a flying robot. In *Proc CARPI'10*, pages 1–6, 2010.

Familiarization to Robot Motion

Anca D. Dragan
Carnegie Mellon University
adragan@cs.cmu.edu

Siddhartha S. Srinivasa
Carnegie Mellon University
siddh@cs.cmu.edu

ABSTRACT

We study the effect of *familiarization* on the *predictability* of robot motion. Predictable motion is motion that matches the observer's expectation. Because of the difficulty robots have in learning motion from user demonstrations, we explore the idea of having *users* learn from *robot* demonstrations — how accurate do users get at predicting how the robot will move? We find that although familiarization significantly increases predictability, its utility depends on how natural the motion is. Overall, familiarization shows great promise, but needs to be combined with other methods that generate appropriate motion with which to be familiarized.

1. INTRODUCTION

We are interested in generating robot motion in the presence of an observer. Imagine a robot like HERB from Fig.1 collaborating with a human on a manipulation task like cleaning up the dining room table. Our goal is to make the motion *predictable*:

DEFINITION 1. *Predictable motion is motion that matches the observer's expectation of how the robot will move [9].*

Predictability is desirable in any interaction, and is especially important for human-robot collaboration [2, 4], where it serves two *goals*: 1) it enables the collaborator to predict how the robot will move (by its very definition), which enables them to plan their own motion accordingly and move simultaneously with the robot; and 2) it increases their *comfort* with the robot (we test this in our experiments).

As the definition implies, to generate predictable motion we must know how an observer expects the robot to move. The traditional paradigm for solving this problem is Learning from Demonstration (LfD), where the observer provides several examples of how they expect the robot to move. The robot learns from these examples using techniques like Gaussian Mixture Models [6], Dynamic Movement Primitives [20], or Inverse Reinforcement Learning [28].

These have shown great success for learning particular skills, or learning general motion in low-dimensional spaces, but suffer in two critical ways: they become computationally intractable in high-dimensional spaces [19], and novice users find it difficult to provide good demonstrations [1].

In this paper, we study the opposite teacher-learner relationship: rather than focusing on the robot learning from the user's demonstrations, we explore the idea of the user learning from the robot's demonstrations, via *familiarization*:

HRI'14, March 3–6, 2014, Bielefeld, Germany.
Copyright 2014 ACM 978-1-4503-2658-2/14/03 ...$15.00.
http://dx.doi.org/10.1145/2559636.2559674.

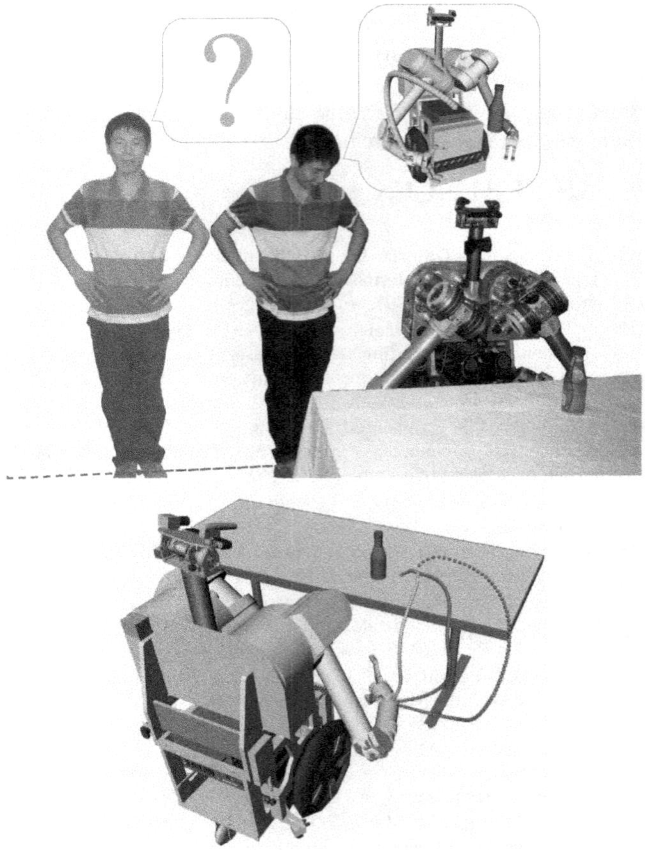

Figure 1: (Top) One of our users getting more comfortable with working/standing next to the robot after familiarization, as he can better predict how the robot will move. (Bottom) Users identify the robot's actual trajectory (we plot here its end effector trace only, in green, but show users the robot actually moving along it) as the one they expect more often after familiarization.

DEFINITION 2. *Familiarization to robot motion is the process of exposing the observer to how the robot moves in different situations.*

Many times, we take for granted that familiarization works. Familiarization is often used in studies prior to experimental conditions [13], under the assumption that it will adapt the user's mental model of the robot. Studies on sensemaking [27] support this assumption [21, 18, 3, 14, 23], as does the remarkable adaptability of humans: we learn new languages [17], adapt to new ways of communicating [24], and even remap existing sensors like our tongues to new senses, like vision [26].

Here, we study the effects of familiarization to *motion*. On the one hand, the breadth of human adaptability suggests that with familiarization, the robot's motion will become significantly more predictable. On the other hand,

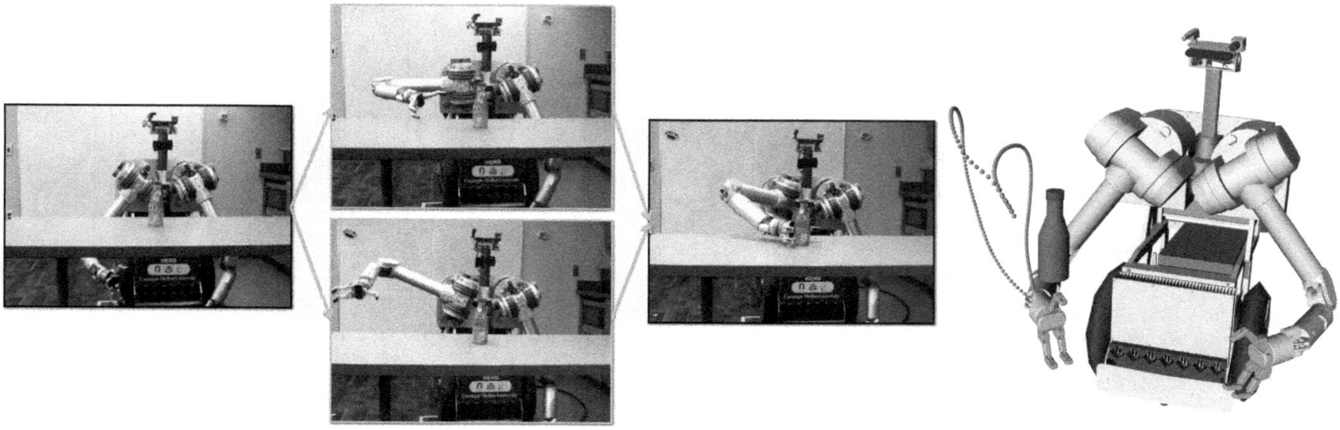

Figure 2: For the same situation, the trajectories for the more natural motion in Sec. 3 (top, green), and for the less natural motion in Sec. 4 (bottom, orange).

the same obstacles robots face when learning motion — the high-dimensionality and complexity of the space — might induce similar limitations in humans.

We ran a series of three experiments investigating the effect of familiarization to two different types of motion, on both the users' ability to predict how the robot moves (Goal 1), as well as the users' comfort with the robot (Goal 2).

Our first experiment (Sec. 3) analyzed familiarization to motion produced by a state-of-the-art trajectory optimizer. We evaluated predictability before and after familiarization by testing whether users identify the actual robot motion as the one they expect it to execute (from a set of different motions, see Fig.1, bottom), as well as asking users to rate the motion on a subjective predictability scale.

Our results do support the utility of familiarization — *the motion became significantly more predictable.* However, we came across unexpected limitations of familiarization. We found that despite improving predictability, familiarization can fail to make the motion fully predictable, and can fail to generalize to new situations.

Next, we tested familiarization on a different type of motion. The initial study indicated that the optimizer-generated motion was moderately natural:

DEFINITION 3. *Natural motion is motion that is predictable without (or prior to) familiarization.*

This finding raised an interesting question: would familiarizations still have an effect when the motion is less natural? In a second experiment (Sec. 4), we found that some unnatural motion may *never* reach a high predictability level, even when exposed to over twice the number of motions, suggesting that familiarization saturates.

Next, we tested the practical effects of increasing predictability (Sec. 5) — does the user comfort with working or standing next to the robot also increase? We found a significant effect of familiarization on comfort. However, a lot of users over-trusted the robot, moving closer to it than would be safe. This has a surprising implication: less predictable motion might actually be safer in some situations, as it might prevent over-trust.

Overall, familiarization is an essential aspect of human-robot interactions, and it is important to study it and understand its limitations — sometimes, we cannot rely solely on human adaptability. Our data suggests that familiarization to motion helps, but *cannot be used exclusively for generating predictable motion.* The robot still has the burden of producing motion that is not too unnatural — motion *with which it is easy to familiarize.* However, given such motion, familiarization shows great promise for significantly improving predictability and ultimately enabling better human-robot collaboration.

2. GENERATING MOTION

Predictable motion matches what the observer expects. The theory of action interpretation suggests that humans apply the principle of rational action when observing other humans [10], as well as when observing robots [12]: they expect the most efficient action to achieve the goal.

In our previous work, we translated the principle of rational action to robot motion in the form of cost optimization [9]: if humans expect efficient motion, then they expect the robot to optimize some cost function defining efficiency.

Thus, generating predictable motion has two requirements: optimizing cost, and finding the cost to optimize.

Generating Motion by Optimizing Cost. We optimize cost functions over motion by functional gradient optimization [29]. We treat motion trajectories as functions mapping time to robot configurations, $\xi : [0,1] \to \mathcal{Q}$. Given a cost functional C defined over the space of trajectories Ξ,

$$C : \Xi \to \mathbb{R}^+ \tag{1}$$

we iteratively improve an initial trajectory ξ_0.

At every iteration, we minimize a first-order approximation of C about the current trajectory, subject to a regularization term which penalizes distances with respect to a metric A on Ξ:

$$\xi_{i+1} = \arg\min_{\xi \in \Xi} C[\xi_i] + \nabla C_{\xi_i}^T(\xi - \xi_i) + \frac{\eta}{2}||\xi - \xi_i||_A^2 \tag{2}$$

We iterate until convergence. For state of the art optimizers like CHOMP, this is typically in the order of 1-2 seconds.

The Cost Function. The main challenge in generating predictable motion is finding the cost functional C that the human observer expects. In this paper, we test how well the robot can adapt the observer to its own C, through familiarization.

We test familiarization with a typical cost functional used in CHOMP [29]. This functional is composed of two terms: C_{prior} which measures the efficiency of the motion, and C_{obs} which measures how safe the trajectory is in staying away from obstacles:

$$C[\xi] = C_{prior}[\xi] + \lambda C_{obs} \tag{3}$$

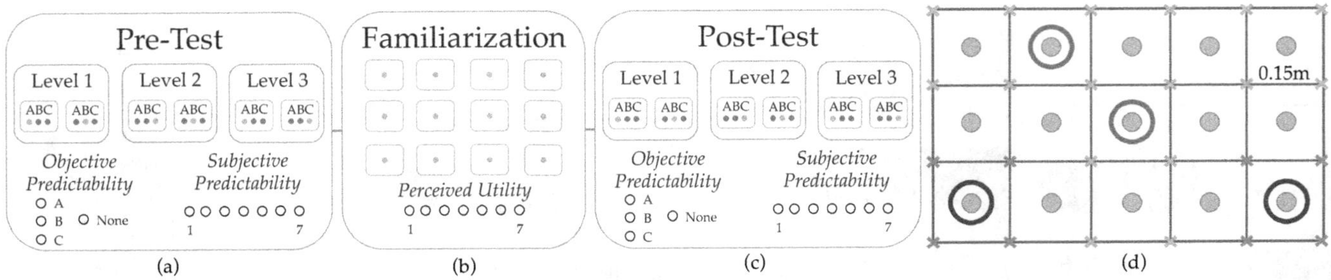

Figure 3: The overall experimental procedure, consisting of a familiarization phase (b), and a pre- and post-test for predictability (a and c). The tests involve three types of examples (`Levels 1-3`), each with two instances to aid robustness. For each example, we show users three trajectories and ask them to identify which one they expect the robot to perform, as well as rate each on a predictability scale. The grid in (d) depicts target object placements on the table (shown in Fig.1 and Fig.2) to produce the familiarization examples. The ones we re-use for testing (`Level 1`) are highlighted in blue, and the ones we set aside for testing-only (`Level 3`) are highlighted in brown. The crosses represent additional example locations we use in Sec. 4.3.

Our implementation of CHOMP uses path length as the measure of efficiency:

$$C_{prior}[\xi] = \int ||\xi(t)'||^2 dt \tag{4}$$

We use CHOMP-generated motions in Sec. 3, when we test how useful familiarization is for state-of-the art generated motion. Fig.2 (top, green) shows one of the example motions. We find that they are moderately natural, i.e. have good levels of predictability even before familiarization, and that familiarization increases their predictability further. This prompts us to test familiarization for less natural motion in Sec. 4 — would it still work?

A Less Natural Alternative. To test familiarization on less natural motion, we changed the cost function. Rather than using CHOMP's notion of efficiency from (4), which uses the same weight on each of the robot's degrees of freedom, we weigh different degrees of freedom differently:

$$C_{prior_W}[\xi] = \int ||\xi'(t)||^2_W dt = \int \xi'(t)^T W \xi'(t) dt \tag{5}$$

By choosing a W with lower values for the shoulder joints and higher values for the wrist joints, the robot starts penalizing motion in the wrist, and starts moving it less at the expense of moving the shoulder more. This is contrary to what human motion does in reaching tasks [15], which suggests it will also make the robot's motion less natural. Our results in Sec. 4) support this.

Fig.2 shows a comparison between the original CHOMP cost function and this modified version (bottom, orange).

3. DOES FAMILIARIZATION WORK?

We designed a user study to test the utility of familiarization to robot motion. Does exposing the users to how the robot moves *help* them form the right expectations in the future? And if so, *how good* do users get at predicting the robot's motion?

3.1 Methods

We exposed users to examples of the robot's motion (Fig.3, b), and measured improvement in predictability by administering a pre- (Fig.3, a) and post-test (Fig.3, c), using both objective and subjective measures. We detail our procedure below.

3.1.1 Design Decisions

The complexity and high-dimensionality of robot motion are the key obstacle to the utility of familiarization. *We designed our experiment to alleviate this issue: we focus on familiarization by training.*

We made familiarization a targeted learning experience, rather than treating it as exposure to the robot "in the wild". We chose a narrowly scoped task, structured the examples users see by parametrizing the task, and presented users with many examples comprising a good task discretization.

Robot Platform. We use the robot HERB [22] from Fig.1 as a platform, a bi-manual mobile manipulator with a total of 24 degrees of freedom.

HERB is a good choice for testing familiarization because it is not too anthropomorphic (antropomorphic robots could inherit the biases of human motion, hindering the effectiveness of familiarization), yet it still has a familiar structure, with a head and two arms. Each arm has 7 DOF, much like human arms: three in the shoulder, one in the elbow, and one in the wrist.

Robot Task. Rather than showing users a snippet of a daily activity, we chose to show them structured examples that better support learning. To do so, we narrowed the scope of our study to a single type of task, and extracted examples by parameterizing the task and discretizing the parameter space.

Of all possible tasks, we focus on *reaching motions.* Reaching for an object (and grasping it) is one of the most common manipulation tasks state-of-the art robots perform (along with placing): we see it in manufacturing environments [11] as well as in personal [22, 5] and assistive robotics [16].

We designed a typical reaching task, where HERB uses its right arm to reach for a target object on the table (see Fig.2). We parametrize the task by a starting configuration for the arm, a goal configuration where the robot can grasp the target object, and obstacles in the environment which the robot's motion must not collide with.

We selected these parameters by replicating a scenario in which HERB drives up to the table and reaches for the bottle: we selected HERB's typical driving configuration as the start, and kept the table in place as the obstacle.

Example Number and Order. We generated examples by varying the goal parameter. We varied the location of the target object on the tabletop, as depicted in Fig.3 (d). To aid familiarization, we discretized this space *finely*, forming a 5×3 grid with 0.15m resolution for where the bottle can be placed. This creates a space of 15 possible examples, 2 of which we kept aside for our pre- and post- test `Level 3` (details in Sec. 3.1.2, "Manipulated Factors").

We followed human teaching patterns and presented the examples to the users in the order from most simple to most complex [25]. Here, we defined simplicity based on how efficient each trajectory was relative to the distance between the starting configuration and the goal.

User Instructions. We decided to specifically instruct the users to actively try to learn how the robot moves, in line with our decision of making this a learning task rather than a passive observation task.

3.1.2 Design Overview

Manipulated Factors. We manipulate two factors: `familiarization` and `difference level`.

We manipulate `familiarization` by testing the predictability of motion both `before` and `after` exposing the users to the examples. We use recordings of HERB executing the CHOMP-generated motions.

With `difference level`, we look at test situations that relate in different ways to the examples.

We select two of the 13 possible scenarios the user will see during training and identify these as `Level 1` situations. Next, we select one of the two and change the start configuration or add another obstacle, and identify these as `Level 2` situations. Finally, the user is shown the two scenarios that will not be shown as part of the training set. These scenarios are `Level 3` situations.

Fig.4 (a-c) shows an example situation for each level. Since there is no clear ordering in terms of difficulty between levels 2 and 3, we keep this variable as nominal (as opposed to ordinal) in our analysis below.

We use two situations for each difference level (as opposed to only one) in order to alleviate the risk of introducing confounds in the manipulation. This leads to a total of 6 test situations, which we present to the users in a randomized order both before and after familiarization.

Dependent Measures. We measured the predictability of the robot's motion in the 6 test situations using both an *objective*, as well as a *subjective* metric.

Objective Predictability. For our objective metric, we measured the accuracy with which users can identify the robot's actual motion from a set of different motions. This is a way of of objectively measuring whether users expect the motion that the robot would execute.

For each test situation, we first presented the users with an image of the robot in the starting configuration, with the bottle placed in the corresponding location. We asked them to spend a minute imagining how they expect the robot to move his arm. To make sure they think the task through, we asked them to describe the motion.

Next, we showed them video recordings of HERB executing three motion trajectories (in randomized order). One of these is the actual trajectory (represented by a green dot in Fig.3 (a) and (c)) produced according to the procedure outlined in Sec. 2.

We selected the other two motions (by varying the goal configuration) such that they are spatially similar either to the actual trajectory from the same situation, or to the actual trajectory from one of the example situations.

We imposed a minimum distance requirement on the test motions: they have to achieve a minimum distance (either at the end effector or at the elbow) from one another. We choose a threshold (of 0.2m) to signify "practical difference": if the users cannot distinguish among motions that are too similar, this has no practical side effect — at the limit, differences among motions will not even be observable to the naked eye; on the other had, if users mistake the motions for one in which the robot's arm reaches a different part of the space, this can have severe practical consequences when working next to the robot.

These two motions are represented as red dots in Fig.3 (a) and (c). Fig.1 (bottom) shows the end effector traces for the three candidate trajectories in one of the test situations.

After seeing the three trajectories, we asked the users a multiple-choice question: "Which of the trajectories matched the one you expected?". The choices were trajectories 1-3. as well as a "None" option (which, despite the strong wording in the question of having "matched" the expected trajectory, was only used in 12% of the cases).

Subjective Predictability. For our subjective metric, we designed a scale for predictability, comprised of three 1-7 Likert scale statements shown in Table I.

TABLE I: PREDICTABILITY SCALE.

Trajectory 'x' matched what I expected.
Trajectory 'x' is predictable.
I would be surprised if the robot executed Trajectory 'x' in this situation.

We asked users, after seeing all three trajectories, to indicate their level of agreement with each statement, for each trajectory (in order to not give away which trajectory HERB would actually execute). In our analysis below, we show that the scale has internal reliability, and combine the ratings for HERB's actual trajectory (with the third statement reverse-coded) into our subjective metric.

Aside from measuring the motion's predictability before and after familiarization, we were also interested in two additional measures: whether the users thought that familiarization helped, and what they thought of the robot's motion.

Perceived Utility. After we showed them the motion examples, users did Likert self reports on utility (whether seeing how HERB moves helps them predict how HERB would move in a new situation), on improvement (whether they are better now at predicting how HERB would move than they were originally), and on confidence (whether they are confident they can predict how HERB would move).

Motion Attributes. We also asked them about the motions that they saw. We were interested in whether the CHOMP motions made sense to them, whether they were more fluid or more machine-like than they originally expected, and whether they would be comfortable working next to the robot if it moved in the way they saw.

Subject Allocation. We opted for a within-subjects design. We explicitly wanted to measure predictability for the same user before and after `familiarization` in order to avoid additional variance. Furthermore, users never get to see what the right answer to the test situations are. This enables us to treat `difference level` as a within-subjects factor as well.

We recruited 25 users (11 female and 14 male, with ages between 19 and 56, $M = 34.68$, $SD = 10.29$, and only 5 reporting having a technical background) via Amazon Mechanical Turk. They performed the study in an average of 50 minutes. To avoid rushed responses, we prevented users from advancing in the task without watching all videos and answering all questions, and we asked control questions at the end to verify attention.

Hypothesis. *Familiarization significantly improves the predictability of motion, as reflected by both the objective accuracy metric, as well as the subjective user ratings.*

3.2 Analysis

Accuracy (objective). Supporting our hypothesis, `familiarization` had a significant effect on the users' accuracy in recognizing HERB's actual motion, as indicated by a logistic regression using `familiarization` and `difference level` as factors ($\chi^2(1, 300) = 8.53$, $p = .0035$). There was

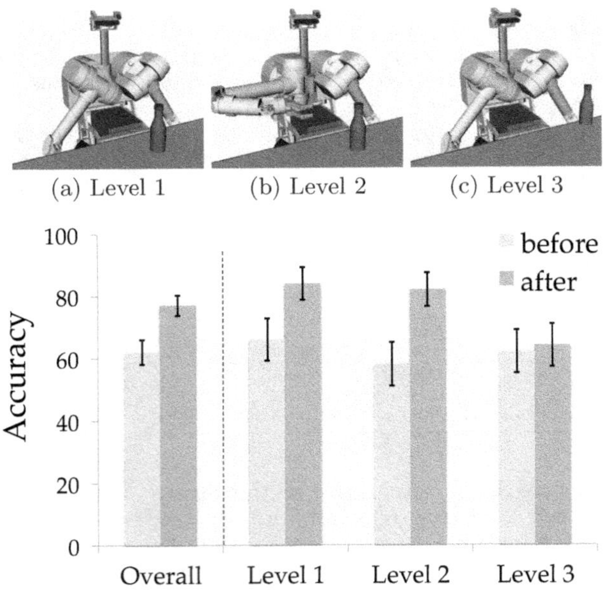

Figure 4: Overall, familiarization significantly improves the accuracy in recognizing the robot's motion (left). Different test situations, however, show different improvements (right). Error bars show standard error.

no main effect for `difference level`, and no interaction effect. A factorial repeated-measures ANOVA treating accuracy as a 0-1 continuous variable ($F(1, 270)$, $p = .0039$) confirmed the significance of `familiarization`. This test has the advantage of allowing a treatment of the user ID as a random variable, and is considered to be robust to dichotomous data[7]. These results are encouraging, indicating that:

RESULT 1. ***Familiarization can make motion more predictable.***

Prior to familiarization, users already had a 62% accuracy (significantly higher than the 33% random choice, Pearson $\chi^2(1, 150) = 55.47$, $p < .0001$), suggesting that the CHOMP-generated motions were *moderately natural.*

Familiarization did significantly increase accuracy, but, surprisingly, only to 77%.

Although familiarization helps make the CHOMP motion more predictable, our data suggest that it has important limitations: despite the test situations coming from the same task as the training ones, and despite the fine discretization of the task space, users were not able to always identify the correct trajectory from other (spatially different) trajectories. For distance `Level 1`, i.e. testing situations that were also present in the training examples, the accuracy was highest, at 84%.

Fig.4 shows the accuracy improvement after familiarization, both across tasks as well as split by the `difference level`: accuracy is highest on testing on situations that were also used as training examples (`Level 1`), as well as on situations with the same target location as a training example, but different starting/obstacle locations (`Level 2`). The test situations that were at the limits of the task (`Level 3`) did not see an improvement with familiarization (Fig.4, right), suggesting that familiarization can have limited generalization.

RESULT 2. ***Familiarization does not always make the motion fully predictable, and can have limited generalization ability.***

Predictability Rating (subjective). Our scale for predictability comprised of ratings for expectedness, predictability, and surprise (reverse-coded) showed internal reliability (Chronbach's $\alpha = 0.91$), leading to a combined score for predictability based on the three ratings. This score is correlated with the accuracy (Pearson's $r(288) = .73$, $p < .0001$).

To test the effects of `familiarization` and `difference level` on this score, we ran a factorial repeated-measures ANOVA. This showed a significant main effect for `familiarization` ($F(1, 270) = 10.17$, $p = .0016$), but not for `difference level` (and no interaction effect). These results are consistent with our findings for accuracy, and strengthen the utility of familiarization to robot motion.

TABLE II: UTILITY OF FAMILIARIZATION RATINGS.

Utility Type	M	SD	$t(24)$ for $M \neq 4$	p
example helpfulness for prediction	5.76	1.09	8.06	<.0001
improvement in prediction capability	5.6	1.32	6.04	<.0001
confidence in prediction capability	5.76	0.97	9.07	<.0001

Perceived Utility. Table II shows the responses for the perceived utility of familiarization. Participants thought that seeing the videos helps them predict how HERB will move in a new situation, that they are better at predicting how HERB will move in a new situation than they were before seeing the videos, and were confident they can make this prediction accurately. These ratings are significantly different from the neutral stance of 4 (1-7 scale), even after Bonferroni corrections for multiple comparisons.

TABLE III: MOTION RATINGS.

Motion Attribute	M	SD	$t(24)$ for $M \neq 4$	p
makes sense	6.56	0.71	17.98	<.0001
more fluid than expected	5.52	1.66	4.57	<.0001
more machine-like than expected	2.32	1.62	-5.17	<.0001
comfort for collaboration	5.8	1.15	7.79	<.0001

Motion Attributes. Table III shows the responses for the motion attribute questions, together with the results of a t-test against the neutral mean of 4. Participants strongly agreed that HERB's motion made sense. They also agreed that the motions are more fluent than they originally expected, and disagreed that the motions were more machine like. All participants but one reported that they would be comfortable collaborating with HERB on a close-proximity task if it moved in the way they saw. The means are significantly different from the neutral stance, and remain significant after Bonferroni corrections.

These findings, together with the initial accuracy on CHOMP motions, suggest that CHOMP makes a good starting choice for familiarization. The next section will put familiarization to a more difficult test. It will study the effect of familiarization for less natural motions — does it still work, and how predictable do these motions become?

4. FAMILIARIZATION TO UNNATURAL MOTION

Our results showed an improvement with familiarization when the motions are moderately natural. This led us to wonder: what if the robot moved in an unnatural way? Would familiarization still increase predictability?

4.1 Methods

To investigate the effect of familiarization on less natural motion, we ran the same study, replacing the type of motion performed by the robot with the less natural version from Sec. 2, also depicted in Fig.2 (bottom, orange).

For the testing situations, we were interested in whether familiarization would change the users' model and make them select the actual trajectory against the more natural CHOMP one. Thus, we selected the original CHOMP trajectory as one of the alternatives whenever possible, i.e. whenever it was practically different (using our definition from Sec. 3.1.2 of having a difference in the end effector or elbow locations of above 0.2m).

We recruited 25 new users via Amazon Mechanical Turk, and eliminated 1 for failing to answer the control questions correctly, leading to 11 male and 13 female users, with ages between 19 and 45 ($M = 29.16$, $SD = 7.12$).

Hypothesis. *Familiarization significantly improves the predictability of the less natural motion. Furthermore, it brings the less natural motion to the same predictability level as the more natural motion.*

4.2 Analysis

Manipulation Check. The initial accuracy this time was only 34% (close to the random choice mark of 33%[1]). This confirms that the motions were less natural (less predictable before familiarization) than the CHOMP motions from the previous section ($\chi^2(1, 588) = 47.38$, $p < .0001$). We call this type of motion *moderately unnatural*: low accuracy without going below the random choice threshold.

Accuracy and Rating Fig.5(left) shows the accuracy before and after familiarization, as compared to the data from the more natural motions in the previous section. Consistent with our previous findings, and with our hypothesis, `familiarization` has a significant positive effect on accuracy, as evidenced by a logistic regression with our two factors ($\chi^2 = 6.95$, $p = .0084$).

Despite this improvement, the accuracy after familiarization is merely 48% — familiarization fails to bring this motion to the same predictability level that it brings the CHOMP motion (i.e. 77% accuracy). This is also supported by the ratings on our predictability scale: although familiarization has a positive main effect on the score ($F(1, 286) = 5.09$, $p = .0248$), the score after familiarization is significantly lower than for the CHOMP motion, as seen in Fig.5(center).

Furthermore, for the test situations where a CHOMP trajectory was one of the options, more users chose the CHOMP trajectory (48%) than the trajectory generated by the cost function with which they were familiarized (43% on these situations).

Given that the initial accuracy on these tests was 29%, familiarization did change the users' model of how the robot moves, *but was not enough to make the true model more likely in their view than the more natural CHOMP model.*

Combined Analysis. The difference between the moderately natural and the moderately unnatural motions is also reflected when looking at the data overall. A logistic regression with `naturalness` (low versus high), `familiarization`, and `difference level` as factors shows significant main effects for all three factors (`naturalness` $\chi^2(1, 588) = 49.71$, $p < .0001$; `familiarization` $\chi^2(1, 588) = 15.46$, $p < .0001$; `difference level` $\chi^2(2, 588) = 14.26$, $p = .0008$). It also shows an interaction effect between difference level and initial predictability ($\chi^2(2, 588) = 10.19$, $p = .0061$).

A factorial repeated-measures ANOVA yielded the same results, and the Tukey HSD post-hoc analysis on the interaction effect revealed that all conditions for the moderately natural motions had significantly better accuracy than all moderately unnatural conditions, with the exception of difference level 2. The tests in this level maintained high accuracy, possibly due to a similarity in the motion for the test situations in this difference level).

[1]this is 25% if we take the "none" option into account

Overall, we see that lower naturalness of motion results in lower predictability even after familiarization. This suggests a second limit:

RESULT 3. ***Familiarization can fail to bring less natural motion to the same predictability levels it brings more natural motion.***

4.3 Follow-Up: Do we just need more examples?

Upon finding this limitation, we wondered: could we bring predictability levels as high as for the more natural motion by simply increasing the number of examples? Is this limitation caused by the amount of familiarization?

Methods. We tested this in a follow-up study. We created more examples by discretizing the space further, as shown by the grid crosses in Fig.3. After eliminating the ones close to the testing situations from `Level 3` (shown in gray in the figure), we obtained 16 new examples (leading to a possible total of 13+16=29).

We replicated our previous study, manipulating one additional factor — the `number of examples` — with 3 levels: 13 (previous study), 21, and 29. We added the additional examples after the original ones, maintaining their order and thus avoiding the order of the examples as a confound.

The `number of examples` factor was between-subjects. This was necessary in order to manage the different number of examples in the familiarization stage. We recruited 25 users per level of examples.

Analysis. Fig.5 (right) shows the accuracy before and after familiarization for each case.

RESULT 4. ***Familiarization can saturate: final predictability does not increase with the number of examples.***

Surprisingly, accuracy decreases in the last case, with the largest number of examples. This decrease is significant in a logistic regression over all example levels, which shows a main effect for `number of examples` ($\chi^2(2, 876) = 6.85$, $p = .0325$), and marginally significant in a factorial repeated-measures ANOVA ($F(2, 70) = 2.80$, $p = .0675$).

The accuracy after familiarization with 29 examples is consistently smaller than with 13 or 21, in particular for difference level 1, i.e. tests that appear in the training data.

This could imply that with more examples to learn from, users are more focused on a general model and less able to keep in mind particular cases. Rather than over fitting to the limited number of examples, users might be fitting a more general but less accurate model. There can also be something specific to the examples added that adds confusion. Further investigation is needed in order to understand this drop, and verify it is not produced by chance.

5. FAMILIARIZATION AND COMFORT

In the previous sections, we found that familiarization increases the motion's predictability. Here, we are taking a first step towards analyzing the practical consequences of improved predictability to human-robot collaboration. In particular, does familiarization improve the users' comfort with working next to the robot?

5.1 Methods

We designed an experiment where we evaluated user comfort before and after familiarization, using both an indirect, objective metric, as well as a direct, subjective metric.

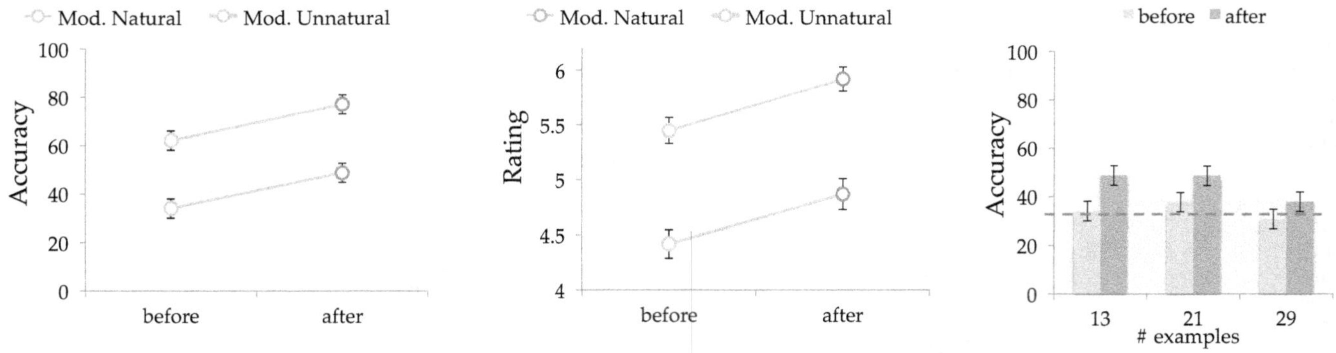

Figure 5: Left and Center: Results for familiarization to a less natural motion, as compared to the more natural CHOMP motion from Fig.4. The error bars represent standard error on the mean. Familiarization does improve predictability, but not to the level of the CHOMP motions. Right: This limitation is not due to the number of examples, since more examples fail to improve performance.

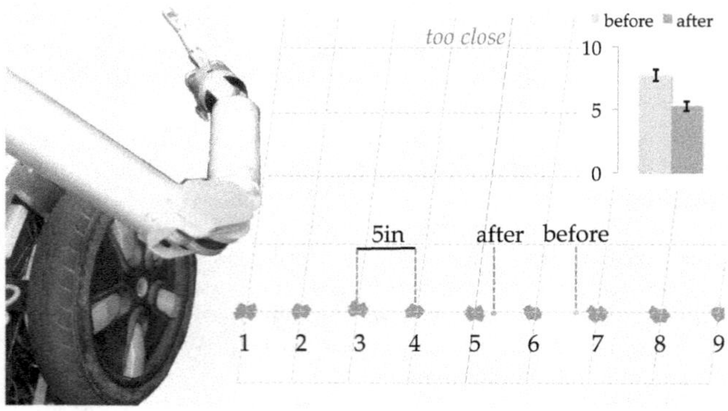

Figure 6: Markers measuring distance to the robot are spaced 5 inches apart. Familiarization brought users 7.35 inches closer to the robot.

Manipulated Factors. We manipulated two factors: `familiarization` and `naturalness` of the motion. We used the same familiarization procedure as before, and the two motions from Sec. 3 and Sec. 4.

We decided against manipulating the `difference level` factor in this study, and only used a `Level 1` situation. We could not use `Level 3`, as familiarization had no effect on the predictability of motion in situations from this level. Furthermore, our pilot for this study (with 6 users) showed no differences between `Level 1` and `Level 2`.

Dependent Measures. We evaluated comfort in two ways:

Objective Comfort. The robot was set in a `Level 1` situation, in the starting configuration. The experimenter told the users that the robot will move to reach for the target object, and asked them to stand side-by-side with the robot, as close as possible, but far enough away that they felt confident that the arm would not hit them as it moves during the reach (Fig.1).

We marked the floor with 18 marks, starting right next to the robot and moving outward, placed every 5 inches (Fig.6). We measured the distance (marker ID) from the user to the robot.

Although indirect, this metric is of high practical relevance for collaboration: we want users to be comfortable enough to get close to the robot as it is working, in oder to be able to do their own tasks simultaneously.

Subjective Comfort. We also directly asked users to indicate (on a Likert scale from 1 to 7), their level of agreement with the statement: "I would feel comfortable working side by side with the robot on a close-proximity task like cleaning up the dining room table." (which we augmented with "if it moved in the way I saw" after familiarization).

Subject Allocation. We used a mixed design. We kept `familiarization` within-subjects, measuring improvement in comfort before and after exposure to the robot's motion. However, `naturalness` was between-subjects, as each user could only familiarize with one type of motion (to avoid confusion and ordering effects).

We recruited 16 users from the local community (9 female and 7 male, with ages between 20 and 64, $M = 36.68$, $SD = 16.6$, with 7 reporting having a technical background).

Hypothesis. *Familiarization significantly improves comfort with working next to the robot, as indicated by both the objective and subjective metrics.*

5.2 Analysis

We were very surprised by how comfortable users were with the robot to begin with: with no prior knowledge of how HERB moves, users stood only 33 inches from the robot's arm, while the arm could touch them even at 45 inches away. A particularly trusting user stood only 20 inches away, which makes it very difficult for the robot to avoid them even when it knows exactly where they are. Users also rated their comfort with the robot very highly ($M = 6.52$, $SD = 0.61$).

A factorial ANOVA showed a significant main effect for `familiarization` on our objective metric ($F(1, 14) = 12.68$, $p = .0031$): in line with our hypothesis, users were willing to stand closer to the robot after familiarization ($M = 5.28$, $SD = 1.49$) than they were initially ($M = 6.75$, $SD = 1.84$) – a difference of $1.47 \times 5 = 7.35$ inches, indicating that:

RESULT 5. ***Familiarization can increase comfort with working side-by-side with the robot.***

We found no effect of `familiarization` on our subjective metric. The mean improved ever-so-slightly ($M = 6.56$, $SD = 0.51$).

Although there was no significant effect for `naturalness`, the means for the objective metric reveal that users did stand slightly further away in the unnatural condition. The means very closely matched the actual safe distances (5.06 for the natural case, and 5.5 for the unnatural case) – users were surprisingly good at estimating the correct spot on which stand, on average.

However, this has an interesting side-effect: familiarization made a lot of users *over-trust* the robot, in that it made them stand *too close* to it (5 out of 8 in the natural condition, and 3 out of 8 in the unnatural condition). Overall, `familiarization` had a marginally significant effect on whether users over-trusted the robot ($\chi^2(1,32) = 3.56$, $p = .0592$), which could have a startling implication:

Less predictable motion might actually be safer in some cases, in that it might prevent over-trusting the robot.

This echoes findings in the trust literature: unreliable behavior increases trust [8]. However, when the robot needs to be conservative about safety (e.g., in the case of industrial arms), this can be a desired effect.

6. DISCUSSION AND LIMITATIONS

In this paper, we explored the effects and limits of familiarizing users to robot motion.

On the one hand, human adaptability would suggests that users would have no issues adapting to any robot motion, as long as it is consistent. We did find that motion becomes more predictable after familiarization, at least when the familiarization process is presented as a learning task.

On the other hand, motion often lies in a complex, high-dimensional space — a possible hindrance for the utility of familiarization. We found that familiarization is not always enough to enable users to identify the robot's motion (despite choosing among spatially different trajectories), and that less natural motion reaches lower predictability levels. Our data suggests that this limitation can not (at least not always) be overcome by increasing the familiarization length: familiarization can saturate.

Furthermore, our experiments used a pre-test, which could prompt the users' learning toward test situations, and inflate the effect of familiarization. Predictability after familiarization could be even lower than our measurements indicate.

Our results suggest that users are more comfortable (or more trusting) with the robot after familiarization. However, this could be confounded by the users' ability to make the translation from the video space to which they familiarize to the physical space in which they are tested.

Of all the factors that could affect the utility of familiarization, our experiments touched upon two: the naturalness of motion, and the number of examples the robot gives the users. Many other factors could impact familiarization: the anthropomorphism of the robot (would users have a harder time with less anthropomorphic robot?), the dimensionality of the space (would they have an easier time with robots with fewer DOF?), the convexity of the cost function the robot optimizes (does non-convexity affect humans as it does machines?), the breadth of examples (one task vs. many), as well as the order or the examples. All of these make very exciting questions for future research.

Although our studies were controlled and focused, they revealed surprising limitations of familiarization. Given that we made optimistic choices for the factors we did not manipulate, aiding familiarizations, we expect to see similar limitations when performing familiarization "in-the-wild": familiarization improves predictability, but the robot still faces the challenge of producing good motion with which to familiarize.

Acknowledgements

We thank Henny Admoni and the members of the Personal Robotics Lab for their advice. This material is based upon work supported by NSF-IIS-0916557, NSF-EEC-0540865, ONR-YIP 2012, and the Intel PhD Fellowship.

7. REFERENCES

[1] B. Akgun, M. Cakmak, J. W. Yoo, and A. L. Thomaz. Trajectories and keyframes for kinesthetic teaching: a human-robot interaction perspective. In *HRI*, 2012.

[2] R. Alami, A. Albu-Schaeffer, A. Bicchi, R. Bischoff, R. Chatila, A. D. Luca, A. D. Santis, G. Giralt, J. Guiochet, G. Hirzinger, F. Ingrand, V. Lippiello, R. Mattone, D. Powell, S. Sen, B. Siciliano, G. Tonietti, and L. Villani. Safe and Dependable Physical Human-Robot Interaction in Anthropic Domains: State of the Art and Challenges. In *Workshop on pHRI*, 2006.

[3] A. Arita, K. Hiraki, T. Kanda, and H. Ishiguro. Can we talk to robots? ten-month-old infants expected interactive humanoid robots to be talked to by persons. *Cognition*, 95, 2005.

[4] M. Beetz, F. Stulp, P. Esden-Tempski, A. Fedrizzi, U. Klank, I. Kresse, A. Maldonado, and F. Ruiz. Generality and legibility in mobile manipulation. *Autonomous Robots*, 28:21–44, 2010.

[5] D. Bertram, J. Kuffner, R. Dillmann, and T. Asfour. An integrated approach to inverse kinematics and path planning for redundant manipulators. In *ICRA*, 2006.

[6] S. Calinon, F. Guenter, and A. Billard. On learning, representing, and generalizing a task in a humanoid robot. *IEEE Trans. on Systems, Man, and Cybernetics*, 37(2):286–298, 2007.

[7] R. B. D'AGOSTINO. A second look at analysis of variance on dichotomous data. *Journal of Educational Measurement*, 8(4):327–333, 1971.

[8] M. Desai, M. Medvedev, M. Vázquez, S. McSheehy, S. Gadea-Omelchenko, C. Bruggeman, A. Steinfeld, and H. Yanco. Effects of changing reliability on trust of robot systems. In *HRI*, 2012.

[9] A. Dragan, K. Lee, and S. Srinivasa. Legibility and predictability of robot motion. In *HRI*, 2013.

[10] G. Gergely, Z. Nadasdy, G. Csibra, and S. Biro. Taking the intentional stance at 12 months of age. *Cognition*, 56(2):165 – 193, 1995.

[11] T. Huang, Z. Li, M. Li, D. G. Chetwynd, and C. M. Gosselin. Conceptual design and dimensional synthesis of a novel 2-dof translational parallel robot for pick-and-place operations. *Journal of Mechanical Design*, 126:449, 2004.

[12] K. Kamewari, M. Kato, T. Kanda, H. Ishiguro, and K. Hiraki. Six-and-a-half-month-old children positively attribute goals to human action and to humanoid-robot motion. *Cognitive Development*, 20(2):303 – 320, 2005.

[13] C. D. Kidd and C. Breazeal. Human-robot interaction experiments: Lessons learned. In *Proceeding of AISB*, volume 5, pages 141–142, 2005.

[14] T. Komatsu and S. Yamada. Adaptation gap hypothesis: How differences between users' expected and perceived agent functions affect their subjective impression. *Journal of Systemics, Cybernetics and Informatics*, 9(1):67–74, 2011.

[15] F. Lacquaniti and J. Soechting. Coordination of arm and wrist motion during a reaching task. *J Neurosci.*, 2:399–408, April 1982.

[16] D. P. Miller. Assistive robotics: an overview. In *Assistive Technology and Artificial Intelligence*, pages 126–136. 1998.

[17] R. Mitchell and F. Myles. *Second language learning theories*. 2004.

[18] B. Mutlu and J. Forlizzi. Robots in organizations: the role of workflow, social, and environmental factors in human-robot interaction. In *HRI*, 2008.

[19] N. Ratliff, J. A. Bagnell, and M. Zinkevich. Maximum margin planning. In *ICML*, 2006.

[20] S. Schaal. Dynamic movement primitives-a framework for motor control in humans and humanoid robotics. In *Adaptive Motion of Animals and Machines*, pages 261–280. 2006.

[21] R. M. Siino and P. J. Hinds. Robots, gender & sensemaking: Sex segregation's impact on workers making sense of a mobile autonomous robot. In *ICRA*, 2005.

[22] S. Srinivasa, D. Berenson, M. Cakmak, A. Collet, M. Dogar, A. Dragan, R. Knepper, T. Niemueller, K. Strabala, M. V. Weghe, and J. Ziegler. Herb 2.0: Lessons learned from developing a mobile manipulator for the home. *IEEE*, 2012.

[23] K. Stubbs, D. Wettergreen, and I. Nourbakhsh. Using a robot proxy to create common ground in exploration tasks. In *HRI*, 2008.

[24] K. Sundin, L. Jansson, and A. Norberg. Communicating with people with stroke and aphasia: understanding through sensation without words. *Journal of clinical nursing*, 9(4):481–488, 2000.

[25] A. L. Thomaz and M. Cakmak. Learning about objects with human teachers. In *HRI*, 2009.

[26] S. Upson. tongue vision. *Spectrum, IEEE*, 44(1):44–45, 2007.

[27] K. E. Weick. *Sensemaking in organizations*, volume 3. 1995.

[28] B. D. Ziebart, A. Maas, J. A. Bagnell, and A. Dey. Maximum entropy inverse reinforcement learning. In *AAAI*, 2008.

[29] M. Zucker, N. Ratliff, A. Dragan, M. Pivtoraiko, M. Klingensmith, C. Dellin, J. A. D. Bagnell, and S. Srinivasa. Chomp: Covariant hamiltonian optimization for motion planning. *IJRR*, 2013.

A Mixed-Method Approach to Evoke Creative and Holistic Thinking about Robots in a Home Environment

Praminda Caleb-Solly, Sanja Dogramadzi,
David Ellender, Tina Fear
Bristol Robotics Laboratory
University of the West of England, UK
Telephone: +44 (0) 1173283178
Praminda.caleb-solly@uwe.ac.uk

Herjan van den Heuvel
Smart Homes,
Eindhoven, Netherlands
Telephone: +31497-514984
h.vdheuvel@smart-homes.nl

ABSTRACT
Discovering older adults' perceptions and expectations of domestic care service robots are vital in informing the design and development of new technologies to ensure acceptability and usability. This paper identifies issues that were elicited from older adults using different methods to promote creative thinking about domestic robots at an emotional level, as well as pragmatic level. These included exploring people's ideal embodiment preferences and requirements for a domestic care service robot, and also what embodiments and functional aspects will not be acceptable. We analysed our findings using relevant constructs from the Unified Theory of Acceptance and Use of Technology, and Technology Acceptance models. In addition to some already well-established findings, we discovered some surprising aspects concerning interaction, behaviour and appearance and the ability for the robot to fit the relevant context, both physically and conceptually.

Categories and Subject Descriptors
Assistive technologies for persons with disabilities, Requirements Elicitation

General Terms
Design, Human Factors

Keywords
Domestic Robots, Requirements Elicitation

1. INTRODUCTION
Going hand-in-hand with technical research into the use of robots to assist older adults in a home environment is research into the user experience aspects of this technology. Discovering older adults' perceptions, expectations and impressions of domestic robots is vital in informing the design and development of these technologies. Using different approaches to elicit issues helps to prompt participants to focus on different aspects, therefore for creating a holistic understanding it is vital to use a range of methods.

HRI'14, March 03–06, 2014, Bielefeld, Germany.

http://dx.doi.org/10.1145/2559636.2559681

Recently there have been a number of research projects that involve the use of robots for providing physical and cognitive assistance to older adults. These include *Hobbit*, a socially assistive robot to support older adults in their home for tasks such as picking up objects and detecting emergency situations [1], *Care-O-Bot*, a mobile service robot focussed on the execution of fetch-and-carry tasks to support personnel of nursing homes in their daily tasks [2], *RoboCare,* a multi-agent human assistance system composed of a robotic agent, sensors for continuous monitoring, and reasoning systems [3], *K-SERA,* developing a social robot that monitors, helps and alerts persons with chronic obstructive pulmonary disorder, to facilitate effective self-management of their disease [4], *Florence*, developing a robot with local and remote communication services to improve home care for older persons [5], and *CompanionAble*, providing people suffering from mild cognitive impairments (MCI) with a cognitive assistive companion to support their wellbeing [6].

The research described in this paper is being conducted as part of a EU FP7 project MOBISERV [7], which comprises a range of integrated assistive technology solutions to support nutrition, physical wellbeing, cognitive stimulation, smart home control and social contact, which have been combined into an intelligent system with also a robot as a front-end interface for users. The design of the MOBISERV system is being undertaken with the participation of older people, as well as a range of other stakeholders – including professional carers, social carers, informal carers, and policy makers.

A mobile robotic platform, Kompaï [8] shown in Figure 1, serves as the interface to accessing and controlling the different components. This physical robotic unit can move autonomously around an older person's house. Its mobility enables pro-active initiative by the system to prompt and support the person wherever they are in their home, thus offering increased availability, awareness, and access as compared to a static system.

A robot as the interface also has the potential to offer a more social and entertaining interaction experience. The use of voice recognition and speech synthesis, gesture recognition and sensor information from ambient intelligent environments and smart garments, enables more natural interactions. However, successful interaction with the robot also includes the willingness of an individual to engage with this type of technology, accept it into their personal environment and use it on a regular basis, is dependent on a number of contextual and psychological factors.

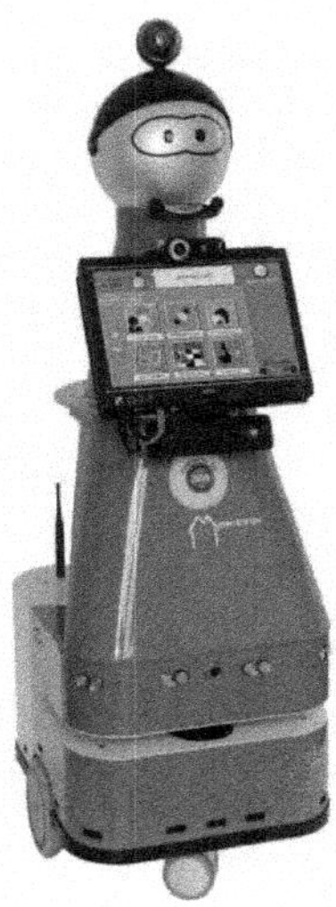

Figure 1. Mobiserv-Kompaï mobile robot from ROBOSOFT used for interaction

This paper reports research conducted to explore older adults' requirements for a domestic robot, investigating aspects such as ideal embodiment preferences and, and also what embodiments and functional aspects will not be acceptable. We start by describing related research on end-user perspectives, followed by a description of our methodology involving a range of techniques, which were implemented to attempt the surfacing of different perspectives and creative ideas of how a domestic robot would function, look and behave. We then analyse our findings and discuss a range of emerging issues related to ensuring improved understanding of user needs.

In addition to providing guidance for researchers to shape future developments of the technology, these findings can also guide the perspectives and agenda for public engagement and dissemination to promote further conversations and discussions about how this technology can be designed. The range of findings emerging from using different techniques for stimulating creative thought, also illustrate the importance of a mixed-method approach.

2. RELATED WORK

This section consists of a brief review of related studies in understanding end-user perspectives regarding robots.

When considering embodiments, there needs to be an understanding of the scope of what this relates to. Embodiments go beyond just the physical appearance, as they also encompass behavioural and interaction aspects afforded by the specific physical appearance. In one of the early studies Mataric [9] draws upon prior research that suggests that people will assign personality, emotions, intentions and objectives towards machines no matter how complex or simple they might be. This process is affected by various factors including an individual's background or culture. Different people will experience the interaction with a robot differently as their personal experience will also be influenced by their expectations, previous experiences and attitudes.

In order to successfully develop robotic solutions for a highly complex domain such as care for older people, it is necessary to take into account these issues to ensure confident and engaging interaction with the technology. However it is also important to note that interaction over a period of time will influence people's expectations and attitudes, which in turn will change their experience. Product attachment, as discussed by Zimmerman [10], results from a product playing a significant role in a person's life. So a formally ambivalent attitude can be transformed through continued use and thus increased dependency. In addition, citing the work of Belk (1988), Zimmerman states that people develop a reflective sense of self in relationship to a thing from observing how other people react to it. So others' responses also play an important role in people's own perceptions and attitudes.

An example of how the physical embodied presence of a robot influences a person's relationship and interaction with it, can be seen with the Paro robot [11], which is a robotic baby seal. The soft and fluffy feel of the seal pup, with large dark eyes and cooing sounds, evokes a human emotion of wanting to take care and cuddle it. It is therefore being successfully used for social companionship and emotional engagement.

Ongoing research conducted by Mataric also includes modelling empathy. Empathy is a key aid used by healthcare professionals in regards to providing care for older people. However imbuing empathy in a robot assistant raises ethical issues related to an older person's vulnerability, and the extent to which they can be manipulated on account of cognitive decline.

The development of domestic robots, which can move, gaze and talk in human-like ways are also raising particular issues related to the way the robots should physically position and move around people. This is known as proxemics, following a framework of social spatial zones of human-human behaviour proposed by Hall [12]. These zones were based on research into the ways people physically and psychologically mediate their position in relation to other people. Current research into human-robot proxemics by Mumm and Mutlu [13] has been limited to laboratory studies of a static robot concerning gaze, likeability, self-disclosure and distancing. Recent research by Walters *et al.* [14], suggests that individual differences play a large role in determining how close people feel it is appropriate for robots of differing embodiments to come near them.

Another study involving user preference regarding robots include the research conducted by Hendriks *et al.* [15] which involved using 30 personality traits and characteristics from the Five-Factor Model to consider the preferred personality aspects of a robot vacuum cleaner. This model organizes personality traits in terms of five basic dimensions: neuroticism, extraversion, openness to experience, agreeableness and conscientiousness (McCrae and Costa (1987) as in Hendriks *et al.*). The results suggested that the participants wanted a polite, efficient and calm robot vacuum cleaner, which was capable of completing its primary function. Participants did not want a highly sophisticated "fancy gadget" to perform the task of a vacuum cleaner. Task based feedback in regards to the personality of the robot resulted with the majority of participants stating the robot was calm, cooperative, systematic and routine driven. The robot was generally described as polite. Hendriks *et al.* conclude that end users anthropomorphise the robot vacuum cleaner and as a result apply various personality characteristics and traits based upon its demonstrated behaviour. They also state that developers can use this as a mean to improve human-robot interaction and user experience by creating a specific personality for the robot which helps the end user develop a conceptual model of how to interact with the robot within the home.

In addition to the embodiment of the robot, the utility of the tasks it performs are a component of user acceptance. In a study aimed at identifying useful tasks for robots to assist residents of a retirement village, and preferences for the appearance and features of healthcare robots, Broadbent *et al.* [16] used a mixture of questionnaires and interviews to discuss preference for the robot's colour, shape, design and size. From a questionnaire, 30 tasks were prioritised from most useful to least useful using an average of the participants' responses. Those tasks rated highest by the residents were detecting falls and calling for help, switching on and off appliances, cleaning, making phone calls to a doctor or nurse, lifting heavy things, monitoring the location of people, and reminders to take medications. The results indicated that residents prioritized healthcare related functions while staff prioritized tasks related to their care roles. On being shown images of different shaped and coloured robots, the participants showed a preference towards a robot with a screen held on the body compared to a screen on the head. There were no major differences between a humanoid or rounded, box shaped embodiments and 1.25m was the preferred height. Both carers and residents stressed the need for the robot to be non-intrusive yet tall enough to perform bed related tasks. Bright colours were preferred with silver as the most popular followed by gold and white. These criteria fit well with the uncanny valley assumption [17] that there is a relationship between an object's appearance or motion and how people perceive the object. Even if this research conducted in 1970 by Prof Masahiro Mori was not validated, it is commonly admitted in the community and regularly updated with regard to the technology progress [18]. Thus, participants preferred a non human-like robot appearance or behaviour, a friendly toy aspect being preferred.

In addition to focusing on functional aspects, research indicates that considering non-functional aspects can also raise the level of enjoyment for elderly users. Heerink *et al.* [19] explored the concept of enjoyment as a possible factor, which might influence acceptance of robotic technology by older adults. They conducted an experiment with a conversational robot, iCat [20], on 30 users, which incorporated both a test session with an interactive robot and a long-term user study. Their study confirmed the role of enjoyment as a positive factor influencing robotic technology acceptance by older adults which also indicates that a social robot is not just for assistance, but also a welcome companion.

Achieving a balance between relevant functions and aesthetics is key. A study by Forlizzi *et al.* [21] found that older people generally want products that match their aesthetic desires and use products that support their functional needs and abandon those that don't. Also the most important products are the ones that support their values of personal identity, dignity and independence.

Summary

Previous studies from literature helped to identify the following issues related to embodiments of robot assistants:

- The individual's background and culture, and ensuring that these aspects are considered when making decisions regarding the embodiment and location of the robot in a shared physical space.
- Importance of incorporating a component of empathy in the robot's responses and interactions
- A level of customisability in the physical appearance to suit individual preferences.
- An embodiment that evokes friendliness (polite, calm) and includes features to enhance enjoyment.

All the studies reviewed used quite focussed methods which helped to identify a range of issues, which related mostly to aesthetics and behaviour, but did not particularly consider fears or anxieties, or other modalities of communication that might be useful.

3. RESEARCH METHODOLOGY

For this project we have used a range of methods whereby we hoped to get a rich montage of perspectives that highlighted a range of concerns. A combination of a cultural probe study, workshops and a survey were used as a means of primary data gathering. The cultural probe study [22] found that the value of getting participants to use disposable cameras helped to shift the focus from what the researchers thought was relevant, to what the participants flagged as important in their lives and were found to be more candid and open about discussing personal issues as a result. Following this, two types of workshops were organised, **Embodiment workshops**, using multi-modal stimuli, where the focus was on understanding the nature of a robot as interface that would appeal to people and what would not, and **Scenario-focussed workshops**, which were part of the evaluation phase of the project, exploring issues related to user acceptance from a more functional perspective as in relation to the context of use and MOBISERV system functions which includes reminders and encouragement for eating, drinking and exercise, social interaction using Skype and control of lights, window blinds, temperature and front door entry.

3.1 Embodiment Workshops

The embodiment workshops were carried out in the UK. We decided to run single-gender group workshops to encourage more open discussion of certain issues such as personal care and reduce the level of inhibition in discussing personal matters. Each of the embodiment workshops was organised into three main parts with comfort breaks in-between.

In the first part of the workshop the participants brainstormed their "ideal robot assistant". To stimulate and provoke ideas amongst the participants, a "mystery bag" of objects was brought to the session. Cruz and Gaudron [23] describe a similar approach called "Open-ended objects" as a tool for use in the process of brainstorming. The significance of objects in peoples' lives are considered in a series of essays in a book edited by Turkle [24], Evocative objects: things we think with, which provides an insight into the potential power of objects to provide a link between emotion and intellect.. Some of the objects in our workshops were selected to provide a tactile impression to users in order to stimulate thoughts on different embodiment forms and materials. Other objects were chosen to be more technical with communication abilities and some level of autonomous behaviour that would suggest functional abilities of assistive devices. The following objects were included: four animated stick figure electronic toys, an electronically controlled butterfly in a jar toy, a miniature toy robot, an Xbox controller and wireless headset, a toy 6 legged robot beetle, an interactive toy doll, some smart garments embedded with sensors to monitor heart-rate, breathing and temperature, a hand-held head massage tool, a Roomba robotic vacuum, a Robosapien humanoid robot toy; references for each item are available in a supplementary document [25]. It should be noted that the participants had also seen the Kompaï robot in a previous project dissemination session.

Prior to the brainstorming, the objects were passed around the group and the participants were left for 20 minutes to feel, play with, and discuss the objects with the people sitting next to them. For the brainstorming, participants were asked to consider and discuss the following questions:

- *If you could have a robot in your home,*
  - *What would you want it to do?*
  - *How would you want it to look?*

In the second part of the workshop, participants were asked to spend some time writing down ideas and discussing with each other the following questions:

- *What would your nightmare robot be?*
  - *What would it do?*
  - *How would it look?*

In the third part of the workshop, in order to generate further discussion of domestic care robots amongst the participants, a short video documentary compiled by MOBISERV researchers on the existing state of the art in robotics in a range of industrial and health-care applications was played to inform the participants of the latest robot developments and capabilities. A list of videos from which clips for the documentary were extracted can be found in [25]. The video documentary was divided into three main sections as follows:

1. Overview of industrial robots
2. State of the art of service robots
3. Care robot developments in recent years

After the participants had watched the robot video documentary, the facilitator asked each of the participants what aspects of the robots that they had viewed were preferred and why. This was followed by further discussions using cue cards with images of the care robots on the video to aid recall of the robots seen.

3.2 Scenario-focused workshops

These workshops were carried out in the UK and the Netherlands. They were conducted in smaller groups or individually (depending on participant's availability) and included older adults, formal and informal carers, occupational therapists, a dietician, a medical doctor and a care-home manager.

Participants were introduced to short scenarios relating to hydration and nutrition support, voice/video calling, an exercising coach, and front door control. The scenarios included a description of the functionality offered and how a person might use and benefit from it. The scenarios were presented both verbally and on paper. The descriptions of the scenarios used are available in the supplementary document with more details [26].

Key discussion points included the following points:

- What is good?
- What is bad?
- What is the effect of this situation?
- Is it right or wrong?
- How could this scenario be different? (E.g. extend it, change it).

3.3 Survey

A questionnaire was prepared and distributed at the Celebration of Age Festival in Bristol, UK. This is a community facing event, organised with exhibits from a range of private and charity services for older adults, together with a programme of health and well-being activity taster sessions for older adults Prior to distributing the questionnaire we showed concept videos of the MOBISERV system to the attendees to our project exhibit and gave a demonstration of existing functionalities available via the robot's interface, such as preparing a shopping list via speech interaction, emailing, and getting weather forecasts. This was followed by individual and small group hands-on sessions where the participants had an opportunity to try out interactions with the robot as demonstrated. Participants were then asked to fill out the questionnaire. The questionnaire focussed on the Kompaï robot and covered issues ranging from whether people would mind having a robot like this supporting them and moving about in their house, to the size, appearance and behaviour of the robot, as well as the preferred communication mode and non-acceptable tasks.

3.4 Analysis of Findings

All the workshops were audio-taped and/or videoed with consent from participants. The qualitative discussion data was transcribed and content analysed to extract themes [27] and cluster reoccurring ones. In analysing the themes, we have chosen to use the UTAUT (Unified Theory of Acceptance and Use of Technology) Toolkit [28], developed to assist in the evaluation of a user's acceptance of social robots. This model enables formalising the method of interpretation, which is necessary for this type of multidisciplinary research. UTAUT constructs that were found to be applicable here include Anxiety, Attitude and Facilitating Conditions and the 'classic' TAM (Technology Acceptance Model) [29] constructs which are Perceived Ease of Use and Perceived Usefulness. These constructs are shown to have a degree of interrelationship. Although used in this study to analyse technology acceptance, they could also be used to gauge a user's or carer's anticipated level of technology acceptance when eliciting non-functional requirements for the system.

4. RESULTS

4.1 Embodiment workshops

There were three separate embodiment workshops focusing on the views of older adults - workshop 1 comprising 3 males, workshop 2 comprising 10 females and workshop 3 comprising 5 males (ages ranges across all three groups was 60 – 93 years old with a mean age of 76).

Suggestions made by participants regarding what they would find acceptable for their "ideal robot assistant" were categorised into

- Desirable functionality

These included memory-associated tasks (6 tasks), cleaning tasks (11 tasks) and assistive tasks (34 tasks). All participants contributed with ideas relating to one or more of these tasks. Women made more specific suggestions for memory related tasks (5 tasks out of 6) and the cleaning tasks suggested were more diverse and specific such as 'cleaning corners', 'under chairs' while men made more general references to house cleaning.

The participants identified tasks that are similar to those used by Beer *et al.* [30] in their questionnaire which corroborate their results indicating how people perceive the robot as being useful for manual cleaning tasks.

- Behaviour and appearance

Here there were some particular notable differences between male and female perspectives.

Figure 3. Workshop with Group 2

Female participant views:

The desire for characteristics relating to social companionship were a key aspect that emerged in the female group. Here is one specific quote from a female participant that communicates this particularly poignantly: *"...it would be comfortable and nice and maybe make me think of my younger days and my family...that would be very nice and companionable and if I can't have something living, I'll have that doll...it's the feeling of comfort. I think comfort is very important, extremely important."*

Other features relating to social companionship that were suggested included that they would like a robot to ask how they were feeling, have a happy appearance: *"I wouldn't mind how it looked but happy perhaps?"*

Appearance was discussed in more depth and this included characteristics such as voice and behaviour. Some suggested that the robot should sing while it worked like: "*Frank Sinatra*" or "*George Formby*", wake them up with a smiling face and smell of a human.

It was suggested that the preferred voice for the robot should be female with a Scottish or Irish woman's accent and not computer generated like a satellite navigator.

It was also suggested that the robot should make soft music like a Viennese waltz or another noise like a washing noise when approaching.

There was agreement that it should not look life-like and more like a machine or a doll. Natural materials like wood were suggested and a dome-shape was preferred.

Male participant views:

Social companionship and appearance was not a priority for the male groups. Some suggested that it should merge into the surroundings, similar to the furniture (table), although a human form was considered as it might enable certain functionality such as picking things up. Functionality over appearance dominated the discussions and suggestions such as a system with attachments that could be swapped depending on the tasks, with clean lines and being easy to clean being put forward.

The male participants also had more concerns regarding costs than the female participants, with two indicating that cost was their main priority and that the embodiment and aesthetics were not of interest. Here is a quote from one of them: *"...I am not interested in what it looks like. All that I am interested in is what it costs....Being a finance bloke all I am interested in is the cost."*

The male participants also preferred a robot to have a female voice and one suggested that the robot play music or whistle while performing tasks.

In total there were 17 distinct references to desirable behaviour and appearance by women, as opposed to 7 by the men - all of which related to the form following functionality.

In the second part of the workshops, getting the participants to consider aspects that would not be acceptable to them was found to be a useful method to surface existing fears and apprehensions. A total of 20 issues of distinct concerns or unacceptable behaviour and appearance were expressed.

Loss of control over the robot remains an innate fear, as does the potential for the system being unreliable or a safety hazard. The following two comments capture the above concerns that were frequently echoed by female participants: *"...it would be a nightmare, what would happen to you if the tablets were there to order...that would be my greatest worry ...that something would go wrong with it and something that I was depending on for medication wouldn't be available and it could be quite damaging."*

"...that it would run amuck...and that you wouldn't be able to know how to stop it making horrible harsh noises...frightening noises."

From a psychological perspective, concern over the possibility of becoming dependent on it was also expressed.

In the third part of the workshops, the documentary and cue cards prompted a host of more specific issues such as the introduction of a robot-based system before it was needed so that people could get used to it, the physical size and terrain of the home and ability of the robot to navigate and fit without taking up too much space. Seeing the robots perform various functions inside and outside the house also led to discussions regarding a feeling of loss of purpose. As one male participant put it: "*What would I do with myself though if all these little beasties are doing everything for me, because it's part of my world to do the gardening and everything. If it's all done for me I might as well climb into a box and ...that would be a problem.*"

Some female participants saw the videos of the industrial robots as "*confidence builders*" in relation to reliability.

4.2 Scenario-focused workshops

Ten scenario-focussed workshops were held in total with three workshops in the Netherlands and seven workshops in the UK. The numbers of participants in each of the ten workshops varied according to availability and ranged from 1 to 4 participants in each workshop. In the Netherlands there were a total of 9 participants over all the three workshops (3 older adults and 3 formal carers 1 dietician, 1 medical doctor and 1 care home manager) and in the UK there were a total of 13 participants over all the seven workshops (5 older adults, 4 formal carers, 2 informal carers and 2 occupational therapists). In the UK three workshops were conducted via telephone with individuals. Overall there was an equal mix of genders. The age range of the older adults was 65 to 74 years old.

People in the Netherlands and UK expressed similar views and concerns. The scenarios provided a tangible framework to consider the utility of the functionalities, while providing scope for probing the pragmatics of the scenarios.

The professionals in the Netherlands noted that the amount a person has eaten would be of interest as part of their care regime, however care home staff have are unlikely to have time to monitor all patients in exact detail.

Older adults responded positively to the concept of talking to the robot (in the manner that they talked to their pet). It was noted that voice interaction with robot could lead to it becoming a *"little friend"*, according to one informal carer and *"the next best thing [to human contact]"*. But there was a strong concern that a robot care assistant might start to be used as a replacement for human contact (namely by carers) and as such, reduce the frequency of human contact with a carer.

Carers felt that the robot should be an addition to their team, not a replacement of them. Furthermore, they see potential in a pro-active robot that takes the initiative to activate and engage users.

Similarly, it was felt by some people that in some instances, instead of the robot just having a passive role, listening to the users' commands without discussion, it should demonstrate a bit of personality and occasionally and playfully override user's control. For example, if a person had not done any exercise and selected a smart home control, the robot might say *"you have not been very active, may I suggest that you close the curtains yourself"*.

As in the embodiment workshops, there was strong concern about the costs of running a MOBISERV system that included a robot. Older adults reported financial worries leading to a review of spending habits, such as whether they should carry on paying for internet access. Also, worries about spending their time trying to troubleshoot or delegate any technical problems was reported to be off-putting. Older people and carers wondered what the added value of the robot was, compared to other possibilities and whether the costs are justifiable and if it was financially viable to have a robot at home. Dependency on the system was also cited as a possibility with the potential to start ignoring the prompts from the robot when their levels of self-motivation started to deteriorate.

Personalisation and customisation were felt to be very important, such as choosing the voice and name of the robot. Carers, doctors, and therapists see that maybe the robot should be different depending on where they are to be used and by whom.

The relationship between form and function also emerged again, with older people noting that drinking and eating reminders were 'human' activities (in the sense that these were tasks that people would normally do) and they expected these reminding activities to be undertaken by a robot that looked more human. This is interesting to note in the context of the "uncanny valley" discussed earlier.

An interesting perspective on the interaction style was reported by a carer, based on their experience of working with older people with minimal or no experience of using technology. They stated that for a person with minimal experience of technology, technologies that require implicit user input, rather than explicit user interaction would be more acceptable. In this sense, room sensors and wearable garments would be acceptable, whereas interacting with a robot via voice or touch would not.

4.3 Survey

The survey was completed by 28 participants, 6 male and 22 female, between the ages of 50 and 90 years old, mean age 74.

It was found that people who reported as living alone, were more accepting of Kompaï's size, compared to people living with others. Four older people reported that it should be half-size or slimmer, due to constraints of their physical environment ("I have a narrow hallway"). One older person reported that the small size of her house was a reason to not want one. This also corresponds with similar views expressed in the embodiment workshop where one of the participants noted: "*... I wouldn't want it looming over me....It should not dominate the room"*

Some older people noted that it was important that the robot did not enter certain rooms in the house (bedroom, bathroom). Interestingly, this is a point where people have been found to have quite different views, as some have stated that the robot should be able to go to these rooms, as these are the locations where accidents happen.

People aged 50-79 years old all showed a preference for wanting to change the appearance of the robot. Being able to change or customise or configure the robot appearance may be a key user requirement and an important aspect of acceptability.

People living alone preferred a pet-like appearance and wanted to interact by talking. Irrespective of living status, this preference seems to increase with age. People living alone also wanted the robot to perform care-related tasks.

People aged 80-90 years old wanted the robot to be like a social companion.

Some older people noted that they did not want the robot to think for them, give opinions or move without being instructed.

5. DISCUSSION

User acceptance of robots to assist active ageing in a home environment is closely bound to the level of utility that is offered. In situations where age has impaired the ability to carry out tasks that require physical agility or memory, solutions that enable a person to continue with these tasks will always have a high degree of user acceptance. It should however be noted that often people are unable to accept their physical and cognitive decline, choosing to conceal their increasing frailty as noted in Sixsmith *et al.* [31]. Therefore a robot assistant or companion could make the admission of need too real for people to accept, which could also be seen as a social stigma. Together with the influence of people's social identity in selecting new products (Kleine *et al.*, as in Zimmerman), this can be a compounding factor.

Applicable UTAUT and TAM constructs are used to discuss the implications of the findings in more detail in following sections.

5.1 Anxiety in relation to robots

The discussions related to embodiments revealed some intrinsic fears and misconceptions, which are a barrier to user acceptance and need to be addressed by higher levels of engagement, education and training. In addition to adequate training, in the form of videos, instruction leaflets, pictorial cards, addressing different learning needs, and brief introductory interactions spaced over a period of time, which would make the system seem more familiar to the person, people could be encouraged to consider the use of the robots in relation to their own scenarios of use. This could not only aid acceptability but could also help to surface fears, which could then be openly addressed. People want to feel in control of the robot at all times, and are concerned that it might not be able to be stopped, become uncontrollable or there will be serious situations when it overrides them. Demonstrable assurance of operational safety, reliability and transparency of override functions are vital for user acceptance.

5.2 Perceived usefulness and attitude towards autonomy

It is interesting to note that some people found it difficult to consolidate the need for semi-autonomous behaviour by a robot to provide active assistance with tasks, and their need for controlling the autonomous behaviour of the robot.

Some older people noted that they did not want the robot to go in certain rooms in the house. This suggests that a user's interaction with the robot is highly contextualised: where possible the user's preferences about the physical environment should be respected (e.g. the user is asleep in bed) but where the need arises sometimes the system should override these preferences (e.g. the user has fallen in bathroom). We need to consider in more depth how we can design acceptable robotic solutions for contexts where overall control may dynamically change from user to system. Our basis for this is a user model – a framework in which preferences and context combine to form appropriate system responsiveness. However, achieving the correct balance between having a robot supporting active ageing, which might require monitoring to enable prompting and reminders, while still enabling the person to feel in control, could be potentially challenging. It may even be that designing acceptability for these conflicts is not possible using traditional means of fixing requirements in advance. Perhaps instead we must make designs that enable conflicts to be managed and negotiated dynamically. One way to achieve this will be through participatory design and user control and freedom of setting the robot's features and behaviour to suit personal preferences, goals and motivations. This could also be achieved through providing a means for people to create their own rules about how and when the robot should perform certain functions and generate meaningful interpretations of the information that it collects and uses to make decisions. However this requires a high level of self-awareness of needs, but assistance in setting the system up could be provided from carers or relatives who knew the older person well.

5.3 Facilitating Conditions

There are a number of facilitating conditions that are key to acceptance of the wide range of functionality offered by a domestic care robot as within the MOBISERV system. These can be categorised into cognitive, physical and social as follows:

Cognitive – There is an assumption that if a person is being reminded or encouraged to drink (tea for instance) to prevent dehydration, then they should also know where the tea is and how to make it. Otherwise the robot would also need to help them by giving structured guidance and support them in making the tea. Or, in another example scenario, if they have a video-linked secured entry system, then they are also able to recognise a familiar face at the door, or if not, be reminded of who the person is, or have the system control the entry based on pre-set rules. If they don't need the enhanced guidance or control, then it is questionable whether they require a robot at all. In the situation of reduced cognition there is more need for support, increasing the acceptance of a solution if it offers continued independence.

Physical – Being reminded of tasks related to activities for daily living assumes a degree of physical mobility, i.e. the person can stand at the cooker to prepare a meal, they can lift a drink to their mouth, or they can use the toilet independently. If this additional support is needed, then just the facility to remind is inadequate.

Social – The provision of social media tools assumes that the person has family and friends who are alive and/or available to be called.

The facilitating conditions which determine the utility of available functionality, and hence the acceptance of technology, is itself highly contextualised. There is a narrow range of user characteristics, capabilities and social pre-conditions, during which specific functionality is particularly relevant. Given that older people's functional capabilities and impairments do change over time (typically as a decline), this suggests that designers need to consider how they handle this decline. Adaptive systems, which can tell when functionality is no longer appropriate, or can change to accommodate for growing or altered needs, are therefore likely to be most acceptable.

5.4 Ease of Use

We also need to emphasise and illustrate that a robot potentially provides a more engaging, enjoyable and sociable interface, enhancing the quality of the user-experience. Considering ways of making the interaction with the system enjoyable and engaging as well as ensuring utility of the functionality is important. It is therefore also vital to investigate whether assistive service robots and technology are better presented as "aids" rather than "carers", and to what extent the image of being "cared for" by a machine affects a person's concept of dignity and independence.

6. CONCLUSIONS

User acceptance will depend on the way we respond to, and address, the concerns and issues highlighted in this paper, through our communications with all stakeholders and the external design of the system, always aiming for a flexible, customisable solution, rather than trying to shoehorn a plethora of requirements into one solution. It was noted that if people were not able to understand the system's benefit in relation to their perceived needs, they would reject it before the demonstration. Additionally, one of the key aspects in relation to user acceptance relates to the process of introduction of a robot into a person's life. A phased approach is recommended which would need to include initial demonstrations describing concept and benefits, followed by numerous sessions of guided practice to build confidence, before trialling independently.

One of the aspects of using a range of methods that struck us was while the techniques surface some common, and known responses in regards to domestic service robots, there were some creative and unexpected ideas, such as the robot could have a smell, or that it should sing aloud as it went about its routines. However, there was an interesting incongruity in the responses from the embodiment workshops, which on one hand indicated a desire for anthropomorphic behaviour, identifying a possible need for companionship, while not looking "life-like." In contrast, where the participants were given a more functional focus, via the use of scenarios, the expectations of form that facilitated related functional behaviour, seemed to be more open to humanistic features. This highlights the importance of adopting a range of approaches to get an equally broad range of perspectives, but also cautions against interpretation of results without considering the context in which they were elicited.

7. ACKNOWLEDGMENTS

This work was developed within the MOBISERV project partially funded by the European Commission under the 7th Framework Programme (FP7-248434). The authors wish to thank the all project members, particularly J.P. Vargheese for his work on the Embodiment Workshops, and the participants for their support.

8. REFERENCES

[1] Hobbit, 2011, http://hobbit.acin.tuwien.ac.at/index.html

[2] Graf, B., Reiser, U., Hagele, M., Mauz, K., & Klein, P. (2009). Robotic home assistant Care-O-bot® 3-product vision and innovation platform. In Advanced Robotics and its Social Impacts (ARSO), pp. 139-144. IEEE.

[3] Cesta, A., Cortellessa, G., Giuliani, V., Pecora, F., Scopelliti, M., & Tiberio, L. (2007). Psychological Implications of Domestic Assistive Technology for the Elderly. PsychNology Journal, 5(3), 229-252.

[4] KSERA, http://ksera.ieis.tue.nl

[5] Meyer, J., Brell, M., Hein, A., Gessler, S. (2009) Personal Assistive Robots for AAL at Home - The Florence Point of View, IoPTS workshop, Brussels.

[6] Badii, A., Etxeberria, I., Huijnen, C., Maseda, M., Dittenberger, S., Hochgatterer, A., & Rigaud, A. S. (2009). CompanionAble: Graceful integration of mobile robot companion with a smart home environment. Gerontechnology, 8(3), 181.

[7] MOBISERV project. http://www.mobiserv.info

[8] Robosoft, Kompaï http://www.robosoft.com/robotic-solutions/healthcare/kompai/index.html

[9] Mataric M J. (2005) The Role of Embodiment in Assistive Interactive Robots for the Elderly, AAAI Fall Symposium on "Caring Machines: AI for the Elderly", Arlington VA.

[10] Zimmerman, J. (2009). Designing for the self: making products that help people become the person they desire to be. In Procs. of the SIGCHI Conference on Human Factors in Computing Systems (pp. 395-404). ACM.

[11] Chang, W. L., Šabanovic, S., & Huber, L. (2013). Use of seal-like robot PARO in sensory group therapy for older adults with dementia. In Procs. of the 8th ACM/IEEE international conference on HRI (pp. 101-102). IEEE Press.

[12] Hall, E. (1968) *Proxemics*. Current Anthropology. 9 (2-3) pp.83-108.

[13] Mumm, J., & Mutlu, B. (2011). Human-robot proxemics: physical and psychological distancing in human-robot interaction. In Proceedings of the 6th international conference on Human-robot interaction (pp. 331-338). ACM.

[14] Walters, M. L., Dautenhahn, K., Te Boekhorst, R., Koay, K. L., Syrdal, D. S., & Nehaniv, C. L. (2009). An empirical framework for human-robot proxemics. Procs of New Frontiers in Human-Robot Interaction.

[15] Hendriks, B., Meerbeek, B., Boess, S., Pauws, S., & Sonneveld, M. (2011). Robot vacuum cleaner personality and behavior. International Journal of Social Robotics, 3(2), 187-195.

[16] Broadbent, E.; Tamagawa, R.; Kerse, N.; Knock, B.; Patience, A.; MacDonald, B. (2009) Robot and Human Interactive Communication, RO-MAN. 18th IEEE International Symposium on, Page(s): 645 – 650.

[17] M. Mori, (1970), Uncanny Valley. Energy. **7**(4).

[18] Gee, F. C., Browne, W. N., & Kawamura, K. (2005). Uncanny valley revisited. In Robot and Human Interactive Communication, 2005. ROMAN 2005. IEEE International Workshop on (pp. 151-157).

[19] Heerink, M., Kröse, B., Wielinga, B., & Evers, V. (2008) Enjoyment intention to use and actual use of a conversational robot by elderly people. In Procs of the 3rd ACM/IEEE international conference on HRI (pp. 113-120). ACM.

[20] iCat,Philips Research. http://www.research.philips.com/technologies/projects/robotics/index.html

[21] Forlizzi, J., DiSalvo, C., & Gemperle, F. (2004). Assistive robotics and an ecology of elders living independently in their homes. Human-Computer Interaction, 19(1), 25-59.

[22] Caleb-Solly, P., Flind, A., Vargheese, J.P. (2011) Cameras as cultural probes in requirements gathering — Exploring their potential in supporting the design of assistive technology. 24th International Symposium on Computer-Based Medical Systems (CBMS), doi: 10.1109/CBMS.2011.5999158.

[23] Cruz, V., & Gaudron, N. (2010). Open-ended objects: a tool for brainstorming. In Proceedings of the 8th ACM Conference on Designing Interactive Systems (pp. 85-88). ACM.

[24] Turkle S (2007) Evocative objects: things we think with. MIT Press, Boston.

[25] Caleb-Solly, P., Dogramadzi, S., Ellender, D., Fear, T., Herjan v.d. H., (2014) Supplementary Document for HRI 2014 paper - A Mixed-Method Approach to Evoke Creative and Holistic Thinking about Robots in a Home Environment: Items used for "mystery bag" and Videos used for video documentary in the Embodiment Workshop. https://docs.google.com/document/d/1_WHY6So-KahUH5NG-cNuuDNggCYZwcCLCBXziH0_IJY/edit?usp=sharing

[26] Caleb-Solly, P., Dogramadzi, S., Ellender, D., Fear, T., Herjan v.d. H., (2014) Supplementary Document for HRI 2014 paper - A Mixed-Method Approach to Evoke Creative and Holistic Thinking about Robots in a Home Environment: Scenarios used for the Scenario-based Workshop. https://docs.google.com/document/d/14EwNGQz-PS0IaUHl9SfKdFGB9HHLACtBZXRCAkCw280/edit?usp=sharing

[27] Braun, V., & Clarke, V. (2006). Using thematic analysis in psychology.Qualitative research in psychology, 3(2), 77-101.

[28] Heerink, M., Krose, B., Evers, V., & Wielinga, B. (2009). Measuring acceptance of an assistive social robot: a suggested toolkit. InRobot and Human Interactive Communication, 2009. RO-MAN 2009. The 18th IEEE International Symposium on (pp. 528-533). IEEE.

[29] Davis, F. D. (1989). Perceived usefulness, perceived ease of use, and user acceptance of information technology. *MIS quarterly*, 319-340.

[30] Beer J.M., Smarr, C-A, Chen T.L., Prakash, A., Mitzner T.L., Kemp, C.C., Rogers, W.A. (2012) The domesticated robot: design guidelines for assisting older adults to age in place. In: 7th ACM/IEEE int. conf. on HRI, Boston, MA, March 2012, pp 335–342.

[31] Sixsmith, A., Sixsmith, J. Ageing in Place in the United Kingdom, Ageing Int (2008) 32:219-235, Springer.

Social Engagement in Public Places: A Tale of One Robot

Lilia Moshkina
NRC Post-Doctoral Fellow
Naval Research Laboratory
Washington, DC 20375 USA
lilia.tsvetik@gmail.com

Susan Trickett
ITT Exelis
Boulder, CO 80301 USA
+1-703-577-6035
sbtrickett@gmail.com

J. Gregory Trafton
Naval Research Laboratory
Washington, DC 20375 USA
+1-202-767-3479
greg.trafton@nrl.navy.mil

ABSTRACT
In this paper, we describe a large-scale (over 4000 participants) observational field study at a public venue, designed to explore how social a robot needs to be for people to engage with it. In this study we examined a prediction of Computers Are Social Actors (CASA) framework: the more machines present human-like characteristics in a consistent manner, the more likely they are to invoke a social response. Our humanoid robot's behavior varied in the amount of social cues, from no active social cues to increasing levels of social cues during story-telling to human-like game-playing interaction. We found several strong aspects of support for CASA: the robot that provides even minimal social cues (speech) is more engaging than a robot that does nothing, and the more human-like the robot behaved during story-telling, the more social engagement was observed. However, contrary to the prediction, the robot's game-playing did not elicit more engagement than other, less social behaviors.

Categories and Subject Descriptors
K.4.0 [**Computing Milieux**]: Computers and Society – *general.*

General Terms
Experimentation, Human Factors.

Keywords
Field experiment, CASA, engagement, human-robot interaction.

1. INTRODUCTION
Interest in social robot behavior has exploded in recent years, in part due to the Computers Are Social Actors (CASA) paradigm, advanced in Media Equation [1]. The CASA framework has been widely accepted in HCI and supported in a large set of experiments [2]. It claims that people will respond to a computer as a social partner, provided appropriate social cues are produced by the computer. This powerful concept extends to robotics as well, and it has been shown that human-like, social non-verbal behaviors can be advantageous in a robot. Breazeal et al. [3] found that implicit use of non-verbal behaviors, such as gaze shifts, shoulder shrugs, facial expressions, etc., was instrumental in human-robot team work. Sidner et al. [4] showed that a penguin robot that performed a few gestures was more engaging than its motionless version. Moshkina [5] reported that non-verbal expressions of anxiety and fear on a small humanoid robot Nao resulted in subjects' greater compliance with the robot's request to evacuate. Similarly, Chidambaram, Chiang, & Mutlu [6] discovered that presence of nonverbal bodily cues, such as gestures and gaze, increased a robot's persuasiveness. It has also been shown that robot form has an impact on human perception of robots: Groom et al.'s [7] self-extension experiment suggests that people are more likely to perceive a humanoid robot as a separate entity rather than an extension of themselves, as compared to their treatment of a robot car.

HRI'14, March 3–6, 2014, Bielefeld, Germany.
Copyright © 2014 ACM 978-1-4503-2658-2/14/03…$15.00.
http://dx.doi.org/10.1145/2559636.2559678

The CASA framework predicts that people will respond to robots in much the same way as people respond to other people as long as the robot presents human-like social cues (for a review, see Fong, Nourbakhsh, & Dautenhahn [8]). The CASA framework also predicts that as a system's social cues increase in number or fidelity in a technologically-consistent manner [9], people should find the system more socially appealing. To explore this issue, we focus on social engagement towards an autonomous robot.

Social engagement is a core social activity that refers to an individual's behavior within a social group [10]. In this study, we are interested in short term social engagement of individuals, and specifically what aspects of a robot's behavior will increase people's engagement. Because most previous studies of the CASA framework have been performed in the laboratory and we are interested in how to elicit social behavior from groups of people, we ran a large-scale observational study with over four thousand of participants in which we increased the social behavior of our robot. We then examined how different levels of the robot's social behavior impacted short term social engagement (listening to a robot tell a story).

2. STUDY DESIGN AND PROCEDURE
To examine the extent to which the presence of social cues in an anthropomorphic robotic platform influences social response in humans, an observational field study involving over 4000 of participants was conducted. In this study, attendees of a large public event had an opportunity to stop and listen to a humanoid robot recite a short story, as they were passing from one exhibit to another. For this study, we kept the verbal behavior the same, but changed non-verbal behavior across conditions, because previous studies found a strong impact of robot gestures on human social behavior [4, 6, 11], and paralinguistic cues had a much smaller or negligible impact on social behavior [6].

Our observational study followed a 2x4 between-subject design, where the first independent variable was Story Type (Informative vs. Humorous) and the second the level of social cues (Social Cues) produced by the robot, ranging from none (no movement) to full body movement. The level of Social Cues was increased incrementally between conditions, where the next level subsumed all the previous levels and added a new layer. The four conditions of Social Cues levels were as follows, in the order of increasing presence of social cues:

- Voice only – the robot produced no movement, just the narrative (Voice hereafter).
- Voice + lips – the robot's lips were making movements in sync with speech (Lips hereafter). Lip movements present a minimum level of motion expected from a talking creature.
- Voice + lips + facial expressions – in addition to lip-sync, the robot produced story-appropriate facial expressions (Face hereafter).
- Voice + lips + facial expressions + gestures – the previous condition was augmented with a variety of story-appropriate gestures and posture changes (Gestures hereafter).

The two Story Types were: Informative, in the form of a short, engaging lecture about the robot's capabilities, and Humorous, in the form of a short joke ending in a punch line. These two styles naturally elicit different social response in humans: nods during lectures [12], and smiles and laughter after jokes. Because of the differences in expected social behavior and content, they were placed in different conditions.

Two stand-alone conditions were also run. The first was a baseline condition where the robot was "in between acts" and was doing nothing – no movement, no talking, not being moved, etc.

In addition to our study, a robotics perception experiment was conducted using the same robot during the same public event [13]. In this experiment, volunteers interacted with the robot during a stylized game, in which the robot asked volunteers questions in an attempt to identify them. As game-playing is a very social activity, this experiment presented an additional comparison point to the original study by adding an interaction element. The robot's behavior here can be construed as exhibiting the most human-like, social behavior (as compared to robot story-telling), and was treated as the second stand-alone condition.

2.1 Stimuli and Robotic Implementation

Two vignettes of each Story Type were devised. All the stories were told in the first person singular; the robot talked about itself or a firefighting project it was involved in (informative stories), or told one of two inoffensive jokes: one about Sherlock Holmes and Dr Watson (relevant due to a recent movie), and another set in a zoo, which would appeal to any audience. All the stories were similar in length, within 10% both in the number of words and duration, and lasted, on average, 66 seconds. The last sentence in all the stories was always the same: "Thank you for listening to me!", and was preceded by a 3-second pause to signify the end of the narration. There were 16 variations total, with two vignettes per each condition. Appendix A contains the text of each vignette.

The Xitome Mobile-Dexterous-Social (MDS) humanoid robot platform was programmed to deliver the stories. The robot (referred to as "Octavia" in this study) was designed for human-robot interaction as an upper-body humanoid on a two-wheel Segway base, sized similarly to a larger adult. Octavia has a total of 41 DoFs (Degrees of Freedom), allowing a wide variety of human-like gestures and facial expressions. Figure 1 provides a close-up look at Octavia's head and a hand. The robotic implementation is described in the next subsections.

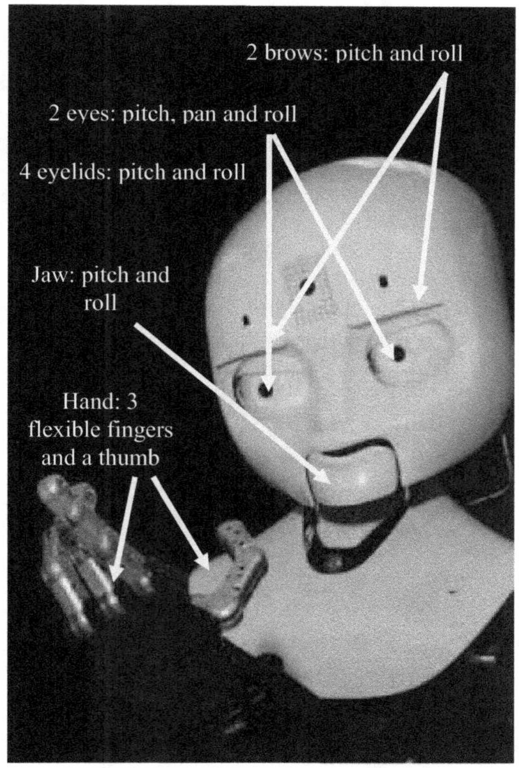

Figure 1: A close-up of Octavia's head and a hand.

2.1.1 Voice

Cepstral voice Allison was used to produce text-to-speech translation of the stories. Any mispronounced words by the TTS engine were manually adjusted to sound correct. The resulting speech was intelligible, though clearly computer-generated. The speech was transmitted through two speakers positioned on both sides of the robot. Figure 2 displays Octavia in a neutral position, which remained unchanged in the Voice condition: head up; eyes open and alert; arms and hands in a non-threatening position in front of the torso; body and head facing the audience.

Figure 2: Octavia in neutral position in Voice condition: head up, eyes open and alert, arms and hands in a non-threatening position, body and head facing the audience.

2.1.2 Lips

Octavia has a movable jaw, allowing its mouth to open or close. Octavia's jaw has two DoFs: pitch (up or down) and partial roll (where corners of the mouth can be made to appear at different heights, as in expressing a smirk). Pitch was used to vary how wide the robot's mouth was open, to correspond with more or less open sounds; the mouth was closed during pauses or between words. The jaw movements were manually synchronized for each vignette. Figure 3 (left) shows Octavia's mouth closed, and Figure 3 (right) open, with all other features in neutral position and unchanged throughout the story.

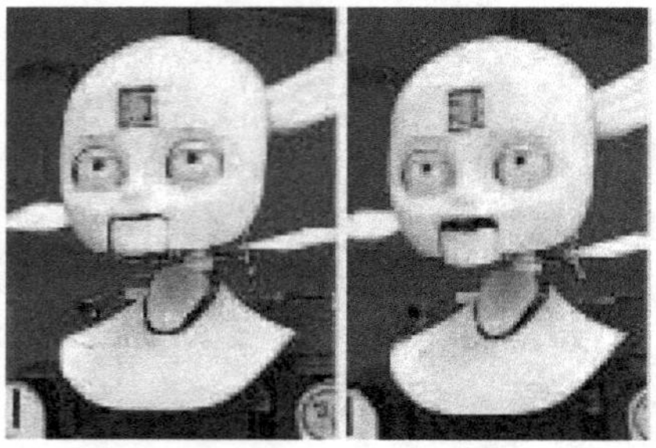

Figure 3: (Left) Mouth closed, as during a pause. (Right) Mouth half-open, pronouncing a phoneme (e.g. "ai").

2.1.3 Face

Octavia's face has nine movable parts which can be used to produce primitive facial expressions: two eyes, two eyebrows, two upper and two lower eyelids, and a jaw. Each eye has 3 DoFs: pitch for up or down, pan for side-to-side movement, and roll. Gaze shifts were used continuously throughout the story-telling to maintain the illusion of connecting with the audience; additionally, eye pitch and pan were used in producing gaze gestures accompanying the words indicating direction (e.g., up, high, there, etc.). Each eyebrow had two DoFs, pitch for up or down, and roll; both were used in production of facial expressions. The combination of upper and lower eyelids was instrumental in producing various degrees of eye closure, from fully closes as if sleeping, to fully open as in surprise; as well as periodic closing and opening of the eyelids was used to emulate blinking. Please note that head and neck positions were not changed in this condition, only facial features were varied. Figure 4 provides a few examples of Octavia's facial expressions used during the experiment: on the left, the eyes are shifted to imitate following individual attendees, in the middle, Octavia expresses surprise/anticipation, and the snapshot on the right shows skepticism.

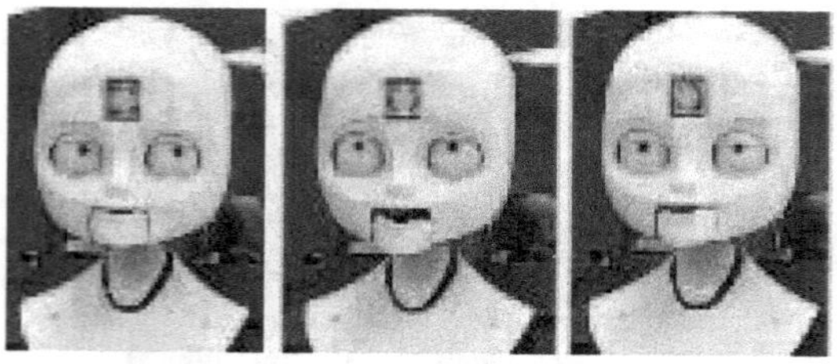

Figure 4: (Left) Eye shift to the right to connect with the audience; (Middle) Expression of surprise/anticipation; (Right) Expression of skepticism.

2.1.4 Gesture

The dexterous upper torso (two arms with shoulders, elbows, and hands with 3 fingers and a thumb) and head (head pitch, pan, roll, as well as neck pitch) allowed us to compose a variety of iconic, metaphoric and deictic gestures. For example, a pointing gesture would involve an extended arm, a turn of the head, and a turn of the torso; and a thumbs-up gesture had the fingers in a fist, a thumb up, and an arm half-extended in front of the torso. Each gesture was designed to correspond to the particular story being recited; in addition, head movements were used to accompany gaze shifts or arm gestures. Figure 5 displays examples of iconic (left), metaphoric (middle), and deictic (right) gestures performed by Octavia.

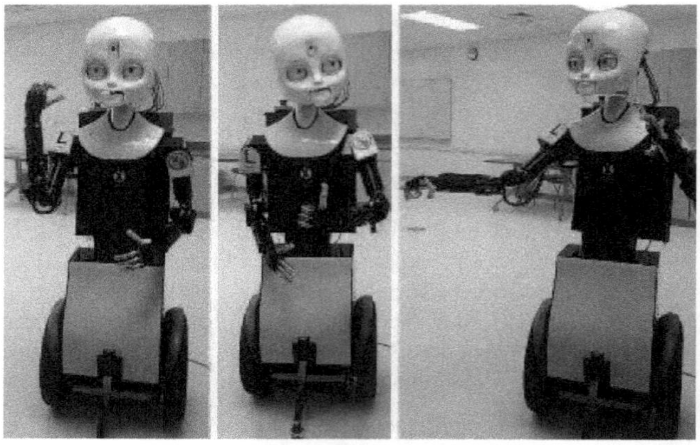

Figure 5: (Left) Octavia's arm gesture accompanies the phrase "when the fence was 40 feet high"; (Middle) Octavia shows a "thumbs up" gesture as she says "Mission accomplished!"; (Right) Octavia points to a hypothetical fire location.

2.1.5 Interactive Game

During the interactive game, 3 volunteers from the audience played a stylized version of a "shell" game with Octavia. In this game (with the goal of person identification) the robot asked each volunteer a question by which it could name them later (e.g., "What is your favorite ice-cream?"), then requested the participants to exchange places while it kept its eyes closed, and finally identified each of the participants by their answer-name (e.g., "You are vanilla, right?"), to the audience's general delight and cheering. The robot in this experiment was completely autonomous; it spoke with the participants and tracked them with its head, gaze and torso as it was addressing them.

2.1.6 Baseline control

In this control condition, the robot was positioned behind the stanchions, but performed no actions: neither speech nor movement. The experimenters were present at the exhibit, but were not manipulating the robot.

2.2 Hypotheses and Measures

The Computers Are Social Actors framework makes several clear predictions in this study. First, as a robot's behavior becomes more and more human-like, the more people should respond socially to it; in this case, we define social engagement as observing the robot for a minimum amount of time (described below). According to CASA, more people should observe or engage the robot as the social cues of the robot increase. Specifically, Idle < Voice < Lips < Face < Gesture < Game. The game should be the most engaging because the robot not only moved and spoke, but it was actively engaging with people and solving problems – very human-like behavior.

A weaker hypothesis concerns the two types of stories the robot told: jokes should be more engaging than informational talks, though people may perceive that robots should be informative over having a sense of humor.

Our primary measure in this study concerned the number of people that observed the robot for a specific length of time (15 seconds, or about ¼ of the length of the story) or that stayed for the entire story. Because the number of people in a public group can also impact whether new people will join the group (e.g., a small group may not look very interesting, but a large group may be too crowded), we also tracked the flow of people who walked by, but did not stay or observe the robot. These types of retention measures have been used successfully by other researchers [14].

2.3 Setting and Procedure

The study was conducted during Fleet Week 2012 in New York City, an annual event organized by the U.S. Navy to showcase its latest technology and allow civilians to tour their ships. A large number of exhibits were setup under a pier in Manhattan, where the general public could walk through and take a look at anything of interest. The exhibition area was located between the entrances to two modern US Navy ships, an assault ship USS Wasp which could be visited prior to entering the exhibits, and a destroyer USS Roosevelt which could be visited right after exiting the exhibits.

The attendees varied greatly in their age (both children and elderly were present), ethnic and language background, occupation (military vs. civilian) and gender from session to session. In addition to being diverse in their composition, the attendees also varied greatly in their current agenda: they could be leisurely strolling by or hurrying to climb onto USS Roosevelt or to the exit; interested in exhibits or just waiting for their companions; having a meal/snack, talking between themselves, or pointing out the robot to each other as it caught their interest.

Our exhibit occupied an approximately 20x15' area, the last one before the exit from the exhibit area, on the way to either USS Roosevelt or the exit from the entire Fleet Week area. Thus, Octavia had to vie for attention not only from other exhibits, many of which were interactive, but also with a tour of an impressive modern destroyer, currently in commission in the US Navy.

Within our exhibit, the robot was cordoned off from the public by stanchions, though it was fully visible. The area in front of the robot and to the left of it (as viewed on camera) was videotaped during the storytelling sessions, as well as a few seconds before and after; the view to the right, as the attendees were leaving the exhibit towards USS Roosevelt and the exit, was limited. Figure 6 provides a snapshot of a recorded session. Each session was started wirelessly; once started, each session ran autonomously.

The traffic (flow of people) through the exhibition area varied greatly throughout each day, from under 10 people passing in front of the robot over a 60-second period to over 70. Whenever there were at least 2 people present and the robot was not engaged in other activities, a session was initiated based on a pre-randomized order; there were at least 2 minutes between the end of one and the beginning of another session, to reduce the number of repeat participants.

Figure 6: View from the camera of attendees passing by the exhibit during a story session; the robot is positioned just out of the camera view, beyond the stanchions; another exhibit is located directly to the left, and the way to the exit is to the right.

As people were passing by the robot, they could choose to: ignore the robot completely (no gaze towards the robot), attend briefly (look at the robot for a few seconds), stay for a portion of a story, or stay for the entire story. Figure 7 shows the participants attending to robot, as opposed to simply passing by (Figure 6). The study was not announced as such, and no incentives were given for participation.[1] A total of 149 sessions were conducted and videotaped during a 6-day period.

Figure 7: Attendees watching Octavia present a story.

The interactive game sessions were videotaped as well from the same camera position. In order to make the interactive game clips comparable to the story sessions, the first 66 seconds (average story duration) of 23 game clips were extracted, as the games were longer in duration.

Finally, as the video recording was going on continuously for a large portion of the exhibit duration, it was possible to extract a number of clips during which the robot remained idle.

2.4 Video Coding

The measures that were used in the analysis were related to engagement: full engagement and attending to the robot for at least 15 seconds (partial engagement). The 15 second interval was deemed to sufficiently reflect observers' interest in the robot's performance. It took approximately 10 seconds to slowly traverse the length of our exhibit; therefore, a 10-second interval would be too small to judge engagement, and there were 2-4 gestures and

[1] IRB approval for this study was received by NRL.

facial expressions produced by the robot in each 15 second period to sufficiently differentiate between the conditions.

From the story sessions, a total of 93 clips (23 for each Social Cue condition, except for Facial Expressions, which had 24 sessions) have been video coded. In particular, the following measures were extracted:

- Full engagement: the number of people who were present and attending to the robot (looking at or actively listening to) for the entire story; this reflects engagement with the robot's storytelling;
- Partial engagement: the number of people attending for 15 seconds or more during the storytelling. People who were present, but not attending to the robot (e.g., engaged in a conversation) were not counted;
- Traffic: the total number of people who passed by the exhibit during the storytelling; included those present at the beginning of the story, and those who entered the exhibit area during the story.

In these 93 clips, 3314 was the total number of people who passed by the exhibit, and of those, 2165 passers-by at least looked at the robot. 15% of these clips were double-coded, and the inter-rater reliability, as expressed by Pearson's R was as follows: Traffic at 0.97, Partial engagement at 0.97, and Full engagement at 0.89.

To compare the story-telling with the interactive shell game, 23 excerpts from interactive games were coded in the same manner. Finally, we also coded 7 excerpts of 66 seconds each, where the robot was completely idle: not performing any task either autonomously or with the help of the experimenters. The combined total was 123 clips, in which 4222 observers passed by the robot.

3. ANALYSIS AND DISCUSSION

We present our results in two primary sections: analysis of the story-type x social cues data, and then compare those results with the two additional conditions. Recall that CASA predicts that as social cues increase, there should be more engagement with the robot. Additionally, CASA predicts that the idle robot with very little social activity beyond its anthropomorphism should be the least engaging and the interactive game with should be the most engaging.

3.1 Story-Telling

On average, 36 people passed by Octavia during a single vignette. Traffic did not differ across either story type, $F(1, 84) < 1$, $MSE = 0.74$, n.s., or social cues, $F(3, 84) < 1$, $MSE = 135.14$, n.s., nor was there an interaction, $F(3, 84) < 1$, $MSE = 92.54$, n.s..

These results show that one condition or another was not systematically run during a higher concentration of people. However, because traffic did differ greatly across sessions, we used traffic as a covariate in all future analyses.

3.1.1 Full Engagement

As suggested by Figure 8, the type of story did not have an impact on the number of people who stayed for the entire story, $F(1, 76) < 1$, $MSE = 0.19$, n.s., nor did it interact with social cues, $F(3, 76) < 1$, $MSE = 2.47$, n.s., or Traffic $F(3, 76) < 1$, $MSE = 6.05$, n.s..

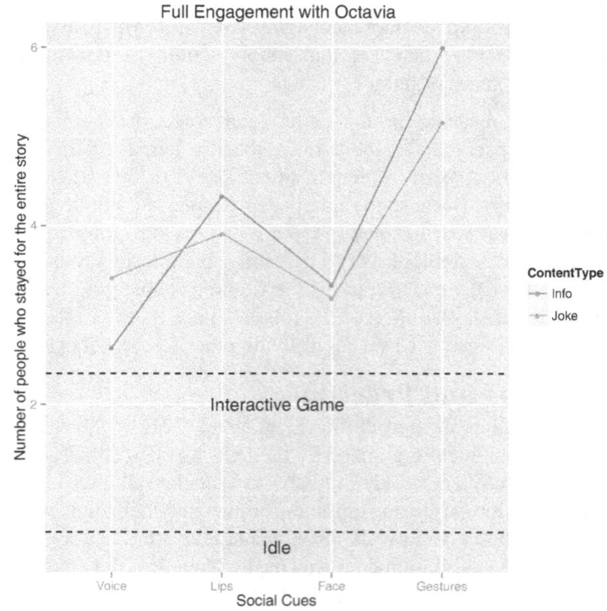

Figure 8: Full Engagement. The number of people who listened to the entire story increases with higher levels of Social Cues; no difference between Story Types is observed.

Not surprisingly, there was an effect of traffic: as traffic increased, more people stayed to watch the robot, $F(1, 76) = 29.40$, $MSE = 198.82$, $p < 0.05$, partial eta squared = 0.28. Traffic did not interact with the level of social cues, $F(1, 76) < 1$, $MSE = 6.05$, n.s.. Our explanation for traffic is straightforward: as more people walked by, more of them were likely to stay to watch the robot.

As predicted by CASA, the level of social cues did have an overall impact on the number of people who stayed for the entire story, omnibus $F(3, 76) = 4.04$, $MSE = 27.34$, $p < 0.05$, partial eta squared = 0.1. Because CASA predicts a specific pattern (an increasing trend), we used a contrast. As predicted by CASA, the contrast showed that as the level of social cues increased, the number of people also increased, $p < 0.05$.

3.1.2 Partial Engagement

Full engagement showed support for CASA. However, the full engagement measure required people who happened to be near the robot at the beginning of the story to stay for the entire story. It could be that a better or stronger measure of engagement would be to look at partial engagement (staying for at least 15 s). This partial engagement measure may show a stronger trend than the full engagement measure.

As suggested by Figure 9 (Partial Engagement) and similar to full engagement, the type of story did not have an impact on the number of people who stayed for at least 15s, $F(1, 76) < 1$, $MSE = 5.8$, n.s., nor did it interact with social cues, $F(3, 76) < 1$, $MSE = 8.2$, n.s., or traffic $F(3, 76) < 1$, $MSE = 2.4$, n.s..

Also similar to the full engagement analysis, there was an effect of traffic: as traffic increased, more people stayed to watch the robot, $F(1, 76) = 65.72$, $MSE = 645.7.82$, $p < 0.05$, partial eta squared = .46. Traffic did not interact with the level of social cues, $F(1, 76) = 1.32$, $MSE = 12.9$, $p > 0.05$. We interpret this finding in a straightforward manner: as more people walked by, more of them were likely to stay to watch the robot.

Similar to the full engagement analysis and as predicted by CASA, the level of social cues did have a strong impact on the number of people who watched for at least 15s, omnibus $F(3, 76) = 8.87$, $MSE = 87.1$, $p < 0.05$, partial eta squared = .18. We also performed a trend analysis for partial engagement and again found that as the level of social cues increased, the number of people who watched the robot also increased, $p < 0.05$.

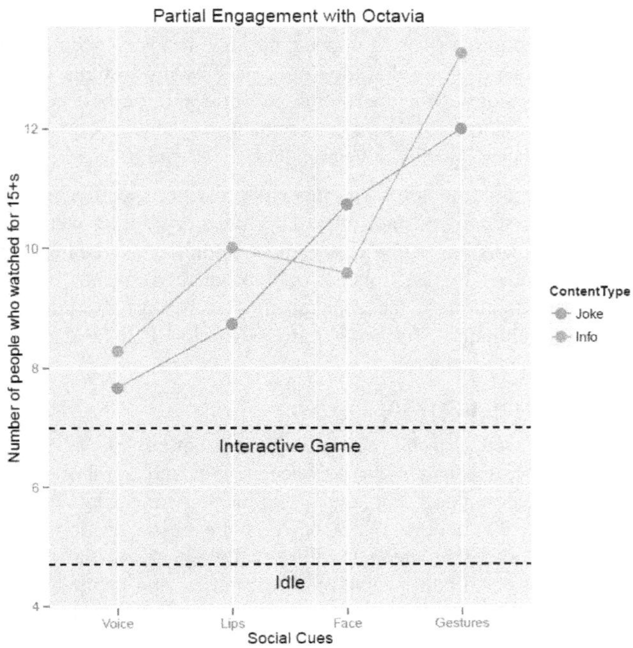

Figure 9: Partial Engagement. The number of people who attended to Octavia's story-telling for 15+ seconds increases with higher levels of Social Cues; no difference between Story Types is observed.

3.1.3 Idle Control

As described above, we also coded video excerpts when the robot was completely idle and there was no one interacting with the robot. The robot had almost no social appeal at all. In fact, the only interesting aspect about it was that it was a robot. CASA predicts that, because this robot was behaving in the least social manner, people should be the least engaged toward it compared to other conditions.

As both Figures 8 and 9 suggest, the idle robot was far less engaging than any of the other more interactive conditions. To test this statistically, we performed two different tests. We first compared the idle condition to all the story-telling conditions, collapsed across content type (since the idle condition obviously did not have that factor). We found that for the full engagement measure, fewer people watched the robot for a full minute when it was idle than when it was telling a joke or being informative, $F(1, 95) = 20.1$, $MSE = 137.2$, $p < 0.05$, partial eta squared = 0.16. Similarly, there was a strong effect for partial engagement: the idle robot was less engaging than when it was telling a story, $F(1, 95) = 15.9$, $MSE = 183.2$, partial eta squared = 0.12. As in previous analyses, traffic did not differ between conditions ($p > 0.05$) and it did have a positive effect on the number of people who engaged with the robot, $F(1, 95) = 34.9$, $MSE = 238.3$, $p < 0.05$, partial eta squared = 0.27 for full engagement and $F(1, 95) = 68.0$, $MSE = 783.7$, $p < 0.05$, partial eta squared = 0.41 for partial engagement.

We also performed a more conservative test where we compared the idle condition to the least interactive story-telling condition, the Voice condition. We found that for the full engagement measure, fewer people watched the robot for a full minute when it was idle than when it was telling a story with its voice only, $F(1, 26) = 26.7$, $MSE = 71.34$, $p < 0.05$, partial eta squared = 0.52. Similarly, there was a strong effect for partial engagement: the idle robot was less engaging than when it was telling a story with its voice alone, $F(1, 26) = 7.0$, $MSE = 56.4$, partial eta squared = 0.22. As in previous analyses, traffic did not differ between conditions ($p > 0.05$) and traffic did have a positive effect on the number of people who engaged with the robot, $F(1, 26) = 11.2$, $MSE = 30.0$, $p < 0.05$, partial eta squared = 0.30 for full engagement and $F(1, 26) = 15.1$, $MSE = 121.08$, $p < 0.05$, partial eta squared = 0.37 for partial engagement.

As predicted by CASA, the idle robot was less engaging socially than a story-telling robot.

3.2 Interactive Game

While the idle condition was predicted by CASA to be the least engaging, the interactive game was predicted to be the most engaging. In this condition, the robot spoke to people playing a game, telling people to move around, and of all the conditions discussed so far, was the most human-like. CASA predicts that, because it is the most human-like, people should be engaged with it more than any other condition.

However, as Figures 8 and 9 suggest, the interactive game was actually **less** engaging than when the robot told stories. The statistical tests in this case will be limited because the direction of the prediction is opposite to what the data shows. We found that for the full engagement measure, people were less engaged with the interactive game robot than a robot telling a story, $F(1, 111) = 9.3$, $MSE = 72.8$, $p < 0.05$, partial eta square = 0.03. Similarly, for partial engagement people were less likely to watch the interactive game than the robot telling a story, $F(1, 111) = 11.9$, $MSE = 163.2$, $p < 0.05$, partial eta squared = 0.03.

Please note again that these results are in the opposite direction to that predicted by CASA.

3.3 Engaged vs. Unengaged

While there was general support for CASA as the robot told stories, there is another measure that should be looked at: unengaged people. As Figures 8 and 9 suggest, and earlier analyses confirm, the number of people who engaged with the robot showed a reliable and robust increasing trend across levels of social cues. However, it is also possible to look at the number of people who were not engaged, or who left without paying attention to the robot. This analysis used the full engagement analysis: people who stayed for the entire story or people who left mid-way through. We collapsed across story type because there was no statistical difference between joke or information in any of our analyses.

As Figure 10 suggests, twice as many people were unengaged and left ($M = 8.8$) than were engaged and stayed ($M = 4.0$), $F(1, 176) = 61.8$, $MSE = 1037.9$, $p < 0.05$, partial eta squared = 0.26. A similar finding occurs for the partially engaged measure.

It is surprising that more people decided to leave than stay, and somewhat counter to the general CASA framework.

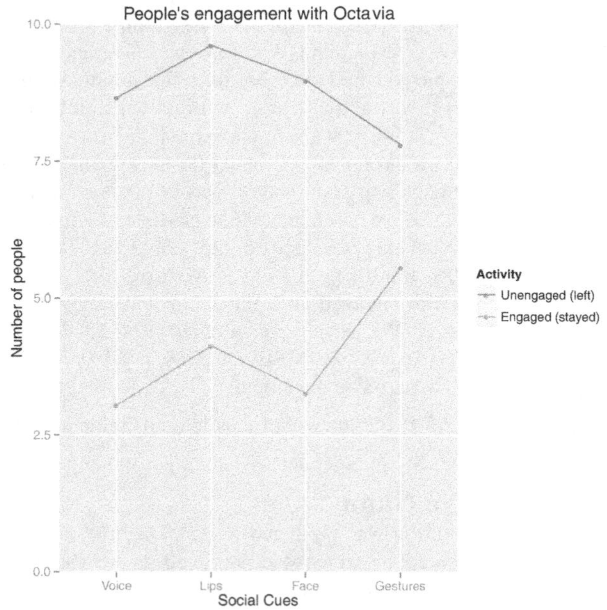

Figure 10: Number of the attendees who stayed for the entire story (fully engaged) vs. those who left (unengaged).

4. GENERAL DISCUSSION

In this paper, we explored one of the fundamental questions of human robot interaction: how to encourage people to engage with a robot. We addressed this question in a very theoretical manner. We used the Computers Are Social Actors (CASA) framework to create robotic interactions that varied in their social cues, from absolutely no active social cues (our idle condition) to increasing levels of social cues (Voice, Lips, Face, Gesture) to full human-like game-playing interaction (interactive game).

We collected data in a naturalistic setting and had the opportunity to examine how "normal" people would engage with a novel robotic platform. Because data collection occurred in a public venue, we were able to collect data on over 4000 individuals as they made a simple choice: should they stay and engage with our robot.

We found several strong aspects of support for CASA. First, we found that a robot that provides even minimal social cues (e.g., talking) is more engaging than a robot that does nothing. While seemingly obvious, it should be noted that the robot that was used in this study was an actual physical robot, and most people in the US have not seen or interacted with a robot before, so the novelty was quite high.

Second, we found that as the robot's social cues increased, people's engagement also increased. Specifically, we found that, while the robot told a story, people were more engaged and interested in the robot if it acted more human-like – if it gestured while making faces and moved its lips as it spoke. People became progressively less engaged with the robot as each of those features was removed.

However, we also found some reasons to question whether CASA is the best or only framework to use in order to increase social engagement with robots. The biggest concern we found was that the robot that had the most human-like social behaviors – conversational talking, movement, game-playing – did not elicit more social engagement from people than other conditions. If anything, the game playing robot engendered **less** social engagement than other, less social interactions. This finding is in direct opposition to CASA.

Another concern is that, even when the robot was telling a story, more people left than stayed to watch the robot. Perhaps this finding is not completely surprising: people at this event had varied agendas and may not have been interested in engaging or watching a robot. However, if one of the goals of the human-robot interaction field is to understand how and why people and robots interact the way that they do, it is sobering to think that a lab, using a state-of-the-art robotic platform and the best current theory on how to elicit social engagement, was able to capture, at most, less than 33% of a naïve population's attention.

Finally, it should be noted that this study did not specifically test whether the social cues accompanying the story-telling were the primary explanation of the engagement findings, or whether just random motion by the robot would produce a similar effect. Given the duration of the engagement, we believe the latter is unlikely, although further studies would be needed to disambiguate this notion.

5. CONCLUSION

This paper used a strong methodology in a naturalistic setting to examine social engagement between people and a robot. We found mixed support for the Computers Are Social Actors framework. We believe that CASA is the best current theory about how and why people will socially engage with robots. However, we also believe that more theoretical and applied work needs to be done to improve or replace the current framework.

6. ACKNOWLEDGMENTS

Our thanks go to those who conducted the experiment during the Fleetweek and made sure the robot behaved properly, namely Magda Bugajska, Eric Martinson, Ed Lawson, Bill Adams, Anthony Harrison, Laura Hiatt and Sunny Khemlani. This research was supported by a grant to JG Trafton from the Office of Naval Research.

7. REFERENCES

[1] Reeves, B., & Nass, C. (1996). The Media Equation: How People Treat Computers, Television, and New Media Like Real People and Places. Cambridge University Press.

[2] Nass, C., & Moon, Y. (2000). Machies and Mindlessness: Social Responses to Computers. Journal of Social Issues (56), pp. 81-103.

[3] C. Breazeal, C. Kidd, A. Thomaz, G. Hoffman, and M. Berlin. (2005) Effects of nonverbal communication on efficiency and robustness in human-robot teamwork. In Intelligent Robots and Systems, IEEE/RSJ International Conference on, pages 708–713.

[4] Sidner, C., Kidd, C., Lee, C., & Lesh, N. (2004) Where to Look: a Study of Human-Robot Engagement. In Proceedings of the 9th International Conference on Intelligent User Interfaces.

[5] Moshkina, L. (2012). Improving Request Compliance through Robot Affect. In Proceedings of Twenty-Sixth AAAI Conference on Artificial Intelligence, Toronto, Canada.

[6] Chidambaram, V., Chiang, Y.-H., & Mutlu B. (2012). Designing Persuasive Robots: How Robots Might Persuade People Using Vocal and Nonverbal Cues. In Proceedings of the 7th ACM/IEEE Conference on Human- Robot Interaction (HRI 2012)

[7] Groom, V., Takayama, L., Ochi, P., & Nass, C. (2009) I am my robot: The impact of robot-building and robot form on operators. In Proceedings of the Human-Robot Interaction Conference: HRI 2009, San Diego, CA.

[8] Fong, T., Nourbakhsh, I., & Dautenhahn, K. (2003) A survey of socially interactive robots. Robotics and Autonomous Systems, 42(3-4), pp. 143-166.

[9] Nass, C., & Gong, L. (1999). Maximized Modality or Constrained Consistency? In Proceedings of the International Conference on Audio-Visual Speech Processing (AVSP'99), Santa Cruz, CA

[10] Avison , W.R., McLeod, J.D., & Pescosolido, B.A. (Eds.) (2007) Mental Health, Social Mirror. New York: Springer.

[11] Huang, C.-M., & Mutlu, B. (2013). Repertoire of Robot Behavior: Enabling Robots to Achieve Interaction Goals through Social Behavior. *Journal of Human-Robot Interaction, 2(2), 80–102.*

[12] Helweg-Larsen, M., Cunningham, S. J., Carrico, A., Pergram, A. M. (2004) To Nod or Not to Nod: An Observational Study of Nonverbal Communication and Status in Female and Male College Students, Psychology of Women Quarterly, 28(4), pp. 358-361.

[13] Martinson, E., Lawson, W.E., & Trafton, J.G. (2013). Identifying People with Soft Biometrics at Fleet Week. In Proceedings of the 8th ACM/IEEE Conference on Human-Robot Interaction (HRI 2013).

[14] Kiesler, S., Powers, A., Fussell, S. R., & Torrey, C. (2008). Anthropomorphic Interactions with a Robot and Robot-Like Agent. Social Cognition (26:2, pp. 169-181).

8. Appendix A: Text of the Vignettes Used in the Study

8.1 MDS Vignette (Informative)

Hello! My name is Octavia. I work at the Navy Center for Applied Research in Artificial Intelligence. I am an MDS robot. M is for mobile. D is for dexterous. S is for social. I was designed so that it would be easy to work with me, just like with people. I have two video cameras in my eyes; and a special infrared camera in my forehead that let me see shapes. I have four microphone ears that allow me to hear you and help me figure out where sounds are coming from. I have a laser range finder on my base. It helps me avoid obstacles. I have a wide range of motion in my arms and hands. My face is also very expressive. Thank you for listening to me!

8.2 Firefighting Vignette (Informative)

Hello! My name is Octavia. I work at the Navy Center for Applied Research in Artificial Intelligence. I am an MDS robot. M is for mobile. D is for dexterous. S is for social. Our latest project was developing robots that can fight fires on board navy vessels. A real fire was set up in our lab. First, I found my team leader with the cameras in my eyes. Next, he showed me where the fire was. A special camera, in my forehead, helped me recognize a few gestures, like pointing, and come here. Then, I found the fire using two infrared cameras. Finally, using a hose, attached to my left arm, I sprayed the fire with a stream of water. The fire was extinguished - mission accomplished! Thank you for listening to me!

8.3 Kangaroo Vignette (Joke)

Hello! My name is Octavia. I work at the Navy Center for Applied Research in Artificial Intelligence. I heard a funny joke yesterday at fleet week - I hope you like it! Here it is. A kangaroo kept getting out of his enclosure at the zoo. Knowing that he could jump high, the zoo officials put up a ten-foot fence. He was out the next morning, just roaming about the zoo. A twenty-foot fence was put up. He got out, again. When the fence was forty feet high, a camel in the next enclosure asked the kangaroo: How high do you think they'll go? The kangaroo said: About a thousand feet, unless somebody shuts the gate at night! Thank you for listening to me!

8.4 Sherlock Holmes Vignette (Joke)

Hello! My name is Octavia. I work at the Navy Center for Applied Research in Artificial Intelligence. I heard a funny joke yesterday at fleet week - I hope you like it! Here it is. Sherlock Holmes and Dr. Watson are going camping. They pitch their tent under the stars and go to sleep. Sometime in the middle of the night, Holmes wakes Watson up: Watson, look up at the stars, and tell me what you deduce! Watson says: I see millions of stars, and even if a few of those have planets, it's quite likely there are some planets like Earth, and if there are a few planets like Earth out there, there might be life. Holmes replies: Watson, you idiot, somebody stole our tent! Thank you for listening to me!

Automatic Analysis of Facial Expressions

Maja Pantic
Imperial College London
m.pantic@imperial.ac.uk

ABSTRACT

Facial behaviour is our preeminent means to communicating affective and social signals. This talk discusses a number of components of human facial behaviour, how they can be automatically sensed and analysed by computers, what is the past research in the field conducted by the iBUG group at Imperial College London, and how far we are from enabling computers to sense and recognise human facial expressions and behaviour.

Categories and Subject Descriptors

H.1.2 User/Machine Systems

Keywords

ACM SIGCHI; computing; human-robot interaction; human behavior understanding; affective computing

Bio

Maja Pantic obtained her PhD degree in computer science in 2001 from Delft University of Technology, the Netherlands. Until 2005, she was an Assistant/Associate Professor at Delft University of Technology. In 2006, she joined the Imperial College London, Department of Computing, UK, where she is Professor of Affective & Behavioural Computing and the Head of the iBUG group, working on machine analysis of human non-verbal behaviour. From November 2006, she also holds an appointment as the Professor of Affective & Behavioural Computing at the University of Twente, the Netherlands.

In 2007, for her research on Machine Analysis of Human Naturalistic Behavior (MAHNOB), she received European Research Council Starting Grant (ERC StG) as one of 2% best junior scientists in any research field in Europe. She was also the Scientific Director of the large European project on Social Signal Processing (2009-2013). In 2011, Prof. Pantic received BCS Roger Needham Award, awarded annually to a UK based researcher for a distinguished research contribution in computer science within ten years of their PhD.

She is the Editor in Chief of the Image and Vision Computing Journal (IVCJ/ IMAVIS), Associate Editor of the IEEE Transactions on Systems, Man, and Cybernetics - Part B: Cybernetics (IEEE TSMC-B), Associate Editor of the IEEE Transactions on Pattern Analysis and Machine Intelligence (IEEE TPAMI), and a member of the Steering Committee of the IEEE Transactions on Affective Computing. She is an IEEE Fellow.

Prof. Pantic is one of the world's leading experts in the research on machine understanding of human behavior including vision-based detection, tracking, and analysis of human behavioral cues like facial expressions and body gestures, and multimodal analysis of human behaviors like laughter, social signals, and affective states. She is also one of the pioneers in design and development of fully automatic, affect-sensitive human-centered anticipatory interfaces, built for humans based on human models. She has published more than 150 technical papers in the areas of machine analysis of facial expressions and emotions, machine analysis of human body gestures, and human-computer interaction. Her work is widely cited and has more than 25 popular press coverage (including New Scientist, BBC Radio, and NL TV 1 and 3).

HRI'14, March 3–6, 2014, Bielefeld, Germany.
ACM 978-1-4503-2658-2/14/03.
http://dx.doi.org/10.1145/2559636.2566688

Spatial and Other Social Engagement Cues in a Child-Robot Interaction: Effects of a Sidekick

Marynel Vázquez[1,3], Aaron Steinfeld[1], Scott E. Hudson[2,3], Jodi Forlizzi[2,3]

[1]Robotics Institute
Carnegie Mellon University
5000 Forbes Ave, USA
Pittsburgh, PA 15213
{marynel,steinfeld}@cmu.edu

[2]HCI Institute
Carnegie Mellon University
5000 Forbes Ave
Pittsburgh, PA 15213
{scott.hudson,forlizzi}@cs.cmu.edu

[3]Disney Research Pittsburgh
4720 Forbes Ave
Lower Level, Suite 110
Pittsburgh, PA 15213

ABSTRACT

In this study, we explored the impact of a co-located sidekick on child-robot interaction. We examined child behaviors while interacting with an expressive furniture robot and his robot lamp sidekick. The results showed that the presence of a sidekick did not alter child proximity, but did increase attention to spoken elements of the interaction. This suggests the addition of a co-located sidekick has potential to increase engagement but may not alter subtle physical interactions associated with personal space and group spatial arrangements. The findings also reinforce existing research by the community on proxemics and anthropomorphism.

Categories and Subject Descriptors

H.4.m [**Information Systems Applications**]: Miscellaneous; H.1.2 [**Models and Principles**]: User/Machine Systems—*human factors*

Keywords

Human-robot interaction; children; proxemics

1. INTRODUCTION

In this work, we explored the idea of a sidekick from a human-robot interaction perspective. A sidekick is closely associated with another, primary character, and regarded as a subordinate or partner. Sidekicks are popular in various forms of narrative, where they are often used as comic relief or to introduce an accessible character to increase audience engagement [38, 30, 14]. Likewise, sidekicks can act as a vehicle for raising an obvious concern to the primary character from the audience. For example, a sidekick may yell, "Look out!" to the hero when a villain appears on screen.

In support of larger goals, we developed a platform for exploring entertainment engagement in general from a human-robot interaction perspective. This robot is Chester, a child-sized robot in the form of a small, but mobile, piece of furniture. Although Chester is intended to be friendly and inviting, we worried that some children would be uncomfortable with its physical appearance. Chester is big with respect to young children, has pronounced corners, and moves rigidly. Thus, we decided to explore how the beneficial aspects of a sidekick might mitigate apprehension and fear.

Robots provide a novel opportunity for sidekicks since it is possible, and reasonable, for the sidekick to be co-located with the primary character – this would be unusual for a human sidekick. Hence, we added an interactive lamp, named Blink, on top of Chester to examine this interaction (Figure 1). This lamp performs the functions of a sidekick, being smaller in size and dependent on Chester for mobility. Blink is smarter and speaks its own language which, much like R2-D2 in Star Wars, only Chester understands.

We conducted an exploratory study with our characters, and predicted that the addition of Blink would lead children to be more engaged in the interaction and treat Chester in a more sociable manner. Besides showing the effects of a sidekick, we also characterize the behavior of children that interacted with our characters. Our work confirms that furniture robots are a plausible design for children.

Figure 1: Chester and Blink. Chester is a mobile robot that looks like a chiffonier. Blink, the lamp, is Chester's sidekick.

HRI'14, March 3–6, 2014, Bielefeld, Germany.

ACM 978-1-4503-2658-2/14/03 ...$15.00.
http://dx.doi.org/10.1145/2559636.2559684.

2. RELATED WORK

Research focused on the interaction between humans and multiple robots suggests that watching two robots interact facilitates interaction along a number of dimensions. First, people can better understand robot utterances when observing two robots interact with each other and with their environment [16]. Furthermore, there is evidence that suggests that the interaction between two robots attracts people's attention, and helps convey information to others. Shiomi et al. [27] noticed this effect at a museum exhibition, and Hayashi et al. [10] highlighted the potential of a pair of robots as a *passive-social medium* to communicate information in the context of Japanese Manzai. Hayashi et al. [9] later evaluated the idea of using robots as a non-interactive communication medium at a railway terminal station in Japan. People that observed two robots interact with each other at the station paid more attention to the content of their dialogues, compared to when one or two robots, with limited realistic interactivity, tried to convey the same information directly.

Models for measuring engagement with a robot typically consider gaze, head pose, turn-taking, human-robot kinesics, and spatial information [21, 4, 24, 25]. The latter is particularly popular for social human-robot interaction analyses, because spatial information can easily be compared with Hall's seminal work on proxemics [7]. According to Hall, the distance people keep with each other can be categorized in four main classes: intimate, personal, social, and public. As Hall noted, the specific distance chosen at a time depends on the relationship of the interacting individuals, how they feel, what they are doing, environmental factors, and culture. Given all these factors, more recent proxemic analyses [5, 37] cluster measured interactant distances first and then compare this result with Hall's, rather than directly categorizing distances into one of the four classes [35, 12]. We use the latter strategy in our proxemics analysis.

Eberts and Lepper found that children have already developed stable patterns of proxemic behavior in their interaction with others by the age of four or five [6], which suggests the utility of Hall's concepts for analyzing the spatial behavior of young children. Moreover, they observed that eye contact affected children's initial interaction distance when approaching one of the experimenters. Other observations, mainly on pairs of children, have revealed that children tend to use more space as they grow older [1, 19, 36].

Bailey et al. [3] provided support for the notion that personal space behavior of fifth and sixth graders can be manipulated via the principles of modeling. Both girls and boys tended to stay close or far from an object person as a function of a confederate's behavior.

Much of the research on the human dimensions of human-robot interaction proxemics is summarized in [31]; we only mention the more relevant work for our study in this paper. Walters et al. [34] found that children tended to stand further away from a PeopleBot robot, compared to adults. Mumm and Mutlu [22] showed in a controlled experiment that participants that disliked a robot tended to maintain a greater distance from it when mutual gaze was established. In addition, the distance participants kept from this robot was affected by participants' gender, and pet ownership.

Important prior work for this effort included Yamaji et al. [37], which examined how children interacted with Sociable Trash Box (STB) robots. Like Chester and Blink, these robots were mobile, expressive furniture. Yamaji et al. found that proxemic distances differed depending on how the robots were behaving. When the robotic trash boxes were moving individually, children exploited two spaces to interact with them: "personal-social" and "public" – in reference to Hall's spatial zones. However, when the robots interacted in groups, as swarms, the authors noted three kind of spaces ("personal", "social", and "public"). Chester and Blink are different since they are co-located, have faces with moving eyes, and can speak. There are logical reasons for different proxemics when robots are independent, but it is unclear whether co-location impacts proxemics.

The way people configure themselves with respect to a robot has also been studied in human-robot interaction [26]. A classical model for this kind of spatial analysis is Kendon's *F-formation* system [17], which considers clusters of people arranged in lines, circles, and other patterns. These formations arise when interactants form a shared space between them to which they have equal and exclusive access. McNeill [20] further categorized F-formations into two kinds of social interactive configurations: *social* and *instrumental*. In the former case, the elements of the formation are other individuals (Kendon's original version). In the latter, two or more people gaze at a common event or object in space. F-formations were directly applied to human-robot interaction by Huettenrauch et al. [13], who found that people sustained "viz-à-viz", "L-shape", and "side-by-side" formations with a PeopleBot. Kuzuoka et al. [18] explored changing a robot's body orientation to actively reconfigure an F-formation sustained with another person.

Other related research focuses on children-robot interaction. Robins et al. [25] showed that a rich contextual environment can encourage children to initiate interaction with a robot. Kanda et al. [15] examined the proposition that robots could form relationships with children, and that children might learn from robots. The results from their field trial suggested that robots may be more successful in establishing common ground and influence children when they share commonalities with their users. Additionally, behavioral observation of the interaction between toddlers and robots by Alač et al. [2] suggested that a robot's social character extends beyond its physical body. The social character includes the robot's positioning in space, the arrangement of other actors around it, and its interlocutors' talk, prosody, gestures, visual orientation, and facial expressions.

3. METHOD

We conducted an exploratory laboratory study as part of the *Summer Games* carried out at Disney Research Pittsburgh, in which groups of children participated in a collection of activities and interacted with different kinds of characters. We used two embodied characters in our study, Chester and Blink (the sidekick), to investigate the effect of a sidekick in a Wizard of Oz fashion. In keeping with good HRI principles, we are attempting to identify appropriate robot behaviors en route to implementing autonomy [29]. Our intent is to progress towards autonomous robot behaviors in future studies.

Participants only experienced one of two conditions: *without sidekick* (C) or *sidekick* (S). Only Chester was active in the control (C) case, while both Chester and Blink interacted with the participants in (S). The interactions were scripted and designed to be as similar as possible.

3.1 Participants

Twenty groups of 3 or 4 children interacted with Chester and Blink. Participants were 4 to 10 years old, some were siblings, and were accompanied by at least one adult. Adults were allowed to observe upon request, but were asked to avoid interrupting the activities of the Summer Games. The latter included trying to stay as far back as possible from the interaction location of our study (Figure 2).

Some kids expected to see a robot because the Summer Games' recruitment flier said that "we study how children (...) interact with toy, animated, and robotic characters". However, kids were unaware of our robot character appearances prior to the study. Both Chester and Blink were kept out of public sight until the interaction.

3.2 Chester and Blink

Chester is a child-sized, mobile chiffonier robot, with wood casing, actuated drawers, and a hidden 1D laser measurement system (Figure 1). Chester has back-projected eyes and mouth. Its eyes are expressive and were programmed to convey awareness. The eyes automatically moved after being steady for a short period of time, or blink every once in a while, as typically done for 2D animations [32]. Chester also has hidden speakers, near its mouth, that allow it to verbally communicate with others. When Chester "speaks", the mouth becomes white, in synchrony with the amplitude of the sounds it emits. Like the eyes, this increases the anthropomorphism of the robot.

Blink is the lamp on top of Chester, which also has back-projected animated eyes. Blink produces nonverbal sounds through a small speaker inside its shade, and has a hidden Xtion Pro Live depth and RGB camera in its base.

Blink is Chester's close companion – its sidekick. As a character Blink is intended to be funny, but more mature and with better judgment in practical matters than Chester.

3.3 Procedure

Children first participated in a virtual "mix and match" game, where they picked apparel and accessories to change a character's look. Kids were able to take a picture of the character whenever they wanted and, at the end of the game, each got to pick their favorite image. The selected pictures were printed afterwards, and stored inside of Chester's drawers without participants' knowledge. Chester's mission was to give these pictures to the kids.

Figure 2: Sketch of the environment in which the interaction happened. The wizard was seated at the end of the table in the dining area (1). Chester was at (2) when children started to approach from the conference room at the end of the hall (3). Parents were asked to remain near (3).

The physical space where the interaction occurred is depicted in Figure 2. The robot wizard was in the same room as the participants due to safety concerns, since this was our first experiment with the platform. She pretended to be working with a laptop at a table nearby (1) for about 1 hour before the interaction. This allowed participants to familiarize with her presence.

An experimenter brought the kids into a conference room prior to the interaction ((3) in Fig. 2). Subsequently, Chester (and Blink) was secretly positioned against the wall in the dining area (2). The experimenter in the conference room then brought the children out and down the hall, with the premise of getting their pictures. The wizard started controlling the characters at this point, using a PlayStation 3 gamepad to surreptitiously command Chester's motions, open and close its drawers, and activate pre-recorded animations for both characters (utterances and associated facial expressions). No participant discovered that the wizard was controlling the robots with the gamepad under the table.

The interaction followed Phases in the (S) condition:

1. *Acknowledgment.* The participants were acknowledged. Blink and Chester looked towards the end of the hall, and realized that the children were coming. As participants approached, Chester and Blink verbally indicated that they were checking if they had the photos.
2. *Greeting.* Chester greeted the participants, and introduced Blink.
3. *How are you?* Chester asked the participants how they were doing and if they liked being at our research facility.
4. *Remember.* Chester asked the children if they remembered the pictures they took during the earlier game. Chester told them that the photos were in its drawers.
5. *Stuck.* Participants experienced the rising action part of the story: Chester realized its drawers were "stuck" and, after conferring with Blink, said that they may need oil.
6. *Bump.* Chester indicted that he thought that bumping into a wall was a good way of fixing the problem, but Blink dissuaded Chester to prevent him from damaging the wall.
7. *Spin.* Chester asked participants to step back and spun around in an attempt to unstick the drawers, but was unsuccessful.
8. *Shaking.* Chester shook, following Blink's advice, and finally got the drawers unstuck.
9. *Opened drawers.* Chester told the participants to "come grab your pictures", and
   (a) Participants grabbed the pictures, or
   (b) If participants did not want to grab the pictures, then the experimenter removed the pictures and gave them to the participants.
10. *Visit again?* Chester asked the participants if they liked the pictures, if they would come to visit again, and if they had to leave.
11. *Goodbye.* Chester and Blink said goodbye to the children, retreated to a safe location, and closed their eyes.

After the characters closed their eyes, the experimenter with the participants told them that they could take stickers of Chester and of the two other robots from the earlier mix and match game. Children then picked the stickers they wanted from a nearby table, and were brought back to the conference room or to another Summer Games activity.

The interaction in the control (C) condition was similar to the interaction in the (S) condition, except that the lamp on top of Chester was not a character, but just a lamp. Blink's eyes were not visible in (C), and it did not emit any sounds. Since Blink was not there to help, the script was modified such that Chester realized that bumping into a wall was a bad idea by itself. Also, it occurred to Chester (not to Blink) that shaking may unstick the drawers.

The wizard had three special buttons in the controller, that scheduled animations to help continue with the flow of the script in case of potential deviations. When one of the buttons was pressed by the wizard, Chester said "No! No! Let me do it myself" in response to situations in which children wanted to open the drawers with their hands. The other two buttons activated animations for "Ouch!" with a sad face and "Don't poke me" with an angry face. These were prepared to prevent very outgoing kids from touching the robot in dangerous ways, e.g., leaning on the top, or sticking fingers in the laser scanner slot.

Participants were free to approach our robots as desired. The experimenter that brought the kids from the conference room stopped approaching our robots about 4 meters away to reduce potential bias on the children's proxemic behavior.

3.4 Data collection and coding

Participants were equipped with a wireless microphone, attached to their clothes, for the duration of their participation in the Summer Games, and were recorded throughout the whole interaction. Video was captured from the Xtion Pro Live sensor inside of Blink's base, a Kinect sensor mounted on the ceiling of the dining area, and a standard camcorder positioned on a tripod in the back of the room (next to the sofa in the right side of Figure 2).

Two professionals transcribed with ELAN [28] when participants spoke, touched the robot, turned their head away from it, and laughed. At the beginning of the process, the transcriptions were evaluated twice for procedural errors. After the process completed, the intercoder reliability was computed for 16 participants (22%) that were transcribed by both people. Cronbach's alpha was 0.90 for number of utterances directed at the characters. Cohen's kappa was 0.87 and 0.93 for touching and head turning, respectively. Coders differed only by 1 annotation for laughing.

One transcriber also annotated when participants sat on the ground, and marked down their location and Chester's top corners in the video collected from the Kinect in the ceiling (as showed in Figure 3). These positions were converted to 3D using depth data, and projected into the ground plane for 2D spatial analysis. To confirm precision, we computed the distance between Chester's top-front corners (in the ground plane) and compared it with the real width of the robot. The difference was 2.3cm on average ($SD = 2.3$cm).

When a participant was not visible from the top view, then his or her position was marked on the camcorder video that was captured from the back of the room. These locations were mapped to the top view using a homography on the ground plane [8], and used for the spatial analysis as well.

Figure 3: Top view of the scene.

4. RESULTS

Our analysis focused on the interactions starting with the beginning of the script up to when Chester gave the pictures. We did not analyze most interactions beyond this point since a significant number of participants were distracted by the pictures. Children typically forgot which pictures they requested and became preoccupied with finding their own.[1]

4.1 Demographics

There were 74 participants total, belonging to 47 families, which were split into 20 groups. Ten groups (37 children) experienced the (C) condition, while 10 groups (37 children) experienced the (S) condition. The average age for each group was 6.8 and 6.9 years old, with standard deviations of 2.1 and 2.1, respectively. Ages were split into three categories: A1 for 4-5 years old, A2 for 6-8 years old, and A3 for 9-10 years old. The number of participants per condition and age group was roughly similar. We had 12, 16, and 9 children in A1, A2 and A3 of (C), and 12, 14, and 11 in (S).

Even though we tried to balance for gender, the proportion of boys with respect to girls was greater in (S) than in (C). We had 23 boys in the *sidekick* condition (62% of that group), but 18 boys in the *without sidekick* condition (49%).

4.2 Proxemics

We mapped the 3D positions of the participants from the top view of the scene to the ground plane. These positions were then transformed from the global frame of reference on the ground to a frame of reference originating from the middle of the front of Chester (Figure 4).

We plotted the distances computed with respect to the robot per interaction phase, since we expected participants' proxemic behavior to change based on activity (Figure 5). We considered the first 9 phases up to when the robot handed out the pictures. The boundaries between these phases was set based on robot utterances. For example, the Greeting phase started when the robot said "Hello".

[1]Experience with the mix and match game did not suggest that children cared about which pictures were theirs, but it mattered in our study. We recommend giving the same object to all participants to avoid distraction and arguments.

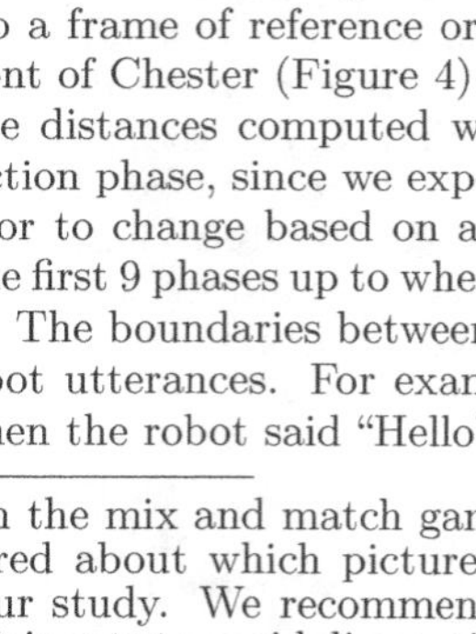

Figure 4: Frame of reference with respect to the robot.

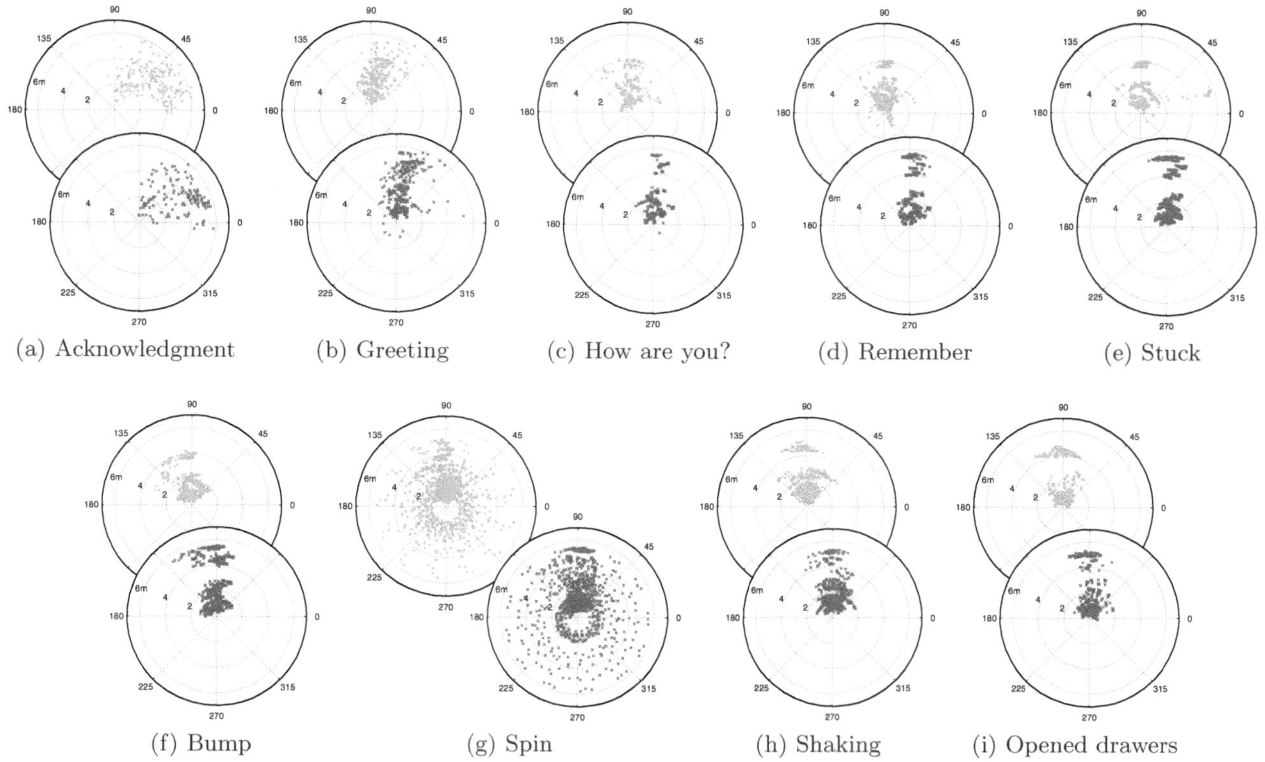

(a) Acknowledgment (b) Greeting (c) How are you? (d) Remember (e) Stuck

(f) Bump (g) Spin (h) Shaking (i) Opened drawers

Figure 5: Polar plots of the position of the participants with respect to the robot. Data is grouped by interaction phase, with the frame of reference set with respect to the front face of Chester (Fig. 4). The gray marks indicate the position of the participants in the (C) condition, and the purple marks indicate the position in (S). Distance unit is meters.

Angular data showed that participants tended to interact with the robot by standing in front of its face, not to its side, nor behind it. The angular range [0, 180] contained 99.7% of all the angles computed for the participants with respect to the robot, excluding when Chester spun. The distribution of these angles followed a bell curve, with the maximum, central peak near 90 (i.e., *face on*).

We inspected the distribution of distances between the participants and the robot(s), and noticed that the first two phases of the interaction (Fig. 5a and 5b) were more chaotic and did not provide as much insight on proxemic behavior as the rest. Additional inspection of the data revealed that many children did not realize that Chester was talking during this time, or were still approaching it. Thus, we excluded this data from further analysis, and focused on phases (c-i).

We found that three normal distributions closely fit the participant distances in logarithmic scale during the time between when Chester said "How are you?" until pictures were distributed. We converted the distances in meters to log scale in order to reduce the bias of close encounters, as in [33]. We used $f(x) = log(x+1)$ to transform the data, and then followed a standard Expectation Maximization procedure to fit a mixture of Gaussian distributions (Fig. 6). The means and variances of the Gaussians in log scale were $\mu_1 = 0.48, \sigma_1 = 0.11, \mu_2 = 0.94, \sigma_2 = 0.23, \mu_3 = 1.71, \sigma_3 = 0.11$.

Table 1 shows the spatial zones obtained after converting the classification boundaries of the mixture of Gaussians back to meters. The first spatial zone, from 0.1 to 1.1 meters, encompasses Hall's intimate and personal spaces [7]. This ranges from 0.15 to 1.2 meters, in principle, though variations may typically occur due to culture and activity type. The second zone we found for Chester ranged from 1.1 to 3.3 meters, and was similar to Hall's social space (1.2 to 3.7 meters). Finally, our third zone extended beyond 3.3 meters. We believe this is similar to Hall's public space, which starts at 3.6 meters. Interestingly, the boundary between our zones 1 and 2 was close to the boundary between distance clusters for STBs that move towards children [37].

We computed the proportion of time spent in each of Chester's spatial zones, based on participant and interaction phase group. Phase group distance distributions showed similarity within logical activity sequences. Phase group P1 included "How are you?", "Remember", "Stuck" and "Bump" (before the participants were asked to move back). Phase group P2 aligned with the phases "Spin" and "Shaking", while "Opened drawers" was P3 (invited to retrieve pictures).

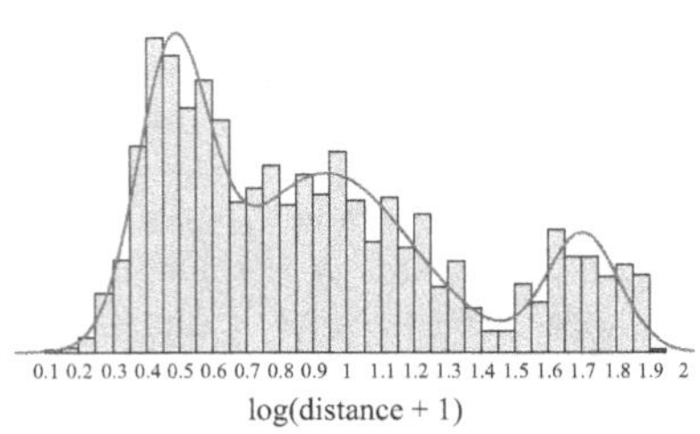

Figure 6: Histogram of the distances with respect to the robot in logarithmic scale. The red line shows the approximation found by fitting a mixture of Gaussians.

Zone	Range (m)	Hall	STB
Zone 1	0.1 - 1.1	Intimate, Personal	Cluster 1
Zone 2	1.1 - 3.3	Social	Cluster 2
Zone 3	3.3 or more	Public	Cluster 2

Table 1: Spatial zones found for Chester, similar social distances by Hall [7], and similar distance clusters found for Sociable Trash Boxes (STB) moving towards children [37].

A regression with Condition (S, C), Age Group (A1: 4-5 years old, A2: 6-8, A3: 9-10), spatial Zone (1, 2, or 3), and Phase Group (P1, P2, P3) showed significant differences for Zone on proportion of zone occupancy, $F[2, 663] = 54.71$ ($p < 0.001$). Occupancy occurred significantly more in Zone 1 ($M = 0.49$, $SE = 0.03$) than in other Zones. Occupancy was also significantly larger in Zone 2 ($M = 0.36$, $SE = 0.03$) than in Zone 3 ($M = 0.14$, $SE = 0.02$). The interaction between Zone and Age Group was significant as well, with $F[4, 661] = 12.81$, $p < 0.001$. A Tukey HSD post-hoc revealed that younger participants (A1,A2) spent significantly more time in Zone 1, while older participants (A3) spent more time in Zone 2, compared to the rest. The interaction between Phase Group and Zone was also significant, $F[4, 661] = 29.16$, $p < 0.001$. Phase Group 1 had significantly more occupancy in Zones 1 and 2, than in Zone 3. As instructed by the robot, the majority of the participants then moved to Zone 2 in Phase Group 2 (when the robot spun around and shook) and moved back to Zone 1 in Phase Group 3 (when the pictures were given). Condition was not significant, nor any interactions with Condition.

4.3 Reactive Behavior

We computed how far the participants moved away from Chester when he said "step back", right before spinning around. The average distance participants moved back per Condition was $M = 2.67$ ($SE = 0.36$) for (C), and $M = 3.41$ ($SE = 0.47$) for (S). Further inspection of the data showed that the distribution of these distances in the control condition looked unimodal and skewed towards small distances. However, the distribution in the sidekick condition looked bimodal with a gap close to 4 meters. A logistic regression on whether participants stepped back more than 4 meters with Condition and Age Group as main effects showed significant differences for Condition only, $\chi^2(1, 74) = 8.18$, $p = 0.004$. The proportion of participants that stepped back more than 4 meters was 13.5% in (C), and 38% in (S). The interaction between Condition and Age Group was not significant.

4.4 Group arrangements

We measured the spread of spatial arrangements during the interaction based on (*i*) the angle spanned by children in front of the robot, and (*ii*) the average and (*iii*) the standard deviation of the distances between participants per frame (1Hz). We grouped the data by Phase Group, once again, based on the distance distribution of the interaction phases.

A REML analysis on the above measures per frame with Condition and Phase Group as main effects, and participants' Group as Random effect, provided significant results for Phase Group, $F[2, 2667] = 406.67$ ($p < 0.001$). A post-hoc test for angle span based on Phase Group showed that the span was significantly higher when participants grabbed their pictures (P3), which is logical since they tended to group around the robot when reaching into the drawers. Average angle span was also significantly reduced when the robot spun and shook (from P1 to P2). This was expected since Chester said "step back" right before spinning.

The interaction results for Condition and Phase Group on the average and standard deviation of interpersonal distance were interesting. Both of these interactions were significant, with $F[2, 2667] = 13.18$ ($p < 0.001$) and $F[2, 2667] = 6.8$ ($p = 0.001$), respectively. However, the average interpersonal distances showed no functional differences, as they were small enough to be attributable to possible location measurement error.

A Tukey HSD post-hoc test for the standard deviation of interpersonal distances revealed that participants in (C) varied their interpersonal distances significantly more in P1 ($M = 0.39$, $SE = 0.02$) and P2 ($M = 0.38$, $SE = 0.02$), compared to P3 ($M = 0.25$, $SE = 0.01$). The latter difference was not observed for (S), with $M = 0.28$, $M = 0.27$ and $M = 0.24$ for P1, P2, P3, with standard errors below 0.01. This tells us that the spatial arrangement of participants in the Sidekick condition tended to be more uniformly spread (i.e., with similar distances between participants) compared to the Control condition. Even when participants stood apart from the robot during P2, the standard deviation of interpersonal distances did not significantly change in (S).

We found it hard to annotate F-formations [17] in our data, since participants did not seem to cooperate and maintain a space between them where all had direct and exclusive access. While we did see some evidence of F-formations, the children's position variability and impulse control made labeling difficult. Spatial arrangements seemed to be based on other factors. This is not surprising given the age range of our participants. Children frequently adopt postures and positions not used by adults and the lack of an authority figure during the experience may have increased the amount of impulsive body motions. We also investigated several methods for quantifiably classifying participants into formation types described in the F-formation literature. None of these approaches proved tractable due to challenges with edge conditions, but we feel such approaches are worth exploring further and may be easier with adult participants.

Children often exhibit hiding behavior and defensive positioning when encountering new things, so we examined how often a participant was occluded by a fellow participant for Condition and Phase Group. This was inconclusive and there were no significant differences.

4.5 Physical contact

We did not find significant differences on how much participants touched the robot between Conditions, but there were differences between Age Groups. We found the proportion of participants who grabbed pictures from Chester's drawers significantly increased with age, $\chi^2(2, 74) = 7.47$ ($p = 0.02$). In particular, 62%, 77% and 95% of A1, A2 and A3 grabbed pictures. Interestingly, very different proportions were found for touching Chester's face, above the drawers, for Age Group, $\chi^2(2, 74) = 10.50$ ($p < 0.01$). No participant in A3 touched Chester's face, while 17% and 30% of A1 and A2 did. Further inspection of when participants first touched the robot using interaction phase as ordinal data (1 to 9) showed the first touch for A3 ($M = 8.6$) happened significantly later than the first touch for A1 ($M = 7.06$) and A2 ($M = 7.08$), $\chi^2(2, 60) = 6.38$ ($p = 0.04$). Participants in A1 and A2 appeared to be more exploratory and less inhibited than their older peers (A3).

4.6 Focus of Attention

As mentioned before, we annotated when participants oriented their head away from the characters. These annotations were labeled as "Participant", "Experimenter" (the person who brought the children to the interaction area), or "Other" based on the target they focused their attention on. In general, participants did not turn their heads away for long: 11% of the turn away annotations ended in less than 1sec, 74% ended in less than 5sec, and 14% lasted for longer.

A regression on the length of the turn aways (in seconds) with distraction Target, Condition, Age Group, and interaction Phase Group provided significant differences. As expected, participants were looking away from the robot for significantly longer time during phase group P3, $F[2, 619] = 12.29$ ($p < 0.001$). The post-hoc test on the interaction between Phase Group and distraction Target showed that participants turned away their heads for a significantly longer time at some "other" target during P3, $F[4, 617] = 5.48$ ($p < 0.001$). This was not surprising since many participants were curious about others' pictures, and there were sometimes arguments about which pictures belonged to who. Moreover, the interaction between Phase Group and Age Group revealed that participants of age 6-8 (A2) turned their heads away from the robot significantly more time in P3 than in the P1 and P2, $F[4, 617] = 2.7$ ($p = 0.03$). The latter difference was not significant for participants in A1 and A3. Finally, there was an interaction between distraction Target and Condition, $F[2, 619] = 3.13$ ($p = 0.044$). A Student's t post-hoc test showed that, on average, participants in the control condition turned their heads towards the experimenter for significantly shorter periods of time ($M = 1.7$, $SE = 0.2$) than participants in the sidekick condition ($M = 3.4$, $SE = 0.8$).

4.7 Audio analyses

We used audio transcription to count participants' utterances and laughter and performed logistic regressions with Condition and Age Group as main effects on these metrics. The number of participants with at least one utterance directed to the characters was significantly different for Age Group ($\chi^2(2, 74) = 7.02$, $p = 0.03$). Only 75% of the children in the youngest age group (A1) spoke to the robot, while 97% and 85% of A2 and A3 did. The interaction between Age Group and Condition was also significant ($\chi^2(2, 74) = 7.01$, $p = 0.03$). The participants in the age group A1 made fewer utterances to the characters when the sidekick was present ($M = 0.67$ versus $M = 0.83$), while those in A3 talked more ($M = 1.0$ versus $M = 0.67$).

We also found that the number of participants that laughed at least once was significantly greater in (S) than in (C) ($\chi^2(1, 74) = 4.98$, $p = 0.03$). The average percentage of participants that laughed was 0.46 ($SE = 0.08$) and 0.22 ($SE = 0.06$), respectively.

4.8 Other Findings

About 19% of the participants sat on the ground near Chester while interacting ($N = 7$ for each condition). These children tended to stay on the ground for long periods, $M = 74.3$ seconds ($SE = 11.4$). This suggests that these participants felt comfortable in close proximity with the robot.

Additional analysis of the utterances pronounced by the participants revealed interest in the sidekick. For example, one participant said the following when Chester was about to turn: *"I feel bad for the lamp. I hope you are going to be OK"*. After the interaction, another children told Chester: *"Oh, by the way, your friend (Blink) kind of sounds like R2-D2"*. While this data is sparse, it reinforces earlier findings showing greater engagement when the sidekick was present.

5. DISCUSSION

Limitations. Our work was limited in several ways. Our robots sometimes fell short in responding adequately to children due to limited verbal abilities. The beginning and the end of the interaction were often chaotic, because the participants were not expecting Chester and frequently got distracted with the pictures. This limited our spatial analysis, and clearly reduced engagement at times. Also, results were obtained with a co-located sidekick, and further testing is needed to confirm these findings in another setting.

Sidekick effects. We found that our sidekick did not alter proximity, but increased attention to spoken elements of the interaction. This suggests that a sidekick has potential to increase engagement in human-robot interactions, though it may not alter subtle physical interactions associated with personal space and spatial arrangements.

For spoken elements, differences were found in verbal utterances, laughter, visual attention, and reactive behavior. For example, more participants moved way back in (S) than in (C) when Chester said "step back". For language metrics, Blink influenced age groups differently. Younger children spoke to the robots less while older children spoke more. Blink clearly had a positive entertainment effect, resulting in twice as many participants laughing at least once during the experiment session. The sidekick relationship in the literature and entertainment media often creates comic relief. Our evidence suggests that this effect can be translated to robots, even when the robots are co-located.

Spatial behavior. While there were no differences between conditions for physical positions, our data supported three spatial zones with respect to the front of the robot. This reinforces earlier findings with other robots [37]. We relied on radial distance measurements for this categorization since participants rarely stood on the sides or the back of Chester. However, we expect these spatial zones to change as people approach the robot from the sides or the back [11], in which case we suggest measuring distances with respect to the closest point on the casing of the robot [33].

Design implications. An early design goal was to create a robot and experience that was friendly and interesting to children. In this regard, our results show excellent engagement in general. The participants routinely entered Hall's Intimate and Personal zones [7], positioned themselves square with Chester, and spoke to and laughed at the characters. While some children maintained a healthy distance from the robots, the overall appearance and behavior of Chester and Blink were positive. These findings reinforce the STB results showing furniture to be a good robot design for children [37]. We are also able to generalize Osawa et al.'s [23] findings that the anthropomorphization of household objects can produce positive engagement effects.

6. ACKNOWLEDGMENTS

We would like to thank J. Lehman for organizing the Summer Games, as well as R. Risden, R. Martincic, C. Enrietti, J. Menge, J. A. Parker, and S. Zhao for helping with data collection. We would also like to acknowledge K. Miller's assistance with data transcription, and A. Stambler for providing the voice for Chester. Special thanks to M. Glisson for helping build the robots, as well as to J. Hodgins and M. Mahler for their feedback and design suggestions. We are thankful to Disney Research and The Walt Disney Corporation for continued support of this research effort.

References

[1] J. Aiello and T. Carlo Aiello. The development of personal space: Proxemic behavior of children 6 through 16. *Human Ecology*, 2(3):177–189, 1974.

[2] M. Alač, J. Movellan, and F. Tanaka. When a robot is social: Spatial arrangements and multimodal semiotic engagement in the practice of social robotics. *Social Studies of Science*, 41(6):893–926, 2011.

[3] K. G. Bailey, J. J. Hartnett, and H. W. Glover. Modeling and personal space behavior in children. *The Journal of Psychology*, 85(1):143–150, 1973.

[4] R. Boekhorst, M. Walters, K. Koay, K. Dautenhahn, and C. Nehaniv. A study of a single robot interacting with groups of children in a rotation game scenario. In *Proc. CIRA*, 2005.

[5] M. Cristani, G. Paggetti, A. Vinciarelli, L. Bazzani, G. Menegaz, and V. Murino. Towards computational proxemics: Inferring social relations from interpersonal distances. In *Proc. PASSAT and SocialCom*, 2011.

[6] E. H. Eberts and M. R. Lepper. Individual consistency in the proxemic behavior of preschool children. *J. Pers. Soc. Psychol.*, 32(5):841–849, Nov. 1975.

[7] E. Hall. *The hidden dimension.* Doubleday, 1966.

[8] R. Hartley and A. Zisserman. *Multiple View Geometry in Computer Vision.* Cambridge UP, 2 edition, 2004.

[9] K. Hayashi, T. Kanda, H. Ishiguro, T. Ogasawara, and N. Hagita. An experimental study of the use of multiple humanoid robots as a social communication medium. In *Proc. UAHCI. Applications and Services*, volume 6768 of *Lect. Notes Comput. Sci.*, pages 32–41. Springer Berlin Heidelberg, 2011.

[10] K. Hayashi, T. Kanda, T. Miyashita, H. Ishiguro, and N. Hagita. Robot manzai - robots' conversation as a passive social medium. In *Proc. Humanoids*, 2005.

[11] L. A. Hayduk. The shape of personal space: An experimental investigation. *Can. J. Behav. Sci.*, 13(1):87, 1981.

[12] H. Huettenrauch, K. Severinson Eklundh, A. Green, and E. Topp. Investigating spatial relationships in human-robot interaction. In *Proc. IROS*, 2006.

[13] H. Huettenrauch, K. Severinson Eklundh, A. Green, and E. Topp. Investigating spatial relationships in human-robot interaction. In *Proc. IROS*, 2006.

[14] K. Isbister. *Better Game Characters by Design: A Psychological Approach.* CRC Press, 2006.

[15] T. Kanda, T. Hirano, D. Eaton, and H. Ishiguro. Interactive robots as social partners and peer tutors for children: a field trial. *Hum.-Comput. Interact.*, 19(1):61–84, June 2004.

[16] T. Kanda, H. Ishiguro, T. Ono, M. Imai, and K. Mase. Multi-robot cooperation for human-robot communication. In *Proc. RO-MAN*, pages 271–276, 2002.

[17] A. Kendon. *Conducting Interaction: Patterns of Behavior in Focused Encounters.* Studies in Interactional Sociolinguistics. Cambridge UP, 1990.

[18] H. Kuzuoka, Y. Suzuki, J. Yamashita, and K. Yamazaki. Reconfiguring spatial formation arrangement by robot body orientation. In *Proc. HRI*, 2010.

[19] J. Lomranz, A. Shapira, N. Choresh, and Y. Gilat. Children's personal space as a function of age and sex. *Develop. Psychol.*, 11(5):541–545, Sept. 1975.

[20] D. McNeill. Gesture, gaze, and ground. In *Machine Learning for Multimodal Interaction*, volume 3869 of *Lect. Notes Comp. Sci.*, pages 1–14. Springer Berlin Heidelberg, 2006.

[21] M. Michalowski, S. Sabanovic, and R. Simmons. A spatial model of engagement for a social robot. In *Proc. IEEE Intl' Workshop on Adv. Motion Control*, pages 762–767, 2006.

[22] J. Mumm and B. Mutlu. Human-robot proxemics: Physical and psychological distancing in human-robot interaction. In *Proc. HRI*, 2011.

[23] H. Osawa, J. Orszulak, K. Godfrey, and J. Coughlin. Maintaining learning motivation of older people by combining household appliance with a communication robot. In *Proc. IROS*, 2010.

[24] C. Rich, B. Ponsler, A. Holroyd, and C. Sidner. Recognizing engagement in human-robot interaction. In *Proc. HRI*, 2010.

[25] B. Robins, K. Dautenhahn, C. Nehaniv, N. Mirza, D. Francois, and L. Olsson. Sustaining interaction dynamics and engagement in dyadic child-robot interaction kinesics: lessons learnt from an exploratory study. In *Proc. RO-MAN*, 2005.

[26] C. Shi, M. Shimada, T. Kanda, H. Ishiguro, and N. Hagita. Spatial formation model for initiating conversation. In *Proc. RSS*, 2011.

[27] M. Shiomi, T. Kanda, H. Ishiguro, and N. Hagita. Interactive humanoid robots for a science museum. *IEEE Intelligent Systems*, 22(2):25–32, 2007.

[28] H. Sloetjes and . P. Wittenburg. Annotation by category - ELAN and ISO DCR. In *Proc. LREC*, 2008.

[29] A. Steinfeld, O. Jenkins, and B. Scassellati. The Oz of Wizard: Simulating the human for interaction research. In *Proc. HRI*, 2009.

[30] M. Stepp. *Quick Guide to Writing Fiction.* Old American Publishing, 2012.

[31] L. Takayama and C. Pantofaru. Influences on proxemic behaviors in human-robot interaction. In *Proc. IROS*, 2009.

[32] F. Thomas and O. Johnston. *The illusion of life: Disney animation.* Hyperion, 1995.

[33] T. van Oosterhout and A. Visser. A visual method for robot proxemics measurements. In *Proc. Metrics for Human-Robot Interaction: A Workshop at HRI 2008*, 2008.

[34] M. Walters, K. Dautenhahn, K. Koay, C. Kaouri, R. Boekhorst, C. Nehaniv, I. Werry, and D. Lee. Close encounters: spatial distances between people and a robot of mechanistic appearance. In *Proc. Humanoids*, 2005.

[35] M. Walters, K. Dautenhahn, R. te Boekhorst, K. Koay, C. Kaouri, S. Woods, C. Nehaniv, D. Lee, and I. Werry. The influence of subjects' personality traits on personal spatial zones in a human-robot interaction experiment. In *Proc. RO-MAN*, 2005.

[36] F. N. Willis, R. Carlson, and D. Reeves. The development of personal space in primary school children. *Environtal Psychology and Nonverbal Behavior*, 3(4):195–204, 1979.

[37] Y. Yamaji, T. Miyake, Y. Yoshiike, P. Silva, and M. Okada. Stb: Child-dependent sociable trash box. *Intl' J. Soc. Robotics*, 3(4):359–370, 2011.

[38] D. A. Zimmerman. *Comic Book Character: Unleashing the Hero in Us All.* InterVarsity Press, 2004.

Telepresence Robot Helps Children in Communicating with Teachers who Speak a Different Language

Fumihide Tanaka
The University of Tokyo
7-3-1 Hongo, Bunkyo-ku
Tokyo 113-8656, Japan
fumihide.tanaka@gmail.com

Toshimitsu Takahashi
University of Tsukuba
1-1-1 Tennodai, Tsukuba-shi
Ibaraki 305-8573, Japan
10432.t@gmail.com

Shizuko Matsuzoe
University of Tsukuba
1-1-1 Tennodai, Tsukuba-shi
Ibaraki 305-8573, Japan
shi25tty@gmail.com

Nao Tazawa
University of Tsukuba
1-1-1 Tennodai, Tsukuba-shi
Ibaraki 305-8573, Japan
s1320839@u.tsukuba.ac.jp

Masahiko Morita
University of Tsukuba
1-1-1 Tennodai, Tsukuba-shi
Ibaraki 305-8573, Japan
mor@bcl.esys.tsukuba.ac.jp

ABSTRACT

This study reports the advantages of using a child-operated telepresence robot system for the purpose of remote education. Video conferencing is already common in educational settings, where a foreign language is taught by a native teacher from a remote location; however, there is a serious issue in that children tend to have difficulties or freeze when facing teachers who speak a different language over a monitor. We hypothesize that a child-operated telepresence robot that offers physical participation and operability will help to address this issue. To investigate this hypothesis, we conduct a field experiment with 52 participants (4–8 years old) in classroom environments, and the use of a telepresence robot system is compared with a baseline Skype condition. The results show the advantages of the telepresence robot system for both children and teachers.

Categories and Subject Descriptors

I.2.9 [**Artificial Intelligence**]: Robotics; H.4.3 [**Information Systems Applications**]: Communications Applications—*Computer conferencing, teleconferencing, and videoconferencing*

General Terms

Design, Human Factors, Verification

Keywords

Telepresence robot, telerobotics, distant education, remote communication, children, video conferencing, foreign language teaching, communication difficulties

HRI'14, March 3–6, 2014, Bielefeld, Germany.
Copyright 2014 ACM 978-1-4503-2658-2/14/03 ...$15.00.
http://dx.doi.org/10.1145/2559636.2559654.

1. INTRODUCTION

With the increasing popularity of video conferencing, many educational organizations have considered its use for the purpose of remote education. In addition to one-to-many lecture-style settings, it is also employed in one-to-one settings. An example of such a one-to-one setting is the teaching of foreign languages by native speakers who give lessons from distant locations. In fact, in countries such as Japan, there is a big demand for foreign language education by native speakers, and many language schools are introducing video conferencing in their lessons. However, classroom teachers often complain that video conferencing may not be ideal for teaching young children because they easily encounter difficulties and freeze when facing a teacher who speaks a different language over the monitor. As discussed in previous studies [1, 2], the use of video conferencing provides children with very limited communication options. Teachers have also reported experiencing some difficulty, which was observed from their behavior when using video conferencing to teach children [3].

The use of telepresence robots may provide a useful solution for the above-explained issue. In contrast with standard video conferencing, where remote communication involves only audio and video, telepresence robots enable operators to physically interact with remote environments that include persons. Because physical interactions, such as handing objects to each other, play an important role in classroom activities involving young children, the use of telepresence robots could enable young children to communicate with teachers who speak a different language. This study explores this hypothesis by conducting a field experiment. The study is expected to become practically important from an educational perspective while providing a useful application for telepresence robots.

In Section 2, we begin by reviewing existing studies involving the use of telepresence robots for children. In fact, there are few studies involving telepresence robots that specifically target child users. When we started our initial project in 2009, there had been no previous attempts for developing a telepresence robot system that is operable by young children. Then, we developed several prototypes of telepresence robots that were operable by young children including the one used for the experiment reported in this study (see Section 2). In Section 3, we briefly report about pilot observations we made in schools before the experiment started. In Section 4, we present the original contribution of this study, which describes

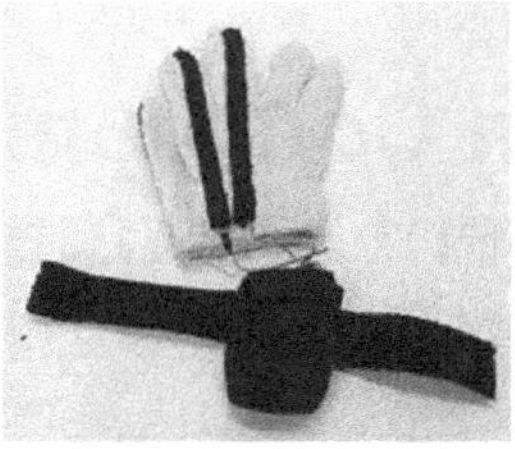

Figure 1: **Data glove equipped with bending sensors extending along the fingers and a motion sensor that was attached on the wrist together with a Bluetooth circuit.**

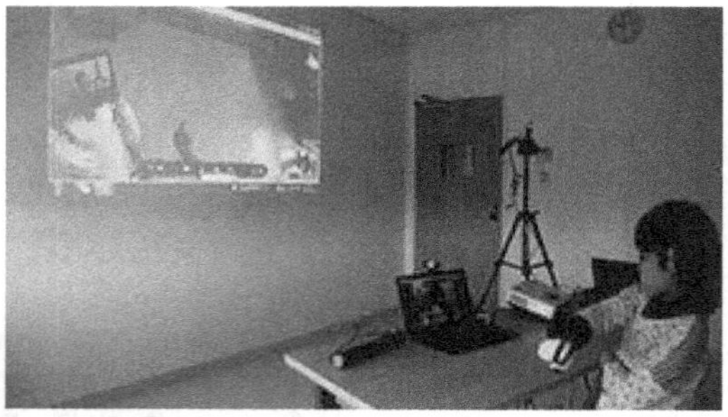

Figure 2: A child remotely controlling the telepresence robot using the data glove shown in Figure 1.

Figure 3: A teacher interacting with the telepresence robot that was remotely controlled by a child.

Figure 4: Teacher's view of the child operator on a Skype monitor mounted on the neck of the robot.

the field experiment mentioned in the previous sentence and the results obtained from the experiment. The experiment was conducted considering two conditions. In one condition, participants used only Skype monitors to join a lesson that was remotely conducted by a teacher who spoke a different language. For the other condition, participants were given both the Skype monitors and a remote-control interface for a telepresence robot that was placed in a room on the teacher's side. A total of 52 Japanese children (4–8 years old) participated in the experiment. The results (Section 4.3) show that the children's responses toward the teachers were significantly improved by the introduction of the remote-control interface. Furthermore, we found that the teachers also became more comfortable with the robot condition, and they were able to introduce a wider variety of teaching styles than with the baseline Skype condition. In Section 5, we discuss these results, and we provide a summary in Section 6.

2. TELEPRESENCE ROBOT FOR CHILDREN

Telepresence robots are gaining increased attention as new media for remote communication. Their application domain has been expanding, and companies have already commercialized telepresence robot products for use in areas such as healthcare, remote collaboration, and education [4, 5, 6, 7, 8, 9]. In academia, studies have been conducted by the human-robot interaction (HRI) community to investigate the use cases and their potential impact on human users [10, 11].

Regarding the use of telepresence robots for educational purposes, one study discussed the development of a telepresence robot, which was remotely controlled by an adult teacher who gave lessons from a remote location using the robot [12]. The goal was to compensate for the shortage of native English teachers in South Korea. The research group developed a user interface for the teacher to remotely control the robot semi-autonomously. Also, a pilot study was conducted in English classrooms, and positive feedback was received from teachers. In contrast, our previous study [3] attempted to develop a telepresence robot system that was remotely controlled by children. The main contribution of that study was the development of a tricycle-style operation interface, which enabled children as young as 3 years old to remotely control a robot placed in a remote location. Then, we also conducted an international field trial, which involved connecting two classrooms in Australia and Japan using the system [13]. As will be explained in Section 3, we observed that children enjoyed interacting with other children in foreign countries, and it appeared that the idea of using telepresence robots would work well for remote education. However, it remained unclear whether the introduction of a child-operated telepresence robot system would make a difference in remote education compared with standard video conferencing. Thus, we decided to perform additional studies in this area.

Considering the age range (4–8 years old) of participants for the experiment that will be described in Section 4, we improved the operation interface so that the operator could remotely control the movement of a telepresence robot using only one hand. Figure 1 shows the newly developed operation interface, which is a small-sized data glove equipped with a motion sensor (ZMP IMU-Z) with which the child operator can remotely control the movement of the robot base (forward, backward, left, and right) and the opening/closing of its gripper hand. Figures 2 and 3 are snapshots taken during the experiment. The telepresence robot (Figure 4) used in this experiment was based on Robovie-R3, which is commercially available from Vstone Co., Ltd. A tablet PC and a monitor camera were mounted on the neck of the robot to enable a video conferencing function. The right hand was fixed in the forward position, and its gripper was remotely controlled by the data glove mentioned above. The robot base could move in forward, backward, right, and left directions, and it was remotely controlled by detecting the gestures of the participants, as explained above. Control signals sent from the operation interface were routed through a server PC and delivered to the telepresence robot. All of these signals were encrypted using SSH tunneling.

3. PILOT OBSERVATIONS IN SCHOOLS

In 2011 and 2012, we paid regular visits to an English learning school for Japanese children and four public classrooms in an elementary school and kindergartens in Tsukuba city, Japan. From discussions with teachers at those schools, we confirmed the importance of helping children at English lessons given by video conferencing. We also tried a pilot trial in which we asked four children to each play with a foreign teacher over a Skype monitor. Then, we found that with the exception of one child who had previously experienced living abroad, most of the children got stuck early in communication with the teacher, and eventually they were unable to do anything in front of the monitor. This confirmed what we had previously heard about the use of video conferencing for teaching young children.

We were also simultaneously working on another project of connecting two classrooms in Australia and Japan using a telepresence robot system. Although the goal was to provide an opportunity for international exchange by allowing children on both sides to interact with each other, we observed that even shy children could enjoy communicating with others on the remote side when a different language was used [13]. However, the participants of this international trial were older than our target children described above. Therefore, we modified the operation interface of the telepresence robot system, as explained in Section 2. Together with the feedback and suggestions received from the school teachers, we prepared the experiment that is explained in Section 4 below.

4. EXPERIMENTS

4.1 Goal

This experiment explores the effect of introducing a telepresence robot system into a remote English conversation involving Japanese children. In particular, we investigated the effect by comparing the system with a controlled condition in which a standard video conferencing technology (Skype) was used, which is a style that is commonly embraced by many English conversation schools in Japan. It is known that children often get stuck and freeze in front of teachers who speak only English while giving video conferencing lessons. We hypothesized that by introducing the telepresence robot system, children would be better equipped to interact with their teachers, and the teachers would also find it easier to give their lessons compared with using only video conferencing. The experiment was designed to explore this hypothesis.

4.2 Method

4.2.1 Participants and Apparatus

The experiment was conducted by connecting two rooms via the Internet. One room (Figure 3) was located at the University of Tsukuba, from where teachers gave English lessons to children in remote locations. A telepresence robot (Figures 3 and 4) was placed in the room, and the children remotely controlled the robot, as explained below. The other room was located at either an elementary school (Kasuga Elementary School) or at two kindergartens (Sakura Kindergarten and Higashi Kindergarten) in Tsukuba city, Japan, from where children operators (one child at a time) remotely controlled the robot. The experimental settings of these three locations were setup such that they were as similar as possible. As seen in Figure 2, the operator was given two Skype monitors: one projected on the wall provided a bird's-eye view and the other on a laptop PC placed in front of the operator provided the view from a camera mounted on the neck of the telepresence robot. In the experimental condition in which the operator had access to remotely control the robot, the operator was given a control interface (Figure 1), which was explained in Section 2. Using the control interface, the operator could control the movement of the robot base (forward, backward, left, and right directions) and the opening/closing of the robot's right hand.

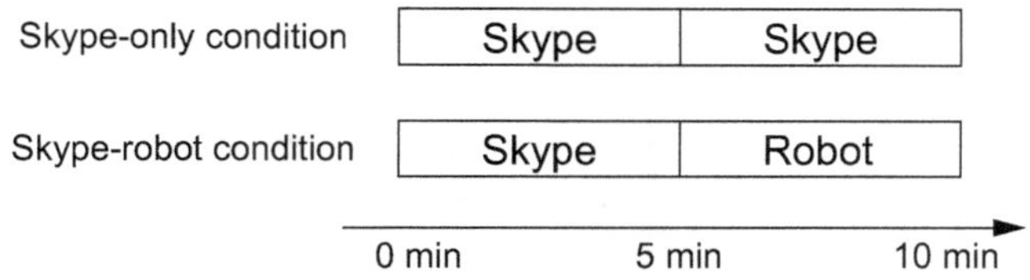

Figure 5: Between-participants design: participants were divided into either of the two condition groups.

A total of 52 Japanese children (4–8 years old, 25 males and 27 females) participated in the experiment. After we received approval for this experiment from the Ethical Committee of the University of Tsukuba, we began to recruit participants by explaining and advertising our research goals to the parents of the children. After obtaining written consent from each parent, we started the experiment. Two experimenters were involved. Experimenter #1, who was on the side of the children operators, gave an instruction to each of the children and maintained safety during the experiment. This individual also interviewed the children before and after each experimental session. Experimenter #2, who was on the teacher side, gave instructions to the teachers and monitored the time during the experiment. The teachers were six native speakers of English at the University of Tsukuba. All of them were international students, and they were paid for helping with the experiment.

4.2.2 Design

We decided to adopt an experimental scenario in which each participant was asked to participate in a story-telling game (lesson) guided by a remote teacher who spoke only English. The lesson was given by video conferencing (Skype); however, half of the participants were provided with the remote-control interface (Figure 1) in the middle of the lesson with instructions about the telepresence robot placed on the teacher's side. This is an experiment using between-participants design, in which half of the participants were allocated a Skype-only condition, and the other half were allocated a Skype-robot condition (Figure 5). In this experiment, we decided to focus on an experimental variable, namely, the presence or absence of the control interface on the operator's side. The telepresence robot was always present on the teacher's side, and it moved only during the period in which the operator had access to the control interface. All of the teachers were deployed so that they experienced both of the conditions equally.

4.2.3 Procedure

Each experimental session involved one participant. At the beginning of the session, Experimenter#1 took a short test to check the level of the participant's oral English. Experimenter #1 greeted and talked to the participant in English for several minutes and observed the participant's reaction. Most of the participants (80–90%) could not respond in English; however, there were some par-

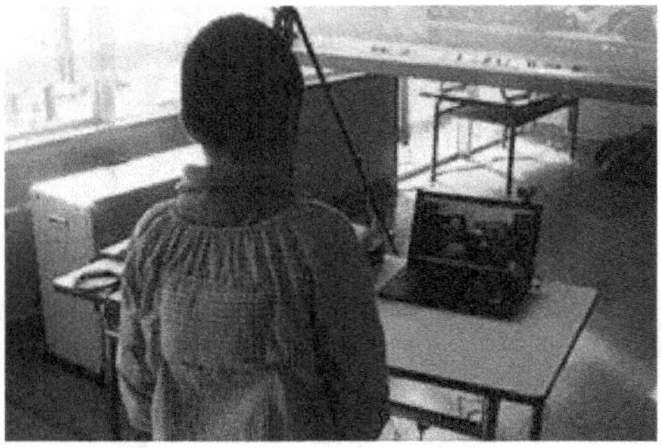

Figure 6: A participant completely stopping his movement (freezing) in front of Skype monitors: similar cases were frequently observed during the Skype period.

ticipants (10–20%) who could respond in limited English. Then, Experimenter #1 allocated the participant to either the Skype-only condition or the Skype-robot condition so that there was an almost equal distribution of participants for both conditions based on their levels of spoken English.

Each session lasted for 10 min. If the participant belonged to the Skype-only condition group, he/she was told to join a story-telling game (lesson) guided by a native English teacher in a remote location using Skype monitors for 10 min. On the other hand, if the participant belonged to the Skype-robot condition group, he/she was told to join the same lesson for 5 min using only the Skype monitors and then for another 5 min using the telepresence robot system (Figure 5). In the Skype-robot condition, Experimenter #1 gave the participant the remote-control interface (Figure 1), along with instructions regarding its use when the first 5 min half ended.

The teacher conducted a story-telling conversation lesson in English from within a room located at the University of Tsukuba (Figure 3). At the beginning of each session, Experimenter #2 gave three randomly chosen objects, e.g., stuffed animals, to the teacher. The teacher was instructed to improvise during the story-telling conversation lesson using the objects. The teacher was also instructed to use only English throughout the session, even if the participant did not understand the teacher's speech at all and got completely stuck.

Finally, at the end of the session, Experimenter #1 performed a brief interview with the participant, asking about the experience of participating in the trial. The participants of the Skype-robot condition group were also asked about the type of lesson (Skype/Robot) that he/she preferred.

4.3 Results

4.3.1 Behavioral Analyses of Children

As expected, based on feedback received from professional teachers in private and public schools, in this experiment, we also encountered many situations in which participants completely stopped their movements in front of Skype monitors despite efforts made by the teacher in remote locations to encourage them to engage in the lesson (Figure 6). We quantified those situations by analyzing videos taken during the experiment. The first analysis was about the participants' responses toward the teacher. During the lesson, the teacher talked to each of the participants in various ways, and most of those actions were selected such that there was an expectation of some type of response from the participant. Using the videos, we extracted all of those actions using 14 human coders (coding reliability measurement: $\kappa = 0.78$).

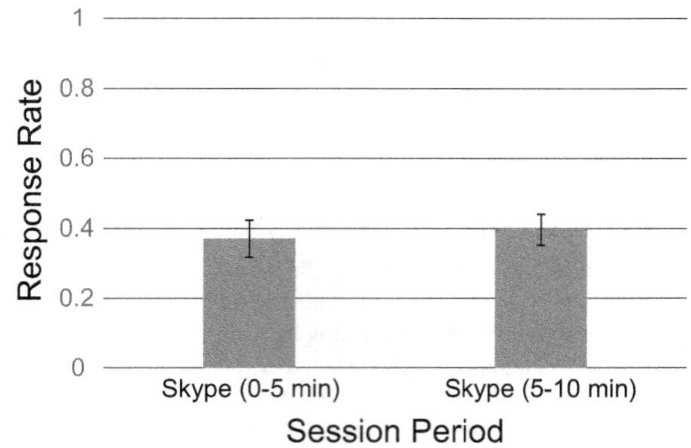

Figure 7: Average response rates of 24 participants allocated to the Skype-only condition toward the teacher's actions that were directed toward the participant. The rate did not change even if the teacher spent more time (> 5 min) focusing on teaching.

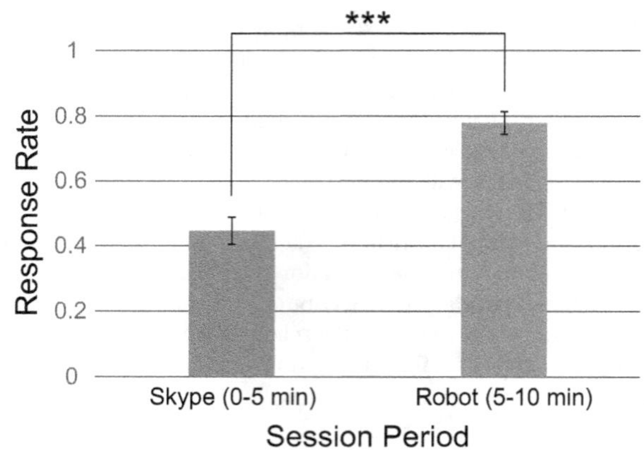

Figure 8: Average response rates of 28 participants allocated to the Skype-robot condition toward the teacher's actions that were directed toward the participant. The rate was significantly improved during the robot period (Wilcoxon signed-rank test was conducted: $Z(28) = -4.60, p < 0.001$).

As shown in Figure 7, the participants' response rates were consistently low in the Skype-only condition. Even if the teacher spent more time, which can be seen from the right bar (5–10 min), the average rate of the participants' responses did not change. In contrast, in the Skype-robot condition (Figure 8), at first, the response rate was nearly the same as that in the Skype-only condition; however, it then significantly improved for the robot period in which the participant was able to remotely control the telepresence robot.

In fact, we observed that many of the participants, even if they could not respond at all to the teacher in the Skype period, could move the robot and successfully communicate their intentions to the teacher during the robot period. Figure 9 shows an example. The participant on the left side of the pictures made almost no response toward the teacher during the first half of the session (the Skype period). However, in the latter half of the session (the robot period), the participant was able to follow each of the instructions given by the teacher (e.g., grabbing a banana and bringing it to a location), and he/she eventually spoke and learned the new word "banana." In general, a 5-min session appeared to be too short to enable all participants to reach this stage; however, for eight par-

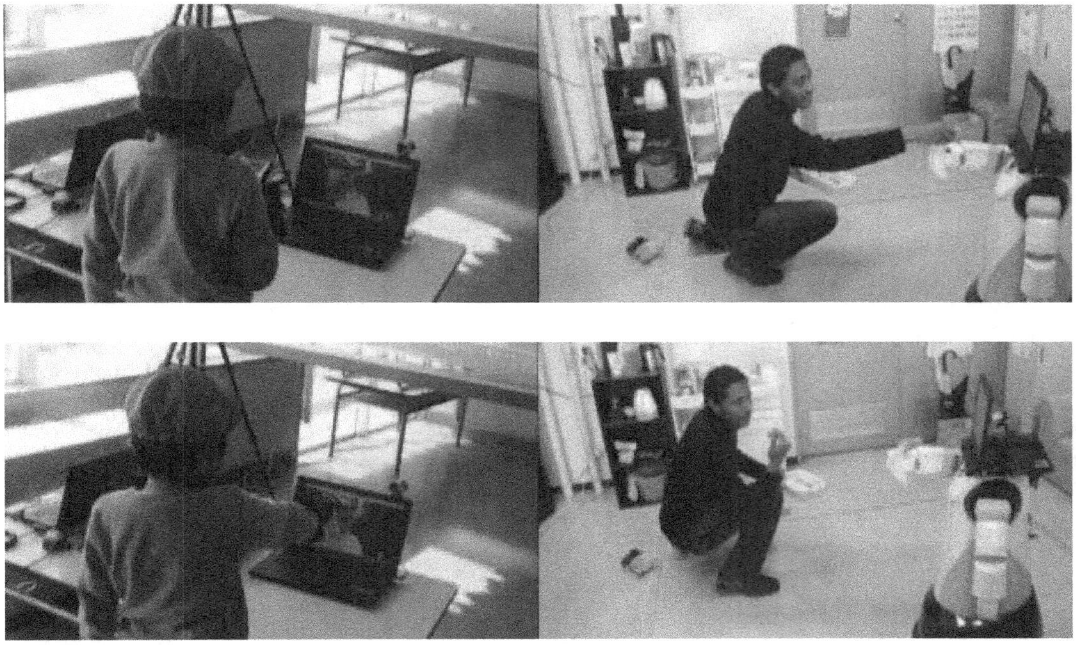

Figure 9: Example from the robot period: the participant on the left side of the images was grabbing a banana (top image) and then bringing it into a location (bottom image) while following the instructions of the teacher to the right side of the pictures. This participant made almost no response to the teacher during the Skype period. However, after interacting with the teacher by remotely controlling the robot, the participant spoke and learned words such as "banana," which was not observed during the Skype period.

ticipants, we confirmed that during the session, they were able to make clear utterances of newly learned English vocabulary. This was not observed during any of the Skype periods.

In addition to the positive changes observed in children during the robot period, teachers also became more comfortable in giving lessons in the robot period because they could better understand the intentions of the participant based on robot movement, and could thus create further teaching actions. We will discuss this point in detail in the next section.

4.3.2 Behavioral Analyses of Teachers

During the experiment, we noted that teachers also became more comfortable while giving their lessons during the robot period. One indication of this was that the teachers appeared to make positive utterances such as praising the participants many times during the robot period. To verify this, we conducted behavioral analyses on the teachers, as we did on the children, using videos taken during the experiment. Figures 10 and 11 show the results. Consistent with our initial impression, the results show a significant increase in the frequency of the teachers' positive utterances (such as praising the participant) during the robot period. It was also observed that in those situations, the participant understood the intention of the teacher and acted in a way desired by the teacher. The increase in the number of positive utterances was considered to be related to the satisfaction level of the teacher. Also, it means that the teacher was able to proceed to the next stage in the lesson, which is significantly different from the "stuck" situation that was frequently observed during the Skype period.

Next, we investigated the teaching styles of the teachers who participated in the experiment. By repeatedly observing the videos taken during the experiment, we found that the four categories listed below covered most of the teaching styles employed by the teachers:

One-way style: This was a style of teaching where the teacher talked to the participant unilaterally, i.e., continued to speak or explain something to the participant without prompting for any interaction such as asking him/her to answer questions.

Yes/No style: The teacher made an inquiry to the participant in a simple manner, asking yes or no.

5W1H style: The teacher made an inquiry to the participant in a manner using a 5W1H (when, where, who, what, why, and how) question.

Repetition style: The teacher made the participant repeat what the teacher was saying (e.g., "Say banana.")

The videos were coded by 14 human coders using these categories ($\kappa = 0.83$). Figure 12 shows the results obtained for the second Skype period (5–10 min) in the Skype-only condition. We also obtained the results from the first Skype period (0–5 min) for both the Skype-only and Skype-robot conditions, and those results were very similar to the one shown in Figure 12. As observed from the results, in the Skype period, the style that was most commonly used by teachers was the one-way style of teaching. However, after the experiment, many of the teachers told us that they had wanted to make the lessons more interactive, as opposed to mainly unilateral (one-way style), to attract the participants' interest. According to the teachers, this was not possible because of the unresponsiveness of the participants during the Skype period, and thus, the frequency with which the one-way style was used inevitably increased. In fact, some teachers had tried to use behaviors such as showing objects similarly to the way used during the robot period; however, it was not effective and then they eventually gave up (:these were considered as "Others" in Figure 12). In contrast, during the robot period, the use of the one-way style of teaching was significantly decreased (from 34% to 15%), and styles of teaching that utilized

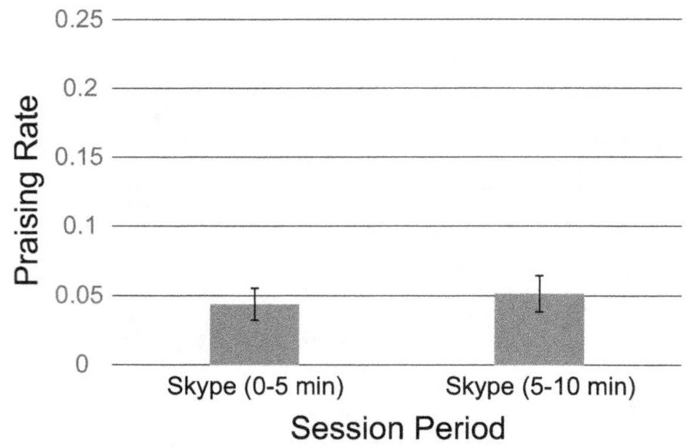

Figure 10: Average accumulated time during which teachers were making positive utterances such as praising in the Skype-only condition. A total of six teachers participated in the experiment. The results were normalized by the time length of each session.

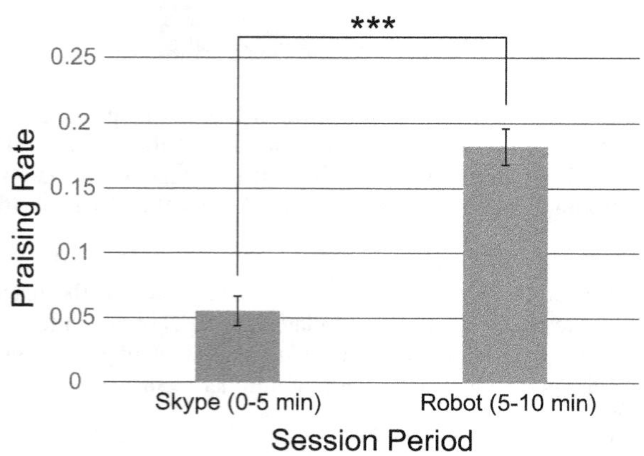

Figure 11: Average accumulated time during which teachers were making positive utterances in the Skype-robot condition. As was the case with the Skype-only condition, six teachers participated in the experiment, and the results were normalized by the time length of each session. The rate was significantly increased in the robot period (Wilcoxon signed-rank test was conducted: $Z(28) = -4.58, p < 0.001$).

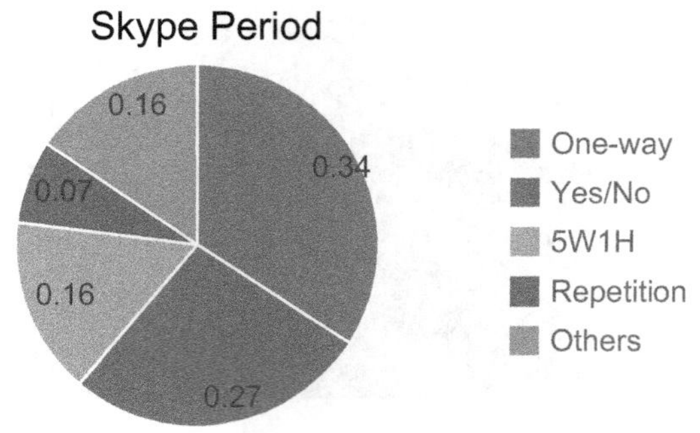

Figure 12: Teaching styles adopted by the six teachers during the Skype period. Rates were calculated on the basis of the amount of time spent utilizing each style. The one-way (unilateral) style and Yes/No style were observed to be dominant.

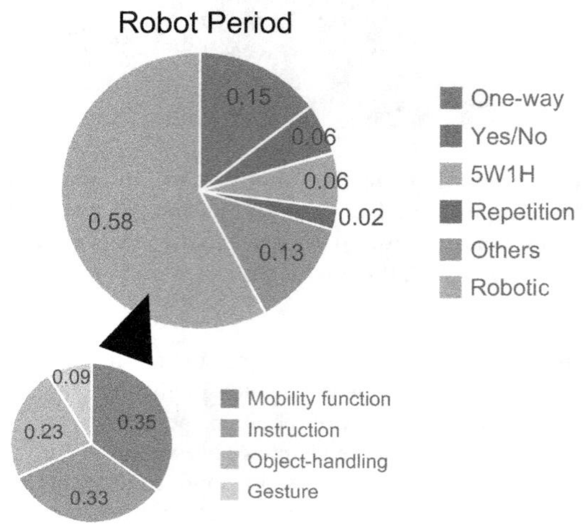

Figure 13: Teaching styles adopted by the six teachers during the robot period. The robotic style included the styles that employed the mobility function, object-handling capability, and gesturing by the robot hand. Using these functions, children were able to physically participate in some stories that were improvised by the teachers.

some functions of the telepresence robot were observed (Figure 13). They included the movement of the robot base, handling of physical objects using the gripper hand, and gesturing. There also observed another style where the teachers gave instructions about how to move the robot. As shown in Figure 9, teachers often used physical objects to let the children physically participate in some improvised stories that were presented by the teachers. This physical participation, which involved moving their bodies, appeared to have positively affected both the children and teachers.

4.3.3 *Interviewing Children and Teachers*

When each session ended, we interviewed the participant. To participants from the Skype-robot condition group, we asked which situation (Skype only or Skype with an access to the telepresence robot) he/she preferred. To all participants including the ones from the Skype-only condition, we asked if he/she enjoyed the lesson and if he/she became nervous about it. There was one participant from the Skype-robot condition whose answer was incomprehensive; thus, we excluded the data from the results. The results show that all the 27 valid participants in the Skype-robot condition preferred the use of the telepresence robot interface. All the participants enjoyed the lesson; however, 10 participants (37%) in the Skype-robot condition and 9 participants (38%) in the Skype-only condition said they became nervous during the session.

We also interviewed teachers after the experiment. It was performed by asking them to fill in a survey form, which consisted of two questions and a free description part about the experience of participating in the experiment. The two questions were as follows:

- Q1: Which condition did you feel easier to communicate with children?
- Q2: If you were a classroom teacher, which style do you think you'd like to use?

The results show that five (out of six) teachers chose the robot option for both Q1 and Q2. There was one teacher who chose the

Skype option, the reason for which was described in the free description part that is reported below (T4).

The list below has some positive comments extracted from the free description part in the survey form given to the teachers:

T1: *"Children were active during the robot condition as they felt at ease when interacting with the teacher supported by the robot. The robot condition encouraged children to follow the lesson as they felt excited when they were able to control the robot. In such a situation, the lesson was conveyed in a showcase system instead of just question and answer. Thus, it allowed the teacher to arouse children's interest by connecting the lesson with the movements of the robot. The other advantage was that the robot condition could be used among physically disabled students where the Skype-only condition might fail to do so."*

T3: *"The participants actively participated in the story-telling activity when the robot was used than when only Skype was used. I think this just confirms that despite most children not understanding English, they enjoy learning through some kind of physical participation. Furthermore, this makes them feel they are part of whatever is happening, and I believe this even helps the children to learn about different things, including a language, faster."*

T5: *"As a foreigner living in Japan, I get to see this kind of reactions very often, especially in kids, when I try to say hi, and they just freeze, not knowing how to respond, they tend to remain quiet and don't talk. This type of reaction is not only seen in little kids but I have experienced with young people and adults. Japanese people are very kind and willing to help, but when there is a barrier, like language in this case, and they are not prepared for it, they tend to freeze and wait for the situation to be solved by itself. (...) In the robot condition, the communication with the kid was also difficult, but the body language gained a new dimension as it was not just me moving, but I was able to ask the kid to perform an action by showing him, and he could respond. Like, for example, I could ask the kid to follow me to the left, then point to the left, then walk to the left, and so the kid could follow me, even if he didn't understand the word 'left,' he could follow. I felt that the fact that the kid was 'forced' to not be static, made him feel more comfortable and less stressed about the situation of not understanding me. Also, the idea of being playing with a robot controlled at distance seems very exciting for them, and I agree with them, I would also be excited."*

Next, listed in below are some negative comments that were also extracted from the survey form. Teacher T4 chose the Skype option for the questions, Q1 and Q2. Teacher T6 chose the robot option for both of the questions.

T4: *"In my opinion, the children seem to enjoy the robot condition more because the robot activity makes the process more interesting. On the other hand, as an English teacher, with the robot, it was hard to coordinate story-telling and robot movements. It was hard to make the two go in sync; therefore, I would find myself having difficulty with coming up with a story that matched the robot movement, so I ended up telling the child to close and open their hand or move forward and backward, etc."*

T6: *"Only stress (with the robot) was that when children didn't break, I didn't know how to operate to stop it. Should I use strength or can I lift it up to make it change direction? If I didn't receive assistance, probably the robot could hit something or someone. I think that the robot can have some sounds when making directions. Like, for example, a little sound (or music) when moving forward so kids can associate the movement with the glove position and learn easier."*

In fact, the warning given by teacher T6 is very important from a practical perspective. In this experiment, we dealt with such a safety concern by deploying an experimenter who was in charge of maintaining safety, but in practice, we will be required to incorporate more safety functions into the robot so that this technology is used in realistic scenarios.

5. DISCUSSIONS

From the field experiments described in this paper, we confirmed that the issue of children "freezing" did in fact exist in the context of remote communication using a different language and that the use of a telepresence robot system was effective in promoting their communication. It should be noted that both the children and teachers in the remote location had good impressions when using the system for the purpose of remote education.

We explained some results that showed clear advantages of the system such as improvements in the responses of the children. However, to confirm its actual impact on children's learning, a single 5–10 min session is insufficient. However, as discussed in Section 4.3.1, in eight of the participants, we observed that there was rapid learning even within such a short period of time. Considering the interview results, where all of the participants in the Skype-robot condition said that they enjoyed the robot (and most of them wanted to have more lessons), we are optimistic at the prospect of conducting longer or more sessions.

Overall, the experimental results appear to be as expected; however, when we started this research project in 2009, it was not a trivial issue, and many classroom teachers including persons working in professional language schools had high expectations for this project. In this sense, as a case study that was conducted in an actual school environment, the results and knowledge obtained from the experiment are significant.

In this study, we chose a standard video conferencing technology such as Skype as a baseline method and compared it with the telepresence robot system. There are more advanced video conferencing systems that have recently been developed [14, 15, 1], which offer more interaction capability (e.g., sharing a display) than the conventional video conferencing approach. Although the telepresence robot system still has an advantage because of the ability to realize physical participation in remote environments, there is a need to make further comparisons of these technologies.

It should be noted that multiple elements (factors) are required to form a telepresence robot system. In this study, we focused on only one factor, namely, the operability of the robot provided with the operator by a control interface. However, there are other factors such as the physical appearance of the robot, which was fixed to ensure consistency in our experiment. To provide a more detailed assessment of the effectiveness of a telepresence robot system for remote communication, the roles of these other factors should also be investigated.

It should be noted that the novelty effect may have affected the results that were obtained in this study. The experiment did not completely eliminate this factor, and the results should be evaluated with this limitation in mind.

Regarding the experiment design, we introduced the initial Skype period (0–5 min) in both conditions so that all participants had the same understanding about the nature of a lesson given by a teacher in a remote location. We have been studying child-robot interactions for about 10 years, and we are aware that individual differences often become an issue, particularly in experiments involving young participants. The introduction of a baseline session is a good way to remedy this issue. It was also useful to verify that the two experimental groups were unbiased.

This study is related to the field of embodied learning [16], which utilizes embodied experiences offered by HCI (human-computer interaction) technologies to achieve effective learning. The results presented in this paper (Figure 13) showed more varieties of embodied experiences during the robot period than during the Skype period, which would have resulted in the offering of more embodied learning during the robot period than during the Skype period.

6. CONCLUSIONS

This study results suggest that child-operated telepresence robots, which are new to this field, are in fact useful for the purpose of remote education such as teaching foreign languages. We showed that they have the potential to overcome issues encountered during conventional video conferencing, which include the students freezing in front of the monitor, uncertain of what their response should be.

In future, we aim to collaborate with a company that is in the business of teaching English conversation to develop actual lesson plans using the system. Also, we need to investigate the role of other factors in telepresence robots in the context of remote education.

7. ACKNOWLEDGMENTS

The authors would like to acknowledge the support provided by the JST PRESTO program and KAKENHI(24119003). We appreciate the cooperation received from the Kasuga Elementary School, Sakura Kindergarten, Higashi Kindergarten, and Ooho Kindergarten during the experiments. We also thank the participating children and their parents, as well as the students of the University of Tsukuba for their cooperation.

8. REFERENCES

[1] Svetlana Yarosh, Kori Inkpen, and A.J. Bernheim Brush. Video playdate: toward free play across distance. In *Proceedings of the 28th International Conference on Human factors in Computing Systems*, pages 1251–1260, Atlanta, USA, 2010. ACM.

[2] Sasa Junuzovic, Kori Inkpen, Tom Blank, and Anoop Gupta. Illumishare: sharing any surface. In *Proceedings of the 2012 ACM Annual Conference on Human Factors in Computing Systems*, pages 1919–1928, Austin, USA, 2012. ACM.

[3] Fumihide Tanaka, Toshimitsu Takahashi, and Masahiko Morita. Tricycle-style operation interface for children to control a telepresence robot. *Advanced Robotics*, 27(17):1375–1384, 2013.

[4] Anybots, Inc. https://www.anybots.com/

[5] InTouch Health. http://www.intouchhealth.com/

[6] VGo Communications, Inc. http://www.vgocom.com/

[7] Suitable Technologies. https://www.suitabletech.com/

[8] Double Robotics. http://www.doublerobotics.com/

[9] iRobot. http://www.irobot.com/us/

[10] Katherine M. Tsui, Munjal Desai, Holly A. Yanco, and Chris Uhlik. Exploring use cases for telepresence robots. In *Proceedings of the 6th International Conference on Human-Robot Interaction (HRI 2011)*, pages 11–18, Lausanne, Switzerland, 2011. ACM.

[11] Jenay M. Beer and Leila Takayama. Mobile remote presence systems for older adults: acceptance, benefits, and concerns. In *Proceedings of the 6th International Conference on Human-Robot Interaction (HRI 2011)*, pages 19–26, Lausanne, Switzerland, 2011. ACM.

[12] Sangseok Yun, Jongju Shin, Daijin Kim, Chang Gu Kim, Munsang Kim, and Mun-Taek Choi. Engkey: Tele-education robot. In *Proceedings of the 3rd International Conference on Social Robotics*, pages 142–152, Amsterdam, The Netherlands, 2011. Springer-Verlag.

[13] Fumihide Tanaka, Toshimitsu Takahashi, Shizuko Matsuzoe, Nao Tazawa, and Masahiko Morita. Child-operated telepresence robot: a field trial connecting classrooms between Australia and Japan. In *Proceedings of the IEEE/RSJ International Conference on Intelligent Robots and Systems (IROS 2013)*, pages 5896–5901, Tokyo, Japan, 2013. IEEE.

[14] Svetlana Yarosh, Stephen Cuzzort, Hendrik Müller, and Gregory D. Abowd. Developing a media space for remote synchronous parent-child interaction. In *Proceedings of the 8th International Conference on Interaction Design and Children*, pages 97–105, Como, Italy, 2009. ACM.

[15] Lyn Pemberton and Marcus Winter. Collaborative augmented reality in schools. In *Proceedings of the 9th International Conference on Computer Supported Collaborative Learning*, pages 109–111, Rhodes, Greece, 2009. International Society of the Learning Sciences.

[16] David Birchfield, Thomas Ciufo, and Gary Minyard. SMALLab: A mediated platform for education. In *Proceedings of the ACM SIGGRAPH 2006 Educators Program*, number 33, Boston, USA, 2006. ACM.

Adaptive Emotional Expression in Robot-Child Interaction

Myrthe Tielman
TNO / Utrecht University
m.l.tielman@gmail.com

Mark Neerincx
TNO / Delft University of Technology
mark.neerincx@tno.nl

John-Jules Meyer
Utrecht University
J.J.C.Meyer@uu.nl

Rosemarijn Looije
TNO Human Factors
rosemarijn.looije@tno.nl

ABSTRACT

Expressive behaviour is a vital aspect of human interaction. A model for adaptive emotion expression was developed for the Nao robot. The robot has an internal arousal and valence value, which are influenced by the emotional state of its interaction partner and emotional occurrences such as winning a game. It expresses these emotions through its voice, posture, whole body poses, eye colour and gestures. An experiment with 18 children (mean age 9) and two Nao robots was conducted to study the influence of adaptive emotion expression on the interaction behaviour and opinions of children. In a within-subjects design the children played a quiz with both an affective robot using the model for adaptive emotion expression and a non-affective robot without this model. The affective robot reacted to the emotions of the child using the implementation of the model, the emotions of the child were interpreted by a Wizard of Oz. The dependent variables, namely the behaviour and opinions of the children, were measured through video analysis and questionnaires. The results show that children react more expressively and more positively to a robot which adaptively expresses itself than to a robot which does not. The feedback of the children in the questionnaires further suggests that showing emotion through movement is considered a very positive trait for a robot. From their positive reactions we can conclude that children enjoy interacting with a robot which adaptively expresses itself through emotion and gesture more than with a robot which does not do this.

Categories and Subject Descriptors

H.1 [**Information Systems Models and Principles**]: User / Machine Systems

Keywords

adaptive, expressive behaviour, emotion, gesture, robot-child interaction

HRI'14, March 3–6, 2014, Bielefeld, Germany.

ACM 978-1-4503-2658-2/14/03 ...$15.00.
http://dx.doi.org/10.1145/2559636.2559663.

1. INTRODUCTION

One of the most promising fields in human-robot interaction is robot-child interaction. Children like robots, are more forgiving when robots make mistakes and are quicker to ascribe human characteristics to robots [4]. In many applications of robot-child interaction, such as a robot as teacher, this interaction will take place for a longer period of time. Research has shown that for persistent interaction between robot and child, the child has to establish a social bond with the robot [18], and that it is certainly possible for such a bond to exist [29]. Forming a social bond is a complicated process, in which several aspects play a role. One aspect is expressive behaviour, which is important in showing internal states to an interaction partner. Two concrete examples of expressive behaviour are showing emotion and gesturing. Humans show their emotions in various ways and gesture while they speak to clarify their meaning. These expressions are very important in interactions and the forming of social relationships [6, 24]. Research in robotics shows that these processes also hold for human-robot interaction. People react differently to robots depending on their expressions [14]. [22] show that empathy facilitates interaction in robot-child interaction, indicating that human-based expressions can be successfully implemented by robots.

Although much work has been done on expressive behaviour, few studies have integrated both emotional behaviour and gesturing. Moreover, research which takes into account the emotional state of the interaction partner is sparse, especially when taking into account the important role contagion plays in human interaction [23]. This paper presents a study of the role of the adaptive expression of gestures and emotion in robot-child interaction, based on the emotions of the interaction partner and relevant occurrences to the robot. In order to study this issue, the expressions first needed to be developed for the Nao robot. Based on previous research, a model of the adaptive expression of emotion and gestures for the humanoid Nao was designed and implemented. In this paper, we present the results of an experiment using a Wizard of Oz design which was done using this model, where we studied the influence of the expressions on the interaction behaviour and opinions of children.

2. MODEL

The Nao is a 57 cm tall humanoid robot, developed by Aldebaran [1]. It has 25 degrees of freedom in its body, but

[1] http://www.aldebaran-robotics.com/

does not have movable facial features. The Nao is very suitable for robot-child interaction because of its size, appearance, and because it is capable of many different bodily expressions, which also makes it a good platform for expressive behaviour.

2.1 Previous Research

In emotion research, two approaches exist. The first approach distinguishes several basic universal emotions, such as happiness and sadness [13]. The other approach considers each emotion to be a specific combination of arousal, or how exciting the emotion is, and valence, how positive the emotion is [26]. This is also the approach taken in this paper, as the combined use of arousal and valence allows us to design complex emotional states and smooth transitions between the basic emotions.

In order to design human-like expressive behaviour for a robot, it is first important to know how humans express themselves in interactions. We can distinguish three ways in which people express their emotion, namely through facial features, through body movement and through voice. As the Nao robot cannot display facial features, this was not considered. People can recognize emotions from body pose alone, especially the emotions happiness, anger and sadness [11]. These poses have also been implemented in the Nao robot, and were well recognized by both children and adults [2, 3]. When considering body movement, trunk position especially is related to the valence of the emotion felt [12], while head position has a strong influence on both perceived valence and arousal [2]. Both adults and children can also recognize emotion from vocal cues alone [20]. The fundamental frequency of voice, speech rate and speech volume of the voice all seem to be related to the arousal of the emotion felt [1].

Aside from considering how people show emotion, it is also important to look at when they show them. This is crucial as people show emotion tailored to the context and reacting to their interaction partner. They mimic the emotions of others, smile when they smile, frown when they frown [15]. People are also influenced by the emotions of others, emotions are contagious [23]. Although the exact link between mimicking and emotional contagion is not quite clear, both processes clearly exist in human interaction.

Most gestures used by people in interactions are classified as spontaneous gestures, as they are made without conscious thought. Four different types of gestures can be distinguished. Iconic gestures refer to concrete events and are closely related to the semantic content of the utterance. Metaphoric gestures are pictorial like iconic gestures, but represent abstract ideas. Beat gestures are related to the rhythm of speech and deictic gestures are pointing gestures. Not all types of gestures occur equally often, beat and iconic gestures being the most common. Which kind of gesture occurs is also related to the type of clause they occur with. Narratives are subject to sequential constraints, extranaratives are not. Iconic and deictic gestures occur most with narrative clauses, metaphoric gestures most with extranarrative clauses [24].

Gestures serve several purposes, including that they show us what the speaker finds relevant [8]. Related to this is that gestures can tell something about the speaker. In robotics, gestures also serve to make a robot more life-like, as people almost always use gestures when speaking. Most systems

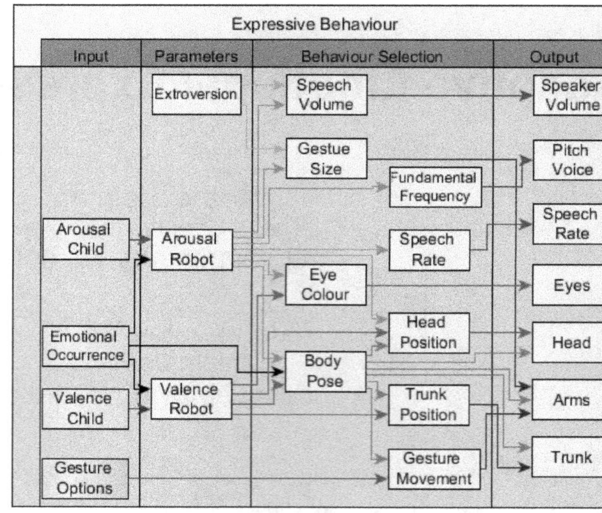

Figure 1: Model for expressive behaviour of the Nao robot

which generate gestures for robots rely on a textural analysis to generate their gestures [9]. The effects of a robot gesturing on the opinions of their human interaction partners is not quite clear. Although some studies find that gesturing is always positive, no matter if it is semantically congruent [27], other results indicate that a robot gesturing might create a cognitive overload [21].

Aside from emotions felt and text spoken, personality also influences how we express ourselves. Extroversion in particular is a trait which influences speech and movement. Extrovert people have a stronger voice, smile more, move quicker and move more than introvert people [5]. Personality is very relevant for robotics, a study using extrovert and introvert robots has shown that people tend to like robots with a personality comparable to their own [17].

There are several ways to implement emotions and gestures in a robot. The most important design choice here is to have either a functional or a biological inspired robot. If the robot reacts directly to input from the environment it is functional, if it reacts according to its internal state, which in turn is influenced by input from the environment the robot is biological inspired. Some studies use a functional approach, such as [28], who employ a state-machine. Most current systems are biologically inspired, however, as the existence of an internal state makes for a more insightful model and can help a robot with long-term interaction and decision making. [7], for instance, use a stimulation model strongly inspired by emotion theory. [16] have developed an architecture based on motives, emotional state, habits of interaction and percepts of interaction.

2.2 Adaptive Emotion Expression

Based on the knowledge from previous studies, it is possible to design a model for the adaptive expression of emotion and gestures for the Nao robot. The full model is presented in Figure 1. It consists of four phases, an input phase, adapting the internal parameters based on this input, reasoning about the correct behaviour and the output to the Nao robot. In this section, all phases will be discussed in more detail.

The model needs *input* from its environment in order to decide on the correct emotional and gesture behaviour. The first kind of input is information about emotional occurrences. The emotions of people are influenced by their environment, so the same should be the case for the robot. For this reason, it is important to know when things take place which influence the emotions. An example is the robot winning a game. The second kind of input is the emotion of the child. As seen in the previous section, people are influenced by the emotions of our interaction partners, so the robot needs to have information about the emotion of the child. The third kind of input are the possible gestures. Based on the text which the robot will speak, several possible gestures can be derived. This will happen outside of this model and is hardcoded in this study.

The model has three *internal parameters*, namely its extroversion, its arousal and its valence. Extroversion of the robot will be based on the extroversion of the child as we have evidence that people like a robot similar in personality. The arousal and valence of the robot are represented on a scale from -1 to 1 and will be influenced by both emotional occurrences and the emotions of the child. Whenever an emotional occurrence takes place, the emotions of the robot will move in the direction of the occurrence. For instance, if a happy occurrence takes place with arousal 0.8 and valence 0.9, the arousal of the robot will move halfway to 0.8 and the valence halfway to 0.9. When no such occurrence takes place, the robot is influenced by the emotions of the child. In this way emotional contagion is considered. The emotions of the child will influence the robot in the same way as emotional occurrences, with the exception of the situation where the emotion of the child becomes too extreme. Whenever the valence or arousal of the child drops too low, or the arousal rises too high, the robot will compensate. This should exclude situations such as the child being very sad and becoming even sadder because the robot is very sad.

Based on the literature, several aspects of *behaviour* have been incorporated in this model. Emotions will be shown by the robot through full body poses as developed and validated by [2, 10] and Aldebaran[2]. These poses will only be executed when emotional occurrences take place, as it is impossible for the robot to constantly use them. The happy pose, for instance, has raised arms, which would make playing a game with a child very difficult. The head position of the robot will be influenced by both arousal and valence, the higher these values the higher the head position. The trunk position will be similarly influenced, but only by valence. The robot also has the possibility of changing its eye colours. Red colours will be associated with high arousal emotions, blue colours with low arousal emotions [19]. The voice of the robot will be influenced by its arousal. The higher arousal, the louder the robot will speak, the higher pitched its voice will be and the higher the speech rate. Speech volume is also influenced by extroversion, the higher the extroversion, the louder the voice. Finally, gesture movement will be chosen based on the type of narrative the gesture relates to and the type of gesture. Knowing how often people use specific kinds of gestures, the model will choose between the options reflecting this. The size of the gesture movement will be influenced by both arousal and extroversion [32].

[2]http://www.aldebaran-robotics.com/

Finally, the model has an *output* module in which the behaviours will be translated into specific voice characteristics and joint values for the Nao robot.

2.3 Implementation

The model was implemented for the Nao robot in the Prolog-based BDI-Agent language GOAL [3]. A GOAL program consists of a knowledge base with static facts, a belief base with changeable beliefs, a goal base with changeable goals, an action base specifying the actions to the environment, a program module specifying which actions to perform and which beliefs to change in which circumstance and an event base which processes the input from the environment. In the implementation of this model, the knowledge base was used to represent the dependencies between specific behaviours and the internal parameters. These parameters, along with information about the environment, were stored in the belief base. The program module specified when to adapt behaviours. Due to technical constraints, it was not practically possible to make gesture and speech perfectly synchronized in the Nao robot. We chose to still work with these imperfect gestures, as research has revealed that incongruent gesturing might still be perceived as more positive than no gesturing at all [27].

3. EXPERIMENT

In order to test the effect of the adaptive expression of emotion and gestures in robot-child interaction, an experiment was done. In this experiment, children played a quiz with a robot that shows the model-based adaptive expressive behaviour and a robot without such a model. We wished to know what the influence of the adaptive expression of emotion and gestures was on the opinions of the children about the robot and on the expressiveness of the children.

3.1 Experimental Method

Experimental Design

We applied a within-subjects design with a two-level independent variable: the adaptive expressive behaviour of the robot. One robot displayed adaptive expressions of emotion, the other did not. Two separate robots were used. From this point, we will call these robots the *affective robot* and the *non-affective robot*. The affective robot adapted its emotions and showed these through voice, body movement, body pose and gesture. The non-affective robot only showed small randomized body movements not related to emotion, such as swaying in the hips and slightly moving the arms. The two dependent variables in this experiment are the opinions of the children and the expressive behaviour of the children when interacting with the robot. During the experiment we also looked at the interpersonal synchrony between the emotions of child and robot, but as these results were of secondary importance, we have chosen to leave them out of this paper. Full results can be found in [30].

Participants and robot settings

All participants were children from the primary school Dalton Lange Voren in Barneveld (group 5 and 6). 18 children participated, mean age was 8.89, SD 0.81. 9 boys and 9 girls participated. The mean extroversion of the children was 69, SD 10. During the interaction, the robot will adopt the ex-

[3]http://mmi.tudelft.nl/trac/goal

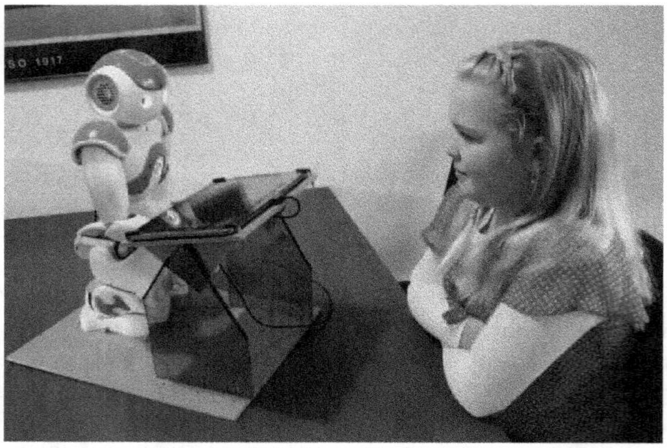

Figure 2: A child playing the quiz with the robot using the tablet and seesaw

troversion of the child as its own. In order to determine the extroversion of the child, the corresponding questions from the BFQ-C questionnaire were used. This questionnaire is validated for children [25] and will give an insight to the extroversion of the children in the form of a score between 0 and 100.

Task

In order to test the effect of the adaptive expression of emotion in robot-child interaction, the child and robot need to interact in a meaningful way. In this experiment the children were told to play a quiz with the robot. In this activity the child and robot are seated across from each other, with a tablet on a seesaw between them projecting the quiz questions as seen in Figure 2. The game starts with the robot asking the child a question and then showing the child the question. The child then has to answer the question, getting two tries. Once an answer is given the turn goes to the robot. A new question will appear on the tablet, including the possible answers, which the child reads to the robot. The robot will then try to answer the question. This procedure is repeated until the quiz stops after 12 questions, 6 posed by each player. All questions are multiple choice with four possible answers. The robot has a 75% chance of answering the question correctly. The quiz questions were either trivia or on health subjects.

Before and after playing the quiz, the robot will have a short conversation with the child. It will first introduce itself, ask the child about its interests, such as hobbies and tell something about itself. At the end of the quiz, the robot will tell the child who has won the quiz, express that it liked playing and say goodbye. The entire experiment was conducted in Dutch.

Measures

A common problem with experiments testing children's opinions on robots is a ceiling effect. Children like all robots so much that it becomes impossible to distinguish between conditions. For this reason, two kind of measures were used in this experiment, video analysis to study the expressive behaviour of the children and questionnaires to get to know their opinions. We have added the video analysis in the hope of getting a better understanding of the unconscious opinions of the children, as conveyed by their behaviour. In order to study this behaviour, all interactions were filmed and the behaviour was analysed. The videos were annotated

Table 1: Expressions and their definitions

Expression	Properties
Smiles	All instances where the mouth of the child angles upwards. As we only count instances and not duration, this was only counted when there was a change. So only when the mouth angles rose upwards.
Laughter	All cases in which the child laughed. Laughter is here classified as those smiles which are accompanied by sound or movement of the chest related to the happy feelings.
Excited bouncing	All cases in which the child either bounced up and down out of obvious excitement, or in which the child made a large excited gesture. An example of the latter is raising both arms, and other such gestures of success.
Positive vocalization	Every positive exclamation not directly related to the dialogue. Common words are *yay* or *yes*.
Frowns	All facial expressions obviously related to thinking, concentrating or misunderstanding. Also all facial expressions where the eyebrows are lowered.
Shrugging & Sighing	Raising the shoulders and dropping them again, or audibly letting out air. These two expressions are seen as signs of boredom
Startle	All signs of involuntary fright from the child, such as it being startled by sudden movement.
Negative vocalization	All negative exclamations not directly related to the dialogue, such as *nou zeg* or *jammer*.

on several specific behaviours, such as smiles and frowns. A full list of the behaviours can be found in Table 1. From these behaviours, we can calculate two measures. The first is the weighed frequency of the expressions of the children, which is calculated by taking the frequency scores of the behaviours and adding them up, counting smiles, frowns and startles once and laughter, bouncing, positive vocalization, shrugging, sighing and negative vocalization double. The second measure is the valence of the expressions, which is calculated by taking the frequency of positive expressions (counting stronger expressions twice) and subtracting the frequency of negative expressions. The corresponding formula is as follows:

Valence expressions = Smiles + 2x (Laughter + Bouncing + PosVocalization) - (Startle + NegVocalization) - 2x (Shrugging & Sighing)

Aside from the behaviour of the children, we also measured their subjective opinions through questionnaires. Although previous work has shown a ceiling effect with questionnaires, we still added them in hopes of being able to compare results between different studies. Two types of questionnaires were used, one questionnaire about an individual robot and one forced-choice questionnaire in which children had to choose between the two robots. Both questionnaires had questions on the same subjects. Table 2. shows the topics of the questions and the number of questions per questionnaire.

Table 2: Topics of questions in questionnaires

Subject	Nr. of questions individual robot	Nr. of questions forced choice
Fun	9	1
Acceptance	3	1
Empathy	3	1
Trust	3	1
Emotions	3	1
Preference	0	1

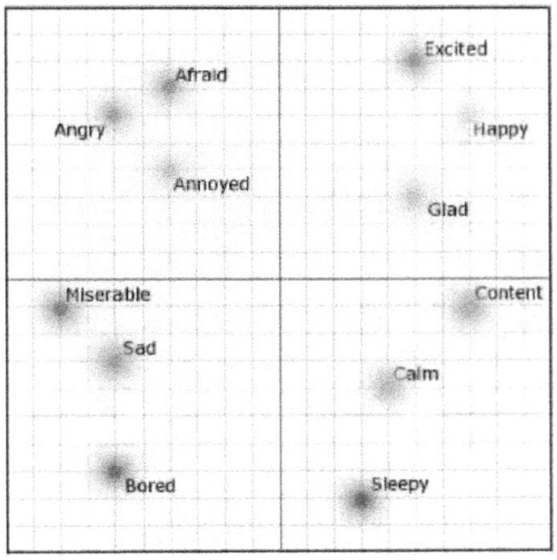

Figure 3: The interface via which the experimenter provided information about the arousal and valence of the child. The horizontal axis represents the valence of the child, the vertical axis the arousal. The coloured dots reference specific emotions as context.

Wizard of Oz

As described in the implementation section, the GOAL language was used to implement the model for the adaptive expression of emotion and gestures. For this experiment, however, a final step was necessary as the model relies on input. In the current experiment, an experimenter provided this information via a Wizard of Oz (WoOz) program. This interface allowed the experimenter to provide the valence and arousal of the child, giving guidelines in the form of specific emotions. Figure 3 shows this WoOz interface. The experimenter also performed the dialogue selection for the robot, all pieces of dialogue were scripted. The emotional occurrences were scripted into the dialogue, as the robot will always say something reacting to these occurrences. For instance, when the robot wins a game it will say *Yay! I've won!*. With selecting this dialogue, the experimenter sends the corresponding input to the model, which will automatically adapt the emotions of the robot accordingly and send a happy pose to the robot. The gesture input was scripted in a similar manner. Whenever a piece of dialogue was selected by the experimenter, the model received input on the possible gestures to display. The model automatically chooses which gesture is actually displayed. During the experiment, the experimenter operating the WoOz was sitting in the same room as the children, as it was necessary to see the child's face to interpret the emotions and the location did not allow for a video set-up.

Materials

The list of materials for this experiment can be divided into two categories, the technical devices and the computer programs. When it comes to the technical devices, two Nao robots were used, a video camera, a Dell laptop and one Samsung Galaxy tablet on a seesaw. The laptop was used by the WoOz and ran the WoOz interface program through which the dialog was managed, the quiz operated and the emotional state of the child communicated to the robot. It also ran the GOAL program which made the decisions on which behaviour to display in the way described in section 2.2. Because the two robots used are identical in appearance, both wore a different little shirt. One robot had a plain orange shirt, the other a striped white and orange shirt. These shirts were used to make sure that the children understood that there were two different robots and help them to keep the robots apart. In addition to keeping the robots apart, it was important that the children remember the names of the robots, as the questionnaires refer to them by the names *Charlie* and *Robin*.

Procedure

The experiment was conducted in two sessions, an introduction session and an experimental session. The introduction session was the same for all participants and took the form of a short classical lesson with the robots. In this lesson, one robot was introduced to the children in order to make them more familiar with robots and to hopefully lessen the ceiling effect where robots are considered so cool that there would be no discrimination between conditions. The robot used in the introduction did not wear a shirt and was given a different name than the robots used in the experimental sessions. After the introductions, all children filled in the BFQ-C questionnaire.

In the experimental session, the first robot was always named Charlie and always used the same dialogue and questions, while the second robot was always named Robin and also always used the same dialogue and questions (different from the first robot, of course). Which robot displayed the adaptive expressions of emotion and gestures was counterbalanced, half of the children played the first quiz with the affective robot, half with the non-affective robot. The children were shown into the room and the experimenter first explained the quiz. In all sessions the first robot started with introducing itself to the child. After a short conversation about their interests, the robot asked if the child still understood the quiz and explained again when necessary. Next, the child and the robot played the quiz. After 12 questions (about 10 minutes), the robot ended the quiz and the interaction. The children were then presented with the questionnaire about the first robot. The first robot was then taken away, but kept in sight, and the second robot was brought to the child. The reason both robots were kept in sight is to ensure that the child viewed the robots as two different entities. The procedure described was repeated, the second robot introduced itself and had a short conversation with the child. The quiz was played for 10 minutes after which the robot ended the interaction and the same questionnaire as before was presented. After this, one more questionnaire about the differences between the robots was presented. The session ended with the possibility for the child to take a picture with one of the robots.

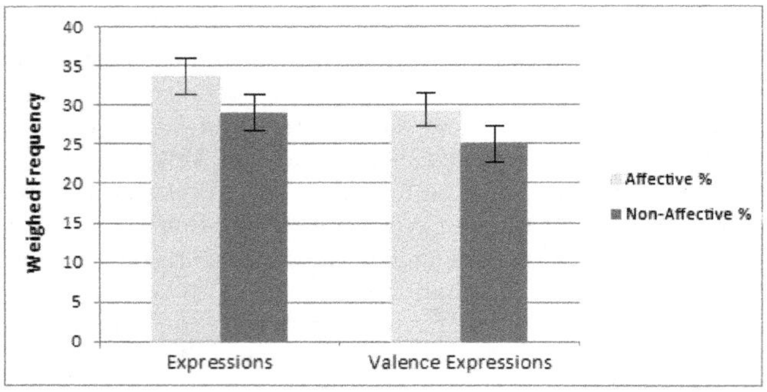

Figure 4: The weighed frequency of the expressions of the children, as well as the valence of their expressions.

3.2 Results

Expressions

The first set of results are those representing the expressions of the children during the interaction. In one session there was a technical problem with the camera, meaning that for one subject no video was available for analysis. The expressions were scored as described in the Measures section, by the experimenter. In order to ensure the objectivity of this scoring method, two children were also scored by a second experimenter. These results show that the differences between conditions are comparable. For instance, experimenter 1 counted 30 smiles with the affective and 14 with the non-affective robot, while the second experimenter counted 24 versus 11 smiles. All other expressions also showed only minor deviations or were identical. Figure 4 shows the weighed frequency scores of expressions of the children when interacting with the affective and the non-affective robot. The results for the expressions of the child for the affective robot (M=33.59, SE=17.34) are significantly higher than for the non-affective robot (M=29.06, SE=13.53), *(*t)(16)=2.156, $p<0.05$, *(*r)= 0.47 (one-tailed). Of course it is important to also consider the valence of the expressions of the children. We would like to know if children react more positively or negatively to the affective robot. These results show that the children had a significantly higher valence in their expressions with the affective robot (M=29.24, SD=16.75) than with the non-affective robot (M=24.94, SD=13.89) *(*t)(16)= 2.251, $p<0.05$, *(*r)= 0.54(one-tailed).

Questionnaires

Figure 5 shows the results from the first questionnaire, about the individual robots. The questions were asked on a scale from 1 to 5, meaning that a score of 100% corresponds to the most positive answer given to every question and a score of 0% to the most negative answer given to every question. Both robots scored very high, the difference between the affective and the non-affective robot is not significant for any of the question topics.

Figure 6 shows the results from the second questionnaire, comparing the robots. Some data were excluded from this dataset, based on the motivations of the answers given. A preference for a robot motivated clearly by reasons which can be contributed to un-planned circumstances was not taken into account. One example is a child disliking one robot because it was slow to answer questions, which was caused by a crash of the program. When considering Figure 6, note

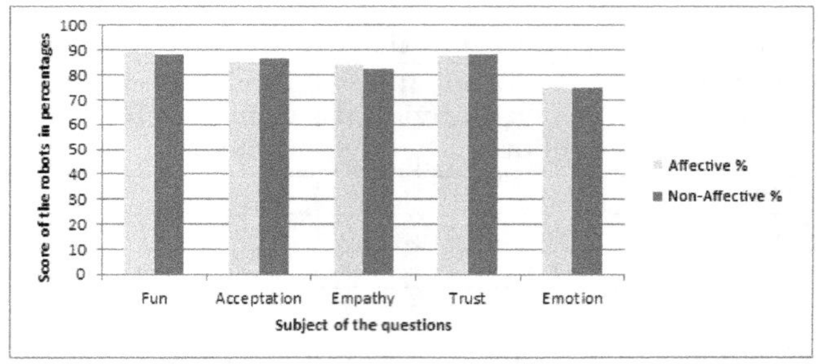

Figure 5: Opinions of the children on both the affective and the non-affective robot on several subjects.

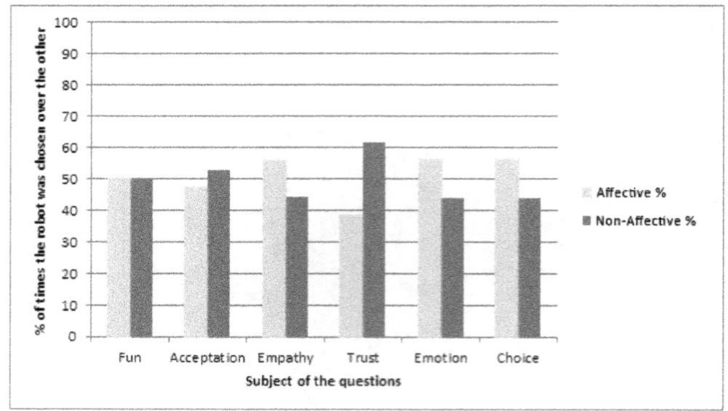

Figure 6: Forced choice between the two robots on several subjects.

that the children had to choose between the robots, meaning that the scores for any subject will add up to 100%. All these scores are based on a single question. Although some differences can be seen, none are statistically significant.

Aside from asking the children about their preference, the final questionnaire also asked for motivations. These motivations can be classified into different categories. Figure 7 shows the number of times that each kind of motivation was given for each robot. This figure also shows how often a child who gave a certain motivation eventually chose the affective robot or the non-affective robot in the final question of the forced-choice questionnaire. This question was which robot they preferred most, so the coordinate gives an indication of the influence of the motivation for the final preference. The most noticeable motivations are clearly that the non-affective robot was more understandable, while the affective robot was preferred most often because it showed emotions.

4. DISCUSSION AND CONCLUSION

Behaviour of the children

When looking at expressiveness scores for children in Figure 4 we can clearly see that children show more expressions when interacting with an affective robot than with a non-affective robot. Moreover, we also see that children behave more positively in their expressions with an affective robot than with a non-affective robot. We can therefore state that when a robot displays adaptive expressions of emotion and gesture, children will also show more, and more positive expressions. Although there are very large differences in weighed expression frequencies between children, the affective robot tends to incite more smiles, more laughs, etc. from children. We already know that expressions from one interaction partner elicit expressions from the other in

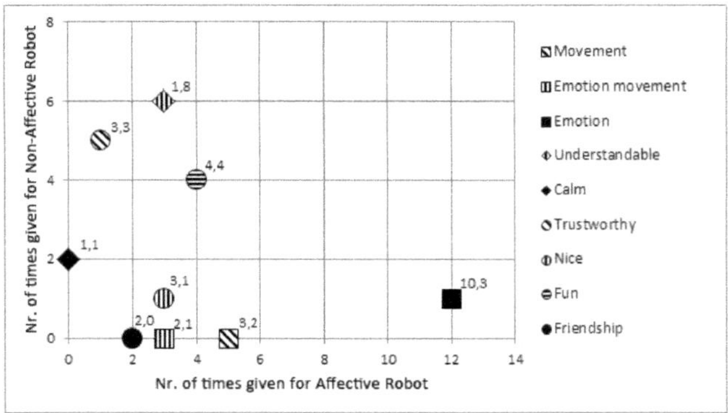

Figure 7: The number of times certain arguments were given as reason to choose one of the robots over the other. The coordinates represent the number of times an argument was given by a child who eventually chose the affective robot (X), or the non-affective robot (Y) as overall preferred.

human-human interaction [15, 23]. From the fact that children show more expressions with a robot showing adaptive emotions than with a non-affective robot, we can conclude that this is also the case in robot-child interaction. This is relevant as it suggests that children interpret robot emotion in the same way as human emotions. It also means that it is possible to influence the behaviour of children by adapting the behaviour of the robot they interact with. As children showed more positive expressions with an affective robot, we can also state that children enjoy themselves more with a robot which shows adaptive emotion expressions and gestures than with a robot which does not.

Opinions of the children

The second dependent variable tested were the subjective opinions of the children. Through questionnaires, we tested if a robot adaptively expressing emotions and gestures elicits different opinions from children than a robot which does not. Looking at the results, we first see that the children are very positive about both robots, they clearly enjoy playing with robots. When asking the children for their opinions of each robot, no significant differences can be found between the robot using the model for adaptive emotion and gesture expression and the robot which did not. One of the possible reasons for this result is that there was a ceiling effect, indicated by the high opinions the children had of both robots. It is possible to make some suggestions about preferences when combining the data from the final questionnaire with the motivations given to the answers. Interesting from Figure 6 is that although the affective robot scores higher on empathy, emotion and general preference, the non-affective scores higher in acceptation and trust. Figure 7 shows an overview of the motivations for choosing either the affective or the non-affective robot over the other, for any of the questions. Looking at these reasons, we see that children particularly like the fact that the affective robot showed its emotions and that it moved more. They also thought this robot was fun and nice and they felt friendship. These reasons are given most often for the questions about fun, empathy and emotion. For the non-affective robot, the strongest argument for choosing it was that it was easier to understand. This can be explained by the fact that this robot had not fluctuations in the pitch of its voice. The fact that this robot moved less might also have contributed, as this leads to less signals to be processed by the child. The children also noted that they found this robot more trustworthy. Additionally, they liked that it was calm, and thought it was fun. All these reasons were given most to the questions about fun, acceptation and trust. We can take these motivations as evidence that the fact that the affective robot scored higher on empathy and emotion and the non-affective robot higher on acceptance and trust is not entirely due to chance. It seems there is some reason to believe that an affective robot increases empathy, but decreases acceptance and trust. Looking at the coordinates for the motivation of emotion, we see that 10 out of 13 children who gave the emotion argument also preferred the affective robot in the end. When asked which robot they thought nicer, one girl motivated her choice for the affective robot with *She showed her feelings and because of this I felt a stronger friendship.* This motivation gives a very clear statement of the positive effect showing emotion can have on robot-child interaction. There is also a downside to the expressive behaviour, however. Especially the voice of the affective robot has proven to make the speech of the robot harder to understand. The questionnaires show that it is very important for children to have a robot which they can understand well. Considering the coordinates with the motivation of understandability, we see that 8 out of 9 children who gave *easier to understand* as reason to choose a robot preferred the non-affective robot in the end. We can conclude that intelligibility is more important to children than emotion when it comes to a robot's voice. Noticeable is that a recent study using the same voice adaptations found no effect on understandability. [31]. As the only difference with this study was that the voice of the robot was constant, we can conclude that the fluctuations in voice might be a bigger problem than that the voice was too high or fast.

Conclusion

In an experiment with children we have shown that children display more expressions when interacting with a robot which displays emotion and adapts its expressions to the child than with a robot which does not. From this, we can conclude that we can influence the expressive behaviour of children by adapting the expressive behaviour of their robotic interaction partner. Moreover, as children showed more positive expressions with an affective robot, we can also state that children enjoy themselves more with a robot which shows adaptive emotion expressions and gestures than with a robot which does not. Data also shows that children particularly like it if a robot shows emotion through movement, while showing emotion through voice has the negative effect of reducing intelligibility. One thing which will have to be explored further in the future is the exact effect of adaptability in the expression of emotion. Because this experiment compared an adaptive affective robot with a non-affective robot, we do not know what part of the results was because of adaptability, and what part because of affect. We believe, however, this work provides a first insight into the relation between adaptive emotion expression and the bond between robot and child.

5. ACKNOWLEDGMENTS

This work is funded by the European Union FP7 ALIZ-E project (grant number 248116). Furthermore the authors would like to thank the teachers and the children of 'Lange Voren' (the school) for their participation in this study.

6. REFERENCES

[1] R. Banse and K. Scherer. Acoustic profiles in vocal emotion expression. *Journal of Personality and Social Psychology*, 70(3):614–636, 1996.

[2] A. Beck, L. Canamero, and K. Bard. Towards an affect space for robots to display emotional body language. In *IEEE RoMan Conference*, 2010.

[3] A. Beck, L. Canamero, L. Damiano, G. Sommavilla, F. Tesser, and P. Cosi. Children interpretation of emotional body language displayed by a robot. In *ICSR 2011*, 2011.

[4] T. Beran, A. Ramirez-Serrano, R. Kuzyk, M. Fior, and S. Nugent. Understanding how children understand robots: Percieved animism in child-robot interaction. *International Journal of Human-Computer Studies*, 69:539–550, 2011.

[5] P. Borkenau and A. Liebler. Trait inferences: Sources of validity at zero acquaintance. *Journal of Personality and Social Psychology*, 62(4):645–657, 1992.

[6] E. Butler, B. Egloff, F. Wilhelm, N. Smith, E. Erickson, and J. Gross. The social consequences of expressive suppression. *Emotion*, 3(1):48–67, 2003.

[7] L. Canamero and J. Fredslund. I show you how I like you-can you read it in my face? *IEEE Transactions on Systems MAN and Cybernetics*, 31(5):454–459, 2001.

[8] J. Cassell. *Nudge Nudge Wink Wink: Elements of Face-to-Face Conversation for Embodied Conversational Agents*, chapter Introduction, pages 29–63. MIT Press, 2000.

[9] J. Cassell, H. H. Vilhjálmsson, and T. Bickmore. Beat: the behavior expression animation toolkit. In *SIGGRAPH 2001*, 2001.

[10] I. Cohen, R. Looije, and M. Neerincx. Child's recognition of emotions in robots' face and body. In *Proc. 6th Int. Conference on Human Robot Interaction 2011*, pages 123–124. ACM, 2011.

[11] M. Coulson. Attributing emotion to static body postures: Recognition accuracy, confusions and viewpoint dependance. *Journal of Nonverbal Behavior*, 28:117–139, 2004.

[12] M. De Meijer. The contribution of general features of body movement to the attribution of emotions. *Journal of Nonverbal Behavior*, 13:247–268, 1989.

[13] P. Ekman. Facial expressions of emotion. *American Psychologist*, 48:384–392, 1993.

[14] R. Gockley, J. Forlizzi, and R. Simmons. Interactions with a moody robot. In *Proc. Conference on Human-Robot Interaction*, 2006.

[15] U. Hess and S. Blairy. Facial mimicry and emotional contagion to dynamic emotional facial expressions and their influence on decoding accuracy. *International Journal of Psychophysiology*, 40(2):129–141, 2001.

[16] J. Hirth, N. Schmitz, and K. Berns. Towards social robots: Designing an emotion-based architecture. *International Journal of Social Robotics*, 3:273–290, 2011.

[17] S. Jung, H. taek Lim, S. Kwak, and F. Biocca. Personality and facial expressions in human-robot interaction. In *Proc. 7th ACM/IEEE Int. conference on Human-Robot Interaction*, 2012.

[18] T. Kanda, R. Sato, N. Saiwaki, and H. Ishiguro. A two-month field trial in an elementary school for long-term human-robot interaction. *IEEE Transactions on Robotics*, 23:962–971, 2007.

[19] N. Kaya and H. Epps. Relationship between color and emotion: a study of college students. *College Student Journal*, 38(3):396–405, 2004.

[20] J. Kessens, M. Neerincx, R. Looije, M. Kroes, and G. Bloothooft. Facial and vocal emotion expression of a personal computer assistant to engage, educate and motivate children. In *3rd IEEE Int. Conference on Affective Computing and Intelligent Interaction*, Amsterdam, the Netherlands, September 2009.

[21] A. Kim, H. Kum, O. Roh, S. You, and S. Lee. Robot gesture and user acceptance of information in human-robot interaction. In *Proc. 7th ACM/IEEE Int. conference on Human-Robot Interaction*, pages 279–280, New York, NY, USA, 2012. ACM.

[22] I. Leite, G. Castellano, A. Pereira, C. Martinho, and A. Paiva. Modelling empathic behaviour in a robotic game companion for children: an ethnographic study in real-world settings. In *Proceedings of the seventh annual ACM/IEEE International conference on Human-Robot Interaction*, pages 367–374, New York, NY, USA, 2012. ACM.

[23] G. McHugo, J. Lanzetta, D. Sullivan, R. Masters, and B. Englis. Emotional reactions to a political leader's expressive displays. *Journal of Personality and Social Psychology*, 49(6):1513Ű1529, 1985.

[24] D. McNeill. *Hand and Mind*. The University of Chicago Press, 1992.

[25] P. Muris, C. Meesters, and R. Diederen. Psychometric poperties of the big five questionnaire for children (bfq-c) in a dutch sample of young adolescents. *Personality and individual differences*, 38(8):1757 – 1769, 2005.

[26] J. Russell. A circumplex model of affect. *Journal of Personality & Social Psychology*, 39(6):1161–1178, 1980.

[27] M. Salem, S. Kopp, I. Wachsmuth, K. Rohlfing, and F. Joublin. Generation and evaluation of communicative robot gesture. *International Journal of Social Robotics*, 4:201–217, 2012.

[28] J. Schulte, C. Rosenberg, and S. Thrun. Spontaneious, short-term interaction with mobile robots. In *Proc. Int. Conference on Robotics and Automation*, 1999.

[29] F. Tanaka, A. Cicourel, and J. Movellan. Socialization between toddlers and robots at an early childhood education center. *Proc. of the National Academy of Sciences*, 104(46):17954–17958, 2007.

[30] M. Tielman. Expressive behaviour in robot-child interaction. Master's thesis, Utrecht University, 2013.

[31] I. Van Dam. Meet my new robot best friend: an exploration of the effects of personality traits in a robot on enhancing friendship. Master's thesis, Universiteit Utrecht, 2013.

[32] J. Xu, J. Broekens, K. Hindriks, and M. Neerincx. Mood expression through parameterized functional behavior of robots. In *22nd IEEE RO-MAN*, 2013.

Effects of Social Presence and Social Role on Help-Seeking and Learning

Iris Howley*[1,2] Takayuki Kanda*[1] Kotaro Hayashi*[1] Carolyn Rosé*[2]

*1 ATR Intelligent Robotics and Communication Laboratory
2-2-2 Hikaridai, Keihanna Science City,
Kyoto, Japan

*2 Carnegie Mellon University
5000 Forbes Avenue
Pittsburgh, PA, USA

ihowley@cs.cmu.edu, kanda@atr.jp, hayashik@atr.jp, cprose@cs.cmu.edu

ABSTRACT

The unique social presence of robots can be leveraged in learning situations to reduce student evaluation anxiety, while still providing instructional guidance. Furthermore, social role of the instructor can also impact the prevalence of evaluation apprehension. In this study, we examine how human and robot social role affects help-seeking behaviors and learning outcomes in a one-on-one tutoring setting. Our results show that help-seeking is a moderator of the relationship between condition and learning, with the "human teacher" condition resulting in significantly less learning (and marginally less help-seeking) than the "human assistant" and both robot conditions.

Categories and Subject Descriptors

H.5.2 **[Information Interfaces and Presentation]**: User Interfaces-Interaction styles. K.3.1 **[Computer Uses in Education]**: Computer-assisted Instruction.

General Terms

Experimentation, Human Factors.

Keywords

Human-robot interaction, Pedagogical agents, Help-seeking, Evaluation apprehension, Educational technology, Social role.

1. INTRODUCTION

The argument has frequently been made that one way to achieve the effectiveness of human tutoring in educational contexts at a dramatically lower cost is by using intelligent tutoring systems, embodied agents, and robots [17]. However, the impact of the technology on learning is often hindered by the negative impact of dysfunctional help-seeking behavior, including limited or non-existent help-seeking [16] possibly due to evaluation apprehension anxiety (the fear of being judged). Addressing this problem with appropriate framing of the technology within the learning setting is an oft neglected endeavor. In this paper, we take an in-depth look at the affordances of educational technology, specifically robots, to reduce this evaluation apprehension through manipulation of the technology's perceived social role and presence..

HRI'14, March 3–6, 2014, Bielefeld, Germany.

http://dx.doi.org/10.1145/2559636.2559667

Help-seeking is a valuable skill that aids students in becoming self-regulated learners. However, past research shows that many students underuse or abuse available help facilities [16]. One of the reasons students may be avoiding the help facilities offered to them is due to a heightened fear of judgment or evaluation apprehension due to the social framing of the learning setting.

Ideally, the framing of the learning situation should reduce potentially harmful effects of social presence for learners with evaluation apprehension without eliminating valuable help resources. For example, if a student is kept alone in a room rather than with others present, there is no additional social presence and no one to deliver evaluation, but then a valuable source of help is also removed. Learning materials still need to be delivered and explained. A solution might be to leverage technology for offering instruction and help while reducing the level of evaluation apprehension through a reduction in perceived social presence as compared to human instructors. Robots carry more social presence than virtual agents, but their ability to interact with the physical world increases their pedagogical potential.

The level of evaluation apprehension of both robot and human tutors alike might be further reduced through manipulations in the social role of the instructor. We often think of human teachers as the ideal instructor, but they also carry considerably more potential for evaluation apprehension. Casting the help source in the social role of a learning assistant rather than a teacher should reduce this evaluation apprehension and thus result in a change in the learner's behavior. In this paper, we investigate how human and robot social role affects help-seeking behaviors and learning outcomes in a one-on-one tutoring setting, shown in Figure 1.

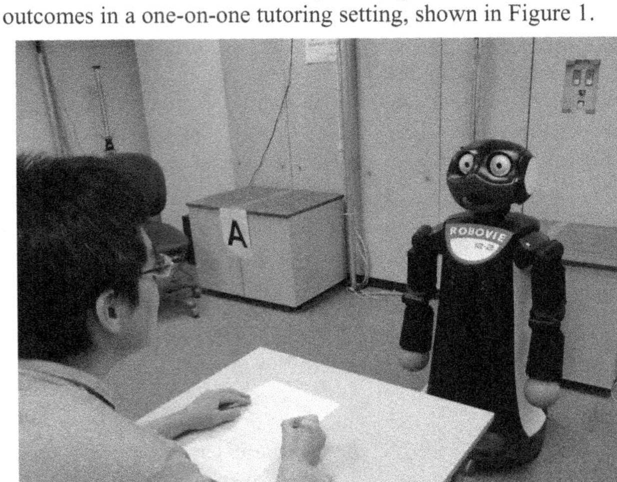

Figure 1. The laboratory setup for the robot tutor condition. The human tutor sat in a chair in the same location.

2. PRIOR WORK

The work of Taylor and Robert [35] provides a conceptual frame for our work. Ten years ago they proposed that the role of computers in education could take the form of tutor, tool, or tutee. More recently, robots have begun to take up all of these roles as well. Where there is a need for personalized, one-on-one tutors, embodied agents and robots are filling those gaps. As we see this shift occurring, it is critical to ask which role(s) should these educational robots appropriate (tutor, tool, or tutee) and how might that role taking affect student behavior and learning?

2.1 Educational Robots

There is a well-established literature on the benefits of virtual agents and intelligent tutoring systems to student learning [17]. These virtual tutors take the physical appearance of everything from text-only agents in a chat room [5]to animated and three-dimensional characters [13]. Many of the benefits of animated pedagogical agents, including increases in student engagement, motivation, and increased nonverbal communication, can be anticipated for pedagogical robots as well, perhaps even more so. However, robots, by existing in the physical world, bring a multitude of additional factors and abilities to learning activities.

One of the factors that pedagogical robots share with pedagogical computer agents is what purpose the robot serves. Robots used as educational tools are effective, such as the Lego Mindstorms robotic construction kits which are popular with the engineering education community [15]. By constructing a robot from the Lego Mindstorms kit, a student can learn programming concepts and embedded system design. Work on the robot-as-tutee also exists, although it has only just begun, with the user-centered design research of a teachable geometry robot described by [32].

Evaluation studies show that robot tutors have measurable advantages over some other approaches. For example, students working with personal robotic tutors that teach English outperform students using audio books and web-based instruction [9]. In this study, children in the robot learning group also exhibited significantly higher levels of concentration and self-reported interest than those in other conditions. Another study [14] examined the robot-tutor from a more social, peer-tutoring perspective and found that young students who interacted more with an English tutor robot during the second week of deployment achieved greater English skills. Beyond the general positive effect of interaction with social robots on learning in this study, the authors also found that having something in common with the robot helped to increase the chances of interaction. Both of these papers point to increased student engagement with the robot as the reason for the success over traditional learning methods.

While robots already exist as educational tutors, tools, and tutees, little work exists within education settings to examine how differences in these roles might affect the learning process.

2.2 Social Presence

One of the paths through which both human and robot social role might have an impact on interaction is through varying amounts of evaluation apprehension, or a person's concern about being evaluated [8]. For this study and future work, we are operationalizing social presence as the extent to which a social other is located in a room with a social being. For instance, one is less likely to be afraid of being judged by a computer agent, than a robot, than a single human, than multiple humans. Collocation and physical embodiment may be another dimension of this social presence continuum that some prior literature explores.

Powers et al [22] examined the impact of computer agents, video-projected robots, and collocated robots on perception of social presence, and how varying the perceived presence of the agent impacted users' behavior and attitudes. The authors found that participants disclosed the least information with the collocated robot, then the remote robot, and then the agent. The authors proposed that a collocated robot causes more evaluation apprehension (fear of judgment) resulting in less information being shared. If we view the collocated robot as causing the most evaluation apprehension and the software agent as causing the least, participants' disclosure behaviors fall nicely along this social presence continuum.

Powers et al.'s continuum did not include a human condition, we can hypothesize that it would occupy a more evaluation apprehension prevalent position than the collocated robot. Other studies point to the same hypothesis. For example, one study examined the extent to which adults hesitated in turning a robot off despite its pleas otherwise [2]. The results suggest that humans afford robots rights somewhere between an inanimate object and another human. So, while robots are viewed as closer to humans than a houseplant, the social presence, and therefore the level of evaluation apprehension caused by the robot, may not be as extreme as another human.

Beyond self-disclosure, Heerink et al (2009) shows that elderly users also experience more enjoyment with an agent with more social presence with preference for a robot over a virtual agent [10]. Being in the presence of social others also impacts performance of many other activities including memorization [33], and other more complex tasks such as seeking help, which is the focus of this paper. Considering some learners view a need to seek help as a sign of their own incompetence [29], it renders them vulnerable to evaluation and judgment, much like self-disclosure of sensitive topics.

In the social and organizational psychology literature, help-seeking is often described as a dilemma in which the help-seeker must weigh not only the potential benefits but also the potentially considerable costs [19]. The perception of these costs depends on an interaction between the learner's individual sensitivity to evaluation apprehension and the actual potential for negative evaluation in that context. For example, previous research shows that a participant is less likely to request assistance when the potential helper is perceived to be of higher status [27], likely due to an increased perception of potential of negative evaluation. It is plausible that a student is less concerned with evaluation from a robot than evaluation from a human, and this reduction in evaluation apprehension can have some important benefits to certain learning processes.

Torrey et al [30] explored the topic of how humans respond differently to different linguistic moves from robot and human experts in the context of baking. While imperative statements from the baking expert were perceived as equally controlling from both humans and robots, the use of discourse markers allowed robots to be viewed as significantly more considerate than humans using discourse markers. This collection of studies shows that human social response to offers of help differs depending on whether the help-giver is a human or a robot. These results, while focusing on help-giving, make it plausible to see similar differences between social responses to human and robot helpers in help-seeking situations.

2.3 Social Role

While the human-robot social presence continuum discussed above provides a foundation for our work, a different and potentially interacting factor to consider in connection with help-seeking and learning is social role. Shirouzu & Miyake [26] explore the use of robots as discussion facilitators and found that students viewed the robot as espousing different conversational roles depending on the experimental condition. In their study, the roles of "co-solver" and "knower" arose naturally as part of the group discussion process, but it is also possible to manipulate roles to better understand what might lead to increases in learning.

Furthermore, when professional service robots are presented as coworkers, human participants take more responsibility for success on a task when the robot is more machine-like, especially when the machine-like robot is presented as a subordinate [11]. This superior-peer-subordinate distinction is important for help-seeking in human-only workplaces as well. For example, Lee [18] observed that doctors and nurses were more likely to seek help from peers rather than superiors or subordinates, when adopting a new computer system within a hospital. Similar roles for a learning setting can be extrapolated from those in a work setting. A "superior" robot could be perceived as a teacher, a "coworker" as a peer, and a "subordinate" as a tool or helper. However, the social expectations and responsibilities assigned to a teacher and learning assistant are different than a workplace boss and subordinate. It is possible that since the role of a learning assistant is slightly less defined than that of a teacher, the help-seeking behaviors will reflect that.

2.4 Help-Seeking

There are additional factors that influence how and when learners seek help, both in the classroom and while using educational technologies. Nelson-Le Gall's model of help-seeking states that a student must (1) first become aware of need for help, (2) decide to seek help from an external source, (3) identify potential helpers, (4) implement strategies for engaging the helper, and (5) reflect upon the help-seeking attempt [21]. Aleven et al. adapt this model of classroom help-seeking to help-seeking within interactive learning environments with minimal adjustments but stop short of exploring help-seeking within robot-enhanced learning environments [1].

Individual differences may affect different student's learning behaviors in different situations. The second step of Nelson-Le Gall's help-seeking theory, "Decide to seek help from an external source," fails to define what processes go into making that decision. There are certainly social and self-perception concerns. Individual learners have varying perceptions of how help-seeking impacts their self-presentation. In some cases, a learner might think that help-seeking means they are incompetent [29] or that seeking help may challenge their autonomy. They may perceive that their potential helper is of too high status from which to request help [7]. Furthermore, while some students may be concerned with self-presentation issues, others may be hesitant for other reasons, or not at all.

3. STUDY DESIGN AND METHODOLOGY

While many factors increase the evaluation apprehension of a situation, we focus on social presence (human versus robot) and social role (teacher versus learning assistant). In order to examine how the social presence of robots and humans impacts help-seeking, we designed two separate conditions, one with a robot tutor and one with a human tutor. To explore the impact of social role on help-seeking, we crossed the social presence factor with two more conditions manipulating the social role by presenting the tutor as either a teacher or a learning assistant.

This 2X2 experiment allows us to better understand how social presence and role of the one-on-one tutor impact conceptual learning and help-seeking behaviors on a human circulatory learning task. From the literature, we constructed a conceptual model of factors impacting a learner's decision to seek help, as shown in Figure 2. From this, we hypothesized:

Hypothesis 1: Participants will be more likely to request help from a robot tutor than a human tutor, due to a decreased prevalence of evaluation apprehension.

Hypothesis 2: Participants will be more likely to request help from a learning assistant than a teacher due to a tutor's elevated social status.

Hypothesis 3: Participants who are extra sensitive to evaluation apprehension will be significantly more impacted by manipulations of evaluation apprehension.

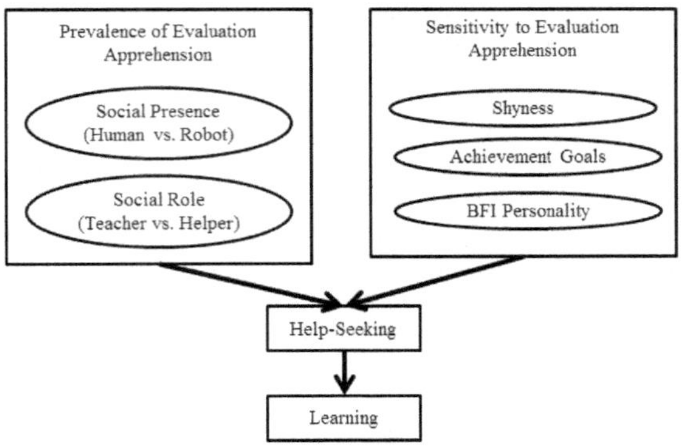

Figure 2. Our conceptual model linking evaluation apprehension to help-seeking and learning.

We recruited 59 students from a local university in Japan for the study: 39 males and 20 females (M = 22 years old, SD = 2.15). Participants were semi-randomly assigned to one of four conditions in a 2X2 factorial experiment: human or robot tutor, and helper or teacher role. In this paper we will refer to the teaching role, either "helper/assistant" or "teacher" as the tutor. 21 participants were assigned to the "robot helper" condition, 20 to the "robot teacher" condition, 9 to the "human helper", and 9 to the "human teacher" condition.

A human operator tele-operated the 110 cm tall ATR Robovie R2 robot through a Wizard-of-Oz interface who also performed the role of the human tutor. Using Wizard-of-Oz techniques ensures that the tutor's social timing and phrasing was kept as similar as possible across all conditions. The Wizard-of-Oz interface was mostly prescripted with standard statements used in helper/teacher conditions, but when a participant's statement could not be answered with the pre-written responses, a text-to-speech interface could be employed to construct a custom statement. Prescripted utterances included welcome remarks, a summary of the learning content, as well as task-related instructions and time announcements. There was also an additional set of responses to anticipated questions, tailored to the helper versus teacher conditions designed specifically for the "worksheet phase" as described in Section 3.2. A voice synthesizer generated the robot's speech.

The tutor (or his chair, for the human tutor) was positioned the same distance from the participant's desk as shown in Figure 1 and Figure 3, while the operator was located in a neighboring room. We placed a small video camera on the wall behind the tutor, and an additional microphone on the front of the participant's desk, where it could not be seen. The participant placed paper materials used during the session into a box located next to the participant's desk.

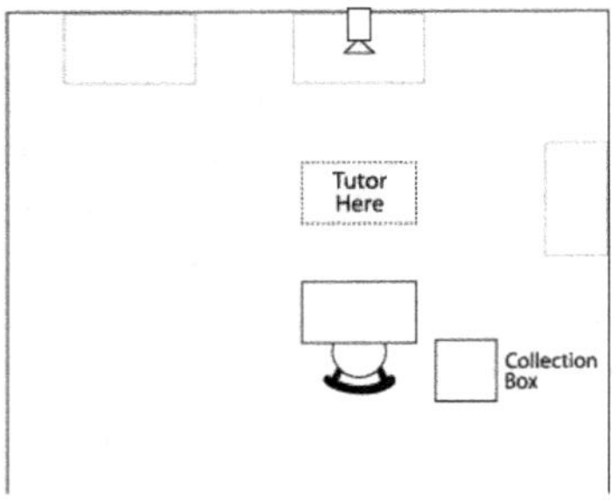

Figure 3. A diagram showing the room set-up of our one-on-one tutoring lab study. The "tutor here" box indicates where either the robot or the human's chair was placed.

The robot remained still throughout the interaction, except for head (three degrees of freedom) and arm movements (4*2 degrees of freedom). We designed the robot's gestures based upon an informal observation of one-on-one tutoring videos, with brief pilot testing to ensure believability. The robot's gaze generally focused on the participant during conversation, and as the participant completed non-interactive tasks (e.g., reading, test-taking) the robot would look away from the participant's desk, and occasionally direct its gaze back towards the participant. After extensive pilot testing and observation of the robot condition, the human tutor attempted to mimic the robot gaze and gesture via limited arm movements and a similar gaze strategy, but it is unlikely that human gesture and gaze was identical to the robot.

While it is possible to simply introduce the robot as a teacher or a helper without differences in behavior, as done in [11], in a real world setting a teacher robot would behave very differently from a helper robot. In this experiment, we expressed this "very different" behavior in the types of help the robot tutor offers. In the "helper" conditions, the tutor introduces himself as a helper for this learning task and mentioned that he preferred giving answers to questions. In the "teacher" tutoring condition, the tutor introduced himself as the teacher and that he preferred providing hints. The tutor's behavior generally followed the experimental condition preference: when participants asked the "helper" a question, they received an answer. The "teacher" answered questions with hints. For more specific questions from the participant, such as confirmation of a fact (i.e., "deoxygenated blood is handled by the right side of the heart?") the tutor would provide the correct answer.

3.1 Learning Materials

The human circulatory system is the domain of interest for this experiment as there is a considerable body of research exploring the topic for learning (see [12] and [4]) which allows us to leverage some of the existing understanding of student conceptions of the human circulatory system. Additionally, as all humans have a circulatory system, and relevant topics such as heart attacks and heart disease appear frequently in the news media [25], the topic of the human cardiovascular system may be seen to be of some intrinsic value for individuals to understand. Furthermore, the human circulatory system is a domain that one can readily learn more than rote facts, but also processes and how multiple systems interrelate, providing an approachable way to explore not just memorization of facts, but procedural knowledge as well.

In this experiment, we adapted learning materials used by Chi et al. in [4] for one-on-one human tutoring of the human circulatory system. The same reading materials from [31] were used, but with some minor adjustments; we removed in-depth explanation of diffusion, as well as references to the names of the valves in the heart, phases of the heartbeat, and subsystems of the cardiovascular system (i.e., coronary circulation, renal circulation, etc.). This simplified some of the vocabulary in the reading, as well as provided the opportunity to test the participants on knowledge they could not gain from the reading.

Potential conceptual knowledge participants had the opportunity to learn included:

- Text-Explicit knowledge: concepts and facts that were explicitly stated in the reading materials.
- Text-Implicit knowledge: concepts that could be acquired by combining multiple sentences in the reading, but were not explicitly stated therein.
- Model-Implicit knowledge: knowledge that relies on the participant having an accurate mental model of the human circulatory system.
- Help-Available knowledge: concepts that the participant cannot find in the reading, but appear on the worksheet and tests that the tutor will provide if the participant asks for help. That is, unless a participant begins the experiment already knowing this knowledge, the participant must otherwise ask her tutor in order to learn these particular concepts.

Text-Explicit, Text-Implicit, and Model-Implicit knowledge are all terms that are borrowed from and described more in depth by [4]. We designed Help-Available knowledge to ensure that even if the participant learned everything possible from the reading, that help from the tutor would still be necessary. These four types of conceptual knowledge vary greatly in difficulty and complexity.

All materials, after being finalized in English, were translated to Japanese and then proofread by another Japanese-native speaker.

3.2 Procedure

Participants first took a dispositional pre-questionnaire and then were led to the experimental lab room by an assistant where they then completed an introductory interaction with their tutor (3 minutes), a pretest (15 minutes), a reading activity (10 minutes), listened to a summary from their tutor (1 minute), and then completed a worksheet (20 minutes), and a posttest (15 minutes) before being led out of the room to complete a post-questionnaire. The *introductory interaction* expressed the tutor's social competence by conversing casually about the participant's experience with learning biology in the past. During the *reading activity*, participants read instructional materials about the circulatory from system by themselves, as discussed in the previous section. The *summary* displayed the tutor's content knowledge. It consisted of a brief summary overviewing the general concepts discussed in the reading. The *worksheet activity* followed the reading phase, and helped the students reflect on concepts they learned from the reading with additional assistant from the human or robot tutor, as needed. Questions on the worksheet were adapted from questions used by one-on-one human tutors in [4]. The worksheet questions were open-ended, and also probed for the four level of knowledge types (e.g., text explicit/implicit, model implicit, and help-available).

The *pretest* and *posttest* were identical and consisted of 23 questions, with 21 being multiple-choice. 6 of these test questions were Text-Explicit, 5 were Text-Implicit, 6 were Model-Implicit, and 4 were Help-Available. The first two questions on the tests probed the participant's mental model of the circulatory system, by having the participant draw the process and explain her drawing. The worksheet consisted of 16 open-ended questions, 4 were Text-Explicit, 2 were Text-Implicit, 7 were Model-Implicit, and 3 were Help-Available.

If participants completed a phase of the experiment early, the tutor encouraged them to check their answers before moving on to the next phase. While this is not strict control of time-on-task, it is a more realistic procedure for one-on-one tutoring interactions.

Participants were informed before the reading and worksheet phase that they could ask their tutor for help.

3.3 Additional Measures

Evaluation apprehension is discussed as an environmental variable to be manipulated, whereas there is no formal measure of one's sensitivity to evaluation apprehension. As proxies for sensitivity to evaluation apprehension, we used scales for Shyness [3], the short Big Five Index [23] personality and Achievement Goal Orientation [6].

The Big Five personality traits consist of: openness to experience, conscientiousness, extraversion, agreeableness, and neuroticism. Of these, extraversion and neuroticism may be the personality traits most relevant to a sensitivity of evaluation apprehension.

Achievement goal orientation consists of three main dispositions: learning orientation (one does an activity for the joy of increasing knowledge), performance-approach orientation (one does an activity to show others how competent they are), and performance-avoidance orientation (one avoids activities to prevent displays of low competence) [6]. So, a person who views help-seeking as a display of incompetence might avoid asking questions, if they are performance-avoidant. In this way, performance-avoidance orientation might be interpreted as highly evaluation apprehensive. Likewise, shyness may be related to evaluation apprehensiveness as well.

Much like the other materials used in this study, questionnaire materials were first formed in English, translated to Japanese, and checked by a second native Japanese speaker for correctness. Since these questionnaire items were not norm-validated for a Japanese sample, this may introduce some issues, although it may allow for better comparison with samples from other locations.

4. RESULTS

Our results suggest partial support for our hypotheses: participants sought marginally less help from human-teachers, with the three remaining conditions statistically indistinguishable. Help-Available question-asking was a marginal moderator on the relationship between condition and Help-Available learning. So while condition only had a marginal effect on the number of questions asked, it was a significant factor, along with help-seeking, in determining student learning.

4.1 Learning

We designed our learning materials to assess learning at several complexity levels including: Text-Explicit, Text-Implicit, Model-Implicit, and Help-Available. As these different conceptual levels vary greatly in difficulty and learning process, we anticipated differences in learning outcomes as well. We measure learning by controlling for pretest scores when predicting posttest scores. An analysis of covariance (ANCOVA) controlling for pretest supports this hypothesis that conceptual type has a significant effect on learning, $F(3, 231) = 5.62$, $p = .001$. Figure 4 shows the differences in percentage improvement from pre- to posttest by conceptual levels, and a post-hoc Student's t-test reveals that participants improved significantly more on Help-Available and Text Explicit, than Text Implicit and Model Implicit. As Text Explicit knowledge requires less cognitive processing than Text Implicit and Model Implicit, these results seem appropriate.

We focus the rest of our analysis on Help-Available knowledge, as this type of knowledge required participants to ask for help to improve. In this way, we can examine how help-seeking and condition interact with learning.

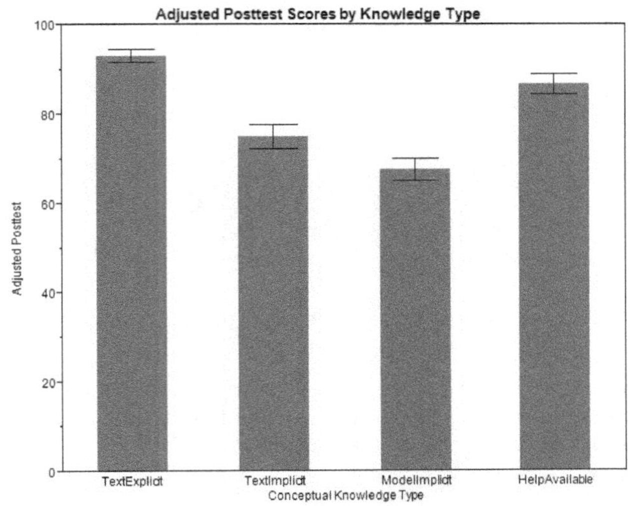

Figure 4. Adjusted posttest scores by conceptual level, with standard error bars.

4.2 Help-Available Knowledge

First, we tested whether tutor condition affected learning of Help-Available knowledge. We performed a nested analysis of covariance (ANCOVA) with condition as the independent variable and Help-Available pretest score and number of Help-Available questions nested within Condition as covariates. Our analysis shows Condition as a significant predictor of learning, $F(3, 50) = 6.74$, $p = .0007$ ($R^2 = 0.17$). Post-hoc comparisons using the Student's t-test reveal that participants in the "human teacher" condition learned statistically significantly less than the other three conditions. Figure 5 shows how adjusted posttest scores differed between the conditions.

4.3 Help-Seeking

In the second step of our nested ANCOVA analysis, we examined the relationship that Help-Available question-asking had on learning, by condition. Help-Available question-asking was a marginal moderator of the relationship between condition and learning, $F(4, 50) = 2.35$, $p = 0.07$, R^2 of 0.30 ($\Delta R^2 = .13$). Looking closer at the relationship between Help-Available question-asking and condition, an ANOVA analysis revealed a marginal effect of condition on Help-Available question-asking, F(3, 55) = 2.45, p = 0.07, as shown in Figure 6. Although a post-hoc Student's t-test reveals that participants in the human teacher condition asked significantly fewer questions about the Help-Available knowledge concepts than the other conditions with the "human helper" condition being not statistically distinguishable from the other conditions. So, being in the Human Teacher condition reduced the number of questions a student asked about Help-Available knowledge (more so than other conditions), which in turn resulted in those participants learning significantly less than the participants in other conditions.

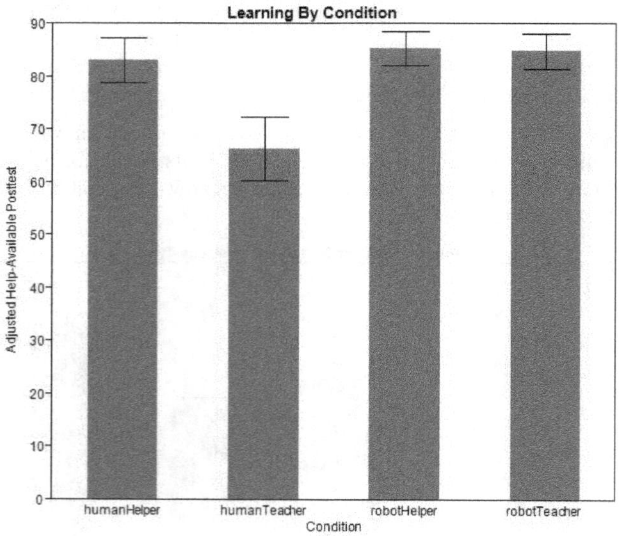

Figure 5. The differences in the learning on Help-Available knowledge items by Condition, with standard error bars.

While the difference in Help-Available questions asked by condition was only marginally statistically different, the overall counts of these questions asked during the 20 minute time period were rather similar: students in the Human Teacher condition asked a median of 0 questions (M = 0.56), students in the Human Helper condition asked a median of 2 questions (M = 1.56), the Robot Helper condition had a median of 2 questions (M = 1.67), and the robot teacher condition also had a median of 2 questions (M = 1.65).

Looking at the quantity of questions that could only be asked during the 20 minute worksheet phase, for each level of conceptual knowledge, there was not a significant difference between conditions. The median number of Text-Explicit questions asked across all conditions was 0 (M = 0.59), Text-Implicit questions had a median of 0 (M = 0.70), Model-Implicit was 2 (M = 2.18), and Help-Available knowledge had a median of 1 (M = 1.48). While it appears that there is an increasing number of questions for increasing difficulty of knowledge, Help-Available knowledge questions does not appear to follow this general pattern.

4.4 Evaluation Apprehension

Examining evaluation apprehension as a situational factor in our study was done through manipulating the social presence and social role of the tutors, however, participants with varying individual factors might be impacted differently by these situational factors. We measured achievement goal orientation, shyness, and the big five index personality scales as proxies for individual sensitivity to evaluation apprehension.

We did not find any relationship between achievement goals and help-seeking. This suggests that perhaps achievement goals are not appropriate proxies for "sensitivity to evaluation apprehension." However, there was a significant negative effect of shyness on number of questions asked when performing a linear regression, F(1, 57) = 19.87, p < .0001 (R^2 = 0.26), although this effect was only marginal when looking specifically at Help-Available knowledge questions, F(1, 57) = 2.86, p = .096. So, while shyness might affect one's overall likelihood to ask questions in this setting, it is only a marginal trend when it comes to Help-Available Questions. This suggests that shyness may have a greater effect on topics where students had exposure to material, and a lesser effect on help-seeking on topics to which they were not previously exposed. Our hypotheses predicted enhancing interactions between Shyness and Condition on Help-Available help-seeking, but there was not a significant relationship.

Supporting our shyness related results, an ANOVA analysis shows that BFI-Extravert was significantly positively related to the number of Help-Available Questions, F(1, 57) = 8.2, p < .006 (R^2= 0.13) and BFI-Neuroticism was significantly negatively related to Help-Available Questions, F(1,57) = 16.24, p < .001 (R^2 = 0.22).

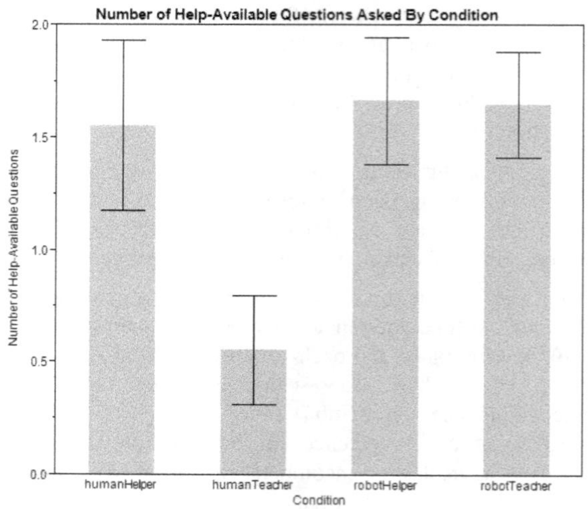

Figure 6. Marginally significant differences in the mean number of Help-Available questions asked by condition.

5. Discussion

Our results show that students learned significantly less from the human teacher, partially due to the fact that they asked the human teacher marginally fewer questions. While students asked marginally fewer Help-Available questions from human teachers than the human helper, we did not see the same distinction made for robot teachers and helpers. So, our Hypothesis 1 (participants will seek more help from robots) appears to only have support when considering human teachers in contrast to robots, and Hypothesis 2 (participants will seek more help from a learning assistant) is only supported if we consider the human teacher separately from the robot teacher condition.

There are a few possible explanations for this, the first being that the robot's perceived social status is so low that the robot teacher did not cause enough evaluation apprehension to affect question asking and learning. Or perhaps perceived social status of robots is still such a novel concept that participants cannot consistently place the robot on the social presence continuum.

Help-seeking was an informative factor as a moderator, but our hypotheses lead us to predict the conditions to result in a stronger effect on help-seeking behavior. One explanation is that social role and presence impacted the kinds of questions asked, rather than the quantity of questions asked, and viewing the questions as an overall sum is obfuscating the more subtle effects these conditions have on help-seeking.

Our learning and help-seeking results are seen only on Help-Available knowledge which could only be learned from asking questions and not from the reading or other materials. That is, we explicitly designed Help-Available content so that in order to see learning gains on those concepts, participants had to ask the tutor questions. This explains why increases in help-seeking result in increases in learning on Help-Available concepts.

Furthermore, while our results touch on proxies for measuring evaluation apprehension, it is clear that a formal measure of "evaluation apprehension anxiety" is important to our hypotheses (Hypothesis 3, sensitive participants will react more strongly to manipulations of evaluation apprehension), but since evaluation apprehension is largely seated in the organizational psychology literature, it is often treated as an environmental factor, and not an individual factor. That is, one can increase (or decrease) the evaluation apprehension prevalence of a situation perhaps by hiring a human tutor instead of a robot tutor, but formal questionnaire measures to directly measure sensitivity to that prevalence do not appear to exist. Instead, we included achievement goal orientation, shyness, and personality scales as potential proxies for evaluation apprehension anxiety. However, these factors did not interact with condition to impact help-seeking. It is possible that people who are shy about asking questions from humans may also be shy about asking questions from robots. More research needs to be done to determine how to best measure sensitivity to evaluation apprehension, and how it might impact help-seeking.

5.1 Limitations

Several factors likely heavily influenced our manipulation of human versus robot including the appearance of both the robot and the human. Since the human tutor operated the robot as well, the personality and gender of the human may also impact this work and different results might possibly occur if a different human operator and tutor are used. Introducing the teacher and helper with two different titles while also giving two different kinds of help, may also affect participant behavior in a way that makes it difficult to distinguish the tutor's introductory role from its behavior. Due to time constraints, the number of participants in the human conditions is not evenly balanced with the robot conditions. Ideally, these conditions would all be equal, and much larger. Furthermore, only using one human or one robot somewhat limits the generalizability of these results to only similar robots and humans.

Also, as this study took place in a suburban area of Japan, results may be limited to similar demographics considering the tremendous impact culture may have on perceived social role. The strong response to only the human teacher condition may not appear the same if this study is redone in other countries.

5.2 Future Work

Future work involves analyzing the types of questions participants asked during the 20 minute worksheet reflection phase. It is possible that the social role and presence of our pedagogical agents impacted whether participants asked simple clarification questions, or more complex questions combining several knowledge components. The types of questions asked may affect learning as well. Only after analyzing participant help-seeking deeper can we determine whether social presence and role had an impact on beneficial help-seeking.

Furthermore, there are many other factors that impact people's decision to seek help, and analyzing a larger, more inclusive model may reveal a more complex and complete story about how using a robot changes participant learning behavior.

The Robovie R2 used in this study was Wizard-of-Ozed, and there are many steps necessary to accomplish before our robot tutor might be autonomous. Advances in language recognition must improve to allow Robovie to parse student questions. Once learner statements can be properly parsed, the robot still needs to be able to answer those questions. For anticipated questions this may not be so difficult, as in this study we most often used pre-written responses for both the human and the robot tutors. However, this can be more complicated for novel questions from learners. Significant training on the participant questions and biology content could help improve the coverage of pre-written questions. Furthermore, once a fully autonomous pedagogical robot exists, it may be difficult to do direct comparisons between this autonomous robot and a human tutor as the social timing may not be the same. Such a study should include a human tutor, a human-controlled robot tutor, and an autonomous robot to properly examine the differences in both embodiment and social cue dimensions. It is possible that less ideal social responses may result in interpreting the robot as less likely to be judgmental, thereby resulting in reduced evaluation apprehension and more question-asking.

6. CONCLUSION

In some learning situations, the use of robot pedagogical agents may be more beneficial to learning than with human pedagogical agents. Our work shows that while learners may not view distinctions in robot social role the same way they view distinctions in human social role, robotic tutors can perform at the same level as our human learning assistants.

While a one-on-one robot or human tutor is not always practical, these same issues with help-seeking, evaluation apprehension, social role, and social presence may all impact the effectiveness of a tutor supervising an entire classroom of students. That is, some of the same concerns we identified in our one-on-one tutoring situation may be applicable to learning situations with larger groups of students.

Even beyond groups of students, help-seeking and learning occur outside of the classroom as well, and dedicated thought should be invested into how social roles are constructed in our workplaces and public spaces so that people may seek help and acquire new knowledge in the best way possible.

7. ACKNOWLEDGEMENTS

This work was supported in part by Graduate Training Grant awarded to Carnegie Mellon University by the Department of Education (# R305B090023) and also by the JSPS Grants-in-Aid for Scientific Research No. 21110008 and 25240042.

8. REFERENCES

[1] Aleven, V., Stahl, E., Schworm, S., Fischer, F., and Wallace, R. 2003. Help seeking and help design in interactive learning environments. *Review of Educational Research 73, 3* (2003), 277-320.

[2] Bartneck, C., Van Der Hoek, M., Mubin, O., and Al Mahmud, A. 2007. "Daisy, daisy, give me your answer do!" switching off a robot. *Proc. Human-Robot Interaction 2007,* IEEE, 217-222.

[3] Cheek, J.M. 1983. *The Revised Cheek and Buss Shyness Scale (RCBS)*, Wellesley College, Wellesley MA, Unpublished.

[4] Chi, M.T.H., Siler, S.A., Jeong, H., Yamauchi, T., and Hausmann, R.G. 2001. Learning from human tutoring. *Cognitive Science 25, 4* (2001), 471-533.

[5] Dyke, G., Howley, I., Adamson, D., Rosé, C.P. 2011. Towards academically productive talk supported by conversational agents. *Proceedings of the 11th International Conference on Intelligent Tutoring Systems*, 531-540

[6] Elliot, A.J., and McGregor, H.A. 2001. A 2 x 2 achievement goal framework. *Journal of Personality and Social Psychology 80, 3* (2001), 501-519.

[7] Fisher, J.D., Nadler, A., and Whitcher-Alagna, S. 1982. Recipient reactions to aid. *Psychological Bulletin 91, 1* (1982), 27-54.

[8] Guerin, B. 1986. Mere presence effects in humans. *Journal of Experimental Social Psychology*, 22, 38-77.

[9] Han, J., Miheon, J., Park, S., & Kim, S. 2008. Comparative study on the educational use of home robots for children. *Journal of Information Processing Systems 4, 4* (2008), 159-168.

[10] Heerink, M., Kröse, B., Evers, V., & Wielinga, B. (2009). Influence of social presence on acceptance of an assistive social robot and screen agent by elderly users. *Advanced Robotics*, *23*(14), 1909-1923.

[11] Hinds, P.J., Roberts, T.L., and Jones, H. 2004. Whose job is it anyway? A study of human-robot interaction in a collaborative task. *Human-Computer Interaction 19, 1* (2004), 151-181.

[12] Jeong, H., and Chi, M.T.H. 1997. Construction of shared knowledge during collaborative learning. *Proc. Computer-Supported Collaborative Learning 1997*, International Society of the Learning Sciences (1997).

[13] Johnson, W. L., Rickel, J. W., & Lester, J. C. 2000. Animated pedagogical agents: Face-to-face interaction in interactive learning environments.*International Journal of Artificial Intelligence in Education, 11,* 1 (2000), 47-78.

[14] Kanda, T., Hirano, T., Eaton, D., and Ishiguro, H. 2004. Interactive robots as social partners and peer tutors for children: A field trial. *Human-Computer Interaction 19, 1* (2004), 61-84.

[15] Klassner, F., and Anderson, S.D. Lego MindStorms: Not just for K-12 anymore. 2003. *Robotics & Automation Magazine 10, 2* (2003), 12-18.

[16] Koedinger, K. R., and Aleven, V. 2007. Exploring the assistance dilemma in experiments with cognitive tutors. *Educational Psychology Review 19, 3*(2007), 239-264.

[17] Koedinger, K. R., & Corbett, A. T. 2006. Cognitive tutors: Technology bringing learning science to the classroom. *The Cambridge handbook of the learning sciences*, 61-78.

[18] Lee, F. 1997. When the going gets tough, do the tough ask for help? Help seeking and power motivation in organizations. *Organizational Behavior and Human Decision Processes 72, 3* (1997), 336-363.

[19] Lee, F. 2002. The social costs of seeking help. *Journal of Applied Behavioral Science 38, 1* (2002), 17-35.

[20] Markus, H. 1978. The effect of mere presence on social facilitation: An unobtrusive test. *Journal of Experimental Social Psychology 14, 4* (1978), 389-397.

[21] Nelson-Le Gall, S. 1981. Help-seeking: An understudied problem-solving skill in children. *Developmental Review 1, 3* (1981), 224-246.

[22] Powers, A., Kiesler, S., Fussell, S., and Torrey, C. 2007. Comparing a computer agent with a humanoid robot. *Proc. Human-Robot Interaction 2007*, 145-152.

[23] Rammstedt, B., and John, O.P. 2007. Measuring personality in one minute or less: A 10-item short version of the Big Five Inventory in English and German. *Journal of Research in Personality 41, 1* (2007), 203-212.

[24] Saerbeck, M., Schut, T., Bartneck, C., and Janse, M.D. 2010. Expressive robots in education: varying the degree of social supportive behavior of a robotic tutor. *Proc. of Human Factors in Computing Systems*, ACM, 1613-1622.

[25] Shankland, Robert. 2013. "US Moves to Ban Trans Fats in Foods" *BBC Online* 7 Nov. 2013: *BBC News* Web. 8 Nov. 2013.

[26] Shirouzu, H. & Miyake, N. 2013. Effects of robots' revoicing on preparation for future learning. *Proc. Of Computer-Supported Collaborative Learning.*

[27] Stokes, S.J., and Bickman, L. 1974. The effect of the physical attractiveness and role of the helper on help seeking. *Journal of Applied Social Psychology 4, 3* (1974), 286-294.

[28] Taylor, I. I., and P. Robert. 2003. The computer in school: Tutor, tool, tutee. *Contemporary Issues in Technology and Teacher Education 3, 2* (2003), 240-252.

[29] Tessler, R.C., and Schwartz, S.H. 1972. Help seeking, self-esteem, and achievement motivation: an attributional analysis. *Journal of Personality and Social Psychology 21, 3* (1972), 318-326.

[30] Torrey, C., Fussell, S. R., & Kiesler, S. 2013. How a robot should give advice. *Proc. Human-Robot Interaction 2013*, 275-282. IEEE.

[31] Towle, A. 1989. *Modern Biology*. New York: Holt, Rinehart and Winston.

[32] Walker, E., and Burleson, W. 2012. User-Centered design of a teachable robot. *Proc. Intelligent Tutoring Systems 2012*, Springer Berlin Heidelberg.

[33] Zajonc, R.B. 1965. *Social facilitation.* Research Center for Group Dynamics, Institute for Social Research, University of Michigan Press.

Personalizing Robot Tutors to Individuals' Learning Differences

Daniel Leyzberg
Yale University
Dept. of Computer Science
daniel.leyzberg@yale.edu

Samuel Spaulding
Mass. Institute of Technology
MIT Media Lab
samuelsp@media.mit.edu

Brian Scassellati
Yale University
Dept. of Computer Science
scaz@cs.yale.edu

ABSTRACT

In education research, there is a widely-cited result called "Bloom's two sigma" that characterizes the differences in learning outcomes between students who receive one-on-one tutoring and those who receive traditional classroom instruction [1]. Tutored students scored in the 95th percentile, or two sigmas above the mean, on average, compared to students who received traditional classroom instruction. In human-robot interaction research, however, there is relatively little work exploring the potential benefits of personalizing a robot's actions to an individual's strengths and weaknesses. In this study, participants solved grid-based logic puzzles with the help of a personalized or non-personalized robot tutor. Participants' puzzle solving times were compared between two non-personalized control conditions and two personalized conditions (n=80). Although the robot's personalizations were less sophisticated than what a human tutor can do, we still witnessed a "one-sigma" improvement (68th percentile) in post-tests between treatment and control groups. We present these results as evidence that even relatively simple personalizations can yield significant benefits in educational or assistive human-robot interactions.

Categories and Subject Descriptors

I.2.9 [**Artificial Intelligence**]: Robotics; J.4 [**Computer Applications**]: Social And Behavioral Sciences—*Psychology*

General Terms

Experimentation

Keywords

Education, Robotics, HRI, Tutoring, Personalization, Assessment, ITS

HRI'14, March 3–6, 2014, Bielefeld, Germany.
Copyright 2014 ACM 978-1-4503-2658-2/14/03 ...$15.00.
http://dx.doi.org/10.1145/2559636.2559671.

1. INTRODUCTION

There is a long-held belief in the HRI community that personalized interactions are likely to be more compelling or more useful than non-personalized interactions. Research in this area has shown that people behave more socially towards a robot that personalizes its interactions based on interaction history [2]. However, relatively little is known about personalization as a means to elicit behavioral change in educational or assistive HRI. To what extent does personalization improve the utility of such robots? Is it difficult or expensive to build systems that tailor their output to individuals' strengths and weaknesses in this context? Does the addition of personalization elicit desirable behavioral changes among users?

To explore these questions we chose a domain in which individual customizations are critical to the success of an interaction. Effective tutoring requires teachers to assess students' individual differences and align their curricula and methods to best suit an individual student's needs. Bloom's "two sigma" result and many years of studies indicate that individually tailored lessons are much more effective than traditional classroom lessons [3]. These results confirm that personalization is important in education, but comparing a classroom learning environment to a one-on-one learning environment leaves open the question of to what extent the difference in learning outcomes can be attributed to personalization alone.

In this work, we compare four conditions, all of which were one-on-one human-robot tutoring interactions. In two conditions, we personalized the lessons participants received based on an online assessment of the individual's skills. The content of each lesson was pre-recorded and identical in both personalized conditions; the only difference was the order in which the lessons were delivered. There are also two control conditions in this study: one with no lessons whatsoever, to establish a baseline of puzzle solving performance in our population, and one with the same pre-recorded lessons as in the two personalized conditions, but where the order is chosen entirely independently of the user's skills.

We find that, despite only changing the order of lessons, participants that received personalized lessons performed "one sigma" better than either control group in post-test puzzle solving time. This result indicates that even relatively simple personalizations can significantly improve the utility of an educational or assistive human-robot interaction.

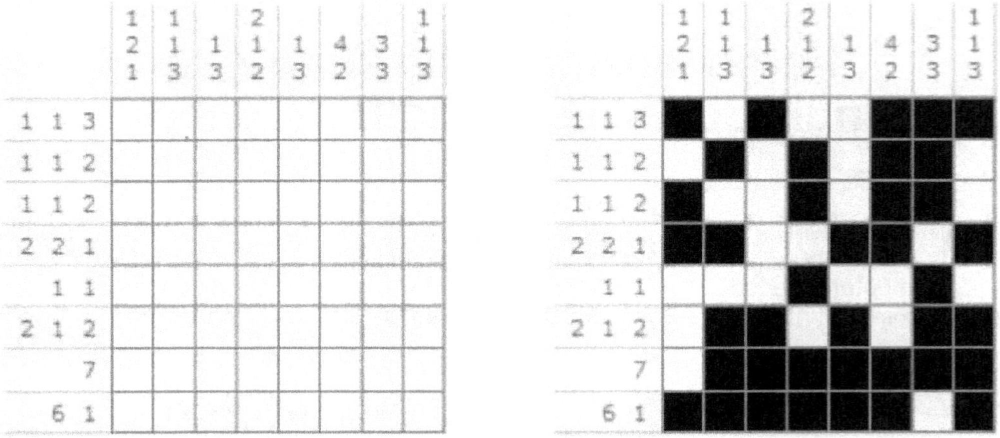

(a) Sample nonogram puzzle, blank.

(b) Sample nonogram puzzle, solved.

Figure 1: A sample nonogram puzzle. The objective of nonograms is, starting with a blank board (see left figure), to find a pattern of shaded boxes on the board such that the number of consecutively shaded boxes in each row and column appear as specified, in length and order, by the numbers that are printed to the left of each row and above each column (see right figure). For a more detailed explanation see Section 3.2.2.

2. RELATED WORK

Bloom's "two sigma" result inspired nearly three decades of research investigating the differences in learning outcomes between one-on-one tutoring and traditional classroom instruction. While there is no debate whether one-on-one tutoring benefits students, a recent review and meta-analysis [3] noted that the average benefit of personalization was closer to one sigma than to two sigma. Whether the benefits are one sigma or two, there is little doubt that individualized instruction has a substantial impact on students' learning gains.

In addition to human tutoring, another active area of research is creating and evaluating computerized tutoring systems [4]. The average effect size across studies evaluating learning gains made via computerized tutoring is that tutored students performed 0.76 sigma better than students who received only traditional classroom education, a close second to the effect of human tutors [3]. These learning outcome results, whether produced by human tutor or computer tutor, underscore the importance of personalization in the education domain. No previous work, however, has isolated the effect of personalization on human-robot interactions in an educational or assistive setting.

Previous work in personalization in HRI has been limited to measures of engagement and user satisfaction. Snackbot, a robot that personalized dialogue in reference to an individual user's history of snack choices, was found to be more engaging on several measures than a non-personalized version of the same robot, including an increased desire to use the robot and an increase in social behavior directed toward the robot [2]. Kidd's robot weight loss coach generates customized dialogue based on the progress of the user [5] but his research does not isolate the effect of personalization. In other work, users that were allowed to decorate, and thus personalize, their Roombas self-reported higher engagement with the robot and more willingness to use the robot in the future [6]. No earlier work, however, isolated the effects of personalization in HRI in an educational or assistive setting.

There has been other work on robot tutoring, however. One such platform is RUBI, a robot tutor designed to interact with 18 to 24 month old children [7]. RUBI is a humanoid with articulated arms, an expressive face, and a tablet embedded in its midsection on which it displays educational content like vocabulary lessons. A study of the iRobiQ, a humanoid similar in design to RUBI, provides some experimentally-derived guidelines for using robot tutors in classrooms [8]. Research has also been done on tutoring robots that operate as museum guides [9] or teleoperated instruments of a human teacher, such as the Huggable robot [10]. A long-term study of elementary students playing chess with an iCat explored how supportive students perceive different versions of the robot tutor to be [11]. No previous robot tutor research, however, isolates the role of personalization.

3. METHOD

To assess the effect of personalization in an educational human-robot interaction, an experiment was conducted in which a robot tutor assisted participants in solving grid-based logic puzzles.

In previous work, the authors demonstrated that physically-embodied robot tutors produce greater learning gains than on-screen virtual agents delivering the same lessons[1] [12]. The present work isolates the effects of personalization in educational/assistive HRI by comparing robot tutors that provide individualized lessons to those that do not.

3.1 Participants

There were 80 participants in this experiment, between 18 and 40 years of age. Most participants were undergraduate and graduate students of Yale University, none of whom

[1]Our earlier work on embodiment [12] used a similar apparatus and some data here were previously presented as part of that work. The current work introduces new data, new algorithms for personalization, and an experimental design that isolates the effect of personalization in educational/assistive HRI.

(a) Participants solve a nonogram puzzle on the computer as the robot (Keepon) analyzes the moves they make and, three times per puzzle, delivers brief lessons (21 – 47 sec.) about gameplay strategies.

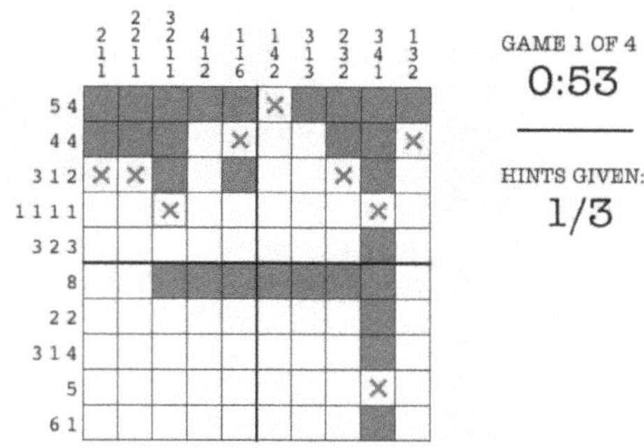

(b) A screenshot of the nonogram puzzle user interface during gameplay. All boards start blank. Participants played four puzzles for a maximum of fifteen minutes per puzzle.

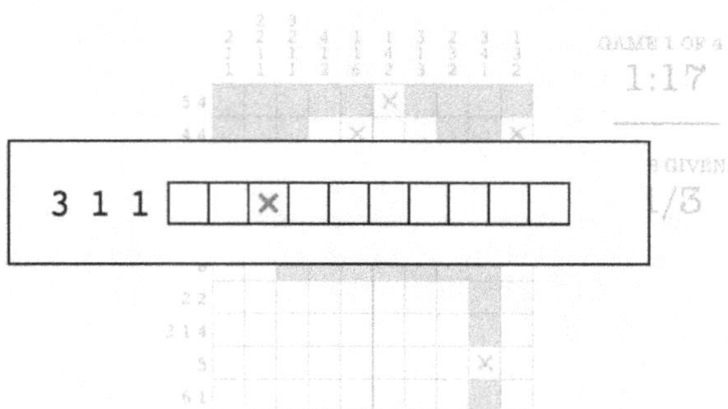

(c) A screenshot of the tutoring user interface. The robot 'speaks' in pre-recorded spoken messages and and moves in pre-recorded motions while coordinated visuals appear on screen.

Figure 2: Experiment apparatus and user interface screenshots.

were pursuing a degree in computer science. This study is a between-subjects design with four groups of 20 participants each, receiving either: (1) no lessons, (2) randomized-but-relevant lessons, (3) personalized lessons chosen by an additive skill assessment algorithm, or (4) personalized lessons chosen by a Bayesian network skill assessment algorithm. Exclusion criteria were a lack of English fluency or prior academic experience with robotics or artificial intelligence.

3.2 Apparatus

Participants in the experiment were asked to solve a set of logic puzzles on a computer. A robot tutor interrupted several times throughout each participants' session to deliver puzzle solving strategy lessons. In the two *personalized lessons conditions*, the robot used one of two skill assessment models (described in Section 4) to choose which among a set of pre-recorded lessons to give the participant, whereas in the *randomized-but-relevant lessons condition* the robot picked a random pre-recorded lesson among those applicable to the current state of the board but independent of the skills of the user. In the *no lessons condition* participants solved the puzzles with no help, the robot merely served as an announcer for the game. We compare the puzzle solving performance between these four groups to evaluate the effects of personalization in educational/assistive HRI.

3.2.1 *Robot*

The robot we used, Keepon, is a small yellow snowman-shaped tabletop robot, 11 inches tall, see Figure 2(a). We chose Keepon because it is particularly well suited to expressive non-threatening social communication [13, 14].

During the experiment, the robot played three roles. First, it refereed and acted as a host: it welcomed participants when they started, told them when they had finished or when they had run out of time, and told them when the experiment was over. Second, it "observed" the board during gameplay: the robot's body faced the screen and its head followed the location of the mouse cursor as the participants worked on the puzzles. Third, it delivered short puzzle-solving strategy lessons, three times per puzzle: it turned to face the participant and "bounced" its body up and down while playing one of several pre-recorded spoken messages with accompanying visuals appearing on screen, overlaid onto the puzzle interface, see Figure 2(a). If a lesson was going to be repeated, the robot would first apologize for repeating itself (i.e., "I'm sorry to repeat this hint but I think this will help.").

To focus our efforts on the personalization of the interaction, we did not use a vision system to detect state changes in the puzzle board. Instead, the robot had perfect knowledge of the game state via a software link to the puzzle interface.

3.2.2 Puzzle

To ensure the greatest likelihood of participants starting the study at the same skill level, we chose a puzzle game that is relatively obscure to American audiences: a grid-based fill-in-the-blanks puzzle called "nonograms" (also called "nonogram puzzles") that resemble crossword puzzles or Sudoku. Nonogram puzzles are a relatively difficult cognitive task, one that requires several layers of logical inferences to complete. Solving a nonogram puzzle of arbitrary size is an NP-complete problem [15].

The objective of nonograms is to, starting with a blank board, shade boxes on the board such that the number of consecutively shaded boxes in each row and column appear as specified, in length and order, by the numbers that are printed to the left of each row and above each column. For instance, a row marked as "4 2" must have 4 adjacent shaded boxes, followed by 2 adjacent shaded boxes—in that order, with no other boxes shaded, and with at least one empty box between the sets of adjacent shaded boxes. For a sample puzzle and its solution see Figures 1(a) and 1(b).

We refer to these contiguous sets of shaded boxes as "stretches.". For instance, the row described above requires two stretches, one of length 4, the other of length 2. One has solved a nonograms puzzle when one finds a pattern of blank and shaded boxes such that all of the requirements for each row and column are satisfied. Some nonogram puzzles have more than one solution, but most only have one.

In a typical puzzle, making progress on any row or column depends on the boxes in the rows and columns that it intersects. One must infer some parts of rows or columns based on what one has already established by inference earlier in the game. When a player has reasoned that some box should be shaded, the player shades it; if he or she reasons that a box will definitely *not* be shaded, they mark such boxes with an 'X' for reference.

We created a full-screen nonograms interface that participants used via mouse and keyboard. The user interface included a game timer and a count of how many lessons (called "hints") the participant had received thus far and how many more they would receive for that puzzle, see Figure 2(b).

Participants were asked to solve four puzzles on a ten-by-ten grid with a time limit of fifteen minutes per puzzle. The four puzzles chosen were identical for all participants across all groups. The fourth puzzle was a copy of the first puzzle, though disguised by rotating the puzzle 90°, such that the column requirements were swapped with row requirements. This manipulation enabled us to make within-subjects comparisons about the extent to which each participant improved over the course of the study. There was no indication that any participant became aware of this manipulation.

3.2.3 Skills & Lessons

Three times per puzzle, the robot interrupted the participant, paused the puzzle, and delivered a short lesson about nonograms solving strategies. The lessons ranged from 21 seconds to 47 seconds in length and consisted of a voice recording and a set of animations presented on screen during the lesson as well as a set of coordinated robot motions specific to each lesson.

When beginning a lesson the robot would turn to face the participant and say "I have an idea that might help you," or "Here's another hint for you." During the lesson, the robot faced the participant and bounced up and down except when, in the course of the lesson, it referenced a visual presented on screen, at which point the robot briefly turned to face the screen. For instance, when the robot said "Like in this example..." or "As you see here...," the robot turned briefly to the screen and then back to the participant.

(a) In this row, there must be one long stretch. By the process of elimination one can infer that this stretch must occupy at least the middle six boxes, no matter where in the row it is placed.

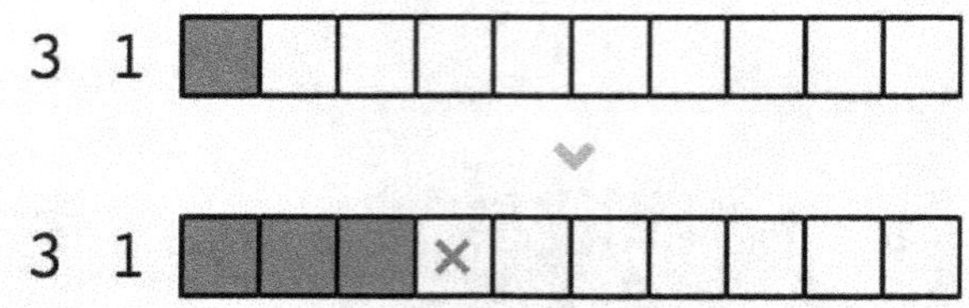

(b) In this row, the first box is already shaded. Given that, and that the first stretch must be 3 boxes long, one can infer that the first three boxes must be shaded and the fourth must be crossed out.

(c) In this row, there is only one short stretch and some boxes are already shaded. One can infer that regardless of where that one stretch is placed, it cannot occupy the first two or the last two boxes in that row.

Figure 3: Examples of nonograms skills. Displayed are the contents of a row before and after each skill is applied. Although only rows are shown here, all nonograms skills apply to columns as well.

Ten puzzle-solving skills were identified based on the subjective experience of the authors. Each skill is defined as a set of row or column states in which one can logically fill in some remaining empty boxes based on what is already filled in. For example, a stretch of length 9 can fit in a blank row or column of 10 boxes in only one of two ways. Either it fills the first box and the next 8, but not the last box, or it fills the same middle 8 boxes and the last box but not the first one. In either case, the middle 8 boxes must be shaded. Following this pattern, one skills defined for this study is that, for an empty row or column with only one stretch requirement, n where $n > 5$, the center $(2n - 10)$ boxes are shaded. For example usages of this skill and two others, see Figure 3.

For each of these ten identified skills, there was one prerecorded lesson. Three lessons were delivered per puzzle, for each of four puzzles; at least two lessons were repeated per participant. Lessons were triggered either when a participant made no moves for 45 seconds or as he or she filled in the 25th, 50th or 75th box on the board of 100. Participants were informed in the user interface of how many lessons were remaining for each puzzle.

The lessons were chosen based on the participant's experimental condition: either the lesson corresponding with the skill that had the lowest internal skill assessment score (in both *personalized lessons conditions*) or randomly chosen from among the applicable lessons to the current game board (in the *randomized-but-relevant lessons condition*). In all conditions, the only lessons eligible were ones that had an available application for the current board. This ensured that each lesson provided information that was actionable at the time the lesson was given.

3.2.4 Isolating Personalization

It was our intention to isolate the effect of personalization in an educational human-robot interaction. To achieve this, the *randomized-but-relevant control condition* chose lessons that were relevant to the participant's current board state but not necessarily the ones that were best suited to their skill level. This is intended to emulate a non-personalized classroom setting in which a teacher chooses an appropriate lesson for the class but not one that is necessarily tailored to any individual student's needs.

4. PERSONALIZED SKILL ASSESSMENT

The skill assessment algorithms presented here are not proposed as optimal solutions to the skill assessment problem more broadly. Instead, we are interested specifically in isolating what effect, if any, relatively simple personalizations have on education/assistive HRI.

To personalize the order of the lessons to suit the skills of individual participants, we created two relatively simple algorithms that assessed students' skills as they solved puzzles. Both algorithms take as input the moves participants make in each puzzle and produce as output a live updated vector of ten elements, each representing the likelihood that the participant has mastered one of ten predefined skills. In both *personalized lessons conditions*, the robot gave users the lesson that corresponded to their lowest scoring skill, of the subset of skills relevant to their current board state. The difference between the two algorithms is how the skill assessment scores were computed.

For our purposes, a skill i is defined as a function s_i that maps a potential state of the world ($w \in W$) from before an application of that skill to all potential resulting states after that skill is applied. A skill is *not* applicable to a state w, if and only if $s_i(w) = \{w\}$.

The skill functions are designed to be used in two ways:

* Skill functions are used to identify successful demonstrations of a skill. Skill i is said to be demonstrated at state w_t if $w_t \in s_i(w_{t-1})$.
* Skill functions are used to identify missed opportunities to demonstrate a skill. Skill i is said to have gone undemonstrated at previous state w_t if no action was taken and $s_i(w_t) \neq \{w_t\}$.

4.1 Additive Skill Assessment

In our first algorithm, we use a simple additive model to update a vector of skill assessments.

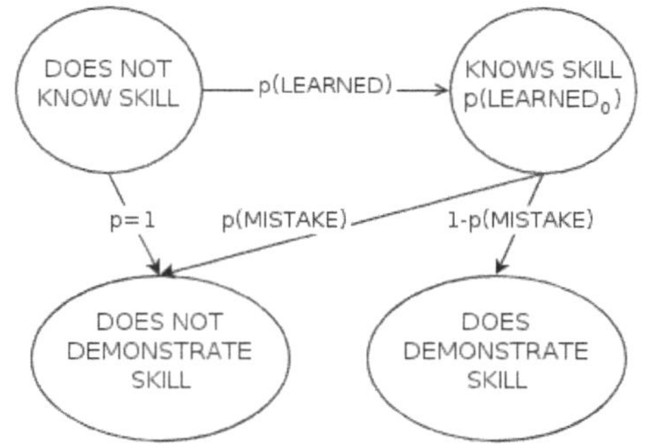

Figure 4: The Bayesian network skill assessment algorithm; an assessment of each skill is determined by an independent network in the form above. The upper nodes are internal states of the algorithm and the lower nodes correspond to the robot's observations of the user. For details see Section 4.2.

Given a set of skill definitions $s_i \in S$, this algorithm produces two internal Boolean functions for each skill i: a positive indicator p_i and a negative indicator n_i. p_i takes as input the previous and current world states and determines whether proficiency in skill i could have been responsible for this state transition ($w_t \in s_i(w_{t-1})$). n_i takes as input a world state and determines whether the ith skill is applicable to that state ($s_i(w_t) \neq \{w_t\}$). The positive indicator functions are evaluated every time the state of the world changes. The negative indicator functions are evaluated every time the state of the world does not change for a given delay, and at regular time intervals thereafter until the user changes the state. In our implementation below, the initial delay was set to 3 seconds and the regular interval was 1 second. These time delays are dependent on the task; the ones used in this paper were chosen based on the authors' subjective experience with the task domain.

The skill assessment $a_{i,t}$ for each skill i is produced at time t as follows:

$$a_{i,t} = d + \sum_{j=0}^{t} (\omega_p p_i(w_{j-1}, w_j) - \omega_n n_i(w_j))$$

Each skill assessment $a_{i,t}$ starts at an initial seed value of $d = 50\%$, and is incremented or decremented by a linear combination of the positive and negative indicator signals. The relative weights of positive indications (ω_p) to negative indications (ω_n) will vary with expected relative frequencies of positive to negative indicators. In this application, we expected positive indications to be rare relative to negative indications; the weights we used were $\omega_p = 50\%, \omega_n = 1\%$. A floor of 0% and a ceiling of 100% is applied to the summed value at each timestep. The weights and seed value used in this algorithm were subjectively derived and fine-tuned based on pilot studies.

4.2 Bayesian Network Skill Assessment

A weakness of the additive skill assessment algorithm is its susceptibility to local maxima and minima. When individual skill assessments reach floor or ceiling, the additive algorithm essentially ignores the participants' performance history. A good human tutor does not forget previous successes or failures in light of more recent observations.

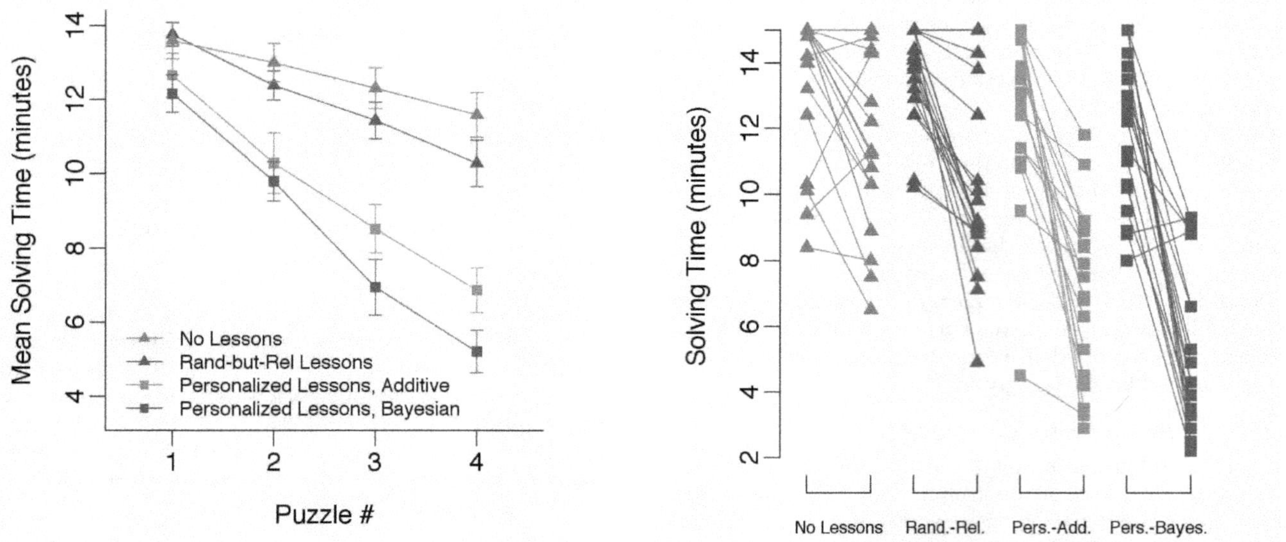

(a) Mean solving time per group, per puzzle. Participants who received personalized lessons solved each puzzle after the first significantly faster than participants in either of the control groups, see Table 1. Participants in both personalized groups performed approximately "one sigma" better on the final puzzle than participants in either control condition.

(b) Pre-test/post-test puzzle solving times for individual participants, separated by group. The fourth puzzle was the same as the first, but disguised by a 90° rotation. Participants receiving personalized lessons improved their same-puzzle solving time significantly more than participants in the control groups, $p < 0.01$.

Figure 5: Personalization produces greater learning gains: (a) Participants whose lessons were personalized solved the last three puzzles faster than participants in either control group. (b) Participants receiving personalized lessons significantly improved their same-puzzle solving time over participants in either control group.

We addressed this weakness by offering a Bayesian network approach. Bayesian networks provide a way of modeling the relationship between observations and skill assessment in probabilistic terms. For each skill, we used the same graph structure with assumed independent variables (see Figure 4). Skills in this representation are categorized as either learned or not learned.

The following equation is used to estimate the student's proficiency with each skill individually:

$$p(L_t) = p(L_{t-1}|w_t) + (1 - p(L_{t-1}|w_t)p(L_0) \qquad (1)$$

where $p(L_t)$ is the sum of the posterior probability that the rule was already learned, regardless of the current world state and the probability that the rule will make the transition to the learned state if it is not learned. In this experiment, we chose not to model the possibility of forgetting a skill. Our application domain was an interaction lasting less than one hour, thus we deemed forgetting a skill to be a relatively unlikely occurrence.

The two parameters are learned based on observations via an Expectation Maximization (EM) algorithm. Expectation Maximization requires starting points for each value it estimates; in the experiment described below, EM was implemented with seed values of 0 for p(LEARNED) and .5 for p(MISTAKE). EM alternates between performing an expectation step, which creates a function for the expectation of the log-likelihood evaluated using the current estimate for the parameters, and a maximization step, which computes parameters maximizing the expected log-likelihood. This method is commonly used to estimate the unknown parameters of a Bayesian network.

For both algorithms, the result is a vector of likelihoods that the tutor has about the users' proficiency with each individual skill. That information is used to select the most appropriate lesson to suit an individual's strengths and weaknesses.

4.3 Procedure

Before participating in this study, participants watched a five minute instructional video describing the rules of nonograms and how to use our computer interface. In this video, participants were encouraged to use logical reasoning to make moves in the game, rather than guessing. Afterwards, any questions were answered by an experimenter.

During the experiment, participants were alone in a room with the robot, the computer, and a video camera positioned behind them, see Figure 2. Participants chose when they were ready to start each new puzzle. Games ended either when the participant solved the puzzle or when fifteen minutes had elapsed, whichever came first.

After the conclusion of the final puzzle, participants were asked to complete a survey consisting of three open-ended questions and five Likert-scale questions. The questions were designed to assess whether participants perceived the lessons to be helpful, clear, and influential, as well as participants' perceptions of the robot. Participants rated how relevant the lessons were to them, how much the lessons influenced their gameplay, how well they understood the lessons, and how "smart/intelligent" and, separately, how "distracting/annoying" they perceived the robot to be.

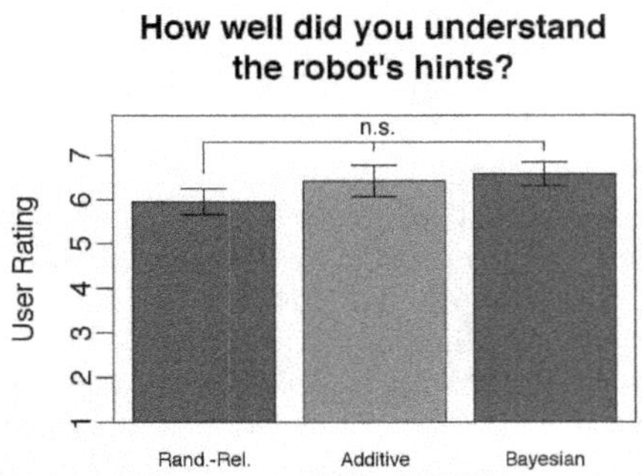

(a) There is no significant difference between groups in how participants rated their understanding of the lessons.

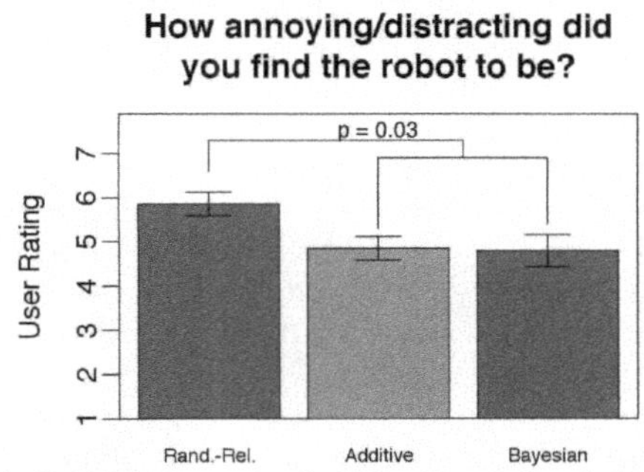

(b) Participants in both *personalized lessons groups* rated the robot as significantly less "distracting/annoying" than those in the *randomized-but-relevant lessons group*, $p = 0.03$.

Figure 6: Results of two survey questions answered by participants upon completing the experiment.

5. RESULTS

The central hypothesis of this study is that personalized educational human-robot interactions will produce measurable behavioral differences when compared to non-personalized interactions. The behavioral measure is the length of time participants took to solve each of the four puzzles. For the purposes of calculating a mean, puzzles that were not completed within the fifteen minute time limit were scored as having been completed in fifteen minutes. The rate of failure was not significantly different between groups for any of the four puzzles, varying from 29% to 38% in the first game to 9% to 17% in the fourth game.

	Game 1	Game 2	Game 3	Game 4
None	13.6 ± 2.2	13.0 ± 2.3	12.3 ± 2.5	11.6 ± 2.7
Rand-Rel	13.8 ± 1.4	12.5 ± 2.0	11.4 ± 2.3	10.3 ± 2.9
Additive	12.7 ± 2.6	10.0 ± 3.5	9.4 ± 3.0	7.6 ± 3.1
Bayesian	12.2 ± 2.3	9.8 ± 2.4	6.9 ± 3.4	5.2 ± 2.6

Table 1: Solving time means and standard deviations, in minutes. In each game except the first game, participants in both *personalized lessons groups* solved the puzzle significantly faster than participants in both the *randomized-but-relevant lessons* and *no lessons* groups ($p < 0.03$ for all).

Participants in both *personalized lessons groups* solved three of four puzzles significantly faster, on average, than those in either the *randomized-but-relevant lessons* or *no lessons* groups, $p < 0.03$ for all, see Table 1 and Figure 5(a). These results confirm the main hypothesis: personalized human robot interactions produced significantly improved user performance than non-personalized interactions.

Between *personalized lesson groups*, the *Bayesian group* did significantly better on the last puzzle than the *Additive group*, $t(37) = 0.05$.

In this study, the fourth puzzle was the same as the first, though disguised by a 90° rotation. There was no indication that any participant became aware of this manipulation. The difference in completion times between the first and fourth puzzles is a within-subjects measure of an individual participant's improvement over the course of the experiment. According to this metric, participants in either *personalized lessons group* improved ($M = 5.8$ minutes, $SD = 3.3$) their same-puzzle solving time significantly more than those in either *control group* ($M = 3.1$ minutes, $SD = 2.4$), $t(31) < 0.01$. See Figure 5(b).

Survey results indicate participants in the *personalized lessons groups* rated the lessons significantly more relevant to them ($M = 4.9, SD = 1.4$) than participants in the *randomized-but-relevant lessons group* ($M = 2.9, SD = 1.1$), $t(33) < 0.001$. There was no significant difference, however, in how participants rated their understanding of the lessons between groups, ($M = 5.4, SD = 1.5$) in the *personalized lessons groups* and ($M = 5.0, SD = 1.4$) in the *randomized-but-relevant condition*, $t(36) = 0.32$. Nor was there a significant difference in how participants self-assessed the degree to which their gameplay was affected, ($M = 4.3, SD = 1.3$) in the *personalized lessons groups* and ($M = 4.1, SD = 1.3$) in the *randomized-but-relevant condition*, $t(36) = 0.31$. Participants in the *personalized lessons groups* rated the robot as smarter or more intelligent ($M = 4.7, SD = 1.8$) than participants in the *randomized-but-relevant condition* ($M = 3.5, SD = 1.6$), $t(36) = 0.03$.

6. DISCUSSION

This study assesses whether personalization in educational or assistive HRI produces beneficial behavioral changes in users. The data indicate that personalization can lead to behavioral differences in users that result in more successful human-robot interactions.

In this puzzle task, we saw a "one sigma," or one standard deviation, improvement in participants final puzzle solving time from those received *personalized lessons* over those receiving *randomized-but-relevant lessons*, see Table 1. One sigma is more than the mean standard deviation effect size that most software Intelligent Tutoring Systems produce compared to classroom education alone, 0.76 sigma [3]. This may be due to the nature of the puzzle game that was used for this experiment. Success in nonograms requires several layers of logical inference, to which participants who received personalized lessons caught on more quickly than those in the control groups. An early lead allowed these participants to progress faster and perhaps feel more motivated.

The self-report survey data indicate that participants did not report having more difficulty understanding the lessons presented to them in the *randomized-but-relevant lessons group* than in either *personalized lessons group*. All three groups rated their level of understanding fairly highly: a mean of 5.4 across *personalized lessons groups* and 5.0 in the *randomized-but-relevant lessons group* out of 7, $t(36) = 0.32$, see Figure 6(a). It is notable that the *randomized-but-relevant lessons group* reported a relatively high understanding of the lessons despite performing poorly. This may indicate that this population was reluctant to admit when they did not understand something.

Judging by survey free-response data, participants in this study ranged greatly in their own evaluation of the usefulness of the lessons. One participant in the *randomized-but-relevant lessons group* reported that: "Lessons were repetitive and a little distracting, even frustrating." In the *personalized lessons conditions*, some reported positive feedback while others reported only frustration. A participant who received personalized lessons, in response to a question about whether the lessons affected his/her gameplay replied, "Not really. I just learned by seeing what worked & what did not." However, judging by performance data, many participants who reported disregarding the content of the lessons, seemed to benefit from them just as much as the others. Some participants in the personalized groups claimed to be unaffected by the lessons but applied a lesson's content more frequently immediately after receiving lessons. From these survey results we conclude that a student's perceived value of a lesson may contradict with the lesson's measurable impact.

The free-response survey data also offers insight into the perception and impact of "easy" lessons. Many participants reported that they found some lessons "easy," "obvious," or "very obvious;" however, providing those lessons may not have been a waste. Eight participants reported a variant of the following sentiment: "Most hints I had previously explicitly figured out, though I found myself more actively seeking the pattern(s) suggested by a hint." This result highlights the benefit of personalization based on behavior rather than self-reported preferences.

7. CONCLUSION

In this paper we investigate the role of personalization in educational/assistive HRI. We compare participants' puzzle solving times across four one-on-one robot tutoring conditions, two of which were personalized to the learning progress of individual participants and two which were not personalized. We find that participants who received personalized lessons outperformed participants who received non-personalized lessons in a pre-test/post-test performance metric. We present these results as evidence that relatively simple personalizations can yield significant benefits in educational/assistive human-robot interactions.

8. REFERENCES

[1] B. S. Bloom, "The 2 sigma problem: The search for methods of group instruction as effective as one-to-one tutoring." *Educational Researcher*, vol. 13, no. 6, pp. 4–16, 1984.

[2] M. K. Lee, J. Forlizzi, S. B. Kiesler, P. E. Rybski, J. Antanitis, and S. Savetsila, "Personalization in HRI: a longitudinal field experiment." *7th ACM/IEEE International Conference on Human-Robot Interaction*, pp. 319–326, 2012.

[3] K. VanLehn, "The relative effectiveness of human tutoring, intelligent tutoring systems, and other tutoring systems," *Educational Psychologist*, vol. 46, no. 4, pp. 197–221, 2011.

[4] R. Nkambou, J. Bourdeau, and V. Psyché, "Building Intelligent Tutoring Systems: An overview," *Advances in Intelligent Tutoring Systems*, pp. 361–375, 2010.

[5] C. D. Kidd and C. Breazeal, "Robots at home: Understanding long-term human-robot interaction," *2008 IEEE/RSJ International Conference on Intelligent Robots and Systems*, pp. 3230–3235, 2008.

[6] J.-Y. Sung, R. E. Grinter, and H. I. Christensen, ""Pimp My Roomba": designing for personalization." *Proceedings of the SIGCHI Conference on Human Factors in Computing Systems*, pp. 193–196, 2009.

[7] J. R. Movellan, F. Tanaka, I. R. Fasel, C. Taylor, P. Ruvolo, and M. Eckhardt, "The RUBI project: A progress report," *2nd ACM/IEEE International Conference on Human-Robot Interaction*, pp. 333–339, 2007.

[8] E. Hyun, H. Yoon, and S. Son, "Relationships between user experiences and children's perceptions of the education robot," *5th ACM/IEEE International Conference on Human-Robot Interaction*, pp. 199–200, 2010.

[9] M. Bennewitz, F. Faber, D. Joho, M. Schreiber, and S. Behnke, "Towards a humanoid museum guide robot that interacts with multiple persons," *5th IEEE-RAS International Conference on Humanoid Robots*, pp. 418 –423, dec. 2005.

[10] J. K. Lee, R. Toscano, W. Stiehl, and C. Breazeal, "The design of a semi-autonomous robot avatar for family communication and education," *Robot and Human Interactive Communication, 2008. RO-MAN 2008. The 17th IEEE International Symposium on*, pp. 166 –173, aug. 2008.

[11] I. Leite, G. Castellano, A. Pereira, C. Martinho, and A. Paiva, "Long-term interactions with empathic robots: Evaluating perceived support in children," *Lecture Notes in Computer Science*, vol. 7621, pp. 298–307, 2012.

[12] D. Leyzberg, S. Spaulding, M. Toneva, and B. Scassellati, "The physical presence of a robot tutor increases cognitive learning gains," in *Proceedings of the 34th Annual Conference of the Cognitive Science Society*. Austin,TX: Cognitive Science Society, 2012.

[13] H. Kozima, C. Nakagawa, and Y. Yasuda, "Interactive robots for communication-care: A case-study in autism therapy," *IEEE International Symposium on Robot and Human Interactive Communication*, 2005.

[14] D. Leyzberg, E. Avrunin, J. Liu, and B. Scassellati, "Robots that express emotion elicit better human teaching," in *6th International Conference on Human-Robot Interaction*. New York, NY, USA: ACM, 2011, pp. 347–354.

[15] C.-H. Yu, H.-L. Lee, and L.-H. Chen, "An efficient algorithm for solving nonograms," *Applied Intelligence*, vol. 35, no. 1, pp. 18–31, 2011.

Teaching People How to Teach Robots: The Effect of Instructional Materials and Dialog Design

Maya Cakmak
University of Washington
Dept. of Computer Science and Engineering
mcakmak@cs.washington.edu

Leila Takayama*
Willow Garage, Inc.
68 Willow Road, Menlo Park, CA 94025
takayama@google.com

ABSTRACT

Allowing end-users to harness the full capability of general purpose robots, requires giving them powerful tools. As the functionality of these tools increase, learning how to use them becomes more challenging. In this paper we investigate the use of instructional materials to support the learnability of a Programming by Demonstration tool. We develop a system that allows users to program complex manipulation skills on a two-armed robot through a spoken dialog interface and by physically moving the robot's arms. We present a user study (N=30) in which participants are left alone with the robot and a user manual, without any prior instructions on how to program the robot. Instead, they are asked to figure it out on their own. We investigate the effect of providing users with an additional written tutorial or an instructional video. We find that videos are most effective in training the user; however, this effect might be superficial and ultimately trial-and-error plays an important role in learning to program the robot. We also find that tutorials can be problematic when the interaction has uncertainty due to speech recognition errors. Overall, the user study demonstrates the effectiveness and learnability of the our system, while providing useful feedback about the dialog design.

Categories and Subject Descriptors

I.2.9 [**Artificial Intelligence**]: Robotics; H.1.2 [**Models and Principles**]: User/Machine Systems

Keywords

Programming by Demonstration, Spoken dialog systems

1. INTRODUCTION

General-purpose robots, such as mobile manipulators, are becoming increasingly accessible. Unlike single-purpose robots

*This author is currently affiliated with Google[x]. The work presented in this paper was conducted while both authors were affiliated with Willow Garage, Inc.

HRI'14, March 3–6, 2014, Bielefeld, Germany.
Copyright 2014 ACM 978-1-4503-2658-2/14/03 ...$15.00.
http://dx.doi.org/10.1145/2559636.2559675 .

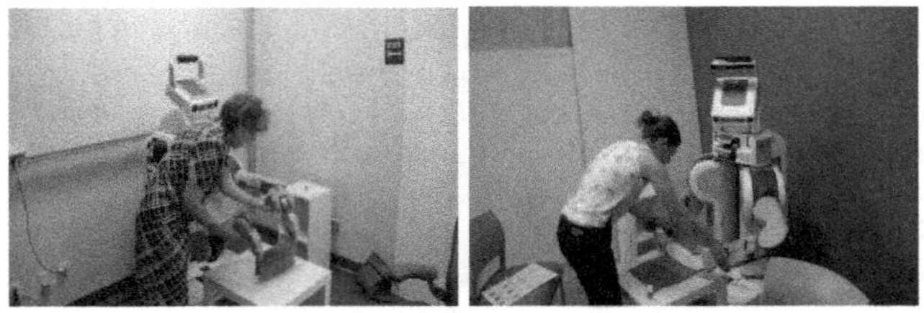

Figure 1: Participants in our user study, programming the PR2 to fold a towel by demonstration.

that are designed and pre-programmed to carry out a particular task, general-purpose robots offer the potential for end-users to program the robot for their unique purposes. This presents several interaction design challenges related to building tools that enable end-users to program new capabilities on their robots. It is crucial for such tools to give as much functionality to the user, while being easy to learn and not requiring in-person training of the end-user. A common method to allow end-users to program new capabilities on a robot is Programming by Demonstration (PbD). This involves demonstrating a desired capability to the robot, allowing it to model and reproduce the capability.

Demonstration is an intuitive way for users to communicate a desired capability. Nonetheless, details of the interaction through which users provide demonstrations might not be directly evident. For instance, even providing a single demonstration requires indicating the start and end of the demonstration, and there can be a number of ways to do that. Existing PbD systems employ vocal commands [2], pedals [18], and buttons on a remote controller [14] or on the robot's arm[1]. All of these methods require instructing users on what to do (*e.g.* which button to press for each functionality). As we start providing more functionalities to end-users (*e.g.* creating multiple actions, browsing actions, executing an action, deleting a previously programmed action, etcetera), the amount of instruction to be given to the users also increase. This makes it difficult for end-users to figure out, on their own, how they can program a robot.

In this work, we set out to design a PbD system for the PR2 robot and instructional materials which would let a naive user to program the robot without any training from an expert. We built a system that allows programming various manipulation skills by physically moving the robot's arms and talking to the robot through a spoken dialog in-

[1] `http://www.rethinkrobotics.com/products/baxter/`

terface (Fig. 1). As instructional materials, we explore the use of a step-by-step tutorial and an instructional video, in addition to a user-manual that specifies all the available commands that can be used. We examine the effects of these in a user study (N=30) which demonstrates superior performance when users are trained with a video and highlights the importance of trial-and-error. Based on the data from this user study, we also characterize the impact of certain design choices related to the dialog system.

2. RELATED WORK

Programming by Demonstration (PbD), also known as Learning from Demonstration, has been studied within robotics for the last three decades [4], with recent work focusing more and more on human interaction problems in PbD [5, 2, 19, 12, 21, 15]. The design choices for the dialog interface of our PbD system are influenced by work on spoken interactions with robots within the human-robot interaction (HRI) literature [7, 8, 21]. Work in the field of human-computer interaction which investigate how the system feedback influences human input [9, 16, 6] also have implications for human-robot dialog, and have been considered in the design of our system.

Our work is also influenced by a long line of research on the role of mental models in learning to operate new devices [11] and methods for effective instructional design for learning complex tasks [20, 1]. Particularly relevant work in this area is by Kamm *et al.* who investigate the influence of tutorials on user expertise with a spoken dialogue system for checking e-mail [10]. In their study, the tutorial significantly reduced task completion times and increased user satisfaction ratings. Although the design of instructional materials have not been explicitly studied in the context of HRI, they are largely employed for user studies evaluating functional systems designed for humans. For instance, work by Nguyen *et al.* employed tutorials to teach RCommander [13]—a tool for creating behaviors for a domestic robot.

3. SYSTEM

3.1 Platform

The robot platform used in this work is PR2 (Personal Robot 2) which is a mobile manipulator with two 7 Degree-of-Freedom (DoF) arms and an omnidirectional base. The passive spring counterbalance system in PR2's arms makes them naturally gravity-compensated, giving users the ability to kinesthetically move the arm within its kinematic range. Each arm has a 1 DoF under-actuated gripper and can carry up to 2.2kg. PR2 has a pan-tilt head with a Kinect sensor mounted on top.

The software written for this work is developed within ROS (Robot Operating System) and was released as an open-source package[2]. Speech recognition for the dialog system is done with Pocketsphinx, using a Shure wireless microphone headset. For text-to-speech on the robot we use Cepstral, with the voice *David*.

3.2 One-shot Keyframe-based Programming by Demonstration

The PbD system presented in this work is based on the keyframe-based PbD framework proposed by Akgun *et al.* [2].

[2]`http://ros.org/wiki/pr2_pbd`

Table 1: Components of the system state.

Dialog state	$d \in \{start,\ programming,\ execution\}$
Robot state	Joint configurations ζ^R, ζ^L, gripper states $g^R, g^L \in \{0,1\}$ and arm stiffnesses $\alpha^R, \alpha^L \in \{0,1\}$
Experiment state	Number of created skills N, current skill index $n \in \{1..N\}$, skills programmed so far $\{\mathcal{S}_i\}_{i=1}^N$ where $\mathcal{S}_i = \{(\zeta^R, g^R, \zeta^L, g^L)_k : k = 1..K_i\}$ and last used command c_{t-1}

We represent a *skill* as a sequence of states that the robot needs to go through: $\mathcal{S} = \{(\zeta^R, g^R, \zeta^L, g^L)_k : k = 1..K\}$, where ζ refers to the robot's 7-DoF arm configurations[3], and g refers to the binary gripper state (open or closed). The superscripts R and L denote right or left end-effectors. Skills are programmed directly with a single demonstration. In other words, the demonstration itself is a sequence of joint states that is used for reproducing the skill. For demonstrations, joint states are manipulated kinesthetically by the user, *i.e.* by physically moving the robot's arms.

To reproduce the skill, the robot moves through recorded states. It moves from one state to the next by first moving both arms with a certain velocity profile and and then changing the gripper states. For instance, if the gripper is closed at step $k-1$ and open at k, the robot will first move to $(\zeta^R, \zeta^L)_k$ with a closed gripper, and then open the gripper. The duration of the movement is determined by the arm that needs to move more. Speeds are adjusted such that both arms reach the next state at the same time.

3.3 Dialog System

The user interaction with the PbD system is done through a simple state-based dialog system with a finite set of input commands. The response to each command differs based on the *system state*. This is the combination of the *dialog*, *robot* and *experiment* states (detailed in Table 1). There are three possible dialog states: *start*, *programming*, and *execution*. The robot state involves the end-effector poses, gripper states (0:closed, 1:open) and arm stiffnesses (0:relaxed, 1:stiff). The experiment state involves the set of skills that have been programmed so far, and the index of the current skill. There are nine different command types (16 unique commands). The commands are listed in Table 2, excluding the two commands TEST MICROPHONE (which has no effect on the system state) and UNDO LAST COMMAND (which reverses the effect of the previous command).

The response to a command involves (i) a change in the system state, (ii) a speech response uttered by the robot, and (iii) a gaze action or head gesture. For example, when the command OPEN RIGHT HAND is used, the robot says "Opening right hand" while the right gripper opens and the robot glances towards the right gripper.

[3]Our system actually represents arm states with the 6-DoF end-effector states and uses the demonstrated 7-DoF arm state to seed the Inverse Kinematics solver. Within the context of this paper, this is equivalent to directly using joint configurations to represent arm states.

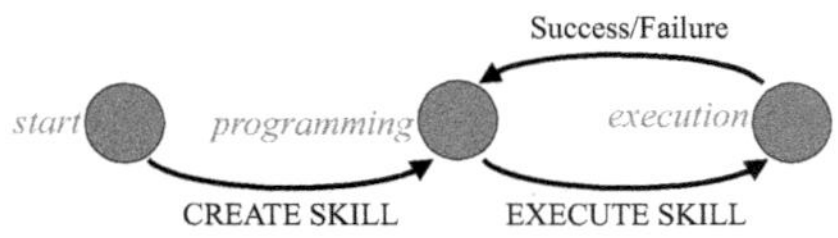

Figure 2: The core finite state-machine for the dialog system.

Table 2: Effect of the commands on the system state. Initialized with $d \leftarrow$ *start*, $N \leftarrow 0$ and $n \leftarrow 0$.

Command (c_t)	Effect of command
RELEASE/HOLD RIGHT/LEFT ARM	$\alpha^{R/L} \leftarrow \neg\alpha^{R/L}$
OPEN/CLOSE RIGHT/LEFT HAND	$g^{R/L} \leftarrow \neg g^{R/L}$
CREATE SKILL	$d \leftarrow$ *programming* $N \leftarrow N+1$, $n \leftarrow N$, $S_n \leftarrow \{\}$
SAVE POSE	**if** (d=*programming*): $S_n \leftarrow S_n \cup (\zeta^R, g^R, \zeta^L, g^L)$
EXECUTE SKILL	**if** (d=*programming*) & ($K_n > 1$) : $d \leftarrow$ *execution*,
CLEAR SKILL	**if** (d=*programming*): $S_n \leftarrow \{\}$
NEXT/PREVIOUS SKILL	**if** ($n > 1$ and $n < N$): $n \leftarrow n \pm 1$

The interaction begins in the *start* dialog state, where the user is allowed to test the microphone, change the stiffness of the robot's arms (released or holding a pose) and change the state of its grippers (open or closed). In the *start* state, the robot's response to the rest of the commands is the utterance "No skills created yet". Similarly, the robot has a speech response in every possible error case. Changes in the system state triggered by the commands are summarized in Table 2.

Creating the first skill moves the dialog state to *programming*. In this state the user can save poses into the current skill, delete poses, create more skills, navigate between the created skills, and trigger executions of the current skill. The commands that change the state of the robot have the same effects as in the *start* state. Once in the *programming* state, the dialog never goes back to the *start* state. The EXECUTE SKILL command, triggers a transition to the *execution* state, which involves moving through the poses of the current skill. In this state, the robot does not respond to any commands. The dialog returns to the *programming* state when the execution is over. The transitions between the dialog states is illustrated in Fig. 2.

4. INSTRUCTIONAL MATERIALS

Our goal in this work is to allow naive users to program the PR2 on their own, without any training from an expert. The complexity of the robot platform and the PbD functionality studied in this work, makes it challenging to accomplish this purely through interface design. We cannot expect participants to know the functionality and guess the right commands to use. To address this challenge we turn to *supplementary materials*, which are modalities outside the

Table 3: Sample command descriptions as worded in the user manual given to participants.

Command	Description in user manual
RELEASE/HOLD R/L ARM	Use these commands to release the robots arms so you can move them around, or to make them hold a certain pose.
CREATE SKILL	Use this command to create a new skill. PR2 will indicate the name of the skill (for example "skill-1") in its response.
CLEAR SKILL	Use this command to delete all the poses and hand actions that have been saved into the skill so far.

interaction that communicate information about the interaction. These are supplementary in the sense that they are not needed for the interaction; *i.e.* an expert user does not use them to program the robot. However, they can have an important role in the interactions of novice users.

In this paper we explore the use of three types of supplementary materials: user manuals, written tutorials and instructional videos. We refer to the latter two also as *instructional* materials, as these are designed with pedagogical intent. Tutorials aim at allowing users to *learn by doing* [17], whereas videos support them to *learn by observing* [3]. In our user study, described later in Sec. 5, we compare these learning paradigms with a baseline in which only a user manual is provided, forcing them to *learn by exploring*, through trial-and-error. We describe the different supplementary materials designed for our the PbD system in the following.

User manual. A user manual (or user guide), is an extensive technical document that assists the user of a particular system—most commonly consumer electronics or computer software. It outlines the different functionalities of the system and provides instructions on how to use them referring to controls (*e.g.* buttons, menus) and states (*e.g.* lights, status bars) that are available to the user.

In this work the user manual communicates the allowed commands in the spoken dialog and explains their function. The manual includes an introductory paragraph that summarizes what the user can do through the interaction, and a table that contains the list of commands and a description of its purpose and effect. Samples from these descriptions are given in Table 3. The whole user manual is one page.

Written tutorial. A tutorial is a set of step-by-step instructions to complete a task. It is intended to teach the use of a certain system *by example*. In some cases the intended task is completed at the end of the tutorial and could be repeated in the future without the tutorial (*e.g.* how to change the strings of a guitar). In other cases, the tutorial involves a special case of a general task that is not exactly the intended task, and it can be transferred to other instantiations of the task (*e.g.* how to write a ROS service).

The tutorial for our system consists of step-by-step instructions to allow the user to program a set of skills, so as to illustrate the effect of the different commands allowed in the dialog. The steps of the tutorial and the commands practiced in each step are given in Table 4. As an example,

Table 4: **Steps of the tutorial for teaching the use of the PbD system.**

Tutorial step	Commands practiced
Getting started	TEST MICROPHONE
Moving the arms	RELEASE/HOLD R/L ARM
Using hand actions	OPEN/CLOSE R/L HAND
Programming a skill: Waving	CREATE SKILL, SAVE POSE, EXECUTE SKILL
Adding a hand action into the skill	OPEN/CLOSE R/L HAND, SAVE POSE, EXECUTE SKILL
Deleting a pose and clearing a skill	UNDO LAST COMMAND, CLEAR SKILL
Navigating skills	CREATE SKILL, PREVIOUS SKILL, NEXT SKILL

the wording of the fourth step in the tutorial is as follows:

1. Say CREATE SKILL and listen to PR2's response.
2. Release PR2's right arm and move it to a waving pose. Say SAVE POSE while holding the arm in place.
3. Move the arm to a different pose to the right of the first pose. Say SAVE POSE while holding the arm in place.
4. Save a third pose slightly to the left of the first pose.
5. Let PR2's arm go and say EXECUTE SKILL. Observe the skill playing out.

Instructional video. An instructional video is a video that instructs the user on how to complete a task by demonstrating it. It allows the user to learn a task by observing someone else do the same task. As with tutorials, users may execute the task themselves as they watch the video step-by-step. Note that videos may not have been made with the intent of teaching, but may still serve this purpose (*e.g.* learning how to play a song on the guitar from a video of someone performing it; learning about the basic functionality of Siri from the iPhone commercial). The instructional video for our PbD system involves a person executing the steps of the tutorial given in Table 4[4]. The length of the video is 3 minutes 36 seconds.

5. EVALUATION

We evaluated the effectiveness of our system (Sec. 3) and the impact of the different instructional materials (Sec. 4) through a user study which we describe in this section.

5.1 Study Design

Our study has three conditions in which participants were given a different combination of supplementary materials.

1. *Baseline:* Participant is only provided with the user manual.
2. *Tutorial:* Participant is provided with the written tutorial in addition to the user manual.
3. *Video:* Participant is provided with the instructional video in addition to the user manual.

[4]http://www.youtube.com/watch?v=Sou_rthgCtE

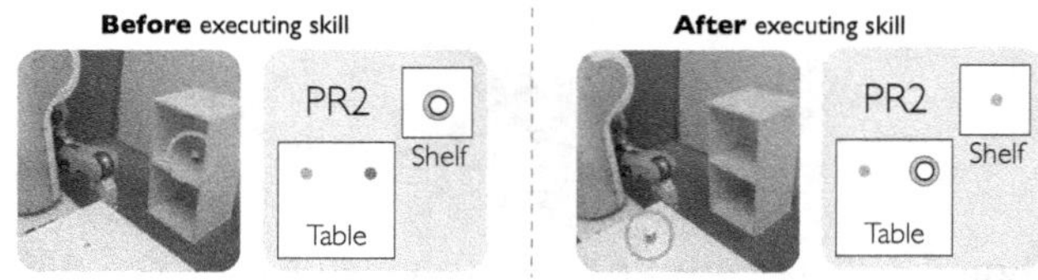

Figure 3: An example skill depiction (*constrained pick-up and place*) from the *skill guide* handed to the participants in the experiment.

We used a between-groups design; *i.e.* each participant was assigned to one of the three conditions. Participants in all conditions were provided with the user manual since a user cannot be expected to know the command set for the dialog. In addition, participants in all conditions were allowed to call the experimenter to ask questions. This is equivalent to calling a *technical support* line to get help on using a product. This was done to measure the occurrence of blockages in the task where the participants felt that the instructional materials were insufficient, while also allowing them to overcome these blockages.

Participants were asked to program four different skills on the PR2. The skills were visually illustrated and explained on the *skill guide* (Fig. 3) which was handed to the participants together with the supplementary materials. The description of the four skills are as follows:

1. Pick-up and place: Pick up the pill bottle from the red dot on the table and place it at the green dot on the table, using the left arm.
2. Constrained pick-up and place: Pick up the pill bottle from the blue dot on the shelf and place it at the red dot on the table, using the left arm (Fig. 3).
3. Pick-up, transfer, and place: Pick up a pill bottle from the green dot on the table with the right hand, transfer it to the left hand, and place it at the red dot on the table.
4. Towel folding: Fold a towel placed on the table (with two corners on the red and green dots) into two.

The second and third skills are progressively more challenging versions of the first one, involving obstacles and coordination of two arms. The last is a transfer task which involves programming a skill with similar constraints as the third skill in a different context. The order of the tasks were maintained across participants.

5.2 Procedure

Participants were scheduled ahead of time for one hour time slots. Upon arrival, they were brought to the experiment area and given an informed consent form to sign. The experimenter briefly stated the long-term goal of the research, and told the participants that their task will be to program new skills on the PR2. The experimenter said that she will not give any instructions on how to program PR2, but that she will provide supplementary materials allowing the participants to figure it out on their own. Next, the experimenter handed the skill guide and went over the four skills by demonstrating them inside the robot's workspace. Depending on the condition, the instructional materials were handed to the participants and explained. In the *video* condition the video was made ready to play on a computer screen inside the experiment area. Participants were told to imagine that they just bought a PR2 knowing that you can program it, and it came out of the box with the given supplementary material. They were told that if they feel they are stuck, they can request tech support by calling the experimenter. Finally, the participant was equipped with the microphone and the experimenter left the experiment area.

The experimenter waited outside the experiment area and responded to tech support requests. If the participant completed all four task within 40 minutes past their arrival, they were told that they have time to program one additional skill of their choice. When done with programming participants were administered a browser-based survey.

5.3 Evaluation Metrics

The experiments were recorded from a video camera overseeing the experiment area. In these recordings, all utterances by the participant directed to the robot were transcribed by two independent coders and categorized as one of the commands or as a wrong command. In addition the recordings were used for measuring (i) success of four skills, (ii) time spent on programming each skill, and (iii) the number of tech support requests.

The exit survey involved five parts. The first part measured the cognitive load index using the NASA-TLX questionnaire, and asked two additional questions to assess the perceived success of each skill they programed, and their difficulty. The second part asked the participant to specify how much the supplementary materials and trial-and-error contributed to their understanding of the different commands. The third part involved questions about the commands and asked the participants to rate their agreement with the following statements about the user manual:

Overall usage	I used the user manual extensively.
Introduction	I carefully read the introductory paragraph of the user manual.
Commands	I carefully read the descriptions of the speech commands.

The fourth part (automatically skipped in the *baseline* condition) asked participants to rate their agreement with statements related to their usage of the tutorial or the video.

Completion	I completed the whole video/tutorial.
Usefulness	The video/tutorial was useful in giving me an understanding of the speech commands.
Redundancy	Parts of the video/tutorial were redundant.
Completeness	The video/tutorial made the user manual unnecessary.

The last part of the survey collected demographic information and information on habits related to technology usage and instructional materials.

6. RESULTS

Our study was completed by 30 participants (15 female, 15 male, gender-balanced across three conditions) in the age range of 19 to 70 (M=39.57, SD=15.53). In the following we present the main findings of the user study grouped in terms of observations relating to the impact of the instructional materials and the design choices of the PbD system used in the study.

6.1 Impact of instructional materials

We first analyze the impact of the instructional materials on the interaction with the robot. We make the following observations.

Video is most effective. Fig. 4(b) shows the number of participants who successfully programmed the four different skills in each condition. For each skill, more participants were successful in the *video* condition than in the other conditions. Participants in this condition are more successful particularly in programming the first two skills. The time spent programming the first skill was significantly reduced by the instructional video as compared to the baseline ($t(18)=3.42$, $p<.05$)(Fig. 4(a)). In addition, the overall time for programming all skills was smallest in the *video* condition (M=25.03 minutes, SD=5.04), although not significantly less than in the *baseline* (M=30.95, SD=7.65) or *tutorial* (M=29.63, SD=12.26) conditions. Thus, the video allowed people to be both more successful and efficient in programming the skills on the robot.

The time that participants spent on the tutorial versus the video prior to programming were about the same (Fig. 4(a)). This was on average longer than the duration of the video, because people either paused the video at times or they watched parts of or the whole video twice. On the contrary, participants tended not to complete the tutorial. Only two out of the 10 participants in this condition executed the tutorial until the last step, whereas all 10 participants in the *video* condition watched the whole video at least once. This was reflected in the survey question that asked participants to rate their agreement with *"I completed the whole tutorial/video."* The rating was significantly higher in the *video* condition (χ^2=-3.06, $p<.005$ in a Kruskal-Wallis test). This means that people got more information out of the video, even though they spent equal time on the tutorial.

The effectiveness of the video was also reflected on the number of tech support requests, which were significantly fewer than in the baseline ($t(18)=8.49$, $p<.01$). Only one participant in the *video* condition made a tech support request, as compared to eight in the *baseline* and four in the *tutorial* condition, where the average number of requests were 2.38 (SD=1.85) and 1.50 (SD=0.58) respectively. We note that the questions asked by participants during tech support did not provide them any information that was not in the user manual. By watching the whole video, participants were exposed to the available functionality even if they might not remember the exact commands or understand exactly how they work.

The usage of UNDO LAST COMMAND is a clear example of the increased awareness about available functionality due to the instructional video. This command allows the user to easily recover from speech recognition errors which were frequent in our experiment. We observed that participants in the *video* condition used this command more frequently (M=4.20, SD=3.79) than those in the *baseline* (M=1.80, SD=1.40) or *tutorial* (M=1.80, SD=2.10) conditions. Part of the reason for the ignorance about the undo command was that it was presented last in the user manual and it was practiced towards the end of the tutorial, which most participants did not get to. Another reason, we believe, was that there were other ways of recovering from errors, al-

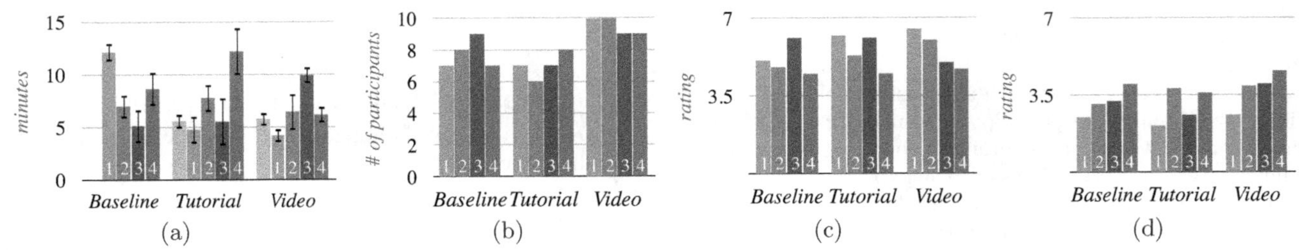

Figure 4: (a) Average time participants spent on the instructional materials and on programming each skill. (b) Number of participants who successfully programmed the four skills in each condition. Participants' average rating of the (c) success and (d) difficulty of the four skills they programmed in each condition.

though these were much less efficient than just undoing the error. For example, when participants accidentally deleted all the poses they had saved so far (a false positive for the CLEAR SKILL command) they would start from scratch, often showing signs of frustration. The participants' increased awareness about this functionally in the *video* condition may have contributed to their efficiency.

We also observed anecdotal examples illustrating how ignorance about the functionality leads to inefficiency. One participant made the arm stiff every time he wanted to save a pose—he gave three commands (HOLD R/L ARM – SAVE POSE – RELEASE R/L ARM) instead of one for each pose, and as a result progressed very slowly.

Tutorials can be problematic. We observed that tutorials were unlikely to be followed until the end (Fig. 5(c)). This could be partly because people felt it was unnecessary and wanted to directly move on to programming the actual skills rather than programming a practice skill (waving) as part of the tutorial. Participants in the *tutorial* condition agreed more strongly that the tutorial had redundant information (Fig. 5(c)), than the participants in the *video* condition did for the same statement regarding the video, although this difference was not significant.

In addition, speech recognition errors were more problematic in the *tutorial* condition than they were in other conditions. The tutorial has a certain progression that assumes errorless speech recognition. Participant are likely to continue following the step-by-step instructions as they appear in the tutorial, even though the robot might not be in the state that it needs to be at each step. They are also less likely to pay attention to the robot's response as they follow these instructions. In our experiment this led to undesirable consequences like participants trying to move the arm while it was stiff or saving poses before successfully creating a skill (which ended up not being saved). Participants who experienced these problems had worse performance than those who did not, resulting in a bi-modal distribution in the *tutorial* condition. This is reflected in the inconsistent progress and the large performance variance observed in this condition (Fig. 4(a)). Nonetheless, we observe some positive effects of the tutorial: in comparison to the *baseline* it significantly reduced the time spent programming the first skill ($t(18)=3.16$, $p<.05$) and had marginally fewer tech support interruptions ($t(18)=4.26$, $p=.054$).

Trial-and-error is essential. As mentioned earlier, programming the first skill took significantly longer in the *baseline* condition as compared to the experimental conditions. Participants in this condition learned and practiced the different commands while programming the first skill. We observe that the time they put into exploring the functionality while programming this simple skill helps them as they move on to more challenging skills. The time they spent programming the subsequent skills is less and less, despite the fact that the skills get more and more challenging (Fig. 4(a)). This points to the importance of trial-and-error in learning to program the robot.

Both the tutorial and the video made participants efficient in programming the first skill, however this effect was lost in more challenging skills. We believe that this was due to the simplicity of the example used in the video and the tutorial (a waving action that involves a gripper state change). This example provides sufficient information for programming the first skill (simple pick up and place) without needing to understand the commands in depth. However, as the skill to be programmed becomes more challenging, the information gained from the video/tutorial becomes insufficient so people spend more time on trial-and-error and referring to the user manual.

Participants in the *baseline* condition stated that 45% of their understanding of the commands came from trial-and-error on average, while the remaining 55% came from the user manual (Fig. 5(a)). In the experimental conditions, the additional instructional material was perceived to have a significant contribution to the participants' understanding (tutorial: 43.5%, video: 49.5%), both more than the other factors that participants rely on in the baseline. We see that the video is complemented more by trial-and-error, whereas the user manual remains more dominant when the primary source of information is the tutorial. The survey indicated consistently higher usage of the user manual by participants in the baseline condition (Fig. 5(b)), however the difference was significant only for the statement regarding the introductory paragraph of the manual ($\chi^2=6.38$, $p<.05$).

Uniform and consistent progress with video. The participants' rating of the difficulty of programming each skill was consistent with our intention—people generally felt that the later skills were more challenging in all conditions ($F(1,26)=14.15$, $p<.01$, Fig. 4(d)). Despite this perception, participants in the *baseline* condition spent most time on the easiest skill (Fig. 4(a)), were more successful in later skills (Fig. 4(b)), and rated the success of their later skills as higher (Fig. 4(c)). This pattern was inverted in the *video* condition, resulting in a more intuitive outcome—participants' perception of the skill difficulty was inversely correlated with their success and efficiency in programming the skill. In other words, participants made consistent and

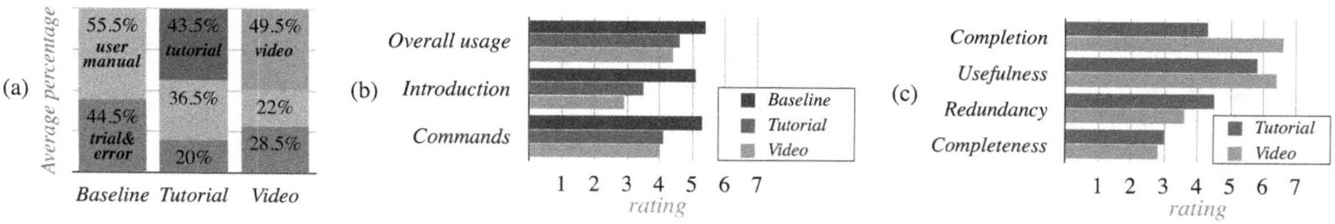

Figure 5: (a) The average contribution of the instructional materials and trial-and-error to the participants' understanding of the commands based on their self-assessment. Participants' self-reported usage of the (b) user manual in all three conditions and (c) tutorial or video in corresponding conditions.

uniform progress, learning more about the functionality as it was needed, as opposed to making most of the progress at the beginning. We believe that the slow progress at the beginning in the *baseline* may result in frustration that might be problematic in other contexts. In our experiment, this was manifested as an increased number of technical support requests.

6.2 System evaluation

The user study demonstrates the success of our system in enabling novice users to program new skills on a robot completely on their own. We saw that all participants in the *video* condition successfully programmed the first two skills and only one participant failed in the following two skills. Only one participant in this condition required technical support. Nine out of the 30 participants also had the opportunity to program a skill that they wanted—this included stacking bowls, high-five, assembling lego bricks, and putting a teddy bear to sleep. The system was also successful at capturing individual variations. Participants programmed various ways of folding a towel—grasping it from the middle versus the edge (Fig. 1), using the edge of the table to lay the towel versus using motion dynamics, *etcetera*.

The study also provided design feedback about different elements of the system interface, that are consistent with the literature and provide insights into how the system could be improved. Some observations relating to this point are given in the following[5]. Addressing some of these issues in the interface are important especially given our finding about the importance of trial-and-error in learning the functionality.

Appropriate feedback reduces learning load. We observed that speech responses by the robot to indicate error cases (*e.g.* "No skills after skill two", "Not enough poses in skill two") were helpful in letting participants know what to do next. For example out of the 14 participants who got the "No skills created yet" error, 10 responded with the command CREATE SKILL within the next ten seconds.

Inaccurate feedback can be problematic. Changes in the robot state in response to user commands may not be noticeable to novice users. For instance, in our experiment, participants did not initially know the difference between the released or holding arm stiffness. The speech response by the robot when this change happened was correct but not precise—it indicated the final state of the arms, without acknowledging whether the arm state had changed or not. It always responded to HOLD RIGHT ARM with "Right arm holding". This resulted in one participant to have an inaccurate understanding of the command. He assumed that the command told the robot to hold a certain pose, and he programed the first skill by forcefully pushing the arm, until he discovered the RELEASE R/L ARM command.

Distinctness of the lexicon is important. The most common invalid command error made by participants was to say "Release right/left hand" with the intent of opening the gripper. This mistake was made by 30 out of the 36 participants at least once. We believe that this was caused by the poor choice of the verb *release* for changing the arm stiffness. Opening the gripper while it has an object results in *releasing* the object. As a result, when participants wanted the robot to drop what it had in its gripper, they were compelled to say *release* instead of *open*.

Inconsistent feedback can be problematic. The second most common error among invalid commands was to use the name of the skill as part of the command; *e.g.* "Execute skill two", "Clear skill two." We believe this was due to the robot's use of the skill names in its feedback, *e.g.* "Starting execution of skill two", "Switched to skill two." The naming of the skill was essential in allowing the user to browse the skill through dialog, however it set the false expectation that the robot would understand name references to skills. This points to the importance of consistency in the input and output lexicon for the dialog.

7. LESSONS LEARNED

In this section we briefly reiterate the findings and observations from our user study in the form of design recommendations and provide examples of how this was applied to the revised design of the system after this user study.

1. **Show a video of the interaction.** Human-robot interactions, especially ones involving physical interactions, may be unique and completely novel to end-users. Showing a video of the intended interaction can efficiently convey the available functionalities and communicate details of the interaction that might not be evident to novices. For instance, in our study, one of the technical support requests in the *baseline* condition was to ask whether the participant was allowed to touch the robot; a video would have quickly mitigated this issue.

2. **User manuals should complement videos.** People are unlikely to read a user manual cover to cover. However videos are not well indexed for searching particular information on demand. Thus, a user manual can complement a video by allowing the user to easily browse information to find details about a functionality that they would have been exposed to through the video.

3. **Do tutorials in a sandbox.** When the interaction has high uncertainty, step-by-step tutorials should be avoided. The uncertainty can be reduced by making the

[5]Refer to video for examples, at `http://www.youtube.com/watch?v=NXZf_JjMAkQ`

robot aware of the tutorial step, or even letting the robot administer the tutorial. Another approach is to have an early step in the tutorial to expose the user to the uncertainty since this is something they eventually learn to deal with through trial-and-error.

4. **Give precise feedback.** The robot should not only indicate state changes, but also acknowledge the lack of state changes in response to commands. As suggested earlier, in our revised system the robot says "Right arm already holding" instead of "Right arm holding" in response to HOLD RIGHT ARM when the command has no effect.

5. **Handle errors with hints.** In response to commands that have no effect in the current state, it is useful to guide users towards states where the command would have an effect. In our system, the response "No skills created yet" was successful in getting participants to create a skill first.

6. **Choose vocabulary carefully.** Commands should not only capture the functionality and be intuitive individually, but also they should be distinct from one another. Commands with potential semantic overlap are likely to be confused since they would all be in short-term memory during the interaction. In the revised command set we have the verb RELAX for changing the arm stiffness, as RELEASE was often used incorrectly to try to open the gripper.

8. CONCLUSION

We present a Programming by Demonstration (PbD) system with a spoken dialog interface and investigate the use of instructional materials to support its learnability. The contributions of this paper are two-fold. We give empirical results regarding the impact of different instructional materials on learning how to program a robot and we present observations and recommendations regarding dialog interface design. Our findings have implications not only for PbD interactions, but also for any end-users interactions with complex robotic functionality. Second, we present a fully autonomous and robust PbD system that captures realistic manipulation tasks and has an intuitive user interface. Our study participants were able to use this system to program complex skills like folding a towel, without any instruction from an experimenter. The results of this experiment are informing the re-design of our PbD system.

9. REFERENCES

[1] S. Ainsworth. Deft: A conceptual framework for considering learning with multiple representations. *Learning and Instruction*, 16(3):183–198, 2006.

[2] B. Akgun, M. Cakmak, K. Jiang, and A. Thomaz. Keyframe-based learning from demonstration. *Journal of Social Robotics, Special issue on LfD*, 4(4), 2012.

[3] A. Bandura. *Social Learning Theory.* General Learning Corporation, 1971.

[4] A. Billard, S. Calinon, R. Dillmann, and S. Schaal. Robot programming by demonstration. In B. Siciliano and O. Khatib, editors, *Handbook of Robotics.* Springer, 2007.

[5] M. Cakmak and A. L. Thomaz. Designing robot learners that ask good questions. In *Proc. of the Intl. Conf. on Human-Robot Interaction (HRI)*, 2012.

[6] L. Dybkjær and N. O. Bernsen. Usability issues in spoken dialogue systems. *Natural Language Engineering*, 6(3&4):243–271, 2000.

[7] K. Fischer. How people talk with robots: Designing dialog to reduce user uncertainty. *AI Magazine*, 32(4):31–38, 2011.

[8] M. E. Foster, M. Giuliani, A. Isard, C. Matheson, J. Oberlander, and A. Knoll. Evaluating description and reference strategies in a cooperative human-robot dialogue system. In *IJCAI*, pages 1818–1823, 2009.

[9] J. Gustafson, A. Larsson, R. Carlson, and K. Hellman. How do system questions influence lexical choices in user answers? In *EUROSPEECH*, 1997.

[10] C. A. Kamm, D. J. Litman, and M. A. Walker. From novice to expert: the effect of tutorials on user expertise with spoken dialogue systems. In *ICSLP*, 1998.

[11] D. E. Kieras and S. Bovair. The role of a mental model in learning to operate a device. *Cognitive science*, 8(3):255–273, 1984.

[12] N. Koenig, L. Takayama, and M. Matarić. Communication and knowledge sharing in human–robot interaction and learning from demonstration. *Neural Networks*, 23(8), 2010.

[13] H. Nguyen, M. Ciocarlie, and K. Hsiao. Ros commander (rosco): Behavior creation for home robots. In *IEEE Intl. Conference on Robotics and Automation*, 2013.

[14] S. Niekum, S. Osentoski, S. Chitta, B. Marthi, and A. Barto. Incremental semantically grounded learning from demonstration. In *Robotics: Science and Systems*, 2013.

[15] N. Otero, A. Alissandrakis, K. Dautenhahn, C. Nehaniv, D. Syrdal, and K. Koay. Human to robot demonstrations of routine home tasks: Exploring the role of the robot's feedback. In *Proc. of the Intl. Conf. on Human-Robot Interaction (HRI)*, 2008.

[16] J. Pearson, J. Hu, H. P. Branigan, M. J. Pickering, and C. I. Nass. Adaptive language behavior in hci: how expectations and beliefs about a system affect users' word choice. In *Proc. of the SIGCHI conference on Human Factors in computing systems*, 2006.

[17] R. C. Schank, T. R. Berman, and K. A. Macpherson. Learning by doing. In C. M. Reigeluth, editor, *Instructional-Design Theories and Models.* LEA, 1999.

[18] J. Schulman, A. Gupta, S. Venkatesan, M. Tayson-Frederick, and P. Abbeel. A case study of trajectory transfer through non-rigid registration for a simplified suturing scenario. In *IEEE/RSJ Intl. Conf. on Intelligent Robots and Systems (IROS)*, 2013.

[19] H. Suay, R. Toris, and S. Chernova. A practical comparison of three robot learning from demonstration algorithms. *Intl. Journal of Social Robotics, special issue on LfD*, 4(4), 2012.

[20] J. J. Van Merriënboer, P. A. Kirschner, and L. Kester. Taking the load off a learner's mind: Instructional design for complex learning. *Educational psychologist*, 38(1):5–13, 2003.

[21] A. Weiss, J. Igelsboeck, S. Calinon, A. Billard, and M. Tscheligi. Teaching a humanoid: A user study on learning by demonstration with hoap-3. In *IEEE RO-MAN*, pages 147–152, 2009.

Which Robot Behavior Can Motivate Children to Tidy up Their Toys? Design and Evaluation of “Ranger”

Julia Fink
Séverin Lemaignan
Pierre Dillenbourg
Computer-Human Interaction in Learning and Instruction Laboratory (CHILI)
Ecole Polytechnique Fédérale de Lausanne (EPFL)
CH-1015 Lausanne, Switzerland
firstname.lastname@epfl.ch

Philippe Rétornaz
Florian Vaussard
Alain Berthoud
Francesco Mondada
Robotic Systems Laboratory (LSRO)
Ecole Polytechnique Fédérale de Lausanne (EPFL)
CH-1015 Lausanne, Switzerland
firstname.lastname@epfl.ch

Florian Wille
Karmen Franinović
Interaction Design (IAD)
Zürcher Hochschule der Künste (ZHdK)
CH-8005 Zürich, Switzerland
firstname.lastname@zhdk.ch

ABSTRACT

We present the design approach and evaluation of our prototype called “Ranger”. Ranger is a robotic toy box that aims to motivate young children to tidy up their room. We evaluated Ranger in 14 families with 31 children (2-10 years) using the Wizard-of-Oz technique. This case study explores two different robot behaviors (proactive vs. reactive) and their impact on children's interaction with the robot and the tidying behavior. The analysis of the video recorded scenarios shows that the proactive robot tended to encourage more playful and explorative behavior in children, whereas the reactive robot triggered more tidying behavior. Our findings hold implications for the design of interactive robots for children, and may also serve as an example of evaluating an early version of a prototype in a real-world setting.

Figure 1: The robotic box “Ranger” aims to motivate children to tidy up their toys on the floor

Categories and Subject Descriptors

H.4 [**Information Systems Applications**]: Miscellaneous; I.2.9 [**Artificial Intelligence**]: Robotics—*Commercial robots and applications*

Keywords

children; domestic robots; field study; human-robot interaction; interaction design; wizard-of-oz experiment

1. THE “ROBJECTS” APPROACH

Designing domestic robots that can enhance daily lives of humans has been a long standing challenge in robotics and still it is not really clear what robots should and could do in the home [9]. User-centered research advocates that domestic robots need to be useful, easy to use, appealing, affordable, energy saving, and compatible with the home environment. Likewise, to ensure long-term adoption, a robot needs to meet user needs and prove its practicality within the “ecosystem” of a home. It is challenging to fulfill all criteria at once. Instead of trying to build novel multi-purpose robots, our approach is to design robotic objects, which we call *“RObjects”*. They integrate robotic functionalities into objects that are already part of our daily lives, and by this are expected to enhance the acceptance of robotic devices in homes. The overall aim of RObjects is to support users in specific daily routines in the domestic environment [11], and create meaningful human-robot interaction (HRI).

In our current project, we focus on robots for daily life in families with children. In a previous study [2], we saw that children generally respond very positively to robots and enjoy interacting with them, which has also been described by others [6, 7, 10, 13]. But where and how could a robot be an added value in a family home? In the initial phase of this project, we explored possible applications for RObjects in homes and identified that tidying up the children's toys is a challenge in a lot of families. We decided to create a RObject out of a toy box in which children would enjoy putting their toys back after playing (Fig. 1). We envisioned that, instead

HRI'14, March 3–6, 2014, Bielefeld, Germany.

ACM 978-1-4503-2658-2/14/03 ...$15.00.
http://dx.doi.org/10.1145/2559636.2559659.

of having a robot carrying out the tidying task for them, it could rather serve as an educative tool and motivate / help children to tidy up themselves. To bring children to tidy up would already be a big help in a lot of families, and could have a positive effect on the family ecosystem.

2. THE ROBOTIC TOY BOX "RANGER"

We call our prototype "Ranger". In French, the verb *"ranger"* means "to tidy up / sort out things" which suits the application of our robotic toy box.

2.1 Design Rationale and Related Work

A robot with an application in a family home must be designed for the entire family [9]. Even if Ranger's main users will be young children, we also need to consider parents, as both might perceive robots differently [14, 15]. Consequently, the robot's design, functionality and interaction should not only be effective and enjoyable for young children but also acceptable for parents. There were several issues to solve, both from a technical and human social side.

One fundamental question was what features Ranger would need to have and whether it should search and load toys itself? On one hand, in a home organization task (such as tidying), a robot is expected to automate the task to disburden humans. On the other hand, it should at the same time still allow people to feel like they have the control [9]. For this, the robot could rely on human-participation. In our tidying scenario the child should therefore remain the most active player, and consequently we did not equip the box with arms or hands that could grasp and load objects.

Another aspect was how Ranger should initiate an interaction and convey its intention to serve as a storage box for toys. To solve this, we can draw on a similar development, the "Child-Dependent Sociable Trash Box (STB)" [16]. This robot, which aims to engage children to collect trash and put it into it, was tested with 108 children (4-11 years old). The authors found three factors that were more effective for interaction and in conveying the STB's intention toward collecting trash: (1) the STB's ability to move (compared to an immobile trash box); (2) the boxes moving toward the trash instead of moving toward the children; and (3) a small group of STB's interacting with the children (compared to one single box). Regarding (3), we could not develop more than one prototype at this time, as we first wanted to find out how well our approach works in a real-world setting. Regarding (1), we equipped Ranger with two motorized wheels to make it mobile, so it could help transferring toys from one place to the other. Regarding (2), we thought about letting the box autonomously move toward a toy, in order to convey to the child to put the toy inside. The trade off of such an autonomous behavior is increasing complexity of the development and cost of the robot. Ranger would need vision and a larger on-board computational power, as well as obstacle avoidance strategies. Is it really necessary to have the robot being *proactive* in searching for and moving toward a toy itself? Could not just the child do this? These considerations led us to our main research question: *How does the robot's "pro-activeness" impact the interaction with the child and the motivation to tidy up?* To investigate this aspect in our case study, we modeled two different robot behaviors: a *proactive* robot that moves toward a toy and a *reactive* robot that responds to actions but more or less remains at one spot in the room.

Further, how should Ranger give feedback when the children put a toy? A similar but immobile toy storage box, called "Bubu Monstry" [8], which aims to encourage children (2-4 years) to return their toys back to it, makes chewing and eating sounds as soon as a toy is put. When all toys are put back, Bubu vibrates and burps. We decided to rather use sound and light cues to give positive feedback. In a study with Roomba [2], we saw that children liked the limited sound cues of the robot. We used interaction design methods to define a set of feedback cues for Ranger.

To let the robot display basic facial expression, movable eyes and eyebrows were added (Fig. 1). The eyes do not only give the robot a front but also a cartoon-like "fac" which can have a positive effect on the interaction [1]. We are aware that the presence of eyes on Ranger might also increase people's expectations. For this reason we avoided a more human-like face.

Finally, for this first design-evaluation iteration, we did not aim at developing a fully autonomous prototype but decided to use a human *"Wizard"* who would operate the robot from the background, following a Wizard of Oz method (Sec. 3.1).

2.2 Pro- and Reactive Systems

One concrete question we explored in this case study is whether a proactive robot triggers more and different kinds of interactions with children than a reactive robot (and in turn is more effective in the given task). The aspect of whether the system or the user takes the initiative is a relevant topic in the design of interactive systems. With being proactive we understand a system that tries to initiate an interaction (system driven) while in a reactive system, the user would take the initiative (user driven). The aspect of initiative- or turn-taking, dialogue, and how to balance the control between user and system is critical and a well studied topic in Human-Computer Interaction, Learning Technologies, Persuasive Technologies, and Interface Design. Ju and Leifer suggest that the degree of proactivity in a system and the required attentional demand from the user side should be adapted to the user's capabilities and need of control, to the situation, and to securtiy factors [5]. One way to balance the interaction in HCI is the implementation of so-called mixed-initiative. In HRI there is yet no common trend how to handle initiative taking, and most research on this deals with how to solve the issue from a technical point of view. Regarding our tidying scenario, the challenge is to find a good balance of the robot proactively trying to trigger interaction while still not pushing the children too much. In human-robot collaboration, it seems that robotic systems that use shared / collaborative control, similar to user-adapted autonomy, can positively impact the performance and the robot's usability [3]. However, there is no clear answer on how active or passive a robot should behave and certainly more research needs to be carried out that investigates the level of activeness in a robot which is beneficial to the human user and effective for the given task.

2.3 The First Prototype of Ranger

The first prototype of Ranger (Fig. 1) is a wheeled box (27 x 37 x 37 cm) with partial wooden surface. Being remote controlled, it can move around a flat surface, move its eyes and eyebrows, display colors (LEDs) and light patterns, and produce a limited set of sounds (integrated speakers).

Figure 2: Study setup in one of the children's rooms; left: camera and embedded computer on a tripod are in one corner of the room; center: before participants entered the room, Ranger was next to the toys on the floor; right: the room after children had tidied up with Ranger and the study was over

During the field study in the children's rooms, Ranger was remote controlled by a human *"Wizard"* in a different room, using a video game controller connected to a laptop computer. The control program sent commands over Bluetooth to the robot's micro-controller. An external computer including a remote camera was placed in the children's room (Fig. 2), and connected to the laptop computer through Ethernet, so that the Wizard could observe the scenario. Fortunately, all the children's rooms were rather small, so that the robot was never out of the camera view and was thus always visible to the Wizard, who beforehand placed and adjusted the camera in the best possible way.

The Wizard followed a pre-defined script to model Ranger's feedback. These low-level robot behaviors were mostly pre-coded, and the Wizard pressed on a specific button of the remote control to execute them. This ensured that Ranger always reacted the same way to the same inputs:

- *Object put in box:* "rewarding" sound and red light pattern, occasionally wiggle-like move in parallel
- *Several objects after each other put in box:* "rewarding" sound, rainbow light pattern, box turns around itself
- *Object removed from box:* "emptying" sound and green light pattern
- *Box is touched or petted:* "blush" with pink light around the area of the "cheeks"
- *Box is kicked or mistreated:* "disturbance" sound and box moves backward
- *Box "finds" a toy on the floor* (only in *proactive* behavior): eyes rotate toward the toy, yellow pulsating light pattern, then after some seconds wiggle-like move, then back-and-forth move

The activity of removing a toy from the box should not be considered as "anti-tidying" because children would probably remove the toys from the box once it was full in order to store them in the drawer or shelf. However, we cannot say if the box was full based on the number of toys because of the different sizes of the objects.

3. METHOD AND PROCEDURE

3.1 Wizard of Oz Approach

We wanted to evaluate an early version of our robot prototype and study human-robot interaction in a realistic setting before developing a fully autonomous robot. To do so, Weiss *et al.* [12] propose the Wizard of Oz approach, in which the robot is not fully autonomous but controlled by a human operator who hides in the background.

Parents (but not children) were told beforehand that the robot was remote controlled. As we are mainly studying children's interaction with the robot, we do not feel that this biased the study. Rather, parents felt assured to have transparency about the functioning of the robot and knew it was safe. During the study, very few children noticed the tripod with the embedded computer and the camera on top of it (Fig. 2). As this "thing" did not resemble a usual camera, children did not notice that they were video-taped. Only two children asked what the "thing" was for and the experimenter replied that Ranger would need this "thing" to work properly. In general, it was the robot and not the tripod with camera that got children's attention, so we do not have the impression that the presence of the camera influenced children's behavior.

3.2 Study Design

We wanted to investigate not only how children use and interact with the robot in general but also whether and how variances in the robot's behavior impact the interaction, and how effective the tidying task was completed. Would a robot that proactively tries to trigger an interaction better motivate children to tidy up their toys, in comparison to a robot that shows rather passive, reactive behavior? To study these aspects, we configured two different robot behaviors:

- *Proactive:* Ranger tries to initiate interaction by driving around the room, searching for toys on the floor. When in front of a toy, it moves its eyes toward it and pulsates in yellow light. After about 5 seconds, if the child does not put the toy inside, Ranger also shows wiggle-like moves, and after 5 more seconds of no toy put inside, it moves a bit back-and-forth, with yellow pulsating light. By this behavior, Ranger proactively tries to trigger the action of putting a toy.

- *Reactive:* Ranger remains at one spot in the room (somewhere close to the toys on the floor) and reacts to the children's actions. The box hardly moves, does neither search for toys itself nor move toward children, but waits until a toy is put, and reacts to it as described above. By this, Ranger only shows a reactive behavior and does not try to initiate an interaction.

In one half of the families Ranger was operated in the *proactive* mode and in the other half in the *reactive* mode. This between-group design allows us to explore how the robot's different level of "activity" impacts the interaction and effectiveness of tidying up. In line with previous findings [16], we imagined that a more active system would trigger more interactions and better encourage children to tidy their toys. We formulated the following research hypothesis:

The proactive robot behavior will be (1) more engaging for children and (2) better motivate them to tidy up their toys (to put and remove objects).

As our analysis includes counting how many toys children put into and remove from the robotic box, we assumed a fairly comparable accumulated amount of toys among the two groups of each 7 families.

Participants

Besides investigating the impact of the robot's activity on task and interaction, we explored children's reaction to the robot and assessed parent's feedback to the design and acceptance of the robot. We tested Ranger in 14 families (1-4 children per family; in total 31 children, 17 parents). Between the two case study groups we balanced the number of children, age, and gender as much as possible. There were 16 boys and 15 girls from 2-10 years ($M = 5.3, SD = 1.98$). We are aware that the large age range implies different developmental stages in children. For this first evaluation of the robot we needed this diversity to explore at which age the robot's features are most effective. However, the large age range also makes it difficult to analyze and interpret data. Therefore we excluded age as a factor in statistical analysis but investigated age differences qualitatively.

Further, we had 16 parents (thereof 12 mothers, 4 fathers, mean age 40.5 years) with whom we conducted post-interviews (together with the children), and who filled in a short questionnaire to evaluate how they experienced and perceived the robot. Through this, we wanted to capture people's first impression of Ranger. Of course, a long-term study is required to study how far people's perception of the robot evolves over time. Still this spontaneous feedback is valuable and can help us to refine the design of this first prototype. The present family members were also asked to name specific aspects they liked and disliked about tidying up, about the robot, and how Ranger could be improved.

3.3 Course of the Study

Two researchers visited each family at their home for about one hour in total:

- *Introduction (~5 min):* Both researchers and the available family members introduced each other in the living room / kitchen. Parents were asked to sign a consent form (agreement that scenario was video-recorded, anonymized, and used for scientific purpose).
- *Pre-interview and preparation of setup (~15 min):* One researcher conducted a short interview with the family about the routine and challenges of tidying up, while the other researcher set up the robot and video recording in the children's room, as well as a remote control station in a different room.
- *Interaction study (max. 30 min):* The family went to the children's room to tidy up the toys with Ranger. No instructions were given on how to use the robot, the only goal was to tidy up the room. Children and parents were free to choose how to interact with Ranger and use it. When more or less all toys on the floor were tidied, the scenario was finished and participants left the room. Otherwise, the scenario was stopped after a maximum of 30 minutes. (Our focus was short-term interaction.)
- *Post-interview and evaluation (~5 min):* Another short interview and evaluation of the interaction and experience with Ranger concluded the visit. Parents evaluated various aspects of the robot and their experience on rating scales, and gave feedback on the design of the robot. The other researcher dismounted the setup.

To thank them for their participation, each child received a little gift at the end of the study before the researchers left the family's place.

3.4 Measurements, Coding and Data Analysis

All tidying scenarios with the robot were video-recorded and interactions analyzed by coding the videos according to a scheme that we developed. In contrast to how Kahn *et al.* [6] segmented behavior, we coded each behavior as one action as long as it continued. If several actions occurred several times within one minute, we coded several actions. Each of the children's actions towards the robot was categorized as one of the following: *exploration* (observing Ranger, trying to find out how it works), *misusage* (hitting or kicking it, poking it in the eye, trying to climb on it), *putting toy*, *removing toy*, using a *gesture* toward Ranger, *touching* it or *playing* with it (e.g. showing a toy, petting). In order to assess the quality of our coding scheme and to measure the reliability of our data, a second coder carried out a second coding pass on one of the 14 videos. We extracted and organized both coders' annotations in a spreadsheet and analyzed agreement on action-category as well as starting-time of the annotation. For this subset a Cohen's Kappa value of $\kappa = 0.74$ was obtained, which indicates a substantial agreement between the two coders. Children's verbal statements were not coded but analyzed qualitatively.

Interviews were audio-recorded for qualitative analysis. Adult participants rated their impression of Ranger in an 11-items questionnaire (Table 1). Most statements are adapted from Heerink *et al.*'s proposed questionnaire to measure the acceptance of assistive social robots [4]. We measured the following constructs: perceived ease of use (PEOU), perceived usefulness (PU), anxiety (ANX), attitude (ATT), intention to use (ITU), perceived enjoyment (PENJ), perceived sociability (PS), social presence (SP), and people's overall impression of the robot. To also get feedback on concrete aspects of the design of Ranger, both children and parents were asked to name 3 aspects they liked and disliked most about the robot, and to make suggestions for improving the robot.

Table 1: **Questionnaire statements to evaluate Ranger (adapted from [4]), participants rated agreement on 5-point scale (1=agree, 5=disagree), mean M and standard deviation SD for each group, n=16 (8 per group)**

	construct	statement	"proactive" M (SD)	"reactive" M (SD)
1.	PEOU	I think Ranger is easy to use.	1.88 (0.83)	**1.00** (0.00)
2.	PU	Ranger is useful.	1.63 (1.06)	**1.50** (1.07)
3.	PU	It would be convenient for me to have the robot.	**1.75** (1.04)	2.00 (1.20)
4.	ANX	I would be afraid to make mistakes with Ranger or to break something.	4.50 (1.07)	**4.29** (1.11)
5.	ATT	I think it's a good idea to use Ranger.	**1.25** (0.46)	1.75 (1.16)
6.	ITU	I think I would use Ranger during the next few days.	**1.25** (0.71)	1.88 (1.13)
7.	PENJ	I think Ranger is boring.	4.88 (0.35)	**4.50** (1.07)
8.	PENJ	I enjoy when Ranger is responding to me.	1.13 (0.35)	**1.00** (0.00)
9.	PS	I think Ranger is nice and pleasant to interact with.	1.50 (1.07)	**1.38** (0.52)
10.	SP	I can imagine Ranger to be a living creature.	2.75 (1.49)	2.75 (1.49)
11.	other	My overall impression of Ranger is: (1 = very good, 5 = very bad)	1.63 (0.74)	**1.38** (0.52)

4. RESULTS

By coding the 14 videos with a total length of about 3 hours, 1740 distinct actions were obtained. The scenario duration varied between 5-27 min ($M = 704\ s, SD = 420\ s$) with no significant difference between the two groups (*proactive* $M = 778\ s$, $SD = 425\ s$; *reactive* $M = 625\ s$, $SD = 415\ s$); ($t(29) = -1.01, p = .32$; independent samples t-test). Thus, overall children did not tidy up quicker in one of the two groups.

4.1 Children's Interaction with the Robot

How Children Approach and Make Sense of Ranger

Children naturally understood how to use Ranger, regardless whether it tried to initiate an interaction itself (*proactive*) or not (*reactive*). They started putting toys into the box on average after 2:22 min ($SD = 245\ s$), with no significant difference with robot behavior ($t(13.4) = -1.5, p = .16$; independent samples t-test, unequal variances). There was the exceptional case of a 4 years old girl who was very shy and hesitated putting something into the robotic box for 27 min. Asked why, she explained that none of her toys would belong into this box but only to a specific place on the shelf.

It seemed that *initially* it was more obvious for the children to put a toy in the proactive behaving robot, as it was actively moving toward the toys. Before putting a toy, most children first shortly explored the robot by looking inside or underneath it, or they touched it to investigate the reaction.

There was a great enthusiasm for the box, and only the youngest children (up to 2 years) were afraid when the robot started to move or wiggle. We observed this reaction of very young children also in our previous work with vacuum-cleaning robots [2]. It seemed that the children up to 2 years could not immediately make sense of the robot. However, after watching how the older brother or sister interacted with the robot, they also approached it, and eventually also put a toy. In general, there were different strategies of making sense of Ranger, as the *proactive* robot enabled more varied interaction and allowed transportation of the toys, for instance. The proactively moving robot helped children in starting and structuring the process of tidying up, which seems to be a major difficulty (*"Where and how do you start sorting out things when there is a huge mess?"*).

In the following, we present the interaction dynamics for one case from each robot behavior. The two examples are not representative for the respective group but were chosen as they are fairly comparable (number / gender of kids; duration of scenario).

Family 1 (boy B (5), girl G (3), *proactive robot*
Ranger moves in front of toys on the floor, both children are attracted and explore the box; B touches Ranger's eyes, puts a toy (after 1 min); B and G are very fascinated by the robot's feedback and start putting a lot of toys in a series (22 toys in 3 min); G watches; there is another toy left on the floor, Ranger moves toward it; this proactive robot behavior motivates B to play a game: B removes a toy from the box and places it somewhere on the floor to make Ranger go there; each time, B jumps happily when Ranger finds the toy on the floor; B eventually puts a toy from box in drawer but still distributes toys on the floor to make the robot go there; [comment: this is playful but not tidying up]; total 50 toys put/removed in 13 min

Family 2 (boy B (8), girl G (3), *reactive robot*
B and G look at Ranger; B waves in front of the robot which doesn't react; B puts a toy (after 1 min,); both kids are fascinated by Ranger's feedback and put a lot of toys (57 toys in 5 min); the box is reasonably full and B starts removing them; also G removes toys and puts them back on the floor; B actually tidies up the toys that G puts on the floor; G continues removing (56 toys in 5 min) and B tidies up the things into drawers and other boxes; B explores the robot; B and G continue until the box is fairly empty again; [comment: kids were focused on tidying but were disappointed that the box didn't move around]; total 122 toys put / removed in 11 min item

Figure 3: Children interacting with Ranger during the field study: The robot's eyes received remarkable attention. Left: first moments of a family exploring together the robot; center: two boys putting toys into Ranger, which displays red lights; right: a girl showing a toy to the robot

How Children Explore and Interact with Ranger

Concerning the total duration of all coded actions, almost half of the time (47 %) children explored the box. Though the differences were not significant, the *proactive* robot was explored almost twice as much as the *reactive* robot. One of the most prevalent interactions was the exploration of Ranger's eyes. Several children touched the robot's eyes or "showed" toys to Ranger before putting it (see Fig. 3). Others waved their hand in front of the robot's face, to find out how it would react and whether the robot would be able to see. With the *proactive* robot, children were fascinated by seeing the box moving around their room and some invented games to let it drive around (e.g. putting a toy on the floor, so that the robot would "search" for it). It seems that children perceived the proactive robot as more "companion-like" and probably this engaged some children in socializing with it. Though we have no real evidence for how "social" children perceived the robot, two boys waved at Ranger and said "bye-bye" when they were leaving the room after the scenario.

We also qualitatively investigated gender and age differences in how children interacted with the robot. It seems that younger children (3-6 years) benefit most from using Ranger. They were more fascinated by the audio and light cues than older children (7-10 years). Children less than 3 years old did not really use the box for tidying but rather watched it or held on it to practice walking around. There were interesting qualitative gender differences. Boys more often mistreated and gestured toward Ranger than girls, who slightly more often petted the robot. For instance, several boys wanted to direct the box around using pointing gestures and verbal comments, such as *"go over there!"* or *"come here"*. Nevertheless, each child has her/his own character and we cannot generalize these findings. However, again, we made similar observations in our previous work with children interacting with vacuum-cleaning robots.

4.2 Tidying up the Toys with Ranger

Concerning the average number of toys put into / removed from the proactive and reactive robot (Fig. 4), there was in general more activity within the first couple of minutes. This could be related to the *novelty effect*. On average children put / removed more toys in the *reactive* robot; even toward the end. An explanation for the rather low activity of putting / removing toys in the *proactive* robot is that children were more playful with the moving robot and seemed less interested in tidying.

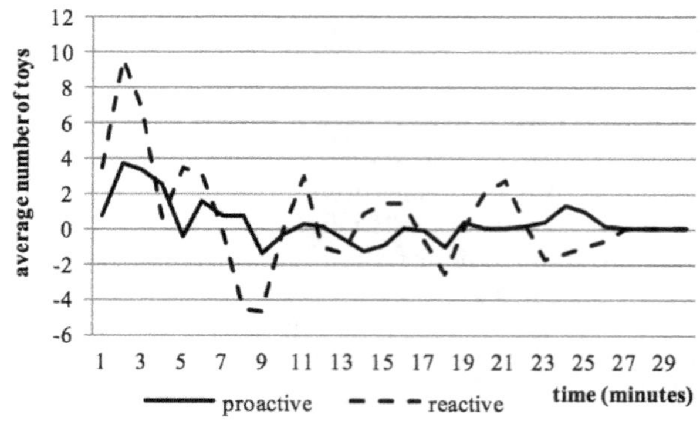

Figure 4: Average number of toys put into and removed from the robotic box per minute; more fluctuations with the reactive robot; in both cases the activities become less over time

Regarding the total number of occurrences of the coded actions, 48 % were "put" and "remove" actions. This generally supports our approach that Ranger can be used to motivate children to tidy up their toys, at least in short term.

Contrary to part (2) of our research hypothesis, data suggests that it was the reactive and not the proactive robot behavior that better motivated children to tidy up: Marginally significantly more toys were put and removed in the *reactive* compared to the *proactive* robot (compared means using ANOVA) (see Table 2). The respective Cohen's d-values indicate moderate effect sizes. Apart from putting or removing toys, all the other actions that were not directly related to tidying up (explore, misuse, touch / play, gestures) were carried out more often with the proactive robot. These differences were not significant, though for "misuse" and "gesture to robot" moderate effect sizes were found. Overall, this result is in line with part (1) of our research hypothesis: The proactive robot seems to be more engaging for children.

More generally, our data suggests that both a proactive and a reactive robot behavior can trigger interactions, however different kinds of interactions. Interestingly, it seems that the *reactive* robot was more effective in enhancing tidying behavior, whereas the *proactive* robot motivated children far more to explore it, misuse it, touch and play with it, and

Table 2: Average number of actions per child carried out with the proactive (n=16) and reactive (n=15) robot; task-related actions (put/remove toy) are carried out more often with the reactive robot, while playful actions (explore, misuse, touch and play, gesture to robot) are more often carried out with the proactive robot; statistical analysis in bottom part; data obtained by coding children's actions from the video recordings

robot behavior	put toy M (SD)	remove toy M (SD)	explore robot M (SD)	misuse robot M (SD)	touch and play M (SD)	gesture to robot M (SD)
"proactive"	9.81 (10.13)	4.94 (6.12)	**18.38** (15.18)	**4.50** (8.08)	**9.81** (11.19)	**2.81** (4.10)
"reactive"	**24.80** (27.41)	**16.13** (23.18)	12.80 (6.33)	0.80 (1.15)	6.80 (5.77)	1.07 (1.28)
F(1,29)	4.18	3.48	1.74	3.09	.869	2.49
p-value	**.05**	.072	.2	.09	.36	.126
Cohen's *d*	**.73**	**.66**	.48	**.64**	.34	.57

use gestures toward it (Table 2). We interpret that a *proactive* system is more fun for children but might distract from the main task (here: tidying). For this, a *reactive* systems seems to be more efficient.

4.3 Evaluation: Acceptance and Design

In the subsequent interview, both parents and children expressed that they liked Ranger and that they enjoyed interacting with it. Parents appreciated that the robot engaged the children in a positive and meaningful way; they liked our general idea of making a RObject out of a toy box, such that it would make tidying up a playful activity.

Overall, parent's ratings (see Table 1) show that Ranger is perceived as very acceptable: there is a general agreement that Ranger is easy to use, useful, and that it would be convenient to have the robot. Parents could also imagine using the robot during the next few days, and they would not be afraid of making mistakes with it or breaking something. The interaction was evaluated as enjoyable, and not boring. Interestingly, participants were undecided about whether Ranger could be considered as a living creature.[1] These ratings did not differ significantly between the two groups (independent-samples t-test). Only for "perceived ease of use", a significant difference was found ($t(7) = 2.97, p = .021$, unequal variances, due to the fact that all participants provided the very same rating (1.0) for the reactive robot) (see Table 1). Surprisingly, participants rated the *reactive* robot as slightly easier to use than the *proactive* one. However, given the limited number of participants who filled in the questionnaire (n=16, 8 in each group), these are not strong results.

There were very few negative remarks. With the *reactive* robot, participants disliked that the robot was hardly moving. One father also criticized that our prototype was very limited because *"it doesn't do things on its own"*. He admitted that he had much higher expectations of "a robot". Contrary, what participants liked most about Ranger were its light and sound cues, the moving eyes, and its simple design (the fact that it was *"just a wooden box"*). This supports our general approach of RObjects. To improve Ranger, participants suggested to include more sounds, and also use verbal statements. Further, more than one box would be useful to sort toys better.

During the conversation, children attributed emotional states to the robot, describing it would be "happy" when they put a toy and "not happy" when it was empty. This shows that yet the limited audio and visual cues were appropriate and perceived as being emotional. It suggests that children viewed the robot as a kind of social agent with mental states. However, the attributions could also be due to a reflection of the child's own feelings and experience.

5. DISCUSSION AND CONCLUSION

We presented the design and evaluation of our robotic toy box prototype "Ranger" that aims to motivate children to tidy up their toys.

Our study is limited by a rather small sample size (which is also critical for the statistical analysis), quite big age differences in the children, and the fact that only one researcher coded the videos and interactions with the robot. Further, we assumed that there was a fairly equal number of toys across the families in the two study groups.

Even though Ranger was able to motivate children to tidy up, parents critically remarked that putting everything in one box or removing toys to put them back on the floor is not tidying. Also, the positive effect might be due to a *novelty effect* during this first interaction. Fascination might fade out quickly and we don't know yet how the interaction changes over time. In the future, long-term studies are needed to investigate how far our results can hold over time.

Several people were surprised that though we consider Ranger a "robot", it does not carry out tasks on its own. However, we do not aim at having a robot carry out a task *for* the family but *with* them. Especially with children, who are developing plenty of different skills and taking responsibility when they tidy up, we believe that it is important to let them do their job themselves, encouraged by a little robot. Still, deploying a robot in a children's room raises ethical questions, in terms of family roles and especially as young children seem to readily engage with robots in a social way.

Findings of our study suggest that both a *proactive* and a *reactive* robot can be engaging for children, however, in a different way. The *proactive* robot triggered more play-

[1] This "neutral" result shows that it is not easy to evaluate something as abstract as the "life-likeness" of a robot. It doesn't seem appropriate to keep asking whether a robot is either "alive" or "not alive" because it might appear to be somehow both. See [6].

ful behavior but also seemed to distract from the tidying task. In contrast, the *reactive* robot triggered more tidying behavior but engaged children less in playing with it. Consequently, we think that probably a robot that tries to balance initiative-taking with the user could result in an engaging but still purposeful behavior (e.g. serious game).

Two further aspects of this project which we are currently investigating are (1) how various kinds of robot behavior (e.g. unexpected robot behavior) impact child-robot interaction, and children's perception of cognitive abilities of the robot, with the goal of sustaining interaction over a longer period of time, and (2) the development of an autonomous version of Ranger which features shared control, such that it is possible to conduct a long-term study with Ranger in family homes.

Acknowledgements

We thank all the families who participated in this study. We also thank Maya Cakmak and the reviewers for their help in refining this article, as well as Frédéric Kaplan and Fanny Riedo for their ideas.

This research was supported by the Swiss National Science Foundation through the National Centre of Competence in Research Robotics.

References

[1] J. Fink. Anthropomorphism and human likeness in the design of robots and human-robot interaction. In S. S. Ge, *et. al.*, editors, *Social Robotics*, no. 7621 in Lecture Notes in Computer Science, pp 199–208. Springer, Jan. 2012.

[2] J. Fink, V. Bauwens, F. Kaplan, and P. Dillenbourg. Living with a vacuum cleaning robot. *International Journal of Social Robotics*, 5(3):389–408, 2013.

[3] T. Fong, C. Thorpe, and C. Baur. Collaboration, dialogue, human-robot interaction. In P. R. A. Jarvis and P. A. Zelinsky, editors, *Robotics Research*, no. 6 in Springer Tracts in Advanced Robotics, pp 255–266. Springer Berlin Heidelberg, Jan. 2003.

[4] M. Heerink, B. Kröse, V. Evers, and B. Wielinga. Measuring acceptance of an assistive social robot: a suggested toolkit. *RO-MAN 2009*, pp 528–533. IEEE, Sept. 2009.

[5] W. Ju and L. Leifer. The design of implicit interactions: Making interactive systems less obnoxious. *Design Issues*, 24(3):72–84, 2008.

[6] P. H. Kahn, Jr., B. Friedman, D. R. Pérez-Granados, and N. G. Freier. Robotic pets in the lives of preschool children. *Interaction Studies*, 7(3):405–436, Jan. 2006.

[7] T. Kanda, T. Hirano, D. Eaton, and H. Ishiguro. Interactive robots as social partners and peer tutors for children: a field trial. *Hum.-Comput. Interact.*, 19(1):61–84, June 2004.

[8] The Interaction Lab - Holon Institute of Technology. Bubu Monstry, URL: http://interaction.hit.ac.il/bubu-monstry/.

[9] C. Pantofaru, L. Takayama, T. Foote, and B. Soto. Exploring the role of robots in home organization. *HRI 2012*, pp 327–334, New York, NY, USA, 2012. ACM.

[10] B. Robins, K. Dautenhahn, C. L. Nehaniv, N. A. Mirza, D. François, and L. Olsson. Sustaining interaction dynamics and engagement in dyadic child-robot interaction kinesics: lessons learnt from an exploratory study. *ROMAN 2005*, pp 716– 722. IEEE, Aug. 2005.

[11] F. Vaussard, M. Bonani, P. Rétornaz, A. Martinoli, and F. Mondada. Towards autonomous energy-wise RObjects. In D. Hutchison, *et. al.*, editors, *Towards Autonomous Robotic Systems*, vol. 6856, pp 311–322. Springer Berlin Heidelberg, 2011.

[12] A. Weiss, R. Bernhaupt, D. Schwaiger, M. Altmaninger, R. Buchner, and M. Tscheligi. User experience evaluation with a wizard of oz approach: Technical and methodological considerations. *Humanoids 2009*, pp 303–308. IEEE, Dec. 2009.

[13] A. Weiss, D. Wurhofer, and M. Tscheligi. "I love this Dog"—Children's emotional attachment to the robotic dog AIBO. *International Journal of Social Robotics*, 1(3):243–248, June 2009.

[14] S. Woods and K. Dautenhahn. Child and adults' perspective on robot appearance. *AISB 2005*, pp 126–132, University of Hertfordshire, Hatfield, England, 2005. SSAISB.

[15] S. Woods, K. Dautenhahn, and J. Schulz. The design space of robots: investigating children's views. *ROMAN 2004*, pp 47– 52. IEEE, Sept. 2004.

[16] Y. Yamaji, M. Taisuke, Y. Yuta, R. De Silva, and M. Okada. STB: child-dependent sociable trash box. *International Journal of Social Robotics*, 3:359–370, Oct. 2011.

Can Two-Player Games Increase Motivation in Rehabilitation Robotics?

Domen Novak
ETH Zurich
Tannenstrasse 1, TAN E3
CH-8092 Zurich, Switzerland
+41 44 632 36 38
domen.novak@hest.ethz.ch

Aniket Nagle
ETH Zurich
Sonneggstrasse 3, ML G53.2
CH-8092 Zurich, Switzerland
+41 44 632 87 38
aniket.nagle@hest.ethz.ch

Robert Riener
ETH Zurich
Tannenstrasse 1, TAN E4
CH-8092 Zurich, Switzerland
+41 44 632 66 79
robert.riener@hest.ethz.ch

ABSTRACT

Rehabilitation robots have the potential to greatly improve motor rehabilitation. However, the patient must be properly motivated to actively participate in therapy. Several strategies have been suggested to improve patient motivation, but one element has not yet been explored: playing with other people. We designed a two-player rehabilitation game played by two people using two ARMin III robots. We tested three game modes: single-player (competing against a computer), competitive (competing against a human), and cooperative (cooperating with a human against a computer). All modes were played by 24 healthy subjects who filled out questionnaires about their personality and in-game motivation. Almost all subjects preferred playing the two-player game modes to the single-player one, as they enjoyed being able to talk and interact with another person. However, there were two distinct player groups. One group liked the competitive mode but not the cooperative mode while the other liked the cooperative but not the competitive mode. Subjects who liked the competitive mode also put more effort into it. Finally, subjects' personalities partially predicted what mode they would like. This emphasizes that two-player rehabilitation games have advantages over single-player ones, but that the right game needs to be chosen for each subject. An extended patient study is planned for the near future.

Categories and Subject Descriptors

H.1.2 [**User/Machine Systems**]: Human factors.
H.5.1 [**Multimedia Information Systems**]: Artificial, augmented and virtual realities.
J.3 [**Life and Medical Sciences**]: Health.

General Terms

Design, Experimentation, Human Factors.

Keywords

Rehabilitation robotics; virtual reality; multiplayer games; motivation.

HRI'14, March 3–6, 2014, Bielefeld, Germany.
Copyright © 2014 ACM 978-1-4503-2658-2/14/03…$15.00.
http://dx.doi.org/10.1145/2559636.2559658

1. INTRODUCTION

Robotic interfaces have many benefits for motor rehabilitation. A robot enables repetitive training, provides multimodal feedback and guidance, and supports the assessment of impairment score and functional ability [1]. Such robots are frequently combined with virtual reality, which allows patients to exercise in game-like environments or in simulations of everyday tasks. Training with such a combination of robot and virtual reality can lead to better rehabilitation outcome than using only a robot [2], and reviews of existing clinical evidence have suggested that virtual reality may improve arm function more effectively than equal doses of conventional therapy [3–5].

Providing the patient with a rehabilitation robot and virtual environment is, however, not enough to guarantee a good rehabilitation outcome. The patients themselves must also be motivated to exercise. Patient motivation has frequently been described by professionals as an important determinant of the rehabilitation outcome [6], and patients who receive additional motivation interventions show better compliance with the therapy regimen [7]. Motivation has been highlighted as an additional advantage of robotics and virtual reality, as properly designed virtual environments can be viewed as more fun, engaging and motivating than conventional therapy [8], [9].

Strategies for the design of motivating virtual rehabilitation environments have included automated difficulty adaptation, rich visual and audio elements, score displays, and cognitive challenges to spice up the motor training [8–10]. These design strategies are similar to those used in the related field of exergames: games that try to encourage physical exercise and weight loss by increasing motivation through elements such as high scores. Such games have been demonstrated to be more interesting and enjoyable than conventional exercise for e.g. balance training [11].

There is, however, one element that is commonly found in exergames but nearly absent from robot-aided virtual rehabilitation: playing with other people. A recent exergame review [12] emphasized that exergaming is often a social activity, and cooperative exergame play has been found to significantly increase motivation and energy expenditure [13]. This can be viewed as similar to computer games in general, where the social component is an important motive for playing (see Boyle et al. [14] for a recent review). In fact, playing computer games with or against other people has repeatedly been found to be more engaging and enjoyable than playing against computer-controlled opponents [15–17].

Rehabilitation robotics may also benefit from games that two (or even more) patients could play together in order to increase motivation. However, so far it appears that no two-player games have been developed and evaluated with rehabilitation robots. This may be due to the high cost of a robot, as a result of which few facilities own more than one. Our paper presents the evaluation of the first (to our knowledge) two-player game for robot-assisted motor rehabilitation.

The design of such a two-player game is not trivial, as its features may affect motivation positively or negatively. The main question is whether the players should cooperate to achieve a common goal or compete against each other. Cooperative games have been almost universally found to result in positive experiences, but competitive games can be either fun or frustrating depending on the characteristics of the game and the personality of the players [18], [19]. For example, players who are easily upset may find losing in a competitive game to be very unpleasant, whereas some players may simply not enjoy competing at all [18]. In fact, older people (who are prevalent in e.g. stroke rehabilitation) have been shown to be less competitive than younger people who play computer games for entertainment [20]. While cooperative games may therefore seem to be a safer choice, previous studies have also raised potential benefits of competitive games over cooperative ones. The most notable potential benefit is a more intense gameplay experience [19].

Therefore, we developed and tested a motor rehabilitation game with three game modes: competing against a computer opponent, competing against another human, or cooperating with another human. Our hypotheses are:

- **H1**: Playing with another human (either competing or cooperating) is more motivating than playing alone.

- **H2**: A player's personality is correlated with whether he/she prefers competing or cooperating with the other player.

This paper presents the evaluation of the game with 24 healthy subjects. Clinical evaluation with a patient population is planned as the natural next step.

2. MATERIALS AND METHODS

2.1 Subjects

Twenty-four subjects (16 males, 8 females) with no arm impairment participated in the study. They were between 25 and 53 years old, with a mean of 33.5 years and standard deviation of 7.6 years. Twenty were right-handed and four were left-handed. Subjects were paired together according to gender, handedness, and approximate age (maximum difference 4 years). They were recruited among the staff and students of ETH Zurich, and most subjects in a pair already knew each other to some degree.

2.2 Rehabilitation robots

Our system includes two ARMin III upper extremity rehabilitation robots [21]. The two robots are functionally identical. Each ARMin III has an exoskeletal structure with 7 actuated degrees of freedom, including a hand module. The subject sits at the robot and is connected to it with cuffs on the upper arm and the forearm. The hand is fixed into the handles of the hand module with elastic straps. The lengths of the arm segments, the size of the hand and the height of the device are adjustable to the individual subject. A screen placed in front of the subject displays the game (Figure 1).

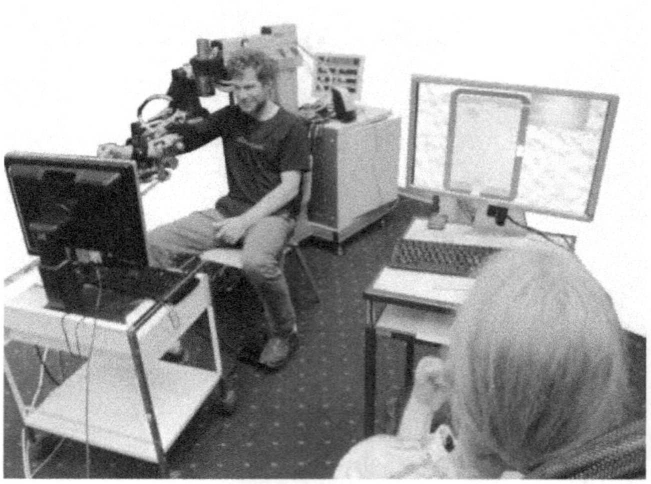

Figure 1. Two subjects playing the air hockey game. The two ARMin robots are attached to the subjects' right arms, and the game is shown on screens in front of each subject.

Each robot provides the player with robotic support in the form of gravity compensation and friction compensation [1]. This support allows the robot to be moved with minimal physical effort, but the robot does not actively move the player's arm in any specific direction. While the robot is capable of also actively assisting a person's movement, this feature was not used in our study. Gravity and friction compensation, however, are essential since the robot is otherwise heavy and tiring to move.

2.3 Game

The game developed for the two ARMin robots is similar to the popular air hockey arcade game. The screen consists of an air hockey board, with goals on the top and bottom of the screen (Figure 2). Each subject controls a mallet in front of his/her own goal. The mallet can be moved left and right by moving the ARMin's end-effector left and right. While the ARMin allows movement in all three dimensions, only left-right movements have an effect on the game.

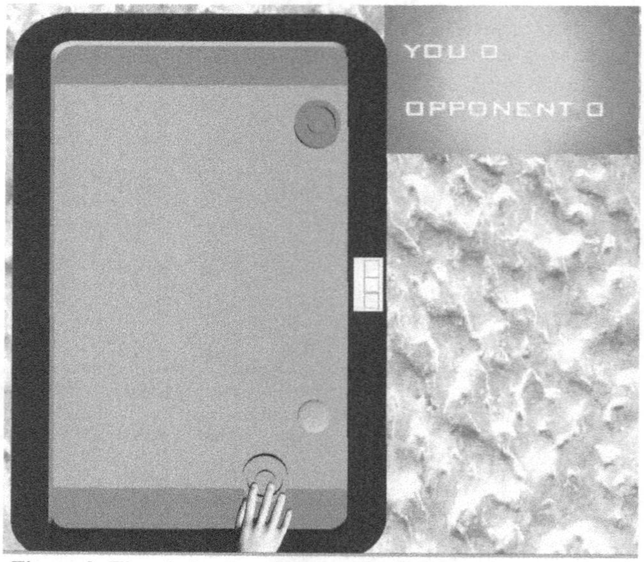

Figure 2. The air hockey game, with the goals, mallets, puck, and score board. The display shown is for the single-player and competitive modes.

At the start of the game, the puck is randomly placed on one player's side of the board, either near the top or near the bottom. When hit with the mallet, the puck moves in a random direction towards the other side. The left and right walls of the board are rigid, and the puck bounces off them. When the puck hits the top or bottom wall, a goal is scored and a point is awarded to the side that scored the goal. The puck then reappears at the center of the board and moves in a random direction, starting a new round. If the puck hits a mallet, it is deflected back toward the other side of the board; players can prevent a goal from being scored by deflecting the puck in this manner.

There are three game modes:

- In the *single-player* mode, the subject controls the bottom mallet while the top one is controlled by the computer. The subject's aim is to score as many points as possible against the computer. Two separate instances of the game run on the two ARMin robots, with no interaction between the subjects.

- In the *competitive* mode, one subject controls the bottom mallet while the other subject controls the top mallet. The subjects play against each other and try to score as many points as possible. The displays on the two computers are appropriately rotated so that for each subject, his/her mallet is on the bottom. The ARMin robots are placed in such a way that the subjects cannot view each other's screens (Figure 1).

- In the *cooperative* mode, the table is twice as wide as in the other two variants. There are three mallets in total: two at the bottom and one at the top of the screen. Each of the two bottom mallets is controlled by one subject while the top mallet is controlled by the computer. Each subject-controlled mallet can only cover half the width of the board while the computer-controlled mallet can cover the entire width of the board. Therefore, the two subjects must work together to score points against the computer – each subject defends his or her half of the board.

2.4 Study protocol

Upon arrival, the experimenter explained the purpose and protocol of the study to the subjects as well as demonstrated the ARMin and the game. They were then seated in the ARMin robots and allowed to briefly practice the single-player variant of the game. Afterwards, the subjects played the game for three 5-minute sessions: once in single-player mode, once in competitive mode and once in cooperative mode. The three modes were played in random order. Subjects were not allowed to talk to each other in the single-player mode, but were told that they could talk as much as they wished in the other two modes.

After each mode, the subjects completed a questionnaire assessing their experience with the particular game mode (section 2.5.1). After completing all three modes, the subjects completed a questionnaire about their overall game experience (section 2.5.2) and a personality questionnaire (section 2.5.3).

2.5 Questionnaires

2.5.1 Experience with last game mode

The subjects' experiences with each game mode were evaluated along four scales: interest/enjoyment, perceived competence, effort/importance and pressure/tension. These were taken from the Intrinsic Motivation Inventory (IMI), which has been previously used to measure subjects' experiences with virtual environments for motor rehabilitation [8], [9]. There are five statements per scale, presented in random order for a total of 20 statements. Subjects indicated how true each statement was on a 7-point scale, with 1 indicating "not at all true" and 7 indicating "very true".

When evaluating the second and third game mode, subjects could see their previous answers. They were asked to focus on differences between modes and avoid giving the same answer to one statement for all three game modes if possible. This instruction is admittedly somewhat problematic from a methodological perspective. It was given since our experiences with the IMI suggest that it does not capture differences between different rehabilitation games well - subjects often repeatedly give the same response unless asked to focus on differences [9].

2.5.2 Overall game experience

The overall experience questionnaire was created specifically for this study. It posed the following questions:

- "What was your favorite game mode? Why?"
- "What was your least favorite game mode?"
- "Which mode did you put the most effort into?"
- "Which mode did you put the least effort into?"
- "Which mode did you feel the most competent at?"
- "Which mode did you feel the least competent at?"
- "Which mode was the most stressful?"
- "Which mode was the least stressful?"

Subjects had to circle one of the three possible modes for each question. For the first question, a blank space was also given so that subjects could write the reason for their choice. It can be seen that the questions are similar to the IMI, except that they ask subjects to specifically rank the three modes rather than evaluate each one independently.

2.5.3 Personality

Each subject's personality was primarily assessed using the Big Five factors: extraversion, agreeableness, conscientiousness, emotional stability, and intellect/imagination. These factors have been used to analyze effects of personality on game enjoyment in a number of studies [22], [23]. They were measured using the 50-item IPIP inventory [24] available at http://ipip.ori.org.

In addition to the IPIP, the Revised Competitiveness Index [25] was used to specifically measure the subject's preference for competitive situations. The index consists of two factors, Enjoyment of Competition and Conscientiousness. Only the Enjoyment of Competition factor (hereafter referred to as 'competitiveness') was used in our study, as Conscientiousness is already measured by the IPIP.

The items of both the IPIP and the Revised Competitiveness Index are brief statements that the subject can agree or disagree with on a 5-point scale from 1 (completely disagree) to 5 (completely agree). All 59 statements (10 for each of the five IPIP factors, 9 for Enjoyment of Competition) were mixed together in a random order. Example items on the questionnaire are:

- Extraversion: "I am comfortable around people."
- Agreeableness: "I sympathize with others' feelings."
- Conscientiousness: "I am always prepared."
- Emotional stability: "I am relaxed most of the time."
- Intellect/Imagination: "I have excellent ideas."
- Competitiveness: "I enjoy competing against an opponent."

2.6 Data analysis

A repeated-measures analysis of variance was first performed on the four IMI scales (interest/enjoyment, competence, effort, and pressure/tension) to find differences in motivation between the three game modes. The model included the within-subject factor of game mode (single-player, competitive, cooperative – the three modes played by each subject) as well as the two between-subjects factors of favorite game mode (single-player, competitive, cooperative – the subject's response to the first question in the overall game experience questionnaire) and competitive winner/loser (whether the subject won or lost in the competitive mode). The Holm-Sidak test was used in all post-hoc tests.

The subjects were then grouped into those who won and those who lost in the competitive condition. The groups' differences in score and the six personality scales were evaluated using t-tests. Afterwards, they were grouped again according to their favorite game mode, and the same differences were analyzed. As mentioned later, very few subjects chose the single-player mode as their favorite, and they were not included in the analysis.

Finally, Pearson correlation coefficients (r) between game score and the four IMI scales, as well as between game score and the six personality scales, were calculated for all three game modes. The threshold for significance was set at $p = 0.05$ in all tests.

3. RESULTS

3.1 Game scores

Eighteen of the 24 subjects scored higher than the computer in the single-player mode, on average scoring 7.2 points more than the computer. There was a negative correlation between age and score ($r = -0.64$, $p = 0.001$).

By definition, 12 subjects won and 12 lost in the competitive mode, with the average difference between two subjects in a pair being 20.6 points. All subjects scored higher than the computer in the cooperative mode, with each of the 12 pairs on average winning by 20.0 points.

3.2 Favorite game modes

The overall rankings for the three game modes are shown in Table 1. Of the 12 subjects who favored the competitive mode, 6 chose single-player and 6 chose cooperative as their least favorite. Of the 10 subjects who favored the cooperative mode, 5 chose single-player and 5 chose competitive as their least favorite.

Table 1. Responses to the overall game experience questionnaire. The numbers indicate the number of subjects who chose a particular game mode on a question.

	single-player	competitive	cooperative
favorite	2	12	10
least favorite	11	7	6
most effort	5	12	7
least effort	12	5	7
most competent	8	8	8
least competent	6	14	4
most pressure	3	20	1
least pressure	13	0	11

Though not all subjects wrote a response to the "Why was this game mode your favorite?" question, some trends can be seen. Subjects who favored the competitive mode (hereafter referred to as 'competitive subjects') generally stated that it was more fun to play against a person, that being able to see and talk to one another during the game was fun, and that beating a person was more satisfying than beating the computer. The human opponent was also praised as being more unpredictable, and was sometimes considered more challenging even by subjects who scored better against the human than against the computer.

Subjects who favored the cooperative mode (hereafter referred to as 'cooperative subjects') also stated that they enjoyed being able to see and talk to the other person, described the computer as an "unattractive opponent", but stated that they preferred to work in a team and win together (as one subject wrote, "we could talk and both beat the computer"). Cooperative subjects had a lower single-player score than competitive subjects ($p = 0.045$).

Interestingly, the two subjects who favored the single-player mode gave their reasoning as "less stress" and "prefer the machine to a human opponent". One of the two had the highest agreeableness and lowest competitiveness score on the personality questionnaire while the other also had an extremely low competitiveness score.

3.3 Motivation in different game modes

3.3.1 Overall

The multivariate test of the effect of game mode on IMI responses found a significant main effect on all four IMI scales. Two overall statements can be made about the three game modes, without taking other factors into account:

- Competence (Figure 3) was higher in cooperative mode than in competitive mode ($p = 0.015$).
- Pressure/tension (Figure 4) was higher in competitive mode than in single-player ($p = 0.021$) and cooperative ($p = 0.024$) modes.

Motivation within the game modes also depended on the score achieved by the subject. In the single-player mode, score was correlated with competence ($r = 0.71$, $p < 0.001$). In the competitive mode, score was correlated with interest/enjoyment ($r = 0.43$, $p = 0.036$), competence ($r = 0.69$, $p < 0.001$) and effort ($r = 0.43$, $p = 0.036$).

3.3.2 Subject subgroups

A significant interaction effect on all four IMI scales was found between game mode and favorite game mode as well as between game mode and competitive winners/losers. We can thus split subjects into subgroups, either into winners and losers or into cooperative and competitive subjects. Statements about the subgroups can be found in Tables 2 and 3. The differences in interest/enjoyment between game modes can also be seen separately for winners and losers in Figure 5.

If we look purely at differences between competitive and cooperative subjects, we find that, compared to competitive subjects, cooperative subjects have:

- lower interest/enjoyment in competitive mode ($p = 0.019$),
- lower competence in all three modes ($p = 0.044$ for single-player, below 0.001 for competitive, and 0.009 for cooperative),
- lower effort in the competitive mode ($p < 0.001$).

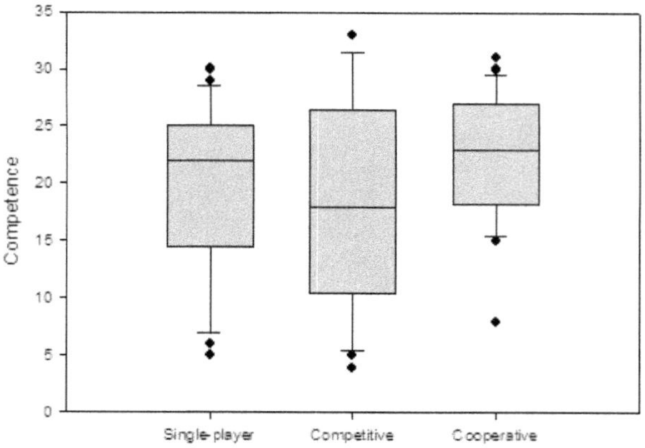

Figure 3. Competence in the three game modes.

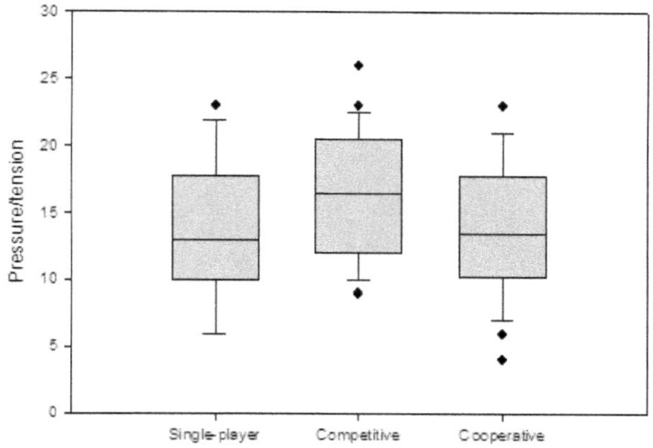

Figure 4. Pressure/tension in the three game modes.

Table 2. Differences between game modes, separately for subjects whose favorite was the competitive mode ('competitive subjects') and for subjects whose favorite was the cooperative mode ('cooperative subjects').

	Competitive subjects	*p*	Cooperative subjects	*p*
Interest / Enjoyment	- higher in competitive mode than in single-player mode	0.028	- higher in cooperative mode than in single-player mode - higher in cooperative mode than in competitive mode	0.049 0.033
Competence	no significant differences between modes		- higher in cooperative mode than in competitive mode	0.017
Effort	- higher in competitive mode than in single-player mode - higher in competitive mode than in cooperative mode	0.001 0.001	no significant differences between modes	
Pressure / Tension	- higher in competitive mode than in single-player mode - higher in competitive mode than in cooperative mode	0.007 0.002	no significant differences between modes	

Table 3. Differences between game modes, separately for those who won in the competitive mode and for those who lost in the competitive mode.

	Winners	*p*	Losers	*p*
Interest / Enjoyment	- higher in competitive mode than in single-player mode	0.008	- higher in cooperative mode than in single-player mode	0.035
Competence	no significant differences between modes		- higher in cooperative mode than in competitive mode	0.008
Effort	- higher in competitive mode than in single-player mode - higher in competitive mode than in cooperative mode	0.001 0.001	no significant differences between modes	
Pressure / Tension	- higher in competitive mode than in cooperative mode	0.007	no significant differences between modes	

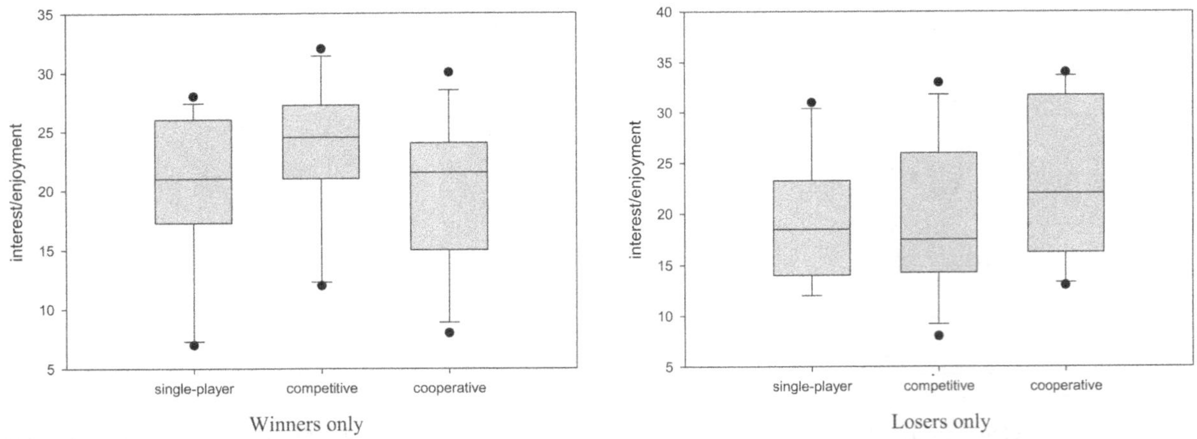

Figure 5. Interest/enjoyment in the three game modes, with subjects split into those who won (left) and those who lost (right) in the competitive mode.

3.4 Effects of personality

As with the IMI, there were significant differences between competitive and cooperative players. Cooperative players had lower emotional stability (p = 0.005) and lower competitiveness (p = 0.011) than competitive players. Furthermore, competitiveness was negatively correlated with age (r = -0.63, p = 0.001).

There were also correlations between personality and score. In the single-player mode, score was correlated with competitiveness (r = 0.58, p = 0.003) and negatively correlated with agreeableness (r = -0.52, p = 0.011). In the competitive mode, score was negatively correlated with agreeableness (r = -0.48, p = 0.021).

4. DISCUSSION

4.1 Influence of game modes on motivation

Two-player rehabilitation games can indeed be more fun than single-player ones, and the majority of players reported that they enjoyed being able to talk to and otherwise interact with another person. However, choosing the right game is not trivial. While 22 of the 24 subjects picked one of the two-player modes as their favorite, those who enjoyed the competitive mode did not necessarily enjoy the cooperative one (and vice versa). A subject's personality allows a rough prediction of what game mode he/she may prefer, particularly the competitiveness and emotional stability. Interestingly, competitive players reported putting more effort into the competitive game mode, suggesting that the right choice of game can not only lead to higher enjoyment, but potentially also to more intensive exercise.

The effect of a particular game mode, of course, depends on both players. The experimenters observed the most positive behavior in subjects who were good friends (as opposed to acquaintances or strictly co-workers) and enjoyed competition, as well as subjects who were evenly matched (achieved similar scores in single-player and competitive modes). Additionally, several subjects who disliked the cooperative mode reported that they did not like depending on a less skilled teammate. One particularly vocal subject emphasized this during the game by repeatedly insulting his teammate due to perceived lack of skill. The effects of the relationship between players have also been noted outside rehabilitation [15], [26]. Overall, an interesting extension of the study would be to create a predictive model of game preference that incorporates the personality, skill and age of the players.

Though the data presented was collected with healthy subjects and the findings are not guaranteed to apply to patients, we can to some degree speculate about what types of patients would benefit from two-player rehabilitation games. For this, we should also take into account the result that competitiveness decreases with age. Therefore, competitive gameplay may be less promising for stroke victims, who are generally older. Stroke victims also often suffer from depression, anxiety and other personality changes (see Taylor et al. [27] for an overview) and may benefit more from cooperative gameplay which would emphasize positive aspects of playing with others without the potential for additional frustration. Competitive gameplay may be more suitable for younger stroke patients and for spinal cord injury patients, who are generally younger than stroke patients and do not suffer personality changes due to the injury itself (as it occurs in the spine and not the brain). It may be particularly suitable for pediatric rehabilitation, especially since some arm rehabilitation robots are now being designed specifically for children (e.g. Keller et al. [28]).

The finding that rehabilitation games should be chosen according to the personality of each subject applies not only to two-player games, but also to virtual environments for rehabilitation in general. During our previous study on including cognitive challenges in motor rehabilitation [9], we observed that some patients enjoy the variety introduced by cognitive challenges while others find them off-putting. It may also explain the findings of Zimmerli et al. [29], who found that computer-controlled opponents did not increase motivation; it is possible that a subset of competitive patients enjoyed competing against opponents and could have benefitted from them. In any case, it may be worth investigating whether patient motivation, and consequently exercise frequency/intensity in rehabilitation, could be improved by tailoring the rehabilitation tasks to each patient's personality.

4.2 Providing active robotic assistance

A major weakness of our study is that the robots act essentially as passive haptic interfaces rather than as active robots, providing no assistance to the subjects other than gravity and friction compensation. The study therefore does not address all the challenges of a two-player robot-aided rehabilitation game. In order to use two-player games with real patients, the rehabilitation robots need to provide active assistance to players. We included this limitation consciously in the study design; for the first study of two-player games, we preferred to focus on the principle of two-player gameplay rather than the active assistance.

Nonetheless, an active robotic assistance algorithm is clearly necessary before the game can be used with patients in rehabilitation. Designing one, however, is not trivial in a two-player game, as it needs to account for the behavior of both players. For instance, an assistive algorithm in a single-player task can be designed so that the patient always succeeds, though just barely. This would be impractical in our game: if both patients always intercepted the puck due to the robot's assistance, the game would be boring. The assistive algorithm should thus ideally be adaptive, taking into account the performance of both patients as well as the energy they put into the game. This problem needs to be investigated with real patients or, failing that, poorly matched healthy subjects. It is particularly problematic in competitive gameplay, as skilled patients may feel cheated if defeated by an unskilled patient who is receiving more robotic assistance.

4.3 Other game possibilities

The game chosen for our study was relatively simple. Unlike many arm rehabilitation games, it involves only movement in the horizontal plane. The two players also do not interact with each other directly, but only through their mallets' effect on the puck. This was intentional; as the aim of the study was to demonstrate that two-player rehabilitation games can be more fun and motivational, the game simplicity should not be an obstacle. A similar game has been previously used to study seniors' experiences with multiplayer games [20]. Nonetheless, we can imagine more complex two-player rehabilitation games. For instance, the two players' avatars (in our case, mallets) could interact directly and e.g. push each other away. They could also interact indirectly via objects in the virtual environment that could be manipulated by both players concurrently.

A second possibility would be a cooperative game played not by two patients, but by a patient and a therapist. The therapist would provide assistance either by 'pushing' the patient's avatar as described in the previous paragraph or even in a master-slave setup: any motion performed by the therapist would be mirrored by the patient's robot, allowing the patient to learn a motion by demonstration. Some feedback could also be given to the therapist, allowing him/her to feel what patients are doing and what mistakes they may be making.

Finally, we must consider that, as previously mentioned, few institutions own more than one rehabilitation robot, and this is unlikely to change in the near future. We should therefore think about potential cheaper alternatives for the future. For instance, it would be possible to connect two robots over the Internet and have patients from different institutions play together. Another possibility would be to have one patient use a robot while another patient (or a therapist, or even a healthy friend of the patient) uses a simpler haptic interface.

4.4 Study weaknesses

Finally, a few additional methodological weaknesses should be mentioned. First of all, in the single-player mode, the subjects could nonetheless see and hear each other, so it was not a completely single-player experience. This was done purely for logistical reasons, but may have affected the results. A possible alternative would have been to either keep a third robot in a separate room for the single-player mode or to place a movable barrier between the players to block their view of each other and perhaps muffle the sound. Another issue is that players always practiced the single-player mode in the beginning, which may have affected results due to differences in novelty.

A problem with the cooperative mode, on the other hand, was that each player's mallet could only cover half the width of the board. While we did not initially realize this was a problem, several subjects later complained that they could not truly cooperate since they could not assist the other player, but could only be hindered by a poor teammate. An easy way to remedy this would have been to allow both mallets to cover the entire width of the board, pushing players to cooperate and communicate more.

5. CONCLUSIONS

Our study showed that most subjects prefer playing a two-player rehabilitation game to a single-player one, as they enjoy being able to talk and otherwise interact with the other person. However, the choice of preferred game mode depends strongly on the subject. Competitive gameplay was preferred by players with a higher competitiveness and higher emotional stability score on the personality questionnaire. Many players who enjoyed the competitive mode did not necessarily enjoy the cooperative mode and vice-versa. Though the study was performed with healthy subjects rather than actual patients, several conclusions may apply to patients. For instance, as stroke victims often exhibit anxiety or depression, they may prefer cooperative gameplay.

The natural next step for our research is to test a two-player game with real patients. However, an algorithm for active robotic assistance needs to be implemented and tested first, as patients may not have sufficient movement ability to play the game unaided. We should also consider more complex two-player games for rehabilitation robots, with features such as physical interaction between the players and even master-slave cooperation between a patient and therapist. The implication that different virtual environments for rehabilitation should be chosen for different patients is also relevant for single-patient rehabilitation, as an optimal choice of virtual environment may increase compliance and exercise intensity.

6. ACKNOWLEDGMENTS

This work was supported by the Swiss National Science Foundation through the National Centre of Competence in Research Robotics and by the Clinical Research Priority Program "NeuroRehab" University of Zurich. The authors would like to thank Urs Keller for his extremely patient technical support and Peter Wolf for fruitful discussions.

7. REFERENCES

[1] Guidali, M., Duschau-Wicke, A., Broggi, S., Klamroth-Marganska, V., Nef, T., and Riener, R. 2011. A robotic system to train activities of daily living in a virtual environment. *Med. Biol. Eng. Comput.* 49, 10 (Oct. 2011), 1213–1223.

[2] Mirelman, A., Bonato, P., and Deutsch, J. E. 2009. Effects of training with a robot-virtual reality system compared with a robot alone on the gait of individuals after stroke. *Stroke* 40, 1 (Jan. 2009), 169–174.

[3] Henderson, A., Korner-Bitensky, N., and Levin, M. 2007. Virtual reality in stroke rehabilitation: a systematic review of its effectiveness for upper limb motor recovery. *Top. Stroke Rehabil.* 14, 2 (Mar. 2007), 52–61.

[4] Saposnik, G., and Levin, M. 2011. Virtual reality in stroke rehabilitation: a meta-analysis and implications for clinicians. *Stroke* 42, 5 (May 2011), 1380–1386.

[5] Laver, K., George, S., Thomas, S., Deutsch, J. and Crotty, M. 2011. Virtual reality for stroke rehabilitation. *Cochrane Database Syst. Rev.*, no. 9, p. CD008349.

[6] Maclean, N. 2002. The concept of patient motivation: a qualitative analysis of stroke professionals' attitudes. *Stroke* 33, 2 (Feb. 2002), 444–448.

[7] Friedrich, M., Gittler, G., Halberstadt, Y., Cermak, T., and Heller, I. 1998. Combined exercise and motivation program: effect on the compliance and level of disability of patients with chronic low back pain: a randomized controlled trial. *Arch. Phys. Med. Rehabil.* 79, 5 (May 1998), 475–487.

[8] Colombo, R., Pisano, F., Mazzone, A., Delconte, C., Micera, S., Carrozza, M. C., Dario, P. and Minuco, G. 2007. Design strategies to improve patient motivation during robot-aided rehabilitation. *J. Neuroengineering Rehabil.* 4, 3 (Jan. 2007).

[9] Mihelj, M., Novak, D., Milavec, M., Ziherl, J., Olenšek, A., and Munih, M. 2012. Virtual rehabilitation environment using principles of intrinsic motivation and game design. *Presence Teleop. Virt.* 21, 1 (Winter 2012), 1–15.

[10] Haringer, M., and Beckhaus, S. 2012. Adaptive generation of emotional impact using enhanced virtual environments. *Presence Teleop. Virt.* 21, 1 (Winter 2012), 96–116.

[11] Fitzgerald, D., Trakarnratanakul, N., Smyth, B., and Caulfield, B. 2010. Effects of a wobble board-based therapeutic exergaming system for balance training on dynamic postural stability and intrinsic motivation levels. *J. Orthop. Sports Phys. Ther.* 40, 1 (Jan. 2010), 11–19.

[12] Staiano, A. E., and Calvert, S. L. 2011. Exergames for physical education courses: physical, social, and cognitive benefits. *Child Dev. Perspect.* 5, 2 (Jun. 2011), 93-98.

[13] Staiano, A. E., Abraham, A. A., and Calvert, S. L. 2012. Motivating effects of cooperative exergame play for overweight and obese adolescents. *J. Diabetes Sci. Tech.* 6, 4 (Jul. 2012), 812–819.

[14] Boyle, E. A., Connolly, T. M., Hainey, T., and Boyle, J. M. 2012. Engagement in digital entertainment games: a systematic review. *Comput. Hum. Behav.* 28, 3 (May 2012), 771–780.

[15] Gajadhar, B. J., De Kort, Y. A., and Ijsselsteijn, W. A. 2008. Shared fun is doubled fun: player enjoyment as a function of social setting. In *Proceedings of the 2nd International Conference on Fun and Games*. Springer-Verlag Berlin, Heidelberg, 106–117.

[16] Lim, S., and Reeves, B. 2010. Computer agents versus avatars: responses to interactive game characters controlled by a computer or other player. *Int. J. Hum.-Comput. St.* 68, 1–2 (Jan. 2010), 57-68.

[17] Weibel, D., Wissmath, B., Habegger, S., Steiner, Y., and Groner, R. 2008. Playing online games against computer- vs. human-controlled opponents: effects on presence, flow, and enjoyment. *Comput. Hum. Behav.* 24, 5 (Sep. 2008), 2274–2291.

[18] Song, H., Kim, J., Tenzek, K. E., and Lee, K. M. 2009. The effects of competition on intrinsic motivation in exergames and the conditional indirect effects of presence. In *Proceedings of the 12th Annual International Workshop on Presence* (Los Angeles, CA, Nov. 11-13, 2009).

[19] Schmierbach, M., Xu, Q., Oeldorf-Hirsch, A., and Dardis, F. E. 2012. Electronic friend or virtual foe: exploring the role of competitive and cooperative multiplayer video game modes in fostering enjoyment. *Media Psychol.* 15, 3 (Jul. 2012), 356–371.

[20] Gajadhar, B. J., Nap, H. H., De Kort, Y. A., and Ijsselsteijn, W. A. 2010. Out of sight, out of mind: co-player effects on seniors' player experience. In *Proceedings of the 3rd International Conference on Fun and Games*. ACM, New York, NY, 74–83.

[21] Nef, T., Guidali, M., and Riener, R. 2009. ARMin III - arm therapy exoskeleton with an ergonomic shoulder actuation. *Appl. Bionics Biomech.* 6, 2 (2009), 127–142.

[22] Weibel, D., Wissmath, B., and Mast, F. W. 2010. Immersion in mediated environments: the role of personality traits. *Cyberpsychol. Behav. Soc. Netw.* 13, 3 (Jun. 2010), 251-256.

[23] Fang, X., and Zhu, M. 2011. Extraversion and computer game play: who plays what games? In *HCII '11 Proceedings of the 14th International Conference on Human-Computer Interaction: Users and Applications*. Springer-Verlag Berlin, Heidelberg, 659–667.

[24] Goldberg, L. R., Johnson, J. A., Eber, H. W., Hogan, R., Ashton, M. C., Cloninger, C. R., and Gough, H. G. 2006. The international personality item pool and the future of public-domain personality measures. *J. Res. Pers.* 40, 1 (Feb. 2006), 84–96.

[25] Houston, J., Harris, P., McIntire, S., and Francis, D. 2002. Revising the competitiveness index using factor analysis. *Psychol. Rep.* 90, 1 (Feb 2002), 31–34.

[26] Peng, W., and Hsieh, G. 2012. The influence of competition, cooperation, and player relationship in a motor performance centered computer game. *Comput. Hum. Behav.* 28, 6 (Nov. 2012), 2100–2106.

[27] Taylor, G. H., Todman, J., and Broomfield, N. M. 2011. Post-stroke emotional adjustment: a modified social cognitive transition model. *Neuropsychol. Rehabil.* 21, 6 (Dec. 2011), 808–24.

[28] Keller, U., Klamroth, V., Van Hedel, H., and Riener, R. 2013. ChARMin□: a robot for pediatric arm rehabilitation. In *Proceedings of the 2013 IEEE International Conference on Robotics and Automation*. IEEE.

[29] Zimmerli, L., Jacky, M., Lünenburger, L., Riener, R., and Bolliger, M. 2013. Increasing patient engagement during virtual reality-based motor rehabilitation. *Arch. Phys. Med. Rehabil.* 94, 9 (Sep. 2013), 1737-1746

Extending Myoelectric Prosthesis Control with Shapable Automation: A First Assessment

Matthew Derry
Northwestern University
Dept. of Electrical Eng. and Computer Science
Evanston, IL 60208
mderry@u.northwestern.edu

Brenna Argall
Northwestern University
Dept. of Electrical Eng. and Computer Science
Evanston, IL 60208
brenna.argall@northwestern.edu

ABSTRACT

For many users of myoelectric prostheses there is a set of functionality which remains out of reach with current technology. In this work, we provide a first assessment of an extension to classical myoelectric prostheses control approaches that introduces simple automation that is shapable, using EMG signals. The idea is not to replace classical techniques, but to introduce automation for tasks, like those which require the coordination of multiple degrees of freedom, for which automation is well-suited. A prototype system is developed in simulation and an exploratory user study is performed to provide a first assessment, that evaluates our proposed approach and provides guidance for future development. A comparison is made between different formulations for the shaping controls, as well as to a classical control paradigm. Results from the user study are promising: showing significant performance improvements when using the automated controllers, and also unanimous preference for the use of automated controllers on this task. Additionally, some questions about the optimal user interaction with the system are revealed. All of these results support the case for continued development of the proposed approach, including more extensive user studies.

Categories and Subject Descriptors

J.3 [**Computer Applications**]: Life and Medical Sciences

Keywords

myoelectric prosthesis control; automation; human-robot interaction

1. INTRODUCTION

Research into the myoelectric control of prostheses has been ongoing since the 1960's [21]. Significant and impressive advances have been made, from the hardware and electronics that enable onboard control, to signal processing

HRI'14, March 3–6, 2014, Bielefeld, Germany.

http://dx.doi.org/10.1145/2559636.2559685 .

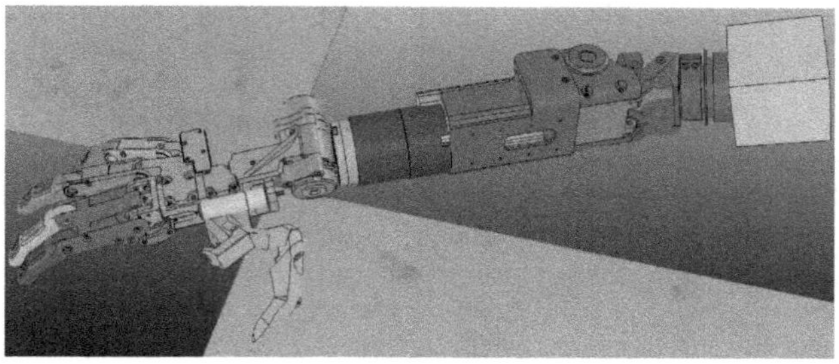

Figure 1: Simulated model of the 5-DoF CBM prosthetic arm (Beta-1 prototype).

techniques that decode the EMG signals. The most common control paradigms employed today are limited however to effectively control one degree-of-freedom (DoF) at a time, and lacking functionality is one reason for low adoption rates [3,4,15,16].[1] For this reason, we hypothesize that the interface between users and their prostheses can be improved, both in capability and in user acceptance, by introducing a set of shapable automated controllers that can provide helpful motions and improved interactions with the device. In particular, tasks requiring the coordination of multiple degrees of freedom are well-suited to automation, but can be a challenge with individual-DoF control paradigms.

In this work, we propose a framework to extend, rather than replace, traditional single-degree-of-freedom control. Our framework incorporates automated controllers, the behavior of which can be shaped online via myoelectric signals. The ability to shape the motion is critically important to the framework, because it allows the controllers to remain simple, and yet generalizable to the needs of a task (e.g. the stroke used with a hammer tends to increase once the nail is set), or to slight differences between tasks (e.g. the hand crank on a fishing rod is smaller than the circular motion you might use whisking pancake batter). The guiding vision is that of a toolbox of simple, shapable, automated motions that can handle a set of critical tasks not achievable with single-DoF control, to improve the user interactions with this important assistive technology. The shaping controls are the interface between the user and the machine, thus exploring different approaches for optimizing these control interactions is of significant interest in this work.

To demonstrate and evaluate the concept of introducing shapable automated controllers to the repertoire of controls

[1]Other reasons for low adoption rates include poor hardware durability, fatiguing interfaces, and user discomfort [4].

available to an upper-limb prosthesis user, this work reports on an early-stage user study within a simulated environment using a model of an upper-limb prosthesis being developed at the Rehabilitation Institute of Chicago (RIC) and controlled by the EMG signals from human subjects (Figure 1). The task, turning a hand crank, was chosen because it requires a motion with hallmark characteristics suitable to automation (e.g. repetition and coordination of multiple DoF). The user study in this work is intended to investigate our hypothesis that performance of a traditionally difficult task can be improved with our framework, and to evaluate the effectiveness of different control interactions between the user and the machine. The information from this user study is intended to help prioritize and guide future development by highlighting the shaping control formulations with potential for high impact for prosthesis users. In addition to the performance aspect, the user study is intended to help gauge how users respond to controlling an automated motion within an alternative control space (i.e. controlling the amplitude and speed of a circular motion, instead of directly).

In Section 2 we present a brief overview of relevant research in to myoelectric prosthesis control and shared human-robot control, and literature assessing the needs of upper-limb prosthesis users. Section 3 introduces our framework and details of the implementation of our prototype system. In Section 4 we describe the methods used for the initial user study, followed by the results in Section 5. Finally, we discuss some insights from the study and areas for future work in Section 6 and conclude the work with Section 7.

2. BACKGROUND

While the use of automated controllers in myoelectric prostheses is a largely open area, it builds on a strong foundation of research and development that has occurred in pursuit of effective myoelectric control of upper-limb prostheses. What follows in this section is a brief overview of relevant research in myoelectric control of upper-limb prostheses, followed by a discussion of some of the important areas of related robotics research.

In early myoelectric prostheses, each degree-of-freedom was controlled by the contraction of a muscle pair, such as the bicep and triceps, where each muscle controls one half of the DoF, such as flexion or extension of the elbow. Switching control between the available DoFs was then accomplished by using a separate signal such as a co-contraction of the muscle pair or a hardware switch [21]. Using an antagonistic muscle pair configuration has the advantage of physiological intuition, but it is also limited in the number of control signals that it can generate.

With an estimated 1.6 million people in the United States alone living with the loss of a limb and an estimated 185,000 who undergo a limb amputation each year [28], the public health impact of advancing the technology of assistive prosthetics is major. A survey [3] of 1,575 prosthesis users in the United States in 1996 points to a want for better control mechanisms (including less visual attention) and the coordinated motion of two joints; characteristics also reflected in their top desired activities (e.g., turning a doorknob). A need for the proportional and simultaneous control of multiple DoF is noted repeatedly [3, 17, 18]. Limited dexterity and unsatisfactory control paradigms are often cited as reasons for the rejection of upper-limb myoelectric prostheses [4, 20]. Also noted is a current lack of non-fatiguing control interfaces for users of myoelectric hands [27], the control of which requires expending a large portion of their energy and concentration [25]. As a result, many electric prostheses often are used only aesthetically, not functionally, and a majority of prosthesis users still prefer body-powered mechanisms or simply using their other hand (for unilateral amputations) [3, 4, 15, 16].

Today, the most innovative techniques are looking at alternate ways to produce control signals; for example, the targeted muscle reinnervation (TMR) approach pioneered by Dr. Todd Kuiken [10, 11]. In the TMR technique, the residual nerves are surgically moved from the residual limb to another muscle (e.g. the pectoral muscle), with the benefit of allowing users to generate the control signals using the same nerve pathways that previously controlled their missing limb, and providing a larger site for electrode placement.

Advances in discriminating control commands from myoelectric signals include most notably pattern matching techniques that classify an array of EMG nodes [20]. The most advanced techniques are able to discern 10-12 motion classes [20, 24], that typically each map to one half of a DoF (one class per motion direction). The most widely used techniques [2, 5, 13, 20, 23, 24] still control each DoF individually and sequentially—e.g., to move the elbow, then the wrist, then close the hand—and asking a user to simultaneously generate signals for more than one class at a time is generally impractical due to high cognitive load [11, 16].

Recent academic work within the field of simultaneous control thus has emphasized alternative mapping paradigms. For example, pattern matching classes that encode multi-DoF motions [22] or force functions for each joint [9]; or direct control within a reduced dimensionality space [14]. Much of this work is motivated by the idea of muscle synergies, that activate in coordination rather than individually.

A small number of works have introduced some element of automation. The lower-level control of hand gripping was automated in the MANUS Hand [19], and different levels of shared human-machine control were evaluated with the CyberHand [6]. Automation was found to make the task less difficult for users, and require less attention.

The partial automation of electric prostheses has much in common with the domain of shared human-robot control. Here the goal is often to find a sweet spot—on the continuum spanning from fully manual (e.g., teleoperation) to fully automated control—that makes the system more capable than at either extreme [7, 8, 12, 26]. Typically the cognitive load on the machine is greatly reduced in shared control paradigms, and the automation consequently is that much more robust. In this work, the prosthesis user and the prosthetic arm operate in concert within a shared human-machine control paradigm with the goal of both enhanced functionality and user acceptance.

3. PROPOSED FRAMEWORK

In order to implement our prosthetic limb control system within a simulation environment, a parameterized automated controller for the prosthesis model and the EMG control system need to be developed for testing the shaping controls. What follows is a discussion of the formulation of each of the subcomponents of our prototype system.

A few notes about convention. When referencing time series elements, τ represents the wall-clock time, so $\Delta\tau$ is the temporal resolution of the simulator (in our case 0.050

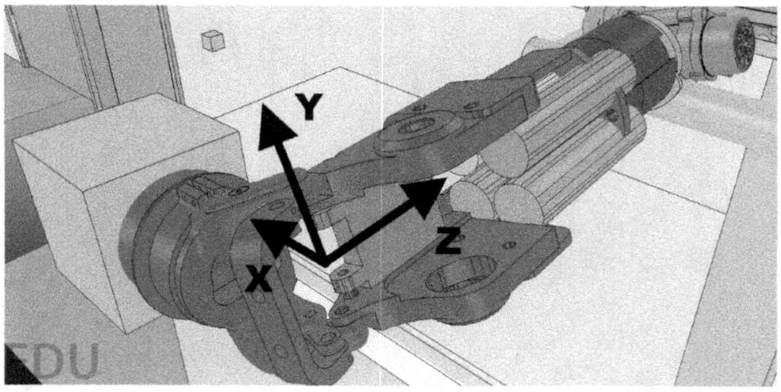

Figure 2: Coordinate frame used for calculating the circular motion of the end effector.

seconds), while t represents the time index. Thus, the difference between t and $t+1$ is $\Delta\tau$. Additionally, bold font is used to represent vectors.

3.1 Automated Controller with Shaping

The automated controller implemented in this work creates a periodic circular motion at the end-effector using a general sinusoidal oscillator, in which the amplitude, α, and angular frequency, ω, are modulated by shaping controls, $\boldsymbol{\theta}$, and the phase, ϕ, is solved for in order to provide smooth transitions between changes in ω.

By choosing an appropriate reference frame relative to the end of the humerus side of the elbow joint at the point of joint rotation (Figure 2), the position $\boldsymbol{p}$ of the target end-effector pose can be made circular regardless of the absolute position of the prosthetic arm in space. An oscillator then updates the x and y components of target end-effector position according to Equations (1) and (2) and the z component is held constant as the length of the forearm segment, l, of the prosthetic arm (Equation (3)).

$$p_x = \theta_\alpha \; cos(\theta_\omega \tau + \phi^t) \tag{1}$$

$$p_y = \theta_\alpha \; sin(\theta_\omega \tau + \phi^t) \tag{2}$$

$$p_z = l \tag{3}$$

In general, a transition occurring due to changes in the amplitude shaping control $\theta_\alpha \in \boldsymbol{\theta}$ is smooth, but changes in the angular frequency shaping control $\theta_\omega \in \boldsymbol{\theta}$ can cause rapid jerks forward or backward around the circle, behaving as a sort of time warp, since the phase is being changed. To smooth out these transitions, a new ϕ^t can be calculated for each new value of θ_ω using the equality described in equation (4) to ensure that the end-effector continues smoothly around the circle despite the change in θ_ω.

$$\theta_\omega^t \tau + \phi^t = \theta_\omega^{t-1} \tau + \phi^{t-1} \tag{4}$$

In order to convert this end effector pose control to velocity commands in the joint space at time t, the target position of the end-effector position is projected forward to time $t+1$. The inverse kinematic (IK) problem for the projected end-effector position $\boldsymbol{p}^{t+1}$ is then solved using a damped least squares IK solver. Finally, the joint velocity commands $\dot{\boldsymbol{\varphi}}^t$ are calculated from the current and projected joint positions $\boldsymbol{\varphi}^t$ and $\boldsymbol{\varphi}^{t+1}$ according to Equation (5).

$$\dot{\boldsymbol{\varphi}}^t = \frac{\boldsymbol{\varphi}^{t+1} - \boldsymbol{\varphi}^t}{\Delta\tau} \tag{5}$$

3.2 The Shaping Controls

With multiple ways to formulate shaping commands for an automated motion, we want to determine which formulation can facilitate more effective interactions between user and machine. To begin to answer this question, this system implements two different formulations for controlling the shaping controls, one discrete and one continuous. In the discrete formulation, the shaping control is adjusted by discrete constant amounts. With the continuous formulation, the proportional value of the muscle activation is mapped to the range of values the shaping control can take on.

Two opposing muscle groups are used in the EMG control system, the right biceps and triceps. One electrode is placed on the skin over each of the muscle bellies. Each channel of the raw signal $\boldsymbol{s}$ is sampled at a frequency of $1000Hz$. The root mean square (RMS) feature, $m(s_i), s_i \in \boldsymbol{s}$, of each channel in the raw signal is calculated according to Equation (6), where the window size N is set to 150.

$$m(s_i) = \sqrt{\frac{1}{N}(s_{i,1}^2 + s_{i,2}^2 + ... + s_{i,N}^2)} \tag{6}$$

Before the EMG control goes online, there is a calibration step in which the subject is asked to relax for some time, and a resting baseline $\boldsymbol{\beta}$ is estimated. $\boldsymbol{\beta}$ is a vector containing the RMS feature calculated for each channel of the signal recorded over that time period, and this resting baseline is subtracted from incoming EMG signals. The RMS feature, less the baseline, is then used to determine if the muscle activation is over the channel threshold λ_i, represented by the binary variable γ_i according to Equation (7).

$$\gamma_i(m_i, \beta_i, \lambda_i) = \begin{cases} 1 & : m_i - \beta_i \geq \lambda_i \\ 0 & : m_i - \beta_i < \lambda_i \end{cases} \tag{7}$$

$$\text{where } i = \{biceps, triceps\}$$

The way $\boldsymbol{\gamma}$ is used is dependent on the formulation (discrete or continuous) of the shaping control, described below.

3.2.1 Discrete Shaping Control Formulation

In the discrete control formulation, the currently selected shaping control is updated by a set increment $\Delta\theta_i$ according to the rule defined by equation (8).

$$\theta_i^t = \begin{cases} \theta_i^{t-1} + \Delta\theta_i & : \gamma_{biceps} = 1 \wedge \gamma_{triceps} = 0 \\ \theta_i^{t-1} - \Delta\theta_i & : \gamma_{biceps} = 0 \wedge \gamma_{triceps} = 1 \\ \theta_i^{t-1} & : otherwise \end{cases} \tag{8}$$

$$\text{where } i = \{\alpha, \omega\}$$

3.2.2 Continuous Shaping Control Formulation

In the continuous control formulation only one muscle group is considered and the value of the shaping control is determined by mapping the proportional value of the muscle contraction to the range of shaping control values, as in Equation (9). Accordingly, there is an additional calibration step to set the full range of muscle activity before the control goes online. In this calibration step the user is asked to flex the controlling muscle (biceps) with maximal effort, m_{max}.

$$\theta^t = \theta_{min} + (\theta_{max} - \theta_{min})\frac{m^t}{m_{max} - \lambda} \tag{9}$$

The prosthesis joint limits and the controller determine the possible range $[\theta_{min}, \theta_{max}]$ of shaping control values.

3.3 Direct Control

We also implement a simplified version of classical single-DoF control (now on referred to as *direct control*), to act as a reference for the performance comparison. The direct control operational mode is formulated in a very similar way to the discrete control of the shaping controls presented in equation (8), with the major exception being that the joint angles are updated directly as opposed to the shaping control values. The two joints involved in the particular task we have implemented are the elbow joint and the wrist extension and flexion joint. With this in mind, a long co-contraction of muscles would initiate a grasp, a short co-contraction would switch which joint was selected for control, and then the activation of biceps and triceps would map to flexion and extension of the active joint respectively.

3.4 Task Execution

In our implementation of a crank turning task, a long (>1.5 second) co-contraction of the biceps and triceps triggers the start of the automated behavior, which begins by grasping the crank handle and starting the rotation. The user then selects the amplitude shaping control θ_α with a short (0.75 to 1.5 seconds) co-contraction of the biceps and triceps; throughout this operating mode, short co-contractions will flip which shaping control (θ_α or θ_ω) is selected. The amplitude can then be tuned: where a biceps contraction increases (and a triceps contraction decreases) the amplitude by modulating θ_α. The angular velocity can also be tuned by modulating θ_ω in the same manner.

Unlike amplitude, the angular velocity can take on both positive and negative values. The shaping control θ_ω thus is formulated to set both rotational speed and direction, smoothly. In particular, a biceps contraction increases the value of θ_ω, and a triceps contraction decreases its value. Thus, when θ_ω is positive (clockwise rotational direction) a triceps contraction slows down the rotation; however, once θ_ω is sufficiently decreased to be negative, the increasingly negative numbers of a triceps contraction will speed up the (counter-clockwise) rotation.

The task we evaluate with our user study is to turn the hand crank 10 revolutions in one direction, followed by 10 revolutions in the opposite direction. This task embodies the type of repetitive, multi-degree of freedom task to which automation is well suited.

4. USER STUDY METHODS

Here we first describe the user demographics, followed by the system implementation and study metrics. For practical purposes relating to fatigue and frustration, the users were given a time limit of eight minutes to complete the task. Each user was given up to 30 minutes to familiarize themselves with the task and the controls. One important note, during the trial using the continuous shaping control formulation, it is the amplitude that is set proportionally; the angular speed is set via the discrete shaping control formulation. The order in which the control formulations were used was randomized to minimize ordering effects.

4.1 User Demographics

This exploratory user study was performed under IRB protocol STU00084001. Participants consisted of five able-bodied users, three male and two female, between 24-32 years old. Each user was instructed to complete the task using all three control formulations (direct, discrete, and continuous). Two of the five users had prior experience with EMG recording. The results and insights gleaned from this initial assessment are meant to guide further investigation with additional subjects and implemented tasks.

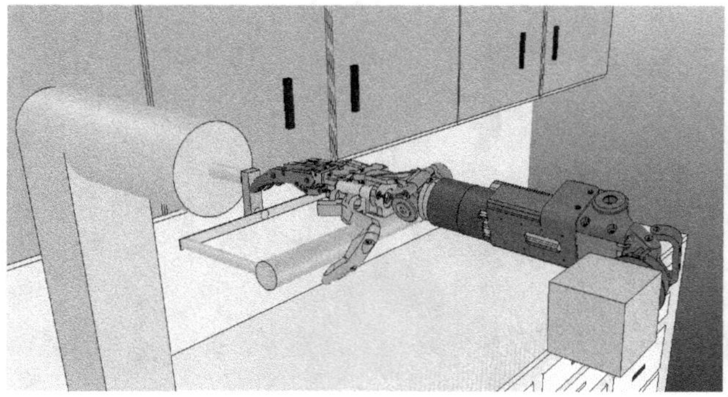

Figure 3: The view of the arm model and hand crank in the simulator for the task of turning the crank 10 times in each direction.

4.2 Virtual Environment

The simulation environment utilized the Virtual Robot Experimentation Platform (V-REP): a 3D physics-based simulation environment, using the ODE and Bullet dynamics engines [1]. We have built a model for an upper limb prosthesis, the 5-DoF CBM prosthetic arm (Beta-1 prototype) from the Center of Bionic Medicine at RIC (Figure 1). The position and orientation of the prosthetic limb was anchored in space, such that the task was achievable given appropriate EMG inputs.[2] The simulator was projected on to a large screen to give a more familiar sense of scale while performing the task. See Figure 4 to see the setup.

A Measurement Computing USB-1408FS DAQ converts the analog signal from an Aurion (now Cometa Systems) ZeroWire EMG system into a digital signal, which is then provided to a PC via USB. Matlab and the Data Acquisition Toolkit interfaces with the DAQ, where the EMG signals are processed and then the commands are passed to V-REP.

4.3 Study Metrics

A number of objective metrics are evaluated. *Task Completion* is a boolean variable indicating whether or not the user was able to complete the task within the eight minute time window. The eight minute task time limit was set to avoid fatigue, which could affect subsequent trials, and limit frustration. *Execution Time* is simply the number of seconds spend on the task, up to 480. *Number of Commands Issued* is a direct count of the number of 150ms time windows in which the user's muscle activity was over the threshold which results in a command being issued. The reason the number of commands metric is important is it is an indirect measure of muscular effort put forth by the user, since increased muscle activity is required to issue a command.

[2]Future work will consider mapping the position and orientation of the user's arm in the real world to the simulated environment to provide a more realistic evaluation. This could be accomplished using tracking from a sensor such as the Microsoft Kinect. However, in this work we anchored the arm to focus on the EMG control alone.

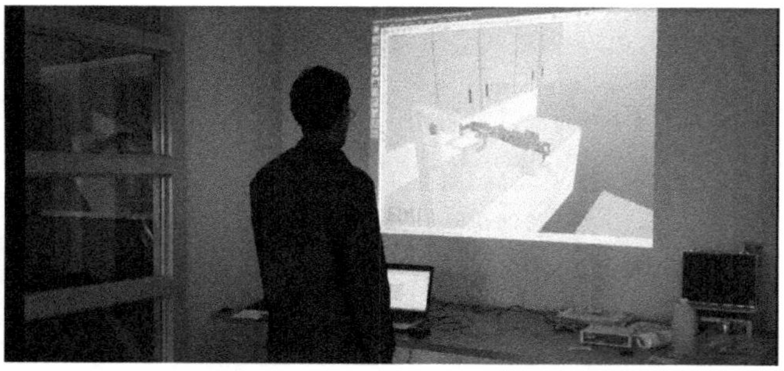

Figure 4: A user completing a task in the virtual environment, by using EMG to shape the motion of the automated prosthesis controller.

Subjective data was gathered via a brief questionnaire (IRB STU00084001) given at the conclusion of the study, to determine user preferences. Subjects were asked if they preferred the direct control or automated control formulation. If automated control was preferred, then they were asked which shaping control formulation they preferred, discrete or continuous. To explore user opinions about their preferred system, they were given six statements and asked to rate each one on a Likert scale according to their agreement with the statement. Where a value of one indicates strong disagreement, a value of four is neutral, and a value of seven indicates strong agreement:

1. **Capability:** The system was able to complete the tasks of the experiment.
2. **Capability:** I think the system would be able to complete other tasks.
3. **Utility:** The system was useful for completing the tasks of the experiment.
4. **Utility:** I think the system would be useful for completing other tasks.
5. **Ease of Use:** The system was easy to use.
6. **Intuition:** The system was easy to learn how to use.

The next portion of the questionnaire consisted of two open-ended questions eliciting suggestions about alternative methods for shaping an automated motion and alternative automated motions that would be useful in their daily tasks. Lastly, there was a question regarding the ability to design their own automated motions. This was a multiple choice question will several possible options, an open-ended 'other' answer, and an answer for 'no interest'.

5. RESULTS

In order to investigate the potential value of the proposed approach, we look at objective performance data, and the subjective perceptions of the users. In this section we present the objective data first to examine the support for the proposed approach, and then the subjective data gathered from our questionnaire.

Table 1: Execution Time (in seconds)
Successful executions in bold.

Subject	Direct	Discrete	Continuous
1	480	**174.9**	**204.5**
2	480	**155.9**	**128.7**
3	480	**125.2**	**141.4**
4	480	**161.4**	**216**
5	480	**107.0**	**129.4**
Mean ± StDev.	480 ± 0	**144.9 ± 25**	**164 ± 38**

5.1 Objective Performance Metrics

The objective metrics both highlighted the potential of our approach for improved task performance and left some open questions regarding the best shaping formulation for improved user interactions.

5.1.1 Task Completion

For task completion, eight minutes was not enough time for any of the subjects to complete the task using the direct control method. Of the five subjects, two were not able to achieve more than one revolution of the hand crank using direct control. The other two subjects were able to nearly complete 10 revolutions of the crank in a single direction before time ran out, and the remaining subject completed two revolutions. By contrast, all five subjects were able to complete the task with the automated control paradigm using either shaping control formulation.

The failures of the direct control stemmed from the fact that, to perform this task, a significant amount of switching had to occur between the two controlled joints. Sometimes there would be unsuccessful switches between the joints due to inadequate muscle activation, causing the actual execution of the movement to get out of sync with the users expectation of what movement their command would elicit.

5.1.2 Execution Time

The time to complete the task is really the most telling metric when it comes to judging the performance of the automated control solutions versus the direct control. While 480 seconds was not enough to complete the tasks using the direct control, both the discrete and continuous shaping control formulations of the automated control required less than half the allotted time to fully complete the tasks (Table 1). While the difference between the automated control methods and the direct control is quite evident, the difference between the discrete and continuous shaping control formulations is less clear. Although the average time with the discrete formulation was lower than the continuous formulation by 18 seconds, this difference is not statistically significant ($p < 0.43$, two-tailed, paired-sample t-test).

5.1.3 Number of Commands Issued

Another metric that provides insight into the performance of these control paradigms is the number of commands issued by the user via EMG. This metric can be useful as an indicator of user effort. In Table 2, the automated controllers again far outperform direct control, requiring fewer commands; moreover, even with issuing more commands, the direct control paradigm never allowed for the successful completion of the task. This result holds even when looking at the average number of commands per second.

Table 2: Number of Commands Issued
Successful executions in bold.
Average number of commands per second in parentheses.

Subject	Direct	Discrete	Continuous
1	343(0.72)	**86**(0.49)	**56**(0.27)
2	320(0.67)	**63**(0.40)	**45**(0.35)
3	161(0.34)	**74**(0.59)	**50**(0.35)
4	196(0.41)	**58**(0.36)	**42**(0.19)
5	301(0.63)	**53**(0.50)	**31**(0.24)
Mean ± StDev.	255 ± 72	**66.8 ± 11.9**	**44.8 ± 8.4**

Interestingly, when comparing the discrete and continuous shaping control formulations, the continuous formulation requires significantly fewer commands ($p < 0.016$). This makes sense when one considers that the amplitude can be set proportionally with a single command using the continuous formulation. As it turns out, there was enough compliance in the task (in the grip of the hand and compliance in the crank handle), that several of the subjects were able to set the amplitude within one or two tries using the continuous formulation. Future work will examine setting the rotational speed and direction using the continuous formulation as well, which could magnify this difference further by reducing the number of commands issued using the continuous formulation.

5.2 Subjective Performance Metrics

To help complete the picture of how well these paradigms perform, a questionnaire was administered following completion of the three task executions. The users were asked two multiple choice questions regarding preference of control paradigms. Additionally, they were asked to give a rating on a Likert scale regarding agreement with statements about ease of use, intuition, capability, and utility. Finally, there were a number of open-ended questions asking for feedback about additional motions that might be useful, additional formulations for shaping controls, and being able to define new motions and their shaping controls.

5.2.1 User Preference

When asked whether users preferred direct control versus automated control in completing this task, the users unanimously chose automated control. This was not surprising given the negative reactions of the users to direct control during the trials. Of more interest was the response to shaping control formulation preference. In this case, the users were again unanimous in that they preferred the discrete formulation to the continuous formulation. This is despite the fact that the continuous formulation required less muscular effort, as noted in Section 5.1.3.

5.2.2 User Opinion

The users were asked to rate several statements (detailed in Section 4.3) on a Likert scale of one to seven. Figure 5 highlights that users had the highest level of agreement with the statements about the capability of their preferred system (statements 1 and 2), believing that the system was capable of completing the task of the study, as well as other potential tasks not included in the study. With respect to the utility of the system (statements 3 and 4), these statements required the user to go beyond just believing that the system could accomplish a task to believing that accomplishing that task would actually be of utility to them. While the agreement weakened slightly, it was still quite positive. Statement 5 related to how easy the preferred system was to use, and in this statement the users were more conflicted, with two users being neutral, one strongly agreeing, and the remaining two falling in between. The result was weak agreement. The sixth and final statement was about how easy it was to learn how to use the system. Once again, there was weak agreement that the system was easy to learn. Seeing as these were users with limited experience and practice with both EMG recordings and the system in general, it makes sense that the lowest scores are related to the ease of use.

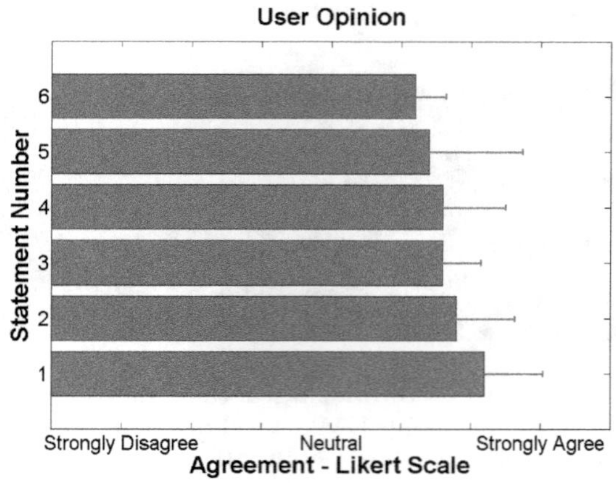

Figure 5: Mean Likert scale values of the user responses to the statements detailed in Section 4.3. Error bars represent one standard deviation.

5.2.3 User Feedback

The questionnaire solicited feedback from the users regarding ideas for additional automated motions that would be useful, alternative methods for shaping the automation, and preferred interfaces for defining their own new automated controllers. These questions proved to be challenging and the responses were minimal. The first question asked "Can you imagine other ways to shape an automated motion?" and only one subject had a response, which was to use muscle groups that were easier to differentiate. The second question asked "Are there other automated motions that would be useful for performing your daily tasks?" One user suggested grasping a phone and bringing it to her head, another user suggested opening the fridge or a door. Another user captured the more general thrust and suggested just being able to grasp and pick something up. In these cases, the suggestions were more task focused, which might be in interesting principle to incorporate in to the framework. Likely, these questions were challenge because each user had full use of their arms and hands, and as such had trouble envisioning the difficulties faced by persons with amputations. We expect these particular questions to be more informative in future studies with individuals with amputations and the clinicians who work with them.

6. DISCUSSION AND FUTURE WORK

As mentioned, the purpose of this study was to provide a first assessment of our proposed system, that will be used to guide future research. The most basic question to assess was whether or not the users would be able to perform the tasks well using our semi-automated control framework. We can say unambiguously that for this task, the user performed much better when using semi-automatic control. This is important support for our proposed framework, which motivates further development and evaluation of user capability. It would be interesting in future studies to go beyond comparisons to other myoelectric control systems, and compare with the capabilities of an expert body-powered prosthesis user as well. In so doing, the advantages of incorporating semi-autonomous behaviors would be tested against the most popular tool for persons with amputations.

Another important question that this user study intended to address related to the user interfacing with the machine; namely, which formulation for shaping controls would be the best. In this, the user study did not differentiate one over the other in a meaningful way. On the one hand, the users were slightly faster with the discrete shaping control formulation. On the other hand, they used less muscular effort with the continuous shaping control formulation. It is not immediately clear the reason for these results, but one possibility is related to the fact that all of these users were able-bodied, novice users of EMG systems. One of the principle strengths of the discrete shaping control formulation is that it allows for a more forgiving experience, because if an erroneous command is provided, it may only change the motion a small amount which can quickly be corrected. With continuous shaping controls, it is very easy to accidentally change the value of the shaping control a large amount, if say a mode change via co-contraction doesn't occur as expected. In a system in which the only feedback is visual confirmation of your command being executed, the higher cost of mistakes present in the continuous shaping control formulation can be daunting for a novice user. However, if a certain level of mastery was achieved using the continuous shaping controls, it is plain to see that significantly fewer commands would be needed, meaning faster execution times and reduced effort on the part of the user.

What this means going forward is that we can not yet throw either formulation out, but an expanded study is warranted to see if the promise of the continuous shaping control formulation pans out within a more experienced target population. It will also be important to see if a general formulation trend is seen across multiple automated controllers and shaping controls. It is possible that users never achieve the level of proficiency with the continuous shaping control formulation envisioned here, due to the noisy signals generated by EMG, and that the formulation thus never achieves a high level of acceptance. Additionally, non-visual feedback is another avenue for study that could tip the scales towards one shaping control formulation or another.

From a more anecdotal perspective, it was interesting to see the users during the initial practice session trying to learn how to control the individual muscles precisely enough to engage the system reliably. Once muscle control was sufficiently "mastered", they would then spend time trying to understand the control methods themselves. During this practice session, users would often verbally express confusion and doubt about the ability to control the motion, but would slowly improve their control. Finally, after having some experience and frustration with the direct control, the response was overwhelmingly positive when then switching back to the automated solutions. The side-by-side comparison between the automated and non-automated solutions we believe can explain the significantly positive views expressed by the users. It will be interesting to see if more experienced users with amputations feel as positively about the system.

With the encouraging results from this user study, there are several avenues for additional work. The first area of work is to improve the realism of the simulation by allowing the user to move the prosthesis around as if it were attached to their upper arm. Work in this area is ongoing. Another area is to identify additional tasks that are of interest to persons with amputations and develop automated solutions within our framework to ensure that the results of this study apply broadly. Finally, studies with more subjects, including persons with an amputation, is the necessary next step to fully asses the value of our proposed framework.

7. CONCLUSIONS

This work has presented a first assessment of a framework for adding automated motion control to myoelectric prostheses, in order to augment classical control methods which only actuate a single degree of freedom at a time. Our proposed framework parameterizes the automated controller so that users may shape the automated motion using the existing EMG control apparatus, by modulating this parameterization. In order to investigate the question of user interfacing with the system, two separate formulations were considered, discrete and continuous, each of which may provide different benefits. Within this work, compelling support for the value of this framework is provided through an early-stage user study which indicates greatly improved performance in a repetitive task requiring the coordinated actuation of multiple degrees of freedom. The users unanimously preferred the automated solution to the classical single-degree-of-freedom control. Additionally, while the novice EMG users in this study overwhelmingly preferred the discrete formulation of the shaping controls, the continuous shaping control did decrease the muscular effort required to set the value, prompting the question of whether an expert user might prefer the continuous shaping control formulation. On going studies will address this question.

8. ACKNOWLEDGMENTS

The authors would like to thank the Center for Engineering and Health in the Feinberg School of Medicine at Northwestern University for providing financial support of this work. We would also like to thank Jon Sensinger and the Center for Bionic Medicine at RIC for providing the CAD model of the 5-DoF CBM prosthetic arm used to build the prosthesis model for this study. Additionally, we would like to thank Ferdinando (Sandro) Mussa-Ivaldi and the Robotics Lab at RIC for providing the EMG system.

9. REFERENCES

[1] The v-rep simulator. `http://www.v-rep.eu`.

[2] A. B. Ajiboye and R. F. ff. Weir. A heuristic fuzzy logic approach to emg pattern recognition for multifunctional prosthesis control. *IEEE Transactions on Neural Systems and Rehabilitation Engineering*, 13(3), 2005.

[3] D. Atkins, D. Heard, and W. Donovan. Epidemiologic overview of individuals with upper-limb loss and their

reported research priorities. *Journal of Prosthetics and Orthotics*, 8:2 – 11, 1996.

[4] E. A. Biddiss and T. T. Chau. Upper limb prosthesis use and abandonment: A survey of the last 25 years. *Prosthetics and Orthotics International*, 31(3):236–257, 2007.

[5] J.-U. Chu, I. Moon, and M.-S. Mun. A real-time emg pattern recognition system based on linear-nonlinear feature projection for a multifunction myoelectric hand. *IEEE Transactions on Biomedical Engineering*, 53(11):2232–2239, 2006.

[6] C. Cipriani, F. Zaccone, S. Micera, , and M. C. Carrozza. On the shared control of an EMG-controlled prosthetic hand: Analysis of user-prosthesis interaction. *IEEE Transactions on Robotics*, 24(1), 2008.

[7] J. W. Crandall, M. A. Goodrich, D. R. Olsen Jr, and C. W. Nielsen. Validating human-robot interaction schemes in multitasking environments. *Systems, Man and Cybernetics, Part A: Systems and Humans, IEEE Transactions on*, 35(4):438–449, 2005.

[8] W. B. Griffin, W. R. Provancher, and M. R. Cutkosky. Feedback strategies for telemanipulation with shared control of object handling forces. *Presence: Teleoperators and Virtual Environments*, 14(6):720–731, 2005.

[9] N. Jiang, K. B. Englehart, and P. A. Parker. Extracting simultaneous and proportional neural control information for multiple-dof prostheses from the surface electromyographic signal. *IEEE Transactions on Biomedical Engineering*, 56(4), 2009.

[10] T. A. Kuiken, G. A. Dumanian, R. D. Lipschutz, L. A. Miller, and K. A. Stubblefield. The use of targeted muscle reinnervation for improved myoelectric prosthesis control in a bilateral shoulder disarticulation amputee. *Prosthetics and Orthotics International*, 28(3):245–53, 2004.

[11] T. A. Kuiken, L. Gi, B. A. Lock, R. D. Lipschutz, L. A. Miller, K. A. Stubblefield, and K. B. Englehart. Targeted muscle reinnervation for real-time myoelectric control of multifunction artificial arms. *The Journal of the American Medical Association*, 301(6):619–28, 2009.

[12] A. E. Leeper, K. Hsiao, M. Ciocarlie, L. Takayama, and D. Gossow. Strategies for human-in-the-loop robotic grasping. In *Proceedings of the seventh annual ACM/IEEE international conference on Human-Robot Interaction*, pages 1–8. ACM, 2012.

[13] M. León, J. Gutiérrez, L. Leija, R. M. noz, J. de la Cruz, and M. Santos. Multiclass motion identification using myoelectric signals and support vector machines. In *Third World Congress on Nature and Biologigally Inspired Computing*, 2011.

[14] G. Matrone, C. Cipriani, E. Secco, G. Magenes, and M. Carrozza. Principal components analysis based on control of a multi-DOF underactuated prosthetic hand. *Journal of NeuroEngineering and Rehabilitation*, 7(16), 2010.

[15] L. V. McFarland, S. L. H. Winkler, A. W. Heinemann, M. Jones, and A. Esquenazi. Unilateral upper-limb loss: Satisfaction and prosthetic-device use in veterans and servicemembers from vietnam and oif/oef conflicts. *Journal of Rehabilitation Research & Development*, 27(2):299–316, 2010.

[16] S. Micera, J. Carpaneto, and S. Raspopovic. Control of hand prostheses using peripheral information. *IEEE Reviews in Biomedical Engineering*, 3:48–68, 2010.

[17] P. Parker, K. Englehart, and B. Hudgins. Myoelectric signal processing for control of powered limb prostheses. *Journal of Electromyography and Kinesiology*, 16:541–548, 2006.

[18] B. Peerdeman, D. Boere, H. Witteveen, R. H. in 't Veld, H. Hermens, S. Stramigioli, H. Rietman, P. Veltink, and S. Misra. Myoelectric forearm prostheses: State of the art from a user-centered perspective. *Journal of Rehabilitation Research & Development*, 48(6):719–738, 2011.

[19] J. Pons, E. Rocon, and R. Ceres. The manus-hand dextrous robotics upper limb prosthesis: Mechanical and manipulation aspects. *Autonomous Robots*, 16:143–163, 2004.

[20] E. Scheme and K. Englehart. Electromyogram pattern recognition for control of powered upper-limb prostheses: State of the art and challenges for clinical use. *Journal of Rehabilitation Research & Development*, 48(6):643–660, 2011.

[21] E. D. Sherman. A russian bioelectric-controlled prosthesis: Report of a research team from the rehabilitation institute of montreal. *Canadian Medical Association Journal*, 91(24), 1964.

[22] K. Shima and T. Tsuji. Classification of combined motions in human joints through learning of individual motions based on muscle synergy theory. In *Proceedings of the IEEE/SICE International Symposium on System Integration (SII '10)*, 2010.

[23] A. M. Simon, L. J. Hargrove, B. A. Lock, and T. A. Kuiken. Target achievement control test: Evaluating real-time myoelectric pattern-recognition control of multifunctional upper-limb prostheses. *Journal of Rehabilitation Research & Development*, 48(6):619–628, 2011.

[24] F. V. G. Tenore, A. Ramos, A. Fahmy, S. Acharya, R. Etienne-Cummings, and N. V. Thakor. Decoding of individuated finger movements using surface electromyography. *IEEE Transactions on Biomedical Engineering*, 56(5):1427–1434, 2009.

[25] R. Weir, C. Heckathorne, and D. S. Childress. Cineplasty as a control input for externally powered prosthetic components. *Journal of Rehabilitation Research and Development*, 38:357–363, 2001.

[26] E. You and K. Hauser. Assisted teleoperation strategies for aggressively controlling a robot arm with 2d input. *Robotics: Science and Systems VII*, page 354, 2012.

[27] M. Zecca, S. Micera, M. C. Carrozza, and P. Dario. Control of multifunctional prosthetic hands by processing the electromyographic signal. *Critical Reviews in Biomedical Engineering*, 30(4-6):459–485, 2002.

[28] K. Ziegler-Graham, E. J. MacKenzie, P. L. Ephraim, T. G. Travison, and R. Brookmeyer. Estimating the prevalence of limb loss in the united states: 2005 to 2050. *Archives of Physical Medicine and Rehabilitation*, 89(3):422–429, 2008.

A Remote Social Robot to Motivate and Support Diabetic Children in Keeping a Diary

Esther J.G. van der Drift, Robbert-Jan Beun
Utrecht University
P.O. Box 80.089
3508 TB Utrecht
evddrift@gmail.com, r.j.beun@uu.nl

Rosemarijn Looije, Oliver A. Blanson Henkemans
TNO
P.O. Box 23
3769 ZG Soesterberg
rosemarijn.looije, olivier.blansonhenkemans@tno.nl

Mark A. Neerincx
Delft University of Technology
Faculty of EEMCS
Mekelweg 4
2628 CD Delft
m.a.neerincx@tudelft.nl

ABSTRACT
Children with diabetes can benefit from keeping a diary, but seldom keep one. Within the European ALIZ-E project a robot companion is being developed that, among other things, will be able to support and motivate diabetic children to keep a diary. This paper discusses the study of a robot supporting the use of an online diary. Diabetic children kept an online diary for two weeks, both with and without remote support from the robot via webcam. The effect of the robot was studied on children's use of the diary and their relationship with the robot. Results show that children shared significantly more personal experiences in their diaries when they were interacting with the robot. Furthermore, they greatly enjoyed working with the robot and came to see it as a helpful and supportive friend.

Categories and Subject Descriptors
H.1.2 **[User/Machine Systems]:** Human factors; I.2.9 **[Robotics]:** Operator Interfaces; J.4 **[Computer Applications]:** Social and Behavioral Sciences.

General Terms
Design, Experimentation, Human Factors, Verification.

Keywords
Social robot; remote robot; diabetes; diary; embodiment; adherence; compliance; bonding; engagement; relationship; child-robot interaction; human-robot interaction.

1. INTRODUCTION
It is estimated that worldwide more than 490 thousand children between the ages of 0-14 suffer from diabetes mellitus type 1, and this number continues to rise explosively [1]. Diabetes is a chronic illness that impacts a child's life in almost every aspect. Effective self-management of diabetes is complex and involves many varied activities related to dosing insulin, monitoring metabolic control and regulating diet and exercise to name just a few. This can be especially challenging for children that are diagnosed at a very young age. They frequently have trouble coping with their diabetes [2], and are at risk for developing depression, anxiety disorders or eating disorders [3, 4, 5]. Health care providers advise children to keep a diary to monitor their health and how they feel on a daily basis so that appropriate treatment adjustments can be made [6]. Keeping a diary can significantly contribute to the quality of life of children with diabetes. A diary provides insight into patterns between blood glucose values and daily activities so that the child can better manage his/her diabetes. But despite this advantage of keeping a diary, children rarely take the time to do it or they do not see the value of keeping a diary. Digital diaries have been found to yield better compliance and accuracy in diary recording compared to paper diaries [7], but the problem of motivating children to start using these diaries still exists.

HRI'14, March 3-6 2014, Bielefeld, Germany.

ACM 978-1-4503-2658-2/14/03...$15.00.
http://dx.doi.org/10.1145/2559636.2559664

Figure 1. NAO robot by Aldebaran Robotics

The EU-funded ALIZ-E project www.aliz-e.org aims to develop a social robot to support chronically ill children in their self-management. The scenario in which the robot is being tested is based on a medical setting where children recently diagnosed with diabetes spend one or two weeks in the hospital. During this time, the child and its parents are intensively trained and educated to manage the child's diabetes. But of course self-management of diabetes does not end there. It is an active and lifelong process that involves shifting and sharing responsibility for care tasks and decision-making between parents and child. The ALIZ-E project focuses on the potential role of a robot (Figure 1) in this process as an educator, motivator and companion that remains interesting to the child on the long term [8].

This paper describes an experiment which aims to improve children's diary adherence by means of a social robot. We created a scenario in which diabetic children keep a diary from home for two weeks, intermittently interacting with the robot via video-conferencing software. We studied the effect of the robot on the children's diary adherence, their engagement in the activity and their relationship with the robot.

2. RELATED WORK

Social robots are increasingly designed to be our pets, assistants, teachers and even emotional companions [9, 10]. They can positively affect people's motivation and compliance in areas such as education, health and well-being [11, 12]. The effectiveness of a social robot as a motivator largely depends on its ability to persuade its user. Persuasion is defined as "an attempt to shape, reinforce, or change behaviors, feelings, or thoughts about an issue, object or action" [13]. In this study, the issue we are addressing is the low diary adherence of children with diabetes. The robot attempts to persuade the child to keep a diary by using a variety of means that have been proven to be effective in human-robot interactions. Directly coercing the child into better keeping a diary is not an option for two reasons: first, coercion often has the opposite effect and causes the child to rebel even more [14]; and second, from a practical standpoint it is impossible to uphold this approach because the parents will not always be around to check up on their child. Rather than making active attempts to change the child's attitude and behavior, the focus should be on positively reinforcing the child's actions and utilizing the potential bond between the robot and the child as an incentive for the child to keep a diary.

To cultivate long-term relationships with users, the robot needs to engage in social behavior and dialogue [15]. Social dialogue includes things like greetings, chatting about general topics like the weather, and exchanging personal preferences [16]. Self-disclosure and empathy are known to greatly contribute to the closeness between conversational participants [17, 18, 19]. This effect is stronger with a physically embodied robot than with a virtual agent. There are many other factors we could consider which have the potential to positively influence children's diary adherence and long-term relationship with the robot. However, we feel that a robot which exhibits self-disclosure, empathy and physical embodiment provides a good starting point for this formative evaluation. These aspects can easily be implemented into the robot's dialogue and behavior.

2.1 Self-disclosure

Studies have shown that self-disclosure plays a central role in the development and maintenance of relationships as well as psychological well-being [17, 20, 21, 22]. Self-disclosure is defined as "sharing information with others that they would not normally know or discover" [23]. Once a person engages in self-disclosure, it is implicitly expected that the other conversational partner will also disclose information (norm of reciprocity). Self-disclosure has been linked to a person's likeability [20]. People who engage in intimate disclosures tend to be liked and trusted more than people who disclose at lower levels. People tend to also like robots better when they disclose affective rather than task-related information in collaborative tasks [24]. Mutual affective self-disclosure between the child and the robot can contribute to the depth and quality of their interaction, and ultimately their relationship. Self-disclosure also contributes to the diabetes self-management of the child. Sharing daily experiences in the diary and reflecting on this information can help the child gain insight into how they can better manage or cope with their diabetes and ultimately improve their quality of life. In order to encourage the child to disclose information, we propose to utilize the reciprocal nature of self-disclosure and have the robot frequently disclose information about itself in order to encourage the child to do the same.

2.2 Empathy

Empathy plays a key role in patient-centered therapy, because it implies the apprehension of another's inner world and a joint understanding of emotions [25]. One of the most comprehensive definitions of empathy is by Davis [26], who defined it as "the capacity to take the role of the other, to adopt alternative perspectives vis-à-vis oneself and to understand the other's emotional reactions in consort with the context to the point of executing bodily movements resembling the other's". Robots cannot feel empathy, but they can emulate it in their behavior, for example by:

- Showing empathic concern for others;
- Taking the perspective of another;
- Emotionally identifying with fantasy characters in books, films, etc.;
- Expressing negative feelings in response to the distress of others.

We propose to incorporate empathy in the robot's behavior by showing sympathy or concern when the child says to be feeling down, and by reacting positively when the child is in good spirits. The robot also expresses its concern in asking the child how he or she handles certain issues related to diabetes (i.e. fear of exercising or pricking insulin in public).

2.3 Embodiment

Social robots do not necessarily need a physical body to interact with their users. Their tasks can often be performed just as well by a virtual 3D representation or avatar of the same robot, which costs considerably less and is much more robust. But having a physical form does offer substantial benefits compared to virtual robots. Embodied robots (robots with a physical presence) are more appealing and perceptive of the world around them than non-embodied robots [27]. Participants' impression of the robot's watchfulness, helpfulness, and enjoyableness is significantly affected by embodiment. In a study on a socially assistive robot exercise coach for the elderly [28], participants strongly preferred a physically embodied assistive robot over the virtually simulated one. The interaction with the physical robot was rated as more enjoyable and useful. Physical embodiment has also been found to evoke a higher degree of user engagement and presence [29].

The positive effects of having a physical body were shown to still be prevalent when the robot is shown remotely via a camera. The social presence of a remote physical robot was almost the same as a robot that was located physically near the user [30]. A remote projected robot and a physically present robot were found to be equally engaging and elicited equal disclosure from the user.

The ALIZ-E project develops a robot for long-term interaction with chronically ill children undergoing treatment. It is important that the children interact with the same robot throughout this entire period to provide a consistent experience. They interact first with the physical robot in the hospital, and later continue with the same robot shown remotely from home.

2.4 Hypotheses

The bond between the robot and the child can serve as an incentive for the child to keep a diary. To this end, the robot engages in self-disclosing behavior and encourages the child to do the same. It also shows emulated empathy and concern for the child. And because people generally find interaction with a (remote) physical robot the most rewarding experience, we choose to study the effect of the robot on the child's self-disclosure in the diary, engagement in the activity, and bonding with the robot. This leads us to the following hypotheses:

1. Adherence: the robot encourages the child to self-disclose more information in their diaries.
2. Engagement: the robot has a positive effect on the child's engagement in the activity.
3. Bonding: the robot conveys a sense of trust and understanding of the child.

In order to test these hypotheses an experiment in a real-world setting was conducted.

3. IMPLEMENTATION

3.1 Robot

The NAO robot (developed by Aldebaran Robotics) was used in this experiment. NAO is well-suited for interaction with children largely due to its friendly childlike appearance. Although its face lacks the capability to display emotions, the robot is able to show a wide array of emotions through its body language. The expressions used in this experiment were idle behavior and emotional expressions that were pretested in [31]. The authors found that the recognition rates for these basic emotions (e.g. happiness, sadness and surprise) were relatively high, between 68% and 99% accuracy. Idle behavior consisted of small body movements such as moving the head and hand positions while speaking or waiting for the user to answer. The robot in the experiment was given the unisex name "Charlie" in order to appeal to both boys and girls. A background story was written for the robot to answer basic questions about its likes and preferences, and about its reason for participating in the experiment. In the story Charlie is a hospital care robot in training and it hopes the child can help it learn more about diabetes by keeping a diary together. When the robot engages in self-disclosure, it does so keeping this background story in mind. The robot has an inquisitive character, and regularly asks the child about what it is like having (and coping with) diabetes.

3.2 Dialogue model

A dialogue model was developed that structured the robot dialogue in an orderly fashion. The model consisted of two parts: the diary-related dialogue, and the interpersonal dialogue.

1. Diary-related dialogue: any dialogue related to the task of keeping a diary. This includes the login process, explaining of diary sections and filling in the diary itself. This part of the dialogue was very structured, and did not allow for much flexibility other than the child choosing what section he/she wanted to start with. Essentially this part of the dialogue was the same for every child.
2. Interpersonal dialogue (or 'small talk'): any dialogue not directly related to the task. There were two different types of small talk.
   - Self-disclosure small talk was used for the robot to share information about itself and optionally ask the child to do the same. For example, the robot told the child about its favorite pets, and then asked the child if he/she has any pets.
   - Diabetes-related small talk was used for the robot to talk about what it learned in school about diabetes (e.g. doing sports when having diabetes) and ask the child some basic questions about this topic (e.g. "How do you handle your diabetes when you do sports?"), and if he/she has any fears related to his/her diabetes (e.g. fear to prick blood glucose, or fear to exercise).

The small talk was used to enrich the dialogue between the robot and the child, with the goal of creating a bond between them.

3.3 Wizard of Oz

The main deliverable of the ALIZ-E project is an integrated and autonomous system comprising different modules. But because this system is developed incrementally and not all features have fully matured, some of the robot's functionality is simulated. The participants interacted with the robot which they believed to be autonomous, but which was actually controlled by the experiment leader in a Wizard of Oz (WoOz) setup. The NAO robot was capable of performing some actions autonomously, such as movements while speaking, 'blinking' of the eyes by switching LEDs on and off, and speaking (text-to-speech). Other actions could not be performed autonomously and needed human intervention. The experiment leader interpreted the user input (speech, gestures, and actions) to respond to the user by choosing the relevant remarks from the dialogue model. Certain movements such as cheering or nodding were initiated by the experiment leader by clicking the corresponding button in the WoOz interface. Updating the user model was also done by hand when the user provided new information. The dialogue was scripted in the dialogue model. In rare incidents, the experiment leader could type a response and have the robot say it via the text-to-speech module. The timing of interpersonal dialogue was largely up to the experiment leader. She could choose from one of the pre-scripted small talk phrases whenever a related topic was mentioned, or when there was a moment of silence.

3.4 Diary

The study required a diary that allowed the children to not only record their measured values, but that also had room for them to express how they feel. This allows the robot to respond empathetically to the emotional content of the diary. To this end, we chose to adapt an online diary for use in our experiment. Mijn Zorgpagina (literally 'my care page') is an initiative from Diabetesvereniging Nederland (DVN), the Dutch Association for Diabetes. In cooperation with DVN there were extra sections added to the diary to record the child's emotional well-being. The diary consisted of three different sections (see Figure 2): the 'values' section which consisted of different 'lines' for the recording of blood glucose values, carbohydrate intake, insulin doses and exercise; the 'emotions' section in which the child could rate his/her appetite, energy and mood levels using three sliders; and finally the 'daily activities' section which was a text box in which the children could write anything they wanted to share about their day.

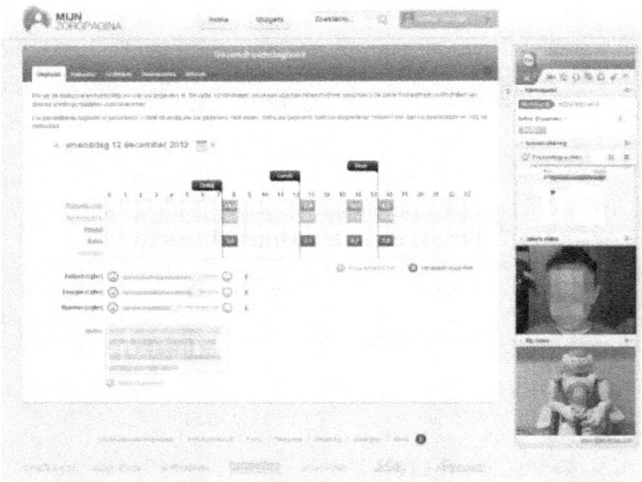

Figure 2. Screen as seen by the child showing diary and video conferencing software

In Figure 2, the video conferencing software (TeamViewer) we used is shown on the right-hand side of the screenshot (face of the child is blurred for privacy reasons). We used TeamViewer to enable desktop-sharing and communication via webcam and audio. Although the children could log into the diary from anywhere, we chose to provide each of them with a laptop that was stripped down to the bare minimum. The main reason for this was that we wanted to make sure all diaries were accessed from the same platform so that there would be no technical difficulties on their end. The children's accounts were set up in a way so that they would automatically log in when there was an internet connection. The child could then invite Charlie for a session. The sessions were all scheduled in advance. If they encountered any issues while attempting to log in or connecting to Charlie, the children could refer back to the child-friendly user manual that we provided or contact the experiment leader.

4. METHODS

4.1 Participants

Six children affiliated with Dutch hospital Rivierenland in Tiel participated in the formative evaluation. They were recruited with the help of a diabetes nurse who informed the children and their parents of the experiment. Interested parents were contacted and they received further information. They could then decide whether they wanted their child to participate. The group consisted of two girls and four boys, aged 9-12 (M=10.8, SD=1.3). All children were diagnosed with diabetes mellitus type 1. On average, they had diabetes for six years. None of the children had any prior experience in keeping a digital diary.

4.2 Experiment design and procedure

One week before the start of the experiment, we visited each of the children individually at home to introduce them to the robot. We explained the goal of the research and there was an opportunity to ask questions. The robot then introduced itself and asked the child to do the same. After that, we scheduled the sessions with the robot for the following two weeks. Children who forgot their appointments with Charlie were called to remind them. We feared that without reminders, children would forget their study participation, at the cost of valuable data. The goal of this experiment was gathering knowledge on the target group and their use of an online diary with or without the robot. As such the experiment can be seen as a formative evaluation. The number of participants was small and there was only limited time available for interaction with the robot. Therefore we decided to do a within-subjects design; this entails that all children kept a diary both with and without the robot. They did this for a total of 11 days. This allowed us to clearly see the differences in diary use for the same children in both conditions. We made two groups of three participants to spread the workload. This means that half of the children started on day 1 and finished on day 11, whereas the other half started on day 2 and finished on day 12. The sessions with and without the robot alternated every day. This excluded the weekends, which were always without the robot because access to the facility where the robot was stored was not possible. The children participated while in the comfort of their own homes using video conferencing software to contact the robot.

4.3 Measures

Below we present the metrics used for each of the three hypotheses.

1. *Adherence:* In this context adherence is defined as the extent to which children keep an accurate account of their values, mood and activities in their diaries on time (meaning on the same day the values were measured). If the robot has a positive effect on diary adherence, we expect to see 1) more completed diary entries with the robot, and 2) richer diary content (experience sharing/self-disclosure). We determine whether this is true by logging children's use of the diary and comparing the contents of the diary between sessions with and without support from the robot. Furthermore, we measure likeability and trust, because literature found these to be contributing factors for self-disclosure.

2. *Engagement:* An engaged child typically spends more time and is focused on the activity, and takes an active role in the activity. Comparing the time spent on the diaries between sessions with and without the robot can tell us what the influence of the robot on engagement is. Active participation and attention are measured by the experiment leader by observing the child's interaction with the robot via the webcam. A child is thought to take an active role in the conversation whenever he/she asks or tells the robot something of his/her own accord instead of waiting for the robot to ask something first. We can determine attention by observing the child's gaze direction. When the child looks away from the diary and the robot, he/she is distracted.

3. *Bonding:* A bond between two conversational partners is characterized by emotions such as affection and trust. To investigate to what extent interaction with the robot created a bond, we used a post-condition questionnaire which focused on the degree of relatedness the children experienced with the robot. When a child trusts the robot, believes it has feelings, and thinks that it can truly understand him/her, the feeling of relatedness is strong.

4.4 Instruments

The children were asked to complete a total of 7 questionnaires. The questions were phrased in simple terms and emoticons were added to Likert-scale questions for clarification (cf. [32]). The pre-condition questionnaire was answered prior to the experiment, and inquired about demographic information, interests and expectations. We used this questionnaire to learn more about our participants and whether they understood the experiment correctly. After each interaction session (5x) with the robot, the children were again asked to fill in a questionnaire. This questionnaire only contained two questions which inquired about the children's ratings of the robot and the diary. This data can be used to determine whether there are any changes over time. Finally, the children answered a post-condition questionnaire after all the sessions were completed. In this questionnaire we asked them about their overall judgment of the robot and the diary, the degree of relatedness with the robot, and feelings towards the robot. These data were mostly used to determine the extent of the relationship between the child and the robot.

Furthermore, we also made use of three different types of logs. The diary logs were provided by MijnZorgpagina and provided insight into the children's use of the diary on days when the robot was not present. The WoOz logs were automatically generated whenever a command was sent to the robot. We used these to determine use of the diary with the robot. Lastly, the experimenter leader's observation logs were used to note any changes in experience sharing, active participation and attention of the children during the sessions. Miscellaneous observations were also noted in these logs.

Initially we had planned to record all interaction sessions on video to carefully note any changes in active participation and attention. However, due to a technical problem, the video conferencing software crashed when the recording software was started. We came to rely on the experiment leader's observations for data regarding the children's engagement.

4.5 Setup

Figure 3 provides a schematic overview of the experimental setup. To mimic the natural sitting position of humans during video calls, the robot (1) was seated in a chair during the interaction sessions. The webcam (2) was aimed at the robot from an angle slightly higher than eye level because we wanted the children to believe it was operating its own laptop. During the interaction sessions, the experiment leader (3) was seated out of view. She was in control of the robot's actions using a laptop and an extra screen (4). She was also able to see the screen and webcam of the child using the video conferencing software (5) on a second laptop. The experiment leader made as little noise as possible so as not to alert the child to her presence. To this end, we used a silent mouse (6) that lacked the "click" sound when a button was pressed.

Figure 3. Experimental setup

5. RESULTS

All six children completed the full experiment and the associated questionnaires. Diary use prior to the experiment was found to be very low; none of the children kept a diary on a daily basis. Five out of six children used an insulin pump and three of them indicated they did not keep a diabetes diary (anymore) because they were able to read out values from their pumps if needed. Only one child said that he currently kept a diary all by himself, but after enquiring about his diary use he admitted to only doing it once every three months when it was required for a hospital consultation. All of the children said to be at least moderately interested in technological advances such as robots or gadgets.

5.1 Adherence

The log data from the diary revealed that not all children completed their diaries on time (meaning on the same day the values were measured). When a diary entry was not completed on time, it was usually completed the day after. When they were not interacting with the robot, two of the children sometimes neglected to keep their diary. One of them missed all (6) entries, the other left only 2 entries uncompleted. Three children logged on multiple times (1, 2 and 8 times) to supplement values as new information became available. The differences between the conditions in filling out the diary were not significant due to the high interpersonal variation. Figure 4 shows the differences in diary completion between conditions in percentages of the total actions performed. For example, all children fully completed the diary in the robot condition, but some of them also supplemented the diary with extra information when it became available in this condition. The total of all these actions adds up to 100 percent.

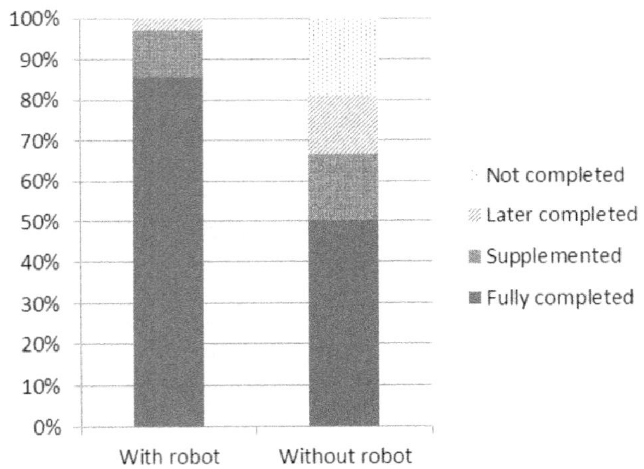

Figure 4. Diary actions performed with and without robot

We compared the amount of characters used in the daily activity logs between the days with the robot and without the robot as an indicator for experience sharing. It was found that children wrote significantly more in their logs when they were interacting with the robot (M=83.10, SD=43.96) than without the robot (M=36.8, SD=54.31); t(5)=4.13, p=.009; but there were clear differences between participants. In table 1 it is evident that one participants (5) always filled in high quantities of data, whereas some others filled in less on days without the robot (2 and 3), or nothing at all when the robot was absent (1 and 4).

Overall, the children rated the diary positive throughout the experiment. The diary received an average rating of 3.9 on a scale from 1 to 5.

6.2 Embodiment and children's engagement

From the log data we gathered that the time taken to fill in the diary dramatically decreased after the first two sessions. This can be explained by the fact that during the first session the children listened to the robot explaining every diary section, while in subsequent interactions this explanation was optionally accessible (and rarely asked for). Due to the failed recordings of the sessions, the data on children's interaction behavior was elicited from notes made by the experiment leader during the study. These notes were taken systematically and helped explain some of the results, but unfortunately they could not be statistically validated. The observations showed a strong difference in active participation between the younger children, who were very open and talkative, and the older children who were less open and talkative. Possibly, the background story for Charlie was not convincing or appealing enough for the older participants in this study. This is in line with the commentary we received from an older child (13) during the pilot study we performed prior to the experiment ("I think the story is too childish for 11-12 year olds"). Overall, the experiment leader had the impression that the children paid close attention to the robot and the diary. They did not allow themselves to be distracted by background noises, siblings or parents. While some parents chose to supervise their child during the sessions, they did not appear to be a distracting factor. We did however see some mixed results in the answers on the question whether it was difficult to focus when they were keeping a diary with Charlie (in the post-condition questionnaire). But this might also be due to the slow internet connections of some children. Occasionally there were very large delays in the sound transmission, which made it difficult to understand what Charlie was saying. Since we did not have sufficient data on the children's engagement with the diary without the robot present, it is difficult to say whether the robot had a positive effect on the child's engagement in the activity. Therefore we cannot confirm the second hypothesis.

6.3 Robot's understanding and trust

Overall, the robot was received very well by the children. They greatly enjoyed interacting with Charlie. They believed it had feelings, was able to understand them, and that it behaved human-like, which are signs of empathy. However, we have to be careful in saying the conveyed sense of trust and understanding of the child was because of the robot (hypothesis 3), because occasionally part of the dialogue was typed by the experiment leader directly and converted to speech by the robot when there was no suitable answer in the dialogue model. Although most of the dialogue used was in fact pre-scripted, the comments that were made on the fly could have still somewhat skewed our results.

6.4 Future work

Future work in the area of robot-driven diary support could benefit from sentiment analysis, which refers to the use of natural language processing, text analysis and computational linguistics to identify and extract subjective information from source materials (i.e. the diary). Sentiment analysis would allow the robot to more accurately predict and interpret the emotional state of the child and choose the appropriate response. In our experiment, a human actor had to interpret the data and 'translate' this for the robot. Ultimately the goal of the ALIZ-E project is an integrated system which operates without human intervention. There still needs to be done a significant amount of work in the area of speech recognition and interpretation to achieve this goal.

This paper presented a first experiment in which we succeeded to include six children with diabetes, who interacted with the application over an extended period of time. Due to the small number of participants, a within-subjects design was applied. Based on the results, we will be able to get other hospitals interested and conduct a between-subjects experiment with more participants. Participation of diabetic children remains crucial, because children without diabetes do not have the intrinsic motivation or ability to fully complete a diabetes diary.

In the current experiment there was no explicit feedback about the relationship between blood glucose, mood and daily activities. In future work it would be interesting to add this type of feedback to the dialogue and to discover patterns together with the robot. We see opportunities for two follow-up experiments: (1) comparing children who keep a diary either with or without the robot, and (2) comparing their diary usage for a robot which does or does not exhibit self-disclosure, empathy and embodiment. Last but not least, the bonding effects of co-located and remote interactions should be tested: How the bonding transfers or evolves from co-located experiences with the robot in the hospital to remote interactions via webcam, and vice versa.

7. CONCLUSION

This paper investigated the contribution of a social robot to keeping an online diary together with diabetic children. A social robot can enhance the pleasure of the activity, and therefore the motivation of the child. Especially once the robot and the child really get to know each other, the child starts to consider the robot as a friend and he/she really opens up to it. Keeping an online diary together with a social robot can contribute to a better diary adherence. The robot utilizes aspects of physical embodiment, self-disclosure and empathy in its behavior and dialogue to achieve this goal. When we take into account that the diary use prior to this study was almost non-existent, this is a considerable improvement. Keeping a record of the values, emotional well-being and the daily activities allows the child to make meaningful inferences about the relationship between these three variables. This positively influences the child's self-reflection capabilities, which in turn contributes to his/her self-management. The robot could help the children overcome the initial hurdles of taking charge of their own diabetes self-management. The addition of a robot does not have to be detrimental to the children's feeling of independence, which becomes increasingly important as they reach puberty. This study provides a sound foundation for future research into robot characteristics and their effect on emotional support for chronically ill children.

8. ACKNOWLEDGMENTS

This work is funded by the EU FP7 ALIZ-E project (grant 248116). We would like to thank the diabetic children and medical staff from the ZRT hospital in Tiel (the Netherlands) and Diabetesvereniging Nederland (DVN) for their cooperation.

9. REFERENCES

[1] International Diabetes Federation. 2012. IDF diabetes atlas. Retrieved August 13, 2013 from http://www.idf.org/diabetesatlas/5e/diabetes-in-the-young

[2] Whittemore, R., Kanner, S. and Grey, M. 2004. The influence of family on psychological and psychosocial health in youth with type 1 diabetes: a systematic review. In Melnyk, B.M. & Fineout-Overholt. *Evidence-based practice*

in nursing and healthcare: a guide to best practice, Williams & Wilkins, Philadelphia, CD22-73-CD22-87.

[3] Grey, M., Whittemore, R. and Tamborlane, W. 2002. Depression in type 1 diabetes in children: natural history and correlates. *Journal of Psychosomatic Research, 53*, 4, 907-11.

[4] Kovacs, M., Goldston, D., Obrosky, D.S. and Bonar, L.K. 1997. Psychiatric disorders in youths with IDDM: rates and risk factors. *Diabetes Care, 20,* 36-44.

[5] Affenito, S.G. and Adams, C.H. 2001. Are eating disorders more prevalent in females with type 1 diabetes mellitus when the impact of insulin omission is considered? *Nutrition Reviews, 59,* 179-182.

[6] Rosenthal, S.M. 2008. *The Canadian Type 2 Diabetes Sourcebook*. John Wiley & Sons Inc, Hoboken (New Jersey), 72-73.

[7] Palermo, T.M., Valenzuela, D. And Stork, P.P. 2004. A randomized trial of electronic versus paper pain diaries in children: impact on compliance, accuracy, and acceptability. *Pain, 107*, 3, 213-219.

[8] ALIZ-E. 2013. ALIZ-E research. Retrieved September 6, 2013 from http://www.alize.org

[9] Lee, K.M., Peng, W., Jin, S. and Yan, C. 2006. Can Robots Manifest Personality? An empirical test of personality recognition, social responses, and social presence in human-robot interaction. *Journal of communication, 56*, 4, 754-772.

[10] Okita, S.Y. 2013. Self-Other's Perspective Taking: The Use of Therapeutic Robot Companions as Social Agents for Reducing Pain and Anxiety in Pediatric Patients. *Cyberpsychology, Behavior, and Social Networking, 16*, 6, 436-441.

[11] Chidambaram, V., Chiang, Y.H. and Mutlu, B. 2012. Designing persuasive robots: how robots might persuade people using vocal and nonverbal cues. In *Proc. HRI 2012*, ACM Press (2012), 293-300.

[12] Blanson Henkemans, O.A., van der Boog, P.J.M., Lindenberg, J., van der Mast, C.A.P.G., Neerincx, M.A. and Zwetsloot-Schonk, B.J.H.M. 2009. An online lifestyle diary with a persuasive computer assistant providing feedback on self-management. *Technology and Health Care, 17*, 3, 253-267.

[13] Fogg, B.J. 2003. *Persuasive technology: using computers to change what we think and do*. Morgan Kaufmann Publishers, Amsterdam.

[14] Lask, B. 2003. Motivating children and adolescents to improve adherence. *The Journal of Pediatrics, 143*, 4, 430-433.

[15] Baxter, P., Belpaeme, T., Cañamero, L., Cosi, P., Demiris, Y. and Enescu, V. 2011. Long-Term Human-Robot Interaction with Young Users. In *Proceedings of HRI Workshop 2011*, Lausanne.

[16] Higashinaka, R., Dohsaka, K. and Isozaki, H. 2008. Effects of self-disclosure and empathy in human-computer dialogue. In *IEEE Spoken Language Technology Workshop 2008*, Goa, India.

[17] Altman, I. and Taylor, D. 1973. *Social penetration: The development of interpersonal relationships*. Holt, Rinehart & Winston, New York.

[18] Reis, H.T. and Shaver, P. 1988. Intimacy as an interpersonal process. In Duck, S. *Handbook of personal relationships*, Wiley, Chichester, England, 367-398.

[19] Moon, Y. 2000, Intimate exchanges: using computers to elicit self-disclosure from consumers. *The Journal of Consumer Research, 26*, 4, 323-339.

[20] Collins, N.L. and Miller, L.C. 1994. Self-Disclosure and Liking: A Meta-Analytic Review. *Psychological Bulletin,* 116, 3, 457-475.

[21] Jourard, S.M. 1964. *The transparent self.* Van Nostrand, Princeton.

[22] Laurenceau, J.P., Feldman Barrett, L. and Pietromonaco, P.R. 1998. Intimacy as an interpersonal process: the importance of self-disclosure, partner disclosure, and perceived partner responsiveness in interpersonal exchanges. *Journal of Personality and Social Psychology, 74*, 5, 1238-1251.

[23] Borchers, T. Self-Disclosure. 1999. Retrieved March 16, 2012 from http://www.abacon.com/commstudies/interpersonal/indisclosure.html

[24] Siino, R.M., Chung, J. and Hinds, P.J. 2008. Colleague vs. Tool: effects of disclosure in human-robot collaboration. In *17th IEEE International Symposium on Robot and Human Interactive Communication 2008*, Münich.

[25] Tapus, A. and Mataric, M.J. 2007. Emulating Empathy in Socially Assistive Robotics. In *AAAI Spring Symposium: Multidisciplinary Collaboration for Socially Assistive Robotics 2007,* Palo Alto, California.

[26] Davis, M.H. 1983. Measuring individual differences in empathy: evidence for a multidisciplinary approach. *Journal of Personality and Social Psychology, 44*, 113-126.

[27] Wainer, J., Feil-Seifer, D.J., Shell, D.A. and Mataric, M.J. 2007. Embodiment and Human-Robot Interaction: A Task-Based Perspective. In *16th IEEE International Conference on Robot & Human Interactive Communication 2007*, Jeju, Korea.

[28] Fasola, F. and Mataric, M.J. 2011 *Comparing Physical and Virtual Embodiment in a Socially Assistive Robot Exercise Coach for the Elderly.* Center for Robotics and Embedded Systems, Los Angeles, CA.

[29] Deshmukh, A., Aylett, R., Kriegel, M. and Vargas, P.A. 2012. Multiple embodiments for robots in heritage applications. In *First international conference robotic innovation for cultural heritage 2012*, Venice, Italy.

[30] Powers, A., Kiesler, S., Fussell, S. and Torrey, C. 2007. Comparing a Computer Agent with a Humanoid Robot. In *HRI 2007*, Arlington, Virginia.

[31] Cohen, I., Looije, R., Neerincx, M.A. Child's perception of robot's emotions: effects of platform, context and experience. *International Journal of Social Robotics* (in press).

[32] Read, J. and MacFarlane, S. 2002. Endurability, Engagement and Expectations: Measuring Children's Fun. In *Interaction Design and Children*, Vol. 2. Shaker Publishing, Eindhoven.

Destination Unknown: Walking Side-by-Side without Knowing the Goal

Ryo Murakami, Yoichi Morales, Satoru Satake, Takayuki Kanda, and Hiroshi Ishiguro
ATR Intelligent Robotics and Communication Laboratories
2-2-2 Hikaridai, Seika-cho, Souraku-gun, Kyoto, Japan
{murakami, yoichims, satoru, kanda, ishiguro}@atr.jp

ABSTRACT

Walking side by side is a common situation when we go from one place to another with another person while talking. Our previous study reported a basic mechanism for side-by-side walking, but in the previous model it was crucial that each agent knew where he or she was going, i.e. *the route to the destination*. However, we have recognized the need to model the situation where one of the agents does not know the destination. The extended model presented in this work has two states: *leader-follower state* and *collaborative state*. Depending on whether the follower agent has obtained a reliable estimate of the route to follow, the walking agents transition between the two states. The model is calibrated with trajectories acquired from pairs of people walking side by side, and then it is tested in a human-robot interaction scenario. The results demonstrate that the new extended model achieves better side-by-side performance than a standard method without knowledge of the subgoal.

Categories and Subject Descriptors

H.5.2 [Information Interfaces and Presentation]: User Interfaces - *Interaction styles*; I.2.9 [Artificial Intelligence]: Robotics

General Terms

Design, Experimentation, Human Factors.

Keywords

Human-robot interaction, anticipation, intention prediction, side-by-side walking.

1. INTRODUCTION

There are various social robots considered for the future use, many of which involve scenes where people and robots walk together. For instance, a museum guide robot would provide a tour guide [25], in a nursing home, robots would take elderly residents between facilities [20], in a supermarket a robot would take a user to a specific item shelf [9], and in a shopping mall a robot would take users to the target shops [6]. It would be great that if such robots could walk in a side-by-side formation like people do when they walk together while talking.

In our previous work, we have revealed that reproducing side-by-side formation is not a trivial problem. We found that it is not a simple computation to be "beside" a partner, but it involves consideration of side-by-side position as well as going toward a destination [19]. In scenarios like tour guide and direction giving, it is the robot that knows the destination, and thus our assumptions about the scenario were satisfactory. In contrast, we have found that such constraints cause problems for a "robot as partner" scenario. For instance, in a scene of window-shopping, people often do not have a pre-determined destination with a shopping partner [12]. Instead, depending on their interest, they sometimes change course. When one person decides whether to go left or right at an intersection (Fig. 1), how would her partner know the direction, and how could she continue to walk side by side?

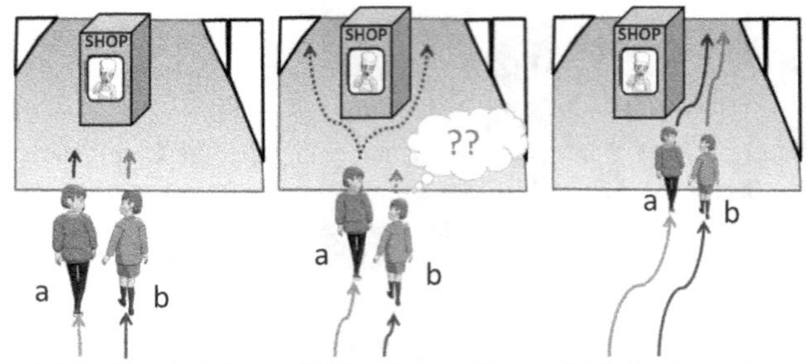

(a) Going straight (b) Leader guiding (c) Inferring subgoal

Figure 1. People walking side by side facing an intersection.

This paper presents a method for a robot to maintain side-by-side walking when it does not know the destination, which reflects quite common situations in our daily interactions, such as window-shopping, strolling, and walking. We build a model in which the robot estimates the local destination (referred to as the subgoal) from the behavior of the user.

2. RELATED WORKS

2.1 Spatial Configuration in Social Robotics

Proxemics is one of the actively studied topics. In Hall's seminal work, he reported that human's interaction distance varies along with their social context [10]. There is a study about formation during conversation while stopped but not walking [14]. It was revealed that people keep social distance even with a robot [26]. Recent studies reported that such social distance is influenced by robot's gaze [24] and height [21]. Distance with a robot is used for estimating engagement [16] and situation of interaction [5].

While the above studies focused on static situations, some research works have addressed dynamic situations. Gockley and her colleagues developed a planner for following its user from behind [7]. Sisbot and his colleagues developed a path-planning algorithm that considers people's comfort [23]. Satake and his colleagues developed an approaching behavior, in which anticipation of the target person's motion was indispensable [22].

2.2 Side-by-side Walking

People tend to walk in a side-by-side formation [4], particularly when they are socially interacting within a group. The importance of side-by-side walking for HRI has already been discussed [13].

HRI'14, March 3-6, 2014, Bielefeld, Germany.

http://dx.doi.org/10.1145/2559636.2559665.

In the literature, only few studies have addressed side-by-side walking [15][19]. The key features of these studies are summarized in table 1. One common idea is *velocity-based prediction*. A robot predicts the partner's position and then tries to simply move to be at the "side" of the predicted position of the partner. For instance, Kobayashi and his colleagues developed a wheel-chair robot that moves alongside a care-giver, basically modeling the situation where it needs to avoid obstacles while trying to move at the "side" of the partner [15].

In contrast, instead of solely relying on the partner's current velocity, we developed a model that learns from people walking in a side-by-side formation [19]. The model computes the utility of an agent that aims to go to the "side" of the partner while avoiding obstacles and moving toward the destination. It enables the robot to *anticipate the partner's motion utility* in addition to its own. In other words, the model is based on the idea that two agents (e.g. a person and a robot) plan for what is best for both. Such anticipation made the robot's behavior natural and smooth.

However, our previous work had a shortcoming. It assumes that both agents know the 'subgoals,' the local destinations that they move to. This information is crucial if we want to anticipate the partner's future motion; consequently, our previous method does not work without *knowing a predefined route*. Such situations often occur. For instance, if a user is window-shopping, he may not have any idea of where to go next, and thus a companion robot may not have any chance to know the path in advance.

We aim to overcome the above fundamental shortcoming. The methods with *velocity-based predictions* are also free from constraints of *knowing a predefined route*, but have weaknesses due to the lack of the partner's motion anticipation. This paper presents a method with the dual capabilities of *anticipating the partner's utility, without knowing a predefined route*.

Table 1: Comparison of methods for side-by-side walking

	Anticipate partner's utility	Without knowing a predefined route
Velocity-based prediction	No	Yes
Previous work [16]	Yes	No
This study	**Yes**	**Yes**

3. DATA COLLECTION

3.1 Purpose

The objective of collecting human trajectory data is to observe how pairs of humans walk together if one of them is not informed about the path. For this purpose, we collected information from pairs of humans walking together in a scenario where one of them knows the destination (*leader*) but the other one (*follower*) does not. This effort involves two key questions:

- Can they continue walking in a side-by-side formation?
- If so, how does the follower acquire the information about the next subgoal? Does the follower need to verbally or non-verbally ask the leader for this information?

3.2 Procedure

The data collection was performed in an indoor corridor environment in an office. Figure 2 shows a map of the environment. The corridor is 2 *m* wide, and there is an intersection in the middle. We defined a start location and two possible goal locations, one that could be reached just by going straight and the other one by turning left.

We placed a set of six laser scanners around the environment to track the positions of humans. The data were processed with a sampling rate of 0.025 seconds. We applied a low-pass filter to the data to smooth the trajectories.

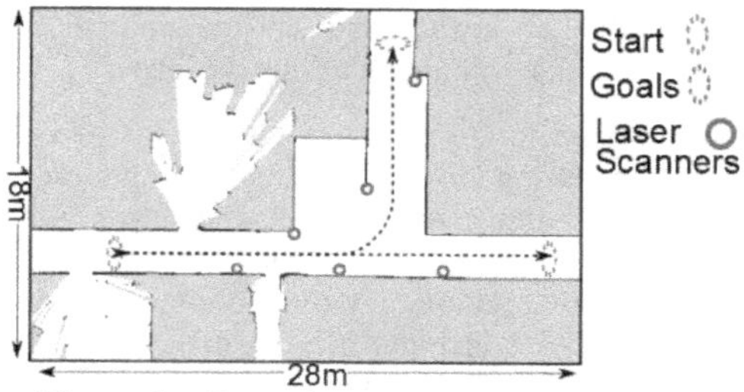

Figure 2. Experimental environment map

There were six pairs of participants (5 females and 7 males, average age 31.1), all members of our laboratory. We carefully paired them according to similar social status in the laboratory.

We did not inform them that we wanted to observe their walking trajectories but only asked the m to walk together side by side as they normally do while having a conversation, and we told them they were free to talk. The goal location was only given to one of the participants (leader), whereas the second one (follower) was asked to keep walking alongside the partner.

Every participant walked ten times as leader and ten times as follower. We collected 20 trajectories per pair, totaling 120 trajectories. We used this 'trajectory dataset' to establish a computational model of 'walking alongside without being informed of the destination.

3.3 Observations

We found that they kept walking side-by-side although we did not tell the followers about the destination. For instance, Fig. 3 shows one of the scenes in which the person walking on the right is the *leader* and the person walking on the left is the *follower*. At first sight, one might be unable to tell which one is the leader as they walked in a similar way, as if both of them knew the subgoal.

How does the follower know where they will go? As we randomly changed their goals, it was difficult to guess. We did not observe any case where they communicated the direction verbally (e.g. saying "let's turn left") or explicitly non-verbally (e.g. pointing in the direction). In our daily life, we sometimes explicitly communicate the direction, but perhaps because they were asked to engage in a normal conversation, these participants did not. The important point is that they were able to walk side by side without explicit communication of the subgoal.

(a) Walking straight (b) Only *leader* turns (c) Both turn

Figure 3. Walking together at an intersection

The crucial moment was captured in the center photo of Fig. 3, where the motion direction is illustrated with arrows. At this moment, we can observe that the leader starts walking left, while the follower continues walking straight. It is also notable that the follower has already opened space for the leader to turn left. If the follower just mindlessly kept walking straight in a strictly side-by-side formation, it would be very difficult for the leader to turn left; if he tries to turn, they would collide or push each other. Then, after this moment, the follower very quickly understood the current subgoal (i.e. toward the corridor on the left) and readjusted to continue walking alongside the leader.

Figures 4 and 5 show the trajectories of a pair of people in a similar situation. In the figures, timestamp points are shown in boldface numbers, indicating people's relative positions at different points in time. In both cases, from the start until the point around the intersection, they walked directly side-by-side ($t \leq 5.3$ in figure 4, $t \leq 5.2$ in Figure 5), meaning that their relative angle (angle toward the *follower* from the *leader's* motion direction) was very close to 90 degrees (89.1 degrees, s.d.=4.5). At these moments, it would have been easy for the follower to understand that they were walking along the path of the corridor. Thus, even though the destination was not given, the current subgoal during these moments was apparent to the follower. We named this situation the *collaborative state*.

However, around the area where there is a choice of route (whether to go straight or turn), their behavior changed (t=7.0 in Fig. 4, t=7.0 in Fig. 5). While the leader (solid line) kept walking toward the goal, the follower (dotted line) walked slightly behind. As discussed above, Fig. 3 captured the moment around this area. This approx. 10 degrees of offset of relative angle from 90 degrees (toward the *follower* from the *leader's* motion direction, in all trajectories, avg. 99.2 degrees, s.d.= 7.9) has two effects: It enables the follower to observe the leader's moving direction, and it also enables the leader to easily turn without obstructing the follower's walking. We named this state *leader-follower* state.

Their recovery from the *leader-follower* state is quite fast. In the case of Fig. 5, by t=10.5, the follower is already directly beside the leader. In Fig. 4, this recovery occurred more slowly, but by t=14.0, we can see that their formation has finally returned to a direct side-by-side position. After knowing whether the leader is turning or not, the current subgoal should again be apparent to the follower. Thus, this situation is also the *collaborative state* we designated above.

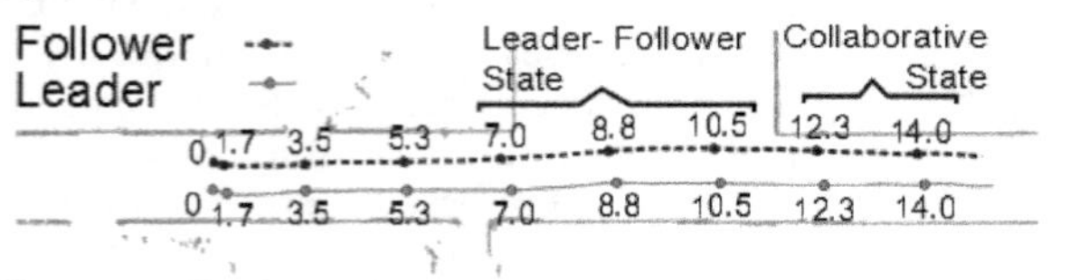

Figure 4. Trajectories when participants walked straight.

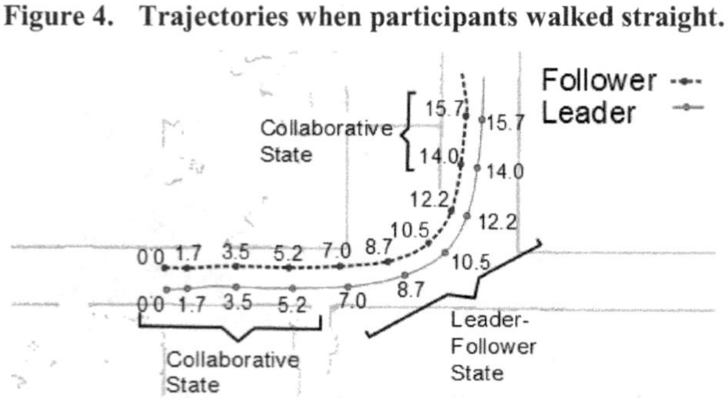

Figure 5. Trajectories when participants turned left.

4. MODELLING

4.1 Overview

In the previous section we found the existence of two states in the pair's motion, *collaborative* and *leader-follower* states. We built a model using these states for "walking side by side when a person does not know the goal". Our target is to reproduce the follower's motion in a human-like manner for a robot. Following the findings of Section 3.4 the assumptions of the model are:

- The follower agent (robot) is not informed about the current destination (subgoal) in advance.
- Follower still maintains a side-by-side formation, which is very important while engaging the partner in conversation.
- Leader and follower agents do not explicitly communicate about the subgoal.

Regarding the third assumption, we believe that it is possible for the leader agent to explicitly provide information about subgoals to the follower, although it was not observed in the data collection. Our model can be easily extended to the case of such explicit communication because the state transition to the *collaborative state* occurs if the follower agent becomes sure of the subgoal. In this study, we focus on the case where the subgoal is not explicitly communicated, and thus the follower agent must identify it from the motion of the leader.

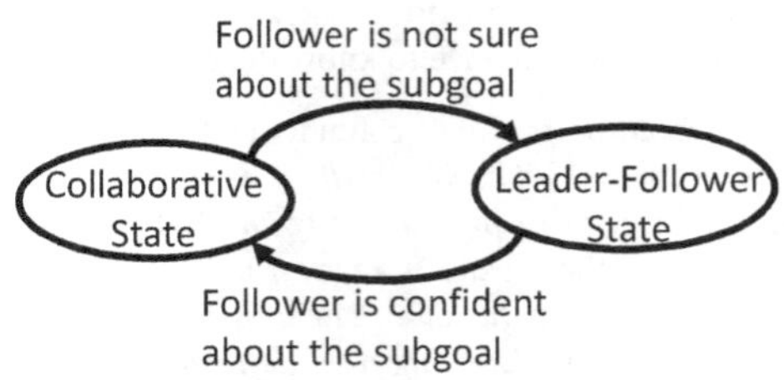

Figure 6. *Collaborative state* and *leader-follower state.*

Figure 6 illustrates this transition. Both agents walk in collaborative state (detailed in section 4.2) when both know the location they are heading toward (subgoal). When only one of the walking partners knows the path (i.e. at an intersection), they walk in a leader-follower state (detailed in section 4.3). The state transition occurs based on whether the follower agent knows the current subgoal. The mechanism of subgoal estimation is explained in section 4.4.

Note that we use the term 'subgoal' as the point in the environment where an agent is heading. There is a technique to estimate the subgoal locations in a real environment if we can observe a number of trajectories from pedestrians [11].

4.2 Collaborative State

This state (Figure 7) was observed before and after the area where there are choice of subgoals. Identical to the situation in previous work [19], both agents know (or successfully inferred) the current subgoal, while both agents try to act collaboratively to maintain their relative positions. Thus, for this state, we simply applied our previous model.

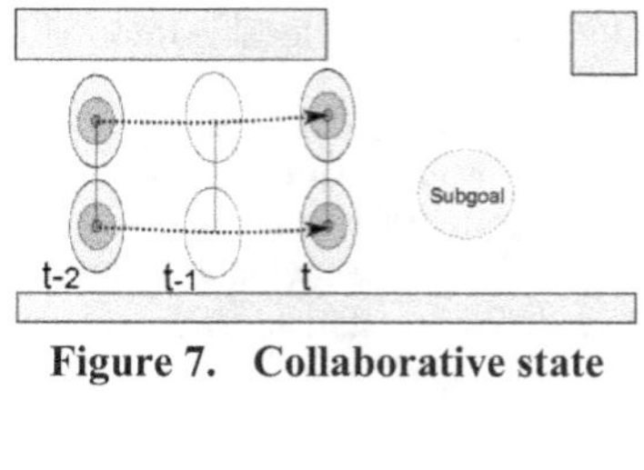

Figure 7. Collaborative state

moment, we can observe that the leader starts walking left, while the follower continues walking straight. It is also notable that the follower has already opened space for the leader to turn left. If the follower just mindlessly kept walking straight in a strictly side-by-side formation, it would be very difficult for the leader to turn left; if he tries to turn, they would collide or push each other. Then, after this moment, the follower very quickly understood the current subgoal (i.e. toward the corridor on the left) and readjusted to continue walking alongside the leader.

Figures 4 and 5 show the trajectories of a pair of people in a similar situation. In the figures, timestamp points are shown in boldface numbers, indicating people's relative positions at different points in time. In both cases, from the start until the point around the intersection, they walked directly side-by-side ($t \leq 5.3$ in figure 4, $t \leq 5.2$ in Figure 5), meaning that their relative angle (angle toward the *follower* from the *leader's* motion direction) was very close to 90 degrees (89.1 degrees, s.d.=4.5). At these moments, it would have been easy for the follower to understand that they were walking along the path of the corridor. Thus, even though the destination was not given, the current subgoal during these moments was apparent to the follower. We named this situation the *collaborative state*.

However, around the area where there is a choice of route (whether to go straight or turn), their behavior changed (t=7.0 in Fig. 4, t=7.0 in Fig. 5). While the leader (solid line) kept walking toward the goal, the follower (dotted line) walked slightly behind. As discussed above, Fig. 3 captured the moment around this area. This approx. 10 degrees of offset of relative angle from 90 degrees (toward the *follower* from the *leader's* motion direction, in all trajectories, avg. 99.2 degrees, s.d.= 7.9) has two effects: It enables the follower to observe the leader's moving direction, and it also enables the leader to easily turn without obstructing the follower's walking. We named this state *leader-follower* state.

Their recovery from the *leader-follower* state is quite fast. In the case of Fig. 5, by t=10.5, the follower is already directly beside the leader. In Fig. 4, this recovery occurred more slowly, but by t=14.0, we can see that their formation has finally returned to a direct side-by-side position. After knowing whether the leader is turning or not, the current subgoal should again be apparent to the follower. Thus, this situation is also the *collaborative state* we designated above.

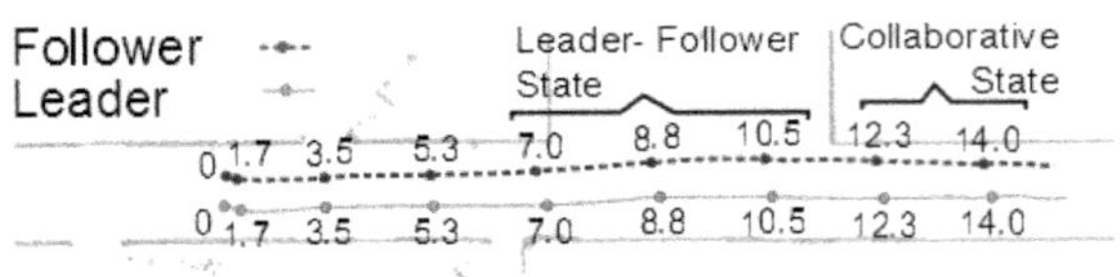

Figure 4. Trajectories when participants walked straight.

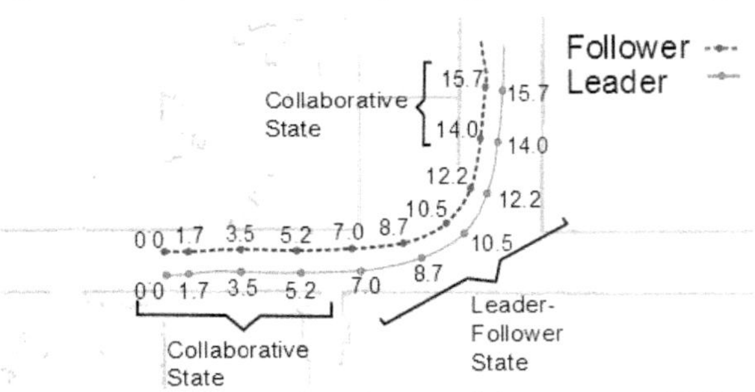

Figure 5. Trajectories when participants turned left.

4. MODELLING

4.1 Overview

In the previous section we found the existence of two states in the pair's motion, *collaborative* and *leader-follower* states. We built a model using these states for "walking side by side when a person does not know the goal". Our target is to reproduce the follower's motion in a human-like manner for a robot. Following the findings of Section 3.4 the assumptions of the model are:

- The follower agent (robot) is not informed about the current destination (subgoal) in advance.
- Follower still maintains a side-by-side formation, which is very important while engaging the partner in conversation.
- Leader and follower agents do not explicitly communicate about the subgoal.

Regarding the third assumption, we believe that it is possible for the leader agent to explicitly provide information about subgoals to the follower, although it was not observed in the data collection. Our model can be easily extended to the case of such explicit communication because the state transition to the *collaborative state* occurs if the follower agent becomes sure of the subgoal. In this study, we focus on the case where the subgoal is not explicitly communicated, and thus the follower agent must identify it from the motion of the leader.

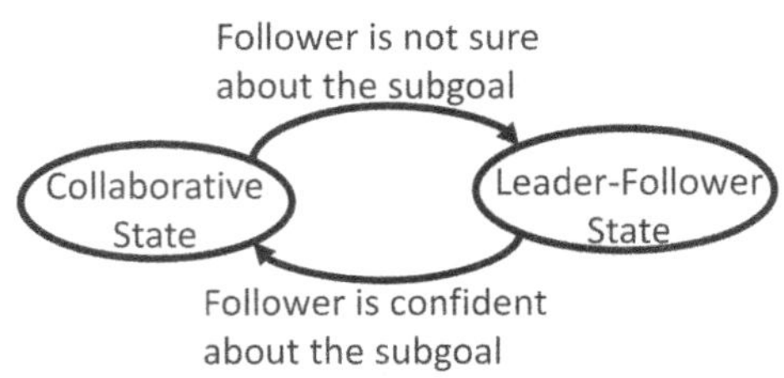

Figure 6. *Collaborative state* and *leader-follower state*.

Figure 6 illustrates this transition. Both agents walk in collaborative state (detailed in section 4.2) when both know the location they are heading toward (subgoal). When only one of the walking partners knows the path (i.e. at an intersection), they walk in a leader-follower state (detailed in section 4.3). The state transition occurs based on whether the follower agent knows the current subgoal. The mechanism of subgoal estimation is explained in section 4.4.

Note that we use the term 'subgoal' as the point in the environment where an agent is heading. There is a technique to estimate the subgoal locations in a real environment if we can observe a number of trajectories from pedestrians [11].

4.2 Collaborative State

This state (Figure 7) was observed before and after the area where there are choice of subgoals. Identical to the situation in previous work [19], both agents know (or successfully inferred) the current subgoal, while both agents try to act collaboratively to maintain their relative positions. Thus, for this state, we simply applied our previous model.

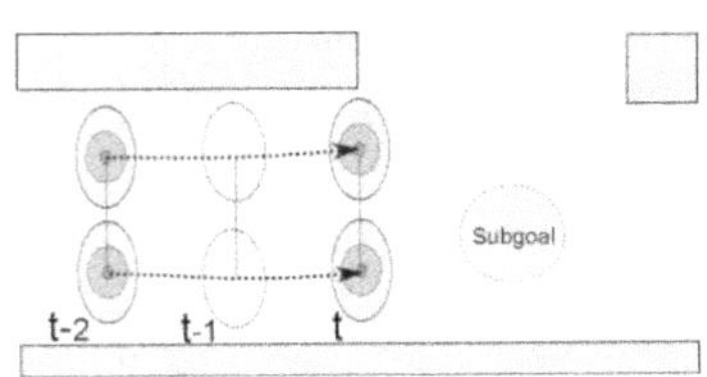

Figure 7. Collaborative state

Here we will briefly introduce our previous work. More details are available in the earlier paper [19]. The primary idea is to represent the goodness of future locations as a *utility* function. We combined eight different factors for this utility. Figure 8 illustrates all eight factors. From the perspective of the 'agent, its utility is high if it moves toward the subgoal (represented by *subgoal utility* E_S), if it is far from obstacles (*obstacle utility* E_O), if its relative position is precisely alongside the partner (*relative utilities:* R_a, R_d, and R_v), and if its motion is sufficiently smooth (*motion utilities:* M_a, M_w, and M_v). In concrete terms, given the agent's position at time *t* denoted as p_t^i, each utility is defined as follows:

Obstacle utility (E_O). This is modeled as the following function, which is often used to represent the potential field for obstacles:

$$f_o(x) = -\left|\left(\frac{x}{a}\right)^{-2b}\right| \tag{1}$$

E_O is defined as $f_o(d_{closest}(p_{t+1}^i))$, where $d_{closest}(p)$ returns the distance to the closest obstacle at position p. The utility will be higher if the distance to the obstacle is farther.

All other utility functions are modeled as power functions (Eq. 2) because their distribution has a peak and is roughly symmetrical.

$$f(x) = -\left|\left(\frac{x-c}{a}\right)^{2b}\right| \tag{2}$$

This power function has three parameters. Parameter "a" is related to the tolerance of the function, parameter "b" corresponds to the curve steepness factor, and parameter "c" is the curve's center where the function yields the maximum value.

Subgoal utility ($E_S(S)$): This computes the utility for moving toward the given subgoal S, which is defined as $f(\text{angle}(\overrightarrow{p_{t+1}^i p_t^i}, \overrightarrow{Sp_{t+1}^i}))$ where $\text{angle}(\vec{p},\vec{q})$ is a function that returns the relative angle of vectors $\vec{p}$ and $\vec{q}$. A better utility is provided if the motion vector heads towards the subgoal.

Motion utilities: These represent the smoothness of the motion. Given that velocity $v_{t+1}^i = (p_{t+1}^i - p_t^i)/\Delta t$, three utilities are defined as preferred velocity utility $M_v = f(v_{t+1}^i)$, angular velocity utility $M_w = f((\theta_{t+1}^i - \theta_t^i)/\Delta t)$ and acceleration utility $M_a = f((v_{t+1}^i - v_t^i)/\Delta t)$. These utilities are high if the agent moves straight at a constant speed.

Relative utilities: These represent the goodness of position relative to the partner. They include relative distance $R_d = f(|p_{t+1}^i - p_{t+1}^j|)$, relative angle $R_a = f(\text{angle}(\overrightarrow{p_{t+1}^i p_t^i}, \overrightarrow{p_{t+1}^i p_{t+1}^j})$ and relative velocity $R_v = f(v_{t+1}^i - v_{t+1}^j)$. The highest utilities are obtained if the partners are strictly alongside at the same velocity.

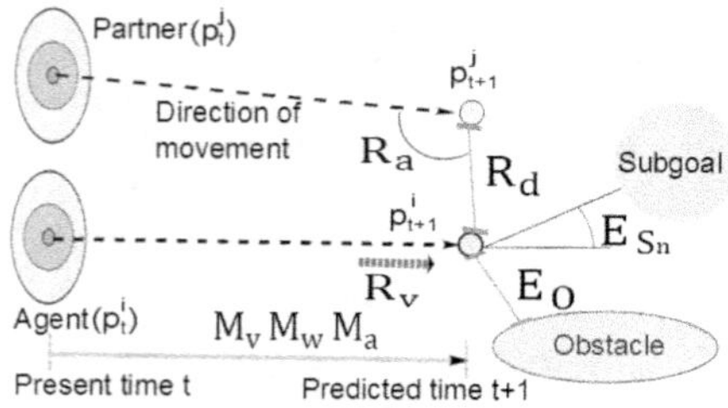

Figure 8. Utility function's factors

The overall utility U_C for agent *i* positioned at point p_i toward its partner's position p_j and moving toward a subgoal S is given as:

$$U_C(p^i,p^j,S) = k_{E_O}E_O + k_{E_S}E_S(S) + k_{R_d}R_d + k_{R_a}R_a + k_{R_v}R_v + k_{M_a}M_a + k_{M_v}M_v + k_{M_w}M_w \tag{3}$$

where constants k_x are parameters that represent the weight of utility x (e.g. $E_O, R_d, \ldots$). The next desired position of agent p^i walking with partner p^j and toward a subgoal S_n is chosen to maximize the utility calculated by the following expression:

$$\hat{p}_{t+1}^i = \text{argmax}_{\{p^i|P^i\},\{p^j|P^j\}}\{U_C(p^i,p^j,S_n) + U_C(p^j,p^i,S_n)\} \tag{4}$$

where P^i and P^j are sets of neighboring locations each agent could move to. This equation represents the agent maximizing its own utility as well as that of its partner. In short, the planning chooses the next location to be the best for both agents.

4.3 Leader-follower State

In section 3, we described how the leader continued walking with no change in behavior when entering the decision area, while the follower slowed down and walked slightly behind the leader.. The leader-follower state (Fig. 9) models this situation.

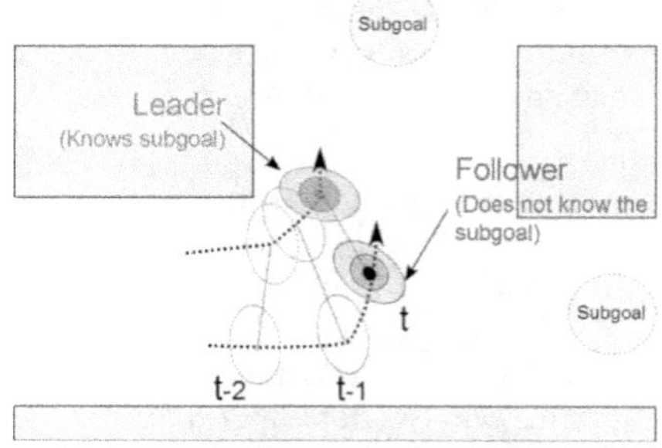

Figure 9. Leader-follower state

4.3.1 Model of Leader

Our primary focus is to reproduce the *follower* agent in a robot; however, to compute the utility for its partner, we also need to develop the model of the *leader*.

The *leader* agent knows the goal, and thus knows the local subgoal toward which they are heading. We analyzed the trajectories obtained in the data collection and compared the velocities of the leader agents. The average velocity computed from all trajectories was 1.09. m/s (s.d. 0.11) during *collaborative* state and 1.11 m/s (s.d. 0.10) during *leader-follower* state. This means that the leader agent walks at a constant pace regardless of the state. From this fact, we infer that the leader's behavior can be approximated as equal between the two states (*collaborative state* and *leader-follower state*).

Accordingly, the leader agent's planning is based on Eq. (4). In the equation, it is assumed that both partners know the subgoal (in reality the follower does not); however, our first approximation is that in *leader-follower* state, the leader behaves in the same way as in the case where the partner knows the subgoal. This assumption implies that the leader does not pay special attention to whether the follower knows the subgoal or not.

4.3.2 Model of Follower

The *follower* agent does not know the subgoal when there is a choice of routes. As we modeled it, until the follower becomes sure about the next subgoal, the state stays in this *leader-follower state*. An important feature of the follower's motion is what we call an *opening-space* behavior. That is, the follower's motion is adjusted so as not to obstruct the leader's possible turning motion (as reported in section 3.3). We interpret this as the follower considering all possible subgoals and thus making space for the *leader*. In addition, the follower temporarily chooses the most likely subgoal for the computation of subgoal utility (E_S).

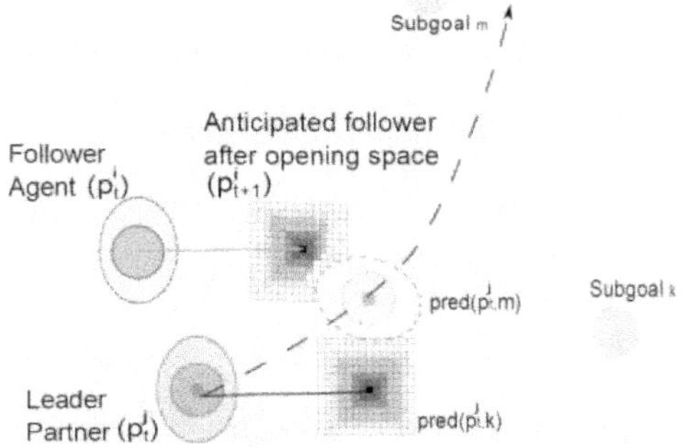

Figure 10. Computation of follower agent

Figure 10 illustrates this follower model. We modeled the above opening-space behavior by adding a new utility named *opening-space utility* (E_{OS}), which is denoted as:

$$E_{OS} = f_o(\min_{\{S_k | S_{visible}\}} |p^i_{t+1} - pred(p^j_t, S_k)|)) \quad \textbf{(5)}$$

where $S_{visible}$ is a set of visible subgoals (computed in the next subsection's Eq. 10) and $pred(p^j_t, S)$ denotes the predicted position of the leader agent located at p^j_t who is assumed to move toward subgoal *S*. This is computed using Eq. 3 and defined as

$$pred(p^j, S) = \operatorname{argmax}_{\{p^i|P^i\},\{p^j|P^j\}}\{U_C(p^i, p^j, S) + U_C(p^j, p^i, S)\} \quad (6)$$

Based on this, the follower's overall utility U_F is computed as:

$$U_F(p^i, p^j, S) = k_{E_{OS}}E_{OS} + k_{E_O}E_O + k_{E_S}E_S(S) + k_{R_d}R_d + k_{R_a}R_a + k_{R_v}R_v + k_{M_a}M_a + k_{M_v}M_v + k_{M_w}M_w \quad (7)$$

Finally, the next location is decided based on the following equation:

$$\hat{p}^i_{t+1} = \operatorname{argmax}_{\{p^i|P^i\},\{p^j|P^j\}}\{U_F(p^i, p^j, S_E) + U_C(p^j, p^i, S_E)\} \quad (8)$$

where S_E is the subgoal esimated by the follower agent (we explain this later with Eq. 9).

This equation expresses that the follower agent also maximizes its own utility as well as that of the leader, in a similar way as defined in Eq. 4; however, the difference is that the follower agent's utility is replaced with U_F. In short, follower made additional effort is made to open space for the leader.

4.4 Subgoal Estimation

Since the subgoal is considered the location where people are heading toward [11], we estimated the current subgoal using the *leader*'s moving direction. However, we did not directly compare it with the directions of subgoals. Instead, in order to quickly detect the switching of subgoals, we checked whether the *leader* started to change her motion towards the subgoals.

Figure 11 illustrates this subgoal estimation process. For instance, at the moment illustrated in the figure, the *leader*'s motion direction is still very close to the direction of subgoal S_1, but it has already started to go towards subgoal S_2. Thus, by comparing it with the predicted locations $\hat{p}^j_t(S_1)$ and $\hat{p}^j_t(S_2)$, its real position p^j_t is quite similar to $\hat{p}^j_t(S_2)$; consequently, the system estimates the *leader's* subgoal to be S_2.

Concretely, the estimated subgoal, S_E, is defined as:

$$S_E = \operatorname{argmin}_{\{S_k|S_{visible}\}}\{\text{angle}(\overrightarrow{p^j_{t-\Delta}p^j_t}, \overrightarrow{p^j_{t-\Delta}\hat{p}^j_t(S_k)})\} \quad (9)$$

where $p^j_{t-\Delta}$ is the position of the leader at time $t-\Delta$. $\hat{p}^j_t(S)$ represents the predicted position at time $t-\Delta$ using Eq. 4, assuming that the *leader* agent moves toward subgoal S. We set $\Delta = 1.5$ sec. The set of subgoals $S_{visible}$ contains all subgoals that are visible from the *leader*, defined as:

$$S_{visible} = \{S_k | \text{angle}(\overrightarrow{p^j_{t-\Delta}p^j_t}, \overrightarrow{p^j_t S_k}) < 90\}\} \quad (10)$$

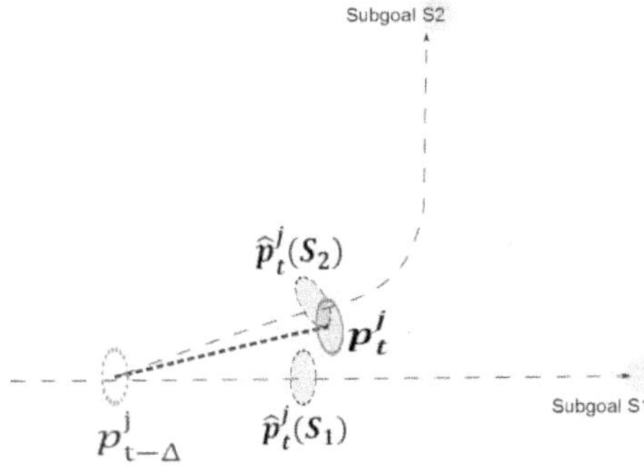

Figure 11. Subgoal estimation

4.5 State-Transition

The state transition is based on how confident the follower agent is of the next subgoal. We simplified this computation by assuming that the *follower* agent is sure about the current estimate of the subgoal if there is only one candidate in the set of candidates $S_{visible}$. In this case, it transitions to the *collaborative state*. Otherwise, if there are two or more candidates, the *follower* agent is unsure about the current subgoal, and thus it stays in the *leader-follower state*. To summarize, transitions occur with the following rules:

Collaborative to *leader-follower* state: if $S_{visible}$ contains two or more elements.

Leader-follower to *collaborative* state: if $S_{visible}$ contains only one element.

4.6 Parameter calibration

We calibrated the parameters for utility in expressions 3 (collaborative state) and 7 (follower state) from the logged data of Section 3. Then, the data set was used for evaluation of the two models. We took the following steps for parameter calibration:

1. Setting the initial parameters:
   We set the initial parameters of each utility function to satisfy the probability distribution of the observation.

2. Calibration of parameters for each utility function:
   We used the collected data to run a simulator and adjust the value of parameters *a*, *b*, and *c* for each component of the utility function. In the simulator, for every time step *t*, the current position of follower and leader agents (p^i_t, p^j_t) are read from recorded trajectories, the next position of follower agent at ($\hat{p}^i_{t+1}$) is predicted (using eqs. 4 or 8, based on the state, and state is computed with eqs. 9 and 10), and prediction error ($|\hat{p}^i_{t+1} - p^i_{t+1}|$) is computed comparing with the position in the recorded trajectory p^i_{t+1}. This process was done for all pairs of trajectories. The parameters that minimize sum of errors from all trajectories are chosen.

3. Calibration of integration parameters:
   Finally, the set of weighting parameters k_x was adjusted. Among possible parameters k_x, the parameters that minimize

sum of errors from all trajectories were chosen. These constants determine the relative importance of the utility functions.

Table 2: Comparison of methods for side-by-side walking

	Collaborative				Leader-Follower			
	a	b	c	k_x	a	b	c	k_x
R_d	350	2.0	750	2.5	350	2.0	750	2.5
R_a	0.08	1.2	$\pi/2$	3.2	0.30	1.2	$\pi/2$	3.1
R_v	200	2.5	0	0.1	200	2.5	0	0.5
E_O	400	500	-----	2.0	400	500	-----	2.0
E_S	0.3	1.5	0	1.5	0.3	1.5	0	0.8
M_v	450	1.3	1100	0.1	450	1.3	1100	0.1
M_w	0.3	3.0	0	0.5	0.3	3.0	0	0.5
M_a	300	1.2	0	0.5	300	1.2	0	0.2

5. IMPLEMENTATION

5.1 System configuration

The model from Section 4 was used for planning future motions. The inputs of the model are the robot and human global positions, velocities and angular velocities together with a map and a list of subgoals. The output the robot's highest utility next position $\hat{p}^i_{t+1}$. Data flow is shown in Figure 12.

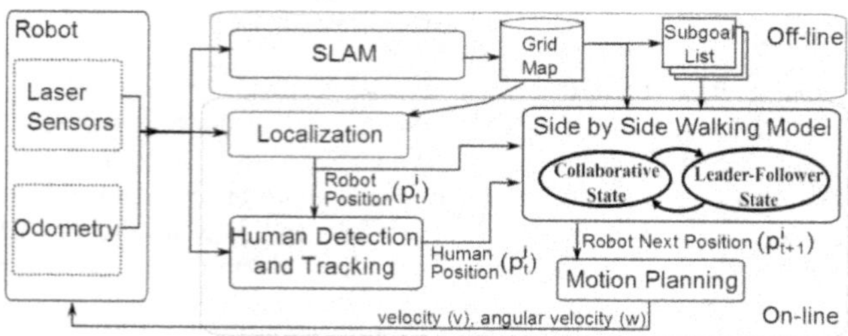

Figure 12. System data flow overview

We used a differential drive robot (Pioneer 3 mobile platform from Adept MobileRobots) with maximum velocity of 1.1 m/sec. This velocity of the robot is much higher than the one used in our previous study [19] (0.5 m/sec), and similar to people's normal walking speed. The mobile platform has a 20 cm tall human-like robot on top, which speaks with synthesized voice (Fig. 13). The robot is equipped with two laser sensors (UTM-30LX from Hokuyo) covering 360° around the robot. We used state of the art algorithms for building a grid map with 0.05 m resolution. We used a particle filter based method for localization with the grid map. Subgoals were generated extracting the topology of the environment using an extended Voronoi approach on the grid map [18] and manually adjusted. Laser sensor data was used for human detection and tracking. The human's legs clusters were detected and the human position was tracked with a particle filter (more details can be found in [19]). For planning a set of 7x7 0.20 m grids were placed in locations according to possible future locations given by current pose, velocities and constraints of the robot where the time for prediction (Δt) is set to 1 second. The grids were used for P^i and P^j in eq. 4, 6, and 8 and the planning was conducted every 50 ms.

5.2 Scene of interaction

To introduce how the system works, we present a typical example. Figure 13 (a) shows a person interacting with the robot. They were about to turn to the left. At the moment of t=1, the robot's state switched to *follower-state* because subgoal S_3 became visible. The robot is directly beside the user at this moment.

Figure 13 (b) shows the result of subgoal estimation at t=2, and the predicted positions $\hat{p}^j_t(S_2)$ and $\hat{p}^j_t(S_3)$ are denoted there. It is just a start of turning, thus the user's motion direction was still rather oriented to S_2 rather than S_3, but the location p^j_t is already similar to $\hat{p}^j_t(S_3)$ rather than $\hat{p}^j_t(S_2)$; consequently the robot started to assume they were going to S_3.

In Fig. 13 (a) at t=2, we can confirm that the robot slowed down and opened space for the user to turn left, even while the robot was heading to S_2. Figure 13 (c) highlights the computation performed at t=1 . While it anticipated that the user would move towards S_2 (red grids show estimated utility), her path to $\hat{p}^j_t(S_3)$ (shown with a red line) was considered in *opening-space utility* (E_{OS}), which suppress the robot's utility around her path and made the robot stay slightly behind her.

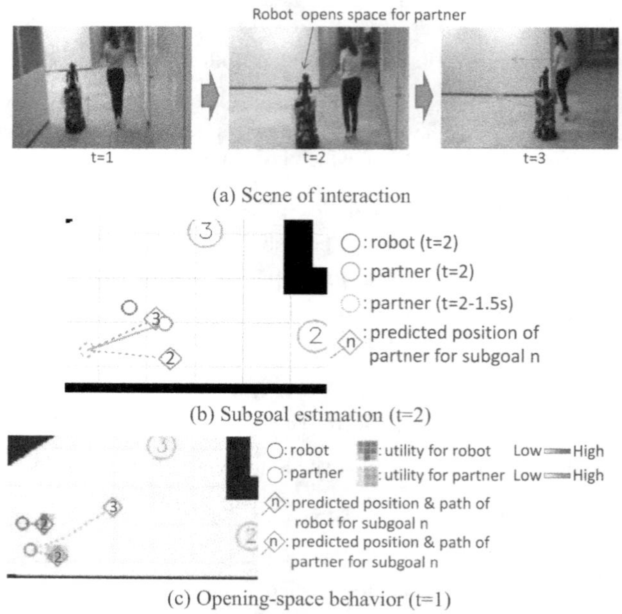

Figure 13. Scene of interaction and processing in the robot

6. USER EVALUATION

6.1 Hypothesis and Prediction

As summarized in Table 1 in Section 2, there are mainly two other approaches to side-by-side walking. One is our previous work [19], where anticipation was proposed; however, it requires the robot to know the subgoal in advance. Therefore, it is not applicable for the *follower* robot.

The other approach is *velocity-based-prediction*, in which a robot is controlled to go alongside the projected position of its partner. Previous studies only proposed a method with linear extrapolation of velocity without proposing a way to anticipate either the robot's or its partner's position. We compared the proposed model with this *velocity-based-prediction*.

However, as our previous work [19] revealed, without having appropriate anticipation of the future utility of both oneself and the partner, the interaction is not natural. Thus, if our new model is appropriately prepared, it should permit appropriate anticipation of the future utility, and thus provide more natural interaction compared with the previous approaches.

In addition, the proposed model contains *opening-space utility* E_{OS} (Eq. 5), which prevents a following robot from obstructing the leader's walking around the intersection; otherwise, they would collide, which cause dangerous situation with a robot. Thus, this feature should contribute to safe walking. Based on this idea, we made this prediction:

Prediction: A robot with the *proposed method* will provide a more natural impression and will be perceived safer, and thus better in its overall evaluation than a robot with *velocity-based-prediction*.

6.2 Method

6.2.1 Participants

Participants were 20 Japanese people (11 males and 9 females, average age 20.9 years), who were paid for their participation.

6.2.2 Conditions

We prepared a within-subject experiment with one factor, *control method*. Two conditions were prepared:

Proposed Model: The robot navigated with the proposed model (Eq. 8) described in Section *4.3.2*.

Velocity-based prediction: The robot navigated with *velocity-based-prediction*. The partner's future position is predicted from linear extrapolation of velocity, and the robot is controlled to move alongside the predicted position. Concretely, it is computed as:

$$\hat{p}^{j}_{t+1} = p^{j}_{t} + v^{j}_{t} \cdot \Delta t \tag{11}$$

where $\hat{p}^{j}_{t+1}$ is the predicted position of partner j at the next time step $t+1$ and p^{j}_{t} and v^{j}_{t} are the observed position and velocity at time step t. The utility $U_V(p_i, p_j)$ is defined as:

$$_{V}(p^{i},p^{j}) = k_{E_O}E_O + k_{R_d}R_d + \\ +k_{R_a}R_a + k_{R_v}R_v + k_{M_a}M_a + k_{M_v}M_v + k_{M_w}M_w \tag{12}$$

where constants k_x are parameters that represent the weight of utility x. All parameters are calibrated to best fit the trajectories collected in the data collection, in the same way we did for the proposed method (section 4.5).

Among all possible positions *P*, the next position is selected to maximize utility $U_V(p_i, p_j)$ in (Eq. 5):

$$\hat{p}^{i}_{t+1} = \text{argmax}_{\{p^{i}|P^{i}\}} U_V(p^{i}, \hat{p}^{j}_{t+1}) \tag{13}$$

6.2.3 Procedure

The experiment was conducted in the same indoor environment with straight corridors and a "T" intersection where we had conducted the data collection (Fig. 2).

For each condition, each participant was asked to walk with the robot in a side-by-side formation while the robot talked to her. For experimental simplicity, we limited the conversation to be one-way only from the robot. They were informed of the destination (but not each of the subgoals). They also knew that the robot was not informed of the destination. There were two destinations, and for each destination they walked with the robot. In addition, we tested two starting formations: when the robot was on the left side of the participant and when it was at the right side of the participant. In total, there were four walks per session, and the order was counter-balanced.

6.3 Measurements

After each session, we asked participants to rate the following items on a 1–7 point Likert scale in a questionnaire:

- **Naturalness**
- **Perceived safety**
- **Overall evaluation**

A brief interview was conducted at the end of each experiment, in which we asked their impressions of two robots.

6.4 Results

6.4.1 Verification of the prediction

Figure 14 shows the results. A repeated-measures ANOVA was conducted. A significant main effect was revealed in *naturalness* ($F(1,19)=5.147$, $p=.035$, $\eta^2=.213$), perceived *safety* ($F(1,19)=16.276$, $p=.001$, $\eta^2=.461$), and *overall evaluation* ($F(1,19)=18.948$, $p<.001$, $\eta^2=.499$). These results show that the robot with the *proposed method* provided a more natural and safe impression, and it was perceived as better in its overall evaluation, than the robot with *velocity-based-prediction*. Thus, our prediction was supported.

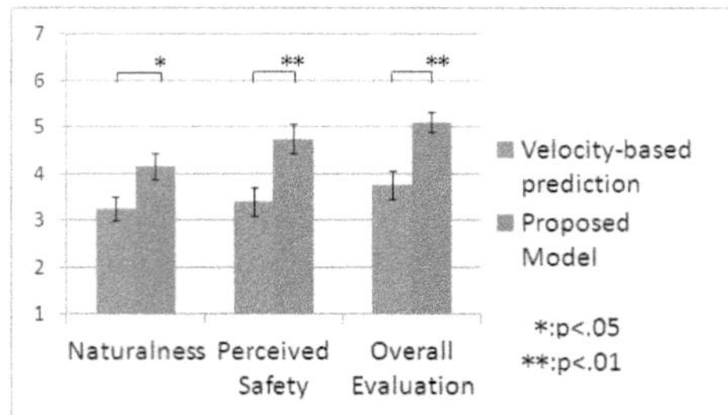

Figure 14. Evaluation results

6.4.2 Interview Results and Observations

We analyzed the feedback from the interviews. Many of them characterized the *velocity-based prediction* as being sensitive to their motion. A few of them (3 persons) thought this was a good feature since the robot reacted well to their motion; however, the majority of them (15 persons) reported that it provided a dangerous impression because the robot did not move straight to down the corridor but in a rather zigzag way. This is because the *velocity-based prediction* method only reacts to the user's velocity. Once participants tried to adjust their walking style to the robot, which many of them did, their motion direction and speed frequently changed. As a result, the robot frequently changed speed and motion direction.

The *proposed method* is, in contrast, rather stable regardless of how participants walk. Therefore, none of the participants commented on any problem related to stability. Further, some of them noticed that the robot opened space for them when they turned, which they thought was useful (7 people). In fact, thanks to this opening-space capability, the robot did not cause any dangerous situation; in the *velocity-based prediction* method, we observed a few cases in which the participants almost collided with the robot when they tried to turn.

The subgoal estimation method might require further improvement. Actually, 5 participants commented that the robot in the proposed method moved slowly and turned late when they turned at the intersection. This was probably caused by the delay in subgoal estimation. Currently, it takes approximately 1.5 seconds to detect the start of user's turning.

7. DISCUSSION

The model has so far only been tested in an indoor office where the candidates of next subgoals are limited to the directions of the corridors. We believe that the system would work similarly in well-structured environments, such as office corridors, streets in shopping malls, and sidewalks. On the other hand, there are some environments that are much more complicated, and thus possible subgoals might be rather difficult to infer, e.g. wide hallways and parks. Our subgoal estimation algorithm is perhaps too simple for such environmental situations.

Let Me Tell You!

Investigating the Effects of Robot Communication Strategies in Advice-giving Situations based on Robot Appearance, Interaction Modality and Distance

Megan Strait
Tufts University
Medford, MA 02155
megan.strait@tufts.edu

Cody Canning
Tufts University
Medford, MA 02155
cody.canning@tufts.edu

Matthias Scheutz
Tufts University
Medford, MA 02155
matthias.scheutz@tufts.edu

ABSTRACT

Recent proposals for how robots should talk to people when they give advice suggest that the same strategies humans employ with other humans are effective for robots as well. However, the evidence is exclusively based on people's *observation* of robot giving advice to other humans. Hence, it is not clear whether the results still apply when people *actually participate in real interactions with robots.* We address this shortcoming in a novel systematic mixed-methods study where we employ both survey-based subjective *and* brain-based objective measures (using functional near infrared spectroscopy). The results show that previous results from observation conditions do not transfer automatically to interaction conditions, and that robot appearance and interaction distance are important modulators of human perceptions of robot behavior in advice-giving contexts.

Categories and Subject Descriptors

H.4 [**Information Systems Applications**]: Miscellaneous

Keywords

Natural language, politeness, presence, interaction modality, human-likeness, functional near infrared spectroscopy

1. INTRODUCTION

Social robots capable of natural language-interactions with humans have to be sensitive to how humans use natural language in communicative situations. Being "sensitive to humans natural language use", however, is a complex multifaceted problem that ranges from low-level algorithmic processing details (i.e., the incrementality of information integration [6]) to high-level pragmatic principles (e.g., social etiquette for how to respond to formulate and respond to requests in a polite manner based on social status [7]). Additional complications for understanding human communicative strategies and implementing them on robots arise from the fact that verbal communicative behavior is modulated by various aspects of the interaction scenario such as interaction distance (e.g., [38]), social role (e.g., [28]), and the nature and purpose of the interaction, among others. For example, humans frequently employ *indirect speech acts* [7, 16] together with various *politeness strategies* in their verbal communication modifications both to live up to and conform with social expectations and to mitigate threat and insult [9]. And while various attempts have been made to implement such strategies in robotic architectures (e.g., [7, 37]), it is currently unclear whether such strategies would work equally well in human-robot interaction (HRI) contexts.

HRI'14, March 3–6, 2014, Bielefeld, Germany.
Copyright 2014 ACM 978-1-4503-2658-2/14/03 ...$15.00.
http://dx.doi.org/10.1145/2559636.2559670.

Recent results regarding how robots should talk to people when they give advice suggest that the same strategies humans employ with other humans are effective for robots as well [33]. However, this evidence is exclusively based on people's *observation* of a robot giving advice to another humans, hence it is not clear whether the results still apply when people *participate* in *real* interactions with robots.

In this paper, we report results from a systematic evaluation of the question of whether robots should use indirect speech acts as a communication strategy when giving advice to humans. In addition to the effects of different *communication strategies* (direct versus indirect speech), we also investigated effects of *interaction modality* (participation versus observation), *interaction distance* (local versus remote interaction) and *robot appearance* (human-like versus machine-like) based on prior evidence that interaction modality and distance as well as robot appearance can be important modulatory factors in human-robot interactions (e.g., [2, 23, 14]). For the evaluation, we developed a novel mixed-methods study design where we employ both survey-based subjective *and* brain-based objective measures using functional near infrared spectroscopy [10] to evaluate the influence of the four dimensions on perceptions of the interactions and the robot. Our main finding is that all four dimensions have an important influence on human perceptions of robot behavior in advice giving contexts and that previous results about the preference of indirect speech acts from observations of human-robot interactions do not transfer to actual interaction contexts.

2. RELATED WORK

Politeness theory [9] describes universal ways in which speakers can modify their speech to avoid threat to interlocutors (see Table 1). In HRI, [24] examined situations in which

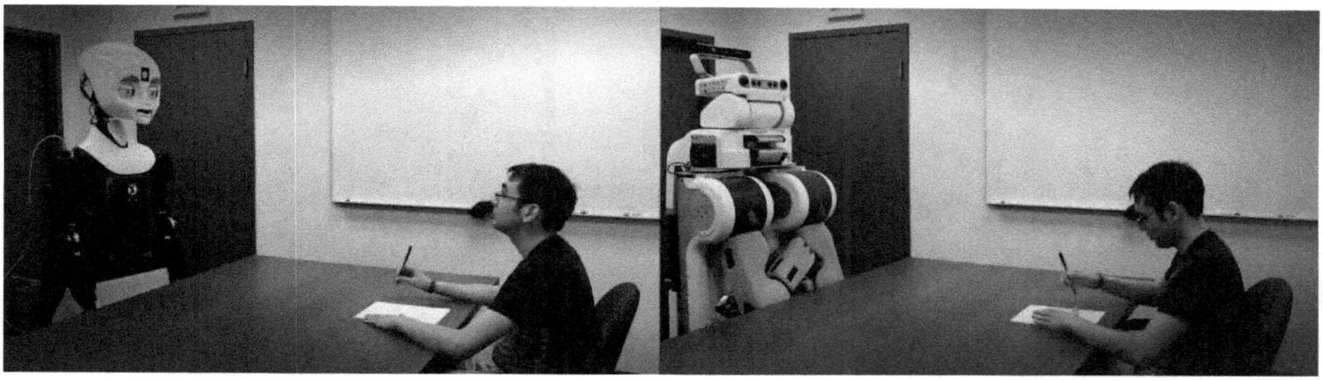

Figure 1: Robot helpers. Left – the MDS (Xitome Design), and right – the PR2 robot (Willow Garage).

natural language dialogue might be helpful for an assistive robot to have. A similar study looked at effects of adaptive dialogue on information exchange, which found that changing dialogue based on the listener's expertise (giving more info to the novices and less to experts) increased social cohesion with the robot [32]. One recent study investigated whether politeness universals for human helpers apply equally for robot helpers [33], which revealed that the presence of politeness modifiers in speech increased perceptions of considerateness and likability, and reduced perceptions of aggression – regardless of agency (whether the speaker was human or a robot). While this served as first steps towards understanding politeness universals for robotic assistants, it is not clear to what extent the results generalize. For instance, another study focused on applying error mitigation techniques drawn from politeness theory to improve perceptions of a robot in the event of an error; however, as to which technique (e.g., apology, compensation, etc.) worked best *depended on the participant's personality* [25]. In contrast, in a multi-social party setting, [15] found that *dialogue efficiency* and *task success* most affected the participant experience most. Hence, in those contexts ([25, 15]), the personality of the participant and as well as *task* success respectively were important in the perceptions of the robot helpers, rather than speech modifications alone.

Beyond natural language and politeness modifications of speech, however, a key aspect of HRI is the way in which the interaction occurs. For example, people are *more likely to perform a task when a robot is physically co-located* than when it is remotely communicating [2, 3, 12, 20, 22]. Moreover, people show more positive perceptions of co-located interactions than remote [4] and are more likely to profit from tutoring with greater levels of embodiment [14]. This suggests that perceptions of speech modifications may vary according to the manner of presentation (e.g., interacting with a physically present robot vs. by telepresence). Furthermore, holding the level of presence of the robot constant, people interacting with a robot from first-person perspective (direct interaction) may consider the interaction more seriously than from a third-person perspective (observing the interaction between another human and a robot) [33].

Finally, people seem to attribute more positive traits to attractive versus unattractive stimuli [8]. Both attractive people and robots are judged as warmer and more sociable than their less attractive counterparts [8, 19]. More importantly, unattractive robots which appear simultaneously very human-like can result in aversive behaviors in human observers [19]. This phenomenon is referred to as the *Uncanny Valley* [26], which posits a mismatch in human-likeness with non-human features results in feelings of unease towards the robot in question [5, 8, 19, 21, 26, 27]. While some have found that increased human-likeness can improve social perceptions of a robot [13, 8], many advise that human-like interfaces should be used with caution and within the appropriate contexts [5, 17, 21].

3. MATERIALS AND METHODS

To investigate the relative effects of communication strategy as modulated by interaction modality and presence as well as the robot's appearance, we conducted a mixed-design experiment. Specifically, speech and human-likeness manipulations were conducted within-subjects (to be consistent with [33]); however, to avoid bias from prior interaction, interaction modality (3rd-person vs. 1st-person remote vs. 1st-person co-located) was manipulated between-subjects.

Table 1: Some politeness strategies and examples.

	Strategy	*Example*
Positive	(a) give praise and	"good job"
	(b) rationale	"to make Y, do X"
	(c) be inclusive	"**we** will now do X"
Negative	(a) use markers,	"now"
	(b) hedges, and	"kind of"
	(c) indirect requests	"**could** you do X?"

Table 2: Example instructions in each communication condition for drawing a koala.

	Example
Direct	"Sketch a vertical oval extending from the space between the eyes down to the snout. This is the nose."
Indirect	"**Great! Now, to add a nose, let's** sketch a vertical oval extending from the space between the eyes down to the snout."

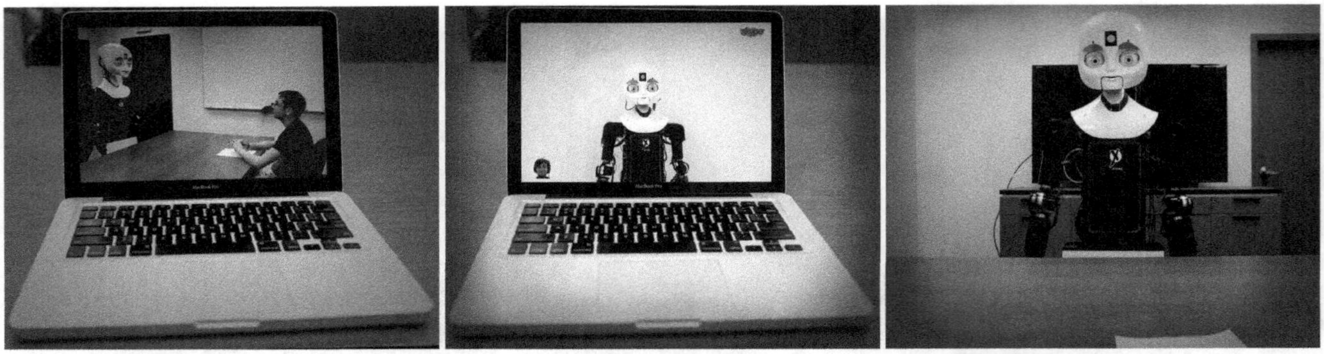

Figure 2: Left – the 3rd-person interaction (3PR) condition (directly replication of [33]). Right and center – the 1st-person protocols, with the robot helper co-located (1PC; right) and remote (1PR; center).

3.1 Design

Participants were informed the purpose of the study was to investigate different communication strategies for robots instructing humans on simple drawing tasks. To avoid habituation effects from repeated stimuli (i.e., the helpers advising on the *same* task), four distinct tasks involving the sketching of a simple object (tulip, koala, etc.) were created. To compare participants' impressions of robot helpers using politeness modifications in their instructions, we used two communication conditions (direct and indirect). Additionally, two robots were selected as representative "human-like" and "mechanical" robotic helpers to investigate how appearance of the helper could influence participant expectations and preferences. Lastly, to examine the effects of participant perspective and robot presence, three interaction conditions[1] were designed (see Figure 2).

Communication Strategies. The two communication conditions used here – *direct* and *indirect* – corresponded to the *no hedges/no markers* and the *hedges plus markers* conditions in [33]. As there was no evidence for additive effects of multiple politeness strategies [33], we expected that the presence of any *or* multiple politeness strategies (see Table 1) would elicit the same increases in liking and perceived considerateness of the helper. Thus we compared only the two communication conditions, where *direct* speech refers to an absence of any and *indirect* contains one or more of the above strategies (see Table 1).

Robot Helpers. Xitome Design's MDS and Willow Garage's PR2 robots were selected as the two helpers for their stereotypical robotic (PR2) and human-like (MDS) appearances. The selection avoided possible effects of height and girth of the helper, as they are nearly equal between the two robots. However, as the two are highly dissimilar in movement and affective capabilities, both robots were kept stationary and un-animated. Audio for the robots' speech was created using the Mac OS X native text-to-speech software, with the male voice, 'Alex', and female voice,'Vicki'. Subjects interacted with either Vicki-MDS/Alex-PR2 or Alex-MDS/Vicki-PR2, and the voice-robot pairing was counterbalanced. To avoid differences between subjects in speech recognition, the audio was controlled by wizard-of-oz: a behind-the-scenes researcher served as a 'human speech recognizer', and was trained to attend to three natural language indicators – *ready* (e.g., "okay, done"), *repeat* (e.g., "could you repeat that?"), or *back* (e.g., "what was the last instruction?"). All tasks were scripted so that the researcher could command the robot with the appropriate instruction immediately upon hearing an indicator. The pacing of the tasks were thus triggered based on these verbal cues.

Interaction Modalities. To measure effects of perspective (first-person vs. third-person) and the robot's presence (co-located vs. remote), three interaction modalities were created: (a) 3rd-person, remote (3PR); (b) 1st-person, remote (1PR); and (c) 1st-person, co-located (1PC) – see Figure 2. The 3PR condition corresponded to the experiment in [33]. Here participants observed video of the robot helpers instructing a human actor on the four tasks. Each video was approx. 2.5 minutes in length and was viewed on a 13" MacBook. The two first-person conditions – 1PR and 1PC – served as comparison for 3PR in order to investigate possible effects based on interaction modality (and distance, in the case of 1PC). They differed from 3PR both in that the participants performed the drawing tasks (rather than observing a video of someone else drawing) and that they interacted directly with the robot helpers.

3.2 Measures

A novel combination of subjective measures of the interaction as well as objective measures of the participants' reactions were used in this study. As human affect has a strong neurophysiological component [35, 36], in order to fully understand participants' unconscious or subconscious emotional reactions to robotic agents (e.g., feelings of unease in response to eerie, human-like robots), it is necessary to probe both conscious appraisal (subjective measures) as well as neurophysiological indicators [29, 35].

Subjective Measures. Immediately following each of the four drawing tasks, participants assessed (a) the interaction difficulty (two questionnaire items) and (b) several characteristics of the robot's communicative behavior (eight questionnaire items). Exploratory factor analysis with varimax ro-

[1]The fourth possible condition with the subject observer co-located with the confederate human interacting with the robot was left out because it was unclear whether minute differences in the live interaction between the confederate and the robot might have important effects on subjects' perception (as it is virtually impossible for human confederates to behave the same in all runs in the employed tasks).

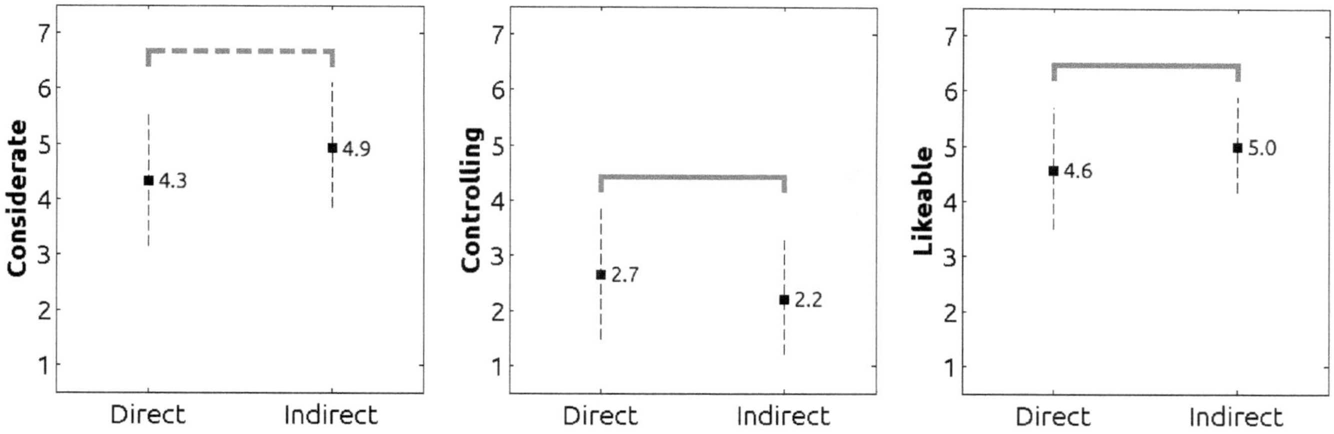

Figure 3: Main Effects of Communication Condition. The *indirect* communication condition significantly increased ratings of considerateness and likability of the robot helper. Moreover, the helper was rated as significantly less controlling in the *indirect* communication condition. *Dashed red comparisons indicate significant interaction effects with other manipulations (e.g., communication condition x interaction modality).

tation was conducted on these eight characteristics, yielding three underlying factors consistent with those found in [33]. Variance explained was used as the criterion for determining the number of factors. Table 3 shows the results of an orthogonal rotation of the solution. We interpreted the three-factor solution to reveal the following latent factors, responsible for 60.4% of the total variance: *considerate* (Cronbach's $\alpha = 0.77$), *controlling* ($\alpha = 0.80$), and *likable* ($\alpha = 0.80$). After participants completed all tasks, they answered a final survey regarding each robot (three items; based on indices by [19] for assessing a robot's appearance) and their preferences for future interaction (two items).

Objective Measures. Functional near infrared spectroscopy (NIRS) was used to measure participants' neural activity (indexed by hemodynamic changes) associated with attention, emotion regulation, and workload. A two-sensor NIRS instrument (ISS Imagent; TR=11Hz) was used to image participants' anterior prefrontal cortices (aPFC) bilaterally. This sensor placement captures the ventromedial prefrontal cortex which holds a key role in emotion regulation [30, 35].

3.3 Population and Procedure

Forty-five Tufts University students and staff were recruited via an affiliate University website and paid \$10/hour for their participation. All subjects reported being healthy, right-handed, and having no history of brain trauma. The subject demographics mostly reflected those of the university, with a 60/40 female-to-male ratio (27 female/18 male participants) and average age of 21.3 years (SD = 3.80). Upon the receipt of informed, written consent, participants were fitted with the NIRS equipment, using a black cap to secure the two NIRS sensors on the left and right aPFC. A five-minute baseline measurement was then sampled for post-hoc conversion of the raw NIRS data into units of hemoglobin. Following, the participant performed the four drawing tasks sequentially (blocked by robot – e.g., first two with the MDS, then two with the other). Tasks were separated with the subjective questionnaires pertaining to the characteristics of communication and interaction difficulty. Lastly, to obtain NIRS measurements of participants' responses to only the appearance of the two robots (no auditory interaction), participants viewed a series of images of the MDS and PR2.

4. RESULTS

We first considered the effects of the interaction and robot helpers on the survey measures, followed by the objective measures of participants neural activity. The dependent measures were analyzed using a type-2 mixed design ANOVA with the following independent variables (IVs): interaction *Modality* (3PR, 1PR, 1PC; between-subjects), participant *Gender* (M, F; between), robot *Voice*-pairing (M-MDS/F-PR2, F-MDS/M-PR2; between), communication *Speech* strategy (indirect, direct; within), robot (PR2, MDS; within), and *Order* of exposure to the robots (1-MDS/2-PR2, 1-PR2/2-MDS; between). Post-hoc comparisons were conducted using Bonferroni-corrected pairwise t-tests.

Task completion. Based on the interaction logs, a 4-way ANOVA on Modality, Robot, Voice, and Gender showed 1PC participants spent significantly more time on the drawings compared to the 1PR condition; $F(1,39)=6.69$, $p=.0123$.[2]

[2]As the 3PR condition involved only observation of the task, it was not comparable in terms of time spent.

Table 3: Factor loadings for the measures of interaction showing a three-factor solution.

	Likable	*Controlling*	*Considerate*
Aggressive	-.324	.644	-.211
Considerate	.276	-.197	.938
Controlling	-.198	.969	-.127
Attentive	.395	-.134	.385
Likable	.667	-.215	.435
Annoying	-.742	.318	-.136
Comforting	.661	-.153	.178
Helpful	-.290	.102	-.127
Eigenvalues	3.82	1.027	.850
Variance	.237	.436	.604

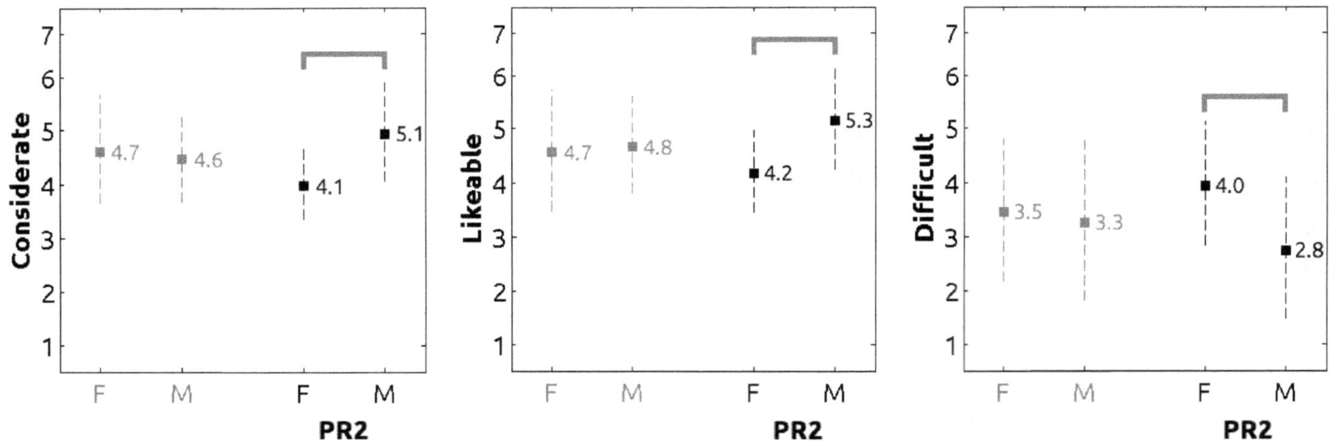

Figure 4: Robot*Voice interaction effects. A male (versus female) voice on the PR2 robot significantly increased ratings of considerateness and likability, and decreased the perceived difficulty of the interaction.

Considerateness, likablity, and aggression. These three factors were analyzed using a 5-way ANOVA with IVS: Modality, Gender, Voice, Speech, and Robot. Here, *indirect* speech significantly increased participants' ratings of liking (main effect; $F(1,33) = 8.56$, $p = .006$) and reduced ratings of control/aggression of the robot helper (main effect $F(1,33) = 12.49$, $p = .001$), see Figure 3. Indirect speech also increased considerateness, but only in the 3PR condition (see Figure 5); interaction $F(2,33) = 4.81$, $p = .014$. Ratings of indirect speech in the 1PC and 1PR conditions were significantly higher than *direct* speech in the 3PR condition ($p = .005$, $p = .024$ respectively), but there was no significant difference between direct vs. indirect within the first-person interaction conditions. Participant preferences also reflected these findings, with participants in the 3PR condition showing a strong preference for indirect speech (12/15) in comparison to the two first-person conditions, which showed instead a slight preference for direct speech (9/15 in both 1PR, 1PC).

An interaction effect was also observed between the Voice and Robot factors on considerateness ($F(1,33) = 7.44$, $p = .010$), liking ($F(1,33) = 11.63$, $p = .002$), and difficulty of the interaction ($F(1,33) = 5.34$, $p = .030$); see Figure 4: with the F-PR2 pairing resulting in significantly reduced ratings of considerateness and liking and significantly increased difficulty than the M-PR2 pairing ($p = .001$). In addition, a four-way interaction effect was found on ratings of aggression between *Interaction*, *Robot*, *Gender*, *Voice*; $F(2,33) = 3.32$, $p = .049$. Subsequent pairwise comparisons showed male participants in the 1PR *Interaction* condition rated the F-MDS as significantly more controlling.

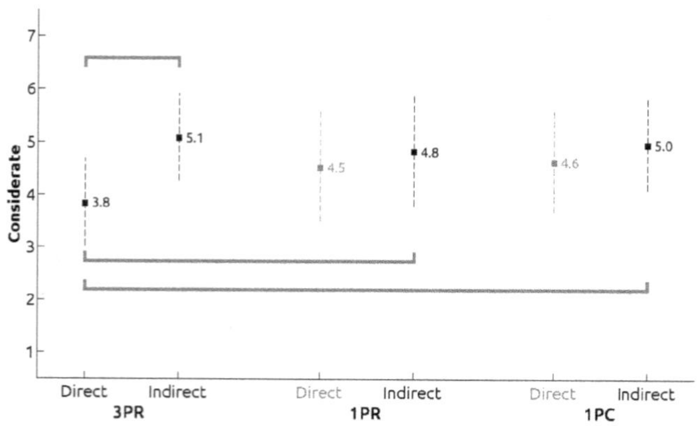

Figure 5: Interaction effect (*speech, modality*).

Human-likeness, warmth, and eeriness. The following three dependent variables were analyzed using a 4-way ANOVA with IVs *Modality*, *Robot*, *Gender*, and *Order*. As expected, the type of robot showed a main effect on ratings of human-likeness; $F(1,39) = 130.92$, $p < .0001$. The robot type (MDS vs. PR2) also showed a significant main effect on ratings of eeriness, $F(1,39) = 6.83$, $p = .013$, with significantly higher eeriness ratings for the MDS compared to the PR2 (see Figure 6). There was no significant effect of the robot on warmth; however, a marginal main effect of interaction *Modality* was observed, $F(2,39) = 2.73$, $p = .078$, with higher warmth ratings in the 1PR than the 3PR condition. Regarding preferences for robot helper, participants in the 1PC showed a strong affinity for the PR2 (10/15 participants) in comparison to the two remote-interaction conditions, which showed roughly 50/50 preferences between the two helpers (7/15 preferred the PR2 in both 1PR, 3PR).

Prefrontal hemodynamics. The NIRS data were preprocessed in the following manner: (1) conversion of raw light attenuation to changes in hemoglobin concentrations, (2) linear detrending to remove signal drift, (3) filtering of systemic artifacts (specifically, cardiac pulsations using a Savitzky-Golay low pass filter with degree 1 and cut-off frequency of 0.5Hz), and (4) correlation-based signal improvement ([11]) to correct motion based on common NIRS preprocessing and filtering techniques [10, 30]. Preprocessing yielded two signals – oxygenated hemoglobin for the left and right PFC – for each agent stimulus (MDS and PR2), for a total of four signals. To normalize the signals for between-subjects analysis, the respective signals for the MDS and PR2 were subtracted to yield one signal: difference in hemodynamic response.

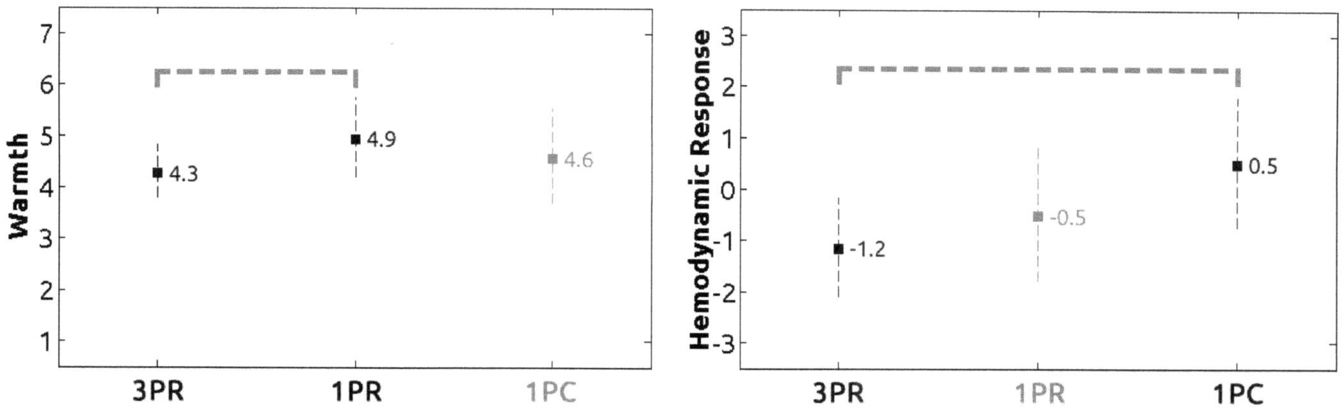

Figure 6: Main effects of Robot helper. As expected, the MDS robot received significantly higher ratings of human-likeness (as well as eeriness) than the PR2.

A type-2 three-way ANOVA revealed a marginally significant main effect of *Modality* on the left prefrontal neural activity ($F(2,39) = 3.12$ ($p = .057$)) with a significant difference between 1PC and 3PR conditions. Specifically: in the first-person interaction condition, the MDS elicited greater overall PFC activity resulting in a net positive MDS-PR2 difference; whereas in the 3rd-person condition, the PR2 elicited greater activity resulting in a net negative MDS-PR2 difference. In the 1PR condition, the MDS-PR2 difference trended towards -.5, falling between the mean differences of the other two conditions (see Figure 7).

5. DISCUSSION

The polite communication strategy (indirect speech) improved ratings of likability and considerateness, and reduced ratings of aggression compared to the communication strategy without any politeness modifiers, consistent with the findings of [33]. However, the effect on considerateness (seen in the interaction effect with interaction modality) was only significant in the 3rd-person modality (3PR). This suggests the effects of politeness modifiers do not necessarily persist in 1st-person human-robot interactions. Participant preferences also substantiate this interpretation, showing affinity for indirect speech *only* in the 3PR condition. Moreover, the preferences for communication condition seem to reverse in the 1st-person interaction conditions, with a slight affinity for *direct* speech. Together, the results show that conclusions from HRI studies that use human subjects solely as interaction observers rather than interaction participants cannot be automatically applied to human-robot interaction scenarios. Hence, it is not only important, but necessary to conduct actual human-robot *interaction* studies as we are ultimately not so much interested in human perceptions as interaction observers, but as interaction participants.

Regarding the influences of appearance, the MDS robot helper was perceived as significantly more human-like but also significantly more eerie than the PR2, both as expected. The difference in human-likeness seemed primarily important when a female synthetic voice was used in combination with the less human-like PR2. The female-voiced PR2 reduced ratings of likability/considerateness and increased perceptions of difficulty. However, these effects might be due more to the mismatch in the relatively male or androgynous appearance of the PR2 with a female voice (e.g., [27]. Although human-likeness did not show effects on perceptions of politeness, the MDS received significantly higher ratings of eeriness which may influence the enjoyment/success of general HRI in other manners (e.g., preferences for future interaction) than measures assessing the agent's politeness. Participant preferences may be revealing of this effect, as 1PC participants strongly preferred the PR2 robot (10/15 participants) over the MDS, whereas the remote condition participants (1PR, 3PR) showed relatively equal preferences for both.

The significant differences in prefrontal hemodynamics in response to the two robots according to the interaction condition further underscores a possible effect of human-likeness and the corresponding perception of eeriness. In the 1PC condition, participants showed markedly greater activity in response to the MDS robot as compared to their level of neural activity in response to the PR2. As prefrontal hemodynamics have been shown to reflect negatively-valenced affect (i.e., [1, 18, 30, 31, 34]), this suggests an emotional response may have been evoked in participants directly interacting with the very human-like MDS. Whereas participants in the remote conditions (1PR, 3PR) showed activity differences closer to zero. Hence, in combination with the subjective responses, these findings suggest there may be emotion-regulatory mechanisms evoked when directly interacting with a co-located, humanoid robot. Whereas, in a removed context such as that of observing video of the two – much like viewing a movie – the fear or anxiety elicited by the MDS' eerie appearance may have been reduced or non-present. The implication here is the same as above: in the context of politeness, it is critical to evaluate modulatory dimensions like robot appearance in real HRI experiments where human subjects *participate* in interactions with co-located robots, for otherwise important effects of such dimensions might be missed or misinterpreted.

Limitations. These results suggest that indirect speech acts – in the context of help-giving – are most appropriate when *observing* human-robot interactions. Whereas in *direct interactions*, although indirect speech improves perceptions of likability and aggression, speech efficiency (directness) and the human-likeness of the robot help-giver are of greater importance. There are several limitations to this study and

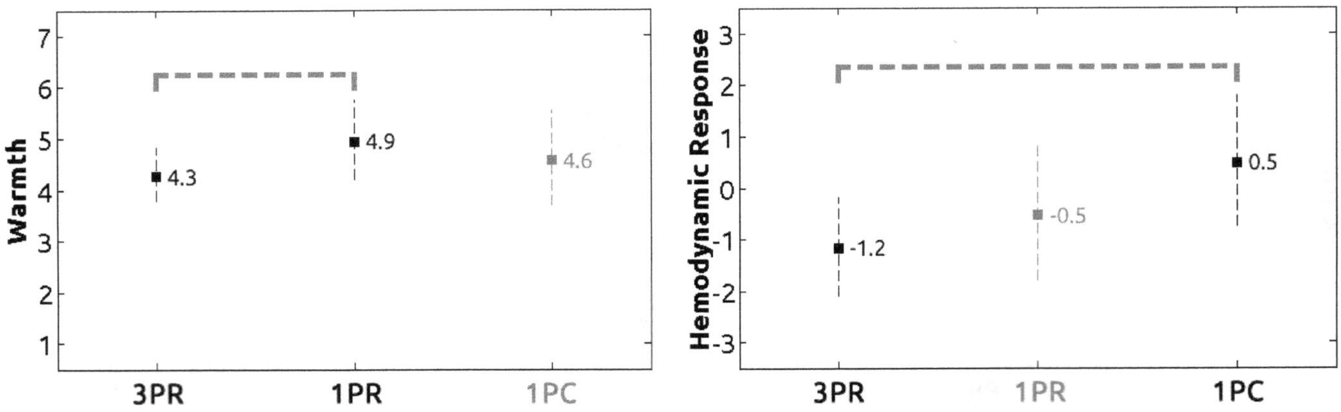

Figure 7: Main effects of *Interaction* modality. Left – the first-person perspective significantly increases ratings of warmth compared to the 3PR condition. Right – a net positive hemodynamic change is observed in the 1PC condition and (significantly lower) net negative change is observed for 3PR (units are micromolar).

its applicability, however. For instance, in situations in which the robot is not giving advice, but rather, receiving it, indirect speech may be more appropriate so as to reflect the superiority of the human help-giver. Whereas, in tasks in which both participants (robot and human) are equally knowledgeable, indirect speech may facilitate collaboration.

Moreover, the lack of nonverbal cues and affective displays (and as a result, the pacing of interactions based solely on verbal cues), as well as unsampled factors of the interactions are considerable limitations of the present work. For instance, the perception of the robots as gendered could indeed influence several of our dependent variables. In particular, it offers an explanation for the effect arising from the female voice-PR2 pairing (that the PR2 may have been perceived as being male in gender). We did not sample this factor here (as to whether the robots or their voices appeared gendered), which does not impact the comparison with the results of [33]; however, it may be an another important modulatory factor. Additionally, it is likely that the results are affected to some extent by the pacing of the interactions, which were triggered solely based on verbal cues (rather than some verbal and nonverbal combination). The observed difference in preferences between 1PC and 1PR conditions despite equal pacing as well as the lack of one between 1PR and 3PR, suggest it is not a major confound when considering differences between interaction modalities. Given the range of nonverbal behaviors and differences in the two robots abilities to execute them, we chose here to keep the robots stationary in order to standardize interactions across the two helpers, but this exclusion warrants further investigation using a combination of verbal and nonverbal behaviors to disentangling their potential contributions.

6. CONCLUSIONS

The aim of this study was to investigate the effects of robot communication strategies such as direct versus indirect speech on humans in advice-giving contexts. Here we specifically included three additional factors – robot appearance, presence, and interaction directness – as they have been shown to modulate the effectiveness of human-robot interactions. The results demonstrate that all four dimensions can have an important influence on perceptions of robot behavior in advice-giving contexts and that prior results regarding indirect speech acts obtained from experiments with human observers watching videos of human-robot interactions do not transfer to actual interaction contexts. Specifically, our results are consistent with prior findings that showed that, from the third-person perspective, a robot's use of polite speech seemed more considerate and likable, and less controlling. But we also found that preferences for indirect speech are not present in first-person interactions. In addition, increasing the presence and human-likeness of the robot engages greater neural activity and severely decreases preferences for future interactions. Lastly, a mismatch in voice and robot appearance results in decreased ratings of liking and increased perceptions of task difficulty. These findings confirm that while politeness modifications (as expressed via indirect speech acts) are important in observational settings of advice giving, other situational factors such as robot appearance and interaction distance might be of greater relevance to the design of effective robotic helpers. Finally, our experimental results also have methodological consequences for the field of HRI in that they suggest that at least for some tasks and contexts actual human-robot interaction experiments, rather than studies with human observers watching pre-recorded human-robot interactions, are necessary for untangling the complex interactions among the many important modulatory factors.

7. ACKNOWLEDGMENTS

This material is based upon work supported by the National Science Foundation under Grant No. ISS-1065154.

8. REFERENCES

[1] R. Aoki, H. Sato, T. Katura, R. Matsuda, and H. Koizumi. Correlation between prefrontal cortex activity during working memory tasks and natural mood independent of personality effects: an optical topography study. *Psychiatry Research: Neuroimaging*, 212(1):79–87, 2013.

[2] W. A. Bainbridge, J. Hart, E. S. Kim, and B. Scassellati. The effect of presence on human-robot interaction. In *RO-MAN*, 2008.

[3] W. A. Bainbridge, J. W. Hart, E. S. Kim, and B. Scassellati. The benefits of interactions with physically present robots over video-displayed agents. *Int. J. of Soc. Rob.*, 3:41–52, 2010.

[4] W. A. Bainbridge, S. Nozawa, R. Ueda, K. Okada, and M. Inaba. A methodological outline and utility assessment of sensor- based biosignal measurement in human-robot interaction. *Int. J. Soc. Rob.*, 4, 2012.

[5] C. Bartneck, T. Kanda, H. Ishiguro, and N. Hagita. Is the uncanny valley an uncanny cliff? In *RO-MAN*, pages 368–373, 2007.

[6] T. Brick and M. Scheutz. Incremental natural language processing for hri. In *HRI*, 2007.

[7] G. Briggs and M. Scheutz. A hybrid architectural approach to understanding and appropriately generating indirect speech acts. In *AAAI*, 2013.

[8] E. Broadbent, V. Kuman, X. Li, J. Sollers, R. Q. Stafford, B. A. MacDonald, and D. M. Wegner. Robots with display screens: a robot with a more humanlike face display is perceived to have more mind and a better personality. *PLOS ONE*, 8(8):e72589, 2013.

[9] P. Brown and S. C. Levinson. *Politeness: Some universals in language usage*. Cambridge University Press, New York, 1987.

[10] C. Canning and M. Scheutz. Functional near-infrared spectroscopy in human-robot interaction. *J. HRI*, 2(3):62–84, 2013.

[11] X. Cui, S. Bray, and A. L. Reiss. Functional near infrared spectroscopy (nirs) signal improvement based on negative correlation between oxygenated and deoxygenated hemoglobin dynamics. *Neuroimage*, 49(3):3039, 2010.

[12] J. Fasola and M. Mataric. A socially assistive robot exercise coach for the elderly. *J HRI*, 2:3–32, 2013.

[13] J. Fink. Anthropomorphism and human likeness in the design of robots and human-robot interaction. *Social Robotics*, 7621:199–208, 2012.

[14] K. Fischer, K. Lohan, and K. Foth. Levels of embodiment: Linguistic analyses of factors influencing hri. In *HRI*, pages 463–470, 2012.

[15] M. E. Foster, A. Gaschler, M. Guiliani, A. Isard, M. Pateraki, and R. P. Petrick. Dynamic multi-party social interaction with a robot agent. In *ICMI*, 2012.

[16] L. Hassell and M. Christensen. Indirect speech acts and their use in three channels of communication. In *Communication Modeling*, 1996.

[17] F. Hegel, F. Eyssel, and B. Wrede. The social robot 'flobi': key concepts of industrial design. In *RO-MAN*, pages 107–112, 2010.

[18] D. Heger, R. Mutter, C. Herff, F. Putze, and T. Schultz. Continuous recognition of affective states by near infrared spectroscopy signals. In *ACII*, 2013.

[19] C.-C. Ho and K. MacDorman. Revisiting the uncanny valley theory: developing and validating an alternative to the godspeed indices. *Comp. Hum. Beh.*, 26, 2010.

[20] L. Hoffman and N. C. Kramer. How should an artificial entity be embodied? Comparing the effects of a physically present robot and its virtual representation. In *HRI*, pages 14–20, 2011.

[21] J. Hou and K. M. Lee. Effects of self-conscious emotions on affective and behavioral responses in hci and cmc. In *SIGDOC*, pages 151–156, 2011.

[22] Y. Jung and K. M. Lee. Effects of physical embodiment on social presence of social robots. In *Presence*, pages 80–87, 2004.

[23] T. Kanda, T. Miyashita, T. Osada, Y. Haikawa, and H. Ishiguro. Analysis of humanoid appearances in human-robot interaction. *IEEE Transactions on Robotics*, 24(3):725–735, 2008.

[24] V. A. Kulyukin. On natural language dialogue with assistive robots. In *HRI*, 2006.

[25] M. K. Lee, S. Kiesler, J. Forlizzi, S. Srinivasa, and P. Rybski. Gracefully mitigating breakdowns in robotic services. In *HRI*, 2010.

[26] K. F. MacDorman and N. Kageki. The uncanny valley. In *IEEE Robotics and Automation*, 2012.

[27] W. J. Mitchell, K. A. Szerszen, A. S. Lu, P. W. Schermerhorn, M. Scheutz, and K. F. MacDorman. A mismatch in the human realism of face and voice produces an uncanny valley. *i-Perception*, 2, 2011.

[28] B. Mutlu, T. Shiwa, T. Kanda, H. Ishiguro, and N. Hagita. Footing in human-robot conversations: how robots might shape participant roles using gaze cues. In *HRI*, pages 61–68, 2009.

[29] R. Rose, M. Scheutz, and P. Schermerhorn. Towards a conceptual and methodological framework for determining robot believability. *Interaction Studies*, 11(2):314–335, 2010.

[30] M. Strait, G. Briggs, and M. Scheutz. Some correlates of agency ascription and emotional value and their effects on decision- making. In *ACII*, 2013.

[31] M. Strait and M. Scheutz. Using near infrared spectroscopy to index changes in affect in realistic human-robot interactions. In *PhyCS OASIS*, 2014.

[32] C. Torrey, A. Powers, M. Marge, S. R. Fussell, and S. Kiesler. Effects of adaptive robot dialogue on information exchange and social relations. In *HRI*, 2006.

[33] C. Torry, S. R. Fussell, and S. Kiesler. How a robot should give advice. In *HRI*, pages 275–282, 2013.

[34] S. Tupak, T. Dresler, A. Guhn, A. Ehlis, A. Fallgatter, P. Pauli, and M. Herrmann. Implicit emotion regulation in the presence of threat: neural and autonomic correlates. *Neuroimage*, 85, 2014.

[35] A. M. R. von der Putten, N. C. Kramer, L. Hoffmann, S. Sobieraj, and S. C. Eimler. An experimental study on emotional reactions towards a robot. *International Journal of Social Robotics*, 5:17–34, 2013.

[36] A. M. R. von der Putten, F. P. Schulte, S. C. Eimler, L. Hoffmann, S. Sobieraj, S. Maderwald, N. C. Kramer, and M. Brand. Neural correlates of empathy towards robots. In *HRI*, pages 215–216, 2013.

[37] S. Wilske. Service robots dealing with indirect speech acts. In *Intelligent Robots and Systems*, 2006.

[38] F. Yamaoka, T. Kanda, H. Ishiguro, and N. Hagita. How close?: Model of proximity control for information- presenting robots. In *HRI*, 2008.

May I Talk about Other Shops Here? Modeling Territory and Invasion in Front of Shops

Satoru Satake, Hajime Iba, Takayuki Kanda, Michita Imai, and Yoichi Morales Saiki
ATR Intelligent Robotics and Communication Laboratories
2-2-2 Hikaridai, Seika-cho, Souraku-gun, Kyoto, Japan
{satoru, iba, kanda, michita, yoichims}@atr.jp

ABSTRACT

This paper models the concept of the "territory" of shops. First, we interviewed three shopkeepers and found that they perceived the space near their shop as their territory and that they interpreted some types of behaviors as invasive. Second, we confirmed that potential visitors share this notion of territory. We also confirmed that the size of the territory depends on the characteristics of a shop's facade. While there is little territory in front of walls, there is more territory in front of shelves and entrances. Our robot traversed around two real shopping malls that included 50 shops and took 3-D scans of their environment shapes. Each shop's facade was analyzed and the shop territory was computed. The computation results match people's perception. The recognition rate accuracy reached 93.5% for the territory areas. User evaluations in a virtual shop environment confirmed that a robot with a territory model behaves better than one without it.

Categories and Subject Descriptors

H.5.2 [**Information Interfaces and Presentation**]: User Interfaces – Interaction styles; I.2.9 [Artificial Intelligence]: Robotics

General Terms

algorithms, design, experimentation, human factors

Keywords

human-robot interaction, social robots, concept of territory

1. Introduction

Previous studies reported several potential uses for robots in public spaces, such as guide at an exposition [18], shopping assistant in a supermarket [5], and an information-gathering tool in an urban environment [25]. In such applications, robots are freely navigating in the space while interacting with people.

What are the capabilities that define such robots as socially acceptable? Identifying them in the short term might not be easy. In the beginning of our tests, people often welcome a robot. However, we have received more actual complaints when we tested robots for longer durations.

Here, we would like to introduce one anecdote that motivated the study reported in the paper. Our robot was setup in a shopping mall wandering around in a corridor among people. We deemed the corridors a kind of public place that people are free to use. As it was not a peak shopping period, we thought there was no risk of congestion and did not expect the robot presence to cause any harm. However, when the robot went back and forth several times along the corridor, a shop-owner complained at the robot disturbing his business. We moved the robot because we agreed that his request was reasonable and logical. However, our robot was not equipped with such common sense. What was it missing ?

Fig. 1 People share a sense of shop territory.

Even though the corridor in front of the shop does not belong to the shop and more closely resembles a kind of public space, the shop people and its customers share a sense that the space in front of the shop is associated with that shop. Thus, when requested, we would follow shop-owner because we thought he can control the use of the space; but, if this occurs somewhere far from the shop, we may not (Fig. 1). That is, we share the sense where shop's territory is. In this paper, we propose computational model of such the *concept of territory* to enable a social robot to recognize the invisible territories formed in a (semi-) public space that is socially shared among people.

2. Related Works

2.1 People's territorial behavior

In an analogy with animals' territorial behavior [4], human beings show territorial behavior, i.e., an individual claiming control over a particular area [17]. People create territory in their daily lives, e.g., in their homes and offices, and even temporarily in public spaces. For instance, research on parking lots revealed that people show territorial responses toward parking spaces even when they are leaving; drivers leave slowly when there is another car waiting, and much slower when the next car shows such invasive behavior as honking [16]. Similar defensive behavior toward invasive acts were found for library aisles [15] and classroom seats [6]. Such defensive behaviors are more significant when invaded by lower-status intruders than higher-status intruders [6, 16].

A stretch of territory to a public space occurred with community consensus [2]. It is reported that people in a local area started to sweep a section of sidewalk, eventually furnishing it with chairs. Via such stretching acts, the territory was generally recognized by the community. People knew that insiders could sit on the chairs on the sidewalk while outsiders could loiter on the sidewalk.

2.2 Robotics research

Robotics research enables robots to navigate around a shopping mall. Safe navigation [19, 23], localization, and map building (e.g.

HRI'14, March 3–6, 2014, Bielefeld, Germany.
Copyright 2014 ACM 978-1-4503-2658-2/14/03 …$15.00.
http://dx.doi.org/10.1145/2559636.2559669

[20]) are fundamental techniques. There are studies for understanding environments. For instance, the human cognition of environments, cognitive maps, has been replicated in a robot so that it understands the topological relationships among locations [27]. Such semantics of locations as "office" and "corridor" are successfully classified from the shapes of geographic maps [13, 21]. Yet, no previous study has addressed *territory* in a public space that people socially share but is not "visually perceivable."

2.3 HRI studies for proxemics behavior

Studies on personal space clearly show that people protect the small space near them [7]. People maintain personal distances toward robots [24]. Michalowski et al. used people's distance to a robot to infer types of interaction [12]. Elena et al. modeled personal space for socially acceptable navigation [22]. Such studies addressed a kind of territorial behavior but only about the space around a person.

In our previous study [10], which partially addressed the concept of territory, we modeled locations where a robot waited for its users and found that unless there is a wall or a high shelf, a robot should not wait within a 2.5 m area of a store. However, except for this, we did not address any other part of our developed concept of territory; e.g., we ignored whether the waiting behavior was profitable for the shop.

3. How Do Shopkeepers Perceive Territory?

3.1 Data collection

We interviewed three male shopkeepers having seen our robot in the past field trial at the shopping mall they work. Each interview was conducted in front of their respective shops to help them answer in their daily context.

We first sought their advice on what our robot in a shopping mall corridor should heed and what it should avoid. We wanted to identify the strain of common sense in their perception of territory and invasive behaviors. We expected that visitors rarely commit invasive behavior because they share feelings of common sense about territory; thus, they would have difficulty providing real experiences of territory invasion. Instead, we used the example from our introduction as a real example where our robot lacked human-like common sense. Then we explained that our robots might commit other behaviors that the shop owners might not want. With this setup, we helped them easily imagine situations where their territory would be invaded. When needed, we explained that our robots could do such tasks as sales, advertising, carrying, and giving directions. The interviews were recorded.

3.2 Analysis

All the recorded utterances were transcribed and analyzed. We manually assigned labels that represent the basic idea in the sentences. We assigned multiple labels, when applicable. Below are some examples of the labels we assigned to the transcribed utterances; assigned labels were highlighted in bold:

- *I think shopkeepers share invisible boundaries in front of a shop* [**facade area, concept of territory**]. *For example, I think the border between that 100-yen store and the furniture place is around that brown line (pointing to a line in the middle of the corridor)* [**facade area**].
- *The front of a store, which is a kind of entrance, is its most important point* [**entrance**]. *Even for window-shopping, if a robot roams around the entrance where visitors might stop, customers are less likely to visit* [**entrance obstruction**]
- *If the robot is near my shelves, I get the impression that it would prevent customers from looking at my shop's items* [**interfering with looking at shop items**]
- *I don't mind if a robot talks here (in front of a wall), but talking here (in front of a shelf) for an hour* [**interfering with looking at shop items**] *would disturb our business* [**hindrance to sales**]

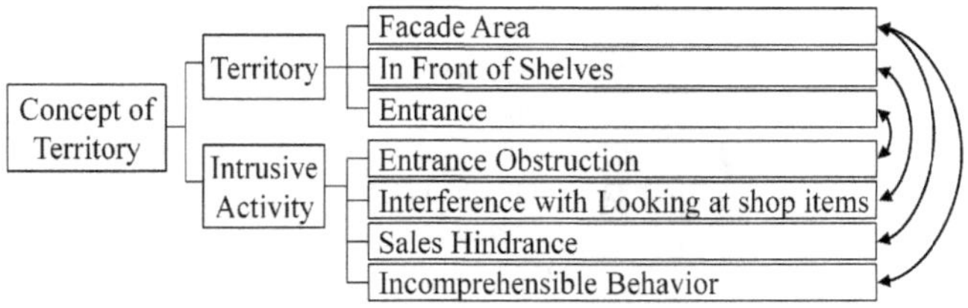

Fig.2 Overview of the concept of territory

Next we repeatedly merged similar labels, established a hierarchical relationship among them, and built a concept (Fig. 2) for which we identified two primary elements: *territory* and *intrusive activities*. *Territory* includes such labels about locations as entrance, in front of shelves, and the facade area that were mentioned in the context of territoriality. For instance, *in front of a shelf* is the location where they would not permit a robot to linger, meaning that they intend to control/protect that space. All the shopkeepers mentioned all three labels, and one shopkeeper explicitly talked about the *concept of territory*.

Intrusive activity includes labels about action and robot behavior that shopkeepers considered interfering, unacceptable, or annoying. They did not use the term *intrusive*, but they expressed the desire to suppress these behaviors if they were conducted in their territory, which we interpret as *intrusive behavior*.

We identified four types of activities: *entrance obstruction, interference with looking at shop items, sales hindrance,* and *incomprehensible behavior*. For instance, one shopkeeper mentioned that shopkeepers would move aside during a talk to avoid interfering with customers who look at shop items. All described these four types of behaviors as intrusive.

In contrast, some activities are considered acceptable even within the territory. One mentioned that if the robot is advertising his shop, operating in front of it is allowed. Another thought that it would be nice to have a guidance robot near a shelf to answer questions about the location of items. In general, if the activity promotes the shop, operating within the territory is acceptable.

In addition, the shopkeepers also commented about the services provided by robots and often stressed that they must be safe enough to avoid collisions. One shopkeeper said that he would put his robot in a conspicuous location to improve sales. We found these comments useful, and we were impressed that they reflect various positive desires about future services from robots; we haven't analyzed them yet because they are beyond this paper's research context.

4. Do Customers Perceive Territory?

We hypothesized that the concept of territory embodies the common sense of humans, and thus it is shared by shopkeepers and customers. To test our idea, we collected data from participants acting as customer.

4.1 Data collection

4.1.1 Environment

Collecting data in actual environments is difficult: Participants must repeatedly intrude on the territories of the stores during shop

Fig. 3 Virtual shop

hours, which means disturbing customers and affecting businesses. Instead, we built a *virtual shop* environment. Using two ultra-short-focus projectors, we projected pictures of facades that matched the actual sizes of the stores (Fig. 3). Virtual reality has been successfully used in spatial cognition research (e.g. [9, 11]). We did not use screen motions for walking [14], but allowed physical motion in front of a large screen.

We took pictures from 50 shops (explained in Section 5.1.1). When they gave us permission, we included the shopkeepers in the pictures that show how they usually work. Large shops were projected using two projectors. For small shops, the second projector projected another shop to imitate a mall's atmosphere.

4.1.2 Participants

Ten members of our laboratory participated (five males, five females, avg. 30.3 years old) in this research without knowing its specific purpose. They routinely visit malls as customers.

4.1.3 Procedure

Since human perceptions of territory are basically unconscious, directly asking people to identify such shop territories would be difficult. Instead, after they performed intrusive activities, we asked them when they felt uncomfortable doing so.

Data collection was done for two activities: *irrelevant* and *shopper chats*. To provide realistic experiences, each participant engaged in each activity with a confederate in front of the virtual shop. In *irrelevant chat*, participants talked for five minutes about which store to visit next. Since such activity matches the shopkeeper's concepts of *entrance obstruction, interference with looking at shop items,* and *hindrance to sales*, people might feel uncomfortable in any territory area. We called the locations where they felt uncomfortable *territory areas*.

In the *shopper chat*, participants chatted for five minutes on a topic related to the shop. They pointed at shop items, looked together, and talked about them. Such activity would be allowed in many areas of the territory; nevertheless, they still match the shopkeeper's concept of *entrance obstruction*; people might feel uncomfortable to do so in some territory areas. We called this the *shopper-restricted area* where they felt uncomfortable.

After they experienced the activity, a participant stood at every location in 50 x 50 cm grids, and we asked whether he/she was uncomfortable if he/she talked there. Every shop was evaluated by two participants. We evenly distributed shops to each pair of participants. Each participant provided reports for ten shops. We collected evaluations for 4170 locations.

4.2 Analysis

Similarity of participant evaluations: We analyzed whether our participants shared similar perceptions of territory. Since every shop was evaluated by a pair of participants, the degree of matches was computed as the κ coefficients for all pairs and averaged them. Although there were some individual differences around the boundary, the κ coefficients showed marginal matches in both *territory* (.592, s.d. .208) and *shopper-restricted areas* (.509, s.d. .290). Fig. 4 shows an example, where matching evaluation are painted respectively in gray and red.

Characteristics of territory concept: We analyzed the relationship between the area size and the facade features of the shop. We divided the space on a shop's facade line into a 50-cm grid (called facade grid in Fig. 8) and manually classified whether

Fig. 4 Evaluation from participants

each cell is an *entrance*, in front of the *shelves* (where items are displayed), or a *wall*. These classifications correspond to the concepts obtained from the shopkeepers (Section 3.2).

We checked the distance from the location at which participants reported uncomfortable feeling to the facade line. Fig. 5 shows the result for the territory area. The horizontal axis represents the distance from the shop, and the vertical axis is the ratio of participants who felt uncomfortable at that distance. The graph shows that the territory is affected by the facade category. Considering having 80% of the participants free from embarrassment as measure criterion, the area in front of the *entrance* is relatively large (as a rough estimate of boundary

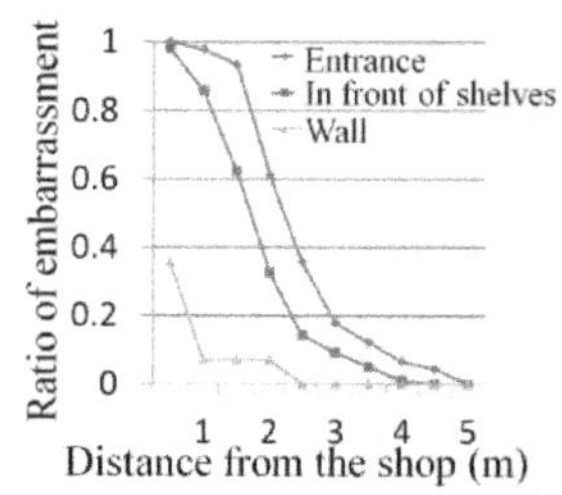

Fig. 5 Territory area

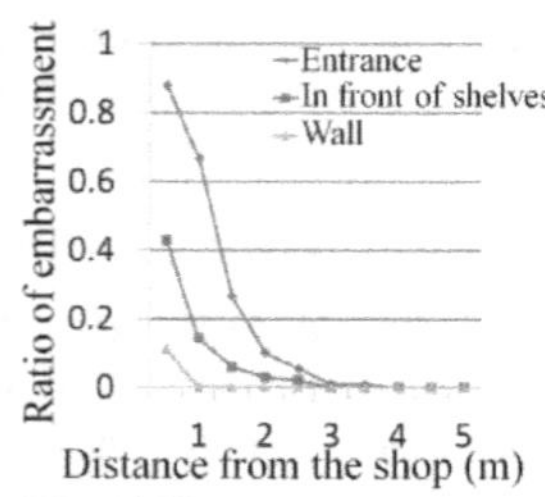

Fig. 6 Shopper-restricted

distance, e.g. we need to keep a 3.0m distance), but it is relatively small in front of the *walls* (1.0 m) and The area in front of the *shelves* in between (2.5m).

Figure 6 shows the result for the shopper-restricted area. This area appears to be smaller than the territory area, and is also influenced by the facade grid. In this case, the area in front of the *entrance* goes up to 2m, 0.5m in front of a *wall* and 1m in front of the *shelves*.

5. Computational Model

5.1 Representation and features

After the analysis in Section 4.2 revealed that territory is influenced by facade types, we decided to let a robot automatically recognize them. So we built a 3D map (Fig. 7 (a)) of a shopping mall and retrieved the relevant features.

5.1.1 Data collection and 3D map-building

We navigated a robot for several corridors in two shopping malls during the mall's business hours. Its mobile base is a P3 mobile platform from Pioneer from which we recorded the odometry information. The robot was equipped with Velodyne HDL-32e, which acquires range scans by a 360° horizontal field of view by a 26.8° vertical field of view in 10 Hz.

We applied 6d SLAM [1]. All odometry information and 3D scans from every 1 m of the robot's movement was used. The 3D map is represented by a set of 10-cm voxels. The frequencies of occupancy and frequencies of scan were counted; and voxels which have low frequencies of occupancy (less than 0.7) were eliminated as mobile entities, like people and baby strollers.

We manually compared the obtained maps with directory maps of two shopping malls, manually defined polygons of the shop

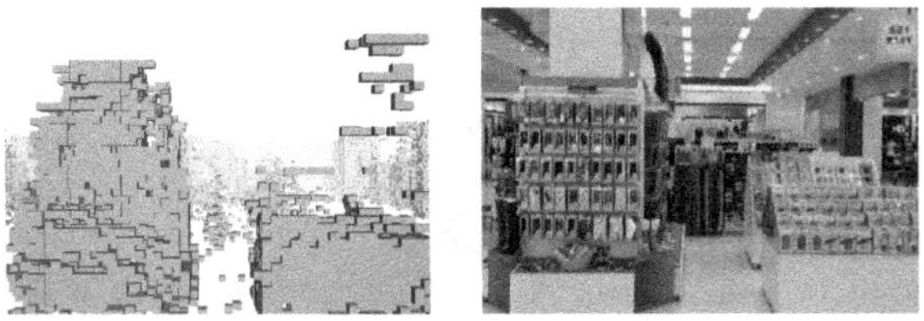

(a) 3D geometrical map (b) Photo from same view

Fig. 7 Example of 3D geometrical map

boundary on the 2D plane, and added facade lines (red lines in Fig. 8) that were defined as lines between corridors and shops. Finally, the maps were divided into individual shops for later processes.

5.1.2 Retrieving facade features

For each shop, we applied *entrance-detection* and *shelf-detection* to compute the facade features from the 3D geometrical map.

Entrance-detection: This idea, which defines the entrance as the area where people can go into the shop, is computed as follows:

Step 1: Scanning non-enterable points in a vertical direction. We put viewpoints on the corridor at a distance of D_{view} from the shop (denoted as *viewpoint* on Fig. 8 (a)). For each *view point*, we applied a simple clustering to the voxels, which exactly exist on the sight direction line from the view point i (Fig. 8 (b)): Occupied voxels were clustered together if distance between them is within C_v. Clusters with N_{v_wall} occupied voxels or more are detected as non-enterable clusters. We moved the viewpoint in the direction of the facade line every 10 cm and repeated the process. At each viewpoint i, the j-th obtained cluster is called $c_{i,j}$. We adjusted the parameters to maximize the overall performance and set them to D_{view}=1.5m, C_v=0.5 m, and N_{v_wall}=4.

Step 2: Merging non-enterable points in a horizontal direction. We merged the result from Step 1 in the direction of the facade line. We applied a simple clustering method again. 'Non-enterable clusters' $c_{i,j}$ were clustered together if their distance was within C_h. Finally, the clusters with W_{wall} length or longer were detected as non-enterable sections. We empirically adjusted the parameters and set them to W_{wall}=0.4 m and C_h =0.2 m.

Step 3: Entrance detection. Finally the sections on the facade line that were not detected as non-enterable over $W_{entrance}$ were labeled as the entrance. $W_{entrance}$ was adjusted to 0.4 m.

Shelf-detection: There are two types of shelves. One is low shelves, including counters and desks. We can see over them into the shop. Another is high shelves, including cases where shop items are displayed on walls or shelves along walls.

We applied the following computation for detecting low shelves:

1. Detection in the vertical direction (Fig. 9): The scan at viewpoint i is labeled as a *low-shelf-candidate* if 'non-enterable cluster' $c_{i,j}$ starts from the floor, and if an enterable space above $c_{i,j}$, which is detected by either (1) no cluster exists above *cluster 1*, or (2) all clusters above $c_{i,j}$ within

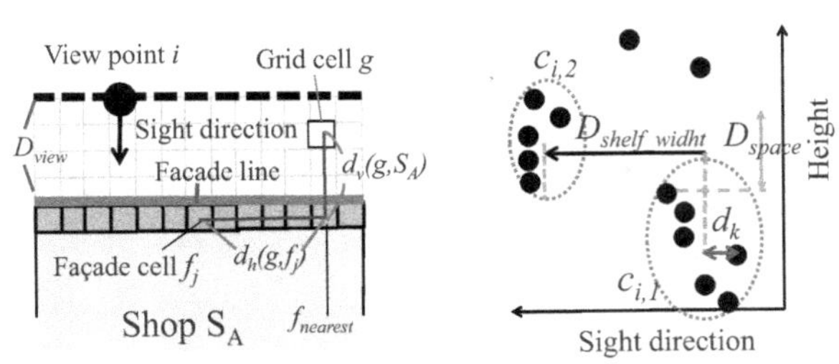

(a) View point (b) Shelf-detection

Fig. 8: Retrieving facade feature

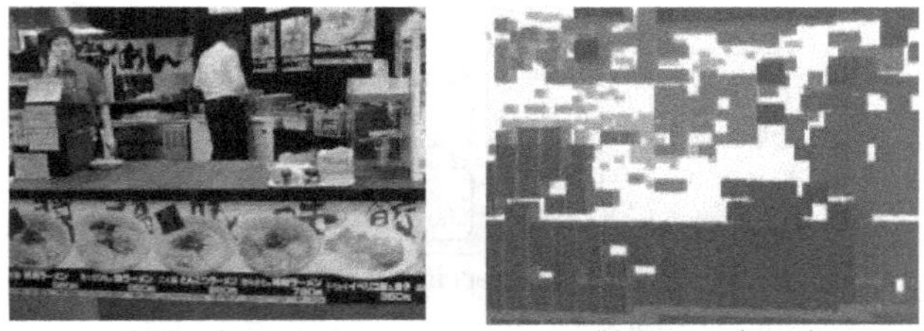

(a) Real scene (b) Detected result

Fig. 9 Examples of low-shelf-detection.

Blue voxels are low-shelf candidates. The open space above the counter allows us to see the shop's interior.

D_{space}, are inside the shop (Fig. 8(b)). The projected distance on the sight direction line with the other clusters above $c_{i,j}$ are larger than D_{shelf_width}, and all these clusters are far enough from the facade line. We adjusted the parameters and set them to D_{space}=0.4 m and D_{shelf_width}=0.8 m.

2. Merging in horizontal direction: If a 0.4 m or longer section along with the facade line is continuously detected as a *low-shelf-candidate*, it is defined as a low-shelf section.

We applied the following computation for detecting high shelves.

1. Detection in the vertical direction (Fig. 10): For non-enterable cluster $c_{i,j}$, which starts from the floor but is not detected as a *low-shelf-candidate*, we checked whether it is a *high-shelf-candidate*. Our idea is that the surface of a high-shelf area is more uneven (e.g. shop items are displayed, and space due to shelf depth) than the surface of plain walls. We checked the distance from the center of the cluster to each member k of its cluster, denoted as d_k (Fig. 8). If d_k is larger than D_{plain_wall} for 40% or more of the member points, it is detected as a high-shelf-candidate.
2. Merging in the horizontal direction: If a 0.4 m or longer section along with the facade line is continuously detected as a *high-shelf-candidate*, it is detected as a high-shelf section.

Walls: All sections on the facade lines, detected as non-enterable but are not detected as low or high shelves, were labeled as *walls*.

5.2 Territory-detection algorithm

The goal of our computation model is to judge if the robot's activity is intrusive for a shop. For that judgment, we computed two types of shop areas: *territory* and *shopper-restricted.*

Figure 11 overviews our territory detection algorithm. Based on the concept of territory (Sections 3.2 and 4.2), we computed three location features (Fig. 11): *distance to shop*, *entrance obstructions, and shelf obstructions*. With the algorithm, we computed whether a location is within the territory of shops every 50 cm x 50 cm grid cell, which is called the *territory grid.* For each cell in the grid, we computed location features. These location features are used as the input for a support vector machine (SVM). We prepared two SVMs, one for deciding whether the target position is intrusive for shop S_n's territory, and another for the shopper-restricted area.

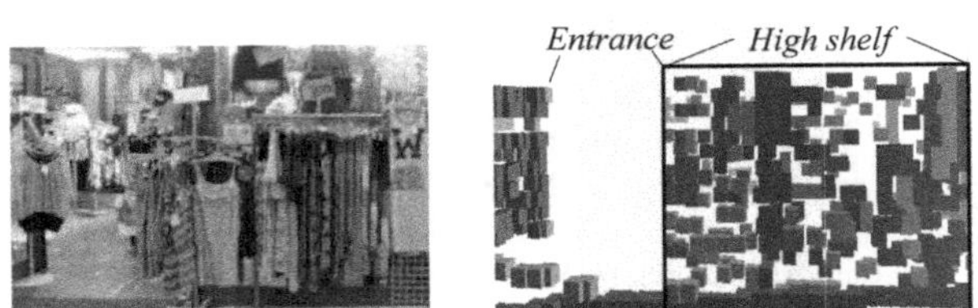

(a) Real scene (b) Detected result

Fig. 10 Examples of high-shelf-detection.

Green voxels are uneven locations that satisfied $d_k > D_{plain\_wall}$

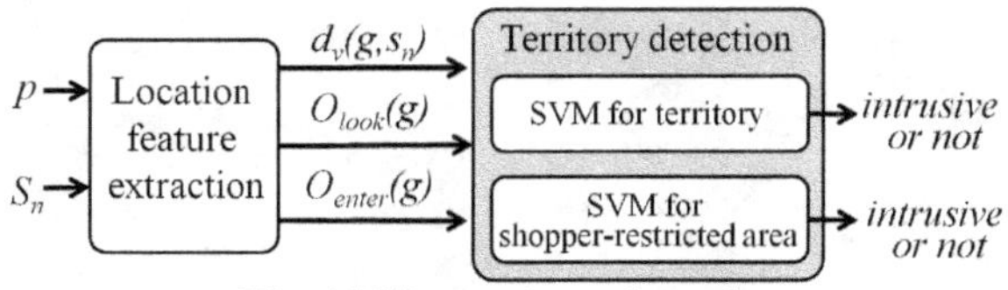

Fig. 11 The territory detection

The location features of grid cell g were computed from nearest shop S_n and its *facade grid* (Figs. 8(a)). In the figures, f_j represents the j-th cell in the *facade grid*, which is classified as *entrance*, *shelf*, or *wall* (based on the algorithm in Section 5.1.2).

First, we define some terms. $d_v(g, S_n)$ represents the distance from grid cell g to shop S_n, which is the shortest distance from grid cell g to the nearest cell in facade grid $f_{nearest}$ of S_n. $d_h(g, f_j)$ represents the distance on the facade line from g to f_j and equals the distance from $f_{nearest}$ to f_j. Below, we explain more details about how we computed each feature.

Distance to shop: This is computed from the shortest distance to the shop's nearest *facade grid* cell, illustrated as $d_v(g, S_n)$.

Entrance obstruction ($O_{enter}(g)$): Our idea is to estimate the entering interference, assuming a person is standing at grid cell g. Since the *distance to shop* feature is also used simultaneously, for this feature we only consider interference regardless of the distance to the shop:

$$O_{enter}(g) = \mathrm{avg}_{\forall f_i, d_h(g,f_j)<D_{enter}}\left(O_{enter}(g, f_j)\right), \quad (1)$$

where D_{enter} is a threshold representing the maximum distance on the *facade line* within which a person influences the entrance. $O_{enter}(g, f_j)$ is an estimate of the degree of interference, if a person stands at g and if another visitor uses f_j to enter the shop:

$$O_{enter}(g, f_j) = \begin{cases} 1.0 - d_h(g, f_j)/D_{enter} & if\ f_j = entrance \\ 0 & otherwise. \end{cases} \quad (2)$$

When the entrance is just in front of grid cell g, the value is the largest, meaning that it causes the most obstruction. We adjusted D_{enter} to 1.0 m.

Shelf obstructions ($O_{look}(g)$): We estimate the degree to which a person standing at grid cell g interferes with other people who want to look at the shelves:

$$O_{look}(g) = \mathrm{avg}_{\forall f_i, d_h(g,f_j)<D_{look}}\left(O_{look}(g, f_j)\right), \quad (3)$$

where D_{look} is a threshold representing the maximum distance on the *facade line* within which a person interferes with looking at the shelves. $O_{look}(g, f_j)$ estimates the degree of interference if a person stands at g and if another visitor looks at the shelves at the cell of *facade grid* f_j:

$$O_{look}(g, f_j) = \begin{cases} (1.0 - d_h(g, f_j)/D_{look} & if\ f_j = \text{shelf} \\ 0 & otherwise. \end{cases} \quad (4)$$

We adjusted D_{look} to 1.0 m.

5.3 Activity-judgment algorithm

Using the computation results for the territory explained in Section 5.2, the system judges whether a planned activity is *intrusive* at a *target position* with two inputs: *target position* (p in fig. 11) and *relevant shop* ($S_{relevant}$). The *target position* is the location where the robot plans to conduct the activity. The *relevant shop* identifies the shop when the activity is beneficial for it; otherwise 'none' is input. The system computes the nearest shop to the *target position* (S_n), and checks the following rules.

1. If $S_n \neq S_{relevant}$, using SVM for territory, it checks whether the *target cell* is inside of (*intrusive* to) the territory of S_n. If so, the activity is judged as *intrusive*.
2. If $S_n = S_{relevant}$, using SVM for shopper-restricted area, it checks whether the *target cell* is inside of (*intrusive* to) the shopper-restricted area of S_n. If so, the activity is judged as *intrusive*..

5.4 Learning from dataset

We used two SVMs (Fig. 11) and implemented them with the libsvm library [3]. The SVM for the territory detection was trained using a dataset built from the *territory area* data (Section 4.1). Since each location was judged by two participants, we only included locations where both evaluations matched. For instance, if both felt uncomfortable to do *irrelevant chat*, the location was included as an inside (*intrusive*) sample in the *territory area*. This avoided using ambiguous locations. Our dataset contains 957 inside (*intrusive*) locations and 2351 outside (*non-intrusive*) locations in the *territory area*.

The SVM for the shopper-restricted area detection was trained using a dataset built from the *shopper-restricted area* data. We only included locations over which both participant evaluations matched. 224 inside and 3406 outside locations were included.

We adjusted the gamma and cost parameters using a grid search algorithm and 2-fold cross-validation where the averaged accuracy per shop was used as the evaluation metrics.

5.5 Evaluation

We compared our proposed model with another model that only used the *distance to shop* feature (explained in Section 5.2) called a *distance model*. We calibrated its SVM parameters and averaged the recognition ratio for each shop. Fig. 12 shows the result for one of the shop. Both results seem reasonably matched.

The proposed model's estimated territory area had 93.5% accuracy and its shopper-restricted area had 96.3% accuracy. Since the distance model had only 69.9% success for the territory area, the developed features contributed well to the estimation. The improvement was relatively small for the shopper-restricted area, since the distance model also successfully estimated 93.7% of the area. Regarding to precision and recall ratio, for territory area, the precision is 86.3% and the recall is 96.5%. There were a few false positives in the proposed model. For shopper-restricted area, the precision is 62.8% and the recall is 74.0%. It looks high false positive (37.2%), but 80.6% of the false positive occurred within 50cm of the real boundary and make the shop-restricted area bigger. Thus we believe the result is reasonable.

6. User Evaluation

6.1 Scenario and robot implementation

Chatting is one fundamental ability of a social robot. People enjoy talking while shopping even with a robot [8]. However, the location of such chatting is important. On the one hand, irrelevant chat in a shop's territory might cause uncomfortable feeling.

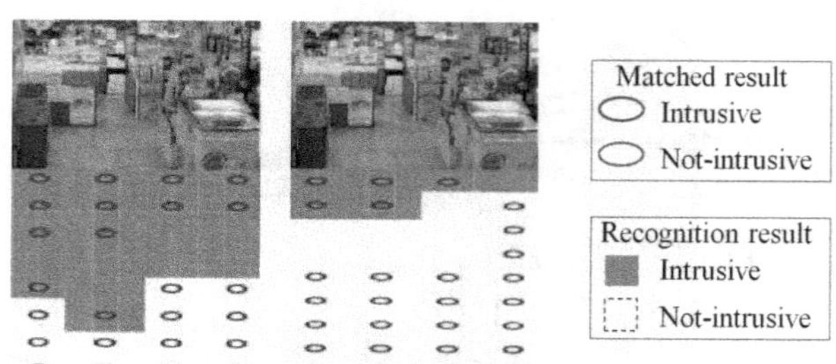

(a) Territory (b) Shopper-restricted area

Fig. 12 The recognized result

When appropriate, a robot should talk about shop items near the shop. Based on such expected needs, we chose a window-shopping scenario where the robot is involved in *shopper* and *irrelevant chats,* which we also consider a good example where the concept of territory is important.

The robot was autonomous. We used Robovie-R3 (Fig. 13), which has two range laser sensors attached at a height of 10 cm. Localization is done with a particle filter and ray tracing on a grid map [20]. Given the geographic map and contents information for chats, it localizes itself, computes the location feature of the target shop, and chooses a location to initiate conversation

For experimental simplicity, the robot spoke and the participants just listened. The location where the robot performed *shopper chat* was computed using the *model of the shoppers' area.* Among the available locations provided by the model, it chose the location closest to the shop center. It moved to the location and performed *shopper chat* for two minutes. The contents were designed using people's chats in relevant situations.

The location for the *irrelevant chat* was computed using a *model of the territory area.* Among the locations judged outside of the territory, it chose the location that minimized the travel distance. It moved there and performed *irrelevant chat* for three minutes.

6.2 Hypothesis and prediction

Because there is no alternative model for computing territory, we compared our method with other possible ideas for navigating the robot for the window-shopping scenario. One idea is to let the robot stay near the shop so that it can easily explain it: the *best-explanation* method. However, we expect that such a robot would intrude on shop territories in irrelevant chats and cause uncomfortable feeling in its user, but not the robot with the territory model. Thus, we made the following prediction:

Prediction 1: The robot with the territory model would choose more comfortable locations for chatting than the robot with the *best-explanation* model

We also compared our model with another idea. We could design a robot that is always careful not to disturb shops and their businesses and thus only operates far away from shops (*far-locations* method). Such a robot would not choose uncomfortable locations, but it would fail to go near shops, when necessary, like the case of shopper chat. Thus, we made the following prediction:

Prediction 2: The robot with the territory model would choose better locations for explaining the shop items than the robot with the *far-locations* model.

If the above hypotheses are true, our proposed model would be preferred more than alternatives. That is,

Prediction 3: The robot with the territory model would be more highly evaluated than the robots with the other methods.

6.3 Method

The experiment was conducted in the virtual shop environment used in the data collection (Section 4.1). We randomly chose three shops from the 50 used in the data collection.

6.3.1 Participants

We paid 24 Japanese people (15 males and 9 females, average age: 20.3 years) for their participation.

(a) Interaction scene (b) Environment

Fig. 13 Scene of user evaluation

6.3.2 Conditions

Three experiment conditions were prepared:

Territory model condition: The robot used the territory model and chose locations for chats as described in Section 6.1.

Best-explanation condition: The best location for explanations is 1.0 – 1.2 m from the target items [26]. We found that it is better to slightly move the robot back for better visibility of many shop items. Finally, we decided the location to be 1.7 m from the center of the facade line of the shop. The robot went there before it started chatting.

Far-location condition: In our data collection, the territory area was at most within 4.5 m; thus, to choose a location far enough outside of territory, we set the distance to 5 m. The robot goes to a location 5 m away from the shop before chatting.

6.3.3 Procedure

We instructed all participants that they are visiting a shopping mall with their assistant robot. As described in Section 6.1, the robot started chats with the participants.

The study was a within-subject design. Participants took part in all three conditions whose orders were counterbalanced.

6.3.4 Measurement

After each session, participants filled out a questionnaire on the following questions on a 1-to-7 point Likert scale, where 1 is the most negative and 7 is the most positive:

- **Comfortableness:** degree of comfortableness – comfortable feeling of chatting at the location to which the robot moved.
- **Ease of understanding:** degree of ease of understanding of the shop items mentioned in the chat.
- **Overall evaluation:** overall rating of the robot.

6.4 Results

The analyses were carried out using linear mixed-effects models having within-participants variables of the experiment condition as a fixed effect and shop as a random effect. Multiple comparisons among conditions were with the Bonferroni method.

6.4.1 Verification of prediction 1

Figure 14 shows the *comfortableness* result. A significant main effect in the territory model condition was revealed ($F(2, 46.000)=4.593$, $p=.015$). The score in the territory model was significantly better than the score in the best-explanation condition ($p=.021$), and no significant difference was found in the far-location condition ($p=1.0$). Thus, as predicted, the participants rated *comfortableness* better for the territory model condition than the best-explanation conditions. Prediction 1 is supported.

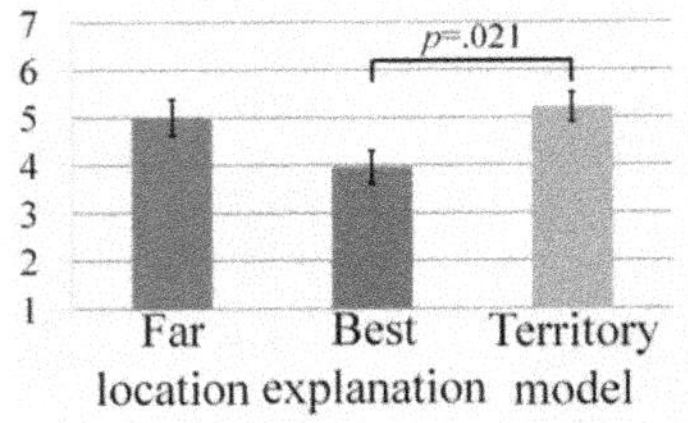

Fig. 14 Comfortableness

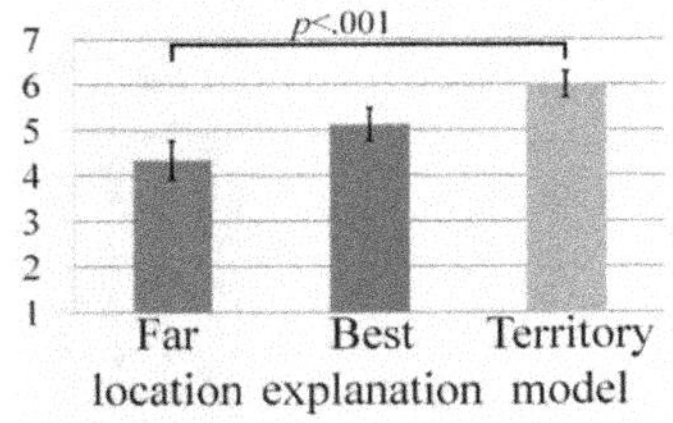

Fig. 15 Ease of understanding

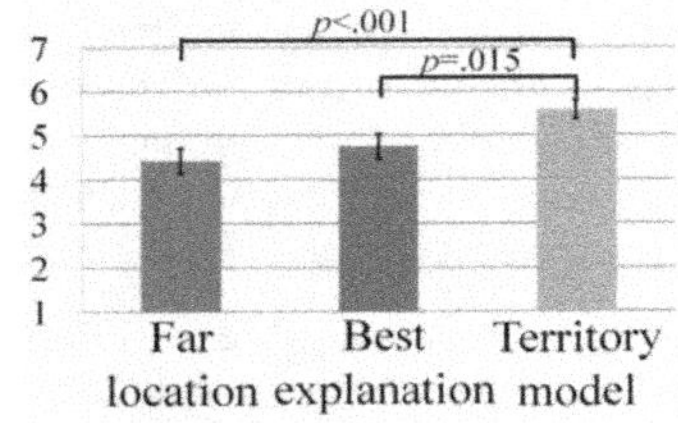

Fig. 16 Overall evaluation

6.4.2 *Verification of prediction 2*

Figure 15 shows the ease of understanding result. A significant main effect was revealed in the territory model condition (F(2, 46.000)=9.285, *p*<.001). The ease of understanding score in the territory model condition was significantly higher than the score in the far-location condition (*p*<.001), and almost significantly higher than the score in the best-explanation condition (*p*=.086). Thus, as predicted, they rated the ease of understanding higher for the territory model condition than the far-location condition. Prediction 2 is supported.

6.4.3 *Verification of prediction 3*

Figure 16 shows the overall evaluation result. A significant main effect was revealed in the territory model condition (F(2, 46.000)=9.061, *p*<.001). The score in the proposed condition was significantly higher than the other conditions (best-explanation: *p*=.015, far-location: *p*<.001). Thus, as predicted, they rated the overall evaluation higher for the territory model condition than the other conditions. Prediction 3 is supported.

7. DISCUSSION

7.1 Brief test in a real environment

Perhaps people's perception is different between virtual and real environments. To test our model's capability in a real shopping mall, we conducted an additional study.

There are 15 Japanese people (8 males and 7 females, average 21.3 years old) participated, for which they were paid. After they practiced *shopper* and *irrelevant chats* with a confederate in the virtual shop environment, they moved to a shopping mall.

To evaluate the *territory area*, for each shop (in total, they visited 10 shops), each participant was asked to stay in two locations. Using the developed territory model, we randomly chose one location from *inside* the territory area and one location from *outside* of it. At each location, we asked the participants whether it was *comfortable* or *uncomfortable* (compared with their own common sense) to do *irrelevant chat*. By this design, we aimed to minimize the intrusion and still acquire evaluation data.

To evaluate the *shopper-restricted area*, we asked each participant for two locations for *shopper chat*, one from inside and another from outside area the shopper-restricted area computed by the model. For both areas, the order of locations (inside or outside of the area) was counterbalanced. 150 points are evaluated in total.

Fig. 17 shows the result. The location that the developed model selected as *not-intrusive* (outside) are almost all judged as *comfortable* by the participants for both areas (94.7% for territory, 99.3% for shopper-restricted area). A chi-squared test revealed significant differences in evaluations between inside and outside area (territory area: χ^2 (1)=133.121, *p*<.001, shopper-restricted area: χ^2 (1)=36.912, *p*<.001). In both areas, outside was more frequently judged as *comfortable* than inside. In short, the result demonstrated that the model selected *comfortable* locations, and the location excluded from the model (i.e., inside the areas) was frequently *uncomfortable* for the task.

This brief evaluation shows that, although the data collection was done in a virtual environment, the locations computed from the model are valid for the real environment. One difference is that participants' evaluation in real world is maybe more tolerant than the evaluation in the virtual shop environment. We asked reasons and found that in case there are multiple entrances in a shop, they less concern the obstruction of the entrances, thus judged as *comfortable* even though the model compute it as *intrusive*.

Note that one would wonder the influence of social pressure in the real environment, e.g. gaze from shopkeepers. However, shopkeepers in Japan tend to avoid actively interact with customers when they just look at shop items, and thus they avoid staring at the customers to not make feel them uncomfortable. Thus, we believe that the participants were not under significant social pressure even in the real environment.

Overall, the result demonstrates that our model can be immediately used in a real environment for a robot to choose *non-intrusive* locations for activities like chatting. Improvement can be possible if we more carefully consider the entrance constraints.

7.2 Applicability

We have not yet fully solved the territory problem for such navigational behaviors reported in the introduction. We must model the territory's area first. Thus, one future work is to establish a model that computes whether the activity is beneficial for a shop and whether it is perceived as *incomprehensible behavior*. For chat behavior, this is not a problem because typically contents are designed by human designers, for whom it is easy to judge whether it can benefit a shop. In contrast, usually since navigational behaviors are the consequence of autonomous behavior, we need a mechanism to automatically compute the perception of intrusiveness. Perhaps we can learn from studies on detecting suspicious behavior, like security camera studies.

7.3 Alternative approaches

A robot might operate without a territory model if it could react well to human behaviors. A robot could stay at an entrance and move only when visitors arrive, chat about irrelevant things near shops, and move away when a shopkeeper is about to complain. That could be a strategy for human visitors. However, because robot perception is not good enough to recognize such human behaviors, it is computationally easier to recognize territory. Even if it were possible, people would get upset by the robot, and such a strategy would not be socially acceptable for long-term use.

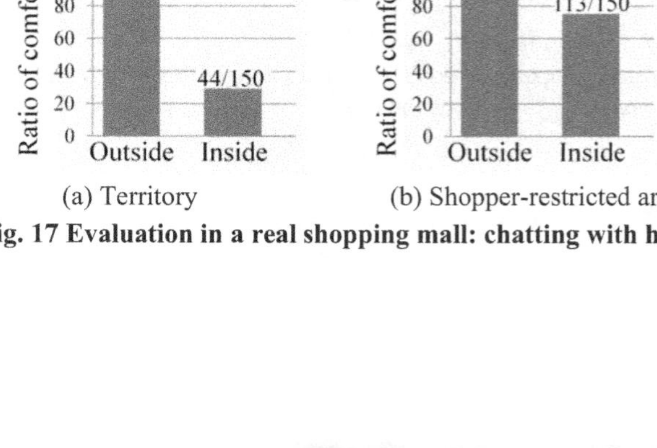

(a) Territory (b) Shopper-restricted area

Fig. 17 Evaluation in a real shopping mall: chatting with human

Perhaps the territory model can be simplified, e.g., only with distance-based thresholds. Such simplification can be useful in some cases. However, as our analysis in Section 5.5 shows, it does not work well for territory areas. For instance, when a corridor is not wide enough, we need to find a space between shops that face the corridor; without knowing a territory's shape, a robot might use a space that is more intrusive.

7.4 Limitations

Our developed model was prepared in a Japanese context and for human-size entity. When it is used in other cultures or a robot that is larger/smaller than human, we might need to extend it or adjust its parameters. When robots will choose locations to talk, we should also consider obstruction to pedestrians, which was not addressed in this study. Long-term relationship (e.g. frequent customers of a shop) would influence to sense of intrusion, but not yet modeled, which would be also important.

8. Conclusion

We developed a model for the concept of territory of shops. This is an important capability so that robots are socially acceptable in shopping malls. Our model uses the features of shop facades, such as the locations of entrances and shelves. It achieved 93.5% accuracy for the territory area and 96.3% accuracy for the shopper-restricted areas. We implemented our system on a robot and tested it in a virtual shop. Participants rated the robot with the territory model superior to the robots that used alternative models.

9. ACKNOWLEDGMENTS

This work was supported by JST, CREST.

10. REFERENCES

[1] Borrmann, D., Elseberg, J., Lingemann, K. and Nuchter, A., 2011, The 3D Hough Transform for Plane Detection in Point Clouds - A Review and A new Accumulator Design, *Journal 3D Research*, vol. 2,

[2] Brower, S. N., 1980, Territory in urban settings, *Culture and Environment. Human behavior and environment*, vol. 4, pp. 179-207.

[3] Chang, C.-C. and Lin, C.-J., 2001, LIBSVM: A Library for Support Vector Machines, ed.

[4] Edney, J. J., 1974, Human Territoriality, *Psychological Bulletin*, vol. 81, pp. 959-975.

[5] Gross, H.-M., Boehme, H.-J., Schroeter, C., Mueller, S., Koenig, A., Martin, C., Merten, M. and Bley, A., 2008, ShopBot: progress in developing an interactive mobile shopping assistant for everyday use, *IEEE Int. Conf. on Systems, Man, and Cybernetics (SMC2008)*, pp. 3471-3478.

[6] Haber, G. M., 1980, Territorial Invasion in the Classroom Invadee Response, *Environment and Behavior*, vol. 12, pp. 17-31.

[7] Hall, E. T., 1966, *The Hidden Dimension*, Doubleday.

[8] Iwamura, Y., Shiomi, M., Kanda, T., Ishiguro, H. and Hagita, N., 2011, Do Elderly People Prefer a Conversational Humanoid as a Shopping Assistant Partner in Supermarkets?, *ACM/IEEE Int. Conf. on Human-Robot Interaction (HRI2011)*, pp. 449-456.

[9] Jansen-Osmann, P. and Berendt, B., 2005, What makes a route appear longer? An experimental perspective on features, route segmentation, and distance knowledge, *The Quarterly Journal of Experimental Psychology*, vol. 58A, pp. 1390-1414.

[10] Kitade, T., Satake, S., Kanda, T. and Imai, M., 2013, Understanding suitable locations for waiting, in *Proceedings of the 8th ACM/IEEE international conference on Human-robot interaction*, ed: IEEE Press, pp. 57-64.

[11] Mallot, H. A., Gillner, S., van Veen, H. A. and Bülthoff, H. H., 1998, Behavioral experiments in spatial cognition using virtual reality, in *Spatial cognition*, ed: Springer, pp. 447-467.

[12] Michalowski, M. P., Sabanovic, S. and Simmons, R., 2006, A Spatial Model of Engagement for a Social Robot, *IEEE International Workshop on Advanced Motion Control*, pp. 762-767.

[13] Mozos, Ó. M., Triebel, R., Jensfelt, P., Rottmann, A. and Burgard, W., 2007, Supervised semantic labeling of places using information extracted from sensor data, *Robotics and Autonomous Systems*, vol. 55, pp. 391-402.

[14] Riecke, B. E., Bodenheimer, B., McNamara, T. P., Williams, B., Peng, P. and Feuereissen, D., 2010, Do we need to walk for effective virtual reality navigation? physical rotations alone may suffice, in *Spatial Cognition VII*, Springer, pp. 234-247.

[15] Ruback, R. B., 1987, Deserted (and Nondeserted) Aisles: Territorial Intrusion Can Produce Persistence, Not Flight, *Social Psychology Quarterly*, vol. 50, pp. 270-276.

[16] Ruback, R. B. and Juieng, D., 1997, Territorial Defense in Parking Lots: Retaliation Against Walting Drivers, *Journal of Applied Social Psychology*, vol. 27, pp. 821-834.

[17] Sebba, R. and Churchman, A., 1983, Territories and Territoriality in the Home, *Environment and Behavior*, vol. 15, pp. 191-210.

[18] Siegwart, R., Arras, K. O., Bouabdallah, S., Burnier, D., Froidevaux, G., Greppin, X., Jensen, B., Lorotte, A., Mayor, L., Meisser, M., Philippsen, R., Piguet, R., Ramel, G., Terrien, G. and Tomatis, N., 2003, Robox at Expo.02: A Large Scale Installation of Personal Robots, *Robotics and Autonomous Systems*, vol. 42, pp. 203-222.

[19] Sisbot, E. A., Marin-Urias, L. F., Alami, R. and Simeon, T., 2007, A human aware mobile robot motion planner, *IEEE Transactions on Robotics*, vol. 23, pp. 874-883.

[20] Thrun, S., Burgard, W. and Fox, D., 2005, *Probabilistic Robotics (Intelligent Robotics and Autonomous Agents)*, The MIT Press.

[21] Topp, E. A. and Christensen, H. I., 2006, Topological Modelling for Human Augmented Mapping, *IEEE/RSJ Int. Conf. on Intelligent Robots and Systems (IROS2006)*, pp. 2257-2263.

[22] Torta, E., Cuijpers, R. H., Juola, J. F. and Van Der Pol, D., 2012, Modeling and testing proxemic behavior for humanoid robots, *International Journal of Humanoid Robotics*, vol. 9,

[23] Trautman, P. and Krause, A., 2010, Unfreezing the Robot: Navigation in Dense, Interacting Crowds, *IEEE/RSJ Int. Conf on Intelligent Robots and Systems (IROS2010)*, pp. 797-803.

[24] Walters, M. L., Dautenhahn, K., Boekhorst, R. t., Koay, K. L., Kaouri, C., Woods, S., Nehaniv, C., Lee, D. and Werry, I., 2005, The influence of subjects' personality traits on personal spatial zones in a human-robot interaction experiment, *IEEE Int. Workshop on Robot and Human Interactive Communication (RO-MAN2005)*, pp. 347-352.

[25] Weiss, A., Igelsböck, J., Tscheligi, M., Bauer, A., Kühnlenz, K., Wollherr, D. and Buss, M., 2010, Robots Asking for Directions: The Willingness of Passers-by to Support Robots, *ACM/IEEE Int. Conf. on Human-Robot Interaction (HRI2010)*, pp. 23-30.

[26] Yamaoka, F., Kanda, T., Ishiguro, H. and Hagita, N., 2009, Developing a Model of Robot Behavior to Identify and Appropriately Respond to Implicit Attention-Shifting, *ACM/IEEE Int. Conf. on Human-Robot Interaction (HRI2009)*, pp. 133-140.

[27] Yeap, W. K., 1988, Towards a computational theory of cognitive maps, *Artificial Intelligence*, vol. 34, pp. 297-360.

Applications for Emotional Robots

Oliver Damm
Applied Informatics
Faculty of Technology
Bielefeld University, Germany
odamm@techfak.uni-bielefeld.de

Christian Becker-Asano
Department of Computer Science
Freiburg University, Freiburg
basano@cs.uni-freiburg.de

Manja Lohse
Human Media Interaction Group
University of Twente, Enchede
m.lohse@utwente.nl

Frank Hegel
Applied Informatics
Faculty of Technology
Bielefeld University, Germany
fhegel@techfak.uni-bielefeld.de

Britte Wrede
Applied Informatics
Faculty of Technology
Bielefeld University, Germany
bwrede@techfak.uni-bielefeld.de

1. MOTIVATION

Based on the success of the previous workshop on applications of emotional robots at HRI2013, we aim to provide a platform to continue the interdisciplinary exchange on this topic at HRI2014.

Human-robot interaction (HRI) research on emotions is motivated by the assumption that social signals (with emotional expressions being one of its components), which are produced by robots, are processed similarly to those accompanying human-human interaction. Therefore, artificial emotions are used in HRI for several purposes. First of all, artificial emotions allow a robot to react in a more believable and natural manner. Furthermore, artificial emotions can serve as a control mechanism [4] or to provide natural user feedback about the robots internal state and its goals.

Over the last years the robotics community has seen a great increase in socially interactive robots. Social robots are designed to interact in a more human and intuitive manner. Some characteristics of this kind of robots are to express/perceive emotions, to communicate with (high-level) dialogues, to learn/recognize models of other agents, establish/maintain social relationships, or develop social competencies. These socially interactive robots are used for different purposes, e.g. as toys, as educational tools or as research platforms.

Depending on the purpose, their capability to express emotions varies. Some robots are quite limited in displaying emotion, e.g., using actuated lips or flashing LEDs [1]. Others have many degrees of freedom and can provide richer movement [6, 2].

From an engineering perspective it is necessary to create robots for specific contexts, requirements, and expectations. In many cases, the context is defined so that it corresponds to the applications. Ever more complex applications require more complex processing steps than just reacting to what is perceived [3, 5]. However, the concomitant expectations differ from one application to the next and it remains a challenging long-term task to identify and formulate general guidelines in this respect. In addition, the limitations and opportunities provided by the integration of emotional aspects into robotic systems need to be carefully investigated as well. With this second full day workshop we aim to continue our discussion of interdisciplinary perspectives on the application of robots that are able to display and perceive emotions, e.g. emotional robots in therapy, in education, in care taking, or in public spaces.

HRI'14, March 3–6, 2014, Bielefeld, Germany.
ACM 978-1-4503-2658-2/14/03.
http://dx.doi.org/10.1145/2559636.2560021.

2. LIST OF TOPICS

Topics include but are not limited to:

- aesthetical design of emotional displays
- multimodal emotional expressions
- emotions in long-term interaction
- modelling emotions and emotional interaction
- acceptance of emotional robots
- role of emotions in applications
- methods to research emotional robots

3. FORMAT OF WORKSHOP CONTRIBUTIONS

We ask researchers, who work on these topics, to submit papers from 4 up to 6 pages. Papers should be formatted according to the IEEE HRI 2014 paper guidelines. They will be presented in 20min talks. Accepted papers will be made available on CD and published on the workshop website. Further publication in a journal is in discussion and depends on the number and quality of the submitted papers.

4. INTENDED ATTENDEES

In order to encourage a discussion facing a large spectrum of usage of emotions in HRI we would like to welcome researches from a broad range of disciplines (e.g. robotics, social sciences, psychology, linguistics).

Table 1: Tentative Schedule.

Time Slot	Duration	Description
09:30 - 10:00	30	Opening by the organisers
10:00 - 11:00	60	Paper Presentations 1
11:00 - 11:30	30	Coffee Break
11:30 - 12:15	45	Paper Presentations 2
12:15 - 13:00	45	Discussion
13:00 - 14:00	60	Lunch
14:00 - 15:30	90	Paper Presentations 3
15:30 - 16:00	30	Discussion
16:00 - 16:30	30	Coffee Break
16:30 - 18.00	90	Discussion & Closing Remarks

5. TENTATIVE SCHEDULE

A tentative schedule is presented in Table 1 (subject to change based on accepted submissions).

6. ABSTRACT FOR HOMEPAGE

In social interaction between humans expressing, recognizing, and understanding emotions is essential. Therefore, artificial emotions are also being exploited to improve human-robot interaction (HRI) and to build robots that interact in a more human-like and intuitive manner. Some characteristics of this kind of robots are to express/perceive emotions, to communicate with (highlevel) dialogues, to learn/recognize models of other agents, to establish and maintain social relationships, and to develop social competencies. These socially interactive robots are used for different purposes, e.g. as toys, as educational tools, or as research platforms. Thus, from an engineering perspective it is necessary to create robots for specific contexts, requirements, and expectations. With this second full day workshop we aim to continue our discussion of interdisciplinary perspectives on the application of robots that are able to display and perceive emotions. We want to develop an idea of how the context influences the characteristics that an emotional robot needs to have and to gain new insights in the role of emotions in HRI.

7. ORGANIZERS

7.1 Oliver Damm

Oliver Damm is a member of the Applied Informatics Group at Bielefeld University. His current research interests includes social factors of human-robot interaction in particular the integration of believable emotions into HRI. His PhD project is to design a computational model for emotional alignment between humans and robots. He received his bachelor of science degree in 2008 and his master of science degree in 2010. In 2010 he joined the CRC 673, Project C2 Communicating Emotions as a research assistant.

7.2 Christian Becker-Asano

Christian Becker-Asano is lecturer in the Foundations of Artificial Intelligence group at Freiburg University, where his research focuses on topics of Affective Computing, Android Science, and Social Robotics. He received his Master's degree and his PhD (Dr. rer. nat.) in Computer Science from Bielefeld University in 2003 and 2008, resp. In 2008, he became post-doctoral fellow of the Japan Society for the Promotion of Science allowing him to join the "Ishiguro laboratory" at the ATR in Kyoto, Japan, for two years. He is co-opted as Cooperative Researcher of this lab.

7.3 Manja Lohse

Manja Lohse is a postdoctoral researcher in the Human Media Interaction group at University of Twente. Until June 2012 she was a member of the Research Institute for Cognition and Robotics (CoR-Lab) in the Hybrid Society Group at Bielefeld University where she received her PhD degree in 2010. Accompanying the thesis work, she obtained a degree in Intelligent Systems. Manja Lohse's research interests are the social aspects of human-robot interaction, evaluation methods, and users' expectations toward robots.

7.4 Frank Hegel

Frank Hegel is postdoctoral design researcher in the Applied Informatics Group (AGAI) at Bielefeld University. He received his Master's degree in Industrial Design from the University of Wuppertal and his PhD (Dr.-Ing.) from Bielefeld University, Germany. From 2006 to 2010 he participated in the CRC 673 "Alignment in Communication" with regard to emotional robots and design of social robots. Since 2010 he is involved in several projects related to the topics of social robotics, conceptual design, industrial design, anthropomorphism, and visual semiotics.

7.5 Britta Wrede

Britta Wrede is heading the research group "Hybrid Society" of the CoR-Lab, Bielefeld University and since 2009 she is temporary head of the Applied Informatics Group. She was awarded a Master's degree in Computational Linguistics and her PhD (Dr.-Ing.) in Computer Science from Bielefeld University in 1999 and 2002, respectively. After her PhD, she received a DAAD Postdoc fellowship in the speech group of the International Computer Science Institute (ICSI) in Berkeley, CA.

8. REFERENCES

[1] H. Ahn, Y. Beak, I. Sa, and W. Kang. Design of reconfigurable heterogeneous modular architecture for service robots. *Intelligent Robots and Systems, 2008. IROS 2008. IEEE/RSJ International Conference on*, pages 1313–1318, 2008.

[2] C. Becker-Asano and H. Ishiguro. Evaluating facial displays of emotion for the android robot Geminoid F. In *IEEE SSCI Workshop on Affective Computational Intelligence*, IEEE 2011 Symposium Series on Computational Intelligence, pages 22–29, 2011.

[3] C. Becker-Asano and I. Wachsmuth. Affective computing with primary and secondary emotions in a virtual human. *Autonomous Agents and Multi-Agent Systems*, 20(1):32–49, January 2010.

[4] C. Breazeal. Designing sociable robots, 2004.

[5] O. Damm, K. Malchus, F. Hegel, P. Jaecks, P. Stenneken, B. Wrede, and M. Hielscher-Fastabend. A computational model of emotional alignment. In *5th Workshop on Emotion and Computing, 2011*, Berlin.

[6] I. Lütkebohle, F. Hegel, S. Schulz, M. Hackel, B. Wrede, S. Wachsmuth, and G. Sagerer. The bielefeld anthropomorphic robot head "Flobi". In *Robotics and Automation (ICRA), 2010 IEEE International Conference on*, pages 3384–3391, 2010.

Socially Assistive Robots for the Aging Population: Are We Trapped in Stereotypes?

Astrid Weiss
Institute of Automation and Control
Vienna University of Technology
weiss@acin.tuwien.ac.at

Jenay Beer
Department of Computer Science & Engineering
College of Social Work
University of South Carolina
jbeer@cse.sc.edu

Takanori Shibata
Institute of Advanced Industrial Science and Technology (AIST)
shibata-takanori@aist.go.jp

Markus Vincze
Institute of Automation and Control
Vienna University of Technology
vincze@acin.tuwien.ac.at

ABSTRACT

Robots caring for the older population in care facilities and at home is an ongoing theme in HRI research. Research projects on this topic exist all over the globe in the USA, Europe, and Asia. All of these projects have the overall ambitious goal to increase the well-being of older adults and to enable them to stay at home as long as possible. In this workshop we want to reflect whether the HRI community is trapped in stereotypes when it comes to socially assistive robots for older adults? Therefore we want to gather and compare findings from user needs analysis, user evaluation studies, as well as interaction scenarios and functionalities of existing care robots. Are our results suggesting similar scenarios? Do older end users in all countries have similar needs and desires when it comes to assistive robots? What are the challenges and opportunities for future assistive robots (maybe for those we develop for ourselves when we belong to the older population...) also on an ethical and legal level? In this workshop we want to escape the stereotype trap what socially assistive robots should do. Can socially assistive robots solve the aging population problem on a societal and individual level? Are older people in general technology opponents? Will robotic helpers be accepted in the home as long as they pretend to be social actors?

Categories and Subject Descriptors

J4 [**Computer Applications**]: Social and Behavioral Sciences – *Sociology; Psychology*

General Terms

Design, Experimentation, Human Factors, Theory.

Keywords

Demographic Change, Aging, Assistive Robotics, Needs Assessment, Older Adults, Service Robotics.

1. INTRODUCTION

In the human-robot interaction (HRI) community there is an ongoing discussion that robots could be one possible solution for caring for the growing aging population and the resulting shortage on qualified healthcare personnel in future. Assistive robots have potential to help older adults staying home longer and supporting them and the personnel in care facilities. However, using robots to assist older adults should not be accepted uncritically as the solution for caring for the aging population. As the recent Special Eurobarometer 382 on "Public attitudes towards robots" [1] revealed the wider public does not want robots to take care of the older population, subsequently in this workshop we want to lean back and reflect: Are we trapped in a stereotypical mindset thinking that assistive technology will automatically ease societal and individual problems (plus boost the economy) and that older adults are reluctant users, but socially assistive robots will convince them of their usefulness.

HRI'14, March 3-6, 2014, Bielefeld, Germany.
ACM 978-1-4503-2658-2/14/03.
http://dx.doi.org/10.1145/2559636.2560022

2. OBJECTIVES

It is the aim of this workshop to reflect on existing assistive robots and ongoing research on HRI with older adults in domestic and care facility contexts. A considerable amount of research has been conducted to understand user needs and desires for "elderly care robots", as well as to build platforms and evaluate them in terms of acceptance and usability, but what have we collectively learned overall as an HRI community? Where are the communalities and differences in our work? In this workshop we want to gather, compare, and combine knowledge gained in various HRI projects with older adults in the US, Europe, and Asia. This should lead to a broader understanding of the target user group as well as of design and implementation challenges of care robots. The following topics should be addressed in the workshop and guide the submission of position papers:

- Identified user needs and desires of older adults at home and in care facilities
- Requirements and constraints of socially assistive robots for older adults
- Functionalities and interaction scenarios of socially assistive robots for older adults
- Moral accountability and legal issues of care robots for the aging population

3. INVITED SPEAKERS

The following invited speakers will present their research in the workshop: Wendy Rogers, Kazuyoshi Wada, Marcel Heerink, Birgit Graf , Selma Sabanovic, Elizabeth Broadbent.

4. TARGET AUDIENCE

The primary audience of the workshop includes researchers in the field of HRI. In particular, researchers working with the aging population on social robotics, user-centered HRI evaluation, and ethical and moral implications will be interested in this workshop. Moreover, researchers from the field of advanced interfaces will be addressed via HCI-related channels, as research on smart homes and ambient intelligences solutions for the older population is a closely related field, but unfortunately underrepresented in the HRI community. As we want to address both sides of the topic, namely the user-centered and the robotic-centered perspective we expect an interdisciplinary audience and also practitioners from health care institutions and robot manufacturers. We also consider the topic as highly interested for mass media and public relations.

5. WORKSHOP FORMAT

This is a one-day workshop with break-out sessions, alternated with a moderated group discussion. The workshop starts with an introduction to the topic, followed by short introductory presentations to get familiar with the participants and their work. After that, the organizers present the common themes of the submitted papers, grouping them into different sessions (following the main topics of the workshop). Two different groups (one from a robot-centered view point and one from a user-centered view point) then reflect in a break-out session on the communalities and differences of their work and how a stereotypical bias may be involved. After the lunch break, the group comes back together to discuss the conclusions of each break-out session.

6. DOCUMENTATION

We will collect all papers and presentations. Additionally we will capture the whole-group discussions in notes in an additional presentation. All material will be presented on the workshop website. An overall whitepaper will also be provided on the website after the workshop.

http://workshops.acin.tuwien.ac.at/HRI2014_Elderly/index.html

7. ORGANIZERS

7.1 Astrid Weiss

Astrid Weiss is a postdoctoral research fellow in HRI at the Vision4Robotics group at the ACIN Institute of Automation and Control at Vienna University of Technology (Austria). She holds a master degree in sociology and a PhD in social sciences from the University of Salzburg. Her current research focuses on user-centered design and evaluation studies for Human-Robot Interaction, with a special interest in the impact technology has on the everyday life and what makes people accept or reject technology. She was involved in the organization of two workshops on social acceptability of robots at Ro-Man2008 and HRI2009, as well as in the HRI Pioneers workshop 2010.

7.2 Jenay Beer

Jenay Beer is the director of the Assistive Robotics and Technology Lab. She is an Assistant Professor with a joint appointment in the Department of Computer Science and Engineering and the College of Social Work at the University of South Carolina. She earned her PhD in Engineering Psychology fro Georgia Institute of Technology in 2013. Her research interests include human factors and aging. With a special interest in Human-Robot Interaction, her research focuses on the application of assistive technology to help future generations of older adults in maintaining their independence. She has studied themes such as user acceptance, emotionally expressive robots, and level of robot autonomy.

7.3 Takanori Shibata

Takanori Shibata is a Chief Senior Research Scientist at Human Technology Research Institute, National Institute of Advanced Industrial Science and Technology (AIST), a Visiting Professor at Tokyo Institute of Technology, and a Visiting Fellow, the AgeLab, Massachusetts Institute of Technology (MIT). He received B.S., M.S. and Ph.D. in Electronic and Mechanical Engineering from Nagoya University in 1989, 91 and 92, respectively. He was a research scientist at AIST 1993 to 98. Concurrently, he was a visiting research scientist at the Artificial Intelligence Lab., MIT from 1995 to 98, and a visiting research scientist at the Artificial Intelligence Lab., Univ. of Zurich in 1996. At the AIST, Dr. Shibata was a senior research scientist 1998-2013. Concurrently, he was the Deputy Director for Information and Communication Technology Policy, Bureau of Science, Technology, and Innovation Policy, Cabinet Office, Government of Japan from 2009 to 10. Since 2013, he has been the current positions.

7.4 Markus Vincze

Markus Vincze received his diploma in mechanical engineering from Technical University Wien (TUW) in 1988 and a M.Sc. from Rensselaer Polytechnic Institute, USA, 1990. He finished his PhD at TUW in 1993. With a grant from the Austrian Academy of Sciences he worked at HelpMate Robotics Inc. and at the Vision Laboratory of Gregory Hager at Yale University. In 2004, he obtained his habilitation in robotics. Presently he leads a group of researchers in the "Vision for Robotics" laboratory at TUW. With Gregory Hager he edited a book on Robust Vision for IEEE and is (co-) author of over 250 papers. Markus' special interests are computer vision techniques for robotics solutions situated in real-world environments and especially homes.

8. PROGRAMME COMMITTEE

The following people serve as PC members: Anglika Peer, Manfred Tscheligi, David Feil-Seifer, Susanne Fernnert, and Kate Tsui.

9. ACKNOWLEDGMENTS

The research leading to the organization of this workshop has received funding from the European Community's Seventh Framework Programme (FP7/2007-2013) under grant agreement No. 288146, Hobbit and from the Austrian Science Foundation (FWF) under grant agreement T623-N23, V4HRC

10. REFERENCES

[1] European Commission. Special Eurobarometer 382 - Public Attitudes towards Robots. 2012.

Workshop on Attention Models in Robotics: Visual Systems for Better HRI *

Michael Zillich
ACIN, Vienna University of Technology
Gusshausstrasse 27-29 E376
A-1040 Vienna, Austria
zillich@acin.tuwien.ac.at

Simone Frintrop
Cognitive Vision Group, University of Bonn
Roemerstrasse 164
D-53117 Bonn, Germany
frintrop@iai.uni-bonn.de

Fiora Pirri
ALCOR Lab, University of Rome
Via Ariosto 25
00185 Roma, Italy
pirri@dis.uniroma1.it

Ekaterina Potapova
ACIN, Vienna University of Technology
Gusshausstrasse 27-29 E376
A-1040 Vienna, Austria
potapova@acin.tuwien.ac.at

Markus Vincze
ACIN, Vienna University of Technology
Gusshausstrasse 27-29 E376
A-1040 Vienna, Austria
vm@acin.tuwien.ac.at

ABSTRACT

Attention is a concept of human perception that enables human subjects to select the potentially relevant parts out of the huge amount of sensory data and that enables interactions with other human subjects by sharing attention with each other. These abilities are also of large interest for autonomous robots, therefore, interest in modeling concepts of human attention computationally has increased strongly in the robotics community during the last decade. Especially in human-robot interaction, the ability to detect what a human partner is attending to and to act in a similar way to enable intuitive communication, are important skills for a robotic system.
Still, there exists a gap in knowledge transfer between researchers in human attention and robotic researchers with their specific, often task-related, problems. Both communities can mutually benefit from each other by sharing ideas. In the workshop, researchers in visual and multi-modal attention can profit from the rapidly growing field of robotics, which offers new and challenging research questions with very concrete applicability to challenging problems. Robotic researchers can learn how to integrate attention to support natural and real-time HRI.

Categories and Subject Descriptors

I.2.m [**Artificial Intelligence**]: Miscellaneous

*The research leading to these results has received funding from the Austrian Science Foundation (FWF) under grant agreement No. TRP 139-N23, InSitu

HRI'14, March 3–6, 2014, Bielefeld, Germany.
ACM 978-1-4503-2658-2/14/03.
http://dx.doi.org/10.1145/2559636.2563723.

Keywords

Visual Attention, Multi-modal Attention, Joint Attention, Saliency, Visual Search

1. ORGANIZERS

Michael Zillich, PhD

Michael Zillich received his PhD degree from Vienna University of Technology in 2007, where he is currently working in the Vision for Robotics group of the Automation and Control Institute. Michael Zillich has collaborated within several European and national projects in the areas of cognitive robotics and vision, with a focus on object segmentation and attention.

Simone Frintrop, PhD

Simone Frintrop received the MS and the PhD degree from the university of Bonn, Germany, in 2001 and 2005 respectively. She is a senior researcher at the Computer Science department at the University of Bonn and is currently heading the Cognitive Vision Group. She has worked for more than 10 years in the field of computational visual attention and saliency detection, with applications for mobile vision systems and robotics.

Prof. Fiora Pirri

Fiora Pirri is full professor at the Department of Computer, Control and Management Engineering, University of Rome, Sapienza. She is head of Alcor Laboratory of Cognitive Robotics and Vision. She has been working on attention for several year and she has patented the Gaze Machine, a device that tracks the point of regard of a subject moving freely in an environment.

Ekaterina Potapova, MS

Ekaterina Potapova received her MS degree *summa cum laude* in Applied Mathematics from National Research Nuclear University MEPhI, Moscow in 2010 and is currently working towards her PhD in Computer Vision at Vienna University of Technology. Her current research interests are in human visual attention and image segmentation.

Prof. Markus Vincze
Markus Vincze received his first degrees from Vienna University of Technology, Diploma in mechanical engineering, 1988, and MS from Rensselaer Polytechnic Institute, USA, 1990. He finished his PhD at Vienna University of Technology in 1993. With a grant from the Austrian Academy of Sciences he worked at HelpMate Robotics Inc. and at the Vision Laboratory of Gregory Hager at Yale University. In 2004, he obtained his habilitation in robotics. Presently he leads a group of researchers in the "Vision for Robotic" laboratory at Vienna University of Technology.

2. OVERVIEW OF THE WORKSHOP

In recent years the robotics vision community has extensively investigated the area of visual and multi-modal attention. Visual attention, as well as attention based on fusing inputs from several modalities plays an important role of prioritizing visual space in robotic scenarios and of deciding what to do next. However, algorithms for visual attention face a wide range of challenges, such as integration of biologically-plausible attention models on robot architectures, developing top-down attention mechanisms and the usage of attention to improve human-robot interactions. We believe, in order to solve these problems, the robotics research community needs greater collaboration and communication with the cognitive science community, as well as with the HRI community. We invite contributions to the following topics: Bottom-up attention and saliency, Top-down attention and visual search, Multi-modal attention and sensor fusion, Joint and shared attention, Application of attention in HRI.
The organizing team has experience in organizing workshops at other venues, such as BVW 2009, IROS 2011, RSS 2013, and BVW 2013.

3. WORKSHOP FORMAT

This half-day workshop will consist of paper presentations, invited talks, panel discussions, and a poster session. We expect to have two oral sessions, two 30 minutes invited talks, 20 minutes contributed paper spotlights followed by 30 minutes discussion. We expect to accept around 8 papers. The workshop poster session will provide space for a detailed discussion of the contributed papers. We have two confirmed invited speakers (see below).

The planned schedule is as follows:

09:00 – 09:10 Introduction

Part 1: Attention in robotics from *human-based* point of view

09:10 – 09:40 Invited talk + questions
09:40 – 10:00 Short presentation (5 minutes each)
10:00 – 10:30 Questions to participants, discussions, posters
10:30 – 11:00 Coffee Break

Part 2: Attention in robotics from *robot-based* point of view

11:00 – 11:30 Invited talk + questions
11:30 – 11:50 Short presentation (5 minutes each)
11:50 – 12:20 Questions to participants, discussions, posters

12:20 – 12:30 Conclusions and final remarks

4. INVITED SPEAKERS

Prof. Verena V. Hafner with the talk *Robot attentional models for intuitive HRI.*

Prof. Daniel T. Levin with the talk *Seeing, thinking, and understanding: The role of visual attention during HRI.*

5. TARGET AUDIENCE

We expect to have papers from the field of HRI, robotics communities, and cognitive science involved in research connected, but not restricted, to human visual attention, multimodal attention, computational models of attention, biologically-plausible attentional mechanisms, theories of attention and attention in robotics visual systems.

6. POSITION PAPER REQUIREMENTS

We will accept papers up to 6 pages long. We encourage submissions with both original work and work that has been already presented at another venue. Each paper will be assigned at least two reviewers. The paper will be evaluated based on the relevance to the workshop topic, technical soundness and significance to the community. We support submissions with both a strong technical contribution and well-described/evaluated integration in working systems. Selected papers will be grouped into two sessions (see above), in order to organize the discussion thematically.

7. DOCUMENTING THE WORKSHOP

We will collect all papers, posters and presentations. Additionally we will record all talks on video. All of those will be placed on the workshop webpage that will be available publicly. We will create a poster during the workshop with the outcome of the presentations and discussions and present it at the poster session during the main conference. We hope that this workshop will serve to broaden the community of people focusing on the proposed research agenda.

8. RECRUITING PARTICIPANTS

Workshop organizers will advertise the workshop. The call for participation for this workshop will be distributed via related mailing lists (e.g. EURON, robotics–worldwide, EUCog). A website will be created in order to provide information about the workshop. Additionally, the organizers have personally invited several speakers and participants.

HRI: A Bridge between Robotics and Neuroscience. From Understanding Humans to Assisting Humans and Back

Alessandra Sciutti
RBCS Dept.,Istituto Italiano di Tecnologia, Via Morego 30
16163 Genova Italy
+39 010 71781475
alessandra.sciutti@iit.it

Katrin Lohan
School of Mathematical and Computer Sciences, Heriot-Watt University, Riccarton, Edinburgh EH14 4AS
katrin.lohan@googlemail.com

Yukie Nagai
Graduate School of Engineering, Osaka University, 2-1 Yamada-oka, Suita, Osaka, 565-0871 Japan
+81 6 6879 4724
yukie@ams.eng.osaka-u.ac.jp

ABSTRACT

A fundamental challenge for robotics is to transfer the human natural social skills to the interaction with a robot. At the same time, neuroscience and psychology are still investigating the mechanisms behind the development of human-human interaction. HRI becomes therefore an ideal contact point for these different disciplines, as the robot can join these two research streams by serving different roles. From a robotics perspective, the study of interaction is used to implement cognitive architectures and develop cognitive models, which can then be tested in real world environments (e.g., [1,2,3]). From a neuroscientific perspective, robots could represent an ideal stimulus to establish an interaction with human partners in a controlled manner and make it possible studying quantitatively the behavioral and neural underpinnings of both cognitive and physical interaction (e.g., [4,5]) . Ideally, the integration of these two approaches could lead to a positive loop: the implementation of new cognitive architectures may raise new interesting questions for neuroscientists, and the behavioral and neuroscientific results of the human-robot interaction studies could validate or give new inputs for robotics engineers. However, the integration of two different disciplines is always difficult, as often even similar goals are masked by difference in language or methodologies across fields. The aim of this workshop will be to provide a venue for researchers of different disciplines to discuss and present the possible point of contacts, to address the issues and highlight the advantages of bridging the two disciplines in the context of the study of interaction.

Website: http://www.macs.hw.ac.uk/~kl360/HRI2014W/index.html

1. ORGANIZERS

Alessandra Sciutti <alessandra.sciutti@iit.it>
Istituto Italiano di Tecnologia

Alessandra Sciutti received her Ph.D. in Humanoid Technologies from the University of Genoa (Italy) in 2010. After an experience of one year at the Robotics Lab of the Rehabilitation Institute of Chicago, she is currently working as a Post Doc at the RBCS Department of the Italian Institute of Technology. Her research activity mainly concerns how motor control and perception laws apply to human- human and human-robot interaction. More information at: http://www.iit.it/people/robotics-brain-and-cognitive-sciences-cognitive-humanoids-lab/post-doc/alessandra-sciutti.html

Katrin Solveig Lohan <katrin.lohan@googlemail.com>
Heriot-Watt University

Katrin Solveig Lohan joined the school of mathematical and computer science at the Heriot-Watt University as a Lecturer in 2013. Previously, she was working at the Istituto Italiano di Tecnologia (IIT), as a junior Post Doc in the RobotDoc project founded by the Marie Curie Fellowship. She obtained her Ph.D. in Engineering at the Bielefeld University, Germany in 2012, where she was associated with the ITALK Project as Ph.D. student. The main research interests are in understanding the learning mechanisms between parents and infant, between adults and adults, and between humans and robots to create a natural interaction with a robot.

Yukie Nagai <yukie@ams.eng.osaka-u.ac.jp>
Osaka University

Yukie Nagai is a Specially Appointed Associate Professor at Graduate School of Engineering, Osaka University. She received her Ph.D. in Engineering from Osaka University in 2004 and then worked as a Post Doc at National Institute of Information and Communications Technology in Kyoto from 2004 to 2006. After working at Bielefeld University in Germany for three and a half years, she came back to Osaka in 2009. Her research interests include the developmental mechanism of human social cognition such as joint attention, imitation, and language use. She investigates how human infants acquire such abilities through interaction with their caregivers by means of constructive approaches. More information at: http://cnr.ams.eng.osaka-u.ac.jp/~yukie

2. OVERVIEW OF THE WORKSHOP

The full-day workshop will be organized along three main perspectives of the study of human robot interaction: 1) *The robot as model* or the robotics perspective; 2) *The robot as stimulus* or the neuroscientific perspective and 3) *The robot as interaction partner*, the result of the integration of the former two. The first perspective addresses the question of how human infants acquire social cognitive abilities by means of constructive approaches.

From this perspective robots are used as a model to implement developmental mechanisms aiming, among other cognitive skills, to learn to communicate naturally with human caregivers. From the second perspective robots are used as displays of social cues to human subjects to investigate and quantify, for example, how humans perceive social signals such as gaze and gestures and whether robots can be accepted as social partners. The third perspective intends to develop robotic interaction partners based on

HRI'14, March 3–6, 2014, Bielefeld, Germany.
ACM 978-1-4503-2658-2/14/03.
http://dx.doi.org/10.1145/2559636.2560024

the knowledge of human social cognition derived from the previous two approaches. The three approaches mutually facilitate the understanding and the development of human social cognition.

Figure 1: The robot as a model, a stimulus, and an interaction partner to investigate human social cognition through HRI experiments.

The full-day workshop will consist of an introduction to the three perspectives by the organizers (20min each), a few keynote talks from speakers representative of the different disciplines involved (30min each) and oral and poster presentations of participants' contributions. In addition to the poster session, the authors will have the possibility to briefly introduce their work as spotlight presentations during the oral session. The workshop will also feature a whole-group final discussion about the topic of the day.

Keynote speakers	Affiliation	Topic
Giulio Sandini	Istituto Italiano di Tecnologia	Use and development of interactive humanoids
Brian Scassellati	Yale University	Computational models of human social behavior
Malinda Carpenter	University of St Andrews; Max Planck Institute for Evolutionary Anthropology	Social cognition in children and apes
Luciano Fadiga	Istituto Italiano di Tecnologia; University of Ferrara	Neurophysiology in monkeys and humans

3. TARGET AUDIENCE

The workshop is targeted to HRI researchers who are interested in interdisciplinary approaches. In particular, in order to encourage a discussion, we would like to welcome researchers from a broad range of disciplines such as robotics, neurosciences, social sciences, psychology and computer science.

4. POSITION PAPER REQUIREMENTS

Prospective participants are required to submit short (2 pages) or full papers (8 pages). Submissions must be in pdf, following the HRI conference style. All contributions will be subject to a peer review process. Position paper should discuss how HRI techniques can be used to bridge the gap between multiple disciplines (e.g., robotics, neuroscience, cognitive science, etc.) and/or provide examples of research along one of the three perspectives indicated before. In addition to the submission participants have to answer one of the following questions:

- Which outcomes should provide neuroscientific research to be useful to robotics?
- How can robotics influence neuroscience and psychology?
- Where the bridge between these disciplines is more useful, and where is it not (or less)?
- How this bridge should be built? At the level of the single individual, of the group, of the department?

Those answers will be used to "drive" the final discussion.

5. PLAN FOR DOCUMENTING THE WORKSHOP

All papers, posters and presentations will be archived after the workshop. Moreover, the whole-group discussions will be captured in notes. After the event, we will update the workshop webpage with a summary of the discussion that will be available publicly. Depending on the overall quality of the contributions, we might consider proposing a special issue to the Journal of Human-Robot Interaction or the Journal of Social Robotics in which extended versions of the submitted manuscripts might be included.

6. APPROACH FOR RECRUITING PARTICIPANTS

The workshop will be advertised on the HRI website and on mailing lists of different disciplines (e.g., robotics-worldwide, connectionist, visionlist). Additionally, the organizers will communicate with their communities (e.g., ICDL-EpiRob) and will personally invite a series of speakers spanning the spectrum of research from neuroscience to robotics.

7. REFERENCES

[1] Lohan, K., Rohlfing, K. J., Pitsch, K., Saunders, J., Lehman, H., Nehaniv, C. L., Fischer, K. and Wrede, B.: Tutor spotter: Proposing a feature set and evaluating it in a robotic system, International Journal of Social Robotics, 2011.

[2] Nagai, Y., Asada, M., and Hosoda, K.: Learning for joint attention helped by functional development, Advanced Robotics, vol. 20, no. 10, pp. 1165-1181, September 2006.

[3] Nagai, Y., Kawai, Y., and Asada, M.: Emergence of Mirror Neuron System: Immature vision leads to self-other correspondence, in Proceedings of the 1st Joint IEEE International Conference on Development and Learning and on Epigenetic Robotics, August 2011.

[4] Sciutti, A., Patanè, L., Nori, F. and Sandini, G.: Do humans need learning to read humanoid lifting actions? Third Joint IEEE International Conference of Development and Learning and on Epigenetic Robotics 2013, Osaka, Japan, August 18-22, 2013.

[5] Sciutti, A., Bisio, A., Nori, F., Metta, G., Fadiga, L., Pozzo, T. and Sandini G.: Measuring human-robot interaction through motor resonance. International Journal of Social Robotics, 2012.

Workshop on Algorithmic Human-Robot Interaction

Brenna Argall
Northwestern University
+1 847 467 0862
brenna.argall@northwestern.edu

Sonia Chernova
Worcester Polytechnic Institute
+1 508 831 6547
soniac@wpi.edu

Kris Hauser
Indiana University
+1 812 856 7496
hauserk@indiana.edu

Odest Chadwicke Jenkins
Brown University
+1 401 863 6055
cjenkins@cs.brown.edu

ABSTRACT

Intelligent behavior in robots is implemented through algorithms. Historically, much of algorithmic robotics research strives to compute outputs that achieve mathematically rigid conditions, such as minimizing path length. But today's robots are increasingly being used to empower the daily lives of people, and experience shows that traditional algorithmic approaches are poorly suited for the unpredictable, idiosyncratic, and adaptive nature of human-robot interaction. This raises a need for entirely new computational, mathematical, and technical approaches for robots to better understand and react to humans. The human-friendly robots of the future will need new algorithms, informed from the ground up by HRI research, to generate interpretable, ethical, socially-acceptable behavior, ensure safety around humans, and execute tasks of value to society.

Categories and Subject Descriptors

I.2.9 [**ARTIFICIAL INTELLIGENCE**]: Robotics – *operator interfaces.*

General Terms

Algorithms, Human Factors, Theory.

Keywords

Human-robot interaction, algorithms, activity recognition, learning from demonstration, safety.

1. INTRODUCTION

This workshop brings together computational and social science perspectives to discuss recent HRI-related algorithmic developments and studies, and catalyze closer ties to make progress toward the mutual vision of human-friendly robots. Of particular interest are works that advance our understanding of one or more of the following areas:

- How are existing algorithms limited in their ability to deliver high-quality HRI? How can these limitations be overcome?
- What assumptions are made in computational research about human behavior and how valid are they?
- What assumptions are made in behavioral research about algorithmic capabilities, and how valid are they?
- How can computational researchers develop algorithms to better support the needs of HRI research?
- What techniques help narrow the gap between the results of HRI studies and their implementations in robots deployed in the real world?

The intended audience includes technical researchers interested in HRI applications as well as social scientists interested in technical implementations. Both academic and industrial perspectives are welcome.

2. CONTRIBUTED PAPERS

Contributed papers will include a mix of position papers and technical papers. Papers will be limited to 6 pages in IEEE conference format.

Topics of technical papers may include, but are not limited to:

- Human behavior modeling and activity recognition
- Learning from human teachers
- Human-robot collaboration
- Safe navigation around humans
- Planning and decision-making under uncertainty
- Human intent recognition
- Software tools for HRI social scientists

Authors are encouraged to submit preliminary work in progress as well as surveys of existing work.

3. WEBSITE

More information is available at the workshop website at http://ahri2014.soic.indiana.edu/.

HRI'14, March 3–6, 2014, Bielefeld, Germany.
ACM 978-1-4503-2658-2/14/03.
http://dx.doi.org/10.1145/2559636.2560024

Cognitive Architectures for Human-Robot Interaction

Paul Baxter
Centre for Robotics and Neural Systems
Cognition Institute
Plymouth University, U.K.
paul.baxter@plymouth.ac.uk

Greg Trafton
Center for Applied Research in
Artificial Intelligence
Naval Research Laboratory
Washington DC, USA
greg.trafton@nrl.navy.mil

ABSTRACT

Developments in autonomous agents for Human-Robot Interaction (HRI), particularly social, are gathering pace. The typical approach to such efforts is to start with an application to a specific interaction context (problem, task, or aspect of interaction) and then try to generalise to different contexts. Alternatively however, the application of Cognitive Architectures emphasises generality across contexts in the first instance. While not the "silver-bullet" solution, this perspective has a number of advantages both in terms of the functionality of the resulting systems, and indeed in the process of applying these ideas. Centred on invited talks to present a range of perspectives, this workshop provides a forum to introduce and discuss the application (both existing and potential) of Cognitive Architectures to HRI, particularly in the social domain. Participants will gain insight into how such a consideration of Cognitive Architectures complements the development of autonomous social robots.

Categories and Subject Descriptors

C.0 [**Computer Systems Organization**]: General; I.2.0 [**Artificial Intelligence**]: General—*cognitive simulation*

General Terms

Design, Human Factors, Theory

Keywords

Cognitive Architecture, Cognitive Modelling, Social HRI

1. INTRODUCTION

In creating autonomous robots for (particularly social) HRI, there are numerous technical challenges to be overcome, such as multi-modal information integration, decision making, behaviour timing, etc [2]. Typically, starting from a specific application domain (a particular interaction task for example), a system is constructed using the most convenient computational means available and then evaluated, with attempts than made to generalise the results to other contexts. Alternatively, an approach starting from a Cognitive Architecture could be used.

One definition (from multiple possibilities) of Cognitive Architecture is that it is an:

> *"...overall, essential structure and process of a broadly-scoped domain-generic computational cognitive model, used for a broad, multiple-level, multiple-domain analysis of cognition and behavior..."* ([4], p341)

Constructs of this type (encompassing both theory and models) seek to account for cognition over multiple time-scales using a set of domain-general structures and mechanisms. Typically inspired by human cognition, the emphasis is on deriving a set of *principles of operation* not constrained to a specific task or context [3]. This therefore presents a holistic perspective: it forces the system designer to initially take a step back from diving into computational mechanisms to achieve a specific task, and instead consider what sort of functionality needs to be present, and how this relates to other cognitive competencies. The very process of applying such an approach to HRI therefore yields benefits – e.g. the integration of evidence from the human sciences, the facilitation of comparison of different systems in a principled manner, and as a more principled manner to verify and refine the resultant autonomous systems.

For HRI, such an approach to building autonomous systems based on Cognitive Architecture – *cognitive integration* – would emphasise first those aspects of behaviour that are common across domains, before applying these to specific interaction contexts for evaluation. Furthermore, given inspiration from human cognition, it can also inherently take into account the behaviour of the humans with which the system should interact, with the intricacies and sub-optimality that this entails (e.g. [5]). However, Cognitive Architectures typically emphasise the role of cognition in the individual. For application to HRI (particularly social), there is a need to expand this scope to interactions, which leads to a re-interpretation of what cognitive processing in the individual needs to account for [1]. One of the issues to be addressed in this workshop is how to balance these (at times) competing considerations.

To date, there have been relatively few efforts to apply the Cognitive Architecture perspective to the context of HRI.

HRI'14, March 3–6, 2014, Bielefeld, Germany.
ACM 978-1-4503-2658-2/14/03.
http://dx.doi.org/10.1145/2559636.2560026.

The aim of this workshop is therefore to provide a forum to discuss the reasons and potential for the application of Cognitive Architectures to autonomous HRI systems. It is expected that by attending this workshop and engaging in the discussions, participants will gain insight into how a consideration of Cognitive Architectures could complement the development of autonomous social robots, and contribute to the cross-fertilization of ideas in this exciting area.

2. OUTLINE OF WORKSHOP

The primary contribution to this workshop is from invited speakers, who will provide a range of perspectives on how concepts of Cognitive Architecture may be beneficial for HRI. The invited speakers have been chosen to provide a balanced range of views and approaches. However, a particular emphasis is placed on having all participants engage in discussions; submitted position papers will be used by the organisers to shape this discussion.

This workshop is aimed at researchers from a wide range of backgrounds who may be interested in applying concepts from Cognitive Architectures to their work, specifically Social HRI. Participation in this workshop will be open to all interested researchers. However, in order to facilitate participant involvement, all participants are encouraged to submit a position paper that will ideally be based on the participant's research, and contain a comment on their views on the application of Cognitive Architectures to Human-Robot Interaction. These submissions will be integrated by the organisers prior to the workshop into a list of perspectives that will form the basis of the workshop discussions.

Outline of the workshop programme:

1. *Introduction*: a brief introduction to the workshop and participants *(led by organisers)*.

2. *Context*: introduction to Cognitive Architectures, their potential application to HRI, and participant perspectives *(led by organisers)*.

3. *Applications*: a number of invited talks from different perspectives on the application of Cognitive Architectures to HRI, each of which will be followed by a brief discussion *(led by invited speakers)*.

4. *General Discussion*: whole group discussion, with speakers and organisers taking a leading role, encompassing basic concepts of Cognitive Architectures, the utility of applying these to HRI (including limitations), and the participant perspectives *(involving all participants)*.

5. *Conclusion*: summary remarks *(led by organisers)*.

The participants' submissions will be archived on the workshop website[1] as a reference for the workshop. The derived list of perspectives and the outcomes of the workshop discussions will also be archived here to serve as a reference for both participants and other interested researchers.

3. ORGANISERS

Paul Baxter is a Research Fellow at Plymouth University (UK) in the Centre for Robotics and Neural Systems, and the Cognition Institute, having obtained a PhD in Developmental Cognitive Robotics from the University of Reading (UK). His current research work involves the application and evaluation of a memory-centred perspective on cognition to social Child-Robot Interaction, conducted as part of the EU FP7 ALIZ-E project. Contact: (email) paul.baxter@plymouth.ac.uk, (website) www.plymouth.ac.uk/staff/pebaxter/

Greg Trafton is a Cognitive Scientist at the Naval Research Laboratory in Washington, DC, USA. He has degrees in both Computer Science (Trinity University) and Psychology (Princeton University) and works on Human-Robot Interaction from a cognitive modeling / architectures perspective. Contact: (email) greg.trafton@nrl.navy.mil, (website) www.nrl.navy.mil/aic/iss/aas/poc-trafton.php/

4. REFERENCES

[1] T. Belpaeme et al. Child-robot interaction: Perspectives and challenges. In *ICSR'13*, volume 8239, pages 452–459. Springer, 2013.

[2] K. Dautenhahn. Socially intelligent robots: dimensions of human-robot interaction. *Philosophical transactions of the Royal Society of London, Series B: Biological sciences*, 362:679–704, 2007.

[3] P. Langley et al. Cognitive architectures: Research issues and challenges. *Cognitive Systems Research*, 10(2):141–160, 2009.

[4] R. Sun. Desiderata for Cognitive Architectures. *Philosophical Psychology*, 17(3):341–373, 2004.

[5] J. G. Trafton et al. ACT-R/E : An Embodied Cognitive Architecture for Human-Robot Interaction. *Journal of Human-Robot Interaction*, 2(1):30–54, 2013.

[1]http://www.tech.plym.ac.uk/socce/staff/paulbaxter/cogarch4hri/

Humans and Robots in Asymmetric Interactions

Anna-Lisa Vollmer
Plymouth University
UK
anna-lisa.vollmer
@plymouth.ac.uk

Lars Schillingmann
Osaka University
Japan
lars
@ams.eng.osaka-u.ac.jp

Katharina J. Rohlfing
Bielefeld University
Germany
kjr
@uni-bielefeld.de

Britta Wrede
Bielefeld University
Germany
bwrede
@techfak.uni-bielefeld.de

1. MOTIVATION

Robots are not human. They might in some cases have a similar appearance but different behavioral and cognitive strengths and limitations. In this sense, an interaction with a robot is asymmetric. When interacting with a robot one is unsure what behavior to expect as the appearance does not necessarily make the abilities of the robot transparent. In human-human interaction, we can also find asymmetric interactions to occur. For example, in an interaction with a child, adults have to adapt to the learner's capabilities and understanding. Similarly, in interactions with special populations such as persons with autistic spectrum disorders (ASD), asymmetry occurs as specific information seems to be processed differently.

In this half-day interdisciplinary workshop, we will discuss how partners cope with asymmetry to succeed in interaction. Our discussion will be motivated by linguistic and non-linguistic interaction strategies that are developed online in human-human as well as human-robot asymmetric interaction. Persons for example are often guided by their expectations and expected abilities in the interaction partners resulting in difficulties in asymmetric interactions with robots and even toward humans. Our aim is to determine factors as well as methods that are capable of supporting communication in asymmetric interactions.

By bringing together researchers working on the area of asymmetric interaction concerning both human-human and human-robot interaction, this workshop aims to develop novel views on interaction understanding and modeling as well as insights into alignment processes.

HRI'14, March 3–6, 2014, Bielefeld, Germany.
ACM 978-1-4503-2658-2/14/03.
http://dx.doi.org/10.1145/2559636.2560027.

Categories and Subject Descriptors

H.1.2 [**Information Systems Applications**]: User/Machine Systems; K.4.2 [**Computers and Society**]: Social Issues

General Terms

Design, Experimentation, Human Factors, Measurement

Keywords

Asymmetric Interaction; Alignment; Expectations; Autistic Spectrum Disorder; Adult-Child Interaction; Social HRI

2. LIST OF TOPICS

- interaction/behavioral strategies and their online generation
- grounding, alignment, adaptation, achieving mutual understanding
- learning (related to the workshop's topic)
- recognition of the interaction partner's state (of understanding, emotional state, limitations etc.)
- (automatic) understanding of partner's abilities
- expectations
- recognition, understanding and communication of own state
- communication of own impairments
- recognition and measurement of the extent of asymmetry of an interaction
- solving the correspondence from the partner's to the own physiology
- informing HRI with findings from human-human asymmetric interaction (parallels)
- support-systems for communication

3. WORKSHOP OVERVIEW

This half-day workshop features six 20 minute talks and a one hour discussion session. The interdisciplinary target audience includes researchers interested in novel methods that operate in the area of asymmetric interactions and researchers interested in interaction understanding and modeling in asymmetric interactions. Accepted 4-6 page full papers and 2 page abstracts, as well as a summary of the discussion session will be published on the workshop website [1].

4. ORGANIZERS

Anna-Lisa Vollmer

Anna-Lisa Vollmer studied Mathematics at Bielefeld University, Germany and the University Pierre and Marie Curie in Paris, France. She received her diploma from Bielefeld University in 2007. Then she became a member of the research group for Applied Informatics and the Research Institute for Cognition and Robotics (CoR-Lab) at Bielefeld University, where she investigated interactive behavior in tutoring action with children and robots and received her Ph.D. degree in 2011. She is currently working as an Experienced Researcher in the Marie Curie ITN "Robotics for Development of Cognition" (RobotDoC), at Plymouth University, UK, where she is doing research on dialogue and interactive alignment in human-robot interaction.

Lars Schillingmann

Lars Schillingmann received the diploma in computer science from the Bielefeld University, Germany, in 2007. Subsequently he joined the research group for Applied Informatics (Angewandte Informatik) at the University of Bielefeld, Germany. He worked for the BMBF Joint-Project DESIRE. Subsequently he worked in the iTalk EU-Project on the topic of Acoustic Packaging. On this topic he received the Ph.D. degree in 2012. Subsequently he was working in the EU-Project HUMAVIPS at the CoR-Lab, which aims at developing adequate robot behavior for interacting with a group of people. Since April 2013, he works at the Emergent Robotics Lab., Graduate School of Engineering, Osaka University, Japan. His research interests include learning and feedback processes embedded in human-robot interaction.

Katharina J. Rohlfing

Katharina Rohlfing Katharina J. Rohlfing received the Masters degree in Linguistics, Philosophy and Media Studies from the University of Paderborn, Germany, in 1997. From 1999 to 2002 she was a member of the Graduate Program Task Oriented Communication. She received the Ph.D. degree (Dr. phil.) in Linguistics from the Bielefeld University, Germany, in 2002. Her postdoctoral work at the San Diego State University, the University of Chicago and Northwestern University was supported by a fellowship within the Postdoc-program of the German Academic Exchange Service (DAAD) from November 2002 to December 2003 and by the Emmy Noether-Programme of the German Research Foundation (DFG) for 2004. She joined the Applied Computer Science Group in 2005. 2006 she became a Dilthey-Fellow (Funding initiative "Focus on the Humanities"), and her research is supported by the Volkswagen Foundation. Since May 2008, she is head of the Emergentist Semantics Group within Center of Excellence Cognitive Interaction Technology, Bielefeld University. Katharina Rohlfing is interested in learning processes. In her research, she is investigating the interface between early stages of language acquisition and conceptual development.

Britta Wrede

Since 2010 Britta Wrede is interim head of the Applied Informatics Group at Bielefeld University and since 2008 head of the research group "Hybrid Society" of the CoR-Lab. After receiving her M.A. and PhD title from the Faculty of Linguistics in 1999 and from the Technical Faculty in 2002 respectively, both in the area of automatic speech recognition, she spent one year as DAAD fellow at the International Computer Science Institute (ICSI) in Berkeley, USA, working on the analysis of prosodic cues for emotional speech or "Hot Spots". Since rejoining the Applied Informatics Group she has been working on human-robot dialog modeling, emotion recognition and modeling in HRI, developmentally inspired speech recognition approaches, visual attention modeling, the analysis of tutoring behavior towards children and robots and the modeling of the perception of multi-modaltutoring behavior for learning. She is Principal Investigator in several EU projects and national projects. Her research is driven by the question how to equip robots with a better understanding of their environment and is strongly inspired by human development. It follows the hypothesis that learning needs to be embedded in social interaction.

[1] https://aiweb.techfak.uni-bielefeld.de/hri2014_workshop_asymmetric_interactions

Culture-Aware Robotics (CARs)

Matthias Rehm
Aalborg University
Sofiendalsvej 11
DK-9000 Aalborg
+45 9940 8789
matthias@create.aau.dk

Maja J. Mataric
University of Southern California
3650 McClintock Avenue, OHE 200
Los Angeles, CA 90089-1450 USA
+1 213 740 4520
mataric@usc.edu

Bilge Mutlu
University of Wisconsin–Madison
1210 W. Dayton St. Room 6381
Madison, WI 53706-1685 USA
+1 608 262 6635
bilge@cs.wisc.edu

Tatsuya Nomura
Ryukoku University
1-5, Yokotani, Setaohe-cho, Otsu,
Shiga 520-2194, Japan
+81 77 544 7136
nomura@rins.ryukoku.ac.jp

Categories and Subject Descriptors
H. Information Systems: H.5 Information Interfaces and Prsentation (I.7): H.5.2 User Interfaces (D.2.2, H.1.2, I.3.6)

General Terms
Design, Experimentation, Human Factors.

Keywords
Culture Aware Robotics, HRI, Behavior Modeling, Social Signal Processing.

1. INTRODUCTION

Culture is not the first aspect that comes to mind when discussing human robot interaction. But our cultural upbringing does to a large degree influence our patterns of behavior and interpretation. Thus, culture is present in the development of robotic systems right from the start, unconsciously influencing how robots look, what we envision with them to do, and how they are programmed to interact with the user. The area of culturally aware robotics is currently emerging as a subfield in the HRI community, which can be seen in the increasing number of publications related to this topic. This becomes increasingly important when robots start to move into the users' environment, fulfilling tasks that have so far been viewed as "human" tasks.

HRI'14, March 3–6, 2014, Bielefeld, Germany.
ACM 978-1-4503-2658-2/14/03.
http://dx.doi.org/10.1145/2559636.2560028

The main research area of the activity is human-robot interaction (HRI), which is dedicated to understanding, designing, and evaluating robotic systems for use by or with humans, tightly focusing on the realization of meaningful and task-oriented communication between robots and humans. The sub-field of social robotics investigates robots that are designed to interact with people in a natural, interpersonal manner – often to achieve social-emotional goals within the social environment they are deployed in. The scientific focus of the workshop more specifically is directed to culturally-aware robotics, which refers to a brand-new area in social robotics and human robot interaction and is closely related to the emergence of the field of culture aware computing in computer science and related disciplines. The main focus is on understanding the influence of culture on many human processes that affect human-robot interactions be it directly or indirectly. Culture aware robots can thus be defined as robotic systems, where culture-related information has had some impact on its design, runtime or internal processes, structures, and/or objectives.

Workshop Goal: The main goal of this workshop is to establish awareness for the emerging field of CARs while at the same time allowing researchers interested in this area to connect and explore collaboration possibilities, which is especially important in a field relying on cross-cultural evaluations.

Timing in Human Robot Interaction

Guy Hoffman
Media Innovation Lab
IDC Herzliya
hoffman@idc.ac.il

Maya Cakmak
Computer Science & Engr.
University of Washington
mcakmak@cs.washington.edu

Crystal Chao
College of Computing
Georgia Inst. of Technology
cchao@gatech.edu

1. WEBSITE

`http://milab.idc.ac.il/timinghri/`

2. INTRODUCTION

Timing plays a role in a range of human-robot interaction scenarios, as humans are highly sensitive to timing and interaction fluency. It is central to spoken dialogue, with turn-taking, interruptions, and hesitation affecting both efficiency and emotional response [1, 2]. Nonverbal behavior such as gestures, gaze, and other communicative cues is similarly sensitive to timing [3, 4]. Beyond communication, the temporal synchronization of functional actions is necessary for sharing resources and physical space, and also affects human perception of robotic teammates [5, 6]. Timing is thus crucial to the success of a broad spectrum of HRI applications, including but not limited to situated dialogue; collaborative manipulation; performance, musical, and entertainment robots; and expressive robot companions [7, 8].

3. WORKSHOP GOAL AND TOPICS

Recent years have seen a growing interest in the HRI community in the various research topics related to human-robot timing. This workshop aims to explore and discuss theories, computational models, systems, empirical studies, and interdisciplinary insights related to the notion of timing, fluency, and rhythm in human-robot interaction.

Our call for papers will solicit submissions on the following topics:

- Timing models and systems implemented in real-time domains, including:
  - human-robot teamwork
  - spoken and situated dialogue
  - performance, entertainment, and musical robots
- Action synchronization and coordination between modalities and agents
- Behavior and interaction planning with time-sensitive constraints
- Incremental perception and behavior generation
- Theories and models with timing-specific elements
- Empirical studies on the effects of human and robot timing

HRI'14, March 3–6, 2014, Bielefeld, Germany.
ACM 978-1-4503-2658-2/14/03.
http://dx.doi.org/10.1145/2559636.2560029.

4. CONTENT AND STRUCTURE

"Timing in Human-Robot Interaction" is a full-day workshop with contributions which will be peer-reviewed by two reviewers. Contributed papers will be presented in five-minute segments, interleaved with 20-minute invited talks, spanning the workshop topics. As timing-related issues are often best illustrated visually, attendees are encouraged to present a short video of their work when introducing themselves. Examples of video documentation could be: a robot system, human study, live performance, etc. These videos will help attendees understand interaction phenomena from disparate fields and serve as common ground for discussions.

4.1 Themes and Invited talks

The workshop is divided into four sessions along four themes, each led by an invited session talk:

Session I: Computational Models and Algorithms
Invited Speaker: Julie A. Shah
Assistant Professor of Aeronautics and Astronautics, MIT
Dynamic Scheduling of Interactions for Human-Robot Collaboration in Manufacturing

Session II: Timing in Human Brains and Bodies
Invited Speaker Natalie Sebanz
Associate Professor of Cognitive Science, Central European University
Non-verbal Coordination Mechanisms in Human Joint Action

Session III: Timing in Human-Robot Dialog
Invited Speaker: Charles Rich
Professor of Computer Science, Worcester Polytechnic Institute
Real-Time Challenges for Conversational Agents and Robots: Beyond Turn-Taking

Session IV: Perspectives from the Arts
Invited Speaker: Scott Barton
Assistant Professor of Music, Worcester Polytechnic Institute
Off the Integer Grid: Using Robots to Create New Rhythmic Identities

4.2 Discussion sessions

We will organize two discussion sessions, one at the end of each two of the sessions. The discussion sessions are set up so that ideas from two disparate fields will be related by workshop participants. For example: The first discussion session will relate ideas from computational models and algorithms on the one hand, with findings from human timing mechanisms on the other. The second session will integrate ideas from human-robot dialog with perspectives from the arts.

This way, participants from different fields (e.g. human-robot dialog, teamwork, music robots, cognitive psychology, etc.) will have the opportunity to find connections between these issues and opportunities for cross-pollination between fields.

5. TARGET AUDIENCE

We particularly want to encourage an interdisciplinary dialog on the topic of timing, encouraging submissions and invited talks from research fields outside the robotics community. Thus, in addition to distributing calls for papers in the robotics and HRI communities, we will seek participation from the psychology, linguistics, humanities, and arts communities for their point of view on timing in humans, as it relates to human-robot interaction.

6. ORGANIZERS

Guy Hoffman is Assistant Professor in the School of Communication at IDC Herzliya, and co-director of the IDC Media Innovation Lab. Before, he was a research fellow at the Georgia Institute of Technology and at MIT. Hoffman holds a Ph.D from MIT in the field of human-robot interaction, and and M.Sc. in Computer Science from Tel Aviv University. His research deals with human-robot collaboration, embodied cognition for robots, anticipation and timing in HRI and multi-agent MDPs, nonverbal communication in HRI, and theater and musical performance robotics. His papers received several academic awards, including Best Paper at HRI and robotics conferences in 2006, 2007, 2008, and 2010.

Maya Cakmak is an Assistant Professor in Computer Science and Engineering at the University of Washington. She received her Ph.D. in Robotics from the Georgia Institute of Technology in 2012 and she was a post-doctoral research fellow at Willow Garage afterwards. Maya's research aims to develop functionalities and interfaces for personal robots that can be programmed by their end-users to assist everyday tasks. Her work has been published at major Robotics and AI conferences and journals and has been featured in numerous media outlets.

Crystal Chao is a Ph.D. candidate in Robotics at Georgia Tech, where she is member of the Socially Intelligent Machines Lab directed by Dr. Andrea L. Thomaz. Her research focuses on the timing of multimodal turn-taking in human-robot collaboration. She received a B.S. in Computer Science from MIT in 2008.

7. DOCUMENTATION

We intend to document the workshop in the following ways: On the workshop's website we will post the accepted papers and submitted videos, as an online archive of the workshop's contributions. The organizers will collect and document the breakout and discussion section outcomes and then publish the findings from these discussions as an article, together with the submitted papers as post-workshop proceedings. Depending on the range of contributions, we are also considering suggesting a special issue for the Journal of HRI with more in-depth articles on the contributed topics by workshop participants.

8. REFERENCES

[1] Chao, C., & Thomaz, A. L. (2012). Timing in Multimodal Turn-Taking Interactions : Control and Analysis Using Timed Petri Nets. *Journal of Human-Robot Interaction*, 1(1), 4–25.

[2] Okuno, Y. (2009). Providing Route Directions : Design of Robot's Utterance , Gesture , and Timing. *In Proceeding of the ACM/IEEE international conference on Human-robot interaction: HRI'09* (pp. 53–60).

[3] Crown, C. L. (1991). Coordinated Interpersonal Timing of Vision and Voice as a Function of interpersonal Attraction. *Journal of Language and Social Psychology*, 10(1), 29–46.

[4] B. Mutlu, J. Forlizzi, I. Nourbakhsh, J. Hodgins, The use of abstraction and motion in the design of social interfaces. *In Proc. Of DIS'06*, ACM Press (2006)

[5] Cakmak, M., Srinivasa, S., Kyung Lee, M., Kiesler, S., & Forlizzi, J. (2011). Using spatial and temporal contrast for fluent robot-human hand-overs. *Proceedings of the 6th international conference on Human-robot interaction - HRI'11*, 489.

[6] Hoffman, G., & Breazeal, C. (2009). Effects of anticipatory perceptual simulation on practiced human-robot tasks. *Autonomous Robots*, 28(4), 403–423.

[7] Kozima, H., Michalowski, M. P., & Nakagawa, C. (2009). Keepon: A playful robot for research, therapy, and entertainment. *International Journal of Social Robotics*, 1(1), 3–18.

[8] Weinberg, G., & Driscoll, S. (2006). Toward Robotic Musicianship. *Computer Music Journal*, 30(4), 28–45.

[9] It's All in the Timing, *2010 AAAI Spring Symposium*, Stanford, California, USA, March 22-24, 2010.

Experimenting in HRI for Priming Real World Set-ups, Innovations and Products

Paolo Barattini
Ridgeback s.a.s.
via S. Francesco da Paola 6
10123 Torino - Italy
+39 0172 575087
paolo.barattini@sharika.eu

Gurvinder S Virk
University of Gävle
Kungsbäcksvägen 47
801 76 Gävle, Sweden
+46 26 648704
gurvinder.virk@hig.se

Nicole Mirnig
University of Salzburg
ICT&S Center, Sigmund-Haffner-Gasse 18, 5020 Salzburg, Austria
+43 662 8044 4836
nicole.mirnig@sbg.ac.at

Maria Elena Giannaccini
Bristol Robotics Laboratory
University of the West of England,
Coldharbour Lane, Bristol BS16 1QY
+44 (0) 117 32 83394
maria.elena.giannaccini@brl.ac.uk

Adriana Tapus
Robotics and Computer Vision Lab
ENSTA-ParisTech
828 Blvd des Marechaux
91120, Palaiseau, France
+33(0)1 81 87 20 44
adriana.tapus@ensta-paristech.fr

Fabio Bonsignorio
Universidad Carlos III de Madrid
Avda. Universidad, 30
28911 Leganés, Spain
fabio.bonsignorio@gmail.com

ABSTRACT
Robotics is moving towards real world applications, beyond the well-structured environment of industrial robotics. In the world of assistant robots and medical robots, Human-Robot Interaction is essential. Also in emerging industrial scenarios there is a need of the human to be closely included in the loop. The companies are confronted with the lack of guidelines and of standards on how the higher features of HRI may be safely incorporated. Although the scientific research is burgeoning and worthy of praise, it is clear that its results are scattered and not capable of giving a clear input to be easily taken up by companies and standardization organizations like ISO and IEC. The workshop aims at the integration of empirical findings into complex real world robot systems by focusing on three typical sectors (industrial, service and medical) to develop systematic approaches to benchmark and evaluate experimental systems so that normative results can be realized rapidly. The present workshop focuses on bringing together scientists, representative of robotics companies and of standardization working groups to foster discussion in the definition of experimental scenarios and protocols in HRI, so to be able to prime real world set-ups and help realize the robotic products of the future.

Keywords
Human-robot interaction, HRI safety, robot application domains, robot scenario specification, benchmarking, normative results.

1. MOTIVATIONS AND OBJECTIVES
The main motivation is to bring together an interdisciplinary team of scientists (both engineering and social psychology), from robotics companies, involved in robot competitions, standardization and benchmarking activities.

HRI'14, March 3–6, 2014, Bielefeld, Germany.
ACM 978-1-4503-2658-2/14/03.
http://dx.doi.org/10.1145/2559636.2560030

This will foster discussion in the definition of experimental scenarios and protocols in HRI, and prime real world set-ups and products as follows:

- How to design evidence-based HRI for real world products?
- How to make a trade-off between the laboratory-based scenarios (lack of realism) and the real world ones (lack of repeatability)?
- What scientific results are available to give normative rules or recommendations?
- Shall the scientific community influence or contribute to the international standardization efforts? If so, how?
- What are the areas lacking the needed evidence?
- Are research-based HRI design and testing normative guidelines needed?
- How will ISO adopt testing procedure for higher level safety features of social and assistive robots (communication, feedback, vocal and gestures, etc.)?
- How big is the gap between the vision of omniscient robots that adapt to any language or user and the contextual/technical constraints, or market vision, or technical standards and regulatory framework?

2. ORGANISERS
G. S. Virk
http://www.hig.se/Ext/Sv/Organisation/Akademier/Akademin-for-teknik-och-miljo/Personalsidor/Gurvinder-Virk/Gurvinder-S.-Virk.html
He is Chairman of: ISO TC 184/SC2/WG7-Personal care robot safety and IEC SC62A & ISO TC184/SC2 JWG9-Medical robots) and Professor of Robotics and the Built Environment Univ. of Gävle and KTH, Sweden. He is also Chairman, Board of Trustees of the UK charity CLAWAR Association Limited (www.clawar.org).
Email: gsvirk@clawar.org.

A. Tapus
http://www.ensta-paristech.fr/~tapus/eng/cv.html
Full Professor, (ENSTA - ParisTech), France.
She is a leading scientist in Assistive HRI.
Email: adriana.tapus@ensta-paristech.fr

N. Mirnig & Manfred Tscheligi
http://www.icts.sbg.ac.at/nicole.mirnig
http://www.icts.sbg.ac.at/manfred.tscheligi
N. Mirnig is Researcher at the HCI & Usability Unit, Univ. of Salzburg . Email: nicole.mirnig@sbg.ac.at
M. Tscheligi is Professor for HCI & Usability at Univ. of Salzburg. He is a member of several expert groups and program committees, and editorial boards in the field of HCI.
Email: manfred.tscheligi@sbg.ac.at
M. E. Giannaccini
Researcher in Bristol Robotics Laboratory, UK
Her research focuses on physical HRI, soft robotics and hazard analysis in service robotic applications.
Email: maria.elena.giannaccini@brl.ac.uk
F. Bonsignorio
http://roboticslab.uc3m.es/roboticslab/persona.php?id_pers=95
Professor at the Carlos III Univ. of Madrid, He co-chair IEEE-TC PEBRAS and coordinates EURON SIG GEM Special Interest Group on Good Experimental Methodology and Benchmarking in Robotics. CEO and Founder HeronRobots.
Email: fabio.bonsignorio@uc3m.es
P. Barattini
CTO of Kontor46 sas, Italy. Email: paolo.barattini@kontor46.eu
B. Matthias
Senior Principal Scientist – Robotic Automation- ABB
Email: bjoern.matthias@de.abb.com
C. Woegerer & A. Pichler
C. Wögerer is at PROFACTOR GmbH Andreas Pichler is the Technical Director for HRI Topics. http://www.profactor.at/.

3. LIST OF TOPICS

- Current status of ISO/IEC robot standardization activities development and future directions in HRI
- Safety, physical contacts, technical aspects and limitations, regulations influencing HRI design
- Testing scenarios and protocols for HRI to produce normative definitions and data to prime real world products
- Role of Benchmarking and Robotics competition in advancing standardized testing procedures
- Robotics scientific community's input to standardization bodies
- Benchmarking: objectively and quantitatively evaluating performance of robots. Measuring autonomy or information metrics of intelligent systems; replicability/benchmarking of research results in robotics needs global agreements.
- Scientific methods to study and quantitatively evaluate the performance in affective and social robotics
- Design guidelines and testing procedures for evidence-based HRI: toward a consensus position paper.

4. SCHEDULE

08:30 – 10:00 Invited speakers
10:00 – 10:30 Coffee Break
10:30 – 11:30 Poster session
11:30 - 13:00 Topic Split Sessions
Topic 1 – Service Robotics scenario HRI requirements
Topic 2 – Industrial Robotics scenario HRI requirements
Topic 3 – Medical Robotics scenario HRI requirements
13:00 – 14:00 Lunch Break
14:00 - 15:30 Topic Split Sessions
15:30 - 16:00 Coffee break
16:00 - 18:00 Plenary Session & Minutes
18:15 End of workshop

5. ORAL PRESENTATIONS

G. S. Virk
ISO/IEC safety standardization in close HRI in medical and non-medical applications
V. Evers
Human Robot Evaluation, cultural aspects and context vs standardization
F. Ferro – PAL robotics
Path to robot certification
R. Gelin - Aldebaran
Social robots: from research and education to market products
B. Matthias - ABB
Safety Requirements for Collaborative Robots and Applications
P. Heiligensetzer - founder and CEO of MRK-Systeme GmbH
Industrial Applications of Collaborative Robots - Experiences and Perspectives
F. Bonsignorio
Hidden challenges in HRI metrics
T. Haidegger
IEEE ORA WG, Standard Ontologies for Robotics and Automation Application for Service Robotic and HRI
D. Nardi
Benchmarking and performance evaluation for service robots

6. TARGET AUDIENCE

Primary Audience: scientists and young researchers involved in HRI with possible real world application.

Secondary Audience: experts and organizations/institutes supporting research and technology transfer to industry and those with relations to Standardization and Regulatory Institutions.

7. SUBMISSIONS

The workshop is intended for lively discussion therefore only posters can be submitted until 15.02.2014 to hri2014wks@kontor46.eu, in PDF format and conform to the conference proceedings specifications. A proposal for a special issue on the topic will be submitted to the Journal of Social Robotics to document the workshop discussions.

8. DOCUMENTATION

During the workshop, minutes will be written and they will be published on the CLAWAR web site http://www.clawar.org that hosts the working group activities.

9. NOVELTY WITH RESPECT TO PREVIOUS WORKSHOPS

It is rare for workshops to be organized bringing together key communities in robotics, comprising the research, industrial and standardization sectors in the frame of formalizing the need of establishing normative results for HRI to allow robots to enter the global market place.

Author Index

www.ingramcontent.com/pod-product-compliance
Lightning Source LLC
LaVergne TN
LVHW082020200926
848481LV00010B/2892